T0081378

NEW INTERNATIONAL VERSION

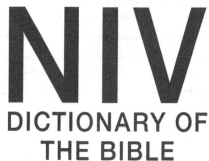

DICTIONARY OF
THE BIBLE

J. D. DOUGLAS & MERRILL C. TENNEY

ZONDERVAN®

ZONDERVAN

The NIV Dictionary of the Bible
Copyright © 1989 by Zondervan

Previously published as the *NIV Compact Dictionary of the Bible*.

Requests for information should be addressed to:
Zondervan, 3900 *Sparks Dr. SE, Grand Rapids, Michigan 49546*

ISBN 978-0-310-53489-1

All Scripture quotations, unless otherwise indicated, are taken from The Holy Bible, New International Version®, NIV®. Copyright © 1973, 1978, 1984 by Biblica, Inc.® Used by permission of Zondervan. All rights reserved worldwide. www.Zondervan.com. The "NIV" and "New International Version" are trademarks registered in the United States Patent and Trademark Office by Biblica, Inc.®

Any Internet addresses (websites, blogs, etc.) and telephone numbers in this book are offered as a resource. They are not intended in any way to be or imply an endorsement by Zondervan, nor does Zondervan vouch for the content of these sites and numbers for the life of this book.

All rights reserved. No part of this publication may be reproduced, stored in a retrieval system, or transmitted in any form or by any means — electronic, mechanical, photocopy, recording, or any other — except for brief quotations in printed reviews, without the prior permission of the publisher.

Edited by Claire Hughes
"Survey of the Bibile and Bible Times" and Topical Index prepared by Claire Hughes
Picture selection and layout: Rachel Hostetter
Compositor: Nancy Wilson

Printed in the United States of America

Contents

How to Use This Book

The *NIV Compact Dictionary of the Bible* consists of four parts:

1. Survey of the Bible and Bible Times. This introductory article will provide you with an overview of the Bible and its background and will gave you a framework for studying individual topics in more depth with the help of the Topical Index (see below).

2. The Dictionary Proper. Arranged alphabetically, the definitions in the *NIV Compact Dictionary of the Bible* will help you understand the meaning of specific words and terms in the Bible, as well as the Bible's background and teachings. The length of the articles reflects the relative importance of the various topics: the longer articles usually cover broader or more important topics such as "God," "Moses," "Animals," "Occupations." The illustrations, charts, and maps in the *NIV Compact Dictionary of the Bible* will help you picture everyday life in Bible lands. Many of the illustrations provide information that is not covered in the text because it is easier to understand in visual form.

3. Names Not Listed in the Dictionary. The names of people and places that are found only once in the Bible are not listed in the main dictionary if nothing is known about them beyond the mere mention of the name—quite a few names in the genealogies fall in this category. (In some cases names that are found twice but that are otherwise unknown are also included in this list.)

4. Topical Index. This index lists alphabetically some 125 topics, from "Agriculture" to "Writing," each followed by a list of the articles in the main dictionary that relate to that topic. The index will help you discover the wide variety of information that is available in the dictionary on various topics. For example, by looking up "Archaeology" in the index, you will be able to move from the general level (an article on "Archaeology") to the specific level (e.g., an article about the "Moabite Stone").

The *NIV Compact Dictionary of the Bible* can thus be used in three ways:

1. As a dictionary for quick reference, by using the main dictionary.

2. As an encyclopedia for a more in-depth study of a particular topic, by going to the Topical Index and reading some or all of the articles that are listed under a main heading.

3. As a basic course of study, by reading through the "Survey of the Bible and Bible Lands," looking up in the Topical Index the words and terms in the "Survey" that have an asterisk (*) in front of them, and then reading in the dictionary proper the articles that are listed under the main heading. (The "Survey" covers seven main topics: the Bible as a whole; the Old Testament; the time between the Testaments; the New Testament; the Lands of the Bible; the People of the Bible; and Religion and Worship in the Old and New Testaments

The *NIV Compact Dictionary of the Bible* is a condensed version of *The New International Dictionary of the Bible.* Although the *NIV Compact Dictionary of the Bible* is based on the New International Version of the Bible (NIV), it contains frequent comparisons with the King James Version (KJV).

Survey of the Bible and Bible Times

This survey provides an overview of the Bible itself as well as an overview of the different kinds of information about the Bible that the *NIV Compact Dictionary of the Bible* contains. By systematically looking up in the Topical Index the main topics mentioned in the survey and then reading the articles listed under the main heading in the topical index, the reader can actually pursue a course of study on the Bible and its background.

In the following material, an asterisk (*) before a word indicates that there is an article about that word in the dictionary. **Bold-faced** words in parentheses refer to a main entry in the Topical Index found at the end of the dictionary.

What Is the Bible?
I. The Bible as the Word of God
II. The Bible as Literature
  A. Poetry
  B. Law
  C. History
  D. Prophecy
  E. Apocalyptic Writing
  F. Wisdom Literature
  G. Gospel
  H. Epistles

How Was the Bible Written?
I. Languages
  A. Hebrew
  B. Aramaic
  C. Greek
II. Texts and Versions
III. Canonicity

The Old Testament
I. Pentateuch
II. Historical Books
III. Poetic Books
IV. Major Prophets
V. Minor Prophets

The Time Between the Testaments
I. History
II. Literature
III. Social Developments

The New Testament
I. Gospels
II. History
III. Epistles

The Lands of the Bible
I. Israel
  A. Names
  B. Geography
  C. Climate
  D. Plants
  E. Animals
II. Israel's Neighbors

The People of the Bible
I. The Home
II. The Family
III. Economic Life
IV. Political Life and the Law
V. Culture

Worship and Relation with God
I. The Old Testament—Israel's Faith
  A. Covenant
  B. Worship and Ritual
  C. Jewish Religious Leaders
II. The New Testament—Christianity
  A. Christ
  B. The Church

WHAT IS THE *BIBLE?

I. THE BIBLE IS THE WRITTEN WORD OF *GOD—THE BIBLE AS DIVINE REVELATION.

In some respects, as Jesus *Christ is the Son of God in the flesh (Matt 1:23), so the Bible is the Word of God in the words of men. *Paul thanked God continually for the Thessalonians who received the word of God from Paul but "accepted it not as the word of men, but as it actually is, the word of God" (1 Thess 2:13). Although the words of the Bible are truly human, they are not *merely* human. As Paul said: "All Scripture is God-breathed" (2 Tim 3:16)—breathed out by God through the mouths and pens of men. The church has always accepted Scripture as having come from God. Thus it is true: What the Bible says, God says.

Jesus is the divine Word (John 1:1–5) who became flesh (John 1:14), and the words of the Bible are divine words that were spoken by men who were "carried along by the Holy Spirit" (2 Pet 1:21) in their thinking, speaking, and writing. As the one and only Son of God (John 3:16), Jesus is without parallel; as the only divine-human book, the Bible is unique. (See * Inspiration; Bible.)

Just as Jesus is true man and true God and was in the world with a task to perform, so the Bible is God's infallible (unfailing) Word to us. "So is my word that goes out from my mouth: It will not return to me empty (Isa 55:11). Because the words of the Bible are God's words, the Bible is God's message to us. Like God, then, the Bible is trustworthy and true. Everything the Bible teaches, affirms, commands, and says concerning God's kingdom is trustworthy and true! As Jesus said to his Father: "Your word is truth" (John 17:17). Jesus promised that the "Spirit of truth" (John 14:17; 15:26; 16:13; 1 John 4:6; 5:6) would guide Christians into all truth (John 16:13) by testifying about Jesus.

Since the Bible conveys God's message to us, it is authoritative. This places three requirements on the Lord's followers. (1) Christians are to trust and obey every word of God (Matt 14:31; 21:21; Luke 8:11–13; John 3:18). (2) Christians are to be totally loyal to the Word of God. They are to live by every word that comes from the mouth of God (Deut 8:3; Josh 1:8; Ps 40:6–8; Matt 5:17–20). They cannot serve two masters (Matt 6:24); the double-minded man is unstable in all his ways (James 1:8). (3) God's Word is to govern every area of their lives (Pss 1:1–3; 119; 2 Tim 3:16–17). It is to be the standard by which they judge all that they feel and imagine, believe and think, say and hear, see and read, do and desire (Lev 18:1–5; Mark 7:13; Rom 12:2; 2 Cor 10:5).

II. THE BIBLE IS THE WORD OF MAN—THE BIBLE AS LITERATURE.

The Bible consists of sixty-six books that were written over a period of more than a thousand years by many different men. Because these men were guided in their thinking and writing by the *Holy Spirit (2 Pet 1:21), the sixty-six individual books are fundamentally unified in theme and content. (See Literature.)

One of the Bible's main themes is the lordship of God in * creation and * redemption. The Almighty God is the Lord of heaven and earth. God's lordship is seen in his sovereign rule over all things.

* Adam and * Eve were created to rule for God by establishing his kingdom on earth for God's glory and humanity's good. Where the first Adam disobeyed and failed to establish God's kingdom, the Second Adam, Jesus Christ, succeeded. (See Fall, The; God; Redemption.)

The Bible is the unfolding drama of the development of the * kingdom of God. It is the story of how the sovereign Lord acted in human history to establish his kingdom to save man and glorify himself. Thus the main focus of the Bible is on God's redeeming historical activity. (See Kingdom of God.)

Jesus Christ is the center of that activity. He is the Redeemer promised to Adam and Eve who will defeat * Satan and save God's people (Gen 3:15). The Mosaic laws, the sacrificial system, the kingdom of * Israel, and the * OT prophecies all point forward to Christ, the messianic Redeemer.

Throughout this unfolding drama of redemption, the Bible addresses the important and practical issues of life: love, hate, fear, hope, need, desire, family, money, work, play, war, peace, and so on. The Bible consists of real history about real people who shared the same type of concerns that we face today, though of course there are differences between then and now. The NIV Compact Dictionary of the Bible can help bridge the differences between people of Bible times and people of today and thus help us understand how the teachings of the Bible apply to our needs and concerns today.

The Bible contains many different types of literature: history, * poetry, * genealogy, and official records—to name a few. By and large, however, the Bible consists of history and poetry. We will now discuss some of the special features of biblical literature.

A. Poetry. The majority of biblical poetry is found in the Old Testament. A few features of Hebrew poetry are similar to modern poetry, though in many ways Hebrew poetry is quite different. Modern poetry is usually based on rhythm or sound; Hebrew poetry is based on rhythm of ideas or meaning. The first line of a Hebrew poem often expresses a thought that is repeated in another way in the second line. This technique is called parallelism, and it is one of the most important characteristics of Hebrew poetry. Other kinds of parallelism use contrast or further develop and build on the first idea.

Some biblical books are all poetry

(Psalms, Song of Songs, and Lamentations), and others contain poetry (many of the *prophets). In modern translations such as the NIV, poetry and prose may easily be distinguished by the way they are printed. In the *NT, the easiest poems to recognize are all found in Luke (1:46b–55, 68–79; 2:14, 29–32), and they echo Hebrew poetry. Other NT books contain parts of what may be Christian hymns (Eph 5:14; 1 Tim 1:17; 3:16; 6:16). (See Poetry.)

B. *Law. God's laws are an expression of his holy character and sovereign will. Through Moses, God provided the nation of Israel with many laws. These laws defined Israel's relationship with God and the Israelites' relationships with one another and with outsiders. The *Ten Commandments (Exod 20:2–17) summarize God's laws that teach us how to love God and one another. Exodus, Leviticus, Numbers, and Deuteronomy contain many additional laws that explain how the broad principles of the Ten Commandments were to be applied in Israel to worshiping God, governing the nation, in individual behavior, and in social interaction. In the NT in the *Sermon on the Mount, Jesus affirmed, repeated, and deepened the demands of the Ten Commandments. Throughout the NT, additional laws and principles are given to the church. The NT emphasizes the Holy Spirit's role of writing God's laws on our hearts and thus making us sensitive to God's will. (See Civil Law; Crimes; Law; Legal System; Punishment.)

C. History. Almost every OT book includes historical information. In the English Bible, however, certain OT books (Joshua–2 Chronicles) are grouped together and commonly referred to as the historical books, since they focus on history. These books cover the period of history from the time of the judges through the Persian Empire. In the NT, the Gospels and Acts contain the majority of the historical information about the early church, though the epistles also are important in this regard.

The Bible does not record all the major events of the historical periods it covers. It includes only those events where God reveals himself by acting in history to redeem his people. God's actions in history reached their climax in the person and work of Jesus Christ.

D. Prophecy. Prophecy is a type of literature found not only in the OT books of Isaiah through Malachi but in the NT as well. Biblical *prophets proclaimed

God's words and predicted the future. They also exposed the sin of God's people and called for *repentance and *obedience, showing how God's law applied to specific situations and problems. (See Eschatology; Prophets.)

A prophecy may have both an immediate and a long-term reference. A prediction that was fulfilled in a prophet's lifetime or soon thereafter may also point to a future fulfillment in the life, death, resurrection, and return of Christ.

E. *Apocalyptic Writing. Apocalyptic writing is a type of prophetic literature that depicts political and spiritual future events in a hidden or secret way through the use of symbols and vivid imagery. The meaning of an apocalyptic writing may not be immediately apparent. Frequently, time is presented as a series of events that are repeated in different ages that eventually culminate in the Day of the Lord, the time when God will end the history of the present earth by establishing a new order. Apocalyptic writing is found in Isaiah, Daniel, Ezekiel, Zechariah, and Revelation. (See Apocalyptic Literature.)

F. *Wisdom Literature. The wisdom books, which are associated with a group of people called "wise men," focus on questions concerning the meaning of life (Job, Ecclesiastes) and on practical, day-to-day living (Proverbs). These writings contrast human wisdom, which brings grief and frustration (Eccl 1:14, 17–18), with divine wisdom, which comes from God (Prov 2:6) and enables people to live lives pleasing to him. The truly wise man is the truly good man. Certain psalms also belong in the category of wisdom literature. (See Wisdom Literature.)

G. *Gospel. The word gospel means "good tidings"—the good news that God has given us salvation through his Son, Jesus. When that message was first written down, it was a brand new type of literature. Although the four Gospels contain biographical and historical information, their purpose is to create faith in Christ on the part of their readers, not to serve as full histories or biographies of Jesus. Each gospel presents the ministry, teachings, death, and resurrection of Jesus in a distinctive way for a specific audience.

H. *Epistles. Although the Bible contains many different examples of letters, the term epistles specifically refers to the twenty-one epistles of the NT. They share the features of other letters of their time. They begin with the name of the writer and the recipient, followed by a greeting, the central message, and (usually) a closing reference to the author's name.

NT epistles deal with situations that needed immediate doctrinal or pastoral attention. Sometimes epistles were written in response to information from messengers or in response to another letter. The teachings of the epistles apply to believers as individuals and to the church as a whole.

HOW WAS THE BIBLE WRITTEN?

As we noted earlier, the Bible was written over a period of more than a thousand years by many different men. The OT and NT together form the Christian Scriptures; the OT alone forms the Hebrew Bible. In the OT, God's people were related to him on the basis of the Mosaic *covenant and its sacrifices for sin. In the NT, God's people are related to him on the basis of the new covenant, which was established by Jesus' sacrificial life, death, and resurrection.

Some of the OT writers used older written records (Josh 10:13; 2 Sam 1:18), oral tradition (information faithfully and accurately passed from one generation to another by word of mouth; Deut 6:20–25; 26:5–9), words dictated by God (Exod 20:1–17; Deut 10:4; Isa 8:1, 11), and information based on God-given *visions (Isa 1:1; 2:1; 6:1; Rev 4:1–2). Throughout the ages, *scribes carefully preserved these writings. (See Old Testament.)

The NT was composed by fewer authors over a period of less than one hundred years. The letters of Paul are probably the earliest writings. The story of Jesus' death and resurrection was written down in the form of gospels. The writers of the NT also relied on information from other eyewitnesses, on oral tradition (2 Thess 2:15; 1 Cor 15:1–9), and on other written accounts (Luke 1:3). (See New Testament.)

I. LANGUAGES.

A. *Hebrew.* Hebrew is the main language in which the OT was written. Hebrew is a Semitic language that was spoken by the Jews until the Exile and that much later (1948) was revived and adopted as the official language of the modern State of Israel. The ancient Hebrew text of the OT contained only consonants. Vowel signs were added in the sixth century A.D. by Jewish scholars called Masoretes to preserve the pronunciation and meaning of the text. Below is the Hebrew text of the first words of Genesis 1:1; the large letters are the consonants, the small dots and lines

above and below the consonants are the vowels and various pronunciation helps.

בְּרֵאשִׁית בָּרָא אֱלֹהִים אֵת

*** God he-created in-beginning

הַשָּׁמַיִם וְאֵת הָאָרֶץ:

the-earth and the-heavens

B. *Aramaic.* Aramaic was the international language at the end of the OT era and the spoken language in Palestine during the time of Christ. A few passages in Ezra, Daniel, and Jeremiah are written in Aramaic, as well as a few words and phrases in the Gospels. Aramaic looks like Hebrew when written or printed.

C. *Greek.* The NT was written in "common" Greek, the everyday business language used throughout the Greek-speaking part of the Roman Empire. This common Greek, which also is known as "Koine" (from the Greek word for "common") or Hellenistic Greek, was a simplified version of classical Greek and was spread by Alexander the Great throughout the Mediterranean world. (See Languages.) Below are the first words of John 3:16 in Greek.

Ἐν ἀρχῇ ἦν ὁ λόγος,
In [the] beginning was the Word,

καὶ ὁ λόγος ἦν πρὸς τὸν
and the Word was with –

θεόν, καὶ θεὸς ἦν ὁ
God, and God was the

*II. *TEXTS AND VERSIONS.*

The OT was originally written on animal skins (called vellum or parchment) or on *papyrus (a writing paper made from the papyrus plant). Because the OT was considered the sacred Word of God, scribes carefully preserved every letter and word of the original text when making new copies. Before the discovery of the Dead Sea Scrolls, the earliest Hebrew manuscripts dated from about A.D. 1,000. Beginning in about A.D. 500, scribes called Masoretes added a system of vowels to the consonantal Hebrew text (see above) to produce the *Masoretic Text*. This text is the basis for modern "critical" editions and English translations of the Hebrew Bible.

The *Dead Sea Scrolls*, which date from 200 B.C. to A.D. 100 and were discovered in 1947, include entire copies or fragments of every OT book except Esther.

The *Septuagint* is the name for a Greek translation of the OT that was made between 250 and 150 B.C. This is a valuable tool for Bible translation. Coptic and Syriac translations of the Bible appeared during the second and third centuries A.D.

The original *Greek NT* was probably written on papyrus and either rolled into a *scroll or folded to form a codex (book). There are numerous copies and fragments of the Greek NT, many of them quite early. Codex Vaticanus dates from the middle of the 4th century A.D. and contains most of the OT and NT. Codex Sinaiticus dates from the fourth century and contains a fragment of the OT and the complete NT. Codex Alexandrinus dates from the fifth century and contains most of the NT.

Latin versions of the complete Bible were available by A.D. 250, though in general their quality was poor. In A.D. 382 a scholar named Jerome began making a Latin translation of the Bible. Due to its widespread acceptance, this translation came to be known as the Vulgate ("common") version. Jerome translated directly from the Hebrew text with references to the Septuagint. By A.D. 405 he had completed his work. The Vulgate version remained the authorized Roman Catholic Bible for 1,200 years. (See Texts and Versions.)

John Wycliffe made the first complete *English translation* of the Bible in 1382. Wycliffe's translation was based on Jerome's Latin Vulgate. After the invention of the printing press, William Tyndale decided to make a translation of the Bible from the original Greek and Hebrew. Tyndale's NT appeared in 1525, and parts of the Pentateuch appeared in 1530. Tyndale's translation was so accurate that the translators who made the King James Version adopted about 90 percent of his translation of the NT. In 1604, King James of England commissioned a group of scholars to make a new

English translation that was based on the best available Greek and Hebrew manuscripts. This translation, which came to be known as the King James or Authorized Version, was first published in 1611. (See BIBLE, ENGLISH VERSIONS.)

The English Revised Version, made in 1881, updated the English used in the King James Version. This new translation was made using older Greek manuscripts than those that were available to the King James translators, and with a better understanding of the Hebrew language. An American Standard Version of the English Revised Version was published in 1901 for an American audience.

Modern translators in the twentieth century have used recent discoveries, such as the Dead Sea Scrolls, and an improved understanding of Hebrew to produce English translations in everyday language. Some of these recent translations include the Revised Standard Version (1946), the New English Bible (1961), the New American Standard Bible (1971), and the New International Version (1978), which is the basis for this dictionary.

III. *CANONICITY.

The sixty-six books in the Protestant Bible are referred to collectively as "the canon," a term that comes from a Greek word that means "rule" or "measure." These books were accepted as authoritative and thus as the "rule" for faith and life. (The Roman Catholic and Eastern Orthodox canons add several other books, known as the Apocrypha.)

The Jews divided the OT canon into three sections: the Law, the Prophets, and the Writings. Joshua recognized the first section (the *Pentateuch) as the authoritative Word of God (Josh 1:7–8). By 400 B.C. Jewish scholars officially confirmed the books of the Law as canonical. By 200 B.C. they confirmed the Prophets, and by 100 B.C. they confirmed the Writings. Long before these official confirmations, however, the Jews had accepted the majority of the writings as canonical. Authorship by a prophet or other recipient of divine revelation was one of the main criteria for accepting a work as canonical. The Dead Sea Scrolls (see below) confirm an early acceptance of all the OT books as canonical (with the possible exception of Esther).

From as early as the second century A.D. there is a large body of evidence that shows that most or all of the sixty-six canonical books were used as authoritative in the early church. All of the NT books were accepted as written by apostles or by those who had close contact with apostles (such as Mark's close association with Peter). The books of the NT were officially listed by the church coun-

cil at Carthage in A.D. 397, though Christians had agreed on which writings belonged to the NT canon well before that.

THE OLD TESTAMENT

The *Old Testament contains thirty-nine books. These books cover the period from the creation of the world until the time of Ezra and Nehemiah (about 400 B.C.). Most of the OT is a history of the people of Israel. This history begins with *Abraham and continues through the return from the *Exile. Christians arranged the books of the OT by subject matter and type of writing, not by chronological order. In the Christian Bible, the books of the OT are divided into the following five groups: Pentateuch, history, poetry, major prophets, and minor prophets. In the Jewish Bible, there are three groups of books: the Law (Torah), the Prophets (Nebi'im), and the Writings (Kethub'im). Because it combines certain books that are separated in English translations, the Hebrew Bible consists of twenty-two books.

I. PENTATEUCH.

The first five books of the OT (the Pentateuch) describe the beginning of the world and the beginning of the Jewish nation. The Jewish people call these books the Law. *Moses is considered their author.

*Genesis is the book of beginnings. Chapters 1–11 cover creation, the *fall of man, the *Flood, and the growth of the nations. In chapter 12, God chose Abraham to be the father of the Jewish race. The rest of Genesis is the story of Abraham and his descendants *Isaac, *Jacob, and *Joseph (the *Patriarchs) and the birth of the *Jews.

*Exodus gives the history of the Jewish people from their stay in *Egypt until the giving of the *Law at Mt. Sinai. God chose *Moses to lead the people out of bondage and gave him the laws that were to be the foundation of the nation. These laws are summarized in the *Ten Commandments.

*Leviticus gives additional, detailed instruction about Israel's worship, especially the *priesthood and *sacrifices. God called his people to be holy and to live for him.

*Numbers describes Israel's time in the wilderness, from Mt. Sinai, where God gave the Law, to Kadesh Barnea, where

only two spies wanted to obey God and enter the Promised Land, as well as the forty years of wilderness wandering that resulted from Israel's disobedience.

*Deuteronomy is a series of speeches given by Moses to the Israelites as they were about to enter the Promised Land. Moses reminded the people of the laws God had given them, of their disobedience to God, and of their need to obey God in the Promised Land by keeping his law.

II. HISTORICAL BOOKS.

The next group of twelve books tells the history of Israel from the time the nation entered the Promised Land until about 400 B.C.

*Joshua describes the conquest of the land under Moses' successor, Joshua. Under his leadership, the land was settled and divided among the twelve *tribes.

*Judges covers the period between Joshua's death and the crowning of King *Saul. During this era, God raised up leaders known as judges to lead the Israelites against their enemies. After each victory, however, the people forgot God.

*Ruth is a story about family loyalty that is set during the time of the judges. Because of her loyalty to her mother-in-law, Ruth became part of the family of God, though she was a Gentile. Ruth was an ancestor of Jesus.

*First Samuel covers the history of Israel from the birth of *Samuel, the prophet who anointed Israel's first two kings, to the death of Saul.

*Second Samuel describes the reign of King *David, beginning with the civil war that followed Saul's death. David established *Jerusalem as his capital.

*First Kings begins with the reign of *Solomon and the building of the *temple. After Solomon's death, the kingdom was divided into two nations: the northern kingdom (*Israel—ten tribes) and the southern kingdom (*Judah—two tribes).

*Second Kings is the continued history of Israel and Judah. Because of her unfaithfulness, Israel was defeated by the *Assyrians and taken captive in 722 B.C., and Judah was taken captive by the Babylonians in 586 B.C.

*First Chronicles was written from a priestly viewpoint (probably that of *Ezra the scribe). First Chronicles emphasizes David's important role in developing worship in Israel and the need for obeying God to receive his blessing.

*Second Chronicles describes Solomon's reign, the temple that he built, and the worship that took place there. The last chapters (10–36) are devoted to the history of Judah.

*Ezra tells about the return of the Jews from *Babylon under *Zerubbabel and their worship in the rebuilt temple. The last four chapters describe the second group of *exiles who returned with Ezra and his religious reforms.

*Nehemiah returned with the third group of exiles and helped rebuild Jerusalem's walls. After Ezra's public reading of the law (the Pentateuch), the people confessed their disobedience to God and promised to obey him in the future. These were the last historical events recorded in the OT.

*Esther is the story of Esther, a Jewish girl who became queen of Persia and who was able to prevent a plot to destroy the Jews. The *Feast of Purim celebrates Israel's deliverance through Esther's faithfulness and God's grace.

III. POETIC BOOKS.

The poetic books of the OT have much to say about the problem of suffering, the need for praise, and how to live daily in relation with God.

*Job concerns the struggle between the experience of suffering and faith in the love and justice of God. God allowed Satan to test Job by making him suffer. Job's three friends offered various reasons for his suffering. After God spoke to Job, he realized that he must trust in God's sovereign love in the midst of his troubles.

*Psalms was Israel's songbook. It contains sacred songs, poems, and prayers, written by David, Solomon, and others. The poems describe how people felt in times of thanksgiving, joy, sorrow, and trouble.

*Proverbs is the best example of *wisdom literature in the Bible. The theme of this book is stated in Proverbs 1:7: "The fear of the LORD is the beginning of knowledge." This practical book teaches how to obey God in our dealings with one another.

*Ecclesiastes examines all that life has to offer. The author discovered that life apart from God is meaningless and urged

us to fear God and obey him. Only then will we find purpose and satisfaction.

*Song of Songs is a poem about the beauty of *love between a man and a woman. God intends that such love be a normal part of *marriage in his good creation.

IV. MAJOR PROPHETS.

In this context, "major" refers to the length of the books, not to their importance. Through the major prophets, God warned Israel that he would judge her if she did not turn from sin and worship and obey the Lord. These prophets lived from about 740 to 540 B.C.

*Isaiah prophesied from 740 to 680 B.C. and is the most frequently quoted prophet in the NT. The first thirty-nine chapters of Isaiah contain a number of prophetic poems concerning God's impending judgment against foreign nations and Israel. During Isaiah's ministry, the northern kingdom was taken captive by Assyria. Even Judah was threatened (chs. 36–37), but God miraculously protected his people. Chapters 40–66, sometimes called the Book of Comfort, reveal the return of the people from Exile in Babylon, the coming of the *Messiah, and everlasting deliverance for God's people.

*Jeremiah was the last prophet God sent to Judah before she fell to the Babylonians and Jerusalem was destroyed. Jeremiah announced God's coming judgment and called the people to repent and submit to God.

*Lamentations is a *funeral song (probably written by Jeremiah) concerning the destruction of Jerusalem. Although mourning deeply over the city, the prophet knew that God's judgment was a result of the people's sin. In calling the people to repentance, he reminded them that God's compassion never fails.

*Ezekiel was taken to Babylon in 597 B.C. as a captive. There he prophesied to the exiles about the coming destruction of Jerusalem (which occurred in 586 B.C.) and about God's judgment of other nations. Ezekiel emphasized God's lordship over all people and nations. He wrote about a new covenant in which God would give his people a new heart and they would be indwelt by the Holy Spirit.

*Daniel, another prophet exiled to Babylon, served in the king's court but remained faithful to God. His visions depict the future, triumphant outworking of God's redemptive plan for history. Daniel predicted the return from exile, the coming of the *Messiah, and other future historical events.

V. MINOR PROPHETS.

The "minor" prophets are twelve prophets who wrote from about 800 to 400 B.C. during three periods: the period of Assyria's power (*Hosea, *Joel, *Amos, *Obadiah, *Jonah, *Micah), the period of Assyria's decline (*Nahum, *Habakkuk, *Zephaniah), and the post-exilic era (*Haggai, *Zechariah, and *Malachi). These writings are grouped together and referred to as "minor" because they are shorter than those of the major prophets, not because they are of minor importance.

*Hosea was written in the final days of the northern kingdom before the Assyrian captivity. Hosea likened his wife's unfaithfulness to Israel's unfaithfulness to God, her covenant husband and Lord. Hosea proclaimed God's love and compassion for Israel, his bride, and his desire for her repentance.

*Joel, a prophet to Judah, likened God's then-current judgment of a terrible locust plague to the coming *Day of the Lord, when God would judge all people. Joel urged repentance and promised that one day God would pour out his Spirit on all flesh.

*Amos was a man of Judah whom God sent to prophesy against the northern kingdom at the height of its power under *Jeroboam II. Amos accused the wealthy of mistreating the poor, condemned their outward show of worship, and predicted their future *judgment.

*Obadiah predicted God's judgment on the nation of *Edom, the people who were descended from *Esau. In the past this nation had persecuted Israel, but in the future Israel would be delivered; God's kingdom would triumph.

*Jonah, a contemporary of Amos, was sent by God to warn the people of *Nineveh to repent. Nineveh was the capital of Assyria, Israel's main enemy. Because of Jonah's preaching, the Ninevites repented. This taught Jonah that God loves all people, not just Israel.

*Micah prophesied the downfall of the northern kingdom and future judgment on disobedient Judah. Micah predicted that glory would return to *Zion through the coming of the Messiah.

*Nahum predicted the downfall of Nineveh, the capital of Assyria, as God's judgment for her cruelty. The prediction was fulfilled in 612 B.C. when Babylon conquered Assyria.

*Habakkuk, a prophet to Judah, learned that God would use Babylon to punish wicked Judah and then in turn would judge Babylon. Habakkuk concluded that no matter what happened, he would trust in God's unfailing love and faithfulness.

*Zephaniah was a prophet in Jerusalem during the reign of Josiah. He announced the coming of the Day of the Lord, when God would punish Judah and the nations, and prophesied a future restoration of Israel.

*Haggai, a contemporary of Zechariah, encouraged the Jews who had returned from exile to finish rebuilding the temple. Haggai promised that God once again would fill the temple with his glory, as he had in the days of Solomon.

*Zechariah was another prophet who returned from exile and whose apocalyptic visions (1:7–6:8) served as an encouragement to God's people to complete the temple. The final chapters of this book (9–14) are visions of the Messiah's future coming, his rejection, and his ultimate victory.

*Malachi rebuked the Jews for their careless worship and urged them to return to God and obey his law. Malachi predicted the coming of the Messiah, who would cleanse and purify his people.

THE TIME BETWEEN THE TESTAMENTS

I. HISTORY.

Great changes occurred within the nation of Israel after being conquered and subjected to different world powers. Many of these changes took place during the approximately four hundred years that separate Nehemiah from the birth of Christ, a time commonly known as the intertestamental period (c. 432 to 5 B.C.). (See Intertestamental Period.)

Following their return from Babylon, the Jews enjoyed relative religious freedom under *Persian rule. *Alexander the Great conquered Palestine in 332 B.C. and began a process known as Hellenization. Alexander wanted to unite his empire by spreading the language and culture of *Greece to every country he had conquered. When Alexander died in 323 B.C., his empire was divided among his generals. Two of these generals founded dynasties that controlled Palestine—the *Ptolemies of Egypt followed by the

*Seleucids of Syria and Mesopotamia. (See **Greece; Persia; Ptolemy; Seleucids.**) Under the Ptolemies, the Jews were allowed to practice their own religion. Even when the Seleucids took control in 198 B.C., the Jews still enjoyed religious freedom. *Antiochus Epiphanes (175– 164 B.C.) drastically changed this policy. He decided to unite his failing kingdom by forcibly Hellenizing the Jews. In order to destroy the national identity and religion of the Jews, Antiochus forbade the Jews to circumcise their children. He destroyed as many copies of the OT as he could find, erected a statue of Zeus in the Jerusalem temple, and sacrificed a pig on the altar.

A Jewish family known as the *Maccabees led the opposition to Antiochus. A priest named Mattathias killed an official of Antiochus and destroyed the Greek altar. This started the Maccabean revolt, a 24-year war (166–142 B.C.). Mattathias and his five sons (Judas [Maccabeus], Jonathan, Simon, John, and Eleazar) led the revolt from the hills. After Mattathias died and his sons Eleazar and John were killed in the fighting, the revolt was led by his remaining sons: Judas, Jonathan, and Simon. Eventually Simon was able to attain Judah's independence in 142 B.C., which lasted until 63 B.C. As both high priest and civil governor he ruled Judah until his death.

After Simon's death, his sons, Israel's new leaders, became very attached to Greek culture. They looked with disfavor on those pious Jews who had previously supported the Maccabean cause. When a civil war broke out over the succession to the throne, Rome intervened. In 63 B.C. Pompey conquered Jerusalem, massacred the priests in the temple, and entered the Most Holy Place. The Jews would neither forgive nor forget this sacrilege.

II. LITERATURE.

The Apocrypha is a collection of fifteen books, most of which were written during the intertestamental period. These books provide valuable information about the history and beliefs of this period and include a history of the Maccabean revolt, additions to biblical books such as Esther and Daniel, legends, and wisdom literature. Frequently, apocryphal writings contain exaggerated stories and contradict the teachings of Scripture. Jews did not accept these works as canonical but understood them as popular, distinctive, and important religious writings. Jerome placed them in a separate section in his Latin Vulgate, which shows that

the church of his day did not accept them as canonical but did accept them as more important than other noncanonical writings. Although the church disagreed over the value and place of these writings, the Apocrypha continued to be used until the Reformation. Protestants recognized as canonical only those OT books that were part of the Jewish canon and those NT books that long had been accepted by the church. At the Council of Trent (1545– 63), however, the Roman Catholic Church accepted twelve of the apocryphal books as canonical.

III. SOCIAL DEVELOPMENTS.

During the intertestamental period a number of important developments occurred that changed the way Jews worshiped. These changes are important for our understanding of the time of Jesus.

In Palestine, Greek culture influenced the *Sadducees, a group of wealthy priests who were loyal to the Roman government. They are understood to have accepted only the *Pentateuch as God's Word. They did not believe in the resurrection of the dead, in *angels, or in spirits. Although few in number, the Sadducees were the most powerful Jewish political party in Palestine. Usually the high priest was chosen from among the Sadducees.

During the Exile the Jews assembled for worship and the study of God's Word (Ezek 8:1; 14:1; 20:1). Although they could not offer sacrifices at the temple in Jerusalem, they tried to live lives that were pleasing to God by obeying his laws and by offering prayers instead of and in place of sacrifices. Sometime after the Exile, Jewish assemblies developed into *synagogues, an institution that spread throughout the Roman Empire wherever Jews were found. Each synagogue had a copy of the Hebrew Bible in the form of a scroll, which was kept in a wooden box. At the synagogue, the people prayed, worshiped, and listened to the reading of God's Word. These services emphasized a personal relationship with God.

The *Pharisees were the strictest and most important group of Jews. They emphasized rigid and complete obedience to the law, which for them included the OT law and their own interpretations, traditions, and laws. Thus in their teachings and requirements, the Pharisees added laws to those found in the OT. The Pharisees were separatists. They hated the Romans and the influence of Greek thought. They emphasized the importance of the nation of Israel. They felt superior to anyone who did not follow their beliefs and kept themselves separate from Gentiles and from Jews who were not Pharisees.

The scribes as a well-defined group developed in the days following the Exile when Ezra the scribe taught God's law to the Jews who returned to Palestine. The scribes were learned men who spent their time studying God's laws, copying the Scripture, and teaching the common people. Over the years their interpretations and traditions became as important to them as God's Word itself. Because they were considered experts in the interpretation of the law, they served as judges.

THE NEW TESTAMENT

I. *GOSPELS.

The first four books of the New Testament recount the life of Christ—his ministry, death, and resurrection. Each gospel depicts Jesus' life and ministry from a particular viewpoint, for a particular audience, and for a particular purpose. Matthew, Mark, and Luke are called the Synoptic Gospels ("seen together"), because many of the same events and teachings appear in all three. John often relates events and sayings of Jesus not found in the other three.

*Matthew wrote his gospel for Jewish readers to show how Jesus fulfilled Old Testament prophecy and to prove by this that Jesus was the promised Messiah and King.

*Mark, the shortest gospel, was written by *John Mark for *Gentile readers and includes material received from *Peter. This gospel is a fast-moving, vivid report of Jesus' ministry from his *baptism through the *resurrection. It emphasizes Jesus' actions rather than his teachings.

*Luke was a Gentile physician who wrote his gospel for educated Gentiles, perhaps for those who had been associated with the synagogues but who had not converted to Judaism. Luke presented a complete, orderly account of Christ's life from his *birth to his *ascension. Luke emphasized the works and teachings of Jesus that explain the way of *salvation and the universal appeal of the Gospel.

*John, which is usually understood to have been written by the apostle John, is a more reflective gospel that focuses on Jesus as the Christ, the *Son of God. John wrote so that his readers might "believe that Jesus is the Christ" and therefore have life in his name (20:30–31). John included many details not found in the other Gospels.

II. HISTORY.

*Acts was written by Luke as the second volume of his two-part work

Luke-Acts. Acts is an account of the early church as it grew from a small, frightened band of disciples to a group of believers spread throughout the Roman Empire. Acts centers around the work of Peter (with the Jews) and Paul (with the Gentiles).

III. *EPISTLES.

The twenty-one epistles of the New Testament were written by five or six authors to individual churches, to groups of churches, or to individuals. These authors are *James, John, *Jude, Paul, Peter, and the author of Hebrews. Paul wrote the greatest number (thirteen or fourteen) of the epistles. His writings include much teaching about the Christian faith, as well as encouragement to put that faith into practice in daily living.

*Romans is one of the most important books in the Bible because it comprehensively explains God's plan of salvation for Jews and Gentiles (1:16–17). In Romans, Paul taught the great doctrines of Christianity in a systematic fashion.

*First Corinthians was written by Paul to the church at Corinth during his third missionary journey. The Corinthian church was plagued with problems in Christian conduct. Paul emphasized the Corinthians' need to grow in *sanctification—the continuing development of a holy, Godlike character.

*Second Corinthians was written as a response to untrue accusations made against Paul by false teachers. In this intensely personal epistle, Paul defended his apostleship and urged the Corinthians to prepare for his upcoming visit by completing their collection for the church in Jerusalem and by dealing with the false teachers.

*Galatians was written by Paul to the churches in Asia Minor to remind new Christians that salvation comes by faith alone in Jesus Christ, not by obedience to the Jewish ceremonial law, as was falsely being taught by some. Paul urged his readers to live lives controlled by the

Spirit, lives that produce the fruits of righteousness.

*Ephesians was probably written to a group of churches in Asia Minor that included Ephesus. In this epistle, Paul focused on the doctrines of union with Christ and the church as the body of Christ. Paul urged Christians to achieve unity in doctrinal and practical matters by speaking the truth in love and by standing against Satan, the Christian's enemy.

*Philippians is a joyous epistle that Paul wrote to the church in Philippi to thank them for their gifts and to encourage them to stand firm when persecuted. In this epistle, Paul reminded the Philippians of Christ's humility and suffering on their behalf, and he urged them to rejoice with him in the Lord.

*Colossians was written to the church at Colosse to correct two types of false teaching: (1) a Jewish emphasis on ceremonial law and feast days and (2) a philosophy that included claims to secret knowledge and the worship of angels. In contrast to the emptiness of human philosophy, Paul emphasized the complete adequacy of Christ—Jesus alone deserves our worship and obedience. (See False Teaching.)

*First Thessalonians is one of Paul's earliest letters and was written to a church that he started on his second missionary journey. In this epistle, Paul encouraged the persecuted young Christians to live godly lives, and he corrected some of the false ideas they had, especially ideas concerning Christ's second coming.

*Second Thessalonians was written shortly after First Thessalonians and deals with the same topics. Paul encouraged the Thessalonians to remain true to Christ, even when persecuted. He also provided additional teaching about *eschatology (the doctrine of last things). He described the *apostasy that will precede Christ's coming in judgment and urged the Thessalonians to stand firm in the faith.

*Pastoral Letters. First and Second Timothy and Titus are called Pastoral Letters because they contain Paul's encouragement and instruction to *Timothy and *Titus, who were responsible for overseeing the churches in *Ephesus and on *Crete.

First Timothy is a personal letter to Timothy about the administration of the Ephesian church. Paul wrote it between his first and second imprisonments. It includes a discussion of the qualifications for elders, instructions for conducting worship, and warnings against false teachers.

Second Timothy, which was written from prison, is Paul's last known letter. In this letter, Paul encouraged Timothy to remain faithful in the face of increasing persecution and false teaching and to preach sound doctrine and live a godly life.

Titus also received instructions from Paul about the qualifications for church leaders, as well as warnings about false teachers who professed to know God but who denied him by their deeds. Paul emphasized the need for believers to live holy lives (sanctification).

*Philemon is a short letter in which Paul urged a fellow Christian, Philemon, to accept the return of his runaway slave Onesimus, who had become his brother in Christ.

*Hebrews is an unsigned letter, and various suggestions have been made as to its authorship (Barnabas, Apollos, Priscilla). Hebrews was written to Jewish Christians to remind them that Christ was greater than angels, Moses, the Old Testament priests, and the Law. Jesus is the highest revelation of God. The author urged his readers to be faithful to their commitment to Christ in the face of persecution.

*James was probably the half brother of Jesus. He reminded Christians that they must do more than just say they belong to Christ—they must live and act accordingly. True saving faith will produce Christian actions.

First Peter is Peter's message of hope to encourage Christians who were suffering persecution from outsiders. Peter encouraged his readers to behave in a godly manner, knowing that their salvation is certain, and to look for the glory that is to be revealed.

Second Peter is a more general letter than 1 Peter. It warns Christians of the dangers of false teachers inside the church, encourages them in their Christian growth, and exhorts them to be watchful because Christ is coming again.

First John was written to assure believers of the reality of the *Incarnation and to warn against false teachers who claimed to be perfect (though they were immoral) and who taught that Jesus was not really a man. John stressed the need for Christians to love God and each other.

Second John was addressed either to a church or to a particular woman and encourages Christians to love one another and to beware of false teachers.

Third John was written to Gaius, a

leader in the church, to praise him for welcoming traveling teachers sent by John. Another leader, Diotrephes, rejected both John and these teachers.

Jude was probably written by one of Jesus' half brothers. Jude warned his readers to beware of false teachers who taught that being saved by grace meant that people could live any way they pleased. Jude urged Christians to keep themselves in God's love until Christ returns.

* Revelation, the last book in the Bible, is the only New Testament book that is primarily prophetic. Revelation belongs to the category of apocalyptic literature because John received his message by means of a vision. John wrote to encourage Christians to refuse to give in to outside pressures. In the future final showdown between God and Satan, Christians must stand firm against Satan's persecution. Christians will be vindicated when Christ returns, destroys the wicked, fully establishes his kingdom, and ushers in the new heaven and new earth. (See **Eschatology.**)

THE LANDS OF THE BIBLE

I. * ISRAEL

A. Names. Different names have been used to describe the land in which most of the events described in the Bible occur. The oldest name, * Canaan (Gen 10:19; 12:6), came from the people who originally occupied the land, the Canaanites. Later, God gave this country to his chosen people, Israel, and it came to be called by that name. After Solomon's death, the nation split into the northern ten tribes, which retained the name Israel (or * Ephraim), and the southern kingdom, which was called Judah. Later, the Romans divided the land into the provinces of * Judea, * Samaria, and * Galilee. Finally, about the fifth century A.D., the land of the Bible came to be called * Palestine, a word that originally meant "land of the * Philistines" and that referred to the people who once lived along its SE coast. Archaeologists have shown that people have inhabited this land since the earliest times. * Jericho, for example, is the oldest continuously lived-in city in the world. (See **Archaeology.**)

B. Geography. Although its borders have varied somewhat, Palestine is small—approximately 150 miles long and between 25 and 85 miles wide—about the size of Vermont. This land of contrasts has four distinct geographical areas: the coastal plain, the hills and mountains, the Jordan Valley, and the Transjordan.

During biblical times, the edge of the coastal plain was lined with high sand dunes that prevented streams from flowing into the ocean. This caused swamps and marshes to form during the rainy season. The straight coast has no natural harbors.

The coastal plain gradually gives way to the hills and mountains of the central region, which includes three mountain ranges. The northern range begins with Mt. * Hermon (the tallest mountain at 9,232 feet) and the hills of Galilee. The central, or Samaritan, range includes Mt * Ebal (3,077 feet) and Mt. * Gerizim (2,849 feet). The southern, or Judean, range includes * Jerusalem (2,592 feet) and * Hebron (3,370 feet). Two important valleys that cut across these ranges are the Valley of * Jezreel in the north and the Valley of * Sorek in the south. In biblical times, most of Israel's cities and people were located in the mountainous regions and valleys.

The eastern slopes of the mountains drop sharply down into the Jordan Valley, which itself is part of a deep fault known as the Great Rift. The Jordan Valley includes the lowest areas in Palestine. From the Sea of * Galilee (650 feet below sea level) in the north, the * Jordan River flows 200 miles south to the * Dead Sea, which is 1,286 feet below sea level — the lowest point on the surface of the earth! East of the Jordan Valley, the land rises to the plateau of the * Transjordan area. (See **Geography.**)

C. Climate. The single most important factor in the Palestinian climate is rainfall. Palestine has both rainy and dry seasons, the rainy seasons occurring in autumn and spring. The autumn rains begin in mid-October, with the heaviest rains occurring in December and January. The spring rains occur in April and are necessary for the development of crops. During the summer, dew and morning mist provide needed moisture along the coastal plains and in the central region. The amount of annual rainfall depends on winds from the west and varies from year to year. The coast, the western slopes of the central hills, the north (Galilee), and the Transjordan receive most of the rainfall. The eastern slopes and the south are drier and include deserts. In biblical times, the best *farming land was found in Galilee, the Valley of Jezreel, and the western and central regions.

For such a small region, Palestine has a surprisingly wide range of temperatures. Not only does the temperature vary from noon to midnight by as much as 36° (20° C.) but from region to region. The Jordan Valley is the hottest region, and its tropical temperatures can reach 122° (50° C.) in the summer. The coastal regions tend to have a more moderate climate, and the mountainous areas, such as Jerusalem, are warmer. (See **Climate; Weather.**)

D. *Plants. Plant life in Palestine has changed a great deal since the time of Genesis. At one time, thick forests covered Galilee and the Transjordan, and the coastal plains consisted of sand dunes, salt marshes, and forests. The fertile plains of the northwest and central areas provided the best land for *agriculture.

Palestine's three basic types of plant life (desert, tropical, and subtropical) correspond to the three different types of climate. Subtropical trees include oaks, terebinths, carob, box, and some pine trees. Tropical plants, such as the palm tree, grow in the hotter temperatures of the Jordan Valley. The acacia, broom tree, nettle, and thorns are found in the desert.

When the spring rains come, the land blossoms with flowers, such as the crocus and anemone, but these quickly fade and die (Matt 6:28). In biblical times, three main fruit-bearing trees were so characteristic of the land that they were used to symbolize Israel: the olive, the fig, and the vine. Wheat, barley, and millet were Israel's primary grain crops and a chief source of food. In biblical times, vegetables such as beans, lentils, and cucumbers were cultivated. Because of its poor soil and climate, the land rarely produced grasses suitable for grazing animals. (See **Plants.**)

E. *Animals. Farming and raising animals were so important in OT times that a man's wealth was calculated by counting the number of cows, horses, sheep, oxen, and camels that he owned. These tame animals provided milk, meat, transportation, tent coverings, and clothing. Some of these animals were offered as sacrifices in the temple or on pagan altars. Palestine was the home of a large number

of wild animals; the lion, leopard, wolf, jackal, fox, rabbit, and deer. The dog was almost wild and was described as a snarling, dirty creature. (See **Animals.**)

Over fifty kinds of *birds are mentioned in the Bible. Birds of prey, such as the eagle, vulture, owl, and hawk, were found in Israel. The heron, bittern, osprey, partridge, dove, pigeon, stork, and sparrow were common. Numerous kinds of fish similar to those found in Egypt were plentiful, especially in Galilee, and were an important source of food. The insect population included bees, grasshoppers, and locusts. The Book of Joel describes a terrible locust invasion. (See **Birds.**)

II. ISRAEL'S NEIGHBORS.

Palestine was located between the two greatest early civilizations in the Mediterranean area—Mesopotamia and Egypt. The trade routes that linked these two civilizations ran north and south through Palestine. Additionally, Palestine offered the only east-west land route between the Mediterranean Sea and the deserts of Arabia. Therefore Palestine was an important piece of real estate that was desired and fought over by many world powers.

The Sumerian culture forms the background of the early chapters of Genesis. The Sumerians were a *Semitic people who lived in the land of the *Tigris and *Euphrates rivers. They developed the first truly independent culture, which dates from 4500 B.C. The Sumerians were quite advanced. They developed writing (about 3200 B.C.) and were known for their literature, law, and science. *Ur, the largest Sumerian city, was a center of learning and included libraries, schools, and numerous temples to pagan gods. Abraham came from Ur.

Egyptian civilization, which dates from about 3000 B.C., centered around the *Nile River. The Nile, which flows from south to north through Egypt, provided the Egyptians with a central means of transportation. And the Nile and its fertile valley allowed the Egyptians to be the breadbasket of the ancient world. Because Egypt was organized around a single ruler, known as a *pharaoh, who held supreme political power and who was considered to be a god, it was possible for massive buildings (pyramids) to be constructed. Egypt was the birthplace of the nation of Israel. Later, as Egyptian power declined, Egypt sometimes allied herself with Israel or even invaded the land. (See **Egypt.**)

The *Canaanites were the primary

racial group in Palestine at the time of the Conquest and were composed of several different tribes, including the Jebusites, Amorites, and Hivites. The Canaanites lived in small city-states or fortress towns. Israel failed to conquer the Canaanites completely, as God had commanded them to do, and absorbed the remaining Canaanites into the nation. Later the pagan religion of these people, especially the worship of Baal, had a disastrous influence on Israel. (See Idols; Idolatry.)

Originally the *Philistines were a seafaring people, perhaps from *Crete, who settled in five major cities (*Gaza, *Ashkelon, *Gath, *Ashdod, and *Ekron) along the south coast of Palestine. The Philistines were more advanced than the Israelites and were skilled metal workers. Their superiority in weaponry and tool making helped them dominate Israel during the period of the *judges. The Philistines were finally defeated by *David. (See Philistines.)

*Syria is the region to the north of Israel that the Bible refers to as *Aram. Syria is a fertile land of many rivers. The most important Syrian cities were *Damascus and *Antioch. Syria's relationship with Israel was characterized by wars, alliances, and periods of peace. (See Syria.)

From the eighth century B.C., five great world powers successively dominated Palestine: Assyria, Babylon, Persia, Greece, and Rome. Assyria, the first great power, was located in northern *Mesopotamia. After extended warfare, Assyria conquered the northern kingdom (Israel) in 722 B.C. The Assyrians were a cruel military power who subdued conquered nations by deporting their peoples and making them resettle outside of their homelands. This policy of forced deportation and resettlement destroyed the national identities of conquered peoples. The Assyrian's capital was *Nineveh, the city to which God sent the prophet Jonah. The Assyrians were conquered by the Babylonians in 612 B.C. (See Assyria.)

The second world power to control Palestine was Babylon. The Babylonian king *Nebuchadnezzar conquered Assyria and the southern kingdom of Judah in 586 B.C. Many Jews (including the prophets *Ezekiel and *Daniel) were deported and exiled to Babylon. The Babylonians were conquered by the Persians in 539 B.C. (See Babylon.)

The third world power to control Palestine was Persia. The Persian Empire extended from the Tigris Valley on the west and south to the Indus Valley on the east, an area that includes most of modern Iran. Because they encouraged subject nations to continue their own religion and culture, the Persians permitted the Jews to return to their land and rebuild the temple. The Persians were conquered by Alexander the Great in 331 B.C. (See Persia.)

The fourth world power to control Palestine was Greece (*Grecia). *Alexander the Great began this empire by conquering most of the then-known world. Alexander's policy of spreading Greek culture and language to all parts of his empire greatly affected Israel. After Alexander's death, his four generals divided the territory he had conquered. At first, Palestine was controlled by *Ptolemy of Egypt and then by the *Seleucids. (See Greece; Ptolemy; Seleucids.)

The final world power to conquer Palestine was Rome. This occurred in 63 B.C., when the Roman general Pompey made Syria a Roman province. Jesus Christ was born during the reign of the Roman emperor *Augustus. The worldwide peace and the vast network of roads that resulted from Roman rule enabled early Christians to spread the Gospel throughout the Roman Empire. Many Jews continually resisted Roman oppression. Jewish resistance finally resulted in the Jewish Revolt against the Roman occupation of Palestine. In A.D. 70 the Romans crushed the revolt and destroyed the temple of Jerusalem. (See Roman Empire.)

THE PEOPLE OF THE BIBLE

I. THE HOME.

In biblical times, the typical *house looked much like a box. It had a flat roof and thick walls made of stone or brick. (See Building Materials.) When entering such a house from the street, a person would pass through a *door into a small courtyard that often served as a kitchen. A second door opened onto a living room that had two small bedrooms behind it. In the homes of common people, the floors were packed *clay. In the homes of wealthy persons, the floors were *stone. Doors were made of wood, cloth, skins, or woven rushes. The windows were small and high. There were no chimneys, so smoke from the indoor stoves had to escape through windows or doors. In hot weather, the flat roofs were used for sleeping, extra living space, work, and worship. Sometimes an outside staircase led to an enclosed area on the roof called the "upper room." Houses might be part of a city wall, or they might share a wall with a neighboring house. In cold weather a family's animals might stay in the lower part of their living room. Furniture consisted of a table for eating, mats or beds for sleeping, and sometimes seats or couches. (See **House; Furniture.**)

Men and women wore similar kinds of clothing, though the women's *dress tended to be more colorful, and there were differences in embroidery and needlework. In cooler weather, both men and women wore long cotton undershirts that reached to the knees or even to the feet. The close-fitting tunic-coat was made of wool that was lined with cotton (so it would not irritate the skin) and had either long or short sleeves. These tunics were long, came in a variety of colors, and were tied at the waist with a wide sash called a girdle. Cloth girdles also formed a kind of pocket for carrying things; leather girdles were used by soldiers and herders to carry swords, daggers, or valuables. The cloak or mantle often was worn outside other clothes and was used both as a coat and as a blanket in cold weather.

Poor men wore cotton or wool caps. Others wore turbans of linen wrapped around the head or head scarves that were folded into triangles and tied with a cord. Women wore head scarves or shawls that often were pinned over a stiff cap and decorated with pearls, silver, or ornaments. Sometimes these scarves were used to form a veil that covered part of the face and upper *body. Sandals were made of stiff leather for longer wear, and shoes were made of soft leather for greater comfort. (See **Dress.**)

Both men and women wore *jewelry such as earrings, nose rings, finger rings, bracelets, and anklets made of gold and silver and set with precious stones. (See also **Jewel, Jewelry; Minerals.**)

Personal hygiene and cleanliness were an important part of worship for Jewish people. The priests had to wash themselves before offering sacrifices. When people or things became unclean, they had to be washed to be considered clean again. Although public baths did not become common until the Greek and Roman periods, people sometimes washed in streams or in fountains. In the hot, dusty Palestinian climate, people washed their feet before they came into a home, and they washed their faces and hands before they ate. (See **Personal Hygiene.**)

Because *water was scarce and people took few *baths, *ointments and perfumes were frequently used as deodorants. Originally these sweet-smelling spices and oils were used in the temple as incense during worship. They also were used to embalm the dead. Women used *cosmetics to paint their eyes and to make themselves more attractive in other ways, though the Bible often discourages the use of cosmetics. (See **Water.**)

Care of the *hair was considered important. Unkempt hair indicated mourning or sadness. Some people known as *Nazirites made vows that involved not cutting their hair. In OT times, long hair was a sign of beauty for men and women. In NT times, men's hair was shorter, and the women's longer hair often was braided and adorned. *Beards were common among the Jews and accepted as a sign of dignity; in fact, priests and Nazirites were forbidden to shave. (See **Hair.**)

The most common *food for an Israelite was bread, which was made from wheat or barley. Roasted meat, especially *lamb or kid, was served for *feasts or for religious celebrations. Because there was no refrigeration, people did not drink much milk, and meat had to be eaten soon after the animal was killed. Milk from cows and goats was used to make cheese and yogurt. Beans and lentils were used to make soups. Grapes, the most common fruit, were often used to make wine. Jews usually drank water with their meals. Olives were made into oil that was used in cooking. Figs, pomegranates, melons, dates, oranges, and lemons were eaten raw.

Israelites generally ate two *meals a day. The times these meals were served varied greatly. The first meal, which usually was lighter than the second, was served any time between early morning and noon. The second meal was the evening meal and usually was eaten at night. During this meal, guests might be entertained at a *banquet or a *feast. The wealthy enjoyed meat, but, except for special occasions, it was too expensive for common people. The main diet of the poor consisted of bread made from barley. Women and girls prepared meals over open *hearths or in firepots, using various *spices to add flavor to the dishes they prepared. Different types of vessels were used for cooking and eating. Generally speaking, knives, forks, and spoons were not used. The main dish was cooked in a large pot into which everyone dipped their bread. In OT times, people usually sat on the ground to eat. In NT times, they stretched out on the floor or on *couches around three sides of a large, low table. (See Food; Vessel.)

II. THE *FAMILY.

In Abraham's time, the extended family included the husband, wife, children, grandparents, *uncles, aunts, cousins, servants, friends, and visiting guests. God called Abraham's family to be his special people, the Jews. From the twelve sons of Jacob, Abraham's grandson, God formed the nation of Israel. Members of a family in OT times called each other *brothers and sisters and worked together to support, protect, and provide for their extended family, thus appearing more like a small village. During this period, the Jews followed some of the marriage practices of the surrounding nations and had more than one wife, a practice known as polygamy. This often led to problems.

In NT times, families were smaller and consisted of a husband, a wife, and children. During this period, families often lived in a small house in a city. Jesus encouraged family members to respect and love one another. The NT uses the family relationship to describe the close and intimate relationship Christians have with God. (See Family.)

In biblical times, *marriage customs were quite different from what they are today. Marriages usually were arranged by the parents. The future husband would pay a price for his bride (mohar), and the future father-in-law would provide a dowry. These fees could be paid either in money, goods, or labor. Once the couple became engaged, they were legally bound to each other, though they did not live together. After a period of time (perhaps a year), the *wedding took place. The groom brought his bride and her bridesmaids to his parents' home. The whole town helped to celebrate the wedding by enjoying a feast that lasted up to a week. (See Marriage.)

The husband was the head of the household—the father, teacher, and provider. He was responsible for the spiritual and physical welfare of his family. The wife was subject to her husband and was considered his property. She was responsible for preparing the meals and making clothing. Her role as a mother

was especially important, for *children were seen as a sign of blessing from God. Children were to obey their *parents. The *firstborn child belonged to God and received a double share in the *inheritance. Girls helped their mothers with household chores or in caring for animals; boys learned their work or trade from their fathers. A man could *divorce his wife in certain circumstances, but a wife could not divorce her husband. Usually, however, Jewish families were strong units that were not easily broken. Not only were parents to help their children develop skills necessary for living, they were also constantly to teach their children about God's great acts in history (e.g., the Exodus) and what God required of them. Learning always centered around God, his works, and his Word. After the Exile, *synagogue *schools taught boys to read, write, and understand the OT.

*Diseases and sickness were common. Often the Bible describes the symptoms rather than naming the disease. Health problems affected both the *mind (epilepsy, madness) and the *body (skin infections, fevers, plagues, blindness, deafness, etc.). To help prevent the spread of disease, God's laws provided special instructions about washing and the preparation of foods. Oil mixed with herbs, ointments, and wine were used as medicines. (See Health.)

When *death occurred, the family and friends *mourned the loss of their loved one. Because of the hot climate, the *funeral took place quickly. *Burial preparations included washing the body, anointing it with perfume and ointments, and wrapping it in *grave clothes. The body was then placed in a *tomb or cave. Israel rejected every form of worship of the dead, and Israelite funeral rites never included *magic. The OT says little about the fate of the dead, though it does teach that dead persons go to a place of shadows called Sheol, and that the righteous dead may look forward to glory (Ps 73:23–24). By the time of the NT, the Pharisees believed in a bodily resurrection. Not until the teaching of Jesus, however, were the concepts of eternal life with God and of bodily resurrection fully developed. (See Death; Magic.)

III. ECONOMIC LIFE.

*Occupations in the Bible mostly centered around the land—farming, fishing, animal tending, and mining. Other jobs included building, government, armies and defense, and religious life. Often people worked at several different jobs to support their families. There were few big businesses—most operated out of the home.

*Farming was both the primary occupation and the oldest one (Adam tended the Garden of Eden). But the dry climate, rocky soil, plant diseases, and insects made farming in Palestine difficult. Farmers had few *tools. Everyone had to help at harvest time. Tending animals (shepherds, herders) and fishing provided food and the raw materials for clothing and tents. Palestine had few *minerals. Near Ezion Geber, iron and copper were mined and worked by metal workers and coppersmiths.

Craftsmen provided goods that were needed for daily life and passed on their trades to their sons. Craftsmen produced clothing (weavers, tailors) and household and agricultural equipment (welders, potters). (See also **Pottery; Vessels; Tools.**) They built and repaired homes and buildings (stonemasons, carpenters, brickmakers), and they provided *jewels and objects used in worship (goldsmiths, jewelers). The lawyers, rabbis, scribes, and judges formed the legal profession. Priests, singers, and musicians assisted in worship and ministry in the temple. Prophets often served as advisers to kings (e.g., Nathan). Israelite government officials and rulers were later replaced by foreign rulers who used their own officers (the NT is full of references to Roman rulers). Soldiers and military officers were occupied with defending Israel. (See **Occupations; Warfare; Weapons.**)

Under Solomon and in cooperation with Tyre and Sidon, Israel began to trade with her neighbors. After Solomon's death, however, this trade declined. Although merchants crossed Palestine on her important trade routes, trade remained largely in the hands of Israel's conquerors, especially the Greeks and the Romans. *Trade guilds in NT times covered all the trades and professions and were largely social in nature. These guilds were often a source of opposition to the early church. (See **Trade and Travel; Weights and Measures.**)

In ancient times, *money was made of metal, often in the shape of jewelry. The first coin mentioned in the OT is the shekel, which means "weight." It was not until 700 B.C. that coins with some imprint or stamp began to be used. At first the Hebrews used the coins of their conquerors—the Assyrians and Babylonians. The NT mentions a Roman coin (denarius), Greek coins (drachma, far-

thing), and Jewish coins (mite, pound, shekel, and talent).

Although banks as we know them did not exist, the money changers in the temple exchanged foreign coins for Jewish currency. The practices of borrowing and lending were covered in some detail in the Mosaic Law—especially to protect the rights of the poor. Jews were not allowed to charge interest (*usury) to each other, though they could do so to foreigners. A *pledge of property or clothing was often given to prove that a *debt would be repaid. The OT law even defined what kind of property could be used as a pledge. The prophets often denounced the rich for their mistreatment of the poor. After the Exile, the OT laws were largely ignored. In NT times usury, *interest, *borrowing, and lending were common. Sometimes people had to sell their children and wives into slavery to pay their debts. (See **Economic Life; Money.**)

IV. POLITICAL LIFE AND THE LAW.

Abraham, the father of the Jewish nation, began his life in the Promised Land living in tents and moving with his family, servants, and animals from place to place. The twelve sons of Jacob, Abraham's grandson, became the twelve tribes of Israel that God later called out of Egypt under the leadership of Moses. Under the leadership of Joshua, Moses' successor, Israel conquered the land of Palestine, and each tribe settled into its separate inheritance, living in small farming communities or villages. Each village contained only 150–200 houses and had no defense. During this time, the Israelites were ruled by *judges whom God raised up to help them defeat their enemies.

Israel was a *theocracy, a nation ruled by God and his law. But the Israelites wanted to have a king such as the other nations had. Although the prophet *Samuel warned Israel about the consequences of having human kings, he anointed Saul and later David as kings of Israel. Under David and his son Solomon, Israel extended her borders and became a powerful nation. During this time, people lived together in *cities that had high walls for protection and *gates that were closed at night.

After Solomon's death, the kingdom divided into two nations (Israel in the north, Judah in the south), each with its own king. The Jews' disobedience to God eventually resulted in the conquest of each kingdom by foreign powers (Israel by Assyria, Judah by Babylon). From the time of those two conquests, Israel was ruled by a succession of empires, each of which appointed its own rulers. The Jews were able to use some of their own officials, and the *priests grew in political power.

Under the Romans, Palestine was allowed a certain amount of self-rule. During Christ's ministry, *Herod Antipas was the king of Galilee, and Judea was governed by *procurators who were appointed by the emperor. There were military leaders in areas where Roman troops were stationed. (See Civil Life; Civil Leaders.) *Taxes were collected from the Jews by the government and by the religious authorities. The first fixed tax was the poll, or temple, tax (a half-shekel), which supported temple worship and continued to be paid during the NT era. The people also gave a tithe, or one-tenth, of their income to support the priests, Levites, and needy people.

It was under Solomon that the Jews first paid taxes to the government. (This was one of the consequences of human kingship that Samuel had warned the Jews about earlier.) These taxes were used to finance Solomon's extensive building program. Taxes continued to be collected by the kings who reigned after Solomon. After Israel was conquered, the Israelites paid taxes to a succession of ruling powers. These taxes were often very high, and their collection was open to abuse. The Romans levied direct taxes on real estate, property, and people (the head tax) and indirect taxes in the form of *custom and town dues. Heavy taxation often led to rebellion. (See Taxes.)

From the time of Moses, judges were elected to settle disputes among the people. The judges used the OT law as the basis for their decisions. After the land was settled, cases were heard at a city's main gate. Following the Exile, a group of professional legal experts known as *scribes arose. The scribes devoted their lives to the study and interpretation of the OT law. Consequently, they were often asked to serve as judges in Jewish courts. Under the Romans, the highest Jewish court was the Sanhedrin, which was located in Jerusalem and was composed of *elders (tribal heads), priests (the family of the chief priest), and scribes (mainly Pharisees). The judgment of the Sanhedrin was final, except in the case of the death penalty, which required the approval of the Roman procurator. The OT includes civil and criminal laws. Civil laws governed marriage, inheritance, the right of the *firstborn, buying and selling, *wages, debts, and interest. Criminal law

specified the punishment that was to be given for certain crimes. The most serious crimes were those against God or against the holiness of God's people, crimes such as *blasphemy, *idolatry, *magic, *murder, and *adultery. (See Civil Law; Crimes; Punishment.)

V. CULTURE.

Because wisdom and understanding come from God, learning and knowledge in Israel centered on the Bible. The Greek idea of knowledge for its own sake was foreign to the Israelites' way of thinking. All teaching and learning focused on the Bible, whether the topic was reading, writing, geography, or history. Other topics were not studied independently but were developed from a religious perspective. For example, *astronomy was used in determining the religious *calendar, and *numbers had a special symbolic value in Jewish writings. The *arts, too, were developed with a religious focus.

Literature was Israel's highest cultural achievement. Hebrew poetry is beautiful and uses concrete examples drawn from daily life. It depicts man's feelings, his longing for a relationship with God, God's redemptive plan, and the glory of the Creation. The Bible contains many different types of literature (*fable, *allegory, gospel, apocalyptic literature, wisdom literature) that focus on man and his relationship to the living God. In its treatment of those topics, the Bible is unsurpassed by any other ancient writings. (See "The Bible as Literature"; also see Bible; Literature.)

*Music also was an important part of Israel's culture. Music was used to celebrate, to mourn, to praise God, and to praise Israel's heroes. David originated Hebrew music and the musical service in the temple. He wrote many psalms (the songs of the Bible) and invented several musical instruments (1 Chron 23:5). The Psalms are the songbook of Israel, but other songs appear throughout the Bible. The temple had an orchestra, and the Levites served as singers and musicians. A variety of different musical instruments were used. (See Music and Musical Terms.) *Dancing and music frequently occurred together. Both children and adults danced, though men and women did not dance together. Dancing was used to celebrate military victories and took place at religious feasts, weddings, and sometimes worship (Ps 149:3).

Israel was forbidden to make images of God (Exod 20:4) and, probably because of that, never developed painting and sculpture. Although *pottery was an important craft, most of Israel's artistic efforts focused on the temple, for example, on the ark of the covenant and on the embroidered curtains. Because *architecture was not very developed in Israel, Solomon imported Phoenician craftsmen to build the temple and his palace. The Greeks produced the most beautiful buildings in the ancient world. Later the Romans borrowed from the Greeks and became famous for their extensive numbers of arches, theaters, and marketplaces throughout their empire. (See Architecture; Art.)

Israel's entertainment centered on her religious feasts, though some ancient board *games and children's games are alluded to in the Bible. The Greeks introduced *races and other kinds of athletic competition to Israel, but the cruel and violent Roman games were unknown. Because Israel produced no drama, there were no *theaters until Herod the Great introduced them at Caesarea and Jerusalem. Because they were so large, these open-air structures were often built on the sides of hills and were used for public assemblies. (See Entertainment.)

WORSHIP AND RELATION WITH GOD

I. THE OLD TESTAMENT–ISRAEL'S FAITH.

A. The Covenant. The covenant was the heart of God's love relationship with his people in the Old Testament. In ancient times, a *covenant was a treaty between two parties. There were two kinds of covenants: a voluntary agreement between equals (as with David and Jonathan, 1 Sam 18:3) and treaties of loyalty between a great king and a lesser king (his vassal). In the Bible, covenants between God and his people are always of the second type. God always dictates the terms of his covenants, which assert his sovereignty and kingship and the people's obligation of faith and obedience. God's plan to redeem his people is progressively revealed through his covenants with *Abraham, *Moses, and *David. Under the terms of the Abrahamic covenant, God promised Abraham a land (Canaan), a nation (Israel), and that he would be a blessing to all people (Gen 15:9–21; 17). Abraham believed God's promises and faithfully obeyed God by submitting to the covenant sign of *circumcision, an act that symbolized separation from sin and holiness toward God. Under the terms of the Mosaic covenant (Exod 19–24), God promised to be Israel's God—her protector and defender—and Israel swore to be God's faithful people. Obedience meant blessing and life (Deut 30:19–20); disobedience would result in curses and death. Under the terms of the Davidic covenant, God promised David's family an eternal throne and kingdom (2 Sam 7:5–16). This covenant pointed to the future Messiah, David's greater Son Jesus, who would finally fulfill all God's promises of redemption. (See Covenant; Judaism; Old Testament.)

The *Law (Torah) (See "The Bible as Literature") defined the substance of God's covenant with Moses and Israel. The *Ten Commandments, which state one's basic duties to God and to one's neighbor, are the general principles of this covenant. After giving the Ten Commandments, God gave a number of specific regulations about worship and about his people's political and social lives. Circumcision was to remind the Israelites of their dedication to God. Although circumcision was a sign of the Abrahamic covenant, it was mandatory under the Mosaic covenant as well (Exod 4:25–26; 12:44, 48), since in part it symbolized belonging to God. The specific sign of the Mosaic covenant was the *Sabbath (31:12–17). The food laws stated what kind of animals, birds, and fish could be eaten and how these were to be killed and cooked. The food laws became especially important as a test of loyalty during the time of the Maccabees. (See Law.)

B. *Worship and Ritual.

1. Places of Worship. God gave specific instructions for building the *tabernacle, the place where he dwelt among his people. This tent could be moved wherever the people went and was used for worship and sacrifice until the time of Solomon. It contained the *ark of the covenant, in which Moses placed the two tablets of the Law. On top of the ark was a golden atonement cover known as the mercy seat, with a winged cherubim at either end. This symbolized the exact place where God was enthroned.

God's permanent residence was the *temple in Jerusalem, which Solomon built in the tenth century B.C. (1 Kings 6–8). The temple was small and resembled the tabernacle. When Babylon conquered Judah, the temple was destroyed in 586 B.C. Zerubbabel and other returned exiles rebuilt a simple and less expensive version of Solomon's temple in 515 B.C. Continued invasions robbed the temple of its furnishings, and it fell into disrepair. Piece by piece, Herod the Great began rebuilding the temple in 20 B.C. This restoration was completed in A.D. 64, but the temple was completely destroyed in A.D. 70 by Roman armies. (See **Jewish Places of Worship; Temple.**)

During the Exile the Jews gathered in synagogues to pray and read the Scriptures. Synagogues served as centers of worship, education, and justice. Following the destruction of the temple in Jerusalem, synagogues became the focus of Jewish religious life. (See the section on the intertestamental period.)

2. Ritual—Acts of Worship. Although sacrifice is as old as Cain and Abel, it was not until the covenant at Sinai that God defined the nature of sacrifice and the various kinds of sacrifices that he required. There are several kinds of sacrifices: sin, guilt, grain, fellowship, and burnt offerings. In sin and guilt offerings, the sacrificial animal provided a way for God to forgive sin: the animal died in place of the sinner and as a substitute for his sin. The animal's shed blood (*death) meant life for the offerer and pointed toward the final fulfillment in Christ, the once-for-all Sacrifice who brings forgiveness and salvation to all who trust in him. Grain and fellowship offerings expressed gratitude and thankfulness to God for his provision. Burnt offerings expressed devotion and wholehearted dedication to God. (See **Sacrifices and Offerings.**)

The *feasts and festivals of the Hebrew calendar reminded Israel of God's past mercies and of her need for forgiveness. They also looked forward to Israel's future deliverance. God commanded these special times of joy and gladness to focus the nation's attention on him. God gave the Jews the Sabbath, a weekly holy day set aside for rest and worship, as a sign of the Mosaic covenant (Exod 31:12–17). The Sabbath was celebrated on the seventh day of the week by families and by small groups worshiping together. After the Exile, the Sabbath was celebrated in the synagogue.

Each year every male Jew was required to attend three pilgrim feasts in Jerusalem. These were the Passover, the Feast of Pentecost, and the Feast of Tabernacles. Passover, the most important feast, was to remind the Jews that God had delivered them from slavery in Egypt and had formed them into his own nation. God "passed over" the houses of the Jews because their doorposts had been smeared with blood, but he brought judgment and death to the unprotected homes of the Egyptians. Passover was celebrated in mid-April, along with the Feast of Unleavened Bread, which lasted seven days. Jesus' last supper with his disciples was a Passover meal. At that meal Jesus gave the Passover new meaning by identifying himself as the Lamb of God who takes away the sins of the world. The Feast of Pentecost (also known as the Feast of Weeks or Harvest) was a one-day celebration at the end of the wheat harvest and was held fifty days after Passover. After the Exile, the Feast of Pentecost also celebrated the giving of the Law. Jesus' disciples received the promised Holy Spirit on this day (Acts 2). The Feast of Tabernacles (or Booths) was an eight-day celebration that took place in the autumn at the final harvest of olives and fruits. It was similar to our Thanksgiving. During this feast, the people made shelters, or "booths," to remind them of Israel's time in the wilderness when the nation lived in tents.

The *Day of Atonement was the most important and solemn day of the Jewish religious calendar. On this day the high priest sacrificed a goat for the sin of the nation, entered the Holy of Holies, and sprinkled the animal's blood on the mercy seat, thereby making atonement for Israel's sins. Atonement means to cover sin by paying for it with a sacrifice that represents and substitutes for the sinner. According to the Bible, an atoning sacrifice brings together and reconciles God and man, enemies who had been separated by sin. After making atonement, the high priest confessed the sins committed during the past year over the head of a second goat, thereby identifying the goat with the people's sins. This goat was then sent out into the wilderness to symbolize the removal of Israel's sins. The Day of Atonement had to be repeated each year, and this showed that a better, permanent solution for sin was needed. Jesus' death on the cross was the final and complete atoning sacrifice for sins. (See **Calendar; Feasts; Holy Days; Jewish Religious Practices.**)

C. Jewish Religious Leaders. The *priests in the Old Testament served as the links between a sinful people and a holy God. At Mt. Sinai, God appointed three groups within the tribe of Levi to serve in Israel's worship. *Aaron was chosen to be the high priest. His most important role came on the Day of Atonement, when he offered the blood in the Holy of Holies. *Eleazar, Aaron's son, became the next high priest. All future high priests were to be chosen from his family. In the NT Jesus is the great High Priest who offers himself for the sins of his people.

The remainder of Aaron's family also were from the tribe of Levi. They, too, were appointed as priests. They were divided into twenty-four groups, and they offered sacrifices and served in the tabernacle. The remainder of the *Levites were chosen to help the priests care for the tabernacle and later for the temple. They were responsible for taking care of the furnishings of the tabernacle and for putting it up and taking it down. Later, when the temple was built, they served as singers, musicians, porters, gatekeepers, and assistants to the priests. The Levites received their support from the people who were to give them a *tithe (one-tenth) of their income. The Levites in turn gave one-tenth of this tithe to the priests. (See **Priests.**)

*Prophets in the OT were God's spokesmen. They proclaimed God's words, predicted the future, promised future deliverance through the Messiah, and called the people to repentance and obedience to the law. Sometimes prophets received their message from God in dreams or visions. Sometimes God spoke to them directly. Prophets often were unpopular with the people because they exposed their sin and predicted judgment on both Israel and other nations. In Deuteronomy 18 God gives the test of a true prophet: his words will come true. Ultimately Jesus Christ fulfilled the message of the prophets. (See **Prophets.**)

Other religious leaders arose during the history of Israel. The scribes were originally court recorders who were responsible for keeping the records of state. During the Exile, they became teachers of the law, which they interpreted for the people and preserved by carefully copying the manuscripts. For more information on the significance of the scribes in later Judaism and on the roles of the Sadducees and Pharisees, see the section on the intertestamental period. (See **Jewish Religious Leaders.**)

II. THE NEW TESTAMENT — CHRISTIANITY.

The NT focuses on the life, ministry, death, resurrection, and teachings of Jesus Christ. His coming fulfilled the promises of the OT and ushered in the kingdom of God. God's promise to bless all nations through Israel was fulfilled in God's only Son Jesus, a Jew of David's line, who makes salvation available to every Jew and Gentile who puts his trust in him. (See **Christ, Jesus.**)

A. Jesus Christ.

1. The Covenant. Jeremiah prophesied of a new covenant (Jer 31:31–34) under which the Law would be written on people's hearts and God would forgive their sin on a permanent basis. This helped to revive Israel's interest in the idea of God's covenant. At his last Passover meal, Jesus referred to his body as bread and to his blood as wine—he was the Passover Lamb who was symbolically eaten by his disciples as a covenant meal. His death on the cross the following day was the basis for the new covenant. The Mosaic, or old, covenant was established when the Israelites promised to obey its terms and Moses sprinkled animal blood on them—the blood of the covenant (Exod 24:5–8). The new covenant was established with Jesus' blood (Matt 26:28). He is a sacrifice that in every way is superior to animal sacrifices (Heb 9:12–14). Israel was under God's curse because of her own sinfulness. She was never able to obey God's law perfectly. On the cross Jesus took the curses of the law on himself to redeem sinful humanity (Gal 3:13). By his once-for-all sacrifice, Jesus removed sin from his people and established a new covenant (Heb 9:15, 26). Because God raised Jesus from the dead and seated him at his right hand (Eph 1:20–23), Jesus is the fulfillment of God's covenant promise to David (2 Sam 7:11–16; Acts 2:22–36; 13:32–37).

2. The Messiah. In the OT the Messiah is described as God's anointed King (Dan 9:25–26; Ps 2:2–9), who would accomplish God's redemptive work, judge Israel's enemies (Ps 110:1–7), and establish God's kingdom (Isa 9:2–7; 11:1–9; Mic 5:3–4). By intertestamental times the Jews pictured the Messiah primarily as a political leader who would overthrow their enemies and establish a physical kingdom. Both Jews and Samaritans believed the Messiah also would be a prophet like Moses (Deut 18:15–16; John 6:14; Matt 21:11; Luke 7:16) and would be the mediator of a new covenant.

Because of these political expectations, Jesus did not openly refer to himself as the Messiah during his ministry, though he emphasized that he fulfilled OT promises. Instead, he taught his disciples that he would fulfill the OT predictions of a messianic, Davidic king (Ps 2:7) by obedience, suffering, death (the Servant of the Lord—Isa 41:1; 53), and resurrection. His entry into Jerusalem (Zech 9:9–10) reminded the people that the Messiah was a humble king who came to bring peace, not war. Jesus referred to himself as the Son of Man. Because this title was not used by the Jews to refer to the Messiah, Jesus could give it his own meaning.

Because Jesus was not the political deliverer the Jews expected, he was largely rejected by his own people. The Sadducees wanted to maintain their political power. The Pharisees resented Jesus' rejection of their traditions, especially his view of the Sabbath (Matt 12:2–14), and considered his claims to be God blasphemous (Luke 5:21). Both of these groups united to bring about his death (Mark 11:18).

Following his death and resurrection, when earthly political hopes for him had vanished, Jesus' identity as the Messiah became the focus of early Christian preaching. By raising Jesus from the dead, God proclaimed him to be the Messiah, the promised deliverer, and the Son of God (Acts 2:31, 36; 3:18). Jesus is now seated at God's right hand (Ps 110:1), the ruler of an eternal and heavenly kingdom that far surpasses the merely national kingdom for which the Jews hoped in Christ's day. One day, however, Jesus will return and exercise political power on earth. At his second coming he will continue to fulfill the Messiah's role as king by judging the enemies of God and the church and by establishing a worldwide, political kingdom in which righteousness and justice triumph in human relationships. This future coming is described in the Book of Revelation and in other passages in the NT. (See **Eschatology.**)

B. The Church. Following Jesus' ascension, his small band of disciples were gathered in Jerusalem. There, at the Feast of Pentecost, they received the promised * Holy Spirit (Acts 2:1–4). The Holy Spirit is the third person of the * Trinity (2 Thess 2:13–14; 1 Peter 1:2). In the NT God revealed that there are three persons in one Godhead: God the Father; Jesus, who is God the Son; and the Holy Spirit, who because of Christ's completed sacrifice for sin now indwells all believers, as Ezekiel and other OT prophets promised. The Holy Spirit provides the power to obey God's laws, produces fruits of righteousness in the lives of Christians (Gal 5:22–23), and gives gifts to the church (1 Cor 12; Rom 12:6–8). (See **Christian Virtues; Church; Holy Spirit; Gifts (Spiritual); Religious Practices.**)

The church was born on Pentecost, when many Jews responded to Peter's preaching by repenting and trusting in Christ as the Savior and Messiah (Acts 2:40–41). These Jewish Christians met together to sing, pray, listen to the teaching of the apostles, and encourage one another in the faith (vv. 42–47). But as the church continued to grow, mounting opposition from Jewish leaders forced the Jewish Christians to leave Jerusalem (8:1–4). Everywhere these Jewish Christians went, they preached the gospel. As a result, many Gentiles and Jews responded by trusting Christ. From Jerusalem, the church first expanded to Samaria (8:14–17). Then it spread outside of Palestine to Antioch (11:19–30), and then to Asia Minor, Greece, and Rome, in fulfillment of Christ's commission to tell other nations the Good News.

One of the fiercest opponents of the early church was Saul, a devout Jew. While Saul was traveling to Damascus to persecute Christians, Jesus appeared to him and called him for a special work. Saul became * Paul, Jesus' special missionary to the Gentiles. As he traveled from town to town, Paul proclaimed the message of salvation not only to Jews in the synagogues but also to Gentiles (Acts 9:15–16). During Paul's three missionary journeys he spread the gospel throughout the Roman Empire. The kingdom of God that began during the ministry of Christ spread throughout the world to all people, Jew and Gentile alike.

At first after their conversion, Jewish Christians continued to attend the temple services and to celebrate the Jewish festivals. Jewish and Gentile Christians met in homes for worship on Sunday, the first day of the week, since Jesus' resurrection occurred on that day (Acts 20:7; 1 Cor 16:2). With the destruction of the temple in A.D. 70, Jewish Christians no longer celebrated the Sabbath—Sunday became the recognized day of worship. The worship service of these early Christians was very similar to the synagogue service.

Two * sacraments were observed by the early church: the * Lord's Supper and * baptism. The Lord's Supper is a new covenant meal celebrated with bread (symbolizing Christ's body) and wine (symbolizing Christ's blood). The Lord's Supper points backward to Christ's final sacrifice for sin and forward to his return in glory. John the Baptist used baptism as a sign of repentance. After Pentecost, new Christians were baptized as a sign of their new life in Christ. Christians have died to sin and are alive in Christ (Rom 6:4). (See **Sacrament.**)

-A-

AARON (âr'ŭn, Heb. *'ahărôn,* meaning uncertain). The oldest son of Amram and Jochebed, of the tribe of Levi, and brother of Moses and Miriam (Exod 6:2; Num 26:59). He was born three years before Moses and before Pharaoh's edict that all male infants should be destroyed (Exod 7:7). His name first appears in God's commission to Moses. When Moses protested that he did not have sufficient ability in public speaking to undertake the mission to Pharaoh, God declared that Aaron should be spokesman for his brother (4:10–16). So Aaron met Moses at "the mountain of God" (4:27) after 40 years' separation, took him back to the family home in Goshen, introduced him to the elders of the people, and persuaded them to accept him as their leader. Together Moses and Aaron went to Pharaoh's court, where they carried on the negotiations that finally ended the oppression of the Israelites and precipitated the Exodus.

Aaron married Elisheba, daughter of Amminadab and sister of Nahshon, a prince of the tribe of Judah (Exod 6:23; 1 Chron 2:10). They had four sons: Nadab, Abihu, Eleazar, and Ithamar (Exod 6:23). After Israel left Egypt, Aaron assisted Moses during the wilderness wandering. On the way to Sinai, in the battle with Amalek, Aaron and Hur held up Moses' hands (17:9–13), in which was the staff of God. Israel consequently won the battle. With the establishment of the tabernacle, Aaron became high priest in charge of the national worship and the head of the hereditary priesthood.

In character he was weak and occasionally jealous. He and Miriam criticized Moses for having married a Cushite woman (Num 12:1–2), perhaps an intentionally insulting reference to Zipporah (Hab 3:7–Cush linked with Midian). Behind this personal slight lies a more serious threat to Moses' position. Aaron, as high priest, was the supreme religious leader of Israel; Miriam was a prophetess (Exod 15:20). The great issue is not whom Moses had married but whether Moses could any longer be considered the sole, authoritative mouthpiece of God. As Aaron and Miriam said, "Hasn't he also spoken through us?" (Num 12:2). Recognizing this basic challenge to Moses' God-given status explains God's prompt and dramatic response (12:4ff.).

Aaron's own authority as priest did not go unchallenged. It becomes clear that

Mt. Hor (Jebel Haroun), just west of Petra, one of the traditional sites associated with the death and burial of Aaron. Courtesy Garo Nalbandian

when Korah and his company (Num 16) challenged Moses' leadership, Aaron's priesthood was also called into question. By the miraculous sign of the flowering and fruitbearing staff, the Lord identified Aaron as his chosen priest (17:1–9) and accorded him a perpetual priesthood by ordering his staff to be deposited in the sanctuary (17:10).

When Moses went up Mt. Sinai to receive the tables of the law from God, Aaron acceded to the people's demand for a visible god that they could worship. He melted their personal jewelry in a furnace and made a golden calf similar to the familiar bull-god of Egypt. The people hailed this image as the god who had brought them out of Egypt. Aaron did not remonstrate with them but built an altar and proclaimed a feast to the Lord on the next day, which the people celebrated with revelry and debauchery (Exod 32:1–6). When Moses returned from the mountain and rebuked Aaron for aiding this abuse, Aaron naïvely replied: "They gave me the gold, and I threw it into the fire, and out came this calf!" (32:24). Perhaps Aaron meant to restrain the people by a compromise, but he was wholly unsuccessful.

Two months later, when the revelation of the pattern for worship was completed, Aaron and his sons were consecrated to the priesthood (Lev 8–9).

At the end of the wilderness wandering, Aaron was warned of his impending death. He and Moses went up Mt. Hor, where Aaron was stripped of his priestly robes, which were passed in succession to his son Eleazar. Aaron died at age 123 and was buried on the mountain (Num 20:22–29; 33:38; Deut 10:6; 32:50). The people mourned for him 30 days.

The Psalms speak of the priestly line as the "house of Aaron" (115:10, 12; 118:3; 135:19), and Hebrews says that Aaron was called by God (Heb 5:4)—though the eternal priesthood of Christ is stated explicitly to be derived from Melchizedek, not from Aaron (7:11).

AARONITES (âr′ŭn-īts). Descendants of Aaron who fought with David against Saul (1 Chron 12:27). They were distinguished from the Levites (27:17).

AB The fifth month of the Hebrew year, coinciding approximately with mid-July to mid-August (Num 33:38).

ABADDON (à-băd′ŭn, Heb. ʾăvaddôn, *ruin, perdition, destruction*). Its six OT occurrences (Job 26:6; 28:22; 31:12; Ps 88:11; Prov 15:11; 27:20) have the idea of "ruin." Found once in the NT (Rev 9:11), it refers to the angel who reigns over the infernal regions.

ABANA (à-băn′à, Heb. ʾăvānâ). Mentioned in the Bible only in 2 Kings 5:12, this river flows through Damascus, making the city, though bordering on a desert, one of the loveliest and most fertile on earth.

ABARIM (ăb′à-rĭm, Heb. ʾăvārîm, *those beyond*, or *on the other side*). Either the region east of the Jordan or the name of a mountain range NW of Moab. The Israelites encamped here just before crossing the Jordan (Num 33:47), and from one of its peaks Moses saw the Promised Land (27:12).

ABBA (ăb′à, Heb. ʾabbāʾ). Aramaic word for *father*, transliterated into Greek and thence into English. It is found three times in the NT (Mark 14:36; Rom 8:15; Gal 4:6). The corresponding Hebrew word is *Ab*.

ABDA (ăb′dà, Heb. ʾavdāʾ, probably *servant of God*). 1. The father of Adoniram (1 Kings 4:6). 2. A Levite, the son of Shammua (Neh 11:17), called "Obadiah the son of Shemaiah" (1 Chron 9:16).

ABDI (ăb′dī, Heb. ʾavdî, probably *servant of Jehovah*). 1. A Levite, father of Kishi, the grandfather of David's singer Ethan (1 Chron 6:44; perhaps 2 Chron 29:12). 2. One of Elam's sons who married foreign wives (Ezra 10:26).

ABDON (ăb′dŏn, Heb. ʾavdôn, meaning uncertain, may be *servant, service,* or *servile*). 1. The eleventh judge of Israel who judged for eight years (Judg 12:13–15). 2. One of the sons of Shashak, a Benjamite, living in Jerusalem (1 Chron 8:23, 28). 3. The son of Jeiel of Gibeon (8:30; 9:35–36). 4. An official that King Josiah sent to Huldah the prophetess (2 Chron 34:20; called Acbor in 2 Kings 22:12).

ABDON One of four Levitical cities in the tribe of Asher (Josh 21:30; 1 Chron 6:74). It may be the same as "Hebron" in Joshua 19:28. Now called Abdeh, near the Mediterranean and about 15 miles (25 km.) south of Tyre.

ABEDNEGO (à-bĕd′nē-gō, Heb. ʾăvēdhneghô, *servant of Nego*). One of the three Hebrews overseeing the affairs of the province of Babylon; he was saved from the fiery furnace (Dan 3:12–30).

ABEL (ā′bĕl, Heb. *hevel*). A Hebrew word of this spelling means "breath," "vapor," that which is "insubstantial"; but more likely the name should be linked with an Accadian word meaning "son." He was Adam and Eve's second son, who was murdered by his brother Cain (Gen 4). Disaffection between the two brothers arose when Cain brought a vegetable offering to the Lord, and Abel brought a lamb. Perhaps God had previously (at 3:21?) revealed that man must approach him with blood-sacrifice. God accepted Abel's offering because it was an animal sacrifice and or because of the spirit ("by faith," Heb 11:4) in which it was offered (Gen 4:4–5). Thus Abel became the first exemplar of the way of righteousness through faith (Matt 23:35; 1 John 3:12).

ABEL (ā′bĕl, Heb. ʾāvēl, *a meadow*). 1. The name of a city involved in the rebellion of Sheba (2 Sam 20:14, 18); the same as Abel Beth Maacah (20:15). 2. "The great stone of Abel" (1 Sam 6:18 KJV; NIV has "the large rock").

ABEL BETH MAACAH (ā′bĕl bĕth mā′à-kà, Heb. ʾāvēl bêth maʾăkhâh). *Abel* ("meadow," perhaps "brook") *of Beth-Maacah* (KJV "Maachah")—i.e., near Beth Maacah—was in the extreme north of Palestine, in the tribe of Naphtali (2 Sam 20:15; 1 Kings 15:20). Sheba, son of Bicri, fled to it when his revolt against David failed. The town was saved from assault by Joab when, with its proverbial shrewdness, it followed the advice of "a wise woman" that the people sacrifice Sheba (2 Sam 20:14–22). About 80 years

The large, ancient mound of Abel Beth Maacah, looking north-northeast. In the days of David, it was a fortified place and "a city that is a mother in Israel" (2 Sam 20:19). Courtesy Duby Tal

later Benhadad seized it (1 Kings 15:20) and in 734 B.C. Tiglath-Pileser carried off its inhabitants to Assyria (2 Kings 15:29).

ABEL MEHOLAH (ā'bĕl mē-hō'là, *meadow of dancing* or *brook of dancing*). Town where Elisha was born and lived (1 Kings 19:16). The Midianites routed by Gideon fled there (Judg 7:22).

ABEL MIZRAIM (ā'bĕl mĭz'rā-ĭm, Heb. *'āvēl-mitsrayim, meadow* or *mourning of Egypt*). A place east of the Jordan at which the funeral procession of Jacob stopped to mourn for seven days before entering Canaan to bury him (Gen 50:11). Previously called the "threshing floor of Atad," the Canaanites now called it the "mourning of (funeral from) Egypt" because the Egyptian nobility and soldiers took part in the funeral rites.

ABEZ (See EBEZ)

ABIA (See ABIJAH)

ABI-ALBON (See ABIEL)

ABIATHAR (à-bī'ă-thàr, Heb. *'evîāthār, father of abundance*). Son of Ahimelech, who with 84 other priests was killed at Nob on Saul's instructions, after Doeg had told the king that Ahimelech had helped David by inquiring of the Lord for him and by giving him Goliath's sword (1 Sam 22). Abiathar somehow escaped the slaughter and joined David, bringing the oracular ephod with him (22:20ff.). Abiathar and Zadok were in effect joint high priests when David brought the ark to Jerusalem (1 Chron 15:11f.). This situation continued through David's reign (e.g., 2 Sam 15:24, 27, 29). Abiathar did not, however, give the same loyalty to Solomon, but associated himself with the cause of Adonijah, the eldest surviving son of David (1 Kings 1:7, 19, 25). It would appear that, even after the failure of Adonijah's attempt to succeed David, Abiathar was in some way still linked with him, for when Adonijah was executed on suspicion of plotting a coup, Abiathar was banished from Jerusalem (2:22–27). This terminated the joint priesthood of Zadok and Abiathar, as referred to in 1 Kings 4:4, and also fulfilled the prediction, made 150 years earlier, of the end of the priestly rule of the house of Eli (1 Sam 2:31–35).

ABIB (ā'bĭb, Heb. *'āvîv, an ear of corn*). The preexilic name for the first month (March April) of the year (Exod 13:4; 23:15; 34:18)–called Nisan after the Exile.

ABIDAN (à-bī'dăn, Heb. *'ăvîdhān, the father is judge*). A prince chosen to represent the tribe of Benjamin at the census in the wilderness of Sinai (Num 1:11; 2:22). At the dedication of the tabernacle he made an offering as one of the heads of Israel (7:60, 65).

ABIEL (ā'bĭ-ĕl, Heb. *'ăvî'ēl, the father is God,* or *God is father*). 1. The grandfather of Saul and Abner (1 Sam 9:1; 14:51). 2. One of David's mighty men (1 Chron 11:32), also called Abi-Albon (2 Sam 23:31).

ABIEZER (ā'bī-ē'zêr, Heb. *'ăvî'ezer, father of help,* or *father is help*). 1. Head of the family in Manasseh to which Gideon belonged (Judg 6:11–12; 8:2, 32). 2. One of David's mighty men (2 Sam 23:27; 1 Chron 11:28; 27:12).

ABIGAIL (ăb'ĭ-gāl, Heb. *'ăvîghayil, father is rejoicing*). 1. The wife of Nabal and, after his death, wife of David (1 Sam 25:3, 14–44; 27:3; 2 Sam 3:3), to whom she bore his second son, Kileab (or, 1 Chron 3:1, Daniel). 2. Hebrew *'ăvîghal.* A sister or stepsister of David, daughter of Nahash, wife of Jether, and mother of Amasa (2 Sam 17:25; 1 Chron. 2:16–17).

ABIHAIL (ăb'i-hāl, Heb. *'ăvîhayil, the father is strength*). 1. A Levite, the father of Zuriel, who in the wilderness was the head of the house of Merari (Num 3:35). 2. The wife of Abishur of the tribe of Judah (1 Chron 2:29). 3. A Gadite who lived in Gilead of Bashan (5:14). 4. The wife of Rehoboam and daughter of Eliab, David's oldest brother (2 Chron 11:18).

5. The father of Queen Esther (Esth 2:15; 9:29).

ABIHU (à-bī'hū, Heb. *'ăvîhû, the father is he*). Second son of Aaron (Exod 6:23). With Aaron, Nadab his brother, and the 70 elders he went with Moses up Mt. Sinai for a limited distance (24:1) and saw God (24:9-11). Subsequently Abihu died under divine judgment because he offered "unauthorized fire before the LORD" (Lev 10:1).

ABIJAH (à-bī'jà, Heb. *'ăvîyâh* or *'ăvîyāhû, Jehovah is father*). **1.** The wife of Judah's grandson Hezron (1 Chron 2:24). **2.** The seventh son of Beker, the son of Benjamin (7:8). **3.** The second son of Samuel who was appointed a judge by his father and became corrupt (1 Sam 8:2; 1 Chron 6:28). **4.** A descendant of Aaron. Of the 24 groups of priests (1 Chron 24:10), he was the ancestral head of the group to which the father of John the Baptist belonged (Luke 1:5). **5.** A son of Jeroboam I (1 Kings 14:1-18). He died from illness when still a child, in fulfillment of a prediction by the prophet Ahijah and as a judgment for Jeroboam's apostasy. **6.** King of Judah, the son and successor of Rehoboam. He made war on Jeroboam in an effort to recover the ten tribes of Israel. Before one battle he appealed to Jeroboam not to oppose God, who had given the kingdom to David and his sons forever; Abijah, though greatly outnumbered, gained a decisive victory. He married 14 wives and followed the evil ways of his father. He reigned three years (2 Chron 12:16-14:1). **7.** Hezekiah's mother (29:1), "Abi" in 2 Kings 18:2 (KJV, NASB, NEB, RSV). **8.** A chief of the priests who returned from Babylon with Zerubbabel (Neh 12:4, 17). **9.** A priest of Nehemiah's time (10:7).

ABILENE (ăb'ĭ-lēn, Gr. *Abilēnē*, probably from Heb., *meadow*). The tetrarchy of Lysanias (Luke 3:1) near Anti-Lebanon.

ABIMELECH (à-bĭm'ĕ-lĕk, Heb. *'ăvîmelekh*, probably either *the father is king* or *the father of a king*). **1.** The name (or dynastic title) of a Philistine king of Gerar to whom Abraham said that Sarah was his sister. Struck by her beauty, Abimelech took her to marry her, but, warned by God, he immediately returned her to Abraham (Gen 20:1-18). Later, when their servants contended over a well, the two men made a covenant (21:22-34). **2.** A second king of Gerar, probably the son of the first-mentioned Abimelech. At his court Isaac tried to pass off Rebekah as his sister (26:1-11). Later their servants

quarreled, and they made a covenant, as Abraham and the first Abimelech had done. **3.** The son of Gideon by a concubine (Judg 8:31; 9:1-57). After Gideon died and aspiring to be king, he murdered 70 sons of his father. Only Jotham escaped. Abimelech was then made king of Shechem. After three years, rebellion broke out against him; he attacked and destroyed his own city of Shechem. Later he was killed while besieging nearby Thebez. **4.** A Philistine king mentioned in the title of Psalm 34. He is very likely the same as Achish, king of Gath (1 Sam 21:10-22:1), with whom David sought refuge when he fled from Saul. **5.** A priest in the days of David, a son of Abiathar; also called Ahimelech (1 Chron 18:16; 24:6).

ABINADAB (à-bĭn'à-dăb, Heb. *'ăvînādhāv, the father is generous*). **1.** A man living in Kiriath Jearim to whose home the ark was brought from the land of the Philistines. About a century later, David removed the ark to Jerusalem (1 Sam 7:1-2; 2 Sam 6:3; 1 Chron 13:7). **2.** The second of Jesse's eight sons. He was in Saul's army when Goliath gave his challenge (1 Sam 16:8; 17:13; 1 Chron 2:13). **3.** A son of Saul killed with his father by the Philistines at Mt. Gilboa (1 Sam 31:2; 1 Chron 8:33; 9:39; 10:2). **4.** The father of a son-in-law of Solomon (1 Kings 4:11).

ABIRAM (à-bī'răm, Heb. *'ăvîrām, the father is exalted*). **1.** A Reubenite who with his brothers Dathan and Korah conspired against Moses and was destroyed by God (Num 16). **2.** Eldest son of Hiel (1 Kings 16:34).

ABISHAG (ăb'ĭ-shăg, Heb. *'ăvîshagh, the father wanders, or errs*). A Shunamite woman who nursed David in his old age (1 Kings 1:3, 15). Solomon had Adonijah, his elder half-brother, executed for asking permission to marry her (2:17ff.), possibly because by marrying the household woman of a former king Adonijah would have been making a claim to the throne.

ABISHAI (à-bĭsh'ā-ī, Heb. *'ăvîshay*, meaning is doubtful). Son of David's sister Zeruiah, and brother of Joab and Asahel. He was impetuous and courageous, cruel and hard to his foes, but always intensely loyal to David. He counseled David to kill the sleeping Saul (1 Sam 26:6-9). He aided Joab in the murder of Abner, who had slain their brother Asahel (2 Sam 3:30). He was loyal to David when Absalom and Sheba revolted, and he wanted to kill Shimei for cursing David (16:5-14). He defeated a large army of Edomites (1 Chron 18:12–13). Late in David's life he rescued the king in the fight with Ishbi-Benob, the Philistine giant (2 Sam 21:17).

ABISHALOM (See ABSALOM)

ABISHUA (à-bĭsh'ū-à, Heb. *'ăvîshûa'*, perhaps *the father is salvation* or *noble*). **1.** The son of Phinehas the priest (1 Chron 6:4–5, 50; Ezra 7:5). **2.** A Benjamite (1 Chron 8:4).

ABNER (ăb'nêr, Heb. *'ăvnēr, the father is a lamp*). The son of Ner, who was the brother of Kish, the father of King Saul. Abner was the commander-in-chief of Saul's army (1 Sam 14:50). He brought David to Saul following the slaying of Goliath (17:55–58). Later, David rebuked Abner for his failure to adequately guard Saul while he was pursuing David (26:5–16).

At Saul's death, Abner had Saul's son Ish-Bosheth made king over Israel (2 Sam 2:8). David's servants overwhelmingly defeated Abner and his men. During the retreat from this battle, Abner killed Asahel, Joab's brother, in self-defense (2:12–32).

After Abner and Ish-Bosheth had a quarrel over Saul's concubine, Abner joined David, but Joab (pretending to believe he was a spy) murdered him to avenge the death of his brother (2 Sam 3:6–27). David composed a lament for the occasion (3:33–34).

ABOMINATION, ABOMINATION OF DESOLUTION The word *abomination* occurs rarely in the NIV (e.g., Prov 26:25; Isa 66:3; Dan 9:27; 11:31; 12:11; cf. "abominable," Isa 66:17; Jer 32:34). The idea is, however, much more widespread, most often expressed in the NIV by *detest* and the *detestable*. Two main Hebrew words are involved: (1) *shiqqutz*, used of idols, of the gods represented by idols, of forbidden practices, and generally of anything contrary to the worship and religion of the Lord. The related noun *sheqetz* is used of idols in animal form, forbidden foods, and generally of anything bringing ceremonial defilement. (2) *Tô'evah* , often synonymous with *shiqqutz*, is also used in wider areas of life—things related to idols, false gods themselves, forbidden sexual practices, prophecy leading to the worship of other gods, offering blemished animals in sacrifice, and heathen divination (or anything that challenges God's authority).

Interpreters differ on the references of Daniel to some notable and frightful abomination (Dan 9:27; 11:31; 12:11). Many continue to hold that Daniel 11:31

was fulfilled in 186 B.C., when the Syrian Antiochus Epiphanes set up an altar in the Jerusalem temple and sacrificed a pig on it. But Matthew 24:15 and Mark 13:14 make it clear that Jesus understood the "abomination" as still to come. Some understand the Lord to refer to some horrifying act of sacrilege during the period of the Jewish revolt and the sack of Jerusalem by the Romans in A.D. 70. The reference may be to Jewish zealot rebels who actually set up their military headquarters in the Holy Place. Other interpreters, however, understand the Lord to be speaking not of the fall of Jerusalem but of the end-time itself, immediately prior to his own coming; and they link the setting up of the abomination with the appearance and activity of the man of sin (2 Thess 2:3–4, 8–9).

Ancient Oak of Mamre, about two miles north of Hebron, thought to be the site where Abram pitched his tent (Gen 13:18). The picture was taken around the turn of the century. From the private collection of the Ottoman Sultan Abdul-Hamid (1876–1909). Courtesy University Library, Istanbul

ABRAHAM (ā'brà-hăm, Heb. *'avrāhām, father of a multitude;* earlier name Abram, Heb. *'avram, exalted father*). Son of Terah, founder of the Hebrew nation and father of the people of God, he descended from Noah through Shem (Gen 11:10ff.) and was called out of an idolatrous background (Josh 24:2). After the death of his brother Haran (Gen 11:28), Abram moved in obedience to a divine vision (Acts 7:2-4) from Ur of the Chaldees in Mesopotamia to the city of Haran in the extreme north of Palestine. He was accompanied by his father, Terah; his wife and half-sister, Sarai; and his nephew Lot (Gen 11:31-32).

Genesis records the development of Abraham's faith—imperfect faith (Genesis 12-13), growing faith (14-17), and mature faith (18-25:10). At age 75 (12:4) Abram was commanded to leave all and go out into the unknown (12:1-3). In faith he obeyed, but, contrary to the command to leave his "father's household," he took his nephew Lot with him, laying the foundation for considerable future trouble (chs 13, 19). When Abram arrived in Canaan (12:6), God confirmed the promise that this was the land Abram's descendants would possess (12:7), but the imperfection of Abram's faith again appeared. Although assured by God that he was in the right place, Abram deserted Canaan for Egypt in a time of famine and, still uncertain whether the Lord could preserve him in trouble, tried to pass off Sarai as his sister, hoping to purchase his own safety at her expense (12:10-20). God protected the chosen family in Egypt (12:17-20) and then, when Abram tried to solve family problems (13:7) by dividing up the Promised Land, reaffirmed (13:14-17) that none but Abram and his descendants could inherit the promises.

In Genesis 14 Abram first opposed the kings (14:13-16) and then refused the world's wealth (14:21-24). The Lord was not slow to respond in both regards (15:1). But the richness of the divine response provoked Abram to question the point of it all, for he had no son to inherit what the Lord would give him. This leads to that high moment of faith when Abram, fully aware that every human aspect of the situation was against him (Rom 4:18-21), rested wholly and absolutely on God's promise; this is the faith that justifies (Gen 15:4-6).

The Lord confirmed his promises of children and land in a great covenant sign (Gen 15:7-21), but Abram and Sarai, tired of waiting (ch 16), turned from the way of faith to a human expedient that was permitted—even expected—by the laws of the day: a childless couple might "have children" through a secondary wife. In gentle grace God picked up the pieces of Hagar's broken life (16:7-16) and reaffirmed his covenant with Abram (17:1ff.).

Genesis 17:17-22:19 is the tale of two sons. Abraham deeply loved his sons Ishmael and Isaac (17:18; 21:11-12), yet

he was called to give them both up—in faith that the Lord would keep his promises concerning them (21:11-13; 22:1-18). The Lord did not spring these great decisions on Abraham but prepared him for them by his experience over Lot and Sodom (chs 18-19).

Quietly the underlining of the maturity of Abraham's faith proceeds: Sarah was laid to rest within the Promised Land by her husband, who was planning to be buried there himself, awaiting the fulfillment of the promise of possession. Sternly Abraham's servant was forbidden to move Isaac away from the place of promise (Gen 24:6-7), for even if Isaac had to marry a Canaanite girl (24:8), he was not to leave the land designated by God.

In the NT Paul stresses Abraham's faith as simple trust in God's promises (Rom 4:18-22); Hebrews notes the patience of faith (11:8-16; cf. 6:11-13); and James brings out the obedience of faith (2:21-23).

ABRAHAM'S SIDE (Luke 16:22-23; "Abraham's bosom" in JB, KJV, NASB, and RSV) indicates *blessedness after death*, since closeness to the founder of the Hebrew nation was considered the highest honor.

ABRAM (See ABRAHAM)

ABSALOM (ăb'sà-lŏm, Heb. *'avshālôm, father [is] peace*, written Abishalom in 1 Kings 15:2, 10). Third son of David, by Maacah (2 Sam 3:3; 1 Chron 3:2). Amnon, David's eldest son and Absalom's half-brother, raped Absalom's sister Tamar (2 Sam 13:1-19). David, though greatly angered, never punished Amnon (13:21). Absalom nursed his hatred for two years, then treacherously plotted Amnon's assassination (13:22-29). Absalom fled to his grandfather and remained with him three years (13:37-38). Then Joab by stratagem induced David to recall Absalom, but David would not see him for two years more (14:1-24). Absalom was finally restored to favor after he tricked Joab into interceding with David (14:28, 33).

"In all Israel there was not a man so highly praised for his handsome appearance as Absalom," and for the abundance of his hair (2 Sam 14:25-26). He had three sons and a daughter, whom he named Tamar after his sister. Absalom now began to act like a candidate for the kingship (15:1-6), parading a great retinue and subtly indicating how he would improve the administration of justice in the interests of the people.

The so-called Tomb of Absalom, located in the Kidron Valley in Jerusalem. Built by wealthy citizens of Jerusalem in the Herodian period. In its lower part, hewn out of rock, was the burial chamber, on top of which was constructed the cone-shaped memorial. In due course, this tomb came to be associated with such notables as the kings of the House of David. Although popularly identified with Absalom, son of King David, this attribution is only legend.
Courtesy Zev Radovan

At the end of four years Absalom pretended a proper motive for visiting Hebron and there proclaimed himself king and attracted the disaffected to his standard (2 Sam 15:7–14). David hastily left Jerusalem (15:13–18). Ahithophel advised Absalom to attack David at once, before he could gather a large following (17:1–4). Hushai (secretly loyal to David) advised delay until all the military power of the realm could be gathered under the command of Absalom himself, to make sure they had a force large enough to defeat the warlike David and his loyal soldiers (17:5–14). Absalom, following a compromise plan, was disastrously defeated (18:1–8); he was caught by his head in the branches of an oak, and the mule he was riding left him dangling helpless there. Killed by Joab and his men, Absalom was buried in a nearby pit (18:9–17).

David's great and prolonged grief over the death of his son nearly cost him the loyalty of his subjects (2 Sam 18:33–19:8). David's failure to fairly rule the entire nation may be seen in the ease with which Absalom attracted the northern tribes (later Israel), and boded ill for the future of a united kingdom.

ABSTINENCE (ăb'stĭ-nĕns, Gr. apechomai). The verb abstain occurs six times and means "hold oneself away from." The noun abstinence occurs once in the KJV (Gr. asitia, Acts 27:21) and means abstinence from food. The decree of the Jerusalem council (15:20, 29) commanded abstinence from practices abhorrent to Jewish Christians. Believers are to abstain from idolatry, fornication, all appearance of evil, and sinful desires (Rom 14:21; 1 Cor 8:4–13; 1 Thess 4:3; 5:22; 1 Peter 2:11). The injunctions regarding drunkenness and sobriety (1 Cor 5:11; 6:9–10; Eph 5:18; 1 Tim 3:3, 8; Titus 2:2–4) point to the wisdom of total abstinence from alcoholic beverages if one would be at his best for the Lord.

ABYSS (à-bĭs', Gr. abyssos). In the NT it refers to the world of the dead (Rom 10:7) or the nether world, the prison of disobedient spirits (Luke 8:31; Rev 9:1–2, 11; 11:7; 17:8; 20:1–3). In classical Greek it meant the primeval deep; in later Judaism it included the interior depths of the earth and the prison of evil spirits.

ACACIA (See PLANTS)

ACBOR (ăk'bôr, Heb. 'akhbôr, mouse). **1.** The father of a king of Edom (Gen 36:38–39; 1 Chron 1:49). **2.** A messenger sent by King Josiah to inquire of the Lord concerning the book found by Hilkiah (2 Kings 22:12, 14; called Abdon in 2 Chron 34:20); father of Elnathan (Jer 26:22; 36:12).

ACCAD (See AKKAD)

ACCO, ACCHO (ăk'ō, Heb. 'akkô, Judg 1:31). The name occurs in some manuscripts and versions of Joshua 19:30. In the NT, Ptolemais; modern Arabic, 'Akka; English, Acre. A seaport near Mt. Carmel. Paul stayed there a day with Christian brethren on his way from Tyre to Caesarea (Acts 21:7). The Ptolemies of Egypt named it Ptolemais; later it was called St. Jean d'Acre by the Crusaders.

ACCUSER (See SATAN)

ACELDAMA (See AKELDAMA)

ACHAIA (à-kā'yà, Gr. Achaia). In NT times a Roman province that included the Peloponnesus and northern Greece south of Illyricum, Epirus, and Thessaly, which were districts of Macedonia. Corinth was the capital. Used together, "Macedonia and Achaia" generally mean all Greece (Acts 19:21; Rom 15:26; 1 Thess 1:7-8). Achaia is also mentioned alone (Acts 18:27; 1 Cor 16:15; 2 Cor 1:1; 9:2; 11:10).

ACHAICUS (à-kā'ī-kŭs, Gr. *Achaikos*). A Corinthian Christian who brought supplies to Paul at Ephesus (1 Cor 16:17-19).

ACHAN (ā'kǎn, Heb. *'ākhān*). An Israelite who disobediently took spoils from Jericho (gold, silver, and a garment), which resulted in Israel's defeat at Ai. By a process of elimination Achan was found out; he confessed, and he and his family were stoned to death in the valley of Achor (Josh 7). Disobedience had consequences for the family (Exod 20:5-6) as well as the people of God. In 2 Chronicles 2:7, he is called "Achar," the man of disaster.

ACHAR (See ACHAN)

ACHAZ (See AHAZ)

ACHBOR (See ACBOR)

ACHIM (See AKIM)

ACHISH (ā'kĭsh, Heb. *'ākhîsh*). King of Gath, to whom David fled twice for protection (1 Sam 21:10-15). First, David pretended insanity; Achish repulsed him, and David fled. The next time David consented to join Achish against Israel, but when the Philistine lords objected, Achish sent David away (29:1-11). He may be the same Achish to whom Shimei's servant fled (1 Kings 2:39-40).

ACHMETHA (See ECBATANA)

ACHOR (ā'kôr, Heb. *'ākhôr, disaster;* see ACHAN). The valley where Achan

was stoned (Josh 7:24-26; cf. 15:7); the subject of prophecy (Isa 65:10; Hos 2:15).

ACHSAH, ACHSA (See ACSAH)

ACHSHAPH (See ACSHAPH)

ACHZIB (See ACZIB)

ACRE (ā'kêr, Heb. *tsemedh*). The average amount a yoke of oxen could plow in a day (1 Sam 14:14; Isa 5:10).

ACROPOLIS (à-krŏp'ō-lĭs, Gr. *akropolis,* from *akros, highest,* and *polis, city*). The upper or higher city, citadel, or castle of a Greek municipality, especially the citadel of Athens, where the treasury was. During Paul's stay in Athens (Acts 17:15-18:1), he was greatly distressed to see the images of gods and heroes that filled the Acropolis. Many NT towns had an Acropolis, which served as the town's civic and religious centers.

ACROSTIC (à-krôs'tĭc, Gr. *akrostichis,* from *okros, topmost,* and *stichos, a line of poetry*). In the common form of acrostic found in OT poetry, each line or stanza begins with a letter of the Hebrew alphabet in order. Each letter may begin a line (Pss 111, 112), a half verse (Pss 25, 34, 145), a whole verse (Ps 37; Prov 31:10-31; Lam 1, 2, 4), or three verses (Lam 3). Psalm 119 is the most elaborate demonstration of the acrostic method where, in each section of eight verses, the same opening letter is used, and the 22 sections of the psalm move through the Hebrew alphabet, letter after letter. Hebrew poetry allows the demands of the sense to take precedence over the demands of form, so there are "broken acrostics" (a letter missing in each of Pss 25 and 34) or acrostics in which letters are taken out of order (Lam 2:16-17).

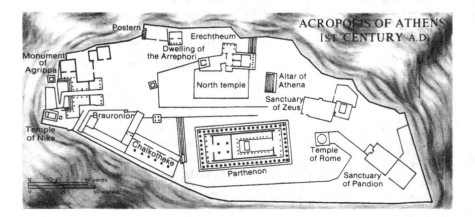

ACROPOLIS OF ATHENS 1ST CENTURY A.D.

Postern
Erechtheum
Dwelling of the Arrephori
Monument of Agrippa
North temple
Altar of Athena
Sanctuary of Zeus
Brauronion
Temple of Nike
Chalkotheke
Parthenon
Temple of Rome
Sanctuary of Pandion

ACSAH (ăk'să, Heb. *'akhsâ, anklet*), The daughter of Caleb, she was given in marriage to Othniel, son of Kenaz, Caleb's younger brother, in keeping with a promise Caleb had made to give his daughter to the one who captured Kiriath Sepher (Josh 15:16). She got Othniel to ask Caleb for a field; after getting it, while riding one day, she met Caleb and asked for and received springs to water the field (Judg 1:12-15).

ACSHAPH (ăk'shăf, Heb. *'akhshāph*). A city (Josh 11:1) that Joshua captured with its king (12:7, 20), on the border of the lot assigned to Asher (19:24-25).

ACTS OF THE APOSTLES The book that selectively gives the history of early Christianity from Jesus' ascension to the end of two years of Paul's Roman imprisonment.

I. Title of the Book. An early MS has the title "Acts" (Gr. *praxeis, doings, transactions, achievements*). Other early titles are "Acts of Apostles," "The Acts of the Apostles," "Acts of the Holy Apostles." Acts narrates actions and speeches chiefly of Peter and Paul. There is some information about Judas (1:16-20), the man chosen to succeed him (1:21-26), John (3:1-4:31; 8:14-17), and James (12:12). The Twelve, except the betrayer, are listed in 1:13. The title "Acts of the Holy Spirit" has often been suggested.

II. Author. Not until A.D. 160-200 do we have positive statements as to the authorship of Acts. From that time onward, all who mention the subject agree that the two books dedicated to Theophilus (Luke and Acts) were written by "Luke, the beloved physician." Only in modern times have there been attempts to ascribe both books to Titus or some other author.

III. Place. The place where Acts was written is not named, though the sudden ending of the book, while Paul is residing at Rome awaiting trial, makes Rome an appropriate choice.

IV. Date. Acts must have been finished after the latest date mentioned in the book, in 28:30. The abrupt close indicates that it was written at that time, c. 61 or 62. Luke's Gospel has an appropriate ending; Acts does not. There is no hint of Paul's release or of his death (nor of how his trial came out).

V. The Speeches in Acts. The style of the speeches in Acts is not Luke's, but that which is appropriate to each speaker: Peter, Stephen, Paul, even the minor characters—Gamaliel (5:25ff.), the Ephesian town clerk (19:35ff.), and

Tertullus (24:2ff.). Similarities between the speeches of Peter and Paul are explained by the fact that Paul explicitly preached the same gospel as Peter did. Speeches by the same person are varied in type, each suited to the occasion.

VI. Summary of the Contents. Introduction, 1:1-26. **1.** The Day of Pentecost, the birthday of the church, 2:1-47. **2.** Pictures of the first church in Jerusalem, 3-7. **3.** The gospel spread to all Judea and Samaria, 8:1-25. **4.** Three "continental" conversions, 9-10. **5.** The Judean mission to the Gentiles and Peter's imprisonment, 11-12. **6.** Paul's first missionary journey, 12:24-14:28. **7.** The Church Council at Jerusalem, 15:1-29. **8.** Paul's second missionary journey, 15:30-18:23. **9.** Paul's third missionary journey, 18:24-21:16. **10.** Paul's arrest and voyage to Rome, 21:17-28:31.

ACZIB (ăk'zĭb, Heb. *'akhzîv, a lie*). **1.** A city of Judah (Josh 15:44). Called Kezib (Gen 38:5) and Cozeba (1 Chron 4:22). **2.** A town in Asher (Judg 1:31; Josh 19:29) on the coast north of Acco. In NT times Ecdippa, modern ez-Zib.

ADAH (ā'dà, Heb. *'ādhâh, ornament*). **1.** One of Lamech's two wives (Gen 4:19-20, 23), mother of Jabal and Jubal. **2.** One of Esau's wives (Gen 36:2, 4, 10, 12, 16), daughter of Elon the Hittite. Basemath is Adah's sister or another name for Adah (Gen 26:34). Adah's son is Eliphaz (36:10), and his sons are called hers (36:12, 16), not Esau's.

ADAIAH (à-dā'yà, Heb. *'ădhāyâh, Jehovah has adorned*, or *pleasing to Jehovah*). **1.** A man of Boscath, father of Josiah's mother (2 Kings 22:1). **2.** A Levite descended from Gershon (1 Chron 6:41-43). **3.** A son of Shimei (8:1, 21). **4.** A Levite of the family of Aaron (9:10-12). **5.** The father of Maaseiah, who helped put Joash on the throne (2 Chron 23:1). **6.** A son of Bani who married a foreign wife during the Exile (Ezra 10:29). **7.** Another of a different Bani family who did the same (10:39). **8.** A descendant of Judah (Neh 11:5). **9.** A Levite of the family of Aaron, likely the same as no. 4 (11:12).

ADAM (Heb. *'ādhām*, Gr. *Adam, of the ground* or *taken out of the red earth*). In Hebrew this is both a personal name (Gen 2:20; 3:17, 21; 4:25; 5:2-3; 1 Chron 1:1) and a general noun ("mankind," over 500 times in the OT). As the first and representative man, Adam was made in God's image, provided with a garden and a wife, and given work to do (Gen 1-2). His rejection of God's authority led to the

Aerial view of the winding course of the Jordan River, with Adam Bridge, the bridge at center, marking the apparent site of the Israelite crossing (Josh 3:16) near the ancient city of Adam. Courtesy Carta, Jerusalem

breaking of communion with God (see FALL), his expulsion from the Garden, and a life of toil (Gen 3). From the physical descendants of Adam and Eve the human race emerged.

Adam is mentioned nine times in the NT (Luke 3:38; Rom 5:14 [twice]; 1 Cor 15:22, 45 [twice]; 1 Tim 2:13–14; Jude 14). Noteworthy truths are the one-flesh union of Adam and Eve, the comparison of the identity and role of Adam with that of Christ, and the submission of woman to man.

ADAM (Heb. *'ādhām, red*). A city near Zarethan (Josh 3:16), 17 miles (28 km.) north of Jericho. At this spot the waters of the Jordan River were stopped to create a dry pathway for Israel to enter Canaan. Now identified with Tell ed-Damiyeh.

ADAMANT (See MINERALS: *Precious Stones*)

ADAR (ā'dàr, Heb. *'āddār*) The twelfth month of the calendar used by the Israelites after the Exile, roughly equivalent to mid-February to mid-March.

ADDAN (See ADDON)

ADDAR (ăd'àr, Heb. *'addār, threshing floor*). Son of Bela, grandson of Benjamin (1 Chron 8:3). Called Ard (Gen 46:21; Num 26:40), counted as a son of Benjamin.

ADDER (See ANIMALS: *Snake*)

ADDON (ăd'ŏn, Heb. *'addān, 'addon*). A place in Babylonia from which exiles named in Ezra 2:59–63 and Nehemiah 7:61–65 returned home.

ADER (See EDER)

ADIEL (ā'dĭ-ĕl, Heb. *'ădhiēl, ornament of God*). 1. A descendant of Simeon (1 Chron 4:36). 2. A priest (1 Chron 9:12). 3. Father of Azmaveth, who was supervisor of David's treasuries (1 Chron 27:25). Perhaps the same as no. 2.

ADIN (ā'dĭn, Heb. *'ādhîn, voluptuous*). 1. One whose family returned from exile with Zerubbabel (Ezra 2:15; Neh 7:20). 2. One whose posterity came back with Ezra (Ezra 8:6). 3. The name of a family sealing the covenant (Neh 10:16). These are all thought to be the same family. The list in Ezra 2 appears to include both exiles who returned with Zerubbabel and some who returned later. The family included "leaders of the people" (Neh 10:14).

ADJURATION (See CURSE)

ADMAH (ăd'mà, Heb. *'adhmâh, red earth*). A city near Gomorrah and Zeboiim (Gen 10:19) with a king (14:2, 8), destroyed with Sodom and Gomorrah (cf. Deut 29:23 with Gen 19:24–28; see Hos 11:8).

ADNA (ăd'nà, Heb. *'adhnā, pleasure*). 1. A son of Pahath-Moab who had married a foreign wife during the Exile (Ezra 10:30). 2. A priest, head of his father's house in the days of Joiakim (Neh 12:12–15).

ADNAH (ăd'nà, Heb. *'adhnāh, pleasure*). 1. A Manassite who joined David at Ziklag (1 Chron 12:20). 2. A man of Judah who held high military rank under Jehoshaphat (2 Chron 17:14).

ADONI-BEZEK (à-dō'nĭ-bĕ'zĕk, Heb. *'ădhōnîvezeq, lord of lightning,* or *of the city of Bezek*). A king of Bezek, captured by the men of Judah and Simeon and taken to Jerusalem, where he was mutilated (Judg 1:5–7; Gal 6:7).

ADONIJAH (ăd'ō-nī'jà, Heb. *'ădhōnîyāhû, my Lord is Jehovah*). 1. The fourth son of David (2 Sam 3:2–4; 1 Chron 3:2). He was a spoiled, handsome lad, who won over Joab and Abiathar the priest to his bid for the throne. His failure to gain Zadok the priest, Nathan the prophet, and David's special guard resulted in the failure of his plan, when instead David proclaimed Solomon king (1 Kings 1:6–53). But after the death of David, Adonijah's attempt to marry Abishag prompted Solomon to have him killed (2:13–25). **2.** A Levite, sent by Jehoshaphat to teach the law (2 Chron 17:8). **3.** A chieftain who with Nehemiah sealed the covenant (Neh 10:14–16).

ADONIKAM (ăd-ō-nī'kăm, Heb. *'ădhōnîqām, my Lord has arisen*). The ancestor of a family, 666 of whom returned from exile with Zerubbabel (Ezra 2:13). Among the chiefs of the people who returned with Ezra are three sons and 60 males of this family (8:13). In the list of exiles whose genealogy proved them Israelites are 667 of this family (Neh 7:18). The Adonijah of Nehemiah 10:16, because of his position among those who sealed the covenant, is thought to be the same as Adonikam.

ADONIRAM (ăd-ō-nī'răm, Heb. *'ădhōnîrām, my Lord is exalted*). He was an officer "in charge of forced labor" under David (2 Sam 20:24) and under Solomon (1 Kings 4:6). Rehoboam sent him to the now rebel tribes of Israel (1 Kings 12:18), who stoned him to death. Another variant of his name, Hadoram, appears in an NIV footnote (2 Chron 10:18).

ADONI-ZEDEK (à-dō'nī-zē'dĕk, Heb. *'ădhōnîtsedheq, lord of righteousness*, or, *my lord is righteous*). Amorite king of Jerusalem (Josh 10:1–27). Having heard how Joshua destroyed Ai and Jericho and how Gibeon made peace with Israel, Adoni-Zedek and four other Amorite kings attacked Gibeon. Joshua came to the aid of Gibeon. God defeated the kings, sending hailstones and causing the sun and moon to stand still. Joshua killed the kings and hanged them on trees. An earlier king of Jerusalem (Salem) bore a name of similar form and identical meaning: Melchizedek, "king of righteousness" (Gen 14:18–20). See also MELCHIZEDEK.

ADOPTION (à-dŏp'shŭn, Gr. *huiothesia* in the NT). Pharaoh's daughter adopted Moses (Exod 2:10) and Mordecai adopted Esther (Esth 2:7, 15). Hadad the Edomite married the sister of the Egyptian queen, and their son Genubath was brought up "with Pharaoh's own children," whether formally adopted or not (1 Kings 11:20). Whether adoption was practiced in the Hebrews' own land is not clear.

Paul is the only NT writer to use the term; with him it is a metaphor derived from Hellenistic usage and Roman law. The legal situation of a son in early Roman times was little better than that of a slave, though in practice its rigor would vary with the disposition of the father. A son was the property of his father, who

(1) was entitled to the son's earnings, (2) could transfer ownership of him by adoption or by a true sale, and (3) could, under certain circumstances, even put him to death. An adopted son was considered like a son born in the family. He could no longer inherit from his natural father. He was no longer liable for old debts (a loophole eventually closed). So far as his former family was concerned, he was dead. Modifications of the rigor of sonship were at intervals introduced into Roman law, and a more liberal Hellenistic view was doubtless in Paul's mind.

Facsimile of papyrus document (from Elephantine, 416 B.C.) in which Zakkur ben Meshullam deeds the slave Yedoniah to Uriah ben Mahseiah for adoption. Courtesy Prof. B. Porten and A. Yardeni

In Galatians 4:1–3 Paul states accurately the Roman law of sonship. God sent his Son to be born into the human condition under law to redeem slaves of sin and give them the full rights of sons (4:4–5). Adoption brought us from slavery to sonship and heirship (4:7).

Adoption is more than a matter of position or status; when God adopted us, he put his Spirit within us, and we became subject to his control (Rom 8:1–15). This involves chastisement (Heb 12:5–11) as well as inheritance (Rom 8:16–18). In Romans 8:23 "our adoption" is spoken of as future, in the sense that its full effects are to be consummated at the time of "the redemption of our bodies," the loosing from all restraints that the limitation of a mortal body imposes.

In Romans 9:4 Paul begins with enumeration of the privileges of Israelites with "the adoption." Israel's sonship (Exod 4:22; Deut 14:1; Hos 11:1) was not the natural relationship by creation (Acts 17:28), but a peculiar one by a covenant of promise, a spiritual relationship by faith, under the sovereign grace of God. Paul expresses God's action that resulted in his adoption of us and enumerates its effects (Eph 1:4–12). This action began with God's election: "For he chose us in him before the creation of the world," using predestination as the mode ("he predestined us"); Christ is the agent (by Jesus Christ); and he himself is the adopting parent (to himself). God's sovereign act is stressed by the concluding phrase of verse 5: "in accordance with his pleasure and will." That adoption is not a mere matter of position is made plain in the statement of the purpose of election: "he chose us . . . to be holy and blameless in his sight" (1:4).

ADORAM (See ADONIRAM)

ADORATION (See WORSHIP)

ADRAMMELECH (ăd-răm′ĕ-lĕk, Heb. *'adhrammelekh, Addar is king*). **1.** The name given to Addar, the god the Sepharvites brought to Samaria when the king of Assyria settled them there, and in the worship of whom children were burned in fire (2 Kings 17:31). **2.** A son of Sennacherib, who, with his brother Sharezer, murdered their father in the temple of Nisroch (2 Kings 19:37; Isa 37–38).

ADRIEL (ā′drĭ-ăl, Heb. *'adhrîēl, God is my help*). Son of Barzillai the Meholathite, to whom Merab, Saul's daughter, was given in marriage, though she had been promised to David (1 Sam 18:19; 2 Sam 21:8). He had five sons, all of whom perished in David's dreadful and sinful acquiescence in the demand of the Gibeonites for scapegoats (2 Sam 21:9).

ADULLAM (à-dŭl′ăm, Heb. *'ădhullām, retreat, refuge*). A city 13 miles (22 km.) SW of Bethlehem; very ancient (Gen 38:1, 12, 20; Josh 15:35); the seat of one of the 31 petty kings conquered by Joshua (12:15). David hid with his family and about 400 men in one of the many limestone caves near the city (1 Sam 22:1–2) at a time when Saul sought his life. It was fortified by Rehoboam (2 Chron 11:7). Because of its beauty it was called "the glory of Israel" (Mic 1:15). It was reoccupied on the return from the Babylonian exile (Neh 11:30).

ADULTERY Sexual intercourse, usually of a man, married or unmarried, with the wife of another. One of the Ten Commandments forbids it (Exod 20:14; Deut 5:18). The punishment for both man and woman was death, probably by stoning (Deut 22:22–24; John 8:3–7). "Adultery" and related words translate deriva-

tives of the Hebrew root *n'ph* (*nā 'aph*), conveying the one plain meaning.

From the earliest times (Gen 39:9), even outside the people of God (26:10), adultery was regarded as a serious sin. Along with other sexual offenses (e.g., Gen 34:7; Deut 22:21; Judg 19:23; 2 Sam 13:12) it is a wicked outrage (Jer 29:23).

The OT finds adultery a ready figure for apostasy from the Lord and attachment to false gods (e.g., Isa 57:3; Jer 3:8–9; 13:27; Ezek 23:27, 43; Hos 2:4).

Jesus quotes the commandment (Matt 5:27–30; 19:18; Mark 10:19; Luke 18:20), broadening its application to include the lustful look. He teaches that such evils as adultery come from the heart (Matt 15:19; Mark 7:21). Jesus declares remarriage of a divorced man or woman to be adultery (Matt 5:31–32; 19:3–9; Mark 10:2–12; Luke 16:18), with one exception (Matt 5:32; 19:9), the interpretation of which differs. Jesus uses the term figuratively of a people unfaithful to God (Matt 12:39; 16:4; Mark 8:38). Paul, without implying any exception, declares it to be adultery to remarry while one's spouse is still alive (Rom 7:3).

The NT treatment of adultery, following the implications of the OT concept, supports marriage as a lifelong monogamous union. Adultery is a special and aggravated case of fornication. In the teaching of Jesus and the apostles in the NT, all sexual impurity is sin against God, against self, and against others. Spiritual adultery violates the union between Christ and his own.

ADUMMIM (à-dŭm′ĭm, Heb. *'ădhummîm, perhaps red spots*). A pass, the ascent of Addummim, on the road between Jerusalem and Jericho (Josh 15:7; 18:17), on the Benjamin–Judah border. It is convincingly held to be the scene of Jesus' parable of the Good Samaritan (Luke 10:30–35).

ADVENT (See ESCHATOLOGY)

ADVOCATE (ăd′vōkăt, Gr. *paraklētos, supporter, Paraclete*). The Holy Spirit is the Advocate of the Father with us, and therefore our Comforter (John 14:16, 26; 15:26; 16:7) who not only consoles but also strengthens, helps, and counsels, with such authority as a legal advocate has for his client. Christ is also spoken of in this way (14:16; 1 John 2:1).

AENEAS (ē-nē′ăs). A paralytic, healed at Lydda by Peter (Acts 9:32–35).

AENON (ē′nŏn; in Aramaic means *springs*). A place near Salim, where John the Baptist was baptizing during the time

Jesus was baptizing in Judea (John 3:22–23). The site of Aenon is unknown.

AEON (ē'ŏn, Gr. *aiōn*). The word *aeon* does not occur in the English Bible. *Aion* originally meant "relative time duration, limited or unlimited," i.e., a period of time, or eternity, and is often translated "world," "age," and "for ever." *Aeon* is sometimes synonymous with Greek *kosmos*, world-order (e.g., Mark 4:19; 1 Cor 1:20; 2:6; 3:19). "The end of the ages" (Heb 9:26) is the period ushered in by the first coming of Christ; "the end of the age" (Matt 24:3; 28:20) is its culmination at his second coming. We live in the in-between period (1 Cor 10:11). "This present age [time]" and "the age [world] to come" are distinguished (e.g., Matt 12:32; Mark 10:30; Rom 12:2; Eph 1:21; 2 Tim 4:10; Titus 2:12; Heb 6:5).

AFRICA Either the whole continent or Roman Proconsular Africa (that is, modern Tunisia, to which were added Numidia and Mauretania). In the OT there are many references to Egypt and a few to Ethiopia (e.g., Isa 45:14; Jer 13:23). In the NT, Egypt, its Greek city of Alexandria (Acts 18:24), Ethiopia (8:27), and the port of Cyrene (in modern Libya) (Mark 15:21) are mentioned primarily because of the Jewish settlements there. Jesus himself went into Egypt (Matt 2:13–14), and Jews from Africa were present on the Day of Pentecost (Acts 2:10).

AGABUS (ăg'à-bŭs). A Jerusalem prophet who correctly predicted a famine over the entire Roman world (Acts 11:27–30). Years later, probably the same prophet warned Paul that he would be put in bonds if he persisted in going to Jerusalem (21:10–11).

AGAG (ā'găg, Heb. *'ăghāgh*, perhaps meaning *violent*). 1. An important king of Amalek whom Balaam prophesied a king of Jacob (Israel) would surpass (Num 24:3–9). This prediction was fulfilled when Saul met Agag in battle and defeated him (1 Sam 15:1–33). See also SAUL.

AGAGITE (See HAMAN)

AGAPE (ăg'à-pā, Gr. *agapē*). The more frequent of two NT words for love, which implies the preciousness of the one loved. It is used in Jude 12 (perhaps also in Acts 20:11; 1 Cor 11:21–22, 33–34; 2 Peter 2:13) of common meals that cultivated brotherly love among Christians. The Lord's Supper properly followed, but was distinct from, the love feast.

AGAR (ā'găr). The Greek name of Sarai's handmaid (Gal 4:24–25). See HAGAR.

AGATE (See MINERALS)

AGE (See AEON)

AGE, OLD AGE Called the reward of filial obedience (Exod 20:12). Respect was to be shown the aged (Lev 19:32). Younger men waited till they had spoken (Job 32:4). God promised Abraham "a good old age" (Gen 15:15; cf. Eccl 12:1–7). Jacob lamented that he had not lived as long as his ancestors (Gen 47:7–9). There are many Hebrew words relating to old age in the OT, showing the honor in which the aged were usually held; yet gray hairs also had their sorrows (44:29–31). Official positions went to older men (elders, e.g., Exod 3:16; Matt 21:23). Aged men and women are given sound advice (Titus 2:2–5). Jesus Christ is portrayed with the white hair of old age (Rev 1:14).

AGONY (Gr. *agōnia*, agony, anguish). The word is derived from the Greek *agōn*, "contest, struggle," and depicts severe conflict and pain. Christ's agony was such that "his sweat was like drops of blood" (Luke 22:44; cf. Matt 26:36–46; Mark 14:32–42; Heb 5:7–8.) His agony was a mixture of his horror at becoming sin on our behalf, the separation which that meant from God the Father, and his struggle with the powers of darkness.

AGORA (ă'gō-rà, Gr. *agora*, marketplace*). In ancient cities the town meeting place, where the public met for the exchange of merchandise, information, and ideas. The agorae of Galilee and Judea were the scenes for many of Jesus'

Remains of the Agora in Athens, the central market place and meeting ground for various public activities. It was here that Paul had his daily disputations with the citizens (Acts 17:17). The temple of Hephaestus is viewed in background. Courtesy Gerald Nowotny.

heallng miracles (Mark 6:56). Here the village idlers, as well as those seeking work, would gather (Matt 20:3); the vain and the proud could parade to gain public recognition (23:7; Mark 12:38; Luke 11:43; 20:46); and the children would gather for play (Matt 11:16–17; Luke 7:32). In Gentile cities, the agorae served also as forums and tribunals. The agora of Philippi was the scene of the trial of Paul and Silas (Acts 16:16ff.). In Athens Paul's daily disputations in the agora led directly to his famed message before the Areopagus (17:17ff.).

AGRAPHA (ăg'rà-fà, Gr. *agrapha, unwritten things*). These are units (few and of little value) of tradition concerning Christ, mostly sayings ascribed to him, transmitted to us outside of the canonical Gospels (Acts 1:4–5; 1:7–8; 11:16; 20:35; 1 Cor 11:24–25; 1 Thess 4:15ff.; James 1:12). Other sources of agrapha include textual variations in ancient NT manuscripts, the patristic literature, and certain Egyptian papyri.

AGRICULTURE Not a Bible word; "husbandry" and "husbandman" are used for the activity and the one who practices it. In the form of horticulture, it is as old as Adam (Gen 2:5, 8–15). Caring for the Garden of Eden became labor after the curse (3:17–19). Nomad and farmer began to be differentiated with Abel and Cain (4:2–4). Noah planted a vineyard (Gen 9:20). Abraham and his descendants were nomad herdsmen in Canaan, though Isaac and Jacob at times also tilled the soil (26:12; 37:7). Agriculture became the basis of the Mosaic commonwealth, since the land of Palestine was suited to an agricultural rather than a pastoral economy.

Viticulture (the cultivation of grapes) is pictured in Isaiah 5:1–7 and Matthew 21:33–41. Some farming procedures are described in Isaiah 28:24–28. The plow was light and drawn by yokes of oxen (1 Kings 19:19). Fallow ground was broken and cleared early in the year (Jer 4:3; Hos 10:11). Seed was scattered broadcast, as in the parable of the sower (Matt 13:1–8), and plowed in afterward, the stubble of the preceding crop becoming mulch by decay. In irrigated fields, the seed was trodden in by cattle (Isa 32:20). Egypt depended exclusively on irrigation, but Palestine depended more on rain (Deut 11:10–12). Sowing varied seed in a field was forbidden (Deut 22:9).

Scripture records the relations of farm laborers, steward (manager or overseer), and owner (Ruth; Matt 20:1–16; Luke 17:7–9). Agriculture was beset with

The Gezer calendar on a tablet of limestone (4 1/4 in. X 3 1/8 in.) that records the annual cycle of agricultural activities. Evidently a schoolboy's exercises from about the time of Solomon. The script is ancient Hebrew. Courtesy Israel Department of Antiquities and Museums

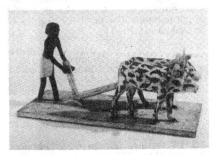

A wooden model of a man guiding a two-handled plow drawn by two oxen. The yoke consists of a bar placed on the necks of the oxen just behind the long horns. From Egypt, c. 2350–2000 B.C. Reproduced by courtesy of the Trustees of the British Museum

pests: locust, cankerworm, caterpillar, and palmerworm (Joel 2:25 KJV), as well

Bronze coin depicting the portrait of King Agrippa I with the Greek inscription, "Of the great King Agrippa the friend of the Emperor." Reverse depicts the city-goddess of Caesarea and the inscription, "Caesarea which is near by the Augustan harbor, year 7 (A.D. 43)." Courtesy Carta, Jerusalem

as blight, mildew, and hail (Hag 2:17). See also FARMING; OCCUPATIONS AND PROFESSIONS.

AGRIPPA I (à-grĭp'à). Known in history as King Herod Agrippa I and in the NT (Acts 12) as Herod. Son of Aristobulus and Bernice and grandson of Herod the Great. Through friendship with the emperors Caligula and Claudius, he gained the rulership first of Iturea and Trachonitis, then of Galilee and Perea, and ultimately of Judea and Samaria. He ruled over this reunited domain of Herod the Great from A.D. 40 until his death in 44 at the age of 54. While owing his position to the favor of Rome, he recognized the importance of exercising great tact in his contacts with the Jews. He killed James to please them, and imprisoned Peter, planning a public trial and execution after the Passover (Acts 12:2–4). Agrippa's sudden death occurred after he had accepted the flattery of being called a god (Acts 12:20–23). His death is fully recorded by Josephus (*Antiq.* 19.8). See also HEROD.

AGRIPPA II (à-grĭp'à). Known in history as King Herod Agrippa II and in the NT (Acts 25 and 26) as Agrippa. The son of Agrippa I, he ruled over only a small part of his father's territory. He went to Caesarea with his sister (and consort) Bernice (Acts 25:23–26:32). He died in 100.

AGUE (See DISEASES)

AGUR (ā'gûr, Heb. *'āghûr, gatherer*). The otherwise unknown author of Proverbs 30. His words are described as "an oracle," thus claiming divine inspiration. Many, however, follow the suggestion of

a place name—"of Massa" (cf. NIV note; Gen 25:14, 16).

AHAB (ā'hăb, Heb. *'ah'āv, father's brother*). **1.** Son of Omri and seventh king of the northern kingdom of Israel, he reigned 22 years (873–851 B.C.). Politically, Ahab was one of the strongest kings of Israel. In his days Israel was at peace with Judah and maintained her dominion over Moab, which paid a considerable tribute (2 Kings 3:4). He went into battle on three different occasions in later years against Ben-Hadad, king of Syria. While he had great success in the first two campaigns, he was defeated and mortally wounded in the third.

Ahab owes his prominence in the OT to the religious apostasy that occurred in Israel during his reign. Of him it is said, he "did more evil in the eyes of the LORD than any of those before him" (1 Kings 16:30) and "There was never a man like Ahab, who sold himself to do evil in the eyes of the LORD, urged on by Jezebel his wife" (21:25). His marriage to Jezebel, daughter of the king of the Zidonians, was politically advantageous but religiously disastrous. Jezebel introduced the idolatrous worship of Baal into Israel as well as the licentious orgies of the goddess Ashtoreth. She also instituted a severe persecution against the followers of the Lord and killed all the prophets of the Lord, except 100 that Obadiah hid (18:4; cf. 19:14). At this critical period in the history of Israel, God raised up Elijah, whose faithful ministry culminated in the conflict with the prophets of Baal on Mt. Carmel (ch 18).

Ahab's religious corruption was equaled by his love of material wealth and display—e.g., his elaborately ornamented ivory palace (1 Kings 22:39). He coveted the vineyard of Naboth and got it (after Jezebel had false witnesses testify against Naboth and then had him stoned to death). For this crime, God said that all of Ahab's posterity would be cut off (21:21), even as had been the case with the two previous dynasties, those of Jeroboam and Baasha. This prophecy of Elijah (21:19) was fulfilled to the letter on Ahab's son Joram (2 Kings 9:24–26) and in part on Ahab himself (1 Kings 22:38). Execution of the sentence was, however, delayed by Ahab's repentance (21:27–29). Ahab also sinned by failing to discern the Lord's will and sparing the defeated Ben-Hadad of Syria (20:20–43). The prediction of his own death (20:42) was fulfilled when he was killed in battle at Ramoth Gilead (22:34).

2. A false prophet who deceived the

Israelite remains of city wall at Ahab's capital, Samaria. The wall was c. 5 feet (1.6 m.) thick and built of fine ashlar masonry laid in headers and stretchers carefully fitted together. Courtesy Israel Department of Antiquities and Museums

Jews in Babylon. Joining with Zedekiah, another false prophet, Ahab predicted an early return to Jerusalem. For this sin and their immoral conduct, Jeremiah prophesied that they would be burned to death by the king of Babylon and that their names would become a byword (Jer 29:21-23).

AHASAI (See AHZAI)

AHASUERUS (See XERXES)

AHAZ (ā'hăz, Heb. *'āhāz, he has grasped*). Reigning over the southern kingdom of Judah, 735-715 B.C., Ahaz was a king of great significance. Historically during his reign and as a result of his policies, the people of God became vassals of Assyria and never again did the throne of David exist in its own sovereign right (although the dominant power changed). Theologically his policies involved a denial of the way of faith (Isa 7:9).

Ahaz gave his country firm and resolute leadership—but in the wrong direction. The 12th king of Judah, he reigned from 735 to 715 B.C. (age 20 to 40), ruling four years as a co-regent with his father Jotham and 16 years as sole monarch. When Rezin of Damascus and Pekah of Israel made a league against Judah, Isaiah promised God's deliverance and told Ahaz to ask for a sign (Isa 7:1-9), but Ahaz refused. Isaiah delivered the prophecy of the virgin conception (7:14). Judah was disastrously defeated (120,000 dying in one day), with many captives taken (2 Chron 28:1-15). Edom and the Philistines also invaded. Ahaz sought help from—but instead was hurt by—Tiglath-

Pileser (28:20). Ahaz turned in vain to worshiping other gods (28:23-25), his apostasy having begun long before this (2 Kings 16:10-18).

2. A great-grandson of Jonathan, son of King Saul (1 Chron 8:35-36).

AHAZIAH (ā'hà-zī'à, Heb. *'āhazyâh, Jehovah hath grasped*). 1. Son of Ahab and Jezebel, 8th king of Israel. He reigned only briefly 851-850 B.C. and worshiped Jeroboam's calves and his mother's idols, Baal and Ashtoreth. The most notable event of his reign was the revolt of the Moabites, who had been paying tribute (2 Kings 1:1; 3:4-5). Ahaziah could not put down the revolt because he was severely injured in a fall. He sent messengers to inquire of Baalzebub, god of Ekron, whether he would recover. Elijah, sent by God, intercepted the messengers and told them that Ahaziah would die. The king tried to capture the prophet, but two groups of 50 men were consumed by fire from heaven in making the attempt. A third contingent implored Elijah to deliver them from the fate of their predecessors (2 Kings 1:13, 14). Elijah then went down to Samaria and gave the message directly to the king, who died shortly afterward.

2. Son of Jehoram of Judah and Athaliah; thus grandson of Jehoshaphat and Ahab, and nephew of Ahaziah of Israel. He was the 6th king of Judah and reigned only one year (2 Chron 22:2), 843 B.C., beginning to reign at age 22. Ahaziah walked in all the idolatries of his mother and the house of Ahab (22:3) and allied with Joram of Israel (22:5). Following his death, his mother Athaliah seized the throne and killed all the royal sons of Judah, except Joash, Ahaziah's son, who had been hidden.

AHI (ā'hī, Heb. *'āhî*). 1. Chief of the Gadites in Gilead (1 Chron 5:15). 2. A man of Asher (1 Chron 7:34).

AHIAH One of the men who set their seal to the covenant drawn up before the Lord in Nehemiah's time (Neh 10:26). See also AHIJAH.

AHIEZER (ā-hī-ē' zêr, Heb. *'āhî'ezer, brother of help*). 1. The head of the tribe of Dan in the wilderness (Num 1:12; 2:25; 7:66). 2. A Gibeonite who joined David at Ziklag (1 Chron 12:3).

AHIHUD (à-hī'hŭd, Heb. *'āhîhûdh, brother is majesty*). 1. Prince of Asher; chosen by Moses to help divide Canaan (Num 34:27). 2. A son of Ehud (1 Chron 8:7).

AHIJAH (à-hī'jà, Heb. *'ăhîyâ, brother of Jehovah*). **1.** One of the sons of Jerahmeel, a great-grandson of Judah and brother of Caleb (1 Chron 2:25). **2.** A descendant of Benjamin, mentioned in connection with an intra-family conflict (8:7). **3.** Son of Ahitub. He was priestly successor to the great priest of Shiloh, Eli, and after the destruction of Shiloh, served as priest under King Saul. He was asked to inquire of the Lord for Saul during the Philistine war (1 Sam 13–14). **4.** The Pelonite, one of the valiant men of David's armies (1 Chron 11:36). **5.** A Levite who was in charge of the treasures of the house of God in David's reign (26:20). **6.** A scribe of Solomon (1 Kings 4:3). **7.** A prophet of Shiloh (11:29–39; 12:15; 14:2; 15:29). He predicted to Jeroboam that he would reign over ten of the twelve tribes, and that his dynasty would be an enduring one if he did what was right in God's eyes. However, Jeroboam did not, so Ahijah foretold the end of Jeroboam's life and line. **8.** The father of Baasha, king of Israel (15:27). See also AHIAH.

AHIKAM (à-hī'kăm, Heb. *'ăhîqām, my brother has risen up*). Son of Shaphan the scribe, sent by Josiah to ask the meaning of the Book of the Law that was found (2 Kings 22:12). Later he successfully pleaded before the princes and elders that Jeremiah should not be put to death for his warnings of impending doom (Jer 26:24). After the deportation to Babylon, Ahikam's son Gedaliah became governor over the people who remained in the cities of Judah (2 Kings 25:22; Jer 40:5).

AHILUD (à-hī'lŭd, Heb. *'ăhîlûdh, a child's brother*). Father of Jehoshaphat the recorder (2 Sam 8:16; 20:24; 1 Kings 4:3; 1 Chron 18:15).

AHIMAAZ (à-hĭm'ā-ăz, Heb. *'ăhîma'-ats, brother of anger*). **1.** The father of Ahinoam, wife of King Saul (1 Sam 14:50). **2.** Son of Zadok the high priest (1 Chron 6:8). During Absalom's rebellion he and Jonathan, son of Abiathar, served as messengers between David and Hushai, David's counselor and spy (2 Sam 15:24–27; 17:15–22; 1 Kings 4:2; 1 Chron 6:8–10).**3.** A son-in-law and commissary officer of Solomon (1 Kings 4:15).

AHIMAN (à-hī'măn, Heb. *'ăhîman, my brother is a gift*). **1.** One of the three giant sons of Anak seen in Mt. Hebron by the spies (Num 13:22) and driven by Caleb from Hebron (Josh 15:14) and killed (Judg 1:10). **2.** A Levite gatekeeper (1 Chron 9:17).

AHIMELECH (à-hĭm'-ĕ-lĕk, Heb. *'ăhîmelekh, brother of a king*). **1.** A priest who assisted David, not knowing that he was a fugitive from Saul. Saul had all the priests at Nob massacred except Abiathar, who fled to David (1 Sam 21–22). **2.** Son of Abiathar and grandson of Ahimelech (2 Sam 8:17; 1 Chron 18:16; 24:6). **3.** A Hittite who, with Abishai, was asked to accompany David to Saul's camp (1 Sam 26:6).

AHINOAM (à-hĭn'ō-ăm, Heb. *'ăhîn-ō'am, my brother is delight*). **1.** Wife of King Saul (1 Sam 14:50). **2.** One of David's wives, a Jezreelitess (25:43), who lived with him at Gath (27:3). She and Abigail were captured by the Amalekites at Ziklag (30:5) but were rescued by David (30:18). They were with David in Hebron (2 Sam 2:2), where Ahinoam bore Amnon, his first son (3:2).

AHIO (à-hī'ō, Heb. *'ahyô, brotherly*). **1.** Son of Abinadab. He and his brother Uzzah accompanied the ark of God from Gibeah on David's first attempt to remove it to Jerusalem (2 Sam 6:2–22; 1 Chron 13:1–14). **2.** A Benjamite (1 Chron 8:14). **3.** A Gibeonite, son of Jehiel (8:31; 9:37).

AHIRA (à-hī'rà, Heb. *'ăhîra', brother of evil*). Prince captain of the tribe of Naphtali (Num 1:15; 2:29; 7:78, 83; 10:27).

AHIRAM (à-hī'răm, Heb. *'ăhîrām, brother of height, exalted brother*). Son of Benjamin (Num 26:38), perhaps the same as Aharah (1 Chron 8:1–2).

AHISAMACH (à-hĭs'à-măk, Heb. *'ăhîsā-mākh, my brother supports*). A Danite, the father of Oholiab (Exod 31:6; 35:34; 38:23).

AHITHOPHEL (à-hĭth'ō-fĕl, Heb. *'ăhî-thōphel, brother of folly*). David's counselor who joined Absalom's conspiracy and was a mainspring of the rebellion (2 Sam 15:12). In his proverbial wisdom (16:23) he urged Absalom to pursue David immediately, smiting the king while he was still weary and underprotected. Ahithophel, seeing his counsel rejected in favor of Hushai's, realized that the cause of Absalom was lost; he went to his home and hanged himself (17:1–23).

AHITUB (à-hī'tŭb, Heb. *'ăhîtûb, brother of goodness*).**1.** Brother of Ichabod, son of Phinehas (son of Eli), and father of Ahiah (1 Sam 14:3) and Ahimelech (22:9, 11, 20). **2.** Son of Amariah and father of Zadok the high priest (2 Sam 8:17; 1 Chron 6:7–8; cf. 9:11 Neh 11:11). **3.** Son of another Amariah and father of another Zadok (1 Chron 6:11–12), or (cf. Ezra 7:1–5) the same as no. 2.

AHLAI (à'lī, Heb. *'ahlay, O would that!*). **1.** The father of Zabad, one of David's soldiers (1 Chron 11:41). **2.** A daughter of Sheshan who married her father's Egyptian slave Jarha. They had a son named Attai (2:31–35).

AHOAH (à-hō'à, Heb. *'ăhôah, brotherly*). A son of Bela (1 Chron 8:4) and the one from whom is derived the term "Ahohite" (2 Sam 23:9, 28; 1 Chron 11:12).

AHOHITE (à-hō'hīt, Heb. *'ăhôhî*). An ancestral name (from the father) given to the descendants of Ahoah: Dodo (2 Sam 23:9), Zalmon (23:28), and Ilai (1 Chron 11:29).

AHOLAH (See OHOLAH)

AHOLIAB (See OHOLIAB)

AHOLIBAH (See OHOLIBAH)

AHOLIBAMAH (See OHOLIBAMAH)

AHUZZATH (à-hŭz'ăth, Heb. *'ăhuzzath, possession*). A "friend" of Abimelech. These men and Phicol, chief of the Philistine army, made a peace treaty with Isaac after they saw that the Lord had blessed him (Gen 26:23–33).

AI (ā'ī, Heb. *'ay, ruin*). A city of central Palestine, east of Bethel also called Aiath (Isa 10:28) and Aija (Neh 11:31). Abraham pitched his tent between Ai and Bethel when he arrived in Canaan (Gen 12:8). Ai figures most prominently in the account of the conquest of the land; it was the second Canaanite city taken by Joshua and Israel (Josh 7–8). The first attack on Ai was unsuccessful because of Achan's sin; but the second successful attack resulted in the total destruction of the city and its inhabitants.

AIAH (ā'yà, Heb. *'ayyâh, falcon*). **1.** A Horite (Gen 36:24; 1 Chron 1:40). **2.** The father of Rizpah, Saul's concubine (2 Sam 3:7; 21:8).

AIJALON (ā'jà-lŏn, Heb. *'ayyālôn, place of gazelles*). **1.** A city of Dan (Josh 19:42), assigned to the Levite sons of Kohath (1 Chron 6:69), mentioned by Joshua (Josh 10:12). **2.** The burial place of the judge Elon, in Zebulun (Judg 12:12).

AIJELETH SHAHAR (ā'jĕ-lĕth shā'hàr, Heb. *'ayyeleth hash-shahar, the hind of the morning*). Term found in the title to Psalm 22. NIV commits itself to the meaning "To the tune of 'The Doe of the Morning.'" But more scholars relate *'ayyeleth* to the word *'ayaluth* (v. 19),

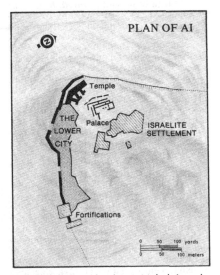

PLAN OF AI

The city captured, after initial defeat, by Joshua and his men (Josh 7:2–8:29). Courtesy Carta, Jerusalem

"strength," or "help." Then the words actually entitle the psalm "Help at Daybreak" suitably, as verses 22–31 show.

AIN (ā'ĕn, Heb. *'ayin, eye, fountain*). **1.** A landmark on the eastern border of the Promised Land; west of Riblah (Num 34:11). **2.** A southern city of Judah (Josh 15:32), later of Simeon (19:7), and still later assigned to the priests (21:16).

AIR In the OT and the Gospels this word is usually found in expressions speaking of the birds or fowl of the air (Job 41:16 is the only exception) and representing words normally translated "heaven." Elsewhere in the NT it stands for *aēr*, the atmosphere. An ineffective Christian is pictured as a boxer "beating the air" (1 Cor 9:26). "Speaking into the air" describes unintelligible language (14:9). Satan is called "the ruler of the kingdom of the air" (Eph 2:2). In the Rapture the church will meet Christ "in the air" (1 Thess 4:17).

AJAH (See AIAH)

AJALON (See AIJALON)

AKELDAMA (à-kĕl'dà-mà, ASV, NIV, RSV; Aceldama, à-sĕl'dà-mà, KJV; Hakeldama, hà-kĕl'dà-mà, JB, NASB; Gr. *Akeldama*). The field purchased by the priests in Judas' name with the money received for betraying Christ (Acts 1:18–19; Matt

Bronze head of an Akkadian ruler thought to represent Niram-Sin of Agade. From Nineveh (c. 2500 B.C.). Courtesy Bildarchiv Foto, Marburg

27:3–10). The field was called "the place of blood" in Aramaic, probably because of the gruesome manner of Judas' death.

AKHENATON (à'kĕn-à't'n, *he who is beneficial to Aton*). The name chosen by Amenhotep IV (1377–1360 B.C.), ruler in the Eighteenth Dynasty of Egypt, when he changed the religion of his country, demanding that all his subjects worship only the sun god under the name Aton. He is credited by many as being the first to worship only one god (a monotheist).

AKKAD (ăk'ăd, Heb. *'akkadh,* Gen 10:10). One of the cities or districts of Nimrod's kingdom, with Babel, Erech, and Calneh. The location of Akkad is uncertain, though it is thought to be identified with Agade, the chief city of a district of the same name in northern Babylonia, which Sargon I made his capital in c. 2350 B.C.

AKKUB (ăk'ŭb, Heb. *'aqqûv, pursuer*). **1.** Son of Elioenai (1 Chron 3:24). **2.** A Levite who founded a family of temple gatekeepers (9:17). **3.** The head of a family of temple servants (Ezra 2:45). **4.** A Levite who helped expound the Law (Neh 8:7).

AKRABBIM (ăk-răb'ĭm, Heb. *'aqrab-bîm, scorpions*). A word always found with *ma'ăleh* (mā'a-la), meaning "the

going up to," "ascent of," or "pass." So "Scorpion Pass" (NIV), rising between the SW corner of the Dead Sea and Zin, was the southern boundary between Judah and Edom (Num 34:4; Josh 15:3) and the boundary of the Amorites (Judg 1:36).

ALABASTER (See MINERALS)

ALAMETH (See ALEMETH)

ALAMMELECH (See ALLAMMELECH)

ALAMOTH (ăl'à-mŏth, Heb. *'ălāmôth, maidens, virgins*). A musical term of uncertain meaning (1 Chron 15:20; Ps 46:1). It may indicate a women's choir, musical instruments set in a high pitch, or instruments played by virgins.

ALEMETH (ăl'ĕ-mĕth, Heb. *'ălāmeth, concealment*). **1.** A son of Beker and grandson of Benjamin (1 Chron 7:8). **2.** Son of Jehoaddah (8:36), Jarah (9:42, JB, KJV, MLB, NASB, NEB, RSV; Jadah NIV).

ALEMETH, ALMON (ăl'ĕ-mĕth, ăl'-mŏn, *hidden*). A priests' city (Josh 21:18; 1 Chron 6:60).

ALEPH (ä'lĕf, *ox*). The first letter of the Hebrew alphabet. Although a consonant, it is the forerunner of the Greek *alpha* and the English *a.*

ALEXANDER (ăl'ĕg-zăn'dêr, Gr. *Alexandros, man-defending*). A common Greek name belonging to five Jews to whom reference is made in the NT: **1.** Son of Simon of Cyrene, the man who carried Jesus' cross (Mark 15:21). **2.** A kinsman of the Jewish high priest Annas (Acts 4:6). **3.** A Jew of Ephesus (19:33). **4.** A false teacher whom Paul handed over to Satan for punishment (1 Tim 1:20). **5.** A metalworker who did Paul harm (2 Tim 4:14)—perhaps the same as no. 3 or no. 4.

ALEXANDER THE GREAT (ăl'ĕg-zăn'dêr, Gr. *Alexandros, man-defending*). Son of Philip, king of Macedon, and Olympias, an Epirote princess; born 356 B.C. Though not named in the Bible, he is described prophetically in Daniel, the "goat" from the west with a notable horn between his eyes. He came against the ram with two horns, who was standing before the river, defeated the ram, and became very great until the great horn was broken and four notable ones came up from it (Dan 8:5–8). The prophecy identifies the ram as the kings of Media and Persia, the goat as the king of Greece, the great horn being the first king. When he fell, four kings arose in his place (8:18–22). The historical fulfillment is striking: Alexander led the Greek ar-

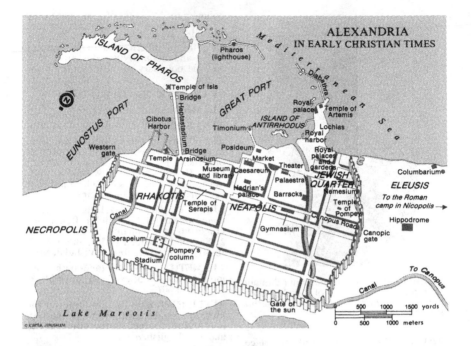

ALEXANDRIA
IN EARLY CHRISTIAN TIMES

The modern port at Alexandria. Courtesy B. Brandl

mies across the Hellespont into Asia Minor in 334 B.C. and defeated the Persian forces at the river Granicus. Moving with amazing rapidity ("without touching the ground," 8:5), he again met and defeated the Persians at Issus. Turning south, he moved down the Syrian coast, advancing to Egypt, which fell to him without a blow. Turning again to the east, he met the armies of Darius for the last time, defeating them in the battle of Arbela, east of the Tigris River. After conquering as far east as India, Alexander died of a fever in 323 at age 33. His empire was then divided among four of his generals.

ALEXANDRIA (ăl′ĕg-zăn′drĭ-à, Gr. *Alexanddreia*). Founded by Alexander the Great, 332 B.C.; successively the Ptolemaic, Roman, and Christian capital of Lower Egypt. Its harbors were suitable for both commerce and war and it was the chief grain port for Rome. Alexandria was also an important cultural center, its university (patterned after the great school at Athens) was noted for mathematics, astronomy, medicine and poetry. The library of Alexandria became the largest in the world with from 400,000 to 900,000 books and scrolls.

The population of Alexandria contained Jews, Greeks, and Egyptians. The Jews flourished here and considered this their metropolis. Here the translation of the OT into Greek, known as the Septuagint, was made in the third century before Christ. It became the popular Bible of the Jews of the Dispersion, generally used by the writers of the NT. The influence of Alexandrian philosophy on the thought of the NT is debatable, but its impact on later theological studies in the Christian church was great.

According to tradition, Mark the evangelist carried the gospel to Alexandria and established the first church there. From this city Christianity spread through Egypt into surrounding countries. A theological school was established here in the second century; Clement and Origen were famous teachers, who were pioneers in biblical scholarship and Christian philosophy.

ALGUM (See PLANTS)

ALIAH (See ALVAH)

ALIAN (See ALVAN)

ALLEGORY (Gr. *allēgoreuein*, from *allos, other,* and *agoreuein, to speak in the assembly*). Literary device used extensively in Scripture (e.g., Isa 5:1–7). To speak allegorically is to set forth one thing in the image of another, the principal subject being inferred from the figure rather than by direct statement. Clarity of inference differentiates between allegory and parable, because the latter usually requires an interpretation for the teaching that it parallels. In the allegory in Galatians 4:24 Isaac, the child of promise, typifies the Christian who is justified in Christ and is free to love and serve his Father; while Ishmael, the child of contrivance, typifies the legalist who is under the law and is bound to serve it and to seek justification in obedience to it.

ALLELUIA (See HALLELUJAH)

ALLIANCES (See COVENANT)

ALLON (ăl'ŏn, Heb. *'allôn, oak*). **1.** A prince of Simeon (1 Chron 4:37). **2.** Otherwise "Elon" (Heb. *'ēlôn*), a town, or *"the large tree* in Zaanannim" (NIV), a southern boundary point in Naphtali (Josh 19:33; cf. Judg 4:11). **3.** *Allon Bachuth,* "the oak of weeping," a tree marking the burial place of Deborah, the nurse of Rebekah (Gen 35:8).

ALMIGHTY (Heb. *shadday,* meaning uncertain). Gr. *pantokratōr, all powerful.* Used with *el, Kurios, Theos,* for identification (Gen 17:1), invocation (28:3), description (Ezek 10:5), praise (Rev 4:8). See also EL SHADDAI.

ALMODAD (ăl-mō'dăd, Heb. *'almôdhādh, the beloved*). First-mentioned of Joktan's 13 sons (Gen 10:26; 1 Chron 1:20). This Arabian name is preserved in El-Mudad, famous in Arabian history as reputed father of Ishmael's Arab wife and as chief of Jurham, a Joktanite tribe.

ALMON (See ALEMETH, ALMON)

ALMOND TREE (See PLANTS)

ALMS (ähms). Kind deeds arising out of compassion, mercy, and pity for the unfortunate. The word itself is not found in the NIV, though the practice repeatedly appears in Mosaic legislation and NT injunction: Greek *eleēmosynē,* also in LXX for Hebrew *tsedhāqâh,* "righteousness," and *hesedh,* "kindness." Matthew 6:1 has *dikaiosynē,* "alms" (KJV), "acts of righteousness" (NIV). The verb *poiein,* "to do, perform," is often used with the noun to convey the meaning of helping the poor and needy (cf. Matt 6:2–3; Acts 9:36; 10:2; 24:17). Mosaic law prescribed gleanings from orchards and

olive groves and from the harvest, the vineyards, and the grain in the corners of the field for the poor (Lev 19:9–10; Deut 24:10–22).

In later Judaism the righteousness of almsgiving became somewhat legalistic and professional. The lame man at the Gate Beautiful exemplified professional begging in that daily he "asked . . . for money" (Acts 3:2–3 NIV; "ask alms" KJV, RSV; "beg alms" MLB, NASB). Perversion in giving alms is seen in benefactors who want "to be seen" (Matt 6:1–2). Almsgiving was of two kinds: "alms of the dish" (food and money received daily for distribution) and "alms of the chest" (coins received on the Sabbath for widows, orphans, strangers, and the poor). The practice of the NT church was foreshadowed in Jesus' admonitions (Luke 11:41; 12:33; cf. 1 Cor 16:2; 2 Cor 8:1–4, 14). A primary function of deacons was to distribute alms (Acts 6).

ALMUG (See PLANTS)

ALOE

ALPHA (ăl'fà). First letter of the Greek alphabet (A). The word "alphabet," indicating a list of elementary sounds in any language, comes from the first two Greek letters, alpha and beta. In contrast is omega, the last letter of the Greek alphabet. Combined with alpha it signifies completeness, as "from A to Z" in modern usage. So God (Christ) is the Alpha and the Omega (Rev 1:8; 21:6; 22:13; cf. Isa 41:4; 44:6).

ALPHABET (See WRITING)

ALPHAEUS (ăl-fē'ŭs, Gr. *Alphaios*). **1.** Father of Levi (Mark 2:14). **2.** Father of James the apostle (Matt 10:3; Mark 3:18; Luke 6:15; Acts 1:13). **3.** Possibly Clopas (KJV Cleophas), husband of the Mary at the cross (John 19:25; cf. Mark 15:40), as *Cleophas* and *Alphaeus* are of Semitic derivation.

ALTAR (Heb. *mizbēah, place of slaughter,* Gr. *bomos,* in Acts only, and *thysiastērion*). In OT times altars were many and varied, their importance seen in the fact that the Hebrew and Greek words appear some 360 times.

The first Hebrew altar we read about (Gen 8:20) was erected by Noah after leaving the ark. Subsequent altars were built by Abraham (12:7–8; 13:4, 18; 22:9), Isaac (26:25), Jacob (35:1–7), Moses (Exod 17:15), and Joshua (Josh 8:30–31)–most for sacrificial purposes, but some were largely memorial (Exod 17:15–16; Josh 22:26–27). Sometimes God stated just how the altar was to be

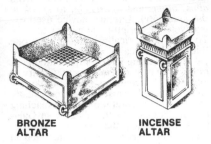

BRONZE
ALTAR

INCENSE
ALTAR

prominent part in most pagan religions. It was the place of sacrifice where God was propitiated and where man was pardoned and sanctified, emphasizing that without the shedding of blood there would be no access to God and no forgiveness of sin (Heb 9:9, 22).

Model of the altar in the main hall of the Canaanite fosse temple at Lachish, thirteenth century B.C. (about the time of Deborah and Barak, Judg 5). This temple was erected in the fosse that has been dug around the mound as a part of the city's outer defense. On and around the altar were placed offering vessels. Courtesy Israel Museum, Jerusalem. Photo Nahum Slapak

built and of what materials (e.g., Exod 20:24-26).

With the erection of the tabernacle, altars were constructed by the Hebrews for two chief purposes: the offering of sacrifices and the burning of incense. Once the fire on this altar was kindled, it was required to burn continually (Lev 6:13).

God also commanded Moses to make an altar for incense (Exod 30:1), sometimes called "the gold altar" (39:38; Num 4:11). Because of its special location—before the veil that separated the Holy Place from the Most Holy Place, midway between the walls (Exod 30:6; 40:5)—it was referred to as "the altar before the LORD" (Lev 16:12).

There are no altars recognized in the NT church. Hebrews 13:10, instead of teaching the contrary, states that Jesus Christ is the true altar of each believer. Inscriptions on altars, such as the one Paul saw in Athens ("TO AN UNKNOWN GOD," Acts 17:23), were common in pagan cultures and are referred to by a number of early writers (see Augustine, *The City of God*, 3:12).

The altar played a leading role in all OT worship of the true God, as well as a

ALTASCHITH (ăl-tăs'chĭth, Heb. *'al tashēth, destroy not*). A title notation in Psalms 57, 58, 59, 75, rightly translated in NIV as "Do not destroy." Perhaps it indicates the melody to be used (cf. Isa 65:8, where it is possibly a snatch from a vintage song). But David's word about Saul, "Don't destroy him" (1 Sam 26:9), and the words of Moses' prayer (Deut 9:26) imply a spirit of trust in the Lord. The title may, therefore, indicate the type of praise that follows. See also AIJELETH SHAHAR.

AMALEK (ăm'à-lĕk, Heb. *'ămālēq*). Son of Eliphaz (eldest son of Esau) by his concubine Timna (Gen 36:12; 1 Chron 1:36). A "chief" of Edom (Gen 36:16).

AMALEKITES (à-măl'ĕk-īts, ăm'à-lĕk-īts Heb. *'ămālēqî*). An ancient and nomadic marauding people dwelling mainly in the Negev from the times of Abraham to Hezekiah, c. 2000-700 B.C.

The first mention of them is among those conquered by Kedorlaomer in the days of Abraham (Gen 14:7). Moses felt their fury in the unprovoked attack on the Israelites at Rephidim, for which God decreed continual war (e.g., Num 14:45; Judg 3:13; 6:3, 33; 1 Sam 12:15; 27:8; 30:18; 2 Sam 1:8ff.; 8:12) and ultimate obliteration (Exod 17:8ff.; cf. 1 Chron 4:43).

In character they were warlike, and usually associated with Canaanites or Moabites. Saul failed to destroy them, but David reduced them to inactivity and the Simeonites at Mt. Seir "killed the remaining Amalekites who had escaped" (1 Chron 4:43).

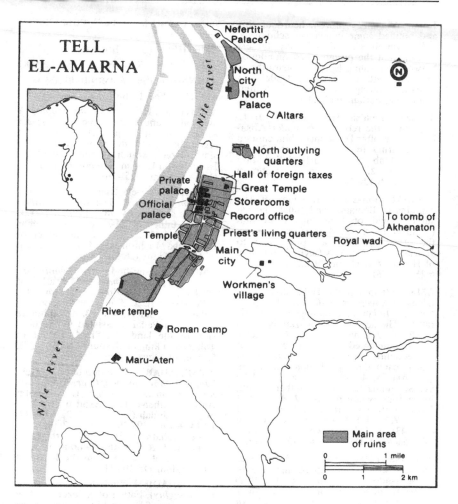

TELL
EL-AMARNA

Nefertiti Palace?
North city
North Palace
Altars
North outlying quarters
Hall of foreign taxes
Private palace
Great Temple
Official palace
Storerooms
Record office
Temple
Priest's living quarters
To tomb of Akhenaton
Royal wadi
Main city
Workmen's village
River temple
Roman camp
Maru-Aten

Nile River

Main area of ruins
0　　　　1 mile
0　　1　　2 km

AMARANTHINE (ăm-à-răn'thĭn, *fades not away*). An inheritance (1 Peter 1:4), glory (5:4). From *amaranth*, a flower that when picked does not wither; the unfading flower of the poets.

AMARIAH (ăm'à-rī'àh). **1.** A Levite and ancestor of Ezra (1 Chron 6:7, 11, 52; Ezra 7:3). **2.** A Levite serving in the house of the Lord under David (1 Chron 23:19; 24:23). **3.** Chief priest under Jehoshaphat (2 Chron 19:11). **4.** A Levite under Hezekiah (31:15). **5.** A man who was guilty of marrying a foreign woman (Ezra 10:42). **6.** A covenant signer (Neh 10:3). **7.** A Levite under Zerubbabel (12:2). **8.** Son of Hezekiah and great-grandfather of Zephaniah (Zeph 1:1; cf. Neh 11:4; 12:13).

AMARNA, TELL EL (tĕll ĕl à-màr'nà, *the hill amarna*). The modern name for the ancient capital of Amenhotep IV (c. 1387–1366 B.C.). In A.D. 1887, a peasant woman, seeking the dust from ancient buildings with which to fertilize her garden, found some clay tablets, which she pulverized and took to her home. Finally an American missionary stationed at

Luxor, Chauncey Murch, heard of this and notified some cuneiform scholars.

Excavation yielded 320 clay tablets that contain the private correspondence between the ruling Egyptian pharaohs at the time and the political leaders in Palestine during the time of Joshua, confirming certain biblical facts.

AMASA (ă-mā'sà, Heb. *'āmāsā'*). **1.** Captain of the rebel forces under Absalom. Later, after David made him captain of the army in place of Joab (2 Sam 19:13), Joab treacherously killed him (20:8–10). **2.** A prince of Ephraim (2 Chron 28:12–13).

AMASAI (à-măs'ă-ī). **1.** Chief of the captains of Benjamin and Judah, he assured David of their loyalty to him (1 Chron 12:18). **2.** A trumpeter among the priests in the ark's procession to Jerusalem (15:24). **3.** A Levite in the time of Hezekiah (2 Chron 29:12; cf. 1 Chron 6:25, 35–36).

AMAZIAH (ăm-à-zī'à, Heb. *'ămatsyâh, whom Jehovah strenghtens*). **1.** Ninth king of Judah and co-regent with his father. The account of Amaziah is found chiefly in 2 Kings 14 and 2 Chronicles 25. He defeated Edom in battle but subsequently worshiped their gods, which resulted in a prediction of his death (2 Chron 25:14–16). His reign lasted 29 years, ending (as had his father's) with his murder by conspirators. **2.** A priest of Bethel during the reign of Jeroboam II (Amos 7:10–17). **3.** A Simeonite (1 Chron 4:34, 43). **4.** A Levite who served in the tabernacle of David's time (6:45, 48).

AMBASSADOR The OT has three Hebrew words that express the idea of "ambassador." (1) *Tzîr* (e.g., Isa 18:2) probably denotes "going," i.e., away from home in a foreign land; (2) *mal'ākh* (e.g., Isa 37:9, 14), meaning "messenger," one sent on higher authority; (3) *lûts*, literally "interpreter" (e.g., Gen 42:23), i.e., one carrying an authorized understanding of his master's mind and policy. The word *ambassador(s)* in the NT (e.g., 2 Cor 5:20; Eph 6:20) is from *presbeuein*, "to be, work, or travel as an envoy or ambassador."

AMBER (ăm'bêr, Heb. *hash-mal*, meaning unknown). Only in description of the color of divine glory (Ezek 1:4, 27; 8:2; NIV "glowing metal").

AMEN (ā-měn, Heb. *'āmĕn*, Gr. *amēn*). English and Greek are both transliterations of Hebrew, from the root meaning "confirm" or "support." The general sense is "so let it be," "truly," "indeed," "verily."

AMETHYST (See MINERALS)

AMIL-MARDUK (See EVIL-MERODAK)

AMINADAB (See AMMINIDAB)

AMMAN (See RABBAH)

AMMI (ăm'ī, Heb. *'ammî, my people*). A symbolic name given to Israel (Hos 2:1 KJV, NASB), it is predictive of God's reconciliation to them, in contrast to sinful Israel, which is represented by Hosea's son Lo-Ammi, "not my people" (1:9; cf. Rom 9:25–26).

AMMIEL (ăm'ī-ĕl, Heb. *'ammî'ēl, my kinsman is God*). **1.** The son of Gemalli and spy sent out by Moses (Num 13:12). **2.** The father of Machir of Lo Debar (2 Sam 9:4–5; 17:27). **3.** The father of Bathsheba (1 Chron 3:5). **4.** The sixth son of Obed-Edom (26:5).

AMMIHUD (ă-mī'hŭd, Heb. *'ammîhûdh, my kinsman is glorious*). **1.** The father of Elishama, chief of Ephraim (Num 1:10; 2:18; 7:48, 53). **2.** A man of Simeon and father of Shemuel (34:20). **3.** A Naphtalite whose son Pedahel assisted in the division of the land (34:28). **4.** Father of Talmai and king of Geshur (2 Sam 13:37). **5.** Son of Omri (1 Chron 9:4).

AMMINADAB (ă-mĭn'à-dăb, Heb. *'ammînādhāv, my people are willing, or my kinsman is generous*). **1.** A Levite, Aaron's father-in-law (Exod 6:23). **2.** A prince of Judah (Num 1:7; 2:3; 7:12, 17; 10:14; Ruth 4:19–20; 1 Chron 2:10). **3.** A son of Kohath (6:22)—perhaps the same as no. 1. **4.** A Kohathite who assisted in the return of the ark from the house of Obed-Edom (15:10–11).

AMMISHADDAI (ăm-ī-shăd'ī, *an ally is the Almighty*). Father of Abiezer, captain of the tribe of Dan in Moses' time (Num 1:12; 2:25; 7:66. 71; 10:25).

AMMON (ăm'ŏn, Heb. *'ammôn, a people*). Or Ben-Ammi, son of Lot by his youngest daughter (Gen 19:38) and the father of the Ammonites.

AMMONITES (ăm'ŏn-īts, Heb. *'ammônîm*). The descendants of Ben-Ammi, or Ammon (Gen 19:38). They were related to the Moabites by ancestry and often appear in Scripture in united effort with them. Because by ancestry they were related to Israel, "children of my people," the Israelites were told by the Lord not to enter into battle with them as they journeyed toward Canaan (Deut 2:19). Many years later the Ammonites made war with Israel in order to extend their

Stone statue of an Ammonite god or king, found in Rabbath Ammon (Amman, capital of Jordan); from Iron Age (c. 1200–300 B.C.). Courtesy Studium Biblicum Franciscanum, Jerusalem

borders farther west. Although this land never really belonged to the Ammonites, they claimed it and gave this as a reason for their aggression (Judg 11:13).

The people were fierce and rebellious and, apart from the period when Nahash was a friendly ally of David's (2 Sam 10:1ff.), hostile to Israel. They threatened to gouge out the right eyes of all in Jabesh Gilead (1 Sam 11:2). They were given to brutal murder (Jer 40:14; 41:5–7; Amos 1:14). Though related to Israel, they refused to help them when asked, and they joined with Moab in securing Balaam to curse them (Deut 23:3–4). Later in Israel's history they united with Sanballat to oppose the work of Nehemiah in restoring the walls of Jerusalem (Neh 2:10–19). They offered human sacrifices to their chief idol, Molech (1 Kings 11:7).

Because of their sins and especially because they constantly opposed Israel, Ezekiel predicted their complete destruc-

tion (Ezek 25:1–7). Their last stand seems to have been against Judas Maccabeus (1 Macc 5:6).

AMNON (ăm'nŏn). **1.** Son of David by Ahinoam. By contrivance he raped his half-sister Tamar as she tended him during a pretended sickness; for this he was later murdered by Tamar's brother Absalom (2 Sam 13:1–29). **2.** A son of the Judahite Shimon (1 Chron 4:20).

AMON (ă'mŏn, Heb. *'āmôn*).**1.** The successor and son of King Manasseh and the father of King Josiah. An evil king who, after two years of reign (642–640 B.C.), was slain by officials of his household (2 Kings 21:19–26; 2 Chron 33:21–25).**2.** The governor of Samaria to whom Micaiah the prophet was committed by Ahab, king of Israel, because he had predicted the king's death (1 Kings 22:15–28).**3.** One of Solomon's servants (Neh 7:57–59), sometimes called Ami (Ezra 2:57).**4.** The name of an Egyptian deity that appears in the OT linked with his city, No (Jer 46:25; Nah 3:8). Better known by its Greek name, Thebes, No was 318 miles (530 km.) south of Cairo and is now known by the names Karnak and Luxor and is famed for its huge city of the dead. During the period of the Theban Dynasties (from 1991 B.C.) Amon became the state god of the Egyptian empire. His city and priesthood came to such glory that Nahum was able to recall its downfall as evidence to great Nineveh that its time of desolation would surely come also.

AMORITE (ăm'ō-rīt, Heb. *'ĕmōrî, mountain dwellers*). Used collectively of that tribe of people who descended from Canaan (Gen 10:16). The Mari tablets throw a flood of light on them, and it is now thought that Amraphel of Shinar (14:1) was one of their kings. When people from the north drove them from this region, they settled Babylonia and brought the entire area under their control, giving to Babylonia one of the richest periods in her history. After several hundred years they were defeated by the Hittites, and they settled throughout a large portion of Canaan. They were apparently a very wicked people, for God told Abraham that his descendants would mete out divine vengeance on them when their iniquity was full (Gen 15:16). Under Moses' leadership this judgment was dealt to Og, king of Bashan, and to Sihon, king of Heshbon—the kings of the Amorites east of the Jordan. Joshua met the Amorites in battle in the united campaign of five kings (Josh 10:1–43). These battles (11:1–14), fought by Joshua under

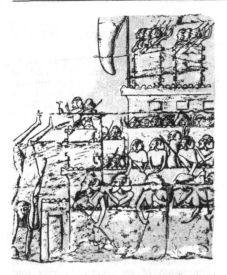

Siege of fortified town in the land of Amurru. The drawing is from relief of Ramses III at Medinet Habu, (c. 1195– 1164 B.C.). The towers and walls of the fortress are manned by Syrian lancers as the chief of the town stands on one of the gate towers at left holding out a brazier as a sign of surrender. Above, two towers, before which is the town's triangular standard hanging from a pole. Courtesy Carta, Jerusalem

divine leadership, ended forever Amorite hostilities against Israel (1 Sam 7:14; 1 Kings 9:20–21).

AMOS (ā'mŏs, Heb. *'āmôs,* Gr. *amos, burden-bearer*). One of the colorful personalities in an era that saw the rise of several towering prophetic figures. His ministry occurred in the reign of Jeroboam II (c. 786–746 B.C.), who enjoyed extended political power before the rise of Assyria. Prosperity was accompanied by an almost unprecedented degree of social corruption (Amos 2:6–8; 5:11–12), caused principally by the demoralizing influence of Canaanite Baal worship.

Amos lived in the small mountain village of Tekoa, south of Jerusalem on the borders of the extensive upland pastures of Judah. A herdsman of sheep and goats (Amos 7:14), he was also engaged in dressing the sycamore-fig tree. Amos protested vigorously against the luxurious and careless lifestyle characteristic of Samaria, castigated the elaborate offerings made at the shrines of Beersheba and Gilgal, and stated flatly that ritual could

never form an acceptable substitute for righteousness. He asserted the moral jurisdiction of God over all nations (Amos 1:3, 6, 9, 11, 13; 2:1, 4, 6) and warned the Israelites that unless they repented of their idolatry and, following a renewed spiritual relationship with God, commenced to redress social inequalities, they would fall victim to the invader from the east. So great was the impact of this vigorous personality that Amos was accused of sedition by Amaziah, the idolatrous high priest of Bethel (7:10ff.). In reply, Amos pointed out that he had no connection with any prophetic order, nor was he linked in any way politically with the house of David.

The style of his book, though simple, is picturesque, marked by striking illustrations taken from his rural surroundings. His work as a herdsman was clearly not incompatible either with a knowledge of history (Amos 9:7) or with an ability to assess the significance of contemporary political and religious trends. The integrity of his book has suffered little at the hands of modern critical scholars.

Analysis (1) The indictment of foreign nations, including Judah and Israel (1–2). (2) The condemnation of Samaria (3:1– 5:17). (3) False security exposed; judgment foretold (5:18–6:14). (4) Five visions of divine forbearance and justice (7:1–9:10). (5) Epilogue—restoration and prosperity (9:11–15).

AMOZ (ā'mŏz, Heb. *'āmôts*). The father of the prophet Isaiah (2 Kings 19:2, 20; Isa 1:1).

AMRAM (ăm'răm, Heb. *'amrām, people exalted*). 1. Father of Aaron, Moses, and Miriam (Exod 6:18, 20; Num 26:59, 1 Chron 6:3). 2. A son of Bani (Ezra 10:34).

AMRAPHEL (ăm'rà-fĕl, Heb. *'amrāphel*). King of Shinar, one of four kings, led by Kedorlaomer, king of Elam, who invaded Palestine to crush a rebellion (Gen 14). After pillaging Sodom and Gomorrah, they took Lot and his goods and departed.

AMULETS Isaiah (3:20) speaks of the women of his day as wearing charms. The Hebrew word, *lāhash,* is used in Ecclesiastes 10:11 and Jeremiah 8:17 specifically of snake-charming (cf. the related verb in Ps 58:4–5). At root it means "a whisper." Isaiah sees the existence of those "instructed in whispering" (i.e., holding whispered communication with the dead, with spirits, or making whispered communication purporting to come from "the other side") as evidence that

Gold amulets (in the shape of an eight-pointed star) and a plaque (representing the goddess Astarte) worn as pendants. Tell el-Ajjul, Late Bronze Age (c. 1550–1400 B.C.). Courtesy Israel Department of Antiquities and Museums

society is about to collapse. The same word (Isa 3:20) also means objects, personal ornaments, into which some magic charm has been whispered, supposed therefore to afford protection or some other "lucky" benefit to the wearer. Archaeology has revealed such practices all over the ancient world. The same Hebrew word is used in Isaiah 26:16 without any overtones of superstition or magic to mean "whisper a prayer."

AMZI (ăm'zī, Heb. *'amtsî*).1. A descendant of Merari and of Levi, and progenitor of Ethan, whom David set over the service of song (1 Chron 6:44–46). 2. Ancestor of Adaiah, a priest in the second temple (Neh 11:12).

ANAH (ā'nà, Heb. *'ănâh*). See Genesis 36:2, 14, 18, 20, 24–25, 29; 1 Chronicles 1:40–41. While all the other references make Anah a male descended from Seir the Horite and in the immediate family of Zibeon, Genesis 36:14 has often been understood to make Anah the daughter of Zibeon. NIV wisely offers "Oholibamah daughter of Anah and granddaughter of Zibeon," for as the word "son" is used in Hebrew of immediate and remote male descendants, so is the word "daughter" here. The family tree, therefore, runs from Seir through the males, Zibeon and Anah, to the female Oholibamah, whom Esau married.

ANAIAH (à-nī'àh, Heb. *'ănāyâh, Jehovah has answered*). 1. A prince or priest who assisted in the reading of the law to the people (Neh 8:4). 2. One of those who, with Nehemiah, sealed the cove-

nant (Neh 10:22). May be the same as No. 1.

ANAK (ā'năk, Heb. *'ănāq, long-necked*). A descendant of Arba (Josh 15:13) and ancestor of the Anakites (Num 13:22, 28, 33).

ANAKITES, ANAKIM (ăn'à-kīts, ăn'à-kīm, Heb. *'ănāqîm*). Also called "sons [children] of Anak." The spies compared them to the giants of Genesis 6:4 (RSV, NIV, Nephilim); also they were reckoned among the Rephaites (Deut 2:11, RSV, NIV). Three chiefs of the Anakites were in Hebron (Num 13:22) from the time of the spies until Caleb took it (Josh 15:13–14). Remnants of them remained in Gaza, Gath, and Ashod (11:21–22).

ANANIAH (ăn'à-nī'àh, Heb. *'ănanyâh, Jehovah is a protector*). 1. The father of Maaseiah and grandfather of Azariah (Neh 3:23). 2. A town of Benjamin (11:32).

ANANIAS (ăn'à-nī'ăs, Gr. form of Heb. *hănanyâh, Jehovah has been gracious*). 1. Husband of Sapphira (Acts 5:1–11). He and his wife pretended to give to the church all they received from a sale of property but kept back part of the proceeds. When Peter denounced his deceit, Ananias fell down dead as a judgment for lying to the Holy Spirit. This severe punishment for the first gross act of disobedience served as a warning to the church. 2. A disciple at Damascus who, obeying a vision, was the means of healing the sight of Saul and introducing him to the Christians in Damascus (Acts 9:10–19; cf. 22:12–16). 3. A high priest before whom Paul was tried in Jerusalem (23:1–5) and who came down to Caesarea in person to accuse Paul before the Roman governor Felix (24:1).

ANATHEMA (à-năth'ĕ-mà, Gr. *anathema*, the rendering in the LXX and NT of the Hebrew *herem, anything devoted*). A thing devoted to God becomes his and is therefore irrevocably withdrawn from common use. A person so devoted is doomed to death—a death implying moral worthlessness (Lev 27:28–29; Rom 3:9; 1 Cor 12:3; 16:22; Gal 1:9). See also DEVOTED THING.

ANATHEMA MARANATHA (à-năth'ĕ-mà mâr'à-năth'à). These words (1 Cor 16:22) have been taken as being a double imprecation (KJV) or as having no necessary connection. It may have been an expression among early Christians to indicate their fervent hope in Christ's early return. See also MARANATHA.

ANATHOTH (ăn'à-thŏth, Heb. *'ănā-thôth*, probably the plural of *anath*, *goddess*). **1.** A city of Benjamin assigned to the priests (Josh 21:18), the native place of Abiathar (1 Kings 2:26), Jeremiah (Jer 1:1) and two of David's distinguished soldiers–Abiezer (2 Sam 23:27) and Jehu (1 Chron 12:3). **2.** A Benjamite, the son of Beker (7:8). **3.** A leader of the men of Anathoth who sealed the covenant (Neh 10:19).

ANCHOR (Gr. *ankyra*). In ancient times every ship carried several anchors that were made of various materials (see Acts 27:13, 17, 29, 30, 40 and Heb 6:19).

ANCIENT OF DAYS God, as he appeared in a vision to the prophet Daniel (Dan 7:9, 13, 22). See DANIEL; SON OF MAN.

ANDREW (ăn'drū, Gr. *Andreas, manly*). The brother of Simon Peter (John 1:44), with whom he lived at Capernaum (Mark 1:29). Andrew was a fisherman and a disciple of John the Baptist, who directed him to Jesus. Convinced that Jesus was the Messiah, he brought Peter to Jesus (John 1:25–42). Subsequently Jesus called Andrew to discipleship (Matt 4:18–19) and appointed him an apostle (Matt 10:2; Mark 3:18; Luke 6:14; Acts 1:13). In the lists of the apostles his name always appears next to that of Philip (also from Bethsaida). At the feeding of the 5,000 he expressed doubt that the multitude could be fed with the lad's five loaves and two fishes (John 6:6–9). According to tradition he preached in Scythia and suffered martyrdom in Achaia, crucified on an X-shaped cross, now called a St. Andrew's cross.

ANER (ā'nêr, Heb. *'ānēr*). **1.** A brother of Mamre the Amorite (Gen 14:13, 24). **2.** A Levitical city in Manasseh (1 Chron 6:70).

ANGEL (Gr. *angelos, messenger*). A supernatural, heavenly being, a little higher in dignity than man. Their creation (Ps 148:2–5; Col 1:16) was certainly before the creation of man (Job 38:7). They are described as "spirits" (Heb 1:14). Their superhuman intelligence and strength is not unlimited (Matt 24:36; 1 Peter 1:12; Ps 103:20; 2 Thess 1:7; 2 Peter 2:11). They are distinct from man (1 Cor 6:3; Heb 1:14), and neither marry nor die (Luke 20:34–36). A vast multitude (Rev 5:11), they are of various ranks and endowments (Col 1:16), but only one—Michael—is expressly called an archangel in Scripture (Jude 9). Both good and bad angels are highly organized

(Rom 8:38; Eph 1:21; 3:10; Col 1:16; 2:15).

Angels were created holy (Gen 1:31; Jude 6), but some fell into sin before Satan tempted Eve (2 Peter 2:4; Jude 6). Their fall was due to a deliberate rebellion against God which resulted in their loss of holiness. They became corrupt and were confirmed in evil. Some are in hell until the Day of Judgment (2 Peter 2:4); others are left free to oppose the work of God for a time (Matt 25:41).

Good angels stand in the presence of God and worship him (Matt 18:10; Heb 1:6; Rev 5:11). They assist, protect, and deliver God's people (Gen 19:11; Ps 91:11; Dan 3:28; 6:22; Acts 5:19; Heb 1:14). They guided Philip to go into the desert (Acts 8:26) and encouraged Paul in Corinth (27:23–24). Sometimes they interpret God's will to people (Dan 7:16; 10:5, 11; Zech 1:9, 13–14, 19), and execute God's will toward individuals and nations (Gen 19:12, 13; 2 Sam 24:16; Ezek 9:2, 5, 7; Acts 12:23). The affairs of nations are guided by them (Dan 10:12–13, 20). God uses them to punish his enemies (2 Kings 19:35; Acts 12:23).

Angels had a large place in the life and ministry of Christ. They appeared to Mary, Joseph, and the shepherds, and ministered to Jesus after the temptation (Matt 4:11). An angel strengthened him in the Garden (Luke 22:43); one rolled away the stone from the tomb (Matt 28:2–7); and they were with him at the Ascension (Acts 1:10–11).

In order to oppose God and to try to defeat his will and frustrate his plans, evil angels endeavor to separate believers from God (Rom 8:38) and oppose good angels in their work (Dan 10:12–13). They hinder man's temporal and eternal welfare by a limited control over natural phenomena (Job 1:12–13, 19; 2:7), by inflicting disease (Luke 13:11, 16; Acts 10:38; 2 Cor 12:7), by tempting man to sin (Matt 4:3; John 13:27; 1 Peter 5:8), and by spreading false doctrine (1 Kings 22:21–23; 2 Thess 2:2; 1 Tim 4:1). They cannot, however, exercise over people any moral power independent of the human will, and whatever power they have is limited by the permissive will of God.

ANGEL OF THE LORD In the OT we often find the phrase "the angel of the Lord." In almost every case, this messenger is regarded as deity and yet is distinguished from God (Gen 16:7–14; 22:11–18; 31:11, 13; Exod 3:2–5; Num 22:22–35; Judg 6:11–23; 13:2–25; 1 Kings 19:5–7; 1 Chron 21:15–17). The

Angel is the Lord himself adopting a visible form (and therefore a human appearance) for the sake of speaking with people (e.g., Judg 13:6, 10, 21). While himself holy as God is holy (e.g., Exod 3:2–5), the Angel expresses the Holy One's condescension to walk among sinners (32:34; 33:3). He is also the executant of divine wrath (e.g., 2 Sam 24:16; 2 Kings 19:35). In all these ways, as we can see from the NT perspective, the Angel is part of the OT preparation for the Lord Jesus Christ.

ANGER The English rendering of at least ten biblical words, of which the most common is Heb. *'aph*, which could also mean "snorting." The OT condemns anger because it encourages folly and evil (Ps 37:8; Prov 14:29) and because vengeance belongs to God (Deut 32:35). Elsewhere it calls for restraint from those confronted by anger (Prov 16:14; Eccl 10:4). In the NT anger is among those emotions that provoke God's wrath (Eph 5:6) and is regarded as alien to godliness (1 Tim 2:8; James 1:19–20). There is righteous anger, however, as when Jesus condemned the misuse of the temple (John 2:12–17), the corruption of children (Mark 9:42), and lack of compassion (3:5). See also WRATH.

ANIMALS This article deals with all kinds of animal life appearing in the Bible, with the exception of birds. The word "animal" itself is used in Genesis 7 in connection with all wild creatures taken into the ark by Noah. See also BIRDS.

Adder. See Snake.

Ant. Ants are an excellent example (Prov 6:6; 30:25), especially to sluggards, of wisdom in preparing for the future.

Antelope. See Gazelle.

Ape. King Solomon's fleet obtained apes (probably the rhesus monkey of India) every three years from Tarshish (1 Kings 10:22; 2 Chron 9:21).

Asp. See Snake.

Ass. See Donkey.

Baboon. The NIV translation (1 Kings 10:22; 2 Chron 9:21) rendered by KJV, NASB, and RSV as "peacock." (Peacocks were for generations an adornment of royal courts.) Baboons are found mainly in Africa, but the Arabian baboon was once considered sacred to the Egyptians.

Badger. The uncertain word for the coverings used in the tabernacle (Exod 25:5; Num 4:6) is rendered in various ways: "fine leather" (JB), "badgers' skins" (KJV), "goatskins" (MLB), "leather" (MOF), "porpoise skins" (NASB),

Ancient clay vessel with spout in the shape of a monkey. Ancient people showed much interest in apes, and Solomon imported them, probably to provide amusement in his court (cf. 1 Kings 10:22).
Courtesy Israel Department of Antiquities and Museums

"porpoise-hides" (NEB), "hides of sea cows" (NIV), and "goats' skins" (RSV).

The coney is confirmed as unclean (Lev 11:5) and is a rock-dweller (hence, perhaps, "rock badger"; see NIV footnote in Lev 11:5; Ps 104:18). It is a vegetarian and looks like a rabbit, except for the absence of a tail and comparatively short legs and ears.

Bald Locust. See Grasshopper, Locust, Cricket.

Bat. The Bible classifies bats as unclean (Lev 11:19; Deut 14:18), while Isaiah's vision of the last days refers to people throwing their various idols made of precious metals to "rodents and bats" (Isa 2:20).

Bear. The bear killed by David (1 Sam 17:34–37) was the Syrian brown bear, *Ursus syriacus*, the species referred to elsewhere in the OT. A female bear robbed of her cubs is ferocious (2 Sam 17:8), perhaps illustrated in an attack on 42 youths who had been jeering at Elisha's bald head (2 Kings 2:23–25). The bear symbolizes national powers in visions given to Isaiah, Daniel, and John.

Beast. This generic description is de-

Young camel quenching its thirst in the Negev. The Bible variety of camel is a single-humped dromedary. Its many chambered stomach is lined with cells that can hold 15–30 quarts of liquid, allowing it to go from 5–25 days (depending on the heat) without drinking. Courtesy Israel Government Press Office

rived from some 13 Hebrew and 5 Greek words, providing the following criteria:

1. A mammal, not including man and clearly different from birds and fishes and sometimes from reptiles also (e.g., Gen 1:30).

2. A wild, undomesticated animal (Lev 26:22; Isa 13:21; 34:14; Mark 1:13).

3. Any of the "inferior" animals, in relation to the Mosaic Law's definition of ceremonially clean or unclean animals or beasts (e.g., Eccl 3:19; Acts 28:5).

4. An apocalyptic symbol of brute force, opposed to God's rule and thereby to man's best interests. In Daniel 7:3 four great beasts symbolize four successive world empires—Babylon, Medo-Persia, Greece and Rome. Many take the beast that comes out of the earth (Rev 13:11–18) to be the Antichrist.

5. Celestial beings that worship God, reflect his qualities, and perform his will (Rev 4:6–9; 5:6, 8, 11, 14; 6:1, 3, 5–7; 7:11; 14:3; 15:7; 19:4).

Bee, Hornet. The description "hornet" applies to several species of large social asps belonging to the family *Vespidae*.

Although there is little evidence that the ancient Hebrews cultivated bees for the manufacture of honey, the link was obvious enough. Bees would be plentiful in any land flowing with milk and honey, as indeed they always have been in Palestine. The abundance of flora in the land insured a large bee community.

Biblical references indicate God's use of the hornet in driving away the enemies of Israel (Exod 23:28; Deut 7:20; Josh 24:12). On occasion, enemies of Israel were compared to a swarm of bees, e.g., the Amorites (Deut 1:44) and other nations (Ps 118:12). Samson found a swarm of bees and honey in a lion's carcass, a discovery that shaped one of the most famous riddles in history (Judg 14:8–14).

Beetle. See Grasshopper, Locust, Cricket.

Behemoth. The graphic description in Job 40:15–24 may refer to the hippopotamus or the elephant.

Boar. See Pig.

Bull. See Cattle.

Butterfly. See Moth, Butterfly.

Calf. See Cattle.

Camel, Dromedary. The importance of the camel to life in Bible lands is confirmed by the many references (over 60) to it in Scripture. Two basic forms are found: the single-humped dromedary and the slower-moving Bactrian camel with its two humps. The dromedary has longer legs and can move considerably faster than the other. With a load that may be up to 400 pounds (182 kg.), the Bactrian camel may cover little more than 30 miles (50 km.) in a single day; a dromedary, lightly burdened, can cover up to 150 miles (250 km.). The two forms are thus complementary: the dromedary for personal travel or the fast conveying of important messages, the Bactrian camel for commerce and trade.

Probably the most familiar biblical reference to the camel is that of Matthew 19:24, in which our Lord compares the difficulty of rich men securing entry into the kingdom of God with that of a camel making its way through the eye of a needle, i.e., the small gate permitting travelers to enter a city after the main gates have been closed. In order to get through the small gateway, the camel had to kneel, be relieved of its load, and then be urged through the gateway on its knees.

Camels feature prominently in OT narrative and are included among Abraham's possessions (Gen 12:16; 24), as well as Jacob's (Gen 30:43), and Job's (Job 1:3; 42:12). The camel was ceremonially unclean (Lev 11:4).

Cankerworm. See Grasshopper, Locust, Cricket.

Caterpillar. See Moth, Butterfly.

Cattle. Cattle are mentioned in the first chapter of the Bible ("livestock" in NIV), symbolic of their importance to the well-being of the human race. The patriarchs were accounted wealthy largely on the basis of their ownership of cattle, as in the case of Abraham (Gen 13:2; cf.32:15). Joseph's destiny was shaped by Pharaoh's dream of seven cows, sleek and fat, succeeded by seven cows, ugly and gaunt (41:1–7), symbolic of years of plenteous harvests followed by bad ones. Joseph's life as prime minister and his relationship to his formerly estranged brothers include reference to their cattle (45:10; 46:34). Moses warned the Egyptians (Exod 9:1–7) of the destruction of their cattle as part of God's judgment. Later, Moses' defeat of the Midianites brought considerable "plunder" including 72,000 cattle (Num 31:33).

Calves (young bulls or cows) were valued for food as well as sacrifice (Lev 9:3, 8) and were worshiped (Exod 32:19). Ashes of the red heifer were used to remove ceremonial uncleanness, as in purification of the leper or of one who had touched a dead person (Num 19:9). A choice, tender calf was chosen by Abraham in entertaining his three mysterious visitors (Gen 18:7). Visions given to Isaiah, Ezekiel, and John included the calf, and Jesus concluded the story of the prodigal's homecoming with a great feast—at which a calf was prepared as appropriate to the celebration.

Oxen, in addition to their use for food and in religious ceremonies, were important working members of the agricultural community. Six covered carts and twelve oxen were presented to the Lord's work at the dedication of the tabernacle (Num 7:3), to "be used in the work at the Tent of Meeting" (7:5). Property rights pertaining to oxen, as well as those relevant to other animals, were defined by the Lord (Exod 22:1). Jesus referred to the care of oxen on the Sabbath (Luke 13:15). Elisha was plowing with twelve yoke of oxen when Elijah encountered him (1 Kings 19:19), just as Amos was following the plow when he heard the call of God. One of Ezekiel's four celestial living creatures had the face of an ox (Ezek 1:10).

The unicorn, distinct from the mythological figure of that name, was probably the extinct auroch. When seen in profile, it gave the appearance of having one horn rather than two and was once a familiar sight in Bible lands. NIV, ASV, and RSV all render "wild ox" to correct the mistranslation in KJV (Num 23:22; Deut 33:17).

Chameleon. See Lizard.

Chamois. See Sheep.

Cobra. See Snake.

Cockatrice. See Snake.

Colt. See Horse.

Coney. See Badger.

Coral. Red Coral, *Corallium nobile*, is native to the central and western Mediterranean and was greatly prized in ancient times. Used in the making of jewelry, coral is mentioned in Job 28:18; Ezek 27:16; Prov 24:7 (where it means "too high").

Cow. See Cattle.

Creeping Thing, Crawling Thing. The description is used in several versions to refer to various land animals.

Cricket. See Grasshopper, Locust, Cricket.

Crocodile. See Lizard.

Deer. Deer could be eaten (Deut 14:5) and were included in Solomon's list of daily provisions (1 Kings 4:23). Special qualities of the deer are praised as models for humans. David compares its feet to his own (2 Sam 22:34), and its panting for streams of water to his thirst for God (Ps 42:1).

The "hart" of KJV and RSV (NIV "deer") was either the red deer of Europe and Asia (*Cervus elephus*) or the Syrian deer (*Cervus barbatus*). The former is similar to the American elk, but smaller. Harts are stags or male deer, the word "stag" appearing only three times (Song of Songs 2:9, 17; 8:14).

Desert Creature. A term used in prophecies against Babylon (Isa 13:21; Jer 50:39), Tyre (Isa 23:13), and Edom (34:14).

Devourer. See Grasshopper, Locust, Cricket.

Doe. See Deer.

Dog. The Bible's 40 references to dogs are not complimentary to these unclean animals. Proverbs 26:11 reflects a contemporary opinion that dogs return to their own vomit. Job had sheep dogs (Job 30:1), and dogs were permitted to eat the crumbs from the master's table (Matt 15:26–27).

Donkey. This small mammal, genus *equus*, with some similarity in appearance to a horse (though usually smaller), has served mankind for thousands of years. Abraham's journey of testing, with his son Isaac, was made with a donkey (Gen 22:3, 5). Balaam's donkey was given the temporary power of speech in order to rebuke the foolish prophet (Num 22:21–33).

Donkeys were a fundamental part of the economy, and a man's wealth was measured by the number he owned. Sometimes donkeys were acquired in battle as plunder, as when the Israelites captured some 61,000 from the Midianites (Num 31:34). But Israelites were commanded neither to covet a donkey nor to attempt to plow with a donkey and an ox together (Deut 5:21; 22:10).

Donkeys undertook heavy work on the farm but were used for personal transportation too. Jesus' triumphal entry into Jerusalem, celebrated on Palm Sunday in the church calendar, fulfilled prophecy (Zech 9:9). Riding a donkey was considered an appropriate choice for a procession of importance (Matt 21:2-7).

The mule is the offspring of a male donkey and a horse mare, and is itself sterile. The Israelites were forbidden to breed mules under a general prohibition on mating different animals (Lev 19:19), but mules were secured in the course of trading and were used for carrying goods, as well as for personal transportation (2 Sam 13:29; 18:9).

Dragon. KJV has some 35 references to "dragon." NASB, NIV, and RSV translate a number of them as "jackal." NIV does not use "dragon" for any OT translation, although it sometimes uses "monster" (Ps 74:13; Ezek 32:2). Satan is characterized as a dragon in Revelation 12:13; 20:2.

Dromedary. See Camel.

Ewe. See Sheep.

Elephant. See Behemoth.

Fallow Deer. See Deer.

Fatling. See Cattle.

Fawn. See Deer.

Fish. In Genesis 1, Adam is instructed to rule over the fish of the sea and many references to fish and the means of catching them are found in the Scriptures. The outline of a fish became symbolic in the early church. Specific species are not mentioned.

Fish were an important part of the diet of Israel (Num 11:5). A great fish (perhaps a whale) swallowed Jonah (Jonah 1:17). Jesus' miraculous feeding of the 5,000 involved the use of two fishes (Matt 14:17). There was a miraculous draught of fish following Christ's resurrection, after the previously daunted fishermen let down their nets at his command (John 21).

Flea. Common throughout Bible lands, as elsewhere in the world, the flea is mentioned in 1 Samuel 24:14; 26:20. The flea is any of the *Aphaniptera* order of small, wingless insects possessing a flattened body and legs highly developed for

leaping. An estimated 500 species of fleas present a threat as well as an irritant to mankind, as their bite can transmit disease, more particularly bubonic plague. Endemic typhus is also transmitted by fleas.

David's rhetorical question (1 Sam 24:14) refers to the folly of pursuing a flea, and later (26:20) he compares the task of looking for a flea with that of hunting a partridge in the mountains.

Fly. This widely occurring species includes not only the house fly, but the tsetse fly and the malaria-carrying mosquito. Ruination of Egypt by flies (possibly mosquitoes, for the original Hebrew word means "to suck") was one of God's judgments described as the plague of flies (Exod 8:20-32), following the plague of gnats described in earlier verses. In addition to threats to health, flies could also ruin crops. Failure of the olive crop (Deut 28:40) was due to the olive fly. Such loss is anticipated by Micah 6:15 (cf. Hab 3:17).

The threat to Egypt prophesied by Jeremiah (Jer 46:20) is described as "destruction" in KJV, but NIV renders the word as "gadfly"—a biting, pestering nuisance. Socrates was described as "the gadfly of Athens," suggesting that the ancients were well aware of the gadfly's persistent attacks.

The gnat was used in one of the judgments on Egypt, though the gnats (Exod 8:16-18) may have been some kind of sandfly with an especially painful sting. Jesus rebuked the teachers of the law for straining at a gnat but swallowing a camel (Matt 23:24). Man's insignificant status is emphasized in Job 25:6 as that of a maggot. Herod's death (Acts 12:23) is described as caused by his being eaten by worms (probably the screw worm) as a judgment arising from his pride and his aspiration to divine status.

The presence of worms on the human body, alive (Job 7:5) or dead (Job 17:14, 21:26; Isa 14:11; 66:24), was a further reminder of the transient nature of life. In hell the worm does not die (Mark 9:48).

Foal. See Horse.

Fox. The nine references in Scripture are to the common fox of Palestine, *Vulpes vulgaris*, a wild carnivore of the dog family, living usually on a diet of small animals and fruit. The craftiness of the fox was emphasized by our Lord's description of Herod (Luke 13:32).

Frog. The frog had some cultic significance to the Egyptians, so the significance of the plague would not have been overlooked (Exod 8; Pss 78:45; 105:30). Revelation 16:13 tells of evil spirits with the appearance of frogs, possibly with the plague narrative in mind.

Gadfly. See Fly.

Gazelle. KJV usually translates "roe" or "roebuck" rather than "gazelle" (see Deer). The Dorcas gazelle was, however, known in Bible lands—a swift-running antelope having its natural habitat in barren wilderness areas. The meat was considered a delicacy (Deut 12:15, 22). Solomon's list of provisions included gazelles (1 Kings 4:23). One of Zeruiah's sons is reported as having been "as fleet-footed as a wild gazelle" (2 Sam 2:18).

The antelope is included among the permitted edible animals (Deut 14:5) as well as the ibex (Deut 14:5).

Gecko. See Lizard.

Gnat. See Fly.

Grasshopper, Locust, Cricket. Grasshoppers are the most frequently mentioned insects in the Bible, and man is sometimes compared to them in terms of his insignificance before great enemies (Num 13:33) or in the sight of God (Isa 40:22). The grasshopper's painful progress points to man's own mortality (Eccl 12:5).

Locusts had significance beyond the natural order, often having been sent as a judgment from God (Exod 10:4). The awesome sight and power of locusts depicted in Revelation 9:3, 7 is beyond anything yet known to man's experience. The author of the book knew well the tradition of locusts as a form of judgment from God. Joel described the utter devastation by locusts (Joel 1:4), picturing them as a great army (2:1–11).

Locusts, however, were not without benefit to the human race and represented a useful diet for the poor—that is, in normal times (Lev 11:21–22). John the Baptist ate locusts and wild honey (Mark 1:6), a diet not considered unusual by his contemporaries. The cankerworm, the larval state of the locust (Joel 1:4; 2:25; Nah 3:15–16), is rendered in NIV as "young locust."

Great Lizard. See Lizard.

Greyhound. See Dog.

Hare. See Rabbit.

Hart. See Deer.

Heifer. See Cattle.

Hind. See Deer.

Hippopotamus. See Behemoth.

Hopper. See Grasshopper, Locust, Cricket.

Hornet. See Bee, Hornet.

Horse. Most of the 150 biblical references concern the use of the horse in warfare, though some religious significance is attached to the appearance of the horse (Rev 6:1–8; 9:17–19). Solomon's accumulation of chariots and horses (1 Kings 10:26) involved importation of horses from Egypt and Kue at considerable expense that, in view of his drift away from his former moral convictions, would have affronted the prophets (Isa 31).

"Well-coiffured" and "crowned" horses, the tribute paid by a Mede to King Sargon of the Persians. This fragment of wall relief was found in Sargon II's palace (722–705 B.C.) at Khorsabad. Courtesy The Metropolitan Museum of Art; gift of John D. Rockefeller, Jr., 1933

Horses were often used in agriculture (Isa 28:24–29), for carrying messages (2 Kings 9:18), in royal processions (Esth 6:8–11) and in sun worship (2 Kings 23:11). Careless Israelites are likened to well-fed, lusty stallions considering their neighbors' wives (Jer 5:8; cf. 50:11). Stallions were large and strong and were used as symbols of enemy power. The Israelites used steeds for battle against Egypt (Jer 46:4) and against the Philistines (47:3).

Horse Leech. See Leech.

Hyena. This carnivorous animal was common in Palestine. Isaiah's prophecy against Babylon speaks of hyenas howling in the strongholds of the fallen city (Isa 13:22)—a fate reserved for the citadels of Edom (34:14; cf. Jer 50:39).

Ibex. See Gazelle.

Katydid. See Grasshopper, Locust, Cricket.

Kine. See Cattle.

Leech. The word is derived from a Hebrew term meaning "sucking" (Prov 30:15). KJV renders "horseleach," though its attentions are not restricted to animals.

Leopard. The reference to "mountain haunts of the leopards" (Song of Songs 4:8) reminds us that these awesome animals were well known in Palestine for their ferocity and intelligence. The leopard was regarded as an instrument of God's judgment on the wicked (Jer 5:6), and was also used figuratively (Dan 7:6; Rev 13:2).

Leviathan. Leviathan was strong and probably very large (Job 41:1), perhaps a creature of the sea (3:8; Pss 74:14; 104:26). Not all allusions to Leviathan concern threatening species, however. Psalm 104:26 refers to its frolicking in the sea, perhaps a reference to the sperm whale.

Lice. See Fly.

Lion. Today found in Africa south of the Sahara and in NW India, in biblical times the lion was far more widespread, found even in Greece as well as in Asia Minor, Iran and Iraq, Syria and Turkey. Lions are associated in Scripture both with God's protection (Judg 14:5–6; 1 Sam 17:34–37; Dan 6) and God's judgment (1 Kings 13:24–28).

The power, speed, and ferocity of the lion were compared to those of Israel's foes; and throughout Scripture the lion is used as a symbol of might. Jacob compared his son Judah to a lion (Gen 49:9), and the Lord Jesus Christ is often called the Lion of the Tribe of Judah (or the Lion of Judah). Daniel described Babylon as a winged lion—a religious symbol used in the ancient pagan world—while Peter warned his contemporaries that the devil prowls around like a roaring lion (1 Peter 5:8).

Lioness. Ezekiel's lament on the princes of Israel refers to the lioness as their mother (Ezek 19:2), whose cubs might be scattered (Job 4:11). Joel's prophecy (Joel 1:6) speaks of the fangs of the lioness as a characteristic of an invading nation.

Livestock. See Cattle.

Lizard. Leviticus 11:29–30 classifies as unclean any kind of great lizard, the gecko, monitor lizard, wall lizard, skink, and chameleon.

Locust. See Grasshopper, Locust, Cricket.

Maggot. See Fly.

Mole. See Rodent.

Monitor Lizard. See Lizard.

Monster. The word formerly meant little more than "large" or "extensive." Job's debate speaks of the monster of the deep (Job 7:12), while other references suggest great wonders of creation rather than any frightening or aggressive beast (cf. Gen 1:21; Lam 4:3).

Moth, Butterfly. Both belong to the order *Lepidoptera*, the moth being distinguished from the butterfly by its nocturnal activity, its threadlike antenna, and

wings that wrap around its body (most butterflies fold their wings vertically).

The moth of Scripture is usually the clothes moth of the large family, *Tineidae*. The frailty of man is like that of the moth (Job 4:19). Man's own wasting away is likened to that of a garment eaten by moths (Ps 39:11; Isa 50:9; 51:8). Man's habitation is akin to that of a moth's cocoon (Job 27:18).

Insignificant and fragile though it is (Hos 5:12), the clothes moth is no less able to destroy those transient possessions that people set their hearts on (Matt 6:19).

Mule. See Donkey.

Ox. See Cattle.

Palmerworm. See Grasshopper, Locust, Cricket.

Peacock. See Baboon.

Pig. The pig, (NASB, NIV; swine, KJV, RSV), though an unclean animal (Lev 11:7; Deut 14:8; Isa 65:4), seems to have been present in considerable numbers in Palestine. Destruction of a large herd occurred when evil spirits entered them following Jesus' healing of a demon-possessed man (Mark 5:1–17; Luke 8:27–39). The parable of the prodigal son demonstrated the desperate plight of the young man, becoming a pig-feeder (Luke 15:15), employment degrading to any self-respecting Israelite.

Jesus advised against throwing pearls before pigs (Matt 7:6), as they are likely to be trampled underfoot by the undiscerning creatures. Solomon compared a beautiful woman devoid of discretion with a gold ring in a pig's snout (Prov 11:22). Peter speaks of a washed sow returning to wallow in the mud (2 Peter 2:22).

The sole reference to "boar" is in Psalm 80:13, where the ravaging actions of wild boars are indicated.

Pygarg. See Gazelle.

Rabbit. The rabbit (hare, KJV, RSV) was classified as unclean (Lev 11:6; Deut 14:7) because it did not have a split hoof.

Ram. See Sheep.

Rat. Rats (mice, KJV, RSV) are unclean animals (Lev 11:29), and appear in the narrative of the plague on the Philistines (1 Sam 6). Isaiah prophesied against those who had followed heathen practices of eating pig's flesh and rats (Isa 66:17).

Red Heifer. See Cattle.

Reptile. See Snake.

Rock Badger. See Badger.

Rodent. In Isaiah 2:20 NIV has "rodents," where KJV, RSV, and NASB have "moles." Isaiah is prophesying that in the Day of the Lord men will throw

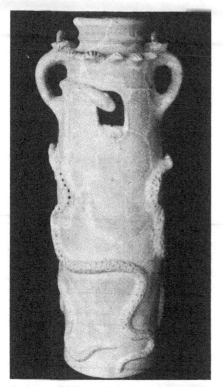

Serpents decorating a pottery stand (c. 60 cm. high), a cult object found in a Canaanite temple at Beth Shan (eleventh century B.C.). Courtesy Israel Department of Antiquities and Museums

their idols of silver and gold away to the lowly rodents. KJV and NASB have "mole" also in Leviticus 11:30 (NIV "chameleon").

Roe. See Gazelle.

Roe Deer. See Gazelle.

Sand Lizard. See Lizard.

Sand Reptile. See Lizard.

Scorpion. Found in the vast, thirsty land of the wilderness journey, the scorpion (Deut 8:15) is notorious for its venomous sting delivered from its long, segmented tail. Rehoboam unwisely threatened to scourge the people with scorpions (1 Kings 12:11, 14). Followers of Jesus were given authority to tread on scorpions (Luke 10:19), an authority related to the work of the kingdom of God. Jesus mentions the scorpion in a rhetorical question (11:12).

Sea Cow. See Badger.

Serpent. See Snake.

Sheep. This animal is the most often mentioned in Scripture, perhaps because of its importance in the economy of the age. The most familiar picture of Jesus Christ is probably that of the Good Shepherd, the most easily recalled parable that of the lost sheep.

In Bible lands sheep were kept for their milk more than for their meat. Religious ceremonies included the sacrifice of sheep, and rams' horns were used to summon the congregation. The life of shepherds and their flocks is reported in several places (Gen 29; Exod 22:1, 4; Num 31:36). Sheep were watered at midday, and the well became an important meeting place. Women also served as shepherds, as in the case of seven daughters of the priest of Midian (Exod 2:16).

Several Hebrew words are translated "ewe," i.e., a female sheep. Seven ewe lambs were presented by Abraham to Abimelech (Gen 21:28, 29) to seal a treaty. Jacob's gift to Esau included 200 ewes and 20 rams (32:14). Use of a female lamb without defect was permitted as a sin offering (Lev 4:32). Nathan's parable (2 Sam 12:3) referred to a man whose "one little ewe lamb" was taken from him by a rich and greedy man.

The list of unclean foods in Deuteronomy 14:5 includes "mountain sheep," KJV "chamois," a ruminant mammal halfway between a goat and an antelope, found usually in mountainous regions of Europe and SW Asia.

The ram, the horned male sheep, was used in breeding. Most biblical references are to the ram's role in priestly ceremony or sacrifice (Gen 15:9; Exod 29; Num 7).

Skink. See Lizard.

Slug, Snail. The action of the slug (KJV, RSV, NASB "snail") is described in Psalm 58:8. The snail is prohibited for food (Lev 11:30).

Snake. The snake has special significance in the OT. One of the signs of authority given to Moses was that of his staff turning into a snake when thrown to the ground (Exod 4:3–4). Venomous snakes invaded the Israelite camp when the people complained about God and Moses. They were healed when they looked at an emblem of a snake cast in bronze by Moses (Num 21). The symbol of the snake on the staff is today an emblem of healing used by the medical profession.

In the millennial age the cobra and the viper will be the harmless companions of children (Isa 11:8)—further confirmation of the reconciliation of man with the natural order following the creation's renewal.

No single species is identified in the word "serpent," but the meaning is that of a crafty and very dangerous creature, albeit a persuasive one. It was a symbol of evil (Gen 3), but God was able to pierce it (Job 26:13). Paul referred to the cunning of the serpent (2 Cor 11:3). KJV prefers the word "serpent" to "snake."

Spider. One who forgets God has hope as fragile as a spider's web (Job 8:14) and finds his own fabrications useless (Isa 59:5). Proverbs 30:28 refers to the presence of spiders in kings' palaces, though NIV here has the word "lizard" rather than "spider."

Sponge. A sponge, an aquatic animal, was filled with wine vinegar and offered to Jesus on the cross (Matt 27:48; Mark 15:36). Such use of a sponge to provide liquid refreshment was common in biblical times.

Stag. See Deer.

Stallion. See Horse.

Steed. See Horse.

Steer. See Cattle.

Swarming Thing. Creatures that swarmed over the earth were among every living thing that perished during the Flood (Gen 7:21). Swarming things were prohibited as food (Lev 11:10).

Swine. See Pig.

Tortoise. See Lizard.

Unicorn. See Cattle.

Viper. See Snake.

Weasel. The weasel is a small, carnivorous mammal classified as unclean (Lev 11:29).

Well Lizard. See Lizard.

Whale. KJV translates as "whale" those words rendered by NIV as "great creatures" (Gen 1:21), "monster of the deep" (Job 7:12), and "monster in the seas" (Ezek 32:2). In KJV, RSV, and NIV the "great fish" describes the animal that swallowed Jonah (Jonah 1:17); KJV and RSV mention "whale" in Matthew 12:40, where NIV keeps to "huge fish."

Wolf. A carnivorous, intelligent mammal, genus *Canis,* the wolf usually hunts in packs and will readily attack more powerful animals. Mentioned 13 times in Scripture, the wolf would have been a familiar threat to shepherds, especially in Palestine with its forest terrain. False prophets were described as "ferocious wolves" in sheep's clothing (Matt 7:15), while the tribe of Benjamin is said to be like the ravenous wolf (Gen 49:27). Isaiah's anticipation of the Millennium includes the wolf living with the lamb (Isa 11:6; 65:25).

Worm. See Fly.

Yearling. See Cattle.

ANISE (See PLANTS)

ANKLET An ornament for the ankles, consisting of metal or glass spangles, worn by women. Sometimes anklets were linked together by ankle chains (Isa 3:20). See also DRESS.

ANNA (ăn'à, Gr. form of *Hannah, grace*). Daughter of Phanuel of the tribe of Asher. Widowed after seven years of marriage, she became a prophetess. At the age of 84, when Jesus was brought into the temple to be dedicated, she recognized and proclaimed him as the Messiah (Luke 2:36–38).

ANNAS (ăn'às, Gr. for Hanan, contraction for Hananiah, *merciful, gracious;* called "Ananos" by Josephus). In his 37th year (c. A.D. 6) he was appointed high priest by Quirinius, governor of Syria. He was deposed c. A.D. 15 by Valerius Gratus, governor of Judea. His five sons became high priests, and he was father-in-law of Caiaphas (John 18:13). He and Caiaphas are described as the high priests when John the Baptist began his public ministry (Luke 3:2), perhaps because as family head Annas was the most influential priest and still bore the title. Therefore when Jesus was arrested, he was led first to Annas (John 18:13), then to Caiaphas (18:24). Similarly, Annas is called the high priest in Acts 4:6 when Peter and John were arrested, although Caiaphas was probably the actual high priest.

ANNUNCIATION (from Lat. *annuntiatio, an announcement*). The word itself is not found in Scripture but is the name given to the announcement made by the angel Gabriel to Mary that she would conceive and give birth to a son to be called Jesus (Luke 1:26–38). The word is used also of the festival held on March 25 (9 months before Christmas Day) to celebrate the visit of Gabriel to the Virgin Mary.

ANOINT To apply oil to a person or thing, a practice common in the East. Anointing was of three kinds: ordinary, sacred, and medical. Ordinary anointing with scented oils was common (Ruth 3:3; Ps 104:15; Prov 27:9). It was discontinued during a time of mourning (2 Sam 14:2; Dan 10:3; Matt 6:17). Guests were anointed as a mark of respect (Ps 23:5; Luke 7:46). The dead were prepared for burial by anointing (Mark 14:8; 16:1). The leather of shields was rubbed with oil to keep it from cracking (Isa 21:5), but this could be called also a sacred anointing — i.e., consecration to the war in the name

Wall painting from tomb of Sebekhotep, Thebes (c. 1421–1413 B.C.), depicting a Syrian envoy carrying an anointing horn, to which has been added a neck and head surmounted by a hand in the form of a spoon. The ointment is apparently passed from the head into the spoon when the flask is turned upside down. Reproduced by courtesy of the Trustees of the British Museum

of whatever god was invoked to bless the battle.

The purpose of sacred anointing was to dedicate the thing or person to God. The stone Jacob used for a pillow at Bethel (Gen 28:18), the tabernacle and its furniture (Exod 30:22–29), prophets (1 Kings 19:16; 1 Chron 16:22), priests (Exod 28:41; 29:7; Lev 8:12, 30), and kings (Saul—1 Sam 9:16; 10:1; David—1 Sam 16:1, 12–13; 2 Sam 2:7; Solomon—1 Kings 1:34; Jehu—1 Kings 19:16) were anointed. The oil symbolized the Holy Spirit, empowering them for a particular work in the service of God. "The Lord's anointed" was the common term for a theocratic king (1 Sam 12:3; Lam 4:20).

Messiah, from the Hebrew word *mashach*, and Christ, from the Greek *chrein*, mean "the anointed one." The word is twice used of the coming Redeemer in the OT (Ps 2:2; Dan 9:25–26). Jesus was anointed with the Holy Spirit at his baptism (John 1:32–33), marking him the Messiah (Luke 4:18, 21; Acts 9:22; 17:2–3; 18:5, 28). His disciples, through union with him, are anointed with the Holy Spirit as well (2 Cor 1:21; 1 John 2:20).

Medical anointing, not necessarily with oil, was customary for the sick and wounded (Isa 1:6; Luke 10:34). Jesus' disciples anointed with oil (Mark 6:13; James 5:14).

ANT (See ANIMALS)

ANTELOPE (See ANIMALS)

ANTICHRIST (Gr. *antichristos, against* or *instead of Christ*). The word *antichrist* may mean either an enemy of Christ or one who usurps Christ's name and rights. The word is found in only four verses of Scripture (1 John 2:18, 22; 4:3; 2 John 7), but the concept appears throughout Scripture. It is evident from the way John and Paul refer to the Antichrist that they took for granted a tradition well known at the time (2 Thess 2:6; 1 John 4:3).

The OT gives evidence of a belief in a hostile person or power who in the end time will bring an attack against God's people—an attack that will be crushed by the Lord or his Messiah (Ps 2; Ezek 38–39; Zech 12–14). The Book of Daniel provides vivid descriptions of the Antichrist that are echoed in the New Testament (cf. 2 Thess 2:4 with Dan 11:36–37; and cf. Rev 13:1–8 with Dan 7:8, 20–21; 8:24; 11:28, 30).

In his eschatological discourse Christ warns against the "false Christs" and the "false prophets" who would lead astray, if possible, even the elect (Matt 24:24; Mark 13:22). He refers to "the abomination that causes desolation" spoken of by Daniel (Matt 24:15).

Paul gives us a very full description of the working of Antichrist, "the man of lawlessness" (2 Thess 2:1–12). He will oppose and exalt himself above God, actually sitting in the temple and claiming to be God. John shows that the coming of the Antichrist was an event generally expected by the church (1 John 2:18).

The beast of Revelation 17:8 recalls the horned beast of Daniel 7–8. He claims and is accorded divine homage and makes war on God's people. For a period of three and one-half years he rules over the earth and is finally destroyed by the Lord in a great battle. With his defeat the contest of good and evil comes to its final decision.

ANTI-LEBANON (See LEBANON)

ANTINOMIANISM (ăn'tĭ-nō'mĭ-ăn-ĭsm Gr. *anti, against; nomos, law*). A theological term (not found in Scripture) for the view that the OT moral law does not apply to Christians, who are under grace. Paul found that this kind of heresy had crept into the church (1 Cor 5-6). Some individuals or groups have sought to combine the spiritual life with moral license, but Scripture makes plain that the new life in Christ means death to the old evil desires (Gal 5:24).

ANTIOCH (ăn'tĭ-ŏk, Gr. *Antiocheia*). **1.** Antioch in Syria, the capital of Syria, built in 301 B.C. by Seleucus Nicator, founder of the Seleucid Empire, which had been the Asiatic part of the vast empire of Alexander the Great. The greatest of 16 Antiochs he founded in honor of his father Antiochus, it was a great commercial center. The city was set in a broad and fertile valley, shielded by majestic snow-covered mountains, and was called "Antioch the Beautiful and the Golden." In 65 the Romans took the city and made it the capital of the Roman province of Syria. Seleucid kings and early Roman emperors extended and adorned the city until it became the third largest in the Roman Empire (after Rome and Alexandria), with a population in the first century A.D. of about 500,000. A cosmopolitan city from its foundation, its inhabitants included many Jews, who were given privileges similar to those of the Greeks. Its citizens were a vigorous and aggressive race, famous for their commercial aptitude, licentiousness, and biting wit.

One of the original deacons of the apostolic church was Nicolas, a proselyte of Antioch (Acts 6:5). The first Gentile church, the mother of all the others, was founded there. Many fugitive Christians, scattered at the death of Stephen, went to Antioch and inaugurated a new era by preaching not only to the Hellenist Jews but to "Greeks also" (11:20). The Jerusalem church sent Barnabas to assist in the work; after laboring there for a while Barnabas summoned Paul from Tarsus to assist him. The disciples were called Christians first in Antioch (11:19-26), a designation probably coming from the populace, who were well known for their invention of nicknames. The church at Antioch sent Paul and his companions out on his three missionary journeys (13:1ff.; 15:36ff.; 18:23), and he reported to it on his return from the first two (14:26ff.; 18:22). It submitted the question of the circumcision of Gentile converts to a council at Jerusalem (Acts 15).

Antioch gave rise to a school of thought distinguished by literal interpre-

tation of the Scriptures. Between A.D. 252 and 380, ten church councils were held there. The city was taken and destroyed in 538 by the Persians, rebuilt by the Roman emperor Justinian shortly afterward, and in 635 was taken by the Muslims, by whom it has since, except for a brief period, been retained. The place, now called Antakiyeh, is unimportant today, with a population of about 42,000.

2. Antioch near Pisidia, a town in southern Asia Minor, founded by Seleucus Nicator. The capital of southern Galatia, and a Roman colony that the Romans made a strong garrison center. Paul and Barnabas preached in the synagogue there on their first missionary journey, but the Jews drove them from the city (Acts 13:14-14:19). On Paul's return journey he revisited Antioch to establish the disciples and probably returned on his second (16:6) and third journeys as well (18:23).

ANTIOCHUS (ăn-tĭ'ŏ-kŭs, Gr. *withstander*). **1.** Antiochus III, the Great (223-187 B.C.), king of Syria and sixth ruler of the Seleucid dynasty. By his victory over the Egyptians in 198 Syria gained control of Palestine. Decisively defeated by the Romans in 190, he lost control over Asia Minor. He was murdered by a mob while plundering a temple. **2.** Antiochus IV (Epiphanes), son of Antiochus III and eighth ruler of the Seleucid Dynasty, 175-163 B.C. (1 Macc 1:10; 6:16). In his attempt to Hellenize the Jews he had a pig sacrificed on the altar in Jerusalem, forbade circumcision, and destroyed all the OT books he could find. These outrages involved him in the Maccabean war in which the Syrian armies were repeatedly defeated by the brilliant Judas Maccabeus. **3.** Antiochus V (Eupator), son of no.2. He reigned as a minor for two years and then was assassinated.

ANTIPAS (ăn'tĭ-păs, Gr. *Antipas*). A contraction of Antipater. **1.** An early Christian martyr of Pergamum, described as "my faithful witness" (Rev 2:13). **2.** Herod Antipas, son of Herod the Great and brother of Philip the Tetrarch and of Archelaus, both of whom, like him, were rulers of parts of Palestine. See HEROD.

ANTIPATER (See HEROD)

ANTONIA, TOWER OF A castle connected with the temple at Jerusalem, rebuilt by Herod the Great and named by him in honor of Mark Antony, his patron. A Roman legion was stationed in the castle to guard against excesses on the part of the people. When Paul was seized

Reconstruction of the Tower of Antonia at the northwest corner of the temple area. Many scholars believe this is the place where Christ was tried before Pilate. Paul was imprisoned here (Acts 21:31 – 22:24). Courtesy Zev Radovan

in the temple by the Jews, he was carried to this castle, from the stairs of which he addressed the people (Acts 21:30ff.; see "the barracks" in 21:34).

ANVIL The Heb. *pa'am* originally meant "strike," "hit." The word occurs in several senses in the OT, only once with the meaning "anvil" (Isa 41:7), in a passage involving the encouragement one workman gives another.

APE (See ANIMALS)

APHEK (ā'fĕk, Heb. *'ăpĕk, strength, fortress*). **1.** A city NE of Beirut, identified with Afqa (Josh 13:4). **2.** A city in the territory of Asher, never wrested from its Canaanite inhabitants (19:30; Judg 1:31). **3.** A town in the Plain of Sharon (Josh 12:18). **4.** A town west of the Jordan in the Plain of Jezreel. The Philistines used it as a base in two important campaigns against Israel (1 Sam 4:1; 29:1). It may also have been the town where a wall fell and killed 27,000 of Ben-Hadad's soldiers (1 Kings 20:26 – 30), and where, according to prophecy, the Syrians were to be destroyed (2 Kings 13:14 – 19).

APHIK (See APHEK)

APHRAH (See BETH OPHRAH)

APHSES (See HAPPIZZEZ)

APOCALYPSE (See APOCALYPTIC LITERATURE)

APOCALYPTIC LITERATURE A type of Jewish and Christian religious writing that developed between the OT and NT and had it roots in OT prophecy. The

word *apocalyptic,* derived from the Greek word *apokalypsis,* means "revelation" or "unveiling" (Rev 1:1), and is applied to these writings because they contain alleged revelation of the secret purposes of God, the end of the world, and the establishment of God's kingdom on earth.

After the days of the postexilic prophets, God no longer spoke to Israel. The prophetic forecasts of the coming of God's kingdom and the salvation of Israel had not been fulfilled. Instead of God's kingdom, a succession of evil kingdoms ruled over Israel: Medo-Persia, Greece, and finally Rome.

The apocalypses were written to meet this religious need. Following the pattern of canonical Daniel, various unknown authors wrote alleged revelations of God's purposes that explained present evils, comforted Israel in her sufferings and afflictions, and gave fresh assurances that God's kingdom would shortly appear. Many modern critics place Daniel in these times, but there are valid reasons for an earlier date.

The outstanding apocalypses are *1 Enoch* or *Ethiopic Enoch,* a composite book written during the first two centuries B.C. that is notable for its description of the heavenly Son of Man; *Jubilees,* an alleged revelation to Moses of the history of the world from creation to the end, written in the second century B.C.; the *Assumption of Moses,* late first century B.C.; *Fourth Ezra* or *Second Esdras* and the *Apocalypse of Baruch,* both written after the fall of Jerusalem in A.D. 70 and reflecting the tragic fall of God's people; *Second Enoch* or *Slavonic Enoch,* date uncertain.

The Testaments of the Twelve Patriarchs and *The Sibylline Oracles* are not strictly speaking apocalyptic literature, which is characterized by (1) alleged revelations of God's purposes, (2) imitation of visions of true prophets, (3) pseudonymity (attributed to some OT saint who lived long ago), (4) elaborate symbolism, and (5) a rewriting of history under the guise of prophecy.

The importance of these apocalyptic writings is that they reveal first-century Jewish ideas about God, evil, and history, and they disclose Jewish hopes for the future and the coming of God's kingdom. They show us what such terms as the "kingdom of God," "Messiah," and the "Son of Man" meant to first-century Jews to whom our Lord addressed his gospel of the kingdom.

APOCRYPHA Fifteen books and chapters interspersed among the OT canonical books in the old Latin Vulgate Bible. In English versions the Apocrypha are usually presented as 15 separate books. At the Council of Trent (A.D. 1546) the Roman Catholic church received as canonical all the additional materials in the Vulgate except for 1 and 2 Esdras and the Prayer of Manasseh. That decision was made in contradiction of the best tradition of even the Roman church itself, in reaction to the Reformers, who recognized only those books that were in the canon of the Jews (cf. esp., Josephus, *Contra Apionem* 1:8), the canon sanctioned by the Lord Jesus Christ. The following books are included in the Apocrypha: 1 and 2 Esdras, Tobit, Judith, Additions to Esther, Wisdom of Solomon, Ecclesiasticus, Baruch, Epistle of Jeremy, The Prayer of Azariah and the Song of the Three Children, Susanna, Bel and the Dragon, The Prayer of Manasseh, and 1 and 2 Maccabees.

APOLLOS (à-pŏl'ŏs, Gr. *Apollōs*). The short form of Apollonius, an Alexandrian Jew, described in Acts 18:24–25 as a man mighty in the Scriptures, eloquent, fervent in the Spirit, instructed in the way of the Lord, but knowing only the baptism of John. He was discipled by Aquila and Priscilla (18:26). Later, he refuted the Jews in Corinth in public debate (18:27–28), and before long an Apollos party arose in the Corinthian church (1 Cor 3:4). There does not, however, appear to have been any feeling of rivalry between Paul and Apollos. Paul urged Apollos to revisit Corinth (16:12), and he also asked Titus to help Apollos, apparently then or when he was on his way to Crete (Titus 3:13). Luther suggested the theory, since accepted by some scholars, that Apollos wrote the Letter to the Hebrews.

APOLLYON (See ABADDON)

APOSTASY (à-pŏs'tà-sē, Gr. *apostasia, a falling away, a withdrawal, a defection*). The Bible has many warnings against apostasy (2 Thess 2:3; Jude) as well as examples of apostasy—Israel (Josh 22:22; 2 Chron 29:19; Jer 2:19), Saul (1 Sam 15:11), Hymenaeus and Alexander (1 Tim 1:19–20), and Demas (2 Tim 4:10). The writer of the Letter to the Hebrews declares apostasy to be irrevocable (Heb 6:4–6; 10:26), and Paul applies it eschatologically to the coming of a time of great rebellion against God (2 Thess 2:3).

APOSTLE (à-pŏs'l, Gr. *apostolos, messenger, envoy, ambassador*). This title is used to describe various men in the NT. (1) Jesus himself is the ambassador of the Father (Heb 3:1). (2) The twelve disciples were chosen and commissioned by Christ (Matt 10:2; Mark 3:14; 6:30; Luke 6:13; 9:10; 11:49; 17:5; 22:14; 24:10). These men (with Matthias replacing Judas) proclaimed the gospel and established churches (Acts 1:26; Acts 4:33; 5:12; 5:29; 8:1, 14–18). (3) Paul was commissioned by the resurrected Christ to be the messenger to the Gentiles (Rom 1:1; Gal 1:1; 2 Cor 11–12; Gal 1; Acts 14:14). There are others who are called "apostles" in the NT. James, the brother of the Lord Jesus (Gal 1:19; 2:9); Barnabas (Acts 14:4, 14); Andronicus and Junias (Rom 16:7); and Silas (1 Thess 2:6).

The teaching contained within the pages of the NT is apostolic teaching, and its authority rests on the relation of the apostles to Christ.

APOSTOLIC AGE The period in the history of the Christian church when the apostles were alive—from the Day of Pentecost to the death of the apostle John near the end of the first century.

APOTHECARY (See OCCUPATIONS AND PROFESSIONS)

APPAREL (See DRESS)

APPEAL No provision was made in the OT for the reconsideration from a lower to a higher court of a case already tried. Exodus 18:26 shows, however, that Moses provided for lower and higher courts. Provision was made for a lower court, under certain conditions, to seek instructions as to procedure from a higher court; but the decision itself belonged to the lower court (Deut 17:8–13).

In NT times the Roman government allowed each synagogue to exercise discipline over Jews, but only the Romans had the power of life and death. A Roman citizen could, however, claim exemption from trial by the Jews and appeal to be tried by a Roman court. Paul did this when he said, "I appeal to Caesar!" (Acts 25:11). In such cases the litigant either pronounced the word *appellō*, as Paul did, or submitted the appeal in writing. In either case the presiding magistrate was under obligation to transmit the file, together with a personal report, to the competent higher magistrate.

APPHIA (ăf'ĭ-à, ăp'fĭ-à, Gr. *Apphia*). Called "our beloved" in KJV, "our sister" in ASV, RSV, NIV, following a different text. A Christian of Colosse, believed to be the wife of Philemon and mother of Archippus (Philem 2).

Ruins of the Roman aqueduct at Caesarea, built during Herod's time. It extended some 5 1/2 miles (9 km.), bringing water to the city from Mount Carmel. Courtesy Israel Government Press Office

APPIAN WAY (ăp'ĭ-ăn). Oldest of the Roman roads, begun in 312 B.C., which originally ran from Rome to Capua and was later extended to Brundisium. Parts of the road are still in use. Paul must have traveled by it from Puteoli to Rome (Acts 28:13–16).

APPIUS, FORUM OF (ăp'ĭ-ŭs). A town on the Appian Way, a day's journey for sturdy travelers, about 40 miles (67 km.) from Rome toward Naples, where Paul was met by Christian brothers from Rome (Acts 28:15, "Market of Appius" in ASV).

APPLE (See PLANTS)

APPLE OF THE EYE (Heb. *'îshôn, little man,* Deut 32:10; Ps 17:8; Prov 7:2; *babhâh, gate,* Zech 2:8). The eyeball or the pupil in its center serves as a symbol of that which is precious and protected.

APRON (See DRESS)

AQABAH, GULF OF (à'kà-bà). The eastern arm of the Red Sea between the Sinai Peninsula on the west and Midian on the east. Solomon's seaport of Ezion Geber is located at its head, where the Wadi Arabah empties into it (1 Kings 9:26).

AQUEDUCT A channel, covered or open, cut in the rock; a waterway built of stone and sometimes faced with smooth cement. Hezekiah excavated the Siloam tunnel (conduit) to bring water into Jerusalem by a way that could not be stopped up in time of siege (2 Kings 20:20; 2 Chron 32:30).

AQUILA (ăk'wĭ-là, Gr. *Akylos,* Latin for "eagle"). A Jew whom Paul found at Corinth on his arrival from Athens (Acts 18:2, 18, 26; Rom 16:3–4; 1 Cor 16:19; 2 Tim 4:19). Aquila and his wife Priscilla are always mentioned together. Having been expelled from Rome, they opened a tentmaking business in Corinth, and later shared their home with Paul. Their willingness to "risk their lives" for him earned them the gratitude of all the churches. Apollos and many others were helped by their spiritual insight. A church met in their house.

AR (Heb. *'ār*). A city or district of Moab (Num 21:15; Deut 2:9, 18, 29; Isa 15:1).

ARABAH (ăr'à-bà, Heb. *'ărāvâh, desert plain, steppe*). The remarkable rift running from Mt. Hermon to the Gulf of Aqabah. It is associated with the Dead Sea and the Sea of Galilee (Deut 3:17; 4:49; Josh 3:16; 12:3; 2 Kings 14:25). The Arabah represents one of the major natural divisions of Palestine in Joshua 11:16, 12:8. The Israelites made stops here in their wilderness wanderings and Solomon got iron and copper from the mines of the Arabah. The name Arabah itself signifies that which is arid or even waste (Isa 33:9).

ARABIA (à-rā'bĭ-à, Heb. *'ărāv, steppe*). The peninsula between the Red Sea and the Persian Gulf. It is first mentioned in the Bible when its king brought gold and spices, either as tribute or in trade, to Solomon (1 Kings 10:15; 2 Chron 9:14). Arabians brought tribute to Jehoshaphat (17:11), and joined the Philistines in defeating Jehoram (21:16–22:1). The kings of Arabia were involved in judgment on the nations after the Babylonian captivity (Jer 25:24). Arabians gave Nehemiah trouble (Neh 2:19; 4:7; 6:1). They were among those present at Pentecost (Acts 2:11). Paul visited Arabia (Gal 1:17).

ARAD (ā'răd, Heb. *'ărādh*). **1.** A descendant of Benjamin (1 Chron 8:15). **2.** A city, now Tell Arad, about 17 miles (28 km.) south of Hebron. When its king opposed Israel, his city was destroyed and renamed Hormah (Num 21:1–3; 33:40; cf. Josh 12:14). Kenites settled in the area (Judg 1:16).

ARAH (ā'rà, Heb. *'ārah, wayfarer*). **1.** A son of Ulla, an Asherite (1 Chron 7:39). **2.** The father of a family that returned from exile (Ezra 2:5; Neh 7:10); perhaps the same as no. 1 above. **3.** A man into whose family Tobiah the Ammonite married (Neh 6:18); this also may be the same as no. 1 above.

ARAM (ā'răm, Heb. *'ărām*). **1.** A son of Shem (Gen 10:22–23; 1 Chron 1:17). **2.** Son of Kemuel, Abraham's nephew (Gen 22:21). **3.** Son of Shamer, of the tribe of Asher (1 Chron 7:34). **4.** In KJV, for the Greek form of Ram (Matt 1:3–4 ASV, RSV, NIV), called Arni in ASV, RSV of Luke 3:33. **5.** A district of the hill country belonging to Gilead (1 Chron 2:23). **6.** Usually appearing as "Syria" in English Bibles, Aram broadly describes the area north of Israel and extending eastward to Mesopotamia. The latter was itself Aram Naharaim, i.e., Aram of the two rivers (Gen 24:10).

ARAMAIC (âr'à-mā'ĭk, Heb. *'ărāmîth*). A West Semitic language, closely related to Hebrew, which developed various dialects. Laban used Aramaic while Jacob used Hebrew (Gen 31:47). Aramaic was the language of Assyrian diplomacy (2 Kings 18:26; Isa 36:11). Aramaic and Hebrew were so different that the people of Jerusalem did not understand the former. Jeremiah 10:11 is in Aramaic, an answer by the Jews to their Aramaic-speaking conquerors who would seduce them to worship idols (also Dan 2:4–7:28; Ezra 4:8–6:18; 7:12–26). Some Aramaic place names and personal names appear in the OT, such as Tabrimmon (1 Kings 15:18) and Hazael (2 Kings 8:8ff.). There are several Aramaic words and phrases in the NT, such as *Talitha koum* (Mark 5:41), *Ephphatha* (7:34), *Eloi, Eloi, lama sabachthani* (Matt 27:46; Mark 15:34), *Maranatha* (1 Cor 16:22), *Abba* (Mark 14:36; Rom 8:15; Gal 4:6). It is probably safe to assert that our Lord habitually spoke Aramaic and occasionally Greek and could read and speak Hebrew.

ARARAT (âr'à-răt, Heb. *'ărārāt*). A country in eastern Armenia, a mountainous tableland from which flow the Tigris, Euphrates, Aras (Araxes), and Choruk rivers. Its mountains rise to as high as 17,000 feet (5,313 m.), the height of the extinct volcano which in modern times is called Mt. Ararat and on which the ark is supposed to have rested, though Genesis 8:4 is indefinite. The region is now part of Turkey.

ARAUNAH (à-rô'nà, Heb. *'ărawnâh*). The Jebusite who owned the threshing floor on Mt. Moriah that David purchased in order to erect an altar. Following the end of a plague (which was the result of David's sin in numbering the people), he presented a costly offering to the Lord at this site (2 Sam 24:15–25). Araunah is called Ornan in 1 Chronicles 21:18–28.

ARBA (âr'bà', Heb. *'arba'*). The father of Anak. He founded the city that bore his name, Kiriath Arba of Hebron (Josh 14:15; 15:13).

ARBATHITE (âr'bà-thīt, Heb. *'arvāthî*). One of David's 30 heroes, a native of the Arabah or of Beth Arabah, called Abi-Albon (2 Sam 23:31) and Abiel (1 Chron 11:32).

ARBITE (âr'bīt, Heb. *'ārbî*). One of David's mighty men in 2 Samuel 23:35 is called Paarai the Arbite. In his place in 1 Chronicles 11:37 is Naarai the son of Ezbai.

ARCHAEOLOGY By definition archaeology is the study of antiquity. In modern times it is a highly scientific discipline, a branch of history that works with the unwritten material remains of antiquity. In addition to excavation, archaeology includes geographical regional surveys, geological analyses, evaluation of artifacts, translation of inscriptions, reconstruction of architecture, examination of human remains, identification of art forms, and construction of ceramic pottery typology for chronological purposes.

Archaeology is biblical only where and when the scientific methodology of general archaeology uncovers something relative to the Bible. The greatest contribution of archaeology to biblical studies is the illumination of our understanding of the cultural settings in which the various books of the Bible were written and which they reflect. That information will, at times, significantly affect our interpretation of relevant sections of the text.

Modern archaeology began with Napoleon's expedition to Egypt (1798), when one of his officers discovered the Rosetta Stone, whose identical inscription in three languages unlocked the mystery of Egyptian hieroglyphs and opened the history of Egypt. Later a British officer named Henry Rawlinson found a trilingual inscription at Behistun, Persia, that unlocked the mysteries of cuneiform.

A number of archaeological discoveries have contributed to the study of the Old Testament including those found at Mari, Nuzi, el Amarna, Ugarit, and Ebla. The period of the monarchy has been significantly touched by the excavations at Hazor, Megiddo, Jerusalem, and Gezer.

The period of the patriarchs has been illuminated by the discovery in 1925 of approximately one thousand clay tablets at Nuzi in Mesopotamia, written in Akkadian cuneiform and dating to the 15th century B.C. Our understanding of the religion of the Canaanites at the time of the conquest has been greatly increased by the discovery of ancient Ugarit and its library.

The Amarna Letters, dating to the reign of Amenhotep IV (Akhenaton) and

The water tunnel at Megiddo, built during Solomon's time. Part of a water system consisting of a pit 81 feet (25 m.) deep, with stairs leading to the horizontal tunnel 224 feet (70 m.) long (viewed here) and to a spring at the foot of the mound. This great engineering feat served to convey water from the spring through the tunnel to the shaft inside the city wall, thus making it safe for the inhabitants to draw water from inside the city in times of siege. Courtesy Israel Government Press Office.

Obverse of the restored stele of Ur-Nammu from Ur, c. 2060–1955 B.C. The top register shows king standing before a deity seated on a throne. Two scenes in second register each show the king offering libations to a deity. What remains of the third and fourth registers shows the king carrying a basket and surveying and building instruments; part of a ladder and bricks (at lower right of fourth register) built into a wall suggest that the subject was the building of a ziggurat. Courtesy The University Museum, University of Pennsylvania

his father in the late 14th century B.C., were written in the Babylonian language and found in Tell-el-Amarna, Egypt, in 1887. They refer to a marauding class of people called Habiru, who may possibly be the Hebrews, though this is not certain.

In 1947 the Dead Sea Scrolls were found on the NW shore of the Dead Sea in a number of caves, deposited there by a sect of Jews generally identified as Essenes. The caves produced tens of thousands of fragments of ancient books including some of every book of the OT. A full copy of Isaiah was found dating to the second century B.C., the oldest copy of a book of the Hebrew Bible. The Essenes' documents were produced between 200 B.C. and A.D. 50. The community, consisting of perhaps 200 members, was destroyed by the Romans about A.D. 68.

In recent decades many papyri contain-ing books of the NT dating into the second and third centuries A.D. have been found; e.g., the Bodmer II papyrus of the complete Gospel of John, the Chester Beatty papyri of Paul's Letters, and the John Rylands fragment of John 18 (which dates to the early second century, making it the oldest surviving piece of any book of the NT).

In 1945 a complete library was discov-

Major Archaeological Finds Relating to the NT

SITE OR ARTIFACT	LOCATION	RELATING SCRIPTURE
ISRAEL		
Herod's temple	Jerusalem	Lk 1:9
Herod's winter palace	Jericho	Mt 2:4
The Herodium (possible site of Herod's tomb)	Near Bethlehem	Mt 2:19
Masada	Southwest of Dead Sea	cf. Lk 21:20
Early synagogue	Capernaum	Mk 1:21
Pool of Siloam	Jerusalem	Jn 9:7
Pool of Bethesda	Jerusalem	Jn 5:2
Pilate inscription	Caesarea	Lk 3:1
Inscription: Gentile entrance of temple sanctuary	Jerusalem	Ac 21:27−29
Skeletal remains of crucified man	Jerusalem	Lk 23:33
Peter's house	Capernaum	Mt 8:14
Jacob's well	Nablus	Jn 4:5−6
ASIA MINOR		
Derbe inscription	Kerti Hüyük	Ac 14:20
Sergius Paulus inscription	Antioch in Pisidia	Ac 13:6−7
Zeus altar (Satan's throne?)	Pergamum	Rev 2:13
Fourth-century B.C. walls	Assos	Ac 20:13−14
Artemis temple and altar	Ephesus	Ac 19:27−28
Ephesian theater	Ephesus	Ac 19:29
Silversmith shops	Ephesus	Ac 19:24
Artemis statues	Ephesus	Ac 19:35
GREECE		
Erastus inscription	Corinth	Ro 16:23
Synagogue inscription	Corinth	Ac 18:4
Meat market inscription	Corinth	1Co 10:25
Cult dining rooms (in Asklepius and Demeter temples)	Corinth	1Co 8:10
Court (bema)	Corinth	Ac 18:12
Marketplace (bema)	Philippi	Ac 16:19
Starting gate for races	Isthmia	1Co 9:24, 26
Gallio inscription	Delphi	Ac 18:12
Egnatian Way	Kavalla (Neapolis), Philippi, Apollonia, Thessalonica	Cf. Ac 16:11−12; 17:1
Politarch inscription	Thessalonica	Ac 17:6
ITALY		
Tomb of Augustus	Rome	Lk 2:1
Mamertime Prison	Rome	2Ti 1:16−17; 2:9; 4:6−8
Appian Way	Puteoli to Rome	Ac 28:13−16
Golden House of Nero	Rome	Cf. Ac 25:10; 1Pe 2:13
Arch of Titus	Rome	Cf. Lk 19:43−44; 21:6, 20

One of the "Amarna Letters," the cuneiform tablets accidently found by a peasant woman in 1887. The tablets, which reflect the socio-political situation of Canaan just prior to the Hebrew conquest, comprise the diplomatic correspondence between Egyptian Pharaohs Amenhotep III and IV (Akhenaton) and the king of the city-states in western Asia. Fourteenth century B.C. Courtesy The Metropolitan Museum of Art, Rogers Fund, 1924

ered at Nag Hammadi, Egypt, that contains many apocryphal NT books along with other books related to the religion of second-century Gnostic sects.

ARCHANGEL (See ANGEL)

ARCHELAUS (är'kĕ-lā'ŭs). Son of Herod the Great, who succeeded his father as ruler of Idumea, Samaria, and Judea in 4 B.C. He was deposed by the Roman government in A.D. 6 (Matt 2:22).

ARCHERS Bowmen, hunters, or warriors with bow and arrows. Ishmael is the first man so named in the Bible (Gen 21:20). Archery plays a part in a crisis in the relations of David and Jonathan (1 Sam 20:17–42). Saul was mortally wounded (1 Sam 31:3) and Josiah was killed (1 Chron 10:3) by archers. Archers were valuable in any army, and their skill was no less useful in hunting.

ARCHIPPUS (är-kĭp'ŭs, *master of the horse*). A Christian at Colosse, conspicuous as a champion of the gospel, a close friend (perhaps the son) of Philemon, an office-bearer in the church (Col 4:17; Philem 2).

ARCHITE (See ARKITE)

ARCHITECTURE This may be defined as the art or science of building. As a form of art, architecture is the effort to make a building aesthetically pleasing as well as useful. The materials of architecture in antiquity were wood, clay, brick (formed of clay, whether sun-baked or kiln-fired), and stone.

Clay bricks seem to have been invented by the Obeid people in Persia before they descended to the Mesopotamian plain early in the fourth millennium B.C. In Egypt early builders experimented not only with clay and brick but also with wood, and then they made a remarkable transition to stone masonry. The genius traditionally connected with this new building technique was Imhotep, the designer and builder of the Step Pyramid at Saqqara in the time of Zoser (or Djoser) of the Third Dynasty (c. 2780 B.C.).

One of the early problems to be faced in building was the construction of the roof, and the solutions led to two main forms of architecture: trabeated and arcuated. The trabeated form is designed and constructed using horizontal beams supported by vertical posts, commonly called "post and lintel." The arcuated form makes use of various modifications of the arch.

Unusual styles of architecture include the pyramid-shaped building. The ziggurat in Mesopotamia is generally believed to be the representative of a mountain; it was built of clay brick with exterior staircases or a sloping ramp and probably a shrine at the top. The pyramids in Egypt were built as tombs and were constructed of stone, having an inner room or rooms. The Egyptians developed great precision in squaring and orienting their pyramids.

Among the Israelites architecture does not seem to have been developed as an art or a skill; rather, Phoenician craftsmen were brought in to build Solomon's palace and temple. Phoenician elements appear to be present also in the buildings of subsequent Israelite periods.

The supreme achievement in architecture is admittedly the Periclean architecture of Greece (460–400 B.C.). This is the Doric order characterized by simplicity and symmetry. The Ionic order achieved its classical form during this same period,

Reconstruction of Mesopotamian ziggurat, a pyramid-shaped building of clay brick with exterior staircases, sloping ramps, and shrine on top. The "Tower of Babel" (Gen 11:1–5) may well have been a ziggurat.
Courtesy Carta, Jerusalem

having originated along the Asiatic coast of the Aegean Sea. The Corinthian order developed toward the end of the fifth and the beginning of the fourth century and reached its zenith in the Greco-Roman period a few centuries later.

Roman architecture owed much to the Greeks but adopted some elements from the Etruscans; among the latter is principally the arch. In general Roman is not as subtle as Greek architecture, but is more utilitarian. The Greeks had developed the skill of masonry to a high degree of perfection and fit marble blocks together with remarkable accuracy without mortar or cement. The Romans, on the other hand, developed the use of pozzolana, a volcanic earth that was mixed with lime to make a hydraulic cement. Using this as mortar, they were able to bond courses of stone without exact precision in masonry, increase the span in arches, and build two-story structures. Roman architecture, even more than Greek, included memorial arches and columns, amphitheaters, theaters, and forums (or marketplaces).

ARD, ARDITE (ärd, är'dīt). Ard is listed as a son of Benjamin in Genesis 46:21, but as a son of Bela, son of Benjamin, in Numbers 26:40; the latter reference mentions also "the Ardite clan." Ard is called Addar (with the Hebrew consonants transposed) in 1 Chronicles 8:3.

AREOPAGITE (See DIONYSIUS)

AREOPAGUS (âr'ē-ŏp'à-gŭs, Gr. *Areios pagos*). The rocky hill of the god Ares, or Mars. A spur jutting out from the western side of the Acropolis at Athens, sepa-

rated from it by a short saddle. To the north directly below was the Agora or marketplace.

Areopagus is also the name of the council that met on Mars Hill, a court charged with questions of morals and the rights of teachers who lectured in public. Paul was brought to the Areopagus (Acts 17:19) to be examined regarding his teaching. Paul's mission in Athens produced numerically scant results, and the founding of no church is recorded; but Dionysius the Areopagite, one of the members of this honorable court, was among those who believed (17:34).

ARETAS (âr'ē-tăs, *pleasing* or *virtuous*). A Nabatean king, father-in-law of Herod the tetrarch, whose deputy sought to apprehend Paul at Damascus (2 Cor 11:32; cf. Acts 9:24).

ARGOB (är'gŏb, Heb. *'argōv, heap,* or *region of clods*). **1.** A well-defined region of Bashan, identified with the kingdom of Og (Deut 3:4, 13–14; 1 Kings 4:13). This land of 60 strong, fortified cities was taken by the Israelites under Moses (Deut 3:4) and was given to the half-tribe of Manasseh (3:13), because Jair of this tribe conquered the region. He gave it his own name, Bashan-Navoth-Jair (3:14). In Solomon's reign, one of his princes, the son of Geber, held Argob (1 Kings 4:13). **2.** The reference in 2 Kings 15:25 is either to a place or to a person. If a place, it may signify the location of one of the king's houses. If a person, he may have been either a follower of Pekahiah, killed with him, or a follower of Pekah who took part in the murder of Pekahiah. The Hebrew text is uncertain. RSV omits mention of Argob here.

ARIEL (âi'ĭ-ĕl, Heb. *'ari'el, lion of God*).**1.** One of an embassy sent by Ezra (Ezra 8:16–17). **2.** In 2 Samuel 23:20 and 1 Chronicles 11:22, where KJV has "two lionlike men of Moab"; ASV conjectures "two sons of Ariel of Moab"; RSV has "two ariels of Moab" (marginally explaining that the meaning of *ariel* is unknown); and NIV renders "two of Moab's best men." The text is uncertain. **3.** A poetic name given to Jerusalem (Isa 29:1–2, 7).

ARIMATHEA (âr'ĭ-mà-thē'à). The city of the Joseph who buried the body of Jesus in his own new tomb near Jerusalem (Matt 27:57; Mark 15:43; Luke 23:51; John 19:38). The location of Arimathea is in doubt but is conjectured to be Ramathaim-Zophim, the Ramah of Samuel's residence, in the hill country of Ephraim,

ARK OF THE
COVENANT

about 20 miles (33 km.) NW of Jerusalem and 6 miles (10 km.) SE of Antipatris.

ARIOCH (ăr'ĭ-ŏk). **1.** The king of Ellasar in Syria and confederate with Kedorlaomer (Gen 14:1, 4, 9). **2.** Captain of the king's guard at Babylon under Nebuchadnezzar (Dan 2:14–25).

ARISTARCHUS (ăr'ĭs-tàr'kŭs, *the best ruler*). A Macedonian of Thessalonica, one of Paul's travel companions. This convert from Judaism was apparently imprisoned for the gospel's sake (Acts 19:29; 20:4; 27:2; Col 4:10; Philem 24).

ARISTOBULUS (ă-rĭstŏ-bū'lŭs, *the best counselor*). A Christian in Rome, whose household Paul greeted. There is a tradition that he was one of the 70 disciples and that he preached in Britain (Rom 16:10).

ARK (Heb. *tēvâh, a chest* or *a vessel to float;* in the Bible the Hebrew word always has the second meaning). It is used of the vessel that God directed Noah to build for the deliverance of himself and his family from the Flood (Gen 6:14–16; Matt 24:38; Luke 17:27; Heb 11:7; 1 Peter 3:20). After Noah abandoned the ark (Gen 8:18–19), what happened to it is unknown, despite many traditions and expeditions. The same Hebrew word is used of the basket of bulrushes in which baby Moses was placed (Exod 2:2–5).

ARKITE (àr'kīt). **1.** A member of the clan of Ataroth in Ephraim (Josh 16:2). One, Hushai, David's friend (1 Chron 27:33), acted as his secret agent in the rebellion of Absalom (2 Sam 15:32–17:23). **2.** People of Arka, a Phoenician town a few miles NE of Tripoli (Gen. 10:17; 1 Chron 1:15).

ARK OF THE COVENANT, ARK OF THE TESTIMONY (Heb. *'ărôn haberîth, chest of the covenant*). The word used for ark is the same as that used of the coffin (mummy case) of Joseph (Gen 50:26); elsewhere of the chest containing the tables of the law, resting in the tabernacle or in the temple. God directed Moses (Exod 25:10–22; Deut 10:2–5) as to the materials and dimensions of the ark. An atonement cover of gold, with two winged cherubim of gold, covered the top of the ark. There God promised to meet and talk with Moses. Moses made the ark after the golden calf was destroyed (Deut 10:1) and set it up in the tabernacle (Exod 40:20).

The ark went before Israel in the wilderness journeys (Num 10:33). It was instrumental in the crossing of Jordan on dry land under Joshua (Josh 3) and in the capture of Jericho (6:7–11). In the days of Eli the ark was in the tabernacle at Shiloh (1 Sam 3:3). Eli's sons took it into battle against the Philistines who captured it. For this reason, it was said, "The glory has departed from Israel" (4:3–22). The ark was returned and later kept in the house of Abinadab until David brought it to Jerusalem (5:1–6:16, 19–21; 7:1–2; 2 Sam 6; 1 Chron 13, 15). When the priests brought the ark into Solomon's temple (1 Kings 8:3–9), there was nothing in it "except the two stone tablets that Moses had placed in it at Horeb" (8:9).

Hebrews 9:4 says that the "ark contained the gold jar of manna, Aaron's staff that had budded, and the stone tablets of the covenant," though perhaps not throughout its history. Jeremiah, writing after the destruction of Jerusalem by Nebuchadnezzar, prophesied that in the time to come the ark would no longer be of significance for worship (Jer 3:16). After the destruction of the first temple, there is no evidence as to what happened to the ark. Synagogues, from our earliest knowledge of them to the present, have had arks in the side wall toward Jerusalem; the scrolls of the Law are stored in them behind a curtain.

The ark was set in the very heart of the tabernacle, the Most Holy Place (Exod 26:34), symbolizing its central significance in Israel. When the high priest, once each year (Lev 16:15; Heb 9:7), penetrated to the innermost shrine, he came into the very presence of the God of Israel (Exod 30:6; Lev 16:1–2). But that presence was not visibly expressed in any image form (Deut 4:12).

ARM Used as a figure for personal, active power, especially God's. The Lord's arm (Isa 53:1) is figurative of his personal intervention. In particular the figure of the "arm" looks back to what the Lord did at the Exodus (Exod 6:6; Deut 4:34; 5:15; Isa 51:9–11).

ARMAGEDDON (ar-mà-gĕd'ŏn, Gr. *Armagedōn*, from Heb., *har-mĕgiddôn*; ASV, Mt. Megiddo). A word found only in Revelation 16:16 for the final battleground between the forces of good and the forces of evil. The Valley of Jezreel and the Plain of Esdraelon at the foot of Mt. Megiddo were the scene of many decisive incidents in the history of Israel: the victory over Sisera sung by Deborah and Barak (Judg 5:19–20); Gideon's defeat of Midian (6:33); Saul's death at the hands of the Philistines (1 Sam 31; cf. 2 Sam 4:4); Josiah's death in battle with Pharaoh Neco (2 Kings 23:29–30); Ahaziah's death when he fled there (9:27). The town of Megiddo guarded the pass that formed the easiest caravan route between the Plain of Sharon and the Valley of Jezreel, and the low mountains around were silent witnesses of perhaps more bloody encounters than any other spot on earth, continuing down to recent times. Hence the appropriateness of this place for the vast conflict pictured in Revelation 16.

ARMENIA (ar-mē'nĭ-à). Occurs only twice in KJV (2 Kings 19:37; Isa 37:38). ASV, RSV, NIV, and KJV elsewhere (e.g., Gen 8:4; Jer 51:27) have Ararat, following the Hebrew and LXX. The same mountainous country, north of Assyria, is meant by both names.

ARMLET, BRACELET An ornament for men and women, usually worn on the upper arm. In seven verses, both KJV and NIV have "bracelets" (Gen 24:22, 30, 47; Num 31:50; Isa 3:19; Ezek 16:11; 23:42); once (Num 31:50) KJV has "chains," NIV has "armlets." "Armlets" appears more in other versions— twice in ASV (Exod 35:22; Num 31:50), four times in RSV (Exod 35:22; Num 31:50; 2 Sam 1:10; Isa 3:20).

ARMOR (See ARMS AND ARMOR)

ARMOR-BEARER One who bears weapons. Abimelech (Judg 9:54), Saul (1 Sam 31:4), Jonathan (14:12), and Joab (2 Sam 23:37) each had one. Cf. Goliath (1 Sam 17:7, 41).

ARMORY Three Hebrew words: *'ôtsār* (Jer 50:25), figurative for the "Lord's means of judgment" rendered also "treasury," "store house"; *nesheq* (Neh 3:19), "storehouse for valuables and arms"; *talpîyôth* (Song of Songs 4:4), used figuratively for "beauty."

ARMS AND ARMOR These are mentioned often in the Bible, both literally and as illustrative of spiritual conflicts. Here only hand weapons and body armor are considered, not chariots or machines used in siege.

A. **Offensive weapons.** (1) *Sword* is the first offensive weapon mentioned in the Bible (Gen 3:24). Hebrew *hereb*, a weapon for killing, is the common sword (27:40; Exod 17:13); a sword for punishment is ascribed to God (Exod 5:3; 22:24). Figurative and literal are united in "a sword for the Lord and for Gideon" (Judg 7:20). Gideon's men were executing the judgment of God. In NT Greek the more common word is *machaira*, short sword, dagger, or saber (Matt 26:27–53; Rom 8:35; 13:4); figuratively "the sword of the Spirit" (Eph 6:17). *Rhomphaia*, once a large, broad sword, occurs with symbolic meaning once in Luke 2:35 and six times in the Book of Revelation (e.g., 1:16). (2) *Rod*, a stick loaded at one end. It could be used for reassurance (Ps 23:4), to count sheep (Lev 27:32), or as a weapon (Ps 2:9). (3) *Sling*, a band of leather, wide in the middle to receive a stone. With the ends held together, it was swung around the head, then one end was released so that the stone could fly to its mark (1 Sam 17:40, 49; Judg 20:16; 2 Kings 3:25). (4) *Bow*, sometimes of bronze (2 Sam 22:35; Job 20:24; Ps 18:34), and *arrows*. Used in hunting (Gen 27:3), the same word is used for the rainbow in Genesis 9:13–16. The practice of archery is described in 1 Samuel 20:20–22, 35–40. The bow is mentioned only once in the NT (Rev 6:2). (5) *Spear, lance, javelin, or dart*, sharp-pointed instruments to be thrust or

A gold helmet that was worn over a quilted cap with laces that passed through the small holes around the rim to hold the helmet in place. Found in the tomb of Meskalamdug, from Ur, 25th century B.C. Goliath (late 11th century B.C.) had a bronze helmet on his head and wore a coat of scale armor weighing about 125 pounds (1 Sam 17:5). Courtesy the University Museum, University of Pennsylvania

thrown (Josh 8:18; Judg 5:8; 1 Sam 17:7; 18:11; Ps 68:30, different Heb. words). Spearmen are mentioned in Acts 23:23, and a Roman lance pierced the body of Jesus on the cross (John 19:34). Flame-tipped darts were used also (Eph 6:16).

B. **Defensive armor.** (1) *Shields* were either small and round, Hebrew *maghēn* (Gen 15:1; Judg 5:8) or large, Hebrew *tsinnâh* (1 Sam 17:7, 41), and were sometimes used for display (2 Chron 9:16), called *thyreos*, "like a door" in Greek (Eph 6:16). (2) *Helmet* (1 Sam 17:5; Isa 59:17), sometimes of bronze (1 Sam 17:38), surrounding the head (Eph 6:17; 1 Thess 5:8). (3) *Coat of mail*, only in 1 Samuel 17:5, 38, called "breastplate" in Isaiah 59:17. In the NT, Greek *thorax* (Eph 6:14; 1 Thess 5:8, figuratively; Rev 9:9, 17, symbolic). (4) *Greaves*, for the legs, only in 1 Samuel 17:6. (5) *Girdle*, or belt from which the sword hung (2 Sam 20:8). Ephesians 6:14 implies it was part of the equipment of a heavily armed soldier; the description of this equipment in Ephesians 6:11–18 is evidently drawn from Paul's intimate contact, as a prisoner, with Roman guards. "The whole armor," Greek *panoplia*, is a technical term for such armament. Note also the detailed description of the armor of Goliath (1 Sam 17:4–7).

ARMY A collection of men armed and organized for warfare. Of the several words used for army, *gedhûdh* (used 32 times) generally means a band of light troops going out on forays (1 Sam 30:8; 2 Sam 22:30), though it was used (2 Chron 25) of Amaziah's great army of 300,000 chosen men of Judah and Benjamin with, at first, 100,000 mercenaries from the northern kingdom. The armies of Israel, when directed and led by God, were uniformly successful (Josh 1:3; 5:14), but when men like Saul (1 Sam 15) and Amaziah (2 Chron 25:14) refused to listen to God, defeat and death followed. *Hayil*, used 231 times and translated "army" 54 times, implies might, valor, wealth, or, in military contexts, warlike resources in general. For some reason, God did not want Israel to use or to depend on cavalry (Deut 17:16; 20:1; Isa 31:1). *Mahăneh*, used over 200 times, generally means "encampment" but is sometimes used of an army in the field (e.g., Judg 4:15).

The word *ma'ărăkhâh* comes from a verb meaning "to set in order" and is used of the army actually drawn up for or involved in battle — "the ranks of Israel" (1 Sam 17:8, 10). The word *tsāvā'* properly means "host," e.g., "Lord God of Sabaoth" (Isa 22:15; NIV "the LORD Almighty") or "LORD God of hosts." It is used nearly 500 times and is rendered "army" 29 times. The word emphasizes the vast number of the soldiers. When used of God's army, the "soldiers" may be people (Exod 7:4), angels (Ps 103:21), or, by implication, locusts (Joel 2). The corresponding Greek word *stratia* is used of angels (Luke 2:13) and of stars and planets (Acts 7:42).

Israel's armies down to Solomon's time were composed mostly of footmen, armed with swords, spears, bows and arrows, and slings, and protected by small shields, with a judge, general, or king at the head.

Israel, on the condition of obedience (Deut 28:1–7), could have become the paramount power of the earth; but when she had gone into hopeless apostasy, God began to raise up great universal world powers (Dan 2) against her. A succession of military powers followed (Babylonian, Persian, Greek and Roman). The Romans had a genius for government and for military organization. Jesus (Matt 26:53) hints at a possible angelic army divided into legions like the Roman army. (See page 50.)

ARNON (àr'nŏn). The swift "roaring stream" and the valley of the same name

Group of model Egyptian soldiers (made of painted wood) armed with spears and shields, from tomb at Asyut (12th Dynasty). Now in Egyptian Museum, Cairo. Courtesy Giraudon

that descend to the east side of the Dead Sea a little north of its center. It is first mentioned (Num 21:13) as the boundary between the Moabites and the Amorites in the time of Moses; Israel encamped on its north side so as not to invade Moab. In Judges 11:18–26 Jephthah tells the Ammonites how Israel had held the land north of the Arnon for 300 years previous to this time (c. 1560–1260 B.C.). For all those years, and for a long time after, the Arnon was the southern boundary of the tribe of Reuben.

ARODI, AROD (àrō'dī, ā'rŏd). A son of Gad (Gen 46:16). Head of the Arodites in the time of Moses (Num 26:17).

AROER (à-rō'êr, Heb. *'aro'ēr, poor, naked, helpless*). The same word is translated "bush" in Jeremiah 17:6; 48:6. **1.** A town on a branch of the brook Jabbok, fortified early by the tribe of Gad (Num 32:34), having been taken from Sihon, king of the Amorites (cf. Josh 13:25). A camping place of Joab (2 Sam 24:5) when taking a census in the days of David. Isaiah speaks of it as being deserted in his

time (Isa 17:2). **2.** A town about 35 miles (58 km.) south of no. 1, on the north bank of the Arnon, located in the tribe of Reuben just across from Moab. Moses took this town also from Sihon (Deut 2:36) and gave it to Reuben (Josh 13:9). Hazael, king of Syria, took it from Israel in the days of Jehu (2 Kings 10:33). Jeremiah scoffs at its inhabitants (Jer 48:19). **3.** A town in the southern part of Judah (1 Sam 30:28).

ARPAD (àr'păd). A town and its surrounding region in the northern part of Syria near Hamath (modern Hamah), with which it is associated in all six biblical references. Rabshakeh, representing Sennacherib before Jerusalem in 701 B.C., boasts that the gods of Arpad could not stand before his master, therefore neither could the Lord deliver Jerusalem (2 Kings 18:34–35). In Jeremiah's time (c. 580) Arpad had lost its power (Jer 49:23).

ARPHAXAD, ARPACHSHAD (àr-făk'săd, Heb. *Arpachshad*). Third son of Shem, c. 2479 B.C., the first birth recorded after the Flood. He lived 438 years and was the ancestor of the Hebrews and of many Arab tribes. In fact, all Semites descend from him except Arameans, Assyrians, Elamites, and Lydians, (Gen 10:22–11:13).

ARROW (See ARMS AND ARMOR)

ARSENAL (See ARMS AND ARMOR)

ART The application of human skills to produce a pleasing effect. The six major arts are music, dance, architecture, sculpture, painting, and literature. The arts can be classified as spatial (architecture, sculpture, painting) and temporal (music, literature), with the dance extending over both categories. Music and, in many cases, literature might be called aural arts, whereas the others are visual arts.

In Israel, probably because of the commandment against representational art (Exod 20:4), there were no great contributions to the arts of painting or sculpturing. The major architectural work in Israel—the temple—is a notable exception, yet even that was constructed with some help from Phoenician craftsmen. References to dance in the OT are extremely limited and afford no information on the form or content. The development of music in Israel, on the other hand, is noteworthy; and to judge from the titles we may assume that many of the psalms, if not all, were sung to music and accompanied by musical instruments. Literature, however, was the most thoroughly developed art in Israel and reached a level not surpassed in all antiquity.

ARTAXERXES (är-tà-zûrk'sēz). A proper name or possibly a title, like *Pharaoh* or *Caesar* for several kings of Persia. It is the name or title of three Persian kings in the OT. **1.** The pseudo-Smerdis of Ezra 4:7–23, a Magian usurper who claimed to be Smerdis. He reigned about seven months and prohibited the Jews from building the temple. **2.** A Persian king (Ezra 7:1–8; Neh 2:1; 5:14; 13:6), nicknamed "Longimanus" who granted the requests of Ezra (Ezra 7:6) in 457 B.C. and of Nehemiah (Neh 2:1–8) in 444 to go to Jerusalem and gave them power, supplies, and authority. **3.** Possibly another king who must have reigned before 516 B.C. (Ezra 6:14).

ARTEMAS (är'tĕ-măs). A companion of Paul at Nicopolis whom Paul expected to send to Crete. He is mentioned only in Titus 3:12. In tradition, he is a bishop of Lystra.

ARTEMIS (Gr. *Artemis,* Lat. *Diana*). Diana was the Roman goddess of the moon. A daughter of Jupiter, she was a twin sister of Apollo, who was associated with the sun, as she was with the moon. She was represented as a virgin huntress and was widely worshiped. When the Greek worship penetrated Italy about 400 B.C., the Italians identified Diana with their Artemis, her Greek counterpart. Her worship was pure compared with the sensual worship of eastern gods and goddesses.

A statue of Artemis, dating from the second century A.D. in Ephesus. This is the Artemis "whom all Asia and the world worship" (Acts 19:27). Courtesy Duby Tal

"Artemis of the Ephesians" is mentioned only in Acts 19:24–35 ("Diana" in JB, KJV, NEB), and her myths were of a very different sort. Her silver "shrines"

(19:24) were little "temples" containing an image of Artemis as imagined by the Asiatics, a combination of the Greek virgin goddess with the many-breasted and lewd Semitic moon goddess Ashtoreth. For the Ephesians, Artemis was the great Asiatic nursing mother of gods, men, animals, and plants, and was the patroness of the sexual instinct. Her images, instead of being artistically beautiful like those of the Greeks, were ugly, more like the lascivious images of India and Tyre and Sidon. Her special worship was centered in the great temple at Ephesus, probably because of the discovery of a very interesting stony meteorite that supposedly fell from heaven (19:35). The feasts of Diana were commercialized, and among the silversmiths there was a large industry dedicated to making shrines and idols for her worship. The preaching of Paul interfered with this commerce and aroused violent opposition.

ARTIFICER (See OCCUPATIONS AND PROFESSIONS)

ARVAD (är'văd). A small island, containing a city of the same name, off the coast of Syria about 40 miles (67 km.) north of Tripoli. Its people are mentioned with Sidonians as rowers of Tyre (Ezek 27:8, 11). They were descendants of Ham through Canaan (Gen 10:18).

ASA (ā'sà, Heb. *'āsā', healer*). 1. Third king of Judah, reigning from 911/10–870/69 B.C. (1 Kings 15:9–24; 2 Chron 14–16). He was the first of the five kings of Judah (Asa, Jehoshaphat, Joash, Hezekiah, Josiah) who were outstanding for godliness. He was the son of Abijah and grandson of Rehoboam. Asa's grandmother was Maacah, a daughter of Absalom and a confirmed idolatress who greatly influenced Judah toward idolatry. She is spoken of as "mother" of both her son, Abijah (1 Kings 15:2) and her grandson, Asa (15:10) in KJV, RSV. Asa began his reign by deposing his wicked and powerful grandmother and by destroying a fearful, impure image that she had set up. He then drove out the male shrine prostitutes and destroyed idols that his fathers had worshiped (15:12), commanding Judah to seek the Lord (2 Chron 14:4).

In the early peaceful days of his reign, he gathered into the temple the dedicated things that he and his father had dedicated to the Lord (1 Kings 15:15). Then about 897 B.C. Zerah the Ethiopian came against him with an immense force. The Lord helped Judah defeat them because

Asa trusted the Lord (2 Chron 14:9–15). Later, c. 895/94, Baasha of the northern kingdom made war against Judah. Instead of trusting the Lord, Asa bribed Ben-Hadad of Syria to break his league with Baasha so as to draw off the forces of Israel. This Ben-Hadad did, but the Lord, through his prophet Hanani, rebuked Asa for trusting in politics rather than in God (1 Kings 15:16–22; 2 Chron 16:1–10). Asa died from a severe disease of the feet because he trusted his physicians rather than the Lord (2 Chron 16:11–14).
2. A Levite among those who had returned from captivity (1 Chron 9:16).

ASAHEL (ăs'à-hĕl, *whom God made*). 1. The youngest son of Zeruiah, David's sister; brother of Joab and Abishai. These three were among the mighty men of David; Asahel was over 24,000 men (1 Chron 27:7). A fast runner, he pursued Abner, Saul's former general (2 Sam 2:18–23), who killed him. 2. A teaching Levite in the reign of Jehoshaphat (2 Chron 17:8). 3. A Levite in Hezekiah's reign, who oversaw the offerings (2 Chron 31:13). 4. Father of a certain Jonathan (Ezra 10:15).

ASAIAH, ASAHIAH (à-sā'yà, ăs'à-hī'à, *whom Jehovah made*). 1. One of Josiah's officers whom he sent to inquire of the Lord concerning the words of the law that Shaphan had read to the king (2 Kings 22:12–14). 2. A Simeonite, c. 800 B.C. (1 Chron 4:36). 3. A Levite of the family of Merari in the time of David (1 Chron 6:30). 4. A Shilonite, one of the first after the Captivity to dwell in Jerusalem (1 Chron 9:5). 5. One of the chief Levites of the family of Merari in David's day (1 Chron 15:6, 11). This may be the same as no. 3 above. He seems to have been the leader of about 220 Levites who assisted in bringing the ark from the house of Obed-Edom.

ASAPH (ā'săf). 1. A Levite of the Gershonite family, appointed over the service of praise in the time of David and Solomon (1 Chron 16:5; 2 Chron 5:12). He led the singing and sounded cymbals before the ark and apparently set up a school of music (Neh 7:44). The twelve psalms credited to Asaph (Pss 50, 73–83) may mean no more than that these psalms constituted an Asaphic collection, begun by him. The psalms of Asaph have certain points in common: God as Judge (50:3–4; 75:8; 76:8–9), a call to true spirituality reminiscent of the prophets (50:7, 14–15, 22–23; 81:8–10), the use of history to teach spiritual lessons (78), and the Lord as Shepherd (74:1; 77:20; 79:13; 80:1). **2.** Father of Hezekiah's recorder (2 Kings 18:18). **3.** An official under Artaxerxes Longimanus, king of Persia (Neh 2:8). **4.** In 1 Chronicles 26:1 read Ebiasaph (cf. 9:19).

ASCENSION OF CHRIST The movement of the eternal Son, in his assumed and glorified humanity, from earth to heaven in order to sit at the right hand of the Father as co-regent. The witness of the NT to the Ascension is of three kinds. First, there is the descriptive material in Mark 16:19; Luke 24:51; Acts 1:9–11. Second, there is the prophetic reference found in John 6:62; 20:17. Third, there is the reference that assumes that Christ is ascended and proclaims his present exalted position or future coming in glory (Eph 4:8–11; Heb 4:14; 6:19–20; Rev 12:1–6). Ascension presupposes bodily resurrection, for it was in his body that Jesus went up (*anabainō*). "Exaltation" covers both resurrection and ascension, while "session" means his sitting at the Father's right hand. As Jesus ascended into heaven, so he will return from heaven to judge the world (Acts 1:11).

ASCENTS (Heb. *ma'ălâh, a going up* or *ascent*, Gr. *tapeinos, low*). The word "ascent" (KJV "degrees") occurs in the titles of 15 psalms (120–134), which are called songs of ascents (KJV, "songs of degrees"). The common opinion regarding the meaning is that they were sung by the pilgrims as they went up to Jerusalem (cf. 1 Sam 1:3; Pss 42:4; 122:4; Isa 30:29). The word is also used in 2 Kings 20:9–10 (translated "steps" in NIV, "degrees" in KJV), where Hezekiah is told that his sundial would go back 10 degrees as a sign that the Lord would heal him. It is also used in a secondary sense of rank or order (1 Chron 15:18; 17:17; Ps 62:9; Luke 1:52; James 1:9).

ASCENTS, SONGS OF The title given to Psalms 120–34. There is uncertainty about the origin of the title. Some Jewish authorities attributed it to the use made of 15 steps leading from the court of men to the court of women in the temple. The Levitical musicians performed with these steps as the stage. Some scholars attribute the title to the way in which the thought advances from step to step, as seen in 121:4–5; 124:1–4, but not all these songs do this. The most logical explanation is that the title was given the series of hymns because they were used by pilgrims *going up* to the three annual pilgrimage feasts of Jerusalem (cf. Ezra 7:9).

ASCETICISM (ǎ-sĕt'ĭ-sĭz'm). Although this word is not used in the Bible, the concept is found frequently. In the sense of self-discipline, asceticism normally occurs in the OT in connection with particular circumstances such as repentance (1 Sam 7:6) or religious regulations (Lev 10:9; Num 6:1–8). In the NT, however, it affects the whole lifestyle, calling for renunciation of everything that hinders discipleship (Matt 19:21–22; Mark 10:29–30). Self-control is a fruit of the Spirit (Gal 5:23). It is demanded of the contestant (1 Cor 9:25), of church elders (Titus 1:8), and of Christians generally (2 Peter 1:6).

ASENATH (ăs'ĕn-ăth). A daughter of Potiphera, priest of On. Pharaoh gave her to Joseph as his wife (Gen 41:45–50), and she bore Manasseh and Ephraim before the famine began.

ASER (See ASHER)

ASHAN (ā'shăn). A town in the tribe of Judah, later given to Simeon because Judah's territory was too large, then given to the priests (Josh 15:42; 19:7; 1 Chron 4:32; 6:59).

ASHDOD (ăsh'dŏd, *stronghold, fortress*). One of the five chief cities of the Philistines: Ashdod, Gaza, Ashkelon, Gath, and Ekron (Josh 13:3). They were assigned to Judah, but Judah failed to drive out the inhabitants "because they had iron chariots" (Judg 1:19). Ashdod was a center of Dagon worship, but when the Philistines thought to honor the ark of the Lord by placing it in the house of Dagon (1 Sam 5:1–7), God cast down and destroyed their idol. The Philistines found by careful testing that their plagues (1 Sam 5–6) were from God, so they sent back the ark with a guilt offering. Uzziah, king of Judah, conquered the city (2 Chron 26:6). Amos predicted Ashdod's destruction (Amos 1:8). About 711 Sargon II of Assyria took it (Isa 20:1). In Jeremiah's prophecy (Jer 25:15–29) Ashdod was to drink the cup of God's wrath. Zephaniah prophesied the destruction of the Philistines (Zeph 2:4), and Zechariah said that "foreigners will occupy Ashdod" (Zech 9:6). In Nehemiah's time (c. 444) the men of Ashdod combined with others to hinder the Jews (Neh 4:7–9). Failing in this, they tried intermarrying with them (13:23–24) to produce a mongrel race, but Nehemiah foiled them. In the LXX and in the NT Ashdod is "Azotus." Philip the evangelist found himself there after the Holy Spirit had taken him away from the Ethiopian eunuch (Acts 8:40).

THE TRIBE
OF ASHER

ZEBULUN

MANASSEH

ASHDOTH PISGAH (See PISGAH)

ASHER, ASER (ăsh'ẽr, ˘a'sêr, *happy*).
1. The second son of Zilpah, the hand-maid whom Leah gave to Jacob; named "Happy" by Leah in her happiness at his birth (Gen 30:13). He had five children (46:17). **2.** The tribe that descended from Asher (Josh 19:24–31). It was given the territory along the Mediterranean in the NW corner of Palestine, but failed to drive out the Canaanite inhabitants and settled down to dwell among them. It was evidently insignificant by David's time, for Asher is omitted in the list of David's chief rulers (1 Chron 27:16–22).

ASHERAH (à-shē'rà). **1.** A goddess of the Phoenicians and Syrians, taken over by the Israelites when they fell into idolatry. **2.** Images representing this goddess whose worship was lewd and associated with Baal (Exod 34:13; 1 Kings 16:29–33).

ASHES The expression "dust and ashes" (e.g., Gen 18:27) is a play on words (*aphar* and *epher*) and signifies the origin of the human body from the ordinary chemical elements. Ashes were sprinkled over a person, or a person sat among ashes, as a sign of mourning (2 Sam 13:19; Job 2:8). The word is often united with "sackcloth" to express mourning (Jer 6:26). **2.** The lovely expression "beauty instead of ashes" (Isa 61:3) is also a play on words. Another word for ashes, *deshen*, is used for the remains of the burnt offering (e.g., Lev 6:10–11).

ASHHUR (ăsh'ẽr). Great grandson of Judah through Perez and Hezron (1 Chron 2:24; 4:5).

ASHKELON (ăsh'kē-lŏn). One of the five chief cities of the Philistines, located on the seacoast about 12 miles (20 km.) NE of Gaza. It was taken by the tribe of Judah shortly after the death of Joshua (Judg 1:18), but was retaken by the Philistines and remained in their hands through much of the OT period. In the eighth century B.C. Amos denounced the city for its complicity with Phoenicia and Edom in their warfare on Israel (Amos 1:6–8). Zephaniah, writing in the dark days before the captivity of Judah (Zeph 2:4, 7) and looking far into the future, saw the restoration of Judah and the Jews occupying the desolate ruins of Ashkelon. Zechariah prophesied that Ashkelon would see the destruction of Tyre and then that Ashkelon itself would be destroyed (Zech 9:5). Apparently it was rebuilt, for Herod the Great was born here and Roman ruins have been found. During the Crusades, the city came to life again, and Richard Coeur de Lion held court there. Later the town reverted to the Saracens.

ASHKENAZ (ăsh'kē-năz). **1.** Great-grandson of Noah through Japheth and Gomer (Gen 10:3; cf. 1 Chron 1:6). **2.** A tribe or nation mentioned once (Jer 51:27) and associated with Ararat and Minni as an instrument of wrath in the hands of God against Babylon.

ASHNAH (ăsh'nà). The name of two villages of Judah, one in the lowland west of Jerusalem and near the tribe of Dan (Josh 15:33), and the other about 27 miles (45 km.) SW of Jerusalem (15:43).

ASHPENAZ (ăsh'pē-năz). Prince of the eunuchs in the court of Nebuchadnezzar. He gave Daniel and his companions their new heathen names (Dan 1:3, 7).

ASHTAROTH, ASTAROTH (ăsh'tà-rŏth). An ancient city in Bashan, where king Og lived. Probably so named because it had a temple to the goddess Ashtoreth. It is generally mentioned with Edrei, and the two were given to Machir of the tribe of Manasseh (Deut 1:4; Josh

9:10; 13:31). It was given in Joshua's time to the children of Gershon of the tribe of Levi (Josh 21:27—here called "Be Eshterah"). Uzzia (1 Chron 11:44), one of David's mighty men, came from this town.

ASHTEROTH KARNAIM (ăsh'tĕ-rŏth kăr-nā'ĭm). A town or region of the Rephaim in Abram's time, conquered by four kings of the East (Gen 14:5). It is located by some east of the Jordan and identified with the Ashtaroth of Bashan (Deut 1:4).

ASHTORETH (ăsh'tō-rĕth). A goddess of the Canaanites, worshiped all along the seacoast from Ras Shamra (Ugarit) southward through Phoenicia and Philistia. The plural Ashtaroth (NIV "the Ashtoreths") is found commonly and refers to the idols representing her. Her male consort was apparently Baal, and the two were worshiped with lewd rites. Israel forsook their God and served "Baal and the Ashtoreths" (Judges 2:11–23). The prophet Samuel brought about a great revival, but before Israel could be saved from the Philistines, they had to give up Ashtoreth and turn to the Lord (1 Sam 7:3–4). Solomon's heathen wives turned him from the Lord to worship of the Ashtoreth and other idols (1 Kings 11:4–8). These idols remained more than 350 years till Josiah defiled and demolished them (2 Kings 23:13–14). Biblical scholar Gesenius related the name Ashtoreth to the Persian word "sitarah" or "star" and connected it with Venus, goddess of love.

ASHUR (See ASHHUR)

The national god Asshur, represented with spread wings and drawn bow and placed within a disc of flames and among rain clouds. This god's name appears as an element in many personal names (cf. Ashurbanipal: "Asshur has created an heir").
Courtesy Staatliche Museen zu Berlin

ASHURBANIPAL (ă-shĕr-bă'nĕ-păl, *Ashur creates a son*). King of Assyria (668 to 626 B.C.) who was the grandson of the famous Sennacherib and son of Esarhaddon. He was a lover of learning and collected a great library of cuneiform tablets (over 22,000 in number) that have given to us most of what we know of Babylonian and Assyrian literature. In Ezra 4:10, his name is also rendered "Asnapper" (KJV, MLB, NEB) and Osnapper (NASB, RSV).

ASHURI (ăsh'ŭr-ē; KJV, RSV, Ashurites). Mentioned as a part of the realm of Ish-Bosheth, son of Saul (2 Sam 2:9 and NIV footnote). Possibly the same as the Asherites or people of Asher (Judg 1:32). The "Asshurites" of Genesis 25:3, mentioned among the Arabian descendants of Abraham through Keturah, may be the same. In Ezekiel 27:6 the Hebrew text reads "daughter of Ashurites."

ASIA Proconsular Asia in NT times was the Roman province that contained the SW part of Asia Minor, including the seven churches of Revelation 1-3. In the NT the word "Asia" occurs 19 times and always refers to this division. Its capital was Ephesus, where both Paul and John labored. Most of its cities have disappeared, but Smyrna (Rev 2:8–11) remains a great city even now (called Izmir, in modern Turkey).

ASNAPPER (See ASHURBANIPAL)

ASP (See ANIMALS)

ASRIEL (ăs'rĭ-ĕl). 1. Grandson of Manasseh and son of Gilead, and head of the family of Asrielites (Num 26:31; Josh 17:2). 2. A son of Manasseh by his Aramean concubine (1 Chron 7:14).

ASS (See ANIMALS)

ASSHUR (ăsh'ûr, Heb. *'ashshûr*). The god of the Assyrians; their reputed human founder; the ancient capital of the country; often the nation Assyria. Asshur is the builder of Nineveh and nearby cities (Gen 10:11 JB, KJV). He comes from the kingdom of Nimrod. ASV, NIV, and RSV render Genesis 10:11 to read that Nimrod went into Assyria and founded Nineveh. For most occurrences of the Hebrew word, KJV has "Assyria," which is the probable meaning in every case.

ASSIR (ăs'êr, *captive*). 1. Moses' first cousin once removed (Exod 6:24). 2. Great-grandson of no. 1 (1 Chron 6:23). 3. A son of Jeconiah (1 Chron 3:17 KJV) or a modifier of "Jehoiachin" ("the captive" NIV).

ASSURANCE The internal and external evidence by which Christians may have confidence to believe that God is their Father and Christ their Savior and Lord. Thus they know that what the gospel declares about Jesus is true and that in Jesus they have a new relationship with God. Christians can have full assurance (Col 2:2; Heb 6:11; 10:22 KJV) and be "fully persuaded" that God is what he says he is and does what he claims to do (Rom 4:21; 8:38; 2 Tim 1:12 KJV).

There is also the internal witness of the Holy Spirit (Rom 8:15–16) as well as the external testimony of a changed life (1 John 2:3–5, 29; 3:9–14, 18–19; 4:7). Because of the presence of the indwelling Spirit, assurance in the new covenant is of a much deeper order than in the old covenant. However, assurance was a reality for believers within the Mosiac covenant (Isa 32:17).

ASSYRIA (à-sĭr′ĭ-à, Heb. ′ashshûr). Originally a land between the upper Tigris and Zab rivers, with its capital first at Assur, later at Nineveh. Assyria was taken over in the third millennium B.C. by Semites from Arabia. First mentioned in the Bible in Genesis 2:14, Assyria and the Assyrians are frequently named, sometimes as Asshur or Assur. By 1900 Assyrian traders had a colony in Hittite territory, at Kanish in Asia Minor. In the 13th century Assyrian military expeditions crossed the Euphrates, and by 1100 they reached the Mediterranean. By 1000 the Aramean kingdom of Zobah reached the Euphrates, but David conquered Zobah and stopped its invasion of Assyria, an irony of history enabling Assyria to become strong. Under Shalmaneser III the Assyrians turned toward Palestine. In 853 they were defeated at Karkar but claimed a victory over Ben-Hadad of Damascus and a coalition including Ahab, king of Israel. They failed to follow up their effort.

After the religious revival under Elijah and Elisha, the coalition of Israel with Syria broke up. When Jehu gained the throne (2 Kings 9–10), Shalmaneser III seized the opportunity to claim tribute from Jehu and to weaken Damascus. Internal difficulties kept Assyria from further Palestinian inroads for nearly a century, until shortly after the middle of the eighth century B.C., when Tiglath-Pileser III invaded the west, divided the territory into subject provinces, and exchanged populations on a large scale to make rebellion more difficult. In 733–732 he conquered Galilee, the Plain of Sharon, and Gilead and made both Israel and Judah pay tribute (15:29; 16:9). Isaiah prophesied that this attempt to subjugate Judah would eventually fail. Shalmaneser V besieged Samaria for three years. He died during the siege, and his successor Sargon II (now called Sargon III) took the city in 721 and carried its more prosperous citizens into exile, replacing them with colonists from other provinces of his empire (17:6–41).

For nearly a century thereafter, Assyria was troubled from all sides—from Babylon, Elam, the Medes, Phrygia, and Egypt. Yet Sennacherib nearly captured Jerusalem in 701–700 B.C. (2 Kings 18:13–19:37; Isa 36–37), the danger ending only when "the angel of the LORD went out and put to death a hundred and eighty-five thousand men in the Assyrian camp" followed by the assassination of Sennacherib. Manasseh, king of Judah, paid tribute to Assyria, except during a short rebellion for which he was carried to Babylon but released after he sought the Lord (2 Chron 33:11–13). The last quarter of the seventh century saw the fall and decline of the Assyrian empire and its subjugation by the Chaldean conquerors of Babylonia with the Medes. Nineveh was taken in 612. For a short time Babylonia replaced Assyria as the great power. The prophets Elijah, Elisha, and Isaiah are largely concerned with Assyria; several other prophets—Jeremiah, Ezekiel, Hosea, Micah, Nahum, Zephaniah, and Zechariah—refer to it. Jonah was actually sent to prophesy to Nineveh, and the revival he unwillingly promoted saved the city from destruction for a long period of time.

The Assyrians early added to their worship of the primitive national god Asshur the Babylonian deities with their cultic apparatus. Wherever they influenced Israel and Judah, the effort was demoralizing, as the historical books of the Bible and the prophets bear abundant witness.

ASTROLOGY, ASTROLOGER In warning his people against Canaanite superstition (Deut 18:10–13), Moses made no reference to astrology or any sort of fortune-telling by means of the stars, for, though this later came into western Palestine, it was essentially a Babylonian or Mesopotamian study. Although the translation "astrologer" appears several times in the English Bible (e.g., Dan 2:2; 5:7 NIV), the only unequivocal reference to the practice and its practitioners is found in Isaiah 47:13 ("those stargazers who make predictions month by month") and in Jeremiah 10:2 (where people are urged

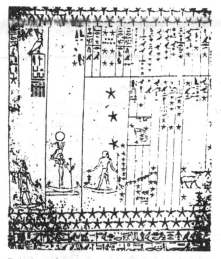

Painting of astronomical chart on ceiling of tomb of Senenmut in the time of Hatshepsut and Thutmose III. The three columns represent (from the left) Jupiter, Sirius, and Orion. The "egg" in the center is probably Pleiades, and the V-shaped constellation between Orion and Pleiades is Ursa Major over Ursa Minor.

not to be "terrified by signs in the sky"). Babylonians and Egyptians pondered the movement of the stars, taking note of variations and conjunctions, so as to predict events on earth. The Hebrew word *'ashshāph* (e.g., in Dan 1:20; 2:2, 10, 27; 4:7; 5:7, 11, 17) has often been translated "astrologer," though not by the NIV. It refers to the general practice of "magic" or the casting of spells and pronouncing of "charms." The NIV does, however, use "astrologer" to represent "Chaldean" in some of these same verses as well as others (e.g., Dan 2:2, 4–5, 10; 5:7, 11), a needless restriction of meaning for a word that covers, for example, philosophy as well as astrology and, in general, refers to educated or knowledgeable people.

ASTRONOMY While the word *astronomy* is not found in the Bible, there are many passages that refer to some aspect of the subject. God made the stars (Gen 1:16), knows their number and names (Ps 147:4), and is glorified by them (Ps 19).

There are hundreds of biblical references to stars, sun, moon, and planets. Evidently the early Bible writers were much better acquainted with the subject of astronomy than are many modern people. When God wished to tell Abraham how numerous his descendants would be, he took him out and showed him the stars (Gen 15:5). Later God compared the number of Abraham's descendants not only with the stars, but also with the sand on the seashore (22:17). Modern discoveries have proved that the total number of stars is approximately equal to the number of grains of sand on the seashore, a number so large it is impossible for the human mind to comprehend.

The Bible refers in a most striking manner to the height of the stars—that is, to their distance from the earth: "Is not God in the heights of heaven? And see how lofty are the highest stars!" (Job 22:12). It turns out that the distances to the most distant stars known are more than one hundred thousand times the diameter of our solar system.

The biblical writers were aware that the stars differ greatly from each other (e.g., 1 Cor 15:41). Astronomers have verified that the stars have different colors, size, density, temperature, and total amount of light emitted. Israel was warned not to worship the sun, the moon, and the stars (Deut 4:19). In spite of such warnings, sun worship often prevailed. Asa and Josiah, kings of Judah, found it necessary to take away the sun images that had been kept at the entrance to the temple.

While there is little evidence in the Bible that the Hebrew people had indulged very much in the study of astronomy, it is very clear that they recognized a sublime order in the movements of the heavenly bodies. They observed carefully the daily rising of the sun, its majestic movement across the sky, and its final setting in the west. This is vividly portrayed in the story of the battle with the Amorites as recorded in Joshua 10, when the sun stood still in the middle of the sky. Many theories have been proposed in an attempt to give a scientific explanation to this "long day of Joshua." None is completely satisfactory, and they will not be discussed here. It is sufficient to add that this is one of many miracles recorded in the Bible to show us that God is the ruler and sustainer of the universe.

More remarkable than the long day of Joshua when the sun apparently stood still, is the story of the return of the shadow on the sundial of Ahaz. In this case the Lord gave King Hezekiah a sign saying, "I will make the shadow cast by the sun go back the ten steps it has gone down on the stairway of Ahaz" (Isa 38:8). This is, indeed, a remarkable miracle. If taken literally, this means not only that the earth stopped rotating on its axis, but that it reversed its direction of rotation for a short time. Again the scientists have no answer to explain such an event.

There are a number of allusions in the Bible to eclipses of the sun and of the moon (Isa 13:10; Joel 2:31; Amos 8:9). Calculated eclipses of the sun that occurred in Palestine during OT times are as follows: July 31, 1063 B.C.; August 15, 831; June 15, 763; May 18, 603; May 28, 585. Very likely the prophets Amos and Joel witnessed the eclipse of August 15, 831. Such an eclipse is vividly described by Amos: "I will make the sun go down at noon and darken the earth in broad daylight" (Amos 8:9).

The subject of astrology has been connected with astronomy since early times. The reference in Judges 5:20 no doubt refers to the influence of the stars in the lives of people. The writer states, "From the heavens the stars fought, from their courses they fought against Sisera." However, the Hebrew people seemed to have had little to do with the subject. In the Book of Daniel there are repeated statements made concerning the astrologers. It is to be noted that Daniel and his three friends, though closely associated with astrologers, are always mentioned as keeping themselves separated and undefiled. Again and again when the magicians and the astrologers were unable to perform a task, it was Daniel who was able to do important things for the king. Thus it is apparent that the Bible condemns the pseudo-science of astrology.

Probably the most fascinating part of biblical astronomy concerns the star of Bethlehem (Matt 2). This miraculous appearance, which is called a star, aroused the curiosity of the wise men to such an extent that they followed it for many miles until finally it pointed out the exact place where they wished to go. Although a variety of theories have been proposed, no attempt by modern science has been able to explain this miracle.

There is much evidence in the Bible that many of the constellations were known to the writers. *Kesil* (Orion) is mentioned in Job 9:9; Isaiah 13:10; Amos 5:8. *Ash* or *Ayish* occurs in Job 9:9; 38:32. Also found in Job 38:32 is the term *Mazzarot*.

ASWAN (ăs'wăn, Heb *sevēnēh*). An Egyptian city, identified as present-day Aswan, at the First Cataract of the Nile, on the east bank of the river, opposite the island of Elephantine. The name Aswan

("Syene" in JB, KJV, MLB, MOF, NASB, NEB, RSV) appears only twice in the OT (NIV—Ezek 29:10; 30:6), both times in prophecies against Egypt, geographically defining the extent of Egyptian territory, from Migdol in the north to Aswan in the south.

ATAROTH (ăt'à-rŏth, *crowns*). **1.** Modern Khirbet-at-tarus, east of Jordan in the territory of Reuben, but fortified by Gad (Num 32:3, 34). **2.** On the border between Ephraim and Benjamin, to the west (Josh 16:2), probably the same as Ataroth Addar (16:5; 18:13). **3.** On the eastern border of Ephraim (Josh 16:7). **4.** Near Bethlehem (1 Chron 2:54; Atroth Beth Joab in NIV). The locations of the last three are uncertain.

ATER (ā'tĕr). **1.** The ancestor of an exiled family (Ezra 2:16; Neh 7:21). **2.** Ancestor of a family of gatekeepers who returned from exile with Zerubbabel (Ezra 2:42; Neh 7:45). **3.** The chief of the people who, with Nehemiah, sealed the covenant (Neh 10:17).

ATHALIAH (ăth'à-lī'à). **1.** The only woman who ever reigned over Judah (see 2 Kings 8:18, 25–28; 11:1–20; 2 Chron 22:1–23:21; 24:7). She was the daughter of Ahab (king of Israel) and Jezebel (a devotee of Baal). Omri (king of Israel) was her grandfather, and Jehoram (king of Judah) was her husband. After the death of their son Ahaziah, Athaliah reigned six years. She put to death all Ahaziah's sons except Joash, who was hidden by Jehosheba, sister of Ahaziah and wife of Jehoiada the priest. Then, in the seventh year, Jehoiada conspired to put Joash on the throne. Coming into the temple to see what the excitement meant, Athaliah found that the coronation had already taken place. She was allowed to leave the temple, that it might not be defiled with her blood, but was killed as she went out the door. **2.** A son of Jeroham, a Benjamite (1 Chron 8:26). **3.** The father of Jeshiah, a returned exile (Ezra 8:7).

ATHENS (ăth'ĕnz, Gr. *Athēnai*). In ancient times the famous capital of Attica, one of the Greek states, now the capital of Greece. The city was named after its patron goddess Athene. It centered around a rocky hill called Acropolis and was 4½ miles (7½ km.) from the sea. According to tradition, the city was founded by Cecrops, who came from Egypt about 1556 B.C.; Athens sent 50 ships to the Trojan War. The city was ruled by kings until about 1068, when archons (magistrates) began to rule. The

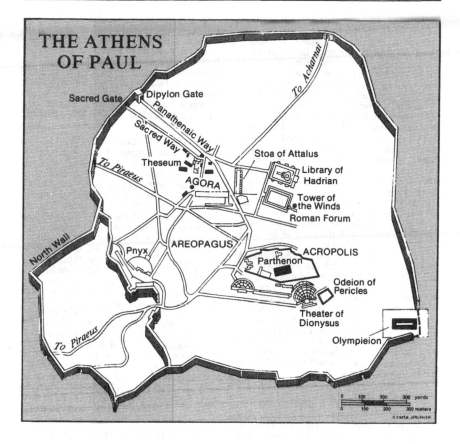

THE ATHENS OF PAUL

Athenians defeated the Persians at Marathon in 490 and again in 480 at Salamis. They then built a small empire, with a powerful fleet for its support. The period of Athens' greatest glory was during the rule of Pericles (459–431), who erected many beautiful public buildings in the city and under whose administration literature and art flourished. The Peloponnesian War (431–404) ended with the submission of Athens to Sparta. Later wars sapped the strength of Athens. Philip of Macedon crushed the city in 338. In 146 the Romans made it a part of the province of Achaea. The Roman general Sulla sacked the city in 86. It subsequently came into the hands of the Goths, the Byzantines, and other peoples. The Turks ruled it from A.D. 1458 until the emancipation of Greece in 1833.

In ancient times Athens had a population of at least a quarter of a million. It was the seat of Greek art, science, and philosophy, and was the most important university city in the ancient world, even under Roman sway. Although politically conquered, it conquered its conquerors with its learning and culture.

Paul visited the city on his second missionary journey and spoke to an interested but somewhat disdainful audience (Acts 17). He reminded them of their altar inscribed with the words "TO AN UNKNOWN GOD," which he had seen in the city, and declared that he could tell them about this God. He made some converts in the city, but there is no record of his establishing a church there or of his returning on any later occasion.

ATONEMENT (ă-tōn′mĕnt). The root meaning in English, "reparation," leads to the secondary meaning of reconciliation, or "at-one-ment," the bringing together into harmony of those who have been separated, enemies.

In the OT, atonement is mainly expressed by the verb *kāphar*, whose root meaning is "to cover over." The noun related to this verb, *kōpher*, is mainly used of the ransom price that "covers" an offense—not by sweeping it out of sight but by making an equivalent payment so that the offense has been actually and exactly paid for (e.g., Exod 30:12, "ransom"; Num 35:31; Ps 49:7; Isa 43:3). Arising from this use of the noun, one whole section of the verb (in Heb. the Piel and Pual forms, *kippēr* and *kuppar*) came to be set aside to express only the idea of removing offense by equivalent payment and so bringing the offender and the offended together. The only secular uses of this word (in Gen 32:20; Lev 5:16; 16:30, 33; 17:11) show also that the means of atonement—the actual price paid as equivalent to the sin committed—was the sacrificial blood, the life laid down in death. See also BLOOD.

In the ritual of the Day of Atonement (Lev 16:15–17, 20–22) the Lord wanted his people to know the significance of what had happened in secret when the high priest sprinkled the blood on the "atonement cover" (Heb. *kappōreth*). Therefore he commanded the ceremony of the live goat so that they might actually see their sins being laid on another and see their sins being borne away never to return again. See also ATONEMENT, DAY OF; LAYING ON OF HANDS.

In Christian theology, atonement is the central doctrine of faith and can properly include all that Jesus accomplished for us on the cross. It was a vicarious (substitutionary) atonement. On the Day of Atonement, the goat that was substituted was in some sense not as valuable as a person, though the goat had never sinned; but God in his matchless grace provided a substitute who was *infinitely* better than the sinner, absolutely sinless and holy, and dearer to the Father than all creation. "The wages of sin is death" (Rom 6:23) and "God made him who had no sin to be sin for us, so that in him we might become the righteousness of God" (2 Cor 5:21).

There are two opposite facts that the ingenuity of the theologians could not have reconciled without God's solution: First, that God is holy and he hates sin, and that by his holy law sin is a capital crime; and second, that "God is love" (1 John 4:8). So the problem was, "How can God be just and at the same time justify the sinner?" (cf. Rom 3:26). John 3:16 tells us that God so loved that he gave his Son. In the eternal counsels of the Trinity, Jesus offered himself to bear our sins (Rev 13:8). He voluntarily emptied himself of the divine trappings of omnipotence, omniscience, and glory (Phil 2:5–8), that he might be truly human. He perfectly fulfilled the law on our behalf (Matt 5:18) and then paid the penalty for our sins in his death for us on the cross. Our Lord's work of atonement looks in three directions: toward sin (1 Peter 1:18–19), toward us (Rom 5:6–11), and toward the Holy Father (1 John 2:1).

ATONEMENT, DAY OF The Jewish feast of Yom Kippur, the tenth day of the seventh month (Sept.), the only day the high priest entered the Holy of Holies. It was a day of fasting, penitence, sacrifice for the whole nation, and abstinence from labor (Lev 16; Heb 9:1–10:25).

The purpose of the Day of Atonement seems to have been at least fourfold: first, to show God's hatred of sin; second, to show the contagious nature of sin; third, to point forward by three types to the death of "the Lamb of God," our blessed Savior; and fourth, by its repetition year after year to signify that the way into the very presence of God had not been made manifest before the death of Christ (Heb 9:7–9). When our Lord offered himself on Calvary, the veil of the temple was torn (Mark 15:38), signifying that from that moment on we were under a new covenant—a covenant of grace. The OT ceremonies were but symbols and types and shadows: the NT records the realities. Today, under grace, we look back to Calvary, when the great Day of Atonement took place once for all.

ATROTH BETH JOAB (See ATAROTH)

ATTAI (ăt'à-ī). **1.** A half-Egyptian member of the tribe of Judah (1 Chron 2:35–36). **2.** A mighty man of Gad who joined David (1 Chron 12:11). **3.** Younger brother of Abijah, king of Judah (2 Chron 11:20).

ATTALIA (ăt'à-lī'à). A seaport of Pamphylia near Perga, mentioned in Acts 14:25. On Paul's first missionary journey he landed at Perga, several miles inland, but on his return he and Barnabas sailed for Antioch in Syria from Attalia, the main seaport on the Gulf of "Adalia," as it is spelled today. The city was founded by and named for Attalus Philadelphus, king of Pergammum from 159 to 138 B.C.

ATTIRE (See DRESS)

AUGUSTUS CAESAR (ô-gŭs'tŭs sē'zêr). Gaius Octavius, whose male ancestors for four generations had the same name, was born in Rome in 63 B.C., and early became influential through his great-uncle

Julius Caesar. He was studying quietly in Illyria when he heard of Caesar's murder in 44. Hastening to Italy, he learned that Caesar had adopted him and made him his heir. Thus in his early manhood by skillful manipulation of his friends, he conquered his rival Antony at Actium. The beginning of the Roman Empire may be reckoned from that date—September 2, 31. By his adoption he had become "Caesar," and now the Roman senate added the title "Augustus." Although he preserved the forms of a republic, he gradually got all the power into his hands. He reigned till A.D. 14. Some of the secular histories omit the most important event in his reign—a Baby was born in Bethlehem! Augustus Caesar is mentioned just once in the NT (Luke 2:1).

AUTHORITY (Gr. *exousia*). The legal and/or moral right to exercise power, or power that is rightly possessed. In the Bible God is presented as the ultimate, personal authority and the source of all authority (Dan 4:34–35; cf. 2:21; 7:13–14; Rom 13:1) God gave authority to Israel's kings, priests, and prophets, and to the written Word of God (Ps 119).

Authority (*exousia*) and power (*dynamis*) are related but different (see Luke 4:36). Jesus is a man under authority and with authority (Matt 7:29; 8:9; Mark 1:27); he empowers his disciples to cast out demons (Matt 10:1; Mark 3:15); he does what only God can do—he forgives sins (Matt 9:6); he has control over nature (Mark 4:41); he exercises power over death (John 10:18); and as the resurrected Lord he has all authority in earth and heaven (Matt 28:18).

After Jesus' exaltation, the apostles developed the theme of the authority of Jesus, presenting him as coregent of the Father and possessing authority over the whole cosmos (Eph 1:20–23; Phil 2:1–11; Col 2:9–10; Rev 17:14).

Other forms of authority delegated by God include that of the state (Rom 13:1ff.), of the apostles as unique pillars of the church and recipients of divine revelation (Luke 6:13; Eph 2:20), and of the husband as head of the family (1 Cor 11:3). The possession of authority and power by Satan (Luke 22:53; Col 1:13) has been abused and will be punished.

AUTHORIZED VERSION (See BIBLE, ENGLISH VERSIONS)

AVA (See AVVA)

AVENGER The Hebrew word *goēl* refers to the "next of kin" who (1) possesses the right to take on himself whatever need may have overwhelmed his kinsman or kinswoman (e.g., Boaz, Ruth 3:13–13; 4:2–10; Jesus, Isa 43:14) and (2) exacts vengeance in the case of murder (Num 35:11–34). This is how the word that means "redeemer" also means "avenger." In the case of murder, where life must be taken for life, the next of kin took up the dreadful duty, carefully restricted in his actions by the clear OT distinction between capital murder and accidental manslaughter and by the limitation of vengeance to the murderer only (Deut 24:16).

AVIM, AVITES (See AVVITES, AVVIM)

AVVA (äv'vȧ). A region in Assyria from which Sargon brought people to populate devastated Samaria (2 Kings 17:24), thought by some to be the Ivvah of 2 Kings 18:34. The people who were brought in worshiped the gods Nibhaz and Tartak (17:31).

AVVITES, AVVIM (ä'vīts, ä'vĭm). 1. An ancient people who dwelled in the region of Gaza before the time of Moses (Deut 2:23). When Joshua was an old man, these people still had not been rooted out (Josh 13:3). 2. Avvim was a city in the tribe of Benjamin (Josh 18:23), perhaps populated by the remains of this ancient tribe.

AZAL (See AZEL)

AZAREL, AZAREEL (ăz'âr-ĕl, ȧ-zä'rē-ĕl, Heb. *'āzar'ēl, God is helper*). 1. A Levite who entered the army of David at Ziklag (1 Chron 12:6). 2. A musician in the temple in David's time (25:18). 3. A captain in the service of David (27:22). 4. A man Ezra persuaded to divorce his foreign wife (Ezra 10:41). 5. A priest who lived in Jerusalem after the Exile (Neh 11:13). 6. A musician who played in the procession when Jerusalem's new wall was dedicated (Neh 12:36).

AZARIAH (ăz'ȧ-rī'ȧ, Heb. *'āzaryahu, Jehovah has helped*). 1. King of Judah. See UZZIAH. 2. A man of Judah of the house of Ethan the Wise (1 Chron 2:8). 3. The son of Jehu, descended from an Egyptian through the daughter of Sheshan (2:38). 4. A son of Ahimaaz (6:9). 5. A Levite of the family of Kohath (6:36). 6. A son of Zadok, the high priest under Solomon (1 Kings 4:2). 7. A high priest and son of Johanan (1 Chron 6:10). 8. Son of Nathan, an officer at Solomon's court (1 Kings 4:5). 9. A prophet, son of Obed (2 Chron 15:1–8). 10. Son of Jehoshaphat (21:2). 11. A son of Jehoram (22:1). 12. Son of Jeroham. He helped to overthrow Athaliah (23:1). 13. Son of Johanan. He helped to get the captives of Judah re-

The large mound of Tell ez-Zakariyeh, identified with Azekah, on the northeastern edge of the Valley of Elah. Courtesy Ecole Biblique et Archéologique Française, Jerusalem

leased (28:12). **14.** A Levite who assisted in purifying the temple in Hezekiah's reign (29:12). **15.** A high priest who rebuked Uzziah's attempt to assume priestly functions (26:16-20). **16.** A son of Hilkiah; a high priest not long before the Exile (1 Chron 6:13-14). **17.** A man of Judah who bitterly opposed Jeremiah (Jer 43:2). **18.** One of the captives taken to Babylon, whose name was changed to Abednego (Dan 1:7). **19.** The son of Maaseiah. He helped repair the walls of Jerusalem (Neh 3:23). **20.** A Levite who assisted Ezra in explaining the Law (8:7). **21.** A priest who sealed the covenant (10:2). **22.** A prince of Judah who marched in the procession at the dedication of the wall of Jerusalem (12:32-33).

AZARIAHU (See AZARIAH)

AZAZEL (See SCAPEGOAT)

AZAZIAH (ăz'à-zī'à, Heb. *'ăzazyāhû, Jehovah is strong*). **1.** A harpist during the reign of David (1 Chron 15:21). **2.** The father of the prince of Ephraim in the reign of David (27:20). **3.** A Levite overseer of the temple in the reign of Hezekiah (2 Chron 31:13).

AZEKAH (à-zē'kà). A town in NW Judah, a place to which Joshua pursued the kings at the battle of Gibeon (Josh 10:10-11; cf. 15:35; 1 Sam 17:1; 2 Chron 11:9; Neh 11:30; Jer 34:7).

AZEL (ā'zĕl). **1.** A descendant of Saul's son Jonathan (1 Chron 8:37-38; 9:43-44). **2.** A place near Jerusalem (Zech 14:5).

AZGAD (ăz'găd, Heb. *'azgādh, Gad is strong*, or *fate is hard*). The ancestral head of a postexilic family (Ezra 2:12; 8:12; Neh 7:17; 10:15).

AZIEL (ā'zĭ-ĕl, Heb. *'ăzī'ēl, God is my strength*). A Levite musician (1 Chron 15:20; Jaaziel in 15:18, Jehiel in 16:5).

AZMAVETH (ăz-mā'vĕth, Heb. *'azmāweth, death is strong*). **1.** One of David's heroes (2 Sam 23:31). **2.** A Benjamite, one of whose sons followed David (1 Chron 12:3). **3.** A man in charge of David's treasures (27:25). **4.** A descendant of Saul's son Jonathan (8:36). **5.** A place north of Amathoth to which some exiles returned (Ezra 2:24; Neh 12:29); also called Beth Azmaveth (Neh 7:28).

AZOTUS (See ASHDOD)

AZRIEL (ăz' rĭ-ĕl, Heb. *'azrî'ēl, God is help*). **1.** A chieftain of Manasseh (1 Chron 5:24). **2.** A Naphtalite of David's time (27:19). **3.** The father of Seraiah of Jeremiah's time (Jer 36:26).

AZRIKAM (ăz'rĭ-kăm, Heb. *'azrîqām, my help has arisen*). **1.** A son of Neariah (1 Chron 3:23). **2.** A descendant of Saul (8:38; 9:44). **3.** A Levite, descended from Merari (9:14). **4.** An officer of Ahaz (2 Chron 28:7).

AZUBAH (à-zū'bà, *forsaken*). **1.** A wife of Caleb (1 Chron 2:18-19). **2.** The mother of Jehoshaphat (1 Kings 22:42).

AZUR (See AZZUR)

AZZAH (See GAZA)

AZZUR (ăz'êr, Heb. *'azzur, helped*). **1.** Father of Hananiah the false prophet (Jer 28:1). **2.** Father of Jaazaniah (Ezek 11:1). **3.** One of the signers of the covenant in the days of Nehemiah (Neh 10:17).

-B-

BAAL (bā'ăl, Heb. *ba'al, lord, posses-sor, husband*). **1.** The word "baal" appears in the OT with a variety of meanings: "master" or "owner" (as in Exod 21:28, 34; Judg 19:22; Isa 16:8) and husband (as in Exod 21:3; 2 Sam 11:26; Hos 2:16). Most often, however, the word refers to the Semitic deity or deities called Baal. Baal became the proper name for the most significant god in the Canaanite pantheon, or company of gods. He was the presiding deity in many localities.

Baal was worshiped on high places in Moab in the time of Balaam and Balak (Num 22:41). In the period of the judges there were altars to Baal in Palestine (Judg 2:13; 6:28–32); and in the time of Ahab and Jezebel, the daughter of the heathen king of the Sidonians, the worship of the Lord was almost supplanted by that of Baal. The struggle between Baalism and the worship of the true God came to a head on Mt. Carmel when the prophet Elijah met the priests of Baal and had 450 of them killed (1 Kings 16:32; 18:17–40). The cult quickly revived, however, and prospered until crushed by Jehu (2 Kings 10:18–28). Jezebel's daughter Athaliah, the wife of Jehoram, gave the worship of Baal a new impulse (2 Chron 17:3; 21:6; 22:2). When she was overthrown, the temple of Baal at Jerusalem was destroyed and the chief priest killed before the altar (2 Kings 11:18). Before long, however, there was another revival of the worship of Baal (2 Kings 21:3; 2 Chron 28:2). Josiah again destroyed the temple of Baal at Jerusalem and caused the public worship of the god to cease for a time (2 Kings 23:4–5). Prophets of Israel, especially Jeremiah, often denounced Baal worship (Jer 19:4–5).

Incense and sacrifice were offered to Baal (Jer 7:9)—even human sacrifice (19:5)—but the worship of Baal was chiefly marked by fertility rites. The main function of Baal was thought to be to make land, animals, and people fertile. To prompt the god to perform these functions, worshipers themselves performed human sexual acts of fertility, and the Baal shrines were staffed with male and female attendants for this purpose. **2.** A descendant of Reuben, the firstborn son of Jacob (1 Chron 5:5). **3.** A Benjamite (8:30). **4.** A town somewhere on the border of Simeon (4:33). **5.** In conjunction with another name it is often the name of a man and not of Baal, e.g., Baal-Manan, a king of Edom (Gen 36:38; 1 Chron 1:49).

BAALAH (See KIRIATH JEARIM)

BAALATH (bā'ălăth, Heb. *ba'allāth*). A town in Dan (Josh 19:44) and a store city of Solomon (1 Kings 9:18; 1 Chron 8:6). In Joshua 15:9 it is identified with Kiriath Jearim.

BAALATH BEER (See RAMAH, RAMA, no. 5)

BAALBEK (bāl'běk, *city of Baal*). A city of Coele-Syria, about 40 miles (67 km.) NW of Damascus, celebrated for its magnificence in the first centuries of the Christian era and famous since then for its ruins. Chief of the ruins is the great Temple of the Sun, built of incredibly huge stones from nearby quarries. (See page 64.)

BAAL-BERITH (bā'ăl-bĭr-īth, *lord of covenant*). A god Israel worshiped after Gideon's death (Judg 8:33). Abimelech was given 70 pieces of silver from the temple of this god, and he used this money "to hire reckless adventurers, who became his followers" (9:4).

BAALE OF JUDAH (See KIRIATH JEARIM)

BAAL GAD (bā'ăl găd, *Gad is Baal*). A place in the Valley of Lebanon at the foot of Mt. Hermon that marked the northern limit of Israel's conquest of Canaan (Josh 11:17; 12:7; 13:5).

BAAL-HANAN (bā'ăl-hā'năn, *Baal is gracious*). **1.** The son of Acbor and king of Edom (Gen 36:38; 1 Chron 1:49). **2.** An official under David (1 Chron 27:28).

BAAL HERMON (bā'ăl hûr'mŏn, *Baal of Hermon*). A town or place near Mt. Hermon marking the NW limit of the half-tribe of Manasseh east of the Jordan (Judg 3:3; 1 Chron 5:23).

BAALIS (bā'à-lĭs, Heb. *ba'alîs*). A king of the Ammonites who reigned soon after Nebuchadnezzar's capture of Jerusalem. He instigated the murder of Gedaliah (Jer 40:14).

BAAL MEON (bā'ăl mē'ŏn, Heb. *ba'al me'ôn, Baal of Meon*). An old city on the frontiers of Moab, assigned to Reuben (Num 32:38), called Beth Meon (Jer 48:23) and Beon (Num 32:3).

BAAL PEOR (bā'ăl pē'ôr, Heb. *ba'al pe'ôr, Baal of Peor*). A Moabite deity,

Coffered ceiling of the peristyle, temple of Bacchus at Baalbek, ancient city in the valley of Beqa'a, which separates the Lebanon and Anti-Lebanon mountains. The ceiling is superbly decorated with intricate carvings and reaches a height of c. 42 feet (14 m.).
Courtesy Stadium Biblicum Franciscanum, Jerusalem

probably Chemosh, worshiped on the top of Mt. Peor. The Israelites, when encamped at Shittim, were induced by Moabite women to the worship of this deity and were severely punished by God as a result (Num 25:1–9; Ps 106:28; Hos 9:10).

BAAL PERAZIM (bā'ăl pē-rā'zĭm, Heb. *ba'al perātsîm, Baal of the breaking through*). A place near the Valley of Rephaim where David had a great God-given victory over the Philistines (2 Sam 5:18–20; 1 Chron 14:9–11).

BAAL-ZEBUB (bā'ăl-zē'bŭb, Heb. *ba'al zevûv, Baal,* or *lord of flies*). The name under which Baal was worshiped by the Philistines of Ekron (2 Kings 1:2, 3, 6, 16). Elijah rebuked Ahaziah for consulting this god to find out whether he would recover from his illness. This is almost certainly the same name as Baalzebub, or Beelzebul in the Greek text. Beelzebub is the prince of the demons (Matt 10:25; 12:24; Mark 3:22; Luke 11:15, 18–19), and is identified with Satan (Matt 12:26; Mark 3:23; Luke 11:18). Beelzebul signifies "lord of the dwelling" (Matt 10:25; 12:29; Mark 3:27).

BAAL ZEPHON (bā'ăl zē'fŏn, Heb. *ba'al tsephôn, lord of the north*). A place near which the Israelites encamped just before they crossed the Red Sea (Exod 14:2, 9; Num 33:7).

BAANA (bā'ȧ-nȧ, Heb. *ba'ănā', son of oppression*). 1. Two officers in the service of Solomon (1 Kings 4:12, 16). 2. The father of Zadok, one of those who helped in rebuilding the wall of Jerusalem in Nehemiah's time (Neh 3:4).

BAANAH (bā'ȧ-nȧ, Heb. *ba'ănā', son of oppression*). 1. A captain in the army of Ish-Bosheth, whom he and his brother murdered. They were put to death as criminals by David (2 Sam 4). 2. The father of Heled, one of David's warriors (23:29; 1 Chron 11:30). 3. A Jew who returned from Babylon with Zerubbabel and was one of those who sealed the covenant (Ezra 2:2; Neh 7:7; 10:27).

BAASHA (bā'ȧ-shȧ, Heb. *ba'shā', boldness*). The son of Ahijah, of the tribe of Issachar. He became the third king of Israel by assassinating Nadab his predecessor. He exterminated the house of Jeroboam and made Tirzah his capital. He ascended the throne in the third year

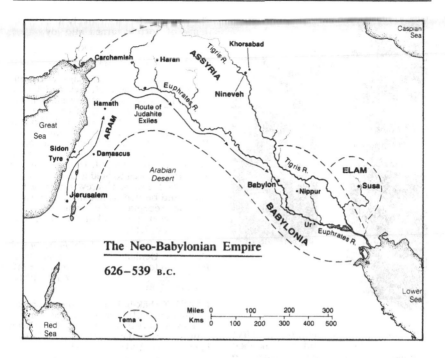

The Neo-Babylonian Empire

626–539 B.C.

of Asa, king of Judah (1 Kings 15–16), and carried on a long war with him. Baasha continued the calf worship begun by Jeroboam. After a reign of 24 years he died a natural death and was succeeded by his son Elah, who, along with every member of the house of Baasha, was killed by Zimri (1 Kings 15–16).

BABEL, TOWER OF (bā'bĕl, *gate of God*). An expression not used in the OT but found popularly for the structure built in the plain of Shinar shortly after the Flood (Gen 11:1–9). The ziggurats may have been imitations of this tower.

BABOON (See ANIMALS)

BABYLON (Băb'ĭ-lŏn). The Greek form of the Hebrew word *bāvel*, which was closely allied to and probably derived from the Akkadian *babilu* or "gate of God." The name referred not only to the city itself but also to the country of which it was the capital. It was situated in central Mesopotamia on the river Euphrates, some 50 miles (83 km.) south of modern Baghdad, capital of Iraq and was in contact with all the most important cultural centers of the ancient Near East.

The date of its foundation is still disputed. The connection between Akkad,

Calneh, Erech, and Babylon (Gen 10:10) indicates a period at least as early as 3000 B.C. The history of Babylon is complicated by the fact that it was governed by rulers from several lands who were successively engaged in struggles for its capture and retention.

The political history of Babylon was bound up with that of Babylonia and Assyria. Under Hammurabi (c. 1704–1662), the last great king of the first dynasty, the Babylonian Empire stretched from the Persian Gulf to the middle Euphrates and upper Tigris regions. From the end of the tenth century Babylon became a vassal of Assyria, controlled by the kings of Nineveh. Nabopolassar founded an independent dynasty in 626, known as the neo-Babylonian, or Chaldean, regime.

Under Nabopolassar (c. 626–605) and his son Nebuchadnezzar II (c. 605–562), ancient Babylon attained the height of its splendor. It was probably the largest and most elaborate city in the ancient world, including the "hanging gardens" (one of the seven wonders of the world) and over 50 temples. In 616 the Babylonians began a military campaign against the middle Euphrates region that ended in the de-

Babylon's Ishtar Gate, set within a 40-feet-high double tower, guarded the northern entrance to the city. The construction here shows the relief figures of bulls and dragons in alternate rows. Brick was the standard building material in a land almost totally lacking in stone. Courtesy Staatliche Museen zu Berlin

struction of the Assyrian Empire. Cyrus conquered Babylon in 539 and set about building up his vast Persian Empire. When the Persian Empire fell to Alexander the Great in 330, Babylon was destroyed. Although remaining an inhabited site, Babylon declined still further in importance under the Parthians (c. 125 B.C.) and was last mentioned on a Babylonian clay tablet dated about 10 B.C. At present the Baghdad-to-Bassorah railway line passes within a few yards of the mound that was once the most splendid city of the world.

Babylon is often mentioned in prophecy (e.g., Isa 13:1, 19; 14:22; 21; 46; 47; Jer 50; 51) and is a NT symbol of opposition to God (1 Peter 5:13; Rev 14:8). (See map on page 67.)

BACA (bā'kà, Heb. bākhā, a balsam tree). KJV, RSV, and NIV in Psalm 84:6 all have "the Valley of Baca" (ASV "the Valley of Weeping" but with a marginal variant "the valley of the balsam trees").

The phrase refers figuratively to an experience of sorrow turned into joy.

BACHRITES (See BEKER)

BADGER (See ANIMALS)

BAG Various kinds of bags are mentioned in the Bible. 1. Hebrew kelî; Greek pēra. This was a kind of haversack made of skin, for the carrying of one or more days' provisions (Matt 10:10). 2. Hebrew kîs, a bag for merchants' weights (Deut 25:13). 3. Greek ballantion, a more finished leather pouch that served as a "purse" (Luke 10:4). 4. Hebrew hārît, a bag large enough to hold a talent of silver (2 Kings 5:23). 5. Hebrew tserôr, a bag that could be tied with a string and was a favorite receptacle for valuables (Gen 42:35; Greek zonē –Matt 3:4; 10:9; Acts 21:11; Rev 1:13; 15:6).

BAHURIM (bà-hū'rĭm, Heb. bahurîm). A place in Benjamin on the road from Jerusalem to Jericho, not far from the Mt. of Olives (2 Sam 16:5; 17:18; 19:16; 1 Kings 2:8)

BAKBUK (băk-bŭk, Heb. baqbûq, bottle [onomatopoeic]). The founder of a family of temple servants (KJV, Nethinim) who returned from the Captivity with Zerubbabel (Ezra 2:51; Neh 7:53).

BAKBUKIAH (băk'bū-kī'a, Heb. buqbuqyâh, flask, or perhaps, the Lord pours out). A Levite in high office in Jerusalem right after the Exile (Neh 11:17; 12:9, 25).

BAKER (See OCCUPATIONS AND PROFESSIONS)

BALAAM (bā'lăm, Heb. bil'ām, perhaps devouring or devourer). The son of Beor, a diviner with a remarkable history (Num 22:22–24:25; 31:8, 16; Deut 23:4; Josh 13:22; 24:9; Neh 13:2; Mic 6:5; 2 Peter 2:15; Jude 11; Rev 2:14). He was employed by Balak, the king of the Moabites, to curse the Israelites. God permitted Balaam to go but warned him (by the strange behavior of his donkey and his encounter with the angel of the Lord) to speak only what God commanded. Balaam, in spite of his own desires, pronounced a blessing on the Israelites instead of a curse. God was protecting his people from harm, even when they were unaware of the danger.

Later Balaam succeeded in turning the people from the Lord. By his advice, the Israelites were seduced into idolatry (Num 31), bringing God's judgment on Israel. By God's command Israel brought vengeance on the Midianites and Balaam perished in the resulting slaughter.

In the NT Balaam is several times held

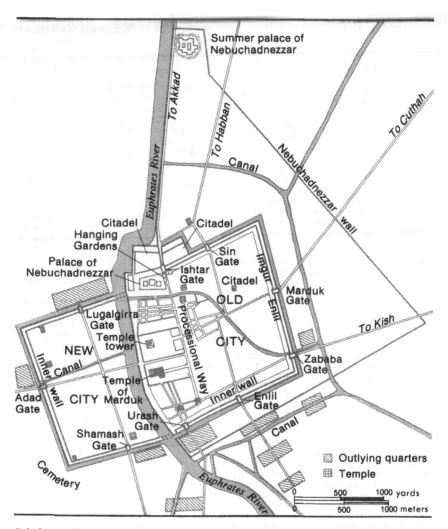

Babylon at the time of Nebuchadnezzar II (605–562 B.C.). Courtesy Carta, Jerusalem

up as an example of the destructive influence of hypocritical teachers who attempt to lead God's people astray (Jude 11; 2 Peter 2:15).

BALAH (bā′là, Heb. *bālâh*). A town in SW Palestine (Josh 19:3), called Bilhah (1 Chron 4:29), perhaps the same as Baalah in Judah (Josh 15:29).

BALAK (bā′lăk, Heb. *bālāq, devastator*). A king of Moab in Moses' day who hired Balaam, a diviner from the Euphrates, to pronounce a curse on the Israelites (Num 22–24; Judg 11:25; Mic 6:5; Rev 2:14). Instead of cursings, he heard blessings; but he achieved his end when he followed Balaam's advice to seduce the people of Israel to idolatry, a sin that resulted in heavy judgment on the chosen people. See also BALAAM.

BALANCE The English word is from the Latin *bilanx* and means "having two scales." Weighing with such balances could be accurately done, but the system was liable to fraud, so that in the OT there is much denunciation of "dishonest scales" (Mic 6:11).

BALD LOCUST (See ANIMALS)

BALDNESS Natural baldness is seldom mentioned in the Bible. It was believed to result from hard work (Ezek 29:18) or disease (Isa 3:17, 24). Baldness produced by shaving the head was a mark of mourning for the dead (Lev 21:5; Isa 15:2; 22:12; Mic 1:16). Shaving the head as a sacrifice to a god was the custom of the heathens in the land, and was forbidden to Israel (Lev 21:5; Deut 14:1). The custom among neighboring nations of shaving all but a small patch in the center of the head was also forbidden (Lev 19:27; 21:5). When a Nazirite completed his vow, the shaven hair was offered as a sacrifice to the Lord (Num 6:18; cf. Acts 18:18; 21:24).

BALM (Heb. *tsŏrî*). A strong-smelling resin perhaps obtained in Gilead (Gen 37:25; Jer 8:22; 46:11) and exported from Palestine. It was used as an ointment for healing wounds (Jer 51:8). See also PLANTS.

BALSAM (See PLANTS)

BAMOTH BAAL (bā'mŏth bā'ăl, Heb. *bāmôth ba'al, high places of Baal*). A place north of the Arnon to which Balak took Balaam (Num 22:41; Josh 13:17; also "Bamoth" in Num 21:19–20).

BAND A company of men or that which holds together (Acts 10:1; 27:1).

BANI (bā'nī, Heb. *bānî, posterity*). **1.** A Gadite, one of David's heroes (2 Sam 23:36). **2.** A Levite whose son served in the tabernacle in David's time (1 Chron 6:46). **3.** A descendant of Judah whose son lived in Jerusalem after the Captivity (9:4). **4.** A Levite and builder (Neh 3:17). **5.** A Levite (9:4). **6.** A Levite who lived before the return from the Exile (11:22). **7.** A Levite who sealed the covenant (10:13). **8.** A leader who also signed the covenant (10:14). **9.** Founder of a family, some of whom returned from Babylonia with Zerubbabel (Ezra 2:10). Some took foreign wives (10:29). **10.** Founder of a house (10:34), a descendant of whom was also named Bani (10:38).

BANK Banking of a primitive kind was known in ancient times among both Jews and Gentiles. Money was received on deposit, loaned out, exchanged for smaller denominations or for foreign money. Israelites were not permitted to charge each other interest (Exod 22:25) but could lend with interest to Gentiles (Deut 23:20).

BANNER (Heb. *nēs, deghel, banner, ensign, standard*). Banners were used in ancient times for military, national, and ecclesiastical purposes, frequently in the figurative sense of a rallying point for God's people (Isa 5:26; 11:10; Jer 4:21).

BANQUET The Hebrews, like other peoples of the ancient East, were very fond of social feasting. At the three great religious feasts, which all males were expected to attend, the family had its feast. Sacrifices were accompanied by a feast (Exod 34:15; Judg 16:23–25), as were birthdays (Gen 40:20; Job 1:4; Matt 14:6), marriages (Gen 29:22; Matt 22:2), funerals (2 Sam 3:35; Jer 16:7), laying of foundations (Prov 9:1–5), gathering grapes (Judg 9:27), and sheep-shearing (1 Sam 25:2, 36). At a large banquet a second invitation was often sent on the day of the feast, or a servant brought the guests to the feast (Matt 22:2ff.; Luke 14:17). The host provided robes for the guests, and they were worn in his honor and were a token of his regard. Guests were welcomed by the host with a kiss (7:45), and their feet were washed because of the dusty roads (Gen 18:4; Judg 19:21; Luke 7:44). The head was anointed (Ps 23:5; Luke 7:46), and sometimes the beard, the feet, and the clothes were also anointed. The head was decorated with garlands (Isa 28:1). The guests were seated according to their respective rank (1 Sam 9:22; Luke 14:8), the hands were washed (2 Kings 3:11), and prayers for blessing on the food were said (1 Sam 9:13; Matt 15:36; Luke 22:17). The most honored guests received either larger portions or more choice ones than the rest (Gen 43:34; 1 Sam 9:23–24). Portions were sometimes sent to friends not attending the feast (2 Sam 11:8; Neh 8:10). Often the meal was enlivened with music, singing, and dancing (2 Sam 19:35; Luke 15:25), or with riddles (Judg 14:12). A great banquet sometimes lasted seven days, but excess in eating and drinking was condemned (Eccl 10:16–17; Isa 5:11–12).

BAPTISM (băp'tĭzm). A term derived from the Greek *baptisma* (antecedent, *baptizō*). The idea of ceremonial washing, or cleansing, appears repeatedly in the Mosaic laws of purification (e.g., Exod 29:4, 17; 30:17–21; 40:12, 30; Lev 1:9, 13; 6:27; 9:14; 11:25; 14:8, 9, 47; 15:5–27; 16:4-28; 17:15–16; 22:6; Num 8:7; 19:7–21; 31:23–24; Deut 21:6; 23:11). The Septuagint uses the word *baptizō* twice (2 Kings 5:14; Isa 21:4). Later Judaism incorporated this meaning of cleansing and purification into its idea

Banquet scene with a bearded figure seated before a table, holding a cup, and attended by servants and a magician, limestone relief from Carchemish, second half of eighth century B.C. Reproduced by courtesy of the Trustees of the British Museum

Baptism scene at the River Jordan. Courtesy Zev Radovan

of the new covenant relation and used baptism as a rite of initiation, as reflected in the Qumran sect and the Dead Sea Scroll communities.

John the Baptist transformed baptism from a rite to a positive moral act, a decisive commitment to personal piety.

But his baptism was, nevertheless, only transitory—the meaning and efficacy of baptism can be understood only in the light of the redemptive death and resurrection of Christ. Christ referred to his death as a baptism (Luke 12:50; Matt 20:22; Mark 10:38). To the act of water baptism Jesus added the promise of the baptism with the Spirit, the means by which his redemptive work is applied to human beings (Matt 3:11; Mark 1:8; Luke 3:16; Acts 1:4ff.; 11:16). Christ made spiritual baptism (by the Holy Spirit) synonymous with the actual application of the virtues of his death and resurrection to sinners (Matt 3:11). Through Spirit baptism the redeemed sinner is incorporated into the spiritual body of Christ.

BAR An Aramaic word for the Hebrew *bēn*, "son." In the NT it is used as a prefix to the names of persons, e.g., Bar-Jonah, "son of Jonah" (Matt 16:17).

BARABBAS (bàr-ăb'ǎs, Gr. *Barabbas,* for Aramaic *Bar-abba, son of the father,* or *teacher*). A criminal chosen by the Jerusalem mob, at the instigation of the chief priests, in preference to Christ, to be released by Pilate on the feast of the Passover. He was a notorious prisoner (Matt 27:16), arrested with others for robbery, sedition, and murder (Mark 15:15; Luke 23:18; John 18:40).

BARACHEL (See BARAKEL)

BARACHIAS (See BEREKIAH, BERAKIAH)

BARAK (bâr'ăk, Heb. *bārāq, lightning*). The son of Abinoam of Kedesh, who was summoned by Deborah the judge to lead the Israelite forces against the Canaanites. A peace of 40 years followed his victory (Judg 4–5). In Hebrews 11:32 Barak's name appears among those who achieved great things through faith.

BARBARIAN (bàr-bâr'ĭ-ăn). Originally anyone who did not speak Greek. Paul uses it in this strict sense in Romans 1:14 (KJV; "non-Greeks" in NIV), where "Greeks" and "barbarians" mean the whole human race. Romans and Jews did not mind being called barbarians in this sense. The word is used of one who spoke in an unintelligible foreign tongue (1 Cor 14:11), of the inhabitants of Malta (they spoke a Punic dialect, Acts 28:2), and of those who did not belong to the cultivated Greek race (Col 3:11).

BARBER (See OCCUPATIONS AND PROFESSIONS)

BAR-JESUS (Gr. *Bariesous, son of Jesus*). A Jewish magician and false prophet in the court of Sergius Paulus when the latter was proconsul of Cyprus. He was struck blind for interfering with Paul's work (Acts 13:6–12).

BARLEY (See PLANTS)

BARNABAS (bàr'nà-băs, Gr. *Barnabas,* explained in Acts 4:36 to mean *son of exhortation* or *consolation*). The surname of Joseph, a Levite from Cyprus, who was an early convert to Christianity. He sold a field and gave the proceeds to help poorer believers in Jerusalem (4:36ff.). He was "a good man and full of the Holy Spirit and faith" (Acts 11:24), who spoke on Paul's behalf to the Jerusalem church (9:27).

The Jerusalem church sent Barnabas to the Antioch church; later he brought back Paul as his associate (Acts 11:22–26). At the end of a year the two men were sent to carry alms from the infant church to the believers at Jerusalem, who were suffering from famine (11:27–30). Returning with John Mark from Jerusalem, they were ordained as missionaries and proceeded on a mission to the Gentiles (13:2–3). Barnabas as well as Paul is called an "apostle" (14:14). Together the two men labored at Cyprus, Antioch in Pisidia, Iconium, Lystra, and Derbe. Up to Acts 13:43 the leadership is ascribed to Barnabas; after that, Paul takes the lead. At Lystra, after a cripple was healed, the inhabitants worshiped Barnabas as Jupi-

ter, and Paul, the chief speaker, as Mercury (13:3–14:28). After their return to Antioch, the church sent them to the council at Jerusalem (15:2). They were commissioned to carry the decrees of the council to the churches in Syria and Asia Minor (15:22–35).

The beginning of a difference between the two men is suggested by Paul in Galatians 2:13, where he says that Barnabas went along with Peter in the latter's inconsistent course. This was followed by a more serious break when, after Paul had suggested a second missionary journey, he refused to take along Barnabas' cousin Mark on the ground that he had left them on their first journey. The two men separated, Barnabas going with Mark to Cyprus, and Paul to Asia Minor (Acts 15:36–41). Paul's allusions to Barnabas in his letters shows that he continued to hold his former associate in high esteem (1 Cor 9:6; Gal 2:1, 9, 13; Col 4:10). Some early church leaders attributed the authorship of Hebrews to Barnabas.

BARSABBAS (bàr-sàb'ăs, Gr. from Aram., *son of Sabbas,* or perhaps, *son of,* i.e., *born on, the Sabbath*). **1.** The surname of the Joseph who with Matthias was nominated by the apostles as the successor of Judas (Acts 1:23). **2.** The surname of Judas, a prophet of the Jerusalem church, sent with Silas to Antioch with the decree of the Jerusalem council (15:22).

BARTHOLOMEW (bàr-thŏl'ŏ-mū, Gr. from Aram., *son of Tolmai* or *Talmai,* Gr. *Bartholomaios*). One of the 12 apostles (Matt. 10:3; Mark 3:18; Luke 6:14; Acts 1:13). There is no further reference to him in the NT, and the traditions concerning him are not trustworthy.

BARTIMAEUS (bàr'tĭ-mē'ŭs, Gr. *Bartimaios, son of Timaeus*). A blind man healed by Jesus as he went out from Jericho on his way to Jerusalem shortly before Passion Week (Mark 10:46–52). A similar account is given by Luke (18:35–43), except that the miracle occurred as Jesus drew near to Jericho. Matthew (20:29–34) tells of Jesus healing two blind men on the way out of Jericho. Various explanations, which may be found in the standard commentaries, have been suggested.

BARUCH (bâr'ŭk, Heb. *bārûkh', blessed*). **1.** Son of Neriah and brother of Seraiah (Jer 36:32), of a princely family. He was the trusted friend (32:12) and secretary (36:4ff.) of the prophet Jeremiah. Jeremiah dictated his prophecies to

Baruch, who read them to the people (ch 36). Later Baruch rewrote the prophet's oracles with additions (36:27–32). After the murder of Gedaliah, the leaders accused him of unduly influencing Jeremiah when the latter urged the people to remain in Judah (43:3), a fact that shows how great Baruch's influence was thought to be over his master. He was taken to Egypt with Jeremiah (43:6). After that, all reliable records about him cease. The high regard in which Baruch was held is shown by the large number of spurious writings that were attributed to him. 2. A man who helped Nehemiah in rebuilding the walls of Jerusalem (Neh 3:20). 3. A priest who signed the covenant with Nehemiah (10:6). 4. The son of Colhozeh, a descendant of Perez (11:5).

BARUCH, BOOK OF (See APOCRYPHA)

BARZILLAI (bàr-zĭl'ă-ī, Heb. *bārzillay, made of iron*). 1. A wealthy Gileadite of Rogelim who brought provisions to David and his army when the king fled from Absalom (2 Sam 17:27–29). After Absalom's defeat, David invited Barzillai to come to live in the capital. Barzillai, who was then 80, refused because of his age but arranged that his son Kimham should go instead (19:31–40). Before his death David charged Solomon to "show kindness to the sons of Barzillai" (1 Kings 2:7). 2. One of the returning exiles living in Ezra's time. He "married a daughter of Barzillai the Gileadite" and adopted his wife's family name (Ezra 2:61–62). 3. A Meholathite, whose son Adriel married Saul's daughter, either Michal (2 Sam 21:8) or Merab (1 Sam 18:19).

BASEMATH (băs'ē-măth, Heb. *bāsmath, fragrant*, "Bashemath" in KJV). 1. One of Esau's wives, daughter of the Hittite Elon (Gen 26:34), also called Adah (36:2–3). 2. Ishmael's daughter (36:3–4, 13, 17), also called Mahalath (28:9). 3. Solomon's daughter, married to Ahimaaz (1 Kings 4:15).

BASHAN (bā'shăn, Heb. *bāshān, smooth, fertile land*). The broad, fertile region east of the Sea of Galilee. In the days of Abraham it was occupied by the Rephaites (Gen 14:5). Og, the last king of the race, was defeated and killed by the Israelites at Edrei in the time of Moses (Num 21:33–35; Deut 3:1–7). The entire district was assigned to the half-tribe of Manasseh (Deut 3:13). It was lost to Israel in the Syrian wars (1 Kings 22:3ff.; 2 Kings 8:28; 10:32, 35). It was celebrated for its cattle (Ps 22:12), its breed of sheep (Deut 32:14), and for its oak trees (Isa 2:13; Ezek 27:6).

BASHAN-HAVOTH-JAIR (see HAVVOTH JAIR)

BASHEMATH (See BASEMATH)

BASIN 1. A wide hollow vessel to hold water for washing and other purposes (John 13:5). 2. A small vessel used for wine and other liquids (Exod 24:6). 3. A shallow vessel used to receive the blood of sacrifices in the temple (Exod 12:22) and for domestic purposes. 4. A large bowl used in the temple for various purposes, especially at the great altar (Zech 9:15).

BASKET Four kinds of baskets are mentioned in the OT. They were made of leaves, reeds, rushes, twigs, or ropes; and they had various shapes and sizes. They were used for carrying fruit (Deut 26:2), bread, cake, and meat (Gen 40:17; Exod 29:2–3), and clay to make bricks, and earth for embankments (Ps 81:6). In the NT two kinds of baskets are referred to. The *kophinos* (Matt 14:20; Mark 6:43; John 6:13) was a relatively small basket that could be carried on the back to hold provisions. The *spuris* was considerably larger (Matt 16:9–10; Acts 9:25).

BASMATH (See BASEMATH)

BASTARD (Heb. *mamzēr*, Gr. *nothos, bastard*, specifically, *child of incest*). In Deuteronomy 23:2 it probably refers to a "child of incest," not simply an illegitimate child (cf. Judg 11:1–2; Zech 9:6 KJV). In Hebrews 12:8 the word is used in its proper sense of born out of wedlock. Bastards had no claim to paternal care or the usual privileges and discipline of legitimate children.

BAT (See ANIMALS)

BATH (See WEIGHTS AND MEASURES)

BATH, BATHING The average Hebrew had neither the water nor the inclination for bathing for physical cleanliness or refreshment. In the Bible bathing stands chiefly for ritual acts—purification from ceremonial defilement because of contact with the dead, defiled persons or things, or things under the ban (Exod 30:19–21; Lev 16:4, 24; cf. Gen 18:4; 19:2; John 13:10; Mark 7:3–4). According to Josephus, the Essenes practiced daily bathing for ceremonial reasons. (See page 72.)

BATHSHEBA (băth-shē'bà, Heb. *bath-sheva', daughter of Sheba*). She was the wife of Uriah the Hittite, a soldier in David's army. During Uriah's absence in the wars David committed adultery with

Interior of a bathhouse at Masada, from Herod's time. Courtesy S. Zur Picture Library

her (2 Sam 11). Uriah was then treacherously killed by David's order (11:6ff.). She became David's wife and lived with him in the palace. They had four sons, including Solomon (5:14; 1 Chron 3:5), after the first child had died (2 Sam 12:14ff.). With the help of the prophet Nathan she defeated the plot of Adonijah to usurp the kingdom and succeeded in having David choose Solomon as his successor. Her sons Nathan and Solomon were both ancestors of Jesus Christ (Matt 1:6; Luke 3:31).

BATHSHUA (băth'shūá, Heb. *bathshûa', daughter of opulence,* or *daughter of Shua*). **1.** In Genesis 38:2 (NIV has "daughter of a Canaanite man named Shua") and 1 Chronicles 2:3, where the name indicates daughter of Shua, wife of Judah. **2.** The mother of Solomon (1 Chron 3:5) in most Hebrew manuscripts, but this is probably a misreading of Bathsheba due to a scribal error.

BATTERING RAM (See WAR)

BATTLE In ancient times a trumpet signal by the commander opened each battle (Judg 7:18), and, when it was over, called the soldiers away from the fight (2 Sam 2:28; 18:16). Priests accompanied the army into war to ascertain God's will (Judg 6:36ff.; 1 Sam 14:8ff.). To make the Lord's help in battle more certain, the ark was taken along. The fainthearted were exempted (Deut 20:8). A force was usu-

ally divided into two attacking divisions, the one in the rear serving as a reserve or as a means of escape for the leader in case of defeat. Most of the fighting was done by footmen. Sometimes the battle was preceded by duels between individuals, and these on occasion determined the outcome of the battle (1 Sam 17:3ff.; 2 Sam 2:14ff.). See also ARMS AND ARMOR; WAR.

BAY TREE (See PLANTS)

BDELLIUM (dĕl'ĭ-ŭm, Heb. *bedhōlah*). A substance (Gen 2:12; Num 11:7) variously taken to be a gum, resin, or a precious stone.

BEALOTH (bē'à-lŏth, Heb. *be'ālôth*). **1.** A town in the south of Judah (Josh 15:24). **2.** A locality in north Israel (1 Kings 4:16).

BEAM It was used in constructing the upper floors and roofs of buildings (1 Kings 7:3) and in a weaver's loom (Judg 16:14). Jesus used the word figuratively (Matt 7:3; Luke 6:41).

BEAN (See PLANTS)

BEAR (See ANIMALS)

BEARD With Asiatics a badge of manly dignity, in contrast to the Egyptians, who usually shaved the head and the face. As a sign of mourning, it was the custom to pluck it out or cut it off. The Israelites were forbidden to shave off the corners of their beards, probably because that act was regarded as a sign of paganism (Lev 19:27). To force a man to cut off his beard was to inflict on him a shameful disgrace (2 Sam 10:4–5).

BEAST (See ANIMALS)

BEATITUDES (bē-ăt'ĭ-tūds, Lat. *beatitudo, blessedness*). The word "beatitude" is not found in the English Bible. It means either (1) the joys of heaven or (2) a declaration of blessedness. Beatitudes occur frequently in the OT (e.g., Pss 32:1–2; 41:1; 65:4). The Gospels contain isolated beatitudes by Christ (Matt 11:6; 13:16; 16:17; 24:46 with the Lukan parallels; John 13:17; 20:29). But the word is most commonly used of the declarations in the Sermon on the Mount (Matt 5:3–11; cf. Luke 6:20–22). The Beatitudes do not describe separate types of Christian character, but set forth qualities and experiences that are combined in the ideal character.

BEBAI (bē'bā-ī, Heb. *bēvay*). **1.** The ancestral head of a family that returned from the Captivity (Ezra 2:11; 8:11; Neh

7:16; 10:15). **2.** One of this family (Ezra 8:11).

BECHER (See BEKER)

BED In the East, in ancient times as now, the very poor slept on the ground, their outer garments serving as both mattress and blanket. In more advanced conditions a rug or a mat was used as a bed. At first it was laid on the floor, usually near a wall; later it was put on an elevation, either a raised part of the floor or a bedstead, which gave rise to the expression "go up into my bed" (Ps 132:3 KJV). Still later, in some cases, a mattress took the place of the mat, and a pillow was also used, along with a blanket of some kind. The giant Og had a bedstead made of iron (Deut 3:11) while Amos speaks of "beds inlaid with ivory" (Amos 6:4). Such bedsteads were sometimes further furnished with posts and a canopy (Song of Songs 3:10), and they had silken cushions on them (Amos 3:12 RV) and rich coverings (Prov 7:16).

BEDAN (bē'dàn, Heb. *bedhān*, perhaps *son of judgment*). **1.** A Hebrew judge who is mentioned as a deliverer of the nation (1 Sam 12:11). **2.** A son of Ulam of the house of Manasseh (1 Chron 7:17).

BEE (See ANIMALS)

BEELIADA (bē'ĕ-lī'à-dà, Heb. *be'el-yādhā', the Lord knows*). A son of King David (1 Chron 14:7); also called Eliada (2 Sam 5:16; 1 Chron 3:8).

BEELZEBUB (See BAALZEBUB)

BEELZEBUL (See BAALZEBUB)

BEER (bē'êr, Heb. *be'ēr, a well*). **1.** A place where the Israelites stopped during their wilderness journey (Num 21:16), perhaps Beer Elim (Isa 15:8). **2.** A place to which Jotham fled from his brother Abimelech (Judg 9:21).

BEERI (bē-ê'rī, Heb. *be'ērî, belonging to the well*). **1.** A Hittite who was the father of Judith, one of Esau's wives (Gen 26:34). **2.** The father of the prophet Hosea (Hos 1:1).

BEER LAHAI ROI (bē'êr là-hī' roi, Heb. *be'ēr lahay rō'î, the well of the living one who sees me*). A well where the Lord appeared to Hagar (Gen 16:7, 14) and where Isaac lived (24:62; 25:11).

BEEROTH (bē-ê'rŏth, Heb. *be'ērôth, wells*). A Canaanite town whose inhabitants succeeded in deceiving Israel by making a covenant with them (Josh 9:3ff.). When the deceit was discovered, they were made slaves by the Israelites

(9:22–23). They were apparently Hivites (9:7).

BEERSHEBA (bē'êr shē'bà, Heb. *be'ēr shēva', well of seven* or *the seventh well*). The most southerly town in the kingdom of Judah. It was allotted to the tribe of Simeon (Josh 19:2). The familiar expression "from Dan to Beersheba" is used to designate the northern and southern extremities of the nation of Israel (2 Sam 3:10; 17:11; 24:2).

Hagar wandered in the wilderness of Beersheba when she fled from Sarah (Gen 21:14). Abraham made a covenant with the Philistine princes here (21:32), and later made this his residence after the "offering up" of Isaac (22:19). Here God appeared to Jacob and promised his continued presence (46:1). Elijah the prophet sought refuge here from the wicked Jezebel (1 Kings 19:3). Amos rebuked its idolatrous tendencies (Amos 8:14). The modern name is Bir Es Seba. (See page 74.)

BE ESHTARAH (See ASHTAROTH)

BEETLE (See ANIMALS)

BEGGAR (See OCCUPATIONS AND PROFESSIONS)

BEHEMOTH (See ANIMALS)

BEKA (See WEIGHTS AND MEASURES)

BEKER (bē'kêr, Heb. *bekher, firstborn,* or *young camel*). **1.** The second son of Benjamin (Gen 46:21; 1 Chron 7:6). Beker's nine sons ultimately had 20,200 male descendants (1 Chron 7:8–9) who lived in the territory of Benjamin. **2.** A son of Ephraim, and founder of a family (Num 26:35, Bachrites in KJV), in 1 Chronicles 7:20 "Bered."

BEL The Baal of the Babylonians, who was described as the supreme ruler, the life-giver, the god of justice, he who holds society together, controller of the elements, particularly fire (Isa 46:1; Jer 50:2; 51:44). See also BAAL.

BELA, BELAH (bē'là, Heb. *bela', destruction, belay*). **1.** A neighboring city of Sodom and Gomorrah that was spared through Lot's intercession (Gen 19:15–30). It was later known as Zoar (14:2; Isaiah 15:5; Jeremiah 48:34). **2.** Son of Beor, an Edomite king (Gen 36:32ff.; 1 Chron 1:43). **3.** Firstborn son of Benjamin (7:6; 8:1). Head of the family of the Belaites (Num 26:40). **4.** Son of Azaz, a Reubenite, an exceptionally wealthy man (1 Chron 5:8–9).

BELIAL (bē'lĭ-ăl, Heb. *belîya'al*, Gr. *Beliar*). Frequent epithet of scorn and

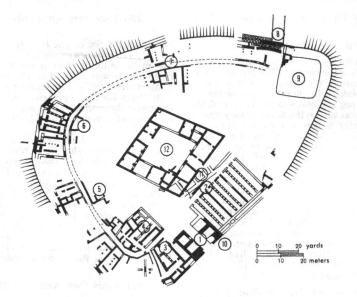

Plan of the excavated areas of Beersheba (Tell es-Seba): (1) city gate; (2) royal storehouses; (3,4) administration buildings; (5) cult area; (6,7) living quarters; (8) deep trench; (9) water system; (10) well; (11) Hellenistic fortress, (12) Roman fortress. Courtesy Carta, Jerusalem

disdain, meaning "worthlessness," and often as "Sons of Belial" (Deut 13:13; Judg 19:22; 1 Sam 2:12). Paul employs the term once (2 Cor 6:15; the only place where the term appears in the NIV) where Belial (Beliar) stands as opposed to Christ, thus approaching the diabolical status of Antichrist. In this later usage it is often used by Jewish apocalyptic writers for both Satan and Antichrist.

BELL (Heb. *metsillôth, pa'amôn*). Bells were attached to the hem of the priestly robes worn by Aaron and his descendants as they performed service in the tabernacle (Exod 28:33ff.; 39:25–26), assuring the worshipers that the high priest remained alive as their intercessor and had not incurred divine wrath. The bell was not used in biblical times for the purpose of religious convocation as today. The use of the bell to summon the worshipers seems to have been introduced by Bishop Paulinus (400 A.D.).

BELLOWS Inflatable skins used to fan a fire (Jer 6:29).

BELSHAZZAR (bĕl-shăz'àr, Heb. *bĕl-sha'tstsar, may Bel protect the king*). Son of Nabonidus and grandson of Nebuchadnezzar. Belshazzar's miserable doom came about at the end of, and largely as a consequence of, a drunken orgy held October 29, 539 B.C. (Dan 5). Suddenly the fingers of a man's hand appeared, writing in fiery letters a message that Belshazzar could not decipher. After the failure of his advisers to decipher the "cryptogram," he summoned Daniel who interpreted the message ("You have been weighed on the scales and found wanting"). The judgment was swift and inevitable. Babylon fell to the Medo-Persians, Belshazzar was killed, and Darius in the name of Cyrus took the throne.

BELTESHAZZAR (bĕl'tĕ-shăz-àr, Heb. *beltsha tstsar, may Bel protect his life*). The name given to Daniel by Nebuchadnezzar's steward (Dan 1:7; 2:26; 4:8; 5:12).

BEN (Heb. *ben*). **1.** In Semite usage a term used to designate a male descendant. It is also used in connection with a clan, in plural only, as in the children of (sons of) Israel, etc. The term is also employed in prefixes of proper names (e.g., Benjamin, Ben-Hadad, etc.) and in connoting a class, as "sons of the prophets" (2 Kings 2:15, NIV "company of the prophets"). **2.** A Levite appointed by David to serve in a musical capacity before the ark of the Lord (1 Chron 15:18).

BENAIAH (bē-nā'yà, Heb. *benāyâh, Jehovah has built*). 1. Son of Jehoiada the priest (2 Sam 23:20; 1 Chron 27:5). A man of exceptional prowess and bravery (2 Sam 23:20, 23), he was appointed over David's personal bodyguard (1 Kings 1:38) and over the coronation of his son Solomon (1 Kings 1:38–39). Benaiah played no part in the rebellion of Adonijah, but remained faithful to the cause of Solomon. He succeeded Joab as captain of the host (2:35; 4:4). **2.** One of David's "valiant Thirty," the Pirathonite, tribe of Ephraim (2 Sam 23:30). **3.** A prince from the tribe of Simeon who drove the Amalekites from the pastureland of Gedor (1 Chron 4:39–40). **4.** A Levite who played the psaltery at the return of the ark to Jerusalem (15:20). **5.** A priest appointed to blow the trumpet on the same occasion (15:24). **6.** Ancestor of Jahaziel the prophet who prophesied for Moab and Ammon in the days of Jehoshaphat (2 Chron 20:14). **7.** One of the overseers for the offerings in the temple in the days of Hezekiah (31:13). **8.** Father of Pelatiah who died as a judgment for false teaching in the days of Ezekiel (Ezek 11:13). **9.** The name of four men, each of whom had taken a foreign wife in the time of Ezra (Ezra 10:25, 30, 35, 43).

BEN-AMMI (běn-ăm'ī, Heb. *ben'ammî, son of my people*). Son of the younger daughter of Lot (Gen 19:38) whom she conceived through her own father following the destruction of Sodom. The progenitor of the Ammonites.

BEN-HADAD (běn-hā'dăd, Heb. *ben hădhadh*). The title (as Pharoah in Egypt) of the rulers of Syria ("son of [the god] Hadad"). The Syrians believed their rulers were lineal descendants of the Syrian god Hadad, the deity of storm and thunder, to be identified with Rimmon (2 Kings 5:18). There are three individuals in the OT called Ben-Hadad.

Ben-Hadad I, a contemporary with Asa (1 Kings 15:18), may be Rezon, the founder of the kingdom of Damascus (11:23–25). At the request of Asa, Ben-Hadad severed his alliance with Baasha of Israel and aligned himself with the southern kingdom (15:16ff.), thereby acquiring treasures and Jewish territory.

Ben-Hadad II, probably the son of Ben-Hadad I, is the Hadadezer of the monuments. He waged war with Ahab, laying siege to the newly constructed capital, Samaria. Ahab refused to capitulate. With divine aid, Ahab routed the Syrian army utterly at the battle of Aphek (1 Kings 20:26ff.). Ahab spared the life of Ben-Hadad, thus never fully realizing the victory that otherwise would have been his.

Ben-Hadad III (796–770 B.C.), son of the usurper Hazael, drastically reduced the fighting personnel of Israel (2 Kings 13:7). Joash was able to defeat Ben-Hadad on three difference occasions and to recover the cities of Israel (13:25).

BEN-HINNOM (See HINNOM, VALLEY OF)

BENJAMIN (běn'jà-mǐn, Heb. *binyāmîn, son of my right hand*, Gen 35:17ff.). The youngest son of Jacob (and his only child born in Palestine), named Ben-oni ("son of my sorrow") by Rachel, his mother, as she died giving birth, but renamed Benjamin ("son of my right hand") by Jacob. He appears as a special object of parental love and devotion. He seems to have played no part in the sale of Joseph into Egypt. The intercession on the part of Judah in behalf of Benjamin (Gen 44:18–34) is one of the most moving speeches in all of literature. 2. A great-grandson of Benjamin, son of Jacob (1 Chron 7:10). 3. One of those who had married a foreign wife (Ezra 10:32).

BENJAMIN, TRIBE OF Named for Jacob's youngest son. The tribe numbered 35,400 at the first census and 45,600 at the second (Num 1:37; 26:41).

Benjamin was assigned the territory between Judah on the south and Ephraim on the north (Josh 11:18ff.)—a strategic position commercially and militarily. The civil war with Benjamin constitutes a sad and strange story (Judg 19–20).

King Saul came from this tribe (1 Sam 9:1ff.). After the death of Saul the forces of David fought the men of Benjamin. Ish-Bosheth, Saul's weak son, was set up as David's rival (2 Sam 2:8). Shimei, who cursed David, was a Benjamite (16:5, 11). After Solomon died and the kingdom divided, the Benjamites joined Rehoboam and the tribe of Judah. Benjamin was included in the restoration. Saul of Tarsus (Paul) was a member of the tribe of Benjamin (Phil 3:5). (See page 76.)

BEN-ONI See BENJAMIN.

BEON (bē'ŏn, Num 32:3, known also as Baal Meon). A town built by the tribe of Reuben, who chose to remain on the east side of the Jordan. Under its new name it was allotted to the Reubenites after the conquest of Canaan (Josh 13:17). See BAAL MEON.

BEOR (See BALAAM)

BERA (bē'rà, Heb. *bera', gift*). King of Sodom, defeated by Kedorlaomer in the

THE TRIBE OF BENJAMIN

Lower Beth Horon
Upper Beth Horon
Aijalon
DAN Kephirah
Kiriath Jearim
Kesalon
EPHRAIM
Ophrah
Bethel
Ataroth Addar
Mizpeh
Ramah
Gibeon
Beeroth
BENJAMIN
Mozah
Gibeah
Waters of Nephtoah
Jerusalem
MANASSEH
Naaran
Gilgal
Jericho
Beth Hoglah
Jordan River
JUDAH
Dead Sea
0 2 4 6 miles
0 5 10 km
© carta, JERUSALEM

days of Abraham at the battle of Siddim (Gen 14:2, 8).

BERACHAIAH (See BEREKIAH)

BERAKIAH (See BEREKIAH)

BEREA, BEROEA (bêr-ē′à, Gr. *Beroia*). A city in SW Macedonia where Paul founded a church (Acts 17:10–15; 20:4). These open-minded people were willing to study the teachings of Paul in the light of the Scripture. However, Jews from Thessalonica arrived, turning the Bereans against the message and forcing Paul to flee to Athens. Silas and Timothy remained there briefly instructing the true believers.

BERED (bē′rĕd, Heb. *beredh, to be cold*). Between Kadesh and Bered was the well-known well of Beer Lahai Roi (Gen 16:14). Bered is located in the region of the Negev and was called Elusa by Ptolemy. It formed a connecting link between Palestine, Kadesh, and Sinai.

BEREKIAH, BERAKIAH (bêr-ē-kī′à, Heb. *Berekhyâh, Jehovah blesses*). **1.** One of David's descendants (1 Chron 3:20). **2.** Father of Asaph the singer (6:39). **3.** A Levite dwelling in Jerusalem (9:16). **4.** A custodian of the ark (15:23). **5.** An Ephraimite who protested the sale of Hebrews to their fellows (2 Chron 28:12). **6.** The father of Meshullam. He was a builder during the days of Nehemiah (Neh 3:4, 30; 6:18). **7.** The father of Zechariah, a prophet of the restoration (Zech 1:1, 7).

BERIAH (bē-rīà, Heb. *berî′âh*, meaning uncertain, perhaps *gift* or *evil*). **1.** A son of Asher (Gen 46:17; 1 Chron 7:30) and

ancestor of the Beriites (Num 26:44). **2.** A son of Ephraim (1 Chron 7:23). If Beriah means "a gift," he was so named because in the face of Ephraim's losses, this son was regarded as a gift from the Lord. **3.** A descendant of Benjamin (8:13, 16) and apparently the ancestor of the people of Aijalon (8:13). **4.** A Levite, the son of Shimei of the Gershonites (23:7–11).

BERIITES (bē-rī′ïts, Heb. *berî′îm*). A people descended from Beriah (Num 26:44) who, in turn, was from the tribe of Asher (Gen 46:17).

BERITES (bē′rïts, Heb. *bērîm, choice young men*). Mentioned only once (2 Sam 20:14), they followed Sheba in his revolt.

BERITH (See EL-BERITH)

BERNICE (bêr-nī′sē, Gr. *Bernikē, victorious*). Referred to three times in Acts (Acts 25:13, 23; 26:30), Herod Agrippa's eldest daughter (12:1), a wicked woman who lived an incestuous life. According to Josephus, she was first married to Marcus. After his death she became the wife of Herod of Chalcis, her own uncle (*Antiq.* 19.5.1; 20.7.1–3). After Herod's death she had evil relations with Agrippa, her own brother, and with him listened to Paul's noble defense at Caesarea. Later after a short marriage to King Ptolemy of Sicily, she returned to Agrippa. She was later the mistress of Vespasian and Titus, who finally cast her aside.

BERODACH-BALADAN
(See MERODACH-BALADAN)

BEROTHAH, BEROTHAI (bē-rō′thà, bē-rō′thī, Heb. *bērôthâh, well or wells*). A town between Hamath and Damascus

Early photograph of the village of Bethany, home of Mary, Martha, and Lazarus, situated just east of Jerusalem. Courtesy Ecole Biblique et Archéologique Française, Jerusalem

(Ezek 47:16), probably the city of Hadadezer that David took (2 Sam 8:8), now identified as Bereitan, north of Damascus.

BERYL (See MINERALS)

BESOR (bĕ'sôr, Heb. *besôr*). A brook 5 miles (8 km.) south of Gaza where David left 200 of his men who were too faint to assist in pursuing the Amalekites (1 Sam 30:9–10, 21).

BETAH (bĕ'tà, *confidence*). A city of Syria that David captured and from which he took much brass, later used by Solomon in making furnishings for the temple (2 Sam 8:8; NIV Tebah, cf. footnote). It is called "Tibhath" in 1 Chronicles 18:8 KJV (Tebah, NIV).

BETH (bĕth, *house*). The second letter of the Hebrew alphabet. Hebrew for the number two, and the most common OT word for house.

BETHABARA (bĕth'ăb'à-rà, *house of the ford*). A place on the east bank of the Jordan where John baptized (John 1:28 KJV), in some manuscripts rendered "Bethany," perhaps Beth Barah (Judg 7:24).

BETHANY (bĕth'à-nē, Gr. *Bethania, house of unripe dates or figs*). **1.** Town east of the Jordan (John 1:28, "Bethabara" KJV). **2.** The home of Mary, Martha, and Lazarus, about 2 miles (3 km.) SE of Jerusalem (John 11:18) on the eastern slope of Mt. Olivet. It was here that Jesus raised Lazarus (John 11) and attended the feast at Simon's house (Matt 26; Mark 14; Luke 7). The ascension took

place in the region of this city (Luke 24:50–51).

BETH ARBEL (bĕth' àr'bĕl, *house of Arbel*). Probably a town in the tribe of Naphtali, mentioned in Hosea 10:14 as the scene of a horrible destruction brought about by Shalmaneser. It is used to illustrate the disaster to come on Ephraim.

BETH ASHBEA (See ASHBEA)

BETH AVEN (bĕth' ā'vĕn, Heb. *bēth'āwen, house of vanity*). A town on the northern mountains of Benjamin (Josh 18:12), beside Ai, east of Bethel (7:2) and west of Michmash (1 Sam 13:5; 14:23). The name is used figuratively by Hosea (4:15; 5:8; 10:5). The house of God (Bethel) had become the house of vanity and idolatry (Beth Aven).

BETH BAAL MEON (bĕth' bā'àl mē'ŏn, Heb. *bêth ba'al me'ôn, house of Baal Meon*). A place in the territory assigned to Reuben, east of the Jordan (Josh 13:17), the same as Baal Meon (Num 32:38) and Beon (32:3). Jeremiah speaks of it as belonging to Moab (Jer 48:23).

BETH BARAH (bĕth' bâr'à, Heb. *beth-barah, house of the ford*). An important ford of the Jordan, perhaps Beth Arabah, appearing in the accounts of Gideon (Judg 7:24), Jephthah (12:5), and Jacob (Gen 32:23).

BETH BIRI (bĕth' bĭr'ĭ, *house of my creator*). A town of Simeon (1 Chron 4:31) in southern Judah, also called Beth

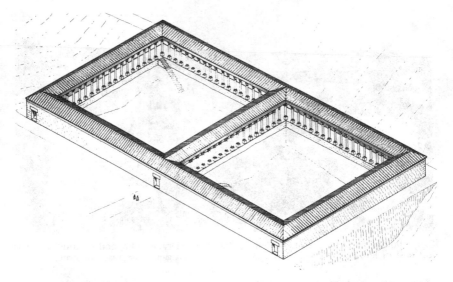

Reconstruction of the pool of Bethesda. According to archaeological evidence, the northern pool (left) was dug first, in the reign of Solomon, and the southern pool was added in the beginning of the second century B.C. (during the Hellenistic period). The drawing is based mainly on Christian sources, and the description given in John 5:1–16. Courtesy Carta, Jerusalem

Lebaoth, "abode of lions," and Lebaoth (Josh 19:6; 15:32).

BETH CAR (bĕth′ kăr′, *house of sheep*). A place west of Mizpah to which Israel pursued the Philistines, "slaughtering them along the way to a point below Beth Car" (1 Sam 7:11). In this area Samuel set up the stone called Ebenezer (7:12).

BETH DAGON (bĕth′ dā′gŏn, *house of Dagon*). 1. A town in the Shephelah of Judah (Josh 15:41), 5 miles (8 km.) from Lydda, perhaps suggesting the worship of the Philistine god Dagon. 2. The name of a town on the border of Asher (19:27).

BETH DIBLATHAIM (bĕth′ dĭb′là-thā′ĭm, *house of a double cake of figs*). A Moabitish town (Jer 48:22), known also as Almon Diblathaim (Num 33:46) and Diblath (Ezek 6:14) and mentioned on the Moabite Stone.

BETH EDEN (See EDEN)

BETHEL (bĕth′ĕl, Heb. *bêth'ēl, house of God*). 1. A town originally known as Luz, 12 miles (20 km.) north of Jerusalem (Gen 28:19), west of Ai. Abraham stopped near this spot on his way to the Negev and offered a sacrifice (12:8; 13:3). Jacob called Luz "Bethel" (28:10–22), since God met him here and confirmed the

Abrahamic covenant to him. Later, Jacob returned and built an altar and worshiped, calling the place El Bethel (35:7). Here Jacob buried Deborah, the nurse of Rebekah who had died (35:8).

Bethel was given to the tribe of Benjamin (Josh 18:21–22), and taken by Joseph's descendants, under the guidance of the Lord (Judg 1:22–26). The ark was kept there during the period of the judges (20:26–28) and Samuel conducted business and worshiped here (1 Sam 7:16; 10:3).

Jeroboam chose Bethel as one of the two centers in which he set up golden calves (1 Kings 12:26–30). Because of these and other sins, Amos cried out against this city (Amos 3:14; 4:4–6). Hosea too pronounced judgment on Bethel, even calling it "Beth Aven," "the house of wickedness" (Hos 4:15). An Israelite priest taught the people resettled here by Assyria about the Lord (2 Kings 17:27–28), but they combined worship of their heathen gods with worship of the Lord (17:33). It was not until Josiah became king that this idolatry was removed from Bethel and the true worship of the Lord was established (23:15–23). When the Jews returned from the Babylonian captivity, Ezra and Nehemiah both record that some returned to Bethel (Ezra 2:28; Neh 7:32) and, as one might suppose, they are listed as Benjamites (Neh 11:31).

2. A city in southern Judah (1 Sam 30:27), also called Bethul (Josh 19:4) and "Bethuel" (1 Chron 4:30).

BETHESDA (bĕ-thĕs'dà, Gr. *Bēthesda, house of grace*). A spring-fed pool at Jerusalem, surrounded by five porches (John 5:2), thought to have healing properties. Here Jesus healed a man who had been sick for 38 years (John 5:1–16). In A.D. 1888, while the church of St. Anne in NE Jerusalem was being repaired, a reservoir was discovered. On the wall is a faded fresco that depicts an angel troubling the water.

BETH GADER (bĕth' gā'dêr, *house of the wall*). A place in Judah (1 Chron 2:51), probably to be identified with Geder (Josh 12:13).

BETH HAKKEREM (bĕth' hă-kē'rĕm, *house of the vineyard*). A Judean town (Neh 3:14), and a vantage site for signaling in time of danger (Jer 6:1).

BETH HOGLAH (bĕth' hŏg'là, *house of a partridge*). A place belonging to Benjamin, lying between Jericho and the Jordan (Josh 15:6; 18:19, 21).

BETH HORON (bĕth' hŏ'rŏn, Heb. *bêth-hôrōn, place of a hollow*). Two towns, the upper and the lower (Josh 16:3, 5; 1 Chron 7:24; 2 Chron 8:5), separated by a few miles. Built by Sherah, a granddaughter of Ephraim (1 Chron 7:24), Beth Horon lay on the boundary line between Benjamin and Ephraim (Josh 16:3, 5), on the road from Gibeon to Azekah (10:10–11). It was assigned to Ephraim and given to the Kohathites (21:22).

It was in this valley that Joshua commanded the sun and moon to stand still while he fought the Amorite kings. Along this route the Philistines fled after they had been defeated at Micmash (1 Sam 14:31), and it was there that Judas Maccabeus overthrew the army of Seron, a prince of Syria (1 Macc 3:13–24). Its towns were fortified by Solomon (2 Chron 8:5).

BETH JESHIMOTH (bĕth' jĕsh'ĭ-mŏth, Heb. *bêth ha-yeshīmō, place of deserts*). A town east of the mouth of the Jordan, next to the last camp of the Israelites (Num 33:49), and assigned to Reuben (Josh 13:20).

BETH LEBAOTH (See BETH BIRI)

BETHLEHEM (bĕth'lē-hĕm, Heb. *bêthlehem, house of bread*). **1.** A town 5 miles (8 km.) SW of Jerusalem, called Ephrath ("fruitful") in Jacob's time; the burial place of Rachel (Gen 35:16, 19; 48:7). After the conquest of Canaan it was called Bethlehem in Judah (Ruth 1:1) to distinguish it from Bethlehem No. 2 (see below). It was the home of Ibzan, the tenth judge (Judg 12:8–10); of Elimelech, father-in-law of Ruth (Ruth 1:1–2), as well as of her husband Boaz (2:1, 4). David was anointed king by Samuel here (1 Sam 16:13, 15), hence it was known as "the city of David" (Luke 2:4, 11). Here the Messiah was born (Matt 2:1; Luke 2:1–7), for whom this town that was "small among the clans of Judah" (Mic 5:2) achieved its great fame. Its male children under two years of age were murdered in Herod's attempt to kill the King of the Jews (Matt 2:16).

2. A town of Zebulun (Josh 19:15), now the village of Beit Lahm, 7 miles (12 km.) NW of Nazareth. (See page 80.)

BETH MAACHAH (See ABEL BETH MAACAH)

BETH MARCABOTH (bĕth' màr'kà-bŏth, Heb. *bêth ha-markāvōth, the house of chariots*). A town of Simeon in the extreme south of Judah (Josh 19:5; 1 Chron 4:31). Possibly one of the cities that Solomon built for his chariots (1 Kings 9:19).

BETH MEON (bĕth' mē'ōn). A city of Moab (Jer 48:23), same as Beth Baal Meon (Josh 13:17).

BETH MILLO (See MILLO)

BETH NIMRAH (bĕth' nĭm'rà, Heb. *bêth nimrâh, house of leopard*). A fortified city of Gad east of the Jordan (Num 32:3, 36). The LXX reading, "Beth-anabra," in Joshua 13:27 has led some to identify this with Bethabara in the NT, whose abundant waters were the scene of John's baptizing (John 1:28).

BETH PEOR (bĕth' pē'ôr, Heb. *bêth pe'ôr, house of Peor*). One of Israel's last campsites (Deut 3:29; 4:46). Here Moses was buried (34:6). A possession of Reuben (Josh 13:20).

BETHPHAGE (bĕth'fà-jē, Heb. *bêth paghah, house of unripe figs*). A village on the Mt. of Olives, on the road going east from Jerusalem to Jericho. The traditional site is NW of Bethany, and it is where the colt was obtained for Jesus' entry into Jerusalem (Matt 21:1–11; Mark 11:1–11; Luke 19:28–40).

BETH REHOB (bĕth' rē'hŏb, Heb. *bêth rehôv, house of Rechob*). An Aramean town and district near the valley contain-

General view of modern Bethlehem, with the Church of the Nativity at top center. Ancient Bethlehem is definitely identified with the modern town located 5½ miles (9 km.) south of Jerusalem. It was a small town that acquired importance when Herod built his fortresses at Herodium and Masada, since it overlooked the roads leading to the fortresses. Courtesy Israel Government Press Office

ing the town Laish or Dan (Judg 18:28), probably to be identified with Rehob (Num 13:21), the northern limit of the spies' search. The Ammonites, having needlessly provoked David, hired the men of Beth Rehob in a futile defense against David's attack (2 Sam 10).

BETHSAIDA (bĕth'sā'ĭ-dà, Gr. *Bēth-saida, house of fishing*). **1.** A village near the Sea of Galilee, the home of Philip, Andrew, and Peter (John 1:44; 12:21). Jesus sent his disciples there by boat after he had fed the 5,000 (Mark 6:45–53). Jesus rebuked Bethsaida, along with Chorazin and Capernaum, for unbelief (Matt 11:20–23; Luke 10:13–15). **2.** Another Bethsaida, NE of the Sea of Galilee and the scene of the feeding of the 5,000 (Luke 9:10). Jesus restored sight to a blind man in Bethsaida (Mark 8:22). Philip the tetrarch enlarged it to be the capital and called it Julias, after Julia, the daughter of Emperor Augustus.

BETH SHAN, BETH SHEAN (bĕth' shăn, bĕth' shē'ăn, Heb. *bêth shan, bêth sheān, house of quiet*). A town of Manas-

seh in the territory of Issachar. The people of Israel were not able to drive the Canaanites out of this town (Josh 17:11–12; Judg 1:27). The Philistines fastened Saul's body to the wall of Beth Shan and put his armor in the temple of the Ashtoreths as trophies of their victory (1 Sam 31:8–12). Later the men of Jabesh Gilead stole the bones of Saul and his sons from the street of Beth Shan; David gave them a proper burial (2 Sam 21:12–14).

Today the site of the city is a mound, called Tell el-Husn ("Mound of the Fortress"). Excavations have yielded rich finds, dating the history of the city from 3500 B.C. to the Christian era. Four Canaanite temples were unearthed at the site, one of which has been identified with the "temple of the Ashtoreths" (1 Sam 31:10), and another with the temple of Dagon where the Philistines fastened Saul's head (1 Chron 10:10).

BETH SHEMESH (bĕth' shē'mĕsh, Heb. *bêth-shemesh, house of the sun*). **1.** A Levitical town of NW Judah near the Philistine border (Josh 15:10; 21:16;

1 Sam 6:12; 1 Chron 6:59). When the Philistines sent back the ark of God (1 Sam 6), it ended up here, where many died for their irreverence. Beth Shemesh was in a commissary district of Solomon (1 Kings 4:9). It was here that Joash, king of Israel, encountered Amaziah, king of Judah, and took him prisoner (2 Kings 14:11–13; 2 Chron 25:21–23). **2.** A city of Issachar (Josh 19:22). **3.** A city of Naphtali (19:38; Judg 1:33), from which the Canaanites were not driven. **4.** An idol city in Egypt (Jer 43:13), the Egyptian On, the Greek Heliopolis.

BETH TOGARMAH (See TOGARMAH)

BETHUEL, BETHUL (bē-thū'ĕl, bĕth'ŭl, Heb. *bethû'ēl, bethûl, abode of God*). **1.** Son of Nahor and Milcah, nephew of Abraham, and father of Rebekah and Laban (Gen 22:22–23; 24:15, 24, 47; 28:2, 5). **2.** A town in the south of Simeon (Josh 19:4; 1 Chron 4:30). It is the same as Kesil (Josh 15:30).

BETH ZUR (bĕth zûr, Heb. *bêth tsûr, house of rock*). One of Judea's strongest natural fortresses (Josh 15:58), fortified by Rehoboam (2 Chron 11:7). Nehemiah, ruler of half of Beth Zur, helped to repair the wall of Jerusalem (Neh 3:16). Known as Bethsura in Maccabean times, it was an important military stronghold, where Judas Maccabeus defeated the Greek army under Lysias (1 Macc 4:28–34). It is now Beit Sur, 4 miles (7 km.) north of Hebron.

BEULAH (byū'là, Heb. *be'ûlâh, married*). A poetic name for the land of Israel in its future restored condition (Isa 62:4).

BEZAI (bē'zā-ī). **1.** Head of a family of 323 men who returned with Zerubbabel (Ezra 2:17; Neh 7:23). **2.** Probably a member of the same family a century later (Neh 10:18).

BEZALEL (bē'zā-lĕl, *in the shadow of God*). **1.** Son of Uri, son of Hur of the tribe of Judah, whom the Lord called by name (Exod 31:2; 35:30) and by his Spirit empowered to work in metals, wood, and stone for the tabernacle. **2.** A descendant of Pahath-Moab, an official of Moab, who in the days of Ezra and Nehemiah was compelled to give up his foreign wife (Ezra 10:30).

BEZEK (bē'zĕk, *scattering, sowing*). **1.** A town in the territory of Judah taken for Israel under Joshua. Its king had either the name or more probably the title Adoni-Bezek (Judg 1:4–5). **2.** The place where Saul numbered his forces before going to relieve Jabesh Gilead (1 Sam

11:8), about 14 miles (23 km.) NE of Samaria.

BEZER (bē'zĕr, Heb. *betser, strong*). **1.** A city of refuge east of the Dead Sea (Deut 4:43) and a home for Merarites of the tribe of Levi (Josh 21:36). On the Moabite Stone, Mesha, king of Moab, claims that he fortified it. **2.** One of the mighty men of the tribe of Asher, known only as a son of Zophah (1 Chron 7:37).

BIBLE The collection of books recognized and used by the Christian church as the inspired record of God's revelation of himself and of his will to mankind.

I. Names. The word "Bible" is from Greek *biblia*, plural of *biblion*, diminutive of *biblos* (book), from *byblos* (papyrus). In ancient times papyrus was used in making the paper from which books were manufactured. The words *biblion* and *biblia* are used in the OT (LXX) and the Apocrypha for the Scriptures (Dan 9:2; 1 Macc 1:56; 3:48; 12:9). By about the fifth century A.D. the Greek church fathers applied the term *biblia* to the whole Christian Scriptures. Later the word passed into the western church, and although it is really a plural neuter noun, it came to be used in the Latin as a feminine singular. Thus "The Books" became by common consent "The Book."

In the NT the OT is usually referred to as "the Scriptures" (Matt 21:42; 22:29; Luke 24:32; John 5:39; Acts 18:24). Other terms used are "Scripture" (Acts 8:32; Gal 3:22), the "holy Scriptures" (Rom 1:2; 2 Tim 3:15), and "sacred writings" (2 Tim 3:15 RSV).

The plural term *biblia* stresses the fact that the Bible is a collection of books. The word's use in the singular emphasizes the unity of the books. That no qualifying adjective stands before it points to the uniqueness of this book.

The names "Old Testament" and "New Testament" have been used since the close of the second century A.D. to distinguish the Jewish and Christian Scriptures. The Old Testament is composed of books produced by writers under God's covenant with Israel; the New Testament contains writings of the apostles (members of God's new covenant people). The term *Novum Testamentum* occurs first in Tertullian (A.D. 190–220). "Testament" is used in the NT (KJV) to render the Greek word *diathēkē* (Lat. *testamentum*), which in classical usage meant "a will" but in the LXX and in the NT was used to translate the Hebrew word *berîth* ("a covenant").

II. Languages. Most of the OT was

Reproduction of a page from the Gutenberg Bible, the first major book to be printed from movable type, c. 1455. This is the opening page of the Book of Proverbs. Courtesy The British Library

written in Hebrew, the language spoken by the Israelites in Canaan before the Babylonian captivity. After the return from exile, Hebrew gave way to Aramaic, a related dialect generally spoken throughout SW Asia. A few parts of the OT are in Aramaic (Ezra 4:8–6:18; 7:12–26; Jer 10:11; Dan 2:4–7:28). The ancient Hebrew text consisted only of consonants, since the Hebrew alphabet had no written vowels. Vowel signs were invented by the Jewish Masoretic scholars in the sixth century A.D. and later.

Except for a few words and sentences, the NT was composed in Greek, the language of ordinary conversation in the Hellenistic world. The papyri found in Egypt have thrown a great deal of light on the meaning of many NT words.

III. Compass and Divisions. The Protestant Bible in general use today contains 66 books, 39 in the OT and 27 in the NT. The 39 OT books are the same as those recognized by the Palestinian Jews in NT times and Jews today. The Greek-speaking Jews of this period, on the other hand, recognized as Scripture a larger number of books, and the Greek OT (LXX), which passed from them to the early Christian church contained, in addition to the 39 books of the Hebrew canon, a number of others, of which 7— Tobit, Judith, Wisdom, Ecclesiasticus, Baruch, 1 and 2 Maccabees, plus the 2 so-called additions to Esther and Daniel — are regarded as canonical by the Roman Catholic church, which therefore has an OT canon of 46 books.

The books in the Hebrew Bible are arranged in three groups: the Law, the Prophets, and the Writings. The Law comprises the Pentateuch. The Prophets consist of eight books: the Former Prophets (Joshua, Judges, Samuel, and Kings) and the Latter Prophets (Isaiah, Jeremiah, Ezekiel, and the Minor Prophets). The Writings are the remaining books: Psalms, Proverbs, Job, Song of Songs, Ruth, Lamentations, Ecclesiastes, Esther, Daniel, Ezra-Nehemiah, and Chronicles. The total is traditionally reckoned as 24, but these correspond to the Protestant 39, since in the latter reckoning the Minor Prophets are counted as 12 books, and Samuel, Kings, Chronicles, and Ezra-Nehemiah as two each.

All branches of the Christian church are agreed on the NT canon. The grouping of the books is a natural one: (1) the four Gospels, (2) the one historical book (Acts), (3) the Epistles (Paul's, then the General Epistles), and (4) Revelation.

IV. Text. The text of Scripture has come to us in a remarkable state of preservation. Until the invention of printing in the middle of the 15th century, all copies of the Scriptures were made by hand. The ancient Jewish scribes copied the OT with extreme care. The Dead Sea Scrolls, some from the 2nd and 3rd centuries B.C., contain either whole books or fragments of all but one (Esther) of the OT books; and they bear witness to a text remarkably like the Hebrew text left by the Masoretes (from A.D. 500 on).

Evidence for the reliability of the NT text is almost embarrassingly large and includes about 4,500 Greek manuscripts, dating from A.D. 125 to the invention of printing; various versions, the Old Latin and Syriac going back to about A.D. 150; and quotations of Scripture in the writings of the church fathers, beginning with

the end of the first century. Among the oldest manuscripts of the Greek NT that have come down to us are the John Rylands fragment of the Gospel of John (c. 125); Papyrus Bodmer II, a manuscript of the Gospel of John dating c. 200; the Chester Beatty Papyri, consisting of three codices containing the Gospels and Acts, most of Paul's Letters, and the Revelation, dating from c. 200; and codices Vaticanus and Sinaiticus, both written c. 350.

V. Chapters and Verses. The Bible originally had no chapters or verses. For convenience of reference, Jews of pre-Talmudic times divided the OT into sections like our chapters and verses. The chapter divisions we use today were made by Stephen Langton, archbishop of Canterbury, who died in 1228. The division of the NT into its present verses is found for the first time in an edition of the Greek NT published in 1551 by a printer in Paris, Robert Stephens, who in 1555 also brought out an edition of the Vulgate that was the first edition of the entire Bible to appear with our present chapters and verses. The first English Bible to be so divided was the Genevan edition of 1560.

VI. Translations. The OT was translated into Greek (the LXX) between 250 and 150 B.C., and other translations in Greek appeared soon after the beginning of the Christian era. Parts, at least, of the OT were rendered into Syriac as early as the first century A.D., and a Coptic translation appeared probably in the third century. The NT was translated into Latin and Syriac c. 150 and into Coptic c. 200. The Bible, in whole or in part, is now available in more than 1,100 different languages and dialects.

VII. Message. Although the Bible consists of many different books written over a long period of time by a great variety of writers, most of whom did not know one another, it has an organic unity that can be explained only by assuming, as the book itself claims, that its writers were inspired by the Holy Spirit to give God's message to man. The theme of this message is the same in both Testaments, the redemption of man. The OT tells about the origin of man's sin and the preparation God made for the solution of this problem through his own Son, the Messiah. The NT describes the fulfillment of God's redemptive plan; the four Gospels telling about the Messiah's coming; Acts describing the origin and growth of the church, God's redeemed people; the Epistles giving the meaning and implication of the Incarnation; and the Book of

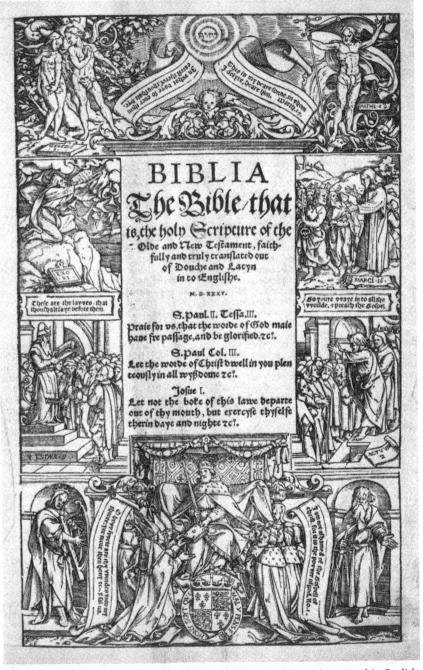

Title page of Coverdale's Bible, dated 1535, the first full Bible to be printed in English.
Courtesy The British Library

Revelation showing how some day all of history will be consummated in Christ. See also NEW TESTAMENT; OLD TESTAMENT; TEXTS AND VERSIONS.

BIBLE, ENGLISH VERSIONS In the earliest days of English Christianity the only known Bible was the Latin Vulgate, made by Jerome between A.D. 383 and 405, and only the clergy and monks could read Latin. It was Wycliffe who first entertained the revolutionary idea of providing ordinary layfolk with the Bible in their own tongue. He was the first to make the whole Bible available in English.

John Wycliffe. Born in Yorkshire about the year 1320, Wycliffe stands out as one of the most illustrious figures of the 14th century. The outstanding Oxford theologian of his day and an ardent ecclesiastical reformer, he is called the "Morningstar of the Reformation." He was convinced that the surest way of defeating Rome was to put the Bible into the hands of the common people, and he therefore decided to make such a translation available. Under his auspices, the NT came out in 1380 and the OT two years later. A number of scholars worked with him on the project, one of them, Nicholas Hereford, doing the greater part of the OT. The translation was made from the Latin, not from the original languages. To help him in his efforts for reform, Wycliffe organized a kind of religious order of poor preachers, called Lollards, whom he sent throughout England to preach his doctrines and to read the Scriptures to all who wished to hear. Foxe reports that the people were so eager to read it that they would give a whole load of hay for the use of the NT for one day.

William Tyndale. William Tyndale, the next great figure in the history of the English Bible, was born about the year 1494 and studied at Oxford and Cambridge. Soon after leaving Cambridge, while working as a chaplain and tutor, he said in a controversy with a clergyman, "If God spare my life, ere many years I will cause a boy that driveth a plough to know more of the Scripture than thou dost." The bishop of London refused to help fund his translation, but a wealthy London cloth merchant finally came to his support; after six months, in 1524, Tyndale left for the Continent after he encountered opposition. He was never able to return to England. He seems to have visited Luther at Wittenberg, and then went to Cologne, where he found a printer for his NT. A priest discovered his plan, and Tyndale was obliged to flee.

In Worms he found another printer, and there, in 1525, 3,000 copies of the first printed English NT were published. By 1530 six editions, numbering about 15,000 copies, were published. They were all smuggled into England—hidden in bales of cotton, sacks of flour, and bundles of flax.

As soon as Tyndale's NT reached England, there was a great demand for it: by the laity that they might read it, and by the ecclesiastical authorities, that they might destroy it! A decree was issued for its destruction. Bishops bought up whole editions to consign to the flames. As a result, only a few imperfect copies survive. Tyndale's English NT was translated from the original Greek, the text published by Erasmus. So well did Tyndale do his work that the KJV reproduces about 90 percent of Tyndale in the NT. He never finished translating the OT from the Hebrew text; he was betrayed in Antwerp by an English Roman Catholic and was condemned to death for being a heretic. He was strangled and his body burned at the stake. His last words were a prayer, "Lord, open the King of England's eyes." Although his NT was burned in large quantities by the church, it greatly increased an appetite for the Bible in English, an appetite the government began to see the wisdom and necessity of satisfying.

Miles Coverdale. While Tyndale was imprisoned in Belgium, an English Bible suddenly appeared in England in 1535. It had come from the Continent. The title page stated that it had been translated out of the German and Latin into English. This Bible was the rendering of Miles Coverdale, although in the NT and in those parts of the OT done by Tyndale, it was no more than a slight revision of the latter's work. It was the first complete printed Bible in the English language. Coverdale used the work of five different translators. His version of the Psalms still appears in the Book of Common Prayer, used daily in the ritual of the Church of England. Two new editions of Coverdale's Bible appeared in 1537, the title page containing the significant words "Set forth with the King's most gracious license." So within a year of Tyndale's death, the entire Bible was translated, printed, and distributed, apparently with royal approval.

Thomas Matthew. In 1537 another Bible appeared in England, this one by Thomas Matthew (a pen name for John Rogers, a former associate of Tyndale's), who was burned at the stake by Queen Mary in 1555. The whole of the NT and

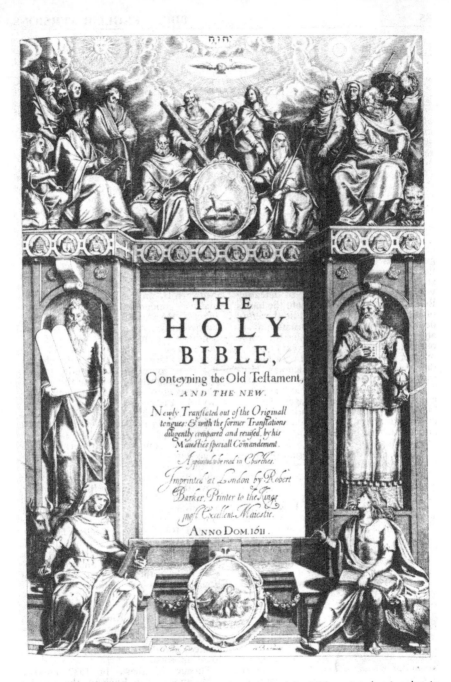

THE
HOLY
BIBLE,
Conteyning the Old Testament,
AND THE NEW.

Newly Tranflated out of the Originall
tongues: & with the former Tranflations
diligently compared and reuifed, by his
Maiefties fpeciall Comandement.

Appointed to be read in Churches.

Imprinted at London by Robert
Barker, Printer to the Kings
moft Excellent Maieftie.

ANNO DOM. 1611.

Title page of the King James (the Authorized Version) of the Bible, printed at London in 1611. Courtesy The British Library

Portrait of King James I, under whose authority the King James Version was prepared (published in 1611). After John de Critz the Elder. Courtesy National Portrait Gallery, London

about half of the OT are Tyndale's, while the remainder is Coverdale's. It bore on its title page the words, "Set forth with the king's most gracious license." This Bible has the distinction of being the first edition of the whole English Bible actually to be printed in England.

The Great Bible. The next Bible to appear was a revision of the Matthew Bible, done by Coverdale. The printing of this was begun in Paris, but the Inquisition stepped in and the work was completed in England. It appeared in 1539 and was called the Great Bible because of its large size and cost. Subsequent editions were called Cranmer's Bible because of a preface he wrote for it. An order was issued in 1538, while this Bible was being printed, that a copy of it was to be placed in every church in the land.

The Genevan Bible. With the accession of Mary in 1553, hundreds of Protestants lost their lives, some closely associated with Bible translation, like John Rogers and Thomas Cranmer. Some English Reformers escaped to Geneva, where the leading figure was John Calvin. One of their number, William Wittingham, who had married Calvin's sister, produced in 1557 a revision of the English NT, the first English NT printed in roman type

and with the text divided into verses. He and his associates then published a revision of the whole Bible in 1560, the Genevan Bible, or the Breeches Bible ("They sewed fig tree leaves together, and made themselves breeches," Gen 3:7).

The Bishops' Bible. Queen Elizabeth, who succeeded Mary Tudor as queen, restored the arrangements of Edward VI. The Great Bible was again placed in every church, and people were encouraged to read the Scriptures. The excellence of the Genevan Bible made obvious the deficiencies of the Great Bible, but some of the Genevan Bible's renderings and the marginal notes made it unacceptable to many of the clergy. Archbishop Parker, aided by eight bishops and some other scholars, therefore made a revision of the Great Bible, completed and published in 1568 and known as the Bishops' Bible, but not as popular as the Genevan Bible.

Rheims and Douai Version. A number of English Romanists left England at the beginning of Elizabeth's reign and settled in NE France, where in 1568 they founded a college. The NT was published in 1582, and was done while the college was at Rheims, but the OT was not published until 1609–10, after the college had moved to Douai. Both were the work of Gregory Martin based on the Latin. The preface warned readers against the then-existing "profane" translations and blames Protestants for casting what was holy to dogs. The Rheims-Douai Bible in use today is a thorough revision made between 1749 and 1763 by Bishop Richard Challoner.

King James (or Authorized) Version. When Elizabeth died in 1603, the crown passed to James I, who authorized a new translation to replace the Bishops' Bible. This would be a translation from the original Hebrew and Greek, without any marginal notes, for the use of all the churches in England.

Forty-seven of the best Hebrew and Greek scholars of the day were divided into six groups: three for the OT, two for the NT, and one for the Apocrypha. In cases of special difficulty, learned men outside the board of revisers were consulted. The revisers, who received no financial remuneration for their work, completed their task in two years; nine more months were devoted to a revision of their work by a special committee consisting of two members from each group. In 1611 the new version was published. Its excellence is shown by the fact that after 375 years it is still used in preference to any other version in the English-speaking Protestant world, for both public and private use.

English Revised Version. In 1870, at the Convocation of Canterbury of the Church of England, a committee was appointed to invite outstanding Hebrew and Greek scholars, irrespective of religious denomination, to join in revising the KJV. Eventually a committee of 54 was formed. American scholars were also invited to cooperate. It was agreed that American suggestions not accepted by the British revisers be recorded in an appendix to the published volume and that the American revisers give their moral support to the new Bible and not issue an edition of their own until at least 14 years later.

Altogether the Greek text underlying the revised NT differed in 5,788 readings from that used by the KJV translators—only about one-fourth of these making any material difference in the substance of the text, though none so seriously as to affect major Christian doctrines. In the English text of the NT there are about 36,000 changes. The new Bible differed from its predecessors in printing poetical passages in the OT as poetry and in grouping verses into paragraphs according to sense units.

The NT was published in 1881, the OT in 1885. The work occupied the NT translators for about 40 days each year for ten years, while the OT group was occupied for 792 days over a period of 14 years. The new version did not meet with immediate approval, nor did it in succeeding years ever surpass the KJV for supremacy among Bible translations.

American Standard Version. The American scholars who cooperated with the English revisers on the ERV were not entirely satisfied with it. They did not disband when the ERV was published, but their revision of the ERV was not published until 1901. It is regarded as being on the whole superior to the ERV, at least for American uses.

Other Twentieth-Century Versions. The discovery at the end of the 19th century of many thousands of Greek papyri in the sands of Egypt, all written in the everyday Greek language of the people, had a revolutionary influence on the study of the Greek of the NT. NT Greek had hitherto presented a vexing problem, since it was neither classical Greek nor the Greek of the Septuagint. Now it was shown to be the Greek of the Papyri, and therefore the colloquial language of Greek-speaking people in the first century. These developments created a keen interest in bringing out fresh translations of the NT in the spoken English of today; and in the next 45 years a number of new modern-speech versions came out, most of them by individuals but a few by groups of scholars.

The first of these to appear was *The Twentieth Century New Testament: A Translation into Modern English Made from the Original Greek* (Westcott and Hort's Text). This was published in 1902 (reprinted 1961) and was the work of about 20 anonymous translators. In 1903 R. F. Weymouth brought out *The New Testament in Modern Speech;* it was thoroughly revised in 1924 by J. A. Robertson. James Moffatt, the well-known Scottish NT scholar, brought out *The Bible: A New Translation* in 1913–14. The American counterpart of Moffatt was *The Complete Bible: An American Translation* (1927, revised 1935). The NT part first appeared in 1923 and was the work of E. J. Goodspeed; four scholars, headed by J. M. Powis Smith, did the OT. *The New Testament. A Translation in the Language of the People,* by C. B. Williams, came out in 1937. *The New Testament in Modern English* (1958) by J. B. Phillips, is one of the most readable of the modern-speech translations. *The Amplified New Testament* (1958), which gives variant shades of meaning in the original, was followed in 1961 by *The Amplified Old Testament.* It was the work of Frances E. Siewert and unnamed assistants. *The Holy Bible: The Berkeley Version in Modern English* (1959) was the work of Gerrit Verkuyl in the NT and of 20 American scholars in the OT. Kenneth Wuest's *The New Testament—An Expanded Translation* appeared complete in 1961. Also in 1961 *The Simplified New Testament* appeared, a new translation by Olaf M. Norlie.

During this period a number of new Roman Catholic versions were brought out also. *The New Testament of our Lord and Saviour Jesus Christ* (1941) was a revision of the Rheims-Challoner NT sponsored by the Episcopal Committee of the Confraternity of Christian Doctrine; therefore it was called the Confraternity Version. It was followed by a translation of the OT in four successive volumes (1948–69), which represented, not a revision of Douai-Challoner, but a new version from Hebrew. This revision appeared in 1970 under the new title *The New American Bible. The Westminster Version of the Sacred Scriptures* appeared under the editorship of Cuthbert Lattey—the NT in 1935, followed by parts of the OT. It was discontinued after

Lattey's death in 1954. R. A. Knox's translation from the Latin Vulgate (NT, 1941, OT, 1949; revision, 1955) is a literary masterpiece. The *Jerusalem Bible* (1966), a scholarly and widely appreciated translation, follows the pattern of the French *Bible de Jerusalem* (1956), produced by the Dominican faculty of the Biblical and Archaeological School in Jerusalem.

Revised Standard Version. This is a revision of the ASV (1901), the NT appearing in 1946 and the OT in 1952. It was sponsored by the International Council of Religious Education and is the work of 32 American scholars. It was designed for use in public and private worship. In this version the language is modernized; direct speech is regularly indicated by the use of quotation marks; and the policy is followed (as in the KJV) of using a variety of synonyms to translate the Greek words where it is thought to be advisable. Special Catholic editions of the RSV appeared in 1965 (NT) and 1966 (complete Bible). But a new edition of the RSV in 1973 was accepted as a "common Bible" for Catholic, Protestant, and Orthodox Christians alike.

New English Bible. This is a completely new translation, not a revision of previously existing versions. It was the joint effort of all the major religious denominations (with the main Bible Societies) in the British Isles, apart from the Roman Catholic church. The NT came out in 1961; the complete Bible (including the Apocrypha), in 1970.

Other Recent Versions. The *New American Standard Bible* (completed 1971) was a revision and modernization of the American Standard Version of 1901. A more recent revision is the *New King James Version* (NT, 1979; complete Bible, 1982), a modernization of the KJV—the OT based on the most recent edition of the Hebrew text, the NT based on the type of Greek text used in 1611.

The Living Bible, a paraphrase into simple English, by Kenneth N. Taylor was completed in 1971. It attained widespread popularity, especially among young people, but has lost ground since 1976 to the *Good News Bible,* completed in that year. The NT part of this latter work had been published ten years earlier under the title *Today's English Version* or *Good News for Modern Man.* The translators had especially in mind the needs of those for whom English is an acquired language as well as those who speak it as their mother tongue.

The New International Version was the work of a team of over 100 evangelical scholars drawn from most of the English-speaking countries—the NT released in 1973, the entire Bible in 1978, and a revision in 1984. Unlike RSV, and like NEB, it is a direct translation from the original languages, not a revision of any existing version.

BIGTHANA, BIGTHAN (bĭg'thă'nà, bĭg'-thăn). One of the chamberlains of King Xerxes (Ahasuerus) who with Teresh had plotted to kill the king. Mordecai heard of the plot and through Esther warned the king, who had the two men hanged (Esth 2:21–23; 6:2).

BIGVAI (bĭg'vă-ī, *fortunate*). **1.** A chief who returned from captivity by permission of Cyrus in 536 B.C. (Ezra 2:2; Neh 7:19). **2.** Ancestor of a family who returned with Zerubbabel from captivity (Ezra 2:14; Neh 7:19). **3.** Probably the same as no. 2 (Ezra 8:14).

BILDAD (bĭl'dăd). One of Job's three "comforters" (cf. Job 2:11–13 with 42:7–10). Evidently a descendant of Shuah (Gen 25:2), a son of Abraham by Keturah, he made three speeches (Job 8, 18, 25) and was a "traditionalist" (8:8–10).

BILGAH (bĭl'gà, *cheerfulness*). **1.** Head of the 15th course of priests in David's time (1 Chron 24:14). **2.** A priest who returned with Zerubbabel (Neh 12:5).

BILHAH (bĭl'hà, *foolish*). **1.** Rachel's maidservant; Jacob's concubine; mother of Dan and Naphtali (Gen 29:29; 30:1–8). **2.** A town in the tribe of Simeon (1 Chron 4:29; "Balah" in Josh 19:3).

BILHAN (bĭl'hăn, *foolish*). **1.** A son of Ezer, son of Seir the Horite (Gen 36:27; 1 Chron 1:42). **2.** An early Benjamite; son of Jediael, son of Benjamin (1 Chron 7:10).

BINDING AND LOOSING The carrying of a key or keys was a symbol of the delegated power of opening and closing. Jesus gave Peter the "power of the keys" (Matt 16:19), and Peter's use of the keys is narrated in what may be called the "three stages of Pentecost." On Pentecost (Acts 2:14–40) Peter opened "the kingdom of heaven" to what became a Hebrew-Christian church; then Peter opened the kingdom to the Samaritans (8:14–17); and later at the house of Cornelius, he opened the kingdom to Gentiles (10:44–48). Thus, the church became universal. The medieval teaching about Peter standing at the gate of heaven to receive or reject souls of men has no basis in biblical teaching.

The partridge (1) is mentioned only twice in Scripture. The sea gull (2), the kite (3), and the heron (4) are all listed in Leviticus 11:13–18 as unclean or "detestable" (v. 13). In Israel, animals were expected to obey covenant law, and these did not. Their eating patterns involved eating flesh with blood in it. Courtesy Carta, Jerusalem

BINNUI (bĭn'ū-ī, *built*). **1.** A Levite, whose son was partly in charge of the silver and gold at Ezra's return (Ezra 8:33). **2.** One of the sons of Pahath-Moab who had married foreign wives (10:30). **3.** A son of Bani who had been similarly guilty (10:38). **4.** One of the rebuilders of Jerusalem in 444 B.C., who also became a covenanter under Nehemiah (Neh 3:24; 10:9). **5.** Alternate spelling of Bani (cf. Ezra 2:10) whose family returned with Zerubbabel. **6.** A Levite who returned with Zerubbabel (Neh 12:8).

BIRDS Palestine is the home of some 375 kinds of birds, of which perhaps 25 are peculiar to that region. The Bible mentions about 50 using Hebrew or Greek names that can sometimes be identified with particular species of the present. Birds are mentioned in more than two-thirds of the biblical books.

Bird of Prey. Predators were described by the Hebrew word *'ayit.* Abraham drove away birds of prey from his sacrifice (Gen 15:11). No bird of prey knew the hidden path of a mine of precious metals (Job 28:7). Birds of prey must also obey the call of God (Isa 46:11).

Bittern. A wading bird of the heron family. With its somewhat mournful call, the bittern was considered a melancholy creature, and therefore likely to live in places far from human habitation, in the wasteland that followed the downfall of Edom (Isa 34:11 KJV), Babylon (14:23 KJV), and Nineveh (Zeph 2:14 KJV). It was translated as "porcupine" in ASV and RSV (Isa 34:11), "hedgehog" in NASB and RSV (Isa 14:23; RSV only: Zeph 2:14), and "owl" in NIV (Isa 14:23; 34:11; Zeph 2:14).

Buzzard. A general description of any of a large number of heavily built hawks included in the list of unclean birds (Lev 11:13; Deut 14:12 NASB, RSV).

Carrion Bird. A variety of flesh-eating birds (Ezek 39:4).

Carrion Vulture. A general reference to vultures. They are unclean because they consume dead flesh (Lev 11:18 NASB; Deut 14:17 NASB, RSV).

Chicken. The hen's care of its chicks is a striking example of Jesus' concern for Jerusalem (Matt 23:37; Luke 13:34).

Cock. In biblical times its early morning crowing was associated with the start of a new day (Mark 13:35), and was also associated with Peter's denial of Jesus (Matt 26:74; Mark 14:30; Luke 22:34, 61; John 13:38; 18:27). NIV always renders the word "rooster."

Cormorant. A diving seabird whose flesh-eating habits made it unclean (Lev 11:17; Deut 14:17).

Crane. A long-necked, long-legged wading bird with a loud honk or croak. Hezekiah's lament over his sickness was compared by Isaiah to the chatter of a crane, as if the king spoke loudly of his affliction, then fell away into muttering (Isa 38:14 KJV). Birds, including the crane, know the time of their coming, i.e., their migratory journey (Jer 8:7 KJV), in contrast to man's often careless view of events. NIV uses "thrush."

Cuckoo. A long, slender bird reaching a length of some 12 inches (31 cm.). An unclean bird in Leviticus 11:16 and Deuteronomy 14:15, both KJV. ASV has "sea mew," RSV "seagull," NIV "gull." The gull is a flesh eater, hence condemned for human food.

Cuckow. See *Cuckoo.*

Desert Owl. See *Owl.*

Dove, Pigeon. The dove is a medium-sized bird of the family Columbidae, to which the pigeon also belongs, the latter being a somewhat larger bird. A white domestic pigeon is usually called "the dove of peace," reproduction drawings showing a twig in its beak, commemorating the dispatch of the dove from the ark by Noah (Gen 8:8–12). The psalmist wrote that he would indeed possess the wings of the dove (Ps 55:6). Believers will share such glory as may be compared to the wings of the dove being sheathed with silver, its feathers with shining gold (68:13). Hezekiah mourned about his illness, like a mourning dove (Isa 38:14), like the people in repentance (59:11). People who escaped the sword in the city would moan like doves of the valley (Ezek 7:16). Yet help was promised to those who flew like doves to their nests (Isa 60:8), their true home being God. The Holy Spirit descended like a dove onto Jesus' head at his baptism (Matt 3:16). Jesus charged his followers to be as shrewd as snakes and as innocent as doves (10:16).

Eagle. For many centuries the eagle has been adopted as a symbol of power and majesty, appropriately, it might be said, in view of its powers and regal appearance. The people of Israel were reminded that they had been borne from Egyptian captivity, as it were, on the wings of eagles (Exod 19:4; Deut 32:11). The psalmist declares that his youth was renewed like that of the eagle (Ps 103:5; cf. Isa 40:31).

Scripture refers to its sudden descent on its prey (Deut 28:49; Job 9:26), its swiftness (2 Sam 1:23; Job 9:26; Jer 4:13), its flight (Prov 23:5), and its power (Ezek 1:10; 17; Dan 7:4).

Falcon. One of the unclean birds (Lev 11:14; Deut 14:13), equipped with long, pointed wings, a powerful hooked beak, and a long tail. Isaiah's prophecy against Edom declared that falcons would gather there following the promised retribution (Isa 34:15).

Fowl. In modern speech "fowl" most often refers to "domestic fowl" and to poultry rather than to birds in general. Humans are wiser than fowl (Job 35:11), and Jesus' followers were worth much more than many birds (Luke 12:24).

The partridge (1 Sam 26:20; Jer 17:11) was a medium-sized game bird, with plump body and a short tail.

Gier Eagle. An alternative translation in KJV (Lev 11:18; Deut 14:17) to "carrion vulture," which elsewhere is translated "osprey" (so NIV).

Glede. A vulture or hawk included in the list of unclean birds (Deut 14:13 KJV).

Great Owl. See *Owl*.

Gull. See *Cuckoo*.

Hawk. A general name applied to several small to medium-sized birds of prey. All hawks were unclean and were not to be eaten (Lev 11:16; Deut 14:15). The impressive flying abilities of the hawk were compared to those of the eagle as the Lord answered Job out of the storm (Job 39:26–27).

Hen. See *Chicken*.

Heron. One of the unclean birds (Lev 11:19; Deut 14:18), the heron is a long-necked, long-legged wading bird.

Hoopoe. A solitary and somewhat timid bird that secures its diet of insects by thrusting its bill into the ground and foraging. This, together with its habit of fouling its own nest, may show why it was considered unclean (Lev 11:19; Deut 14:18 NASB, RSV, NIV).

Horned Owl. See *Owl*.

Ibis. An unclean bird (Lev 11:17 RSV), the ibis was regarded as sacred in ancient Egypt. The Greek historian Herodotus reported that the ibis was considered so sacred that anybody who killed one even accidentally was put to death.

Kite. An unclean bird (Lev 11:14; Deut 14:13), its diet consists mostly of carrion and small birds, though some kites live on insects.

Lapwing. A large, greenish-black and white plover on the list of prohibited birds (Lev 11:19; Deut 14:18).

Lilith. NIV "night creature."

Little Owl. See *Owl*.

Nighthawk. A small-beaked, insect-eating bird with impressive flying abilities appearing in the list of prohibited birds (Lev 11:16 KJV, RSV; Deut 14:15 KJV).

Osprey, Ospray. A large, dark plumed bird of the hawk family that was listed as unclean (Lev 11:18; Deut 14:17).

Ossifrage. See *Osprey*.

Ostrich. The largest of all birds, up to 8 feet (2.5 m.) tall, is noted for its heartlessness (Job 39:16; Lam 4:3) and its life in desolate places (Jer 50:39). Job's essay on the ostrich (Job 39:13–18) confirms the a keen observation of the bird.

Owl. The "great owl," "horned owl," and "little owl" are unclean birds (Lev 11:16–18; Deut 14:15–16). Owls often dwell in ruins (Ps 102:6; Isa 34:11, 15; Jer 50:39). The "little owl" (Lev 11:17; Deut 14:16) was the most common owl in Palestine.

Partridge. Because of their swift and sneaky running, they are excellent game birds. When Saul was hunting him, David compared himself to a partridge (1 Sam 26:20). It was supposed that partridges robbed eggs from other birds and hatched them, a symbol of getting riches unfairly (Jer 17:11).

Peacock. With their brightly colored bodies, peacocks were shown off in any self-respecting court in the ancient world. Large numbers of peacocks were imported for Solomon's palace (1 Kings 10:22; 2 Chron 9:21 KJV, RSV, NASB; NIV "baboon"; cf. Job 39:13).

Pelican. The pelican is one of the world's largest birds. Its flesh diet is one

Terracotta figurine of a pregnant woman, carved in Syrian-Phoenician style, from Aczib, c. seventh century B.C. Courtesy Israel Department of Antiquities and Museums. Exhibited and photographed by Israel Museum, Jerusalem

reason for its inclusion in the list of unclean birds (Lev 11:18; Deut 14:17 KJV, RSV, NASB; NIV has "desert owl"). The pelican was incorporated into church tradition and architecture because it was regarded as pious. When feeding its young, the nesting adult excretes a reddish liquid, emphasized as the bird preens its feathers. It was suggested that the pelican was somehow sustaining its young with its own blood.

Pigeon. See *Dove, Pigeon.*

Quail. A small migratory game bird whose flesh is delicious (Exod 16:13; Num 11:31; Ps 105:40).

Raven. This large unclean bird (Lev 11:15) is a member of the crow family. Noah sent a raven from the ark (Gen 8:7); ravens were used by God to feed Elijah

(1 Kings 17:4); and were themselves fed by the Lord (Job 38:41; Luke 12:24).

Ravenous Bird. See *Bird of Prey.*

Rooster. See *Cock.*

Screech Owl. See *Owl.*

Sea Gull, Sea Mew. See *Cuckoo.*

Sparrow. A small, short-beaked, seed-eating bird—noisy, active, and prolific. Sparrows were protected within the temple precincts (Ps 84:3). Sparrows were so cheap to buy that the purchaser of four would get a fifth free. God knows when any sparrow falls to the ground but values people far more highly than sparrows (Matt 10:29, 31; Luke 12:6, 7).

Stork. A large migratory bird that was prohibited (Lev 11:19; Deut 14:18). It was alert and knew its appointed seasons (Jer 8:7).

Swallow. Scripture refers to its skill in executing maneuvers (Prov 26:2) and its piercing chatterlike call (Isa 38:14 NASB, KJV, RSV).

Swan. A large aquatic bird. In the list of unclean birds it is called "water hen" in RSV, "horned owl" in ASV, and "white owl" in NIV (Lev 11:18; Deut 14:16).

Swift. The swift knew the time of its seasons (i.e., for migration, Jer 8:7, NASB, NIV; cf. Isa 38:14 NIV where KJV, NASB, RSV have "swallow").

Thrush. See *Crane.*

Turtledove. Abundant in number, this bird was used in ceremonial cleansing or sacrifice (Gen 15:9; Lev 12:6–8; Num 6:10).

Vulture. A large unclean bird (Deut 14:12) that eagerly devours carcasses (Matt 24:28; Luke 17:37; NASB, NIV; cf. Isa 34:15).

BIRTH The bringing forth of a separate life into the world, accompanied by rending pain, because of Eve's sin (Gen 3:16). Almost all 40 KJV uses of the word "travail" point to intense suffering (e.g., Jer 13:21; Rom 8:22; Gal 4:19). Birthdays were celebrated (Gen 40:20; Matt 14:6) and ceremonies were observed at childbirth (Lev 12; Luke 2:24). A second birth (the new birth) is necessary (John 3:3–6) to inherit eternal life.

BIRTHRIGHT Among the Israelites God had a special claim on the firstborn, at least from the time of the Exodus, when he destroyed the firstborn of Egypt and claimed those of Israel by right of redemption (Exod 13:2, 12–16). The birthright included a double portion of the inheritance (Deut 21:15–17) and the privilege of priesthood (Exod 13:1–2; 24:5); but in Israel God later set apart the tribe of Levi instead of the firstborn for that service. (Note Num 3:38–51, where the Levites are about the same in number as the firstborn of Israel.) Esau lost his birthright by selling it to Jacob for some stew (Gen 25:27–34; Obad 17–18; Heb 12:16). In Israel, Reuben lost his birthright through sin, and his brothers Simeon and Levi lost theirs through violence; and so the blessing came to Judah (Gen 49:3–10).

BISHOP (Gr. *episkopos, overseer*). Originally the principal officer of the local church, the other being the deacon or deacons (1 Tim 3:1–7). The title "elder" or "presbyter" generally applied to the same man; "elder" referring to his age and dignity, and "bishop" to his work of superintendence. As the churches multiplied, the bishop of a larger church would often be given special honor, and so gradually there grew up a hierarchy, all the way from presiding elders to bishops (over groups of churches), then archbishops.

BITHYNIA (bĭ-thĭn'ĭ-à, Gr. *Bithynia*). A region along the northern edge of Asia Minor fronting on the Black Sea, the Bosphorus, and the Sea of Marmara. Paul and his companions wanted to evangelize Bithynia (Acts 16:6–10), but could not; the Holy Spirit was leading toward Europe. However, there were Christians there in the first century (1 Peter 1:1). The Roman governor Pliny the Younger complained to Trajan concerning the Christians and at the beginning of the second century asked how to deal with them.

BITTER HERBS (See PLANTS)

BITTERN (See BIRDS)

BITUMEN (bĭ-tū'mĕn). A mineral pitch widely scattered over the earth, and one of the best waterproofing substances known. It was used with tar to cover the ark of bulrushes (Exod 2:3) and to waterproof Noah's ark (Gen 6:14). It was also used for mortar in the tower of Babel (11:3), and to represent a curse on Edom (Isa 34:9).

BLACKSMITH (See OCCUPATIONS AND PROFESSIONS)

BLASPHEMY (blăs'fē-mē, Gr. *blasphēmia*). To reproach or to bring a railing accusation against any one is bad enough (Jude 9), but to speak lightly or carelessly of God is a mortal sin. The third commandment, "You shall not misuse the name of the LORD your God" (Exod 20:7), was observed so meticulously by the Jews that they would not speak the sacred name (Jehovah) at all, and so no one knows today for certain how it was pronounced. God prescribed that in Israel the punishment for blasphemy would be death by stoning (Lev 24:10–16). Naboth was falsely charged with blasphemy and was stoned to death (1 Kings 21:10–13), as was Stephen (Acts 6:11). Stoning was also in the minds of those who charged Jesus with blasphemy (Matt 9:3; 26:65; Luke 5:31; John 10:33); what Jesus said about himself would have been blasphemy were it not true. See also UNPARDONABLE SIN.

BLESS, BLESSING (Heb. *bārakh*). 1. God blesses nature (Gen 1:22), humankind (1:28), the Sabbath (2:3), nations (Ps 33:12), classes of people (1:1–3), and individuals (Gen 24:1). 2. Godly people should "bless" God; i.e., they should adore him, worship him, and praise him (Ps 103:1–2). 3. Godly people by words and actions can bestow blessings on others (Matt 5:44; 1 Peter 3:9). 4. Godly men bestowed prophetic blessings on their descendants (Gen 9:26–27; 27:27–29, 39–40; 49; Deut 33). 5. People can bless things by setting them apart for sacred use, e.g., the "communion cup" (1 Cor 10:16).

BLESSING, THE CUP OF (KJV, RSV, ASV, "cup of thanksgiving" in NIV). In the "communion" service, the church blesses the cup set apart for the Lord's Supper (1 Cor 10:16).

BLINDNESS (See DISEASES)

BLOOD The word occurs over 400 times in the Bible and is especially frequent in Leviticus, Ezekiel, and Hebrews. For the most part Bible references are directed toward the practical observation that loss of blood leads to loss of vitality and that a draining away of the blood leads to death. Genesis 9:5 says (literally), "Your blood, belonging to your lives, I will seek . . . from the hand of man . . . I will seek the life of man." "Seek" means, in this verse, "seek requital." In this verse "seeking your blood" is parallel with "seeking the life," and both mean exacting the death penalty. When blood is shed, life is terminated, and the Lord seeks requital for the shedding of blood by demanding the life of the murderer (Gen 9:5; cf. 37:26; 2 Sam 1:16; Pss 30:9; 58:10). Blood is the life of the flesh (Gen 9:4; cf. Lev 17:11) in that flesh and blood in their proper union constitute a living creature, beast or man, but when they are separated death takes place.

BLOOD, AVENGER OF Genesis 9:6 states the biblical law requiring the execution of a murderer. This may involve the courts (e.g., Exod 24:12; Deut 19:15–21). The next of kin of the murdered person was permitted to exact the death penalty. The word questionably translated "avenger" (e.g., Num 35:12) is properly "next of kin" or "redeemer" (go'el). See also REDEMPTION. To prevent the work of the "avenger" from becoming a family vendetta, OT law appointed cities of refuge to which one guilty of manslaughter (not of murder) could flee for safety and where the avenger was not permitted to enter; also the OT insisted that children could not be punished for a parent's crime or vice versa (Deut 24:16).

BLOOD, ISSUE OF (See DISEASES)

BLOODY SWEAT (See DISEASES)

BOANERGES (bō'à-nûr'jēz, *sons of thunder*). A title given by the Lord to James and John, the sons of Zebedee (Mark 3:17), probably because of their temperamental violence (cf. Luke 9:54–56).

BOAR (See ANIMALS)

BOAZ (bō'ăz, Heb. *bō'az*). A well-to-do Bethlehemite in the days of the judges who became an ancestor of Jesus by marrying Ruth, the Moabitess, widow of one of the sons of Elimelech (Ruth 2–4). This was in accordance with the levirate law (Deut 25:5–10); Boaz could marry Ruth only after the nearer kinsman (Ruth 3:12; 4:1–8) had refused the privilege—or the duty. The other refused because if he had married Ruth and had a son, a portion of his property would have gone to the credit of Elimelech's posterity, instead of his own by a former marriage.

BOAZ AND JACHIN (See TEMPLE)

BOCHERU (See BOKERU)

BOCHIM (See BOKIM)

BODY (Gr. *sōma*). The word can refer to a corpse (Matt 27:52), one's physical body (Mark 5:29), and the human self expressed in and through a body (Heb 10:10; 1 Peter 2:24). Paul saw the body as the expression of the whole person (Rom 12:1), and warned against the misuse of the body (1 Cor 6:13ff.), since for the believer it is the temple of the Holy Spirit (6:15, 19). However, the body is affected by sin and so may be called the "body of sin" (Rom 6:6) and "body of death" (7:24).

There is a physical body for this life and a spiritual body for the life after the resurrection (1 Cor 15:38ff.). The present

sinful body will be replaced by one like Christ's resurrection body.

In the Lord's Supper the bread symbolizes the body of Jesus offered as a sacrifice for sin (Mark 14:22; 1 Cor 11:24). Further, the local church is called by Paul a "body" (Rom 12:4–5; 1 Cor 12:12ff.) as is the universal church, "the body of Christ" (Eph 4:12).

BODY OF CHRIST Within the NT this may be understood in three ways: **1.** As the natural, human body of Jesus that the eternal Son made his own in the womb of Mary, and in which he died at Calvary (Heb 10:10). This body was transformed into a spiritual body in resurrection and then taken to heaven in ascension. **2.** As the people of God—the church (local and universal), ruled and sustained by Christ, the Head (Rom 12:5; Eph 4:12; 5:23). **3.** As the bread that symbolically represents Jesus' body in communion (Matt 26:26).

BOIL (See DISEASES)

BONE The phrase "Bone of my bones and flesh of my flesh" (Gen 2:23; 29:14), figuratively shows kinship. Strong chastening is a bone-breaking experience (Ps 51:8), and the terrible writhing on the cross of Calvary literally threw bones out of joint (22:14). Dry bones form a picture of hopeless death (Ezek 37:1–12). The Passover lamb, without a broken bone (Exod 12:46), was a type of the Lamb of God (John 19:36).

BOOK Generally a literary production having more or less unity of purpose. Books may be classified by their forms or subjects, but more particularly by the nature and quality of the written material within. In ancient Assyria and Babylonia much of the writing that was thought to be of value was done in wedge-shaped characters on soft clay that was then baked, and the "libraries" were, in form, almost like piles of brick.

In ancient Egypt, the people early learned to press and glue thin sheets of the papyrus plant into sheets of "paper"; the writing was in narrow columns on sheets of regular size that were then glued together and wound around two sticks, thus forming a "volumen" or roll. Sheets were bound together into a "codex," very similar to our modern books. "Book" in the Bible always refers to a roll or scroll, a word that occurs 14 times in Jeremiah 36. In Pergamum, in the second century B.C., due to the scarcity of paper, people began using parchment, the skin of calves and of kids as a writing material.

In ancient books made of papyrus or

parchment, the writing was generally done on one side of each sheet, but occasionally, owing to afterthoughts, material was written also on the back side (see Rev 5:1). When a book was sealed, the contents were made secret, and when unsealed they were open (Dan 12:4, 9; Rev 5:1–4; cf. Rev 5:5; 22:10).

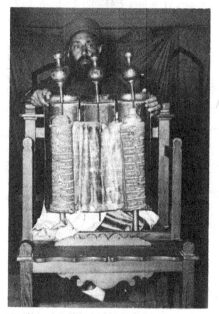

Ancient scroll held by a Samaritan priest.
Courtesy S. Zur Picture Library

The Bible is *the* book, God's Word, and it differs from all other books in that it alone is inspired (God-breathed). The Bible originally had 63 books, as the division of Samuel, Kings, and Chronicles into "First" and "Second" was not originally intended. The larger books were generally written on separate rolls (see Luke 4:17) but sometimes the "megilloth" (Ruth, Esther, Lamentations, Song of Songs, and Ecclesiastes) were bound together, as were also "The Twelve" (i.e., the Minor Prophets). Many books that have been lost are mentioned in the Bible: e.g., "the book of Jashar" (Josh 10:13), "the book of the annals of Solomon" (1 Kings 11:41). The word "book" is also used figuratively, as in "the Lamb's book of life" (Rev 21:27).

BOOTH A simple, temporary shelter generally constructed of tree branches with the leaves left on. It was used by the guardian of a vineyard or vegetable garden when the fruit was fit to be stolen. Sometimes this word describes a larger enclosure (Gen 33:17) such as Jacob built for his cattle.

BOOTY Goods taken from a defeated enemy. In the case of some cities whose people were extremely wicked, everything was to be "devoted" to the Lord, i.e., destroyed absolutely, except for vessels that could be sterilized by fire (Josh 6:18–21). Persons could sometimes be enslaved (Deut 20:14), but in other cases they had to be utterly destroyed (20:16–18). The purpose here was to prevent the pagans from teaching their abominations to God's people Israel (cf. 1 Sam 15, where Saul's hypocritical half-obedience brought ruin on himself and his house).

Booty was divided by custom, as when Abram devoted a tenth of the spoil to the Lord by giving it to Melchizedek (Gen 14:20), and by legislation, as when David ordered that booty be shared equally by those who because of weariness could not continue in battle (1 Sam 30:21–25).

BOR ASHAN (See ASHAN)

BORROW, BORROWING The people of Israel "borrowed" extensively from the Egyptians (Exod 3:22; 11:2; 12:35). The Egyptians, thoroughly cowed by the rigors of the ten plagues, were willing to give generously in order to get rid of their troublesome "guests." God allowed Israel to despoil the Egyptians (Exod 12:36) in order to provide gold and silver for the tabernacle that was to be constructed.

The Law of Moses provided legislation regarding those who borrow, hold property in trust, or are criminally careless in regard to the property of another (Exod 22:1–15). Jesus instructed his followers to not turn away those who wanted to borrow from them (Matt 5:42). Generally the borrower is the servant of the lender (Prov 22:7), but God's judgment can erase differences (Isa 24:2).

BOSCATH (See BOZKATH)

BOSOM The word is generally used in an affectionate sense in Scripture, of closeness and care (Isa 40:11; Luke 16:22–23 KJV; John 1:18 RSV). It can be almost synonymous with "heart" as the center of one's life (cf. Ps 35:13; Eccl 7:9 KJV). Quite commonly, of course, it refers to conjugal love (e.g., Mic 7:5 KJV).

BOTCH (See DISEASES)

BOTTLE 1. A container made of goatskin, sewed up with the hair outside and

Water carrier in Jerusalem bearing a container made from goat skin. Picture taken about the turn of the century. Courtesy University Library, Istanbul

used for carrying water (Gen 21:14–19), for storing wine (Josh 9:4, 13), and for fermenting milk into "leben" or "yogurt" (Judg 4:19). **2.** A container made of baked clay, and therefore very fragile (Jer 19:1–11). **3.** Beautifully designed glass bottles, often found in Egyptian tombs, were used originally for burying some mourners' tears with the deceased (Ps 56:8). **4.** Figuratively, the clouds as the source of rain (Job 38:37; NIV "water jars of the heavens").

BOTTOMLESS PIT (See ABYSS)

BOUNDARY STONES God set careful bounds to the land of his people (Josh 13–21) and provided a curse for those who removed their neighbors' landmarks (Deut 27:17; cf. 19:14). Figuratively, the expression implies a decent regard for ancient institutions (Prov 22:28; 23:10).

BOW (See ARMS AND ARMOR; RAINBOW)

BOWELS In the KJV the word occurs 36 times: **1.** Literally (2 Chron 21:15–19; Acts 1:18). **2.** The generative parts of the body (Gen 15:4; Ps 71:6). **3.** The seat of the emotions (English "heart"—Lam 1:20; Phil 1:8).

BOWL 1. *Sēphel*, a large, flat earthenware dish for holding a liquid (Judg 5:25). **2.** *Mizrāq*, sometimes also translated "basin," large costly bowls (Num 7:13–14). **3.** *Gāvia'*, a large silver bowl like the kind used at banquets to replenish drinking cups (Jer 35:5). **4.** *Gullâh*, the receptacle for oil in a candlestick (Zech 4:3) and the bowl-shaped capitals of the temple pillars (1 Kings 7:41–42; 2 Chron 4:12–13).

BOX TREE (See PLANTS)

BOZEZ (bō'zĕz). A rocky crag near Gibeah (1 Sam 14:4). Because one of General Allenby's officers read this account, the British followed the route of Jonathan and attacked the Turks here in A.D. 1918, conquering them even as Jonathan and his armor-bearer defeated the Philistines.

BOZRAH (bŏz'rà, Heb. *bŏtsrâh, sheepfold*). **1.** An important city of Edom (Gen 36:33; Jer 49:13, 22; Amos 1:12; Mic 2:12). **2.** In Jeremiah 48:24 the word refers to a town in Moab.

BRACELET A circlet for the wrist (Gen 24:22, 30, 47; cf. Isa 3:19; Ezek 16:11; 23:42).

BRAMBLE (See PLANTS)

BRANCH Most notably a title applied to the Messiah as the offspring of David (Jer 23:5; 33:15; Zech 3:8; 6:12).

BRASS (See MINERALS)

BRAY 1. The ass brays when hungry (Job 6:5), and some crude, uncouth people are described contemptuously as braying (30:7). **2.** To pound as in a mortar (Prov 27:22 KJV; NIV "grind").

BRAZEN SEA (See BRONZE SEA)

BRAZEN SNAKE (See BRONZE SNAKE)

BREAD The "staff of life," generally baked from dough made of wheat flour that has been leavened and made into loaves of various shapes and sizes. At the time of the Passover (Exod 12) the Israelites ate unleavened bread because of their haste and remembered this in their annual feast of unleavened bread (12:15–20). In times of distress and of famine most of the people used barley. "Bread" is often used figuratively for food in general (Gen 3:19 KJV; Matt 6:11; cf. John 6:43–59). In the tabernacle and in the temple, the "bread of the Presence" indicated the presence of the Lord, the "bread of life," among his people.

BREAD OF THE PRESENCE (See TABERNACLE)

BREASTPLATE (See ARMS AND ARMOR)

BRETHREN OF THE LORD (See BROTHERS OF THE LORD)

BRICK Building material made of clay dried in the sun. Owing to the prevalence of stone in Egypt and its comparative rarity in lower Mesopotamia, the use of brick for building was much more common in Chaldea than in Egypt, though the record of the bondage of Israel in Egypt (Exod 1:11–14; 5:7–19) shows that at least some cities in Egypt were built of brick rather than of stone. The ancient bricks were generally square instead of oblong and were much larger than ours, about 13 x 13 x 3½ inches (33 x 33 x 9 cm.). Before being baked they were often stamped with the name of the monarch — e.g., Sargon or Nebuchadnezzar. Much of the ancient brickwork was of bricks merely baked in the sun, especially in Egypt, but at Babylon the bricks were thoroughly burned.

BRIDE, BRIDEGROOM (See WEDDING)

BRIDLE The part of a harness that surrounds the head of the beast and connects the bit with the reins. It is used literally (e.g., Pss 32:9 KJV; 39:1 KJV; Prov 26:3 KJV; Rev 14:20) and figuratively (e.g., Isa 37:29 KJV; James 1:26 KJV; 3:2 KJV).

BRIER (See PLANTS)

BRIMSTONE More properly translated "sulfur" in the NIV, the Hebrew word is related to "gopher," a resinous wood that was used in the construction of the ark. It is generally connected with judgment, as when the Lord rained brimstone and fire on Sodom and Gomorrah (Gen 19:24 KJV; cf. Ps 11:6 KJV; Isa 34:9 KJV), and with fire (Rev 20:10 KJV; 21:8 KJV).

BRONZE (See MINERALS)

BRONZE SEA A rather exaggerated figure for the immense laver that Solomon placed in front of the temple for washing the sacrifices and the bodies of the priests (2 Kings 25:13; 1 Chron 18:8; Jer 52:17).

BRONZE SNAKE This snake was made by Moses and set on a pole as a means of recovery from venomous snakebites (Num 21:4-9). It was later worshiped and then destroyed (2 Kings 18:4). Jesus compared it to his death on the cross (John 3:14).

BROOK A small stream—e.g., Besor (1 Sam 30:9 KJV), Cherith (1 Kings 17:3–7), and Kidron (2 Sam 15:23 KJV).

BROOM (See PLANTS)

BROTHER 1. A male person related to another person or other persons by having the same parents (Gen 27:6) or the same father (28:2) or the same mother (Judg 8:19). 2. A man of the same country (Exod 2:11; Acts 3:22 KJV). 3. A member of the same tribe (2 Sam 19:12). 4. An ally (Amos 1:9). 5. One of a kindred people (Num 20:14). 6. One who shares the same religion (Acts 9:17; 1 Cor 6:6); often, Christian disciples (Matt 23:8; Rom 1:13). Someone spiritually akin (Matt 12:50). 7. A fellow office-bearer (Ezra 3:2). 8. Someone of equal rank or office (1 Kings 9:13). 9. Any member of the human race (Matt 7:3-5; Heb 2:17).

BROTHERS OF THE LORD The term is used in the NT in identifying four men: James, Joseph, Simon, and Jude (Matt 13:55; Mark 6:3). It is also used collectively of a group of men whose names are not given (John 7:3; Acts 1:14; 1 Cor 9:5). The precise relationship of these men to Jesus has been much debated, with three different answers offered: 1. Younger children of Mary and Joseph (Luke 2:7). 2. Joseph's children from a previous marriage. 3. Cousins of Jesus, sons of his aunt Mary, wife of Cleopas (John 19:25; Mark 15:40).

BUCKET or PAIL A vessel for drawing or holding water. It is also used figuratively (Num 24:7; Isa 40:15).

BUCKLER (See ARMS AND ARMOR)

BUKKI (bŭk'ī). 1. A prince of the tribe of Dan chosen to help Joshua divide the land (Num 34:22). 2. Son of Abishua, and high priest of Israel (1 Chron 6:5, 51; Ezra 7:4).

BUL (būl). The 8th month of the Jewish religious year (1 Kings 6:38), our November/December. See CALENDAR.

BULL (See ANIMALS)

BULLOCK (See ANIMALS)

BULRUSH (See PLANTS)

BUNNI (bŭn'ī). Three Levites mentioned in Nehemiah had this name: 1. A helper of Ezra (Neh 9:4). 2. An early dweller in Jerusalem (11:15). 3. One of the chief covenanters with Nehemiah (10:15).

BURDEN That which is laid on an animal or person in order to be carried. The word translates eight different words in the OT and three in the NT. Figuratively, it is used in the sense of "responsibility" (Num 11:11; Matt 11:30) or of a "sorrow" (Ps 55:22 KJV; "cares," NIV). The KJV translates "burden" where the NIV

Burial tomb from Jericho, Middle Bronze Age. Skeleton lying on burial bed is surrounded by pottery and other artifact remains. Courtesy Israel Department of Antiquities and Museums

has "oracle" (Isa 15:1; 19:1; 22:1; Zech 12:1; Mal 1:1).

BURIAL The act of placing a dead body in a tomb, in the earth or in the sea, generally with appropriate ceremonies; as opposed to exposure to the beasts, or abandonment or burning. Partly because of God's declaration to fallen man, "For dust you are and to dust you will return" (Gen 3:19), the people of Israel almost always buried their dead, often in one of Canaan's caves. Although God had given to Abraham the deed of the land of Canaan (Gen 15:18–21), the only land that the patriarchs possessed before Joshua's time was the burial places for the original family: a cave at Hebron and a field at Shechem (cf. Gen 23—the burial of Sarah; 49:29–32—Jacob's final request; and Josh 24:32–33—the burial of the mummy of Joseph and the body of Eleazar). In Canaan, in ancient times and in the more primitive parts of the land even today, bodies are buried the same day and without embalming in most cases (Num 19:11-22). In the time of Christ, the bodies were wrapped in clean linen (Matt 27:57–60), and spices and ointments were prepared (Luke 23:56).

BURNING Fire often accompanies God's judgments—e.g., with Sodom and Gomorrah (Gen 19:24–28), Nadab and Abihu (Lev 10:1–6), and the 250 rebels in the wilderness (Num 16:2, 35). The final destruction of this earth is to be with fierce fire (2 Peter 3:7–10, 12).

BURNING BUSH A thorny bush that Moses saw burning and from which he heard the Lord speak (Exod 3:2–3; Deut

The traditional "burning bush" found at St. Catherine's Monastery in the Sinai Peninsula (cf. Exod 3:2). Courtesy Israel Government Press Office

33:16; Mark 12:26). The flame that needs no fuel to maintain it ("the bush . . . did not burn up") represents the eternal, self-sufficient life of God. Where this God is, holiness is, and sinners can draw near only by meeting the conditions God imposes ("take off your sandals"). The unapproachable fire is seen in all its majesty on Mt. Sinai (Exod 19:18), and is reflected in the undying fire on the altar (Lev 6:9). The same God who made the simple provision for Moses to draw nigh (Exod 3:5; cf. Josh 5:13) provided the sacrifices.

BURNT OFFERING (See SACRIFICE AND OFFERINGS)

BUSH (See PLANTS)

BUSHEL (See WEIGHTS AND MEASURES)

BUTLER (See OCCUPATIONS AND PROFESSIONS)

BUTTER "Butter" is mentioned figuratively (Ps 55:21; in KJV, Job 20:17; 29:6, where NIV renders "cream"), as well as literally (Gen 18:8 KJV). Where KJV has "butter," NIV generally renders "curds" (e.g., Gen 18:8; Deut 32:14; 2 Sam 17:29).

BUZ 1. A nephew of Abraham and the second son of Nahor (Gen 22:21). His family apparently settled in Arabia (Jer 25:23). **2.** Head of a family in the tribe of Gad (1 Chron 5:14).

BUZZARD (See BIRDS)

BYBLOS (See GEBAL)

BYWAYS Literally "crooked paths," traveled to avoid danger (Judg 5:6 KJV, RSV; NIV "winding paths").

–C–

CAB (kăb, *a hollow vessel*, ASV "kab"). A measure of capacity, a little less than two quarts (2 Kings 6:25).

CABUL (kā'bŭl). **1.** A city of Galilee, a border city of the tribe of Asher (Josh 19:27). **2.** A name given by Hiram of Tyre to a district in northern Galilee, including 20 cities, which Solomon ceded to him (1 Kings 9:13).

CAESAR (sē'zêr). **1.** The name of a Roman family prominent from the third century B.C., of whom Caius Julius Caesar (c. 102–44) was by far the most prominent. **2.** The title taken by several Roman emperors; e.g., Augustus Caesar, who reigned when Jesus was born (Luke 2:1); his successor Tiberius Caesar, who reigned A.D. 14–37 (3:1); Claudius Caesar, 41–54 (Acts 11:28; 18:2); and Nero, under whom Peter and Paul were martyred, 54–68 (Phil 4:22). It was under Domitian (81-96) that John was exiled to Patmos. "Caesar" is mentioned by our Lord (Luke 20:22–25) both literally as referring to Tiberius and figuratively as meaning any earthly ruler. The name Caesar came to be used as a symbol of the state (Matt 22:17, 21; Mark 12:14, 16–17; Luke 20:22, 25).

CAESAREA (sĕs'à-rē'à). A city built between 25 and 13 B.C. by Herod "the Great" at a vast cost and named in honor of his patron Augustus Caesar. It lay on the coast of the Mediterranean about 25 miles (42 km.) NW of the town of Samaria. Herod intended it as the port of his capital, and a splendid harbor was constructed. Being the military headquarters for the Roman forces and the residence of the procurators, it was the home of Cornelius (Acts 10). It was the place of residence of Philip the evangelist (8:40; 21:8–9). Paul was a prisoner there for two years and preached before King Agrippa (23:31–26:32). The Jewish war that ended in the destruction of Jerusalem had its origin in a riot in Caesarea.

CAESAREA PHILIPPI (sĕs'à-rē'à fĭ-lĭp'ī, *Caesarea of Philip*). A town at the extreme northern boundary of Palestine, about 30 miles (50 km.) inland from Tyre and 50 miles (83 km.) SW of Damascus. Augustus Caesar presented it, with the surrounding country, to Herod the Great, who built a temple there in honor of the emperor. Herod's son, Philip the Tetrarch, enlarged the town and named it Caesarea Philippi to distinguish it from the other Caesarea. It was at a secluded

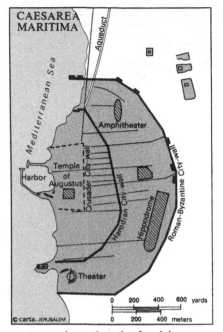

CAESAREA MARITIMA

spot near here that the Lord began to prepare his disciples for his approaching suffering, death and resurrection, and that Peter made his famous confession (Matt 16:13–17).

CAGE A device so-called when used by the fowler to keep his live birds, but "basket" when used for fruit (Jer 5:27; Amos 8:1–2; cf. Rev 18:2 KJV).

CAIAPHAS (kā'yà-fàs). From 168 B.C., when Antiochus Epiphanes desecrated the temple, to 66, when the Romans took over, the high priesthood was almost a political office, the priests still coming from the descendants of Aaron but being generally appointed for worldly considerations.

From 66 B.C. the Romans rulers appointed not only the civil officers (e.g., Herod) but the high priests also, with the result that the office declined spiritually. Annas, father-in-law of Caiaphas (John 18:13), had been high priest by appointment of the Roman governor from A.D. 7 to 14 (Luke 3:2), and though three of his sons succeeded for a short period, Caiaphas held the office from 18 to 36, with Annas still a sort of "high priest emeritus." After Jesus had raised Lazarus from the dead (John 11), many of the Jews believed in him (11:45–46), but some through jealousy reported the matter to the Pharisees. With the chief priests they gathered a council, fearing, or pretending to fear, that if Jesus were let alone many would accept him and the Romans would destroy what was left of Jewish autonomy. Caiaphas (11:49–53) declared that it would be better for Jesus to die than for the whole nation to be destroyed. When our Lord was betrayed into the hands of his enemies, the Roman soldiers and the Jewish officers took him first to the house of Annas, where by night he was given the pretense of a trial (18:12–23). Then Annas sent him bound to Caiaphas, before whom the "trial" continued (18:24–27). Afterward he was delivered to Pilate because the Jews could not legally execute him.

CAIN (kăn). **1.** The first son of Adam and Eve, and a farmer by occupation. As an offering to God, he brought some of the fruits of the ground, while his brother brought an animal sacrifice (Gen 4). Angry when his offering was not received (Heb 11:4 shows that he lacked a right disposition toward God), he murdered his brother. He added to his guilt before God by denying the act and giving no evidence of repentance. He fled to the land of Nod and there built a city, becoming the ancestor of a line that included Jabal. **2.** The progenitor of the Kenites (Num 24:22). **3.** A village in Judah (Josh 15:57, NIV "Kain").

CAINAN (kā-ī'năn). **1.** In NIV, RSV, ASV "Kenan," the fourth from Adam in the messianic line (Gen 5:12-14; 1 Chron 1:2; Luke 3:37). **2.** A son of Arphaxad (Luke 3:36).

CALAH (kā'là). A very ancient city of Assyria on the upper reaches of the Tigris River, built originally by Nimrod or Asshur (Gen 10:6–12). The city was apparently rebuilt by Shalmanezer I (reigned c. 1456–1436 B.C.), then later abandoned for many centuries till Ashurnasirpal, who is pictured as "Ruthlessness Incarnate" (reigned c. 926–902), restored it.

CALAMUS (See PLANTS)

CALCOL, CHALCOL (kăl'kŏl). A son or descendant of Mahol. He was noted for his wisdom, yet Solomon was wiser than he (1 Kings 4:30–31). Calcol was also a son or descendant of Zerah (1 Chron 2:6).

CALDRON A large pot or vessel in which meat is to be boiled (Jer 52:18, 19 KJV; Ezek 11:3, 7, 11 KJV).

Colossal human-headed winged lion that guarded the doorway to the palace of Ashurnasirpal II, 883–859 B.C., at Nimrud (Calah). Reproduced by courtesy of the Trustees of the British Museum

CALEB (kā'lĕb, *dog*). **1.** The son of Jephunneh, the Kenezite; the 40-year-old prince of Judah whom Moses sent with 11 others to spy out the Promised Land (Num 13:6; Josh 14:7). Only Caleb and Joshua encouraged the people to go up and take the land. Because Israel adopted the majority report, God imposed on them 40 years of "wandering" in the wilderness until that generation died out. At age 85, when the land of Canaan was being distributed, Caleb asked for, and received, Hebron and the hill country, home of the Anakim who had terrorized ten of the spies. Later he became father-in-law of Othniel, the first of the "judges," by giving him Acsah his daughter (Judg 1:12–15, 20). **2.** A son of Hezron, son of Judah (1 Chron 2:18–19, 42).

CALEB EPHRATHAH (kā'lĕb ĕf'rà-tà). The place where Hezron died (1 Chron 2:24). The Hebrew and LXX texts differ here, and many scholars prefer the LXX reading, "after the death of Hezron, Caleb came unto Ephrath, the wife of

SYNCHRONIZED JEWISH CALENDAR

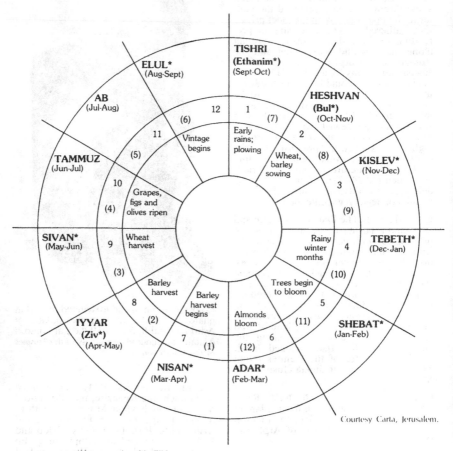

Courtesy Carta, Jerusalem.

*Name mentioned in Bible.
Numbers of months according to Bible. Numbers in parentheses according to Judaism today.
Month Adar II (13) is added every 2 to 3 years in order to align length of Jewish year with solar year.

Hezron, his father." When a son took his father's wife, it signified that he was claiming his father's possessions.

CALENDAR Calendars are devised as a trustworthy means for recording history and determining dates in advance for social, civic, and religious anniversaries, and for economic planning. Comparatively little is known of the calendar of the early Israelites from the patriarchs to the Exile, but a critical study of the biblical records and archaeological discoveries is rewarding.

During the Bible period, time was reckoned solely on astronomical observations. The early Chaldean and Egyptian astrologers became quite learned in the movements of astronomical bodies. Their discoveries, as well as those of other Near Eastern neighbors, made their impact on the Jewish calendar. From earliest times the sun and moon were determinants of periods: days, months, and years.

(1) **Days** in the biblical record of time begin with the account of creation. While

the Babylonian day began at sunrise, the Bible reckoned the 24-hour span from sunset to sunset (Deut 23:11; cf. Neh 4:21; Gen 1:5, 8, et al). Days of the week were not named but were designated by ordinal numbers. "Sabbath" was not the name of the seventh day but a sacred designation. Israel had timing devices (Isa 39:8; cf. 2 Kings 20:9–10). The Crucifixion account mentions the third, sixth, and ninth hours (Mark 15:25, 33, 34; cf. John 11:9), referring to 9 a.m., noon, and 3 p.m. Early Hebrews divided the night into three watches (Exod 14:24; Judg 7:19; Lam 2:19). The Romans divided the night into four watches (Mark 13:35).

(2) **The seven-day week** is of Semitic origin. Though God placed special emphasis on the seventh day at the time of creation (Gen 2:2–3), the first recorded instance of the observance of a sabbath was when the Israelites were gathering manna in the wilderness (Exod 16:23).

When Moses transmitted to Israel the fourth commandment in the Decalogue, "Remember the Sabbath day by keeping it holy" (Exod 20:8), it was designated as a perpetual memorial sign of the covenant between God and his chosen people. It became a distinctive day with successive injunctions to observe it, describing the manner of doing so and the penalties for its desecration (23:12; 35:2–3). Early Christian Jews made a habit of assembling on the first day of the week to commemorate Jesus' resurrection on that day (Luke 24:1); the first day instead of the seventh, became the day of worship and rest in Christendom.

(3) **The Hebrew month** began with the new moon. The early Israelites designated their months by names that they borrowed from the Canaanites or Phoenicians. These names had seasonal connotations—e.g., Abib (Exod 13:4; Deut 16:1), corresponding to Nisan in the later calendar, means "month of the ripening ears." About the end of the kingdom period the calendar was reformed, replacing the old names of the months with ordinal numerals and changing the beginning of the year from fall to spring (cf. 1 Kings 6:1; 8:2; Haggai 1:1; 2:1, 10). The postexilic names of months were, as confirmed by the Talmud, adopted from the Babylonian calendar but not used for civil and historical purposes.

(4) **Years.** The OT calendar contained two concurrent years: the sacred year, beginning in the spring with the month Nisan, and the civil year, beginning in the fall with Tishri. The sacred year was instituted by Moses following the Exodus

while the civil year claims to be reckoned from Creation.

Feasts and fasts were intricately woven into the lunar-solar sacred year. Three great historic feasts were instituted by Moses: "the Feast of Unleavened Bread," "the Feast of Harvest," and "the Feast of Ingathering" (Exod 23:14–16), corresponding roughly to Passover, Pentecost, and Thanksgiving. There were also numerous minor feasts.

(5) **Cycles.** From God's hallowing of the seventh day there arose a special sacredness in relation to the number seven. The sabbath of seven days, Pentecost (at the end of seven weeks after Passover), and the Feast of Trumpets (introducing the sacred seventh month) were all "appointed assemblies" (*mo'adhim*) of the Lord. The sabbatical year was one of solemn rest for landlords, slaves, beasts of burden, and land, and of freedom for Hebrew slaves (Exod 23:10–11; Lev 25:3–7). The Jubilee, every 50th year, following "seven weeks of years," was a hallowed year whose observance included family reunions, canceled mortgages, and the return of lands to their original owners (Lev 25:8–17).

(6) **Eras** in the Bible calendar constitute the whole span of time from the creation of the world to the consummation of the ages. Great events are terminal markers. These mountain peaks of time, in chronological sequence, are Creation, Flood, Abraham, Exodus, Exile, and Birth of Jesus. Consequently, the eras may be designated Ante-Diluvian, Post-Diluvian, Patriarchal, Israelite, Judean, and Christian. (Cf. Matt 1:2–17; Luke 3:23–38.)

CALF (See ANIMALS)

CALF WORSHIP A part of the religious worship of almost all ancient Semitic peoples. At least as early as the Exodus, living bulls were worshiped in Egypt. The Babylonians looked on the bull as the symbol of their greatest gods. Among the Semitic Canaanites the bull was the symbol of Baal. It symbolized strength, vigor, and endurance.

Aaron made a golden image of a male calf in order that the people might worship the Lord under this form (Exod 32:4). The feast held in connection with this worship was a "festival to the LORD" (32:5).

After the division of the kingdom, Jeroboam set up two golden calves in his kingdom, one at Bethel and one at Dan (1 Kings 12:28–29) because he feared that his people might desert him if they continued to worship in Jerusalem. The

Encampment of the Tribes of Israel

Nu 2:1–31 Nu 10:11–33

*Leading tribe of the group

Marching Order of the Tribes

bull images were erroneously supposed to represent God, but in time came to be regarded as common idols (1 Kings 12:30; Hos 13:2).

CALL (Gr. *kaleō, to call*). One of the most common verbs in the Bible, representing over 20 Hebrew and Greek words with four different meanings: **1.** To pray—"Call to me and I will answer you" (Jer 33:3). **2.** To summon or appoint—"I am about to summon all the peoples of the northern kingdoms" (Jer 1:15). **3.** To name a person or thing—"God called the light 'day' " (Gen 1:5). **4.** To invite people to accept salvation through Christ. This last is a call by God through the Holy Spirit; it is heavenly (Heb 3:1) and holy (2 Tim 1:9). This call comes to people in all situations and occupations (1 Cor 1:26; 7:20).

CALNEH (kăl′nė). One of the four cities—including also Babel, Erech (whence "Iraq"), and Akkad—that were founded by Nimrod in the third generation after the Flood (Gen 10:10).

CALVARY (kăl′và-rē, Lat. *calvaria, skull*). A place not far from the walls of Jerusalem where Christ was crucified and near which he was buried (Luke 23:33). The Latin *calvaria* is a rendering of the Greek *kranion,* "skull," which renders the Hebrew *Gulgoleth* and the Aramaic *Gulgulta.* The common explanation is that the name was due to the cranial shape of the hill.

CAMEL (See ANIMALS)

CAMEL'S HAIR Mentioned only in Matthew 3:4 and Mark 1:6, where we are told that John the Baptist wore a garment of camel's hair (probably dressed camel's skin), a garment still used in the Near East.

CAMON (See KAMON)

CAMP, ENCAMPMENT (Heb. *mahaneh*). A group of tents intended for traveling or for temporary residence as in case of war. When the angels of God met Jacob, he exclaimed, "This is the camp of God!" and he named the place "Mahanaim," or "Two Camps," referring to God's host and his own (Gen 32:1–2).

In the wilderness the Israelites were given precise instructions as to the order and arrangements of their camp, both at rest and in traveling (Num 2). The tabernacle in the center indicated the centrality of God in their life and worship.

CAMPHIRE (See PLANTS: *Henna*)

CANA (kā′nà). Cana of Galilee is mentioned four times in Scripture (John 2:1, 11; 4:46; 21:2). It was in the highlands of Galilee, where Jesus performed his first miracle, graciously relieving the embarrassment caused by the shortage of wine at a marriage feast.

CANAAN, CANAANITES (kā′năn, kā′năn-īts). **1.** The son of Ham (Gen 9–10) whose descendants occupied Canaan and took their name from that country (Gen 9:18, 22; 10:6). **2.** Canaan was one of the old names for Palestine (the land of the Canaanites whom the Israelites dis-

possessed), Egyptian inscriptions of c.
1800 B.C. use it for the coastland between
Egypt and Asia Minor. In the Amarna
letters of c. 1400 B.C. the name is applied
to the Phoenician coast. According to
Scripture Canaanites lived throughout the
land (Judg 1:9–10), and included the
whole pre-Israelite population, even east
of the Jordan (Gen 12:6; 24:3, 37; Josh
3:10). The language of Canaan (Isa 19:18)
refers to the group of West Semitic
languages of which Hebrew, Phoenician,
and Moabite were dialects. The continued presence of the Canaanites with their
heathen practices created serious religious problems for the Israelites.

CANAANITE, SIMON THE The KJV
rendering of the name of an apostle (Matt
10:4), distinguishing him from Simon
Peter.

CANDACE (kăn′dȧ-sē, Gr. *Kandakē*).
The queen of Ethiopia (Acts 8:27). The
name seems to have been a general
designation of Ethiopian queens (as
"Pharaoh" was for Egyptian kings, and
"Caesar" for Roman emperors). Her
chief treasurer, a eunuch, went to Jerusalem to worship and was led by Philip the
evangelist to faith in Christ.

CANDLE (See LAMP)

CANDLESTICK (See LAMPSTAND)

CANE (See PLANTS)

CANKER (See DISEASES)

CANKERWORM (See ANIMALS)

CANONICITY (kăn′ŏn-ĭc′i-tē). The word
"canon" originally meant "measuring
rule," hence "standard." In theology its
chief application is to those books received as authoritative and making up our
Bible. The Protestant canon includes 39
books in the OT (as does the Jewish
canon) and 27 in the NT. The Roman
Catholic and Orthodox Canons add seven
books and some additional pieces in the
OT (See APOCRYPHA).

It is commonly said that the Protestant
test of canonicity is inspiration. That is,
Protestants accept into their canon those
books they believe to be immediately
inspired by God and therefore true, infallible, and inerrant, the very Word of God.

I. The Old Testament Canon. The Jewish Talmud of about A.D. 400 names the
books of the Jewish canon in approximately the order found in our Hebrew
Bibles today. The Jewish historian Josephus (in about A.D. 90 in his work against
Apion) wrote that the Jews received 22
books (equivalent to the Protestants' 39),
which they would rather die than alter or

deny. He attributes the authorship of
these books to Moses and the succeeding
prophets from that time to the days of
Artaxerxes (around 400 B.C.). He also
states that other later books, not written
by prophets, were not so highly regarded.

The Dead Sea Scrolls give four places
where the OT is referred to in two
categories, the Law and the Prophets, as
is usual in the NT (e.g., Matt 5:17; 22:40;
Luke 16:16; 24:27; cf. 24:44). That this
twofold canon included all our present
books seems obvious from the fact that
the Qumran community quoted from
most of the OT books, including those
later classified in the third division of
"writings," and has left manuscripts of
all the biblical books except Esther.

The canonicity of the Apocrypha (Tobit, Judith, Wisdom, Ecclesiasticus, Baruch, 1 and 2 Maccabees, and certain
additions to Esther and Daniel) has no
ancient authority and was not recognized
by Christ, the apostles, or the Jewish
people. The distinction between those
books and the canonical OT writings was
generally preserved by the Greek fathers;
it was generally overlooked by the Latin
fathers.

II. The New Testament Canon. Information on the early use of the NT books
has been augmented in recent years both
by the discovery of old portions of the
NT and of early books that quote it.

Some NT books were questioned for a
time for various reasons, but since the
end of the fourth century A.D. there has
been no question among most of the
Christian churches as to which books
belong in the NT. Nearly all branches of
Christendom have accepted the current
27 books as authoritative and canonical,
not because of any arbitrary decree of
church leaders, but because of the witness of the NT itself, the early church
fathers, the truth contained in these
books, and the blessing on those who
believe and obey them.

CANTICLES (See SONG OF SONGS)

CAPERNAUM (kȧ-pŭr′nā-ŭm, Gr. *Ka-
pernaoum*, from Heb. *Kaphar-Nahum,
village of Nahum*). A town on the NW
shore of the Sea of Galilee where Jesus
made his headquarters during his ministry in Galilee (Matt 4:13; Mark 2:1). In
Scripture it is mentioned only in the
Gospels. It was a town of considerable
size: a tax collector had his office there
(Mark 2:14); a high officer of the king
(Herod Antipas) had his residence there
and built a synagogue for the people there
(Matt 8:5–13; Luke 7:1–10). Jesus performed many striking miracles there,

Limestone relief of a line of Syrian captives being led into the presence of Horemheb, on his tomb from Memphis, c. 1350–1300 B.C. Courtesy Rijksmuseum van Oudheden, Leiden, Netherlands

among them the healing of the centurion's palsied servant (Matt 8:5–13), the paralytic who was lowered through a roof by four friends (Mark 2:1–13), and a nobleman's son (John 4:46–54). It was there that Jesus called Matthew to the apostleship (Matt 9:9–13). Many addresses were delivered there, including the one on the Bread of Life (Mark 9:33–50). In spite of Jesus' remarkable works and teachings, the people did not repent, and Jesus predicted the complete ruin of the place (Matt 11:23–24; Luke 10:15). His prophecy was so completely fulfilled that the town has disappeared and its very site is a matter of debate.

CAPH (kàf). The eleventh letter of the Hebrew alphabet, corresponding to our *k*. As a numeral it is eleven.

CAPHTOR (kăf'tôr, Heb. *kaphtôr*). The place from which the Philistines originally came (Amos 9:7). Jeremiah (47:4) calls it an island, probably Crete. There is evidence of ancient connection between Crete and Philistia (Ezek 25:16; Zeph 2:5, where the LXX renders Kerethites "Cretans").

CAPPADOCIA (kăp'à-dō'shĭ-à). A large inland region of Asia Minor. In the latter time of the Persian Empire the region was divided into two territories of which the more northerly was later named Pontus and the southerly Cappadocia, the name it retained in NT times. Jews from Cappadocia (Acts 2:9) were among the hearers of the first Christian sermon, and Peter directed his first letter (1 Peter 1:1) in part to believers there. It is almost certain that many of these Cappadocian Jews were converted on the Day of Pentecost,

and so had the honor of being among the very earliest Christians.

CAPTAIN A word that in KJV translates 16 different terms in the original text, usually expressing leadership but not necessarily in the military (Gen 37:36; 2 Kings 1:9–11; Isa 3:3).

CAPTIVITY The captivity of the northern kingdom of Israel in 722 B.C. and the captivity of Judah (or the southern kingdom) in 586 B.C. After a three-year siege of Samaria, Sargon captured this capital city of Israel and deported the inhabitants to Assyria (2 Kings 17:6–7; 18:11–12). The very poor in Israel were left because they were not considered a threat (25:12). Some time later Sargon's grandson Esarhaddon and his great-grandson Ashurbanipal imported to the region of Samaria some conquered peoples from the East (17:24). When the ten northern tribes were taken into captivity, some undoubtedly were absorbed into the pagan culture surrounding them, but for the most part they retained their identity, some returning to Judah at the end of the Exile, others remaining to become part of the Dispersion.

The captivity of Judah was predicted 150 years before it occurred (Isa 6:11–12; 11:12). Isaiah (11:11; 39:6) and Micah (4:10) foretold that the place of the Captivity was to be Babylonia; and Jeremiah announced that it would be for 70 years (Jer 25:1, 11–12). Nebuchadnezzar came into Jerusalem in 605 and carried off to Babylon the vessels of the house of God and members of the nobility of Judah, among them Daniel the prophet (2 Chron 36:2–7; Jer 45:1; Dan 1:1–3). Jehoiakim was taken in chains to Babylon (2 Chron

36:6). In 597, Nebuchadnezzar carried off Jeholaohin, his mother, his wives, 3,000 princes, 7,000 men of might, and 1,000 artisans (2 Kings 24:14–16). Among them was the prophet Ezekiel. This was the first large-scale deportation of the southern kingdom into Babylonia. In 586 Nebuchadnezzar burned the temple, destroyed the city of Jerusalem, and deported into Babylonia all but the poorest of the land (2 Kings 25:2–21). A third group was taken into Babylonia five years after the destruction of the city (Jer 52:30).

The exiles were not heavily oppressed by their conquerors. They engaged in business, built houses (Ezra 2:65; Jer 29:5–7), and even held high positions in the state (Neh 1:11; Dan 2:48). They were not able to continue their system of sacrifices, but they had with them their priests and teachers (Ezra 1:5; Jer 29:1); and Ezekiel gave them constant encouragement (Ezek 1:1). In 539 B.C., Babylon fell to Cyrus king of Persia, who issued a decree permitting the Israelites to return to Jerusalem to rebuild the temple (Ezra 1:1–4). The next year, about 43,000 returned with Zerubbabel (Ezra 2:64). The rest preferred to remain in Mesopotamia (Zech 6:10). In 458, 1,800 returned with Ezra.

CARAVAN A group of travelers united together for a common purpose or for mutual protection and generally equipped for a long journey, especially in desert country or through foreign and presumably hostile territory. Jacob's "company" (Gen 32–33) was organized to carry a clan to a new home; and the caravan of the Amalekites whom David destroyed (1 Sam 30:1–20) were organized for raiding purposes.

CARAWAY (See PLANTS)

CARCASS, CARCASE The dead body of a person or beast. The word is a translation of six different words in Scripture with root ideas of something fallen, faded, exhausted, or dead (Judg 14:8–9; cf. Lev. 11:8–40).

CARCHEMISH, CHARCHEMISH (kà r'kē-mĭsh). An ancient city of the Hittites located on the west bank of the Euphrates 63 miles (105 km.) NE of Aleppo. It was important commercially and militarily. For many years it paid tribute to the kings of Assyria. When Sargon captured it in 717 B.C., the Hittite Empire fell with it (Isa 10:9). It was the scene of a great victory by Nebuchadnezzar over Pharaoh Neco in 605 (Jer 46:2; 2 Chron 35:20).

CAREAH (See KAREAH)

CARITES (See KERETHITES)

CARMEL (kàr'mĕl, *garden*). **1.** The mountainous promontory jutting into the Mediterranean Sea just south of the modern city Haifa and straight west of the Sea of Galilee. When the word occurs with the definite article, it generally refers to Mt. Carmel and is often used to illustrate a beautiful and fruitful place (Isa 35:2; but see 33:9, which pictures God's judgment). At Carmel, Elijah stood against 450 heathen prophets and defeated them (1 Kings 18). Elisha also visited Carmel (2 Kings 2:25; 4:25). **2.** A very ancient town of Judah about 7 miles (12 km.) almost directly south of Hebron. It is best known as the residence of the very churlish Nabal, who refused kindness to David (1 Sam 25:2–40) and whose life was saved by the tact of his beautiful wife Abigail. Abigail later became a wife of David.

CARMELITE (kàr'mĕl-īt). A native of Judean Carmel. This term was used in reference to David's wife Abigail, who had first married Nabal (1 Sam 27:3 KJV), and to Hezro, one of David's mighty men (1 Chron 11:37).

CARMI (kàr'mē). **1.** One of the sons of Reuben, eldest son of Jacob, and head of the family of the "Carmites" (Gen 46:9; Num 26:6). **2.** An early descendant of Judah (probably great-grandson) and father of Achan (Josh 7:1).

CARNAL Fleshly, with reference to the body as the seat of the desires and appetites; usually used in Scripture in the negative sense, as opposed to the spiritual. In 1 Corinthians 2:14–3:4, Paul divides mankind into two classes—the natural and the spiritual; this corresponds to the classification of people as once-born and twice-born. Then he classifies Christians as "carnal" and "spiritual" (KJV; NIV has "worldly" and "spiritual") and lists the marks of carnality as "jealousy and quarreling" and undue emphasis on personalities: "I follow Paul—I follow Apollos." "Carnal" does not necessarily imply active and conscious sin but is opposed to "spiritual" (Rom 7:14; 2 Cor 10:4; Heb 7:16; 9:10). It describes the dominance of the lower side of human nature apart from God's work in one's life.

The KJV OT uses the expression "lie carnally" to describe adultery (Lev 18:20) and fornication (19:20), but far more often it refers figuratively to idolatry. To take the love that belongs to husband or wife and give it to another is adultery, and to take the love that be-

The renowned caves at Qumran, place where the Dead Sea Scrolls were discovered early in 1947 by a Bedouin goatherd.
Courtesy S. Zur Picture Library

longs to God and give it to another is idolatry (Hos 1–3; Rev 17:18).

CARNELIAN (See MINERALS)

CARPENTER (See OCCUPATIONS AND PROFESSIONS)

CARRIAGE (See CHARIOT)

CARRION (See BIRDS)

CARTS Carts and wagons are light, small, usually two-wheeled vehicles for carrying people or freight. Pharaoh provided carts for Jacob's journey into Egypt (Gen 45:19–21). The Philistines used a cart to return the ark of God to Israel (1 Sam 6); but when David later desired to bring the same ark to his city, he used a cart, and there was a disastrous event connected with that arrangement (see 2 Sam 6:1–11).

CASLUHITES (kăs'lū-hīts). One of the seven tribes descended from "Mizraim," which is the name for Egypt (Gen 10:13–14; 1 Chron 1:11–12). The Philistines are said to have come from this tribe.

CASSIA (See PLANTS)

CASTLE A large fortified building, set of buildings, or encampment, as that of a prince or nobleman. David took the Jebusite castle in Jerusalem and made it his residence (1 Chron 11:5, 7). Castles were built in the cities of Judah by Jehoshaphat (2 Chron 17:12) and in its

forests by Jotham (27:4). Nehemiah erected a "castle" in Jerusalem that later became the Tower of Antonia, where Paul was confined.

CASTOR AND POLLUX (kăs'têr, pŏl'ŭks, Gr. *Dioskyroi, sons of Zeus*). In Greek mythology they were sons of Zeus by Leda, one of his numerous mistresses. Castor was a horseman and Pollux an adept boxer. They were later put in the sky in the constellation known as "Gemini," "the Twins," and were considered as tutelary deities favorable to sailors, a fact that explains why the ship mentioned in Acts 28:11, in which Paul sailed, was named in their honor. St. Elmo's fire used to be credited to Castor and Pollux.

CATERPILLAR (See ANIMALS)

CATHOLIC EPISTLES A term applied to the Epistles of James, Peter, John, and Jude. It goes back to the early church fathers, but how it arose is unknown. The most commonly accepted explanation is that these epistles were addressed, not to individual churches or persons, but to a number of churches. They were addressed to the church at large, i.e., the universal church. The seeming exceptions, 2 and 3 John, were probably included as properly belonging with 1 John and of value to the general reader.

CATTLE (See ANIMALS)

CAVE A hollowed-out place in the earth, whether formed by nature or by man. In Palestine, where there is much limestone, caves are likely to be quite numerous. Caves were often used for regular human habitation, for hiding from the law or from enemies in warfare, for securing precious treasure (such as the Dead Sea Scrolls), for storehouses and cisterns, for stables and cattle, and for burial (Gen 19:30; 1 Kings 19:9).

CEDAR (See PLANTS)

CEDRON (See KIDRON)

CEILING The word appears only in 1 Kings 6:15 (KJV "ceiling"), which says that Solomon built the walls of the ceiling with cedar, referring not to the upper surface of a room, but to the inner walls. The word "ceiled" appears several times, but it usually means to panel the walls of a building.

CELIBACY The state of being unmarried, particularly when this state is deliberately chosen. John the Baptist, for example, was unmarried, but Peter was married. Jesus himself did not marry, but he contributed notably to the wedding celebrations at Cana (John 2:1–11). He realized that some "have renounced marriage because of the kingdom of heaven" (Matt 19:12), and once he warned against wrong priorities if to become married would be a positive hindrance to discipleship (Luke 14:20). Paul recognized the dangers of earthly ties and stressed basic principles: God has an assignment for every life, and whatever our situation, married or single, the main thing is to be able to exercise our God-given gifts to the full (1 Cor 7:7–9, 17, 32–38).

CELLAR A place for storage of wine (1 Chron 27:27, KJV, RSV) or oil (27:28 KJV), not a room under a house, but a place of storage.

CENCHREA (sĕn'krē-à). The eastern harbor of Corinth, and the little town on the harbor. Paul commends to the Roman church a deaconess called Phoebe of the church at Cenchrea (Rom 16:1), a church that Paul may have founded on his second missionary journey. Paul stopped here to have his head shaved in fulfillment of a vow (Acts 18:18).

CENSER A vessel, probably shaped like a saucepan, for holding incense while it is being burned (Num 16:6–7, 39). The same Hebrew word is sometimes rendered "firepan" (Exod 27:3) or "snuffdish." NIV in certain contexts uses "wick trimmer" (Exod 25:28; 37:23; Num 4:9).

CENSUS A numbering and registration of a people. The OT tells of three different occasions when a formal census was taken. The first was at Mt. Sinai, soon after the Israelites left Egypt (Num 1). The second was at Shittim near the end of the 40 years' wilderness wandering. The third was made by David (2 Sam 24:1–9; 1 Chron 21:1–5). The exiles who returned from Babylonia with Zerubbabel were also numbered (Ezra 2). Shortly before the birth of Christ, Emperor Augustus ordered an enrollment in his empire (Luke 2:1).

CENTURION (cĕn-tū'rĭ-ŏn, Lat. *centum*, *one hundred*). A commander of 100 soldiers in the Roman army. The centurion of Capernaum had built a synagogue for the Jews; Jesus healed his servant (Matt 8:5–13; Luke 7:2–10) saying, "I have not found anyone in Israel with such great faith." Cornelius (Acts 10), another centurion, was "devout and God-fearing." Peter was sent to him and "used the keys" to open up salvation for the Gentiles, as he had at Jerusalem for the Jews (Acts 2) and at Samaria for its people (Acts 8:14–17). Another centu-

rion, Julius, of the Imperial Regiment (Acts 27:1–43), had the duty of taking Paul to Rome. He saved Paul's life when the soldiers wished to kill all the prisoners, and Paul by his presence and counsel saved the centurion and all the ship's company. Other centurions are mentioned elsewhere (Matt 27:54; Acts 22:25; 23:17).

CEPHAS (sē'făs, Gr. *Kēphas*, from Aram. *Kepha, rock, or stone*). A name given by Jesus to the apostle Peter (John 1:42). See PETER.

CHAFF The refuse of the grain that has been threshed and winnowed. This is partly dust and dirt, but the real chaff is the hard and inedible coat of the grain. In Isaiah 5:24 and 33:11, the word properly means "dry hay" fit for burning. The word is figuratively used for worthless or godless men (e.g., Ps 1:4— "Not so the wicked! They are like chaff that the wind blows away"). It is used also for godless nations (Isa 17:13). In the preaching of John the Baptist (Matt 3:12; Luke 3:17) our Lord is to save the righteous ("gathering his wheat into his barn") and destroy the wicked ("burning up the chaff with unquenchable fire").

CHAIN The English word represents many Hebrew words meaning "chain, necklace, band, bracelet, clasp, hook, ring, and rope." Chains were used for the following purposes: **1.** As marks of distinction, in the cases of Joseph (Gen 41:42) and Daniel (Dan 5:7, 16, 29). **2.** For ornaments (Exod 28:14, 22; 39:15, 17–18; Num 31:50; Judg 8:21, 26; 1 Kings 6:21; 7:17; 2 Chron 3:5, 16; Ps 73:6; Prov 1:9). **3.** For fetters (Ps 149:8; Isa 45:14; Jer 39:7; 40:1; Lam 3:7; Mark 5:3–4; Luke 8:29; Acts 12:6–7; 28:20; Jude 6; Rev 20:1).

CHALCEDONY (See MINERALS)

CHALCOL (See CALCOL)

CHALDEA (kăl-dē'à). The country of which Babylon was the capital, and which conquered Judah and carried its inhabitants into captivity (e.g., Gen 11:28; Job 1:17; Ezek 23:14–16; Acts 7:4), but sometimes NIV translates it "Babylonia" (Jer 50:10; 51:24, 35; Ezek 11:24; 16:29).

CHAMBERING Repeated or habitual acts of illicit intercourse (Rom 13:13), rendered by NIV as "sexual immorality."

CHAMBERLAIN (See OCCUPATIONS AND PROFESSIONS)

CHAMELEON (See ANIMALS)

CHAMOIS (See ANIMALS)

CHANCELLOR A Persian official in Palestine (Ezra 4:8–9, 17 KJV). RSV translates this word as "commander," NIV "commanding officer."

CHANGERS OF MONEY Men who exchanged one currency for another at a premium. Coins issued by many governments circulated in Palestine; also Jews had to convert their currency into shekels for the temple tax. It was not the trade but the place where they plied it that led Christ to drive them out of the temple court (Matt 21:12; 25:27; Mark 11:15; John 2:14–15).

CHARASHIM (See GE HARASHIM)

CHARCHEMISH (See CARCHEMISH)

CHARCOAL (See COAL)

CHARGER A dish or platter given as an offering for the tabernacle (Num 7:13–85); called "dishes" in Exodus 25:29; 37:16. NIV consistently renders as "plates." Another word (Ezra 1:9) refers to baskets or dishes (SO NIV) belonging to the temple service. The NT word means a wooden dish or platter (Matt 14:8, 11; Mark 6:25, 28).

CHARIOT (Heb. *rekhev* and derivatives, from a root meaning *mount and ride*). A two-wheeled vehicle drawn by two horses mentioned frequently in Scripture (Gen 41:43; 50:9; Exod 14:7–15:19; 1 Sam 13:5; 2 Sam 8:4; 1 Kings 1:5; 9:19; 10:28–29). Both divided kingdoms used chariots in war (16:9; 22:34; 2 Kings 23:30). Elijah was honored by being escorted up to heaven by a chariot of fire (2 Kings 2:11), and his manner of going became a proverb (2:12; 13:14). God is represented as having thousands of chariots, showing his power (Ps 68:17). Trust in chariots is vain compared with trust in God (20:7).

Egyptian war chariot. Courtesy Carta, Jerusalem

CHARITY The KJV translation of the Greek word *agapē* in 28 places. It is translated "love" in 87 places; once it is translated "dear" (Col 1:13). Charity in the Bible never means giving to the poor; it is always a God-given love that includes respect for, and concern for the welfare of, the one loved. See 1 Corinthians 13.

CHARMS (See AMULETS)

CHARRAN (See HARAN)

CHASTE, CHASTITY (See CLEAN)

CHASTISEMENT (chăs'tīz-mènt, Heb. *mûsār*, from the verb *yāsar, discipline, chasten, admonish, correct;* Gr. *paideia, child-training, the formation of manhood*). Both are translated by many English words, exhibiting shades of meaning: the widest sense (Deut 11:2; Isa 53:5); *punishment* (Jer 30:14); *discipline* (Heb 12:8); When *mûsār* is translated "chastening" (KJV), "discipline" (NIV) rather than punishment is meant (Job 5:17; Prov 3:11–12. *Instruction in wisdom* is prominent in Proverbs. The Greek word in Acts 7:22–23; 2 Timothy 3:16 (*learn, teach, instruct*) refers to education. Hebrew *yākah* means child-training (2 Sam 7:14) and the meaning and value of suffering (Job 33:19; Ps 73:14). Chastisement is the process by which God provides a substitute to bear our sins, brings people to put their trust in him, and trains those whom he has received until they reach maturity.

CHEBAR (See KEBAR)

CHEDORLAOMER
(See KEDORLAOMER)

CHEESE The translation of three Hebrew words, each of which occurs only once (1 Sam 17:18; 2 Sam 17:29; Job 10:10). In a warm climate, without refrigeration, it soon curdled. The process used to make cheese can only be guessed from the practices current in the Near East today.

CHELAL (See KELAL)

CHELLUH (See KELUHI)

CHELUB (See KELUB)

CHELUBAI (See CALEB)

CHEMARIM (kĕm'à-rīm, Heb. *kemārîm*). The KJV rendering of a word probably from a root meaning "prostrate oneself" (Zeph 1:4). The Hebrew word occurs also in 2 Kings 23:5 and Hosea 10:5 and always refers to idolatrous priests, thus the reading in RSV and NIV.

CHEMOSH (kē'mŏsh). The god of Moab (Num 21:29, alluded to in Jer 48:7, 13, 46)

"There above the cover between the two cherubim that are over the ark of the Testimony, I will meet with you and give you all my commands . . ." (Exod 25:22). These ivory carvings borrowed from Phoenician art are now understood to be winged sphinxes with human faces. (See also 1 Kings 6:23–29.) Reproduced by courtesy of the Trustees of the British Museum

and perhaps Ammon (Judg 11:24). Solomon introduced the worship of Chemosh into Jerusalem to please a foreign wife, though by doing so he displeased God (1 Kings 11:7, 33). Josiah defiled this high place of Chemosh (2 Kings 23:13), putting an end to its use as a place of worship. Mesha, king of Moab, suffered a great disaster in his rebellion against Israel, in consequence of which he offered his son to Chemosh as a burnt offering (3:4–27).

CHENAANAH (See KENAANAH)

CHENANI (See KENANI)

CHENANIAH (See KENANIAH)

CHEPHAR-HAAMMONI (See KEPHAR AMMONI)

CHEPHIRAH (See KEPHIRAH)

CHERAN (See KERAN)

CHERETHITES, CHERETHIM (See KERETHITES)

CHERITH (See KERITH)

CHERUB, CHERUBIM (chĕr'ŭb, chĕr'ŭbĭm). In other than biblical usage the English plural is cherubs. The cherubim and a flaming sword were placed at the east of Eden to guard the way to the Tree of Life after Adam and Eve were expelled from the Garden of Eden (Gen 3:24). The curtains of the tabernacle were embroidered with cherubim (Exod 26:1). God

directed Moses to place two cherubim of beaten gold on the mercy seat above the ark, where God would commune with Moses in the tabernacle (25:18–22; 37:7–9). God's glory rested between the cherubim (Num 7:89; 1 Sam 4:4; 2 Sam 6:2; 2 Kings 19:15; Pss 80:1; 99:1; Isa 37:16), in both the tabernacle and the temple. The cherubim in the temple were huge figures newly made for the purpose (1 Kings 6:23–28; 2 Chron 3:10–13; 5:7–8). Carved cherubim also ornamented the walls of the temple (1 Kings 6:29). David sings of God riding on a cherub (2 Sam 22:11; Ps 18:10). Psalm 18 pictures a storm with God riding on and speaking from the clouds.

That the cherubim were more than clouds or statues is plain from the description Ezekiel gives (Ezek 9:3; 10:1–22), which shows that they are the "living creatures" of the first chapter. The four faces of each of the cherubim (1:10) stand for the four "excellencies" of the created order: the lion, the greatest of the wild beasts; the eagle, the greatest of the birds; the ox, the greatest of the domestic beasts; and man, the crown of creation. Ezekiel sees, over the heads of the cherubim, the throne of God. Ezekiel's vision explains the OT allusion to the Lord as seated on (or enthroned) between the cherubim (e.g., Ps 99:1); it is a metaphor of his total sovereignty. Likewise when the Lord rides on the cherubim (e.g., Ps 18:10; Ezek 10 passim), the thought is that all creation is subject to his sovereign rule and "intervention," and all its powers are at his disposal.

In Revelation 4:6–9; 5:6–14; 6:1–11; 14:3; 15:7; 19:4 are four "beasts" (Gr. zōa, living creatures; so ASV, RSV, NIV; these are to be distinguished from the Gr. thēria, wild beasts, mentioned, e.g., in Rev 13:1). They are described in terms that identify them with Ezekiel's living creatures or cherubim (Ezek 1, 10).

To sum up: The cherubim are the living chariot or carriers of God when appearing to men. They are heavenly creatures, servants of God in theophany and judgment, appearing in winged human-animal form with the faces of lion, ox, man, and eagle. They are significant in prophecy (Ezekiel) and in the Apocalypse (Revelation). Their service is rendered immediately to God. In Ezekiel's new temple, and in the heavenly sanctuary of Hebrews and Revelation, they are no longer needed, for the redeemed themselves stand in the presence of the living cherubim.

CHERUB (See KERUB)

CHESALON (See KESALON)

CHESED (See KESED)

CHESIL (See KESIL)

CHEST Receptacles for money to repair the temple (2 Kings 12:9–10; 2 Chron 24:8, 10–11). Hebrew ' ārôn is translated "coffin" once (Gen 50:26); elsewhere the "ark" in tabernacle and temple.

CHESTNUT TREE (See PLANTS)

CHESULLOTH (See KESULLOTH)

CHEZIB (See KEZIB)

CHICKEN (See BIRDS)

CHIDON (See KIDON)

CHILD, CHILDREN Among the people of the OT and NT, as in most other cultures, children, especially male, were greatly desired (Gen 15:2; 30:1; 1 Sam 1:11, 20; Pss 127:3; 128:3; Luke 1:7, 28). Among the Hebrews all the firstborn belonged to God and had to be redeemed (Num 3:40–51). Children were sometimes dedicated to God for special service (Judg 13:2–7; 1 Sam 1:11; Luke 1:13–17, 76–79). Male descendants of Abraham were circumcised on the eighth day (Gen 17:12; 21:4; Luke 1:59; 2:21), when the name was given. Weaning often was delayed and then celebrated (Gen 21:8) with a feast. Education was primarily in the home and was the duty of parents

(Exod 12:26–27; Deut 6:7; Josh 4:21–24; Prov 22:6; Eph 6:4; Col 3:21; 2 Tim 3:15). Discipline was to be firm, with corporal punishment (Prov 22:15; 23:13; 29:15). Much was expected of children (Prov 20:11). Obedience and respect to parents was commanded (Exod 21:17; Eph 6:1– 3; Col 3:20; 1 Tim 3:4, 12; Titus 1:6). Favoritism was sometimes shown (Gen 25:28; 37:3). Affection for children is strikingly portrayed in many instances, as in David's love for a child who died (2 Sam 12:15–23); and in the raising of children to life by Elijah (1 Kings 17:17–24), by Elisha (2 Kings 4:18–37), and by Jesus (Matt 9:23–26; Mark 5:35–43; Luke 8:49–56). Jesus' love and concern for children is seen in Matthew 18:1–14; 19:13–15; Mark 9:35–37; 10:13–16; Luke 9:46–48; 18:15–17. Jesus recognized children's play (Matt 11:16). There are many reports of attractive childhood—e.g., Moses (Exod 2:1–10), Samuel (1 Sam 1:20–3:19), Jesus (Luke 2:7–40), Timothy (2 Tim 1:5; 3:14–15).

"Children" is an affectionate address, as in 1 John, of an old man to adults, who are nevertheless expected to act their age (1 Cor 13:11; 14:20). The attention given to the childhood of the Messiah in prophecy (Isa 7:14; 9:6) prepares us for the infancy narratives in Matthew 2 and Luke 2. The Savior came as a helpless babe and apparently had a normal childhood. A return to childlike receptiveness and trust is required of those who would enter the kingdom of heaven (Matt 18:1–14; 19:13–15; Mark 9:35–37; 10:13–16; Luke 9:46–48; 18:15–17).

CHILDBEARING The word occurs in 1 Timothy 2:15 in a passage relating to the proper sphere and conduct of women. "Women will be saved through childbearing" (NIV; KJV, RSV are similar) cannot refer to salvation from sin, which is by grace through faith, but to safekeeping through the pain that became incidental to childbirth through the Fall (Gen 3:16). Hebrew mothers had the assistance of midwives (Exod 1:15–21). Newborn babies had the navel cut, were washed with water, salted, and wrapped in swaddling clothes (Ezek 16:4; Luke 2:7, 12). Purification rites were prescribed after childbirth (Lev 12; Luke 2:22–24).

CHILDREN OF GOD (See SON OF GOD and SONS OF GOD, CHILDREN OF GOD)

CHILEAB (See KILEAB)

CHILION (See KILION)

CHILMAD (See KILMAD)

CHIMHAM (See GERUTH KIMHAM)

The Mount of Temptation with a Greek Orthodox monastery built into its slopes. It is the traditional site where Jesus fasted and prayed for forty days and resisted the temptations of Satan (Matt 4:1–11). Courtesy Israel Government Press Office

CHINNERETH (See KINNERETH)

CHIOS (See KIOS)

CHISLEV (See KISLEV)

CHISLON (See KISLON)

CHISLOTH-TABOR (See KISLOTH TABOR)

CHITTIM (See KITTIM)

CHIUN (kī'ŭn). Possibly Saturn as a god (Amos 5:26 KJV), but the meaning of the Hebrew word is uncertain.

CHLOE (klō'ē). A woman whose people informed Paul of contentions in the Corinthian church (1 Cor 1:11). She was well known to the Corinthian Christians by her personal name.

CHORASHAN (See ASHAN)

CHRIST, JESUS (krīst, jē'zŭs, Gr. *Iēsous*, for Heb. *Jeshua, Jehoshua, Joshua, Jehovah is salvation;* Heb. *māshîah,* Gr. *Christos, anointed*).

I. Comprehensive Life and Work. The various "I Am" sayings of Jesus assert his absolute existence (John 8:58). Scripture affirms his preexistence in terms of fellowship with the Father (1:1), glory (17:5), and designation in advance as the Savior of the world (1 Peter 1:20). All things came into being through him (John 1:3; 1 Cor 8:6; Heb 1:2) and in him continue to have their cohesive principle (Col 1:17). The manifestations of God in the OT are apparently connected with the preincarnate Christ. When Isaiah glimpsed the glory of God, he was seeing Christ (John 12:41). Moses and the prophets spoke of him (Luke 24:27, 44; John 5:46), with special reference to his sufferings and the glories that would follow (1 Peter 1:11). The OT abounds with predictions about Jesus (Gen 3:15; Deut 18:15, 18; Pss 2, 16, 22, 110; Isa 7:14; 9:6, 7; 42:1–4; 52:13–53:12; 61:1, 2; Jer 23:5–6; Mic 5:2). As though in anticipation of the Incarnation, the Son of God showed himself at times to the faithful in visible form as the Angel of the Lord or the Angel of the covenant (Gen 18:1–19:1; Judg 13).

He came in the Incarnation to reveal God (John 1:14, 18), to redeem people from their sins (Mark 10:45), and to relate sympathetically with their needs (Heb 2:17–18). Today the God-man is in heaven, representing the saints before the throne of God (Heb 7:25; 1 John 2:1). By the successful completion of his work on earth he is exalted to be the head of the church (Eph 1:22; 4:15) and by the Spirit directs the life and service of his saints on earth (Matt 28:20).

One purpose of the Incarnation is reserved for his second coming. His kingly rule will then be introduced following his work as judge (Matt 25:31–34). This future coming is one of the major truths set forth in the epistles (Phil 3:20–21; 2 Thess 1:7–10) and is the leading theme of Revelation. After the millennial kingdom, Christ will enter with his people the blessedness of the eternal state, which will be unmarred by the inroads of sin or death.

II. Earthly Ministry. The long-heralded Christ came in the fullness of time (Gal 4:4). God providentially supplied the proper background for his appearing and mission. The birth of the Savior was natural, but his conception was supernatural, by the power of the Holy Spirit (Matt 1:18; Luke 1:35). Augustus was one of God's instruments when he ordered a universal enrollment for taxation, making possible the birth of Jesus in the place appointed by prophetic announcement (Mic 5:2; Luke 2:1–7). The shepherds, by their readiness to seek out the babe in the manger and by their joy at seeing him, became prototypes of the humble souls in Jewry who in coming days would recognize in Jesus their Savior. An intimation of Gentile desire to participate in the Christ may be seen in the coming of the

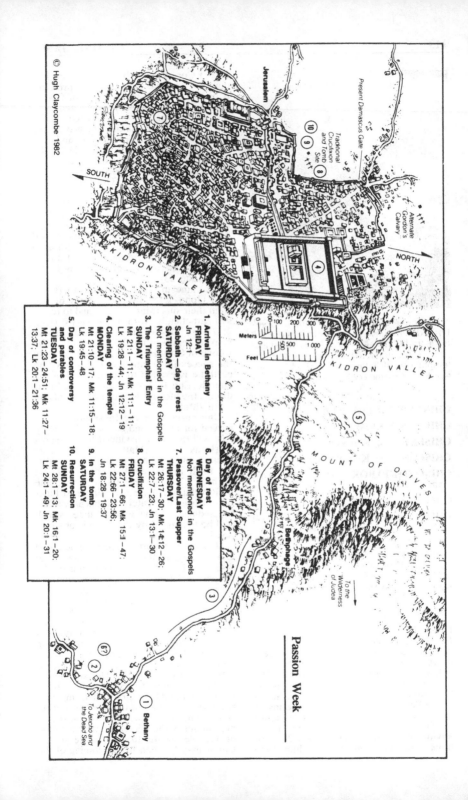

Passion Week

© Hugh Claycombe 1982

1. Arrival in Bethany
   FRIDAY
   Jn 12:1

2. Sabbath—day of rest
   SATURDAY
   Not mentioned in the Gospels

3. The Triumphal Entry
   SUNDAY
   Mt 21:1–11; Mk 11:1–11;
   Lk 19:28–44; Jn 12:12–19

4. Clearing of the temple
   MONDAY
   Mt 21:10–17; Mk 11:15–18;
   Lk 19:45–48

5. Day of controversy
   and parables
   TUESDAY
   Mt 21:23–24:51; Mk 11:27–
   13:37; Lk 20:1–21:36

6. Day of rest
   WEDNESDAY
   Not mentioned in the Gospels

7. Passover/Last Supper
   THURSDAY
   Mt 26:17–30; Mk 14:12–26;
   Lk 22:7–23; Jn 13:1–30

8. Crucifixion
   FRIDAY
   Mt 27:1–66; Mk 15:1–47;
   Lk 22:66–23:56;
   Jn 18:28–19:37

9. In the tomb
   SATURDAY
   Lk 23:56

10. Resurrection
    SUNDAY
    Mt 28:1–13; Mk 16:1–20;
    Lk 24:1–49; Jn 20:1–31

Magi from the East. In the scribes we see the leaders of a nation refusing to receive him when he came to his own.

Christ was not merely a messenger of God, like the ancient prophets, but rather the eternal Son of God now clothing himself with human nature, yet free from any taint of sin. He had a divine and a human nature united in one person. The boy Jesus grew in body and advanced in knowledge and in the wisdom that enabled him to make proper use of what he knew. The scriptural accounts emphasize his progress in the understanding of the OT and affirm his consciousness of a special relation to his Father in heaven (Luke 2:49).

At his baptism Jesus received divine confirmation of his mission and the anointing of the Holy Spirit for the fulfillment of it. By the Baptism he was fulfilling all righteousness (Matt 3:15) in the sense that he was identifying himself with those he came to redeem.

Closely related to the Baptism is the Temptation, for it also includes this representative character. The first Adam failed when put to the test; the last Adam succeeded, though weakened by hunger and harried by the desolation of the wilderness. Jesus overcame Satan's temptations, refusing to be moved from a place of trustful dependence on the Almighty (Matt 4:7, 10).

The public ministry of Jesus was brief. Judging from the number of Passovers (John 2:23; 5:1; 6:4; 13:1), the period was somewhat in excess of two years and possibly more than three. The Synoptists put chief stress on Galilee, along with visits to Tyre and Sidon (Matt 15:21–28), Caesarea-Philippi (16:13ff.), the Decapolis (Mark 7:31; cf. also Mark 5:1–20), Samaria (Luke 9:51–56; 17:11), and Perea (Mark 10:1). John, however, emphasizes Judea.

During his Galilean mission, Jesus made the city of Capernaum his headquarters, conducting tours to outlying towns (Mark 1:38, 6:6; Luke 8:1). His healings and exorcisms were tokens of divine compassion and signs the Promised One had come (cf. Matt 11:2–6; Luke 4:16–19).

Jesus' message was "the kingdom of God," the rule of God in human life and history. The kingdom was both future (Matt 25:31ff.) and present (Luke 11:20). This last reference connects the kingdom with the activity of Jesus in casting out demons. To the degree that Jesus invades the kingdom of Satan in this fashion, the kingdom of God has already come. Doing the will of God was the mainspring of

Jesus' ministry (Matt 6:10; 12:50; Mark 14:36; John 4:34). Entrance into the present aspect of the kingdom comes through faith in the Son of God (John 3:3, 5, 15, 16).

Much of our Lord's teaching was conveyed through parables, usually comparisons taken from various phases of nature or human life. "The kingdom of God is like. . . ." This method of teaching preserved the interest of the hearers until the spiritual application could be made.

The ministry of the Savior was predominantly to the multitudes during its earlier phase (Matt 4:17), but much of Jesus' last year of ministry was given over to instruction of the twelve disciples whom he had chosen (16:21). They understood Jesus as the Messiah and the Son of God (16:16), but they were quite unprepared to receive his teaching on the suffering and death that his earthly life would involve (16:21–23).

In contrast to the Twelve in their attitude to Jesus are the scribes and Pharisees. They were shocked that he would declare men's sins forgiven and claim a special relation to God as Son that others did not have. Because tradition meant more to them than truth, they stumbled in their apprehension of the Christ of God. In the end they plotted with their opponents the Sadducees in order to do away with Jesus.

Even as Christ was engaged in teaching his disciples from the days of the Transfiguration on, he was ever moving toward Jerusalem to fulfill his course at the cross (Luke 9:51). In those latter days some stirring events were unfolded — the triumphal entry into Jerusalem, the cleansing of the temple, the institution of the Lord's Supper, the soul conflict in the Garden of Gethsemane, the arrest and trial, the Crucifixion, the Resurrection, the appearances, the Ascension into heaven. In the Cross man's day erupted in violence and blasphemy. In the Resurrection God's day began to dawn. It was his answer to the world and to the powers of darkness. In it Christ was justified and his claims illuminated.

III. Names, Titles, and Offices. *Jesus* is used mostly in the narratives of the Gospels, and only rarely does it appear in direct address. It means "Savior" (Matt 1:21), being related linguistically to the Hebrew name *Joshua*.

Christ, meaning "anointed one," is the Greek equivalent of the Hebrew word *Messiah*. Our Lord uses it of himself in Luke 24:46. "Christ" was also used as a personal name (Mark 1:1; John 17:3). The prohibition (Matt 16:20; Luke 4:41)

against making Jesus known as the Christ during the days of his ministry was to prevent the people from expecting him to be a political Messiah who would gain their national freedom.

Only once does the name *Immanuel* ("God with us") occur with the conception of Jesus (Matt 1:23). Jesus was often called the *Nazarene* because of his years spent in Nazareth (Luke 24:19).

When Jesus referred to himself, he most often used the title *Son of Man*, occasionally stressing his humanity, but mainly pointing to his transcendence as a heavenly figure (Dan 7:13; Luke 22:69–70). By using this title publicly rather than Messiah, Jesus was able to avoid suggesting that his mission was political in nature, and instead could put into the title his own content.

One of the most familiar designations for Jesus is *Son of God*. Only in John's Gospel does he use it of himself (John 5:25; 10:36; 11:4). But elsewhere he uses its equivalent, the Son (Matt 11:27). Rather frequently in the course of his ministry Jesus was addressed as *Son of David* (Matt 21:9; Luke 18:38), a distinctly messianic title pointing to him as the One who fulfilled the Davidic covenant.

A few passages proclaim outright that Jesus is *God* (John 1:1, 18 [some manuscripts]; 20:28; Rom 9:5; Titus 2:13; Heb 1:8). No term is more expressive of the faith of early believers in Jesus than *Lord* (Acts 2:36; 10:36; Rom 10:9; 1 Cor 8:6; 12:3; Phil 2:11). It denotes the sovereignty of Christ and his headship over the individual believer, the church as a body, and all things.

Some titles pertain to the mission of Christ more than to his person. One of these is *Word* (John 1:1, 14; 1 John 1:1), the revealer of God, who discloses the nature and purposes of the Almighty. Christ is also the *Servant* (Phil 2:7; cf. Matt 12: 17–21; Mark 10:45), the *Savior* (Luke 2:11; John 4:42), *Lamb of God* (John 1:29, 36; 1 Peter 1:19; cf. Rev 5:6), the *High Priest* (Heb 9:11–12), the *Mediator* between God and men (1 Tim 2:5), and the *Last Adam* (1 Cor 15:45; Rom 5:12–21).

This list of names and titles of Christ is not exhaustive. The most satisfying analysis of Christ's ministry divides it into the offices that he fulfills—*prophet, priest,* and *king.*

IV. Character. Certain ingredients of character deserve special mention, but it cannot be said that he was noted for some things above others, for this would involve disproportion and would reflect on the perfection of his being. He had integ-

rity, courage, compassion, humility, and sinlessness.

V. Influence. A life so brief, so confined in its geographical orbit, so little noticed by the world in his own time, has yet become the most potent force for good in all of human history. When he comes into someone's heart by faith, he creates a new point of reference and a new set of values. Sinners feel the touch of Christ and are never the same afterward.

In a more general sense, Christ has mightily affected society in its organized state. He has taught the world the dignity of human life, the worth of the soul, and the preciousness of personality. Under Christian influence, the status of women has steadily been improved, slavery has been abolished, children are recognized as a primary responsibility for the lavishing of love and care, and governments and scientific groups have been stimulated to social service. The arts owe their sublimest achievements to the desire to honor the Son of God. Moralists and philosophers, even when they lack faith in him for the saving of the soul, often acknowledge him as the one great hope for mankind.

CHRISTIAN (Gr. *Christianos*). The biblical meaning is "adherent of Christ." The disciples were formally called Christians first in Antioch (Acts 11:26). Agrippa recognized that to believe what Paul preached would make him a Christian (26:28). Peter accepted the name as in itself a basis for persecution (1 Peter 4:16). The Latin termination *-ianos,* widely used throughout the empire, often designated the slaves of the one with whose name it was compounded. This implication occurs in the NT (e.g., Rom 6:22; 1 Peter 2:16). The apostles wrote of themselves as servants (slaves) of Christ (Rom 1:1; James 1:1; 2 Peter 1:1; Jude 1; Rev 1:1). The NT calls the followers of Christ *brothers* (Acts 14:2); *disciples* (6:1–2); *saints* (9:13; Rom 1:7; 1 Cor 1:2); *believers* (1 Tim 4:12); *the church of God* (Acts 20:28); *all who call on your name* (9:14; Rom 10:12–13).

CHRONICLES, 1 AND 2 These books are called in Hebrew *diverê ha-yāmîm,* "the words [affairs] of the days," meaning "the annals" (cf. 1 Chron 27:24). The church father Jerome (A.D. 400) first entitled them "Chronicles." Originally they formed a single composition but were divided into 1 and 2 Chronicles in the LXX, about 150 B.C. In the Hebrew they stand as the last book of the OT canon. Christ (Luke 11:51) thus spoke of all the martyrs from Abel in the first book

(Gen 4) to Zechariah in the last (2 Chron 24).

Chronicles contains no statements about its own authorship or date. The last event it records is the decree of Cyrus in 538 B.C. that permitted the exiles to return from their Babylonian captivity (2 Chron 36:22); and its genealogies extend to approximately 500 B.C. (1 Chron 3:21). The language, however, and the contents of Chronicles closely parallel that of the Book of Ezra, which continues the history of the Jews from the decree of Cyrus down to 457 B.C. Both documents are marked by lists and genealogies, by an interest in priestly ritual, and by devotion to the Law of Moses. The closing verses of Chronicles (2 Chron 36:22–23) are repeated as the opening verses of Ezra (1:1–3). Ancient Hebrew tradition and the modern scholarship of W. F. Albright therefore unite in suggesting that Ezra may have been the author of both volumes, perhaps around 450 B.C.

The occasion for the writing of Chronicles appears to be Ezra's crusade to bring postexilic Judah back into conformity with the Law of Moses (Ezra 7:10). From 458 B.C., Ezra sought to restore the temple worship (7:19–23, 27; 8:33–34), to eliminate the mixed marriages of Jews with their pagan neighbors (9–10), and to strengthen Jerusalem by rebuilding its walls (4:8–16). Chronicles, accordingly, consists of these four parts: genealogies, to enable the Jews to establish their lines of family descent (1 Chron 1–9); the kingdom of David, as a pattern for the ideal theocratic state (10–29); the glory of Solomon, with an emphasis on the temple and its worship (2 Chron 1–9); and the history of the southern kingdom, stressing in particular the religious reforms and military victories of Judah's more pious rulers (10–36).

As compared with the parallel histories in Samuel and Kings, the priestly annals of Chronicles put a greater emphasis on the structure of the temple (1 Chron 22) and on Israel's ark, the Levites, and the singers (1 Chron 13, 15–16). They omit, however, certain individualistic, moral acts of the kings (2 Sam 9; 1 Kings 3:16–28), as well as detailed biographies of the prophets (17–22:28; 2 Kings 1–8:15), features that account for the incorporation of Chronicles into the third (nonprophetic) section of the Hebrew canon, as distinguished from the location of the more homiletic books of Samuel and Kings in the second (prophetic) division. Finally, the chronicler foregoes discussion of David's disputed inauguration and later shame (2 Sam 1–4, 11–21), of Solo-

mon's failures (1 Kings 11), and of the whole inglorious history of Saul (1 Sam 8–30, except his death, ch. 31), and of the northern kingdom of Israel. The disillusioned, impoverished Jews of 450 B.C. knew enough of sin and defeat; they needed an encouraging reminder of their former, God-given victories (e.g., 2 Chron 13–14, 20, 25).

One of the important theological themes of the books of Chronicles is the necessity of obedience for divine blessing. The chronicler observes that Saul's death was due to unfaithfulness (1 Chron 10:13–14), as was the exile of the southern kingdom (9:1; see also 2 Chron 6:24). On the other hand, obedience will bring blessing to the nation (1 Chron 28:8; 2 Chron 7:14–18). Even the lengthy genealogy that forms the preface to 1 Chronicles contains affirmations of this fact (4:10; 5:1, 25). The narration of selected events from the life of David focuses on the steps of obedience that led to his successful administration of the kingdom. David's role in the establishment of Israelite worship also receives prominence (22:2–5; 23:1–32; 25:1–26:32). The legitimacy of the postexilic temple and its personnel is established by virtue of its continuity with the temple built by Solomon under the sponsorship of David (17:24; 2 Chron 6:7–9).

CHRONOLOGY, NEW TESTAMENT

The science of determining the dates of the NT books and the historical events mentioned in them. NT chronology naturally falls into two parts: the life of Christ and the apostolic age.

I. Life of Christ. The erection of a chronology of the life of Christ turns around three points: his birth, baptism, and crucifixion. Luke's statement of the age of Jesus at his baptism (Luke 3:23) links the first two, while the problem of the length of the ministry links the second and third.

The Christian era, now used for civil chronology, was introduced at Rome by Abbot Dionysius Exiguus in the sixth century. It is now generally agreed that the beginning of the era should have been fixed at least four years later.

According to the Gospels, Jesus was born some time before the death of Herod the Great. Josephus, the Jewish historian who was born A.D. 37, affirms (*Antiq.* 17.6.4) that Herod died shortly after an eclipse of the moon, which is astronomically fixed at March 12–13, 4 B.C. His death occurred shortly before Passover, which that year fell on April 4. Jesus was born at least some months before Her-

Chronological Chart of the New Testament

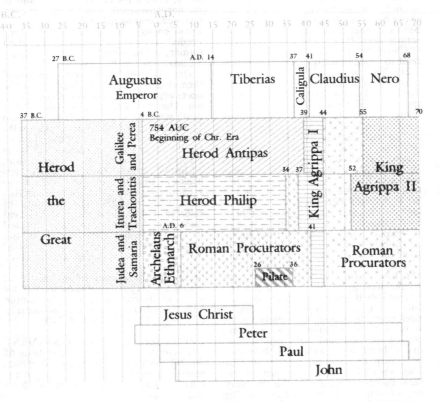

od's death. Christ's presentation in the temple after he was 40 days old (Lev 12:1–8; Luke 2:22–24) means that the wise men came at least six weeks after his birth. The time spent in Egypt is uncertain, perhaps several months. Thus, the birth of Jesus should be placed in the latter part of the year 5 B.C.

Luke gives the age of Jesus at his baptism as "about thirty years" (Luke 3:23). If he was born in the latter part of 5 B.C., his baptism then occurred near the close of A.D. 26 or the beginning of 27. The 40-day period of the temptation, plus the events recorded in John 1:19–2:12 seem to require that the baptism occurred at least three months before the first Passover of his public ministry (John 2:13–22). Since Herod began the reconstruction of the temple in 20 B.C., the "forty and six years" mentioned by the Jews during this Passover, using the inclusive Jewish count, again brings us to A.D. 27 for this first Passover.

The time of the Crucifixion will be determined by the length of the ministry of Jesus. John's Gospel explicitly mentions three Passovers (John 2:23; 6:4; 11:55). If the feast of John 5:1 is also a Passover, as seems probable (a view having the traditional backing of Irenaeus), then the length of the ministry of Jesus was over three years. This places the Crucifixion at the Passover of A.D. 30.

II. Apostolic Age. The death of Herod Agrippa I (Acts 12:23) took place in A.D. 44, the year of Peter's arrest and miraculous escape from prison. The proconsulship of Gallio (18:12) was between May 51 and 52, or May 52 and 53. So Paul's ministry at Corinth began in late 49 or 50. From inconclusive data, advocates have argued for a date as early as 55 and as late as 60 or 61 for Festus' accession as governor. The balance of the arguments seem to point to 60 or perhaps 59. If the latter, the suggested dates should be adjusted accordingly.

CHRONOLOGY, OLD TESTAMENT

The chronological problem of the OT is one of the availability of evidence, of the correct evaluation and interpretation of that evidence, and of its proper application.

I. From the Creation to the Flood. In this period the only biblical data are the ages of the patriarchs in Genesis 7:11 and the genealogical tables of Genesis5. Calculations of the years from Adam to the Flood vary: 1,656 (Masoretic Text), 1,307 (Samaritan Pentateuch), and 2,242 (LXX). Extrabiblical sources for this period are almost completely lacking.

II. The Flood to Abraham. Reckoning the age of Terah at the birth of Abraham as 70 (Gen 11:26), the years from the Flood to Abraham would be 292 according to the MT, 942 according to the Samaritan Pentateuch, and 1,172 according to the LXX. But if the age of Terah at Abraham's birth is reckoned as 130 years (on the basis of Gen 11:32; 12:4; Acts 7:4), the above totals would be raised by 60 years. On this basis, the Hebrew text would give 352 years from the Flood to Abraham, and the Greek would be 1,232. Extrabiblical materials from the Flood to Abraham are of little assistance in the establishment of an absolute chronology for this period. Because of the difficulties involved, it must be admitted that the construction of an absolute chronology from Adam to Abraham is not now possible on the basis of the available data.

III. Abraham to Moses. Since Abraham was 75 years old at the time of his entrance into Canaan (Gen 12:4), and since he was 100 at the birth of Isaac (21:5), there were 25 years from the entry into Canaan to Isaac. Isaac was 60 at the birth of Jacob (25:26), and Jacob was 130 at his entrance into Egypt (47:9, 28), making 215 years from the beginning of the sojourn in Canaan to the beginning of the stay in Egypt. The total length of the sojourn was 430 years (Exod 12:40). Did this involve only the sojourn in Egypt or did it include also the sojourn in Canaan? If Israel was in Egypt 430 years, there were 645 years from the entrance into Canaan to Moses' departure from Egypt. However, if the 430 years includes the time spent by the patriarchs in Canaan, the length of the Egyptian sojourn would have been only 215 years.

On the basis of the OT data it is impossible to give a categorical answer as to exactly what was involved in the 430-year sojourn, nor is it possible to give an absolute date for Abraham's entry into Canaan. Paul regarded the 430 years as beginning at the time when the promises were made to Abraham (Gen 12:1–4) and terminating with the giving of the law at Sinai (Gal 3:16–17). On this basis the date of the entry into Canaan and the beginning of the sojourn was 1875 B.C.

An Exodus date of 1445 calls for 1405 as the beginning of the conquest (Num 33:38; Deut 1:3; Josh 5:6). According to these dates the Exodus took place during the reigns of the famous rulers of Egypt's Eighteenth Dynasty (c. 1570–1325). This fits in well with the Habiru inroads of the Amarna period and with the evidence of Israel's presence in Palestine during the Nineteenth Dynasty (c. 1325–1200). In view of recent evidence of a sedentary occupation of Trans-Jordan from the end of the Middle Bronze Age (c. 1550) to the end of the Late Bronze Age (c. 1250), the view is no longer tenable that nonoccupation of that area from the eighteenth to the thirteenth centuries B.C. makes a fifteenth-century date for the Exodus impossible.

IV. The Conquest to the Kingdom. Many attempts have been made to set dates for the judges, but, with the data now available, absolute certainty regarding the chronology for this period is impossible. Here are the data:

	Years
Oppression under Cushan-Risha-thaim (Judg 3:8)	8
Deliverance under Othniel; peace (Judg 3:11)	40
Oppression under Eglon of Moab (Judg 3:14)	18
Deliverance by Ehud; peace (Judg 3:30)	80
Oppression under Jabin of Hazor (Judg 4:3)	20
Deliverance under Deborah; peace (Judg 5:31)	40
Oppression under Midian (Judg 6:1)	7
Deliverance under Gideon; peace (Judg 8:28)	40
Reign of Abimelech (Judg 9:22)	3
Judgeship of Tola (Judg 10:2)	23
Judgeship of Jair (Judg 10:3)	22
Oppression of Gilead by Ammon (Judg 10:8)	18
Judgeship of Jephthah (Judg 12:7)	6
Judgeship of Ibzan (Judg 12:9)	7
Judgeship of Elon (Judg 12:11)	10
Judgeship of Abdon (Judg 12:14)	8

The Kings of Israel and Judah

ISRAEL			JUDAH		
Ruler	Overlapping Reign	Reign	Ruler	Overlapping Reign	Reign
Jeroboam I		931/30–910/9	Rehoboam		931/30–913
Nadab		910/9 –909/8	Abijam		913 –911/10
Baasha		909/8 –886/85	Asa		911/10–870/69
Elah		886/85–885/84	Jehoshaphat	873/72–870/69	870/69–848
Zimri		885/84	Jehoram	853 –848	848 –841
Tibni		885/84–880	Ahaziah		841
Omri		885/84–880	Athaliah		841 –835
Ahab		874/73–853	Joash		835 –796
Ahaziah		853 –852	Amaziah		796 –767
Joram		852 –841	Azariah	972/91–767	767 –740/39
Jehu		841 –814/13	(Uzziah)		
Jehoahaz		814/13–798	Jotham	750 –740/39	740/39–732/31
Jehoash		798 –782/81			
Jeroboam II	793/92–782/81	782/81–753	Ahaz	735 –732/31	732/31–716/15
Zachariah		753 –752			
Shallum		752	Hezekiah		716/15–687/86
Menahem		752 –742/41	Manasseh	697/96–687/86	687/86–643/42
Pekahiah		742/41–740/39	Amon		643/42–641/40
Pekah		752 –740/39	Josiah		641/40–609
Hoshea		732/31–723/22	Jehoahaz		609
			Jehoiakim		609 –598
			Jehoiachin		598 –597
			Zedekiah		597 –586

Oppression under the Philistines (Judg 13:1)	40
Judgeship of Samson (Judg 15:20 16:31)	20
Judgeship of Eli (1 Sam 4:18)	40
Judgeship of Samuel (1 Sam 7:2)	20

The sum of the above numbers is 470 years. However, it seems clear that we can subtract the 20 years of Samson's judgeship, because that period is included in the 40 years of oppression under the Philistines—he "led Israel for twenty years in the days of the Philistines" (Judg 15:20). This results in the grand total of 450 years for the period of the judges, the same number given by the apostle Paul when he spoke of this period in his speech in the synagogue at Antioch in Pisidia (Acts 13:20).

V. The United Monarchy. Paul says Saul reigned 40 years (Acts 13:21); he must have been very young when he took the throne (1 Sam 13:1–2; 2 Sam 5:4). The reign of David, on the other hand, may be regarded as a full 40 years, for he reigned 7 years in Hebron and 33 in Jerusalem (2 Sam 5:4–5; 1 Kings 2:11; 1 Chron 3:4), and one event is dated in the 40th year (1 Chron 26:31). Solomon began his 40-year reign probably shortly before the death of David (1 Kings 1:32–48).

VI. The Divided Monarchy. An abun-

dance of data and four biblical yardsticks are here provided—the lengths of reign of the rulers of Judah and those of Israel, and the synchronisms of Judah with Israel and of Israel with Judah. Furthermore, a number of synchronisms with the fixed years of contemporary Assyria make possible a check with an exact chronological yardstick and make possible the establishment of absolute years B.C. for the period of the kings. The years of the kings based on the above principles are listed above.

VII. The Exile and Return. Babylon fell to the Persians October 12, 539 B.C., and Cyrus in the first year of his reign issued a decree permitting the Jews to return and rebuild the temple (2 Chron 36:22; Ezra 1:1), 538 or 537 B.C. The temple was completed on the third of Adar, the sixth year of Darius (Ezra 6:15), March 12, 515.

The return of Ezra from Babylon was begun the first day of the first month, in the seventh year of Artaxerxes (Ezra 7:7, 9). Artaxerxes came to the throne in December, 465 B.C., and this would bring the first of Nisan of his seventh year on April 8, 458, according to Persian reckoning, but on March 27, 457, according to Judean years.

Word was brought to Nehemiah of the sad state of affairs at Jerusalem in the month Kislev of the 20th year of Artaxerxes (Neh 1:1), and in Nisan (March/April) 444 B.C. Nehemiah stood before Artaxerxes and received permission to return to Jerusalem to rebuild the city (2:1–8). That was April, 444 B.C. With Nehemiah's return to Babylon in the 32nd year of Artaxerxes (13:6), 433/432 B.C., the chronology of the OT proper comes to a close.

CHRYSOLITE (See MINERALS)

CHRYSOPRASE (See MINERALS)

CHURCH The English word derives from the Greek *kuriakos* (belonging to the Lord), but it stands for another Greek word *ekklēsia* (whence "ecclesiastical"), denoting an assembly. This is used in its general sense in Acts 19:32, but had already been applied in the LXX as an equivalent for the "congregation" of the OT (cf. 7:38), and in this sense it is adopted to describe the new gathering or congregation of Jesus' disciples.

In the Gospels the term is found only in Matthew 16:18 and 18:17. This scarceness is perhaps explained by the fact that both these verses seem to envisage a situation that would follow Christ's earthly ministry. Yet the verses show that Christ has this reconstitution in view, that the church thus reconstituted will rest on the apostolic confession, and that it will take up the ministry of reconciliation.

When we turn to Acts, the situation changes. The saving work has been fulfilled, and the NT church can thus have its birthday at Pentecost. The term is now used regularly to describe local groups of believers. Thus, we read of the church at Jerusalem (Acts 5:11), at Antioch (13:1), and at Caesarea (18:22). At the same time the word is used for all believers (possibly 9:31). From the outset the church has both a local and a general significance, denoting both the individual assembly and the world-wide community.

This twofold usage is also seen in Paul. He addresses his letters to specific churches (e.g., 1 Cor 1:2; 1 Thess 1:1). Indeed, he seems sometimes to localize further by referring to specific groups within the local community as churches, as though sending greetings to congregations within the one city (e.g., Rom 16:5). Yet Paul also develops more fully the concept of a church that consists of all believers in all local churches (1 Cor 10:32; Col 1:18; 1 Tim 3:15; especially Eph). The other NT books give us mostly examples of the local usage (e.g., 3 John 9; Rev 1:4; 2:1).

The church is not primarily a human structure like a political, social, or economic organism. It is basically the church of Jesus Christ (Matt 16:18), of the living God (1 Tim 3:15). It is a building of which Jesus Christ is the chief cornerstone or foundation (Eph 2:20–22), the fellowship of saints or people of God (1 Peter 2:9), the bride of Christ (Eph 5:25–26), and the body of Christ, he being the head and Christians the members (Rom 12:5; 1 Cor 12:12–13; Eph 4:4, 12, 15–17). As the body, it is the fullness of Christ, who himself fills all in all (Eph 1:23).

The church draws its life from Jesus Christ by the Holy Spirit; but it does so through the Word, from which it gets life (James 1:18) and by which it is nourished and sanctified (Eph 5:26; 1 Peter 2:2). Its function is to pass on the Word so that others may also be quickened and cleansed. It is to preach the gospel (Mark 16:15), to take up the ministry of reconciliation (2 Cor 5:19), and to dispense the mysteries of God (1 Cor 4:1).

Finally, the church's work is not merely for the salvation of people; it is primarily to the praise of God's glory (Eph 1:6; 2:7). Hence neither the church nor its function ceases with the completion of its earthly task. There is ground, therefore, for the old distinction between the church triumphant and the church militant. All the church is triumphant in its true reality. But the warring and wayfaring church is still engaged in conflict between the old reality and the new. Its destiny, however, is to be brought into full conformity to the Lord (1 John 3:2). Toward this it moves hesitantly yet expectantly, confident in its future glory when it will be wholly the church triumphant as graphically depicted in Revelation 7:9ff., enjoying its full reality as the bride and body of the Lord.

CHUZA (See CUZA)

CILICIA (sĭ-lĭsh′ĭ-à, Gr. *Kilikia*). A country in SE Asia Minor, bounded on the north and west by the Taurus range, and on the south by the Mediterranean. It had two parts, the western one called the Rugged; the eastern one, the Plain Cilicia, the chief city of which was Tarsus, the birthplace of Paul (Acts 21:39; 22:3; 23:34). It became a Roman province in 100 B.C. One of its governors was Cicero, the orator (51–50). Cilicia is accessible by land only by way of its two famous mountain passes, the Cilician Gates and the Syrian Gates. Jews from Cilicia dis-

The Cilician Gates at Tarsus, a formidable pass through the Taurus range of mountains. Paul and his companions traveled through this pass on their missionary journeys. Courtesy Dan Bahat

puted with Stephen (Acts 6:9). The gospel reached it early (15:23), probably through Paul (9:30; Gal 1:21). On Paul's second missionary journey he confirmed the churches that had been established there (Acts 15:41), and on his way to Rome as a prisoner he sailed over the sea of Cilicia (27:5).

CINNAMON (See PLANTS)

CIRCUMCISION (sĭr'kŭm-sĭ'shŭn, Lat. *a cutting around*). The cutting off of the foreskin, a custom that still prevails among many peoples in different parts of the world—in Asia, Africa, America, and Australia. In ancient times it was practiced among the western Semites— Hebrews, Arabians, Moabites, Ammonites, Edomites, and Egyptians, but not among the Babylonians, Assyrians, Canaanites, and Philistines. There can be no doubt that it was at first a religious act.

Among the Hebrews the rite was instituted by God as the sign of the covenant between him and Abraham, shortly after the latter's sojourn in Egypt. God ordained that it be performed on Abraham, on his posterity and slaves, and on foreigners joining themselves to the Hebrew nation (Gen 17:12). Every male child was to be circumcised on the eighth day. In later times a Hebrew surgeon was called in. The child was also named at the ceremony.

According to the terms of the covenant symbolized by circumcision, the Lord undertook to be the God of Abraham and his descendants, and they were to belong to him, worshiping and obeying only him. The rite effected admission to the fellowship of the covenant people and secured for the individual, as a member of the nation, his share in the promises God made to the nation as a whole. Circumcision reminded the Israelites of God's promises to them and of the duties they had assumed. The prophets often reminded them that the outward rite, to have any significance, must be accompanied by a "circumcision of the heart" (Lev 26:41; Deut 30:6; Jer 9:25–26; Ezek 44:7). Paul used the word *concision* for this outward circumcision not accompanied by a spiritual change. In the early history of the Christian church, Judaizing Christians argued for the necessity of circumcising Gentiles who came into the church; Paul (Gal 5:2) and the Jerusalem Council (Acts 15) insisted that the signs of the old covenant could not be forced on the children of the new covenant.

CISTERN (Heb. *bō'r* or *bôr*). An artificial tank or reservoir dug in the earth or rock for the collection and storage of rain water, or, sometimes, of spring water brought from a distance by a conduit. A cistern is distinguished from a pool by always being covered. Cisterns were very numerous in Palestine. The long, dry, rainless summers, lasting from May to September, and the small annual precipitation, together with a lack of natural springs, made the people largely dependent on rain water. The temple area in Jerusalem had at least 37 great cisterns, one of them holding between two and three million gallons (8 and 11 million liters). Public rock-cut cisterns were made within the city walls so that the inhabitants could hold out in time of siege.

Besides the large public cisterns, there were many smaller private ones. Ancient sites are honeycombed with them. All cisterns had one or more openings for drawing water to the surface. Empty cisterns were sometimes used as prisons. Joseph was cast into one (Gen 37:22), and Jeremiah was let down into one with a muddy bottom (Jer 38:6). Zechariah 9:11 alludes to the custom of confining prisoners in an empty cistern.

Cities
of
Refuge

Kedesh
Acco
•Golan
Dor
Beth
Shan•
•Ramoth
Shechem•
Peniel
Gezer
•Gibeon
•Bezer
Heshbon
Hebron•
The six cities
of refuge are
shown in bold type.
Beersheba•
Miles 10 5 0   10   20
Kms 105 0   10   20   30

CITADEL A fortification in a Hebrew town. The term should probably be applied only to the final defense unit of a city. This might include the palace (1 Kings 16:18) or sometimes the temple (Neh 2:8). See also CASTLE.

CITIES OF REFUGE Six cities, three on each side of the Jordan, set apart by Moses and Joshua as places of asylum for those who had committed manslaughter. Those east of the Jordan were Bezer in Reuben, Ramoth Gilead in Gad, and Golan in Manasseh (Deut 4:41–43); those west of the Jordan were Hebron in Judah, Shechem in Ephraim, and Kedesh in Naphtali (Josh 20:7–8). To shelter the person guilty of manslaughter from the "avenger of blood," provision was made that the principal roads leading to these cities should always be kept open. No part of Palestine was more than 30 miles (50 km.) away from a city of refuge—a distance that could easily be covered in one day. Cities of refuge were provided to protect a person until his case could be properly decided. The right of asylum was only for those who had taken life unintentionally. Willful murderers were put to death at once.

The regulations concerning these cities of refuge are found in Numbers 35; Deuteronomy 19:1–13; and Joshua 20. If one guilty of unintentional killing reached a city of refuge before the avenger of blood could kill him, he was given asylum until a fair trial could be held. The trial took place where the accused had lived. If proved innocent of willful murder, he was brought back to the city of refuge. There he had to stay until the death of the high priest. After that he was free to return to his own home. But if during that period he passed beyond the limits of the city of refuge, the avenger of blood could kill him and not be blamed. See also AVENGER.

CITIES OF THE PLAIN (Heb. *kikkar hayardēn, circle of the Jordan*). Cities near the Dead Sea, including Sodom, Gomorrah, Admah, Zeboiim, and Zoar (Gen 13:10–12). Lot decided to dwell in the cities of the plain and pitched his tent near Sodom. Abraham delivered Lot when the cities were attacked and Lot taken captive (Gen 14). God destroyed the cities because of their wickedness (Gen 19). It is believed that the south end of the Dead Sea covers the site. Sodom and Gomorrah are often used as a warning example of sin and divine punishment (Deut 29:23; Isa 1:9; 3:9; Jer 50:40; Ezek 16:46; Matt 10:15; Rom 9:29).

CITIZENSHIP (Gr. *politeuma, commonwealth*). In the NT the word for citizen often means nothing more than the inhabitant of a country (Luke 15:15; 19:14). Among the ancient Jews emphasis was placed on Israel as a religious organization, not on relationship to city and state. The good citizen was the good Israelite, one who followed not just civil law but religious law. Non-Israelites had the same protection of the law as native Israelites, but they were required not to perform acts hurting the religious feelings of the people. The advantage of a Jew over a Gentile was thus strictly spiritual. He was a member of the theocracy.

Among the Romans, citizenship brought the right to be considered equal to natives of the city of Rome. Emperors sometimes granted it to whole provinces and cities, and also to single individuals for services rendered to the state or to the imperial family, or even for a certain sum of money. Roman citizens were exempted from shameful punishments, such as scourging and crucifixion, and they had the right of appeal to the emperor with certain limitations.

Paul had become a Roman citizen by birth. Either his father or some other ancestor had acquired the right and had transmitted it to his son. He was proud of his Roman citizenship and when occasion demanded, availed himself of his rights. When writing to the Philippians, who were members of a Roman colony and therefore Roman citizens, Paul emphasized that Christians are citizens of a heavenly commonwealth and ought to live accordingly (Phil 1:27; 3:20).

CITRON (See PLANTS)

Sketch of the Roman emperor Claudius, drawn from a statue now in the Vatican in Rome. Claudius is mentioned twice in the New Testament (Acts 11:28; 18:2). Courtesy Carta, Jerusalem

CITY In ancient times cities owed their origin, not to organized manufacture, but to agriculture. Cities were built in areas where agriculture could be carried on, usually on the side of a mountain or the top of a hill, and where a sufficient supply of water was assured. The names of cities often indicate the feature that determined the selection of the site. For example, the prefixes *Beer*, meaning "well," and *En*, meaning "spring," in such names as Beersheba and En Gedi, show a local well or spring was nearby. Names like Ramah, Mizpah, and Gibeah (all from roots indicating height) were very common in Palestine, indicating that a site on an elevation was preferred for a city. A ruling family sometimes gave its name to a city (*Beth*, meaning "house of").

Smaller villages sought the protection of nearby cities. That is the meaning of the expression, added to the name of a city, "and its surrounding settlements" (Num 21:25; 32:42). In return for the protection offered against nomadic attacks, the cities received payment in service and produce.

The chief feature distinguishing a city from a village was that it had a wall (Lev 25:29–30). Walls 20 and 30 feet (6 to 9 m.) thick were not unusual. The wall had one or more gates that were closed during the night (Josh 2:5, 7), and in later times on the sabbath (Neh 13:19). The gates were strengthened with iron or bronze

bars and bolts (Deut 3:5; Judg 16:3) and had rooms overhead (2 Sam 18:24). From the top of the wall or from a tower by the gate, a watchman was on the lookout for approaching danger (Jer 6:17). The gates were approached by narrow roads easy to defend.

Within the walls, the important features of a city were the stronghold or fortress, the high place, the broad place by the gate, and the streets. The stronghold was an inner fort protected by a garrison to which the inhabitants could run when the outer walls were taken by an enemy. The people of Shechem tried unsuccessfully to hold out against Abimelech in such a stronghold (Judg 9:49), and the king was afterward killed by a woman who dropped a stone from the tower within the city of Thebez (Judg 9:50, 53). When David captured the fortress of Zion, the whole city came into his possession (2 Sam 5:7). Sometimes towers abutted the inside of the city wall.

The high place was an important part of every Canaanite city and retained its place in Palestine to the time of Solomon's reign (1 Sam 9:12ff.). There sacrifices were offered and feasts held. Originally they were on an elevation, but the term became the general one for any local sanctuary even when it was on level ground.

Little is known about how city government was organized and administered. In Deuteronomy 16:18 and 19:12 mention is made of elders and judges. Samaria had a governor (1 Kings 22:26). Jerusalem must have had several high officials (2 Kings 23:8).

CITY OF DAVID 1. The Jebusite fortress of Zion that David captured and named the city of David (2 Sam 5:7, 9; 1 Kings 8:1; 1 Chron 11:5, 7; 2 Chron 5:2). It stood on a ridge near the later site of the temple. David made it his royal residence. **2.** Bethlehem, the home of David (Luke 2:4).

CLAUDIUS (klô'dĭ-ŭs). The fourth Roman emperor (A.D. 41–54). He was a nephew of Tiberius, the second Roman emperor. Herod Agrippa I, grandson of Herod the Great, had assisted him considerably in his advancement to the throne, and in consequence was given the whole of Palestine. Claudius gave the Jews throughout the empire the right of religious worship, but later he banished all Jews from Rome (Acts 18:2; cf. Suet. *Claud.* 25). The famine foretold by Agabus took place in the reign of Claudius (11:28).

CLAUDIUS LYSIAS (klô'dĭ-ŭs lĭs'ĭ-ăs). A chief captain who rescued Paul from fanatical Jewish rioters at Jerusalem (Acts 21:31; 24:22). He was a Greek, as his second name shows. He was a chiliarch (i.e., leader of 1,000 men), in charge of the Roman garrison of Jerusalem, stationed in the Castle of Antonia, adjoining the temple. When Paul informed him that he was a Roman citizen and therefore could not legally be scourged, Claudius told Paul that he had purchased his Roman citizenship with a "big price" (22:28). To protect Paul, he soon afterward sent him to Caesarea to see Felix, the Roman governor.

CLAY Clay was widely used in OT times for the making of brick, mortar, and pottery, and, in some countries, for the making of tablets on which inscriptions were impressed (see CLAY TABLETS). Babylon was made wholly of brick, either baked or dried in the sun. Nineveh, the capital of Assyria, was made mostly of brick. The villages of Egypt were constructed of sun-dried clay.

CLAY TABLETS In ancient times writing was done on papyrus, parchment, potsherds, and clay tablets. The latter were made of clean-washed, smooth clay. While still wet, the clay had wedge-shaped letters (now called "cuneiform" from Latin *cuneus*, "wedge") imprinted on it with a stylus, and then was kiln fired or sun dried. Tablets were made of various shapes—cone-shaped, drum-shaped, and flat. They were often placed in a clay envelope. Vast quantities of these have been excavated in the Near East, of which about 500,000 are yet to be read. It is estimated that 99 percent of the Babylonian tablets have yet to be dug. The tablets reveal details of everyday life in the Near East and shed light on customs mentioned in the OT. Some tell the story of the Creation, the Fall, and the Flood. They do much to verify the truth of the biblical record.

CLEAN (Heb. *tahor*, Gr. *hagnos, katharos*). The division found in the OT between clean and unclean was fundamental for Israelites. They were to be physically clean (Exod 19:10ff.; 30:18–21), ritually and ceremonially clean (having offered the right sacrifices and been through the correct ceremonies [e.g., Lev 14:1ff.; 15:1ff.; Mark 1:44; Acts 21:26]), and morally clean (Ps 51:7). The NT emphasis is on the clean heart and pure life. Jesus condemned the obsession with external purity with no related emphasis on internal purity and wholeness (Mark

7:1–23). By his atoning work Jesus cleanses believers from all sin (Eph 5:25–26; 1 John 1:7). As High Priest, Jesus cleanses the heart as well as the body (Heb 10:2, 21–22). So believers are to be pure in heart (Matt 5:8; 1 Tim 1:5) and chaste in life (1 Tim 4:12; 5:2). It is their duty to purify themselves (1 Peter 2:22; 1 John 3:3). See also UNCLEAN.

CLEANTHES (klē-ăn'thēz). Son of Phanius of Assos and head of the Stoic school from 263 to 232 B.C. He taught that the universe was a living being and God its soul. He taught disinterestedness in ethics, and that evil thoughts were worse than evil deeds. His *Hymn to Zeus*, a surviving poem, contains the words quoted by Paul in Athens (Acts 17:28).

CLEMENT (klĕm'ĕnt). A Christian who labored with Paul at Philippi (Phil 4:3). It is uncertain whether he was in Philippi when Paul wrote. Origen identifies him with the church father who afterward became bishop of Rome and wrote a letter to the Corinthian church, but if he is right, Clement must have lived to an extreme old age.

CLEOPAS (klē'ō-păs). One of the two disciples to whom the Lord appeared on the afternoon of the resurrection day. They walked with him on the road from Jerusalem to Emmaus, about 7 miles (12 km.) away (Luke 24:18). He is not to be confused with the Clopas (Cleophas, KJV) mentioned in John 19:25, although some church fathers assumed that the two were identical.

CLEOPHAS (See CLOPAS)

CLERK (See OCCUPATIONS AND PROFESSIONS)

CLOAK (See DRESS)

CLOPAS (klō'păs). Mentioned in John 19:25 (KJV, Cleophas) as the husband of Mary, one of the women who stood beside the cross and who is described as a sister of the mother of Jesus. He is not the same as the Cleopas who walked with Jesus to Emmaus (Luke 24:18).

CLOSET (Gr. *tameion*). This most probably refers to a special storage closet in which bedding was stored during the day. If required, it could also be used as a sleeping-room or for private conference. Our Lord advised that it be used for private prayer (Matt 6:6; Luke 12:3 KJV).

CLOTH, CLOTHES, CLOTHING (See DRESS)

CLOUD Few biblical references suggest that clouds have anything to do with actual weather conditions, because in Palestine the weather is not very varied. There were two recognized seasons: a rainy one from October to April, and one of sunshine from May to September. Most Scripture references to clouds are metaphorical or figurative. They symbolize transitoriness (Job 30:15; Hos 6:4 KJV; "mist" in NIV), mystery (Job 3:5; 38:9; Ps 97:2), the unattainable (Job 20:6; Ps 147:8; Isa 14:14) and God's presence (Exod 19:9; 24:16; 34:5; 40:36; Ps 78:14; Isa 19:1; Nah 1:3). A cloud appeared at our Lord's transfiguration (Matt 17:5) and at his ascension (Acts 1:9), and it has a place in his prediction of his coming again (Matt 24:30; 26:64).

CLOUD, PILLAR OF A symbol of the presence and guidance of God in the Israelites' wilderness journey (Exod 13:21–22). At night it became fire. When God wanted Israel to rest in any place, the cloud rested on the tabernacle above the atonement cover (KJV "mercy seat") (Lev 16:2) at the door of the tabernacle (33:9–10; Num 12:5), or it covered the tabernacle (Exod 40:34–38).

CNIDUS (nī'dŭs). A free city of Caria at the SW corner of Asia Minor, past which Paul sailed on his journey to Rome (Acts 27:7). It had two excellent harbors. Jews lived there as early as the second century B.C. Only ruins are left of a once-flourishing city, especially noted for its temple of Venus and a statue of the goddess by Praxiteles.

COAL Often found in the English Bible, the word never refers to true mineral coal, which has not been found in Palestine proper. The half dozen Hebrew and Greek words rendered "coal" refer either to charcoal or to live embers of any kind. Charcoal was used by the Hebrews to provide warmth in winter (Isa 47:14; John 18:18), for cooking (Isa 44:19; John 21:9), and for blacksmith work (Isa 44:12; 54:16).

Frequently the word is used metaphorically (Prov 26:21). The heaping coals of fire on the head of an enemy (Prov 25:22; Rom 12:20), is not meant to suggest the pain of punishment but the softening of the enemy's heart as he thinks with burning shame of his unworthy hatred. Love will melt and purify.

COAT (See DRESS)

COAT OF MAIL (See ARMS AND ARMOR)

COBRA (See ANIMALS)

COCK (See BIRDS)

COCKATRICE (See ANIMALS)

COCK CROWING When referring to time, this is the third of the four watches into which the Romans divided the night (evening, midnight, cock crowing, and morning)—between midnight and 3 a.m. (Matt 26:34; Mark 13:35). NIV reads "rooster."

COCKLE (See PLANTS)

Thirteenth-century B.C. anthropoid coffin, stylistically similar to the mummy-cases found in Egypt, from Deir el-Balah in the Gaza region. Courtesy Zev Radovan

COFFIN This word is used only in Genesis 50:26; Luke 7:14 (NIV "coffin," KJV has "bier"). Coffins were unknown among the Israelites, who were carried to the grave on a bier, a simple flat board with two or three staves. In Egypt, where Joseph died, the dead were embalmed and put in a mummy case.

COIN (See MONEY)

COL-HOZEH (kŏl-hō'zĕ, *all-seeing one*). A Judahite of Nehemiah's day whose son Shallum rebuilt the fountain gate of Jerusalem (Neh 3:15; 11:5).

COLLAR (See DRESS)

COLONY (Gr. *kolōnia*, a transliteration of the Latin *colonus, farmer*). In the only occurrence of the word in the NT, Acts 16:12, Philippi is mentioned as a colony. A colony was a settlement of Roman citizens, authorized by the government, in conquered territory. The settlers were usually retired Roman soldiers, who settled in places where they could keep enemies of the empire in check. They were the aristocracy of the provincial towns where they lived. Such colonies had the rights of Italian cities: municipal self-government and exemption from poll and land taxes.

COLOSSE (kŏ-lŏs′ē, Gr. *Kolossai*). An ancient city of Phrygia, situated about 11 miles (18 km.) from Laodicea and 13 (21 km.) from Hierapolis. Colosse stood on the most important trade route from Ephesus to the Euphrates and was a place of great importance from early times. The church at Colosse was established on Paul's third missionary journey, during his three years in Ephesus, not by Paul himself (Col 2:1), but by Epaphras (1:7, 12–13). Archippus also exercised a fruitful ministry there (4:17; Philem 2). Philemon was an active member of this church as was Onesimus (Col 4:9). During Paul's first Roman imprisonment Epaphras brought him a report of the religious views and practices in Colosse that called forth his letter, in which he rebuked the church for its errors.

COLOSSIANS, THE LETTER TO A letter written by the apostle Paul when he was a prisoner (Col 4:3, 10, 18), about the year A.D. 62, probably during his first imprisonment in Rome (Acts 28:30–31), though Caesarea (23:35; 24:27) and Ephesus have also been suggested. The external and internal evidence for its genuineness is all that can be desired. The church at Colosse was very likely founded during Paul's three-year stay in Ephesus on his third missionary journey. It appears from Colossians 2:1 that Paul himself had never preached in Colosse. Epaphras, a native of Colosse (Col 4:12), was probably converted under Paul's ministry at Ephesus and was then sent by the apostle to preach in his native city (1:7). The disturbing report of Epaphras on the condition of the church led Paul to write this letter.

In the few years since Paul had been in the province of Asia an insidious error had crept into the church at Colosse. The teaching attacked by Paul (Col 2:8, 16–23) was, at least in part, Judaistic, as is seen in his reference to circumcision (2:11; 3:11), ordinances (2:14), meats and drinks, feast days, new moons, and Sabbaths (2:16). It also contained a strong ascetic element. Special self-denying rules were given (2:16, 20–21) that had as their purpose the mortification of the body (2:23). Some sort of worship of angels was practiced—a worship that continued for several centuries, as we know from the fact that in the fourth century A.D. the Council of Laodicea condemned it in one of its canons, and in the fifth century Theodoret said that the archangel Michael was worshiped in the area. This heresy claimed to be a philosophy and made much of wisdom and knowledge (2:8). Plainly, the Colossians were beguiled by this religious syncretism and even took pride in it (2:8). Some find this teaching in Essenism; others in incipient Gnosticism or in contemporary Judaism with a syncretistic addition of local Phrygian ideas.

Paul met these errors by presenting the counter truth that Jesus Christ is the image of the invisible God (Col 1:15), in whom are hid all the treasures of wisdom and knowledge, and in whom the fullness of the divine perfections find their perfect embodiment (1:19). He is the creator of all, and all power is from him. On the cross he revealed the impotence of all the powers that had tried to thwart his purposes (2:15). Freedom from the corruption of human nature is found in the newness of life that the death and resurrection of Christ provide. The letter to the Colossians may be divided into four parts: (1) The salutation and thanksgiving (1:1–8); (2) the doctrinal section (1:9–2:5); (3) practical exhortations (2:6–4:6); (4) concluding salutations (4:7–18). Toward the end of the letter (4:16), Paul asks that the Colossian church exchange letters with the church at Laodicea, to which he has also written. It is likely that this letter to the Laodiceans is what we know as the letter to the Ephesians, sent as a circular letter to various churches in the Roman province of Asia.

COLT (See ANIMALS)

COMFORTER, THE (See ADVOCATE; HOLY SPIRIT)

COMMANDMENT The word is used in the English Bible to translate a number of Hebrew and Greek words meaning law, ordinance, statute, word, judgment, precept, saying, charge. The idea of authority conveyed by these words comes from the fact that God as sovereign Lord has a right to be obeyed. The instruction of Jesus is as authoritative as what was said by God in OT times, even though Jesus does not always use the word "commandment." What is said of God and Christ is also true of the apostles (1 Cor 14:37).

COMMANDMENTS, TEN The OT is distinctly a religion of law, with creed, cult, and conduct prescribed minutely by God. The Torah is revered because it embodies the will and wisdom of the Creator. Expressing God's own nature, it demands of the creature only what the Creator's holiness requires for fellowship with himself. The climax of Torah is the Decalogue, the Code of the Ten Words, received by Moses on Mt. Sinai. The Decalogue is unique among the several codes found in the OT. Originally spoken by God in a context calculated to produce unforgettable awe (Exod 19:9–25), it was afterward inscribed by his finger on two tables of stone (31:18)—and later on a second pair of stones (Deut 10:1–4). It was placed in the ark of the covenant (Exod 25:21) and thus enshrined at the very center of Israel's worship. It was repeated by Moses (Deut 5:6–21), and all of its precepts, with the exception of sabbath-keeping, are repeated in the NT.

The Ten Words, not numbered by God or Moses, have been numbered in different ways since then. The most common among English-speaking communities sees the first commandment as forbidding the worship of false deities, the second as prohibiting the use of idols, and the tenth as including all the prohibitions of covetousness.

There is uncertainty about how the Ten Words were divided between the two tables. The Roman Catholic church puts three commandments on the first table, seven on the second. The Reformed church adheres to a four and six classification. Josephus, however, gives the traditional five and five arrangement.

Is there any significance to the fact that the Ten Words are inscribed on two tables rather than one? Traditionally the "two tables" were thought to refer to two sections: our duty to God and our duty to man. Recent knowledge of ancient covenant forms has shown that the stipulations of the covenant—the laws imposed by the covenant-lord—were written in duplicate. The covenant-lord retained one copy and deposited the other in the sanctuary of the god of the people on whom he was imposing his covenant. In the case of the Decalogue, Yahweh is both Covenant-Lord and also God of Israel. He, therefore, takes both copies into his care: the whole care, continuance, and maintenance of the covenant relationship rests with him.

This Code was not "a yoke of slavery" (Gal 5:1) but a wise provision that God graciously made for his people—to enable the Israelites to enter into a life of

The Nash Papyrus, a second-century (c. 150) B.C. papyrus fragment written in square Hebrew script. It contains the Ten Commandments and was the oldest biblical text known until the discovery of the Dead Sea Scrolls. Courtesy Encyclopaedia Judaica Photo Archive, Jerusalem

joyful fellowship with their Redeemer. Used lawfully (1 Tim 1:8), this Code, which guided life rather than gave it, was a source of blessing (Pss 19:8–9; 119:54). Except as the NT deepens and extends its principles, the Decalogue represents the high-water level of morality.

CONANIAH (kŏn′ȧ-nī′ȧ, Heb. *kônany-āhû, Jehovah has founded*). **1.** A Levite in charge of tithes and offerings in the reign of Hezekiah (2 Chron 31:12–13; KJV "Cononiah"). **2.** A Levite in Josiah's reign (35:9).

CONCUBINE In the Bible, not a paramour, but a woman lawfully united in marriage to a man in a relation inferior to that of the regular wife. Concubinage is assumed and provided for in the law of

Moses, which tried to prevent its excesses and abuses (Exod 21:7–11; Deut 21:10–14). Concubines enjoyed only the right of lawful cohabitation. They had no authority in the family or in household affairs. Their husbands could send them away with a small present, and their children could, by means of small presents, be excluded from the heritage (Gen 25:6). The children were regarded as legitimate, although the children of the first wife were preferred in the distribution of the inheritance. Prominent OT figures who had concubines were Nahor (22:24), Abraham (25:6), Jacob (35:22), Eliphaz (36:12), Gideon (Judg 8:31), Saul (2 Sam 3:7), David (5:13; 15:16; 16:21), Solomon (1 Kings 11:3), Caleb (1 Chron 2:46), Manasseh (7:14), Rehoboam (2 Chron 11:21), Abijah (13:21), and Belshazzar (Dan 5:2).

CONDUIT (See AQUEDUCT)

CONEY(See ANIMALS)

CONFECTIONER (See OCCUPATIONS AND PROFESSIONS)

CONFESSION (Heb. *yādhâh*, Gr. *homologeō*, and their derivatives). To confess is to acknowledge the truth openly in anything, as in the existence and authority of God or the sins of which one has been guilty (e.g., Matt 5:24; Luke 17:4). Occasionally it also means to concede or allow (John 1:20; Acts 24:14; Heb 11:13), or to praise God by thankfully acknowledging him (Rom 14:11; Heb 13:15).

CONGREGATION (Heb. *'ēdhâh* and *qāhāl*, Gr. *ekklēsia* and *synagōgē*). The Hebrew people, in its collective capacity regarded as God's people or as an assembly of the people summoned for a definite purpose (1 Kings 8:65), or met on a festive occasion (Deut 23:1). Sometimes it refers to an assembly of the whole people, sometimes to a part (Exod 12:6, 47; 19:7–8; Lev 4:13; 8:4; Num 16:3; 25:6; Joel 2:15).

CONIAH (kō-nī'a, Heb. *konyāhû, Jehovah is creating*). A form of the name Jehoiachin, found in Jeremiah 22:24, 28; 37:1. See also JEHOIACHIN.

CONSCIENCE The OT has no separate word for "conscience," but it neither lacks the idea nor the means to express it. It is clear from Genesis 3:8 that the first result of the Fall was a guilty conscience, compelling Adam and Eve to hide from God. David's "heart smote him" (1 Sam 24:5 KJV, MLB, RSV); NIV interprets this as "David was conscience-stricken." In everyday Greek the word *syneidēsis* referred to the pain or guilt felt by persons who believed they had done wrong. Paul, who used the word more than other NT writers, refined and developed this meaning. (1) He described the universal existence of conscience (Rom 2:14–16) as the internal moral witness found in all human beings. (2) He believed that Christians should have clear and good consciences (2 Cor 1:12; 1 Tim 1:5, 19; 3:9). (3) Some Christians have a weak or partially formed conscience (1 Cor 8:1–13 and 10:23–11:1); in certain cases mature Christians are to restrict their liberty of action in order not to offend them. (4) Evil consciences are corrupted by false teaching (1 Tim 4:2; Titus 1:15). A person who rejects the gospel and resolutely opposes God has an evil conscience. (5) As a result of accepting the gospel, people receive a purified, or perfected, conscience (Heb 9:14; 10:22), through forgiveness and the gift of the Holy Spirit. While Paul's use of the word "conscience" is that of the internal witness of the mind and heart judging past actions in the light of Christian teaching, he also appears to suggest that the conscience will guide present and future actions (e.g., Rom 13:3; 1 Cor 10:25).

CONSECRATION An act by which a person or thing is dedicated to the service and worship of God. In the KJV it translates several Hebrew and Greek words of different meanings. (1) Hebrew *hāram*, "devote" (Mic 4:13, NIV "devote"). (2) Hebrew *nāzar, nēzer*, "separate" (Num 6:7, 8, 12, NIV "separation"). (3) Hebrew *qādhēsh*, "to be set apart" (i.e., from that which is common or unclean: Exod 28:3; 30:30; 2 Chron 26:18; 29:33). (4) Hebrew *millē' yadh*, literally, "to fill the hand," a peculiar idiom normally used for the installation of a priest into his office or of the installation offerings put into his hands (Exod 29:9, 29; Lev 8:33, NIV "ordain"). (5) Greek *teleioō*, "to make perfect" (Heb. 10:20, NIV "opened").

CONSOLATION (Gr. *paraklēsis, encouragement, comfort*). In the thought behind this word the "consolation of Israel" looked for by Simeon (Luke 2:25) is linked with the famous "comfort" associated with the fulfillment of the promises (Isa 40:1ff.). Yet "comfort" is more positive than "console," as can be seen in the description of the Holy Spirit as "the Comforter" (John 14:16–17 KJV), and of Barnabas as "Son of Encouragement" (Acts 4:36, RSV, NIV).

CONTEST (Gr. *athlēsis, fight*). The verb form is used in the NT in the sense of "to strive" or "to labor fervently"—in the good fight of faith (1 Tim 6:12), consistent intercessory prayer (Col 4:12), and the struggle to overcome (1 Cor 9:25). Metaphors from the Greek athletic games would appeal particularly to the Corinthians, for games were regularly held in their city.

CONVERSATION A word often used in KJV to translate various terms signifying conduct or manner of life, especially with respect to morals. The Greek words rendered "conversation" in Philippians 1:27 and 3:20 refer to "civil life" or "citizenship" (so NIV).

CONVERSION (Heb. *shûv*, Gr. *epistrophē*). A turning, literal or figurative, ethical or religious, either from God or, more frequently, to God. It implies both a turning *from* and a turning *to* something. In the NT it is sometimes associated with repentance (Acts 3:19; 26:20) and faith (11:21)—negatively turning from sin and positively believing in Christ (20:21). Although conversion is an act of man, it is brought about by the power of God (3:26).

CONVICTION (Gr. *elenchō, to convince or prove guilty*). Conviction is the first stage of repentance. Although the word "conviction" is never used in KJV, both Testaments give many illustrations of the experience. In the OT one of the most notable is found in Psalm 51, where David, realizing he has sinned against God, is overwhelmed with sorrow and cries out to God for forgiveness and cleansing. In the NT the central passage on conviction is John 16:7–11.

CONVOCATION (Heb. *mikrā'*). The word is used in the expression "holy convocation," but it is sometimes used alone (Num 10:2, RSV "congregation," NIV "community"; Isa 1:13). A convocation was a religious festival during which no work could be done. The holy convocations were the Sabbath days (Lev 23:1–3); Pentecost (23:15–21); the first and seventh days of the feast of unleavened bread (Exod 12:16; Lev 23:6–7); the first and tenth days of the seventh month, the latter being the Day of Atonement (Lev 23:24–28); and the first and eighth days of the Feast of Tabernacles (23:34–36). The phrase "solemn assembly" is applied only to the concluding festivals at the end of Passover and the Feast of Tabernacles.

COOS (See COS)

COPPER (See MINERALS)

COPPERSMITH (See OCCUPATIONS AND PROFESSIONS)

COR (See WEIGHTS AND MEASURES)

CORAL (See ANIMALS; MINERALS)

CORBAN (Heb. *qorbān, an offering*). In the Hebrew text of the OT the word refers to an offering or sacrifice, whether bloody or unbloody, made to God (Lev 1:2–3; 2:1; 3:1; Num 7:12–17). It is found in our English versions in the NT in Mark 7:11, where the one who vowed to dedicate money to God might actually keep it in his possession.

CORD (Heb. *hevel, yether, mêthār*, Gr. *schoinion*). Throughout the East in ancient times, ropes and cords were made of goat's or camel's hair spun into threads and then plaited or twisted into the larger and stronger form. Sometimes strips of skin from goats and cows were twisted together. Ropes for temporary fastenings were sometimes made from vines twisted together and also from the bark of the branches of the mulberry tree. Frequently the word is used in a figurative sense in the Bible (Job 36:8; Pss 129:4; 140:5; Prov 5:22; Eccl 4:12; Isa 5:18; 54:2).

CORIANDER (See PLANTS)

CORINTH (Gr. *Korinthos, ornament*). A city of Greece on the narrow isthmus between the Peloponnesus and the mainland. Under the Romans, Athens was still the educational center of Greece, but Corinth was the capital of the Roman province they called Achaia and was the most important city in the country. Land traffic between the north and south of Achaia had to pass the city, and much of the commerce between Rome and the East was brought to its harbors.

In Roman times Corinth was a city of wealth, luxury, and immorality. It had no rivals as a city of vice. "To live like a Corinthian" meant to live a life of profligacy and debauchery. It was customary in a stage play for a Corinthian to come on the scene drunk. The inhabitants were naturally devoted to the worship of Poseidon, since they drew so much of their wealth from the sea, but their greatest devotion was given to Aphrodite, the goddess of love. Her temple on the Acrocorinthus had more than a thousand *hierodouloi*—priestesses of vice not found in other shrines of Greece, and she attracted worshipers from all over the ancient world. The Isthmian games, held every two years, made Corinth a great center of Hellenic life.

Paul visited Corinth for the first time on

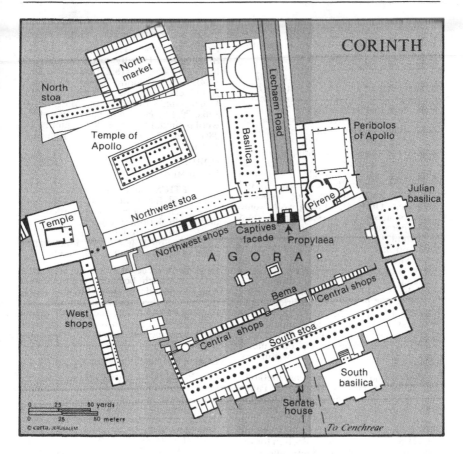

his second missionary journey (Acts 18). He became acquainted with Aquila and Priscilla, fellow Christians and, like himself, tentmakers. During his stay of a year and a half he resided in their home.

After Paul met with strong opposition from the Jews, he turned his attention to the Gentiles (Acts 18:6) and many were converted. The Jews brought an accusation before Gallio against Paul, charging that he was preaching a religion contrary to Roman law. Gallio, however, refused to admit the case to trial and dismissed them. Gallio's action was highly important, for it amounted to an authoritative decision by a highly placed Roman official that Paul's preaching could not be interpreted as an offense against Roman law. Paul left Corinth to go to Jerusalem and Antioch, on his way stopping off briefly at Ephesus.

Apollos was sent from Ephesus to Corinth and exercised an influential ministry there (Acts 18:27–28; 1 Cor 1:12). Paul later wrote two NT Epistles to that church and at least one other letter (1 Cor 5:9). Paul also wrote the letter to the Romans while in Corinth (Rom 16:23).

CORINTHIANS, 1 AND 2 The first letter to the Corinthians was written by Paul in Ephesus on his third missionary journey (Acts 19:1; 1 Cor 16:8, 19), probably in A.D. 56 or 57. He had previously written a letter to the Corinthians that has not come down to us; in it he had warned against associating with immoral persons (5:9). In reply Paul received a letter (5:10; 7:1; 8:1) in which they declared it was impossible to follow his advice without going out of the world altogether, and submitted to him a number of problems on which they asked his opinion. Meanwhile, Paul had heard of factions in the church (1:11). These various circumstances led to the writing of 1 Corinthians.

After the introductory salutation (1 Cor 1:1–9), Paul discusses (1) factionalism, (1:10–3:23), (2) his own ministry (ch 4), (3) incest (ch 5), (4) Christians taking Christians to heathen courts (ch 6), (5) Christian marriage (ch 7), (6) meat offered to idols (chs 8–10), (7) head covering for women (11:2–16), (8) proper observance of the Lord's Supper (11:17–34), (9) the use and abuse of spiritual gifts, especially tongues (chs 12–14), (10) the resurrection of the body (ch 15), and (11) collections for the poor saints in Jerusalem (16:1–3), closing with some remarks about his personal plans and some personal greetings (16:4–24).

Second Corinthians was written by Paul on his third missionary journey somewhere in Macedonia. Judaizing teachers had sought to discredit the apostle and had succeeded in turning the church as a whole against him. This revolt caused Paul to make a brief visit to Corinth (2 Cor 12:14; 13:1–2), but the visit did not restore his authority. Later, Titus brought Paul a report that Paul's authority was acknowledged once more; this report occasioned the writing of 2 Corinthians.

This second letter is the least methodical and the most personal of Paul's writings. It is very autobiographical and falls naturally into three main divisions: (1) some thoughts on the crisis through which the church has just passed (chs 1–7), (2) completion of the collection for the poor in Jerusalem (chs 8–9), and (3) a defense of Paul's ministry against the attacks of his enemies and a vindication of his apostleship (chs 10–13).

CORMORANT (See BIRDS)

CORN (See PLANTS)

CORNELIUS (kôr-nēl'yŭs, Gr. *Kornēlios, of a horn*). A "devout and God-fearing" centurion of the Italian Regiment (Acts 10:1–2). While stationed at Caesarea, in obedience to instructions received in a vision, he sent for Peter to learn from him how he and his household should be saved (11:14). Any doubts that Peter was acting improperly by sharing the message with this first Gentile convert are dispelled by the twofold consideration of Peter's preparatory vision (10:9–16) and the subsequent outpouring of the Holy Spirit on the household of Cornelius (10:44–47). On these grounds,

Peter defended his conduct before his critics at Jerusalem (11:1–18).

CORNERSTONE (Heb. *pinnâh*, Gr. *akrogōniaios*). Usually used figuratively (e.g., Job 38:6; Ps 118:22; Isa 28:16; Zech 10:4). The synoptic Gospels validate Jesus' claim to messiahship by citing Psalm 118:22 (Matt 21:42; Mark 12:10; Luke 20:17). Peter and Paul's use of the word is similar (see Rom 9:33, quoting Isa 28:16 and 8:14, following LXX; Eph 2:20; 1 Peter 2:6).

CORNET (See MUSIC AND MUSICAL INSTRUMENTS)

COSMETICS Any of the various preparations used for beautifying the hair and skin. Such practices were regarded with disfavor in Scripture (e.g., Jer 4:30; Ezek 23:36, 40). Jezebel, Ahab's wicked queen, painted her eyes immediately prior to her death (2 Kings 9:30).

COUCH A piece of furniture for reclining. The couch became so ornate that Amos rebuked the rich for the costly display of their couches (Amos 6:4). Sometimes, however, the couch was no more than a rolled-up mat that could be easily transported (Matt 9:6). See also BED.

COULTER (See PLOWSHARE)

COUNCIL (Heb. *rigmâh*, Gr. *symboulion, synedrion*). A Jewish governing body, more or less informally held (Ps 68:27). The heavenly host who surround the throne of the Lord are sometimes presented as the heavenly council of the Lord (Job 15:8; Ps 89:7). In the NT the "council" usually means the Sanhedrin consisting of 71 members (Matt 26:59; Mark 14:55; Acts 5:21, KJV; NIV renders "Sanhedrin"). The word is also used of other local Jewish courts (Matt 10:17; Mark 13:9) and Roman advisory boards (Acts 25:12).

The meeting of delegates of the church in Antioch with the apostles and elders in Jerusalem (Acts 15; Gal 2:1–10) is usually called the "Council of Jerusalem," though the text does not contain the word "council."

COUNSELOR (See ADVOCATE; HOLY SPIRIT; OCCUPATIONS AND PROFESSIONS)

COURT On Jethro's advice Moses instituted a system of jurisprudence for the Israelites. He appointed judges over tens, fifties, hundreds, and thousands; Moses himself had the final decision in "difficult cases" (Exod 18:25–26). The office of judge was an elective one (Deut 1:13). Under the Romans the supreme legislative and judicial body was the Sanhedrin. Its judgment was final except in cases involving capital punishment, when the consent of the procurator had to be secured. The Sanhedrin met in Jerusalem.

COVENANT This translates the Hebrew noun *berîth*. The verbal root means either "to fetter" or "to eat with," which would signify mutual obligation, or "to allot" (1 Sam 17:8), which would signify a gracious disposition. Compare this with the Hittite "suzerainty covenant," in which a vassal swore fealty to his king out of gratitude for favors received.

In the OT, *berîth* identifies three different types of legal relationships. (1) A two-sided covenant between human parties who both voluntarily accept the terms of the agreement (for friendship, 1 Sam 18:3–4; marriage, Mal 2:14; or political alliance, Josh 9:15; Obad 7). God, however, never "enters in" to such a covenant of equality with men. (2) A one-sided disposition imposed by a superior party (Ezek 17:13–14). God the Lord thus "commands" a *berîth* that man, the servant, is to "obey" (Josh 23:16). In the original "covenant of works" (Hos 6:7 ASV), he placed Adam on probation, bestowing life, should he prove faithful (Gen 2:17). Humanity failed; but Christ, the last Adam (1 Cor 15:45), did fulfill all righteousness (Matt 3:15; Gal 4:4), thereby earning restoration for all who are his. (3) God's self-imposed obligation, for the reconciliation of sinners to himself (Deut 7:6–8; Ps 89:3–4).

The covenant then constitutes the heart of all God's special revelation; when put into writing, the "Book of the Covenant" becomes the objective source for man's religious hope (Exod 24:7). Scripture consists of the "Old Testament" and the "New Testament." For while there can be but one testament, corresponding to the one death of Christ ("my blood of *the* testament," according to the better MSS of Matt 26:28), revelation yet organizes itself under the older testament, with its anticipatory symbols of Christ's coming (Jer 31–32; 2 Cor 3:14), and the newer testament, commemorative of his accomplished redemption (Jer 31:31; 2 Cor 3:6).

God's revelations of his covenant exhibit historical progression (note plural "covenants," Rom 9:4): (1) the Edenic (Gen 3:15), God's earliest promise of redemption, though at the cost of the bruising of the heel of the seed of woman; (2) the Noachian (9:9), for the preservation of the seed; (3) the Abrahamic

(15:18), granting blessing through Abram's family; (4) the Sinaitic (Exod 19:5–6), designating Israel as God's chosen people; (5) the Levitical (Num 25:12–13), making reconciliation through priestly atonement; (6) the Davidic (2 Sam 23:5), with messianic salvation promised through David's dynasty; (7) the present new covenant in Christ, which is internal, reconciling, direct, and with finished atonement (Jer 31:33–34; Heb 8:6–13); and (8) the future covenant of peace, when our internal salvation will reach out to embrace external nature (Ezek 34:25), when direct spiritual communion will become "face to face" (20:35; 37:27), and when divine forgiveness will achieve the goal of peace among all nations (34:28). (A "dispensation" may be defined as a covenantal period during which faith in Christ is manifested by a distinct form of ceremonial obedience.)

COVERING THE HEAD This is mentioned only in 1 Corinthians 11:15, where Paul says that a woman's hair is given her for a covering. In the preceding verses he says that women should have their heads covered in public worship. At that time in Greece only immoral women were seen with their heads uncovered. Paul means that Christian women cannot afford to disregard social convention; it would hurt their testimony. In giving them long hair, a natural veil, "nature" teaches the lesson that women should not be unveiled in public assemblies.

COVETOUSNESS (kŭv'ĕt-ŭs-nĕs). The word has various shades of meaning: (1) The desire to have something (1 Cor 12:31; 14:39); (2) the inordinate desire to have something (Luke 12:15ff.; Eph 5:5; Col 3:5); (3) excessive desire to have what belongs to another (Exod 20:17; Rom 7:7). Outstanding examples of those who coveted in this sense are Achan (Josh 7), Saul (1 Sam 15:9, 19), and Ananias and Sapphira (Acts 5:1–11).

COW (See ANIMALS)

COZ (See HAKKOZ)

CRAFT, CRAFTSMAN (See OCCUPATIONS AND PROFESSIONS)

CRAFTINESS The determination to use any means, however bad, to attain one's purpose; guile; cunning (Luke 20:23 KJV; NIV has "duplicity"; also Eph 4:14).

CRANE (See BIRDS)

CRAWLING THING (See ANIMALS)

CREATION The doctrine is clearly presented in certain key passages (Gen 1–2; Isa 40–51; Heb 11:3; the latter part of

Major Covenants in the Old Testament

COVENANTS/TYPE	REFERENCE	PARTICIPANT	DESCRIPTION
Noahic Royal Grant	Ge 9:8–17	Made with "righteous" (6:9) Noah (and his descendants and every living thing on earth — all life that is subject to man's jurisdiction)	An unconditional divine promise never to destroy all earthly life with some natural catastrophe; the covenant "sign" being the rainbow in the storm cloud
Abrahamic A Royal (land) Grant	Ge 15:9–21	Made with "righteous" (his faith was "credited to him as righteousness," v. 6) Abram (and his descendants, v. 16)	An unconditional divine promise to fulfill the grant of the land; a self-maledictory oath symbolically enacted it (v. 17)
Abrahamic B Suzerain-vassal	Ge 17	Made with Abraham as patriarchal head of his household	A conditional divine pledge to be Abraham's God and the God of his descendants (cf. "As for me," v. 4; "As for you," v. 9); the condition: total consecration to the Lord as symbolized by circumcision
Sinaitic Suzerain-vassal	Ex 19–24	Made with Israel as the descendants of Abraham, Isaac, and Jacob and as the people the Lord has redeemed from bondage to an earthly power	A conditional divine pledge to be Israel's God (as her Protector and the Guarantor of her blessed destiny); the condition: Israel's total consecration to the Lord as his people (his kingdom) who live by his rule and serve his purposes in history
Phinehas Royal Grant	Nu 25:10–31	Made with the zealous priest Phinehas	An unconditional divine promise to maintain the family of Phinehas in a "lasting priesthood" (implicitly a pledge to Israel to provide her forever with a faithful priesthood)
Davidic Royal Grant	2Sa 7:5–16	Made with faithful King David after his devotion to God as Israel's king and the Lord's anointed vassal had come to special expression (v. 2)	An unconditional divine promise to establish and maintain the Davidic dynasty on the throne of Israel (implicitly a pledge to Israel) to provide her forever with a godly king like David and through that dynasty to do for her what he had done through David — bring her into rest in the Promised Land (1 Ki 4:20–21; 5:3–4)
New Royal Grant	Jer 31:31–34	Promised to rebellious Israel as she was about to be expelled from the Promised Land in actualization of the most severe covenant curse (Lev 26:27–39; Dt 28:36–37, 45–68)	An unconditional divine promise to unfaithful Israel to forgive her sins and establish his relationship with her on a new basis by writing his law "on their hearts" — a covenant of pure grace

Job). The Bible teaches that the universe, including all matter, had a beginning and that it came into existence through the will of the eternal God. Some hold that there is a long gap between Gen 1:1 and 1:2, in which God's perfect creation came into chaos through a great catastrophe. God then refashioned creation as we see it now (1:3–31). Hebrew syntax permits such a view but does not require it.

Scholars differ over length of the creative days of Genesis 1. The Hebrew word for "day" may mean a period of light between two periods of darkness, a period of light together with the preceding period of darkness, or a long period of time. On the seventh day (Gen 2:2–3) God ceased from his labors. God refers to this as an example for Israel to have six days of labor followed by one day of rest (Exod 20:11).

Genesis teaches that there are a number (perhaps a large number) of "kinds" of plants and of animals, which cannot reproduce in such a way as to evolve from one into the other. Nothing in the Bible denies the possibility of change and development within the limits of a particular "kind." The creation of Adam is sharply distinguished from other aspects of Creation, and the creation of Eve is described as a distinct act of God.

The two accounts of Creation do not conflict, just as a map of the United States does not conflict with a map of the whole world. Genesis 1 describes the creation of the universe as a whole. Genesis 2:4–25 covers one special segment of that creation.

CREATURE (Gr. *ktisis*). In the NT the word denotes that which has been created (Rom 1:25; 8:39; Heb 4:13). Sometimes it is used with the adjective *kainē* in the sense of the new creation (2 Cor 5:17) or in contrasting the old person with the new person (Gal 6:15).

CREEPING THING (See ANIMALS)

CRETE, CRETANS (Gr. *Krētē, Krētes*, Acts 2:11; Titus 1:12). An island in the Mediterranean Sea with Cythera on the NW and Rhodes on the NE, forming a natural bridge between Europe and Asia Minor.

In mythology, Mt. Ida is the legendary birthplace of Zeus, the head of the Greek Pantheon. King Minos, a half-historical and half-mythological character, alleged son of Zeus, was an early ruler of Crete. The most important of the ancient cities of Crete are Knossos, excavated by Arthur Evans; Gortyna near the Gulf of Messara; and Cydonia. Around 140 B.C. the Jews established a large enough colony on this island to be able to appeal successfully to the protection of Rome.

In the OT the Kerethites (1 Sam 30:14; Ezek 25:16), held to be a group of Philistines, are identified as Cretans. In the NT a number of Cretans are represented as being present on the Day of Pentecost. Paul visited Crete and left his assistant

Major Types of Royal Covenants/Treaties in the Ancient Near East

Royal Grant (unconditional)	Parity	Suzerain-vassal (conditional)
A king's grant (of land or some other benefit) to a loyal servant for faithful or exceptional service. The grant was normally perpetual and unconditional, but the servant's heirs benefited from it only as they continued their faither's loyalty and service (Cf. 1Sa 8:14; 22:7; 27:6; Est 8:1.)	A covenant between equals, binding them to mutual friendship or at least to mutual respect for each other's spheres and interests. Participants called each other "brothers." (Cf. Ge 21:27; 26:31; 31:44–54; 1 Ki 5:12; 15:19; 20:32–34; Am 1:9.)	A covenant regulating the relationship between a great king and one of his subject kings. The great king claimed absolute right of sovereignty, demanded total loyalty and service (the vassal must "love" his suzerain) and pledged protection of the subject's realm and dynasty, conditional on the vassal's faithfulness and loyalty to him. The vassal pledged absolute loyalty to his suzzerain—whatever service his suzerain demanded—and exclusive reliance on the suzerain's protection. Participants called each other "lord" and "servant," or "father" and "son." (Cf. Jos 9:6, 8; Eze 17:13–18; Hos 12:1.)

Commitments made in these covenants were accompanied by self-maledictory oaths (made orally, ceremonially, or both). The gods were called upon to witness the covenants and implement the curses of the oaths if the covenants were violated.

The first dayes worke.   The seconde dayes worke.   The thirde dayes worke.

The fourth dayes worke.   The fifth dayes worke.   The sirte dayes worke.

Woodcuts illustrating the Creation, from Miles Coverdale's Bible of 1535. Courtesy The British Library

Titus in charge. Paul had a low view of Cretans' moral character (Titus 1:12). The first words of this quotation are to be found in the hymn to Zeus by Callimachus. The particular lie of which the Cretans were always guilty was that they said the tomb of Zeus, a nonexistent personage, was located on their island. A storm on his journey to Rome forced Paul's ship into the port of Cnidus (Acts 27:17).

CRIB (See MANGER)

CRICKET (See ANIMALS)

CRIMSON (Heb. *karmîl, tôlā'*). The brilliant red dye obtained from a bug (Isa 1:18). The word is applied to garments (2 Chron 2:7, 14; Jer 4:30 KJV).

CRISPUS (Gr. *Krispos, curled*, Acts 18:7–8; 1 Cor 1:14). Formerly the ruler of the Jewish synagogue at Corinth; con-

verted under the preaching of Paul and subsequently baptized by him.

CROCODILE (See ANIMALS)

CROCUS (See PLANTS)

CROP (Lev 1:16). The enlargement of the gullet of a bird where food is partly macerated, removed by the priest for sacrificial purposes.

CROSS (Gr. *stauros*). Its biblical uses include (1) the wooden instrument of torture, (2) the cross as a symbolic representation of redemption, and (3) death on the cross, i.e., crucifixion. Our English word is derived from the Latin *crux*. The wooden cross existed in four different forms: (1) the *crux immissa*, the type usually presented in art in which the upright beam extends above the cross beam, traditionally held to be the cross on which Jesus suffered and died, (2) the

Anchor-shaped   Byzantine,   C. of Lorraine
                 Eastern Orthodox

Greek   Jerusalem   Latin

St. Anthony's Tau   Swastika   Trefoiles

C. of Malta   Egyptian Ankh   Papal

St. Andrew's   T - shaped   Christograms

Chart showing the various forms of the cross. Courtesy Carta, Jerusalem

crux commissa, or "Saint Anthony's Cross" in the form of the letter "T," (3) the Greek cross, in which the cross beams are of equal length, and (4) the *crux decussata*, or "Saint Andrew's Cross," in the shape of the letter "X."

Crucifixion was one of the most cruel and barbarous forms of death known to man. It was practiced, especially in times of war, by the Phoenicians, Carthaginians, Egyptians, and later by the Romans. So dreaded was it that even in the pre-Christian era, the cares and troubles of life were often compared to a cross. The agony of the crucified victim was brought about by (1) the painful but nonfatal character of the wounds inflicted, (2) the abnormal position of the body, the slightest movement causing additional torture, and (3) the traumatic fever induced by hanging for such a long period of time.

In 1 Corinthians 1:17 the "preaching" (*kērygma*) of the Cross is set forth as the "divine folly" in sharp contrast to earthly wisdom. In Ephesians 2:16 it is presented as the medium of reconciliation. In Colossians 1:20 peace has been effected through the cross. In Colossians 2:14 the penalties of the law have been removed from the believer by the cross. How Paul as a Roman, to whom one crucified was an object of scorn (1 Cor 1:17), and as a pious Hebrew, to whom one hanged was accursed, (Gal 3:13), came to glory (6:14) in the cross would be one of the absurdities of history were it not for the fact that

the apostle held the Crucified as the Christ of God (2:20).

What was the physical reason for Christ's death? Recent medical studies have sought an answer to the question. When a person is suspended by his two hands, the blood sinks rapidly into the lower extremities of the body. Within six to twelve minutes the blood pressure has dropped to half, while the rate of the pulse has doubled. The heart is deprived of blood, and fainting follows. Death during crucifixion is due to heart failure. Victims of crucifixion did not generally succumb for two or three days. Death was hastened by the "crucifragium" or the breaking of the legs. "But when they came to Jesus and found that he was already dead, they did not break his legs" (John 19:33). Sometimes a fire was built beneath the cross that its fumes might suffocate the sufferer.

Among the Jews, a stupefying potion was prepared by the merciful women of Jerusalem, a drink that Christ refused (Mark 15:23). To such a death, the one who was coequal with God descended (Phil 2:5).

CROW (See BIRDS)

CROWN A band around the head to designate honor. There are three main types of crowns: the royal crown, the priestly crown, and the victor's crown. Among the terms used for "crown" in the OT are Hebrew *qodhqōth*, a part of the human anatomy, the "crown" of the head (Deut 28:35; 2 Sam 14:25); Hebrew *zēr*, that which encircles the head; a garland of flowers (Exod 25:11); Hebrew *nezer*, that which is a symbol of dedication to the priesthood; Hebrew ' *ătārâh*, the customary term (1 Chron 20:2; Prov 4:9). In the NT, Greek *stephanos* refers to a garland or chaplet such as worn by a victorious athlete—a figurative term used by Paul and John, symbolizing Christian triumph (2 Tim 4:8; Rev 2:10). The diadem (*diadēma*) was a symbol of the power to rule.

Of special interest is the crown of thorns worn by Jesus (Gr. *akanthinos stephanos*, Matt 27:29; Mark 15:17; John 19:2). It is impossible to determine the particular variety of thorn used here; many words in the Bible are used for the thorny plants, and the Greek word is a generic, not a specific term.

CRUCIBLE A refining pot for silver and gold and other metals, made to resist great heat (Prov 17:3; 27:21).

CRUCIFIXION (See CROSS)

CRUSE A small porous, earthen vessel for holding liquids (1 Sam 26:11–12, 16, NIV "water jug"; 1 Kings 19:6, NIV "jar"). *Alabastron* occurs in Matthew 26:7, Mark 14:3, and Luke 7:37—an alabaster "bottle" (NEB), "box" (KJV), "flask" (MLB, RSV), or "jar" (JB, NIV).

CRYSTAL Both Hebrew and Greek terms can be translated "ice." More likely it means rock crystal or crystallized quartz. The reason for the meaning "ice" is that the ancients believed that crystal was formed by the process of intense cold (Job 28:17; Rev 4:6; 21:11; 22:1). See also MINERALS.

CUBIT (See WEIGHTS AND MEASURES)

CUCKOO (See BIRDS)

CUCKOW (See BIRDS)

CUCUMBER (See PLANTS)

CUMMIN (See PLANTS)

CUP (Heb. *kôs*, Gr. *potērion*). A term used in a literal and figurative sense. Cups were of various forms and designs and were made of a variety of materials: gold (e.g., all of Solomon's drinking vessels, 1 Kings 10:21), silver, earthenware, copper, bronze, etc.

The word *cup* may also signify a laver (Exod 24:6) or goblet (1 Chron 28:17; Song of Songs 7:2). The cup is used as a symbol of prosperity or of the Lord's blessing and, in reverse, of his malediction on the wicked (Pss 11:6; 16:5; 23:5). The cup also represents drunkenness and other illicit pleasures (Prov 23:31; Rev 17:4; 18:6). "Cup of salvation" (Ps 116:13), "cup of thanksgiving" (1 Cor 10:16), and "cup of the Lord" (v.21) are also used. In the latter two passages, Paul is referring to the communion cup, over which the blessing is said prior to the feast that commemorates the Lord's death and burial. The cup from ancient times signified fellowship. Thus when the believer takes the cup of the Lord, he enters into fellowship with him. This is contrasted with "cup of demons" (10:21) in a figurative way, meaning that we cannot have fellowship with Christ and with the forces of darkness at the same time. At heathen feasts the cup was sacred to the name of the god in whose name the feast was being held. Thus, in the communion service, the cup is sacred to the name of the Redeemer who instituted its practice (Matt 26:27; Mark 14:23–24; Luke 22:20). The "cup of his wrath" (Isa 51:17, 22), the "cup that sends all the surrounding peoples reeling" (Zech 12:2), and the "cup of ruin

and desolation" (Ezek 23:33) are among other biblical occurrences of the term.

CUPBEARER (See OCCUPATIONS AND PROFESSIONS)

CURDS (See BUTTER)

CURSE (Heb. *'ālāh*, *me'ērâh*, *qelālâh*, Gr. *katapa*). The reverse of "to bless." On the human level, to wish harm or catastrophe. On the divine, to impose judgment. In the oriental mind the curse carried with it its own power of execution. A curse was imposed on the serpent (Gen 3:14). Noah cursed Canaan (9:25). The curse of Balaam, the pseudoprophet, turned to a blessing (Num 24:10). A curse was pronounced from Mt. Ebal for disobedience to the law of Moses (Deut 27:1–9). The cursing of one's parents is sternly prohibited by Mosaic regulations. Christ commanded those who would be his disciples to bless and not to curse (Luke 6:28). When Peter, at Christ's trial, denied that he knew him, he invited a curse on himself (Matt 26:74). Christ bore the curse of the law for believers (Gal 3:13). The modern Western practice of cursing, i.e., using profane language, is never referred to in the Scriptures. See also BLASPHEMY.

CURTAINS (Heb. *yerî'âh*). 1. The curtains of fine linen and goats' hair that covered the tabernacle (Exod 26:1ff.; 38:9ff.). Gradually the "curtains" gave their name to the entire structure. 2. Employed figuratively by Isaiah (40:22), referring to the heavens. He uses the word *dōq*, literally, "gauze."

CUSH (Heb. *kûsh*). 1. The oldest son of Ham, one of the three sons of Noah (Gen 10:6–8; 1 Chron 1:8–10). Among the descendants were Seba, Havilah, Sabta, Raamah, and Sabtecha. They were mostly located in Arabia. Nimrod is likewise said to be the son of Cush, but the word "son" probably means "descendant." 2. "Cush, a Benjamite," in the title for Psalm 7, viewed as referring to King Saul, the Benjamite, whose father's name was Kish. 3. Cush, the country. The name of the territory through which the Gihon flowed (Gen 2:13; translated "Ethiopia" by KJV, but NIV margin says "possibly southeast Mesopotamia"). The wife of Moses is referred to as a Cushite, making her a target of criticism by Miriam and Aaron (Num 12:1). If this is Zipporah, the wife of Moses mentioned earlier, her origin was that of the land of Midian. The earlier passages seem to indicate Cush as African, the latter as Asian. The precise identification of either the woman or the country is an unsolved problem. See also ETHIOPIA.

CUSHI (kū′shī). A member of the Cushite people. **1.** The man sent by Joab to inform David that Absalom's rebellion was quelled and that the time was ripe for him to return to his throne (2 Sam 18:21–32). **2.** A contemporary of Jeremiah, the great-grandfather of Jehudi (Jer 36:14). **3.** The father of the prophet Zephaniah (Zeph 1:1).

CUSTOM When not referring to a tax, usually means "manner," "way," or "statute" (Gen 31:35; Judg 11:39; Jer 32:11), or heathen religious practice (Lev 18:30; Jer 10:3). In the NT it means "manner," "usage" (Luke 1:9; Acts 6:14), and "religious practices."

CUSTOM, RECEIPT OF (NIV "tax collector's booth"). The post from which Matthew (Levi) was called to follow Christ (Matt 9:9), probably a road toll. The Romans imposed tribute or tax on Jews as on all their subjects for the maintenance of their provincial government. Tax collectors or publicans were despised because of their notorious dishonesty and willingness to work for a foreign power.

CUTHAH, CUTHA, CUTH (kū′tha, kŭth). One of the cities from which Sargon, king of Assyria, brought immigrants to repopulate the area of Samaria that he had sacked in 720 B.C. (2 Kings 17:24–30). Because of their numerical predominance, the inhabitants of Samaria were henceforth referred to as Cutheans. They began a syncretistic form of religion, worshiping both the true God and the gods of the nations they came from. This is one of the explanations for the deep antipathy existing between the Jews and the Samaritans even to NT times (John 4:9).

From the contract tablets found by Rassam at Tel-Ibrahim it now appears that the ancient name of Cuthah was Gudua or Kuta. This city of high culture and commerce lay NE of Babylon and was one of its most important centers. Rassam describes its almost perfect ruins as being about 3,000 feet (937.5 m.) in circumference and 280 feet (87.5 m.) high. In it was a sanctuary dedicated to Ibrahim (Abraham). Both the city and its great temple, the latter dedicated to Nergal, appear to date back to Sumerian times.

CUZA (kū′zà, Gr. *Chouzas*). The steward of Herod Antipas. Luke 8:3 states that his wife, Joanna, Susanna, and many others supported Christ and his disciples out of their own resources. Cuza was undoubtedly a man of rank and means.

CYMBAL (See MUSIC AND MUSICAL INSTRUMENTS)

CYPRESS (See PLANTS)

CYPRUS (sī′prŭs, Gr. *Kypros, copper*). An island in the eastern part of the Mediterranean directly off the coast of Syria and Cilicia. The OT refers to it as the "Isles of Chittim" (*Kittim*, Ezek 27:6; rendered by NIV as the "coasts of Cyprus"). Barnabas, who accompanied Paul on his first missionary journey, was a native of the island (Acts 4:36); with John Mark he returned to evangelize Cyprus after they had left Paul's company (15:36–39). The apostolic party passed through the island from Salamis to Paphos. At Paphos, Sergius Paulus, the imperial deputy of the island, came to believe in Christ (13:12).

CYRENE (sīrē′nĭ, Gr. *Kyrēnē, wall*). A Libyan city in North Africa, west of Egypt, separated from it by a part of the Libyan Desert. A native of Cyrene, Simon by name, was impressed by the Roman soldiers into carrying the cross of Jesus (Luke 23:26). Cyrenians were present in Jerusalem on the day of Pentecost (Acts 2:10). Its Jewish population warranted a synagogue (6:9). Lucius of Cyrene is mentioned in Acts 11:19–20. Archaeology has shown that it was the Greek plan to make Cyrene the "Athens of Africa." The most interesting remains are a great system of tombs cut out of solid rock into the cliff.

CYRENIUS (See QUIRINIUS)

CYRUS (sī′rŭs, Heb. *kôresh*). The son of Cambyses, king of Anshan. With the rise of Cyrus began the renowned Persian Empire that was to continue until the coming of Alexander the Great. Nabonidus was destined to be the last ruling sovereign of the neo-Babylonian Empire, for in the highlands of Iran another kingdom was forging out its own program of conquest. When the Medes and their king, Astyages, were defeated by Cyrus, the realm of Persia began to assume threatening proportions. Cyrus himself announced his genealogy: "I am Cyrus, king of the hosts, the great king, king of Babylon, king of Sumer and Akkad . . . son of Cambyses, the king, king of Anshan; the grandson of Cyrus . . . the great-grandson of Teispes . . . king of Anshan. . . ." In this same inscription Cyrus proceeds to relate how the city of Babylon opened its gates to him without

The famous Cylinder of Cyrus (the Lord's "anointed," Isa 45:1), which tells how he captured Babylon and liberated the prisoners from Babylonia. It was made of baked clay, from Babylon, c. 536 B.C. Reproduced by courtesy of the Trustees of the British Museum

The Tomb of Cyrus, at Pasargadae in Iran. The tomb is constructed of white limestone and rests upon six steps of irregular height. The small entrance leads to a windowless chamber. Courtesy B. Brandl

resistance, confirming the biblical account recorded in Daniel 5 when Darius, acting as vice-regent for Cyrus, took the city of Babylon in the name of Cyrus the Great. The neo-Babylonian Empire was in no condition to resist the advance of Cyrus, and fell easily into the hands of the Persians. The OT sets the framework of reference against the backdrop of Belshazzar's impious feast (Dan 5:1–30).

Cyrus entered Babylon on October 29, 539 B.C., and presented himself in the role of the liberator of the people. He allowed the images of the gods to be transported back to their original cities and instituted a kindly policy of repatriation for captive peoples. His policies of moderation naturally extended to the Hebrews, whom he encouraged to return to Judea to rebuild their temple (2 Chron 36:22–23; Ezra 1:1–6). Isaiah refers to Cyrus as "his [i.e., the Lord's] anointed" (Isa 45:1).

–D–

DABERATH (dăb'ă-răth). An ancient town near the western side of Mt. Tabor; part of the heritage of Issachar given to the Levites (Josh 19:12; 1 Chron 6:72). A strategic location, the probable site of the defeat of Sisera by Barak (Judg 4:14–22).

DAGON (dā'gŏn, Heb. *dāghôn,* probably *fish*). Chief god of the Philistines (e.g., 1 Sam 5). Originally worshiped by the Canaanites before the Philistine invasion of Canaan, as indicated by place-names such as Beth Dagon in Judah (Josh 15:41) and in Asher (19:27). Either a fish god or the god of agriculture, from *Dab,* "fish," or *Dagan,* "grain." Saul's head was placed in a temple of Dagon (1 Chron 10:10). Samson destroyed the temple of Dagon in Gaza (Judg 16:30).

DALAIAH (See DELAIAH)

DALMANUTHA (dăl-mà-nū'thà). A village on the west coast of the Sea of Galilee, adjoining Magdala (Matt 15:39), and the landing place of Jesus after feeding the multitude (Mark 8:10). It is mentioned only in the NT. Considerable ruins near modern Mejdel (Magdala) are considered to be the location.

DALMATIA (dăl-mā'shà, Gr. *Dalmatia, deceitful*). A mountainous province on the east shore of the Adriatic Sea. Christianity, implanted under Titus (2 Tim 4:10), continues until today. It was ruled by Rome as early as A.D. 160. Paul may have visited in the province (Rom 15:19); in his time it was regarded as part of Illyricum.

DAMASCUS (dà-măs'kŭs, Gr. *Damaskos*). For more than 4,000 years the capital of one government after another, a prize for which nation after nation went to war, a city whose boast for centuries has been, "The world began at Damascus, and the world will end there." Damascus is the capital of Syria, a small region of unique geological formation, lying between Mt. Hermon and the Syrian Desert. Caravan routes from the east, west, and south once crossed in the city, carrying treasures of silks, perfumes, carpets, and foods. It was a rich city whose merchandise was far-famed (Ezek 27:16).

Damascus and Syria played an important part in biblical history. By the time of Abraham, Damascus was well enough known to be a landmark (Gen 14:15). Abraham secured a wife for Isaac from Syria, hence Israel is of Syrian ancestry (Gen 24; Deut 26:5). Jacob labored long in Syria for Rachel (Gen 29).

According to Josephus, Hadad was the first king. David subjugated and ruled the city for a time (2 Sam 8:5–6; 1 Chron 18:3–6). There was frequent interaction (sometimes hostile) between Syria and Israel: Rezon and Solomon (1 Kings 11:23–25; cf. 10:29); Ben-Hadad and Asa (15:16–21); Hazael and Elijah (19:15–17); Ben-Hadad and Ahab (20:1–34); Ben-Hadad, Hazael, and Elisha (19:15; 2 Kings 8:7–15); Hazael, Ahaziah, and Joram (8:28; 10:32–33; 13:3); Syrians and Joash (13:14–22); and Ben-Hadad II and Israel (13:24–25). Under Jeroboam, Damascus was taken by Israel (14:28). Ahaz, in order to save his kingdom from Syria, made an alliance with Tiglath-Pileser (Pul) who destroyed Damascus and ended Syria's power for many decades (16:7–9). The city remained of little importance until 333 B.C. when an army of Alexander the Great captured it. Then followed two centuries of rise and fall. In 63 Syria became a province of the Roman Empire.

During NT days, Damascus was an important center, ruled by Arabia under Aretas (2 Cor 11:32). While en route there to arrest the believers in a strong Christian community, Saul was converted (Acts 9:1–18). He escaped his Jewish enemies of the city by being let down from a wall in a basket (9:25; 2 Cor 11:33). After a checkered history under Rome, Damascus was captured by Muslims in A.D. 635 and made the seat of the Muslim world. It remained the center of the Muslim faith until 1918 when it was put under French mandate after World War I. In 1946 it became a free state.

DAMNATION (Heb. *rasha', to hold guilty,* Deut 25:1; Isa 50:9; 54:17; Gr. *krinō, to put under condemnation,* John 3:17–18; Rom 14:22; *katakrinō, to hold to be unpardonable,* Matt 12:41; 20:18; Rom 8:1, 3, 34; Heb 11:7; *krima* and *krisis, judgment, eternal punishment,* Matt 23:33; Mark 12:40; John 5:29; Rom 3:8; 5:16; 13:2; 1 Cor 11:29, 34; *apōleia, destruction, damnation,* 2 Peter 2:3). The penalty for unbelief (2 Thess 2:12), adulterous relations (1 Tim 5:11–12), hypocrisy (Matt 23:14), and treason (Rom 13:2). When referring to the future, the words primarily mean eternal separation from God, which includes awful punishment (Ps 88:10–12; Isa 38:18)—being cast into hell (Matt 5:29; 10:28; 23:33;

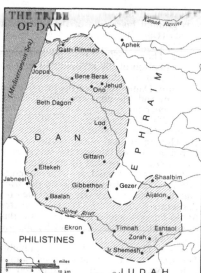

THE TRIBE OF DAN

Kanah Ravine
Aphek
Gath Rimmon
Joppa
Bene Berak
Jehud
Ono
Beth Dagon
Lod
D A N
Gittaim
Eltekeh
Jabneel
Gibbethon   Gezer
Baalah   Aijalon
Sorek River
Ekron   Timnah   Eshtaol
PHILISTINES   Zorah
                    Ir Shemesh
0   2   4   6 miles
0   5   10 km
© CARTA, JERUSALEM
J U D A H
(Mediterranean Sea)
E P H R A I M

24:51; Mark 9:43). The severity of the punishment is determined by the degree of sin (Luke 12:36–48), and it is eternal (Isa 66:24; Mark 3:29; 2 Thess 1:9; Jude 6–7).

DAN Northernmost city of Palestine (e.g., Judg 20:1; 1 Sam 3:20). Originally Leshem (Josh 19:47; Judg 18:29). Captured by Danites and renamed Dan (Judg 18). It was a commercial center at one time (Ezek 27:19). Jeroboam I set up the golden calf here (1 Kings 12).

DAN The tribe to which Dan, the fifth son of Jacob, gave origin, and the territory allotted it in Canaan. The tribe acted as rear guard during the Exodus (Num 10:25). They were given a fertile area lying between Judah and the Mediterranean Sea, occupied by the Philistines (Josh 13:3). Failure to conquer it made the Danites move northward, where by strategy they conquered Leshem (Laish of Judg 18:29) and renamed it Dan (Josh 19:47; Judg 18:1–29).

The heritage of Dan, though small, was productive and, with the acquisition of extra lands, provided for growth. Oholiab and Samson were Danites (Exod 31:6; Judg 13:2, 24). Jeroboam set up a golden calf in Dan and put high places throughout Israel (1 Kings 12:25–33). Menahem stopped Pul (Tiglath-Pileser) by bribery (2 Kings 15:14–20), but eventually Pul returned, overran Israel, and took many Danites into captivity (1 Chron 5:26).

DANCING The Hebrew people developed their own type of dancing, associated in the main with worship. Basically, it was more like modern religious shouting by individuals, or processions of exuberant groups. Three things characterized it. First, the sexes never intermingled in it, except where pagan influences had crept in (cf. Exod 32:19). Second, dancing was usually done by women, (Exod 15:20; Judg 21:19ff.; 1 Sam 18:6; Ps 68:25) with one leading, as in the case of Miriam (Exod 15:20–21). In this incident, as well as on other occasions, a form of antiphonal singing was used. Third, dancing usually took place out of doors. Men danced solo, as in the case of David before the ark (2 Sam 6:14–16), and in groups, as when Israel celebrated the victory over the Amalekites (1 Sam 30:16). Percussion and other noise-making instruments seem to be native to dance (Judg 11:34; Ps 68:25). Job complained against the rich because of their ability to dance (Job 21:11). There was a time for dancing (Eccl 3:4), but sometimes tragedy made singing and dancing out of place (Lam 5:15). The redemption of Israel was to be celebrated by dancing—by virgins, men and boys (Jer 31:13). The Romans introduced the Greek dance to Palestine. Primitive Christian churches allowed the dance, but it soon caused degeneracy and was banned, as is indicated by many of the early Christian writers.

DANIEL (dăn′yĕl, Heb. *dāniyē′l* or *dāni′ēl, God is my judge*). **1.** David's second son (1 Chron 3:1; *Kileab*, 2 Sam 3:3). **2.** A postexilic priest (Ezra 8:2; Neh 10:6). **3.** The exilic seer of the Book of Daniel. The prophet was born into an unidentified family of Judean nobility at the time of Josiah's reformation (621 B.C.); he was among the select, youthful hostages of the first Jewish deportation, taken to Babylon by Nebuchadnezzar in 605, the third year of King Jehoiakim (Dan 1:1, 3).

For three years Daniel was trained in all the wisdom of the Babylonians (Dan 1:4–5) and was assigned the Babylonian name Belteshazzar, "Protect his life!"— an invocation of a pagan deity (4:8). Daniel and his companions, however, remained true to their ancestral faith, courteously refusing "the royal food and wine" (1:8, tainted with idolatry and contrary to the Levitical purity laws). God rewarded them with unsurpassed learning (1:20, qualifying them as official "wise men"; cf. 2:13). On Daniel, moreover, he bestowed the gift of visions and

The traditional tomb of Daniel, marked by the mosque with its conical tower, at Susa. Courtesy B. Brandl

of interpreting dreams (1:17; cf. Daniel's wisdom in the apocryphal stories of *Susanna* and *Bel and the Dragon*).

Near the close of this second year (602 B.C.), Nebuchadnezzar required his fellow Babylonians, who as the ruling strata in society had assumed the position of priestly diviners (Dan 2:2; cf. Herodotus, I.191), to identify and interpret an undisclosed dream that had troubled him the preceding evening (2:5, 8). The hoax of spiritism and astrology was duly exposed; but when judgment was pronounced on the enchanters, Daniel and his companions were included under the death sentence. But the "God in heaven who reveals mysteries" (2:28; cf. 2:11) answered Daniel's prayer for illumination (2:18–19). Daniel revealed both the dream, depicting a fourfold image, and its import of four world empires (Babylon, Persia, Greece, and Rome) leading up to God's messianic kingdom (2:44; see also DANIEL, BOOK OF). Nebuchadnezzar elevated Daniel to be chief over the wise men (2:48 does not, however, state that he became a pagan priest, as inferred by those who would discredit Daniel's historicity). He further offered him the governorship of the province of Babylon, though Daniel committed this latter appointment to his three friends (2:49).

In the latter years of Nebuchadnezzar's reign (604–562 B.C.), Daniel's courage was demonstrated (Dan 4:19; cf. 4:7) when he interpreted the king's dream of the fallen tree (4:13–27). He tactfully informed his despotic master that for seven "times" pride would reduce him to beast-like madness (4:24–25; cf. its historical fulfillment twelve months later, 4:28–33).

In 552 B.C. after the retirement of King Nabonidus to Arabian Teima and the accession of his son Belshazzar, Daniel was granted his vision of the four great beasts (Dan 7) that parallels Nebuchadnezzar's earlier dream of the composite image. Then in 550, at the time of Cyrus' amalgamation of the Median and Persian states and of the growing eclipse of Babylon, Daniel received the prophecy of the ram and the goat concerning Persia and Greece (8:20–21) down to Antiochus IV (8:25). On October 12, 539, Cyrus' general, Gobryas, after having routed the Babylonian armies, occupied the city of Babylon. During the profane revelries of Belshazzar's court that immediately preceded the end, Daniel was summoned to interpret God's handwriting on the wall, and the prophet fearlessly condemned the desperate prince (5:22–23). He predicted Medo-Persian victory (5:28), and that very night the citadel fell and Belshazzar was slain.

When Darius the Mede (presumably Gubaru or another official of similar name) was made king of Babylon by Cyrus (Dan 5:31; 9:1), he at once sought out Daniel as one of his three "administrators" (6:2) because of his excellency, and was considering him for the post of chief administrator (6:3). Daniel's jealous colleagues, failing to uncover a valid charge of corruption (6:4), proceeded to contrive his downfall through a royal edict prohibiting for 30 days all prayers or petitions, except to Darius himself. Daniel was promptly apprehended in prayer to God; and Darius had no recourse but to cast him into a den of lions, as had been prescribed. God, however, intervened on behalf of his faithful servant (cf. 6:16) and shut the lion's mouths, though they subsequently devoured his accusers when they were condemned to a similar fate. It was in this same first year of Darius (6:28; cf. 1:21), as the 70 years of Babylonian exile drew to a close, that the angel Gabriel answered Daniel's prayers and confessions with a revelation of the 70 "sevens" (9:24–27).

The last-known event in the life of Daniel took place in the third year of Cyrus (536 B.C.), when he was granted an overpowering vision of the archangel Michael contending with the demonic powers of pagan society (Dan 10:10–11:1); of the course of world history, through the persecutions of Antiochus IV (11:2–39); and of the eschatological Antichrist, the resurrections, and God's final judgment (11:40–12:4). The vision concluded with the assurance that though Daniel would go to his grave prior to these events, he would yet receive his appointed reward in the consummation

Remains of the palace of Darius I at Persepolis. Courtesy B. Brandl

(12:13). Thus in his mid-eighties, after completing his inspired autobiography and apocalyptic oracles, he finished his honored course.

The history of Daniel the prophet is confirmed both by the words of Christ (Matt 24:15) and by references to his righteousness and wisdom by his prophetic contemporary Ezekiel (14:14, 20; 28:3, in 591 and 586 B.C., respectively).

DANIEL, BOOK OF Although it stands as the last of the major prophets in the English Bible, this book appears in the Hebrew OT (which consists of "the law, prophets, and writings") as one of the "writings." For though Christ spoke of Daniel's *function* as prophetic (Matt 24:15), his *position* was that of a governmental official and inspired writer rather than ministering prophet (Acts 2:29–30).

The first half of the book (chs. 1–6) consists of six narratives on the life of Daniel and his friends: their education (605–602 B.C.), Daniel's revelation of Nebuchadnezzar's dream-image, the trial by fiery furnace, Daniel's prediction of Nebuchadnezzar's madness, his interpretation of the handwriting on the wall (539, the fall of Babylon), and his ordeal in the lion's den (see also DANIEL; SHADRACH). The second half consists of four apoca-lyptic visions predicting the course of world history.

Daniel 7 envisions the rise of four beasts: a lion, bear, leopard, and monster with iron teeth explained as representing successive kings (kingdoms, 7:23). These kingdoms are thought to represent respectively Babylon, Persia, Greece and Rome. The vision further describes the disintegration of Rome into a tenfold balance of power (2:42; 7:24; Rev 17:12, 16), the eventual rise of Antichrist for an indefinite period of "times" (Dan 7:8, 25), and his destruction when "one like a son of man" comes with the clouds of heaven (7:13). This figure is understood by most scholars as the Messiah because Christ applied this imagery to himself (Matt 24:30), although some understand it to symbolize the saints of the Most High (Dan 7:18, 22). The prophecy of the 70 "sevens" in 9:20–27 has received various interpretations.

Daniel 2:4b–7:28 is composed in the international language of Aramaic; the rest is in Hebrew. There are references to the book in the NT (Matt 24:15; Luke 1:19, 26; Heb 11:33, 34). The book was designed to inspire Jewish exiles with confidence in the Most High (Dan 4:34–37).

DARDA, DARA (där'dà, dä'rà). A member of a noted family of wise men. He was either a son of Mahol (1 Kings 4:31) or son of Zerah (1 Chron 2:6).

DARIC (där'ĭk). A Persian gold coin used in Palestine after the return from captivity (1 Chron 29:7; Ezra 8:27). It was worth about five dollars. See also MONEY.

DARIUS (dă-rī'ŭs, Heb. *dāryāwesh*, Gr. *Darios*). A common name for Medo-Persian rulers. *Darius the Mede* is a more mysterious figure who, so far, appears only in the Bible (Dan 5:31; 6:1, 6, 9, 25, 28; 9:1; 11:1). He may have been Gubaru, an officer in Cyrus' army who became governor of the Persian province of northern Babylon, but this may be an alternative title for Cyrus the Persian himself.

Darius Hytaspes was the greatest of the Persian rulers. Under his lenient reign, the Jews restored the walls of the city and rebuilt the temple (Ezra 4:5, 24; 5:5–7; 6:1–15; Hag 1:1; 2:1, 10, 18; Zech 1:1, 7; 7:1). His forces were overwhelmed in the battle at Marathon, 490 B.C.

Darius the Persian (Neh 12:22). This was either Darius Nothus or Darius Codomannus, probably the latter, the last Persian king. (See page 145.)

DARKNESS (Heb. *hōshekh, the dark,* Gr. *skotos, darkness*). Used in the OT and NT both in a literal and in a figurative sense. **1.** To denote the absence of light (Gen 1:2–3; Job 34:22; Isa 45:7). **2.** To depict the mysterious (Exod 20:21; 2 Sam 22:10; 1 Kings 8:12; Ps 97:2; Isa 8:22; Matt 10:27). **3.** As ignorance, especially about God (Job 37:19; Prov 2:13; Eccl 2:14; John 12:35; 1 Thess 5:1–8). **4.** To describe the seat of evil (Prov 4:19; Matt 6:23; Luke 11:34; 22:53; John 8:12; Rom 13:12; 1 Cor 4:5; Eph 5:11). **5.** Presenting supernatural events (Gen 15:12; Exod 10:21; Matt 27:45; Rev 8:12; 16:10). **6.** A sign of the Lord's return (Isa 60:2; Joel 2:2; Amos 5:8; Matt 24:29). **7.** An agency of eternal punishment (22:13; 2 Peter 2:4, 17; Jude 6–7; cf. Job 2:1–5; 20:20). **8.** Spiritual blindness (Isa 9:2; John 1:5; Eph 5:8; 1 John 1:5; 2:8), sorrow and distress (Isa 8:22; 13:10; Ps 23:4), dispelled wherever Christ sheds his light (Col 1:13).

DART (See ARMS AND ARMOR)

DATHAN (dä'thăn). A great-grandson of Reuben (Num 16:1). He, with his brothers Abiram and Korah, rebelled against Moses (16:1–15), for which sin they were swallowed by the earth (16:31–35; see also ch. 26).

DAUGHTER A word of various uses in the Bible. It referred to both persons and things, often without regard to kinship or sex. **1.** Female child (Gen 6:1; 20:12; 24:23; Judg 11:34; Matt 15:28). **2.** Any female descendant, regardless of the nearness of relations (Gen 34:13–17; cf. Ps. 45:12; 144:12; Luke 1:5). **3.** Women in general (Gen 28:6; Num 25:1). **4.** Offspring (Isa 22:4; Jer 9:1; Lam 4:10). **5.** Those who worshiped the true God (Ps 45:10; Song of Songs 1:5; 3:11; Isa 62:11; Zech 9:9; Matt 21:5; John 12:15). **6.** Physical means of making music, the mouth, ears, etc., were called daughters of music (Eccl 12:4 KJV). **7.** City (Isa 37:22). **8.** Citizens (Zech 2:10).

DAVID (dä'vĭd, Heb. *Dāwîdh, beloved* or, as in ancient Mari, *chieftain*). Israel's greatest king, one of the most commanding OT figures (1 Sam 16–1 Kings 2:11; 1 Chron 11–29; many Pss).

David was born in 1040 B.C. (2 Sam 5:4), the youngest son of Jesse of Bethlehem (1 Sam 16:10–11), and developed in strength, courage, and attractiveness while caring for his father's sheep (16:12; 17:34–36). Samuel anointed him as king, and God's Spirit came upon David from that time on (16:13). Saul, meanwhile, summoned David to periodic appearances at court to soothe his own troubled mind by skillful harp-playing (16:18; 17:15). While still in his teens, David gained national renown and the friendship of Saul's son Jonathan (18:1–3; cf. 20:12–16; 23:16–17) through his victory over Goliath (17:45–47). Saul's growing jealousy and four insidious attempts on David's life served only to increase the latter's popularity (cf. 18:13–16, 27). At length, urged on by David's rivals (cf. Ps 59:12), Saul openly sought his destruction; and though frustrated by Samuel and the priests at Nob, he did succeed in driving David into exile (1 Sam 19:11; 21:10).

David fled to Philistine Gath and then to Adullam (1 Sam 21:12; Pss 34:6–8; 56:3; 142:6). On three occasions Saul attempted to seize David (1 Sam 23; 24; 26; Pss 7:4; 54:3; 57:6). Near the end of 1012 B.C., however (1 Sam 27:7), David in despair sought asylum in Gath, feigning vassalage (27:8–28:25). After Saul's death at Mt. Gilboa in 1010 B.C. David's forces advanced inland to Hebron, where he was declared king over Judah (2 Sam 2:1–4). In 1005 B.C. Saul's general, Abner, enthroned Ish-Bosheth, a son of Saul. Only after the death of Ish-Bosheth (ch. 4) did all Israel acclaim David king in 1003 (5:1–5; 1 Chron 11:10; 12:38).

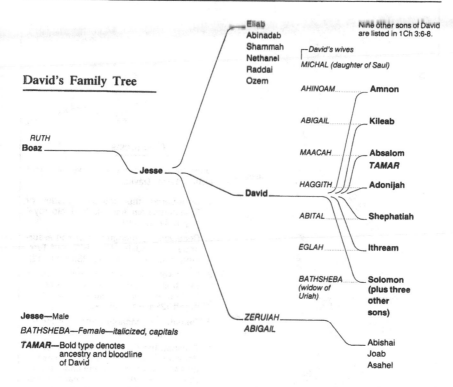

David's Family Tree

Eliab
Abinadab
Shammah
Nethanel
Raddai
Ozem

Nine other sons of David
are listed in 1 Ch 3:6-8.

David's wives

MICHAL (daughter of Saul)

AHINOAM........... Amnon

ABIGAIL............ Kileab

MAACAH........... Absalom
                  TAMAR

HAGGITH.......... Adonijah

ABITAL............ Shephatiah

EGLAH............. Ithream

BATHSHEBA...... Solomon
(widow of   (plus three
Uriah)   other
                 sons)

RUTH
Boaz

Jesse

David

ZERUIAH
ABIGAIL

Abishai
Joab
Asahel

Jesse—Male

BATHSHEBA—Female—italicized, capitals

TAMAR—Bold type denotes
ancestry and bloodline
of David

David, after an initial retreat to Adullam (2 Sam 5:17; 23:13–17), expelled the Philistines in two divinely directed campaigns (5:18–25). He next established a new political and religious capital by capturing the Jebusite stronghold of Jerusalem and installing Moses' ark of the covenant in a tent on Zion (2 Sam 6; Ps 24).

From 1002 to about 995 B.C. David expanded his kingdom on all sides: west against Philistia (2 Sam 8:1), east against Moab, (8:2), north against Syria (10:13, 18; cf. 8:3) to the Euphrates River, and south against stubborn Edom (1 Kings 11:15; Ps 60:10). An alliance with Hiram of Tyre enabled David to construct a palace in Jerusalem (2 Sam 5:11).

Rest from war followed (2 Sam 7:1; 22:1–51; Ps 18), and David proposed a permanent temple for the Lord in Jerusalem, but was denied this privilege (1 Chron 22:8; 28:3). However, God promised to establish David's dynasty through Solomon, who would build the temple, and culminating in the incarnation of God's eternal Son (2 Sam 7:13–14). David composed many psalms concerning this Messiah (Pss 2, 16, 22, 68, 110). Some of David's greatest achievements lie in this literary sphere. Of the 150 canonical psalms, 73 possess titles asserting Davidic authorship.

Yet soon after this, David lapsed into a series of failures including the killing of seven innocent descendants of Saul (2 Sam 21:9), adultery with Bathsheba and the murder of her husband (10–11), and ineffective control over his sons— Ammon's rape of Tamar, Absalom's murder of Amnon (13:23–29) and his revolt and death (13:38; 14:28; 15:7; 16:20–22; 18:9–15).

David's last years (975–970 B.C.) were occupied with Philistine wars (2 Sam 21:15–22), a military census (24:3, 9; Ps 30:6), and the resulting plague (2 Sam 24:15). David subsequently undertook massive preparations for the temple (1 Chron 22). In David's old age, his oldest surviving son, Adonijah, attempted to usurp the throne from Solomon, but David proclaimed Solomon's coronation (1 Kings 1). Thus in 970, after a final charge to his son (2:2–9), David died. His last words were a prophecy of

Euphrates R.

Orontes R.

Hamath

Great Sea

PHOENICIANS

Litani R.

ARAMEANS

• Damascus

Tyre

Kishon R.

GESHUR

Yarmuk R.

Dor •

Megiddo

Taanach

• Beth Shan

Jabbok R.

Jordan R.

• Rabbah

AMMONITES

Jerusalem

Hebron •

Arnon R.

PHILISTINES

MOABITES

AMALEKITES

Zered R.

E D O M I T E S

Eastern arm of the
Red Sea

David's Conquests

Once he had become king over all Israel (2Sa 5:1–5), David:

1. Conquered the Jebusite citadel of Zion/Jerusalem and made it his royal city (2Sa 5:6–10);

2. Received the recognition of and assurance of friendship from Hiram of Tyre, king of the Phoenicians (2Sa 5:11–12);

3. Decisively defeated the Philistines so that their hold on Israelite territory was broken and their threat to Israel eliminated (2Sa 5:17–25; 8:1);

4. Defeated the Moabites and imposed his authority over them (2Sa 8:2);

5. Crushed the Aramean kingdoms of Hadadezer (king of Zobah), Damascus, and Maacah and put them under tribute (2Sa 8:3–8; 10:6–19). Talmai, the Aramean king of Geshur, apparently had made peace with David while he was still reigning in Hebron and sealed the alliance by giving his daughter in marriage to David (2Sa 3:3; see 1Ch 2:23);

6. Subdued Edom and incorporated it into his empire (2Sa 8:13–14);

7. Defeated the Ammonites and brought them into subjection (2Sa 12:19–31);

8. Subjugated the remaining Canaanite cities that had previously maintained their independence from and hostility toward Israel, such as Beth Shan, Megiddo, Taanach, and Dor.

Since David had earlier crushed the Amalekites (1 Sa 30:17), his wars thus completed the conquest begun by Joshua and secured all the borders of Israel. His empire (united Israel plus the subjugated kingdoms) reached from Ezion Geber on the eastern arm of the Red Sea to the Euphrates River.

Miles	0	20	40	60	80	100
Kms	0	20	40	60	80	100 120 140

the future Davidic Messiah and of his own salvation, springing from this covenant (2 Sam 23:5).

DAVID, CITY OF (See CITY OF DAVID; JERUSALEM)

DAY (Heb. *yôm*, Gr. *hēmera*). A word often misinterpreted because of its various uses in the Bible. It often denotes time from sunrise to sunset (Gen 1:5; Ps 74:16). At an early date it was divided into three parts—morning, noon, and evening (Ps 55:17; Dan 6:10). The word also refers to time in general (Judg 18:30; Obad 12). It is also used figuratively, referring to the day of judgment (Isa 2:12; Joel 1:15; Amos 5:18; Rom 13:12), the length of life (Gen 5:4 KJV), the time of opportunity (John 9:4), and any time (Prov 12:16, KJV, ASV, see footnote).

DAY OF ATONEMENT (See ATONEMENT, DAY OF)

DAY OF CHRIST A term used in the NT to indicate Jesus' intervention in human history. Sometimes it is called "that day" (Matt 7:22) and "the Day" (1 Cor 3:13). It refers to the return of Jesus for his own and for the judgment of unbelievers (1:8; 5:5; 2 Cor 1:14; Phil 1:6, 10; 2:16; 2 Thess 2:2–3). It will signal the completion of the redemptive work (2:1, 13), the day of triumph (Phil 2:9–11).

DAY OF THE LORD An eschatological term referring to the consummation of God's kingdom and triumph over his foes and deliverance of his people. It begins at the Second Coming, and will be accompanied by social calamities and physical cataclysms (Matt 24; Luke 21:7–33). It will include the millennial judgment (Rev 4:1–19:6) and culminate in the new heaven and the new earth (Isa 65:17; 66:22; Rev 21:1).

DAYSMAN (Heb *yākhah, to act as umpire*). A mediator or arbitrator—one who has set a day for hearing a dispute. As used in Job 9:33 (KJV; NIV "someone to arbitrate"), the word means an umpire or referee who hears two parties in a dispute and decides the merits of the case.

DAYSPRING (Heb. *shāchar, to break forth*). A poetic name used in KJV for the dawn (Job 38:12; NIV "dawn"), and also in describing the advent of the Messiah (Luke 1:78; NIV "rising sun").

DAYSTAR (Gr. *phōsphoros, light-giving*). The planet Venus, seen as a morning star, heralding the dawn. The prophet compared the splendor of the king of Babylon to Lucifer, "son of the morning" (Isa 14:12 KJV; JB, NASB, RSV "son of the dawn"; NIV "morning star"). Jesus calls himself "the bright Morning Star" (Rev 22:16). He is called the "morning star" in 2 Peter 1:19.

DEACON, DEACONESS (Gr. *diakonos, servant*). Paul used the Greek word of himself (1 Cor 3:5; Eph 3:7). Jesus was declared to be a *diakonos* of the Jews (Rom 15:8). Household servants were *diakonoi* (Matt 22:13). Paul told Timothy how to be a good *diakonos* (1 Tim 4:6). NIV usually renders "servant"; KJV, "minister."

The diaconate, as a church office, is inferred from Acts 6:1–8, but at least two of the seven men were evangelists. Qualifications given in 1 Timothy 3 show that deacons were not considered ordinary lay members of the church. Paul mentions deacons in connection with bishops (Phil 1:1).

The same Greek word is used of Phoebe in Romans 16:1—translated as "servant" (KJV, NASB, NIV) or "deaconess" (JB, RSV). Certain women ministered (*diakonein*) to Jesus (Luke 8:2–3). It does not appear from the Scripture or early church literature that deaconesses were ever church officers.

DEAD SEA Called in Scripture the Salt Sea (Gen 14:3), Sea of the Arabah (Deut 3:17), or the eastern sea (Joel 2:20; Zech 14:8). It has the earth's lowest surface, 1,290 feet (403 m.) below sea level. Occupying a geologic fault that extends from Syria through the Red Sea into Africa, it measures 47 by 10 miles (78 by 16 km.) (approximately 300 sq. mi. [789 sq. km.]). Cliffs rise 1,500–2,500 feet (469–781 m.) on either shore. North of Lisan, "the tongue" (Josh 15:2 ASV footnote), the water's depth attains 1,300 feet (406 m.), though southward it averages less than 10 feet (3 m.). The Sea is slowly expanding, as the muddy Jordan extends its northern delta. Salt concentration reaches 25 percent, four times that of ocean water. Magnesium bromide prevents organic life; the climate is arid, and the heat extreme.

The Dead Sea constituted Israel's eastern border (Num 34:12; Ezek 47:18). At En Gedi, which terminates the principal descent from Judah, a spring provided refuge for David (1 Sam 24:1). The Valley of Salt, south of the Sea, witnessed the victories of David and of Amaziah over Edom (2 Kings 14:7; 1 Chron 18:12) and countermarches in the days of Jehoshaphat (2 Kings 3:8–9; 2 Chron 20:1–2; the "Moabite Stone"). On the east shore above the Arnon, the springs of Callirhoe served Herod the Great during his final

View of the Dead Sea, looking south from the ruins of the Essene community at Qumran. Courtesy S. Zur Picture Library

illness; and at Machaerus his son Herod Antipas imprisoned John the Baptist (Mark 1:14; 6:17). On the west shore, above En Gedi, lies Khirbet Qumran, site of the NT community with its famous scrolls; and opposite Lisan rises Masada, Palestine's finest natural fortress, the refuge of Herod against Parthians in 42 B.C., and the last stand of Jerusalem's zealots in A.D. 70 (*Jewish War* 7.10.1). In modern times the Dead Sea has produced potash; but Ezekiel predicts a healing of its waters, granting abundant life in God's kingdom age (Ezek 47:8–10).

DEAD SEA SCROLLS These were discovered, probably in A.D. 1947, by a Bedouin and brought to the attention of the scholarly world late that year and early in 1948. The discoveries were made in caves located in the cliffs a mile or so (1.6 km.) west of the NW corner of the Dead Sea, at a place known by the modern Arabic name of Qumran.

The scrolls (biblical, deuterocanonical, noncanonical) come from the last century B.C. and the first century A.D. At least 382 manuscripts are represented by the fragments of Cave Four alone, about 100 of which are biblical manuscripts. These include fragments of every book of the Hebrew Bible except Esther. Some of the books are represented in many copies. One of the significant finds concerns the Book of Daniel, fragments of which have been found with the change from Hebrew to Aramaic in Daniel 2:4 and from Aramaic to Hebrew in 7:28–8:1, exactly as in our modern texts of Daniel.

In addition to biblical books, fragments of deuterocanonical writings have been found, specifically Tobit and Ecclesiasticus, as well as fragments of several noncanonical writings. The Thanksgiving Psalms, the Book of Warfare, and the commentaries on portions of Scripture give us insights into the nature and beliefs of the community at Qumran.

Near the cliffs of the Dead Sea is the site of an ancient building known as the "Monastery," which has yielded important data about the nature, size, and date of the Qumran community. From the sect's literature we know that the people of Qumran were Jews who had split off from the Jerusalem (or main) stream of Judaism, and indeed were quite critical of and even hostile toward the priests at Jerusalem. The fact that they used the name "The Sons of Zadok," has suggested to some scholars that they should be connected with the Zadokites or Sadducees; other scholars believe that they are rather to be identified with the Essenes, a third sect of Judaism described by Josephus and Philo. It is not impossible that elements of truth are to be found in both of these theories and that there was originally a split in the priestly or Sadducean line that first joined the movement known as the Hasidim, the forerunners of the Pharisees, ultimately to split again and form a narrow separatist group, part of which located at Qumran. We must await further discoveries before we attempt to give a final answer to this entire problem.

The community devoted itself to the study of the Bible. The life of the community was largely ascetic, and their practices included ritual bathing, sometimes referred to as baptism.

The discoveries of Qumran are important for biblical studies in general. In the matter of the text of the OT, however, the Dead Sea Scrolls are of great importance. The text of the Greek OT (or the Septuagint), as well as the quotations of the OT in the NT, indicate that there were other texts besides the one that has come down to us (the Masoretic Text). The study of the Dead Sea Scrolls makes it clear that there were at least three texts in existence. In relation to the NT, the Dead Sea Scrolls furnish the background to the preaching of John the Baptist and Jesus Christ, as well as the writings of Paul and John. There is no evidence in the Qumran documents that Jesus or John the Baptist were members of the sect, and nothing in the NT requires such a position.

DEAFNESS (See DISEASES)

DEATH (Heb. *māweth*, Gr. *thanatos; nekros*). Both the OT and NT present death as an event belonging to our sinful

Fragment of the Isaiah Scroll found in Cave 1 at Qumran. The column shown here (c. 125–100 B.C.) contains Isaiah 51:13–52:12. Courtesy The Shrine of the Book, D. Samuel and Jeane H. Gottesman Center for Biblical Manuscripts, Israel Museum, Jerusalem

existence, but also in relation to the living God, Creator, and Redeemer. Death means the end of a human life on earth (Gen 3:19). To ponder this may cause a sense of separation from God (e.g., Pss 6:5; 30:9; 88:5); but as death is faced it is recognized that total confidence should be placed in the Lord (Job 19:25–26; Pss 73:23–24; 139:8).

Death is also the absence of a spiritual communion with God. (Deut 30:15; Jer 21:8; Ezek 18:21–22, 31–32.) Death is caused by sin (Rom 5:12; 6:23) and the devil who, in this age on this fallen earth, has power over death—until Christ takes it from him (Heb 2:15). The death of Jesus for the sins of the world is greatly emphasized as is his victory over death in bodily resurrection.

"The second death" (Rev 20:6, 14; 21:8) is experienced by those whose names are not written in the Lamb's Book of Life (20:15) and means everlasting separation from God and his redeemed people.

DEBIR (dē′bêr). A city of Judah, once a center of culture for the Canaanite people. Probably it took its name from the pagan temple in which the oracle occupied the holy place (see 1 Kings 6:5, where the word is translated "oracle" in KJV). It was SW of Jerusalem, some 10 miles (17 km.) west of Hebron, occupied by the Anakim (Josh 11:21; 15:14), captured by Joshua (10:38–39), and captured a second time under Caleb (15:13–17). It later became a priestly possession (21:15; 1 Chron 6:58). **2.** A king of Eglon, who made an alliance with the king of Jerusalem against Joshua and was defeated at Gibeon (Josh 10:1–11). **3.** A town on the border of Gad near Mahanaim (13:25–26). **4.** A town on the border between Judah and Benjamin (15:7), on the road between Jerusalem and Jericho.

DEBORAH (dĕb′ŏ-rà, Heb. *devôrâh, bee*). **1.** Rebekah's beloved wet nurse (Gen 24:59; 35:8), who accompanied her to Palestine. She became attached to Jacob's household and died at great age (cf. 25:20; 35:8) near Bethel. The tree under which she was buried was called "oak of weeping." **2.** The fourth of Israel's judges, a prophetess, a wife of Lappidoth (Judg 4–5). Like most Hebrew "judges," however, Deborah served primarily as a divinely appointed deliverer and executive leader of Israel.

After the death of Ehud, the people lapsed into apostasy, resulting in their subjection to the Canaanites. Then arose Deborah, "a mother in Israel" (Judg 5:7). Summoning Barak of Naphtali, she prophesied that an offensive from Tabor would lure Sisera and Jabin's army to annihilation on the plains, including Sisera's death by a woman (4:8–9). Deborah and Barak accomplished Israel's first united action (5:14–17) since the conquest, 175 years before.

God fought against Sisera (5:20) in a providential storm (cf. 5:4), which turned the plain into a morass, rendering Sisera's chariotry unmaneuverable. They were cut to pieces by Israel's charging foot soldiers, and then swept away by a flash flood (5:21). Sisera fled alone and was killed by the woman Jael at Kedesh (4:11, 17–22). Jabin was destroyed (4:24), and the land rested 40 years (5:31), corresponding to the reign of Rameses III, the last great Pharaoh of Egypt's 20th Dynasty. After the battle Deborah and Barak sang Deborah's song of victory (5:2–31; cf. v. 7).

The Roman ruins of Gerasa (modern Jerash in Jordan), one of the principal cities of the Decapolis, looking northward. In the foreground is shown the south theater and, to its right, the oval forum and colonnaded street. Courtesy Studium Biblicum Franciscanum, Jerusalem

DEBT (Heb. *neshî*, Gr. *opheilēma, a sum owed, an obligation*). Under Mosaic Law Jews were not allowed to exact interest (usury) from other Jews (Exod 22:25). Special laws protected the poor against usurers (22:25–27; Deut 24:12–13). A debtor had to make good his obligation, so land that was pledged (mortgaged) could be seized, but had to be restored during the Jubilee year (Lev 25:28). A house so pledged could be sold, or held in perpetuity if not redeemed during a year, unless it was an unwalled town (25:29–30). The NT mentions bankers, money-changers, interest, and usury (Matt 25:16–27; John 2:13–17). Debtors were often thrown into prison (Matt 18:21–26). Jesus taught compassion toward those in debt (18:23–35).

DECALOGUE (See COMMANDMENTS, TEN)

DECAPOLIS (dē-kăp'ô-lĭs, Gr. *deka, ten* and *polis, city*). A region east of Jordan that had been given to the tribe of Manasseh (Num 32:33–42). A league of 10 cities, consisting of Greeks who had come in the wake of Alexander's conquests, was established after the Romans occupied the area (65 B.C.) According to Ptolemy, the number was later increased to 18. They had their own coinage, courts, and army. Jesus drove the demons into swine near Gadara, one of these cities (Mark 5:1–20), and became popular in the Decapolis (Matt 4:24–25; Mark 7:31–37).

DECISION, VALLEY OF The place where God will some day gather all nations for judgment (Joel 3:2, 12, 14). It is called the Valley of Jehoshaphat (*Jehovah judges*). Some identify it with the Valley of Kidron.

DECREE An official ruling or law. The word refers to laws governing special occasions (Esth 1:20; Dan 3:10; Jonah 3:7), rules for Christian living (Acts 16:4), and God's settled plan and purpose (Exod 32:32; Ps 2:7–10; Dan 4:24; Rev 13:8).

DEDAN (dē'dăn). 1. An Arabian people descended directly from Noah (Gen 10:6–7) and living around the NW end of the Persian Gulf. Dedanites were traveling tradesmen (Isa 21:13) connected with Tyre (Ezek 27:3, 15, 20). The Dedanites were warned to flee (Jer 49:7–8); they would be destroyed with the Edomites (Ezek 25:3). 2. A descendant of Abraham by Keturah (Gen 25:3).

DEDICATION (Heb. *kādhēsh, to sanctify, ḥānukkāh, to consecrate*). The consecration of persons, or (usually) the setting apart of things for God's use. Consecration of the tabernacle (Num 7) was an elaborate ceremony, as was that of the temple (1 Kings 8). Among various dedicated things were: the city wall (Neh 12:27), private dwellings (Deut 20:5), the temple treasure (1 Chron 28:12), children (Exod 13:2), people (Exod 29:4; 1 Sam 16:5), and booty of war (2 Sam 8:10–11). The dedication of Nebuchadnezzar's image (Dan 3:2–3), and of Herod's temple (Jos. *Antiq.* 15.11.6) were elaborate occasions.

DEDICATION, FEAST OF An annual 8-day festival of the Jews celebrating the restoration of the temple following its desecration at the hands of the Syrians under Antiochus Epiphanes (1 Macc 4:52–59; 2 Macc 10:5; cf. Jos. *Antiq.* 12.5.4). Beginning on the 25th of Kislev (Nov/Dec) this feast, also called the "Feast of Lights," was the occasion for Jesus' temple discourse (John 10:22ff.).

DEEP "The ocean" (Neh 9:11; Job 41:31; Ps 107:24; Isa 44:27); "torment" (Ps 88:6); "chaos" (Gen 1:2; 7:11); or "subterranean water" (49:25; Deut 33:13); "mysterious" (Dan 2:22); "depth" or "power" (Lev 13:4, 31; Job 11:8); "water" or "condition" (Luke 5:4; John 4:11; Acts 20:9; 2 Cor 8:2); "sea" (2 Cor 11:25) or "abyss" (Luke 8:31; Rev 9:1; 11:7).

DEER (See ANIMALS)

DEFILE Profane, pollute, render unclean. In the OT defilement was physical (Song of Songs 5:3), sexual (Lev 18:20), ethical (Isa 59:3; Ezek 37:23), ceremonial (Lev 11:24, 17:15), and religious (Num 35:33; Jer 3:1). In the NT it is ethical or religious (Mark 7:19; Acts 10:15; Rom 14:20).

DEGREE (See ASCENTS)

DEGREES, SONGS OF (See ASCENTS, SONGS OF)

DELAIAH (dē-lā'yà, *raised* or *freed by Jehovah*). **1.** A descendant of David (1 Chron 3:1, 24). **2.** A priest of David's time and leader of the 23rd course of temple service (24:18). **3.** A prince who urged King Jehoiakim not to burn Jeremiah's roll (Jer 36:12, 25). **4.** Head of a tribe that returned under Zerubbabel from captivity (Ezra 2:60; Neh 7:62). **5.** The father of Shemaiah who advised Nehemiah to flee (6:10).

DELILAH (dē-lī'là, *dainty one*). A Philistine woman who by her seductive wiles learned the secret of Samson's strength and brought him to his ruin (Judg 16:4–20).

DELUGE (See FLOOD, THE)

DEMAS (dē'mås, Gr. *Dēmas, popular*). A faithful helper of Paul during his imprisonment in Rome (Col 4:14). Paul called him a "fellow worker" (Philem 24). He was probably a citizen of Thessalonica, where he went when he deserted Paul (2 Tim 4:10).

DEMETRIUS (dē-mē'trĭ-ŭs, Gr. *Dēmētrios, belonging to Demeter*). **1.** The disciple whom John praised in his letter to Gaius (3 John 12). **2.** The jeweler of Ephesus who raised a mob against Paul because his preaching had resulted in damage to his lucrative business of making silver images of the goddess Diana (Acts 19:23–27).

DEMONS (Gr. *daimonia*). Evil spirits (Matt 8:16; Luke 10:17, 20; cf. Matt 17:18 and Mark 9:25). The immaterial and incorporeal nature of both Satan and his demon hosts is discussed by Paul (Eph 2:2; 6:12) and John (Rev 16:14).

As purely spiritual beings or personalities, demons operate above the laws of the natural realm and are invisible and incorporeal. However they may be glimpsed (2 Kings 2:11; 6:17). John in apocalyptic vision *saw* the awful last-day eruption of locust-demons from the abyss (Rev 9:1–12), as well as the three hideous frog-like spirits that emanate from the satanic trinity (the dragon, the beast, and the false prophet) in the Tribulation to muster the world's armies to their predestined doom at Armageddon (16:13–16).

As spirit personalities, demons have an intellectual nature through which they possess superhuman knowledge. Scripture features the shrewdness of demons. They know Jesus (Mark 1:24), bow to him (5:6), describe him as "the Son of the Most High God" (5:7), entreat him (8:31), obey him (Matt 8:16), corrupt sound doctrine (1 Tim 4:1–5), conceal the truth of Christ's incarnate deity and sole saviorhood (1 John 4:1–3), and comprehend prophecy and their inevitable doom (Matt 8:29). Demons are consulted by spiritistic mediums, who allow themselves to get under the control of evil spirits for oracular purposes (1 Sam 28:1–25; Acts 16:16), as is seen in both ancient and modern spiritism, erroneously called "spiritualism."

In their moral nature all demons (as fallen angels) are evil and depraved, in distinction to the good spirits (the unfallen angels), who are sinless. They affect

Bronze figure of the Assyrian demon Pazuzu, seventeenth century B.C. Courtesy Réunion des Musées Nationaux

their victims mentally, morally, physically, and spiritually, and are frequently described as "unclean" (Matt 10:1; Mark 1:27; Luke 4:36; Acts 8:7; Rev 16:13 KJV; NIV renders "evil"). They cause fleshly uncleanness and base sensual gratification (Luke 8:27), and gross carnality and sexual sin (2 Tim 3:1–9; Rev 9:20–21).

Demons possess terrible physical strength, imparting it to the human body (Luke 8:29) and binding their victims as with chains and with physical defects and deformities (13:11–17) such as blindness (Matt 12:22), insanity (Luke 8:26–36), dumbness (Matt 9:32–33), and suicidal mania (Mark 9:22).

Demons are of two classes—those who are free, with the earth and the air as their abode (Eph 2:2; 6:11–12; Col 1:13), and those who are imprisoned in the abyss (Luke 8:31; Rev 9:1–11; 20:1–3). The abyss is only the temporary prison; their final end will be the "lake of fire"

(Matt 25:41), the eternal abode of Satan, demons, and unsaved human beings.

DENARIUS (See MONEY)

DEPUTY (Heb. *nitstāv*, Gr. *anthypatos*). One appointed to rule under a higher authority, as a regent in place of a king (1 Kings 22:47) or a Roman consul or proconsul (Acts 13:7, 18:12, 19:38).

DERBE (dûr'bē, Gr. *Derbē*). A city in the SE corner of Lycaonia in Asia Minor. Paul visited it on the first journey after being stoned at Lystra (Acts 14:20), on his second tour (16:1), and probably on the third. Gaius, who accompanied Paul to Jerusalem, was from this city (20:4).

DESCENT INTO HELL The familiar Apostles' Creed affirmation that Jesus descended into hell is based chiefly on two references by Peter, one of which (1 Peter 3:19) is more direct than the other (4:6), supported by implications to be taken from two other NT verses (Acts 2:27; Rom 10:7). The term is in harmony also with the language of Paul (Eph 4:9), and John (Rev 1:17–18). The lowest regions were recognized as the habitation of the disembodied spirits of the dead, but 1 Peter 4:6 may refer rather to fallen angels (cf. Jude 6).

DESERT 1. Hebrew *midbār* and Greek *erēmos,* "a wilderness," yet capable of pasturing flocks (Gen 16:7; 21:20; 1 Sam 17:28; Matt 3:1; Mark 1:13). **2.** Hebrew *'ărāvâh,* "an arid region." When used with the definite article, it denotes the plain of the Jordan and Dead Sea (2 Sam 2:29; Ezek 47:8). **3.** Hebrew *yeshîmôn,* "a waste." With the definite article, it is rendered as a proper name, Jeshimon (Num 21:20). **4.** Hebrew *hārbâh,* "waste, desolate place" (Isa 48:21; Ezek 13:4). The deserts known to the Israelites were mostly latently fertile lands, needing only rain to make them fruitful.

DESERT CREATURE (See ANIMALS)

DESIRE (See PLANTS)

DESIRE OF ALL NATIONS A phrase occurring only in Haggai 2:7 (KJV). Many expositors refer the prophecy to Christ's first advent, and others to the second advent; still others deny a messianic application, holding that the phrase refers to nations' precious gifts (cf. Isa 60:5, 11; 61:6).

DEUEL (dū'ĕl). A Gadite, father of Eliasaph, prince of Gad in the wilderness just after the Exodus from Egypt (Num 1:14; 7:47; 10:20). In Numbers 2:14 most manuscripts of the Masoretic Text read "Reuel."

Deuteronomy 8:5–10, part of a leather scroll (c. first century B.C.) found at Qumran. Courtesy Israel Department of Antiquities and Museums

DEUTERONOMY (dū-têr-ŏn'ō-mē, Gr. *Deuteronomion, second law*). In sight of the Canaan he would not be allowed to enter, Moses gathered the hosts of Israel about him for his farewell addresses. These, set within the historical framework of several brief narrative passages, constitute the Book of Deuteronomy.

The English title is based on the LXX's mistranslation of the phrase "a copy of this law" (Deut 17:18). The Jewish name *debārîm*, "words," derives from the opening expression, "These are the words Moses spoke" (1:1). This title is well-suited because it focuses attention on a clue to the peculiar literary character of the book; the treaties imposed by ancient imperial lords on their vassals began with such an expression. Deuteronomy is the text of "words" of a suzerainty covenant made by the Lord of heaven through the mediatorship of Moses with the servant people Israel beyond the Jordan.

Moses' addresses are dated in the last month of the 40 years of wandering (Deut 1:3), and it is stated that Moses wrote as well as spoke them (31:9, 24; cf. 31:22). Jesus affirmed the Mosaic authorship of the Law, i.e., the Pentateuch (cf. Mark 10:5; 12:26; John 5:46–47; 7:19). Modern orthodox Christian scholars, therefore, join older Jewish and Christian tradition in maintaining the Mosaic authorship of Deuteronomy as well as of the first four books of the Pentateuch.

The unity, antiquity, and authenticity of Deuteronomy are evidenced by the conformity of its total structure to the pattern of Near Eastern suzerainty treaties dating from the second millennium B.C. The classic covenantal pattern consisted of the following sections: preamble, historical prologue, stipulations, curses and blessings, invocation of oath deities, directions for deposit of duplicate treaty documents in sanctuaries and periodic proclamation of the treaty to the vassal people.

This substantially is the outline of Deuteronomy:

I. **Preamble: Covenant Mediator (1:1–5).**

II. **Historical Prologue: Covenant History (1:6–4:49).**

III. **Stipulations: Covenant Life (5–26).**

IV. **Curses and Blessings: Covenant Ratification (27–30).**

V. **Succession Arrangements: Covenant Continuity (31–34).**

In Deuteronomy 1:1–5 the speaker is identified as Moses, as the Lord's representative. Deuteronomy 1:6–4:49 is a rehearsal of God's past covenantal dealings with Israel from Horeb to Moab and serves to awaken reverence and gratitude as motives for renewed consecration. With 5:26 it is made clear that when covenants were renewed the former obligations were repeated and brought up to date. Thus chapters 5–11 review the Decalogue with its primary obligation of fidelity to Yahweh, while chapters 12–26 in considerable measure renew the stipulations of the Book of the Covenant (Exod 21–33) and other Sinaitic legislation, adapting where necessary to the new conditions awaiting Israel in Canaan. In chapters 27–30 directions are first given for the future and final act in this covenant renewal to be conducted by Joshua in Canaan (ch. 27). Moses then pronounces the blessings and curses as reasons for Israel's immediate ratification of the covenant, but also as a prophecy of Israel's future down to its ultimate exile and restoration (chs. 28–30). In chapters 31–34 preparations are made for the continuity of leadership (through Joshua) and for periodic reading of the covenant document and a prophetic song of covenant witness (chs. 31–32). The book ends with the final blessings and the death of Moses (chs. 33–34).

Deuteronomy is the Bible's full-scale exposition of the covenant concept and demonstrates that, far from being a contract between two parties, God's covenant with his people is a proclamation of his sovereignty and an instrument for binding his elect to himself in a commitment of absolute allegiance.

DEVIL (Gr. *diabolos, slanderer*). One of the principal titles of Satan, the archenemy of God and of man. In the NT the word refers to Satan 35 times. The KJV uses the same word about 60 times to render the Greek *daimonion* (ASV and NIV, "demon"). Three times the word *diabolos* is used for ill-natured persons, or "slanderers" (1 Tim 3:11; 2 Tim 3:3; Titus 2:3); in the KJV the last two of these passages have "false accusers." The plural word "devils" occurs four times in the OT (KJV)—twice representing *sa'irim*, which means "he-goats" (Lev 17:7; 2 Chron 11:15), and twice translating *shedim*, or "demons" (Deut 32:17; Ps 106:37).

Apparently God first peopled the universe, or at least our part of it, with a hierarchy of holy angels, of whom one of the highest orders was (or contained) the cherubim. One of them, perhaps the highest of all, was "the anointed cherub that covereth," who was created beautiful and perfect in his ways. This cherub knew that he was beautiful, but pride entered his heart and the first sin in the whole history of eternity occurred. Pride led to self-will (Isa 14:13–14) and self-will to rebellion. This great cherub became the adversary ("Satan") of God and apparently led other angels into rebellion (cf. 2 Peter 2:4; Jude 6). One day Satan and all the other enemies of God will be cast into the "lake of burning sulfur" (Rev 20:10, 15). In the age-long (though not eternal) conflict between good and evil, it sometimes seems as though God has given Satan every advantage. Even so, God's victory is certain.

The devil is called "the god of this age" (2 Cor 4:4), "the ruler of the kingdom of the air" (Eph 2:2), a murderer and a liar (John 8:44), "Abaddon" and "Apollyon" (i.e., "Destroyer," Rev 9:11), "Beelzebub, the prince of demons" (Matt 12:24), and "that ancient serpent . . . the accuser of our brothers" (Rev 12:9). He can be resisted (James 4:7) and defeated (Matt 4:1–11; cf. Eph 6:16).

DEVOTED THING That which is set apart to the Lord. A sacrifice or offering is a voluntary gift from the owner and can be recalled at any time before the ceremony, but not a devoted thing. Achan's sin at Jericho (Josh 6:17–19) was considered far more serious than mere stealing, for he had taken something devoted. Nations, cities, or men who were "devoted" were to be utterly destroyed— e.g., the Amalekites (1 Sam 15).

DEW The moisture condensed from the air that forms in drops during a still, cloudless night on the earth or any warm surface. In Syria and most of Palestine through the cloudless summer and early autumn the dew is a great blessing to the fruits of the land. Dew is often used in

Scripture as a symbol of blessing (Gen 27:28; Mic 5:7) and of refreshment (Deut 32:2; Job 29:19; Ps 133:3; Isa 18:4).

DIADEM (Gr. *diadema*). Properly an emblem of royalty, but in the OT the Hebrew word is generally rendered "mitre" and refers to the turban of the chief priest (Zech 3:5), a royal diadem (Isa 62:3), or a turban (Job 29:14). In the NT the word *diadem* does not occur in the KJV or NIV, but the Greek *diadema* is used three times (Rev 12:3; 13:1; 19:12) as an emblem of absolute power and is to be distinguished from the crown (Gr. *stephanos*) used elsewhere in the NT. Our Lord will wear the diadem (Rev 19:12). See also CROWN.

DIAL Properly, a graduated arc intended to mark the time of day by the shadow of a style or shaft falling on it. The word occurs twice in KJV (2 Kings 20:11; Isa 38:8), referring to the "sun-dial of Ahaz." The Hebrew *ma'alah* is generally translated "dial" is generally "degrees" or "steps" (so NIV), from the root meaning "to go up." It appears that the men of Hezekiah's day judged time by the shadow of a pillar as it ascended or descended the steps leading to the palace. The miracle recorded in connection with the dial can be compared with the "long day" in Joshua's time (Josh 10:12–14) and is equally inexplicable on natural grounds.

DIANA (See ARTEMIS)

DIASPORA (See DISPERSION)

DIBLATH (See DIBLAH)

DIBON, DIBON GAD (dī'bŏn). 1. A place in the high plain of Moab, one of the stations of Israel in its journey toward the Promised Land (Num 33:45–46). It belonged to Sihon, king of the Amorites (21:21–31), who was conquered by Israel under Moses. The city was rebuilt by the tribe of Gad (32:34). It was later taken by Moab under King Mesha, who rebelled against Israel after the death of Ahab 906 B.C. (2 Kings 1:1; 3:4–5). Israel badly defeated Mesha at the ensuing battle (2 Kings 3), but Mesha set up a stele at Dibon (the famous "Moabite Stone") boasting of his defeat of Ahab. 2. A town in Judah, occupied by some Jews who returned with Zerubbabel (Neh 11:25).

DIDRACHMA (See MONEY)

DIDYMUS (dĭd'ĭ-mŭs, *a twin*). Surname of Thomas (John 11:16; 20:24; 21:2).

DILL (See PLANTS)

DINAH (dī'nà). A daughter of Jacob and Leah (Gen 30:21), the only one mentioned in Scripture. While sightseeing (ch. 34) at the city near which Israel encamped, Shechem the prince violated her, for which crime Levi and Simeon, her brothers, destroyed the city.

DINAITE (dī'nà-īt). A member of the tribe of whom Ashurbanipal had brought from Assyria to colonize Samaria (cf. 2 Kings 17:24 with Ezra 4:7–10 KJV).

DIOSCURI (See CASTOR AND POLLUX)

DIOTREPHES (dī-ŏt'rĕ-fēz, Gr. *Diotrephēs, nurtured by Zeus*). A leading member of the church to which Gaius belonged, to whom John wrote his third letter. His domineering attitude (3 John 9) made him an obstacle to the progress of the church.

DISCERNING OF SPIRITS (KJV). The ability given by the Holy Spirit to some Christians to discern between those who spoke by the Spirit of God and those who were moved by false spirits. The phrase occurs in 1 Corinthians 12:10 as one of the gifts of the Spirit. The NIV renders "distinguishing between spirits."

DISCIPLE (Gr. *mathētēs, a learner*). A pupil of a teacher—like the disciples of John the Baptist (Matt 9:14), the Pharisees (22:16), and Moses (John 9:28). Usually, however, it refers to the adherents of Jesus—the twelve apostles (e.g., Matt 10:1; 11:1) or believers in general (Acts 6:1–2, 7; 9:36). Followers of Jesus were not called "Christians" until the founding of the church at Antioch (11:26).

DISCIPLINE (See CHASTISEMENT)

DISEASES The diseases mentioned in Scripture appear largely to have been those that now exist especially in semitropical climates like that of Palestine. Instead of naming the disease involved, however, the Bible often simply mentions symptoms (e.g., fever, itch, sore).

I. Diseases with primary manifestations in the skin were of two kinds. (A) Those requiring isolation were: (1) leprosy (Lev 13); (2) syphilis (Num 25:9; Deut 28:27; cf. Lev 22:4); (3) smallpox (Job 2:7); (4) boils, or carbuncles (2 Kings 20:7); (5) anthrax (Exod 9:3; cf. 9:9), and (6) scabies (Deut 28:27). (B) Diseases not requiring isolation probably include what today are known as eczema, psoriasis, and inflammation (Lev 22:22).

II. Diseases with primarily internal manifestations were of two types: (A) plagues, which included (1) bubonic plague (1 Sam 5; 6:5) and (2) pneumonic plague (perhaps 2 Kings 19:35). (B) Con-

Limestone relief of a blind harpist, c. 1350 B.C., from the tomb of Paatenemheb near Saqqara. Courtesy Rijksmuseum van Oudheden, Leiden, Netherlands

sumption diseases (pestilences) included (1) tuberculosis, (2) typhoid fever, (3) malaria (Lev 26:16; Deut 28:22), and (4) dysentery (Acts 28:8).

III. Diseases caused by worms and snakes included (1) intestinal roundworm infection (perhaps Acts 12:21–23), (2) the Guinea worm, and (3) snake-bite (Acts 28:3, 6).

IV. Diseases of the eyes included (1) epidemic blindness (2 Kings 6:18), and (2) infirmity (Gal 4:13–15; cf. 6:11).

V. Nervous and mental diseases may be indicated in the lives of David (pretended, 1 Sam 21:13–15), Saul, Elijah (1 Kings 19), Jonah (Jonah 4), and Epaphroditus (Phil 2:25–30).

VI. Miscellaneous medical disorders and therapy may be indicated in several passages (Lev 21:20; Luke 1:20–22, 64; 6:6; 8:43–44; 14:2; 22:44; 2 Cor 12:8–10; 2 Tim 2:17; 4:20).

James urges that the church elders be called to pray for the sick. He also directs that they "anoint him with oil in the name of the Lord" (James 5:14). The Greek word used for "anointing" commonly referred to rubbing oil on the skin as a household remedy. The sick one is not only to be prayed for but the commonly accepted remedies are also to be applied as an indication of compassionate concern. Jesus' disciples made similar use of the application of oil to the sick (Mark 6:13).

DISH A receptacle for food made of baked clay (generally) or metal. Orientals ate from a central platter or dish, generally using a thin piece of bread for a spoon and handling the food quite daintily (Matt 26:23 KJV).

DISHON (dī'shŏn). **1.** A chief among the Horites, the name sometimes rendered Dishan (Gen 36:21). **2.** A great-grandson of Seir the Horite (36:25, perhaps the same as #1).

DISPENSATION (Gr. *oikonomia*, law or arrangement of a house). A word that appears in the Bible four times (1 Cor 9:17; Eph 1:10; 3:2; Col 1:25) in a twofold sense: (1) with respect to one in authority, it means an arrangement or plan, and (2) with respect to one under authority, it means a stewardship or administration.

The modern theological use of the term as a "period of time during which man is tested in respect to obedience to some specific revelation of the will of God" (Scofield) is not found in Scripture. Nevertheless, the Scriptures do make a distinction between the way God manifested his grace in what may be called the "Old Covenant" and the way his grace has been manifested since the death of Christ in the "New Covenant," and there are accompanying differences in the requirements that God has for believers. Paul has this in mind when he speaks of God's dispensations in Ephesians and Colossians.

DISPERSION (Gr. *diaspora, that which is sown*). The name applied to the Jews living outside of Palestine and maintaining their religious faith among the Gentiles. God had warned the Jews through Moses that dispersion among other nations would be their lot if they departed from the Mosaic Law (Deut 4:27; 28:64–68). These prophecies were largely fulfilled in the two captivities, by Assyria and Babylonia. Especially from the time of Alexander the Great, many thousands of Jews emigrated for the purposes of trade and commerce into the neighboring countries, particularly the chief cities. By the time of Christ the dispersion must have been several times the population of Palestine. The synagogues in every part of the known world helped greatly in the spread of Christianity, for Paul invariably went to them in every city he visited. The word *diaspora* occurs three times in the NT (John 7:35; James 1:1; 1 Peter 1:1).

DISTAFF A stick used to hold the wool or flax fibers used in the process of spinning (Prov 31:19).

DIVES (dī'vēz, Lat. *rich*). A translation of the Greek word *plousios*, a name applied in the Vulgate to the rich man in the parable of the rich man and Lazarus (Luke 16:19–31).

DIVINATION (dĭv'ĭ-nā'shŭn). The attempt to obtain secret knowledge, especially of the future, either by inspiration (Acts 16:16) or by the reading and interpreting of certain signs called omens. Those who practice divination assume that the gods or spirits possess secret knowledge that they can impart. The classical passage on this subject (Deut 18:10–11) and others (e.g. Lev 19:26; Ezek 8:17; Hos 4:12) severely condemn it in all its forms. There were various modes of divination: by reading omens, dreams, the use of the lot, hydromancy (foretelling from the appearance of water), astrology, rhabdomancy (use of the divining rod, Hos 4:12; Ezek 8:17), hepatoscopy (divination by an examination of the liver of animals), necromancy or consulting the dead, and the sacrifice of children by burning.

DIVORCE (Gr. *apostasion*). A means whereby a legal marriage is dissolved publicly and the participants are freed from further obligations of the matrimonial relationship. It is an ancient device that has varied procedurally over the centuries, but in the main it has been instituted on the initiative of the husband.

Although the Old Testament seems to permit divorce for rather general reasons (Deut. 24:1), it was usually either for adultery or childlessness. Because of the strength of the family unit, divorce was in actual fact not very common among the Hebrews. Nevertheless, in the postexilic period, in order for the purity of the Hebrew faith to be maintained, wholesale divorce was required by Ezra of those Jews who had married foreign wives in Babylonia (Ezra 9:2; 10:3, 16–17).

The NT forbids divorce. Jesus asserts that God had, under the Mosaic Law, allowed divorce as a concession to the hardness of the human heart (Matt. 19:8). Even the remarriage of widows was frowned upon by some in the apostolic period, though 1 Timothy 5:14 seems more lenient on this matter. Although in the early church the husband could not technically divorce an adulterous wife, he could separate from her or "put her away." Under such circumstances, neither party could marry without committing adultery. While a wife might emotionally reject a flagrantly unfaithful husband, she was nevertheless expected to show him an example of Christian love and stay with him if he wanted to continue the marriage. There were rare exceptions where a remarriage was permitted, but usually it was only for the pagan partner in a mixed Christian-pagan marriage. In any event the Christian partner was not permitted to remarry (1 Cor 7:10-15).

DOCTOR (Gr. *didaskalos, teacher*). The word *didaskolos* is rendered "doctor" by KJV only in Luke 2:46. It is usually rendered "master" or "teacher," whether referring to Jesus or other teachers. It is not to be confused with *iatros* ("physician") in certain passages (Matt 9:12; Mark 5:26; Luke 4:23).

DODANIM (See RODANIM)

DODO (dō'dō). 1. A man of Issachar, grandfather of the judge Tola (Judg 10:1). 2. A son of Ahohi, and father of Eleazar the second of David's mighty men (2 Sam 23:9 KJV). 3. A man of Bethlehem whose son Elhanan was one of David's mighty men (23:24).

DOE (See ANIMALS)

DOEG (dō'ĕg). An Edomite whom Saul made chief of his herdsmen. When David, fleeing from Saul, came to Nob, Doeg reported to Saul about the help Ahimelech the priest gave David (1 Sam 21:1-9). In revenge Saul gathered all the house of Ahimelech and Doeg killed them, 85 priests, all the women and children of the village, and even the cattle (22:11-23).

DOG (See ANIMALS)

DONKEY (See ANIMALS)

DOOR (Heb. *pethah, opening, doorway; deleth, door*; Gr. *thyra*). Doors in ancient times moved on pivots turning in sockets above and below and were frequently double doors. The word is often used in the NT in a figurative sense, many times referring to Christ (John 10:1, 2, 7; NIV "gate"; Rev 3:20) and sometimes to opportunity (Matt 25:10; Acts 14:27; 1 Cor 16:9) and freedom and power (Col 4:3).

DOORKEEPER Public buildings, temples, and walled cities had special officers to keep the doors (2 Sam 18:26; Ps 84:10; John 18:17).

DOR (dôr). A very ancient Canaanite city on the coast of Palestine, about 8 miles (13 km.) north of Caesarea. Joshua 11:2 and 12:23 read "Naphoth Dor." Joshua conquered it (11:1-8), but it was one of the towns not occupied by the Israelites (Judg 1:27).

DORCAS (Gr. *Dorkas, gazelle*). An early Christian disciple living at Joppa who was well known for her works of charity. When she died, her friends sent for Peter. He prayed, and she was raised from the dead. As a result, many believed (Acts 9:36-43).

DOTHAN (dō'thăn, Heb. *dōthān*, possibly *two wells*). A place in the boundaries between the tribes of Manasseh and Issachar, about 13 miles (22 km.) north of Shechem. Joseph's brothers cast him into a dry well-pit there (Gen 37:24). Nearly a millennium later, the prophet Elisha (2 Kings 6:13) was dwelling at Dothan when the king of Syria tried to capture him with an army. The king had learned that Elisha was able to tell his plans to the king of Israel, Joram. When Elisha's servant informed him that a great host surrounded Dothan, Elisha prayed that the Lord would open his servant's eyes, and the servant saw angelic hosts defending his master.

DOUGH The soft mass of moistened flour or meal that after baking becomes bread or cake—before raising (Exod 12:34, 39) or (generally) after raising (Jer 7:18; Hos 7:4).

DOVE (See BIRDS)

DOWRY (dou'rē). The price paid by the suitor to the parents of the prospective bride; also the portion that the bride brought to her husband (Gen 30:20; 34:12; Exod 22:17; and 1 Sam 18:25). NIV renders "gift," "bride-price."

DRACHMA (See MONEY)

DRAGON The Hebrew words *tannîm* and *tannîn*, appearing 13 and 14 times respectively in the OT, are translated in different passages and versions as "dragon,"

Bedouin women, probably from Galilee, drawing water by means of lowering buckets tied to ropes. Photo from late nineteenth to early twentieth century. Courtesy University Library, Istanbul

"jackal," "sea-monster," "serpent," "whale," and "wolf." They were evidently large creatures and of frightening aspect. In the NT, Satan is referred to as a dragon (Rev 12:3, 4, 7, 9, 13, 16, 17; 13:2, 4, 11; 16:13; 20:2).

DRAM (See WEIGHTS AND MEASURES)

DRAWER OF WATER The heavy work of bringing water from a well or a spring to the house was generally done by servants (Deut 29:11; Josh 9:23–27), sometimes by daughters (Gen 24:19–25). (See page 159.)

DREAM From the time of Jacob onward God's revelations were more often in dreams (Gen 28:10–17) than in theophany (e.g., Gen 18). He could reveal his will in dreams today, but the written Word of God and the indwelling Holy Spirit have made dreams of this sort unnecessary for added revelation. (Contrast Num 12:6 with Jude 8.) Often in ancient times God spoke in dreams to persons outside the chosen family—e.g., Abimelech (Gen 20:3), Laban (31:24), the butler and baker of Pharaoh (40:8–19), Pharaoh himself (41:36), and Nebuchadnezzar (Dan 2:1–45; 4:5–33). In these dreams the meaning was clear enough to need no interpretation, as in those of Abimelech and Laban, or else God caused one of his servants to interpret the meaning, as in the latter cases. One principle of interpretation seems quite evident: When the symbol is in the natural realm, the interpretation is in the human realm; e.g., when Joseph dreamed of the sun, moon, and eleven stars bowing to him, his brothers immediately knew the meaning as referring to his father, mother, and brothers (Gen 37:9–11). When the symbol is in the human realm (e.g., Dan 7:8), the interpretation is in the spiritual realm. Dreams may lead men astray, but God's Word tells how to deal with this situation (Deut 13:1–3; cf. 1 John 4:1–6). God spoke directly to Mary through Gabriel (Luke 1:26–35); an angel appeared to Joseph in a dream (Matt 1:20–24).

DREGS (See LEES)

DRESS Scripture refers to spinning and weaving cloth of hair, wool, cotton, flax, and eventually silk (Gen 14:23; 31:18–19; 37:3; 38:28; Job 7:6; Ezek 16:10, 13). With certain kinds of cloth and with astonishingly vivid colors of white, purple, scarlet, blue, yellow, and black, the Hebrew people represented the state of their minds and emotions. When joyful and ready to enter into festive occasions, they donned their clothing of brightest array; and when they mourned or humbled themselves, they put on sackcloth—cloth from which sacks were made—which was considered the very poorest kind of dress (1 Kings 20:31–32; Job 16:15; Isa 15:3; Jer 4:8; 6:26; Lam 2:10; Ezek 7:18; Dan 9:3; Joel 1:8).

When a person's heart was torn by grief, the inner emotions were given expression by "rending" or tearing the garments (Mark 14:63; Acts 11:14). To confirm an oath or seal a contract, a man plucked off his shoe and gave it to his neighbor (Ruth 4:8). When Jonathan made a covenant with David, he went even farther and gave him his own garments (1 Sam 18:3–4).

The basic garments used among the men of biblical times seem to have consisted of the *inner-tunic*, the *tunic-coat*, the *girdle*, and the *cloak*. Added to this was the *headdress* and the *shoes* or *sandals*. The girdle is not only a picturesque article of dress but also may indicate the position and office of the wearer. It is sometimes used to signify power and strength (2 Sam 22:40; Isa 11:5; Jer 13:1; Eph 6:14).

The **leather girdle** or belt, was from 2 to 6 inches (5 to 15 cm.) wide, and was the kind of girdle worn by Elijah (2 Kings 1:8) and by John the Baptist (Matt 3:4).

The **simlah**, the large, loose-fitting, sleeveless cloak or mantle, was worn by day and slept in by night; therefore it was not be to taken in pledge unless it was returned by sundown (Exod 22:26). This long outer garment or topcoat was, in all probability, the "mantle" worn by Elijah and Elisha (2 Kings 2:8–14). It was the camel-hair garment worn by John the Baptist (Matt 3:4). Blue tassels on the borders of Jewish garments were to remind them to keep all the commandments and to be holy before God (Num 15.38–40; Deut 22:12).

The word "skirt," found several times in the KJV, usually refers to an article of male, not female, clothing, and has a number of meanings: "corner" (Ruth 3:9; 1 Sam 24:4ff.), "hem" (Exod 28:33), "collar" (Ps 133:2).

The **headdress** was worn chiefly as a protection against the sun and as a finish to a completed costume. It varied from time to time according to rank, sex, and nationality. In the main, however, there were three known types that were worn by the male members of the Hebrew and surrounding nations: the *cap*, the *turban*, and the *head-scarf*.

Shoes were of soft leather, while sandals were of a harder leather and were worn for rougher wear. Shoes were usu-

Egyptian.   Canaanite.   Assyrian.

Persian.   Greek.   Roman.

Artist's rendition of ancient peoples and their dress, based on scenes from history and monuments. Courtesy Carta, Jerusalem

ally removed at the doorway before entering a home, on approaching God (Exod 3:5), and during mourning (2 Sam 15:30). Property rights were secured by the seller pulling off his shoe and giving it to the purchaser (Ruth 4:7).

Women's Dress. Mosaic law forbade either sex to wear the same form of clothing as was used by the other (Deut 22:5). A few articles of female clothing carried somewhat the same name and basic pattern, yet there was always sufficient difference in embossing, embroidery, and needlework so that in appearance the line of demarcation between men and women could be readily detected.

Peter found it necessary to warn Christian women against relying on elaborate braiding of the hair to make themselves attractive (1 Peter 3:3). In the OT there are a number of references to painting the eyes in order to enhance their beauty, but it is always spoken of as a showy and somewhat vulgar device, unworthy of good women. Jezebel painted her eyes (2 Kings 9:30).

In ancient times women especially were much given to various kinds of ornaments. Earrings and nose-rings were especially common. On account of their drop-like shape, earrings are called "chains" (Isa 3:19 KJV) and "pendants" (Judg 8:26). Men also wore such earrings (Gen 35:4; Judg 8:24). The nose-ring or nose-jewel made necessary the piercing of the nostrils. Rings were worn by both men and women. All ancient Israelites wore signet rings (Gen 38:18 KJV; NIV "seal"). Rings were often worn on the toes, anklets (bangles) on the ankles (Isa 3:18), bracelets on the arms and wrists (Gen 24:22; Ezek 16:11).

Beginning about the second century B.C., all male Jews were expected to wear at morning prayers, except on Sabbaths and festivals, two *phylacteries*, one on the forehead, called a *frontlet*, the other on the left arm. They consisted of small leather cases containing four passages of Scripture from the OT (Exod 13:1-10, 11-16; Deut 6:4-9; 11:13-21).

DRINK The most common beverage of the Jews was water—procured chiefly by means of cisterns (2 Sam 17:18; Jer 38:6) and by means of wells. Wine was also widely used, both in the form of new wine (called must) and fermented wine. Next to bread and vegetables, the most important food was milk, both of larger and smaller cattle, especially goat's milk.

DRINK OFFERING (See SACRIFICE AND OFFERINGS)

DROMEDARY (See ANIMALS)

DROPSY (See DISEASES)

DROSS The refuse in impure metals that is generally separated by melting, when the dross rises to the top and may be skimmed off. It is used figuratively of what is worthless (Ps 119:119; Isa 1:22, 25; Ezek 22:18-19).

DRUNKENNESS The Scriptures show that drunkenness was one of the major vices of antiquity, even among the Hebrews. Well-known cases of intoxication are Noah (Gen 9:21), Lot (19:33, 35), Nabal (1 Sam 25:36), Uriah (2 Sam 11:13), Ammon (13:28), Elah (1 Kings 16:9), and Ben-Hadad (20:16). Even the women were guilty (Amos 4:1). The symptoms and effects of strong drink are vividly pictured (Job 12:25; Ps 107:27; Isa 28:7; Hos 4:11). While Scripture condemns intemperance in the strongest terms, it does not prescribe total abstinence as a formal and universal rule. Nevertheless, the principles laid down point in that direction (Matt 16:24-25; Mark 9:42-43; Rom 14:13-21; 1 Cor 8:8-13; Eph 5:18). Drunkenness is sometimes used figuratively (Isa 29:9).

DRUSILLA (drū-sĭl'à, Gr. *Drousilla*). The youngest of the three daughters of Herod Agrippa I, her sisters being Bernice and Mariamme. At the age of 14 she married Azizus, king of Emesa, but left him for Felix, procurator of Judea, who was captivated by her beauty and employed a Cyprian sorcerer to gain her for his wife. When Paul unsparingly preached before Felix and Drusilla of righteousness, temperance, and judgment, Felix trembled (Acts 24:24-25). See also HEROD.

DUKE In general a leader of a clan or a tribal chief. NIV usually translates "chief" (Gen 36:15-16; Exod 15:15; Josh 13:21; 1 Chron 1:51-52).

DUMAH (dū'mà, Heb. *dûmâh, silence*). **1.** One of the 12 sons of Ishmael (Gen 25:14-16) and apparently head of one of the 12 tribes of Ishmaelites in Arabia. **2.** A place unknown but connected with Seir or Edom (Isa 21:11-12). The designation may be symbolic, applying to all Edom and indicating its coming destruction (cf. Obad 15-16). **3.** A village in southern Judah and associated with Hebron in Joshua 15:52-54.

DUMBNESS (See DISEASES)

DUNG The excrement of man or beast. In several of the offerings, under the Levitical priesthood the blood and the fat and the flesh were used, but the skins and the dung were discarded or burnt outside the camp (Exod 29:14; Lev 8:17 KJV; NIV "offal"). The ultimate disgrace was to have one's carcass treated as dung (2 Kings 9:37 KJV; NIV "refuse"). Dry dung was (and is) often used as fuel (Ezek 4:12–15). Paul counted his natural advantages as dung (NIV "rubbish") compared with his blessings in Christ (Phil 3:8).

DUNG GATE One of the 11 gates of Jerusalem in Nehemiah's time (Neh 2:13; 3:13–14; 12:31). It was located near the SW corner of the wall and was used for the disposal of rubbish, garbage, and dung. It led out to the Valley of Hinnom.

DUST (Heb. *'avaq, dust; 'aphar, dust;* Gr. *koniortos, dust; chous, clay, earth*).

In the warm and dry climate of the ancient Near East, dust was a reality that prompted such practices as washing the feet on entering a home (John 13:1–17). Symbolically (1) throwing dust on the head was a common sign of mourning or repentance (Job 2:12; Rev 18:19). (2) Shaking off dust from the feet was a sign of having no further responsibility for the area where the dust was picked up, thus leaving that area to God's judgment (Matt 10:14; Luke 9:5; 10:11; Acts 13:51). In referring to human beings as made of dust (1 Cor 15:47–49) Paul was echoing a strong theme of the OT where man is said to be made from dust and to return to dust (Gen 2:7; 3:19; Job 4:19; 17:16).

DYERS, DYEING (See OCCUPATIONS AND PROFESSIONS)

-E-

EAGLE (See BIRDS)

EAR (Heb. *'ōzen*, Gr. *ous, ōtion, the physical organ of hearing*). In biblical times people spoke to each other's ears; instead of listening they "inclined their ears." God "bowed down his ear" to hear prayer. The ear was sanctified by blood in the consecration of Aaron and his sons to the priesthood (Exod 29:20; Lev 8:24) and at the cleansing of a leper (Lev 14:14). The piercing of the ear of a slave denoted permanent servitude (Exod 21:6; Deut 15:17).

EARNEST (Gr. *arrabōn*). A legal term—denoting the payment of a sum of money to make a contract binding, guaranteeing a further payment to fulfill the contract—used of the Holy Spirit (2 Cor 1:22; 5:5; Eph 1:14). The NIV renders "seal" in the first passage, "deposit" in the two others. The Holy Spirit's gift to believers is the assurance that their redemption will be fully carried out.

EARRING (Heb. *nezem, 'āghîl, hoop*). Men and women wore nose-rings (Gen 24:47; Isa 3:21; Ezek 16:12) and earrings (Gen 35:4; Exod 32:2-3; Ezek 16:12). Rings or hoops in other passages may be either nose-rings or earrings (Exod 35:22; Num 31:50; Judg 8:24-26; Job 42:11; Prov 11:22; 25:12; Hos 2:13).

EARTH (Heb. *'ădhāmâh, ground; 'erets, earth*; Gr. *gē, earth; oikoumenē, inhabited earth; kosmos, orderly arrangement*). The Hebrew word *'ădhāmâh* most commonly means the tilled reddish soil of Palestine. But it is also used to denote a piece of real estate (Gen 47:18ff.), earth as a material substance (2:7), a territory (28:15), or the whole earth (Gen 12:3; Deut 14:2).

The word *'erets* denotes commonly the earth as opposed to the sky (Gen 1:1; Josh 2:11), or "land" in the sense of a country (Gen 13:10; 45:18). In the NT, *gē* means "ground," arable and otherwise (Matt 5:18; John 8:6); "the earth" as opposed to the heavens (Matt 6:10; Acts 2:19); and "territory" or "region" (Luke 4:25; John 3:22). *Oikoumenē* carries the meaning of the inhabited earth or the "world" (Matt 24:14; Luke 4:5), the Roman Empire (Luke 2:1), and all the inhabitants of the earth (Acts 17:6; Rev 3:10). *Kosmos* in a derived sense is used to denote the earth, though it is always translated "world."

EARTHQUAKE (Heb. *ra'ash, quaking;* Gr. *seismos, earthquake*). There are four actual earthquakes recorded in Scripture: the one for Elijah's benefit (1 Kings 19:11); the one referred to by Amos (1:1) and Zechariah (14:5) as occurring in the reign of Uzziah; the one that happened at Christ's resurrection (Matt 28:2); and the one that freed Paul and Silas from prison (Acts 16:26). Earthquakes may be used by God in judgment. All natural phenomenon—earthquake, wind, storm, rain, hail, and the rest—are under divine sovereign control and are part of his armory for ruling the world in righteousness.

EAST (Heb. *qedem* and other forms of this root, *front, aforetime, east; mizrâh, place of the sunrise, east;* Gr. *anatolē, rising, east*). East was a significant direction for the Hebrews. Eden was "in the east" (Gen. 2:8). The gate of the tabernacle was on the east side (Exod 38:13-14). In the wilderness, Moses, Aaron and Judah camped on the east side of the tabernacle, and this area was barred to strangers (Num 2:3; 3:38). The "Beautiful" gate of Herod's temple (Acts 3:2) was the east gate. Ezekiel saw the glory of the Lord leave the doomed temple by the east gate (Ezek 10:19; 11:23). In his description of the Lord's temple, Ezekiel saw the glory of the Lord coming from the east and entering the temple by the east gate (43:2, 4). Job was one of the people of the East (Job 1:3). The Magi came from the east and said they had seen the star of the King of the Jews in the east (Matt 2:1-2).

EASTER The word "Easter" occurs only in Acts 12:4 (KJV). It is the day on which most Christians celebrate Jesus' resurrection. There is no celebration of the Resurrection in the NT. Jewish Christians linked it with Passover and so observed it on the 14th day of Nisan regardless of the day of the week. But Gentile believers celebrated the Resurrection on Sunday. This difference was settled by the Council of Nicea in A.D. 325, which ruled that Easter should be celebrated on the first Sunday after the full moon following the vernal equinox. This is the system followed today, the date of Easter varying between March 22 and April 25.

EAST SEA (See DEAD SEA)

EAST WIND (Heb. *qādîm*). Hot, dry wind from the east came to Palestine over the desert (Jer 4:11). An east wind brought the plague of locusts on Egypt (Exod 10:13) and dried up the sea so that the Israelites could cross over on dry land (14:21). Many references mention the destructive results of the east wind: thin and withered heads of grain (Gen 41:6), broken ships (Ps 48:7; Ezek 27:26), withered plants (17:10), dried fountains (Hos 13:15), Jonah's fainting spell (Jonah 4:8), and judgment by God (Isa 27:8; Jer 18:17).

EBAL (ē'băl, Heb. *'ēvāl,* meaning uncertain). **1.** A son of Shobal (Gen 36:23; 1 Chron 1:40). **2.** A mountain 3,077 feet (962 m.) high, one of the highest points in the land of Samaria, opposite Mt. Gerizim. At its foot was Jacob's well (John 4:20). Shechem was located nearby. When the Israelites first entered the land, Moses commanded them to erect on Mt. Ebal a monument of stones (on which the law was inscribed) and a stone altar for burnt offerings and peace offerings. The law, with its blessings and curses, was recited by the people antiphonally, the blessings from Mt. Gerizim and the curses from Mt. Ebal (Deut 27:4–26; cf. Josh 8:30–35). **3.** In KJV one of the sons of Joktan; rendered Obal in NIV (1 Chron 1:22).

EBED (ē'bĕd, Heb. *'evedh, servant*). **1.** Father of Gaal, the adversary of Ahimelech who unsuccessfully rebelled against this ruler in Shechem (Judg 9:26–45). **2.** Son of Jonathan, one of the 50 men of the family of Adin that came from Babylon under Ezra (Ezra 8:6).

EBED-MELECH (ē'bĕd-mē-lĕk, Heb. *'evedh melekh, servant of the king*). An Ethiopian eunuch who drew Jeremiah up out of a muddy dungeon (Jer 38:7–13). The Lord gave Jeremiah a message for Ebed-Melech, assuring him of safety and

The annual Easter procession along the Mount of Olives in Jerusalem, marking Jesus' resurrection. Courtesy Zev Radovan

protection in the coming destruction of the city (39:15–18).

EBENEZER (ĕb'ĕn-ē'zêr, Heb. *'even-'ezer, stone of help*). **1.** A town of Ephraim near Aphek by which the Israelites camped before fighting a losing battle with the Philistines (1 Sam 4:1). The ark of God was captured by these enemies of Israel, and they brought it from Ebenezer to their city, Ashdod (5:1). **2.** Later, God gave Israel victory over the Philistines. Samuel then took a stone and set it up as a memorial of the occasion, calling it *Eben-ezer,* "the stone of help" (7:12).

EBER (ē'bêr, Heb. *'ever*). This word means "a region across or beyond." The name of the Hebrew people may be derived from Eber, as its form is the same as the word *iberi* (meaning "Hebrew") without the gentilic ending. The Hebrews were a people who came from a region beyond the Euphrates River. **1.** The son of Shelah, a grandson of Shem (Gen 10:24; 11:14; 1 Chron 1:18). He was the father of Peleg and Joktan (Gen 10:25; 11:16; 1 Chron 1:19–25). **2.** The head of a family in the tribe of Gad (5:13). **3.** The oldest son of Elpaal, a Benjamite (8:12). **4.** A son of Shashak, a Benjamite (8:19). **5.** Head of a priestly family that came from Babylon under Zerubbabel (Neh 12:20).

EBIASAPH (ē-bī'à-săph, Heb. *'avî'-āsāph* and *'ĕvî'āsāph, my father has gathered*). A son of Elkanah, a descendant of Kohath, son of Levi (Exod 6:24; 1 Chron 6:23; 9:19).

EBONY (See PLANTS)

EBRONAH (See ABRONAH)

ECBATANA (ĕk-băt'-ă-nà, Heb. *'ahmethā'*). The capital of Media, the summer residence of the Persian kings and later the Parthian capital. It is mentioned in the Bible only in Ezra 6:2 (KJV "Achmetha"), denoting the location of the palace in which the decree of Cyrus authorizing the building of the Jewish temple was found.

ECCLESIASTES (ĕ-klē-zĭ-ăs'tēz, Gr. *Ekklēsiatēs,* Heb., *qōheleth,* meaning probably the official speaker in an assembly). Traditionally the book has been ascribed to Solomon, based on the superscription (Eccl 1:1) and several allusions to the author's wisdom (1:16), his interest in proverbs (12:9; cf. 1 Kings 4:32), and his building projects (2:4–11).

The book presents a pessimistic view of life apart from God. The writer tells us that the endless cycles of nature (Eccl 1:2–11), wisdom (1:16–18; 2:12–17),

The land of Edom, a region of rugged mountains and plateaus that extends from the southern end of the Dead Sea to the Gulf of Aqabah. Courtesy Studium Biblicum Franciscanum, Jerusalem

pleasure (2:1–8), and toil (2:9–11; 2:18–23) are meaningless.

There is a positive life view that emerges from the book that may be called a theology of contentment. In view of the lack of substance and meaning in life, Qoheleth urges his readers to enjoy life, for it is God who gives us that privilege (Eccl 2:24–25). This satisfaction does not belong to all mankind, for the work of the sinner ends in futility (2:26). Godly contentment, however, is not the ultimate good for mankind. Qoheleth reminds us of a future time when God will bring all things into judgment. This is the conclusion of his search for meaning in life (12:14). One is reminded of the counsel of the apostle Paul in view of the futility of life, for like Qoheleth, he looked away from life's meaninglessness to his future redemption (Rom 8:20; cf. vv. 22–25).

Qoheleth urges us to fear God and obey him. Only when God is taken into account (Eccl 12:1) and his will observed (12:13) does life impart purpose and satisfaction.

ECCLESIASTICUS (See APOCRYPHA)

EDEN (Heb. *'ēden, delight*). **1.** The district in which the Lord God planted a garden for the newly created man, Adam. In it grew every tree that was pleasant to see and good for food, including the tree of life and the tree of the knowledge of good and evil. Adam and Eve lived there until they sinned by eating the forbidden fruit and were expelled (Gen 2–3). Later

Scripture writers mention Eden as an illustration of a delightful place (Isa 51:3; Ezek 28:13; 31:9, 16, 18; 36:35; Joel 2:3). **2.** An Eden mentioned by the Assyrians as conquered by them (2 Kings 19:12; Isa 37:12; cf. Ezek 27:23). The house of Eden, or Beth Eden (Amos 1:5), was probably near Damascus. **3.** A Gershonite who lived in Hezekiah's time and served under Kore, the porter of the east gate of the temple, in distributing the holy oblations (2 Chron 29:12; 31:15).

EDER (ē'dêr, Heb. *'edher, floods*). **1.** A city in south Judah near Edom (Josh 15:21). **2.** A son of Mushi, the son of Merari (1 Chron 23:23; 24:30). **3.** A son of Beriah, grandson of Shaharaim, a Benjamite (8:15); KJV, Ader.

EDOM, EDOMITES (ē'dŏm, ē'dŏm-īts, Heb. *'ĕdhōm, 'ădhômîn,* from *'ĕdhōm, red*). The nation and its people who were the descendants of Esau. He founded the country, so his name is equated with Edom (Gen 25:30; 36:1, 8). The country was also called Seir, or Mt. Seir, the name of the territory in which the Edomites lived, the mountain and plateau area between the Dead Sea and the Gulf of Aqabah about 100 miles (167 km.) long and up to 40 miles (67 km.) wide. When Esau departed from Canaan to find room for his cattle and came to Mt. Seir (36:5–8), the Horites had some tribal chiefs reigning in the land (36:29–30). Esau took the daughter of one of these chiefs for a wife, Oholibamah, daughter of Anah

(36:2, 25). Esau's sons and grandsons were also tribal chiefs (36:15-19, 40-43). Probably the Edomites gradually absorbed the Horites, until they disappeared (Deut 2:12, 22).

Eight kings reigned over Edom before the Israelites had any such ruler (Gen 36:31-39). One refused to permit the Israelites to pass through his country (Num 20:14-21). Saul fought against the Edomites (1 Sam 14:47), but David conquered them and put garrisons throughout the whole land (2 Sam 8:14). The Israelite army spent six months cutting off all the men of the kingdom (1 Kings 11:15-16). Solomon made the Edomite cities Ezion Geber and Eloth, on the Gulf of Aqabah, seaports from which his ships sailed to Ophir (2 Chron 8:17-18). Judah lost Edom in the reign of Jehoram (2 Kings 8:20, 22). About 50 years later, Amaziah, king of Judah, inflicted a severe defeat on the Edomites (14:7). About 735 B.C. Rezin, king of Syria, went to war with Judah, captured Eloth, and drove the Jews out (16:6). When Jerusalem was destroyed and Judah depopulated in 586 B.C., the Edomites rejoiced over the affliction of the Judeans and began to take over the southern part of Palestine. Eventually penetrating as far north as Hebron intensified the already smoldering hatred between the Jews and Edomites (see Ps 137:7; Ezek 25:12-14; Amos 1:11; Obad 10-13).

Edom figures prominently in the prophetic Scriptures (Isa 11:14; 34:8ff.; 63:1ff.; Ezek 35:2ff.; Joel 3:19; Amos 9:12; Obadiah). The explanation of this often unexpected appearance of Edom finds its origin in that the conquest of Edom was a unique achievement of David; the overthrow of Edom therefore became a symbol of the reign of the Davidic Messiah.

EDREI (ĕd'rē-ī, Heb. *'edhre'î, strong*). **1.** One of the chief sites of Og, king of Bashan (Deut 1:4; Josh 12:4) where he fought with the Israelites (Num 21:33; Deut 3:1). They defeated him and took his country with its cities, including Edrei (3:10). This town was assigned to the half-tribe of Manasseh (Josh 13:12, 31). It was located about 30 miles (50 km.) east and a little south of the Sea of Galilee. **2.** A fortified city of Naphtali (19:37).

EGG (Heb. *bêtsâ, whiteness*). This appears in the OT only in the plural form (cf. Job 6:6—another Heb word): birds' eggs (Deut 22:6); ostrich eggs (Job 39:14); any kind of eggs (Isa 10:14); snake eggs (59:5).

EGLAH (ĕg'làh, Heb. *'eglàh, heifer*). The name of one of David's wives who was the mother of his sixth son, Ithream (2 Sam 3:5; 1 Chron 3:3).

EGLATH SHELISHIYAH (ĕg'lăth-shĭ-lĭsh'ĕ-yà, the third Eglath). A town near Zoar mentioned in prophecies against Moab (Isa 15:5; Jer 48:34).

EGLON (ĕg'lôn, Heb. *'eghlôn*). **1.** A city of Canaan located between Gaza and Lachish. Joshua captured the city (Josh 10:3, 5, 23, 36-37; 12:12). It was assigned to Judah (15:39). **2.** A king of Moab who captured Jericho, the city of palm trees (Judg 3:12-13). The Israelites served him for 18 years (3:14). Then he was killed by Ehud, whom the Lord had raised up to save the children of Israel (3:21).

EGYPT (ē'jĭpt, Gr. *Aigyptos*). To the Israelites, Egypt was Mizraim (Heb. *mitsrayim*). "Egypt," said Hecateus, echoed by Herodotus, "is the gift of the Nile." In view of the almost complete absence of rain, the annual overflow of the Nile was of great importance to the land, for it watered the soil and provided it with new alluvium and some organic fertilizer. Its waters were used for drinking (Exod 7:18, 21, 24; Ps 78:44), bathing (Exod 2:5), and irrigation (Deut 11:10). It was the main channel of commerce and travel.

The awareness of the dependence of land and people on the resources of the Nile led to the deification of the river, the longest river in the world—4,000 miles (6,667 km.).

The division of the land into Upper and Lower Egypt predates the union into one nation. Lower Egypt included the delta and a short section of the valley southward; the rest of the valley to Aswan was Upper Egypt. The land was protected by natural borders to the south and west and east. On the NE border, fronting Asia, the Egyptians made early use of fortresses and other checkpoints to control invasion from this direction. With such protection, the country was free to develop its culture in comparative security and still to retain a free exchange of goods and ideas with other peoples.

In general, the religion may be described as a complex polytheism, with many local deities of varying importance. Some of the more important divinities included: Osiris and Isis, Ra (Re) and Horus, sun-gods, Set and Amon-Re. There was a preoccupation with death. The influence of Egyptian religion on Israelite religious practice was largely negative.

The Great Pyramid at Giza, built during the reign of Khufu, 4th Dynasty (2575 – 2465 B.C.). The base area is 230 square meters; the original height was 146 meters. Courtesy Zev Radovan

Egypt was the "iron furnace of affliction" during the bondage, but Israelites were so impressed with the might of the Pharaonic kingdom that there were elements in Judah that looked to Egypt for help even when she was dominated by Assyria (cf. 2 Kings 18:21; Isa 36:6). An unreliable ally, Egypt was also a sanctuary for some of Israel's individual enemies. From Egypt, too, came some of the worst occasions for apostasy in Israel. It was an abundant Near Eastern breadbasket and was for centuries the ranking world power.

Egypt appears early in biblical references, since Mizraim (Egypt) is a son of Ham (Gen 10:6). Abram sojourned in Egypt during a famine. The closest Egyptian-biblical relationships may be seen in the narrative of Joseph and the account of Israelite life in Egypt to the time of their Exodus (Gen 37, 39–50; Exod 1–15).

When the Assyrian remnant was making its dying stand and Egypt marched to aid them against the rampaging Babylonians, the Judean Josiah made a fatal effort to stop the Egyptian forces at Megiddo (2 Kings 23:29–30; 2 Chron 35:20–27). After the fall of Jerusalem in 586 B.C. and the subsequent murder of Gedaliah, the Judeans again looked to Egypt as a place of refuge in spite of the prophet's warning. Here they were scattered about, with a group as far south as Elephantine maintaining a temple and

keeping up correspondence with Palestine, as revealed by the Aramaic papyri found at Elephantine.

Most of the NT references to Egypt have to do with Israel's past. Joseph was divinely directed to take the infant Jesus and Mary to Egypt to escape the wrath of Herod (Matt 2:13–15; cf. Exod 4:22; Hos 11:1). Egypt often was a place of refuge or a means of sustaining life. It has the scriptural prediction of a wonderful future (Isa 19:24–25; cf. 19:18–23).

EGYPT, RIVER OF The dividing line between Canaan and Egypt (Gen 15:18; Num 34:5), the southern boundary of Judah (Josh 15:4, 47). It is coupled with the Euphrates River (Gen 15:18; 1 Kings 8:65; 2 Kings 24:7; 2 Chron 7:8) as marking the northern and southern limits of the land given to the Israelites. It is not really an Egyptian river, but a *wadi*.

EHI (e'hī, Heb. *'ēhî*). A son of Benjamin (Gen 46:21); in Numbers 26:38 spelled Ahiram; in 1 Chronicles 8:1 Aharah.

EHUD (ē'hŭd, Heb. *'ēhûdh, union*). 1. A descendant of Benjamin (1 Chron 7:10; 8:6). 2. A judge of the Israelites, a Benjamite, the son of Gera. A left-handed man, he killed Eglon, the king of Moab, and rallied the Israelites against the Moabites. They subdued these enemies, and the land had peace for 80 years until Ehud died (Judg 3:15–30).

EKRON (ĕk'rŏn, Heb. *'eqrôn, eradication*). The most northern of the five chief cities of the Philistines (1 Sam 6:17). Located on the boundary between Judah and Dan (Josh 15:11; 19:43), it was assigned to Judah (15:45). After the Philistines returned the ark from Ekron to escape the wrath of God (1 Sam 6), the Israelites regained possession of Ekron and other cities (7:14). Following David's victory over Goliath, the Israelites drove the Philistines back to Ekron (17:52). The god of this city was Baal-Zebub (2 Kings 1:3). The prophets mention Ekron with other Philistine cities (Jer 25:20; Amos 1–8; Zeph 2:4; Zech 9:5, 7).

EL (Heb. *'ēl, God*). The generic word for God in the Semitic languages: Aramaic *elah*, Arabic *ilah*, Akkadian *ilu*. In the OT, *el* is used over 200 times for "God." El was the chief, and somewhat vague, shadowy god of the Canaanite pantheon, the father of men and of gods (see RAS SHAMRA). A plural term, *'elohim*, was the Hebrews' regular name for God.

ELADAH (See ELEADAH)

ELAH (ē'làh, Heb. *'ēlâh, terebinth*). 1. A descendant of Esau who was a chief of Edom (Gen 36:41). 2. The valley in which David killed Goliath (1 Sam 17:2, 19; 21:9). 3. A king of Israel, the son of Baasha (1 Kings 16:8–14), who reigned two years and was assassinated by Zimri, fulfilling the prediction of Jehu (16:1–4). 4. The father of Hoshea, the last king of Israel (2 Kings 15:30; 17:1; 18:1, 9). 5. A son of Caleb, the son of Jephunneh (1 Chron 4:15). 6. A Benjamite, one of the people who returned to Jerusalem from Babylon (9:8).

ELAM (ē'lăm, Heb. *'êlām*). 1. A son of Shem, thus making Elam a Semitic nation (Gen 10:22; 1 Chron 1:17). 2. A son of Shashak, a descendant of Benjamin (8:24). 3. The fifth son of Meshelemiah, a doorkeeper of the Korahites (26:3). 4. The progenitor of a family of 1,254 members that returned from exile under Zerubbabel (Ezra 2:7; Neh 7:12). 5. Another forefather of a returned family with the same number of members (Ezra 2:31; Neh 7:34). 6. The father of two sons who returned from exile with Ezra (Ezra 8:7). 7. An ancestor of a man who confessed marriage to a foreign woman. Evidently this ancestor was either no. 4, 5, or 6 above (10:2, 26). 8. A chief who sealed the covenant with Nehemiah (Neh 10:14). 9. One of the priests who took part in the dedication of the wall (12:42).

Elamite soldier of the Persian guard holding a spear, on a glazed brick from Susa, fifth century B.C. He is carrying a quiver strapped over his back and an unsheathed bow on his shoulder. Courtesy Réunion des Musées Nationaux

ELAM (ē'lăm, Heb. *'êlām*). A country situated on the east side of the Tigris River opposite Babylonia. Its population was made up of a variety of tribes. Elam was one of the earliest civilizations. In classical literature it was known as *Susiana*, the Greek name for Susa, the capital city of Elam.

Isaiah cites Elam as one of the nations going up with Cyrus against Babylon (Isa 21:2) and joining the Assyrian army against Judah (22:6). Elam was one of the nations forced to drink the cup of God's wrath (Jer 25:25) and doomed to judgment (49:34–39). Elamites were among the peoples brought over to Samaria by the Assyrians (Ezra 4:9–10). Elamite was one of the tongues being spoken by visitors at Jerusalem (Acts 2:9).

ELASAH (ĕl'à-sàh, Heb. *'el'āsâh, God has made*). 1. One of the sons of Pashhur who was guilty of marrying foreign women (Ezra 10:22). 2. Son of Shaphan, one of the men sent by Jeremiah from Jerusalem with a message of advice to the exiles in Babylon (Jer 29:3).

ELATH, ELOTH (ē'lăth, ē'lŏth, Heb. *'êlâth*, or *'êlôth, lofty trees*). A town situated very near to Ezion Geber, Solomon's seaport (1 Kings 9:26). The Israelites passed the area on the way to the Promised Land (Deut 2:8). Azariah (767–740 B.C.) built it up, probably for use as a seaport, when he took it from Edom (2 Kings 14:22; 2 Chron 26:2). During the reign of Ahaz over Judah (736–716), Rezin, king of Syria, joined with Pekah, king of Israel, threatened Jerusalem, and captured Elath (2 Kings 16:5–6).

EL-BERITH (ĕl-bĕr-īth', Heb. *god of the covenant*). An alternate name for the god worshiped at Shechem (Judg 9:46). Some of the people of Shechem sought safety in his temple when Abimelech destroyed the city. Possibly to be identified with Baal-Berith of Judges 8:33; 9:4.

ELDAD (ĕl'dăd, Heb. *'elādh, God has loved*). A man who remained in camp with Medad when the 70 elders received the gift of prophecy at the tabernacle. The spirit of prophecy came to Eldad and Medad in camp, and they prophesied there. When Joshua begged Moses to forbid them, he refused, saying he wished that all God's people were prophets (Num 11:24–29).

ELDER (Heb. *zāqēn*, Gr. *presbyteros*). In ancient times the older men of a community were known as the elders. They governed the community and made all major decisions. Moses called the

elders of Israel together to announce that the Lord had heard their cries for help and had appointed him to lead them out of Egypt (Exod 4:29). Later he called them out to institute the Passover (12:21). At Sinai, 70 elders went up the mountain with Moses and saw the God of Israel (24:9). In the wilderness, to relieve Moses, 70 elders shared his divine anointing (Num 11:25). After the Israelites had settled in Canaan and had a king over them, the elders still functioned (1 Kings 8:1). Each town had its group of elders (Ezra 10:14; cf. 1 Sam 16:4). After the return from exile the elders made up the Sanhedrin, the Jewish governing council.

The elders joined the priests and scribes against Jesus (Matt 27:12). When churches came into being, elders were appointed for each congregation (Acts 14:23). The terms "elders" and "bishops" are used interchangeably in the NT (Acts 20:17, 28; Titus 1:5, 7). These men were required to be blameless in their lives and obedient to the truth in their faith (1 Tim 3:1–7; Titus 1:6–9). Their duties involved spiritual oversight of the congregation and teaching the Word (1 Tim 5:17). Before the first century A.D. had elapsed, the term "bishop" had taken on a special meaning, denoting the one leader of a church. A biblical example of this (both in the Book of Acts and in Paul's letters) is James, the brother of Jesus, who was obviously the leader of the Jerusalem church.

ELEALEH (ē'lē-ā'lĕ, Heb. *'el'ālêh, God doth ascend*). A town near to and always mentioned with Heshbon (Num 32:3, 37). It appears in prophecies against Moab (Isa 15:4; 16:9; Jer 48:34).

ELEASAH (ē'lē-ā-sàh, Heb. *'el'āsâh, God has made*). 1. A Hezronite (1 Chron 2:39–40). 2. A Benjamite, a descendant of Saul (8:37; 9:43).

ELEAZAR (ĕ-lē-ā'zär, Heb. *'el'āzār, God has helped*). 1. The third son of Aaron (Exod 6:23). After the death of the two elder sons, Nadab and Abihu (Lev 10:1–2), Eleazar was designated to be chief priest (Num 3:32). He ministered before the Lord with Ithamar, his brother, helping his father. But the Lord assigned special tasks to Eleazar: gathering up the 250 censers offered to the Lord by rebellious men and hammering them into sheets to cover the altar (16:36–39), and leading the ceremony involving a red heifer (19:3–4). When Aaron died, Eleazar became the chief priest (20:28). He assisted Moses in numbering the people (26:1–2), in dividing the spoil from the slaughter of the Midianites (31:13–54), and in assigning land to the tribes east of the Jordan (32:28). He was divinely appointed to help Joshua divide the Promised Land among the tribes (34:17; Josh 14:1; 19:51). His only son was Phineas (1 Chron 6:4). Eleazar died soon after Joshua's death (Josh 24:33). **2.** The son of Abinadab who was sanctified to keep the ark after it had been brought to his father's house (1 Sam 7:1). **3.** Son of Dodai, one of the three mightiest men of David who gained a great victory over the Philistines (2 Sam 23:9–10; 1 Chron 11:12–14). **4.** A childless son of Mahli (23:21–22; 24:28). **5.** Son of Phineas, a Levite, one of the group to which Ezra delivered the temple treasures for tabulating and keeping for the temple (Ezra 8:32–34). **6.** A priest who took part in the service dedicating the wall (Neh 12:42). **7.** An ancestor of Joseph, the husband of Mary (Matt 1:15).

ELECTION AND PREDESTINATION For God to predestinate (Gr. *proorizō*) is for him to decree or foreordain the circumstances and destiny of people according to his perfect will (Rom 8:29–30; Eph 1:11), a particular aspect of the general providence of God. For God to elect (Heb. *bachar*, Gr. *eklegomai*) is for him to choose for salvation and/or service a people or a person; the choice is based not on merit but on his free, sovereign love (Deut 4:37; 7:7; 14:2; Acts 13:17; 15:7; 1 Thess 1:4). Further, since predestination and election are both presented as acts of God, election cannot be on the basis of God's knowing in advance the reactions of people to his will. Election must be choice flowing only from God's own initiative. Believers were chosen in Christ before the foundation of the world (Eph 1:4).

Election is a prominent theme in the OT. There is the choice of Abraham and his "seed" that in him the nations of the world will be blessed (Gen 12:1ff.; 22:17–18); and there is the choice of (covenant with) the people Israel (Exod 3:6–10; Deut 6:21–23). This nation was chosen by God as those to whom he could reveal himself and his will, and through whom he could exhibit and declare to the world his purposes and salvation (28:1–14; Isa 43:10–12, 20, 21). Further, there was the choice, from within the chosen people, of specific individuals—e.g., Aaron and David—for special roles and tasks (Deut 18:5; 1 Sam 10:24; Pss 105:26; 106:23).

In the NT, Jesus is the Elect One (Luke 9:35), in whom the election of Israel and of the church of God of the new covenant find their meaning and center. Jesus is the elect "cornerstone" of the new building that God is constructing, composed of both Jewish and Gentile believers (1 Peter 2:4–6). God destined us in love to be his sons through Jesus Christ (Eph 1:5). So the church of God is an elect race (1 Peter 2:9). God's election is never presented as a cause for speculation or controversy, but rather to celebrate the free grace of God that grants salvation and also to move believers to constant worship and lives of holiness and goodness. As in the OT there is in the NT the election of individuals for service (e.g., Acts 6:5; 15:22, 25). The Jews are, as a people, still the elect of God (Rom 9–11).

EL ELOHE ISRAEL (ĕl ē-lō'hĕ ĭz'rà-ĕl). An altar erected by Jacob when he settled near Shechem (Gen 33:20). The name means "the God [who is] the God of Israel." Jacob vowed at the beginning of his pilgrimage that if the Lord would bring him safely back again then the Lord would be his God (Gen 28:20–21). He kept this vow, acknowledging his God and believingly incorporating his own new name.

ELEMENTS (Gr. *stoicheia*, *rows*, *series*, *alphabet*, *first principles of a science*, *physical elements*, *planets*, *personal cosmic powers*). In Hebrews 5:12 "elementary truths" (KJV "first principles") is clearly the meaning. Hebrews 6:1 and Galatians 4:3, 9 refer to heathen deities and practices. Colossians 2:8, 20, translated "basic principles" (KJV "rudiments") indicate a more philosophical concept of the elements. Heavenly bodies or physical elements are referred to in 2 Peter 3:10, 12.

ELEPHANT (See ANIMALS)

ELEVEN, THE The eleven apostles (Acts 1:26) or disciples (Matt 28:16) remaining after the death of Judas (Mark 16:14; Luke 24:9, 33; Acts 2:14).

ELHANAN (ĕl-hā'năn). **1.** A son of Jaare-Oregim (called also Jair), a Bethlehemite who killed Lahmi, the brother of Goliath (2 Sam 21:19; 1 Chron 20:5). **2.** A son of Dodo of Bethlehem and one of David's 30 heroes (2 Sam 23:24; 1 Chron 11:26).

ELI (Heb. *'ēlî*). A judge and high priest in Israel at Shiloh in a dwelling adjoining the tabernacle (1 Sam 1–4; 14:3; 1 Kings 2:27). The conduct of Eli's sons, Phinehas and Hophni, in the priest's office gave him grief in his declining years. Eli warned and reasoned with them concerning their shameful ways, but did not rebuke or restrain them (1 Sam 2:23). Although a good man, Eli was weak and indecisive. When the messenger came with the news of the slaughter of his sons and of the taking of the ark, Eli fell off his seat and died of a broken neck.

ELI, ELI, LAMA SABACHTHANI (See ELOI, ELOI, LAMA SABACHTHANI)

ELIAB (ē-lī'ăb, Heb. *'ĕlî 'āv*). **1.** A son of Helon and leader of the tribe of Zebulun when the census was taken in the wilderness (Num 1:9; 2:7; 7:24, 29; 10:16). **2.** A son of Pallu or Phallu, a Reubenite, and father of Nathan and Abiram (16:1, 12; 26:8–9; Deut 11:6). **3.** The eldest son of Jesse and brother of David (1 Sam 16:6; 17:13, 28). Of commanding appearance, he was serving with Saul's army when it was menaced by Goliath, and he resented his younger brother's interference. Eliab's daughter Abihail became one of Rehoboam's wives (2 Chron 11:18). **4.** A Levite in David's time who was a tabernacle porter and musician (1 Chron 15:18, 20; 16:5). **5.** A Gadite warrior who with others came over to David when David was hiding in the wilderness (12:9). **6.** An ancestor of Samuel the prophet; a Kohathite Levite (6:27). Called Elihu (1 Sam 1:1) and Eliel (1 Chron 6:34).

ELIADA (ē-lī'à-dà, Heb. *'elyādhā'*). **1.** One of David's sons (2 Sam 5:16; 1 Chron 3:8). **2.** A Benjamite, a mighty warrior who led 200,000 of his tribe to the army of Jehoshaphat (2 Chron 17:17). **3.** The father of Rezon, captain of a roving band that annoyed Solomon (1 Kings 11:23; KJV Eliadah).

ELIAKIM (ē-lī'à-kĭm, Heb. *'elyāqîm, God sets up*). **1.** A son of Hilkiah, successor of Shebna as the master of Hezekiah's household (Isa 22:15–25). He was spokesman for the delegation from Hezekiah that attempted to negotiate with the representatives of Sennacherib, who was besieging Jerusalem (2 Kings 18:17–37; Isa 36:1–22). When these negotiations failed, Eliakim headed the delegation sent to implore the help of Isaiah the prophet (2 Kings 19:2; Isa 37:2). **2.** The original name of King Jehoiakim (2 Kings 23:34; 2 Chron 36:4). **3.** A priest who helped in the dedication of the rebuilt wall in Nehemiah's time (Neh 12:41). **4.** A grandson of Zerubbabel and ancestor of Jesus (Matt 1:13). **5.** Another earlier ancestor of Jesus (Luke 3:30).

ELIAM (ē-lī'ăm). **1.** The father of Bathsheba, wife of David (2 Sam 11:3), called Ammiel (1 Chron 3:5). **2.** The son of Ahithophel the Gilonite (2 Sam 23:34).

ELIAS (ē-lī'ăs). The Greek form of the name of the prophet Elijah, used in KJV in all NT occurrences of the name.

ELIASAPH (ē-lī'à-săf). **1.** The son of Deuel and head of the Gadites during the wandering in the wilderness (Num 1:14; 2:14; 7:42, 47; 10:20). **2.** A son of Lael, a Levite and prince of the Gershonites during the wilderness wanderings (3:24).

ELIASHIB (ē-lī'à-shĭb, Heb. *'elyāshîv, God restores*). **1.** A priest in David's time from whom the eleventh priestly course took its name (1 Chron 24:12). **2.** A son of Elioenai, descendant of Zerubbabel, a Judahite (3:24). **3.** The high priest at the time of the rebuilding of the city wall (Neh 3:1, 20–21; 13:4, 7, 28). **4.** A Levite and singer who put away his foreign wife (Ezra 10:24). **5.** A son of Zattu who married a foreign wife (10:27). **6.** A son of Bani who also married a foreign wife (10:36). **7.** An ancestor of Johanan who helped Ezra in gathering together the foreign wives, and in other matters during the reign of Darius the Persian (10:6; Neh 12:10, 22–23).

ELIEHOENAI (ĕl'ĭ-hō-ē'nī, *to Jehovah are my eyes*). **1.** A descendant of Pahath-Moab who returned with Ezra (Ezra 8:4). Also called Elihoenai. **2.** Perhaps also the seventh son of Meshelemiah (1 Chron 26:3). See also ELIOENAI.

ELIEL (ē'lĭ-ĕl, ē-lī'ĕl, Heb. *'ĕlî 'ēl, God is God*). A Levite of the family of Kohath and an ancestor of Samuel the prophet (1 Chron 6:34). **2.** A chief man of the half tribe of Manasseh in Bashan (5:24). **3.** A son of Shimei the Benjamite (8:20). **4.** A son of Shashak, a Benjamite (8:22). **5.** A Mahavite and a captain in David's army (11:46). **6.** Another of David's heroes (11:47). **7.** The seventh Gadite who joined David at Ziklag (12:11). Perhaps the same person as no. 5 or 6. **8.** A chief of Judah, a man of Hebron, in David's time (15:9). Perhaps the same man as no. 5. **9.** A chief Levite who helped in the return of the ark from the house of Obed-Edom (15:11). **10.** A Levite overseer of tithes and offerings in Hezekiah's reign (2 Chron 31:13).

ELIEZER (ĕl'ĭ-ē'zêr, Heb. *'ĕlî 'ezer, God is help*). **1.** Abraham's chief servant, named "Eliezer of Damascus" probably to distinguish him from others of the same name (Gen 15:2). Probably the unnamed servant Abraham sent to his own country and kindred to secure a bride for Isaac (Gen 24). **2.** The second son of Moses and Zipporah (Exod 18:4; 1 Chron 23:15, 17; 26:25). **3.** A son of

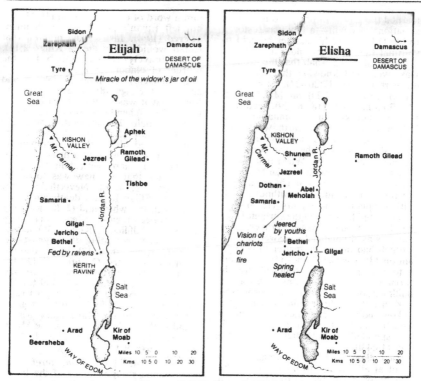

Lives of Elijah and Elisha

Beker and grandson of Benjamin (7:8). **4.** A priest who assisted, by blowing a trumpet, in the return of the ark to Jerusalem (15:24). **5.** Son of Zicri, a Reubenite ruler in David's time (27:16). **6.** The prophet who rebuked Jehoshaphat for his alliance with Ahaziah in the expedition to Tarshish (2 Chron 20:37). **7.** A chieftain sent with others to induce many of the Israelites to return with Ezra to Jerusalem (Ezra 8:16). **8.** A priest who put away his foreign wife (10:18). **9.** A Levite who had done the same (10:23). **10.** One of the descendants of Harim who had done the same (10:31). **11.** An ancestor of Jesus in the intertestamental period (Luke 3:29).

ELIHU (ē-lī'hū, Heb. *'elîhû, he is my God*). **1.** The father of Jeroham and great-grandfather of Samuel the prophet (1 Sam 1:1), also called Eliel (1 Chron 6:34). **2.** A man of Manasseh who joined David at Ziklag (12:20). **3.** A Kohathite of the family of Korah, and a tabernacle porter in David's time (26:7). **4.** A brother of David; he became ruler over Judah

(27:18). Also known as Eliab. **5.** The youngest of Job's friends, the son of Barakel (Job 32:2–6; 34:1; 35:1; 36:1).

ELIJAH (ē-lī'jà, Heb. *'ēlîyāhû, Jehovah is God*). The name of four men in the Bible. **1.** A Benjamite and son of Jeroham, resident at Jerusalem (1 Chron 8:27). **2.** A descendant of Harim who married a foreign wife during the Exile (Ezra 10:21). **3.** An Israelite induced to put away his foreign wife (10:26).

4. The prophet Elijah (1 Kings 17:1–2 Kings 2:12) whose ministry was set in the days of King Ahab (c. 874-852 B.C.) of the northern kingdom of Israel. Elijah was born in Tishbe and is described as one of the settlers in Gilead (1 Kings 17:1). He predicted a drought (17:1) that would last over three years (18:1). God then took Elijah away into three hidden years of apprenticeship (17:3), and miraculously provided for him. In Zarephath Elijah learned that the Lord cared for his obedient servant, and that the Lord's power is superior to all the power of man (18:10). Elijah also learned the power of prayer to transform situations of death—a boy was restored to life (17:22) and his mother brought to spiritual faith and testimony (17:24).

Elijah informed Ahab that the drought was over, and knowing that the Lord answers prayer (17:20–24), proposed a prayer contest (18:24) on Mt. Carmel. The Baal prophets (18:26–29), according to a practice known as "imitative magic," sought to do on earth what they desired their god to do from heaven. Their dance around the altar suggested flicking flames (18:26). When that failed, they slashed their bodies in the hope that the down-pouring blood might prompt the down-pouring of fire, but without result. With simplicity and dignity (18:36–37), Elijah rested his case on the certainty that the Lord would answer prayer. His prayer was dramatically answered.

Elijah had one more matter to occupy him on Mt. Carmel. James (5:18) directs us to interpret Elijah's crouched attitude as one of prayer: he was praying for the fulfillment of what the Lord had promised (1 Kings 18:1). He sent his servant to a lookout point seven times; as soon as even the slightest sign of rain appeared, he responded in active faith to its message (18:43ff.).

The collapse of Elijah (1 Kings 19:1ff.) is not at all difficult to understand. The amount of sleep the Lord insisted on giving Elijah (19:5–6) after his collapse shows the extent to which he had neglected his physical well-being. God gave his servant rest and nourishment (19:5–7), brought him into his own presence (19:8–9), and renewed Elijah's sense of the power of the word of God. The Lord renewed Elijah's commission and gave

him a word of encouragement (19:15–18) but left Elijah's prayer for death unanswered (19:4). Instead, he granted that Elijah would never die (2 Kings 2:11). Elijah bravely rebuked Ahab for the murder of Naboth (1 Kings 21).

Elijah easily felt himself isolated and solitary (1 Kings 18:22), even when he knew that it was very far from the truth (cf. 18:13). When he most needed fellowship and help, he deliberately sought a solitary path (19:3–4), and when the Lord blessed him with the companionable and warm-hearted Elisha, he was unready to share with him the great experience that he knew was to be his (2 Kings 2:2, 4, 6). Nevertheless, the Lord let Elijah bypass death and enter heaven in the whirlwind (2 Kings 2:11). His prophecy regarding Jezebel (1 Kings 21:23) was fulfilled (2 Kings 9:36), as was his forecast regarding the dynasty of Ahab (2 Kings 10:10, 17). Elijah also had a writing ministry (2 Chron 21:12–15). Elijah as the forerunner of the Messiah was prophesied (Mal 4:5–6) and fulfilled in the ministry of John the Baptist (e.g., Matt 11:13–14; 17:9–13). Elijah's greatest privilege in the Bible story was to stand with the Son of God on the Mount of Transfiguration (Matt 17:3–4; Mark 9:4–5; Luke 9:30–33).

ELIM (ē'lĭm, Heb. *'ēlîm, terebinths*). The second stopping-place of the Israelites after they crossed the Red Sea on their exodus from Egypt (Exod 15:27; 16:1; Num 33:9–10).

ELIMELECH (ē-lĭm'ĕ-lĕk, Heb. *'ĕlîmelekh, my God is king*). A man of Bethlehem-Judah who emigrated to Moab during a famine in Judah in the time of the judges (Ruth 1:2–3; 2:1, 3; 4:3, 9). He

Wadi Gharandel, a well-known watering spot with tamarisks and palms, located on the western side of the Sinai Peninsula and thought to be the probable site of Elim. Courtesy Ecole Biblique et Archéologique Française, Jerusalem

and his sons died in Moab. He is remembered because his daughter-in-law Ruth was faithful to his widow Naomi.

ELIOENAI (ĕl'ĭ-ō-ē'nĭ, *to Jehovah are my eyes*). **1.** A son of Neariah of the family of David (1 Chron 3:23–24). **2.** The head of a family of Simeon (4:36). **3.** The head of one of the families of the sons of Beker, son of Benjamin (7:8). **4.** A son of Pashhur, a priest who put away his foreign wife (Ezra 10:22). Perhaps the same person as no. 6. **5.** A son of Zattu who married a foreign wife (10:27). **6.** A priest, perhaps the same person as no. 4 (Neh 12:41). See also ELIEHOENAI.

ELIPHALET (See ELIPHELET)

ELIPHAZ (ĕl'ĭ-făz, Heb. *'ĕlîphaz*, possibly *God is fine gold*). **1.** A son of Esau by Adah, daughter of Elon (Gen 36:4–16; 1 Chron 1:35–36). **2.** The chief of Job's three friends (Job 2:11); from Teman, traditionally famous for its wise men (Jer 49:7). Eliphaz's speeches show clearer reasoning than those of the two other friends (Job 4–5; 15; 22). God addresses Eliphaz as the chief of Job's friends and commands him to make sacrifice in expiation for wrongly accusing Job (42:7–9), saying that Job will pray for them and they will be forgiven.

ELIPHELET (ē-lĭf'ĕ-lĕt). **1.** The last of David's sons born at Jerusalem (2 Sam 5:16; 1 Chron 14:7). **2.** Another son of David born in Jerusalem (3:6). Also called Elpalet (14:5). **3.** A son of Ahasbai, one of David's heroes (2 Sam 23:34). **4.** A son of Eshek and descendant of Saul, a Benjamite (1 Chron 8:39). **5.** A leader of the sons of Adonikam who returned from exile with Ezra (Ezra 8:13). **6.** A son of Hashum who put away his foreign wife (10:33).

ELISABETH (See ELIZABETH)

ELISHA (ē-lī'sha, called *Eliseus*, the Gr. form of Heb. *'ĕlîshā'*, in Luke 4:27 KJV; Elisha in NIV, ASV, RSV), God directed Elijah to anoint Elisha to be his successor (1 Kings 19:16–21). Elijah found Elisha (19:16) plowing with the last of 12 yoke of oxen. The number of oxen indicates the wealth of the family. Elijah cast his mantle on Elisha to indicate his succession. Elisha next appeared in connection with the translation of Elijah (2 Kings 2). He persisted in following Elijah till the latter was carried up to heaven. Because he saw him go, a double portion of Elijah's spirit was given him. Taking the mantle of Elijah, he used it to make a dry path over the Jordan, as his master had done. He then healed the waters at

Jericho and cursed the rabble at Bethel (2 Kings 2:19–25).

Elisha had a long ministry during the reigns of Joram (KJV "Jehoram"), Jehu, Jehoahaz, and Jehoash (KJV "Joash"), kings of Israel. Elisha saved a poor widow from financial distress by miraculous multiplication of her oil supply (2 Kings 4:1–7). A well-to-do woman and her husband in Shunem often provided hospitality for Elisha. In return they were granted a request for a son. When the lad suffered a fatal sunstroke, his mother went for Elisha, who raised their son to life. At Gilgal during a famine (4:38–41), Elisha saved a company of the prophets from death because of eating poisonous vegetables. When a present of food was given him, Elisha set it before 100 men, and the Lord increased the supply to satisfy them (4:42–44). Elisha healed Naaman of leprosy (ch. 5) and rescued a young prophet's borrowed axhead (6:1–7). He gave timely warning, repeatedly saving Israel from defeat by the Arameans (6:23). When the Arameans came to Dothan to capture Elisha, he prayed and his servant was shown the armies of God protecting the city. The Arameans were stricken with blindness, and Elisha led them to Samaria and persuaded the king of Israel to feed and release them.

A man being hastily buried in Elisha's sepulcher touched Elisha's bones and revived (13:20–21). Elisha's ministry was filled with miracles, many relieving private needs, some related to affairs of state. He finished the work of Elijah, destroying the system of Baal worship, completed the tasks assigned to Elijah of anointing Hazael and Jehu, and saw the final ruin of the house of Ahab and Jezebel. The mention of the cleansing of Naaman the Syrian from leprosy in Luke 4:27 perhaps indicates this as the crowning achievement of his career, giving Elisha an influence with the Syrian king that enabled him to help Israel. (See map on page 173.)

ELISHAH (ē-lī'sha, Heb. *'ĕlîshâh, God saves*). The eldest son of Javan, grandson of Noah and founder of a tribal family (Gen 10:4; 1 Chron 1:7). The land from which Tyre got its purple dye (Ezek 27:7).

ELISHAMA (ē-lĭsh'à-mà, Heb. *'ĕlîshāmā', God has heard*). **1.** Grandfather of Joshua, son of Ammihud, prince of the Ephraimites at the outset of the wilderness journey (Num 1:10; 2:18; 7:48, 53; 10:22; 1 Chron 7:26). **2.** A son of David born in Jerusalem (2 Sam 5:16; 1 Chron

3:8). **3.** Another son of David, who is also called Elishua (3:6; cf. 2 Sam 5:15). **4.** A son of Jekamiah, a Judahite (1 Chron 2:41). **5.** Father of Nethaniah and grandfather of Ishmael (2 Kings 25:25; Jer 41:1). This may be the same as no.4. **6.** A scribe or secretary to Jehoiakim (Jer 36:12, 20-21). **7.** A priest sent by Jehoshaphat to teach the people the law (2 Chron 17:8).

ELISHEBA (ē-lĭsh'ē-bà). Amminadab's daughter, sister of Nahshon, captain of Judah (Num 2:3). By marrying Aaron (Exod 6:23) she connected the royal and priestly tribes.

ELIZABETH (Gr. *Elisabet, God is my oath*, KJV Elisabeth). The wife of the priest Zechariah, herself of the lineage of Aaron (Luke 1:5-57). In fulfillment of God's promise, in her old age she bore a son, John the Baptist. She was a woman of unusual piety, faith, and spiritual gifts, whose witness to her cousin Mary must have been an incomparable encouragement. Luke appreciated the significant role of women in the history of redemption and emphasized the agency of the Holy Spirit in the life of Elizabeth.

ELIZAPHAN (ĕl'ĭ-zā'făn, ē-lĭz'à-făn, Heb. *'ĕlîtsāphān, God has concealed*). **1.** The son of Uzziel, chief ruler of the Kohathites (Num 3:30; 1 Chron 15:8; 2 Chron 29:13), also called Elzaphan (Exod 6:22; Lev 10:4). **2.** The son of Parnach, prince of the tribe of Zebulun in the wilderness (Num 34:25).

ELIZUR (ē-lī'zēr). The son of Shedeur, and prince of the Reubenites, who helped in the census Moses took (Num 1:5; 2:10; 7:30-35; 10:18).

ELKANAH (ĕl-kā'nà, Heb. *'elqānâh, God has possessed*). **1.** The father of Samuel the prophet (1 Sam 1:1-2:21). He appears to have been a Levite, descendant of Kohath (1 Chron 6:22-23, 27, 33-34). **2.** A son of Korah, a Levite, descendant of Kohath (Exod 6:23-24; 1 Chron 6:24). The sons of Korah did not die with their father, who perished for rebellion against Moses and Aaron (Num 26:11). **3.** The second in power to King Ahaz, killed by Pekah, king of Israel, when he invaded Judah (2 Chron 28:7). **4.** One of the ambidextrous warriors who came to David at Ziklag (1 Chron 12:6). **5.** In addition, several Levites bear the name Elkanah (6:22-28, 33-38; 9:16).

ELLASAR (ĕl-lā'sàr, Heb. *'ellāsār*). One of the city-states whose king, Arioch (Eri-aku), invaded Palestine in the time of Abraham (Gen 14:1, 9). It is the ancient

Babylonian Larsa, modern Senkereh, SE of Babylon, between Erech and Ur. At first independent, it became subject to Hammurabi (Amraphel of Gen 14:1, 9) or to his successor. Ellasar was at this period a city of a high degree of civilization, a center of sun-god worship, with a temple tower (ziggurat) called "House of Light." Thus the four kings with whom Abraham fought (14:13-16) were no petty chieftains, but sovereigns of flourishing and cultured cities, from one of which Abraham himself had recently emigrated.

ELNATHAN (ĕl-nā'thăn, Heb. *'elnāthān, God has given*). **1.** Father of Nehushta, the mother of Jehoiachin (2 Kings 24:8). **2.** The son of Acbor, sent to Egypt by King Jehoiakim to bring back the prophet Uriah (Jer 26:22). He was one of those who urged King Jehoiakim not to burn the roll that Jeremiah had written (36:12, 25). He may be the same person as no. 1. **3.** The name of three men listed among leaders and men of learning, Levites, sent on an embassy by Ezra (Ezra 8:16).

ELOHIM (ē-lō'hĭm). The most frequent Hebrew word for God (over 2,500 times in the OT). Elohim is plural in form, but is singular in construction (used with a singular verb or adjective). When applied to the one true God, the plural is due to the Hebrew idiom of a plural of magnitude or majesty (Gen 1:1). When used of heathen gods (35:2; Exod 18:11; 20:3; Josh 24:20) or of angels (Job 1:6; Pss 8:5; 97:7) or judges (Exod 21:6; 1 Sam 2:25) as representatives of God, Elohim is plural in sense as well as form. The most likely roots mean either "be strong," or "be in front," suiting the power and preeminence of God. Jesus used a form of the name on the cross (Matt 27:46; Mark 15:34). See next article.

ELOI, ELOI, LAMA SABACHTHANI (à'lē, à'lē, lă'mă sà-băch'thă-nē). The English transliteration of a Greek phrase (Matt 27:46; Mark 15:34), which in turn is a transliteration of either the Hebrew or an Aramaic version of Psalm 22:1. The words are the central of the seven cries of Jesus from the cross, as gathered from all four Gospels. Christ was forsaken by the Father when he bore our sins.

ELON (ē'lŏn). **1.** A Hittite whose daughter Basemath (Gen 26:34) or Adah (36:2) married Esau. **2.** The second of Zebulon's three sons (46:14; Num 26:26). **3.** The Zebulonite who judged Israel ten years (Judg 12:11-12).

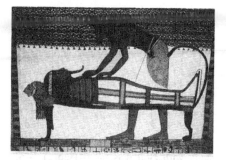

A wall painting from Sennedjem's tomb at Deir el-Medina, c. 1306–1290 B.C., of Anubis, the Egyptian god connected with mummification, preparing a body for burial. Courtesy Seffie Ben-Yoseph

ELON (place). **1.** A town in the territory of Dan (Josh 19:43). **2.** Elon Bethhanan, a town in one of the districts that furnished provisions for Solomon's household (1 Kings 4:9).

ELOTH (See ELATH, ELOTH)

ELPALET, ELPELET (See ELIPHELET)

EL PARAN (See PARAN)

EL SHADDAI (ĕl shăd'à-ī, -shăd'īà). The name of God (translated "God Almighty") by which (Exod 6:3) he appeared to Abraham, Isaac, and Jacob— recorded once to Abraham (Gen 17:1) and four times to Jacob (28:3; 35:11; 43:14; 48:3). Often "the Almighty" (*Shaddai* without *El*) is used as a name of God: in Jacob's deathbed words (Gen 49:25), in Balaam's prophecies (Num 24:4, 16), by Naomi (Ruth 1:20, 21), 30 times by Job and his friends (Job 5:17–37:23), by God himself (40:2), and twice in the Psalms (Pss 68:14; 91:1). The name is rare in the prophets (Isa 13:6; Ezek 1:24; 10:5 ["Almighty God"]; Joel 1:15). "God (the) Almighty" (Gr. *pantokratōr*, "all-powerful") occurs nine times in the NT (2 Cor 6:18; eight times in Revelation).

ELTEKEH (ĕl'tē-kē). A city in the territory given to Dan, on its southern border with Judah (Josh 19:44). With its pasturelands it was given to the Kohathite Levites (21:23).

ELTOLAD (ĕl-tō'lăd). A city in the Negev of Judah toward Edom (Josh 15:30), but assigned to Simeon (19:4). Also (1 Chron 4:29) called Tolad.

ELUL (ĕ-lūl'). The sixth month of the Hebrew year, approximately mid-August–mid-September (Neh 6:15). See also CALENDAR.

ELYMAS (ĕl'ĭmăs, Gr. *Elymas*). A Jew, Bar-Jesus (meaning *son of Jesus* or *Joshua*), a sorcerer who was with Sergius Paulus, the proconsul of Cyprus. He became blind following Paul's curse, causing the proconsul to believe in the Lord (Acts 13:4–13).

ELZABAD (ĕl-zā'băd, ĕl'zà-băd). **1.** A Gadite who joined David at Ziklag (1 Chron 12:12). **2.** The son of Shemaiah and a Korahite Levite (26:7).

ELZAPHAN (See ELIZAPHAN)

EMBALM To prepare a dead body with oil and spices to preserve it from decay. Embalming was of Egyptian origin. The only clear instances of it in the Bible were in the cases of Jacob and Joseph. Joseph ordered his slaves, the physicians, to embalm his father (Gen 50:2–3; a process that took 40 days); and later Joseph himself was embalmed (50:26). The purpose of the Egyptians in embalming was to preserve the body for the use of the soul in a future life. The purpose of the Hebrews was to preserve the bodies of Jacob and Joseph for a long journey to their resting place with Abraham (50:13). In the case of Joseph, centuries elapsed before burial in the ancestral tomb (Exod 13:19; Josh 24:32).

EMBROIDERY, EMBROIDERER The work and worker of ornamental needlework on cloth. For the Hebrews embroidery was used for the hangings of the tabernacle; for the coats, girdles, and ephod of the priests; for royal garments; and for clothing of private persons.

EMERALD (See MINERALS)

EMITES (ē'mīts, Heb. *'êmîm;* KJV, Emim). The original inhabitants of Moab (Deut 2:10–11), a great people—powerful, of advanced civilization, numerous, and tall. In Abraham's time they were defeated by the Mesopotamian invaders in Shaveh Kiriathaim (Gen 14:5), a plain east of the Dead Sea.

EMMANUEL (See IMMANUEL)

EMMAUS (ĕ-mā'ŭs). The village to which two disciples were going on the day of Jesus' resurrection, when he met and was recognized by them as he broke bread at supper (Luke 24:7–35). It was about 7 miles (12 km.) from Jerusalem.

EMMOR (See HAMOR)

EN GANNIM (ĕn găn'ĭm, Heb. *'ên gannîm, fountain, spring of gardens*). **1.** A town in the foothills of Judah, mentioned with Eshtaol and Zanoah (Josh 15:34). **2.** A town in Issachar, assigned to the Gershonite Levites (19:21; 21:29).

EN GEDI (ĕn gē'dī, Heb. *'ên gedhî, spring or fountain of the kid or wild goat*). An oasis on the west coast of the Dead Sea about midway of its length in Judah (Josh 15:62). Here David fortified a refuge from Saul (1 Sam 23:29; 24:1). Jehoshaphat defeated the Ammonites, Moabites, and Edomites from Mt. Seir when they attacked by the narrow paths up the steep cliffs from the shore (2 Chron 20:2). En Gedi is there identified with Hazazon Tamar, occupied by Amorites, which Kedorlaomer invaded in the days of Abraham (Gen 14:7). Its luxurious vegetation, due to warm springs, was famous in the days of Solomon (Song of Songs 1:14). Ezekiel prophesied that fishermen would stand here, in the restored land (Ezek 47:10).

EN RIMMON (ĕn rĭm'ŏn, Heb. *'ên-rimmôn, fountain of a pomegranate*). A place south of Jerusalem (Zech 14:10), 11 miles (18 km.) NE of Beersheba. Alternatively "Ain and Rimmon" (Josh 15:32; 19:7; 1 Chron 4:32). En Rimmon was reinhabited after the Captivity (Neh 11:29).

EN ROGEL (ĕn rō'gel, Heb. *'ên rōghēl, fountain of feet*—so called because washermen trampled cloth with their feet there). It was on the border between Benjamin and Judah (Josh 15:7; 18:16). Here Jonathan and Ahimaaz hid to receive intelligence for David from within the walls (2 Sam 17:17), and Adonijah held his sacrificial feast, expecting to seize the throne (1 Kings 1:9).

EN SHEMESH (ĕn shĕm'ĭsh, *fountain of the sun*). Located about 3 miles (5 km.) east of Jerusalem on the way to Jericho. It is mentioned in Joshua 15:7; 18:17; it served to mark Judah's northern border and Benjamin's southern border.

ENAN (ē'năn). The father of Ahira, of the tribe of Naphtali, who assisted in the Sinai census (Num 1:15; 2:29; 7:78, 83; 10:27).

ENCAMPMENT (See CAMP, ENCAMPMENT)

ENDOR (ĕn'dôr, Heb. *'ên dor, spring of habitation*). A village about 7 miles (12 km.) SE of Nazareth. The hometown of the "witch of Endor," the spiritist medium Saul visited before his last battle with the Philistines (1 Sam 28:8–25).

ENGRAVER (See OCCUPATIONS AND PROFESSIONS)

ENOCH (ē'nŭk, Heb. *hănôkh, consecrated*, Gr. *Henoch*). **1.** Cain's eldest son, for whom the first city was named (Gen 4:17–18). **2.** Son of Jared (5:18) and father of Methuselah (5:21–22; Luke 3:37). Abram walked "before God" (Gen 17:1), but of Enoch and Noah alone it is written that they walked *"with God"* (5:24; 6:9). Walking with God occurred in Eden and anticipates a new paradise (Rev 21:3; 22:3–4). The secret of Enoch's walk with God was faith (Heb 11:5–6). He typifies the saints living at Christ's coming who will be removed from mortality to immortality without passing through death (1 Cor 15:51–52). His translation out of a wicked world was an appropriate testimony to the truth ascribed to him in Jude 14–15.

ENOCH, BOOKS OF A collection of apocalyptic literature written by various authors and circulated under the name of Enoch. First Enoch is an Ethiopic version made through the Greek from the original Hebrew text that was written by the Chasidim or by the Pharisees between 163–63 B.C. It is the best source for the development of Jewish doctrine in the last two pre-Christian centuries. Jude 14–15 may be an explicit quotation from it. Second Enoch was written A.D. 1–50. See also APOCALYPTIC LITERATURE.

ENOSH, ENOS (ē'nŏsh, ē'nŏs, Heb. *'ĕnôsh, mortal*, Gr. *Enos*). Son of Seth and grandson of Adam (Gen 4:26; 5:6–11; Luke 3:38). Attached to his birth is an implication of godly fear. He lived 905 years.

ENVY The Hebrew word *qin'a* is rendered in OT translations as both "envy" and "jealousy," though in English the two are not synonymous terms (e.g., 1 Sam 18:9; Job 5:2; Prov 6:34), and is used with reference to the jealousy of the Lord or for his name (Exod 20:5; Ezek 39:25; Joel 2:18). In the NT two Greek words are found: *phthonos* and *zēlos*. The former always has a bad sense (e.g., Matt 27:18; Gal 5:21; Phil 1:15; James 4:5). While *zēlos* can be used similarly (Acts 13:45), it is more often translated "zeal" (e.g., John 2:17; Phil 3:6; cf. 2 Cor 11:2).

EPAPHRAS (ĕp'à-frăs, Gr. *Epaphras*). A contraction of Epaphroditus, but not the same NT character. He was Paul's "dear fellow servant" and minister to the church at Colosse, perhaps its founder (Col 1:7). He brought to Paul a report of their state (1:4, 8) and sent back greetings to them from Rome (4:12). Commended by Paul for his ministry of intercession, he desired their perfect and complete stand in all the will of God (4:13). Paul also called him "my fellow prisoner." This may mean that he voluntarily shared the apostle's imprisonment, or he may have been apprehended for his zeal in the gospel.

EPAPHRODITUS (ĕ-păf-rō-dī'tŭs, Gr. *Epaphroditos, lovely*). The messenger sent by the Philippian church with gifts to the imprisoned Paul (Phil 4:18). On recovering from a serious illness, Epaphroditus longed to return to his concerned flock. Paul highly esteemed him as "brother, fellow worker and fellow soldier," and sent him back to Philippi with his letter (2:25–30).

EPHAH (See WEIGHTS AND MEASURES)

EPHAH (ē'fà, Heb. *dark one*). **1.** A son of Midian through Abraham's concubine Keturah (Gen 25:4; 1 Chron 1:33; Isa 60:6). **2.** A concubine of Caleb of the tribe of Judah (1 Chron 2:46). **3.** A son of Jahdai of the tribe of Judah (2:47).

EPHAI (ē'fī, Heb. *'ēphay, gloomy*). The Netophathite whose sons were among the captains of the forces left in Judah after the deportation to Babylon (Jer 40:8). After their warning of the plot against Gedaliah went unheeded (40:13–16), they were murdered with him by Ishmael, son of Nethaniah (41:3).

EPHER (ē'fĕr, Heb. *'ēpher, calf*). **1.** Son of Midian and grandson of Abraham (Gen 25:4; 1 Chron 1:33). **2.** Son of Ezra of the tribe of Judah (4:17). **3.** A family head in the half-tribe of Manasseh east of Jordan (5:23–24).

EPHES DAMMIM (ē-fĕs dăm'ĭm, Heb. *'ephes dammîm, boundary of blood*). A place of bloody battles between Israel and the Philistines. It was the Philistine encampment when David killed Goliath (1 Sam 17:1). It is also called Pas Dammim (1 Chron 11:13).

EPHESIANS, LETTER TO THE Generally acknowledged to be one of the richest and most profound of the NT letters. The dignity of its contents have made the Letter to the Ephesians precious to believers in all ages and in all places. Its profound truths and vivid imagery have deeply penetrated into the thought and literature of the Christian church.

Ephesians explicitly claims authorship by Paul (Eph 1:1; 3:1), and its entire tenor is eminently Pauline. Liberal critics have raised doubts as to its origin—based

The library of Celsus, built in the time of Trajan (A.D. 98–117), the most remarkable building to be revealed from the extensive excavations at Ephesus. Below is the façade of the temple of Hadrian, located just southeast of the library and south of the famous theater. Courtesy Top: Duby Tal. Bottom: Dan Bahat

solely on internal arguments drawn from the style, vocabulary, and theology of the letter. These arguments are subjective and inconclusive and offer no compelling reasons for rejecting the undeviating evidence of text and tradition.

Ephesians was written while Paul was a prisoner (Eph 3:1; 4:1; 6:20). The prevailing view has been that it was written from Rome during his first Roman imprisonment (Acts 28:30–31), although some have suggested Caesarea (24:27) or even Ephesus (19:10; 20:18–21, 31; 2 Cor 11:23) as possible locations. However, the traditional Roman origin firmly holds the field.

Along with Colossians and Philemon (Col 4:7–8; Philem 9, 13, 17), the letter was transmitted to its destination by Tychicus (Eph 6:21–22). Thus all three were sent to the Roman province of Asia, but scholars disagree as to the precise destination of Ephesians. The words "at Ephesus" (1:1) are not found in three very ancient copies (the Chester Beatty Papyrus, the Uncials *Aleph* and *B*). But the words are found in all other manuscripts in their uncorrected form and in all ancient versions. With the exception of the heretical Marcion, whom Tertullian accused of tampering with the title, ecclesiastical tradition uniformly designates it as "to the Ephesians." A fair solution would seem to be that the letter was originally addressed to the saints "at Ephesus" but was intentionally cast into a form that would make it suitable to meet the needs of the Asian churches. As transcriptions of the original to the mother church were circulated, the place of destination might be omitted, though they were uniformly recognized as the letter originally addressed to the Ephesians.

Its contents offer no clear indication as to the occasion for the writing of Ephesians. Its affinity to Colossians in time of origin and contents suggests an occasion closely related to the writing of that letter.

Ephesians sets forth the wealth of the believer in union with Christ. It portrays the glories of our salvation and emphasizes the nature of the church as the body of Christ. As indicated by the doxology in 3:20–21, its contents fall into two parts, the first doctrinal (1–3), the second practical and encouraging (4–6). An outline may suggest some of its riches:

I. **The Salutation (1:1–2).**

II. **Doctrinal: The Believer's Standing in Christ (1:3–3:21).**
   A. Thanksgiving for our redemption (1:3–14).
   B. Prayer for spiritual illumination (1:15–23).
   C. Power of God manifested in our salvation (2:1–10).
   D. Union of Jew and Gentile in one body in Christ (2:11–22).
   E. Paul as the messenger of this mystery (3:1–13).
   F. Prayer for the realization of these blessings (3:14–19).
   G. Doxology of praise (3:20–21).

III. **Practical: The Believers' Life in Christ (4:1–6:20).**
   A. Their walk as God's saints (4:1–5:21).
      1. The worthy walk, in inward realization of Christian unity (4:1–16).
      2. The different walk, in outward manifestation of a changed position (4:17–32).
      3. The loving walk, in upward imitation of our Father (5:1–17).
      4. The summary of the Spirit-filled life (5:18–21).
   B. Their duties as God's family (5:22–6:9).
   C. Their warfare as God's soldiers (6:10–20).

IV. **The Conclusion (6:21–24).**

EPHESUS (ĕf'ē-sŭs, Gr. *Ephesos, desirable*). Ephesus was a proud, rich, busy port, the rival of Alexandria and Syrian Antioch. Built near the shrine of an old Anatolian fertility goddess, Ephesus became the seat of an oriental cult. The Anatolian deity had been taken over by the Greeks under the name of Artemis, the Diana of the Romans. Grotesquely represented with turreted head and many breasts, the goddess and her cult found expression in the famous temple, served, like that of Aphrodite at Corinth, by a host of priestess courtesans.

Much trade clustered round the cult. Ephesus became a place of pilgrimage for tourist-worshipers, all eager to carry away talisman and souvenir, hence the prosperous guild of the silversmiths whose livelihood was the manufacture of silver shrines and images of the meteoric stone that was said to be Diana's image "fallen from heaven." Ephesus leaned more and more on the trade that followed the cult, and commerce declined in her silting harbor. Ephesus in the first century was a dying city, given to parasite pursuits, living, like Athens, on a reputation, a curious meeting place of old and new religions, of East and West (Acts 19). Ephesus' decline was mortal sickness, and it is possible to detect in the letter to Ephesus in the Apocalypse a touch of the weariness that characterized the decadent and declining community.

EPHOD (ĕf'ŏd, Heb. *'ēphōdh*). **1.** A sacred vestment originally worn by the high priest (Exod 28:6–14; 39:2–7). On each shoulderpiece was an onyx stone engraved with six names of the tribes of Israel. Attached to the ephod by chains of pure gold was a breastplate containing twelve precious stones. The blue robe of the ephod was worn underneath, having a hole for the head and extending to the feet, with a hem alternating with gold bells and pomegranates of blue, purple, and scarlet (28:31–35; 39:22–26).

Later, persons other than the high priest wore ephods. Samuel wore a linen ephod (1 Sam 2:18), characteristic of the ordinary priests (2:28; 14:3; 22:18). David wore a linen ephod while he danced before the Lord after bringing the ark to Jerusalem (2 Sam 6:14). Abiathar carried off from Nob an ephod that represented to David the divine presence, for of it he inquired the will of the Lord (1 Sam 23:6, 9; 30:7–8).

The ephod was misused as an object of idolatrous worship by Gideon (Judg 8:27) and associated with images by Micah (17:5; 18:14).

2. Father of Hanniel who was the prince of the children of Manasseh (Num 34:23).

EPHPHATHA (ĕf'à-thà, Gr. *Ephphatha* from Aram. *'etpătah*, passive imperative of the verb *petah, be opened*). A word occurring only in Mark 7:34, uttered by Jesus as he was healing a deaf man.

EPHRAIM (ē'frà-ĭm, Heb. *'eprayim, double fruit*). The younger of two sons of Joseph (Gen 41:50–52). The aged Jacob, when he blessed his grandsons Manasseh and Ephraim, adopted them as his own sons. Despite Joseph's protest, Jacob gave the preferential blessing to Ephraim (48:1–22). When Jacob blessed his own sons, he did not mention Ephraim and Manasseh, but he did give a special blessing to their father, Joseph (49:22–26).

Ephraim was the progenitor of the tribe called by his name. Ephraim together with Manasseh and Benjamin camped on the west side of the tabernacle in the wilderness (Num 2:18–24). Joshua, one of the spies and Moses' successor, was an Ephraimite (13:8).

At the division of the land among the tribes, the children of Joseph (except half of Manasseh, which settled east of the Jordan, Num 32:33, 39–42) received the central hill country of Palestine, sometimes called Mt. Ephraim. Ephraim and Manasseh seem to have been bitter rivals (Isa 9:20–21), Manasseh being the larger group (Gen 49:22), but Ephraim asserting the more vigorous leadership. Although they seem to have held their land in common for a time (Josh 17:14–18) it was presently divided between them. Ephraim's portion was well defined and very fruitful, its soil fertile and its rainfall more plentiful than Judah's to the south (Deut 33:13–16).

At Shiloh, in the territory of Ephraim, Joshua pitched the tabernacle (Josh 18:1), and this town remained a religious center for the Hebrews (22:12; Judg 18:31; 21:19; 1 Sam 1:3, 9, 24; 2:14; 3:21) until it was destroyed by the Philistines after the battle of Ebenezer (4:1–11). Samuel was an Ephraimite (1:1).

The Ephraimites contributed their share of the hatred and strife that divided the Hebrew tribes during the dark days of the judges (Judg 8:1–3; 12:1–6). Seemingly, Ephraim, in common with the rest of the central and northern tribes, was never completely reconciled to the rule of Judah (2 Sam 2:8–9; 1 Kings 12:16). Jeroboam I, an Ephraimite (11:26), rebelled against Solomon's son Rehoboam. Ephraim became such a leader in the new northern Hebrew kingdom that in addition to its more common name Israel, the kingdom is also called Ephraim (Isa 7:2, 5, 9, 17; Hos 9:3–16). From this time on

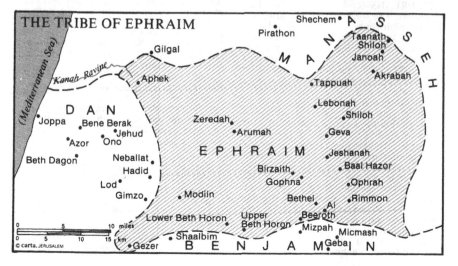

THE TRIBE OF EPHRAIM

the tribe's history is merged with that of this kingdom.

Ephraim is also the name of a city north of Jerusalem (2 Sam 13:23; John 11:54).

EPHRAIM, FOREST OF (Heb. *ya'ar 'eprayim*). Mentioned only in 2 Samuel 18:6 ("wood" [KJV], "woods" [MLB] "of Ephraim"), it was the location in Gilead of the decisive defeat of Absalom.

EPHRAIM, MOUNT OF (Heb. *har 'eprayim*). The mountainous part of Ephraim (Josh 17:15).

EPHRAIMITE (Heb. *'ephrayim*, always in this plural form). A member of the tribe of Ephraim (Josh 16:10; Judg 12).

EPHRAIN (See EPHRON)

EPHRATAH, EPHRATH, EPHRATHAH (ĕf'răth-à, Heb. *'ephrăth, fruitful land*). 1. The place where Rachel was buried (Gen 35:16). 2. Second wife of Caleb, son of Hezron. She was the mother of Hur (1 Chron 2:19–20). 3. The ancient name of Bethlehem or the district around it. This name is attached to that of Bethlehem in the great prophecy of the place of the birth of Christ (Mic 5:2).

EPHRON (ē'frŏn, Heb. *'ephrôn, fawn*). 1. A Hittite from whom Abraham purchased the field of Machpelah for the burial of his wife Sarah (Gen 23:8–9). 2. A mountain on the north border of Judah, located about 6 miles (10 km.) NW of Jerusalem (Josh 15:9). 3. A city taken from Jeroboam by Abijah (2 Chron 13:19; KJV "Ephrain"). It is perhaps identical with Ophrah (Josh 18:23).

EPICUREANS (ĕp-ĭ-kū-rē'ănz, Gr. *Epikoureioi*). The followers of Epicurus, the Greek philosopher who lived 341–270 B.C. He taught that nature rather than reason is the true reality; nothing exists but atoms and void, that is, matter and space. The chief purpose of man is to achieve happiness. He has free will to plan and live a life of pleasure. Epicurus gave the widest scope to this matter of pleasure, interpreting it as avoidance of pain, so that the mere enjoyment of good health would be pleasure. For the philosopher the highest joy is found in mental and intellectual pursuits, but for lesser souls lower goals of sensual satisfaction fulfill the greatest pleasure. Thus the high standards of the founder were not maintained, and the philosophy gained a bad reputation. It was widely held at the time of Christ. Paul met it at Athens when he encountered the philosophers of that city (Acts 17:16–33). They were not impressed by his teaching of creation, judgment, and resurrection, since all these doctrines were denied by the Epicurean philosophy.

EPILEPTIC (See DISEASES)

EPIPHANY From a Greek word meaning "manifestation," the term originally marked a feast to celebrate the baptism of Christ (Matt 3:16–17)—and still does so in the churches of Eastern Orthodoxy. From the fourth century, however, Epiphany has been linked with Christ's manifestation of himself to the Magi, the first Gentiles who believed in him (Matt 2:1–12). In England, it has become customary for the monarch to offer gold, myrrh, and frankincense in the Chapel Royal every year on January 6, the day the feast is observed.

EPISTLE (ē-pǐs'l, Gr. *epistolē, letter, epistle*). Written correspondence, personal or official. The OT abounds with evidence of widespread written letters, among the best known being David's letter to Joab concerning Uriah (2 Sam 11:14–15), Jezebel's letter regarding Naboth (1 Kings 21:8–9), and Sennacherib's letter to Hezekiah (2 Kings 19:14); the NT also abounds (Acts 9:2; Rom 16:1ff.; 1 Cor 7:1).

The term is, however, almost a technical one, referring particularly to the 21 epistles of the NT, written by 5 (possibly 6) writers. Paul wrote 13 (or 14, if Hebrews is by him); John, 3; Peter, 2; James, 1; and Jude, 1. According to the custom of the time, they usually began with the name or title of the writer and that of the addressee or addressees; then followed words of greeting, the message of the epistle; and at the end the author usually gave his name. It was Paul's usual practice to employ a secretary to write from dictation. Seven epistles are called General Epistles, because they were written to the church at large.

The influence of the NT epistles on the literature of Christianity is seen in the writings of the next century, which were mostly epistolary in form. Indeed, heretics wrote epistles in the name of the apostles. Not all of the epistles of the apostles have survived (1 Cor 5:9; Col 4:6).

ER (Heb. *'ēr, watchful*). 1. Eldest son of Judah. He was so wicked the Lord put him to death (Gen 38:3, 6–7). 2. The third son of Shelah, the son of Judah (1 Chron 4:21). 3. An ancestor of Jesus in the maternal line (Luke 3:28).

ERASTUS (ē-răs'tŭs, Gr. *Erastos, beloved*). A name that occurs three times, each time denoting a friend of Paul: (1) an emissary of Paul (Acts 19:22); (2) the treasurer of Corinth (Rom 16:23); (3) probably the same man is designated by 2 Timothy 4:20 as remaining at Corinth.

ERECH (ē'rĕk, Heb. *'erekh*). A city of ancient Babylonia mentioned in Genesis 10:10 as the second city founded by Nimrod. The Babylonian form of the name is *Uruk*, the home of Gilgamesh, the hero of the great Akkadian epic.

ESAIAS (See ISAIAH)

ESARHADDON (ē'sàr-hăd'ŏn, *Ashur has given a brother*). A younger son of Sennacherib who obtained the throne of Assyria after his older brothers murdered their father (2 Kings 19:36–37; 2 Chron 32:21; Isa 37:37–38). His reign (681–669 B.C.) saw important political developments. He restored the city of Babylon, which his father had destroyed. His main achievement was the conquest of Egypt (671 B.C.).

He brought deportees into Samaria (Ezra 4:2), which had already been colonized with pagans by Sargon when he destroyed it in 722 B.C. The Assyrian Empire reached its greatest power with the conquest of Sidon and then 12 kings (including Manasseh of Judah) along the Mediterranean. Manasseh's summons to appear before an Assyrian king (2 Chron 33:11–13) probably took place in the reign of Esarhaddon's successor, Ashurbanipal.

ESAU (ē'saw, Heb. *'ēsāw, hairy*). The first-born of the twin brothers, Esau and Jacob, sons of Isaac and Rebecca (Gen 25:24–25). Before their birth God had told their mother that the elder would serve the younger (25:23). Esau became a man of the fields. He let Jacob have his birthright for a dinner of bread and stew because he was hungry (25:30–34).

At the age of 40 he married two Hittite women (Gen 26:34). He hated Jacob for cheating him out of Isaac's blessing and intended to kill him (Gen 27).

When Esau saw Jacob sent away to obtain a wife he realized that Canaanite wives did not please his father, so he went out and took for himself two additional wives of the Ishmaelites (Gen 28:6–9).

Years later, when Jacob was returning to Canaan (Gen 32:3–5), Esau and 400 men met and welcomed him warmly (32:7–33:15). They soon parted company and Esau went back to Mt. Seir (33:16).

In Hebrews 12:16–17 he is described as a profane person. Long after Esau's death the Lord declared he had loved Jacob and hated Esau (Mal 1:2–3). The apostle Paul used this passage to illustrate how God carries out his purposes (Rom 9:10–13).

Sometimes in Scripture Esau is used as the name of the land of Edom in which his descendants lived (Gen 36:8).

ESCHATOLOGY (ĕs-kà-tŏl'ō-gē, Gr. *eschatos, last* and *logos, ordered statement*). The study of the last things to happen on this earth in this present age. The word is used to cover the study of such important events as the second coming parousia of Christ, the judgment of the world, the resurrection of the dead, and the creation of the new heaven and earth. Related topics include the kingdom of God, the Millennium, the intermediate state, the concept of immortality, and the eternal destiny of the wicked.

Since God controls history (including its end), the believer is to have hope. It is helpful, in order to do justice to the tension within the NT between salvation already (but partially) experienced and salvation not yet (wholly) experienced, to speak of "inaugurated" eschatology and "fulfilled" eschatology. The people of God are living in the last days, but the Last Day has not yet arrived. The new age broke into this present evil age when Christ rose from the dead, but the new has not yet wholly replaced the old. The Spirit of Christ brings into the present age the life of the age to come; so what he makes available is "firstfruits" (Rom 8:23), and he is the "guarantee guarantor" or "pledge" of the fullness of life to come (2 Cor 1:22; 5:5; Eph 1:14).

As the people of the new age yet living in the old world and age, the church is called to engage in mission and evangelism (Matt 24:14; 28:19–20) until Christ's return to earth. Signs of the times—i.e., that the end is sure and near—include the evangelization of the world, the conversion of Israel (Rom 11:25–26), the great *apostasy (2 Thess 2:1–3), the tribulation (Matt 24:21–30), and the revelation of *Antichrist (2 Thess 2:1–12).

I. The Second Coming. Three Greek words—*parousia* (presence, 1 Thess 3:13), *apokalypsis* (revelation, 2 Thess 1:7–8), and *epiphaneia* (appearance, 2:8)—are used of the personal, visible, and glorious return of Jesus (Matt 24:30; Acts 1:11; 3:19–21; Phil 3:20).

II. The Resurrection of the Dead. Christ is the "firstborn" from the dead (Rom 8:11, 29; Col 1:18) and the "firstfruits" of the resurrection of all believers (1 Cor 15:20). Every person who has ever lived will rise from the dead (Dan 12:2; John

5:28–29; Acts 24:15); but the resurrection of the wicked will be the beginning of God's judgment on them, while the resurrection of the righteous will be the beginning of their life in Christ. The resurrection bodies of the righteous will be incorruptible, glorious, and spiritual (1 Cor 15:35ff.) and like Christ's glorious body (Phil 3:21).

III. The Judgment. There are two ways conservative Bible scholars view the doctrine of judgment. One is to say that there will be one future judgment in which Jesus Christ will judge the nations and every person who has ever lived. This judgment is an examination of the motives and deeds of everyone, believer and unbeliever, together with judgment based on this evidence (Matt 11:20–22; 12:36; 25:35–40; 2 Cor 5:10) and on the human response to the known will of God (Matt 16:27; Rom 1:18–21; 2:12–16; Rev 20:12; 22:12). There are spiritual rewards in the age to come for those in this life who have faithfully served the Lord (Luke 19:12–27; 1 Cor 3:10–15; cf. Matt 5:11–12; 6:19–21). The other way of viewing judgment accepts the tenets of the first view but fits them into several judgments—of the sins of believers (at Calvary), of the works of the believer (at the time of the Rapture), of individual Gentiles (before the Millennium), of the people Israel (before the Millennium), of fallen angels, and of the wicked (after the Millennium).

IV. Eternal Happiness in the New Order of Existence (New Heaven and Earth). The old universe will be marvelously regenerated (Isa 65:17–25; 66:22–23; Acts 3:19–21; Rom 8:19–21; 2 Peter 3:12; Rev 21:1–4). Those with resurrection bodies will dwell with their God in a regenerated universe, from which heaven—as God's place and sphere—is not separated but is rather present.

V. Eternal Misery and Punishment in Hell. Jesus himself had more to say about *hell than any NT writer or speaker (e.g., Matt 5:22, 29–30; 10:28; 13:41–42; 25:46). Through a variety of pictures and images, the NT presents a frightening portrayal of the everlasting suffering of those who have rejected the gospel.

VI. Immortality. God alone truly possesses immortality (*aphtharsia*, 1 Tim 6:16), for he is the eternal source of life. Human beings were created for immortality (rather than created with immortal souls); and this immortality, in the sense of receiving and enjoying God's life, is given to the righteous at the resurrection of the dead, in and through the gift of an imperishable and immortal new body

(1 Cor 15:53–55). The wicked are never said to have immortality or to exist eternally in immortal bodies, for the NT use of immortality is to denote the immunity from death and decay that results from sharing in the divine life.

VII. The Intermediate State. The existence of those who die before the Second Coming is often called the Intermediate State. The parable of the rich man and Lazarus (Luke 16:19–31) suggests that there is conscious existence and that this can be of misery or of rest/happiness. Certainly the NT points to the comfort and security of those who die as disciples of Jesus (23:42–43; 2 Cor 5:6–8; Phil 1:21–23; 1 Thess 4:16; see also HADES; PARADISE; SHEOL).

ESDRAELON (ĕs'drā-ē'lŏn, a Gr. modification of *Jezreel*; does not occur in Heb.; is Gr. in form; found only in Revelation). The great plain that breaks the central range of Palestine in two. In the OT it is known as the plain, or valley, of Jezreel. It affords a direct connection between the maritime plain and the Jordan Valley. It lies between Galilee on the north and Samaria on the south.

Esdraelon was the scene of some of the most important battles in Bible history: The victory of Barak over Sisera (Judg 4) and the victory of the Philistines over Saul and his sons (1 Sam 31). Here the Egyptians under Pharaoh Neco killed Josiah (2 Kings 23:29). A great future conflict seems indicated for this area (Rev 16:16).

ESDRAS, BOOKS OF (See APOCRYPHA)

ESH-BAAL (ĕsh'-bā'ăl, Heb. *'esha'al, man of Baal*). The fourth son of Saul (1 Chron 8:33; 9:39). The same man is called Ishbosheth (2 Sam 2:8, 10, 12, et al). He was made king of Gilead by Abner after Saul's death. A few years later he was murdered.

ESHCOL (ĕsh'kŏl, Heb. *'eshkōl, cluster*). **1.** An Amorite who helped Abram defeat King Kedorlaomer and his forces and bring back Lot and his family (Gen 14:13, 24). **2.** A valley near Hebron. The men sent by Moses to spy out the land found a cluster of grapes here that they carried back to the people (Num 13:23–24).

ESHTAOL (ĕsh'tā-ŏl, Heb. *'eshtā'ôl*). A town in the lowlands of Judah on its border with Dan (Josh 15:33; 19:41). In the Book of Judges it is always mentioned with Zorah. Samson was moved by the Spirit of the Lord near Eshtaol (Judg 13:25), and was later buried there (16:31).

The Esdraelon (Jezreel) Valley with a view of the Hills of Mareh in the background. Naboth, the Jezreelite, had a vineyard in this area (1 Kings 21:1). Courtesy Zev Radovan

The Danites sent out five brave men from Zorah and Eshtaol to look for additional living space. Then 600 armed men set forth out of Zorah and Eshtaol to conquer Laish (18:2, 8, 11).

ESHTEMOA (ĕsh'tē-mō-à, Heb. *eshtemôa'*). **1.** A city assigned to the Levites (Josh 21:14), also called Eshtemoah (15:50). It received a share of the spoil of the Amalekites (1 Sam 30:28). **2.** The son of Ishbah (1 Chron 4:17). **3.** A Maacathite, a son of Hodiah (4:19).

ESROM (See HEZRON)

ESSENES (ĕ-sēnz', Gr. *Essenoi* or *Essaioi*). A sect of reportedly 4,000 Jews in Palestine during the time of Christ, but not mentioned in the NT. The Essenes lived a simple life of sharing everything in common. They practiced strict rules of conduct and were mostly unmarried. The majority of them lived together in settlements, but some resided in cities. Apparently they kept their ranks filled by the adoption of other people's children. They did not participate in the temple worship but had their own purification rites. They observed the Sabbath day very strictly and greatly venerated Moses. They

would take no oaths; but new members, after going through a three-year probationary period, were required to swear a series of strong oaths that they would cooperate in every way with the organization and would never reveal to outsiders any of the affairs or beliefs of the sect.

The Dead Sea Scrolls and the monastery called Khirbet Qumran where the scrolls were written give evidence of an organization very similar to what is known about the Essenes. The structure was occupied from the end of the second century B.C. to A.D. 135, the Essenes' period of prominence.

ESTHER (Heb. *'estēr*, perhaps from Akkad. *Ishtar* [Venus], Gr. *astēr*, star). A Jewish orphan maiden in the city of Shushan who became queen of Persia. Her Hebrew name was Hadassah (*myrtle*). Her cousin Mordecai, who was a minor official of the palace, reared her as his own daughter. Xerxes (KJV Ahasuerus), the Persian king, had divorced his wife. When he sought a new queen from among the maidens of the realm he chose Esther. When the Jews in the empire were faced with destruction she

The traditional tomb of Esther and Mordecai, at Ecbatana, modern Hamadan, Iran.
Courtesy B. Brandl

was able to save them. In her honor the book that bears her name is read every year at the Feast of Purim.

ESTHER, BOOK OF The last of the OT historical books, it tells how Esther became queen of Persia and then was instrumental in saving the Jews from Haman's plan to eliminate them. Most scholars today agree that the KJV Ahasuerus was the Xerxes who reigned 486 B.C. to 465 B.C. Probably the book was written about 400. The author is unknown, but it is evident from the details of the record that he was well acquainted with the Persian court life. The Book of Esther has always been accepted as canonical by the Jews.

An undated cuneiform text mentions a certain Mordecai (Marduka) who was a high official at the Persian court of Shushan during the reign of Xerxes and even before that under Darius I. This text came from Borsippa and is the first reference to Mordecai outside the Bible.

Outstanding peculiarities of the book are the complete absence of the name of God, the lack of any direct religious teaching, and no mention of prayer. These remarkable features can have occurred only by deliberate design. Probably the book was written for the Jews in the Persian Empire as an account that could be circulated without danger of offending the people of that land who ruled over many Jews.

ESTHER, ADDITIONS TO (See APOCRYPHA)

ETAM (ē'tăm). **1.** A town and clan in Judah between Bethlehem and Tekoa (1 Chron 4:3), Khirbet-el-Khokh, rebuilt by Rehoboam (2 Chron 11:6); also named in LXX of Joshua 15:59. **2.** A village near En Rimmon in Simeon (1 Chron 4:32). **3.** The rock where Samson lived after a

slaughter of Philistines (Judg 15:8, 11). Perhaps the same as No. 1.

ETERNAL LIFE (See ESCHATOLOGY)

ETHAM (ē'thăm, Heb. *'ēthām*). An uncertain site on Israel's journey out of Egypt (Exod 13:20; Num 33:6–8), seemingly a wilderness district on both sides of the north end of the Red Sea.

ETHAN (ē'thăn, Heb. *'êthan*). **1.** An Ezrahite of Solomon's time, renowned for his wisdom (1 Kings 4:31; Ps 89 title). **2.** A son of Zerah, son of Judah (1 Chron 2:6, 8). **3.** A descendant of Gershon, son of Levi (6:39–43). **4.** A singer, descendant of Merari, son of Levi (6:44; 15:17, 19).

ETHIOPIA (ē'thĭ-ō'pĭ-à, Heb. *kûsh*, Gr. *Aithiopia*). A country extending south of Egypt from the first cataract of the Nile indefinitely, including Nubia, Sudan, and northern if not southern modern Ethiopia. The nation descended from Cush, son of Ham (Gen 10:6–8; 1 Chron 1:8–10). Moses married an Ethiopian woman (Num 12:1). In the reign of Rehoboam, Ethiopians came against Judah with the king of Egypt (2 Chron 12:3); and Asa (14:9–13; 16:7–9) defeated Zerah the Ethiopian and a million men. Tirhakah, an Ethiopian king of a dynasty that had conquered Egypt, came against Judah in the days of Hezekiah and was only driven away by the superior force of Assyria (2 Kings 19:9; Isa 37:9). Henceforth the ultimate ruin of Ethiopia is a theme of prophecy (Isa 11:11; 18:1; 20:3–5; 43:3; 45:14; Jer 46:9; Ezek 29:10; 30:4–5; 38:5; Nah 3:9; Zeph 3:10). Ethiopia in NT times was ruled by a queen whose name or title was Candace (Acts 8:27).

ETHIOPIAN EUNUCH (ē'thĭ-ō'pĭ-ăn yū'nŭk). Treasurer of Candace, queen of the Ethiopians (Acts 8:26–39). As a eunuch he could not be a full member of the Jewish community (Deut 23:1), but he had been worshiping in Jerusalem. He was reading aloud the Book of Isaiah when Philip, sent by the Holy Spirit from Samaria, met his chariot. From Isaiah 53, Philip led the African to faith in Christ, and baptized him.

EUNICE (yū'nĭs, yū-nī'sē, Gr. *Eunikē*). The Jewish wife of a Greek, daughter of Lois and mother of Timothy (Acts 16:1; 2 Tim 1:5). They lived at Lystra, where the two women and Timothy were converted, probably on Paul's first visit (Acts 14:6–20), since Timothy knew of Paul's persecution there (2 Tim 3:11). She brought up her son to know the OT Scriptures (3:15).

EUNUCH (yū'nŭk, IIcb. *sārîs*, Gr. *eu-nouchos*). A castrated male. From the employment of such men as custodians of royal harems the term came to designate an officer, whether physically a eunuch or not (e.g., Gen 37:36; 2 Kings 23:1; Isa 56:3; Jer 29:2). The Mosaic Law forbade those blemished by castration to enter the congregation (Deut 23:1), but Isaiah prophesied of a day when this disability would be removed and their loss compensated (Isa 56:3-5). The Ethiopian (Acts 8:27-39) was a queen's treasurer. Our Lord uses the term and its cognate verb four times in Matthew 19:12; those born eunuchs and those made eunuchs by men are physically incapable of begetting children, while others remain chaste to concentrate on Christ's kingdom (cf. Rev 14:4).

EUODIA (yū-ō'dĭ-à, Gr. *Euōdia, prosperous journey* or *fragrance*). A Christian woman at Philippi, also called Euodias (Phil 4:2). Paul pleads with Euodia and Syntyche to "agree with each other in the Lord."

EUPHRATES (yū-frā'tēz, Heb. *perāth*, from a root meaning *to break forth*, Gr. *Euphratēs*). The longest and most important river of western Asia, frequently in the OT called "the river," "the great river," as being the largest with which Israel was acquainted, in contrast to the soon dried up torrents of Palestine (Gen 15:18; Deut 1:7; Isa 8:7). The promise to Abraham that his seed's inheritance should reach the Euphrates (Gen 15:18; Deut 1:7; Josh 1:4) received a partial fulfillment in Reuben's pastoral possessions (1 Chron 5:9-10); a fuller accomplishment under David and Solomon, when an annual tribute was paid by subject petty kingdoms in that area (2 Sam 8:3-8; 1 Kings 4:21; 1 Chron 18:3; 2 Chron 9:26).

EUROCLYDON (yū-rŏk'lĭ-dŏn, Gr. *Euroklydōn*, from *euros, the east wind*, and *klydōn, a wave*). Extremely dangerous wind (Acts 27:14) translated as "Euraquilo" in NASB and RV and as "Northeaster" in NEB and NIV. It threatened Paul's ship (27:17).

EUTYCHUS (yū'tĭ-kŭs, Gr. *Eutychos, fortunate*). A young man of Troas mentioned in Acts 20:9 who, while listening to Paul preach, was overcome with sleep and fell out of the third story window to his death. Paul then went down and restored him to life.

EVANGELIST (Gr. *euangelistēs, one who announces good news*). Used in a general sense of anyone who proclaims the gospel of Jesus Christ. Sometimes it designates a particular class of ministry (Eph 4:11). The evangelist founded the church; the pastor-teacher built it up in the faith. The evangelist moved about in different localities, preaching the Good News. Apostles (Acts 8:25; 14:7; 1 Cor 1:17) did the work of an evangelist, as did bishops (2 Tim 4:2-5). Philip, one of the seven deacons (Acts 6:5), was also called "the evangelist" (21:8).

EVE (Heb. *hawwâh, life, living*). The first woman, formed by God out of Adam's side. Adam designated her (Gen 2:23) as woman (Heb. *'ishshâh*) for she was taken out of man (Heb. *'ish*). The way in which Eve was created and the designation "woman" emphasize also the intimacy, sacredness, and inseparability of the marital state, transcending even the relationship between children and parents (2:24). While the Scriptures uniformly trace the fall of the race to Adam's sin, the part Eve played in this tragedy is vividly portrayed in Genesis 3. Her greater weakness and susceptibility to temptation are juxtaposed with Adam's willful act of disobedience. Deceived by Satan, she ate of the fruit. Enamored of his wife, Adam chose to leave God for the one he had given him (2 Cor 11:3; 1 Tim 2:13).

EVI (ē'vī, Heb. *'ĕwî*). One of the five kings of Midian killed by the Israelites during their encampment in the plains of Moab (Num 31:8). His land was allotted to Reuben (Josh 13:21).

EVIL (Heb. *ra'*, Gr. *ponēros, kakos*). A term designating what is not in harmony with the divine order. In the Bible, evil is clearly depicted under two distinct aspects: moral and physical. Evil has been permitted by God in order that his justice might be manifested in its punishment and his grace in its forgiveness (Rom 9:22-23). Moral evil, or sin, is any lack of conformity to the moral law of God and is the cause of the existence of physical or natural evil. Moral evil entered the world with Adam and Eve's disobedience. The consequences of their choice affected their lives as well as creation (Gen 3:16-19). In the NT the relationship between moral and natural evil is indicated by Paul in Romans 8:18-22.

EVIL-MERODACH (ē'vĭl-mĕ-rō'dăk). A king of Babylon whose name means "Man of Marduk," Marduk being the chief god of Babylon. The son and successor of Nebuchadnezzar, Evil-Merodach was murdered by his brother-in-law,

Neriglissar (the Nergal-Sharezer of Jer 39:3), a prince who usurped the throne.

Evil-Merodach released Jehoiachin, king of Judah, from his 37-year Babylonian imprisonment and gave him a position of prominence among the captive kings and a daily allowance of food for the rest of his life (2 Kings 25:27–30; Jer 52:31–34).

EVIL SPIRITS (See DEMONS)

EWE (See ANIMALS)

EXALTATION The term covers the sequence of events that begins with the resurrection of Christ and includes his ascension and coming again (Phil 2:8–11; cf. Acts 2:33). The exaltation of Christ places him "at the right hand of God" (Acts 7:55–56; Rom 8:34; Eph 1:20; Heb 1:3; 10:12; 12:2; 1 Peter 3:22).

EXCOMMUNICATION Disciplinary exclusion from church fellowship. The Jews had two forms of excommunication, apparently alluded to in Luke 6:22—"exclude you" [the Jewish *middûy*, for 30, 60, or 90 days] and "reject your name as evil" [the Jewish *hērem*, a formally pronounced, perpetual cutting off from the community]. Christian excommunication is commanded by Christ (Matt 18:15–18), and apostolic practice (1 Tim 1:20) and precept (1 Cor 5:11; Titus 3:10) are in agreement. "Hand this man over to Satan" (1 Cor 5:5; 1 Tim 1:20) seems to mean casting out of the church into the world that lies in the power of the wicked one (Eph 6:12; 1 John 5:19). The object of excommunication is the good of the offender (1 Cor 5:5) and the moral wellbeing of the sound members (2 Tim 2:17). Its subjects are those guilty of heresy or great immorality (1 Cor 5:1–5; 1 Tim 1:20). It is inflicted by the church and its representative ministers (1 Cor 5:1, 3–4; Titus 3:10).

EXECUTIONER An officer of high rank in the East, commander of the bodyguard who executed the king's sentence. Potiphar (Gen 37:36 ASV footnote) was "chief of the executioners." Nebuzaradan (Jer 39:9 ASV footnote) and Arioch (Dan 2:14 ASV) held this office. King Herod sent an executioner to behead John the Baptist (Mark 6:27).

EXILE This usually refers to the period of time during which the southern kingdom (Judah) was forcibly detained in Babylon. It began with a series of deportations during the reigns of the Judean kings, Jehoiakim (609–598 B.C.), Jehoiachin (598), and Zedekiah (598–587). After the destruction of Jerusalem by

Nebuchadnezzar (587) the kingdom of Judah ceased to exist as a political entity. Although there were settlements in Egypt, the exiles in Babylon were the ones who maintained the historic faith and provided the nucleus that returned to Judea after the decree of Cyrus (536). The northern kingdom (Israel) was earlier exiled to Assyria (722). It was the policy of the Assyrian conquerors to move the populations of captured cities, with the result that Israelites were scattered in various parts of the empire and other captives, later known as the Samaritans, were brought to the region around Samaria (2 Kings 17:24). No organized return took place from the Assyrian captivity.

Both theological and political causes are mentioned in the biblical accounts of the Exile. The prophets noted the tendency of both Israel and Judah to forsake the Lord and adopt the customs of their heathen neighbors. These included the licentious worship associated with the Baal fertility cult and the Molech worship that required the offering of human beings in sacrifice to a heathen deity. Politically the Exile was the result of an anti-Babylonian policy adopted by the later kings of Judah.

The Exile worked great hardships on a people who were forcibly removed from their homeland and settled in new territory. The psalmist pictures the exiles weeping in Babylon, unable to sing the songs of Zion in a strange land (Ps 137:4). From Ezekiel, himself present among the exiles (Ezek 1:1–3), we gather that the exiles were organized in their own communities under their own elders (8:1). Ezekiel's own community was situated at Tel Abib (3:15), an otherwise unknown location on the river, or canal, Kebar.

The prophets Ezekiel and Daniel ministered in Babylon during the Exile. Jeremiah, who had urged Zedekiah to make peace with Nebuchadnezzar, was permitted to remain in Judah after the destruction of Jerusalem. The murder of Gedaliah, who had been appointed by Nebuchadnezzar as governor of Judah, precipitated a move on the part of the remaining Judeans to migrate to Egypt. Although tradition suggests that he subsequently went to Babylon, Jeremiah's actual prophetic ministry ends among those who had fled this way to Egypt.

The sacred books of the Jews assumed great importance during the period of the Exile. The law, which had been lost prior to Josiah's reign (2 Kings 22:8), became the subject of careful study. By the time of the return from Babylon, the institu-

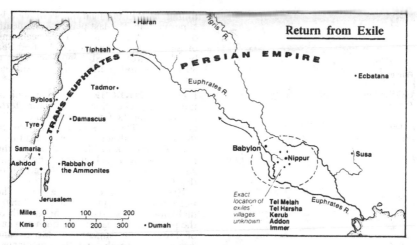

Return from Exile

1. RESTORATION	2. THE TEMPLE	3. EZRA won the	4. CLAY TAB-
of the exiles be-	was consecrated	approval of Arta-	LETS from the
gan under Cyrus	by official permis-	xerxes I (465-424	Murashu archives
(559-530 B.C.),	sion of Darius I	B.C.) to return	at Nippur reveal
who allowed	(522-486 B.C.).	with additional	the presence of
them to return to		exiles; Nehemiah,	Jews remaining a
Judah with the		to rebuild the	half century after
captured temple		walls of Jerusa-	Ezra.
treasures.		lem.	

tion of the scribe was established. Scribes not only made copies of the law, but they also served as interpreters. Ezra is regarded as the first scribe (Neh 8:1ff.). The Sabbath served as a weekly reminder that they had a definite covenant relationship to God.

Successively unifying the Persians, conquering the neighboring Medes and the distant Lydians of Asia Minor, Cyrus marched against Babylon, which he defeated in 539. The governor of Babylon, Gubaru, is doubtless to be identified with "Darius the Mede" (Dan 5; 6). Cyrus issued the decree that permitted Jews to return to Jerusalem to rebuild the temple (Ezra 1:1-4). This may be regarded as the end of the Exile, although many Jews chose to remain in Babylon.

The Exile served to emphasize the fact that God was in no sense confined to Palestine. He providentially cared for his people in Babylon (cf. Ezek 11:16). The experience of life far away from the land, city, and house where the Lord had chosen to dwell, brought to the fore the monotheism of Israel. Their suffering, coupled with face-to-face contact with the realities of false religion, purged the people once and for all of idolatrous desire. Many exiles following the decree

of Cyrus remained in the Persian Empire, with the result that in due time Judaism became international in scope.

EXODUS (Gr. *ex hodos, a going out*). The event that ended the sojourn of Israel in Egypt. The family of Jacob (Israel) voluntarily entered Egypt during a time of severe famine in Canaan. Joseph, who had been sold into slavery by jealous brothers, was then vizier of Egypt and his Israelite brothers were assigned suitable land in the NE section of Egypt known as Goshen (Gen 42-46). When a new dynasty arose "who did not know about Joseph" (Exod 1:8), i.e., forgot what he had done for Egypt, the Israelites were reduced to the status of slaves. Afraid that they might prove sympathetic with foreign invaders, Pharaoh ordered the male children destroyed. The infant Moses, however, was placed in an ark of bulrushes where he was rescued by Pharaoh's daughter (2:1-10). Raised in the royal court, Moses chose to turn his back on the possibilities of advancement in Egypt in order to lead his oppressed people into freedom.

Israel did not take the direct route through the Philistine country to Canaan (Exod 13:17). Had they done so, Israel

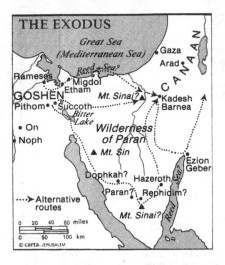

THE EXODUS

Great Sea
(Mediterranean Sea)
Gaza
Arad
CANAAN
Reed Sea?
Rameses
Migdol
Etham
GOSHEN
Pithom
Succoth
Bitter
Lake
Mt. Sinai?
Kadesh
Barnea
On
Noph
Wilderness
of Paran
Mt. Sin
Ezion
Geber
Dophkah?
Hazeroth
Paran?
Rephidim?
Mt. Sinai?
Alternative
routes
0   20   40   60 miles
0   50   100 km
© carta. JERUSALEM

would have had to pass the Egyptian wall
(biblical Shur) that protected the NE
highways out of Egypt. This wall was
guarded and could be passed only with
great difficulty. If they successfully
crossed the border, further opposition
could be anticipated from the Philistines.
The discipline of the wilderness was a
part of God's preparation for his people
before they were to come into open
conflict with formidable foes. Leaving
Rameses (12:37) in the eastern delta, the
Israelites journeyed SE to Succoth (Tell
el-Mashkutah).

They then moved on to Etham "on the
edge of the desert" where they were
conscious of God's guidance in the pillar
of cloud and pillar of fire (Exod 13:21–
22). After passing Pi Hahiroth, Israel
arrived at the Red Sea, the Yam Suph of
the Hebrew text. The direct intervention
of God (Exod 14:21) allowed Israel to
cross from Egypt to the Sinai Peninsula.
When the armies of Pharaoh attempted to
pursue the Israelites, the Egyptians were
destroyed by the waters that returned to
their normal course.

The Exodus has been dated by some
about 1450 B.C. and by others about 1290
B.C.—depending on varying interpretations of the biblical and extrabiblical
data. The 600,000 men who took part in
the Exodus (Exod 12:37) a year later
numbered (over age 20) 603,550 (Num
1:46).

The Exodus period was one of the
great epochs of biblical miracles. The first
nine plagues may have been related to the
natural phenomena of Egypt, but their

timing and intensification were clearly
supernatural. The last plague—the death
of the first-born—signaled the beginning
of the Exodus. God opened the Red Sea
by the "strong east wind" and for a
40-year period miraculously sustained
Israel.

EXODUS, BOOK OF The second book of
the Bible. The title is a Latin term
derived from the Greek word *Exodos*, "a
going out." The book is called *Exodos* in
the LXX. Tradition ascribes the authorship of the book to Moses. It covers the
history of the Israelites from the events
surrounding the Exodus to the giving of
the Law at Sinai.

Exodus has three sections: (1) The
Israelites in Egypt (Exod 1:1–12:36),
including events involving the growth of
the people into a nation, the birth and call
of Moses, the ministry of Moses and
Aaron to Pharaoh, and the ten plagues
which culminated in the death of the firstborn. (2) The journey from Egypt to Sinai
(12:37–19:2), including the institution of
Passover and the Feast of Unleavened
Bread, the consecration to God of every
first-born male, and the escape through
the Red Sea. Although the people frequently complained against God and
Moses, God miraculously provided for
them by giving them manna, quails, and
water out of a rock. (3) The Israelites at
Sinai (19:3–40:38), including the giving of
the Law—the Ten Commandments
(20:2–17), civil and societal laws (21:1–
23:11), and ceremonial laws (23:12–
31:18)—the construction of the tabernacle, and the fashioning of the priests'
garments.

EXORCISM (Gr. *exorkizō, to adjure*).
The expelling of demons by means of
magic charms, spells, and incantations. It
was a common practice among ancient
heathen. In Acts 19:13–16 the profane
use of Jesus' name as a mere spell was
punished when the demon-possessed man
turned on the would-be exorcists; these
"vagabond Jews" were pretenders.
Christ, however, implies that some Jews
actually cast out demons (Matt 12:27)—
some probably by demonical help, others
(in the name of Jesus) without saving
faith in him (7:22). He gave power to cast
out demons to the 12, the 70, and to the
other disciples after the Ascension (Matt
10:8; Mark 16:17; Luke 10:17–19; Acts
16:18). The Bible never mentions Christians "exorcising."

EXPANSE (See FIRMAMENT)

EXPIATION (See PROPITIATION AND
EXPIATION)

EYE (Heb. *'ayin*, Gr. *ophthalmos*). The organ of sight, among the most valued of the members of the body. If a man hit a slave's eye so that it was blinded, the slave was to be released (Exod 21:26). One of the most cruel customs of the heathen nations was that of putting out the eyes of a defeated enemy (2 Kings 25:7). Frequently "eye" speaks of spiritual perception and understanding (Ps 19:8; Eph 1:18). Other expressions speak of the eye as indicative of character (Ps 131:1; Prov 22:9 KJV; Matt 20:15 KJV).

EYES, PAINTING OF The ancient practice of painting the eyelids in order to enhance the beauty of the feminine face (2 Kings 9:30 [Jezebel]; Jer 4:30; Ezek 23:40). Oriental women still paint their eyelids with antimony or *kohl* (a black powder made of the smoke black from the burning of frankincense) to make them look full and sparkling.

EYESALVE (Gr. *kollourion*). A compound used either by simple application or by reduction to a powder to be smeared on the eye (Rev 3:18). When used figuratively it refers to the restoration of spiritual vision.

Fragment (7 cm. wide) from Assyria (late eighth century B.C.) of amulet designed to exorcise demons from the sick. Upper register contains seven demons, each with a different animal's head. The second register shows the horned demon Lamashtu holding a serpent in her hand. To the left is a bed for the sick; to the right is a smaller demon and demonic head. Courtesy Réunion des Musées Nationaux

EZBON (ĕz'bŏn). **1.** One of the sons of Gad (Gen 46:16), also called Ozni (Num 26:16). **2.** First named son of Bela, son of Benjamin (1 Chron 7:7).

EZEKIEL (ē-zēk'yĕl, Heb. *yehezqē'l*, God strengthens). A Hebrew prophet of the Exile. A play is made on this name in connection with the prophet's call (Ezek 3:7–8, 14). Of a priestly family (1:3), Ezekiel grew up in Judea during the last years of Hebrew independence and was deported to Babylon with Jehoiachin in 597 B.C., probably early in life. He was thus a contemporary of Jeremiah and Daniel. Ezekiel was married (24:18) and lived with the Jewish exiles by the irrigation canal Kebar (1:1, 3; 3:15) which connected the Tigris River with the Euphrates above Babylon; Daniel carried out his quite different work in the Babylonian court.

Ezekiel was called to be a prophet in the fifth year of his captivity (Ezek 1:1–2); the last date mentioned is the 27th year (29:17); his ministry therefore lasted at least 22 years, from about 593 to 571 B.C.

When Jerusalem was finally destroyed, some ten years after he arrived in Babylon, Ezekiel entered into the sufferings of his people. On the day on which the final siege began, the prophet's wife became suddenly sick and died. In this he became a sign to the people and was not allowed to go through the customary period of mourning, doubtless to emphasize to them the greater sorrow now coming on the nation. In Babylon the Jews were cured permanently of their idolatry; and Ezekiel, their major religious leader, must be given much credit for that.

The prophet's ministry was divided into two periods. The first ends with the siege of Jerusalem in 587 B.C. (24:1, 27). It was a message of approaching destruction for Jerusalem and of condemnation of her sin. The second period begins with the reception of the news of Jerusalem's fall, some two years later (33:21–22). Now the prophet's message emphasized comfort and looked forward to the coming of the kingdom of God.

Ezekiel is referred to as "son of man" over 70 times in this book, meaning a mortal (Ps 8:4). It is used to emphasize the prophet's weakness and dependence on God for his success. Later the term came to be a messianic designation.

EZEKIEL, BOOK OF The locality of Ezekiel's ministry was Babylon, to which he had been deported in 597 B.C. Ezekiel 8–11 contains a unique vision of events that were transpiring in Jerusalem (cf.

24:1–2). It appears impossible that Ezekiel in Babylon could have known in such detail events in Jerusalem except by divine revelation.

The book is divided into three parts: (1) denunciation of Judah and Israel (Ezek 1–24, dated 593–588 B.C.), (2) oracles against foreign nations (chs. 25–32, dated 587–571), and (3) the future restoration of Israel (chs. 33–48, dated 585–573). The prophecies of the first section were uttered before the fall of Jerusalem. Ezekiel's call to the prophetic work (Ezek 1–3) includes his vision of the divine glory—God's throne borne by an unearthly chariot of cherubim and wheels (1:4–21). The prophet eats the scroll on which his sad message is written (2:8–3:3); and he is commanded to be the Lord's watchman, his own life to be forfeited if he does not cry the alarm (3:16–21; cf. 33:1–9). Ezekiel then predicts the destruction of Jerusalem by symbolic acts (4:7), such as laying siege to a replica of the city (4:1–8) and by rationing food and drink (4:9–17). Next follows the famous vision of Jerusalem's iniquity, for which Ezekiel is raptured in spirit to Jerusalem (chs. 8–11), and sees all kinds of loathsome idolatry being practiced in the temple courts. While he watches the desecration of the house of the Lord, he beholds the divine glory, which had been manifested in the Most Holy Place (8:4), leave the temple and city (9:3; 10:4, 19; 11:22–23), symbolizing God's abandonment of his apostate people. At that moment Ezekiel returns in spirit to Babylon. The rest of the first section (chs. 12–24) records symbolic actions and sermons predicting the fall of Jerusalem. He enacts the departure into exile (12:1–7), preaches against false prophets (chs. 13), and in two deeply moving oracles (chs. 16, 23) depicts the ungrateful people's apostasy. His statement of the individual's responsibility before God (ch. 18) is famous. Finally he announces the beginning of the siege of Jerusalem, in the evening of the same day his wife dies, and he becomes dumb until the fall of the city (ch. 24).

After the prophecies of judgment against foreign nations (Ezek 25–32) comes the climax of the prophet's vision, written after the fall of Jerusalem—the restoration of Israel (chs. 33–48). God will bring back the people to their land, send the son of David to reign over them, and give them a new heart (chs. 34, 36). The vision of the valley of dry bones (ch. 37) is a figurative statement of this regathering of the nation. Then follows Israel's defeat of the Gentile powers, Gog and Magog (chs. 38–39). Finally a great restored temple is pictured (chs. 40–43), its holy services (chs. 44–46), the river of life running from it (ch. 47), and the people of Israel living in their places around the city called "The Lord is there" (ch. 48), to which the glory of the Lord has returned (43:2, 4–5; 44:4).

EZEM (ē′zĕm). A town near Edom assigned to Simeon (Josh 15:29; 19:3; 1 Chron 4:29). Sometimes rendered Azem.

EZER (ē′zêr, Heb. *'ēzer, help*). 1. The son of Seir and a chief of the Horites (Gen 36:21; 1 Chron 1:38). 2. Descendant of Hur, of the tribe of Judah, and the father of Hushah (4:4). 3. An Ephraimite who was killed by men of Gath (7:21). 4. The first of the Gadite men of might who joined David in Ziklag when he was a fugitive from Saul (12:9). 5. The son of Jeshua, ruler of Mizpah. Under Nehemiah, Ezer repaired a section of the wall of Jerusalem (Neh 3:19). 6. One of the Levitical singers who participated in the dedication of the rebuilt walls of Jerusalem under Nehemiah (12:42).

EZION GEBER (ē′zĭ-ŏn gē′bêr, Heb. *'etsyôn gever*). A city near Elath on the Gulf of Aqabah. It was the last stopping place of the Israelites in their wilderness wanderings before Kadesh (Num 33:35–36). The city's period of greatest prosperity was in the time of Solomon, who built a fleet of ships that sailed between Ezion Geber and Ophir, a source of gold (1 Kings 9:26ff.; 2 Chron 8:17–18). There also Jehoshaphat joined with Ahaziah in building ships designed to sail to Ophir, but the fleet was destroyed before leaving port (20:35–36; 1 Kings 22:48–49). The city was located between the hills of Edom on the east and the hills of Palestine on the west. An industrial center as well as a seaport, it had an extensive industrial complex centered on the smelting and refining of copper (chiefly) and iron. The furnace rooms were so placed that they received the full benefit of the prevailing winds from the north, which were used to furnish the draft for the fires. Nearby mines were worked extensively in Solomon's day to supply the ore for these smelters. These operations were an important source of Solomon's wealth.

EZNITE (ĕz′nīt, Heb. *'etsnî*). Designation of Adino, one of David's chief captains (2 Sam 23:8 KJV, MLB, NASB). Some versions (NEB, NIV, RSV) are based on a conjecture that the statement about Adino the Eznite is a corruption of the Hebrew for "he lifted up his spear." A

The Behistun Rock, northeast of Babylon, hewn by order of Darius I (521–486 B.C.), under whose authority the temple at Jerusalem was reconstructed after the Jewish return from exile in Babylonia, as recounted by Ezra. Here the king, followed by two attendants, stands before nine rebels roped together. Above is the figure of the Persian god Ahura Mazda. Accompanying the sculptures is a trilingual inscription in Old Persian, Elamite, and Akkadian. Courtesy B. Brandl

parallel passage (1 Chron 11:11) speaks of Jashobeam, a Hachmonite, who "raised his spear."

EZRA (ĕz'rà, Heb. *'ezrā', help*). **1.** A man of Judah (1 Chron 4:17). **2.** A leading priest who returned from Babylon to Jerusalem with Zerubbabel (Neh 12:1); whose full name is Azariah (10:2). **3.** The famous Jewish priest and scribe who is the main character of the Book of Ezra and the co-worker of Nehemiah (Ezra 7–10; Neh 8–10). Ezra was a lineal descendant from Eleazar, the son of Aaron the high priest, and from Seraiah, the chief priest put to death at Riblah by order of Nebuchadnezzar (2 Kings 25:18–21).

In the seventh year of the reign of Artaxerxes Longimanus, king of Persia (458 B.C.), Ezra received permission from the king to return to Jerusalem to carry out a religious reform. Following the return from Babylonian captivity, the temple had been rebuilt in 516, in spite of much powerful and vexatious opposition from the Samaritans; but after a brief period of religious zeal, the nation drifted into apostasy once more. Many of the Jews intermarried with their heathen neighbors (Mal 2:11); the temple services and sacrifices were neglected (1:6–14); and oppression and immorality were prevalent (3:5). Ezra received a royal edict granting him authority to carry out his purpose. He was given permission to take with him as many Israelites as cared to go; he was authorized to take from the king and the Jews offerings made for the temple; to draw on the royal treasury in Syria for further necessary supplies; to purchase animals for sacrifice; to exempt the priests, Levites, and other workers in the temple from the Persian tax; to appoint magistrates in Judea to enforce the law of God, with power of life and death over all offenders. He left Babylon with 1,800 Jews. Nine days later, they halted at a place called Ahava, and when it was found that no Levites were in the caravan, 38 were persuaded to join them. After fasting and praying three days for a safe journey, they set out. Four months later they reached the Holy City, having made a journey of 900 miles (1,500 hundred km.). The treasures were delivered into the custody of the Levites, burnt offerings were offered to the Lord, the king's commissions were handed to the governors and viceroys, and help was given to the people and the ministers of the temple.

When he had discharged the various trusts committed to him, Ezra entered on his great work of reform. The Jewish people generally, but especially the rulers and princes, had not kept themselves religiously separate from the heathen around them, and had even married heathen wives. A divorce court, consisting of Ezra and some others, was set up to attend to the matter; and after three months, in spite of some opposition, the work of the court was finished and the foreign wives were put away.

The Book of Ezra ends with this important transaction. Nothing more is heard of Ezra until 13 years later in the 20th year of Artaxerxes (446 B.C.), he appears again at Jerusalem, when Nehemiah returned to Jerusalem as governor of Palestine with the king's permission to repair the ruined walls of the city. Since he is not mentioned in Nehemiah's narrative until after the completion of the wall (Neh 8:1), it is probable that Nehemiah sent for him to aid in his work. Under Nehemiah's government his functions were entirely of a priestly and ecclesiastical character. He read and interpreted the law of Moses before the assembled congregation during the eight days of the Feast of Tabernacles, assisted at the dedication of the wall, and helped Nehemiah in bringing about a religious reformation. In all this he took a chief place. His name is repeatedly coupled with Nehemiah's, while the high priest is not mentioned as taking any part in the reformation at all.

Evidence points to Ezra's ministry taking place during the reign of Artaxerxes I (456–424 B.C.). According to Jewish tradition, Ezra is the author of the Book of Ezra and of 1 and 2 Chronicles. Many modern scholars hold that he wrote the Book of Nehemiah as well. First Esdras, a part of the OT Apocrypha, reproduces the substance of the end of 2 Chronicles, the whole of Ezra, and a part of Nehemiah, and was written somewhere near the beginning of the first century A.D. There is also an apocalyptic book known as 2 Esdras, written about A.D. 100, describing some visions supposedly granted to Ezra in the Babylonian exile. Ezra made a lasting impression on the Jewish people. His influence shaped Jewish life and thought in a way from which they never completely departed.

EZRA, BOOK OF So named because Ezra is the principal person mentioned in it; possibly also because he may be its author. It does not in its entirety claim to be the work of Ezra, but Jewish tradition says it was written by him. Chapters 7–10 are written in the first person singular, while events in which he did not take part are described in the third person.

The Book of Ezra continues the narrative after Chronicles and records the return from Babylon and the rebuilding of the temple. The purpose of the author is to show how God fulfilled his promise given through prophets to restore his exiled people to their own land through heathen monarchs, and raised up such great men as Zerubbabel, Haggai, Zechariah, and Ezra to rebuild the temple, reestablish the old forms of worship, and put a stop to compromise with heathenism. All material that does not contribute to his purpose he stringently excludes.

The period covered is from 536 B.C., when the Jews returned to Jerusalem, to 458, when Ezra came to Jerusalem to carry out his religious reforms—although the years between 535–520 and 516–458 are practically a blank.

The Book of Ezra consists of two parts. The first (chs. 1–6) is a narrative of the return of the Jews from Babylonia under Zerubbabel and the restoration of worship in the rebuilt temple; the second (chs. 7–10) tells of a second group of exiles returning with Ezra and of Ezra's religious reforms.

FABLE A narrative in which animals and inanimate objects of nature are made to act and speak as if they were human beings. The word "fable" is not found in the OT, but the OT has two fables (Judg 9:7–15; 2 Kings 14:9). The word "fables" is found in the KJV as the translation of *mythos* in each of its five NT occurrences (1 Tim 1:4; 4:7; 2 Tim 4:4; Titus 1:14; 2 Peter 1:16). NIV has "cleverly invented stories" in 2 Peter 1:16, "myths" elsewhere.

FACE The word is used literally, figuratively, and idiomatically. Often "my face" was nothing more than an oriental way of saying "I." Sometimes it meant "presence" and sometimes "favor." The hidden face was the equivalent of disapproval or rejection (Pss 13:1; 27:9). To spit in the face was an expression of contempt and aversion (Num 12:14). To harden the face meant to harden oneself against any sort of appeal (Prov 21:29 KJV). To have the face covered by another was a sign of doom (Esth 7:8). Falling on the face symbolized prostration before man or God (Ruth 2:10). Setting the face signified determination (Luke 9:51 KJV). To cover the face expressed mourning (Exod 3:6).

FAIR It has the meaning of beautiful, attractive (Hos 10:11; Acts 7:20 RSV; cf. NIV footnote); unspotted, free of defilement (Zech 3:5 KJV); plausible, persuasive (Prov 7:21 KJV); making a fine display (Gal 6:12 KJV); good weather (Job 37:22 KJV; Matt 16:2); honest, just (Judg 9:16; Prov 1:3).

FAIR HAVENS (Gr. *Kaloi Limenes*). A small bay on the south coast of Crete. Paul stayed there for a time on his way to Rome (Acts 27:8–12).

FAITH (Heb. *'emûn*, Gr. *pistis*). Faith has a twofold sense in the Bible: (1) "trust," "reliance" (Rom 3:3), and (2) "fidelity," "trustworthiness."

In the OT the verb "to believe" occurs only 30 times, but this comparative infrequency does not adequately reflect the importance of the place of faith in the OT scheme of things. The NT draws all its examples of faith from the lives of OT believers (e.g., Rom 4:18ff.; Heb 11; James 2:14ff.), and Paul rests his doctrine of faith on the word of Habakkuk 2:4.

When used with a religious application, faith in the OT is sometimes in a specific word or work of God (Lam 4:12; Hab 1:5), or in the fact of God's revelation (Exod 4:5; Job 9:16), or in the words or commandments of God in general (Ps 119:66), or in God himself (Gen 15:6). Faith is put in the word of God's prophets because they speak for him, and he is absolutely trustworthy (Exod 19:9; 2 Chron 20:20). NT writers, especially Paul and the author of Hebrews, show that the faith manifested by OT saints was not different in kind from that expected of Christians.

The terms "faith" and "believe" occur almost 500 times in the NT. A principal reason for this is that the NT makes the claim that the promised Messiah had finally come, and, to the bewilderment of many, the form of the fulfillment did not obviously correspond to the Messianic promise. It required a real act of faith to believe that Jesus of Nazareth was the promised Messiah. It was not long before "to believe" meant to become a Christian. In the NT, faith therefore becomes the supreme human act and experience.

It is in Paul's letters that the meaning of faith is most clearly and fully set forth. Faith is trust in the person of Jesus, the truth of his teaching, and the redemptive work he accomplished at Calvary. Faith is not to be confused with a mere intellectual assent to the doctrinal teachings of Christianity, though that is obviously necessary. It includes a radical and total commitment to Christ as the Lord of one's life.

Unbelief, or lack of faith in the Christian gospel, appears everywhere in the NT as the supreme evil. Not to make a decisive response to God's offer in Christ means that the individual remains in sin and is eternally lost. Faith alone can save him.

FAITHFULNESS (Heb. *ĕmûnâh*). An attribute or quality applied in the Bible to both God and human beings. God is constant and true, faithful in keeping his promises, and unchangeable in his ethical nature. God's faithfulness is usually connected with his gracious promises of salvation. Faithful men are dependable in fulfilling their responsibilities and in carrying out their word. The NT has frequent exhortations to faithfulness. It is one of the fruits of the Spirit (Gal 5:22).

FALCON (See BIRDS)

FALL, THE The Fall of man is narrated in Genesis 3 as a historical fact, not as a myth. It stands in a context of historical facts. Though not alluded to again in the

OT, the NT regards it as a literal, historical event (Rom 5:12–13; 1 Cor 15:22; 1 Tim 2:14). Some philosophers and theologians think the account is an allegory describing the awakening of man from a brute state of self-consciousness and personality—a fall upward, rather than downward, but such an explanation conflicts radically with biblical teaching. There is no doubt that Paul takes the account literally and sees in the Fall the origin of sin in the human race. The scriptural view of sin and of redemption takes the Fall for granted.

The sin that constituted the Fall involved Adam and Eve in disobeying the word of God (Gen 3:1–4) and challenging the goodness of God by imputing to him an ill motive (3:5). But chiefly it consisted in disobeying the law of God. The effect of the Fall, as Genesis 4 and the remainder of the Bible explicitly and implicitly bring out, was not merely immediate alienation from God for Adam and Eve, but guilt and depravity for all their posterity and the cursing of the earth. Redemption from the Fall and its effects is accomplished through Christ (cf. Rom 5:12–21; 1 Cor 15:21–22, 45–49).

FALLOW DEER (See ANIMALS)

FAMILIAR SPIRIT (Heb. *’ôv*, etymology and exact meaning unknown). Used in the KJV to refer to the spirit of a dead person that mediums claimed they could summon for consultation (Deut 18:11). The word "familiar" has in this phrase the sense of the Latin *familiaris*, belonging to one's family, and hence ready to serve one as a servant. Such a spirit was thought to be able to reveal the future (1 Sam 28:7; Isa 8:19). Since the voice seemed to come in a whisper from the ground, the medium was very likely a ventriloquist. Israelites were forbidden by the Lord to consult familiar spirits (Lev 19:31; Isa 8:19). This was regarded as apostasy so serious that those who consulted them were put to death (Lev 20:6). Saul put away mediums early in his reign, but consulted the witch of Endor when he became apostate just before his death (1 Sam 28:3–25; 1 Chron 10:13). Manasseh dealt with familiar spirits (2 Kings 21:6; 2 Chron 33:6), but his grandson Josiah carried out the Mosaic Law against them (2 Kings 23:24). The practice of consulting them probably prevailed more or less to the time of the Exile (Isa 8:19; 19:3).

FAMILY (Heb. *mišpāhāh, bayith, house*; Gk. *oikia, patria, house, clan*). In a patriarchal setting the father was the head of the family, having authority over his wife, children, unmarried daughters, and sometimes married sons and their families, as well as cousins and their families and possibly grandparents and even great-grandparents (Gen 46:8–26). Additional members of the household also included in the designation of family would be concubines, servants, slaves, visitors, and occasionally prisoners of war. Some polygamy was practiced, and this also made the family unit more extensive.

In a wider sense, family could also mean clan, tribe, or village, and phrases such as "house of David" (Isa 7:13) or "house of Israel" (Ezek 9:9; 18:30) show that in broader terms the household could encompass the entire nation. Some families returning from exile in Babylon comprised several hundred members (Ezra 8:1–14).

A common bond of blood bound together the members of the larger family or clan, who referred to each other as "brothers" (1 Sam 20:29). Members of the clan accepted a communal responsibility for assistance, protection, the sharing of work, loyalty, and cooperation for the general well-being of the family. As the focus of the family unit sharpened, the sense of communal responsibility lessened, and biblical reminders concerning obligations toward widows and orphans became more frequent (Isa 1:17; Jer 7:6). Family blood feuds declined as revenge for the honor of members of the wider family was no longer usual, though it was sometimes practiced and expected (2 Sam 3:27; 16:8; 2 Kings 9:26; Neh 4:14).

The religious observances and festivals were frequently family-oriented, particularly the Passover—observed as a religious family meal and thank offering (Exod 12:3–4, 46). In patriarchal times, before worship was centralized in the temple and the later synagogue, it was the fathers that offered sacrifice to God (Gen 31:54).

In the NT, little reference is made to the family, except to reinforce monogamous marriage and to denounce divorce (Matt 5:27–32; 19:3–12; Mark 10:2–12; Luke 16:18). Paul reinforces the duties of the family members (Eph 5:22–6:9; Col 3:18–22). He reiterates the financial responsibility of the members towards each other (1 Tim 5:4, 8) and the importance of teaching religion in the home (Eph 6:4). Also Paul clearly insisted on the subordinate role of women in the family (1 Cor 11:3; Eph 5:22–24, 33; Col 3:18; cf. also 1 Peter 3:1–7). In the early church—

where, in the absence of a church building, services took place in a private home—converts were often entire families (2 Tim 1:5) or all the members of the household (Acts 16:15, 31–34).

The father was responsible for the economic well-being of those over whom he had authority. The entire family could be sold for falling into debt, and uncles and cousins would be expected to prevent family property from passing into outside hands (Lev 25:25; Jer 32:6–15). The teachings of Hebrew history, religion, law, and custom were passed on from father to son in the family setting (Exod 10:2; 12:26; Deut 4:9; 6:7) and reinforced by the many rites celebrated within the house, often associated with the family meal.

The list of a man's possessions included his wife, servants, slaves, goods, and animals (Exod 20:17; Deut 5:21). Even the phrase "to marry a wife" comes from a phrase that means "to become the master of a wife" (Deut 21:13; 24:1). Although she would address the husband in subservient terms, the status of the wife was higher than that of the rest of the household. The primary responsibility of the mother was to produce children, preferably sons. A large number of sons, who became workers from an early age, ensured the future economic prosperity and security of the family.

Throughout her life a woman was subject to the protecting authority of a male relative—as a daughter, that of her father, and as a wife, that of her husband. If she became a widow, her nearest male relative became her protector and (under the levirate marriage provisions) her "redeemer."

The bride-price paid by the betrothed male to his fiancée's father, though not directly a "purchase price," was intended to compensate the father for the loss of his daughter's services (cf. Gen 29:18, 27; Exod 22:16–17; 1 Sam 18:25; 2 Sam 3:14). After the wedding the bride normally went to live with her husband's family. Thus she became part of that extended family group and was subject to its authority. Aside from the primary duty of childbearing (Gen 1:28; 9:1), the wife's main responsibility was the organization of the household—food, clothing, and domestic animals. In many families her opinion was sought in decision making, and her ideas were respected (Exod 20:12; Prov 19:26; 20:20; Ecclus 3:1–16).

By Persian times the status of the wife was showing definite improvement. She had her own position at games, the theaters, and religious festivals. Women sometimes managed property and a business (Prov 31:16, 18, 24; Acts 16:14).

The law of primogeniture provided a double portion of the inheritance as the birthright of the eldest son (Deut 21:17; Gen 25:24–26; 38:27–30; 43:33). The right to primogeniture could be forfeited as a result of a serious offense (35:22; 49:3–4; 1 Chron 5:1), surrendered voluntarily, or sold, as Esau did to his brother Jacob (Gen 25:29–34). David gave his kingdom to his youngest son, Solomon (1 Kings 2:15), despite a law protecting the eldest son from the favoritism of a father toward a younger brother (Deut 21:15–17). In a family that had no sons, property could be inherited by a daughter (Num 27:8).

The inferior status of a daughter in patriarchal society is depicted clearly. She could be sold into slavery or into concubinage and then possibly resold (Exod 21:7–11). Even her very life was at the disposition of her father. Both sons and daughters could be put to death for disobeying the head of the household. Abraham was prepared to sacrifice his son Isaac (Gen 22:1–14). Judah ordered the burning of Tamar on suspicion that she, a widow, was having sexual relations with a man who was not of her late husband's family (Gen 38:11–26), when she should normally have been expected to marry a relative of her husband and was, in fact, promised to his brother.

With the coming of the Mosaic Law, a father could no longer put his child to death without referring the case to the authorities. Thus the elders heard accusations of disobedience, gluttony, and drunkenness, which, on conviction, were punishable with death by stoning (Deut 21:20–21). Children, however, could no longer be held responsible for the crimes of their parents (Deut 24:16). By the time of king David, there was the right of ultimate appeal to the monarch himself (2 Sam 14:4–11).

Frequently, neither sons nor daughters were consulted when marriage partners were being selected for them. A marriage was often an alliance or contract between families, the wishes of the individual being regarded as unworthy of consideration. Although loved and valued, children were not pampered (Ecclus 30:9–12). As family disciplinarian, the father spared neither the rod nor the whip (Prov 13:24; 22:15; 29:15–17). In postexilic times, a son's more formal education took place within the precincts of the synagogue, and just prior to the time of

Agricultural scenes in Theban tomb No. 1 at Deir el-Medina, belonging to Sennedjem, from the reign of Sethos I (1306–1290 B.C.). Sennedjem, accompanied by his wife, is shown reaping grain, plowing with a pair of cattle, and harvesting flax. Courtesy Seffie Ben-Yoseph

Christ a form of general education was introduced into Palestine.

In the OT, the relationship between God and Israel is seen in such family terms as "bride" (Jer 2:2), "daughter" (31:22), "children" (3:14 KJV), or "betrothal" (Hos 2:19f.). The NT uses bridal imagery to describe the relationship between Christ and the church (2 Cor 11:2; Eph 5:25–33; Rev 19:7; 21:9), and the church is referred to as the household of God (Gal 6:10; Eph 2:19; 3:15; 1 Peter 4:17).

FAMINE (Heb. *rā'āv, hunger, famine,* Gr. *limos, want of good*). Famines were produced by lack of rainfall in due season, destructive hail storms and rain out of season, destruction of crops by locusts and caterpillars, and the cutting off of food supplies by a siege (2 Kings 6:25). Pestilence often followed, and the suffering was great. Famines that were the result of natural causes are recorded as occurring in the time of Abraham (Gen 12:10), Joseph (41:56), the judges (Ruth 1:1), David (2 Sam 21:1), Ahab and Elijah (1 Kings 17:1; 18:2), and Elisha (2 Kings 4:38; Luke 4:25). The NT speaks of a famine "over the entire Roman world" (Acts 11:28). Jesus predicted famines in various places (Matt 24:7; Mark 13:8; Luke 21:11), a prophecy believed to be partly fulfilled in the siege of Jerusalem by Titus. Famines are sometimes said to be sent as punishments, and sometimes they are threatened as such (Lev 26:19–20; Deut 28:49–51; 2 Kings 8:1; Isa 14:30; 51:19; Jer 14:12, 15; Ezek 5:16). To be preserved in time of famine is a special mark of God's favor and power (Job 5:20; Pss 33:19; 37:19). Sometimes the word "famine" is used in a figurative sense (Amos 8:11).

FAN (See WINNOWING FORK)

FARMING Agriculture was the background for all the legislation of Israel. At the time of the conquest every family probably received a piece of land, marked off by stones that could not be removed lawfully (Deut 19:14; 27:17; Hos 5:10). The soil of Palestine was generally fertile. Fertilizing was almost unknown. To maintain the fertility of the land, the law required that farms, vineyards, and

A Palestinian farmer plowing his land with a primitive, one-handled wooden plow.
Courtesy S. Zur Picture Library

olive orchards were to lie fallow in the seventh year (Exod 23:10). On the year of Jubilee those who had lost their ancestral estates recovered possession of them. Terracing was necessary to make use of soil on the hillsides. Irrigation was not required, since there was usually sufficient rainfall.

Plowing to prepare the land for sowing was done in autumn, when the early rains softened the ground that had become stone-hard in the summer sun. This was done with a crude wooden plow drawn by oxen or, if the soil was thin, with a mattock. With such implements the surface of the ground was hardly more than scratched—perhaps three or four inches (eight or ten cm.). Little harrowing was done and was probably unknown in Palestine in early times.

The summer grain was sown between the end of January and the end of February. Usually the seed was scattered by hand from a basket, but careful farmers put it in furrows in rows (Isa 28:25). Between sowing and reaping, the crops were exposed to several dangers: (1) failure of the latter rain (in March and April), (2) hot, drying easterly winds (often in March and April—Gen 41:6), (3) hail storms (Hag 2:17), (4) various kinds of weeds (tares, thorns—Jer 12:13;

Matt 13:7, 25), (5) injurious insects, especially the palmerworm, the cankerworm, the caterpillar, and the locust (Amos 7:2), (6) thefts by crows and sparrows (Matt 13:4), and (7) fungus diseases, especially mildew (Deut 28:22). As the harvest season approached, particularly valuable crops were protected by watchmen (Jer 4:17); but the law permitted a hungry person to pick grain when passing by (Deut 23:25; Matt 12:1).

The grain was threshed in the open air, a custom made possible because the harvest season was free from rain (2 Kings 13:7). During the threshing time the grain was guarded by harvesters who spent the nights on the threshing floor (Ruth 3:6). The grain was winnowed by tossing the grain and chaff into the air with a wooden fork or shovel so that the wind might blow away the chaff. This was usually done at night, to take advantage of the night breezes. The chaff was either burned or left to be scattered by the winds. The grain was then sifted (to remove stones and other impurities), and collected into pits or barns (Luke 12:18).

Of the large number of crops the Israelites cultivated, wheat and barley were the most important. They also raised rye, millet, flax, and a variety of vegetables. See also AGRICULTURE.

FARTHING (See MONEY)

FASTING (Heb. *tsûm*, Gr. *nēsteia*, *nēstis*). Abstinence from food and drink is frequently mentioned in Scripture. Sometimes, instead of the single word "fast," the descriptive phrase "to afflict the soul" is used, the reference being to physical fasting rather than to spiritual humiliation (Lev 16:29–31; 23:27; Num 30:13; Isa 58:3, 5, 10).

The only fast required by Moses was that of the Day of Atonement (Lev 16:29, 31; 23:27–32; Num 29:7; Jer 36:6). Many fasts on special occasions were held because of transgression or to ward off present or impending calamity (1 Sam 7:6; Jer 36:9; 1 Kings 21:9, 12; 2 Sam 12:16, 21–23).

After the Captivity, four annual fasts were held in memory of the national calamities through which the nation had passed; they are mentioned only in Zechariah (7:1–7; 8:19). In Rabbinic times the Feast of Purim (Esth 9:31–32) was accompanied by a fast in commemoration of the fast of Esther, Mordecai, and the Jews (4:1–3, 15–17). The OT notes other fasts in which individuals (Neh 9:1; Dan 9:3) or the whole people joined (Ezra 8:21–23; Neh 9:1; Jonah 3:5).

Fasting among the Israelites was either partial or total, depending on the length of the fast. Daniel mourned three full weeks (Dan 10:2–3); a longer fast is mentioned in Nehemiah 1:4; the fast on the Day of Atonement was 24 hours (Lev 23:32). The fasts of Moses and Elijah for 40 days were exceptional (Exod 34:28; 1 Kings 19:8).

Religious fasting was observed as a sign of mourning for sin, with the object of deprecating divine wrath or winning divine compassion. The prophets often condemn the abuse of the custom, for Israelites superstitiously thought that it had value even when not accompanied by purity and righteousness of life (Isa 58:3–7; Jer 14:10–12; Zech 7–8). Fasts were not necessarily religious in nature. They were commonplace when someone near and dear died (e.g., 1 Sam 31:13; 2 Sam 1:12).

The Gospels show that frequent fasts were customary with those Jews who desired to lead a specially religious life (e.g., Luke 2:37; 18:12). Jesus fasted on at least one occasion (Matt 4:2), and he spoke about it on other occasions (Matt 6:16–18; 9:14–17). He warned against making it an occasion for a parade of piety (Matt 6:16–18). Jesus also said that fasting, which is a sign of mourning, would be inconsistent

with the joy that should characterize those who know that the Messiah has finally come and is now with them (Matt 9:14–17; Mark 2:18–22; Luke 5:33–39). On another occasion Jesus said that a certain kind of demon could not be cast out without prayer and fasting, though the word "fasting" is not found in some MSS (Matt 17:21; Mark 9:29). The two other NT references are to voluntary fasting for religious purposes (Acts 13:2–3; 14:23).

FAT (Heb. *hēlev, helev*). **1.** The subcutaneous layer of fat around the kidneys and other viscera, which, like the blood, was forbidden by the Mosaic Law to be used for food but was burned as an offering to the Lord, for a sweet aroma to him (Exod 23:18; Lev 4:31; cf. Gen 4:4). **2.** Sometimes used in the KJV to refer to a wine vat, a receptacle into which the grape juice flowed from the "press" above (Isa 63:2; Joel 2:24).

FATHER (Heb. *'āv*, Gr. *patēr*). **1.** Immediate male progenitor (Gen 42:13). Reverence and obedience by children is prescribed (Exod 20:12; Lev 19:3; Deut 5:16). The Scriptures often set forth the character and duties of an ideal father. See also FAMILY. **2.** Ancestor, immediate or remote. Abraham is called Jacob's father (Gen 28:13), and God tells him he will be the "father of many nations" (17:4). The term is used of the patriarchs (Rom 9:5 KJV) and of heads of clans (Exod 6:14; 1 Chron 27:1). **3.** The word has many figurative and derived uses: a spiritual ancestor (John 8:44; Rom 4:11), the originator of a mode of life (Gen 4:20), one who exhibits paternal kindness and wisdom to another (Judg 17:10), a revered superior (1 Sam 10:12; 1 John 2:13), royal advisors and prime ministers (Gen 45:8), early Christians who have died (2 Peter 3:4), and a source (Job 38:28).

God is Father: as Creator of the universe (James 1:17); as Creator of the human race (Mal 2:10); as one who begets and takes care of his spiritual children (Rom 8:15); and, in a special and unique sense, as the Father of Jesus Christ (Matt 11:26; Mark 14:36; Luke 22:42).

FATHOM (See WEIGHTS AND MEASURES)

FATLING (See ANIMALS)

FAWN (See ANIMALS)

FEAR (Heb. *yir'âh*, Gr. *phobos*). This word has two principal meanings: (1) that apprehension of evil that normally leads one either to flee or to fight and (2) that awe and reverence felt in the presence of a higher authority (be it parent, husband, or especially God). The word "reverend," which occurs only in the KJV of Psalm 111:9 (NIV has "awesome"), means literally "to be feared" and is used only for God.

FEASTS (Heb. *mô'ēdh, an assembling, hagh, dance, or pilgrimage*). The feasts, or sacred festivals, held an important place in Jewish religion. They were religious services accompanied by demonstrations of joy and gladness.

The Weekly Sabbath (Lev 23:3) involved families and other small groups assembled under the guidance of Levites or elders and engaged in common acts of devotion.

The Passover (Lev 23:4–8) was the first of all the annual feasts, and historically and religiously it was the most important of all. It was celebrated on the first month of the religious year, on the 14th of Nisan (our March April), and commemorated the deliverance of the Jews from Egypt and the establishment of Israel as a nation by God's redemptive act.

The Feast of Unleavened Bread began on the day after the Passover and lasted seven days (23:5–8). This feast together with Passover was one of the three times that all male Jews who were physically able and ceremonially clean were required by Mosaic Law to attend (Exod 23:17; Deut 16:16). The other two were the Feast of Weeks, or Pentecost, and the Feast of Tabernacles. These were known as the pilgrimage festivals; on all of them special sacrifices were offered, varying according to the character of the festival (Num 28–29).

The Feast of Pentecost (Lev 23:15–21)—also called the Feast of Weeks, Firstfruits, and Harvests—was celebrated on the sixth day of the month of Sivan (our May/June). The name "Pentecost," meaning "fiftieth," originated from the fact that there was an interval of 50 days between Pentecost and the offering of the wave sheaf after Passover. The characteristic ritual of this feast was the offering and waving of two loaves of leavened bread, made from ripe grain that had just been harvested.

The Feast of Trumpets (Lev 23:23–25) was held on the first day of the seventh month, Tishri (our Sept./Oct.). It corresponded to our New Year's Day, and on it, from morning to evening, horns and trumpets were blown.

The Day of Atonement (Lev 23:26–32) was observed on the tenth day of Tishri. It was really less than a fast, as the distinctive character and purpose of the day was to bring the collective sin of the whole year to remembrance, so that it might earnestly be dealt with and atoned for. On this day the high priest made confession of all the sins of the community and entered on their behalf into the Most Holy Place with the blood of reconciliation.

The Feast of Tabernacles, or Booths, or Ingathering (Lev 23:33–43) began five days after the Day of Atonement (Lev 23:34; Deut 16:13) and lasted seven days. It marked the completion of the harvest and historically commemorated the wanderings in the wilderness. During this festival people lived in booths and tents in Jerusalem to remind themselves of how their forefathers wandered in the wilderness and lived in booths. The sacrifices of this feast were more numerous than at any other.

The Feast of Lights was observed for eight days beginning on the 25th day of Kislev (our Nov./Dec.). It was instituted by Judas Maccabeus in 164 B.C. when the temple, which had been defiled by Antiochus Epiphanes, king of Syria, was cleansed and rededicated to the service of the Lord. During these days the Israelites met in their synagogues, carrying branches of trees in their hands, and held jubilant services. The children were told the brave and stirring deeds of the Maccabees so that they might emulate them.

The Feast of Purim was kept on the 14th and 15th days of Adar (our Feb./Mar.). It was instituted by Mordecai to commemorate the failure of Haman's plots against the Jews (Esth 9:20–22, 26–28). The word Purim means "lots." On the evening of the 13th the whole Book of Esther was read publicly in the synagogue. It was a joyous occasion. See also CALENDAR.

FELIX (Gr. *Phēlix, happy*). He and his brother Pallas were favorites of two emperors, Claudius and Nero (54–68). Tacitus said of him that "he revelled in cruelty and lust, and wielded the power of a king with the mind of a slave." His very title of "procurator" hints at his fiscal duties of procuring funds for Rome, which he seems to have accomplished with all sorts of tyranny. He began his career as procurator of Judea by seducing Drusilla, the sister of Agrippa II and wife of the king of Emesa (modern Homs), and marrying her. Because she was Jewish (at least in part), he learned much of Jewish life and customs. Felix appears in the

Old Testament Feasts and Other Sacred Days

NAME	OT REFERENCES	OT TIME	MODERN EQUIVALENT
Sabbath	Ex 20:8–11; 31:12–17; Lev 23:3; Dt 5:12–15	7th day	Same
Sabbath Year	Ex 23:10–11; Lev 24:1–7	7th year	Same
Year of Jubilee	Lev 25:8–55; 27:17–24; Nu 36:4	50th year	Same
Passover	Ex 12:1–14; Lev 23:5; Nu 9:1–14; 28:16; Dt 16:1–3a, 4b–7	1st month (Abib) 14	Mar.–Apr.
Unleavened Bread	Ex 12:15–20; 13:3–10; 23:15; 34:18; Lev 23:6–8; Nu 28:17–25; Dt 16:3b, 4a, 8	1st month (Abib) 15–21	Mar.–Apr.
Firstfruits	Lev 23:9–14	1st month (Abib) 16	Mar.–Apr.
Weeks (Pentecost)(Harvest)	Ex 23:16a; 34:22a; Lev 23:15–21; Nu 28:26–31; Dt 16:9–12	3rd month (Sivan) 6	May–June
Trumpets (Later: Rosh Hashanah— New Year's Day)	Lev 23:23–25; Nu 29:1–6	7th month (Tishri) 1	Sept.–Oct.
Day of Atonement (Yom Kippur)	Lev 16; 23:26–32 Nu 29:7–11	7th month (Tishri) 10	Sept.–Oct.
Tabernacles (Booths)(Ingathering)	Ex 23:16b; 34:22b; Lev 23:33–36a, 39–43; Nu 29:12–34; Dt 16:13–15; Zec 14:16–19	7th month (Tishri) 15–21	Sept.–Oct.
Sacred Assembly	Lev 23:36b; Nu 29:35–38	7th month (Tishri) 22	Sept.–Oct.
Purim	Est 9:18–32	12th month (Adar) 14, 15	Feb.–Mar.

On Kislev 25 (mid-December) Hanukkah, the Feast of Dedication or Festival of Lights, commemorated the purification of the temple and altar in the Maccabean period (165/4 B.C.). This feast is mentioned in Jn 10:22.

biblical account only in Acts 23:24–25:14. When Paul reasoned before him about "righteousness, self-control and the judgment to come" (24:25), he was terrified. He held Paul for about two years hoping for a bribe. He was then replaced by Festus, a far better man.

FELLOWSHIP (Gr. *koinōnia, that which is in common*). 1. Partnership or union with others in the bonds of a business partnership, a social or fraternal organization, or just proximity. Christians are told not to be unequally yoked together with unbelievers (2 Cor 6:14–18) because such a union, either in marriage, business, or society, is incompatible with fellowship with Christians and with God. 2. Membership in a local Christian church

DESCRIPTION	PURPOSE	NT REFERENCES
Day of rest, no work	Rest for people and animals	Mt 12:1–14; 28:1; Lk 4:16; Jn 5:9; Ac 13:42; Col 2:16; Heb 4:1–11
Year of rest; fallow fields	Rest for land	
Canceled debts; liberation of slaves and indentured servants, land returned to original family owners	Help for poor, stabilize society	
Slaying and eating a lamb, together with better herbs and bread made without yeast, in every household	Remember Israel's deliverance from Egypt	Mt 26:17; Mk 14:12–26; Jn 2:13; 11:55; 1Co 5:7; Heb 11:28
Eating bread made without yeast; holding several assemblies; making designated offerings	Remember how the Lord brought the Israelites out of Egypt in haste	Mk 14:1, 12; Ac 12:3; 1Co 5:6–8
Presenting a sheaf of the first of the barley harvest as a wave offering; making a burnt offering and a grain offering	Recognize the Lord's bounty in the land	Ro 8:23; 1Co 15:20–23
A festival of joy; mandatory and voluntary offerings, including the firstfruits of the wheat harvest	Show joy and thankfulness for the Lord's blessing of harvest	Ac 2:1–4; 20:16; 1Co 16:8
An assembly on a day of rest commemorated with trumpet blasts and sacrifices	Present Israel before the Lord for his favor	
A day of rest, fasting, and sacrifices of atonement for priests and people and atonement for the tabernacle and altar	Cleanse priests and people from their sins and purify the Holy Place	Ro 3:24–26; Heb 9:7; 10:3, 19–22
A week of celebration for the harvest; living in booths and offering sacrifices	Memorialize the journey from Egypt to Canaan; give thanks for the productivity of Canaan	Jn 7:2, 37
A day of convocation, rest, and offering sacrifices	Commemorate the closing of the cycle of feasts	
A day of joy and feasting and giving presents	Remind the Israelites of their national deliverance in the time of Esther	

In addition, new moons were often special feast days (Nu 10:10; 1Ch 23:31; Ezr 3:5; Ne 10:33; Ps 81:3; Isa 1:13–14; 66:23; Hos 5:7; Am 8:5; Col 2:16).

or in *the* church (Acts 2:42). **3.** Partnership in the support of the gospel and in the charitable work of the church (2 Cor 8:4). **4.** That heavenly love that believers have for one another, called *agapē*, a word that seldom appears in classical Greek. This fellowship is deeper and more satisfying than any mere human love.

FERRET (See ANIMALS)

FERTILE CRESCENT A modern description of the territory that may roughly be described as reaching NW from the Persian Gulf through Mesopotamia, then west to the north of Syria, then SW through Syria and Palestine. The land is mostly rich and fertile. A journey in a

THE FERTILE CRESCENT

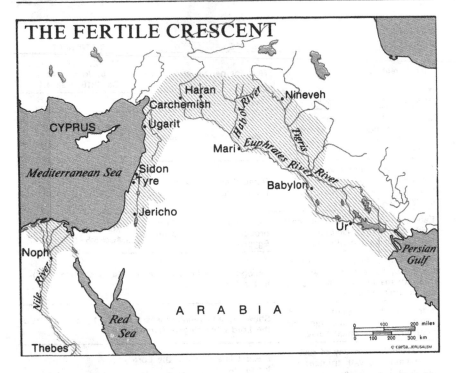

Haran
Carchemish
Nineveh
CYPRUS
Ugarit
Habor River
Mari
Euphrates River
Tigris River
Mediterranean Sea
Sidon
Tyre
Babylon
Jericho
Ur
Noph
Persian Gulf
A R A B I A
Red Sea
Thebes

© carta, JERUSALEM

straight line across the crescent from one end to the other would go mostly through the great Syrian desert, with only an occasional oasis. This configuration of the land explains much of Bible history.

FESTIVALS (See FEASTS)

FESTUS, PORCIUS (Gr. *Porkios Phēstos, festal, joyful*). The Roman governor who succeeded Felix in the province of Judea (Acts 24:27). Almost nothing is known of the life of Festus before his appointment by Nero as procurator of Judea (24:27–26:32). Festus was apparently a far better and more efficient man than his predecessor. At the very beginning of his rule, he took up the case of Paul. Festus evidently knew that Paul was a good man (25:25), but he was unable to understand Paul's reasoning with King Agrippa and thought that Paul had gone mad with much study (26:24).

FETTERS (See SHACKLES)

FEVER (See DISEASES)

FIELD The biblical "field," usually not enclosed, was marked off from its neighbors by stone markers at the corners and sometimes one or two along the sides. Because they were unenclosed, and be-cause of normally unsettled conditions, a watchman was often employed, especially when the crop was nearing maturity. Besides the danger of human intruders, there might be danger from straying cattle or even of cattle driven by rustlers (Exod 22:5).

FIG (See PLANTS)

FIR (See PLANTS)

FIRE (Heb. *'ēsh*, Gr. *pyr*). The first use of the word "fire" in Scripture is in Genesis 19:24 (KJV). Before the Flood, Tubal-Cain (4:22) was the father of smiths. In the account of the Abrahamic covenant (15:17) one reads of a smoking firepot and a flaming torch. In the institution of the Aaronic priestly ceremonies, God sent fire from heaven to consume the first offering (Lev 9:24) to show his acceptance. This fire was to be kept burning continually (6:9). When the two sons of Aaron, Nadab and Abihu, offered "unauthorized fire," probably when intoxicated (10:1, 9–10), God's fiery judgment descended on them and destroyed them. The final destiny of the enemies of God is the "fiery lake" (Rev 19:20; 20:10, 14). This world will some day be consumed by fire (2 Peter 3:7–12).

God uses "fire" not only for judgment but also for testing (1 Cor 3:12-15). God's glory is accompanied by fire (Ezek 1:27). The seraphim are fiery creatures (Isa 6:2), as are the "venomous snakes" of Numbers 21:6 (from the same Hebrew verb *saraph*, "to burn"). Our Lord is pictured with eyes as a flame of fire, hinting at his work of judgment (Rev 1:14). Fire is used to refine gold and to cleanse us (Mal 3:2).

FIREBRAND The KJV rendering of three Hebrew words, meaning: a stick for stirring fire (Isa 7:4; Amos 4:11); brands, sparks (Prov 26:18); and a torch (Judg 7:16; 15:4).

FIREPAN (Heb. *mahtâh*). A vessel used for carrying live coals (e.g., Exod 27:3). The Hebrew word is rendered "censer" many times, and "snuff dish" three times by KJV (e.g., Exod 25:38; Lev 10:1; NIV "wick trimmers").

FIRKIN (See WEIGHTS AND MEASURES)

FIRMAMENT (Heb. *raqia'*). The expanse of sky surrounding the earth, made by God on the second day of creation (Gen 1:6). It corresponds to the "empty space" of Job 26:7. Our English word "firmament" does not correctly suggest the real meaning of the Hebrew word. NIV translates it as "expanse."

FIRSTBORN (Heb. *bekhôr*, Gr. *prôtotokos*). The Hebrew word is used chiefly of men but also of animals (Exod 11:5). Because the first-born of the Israelites were preserved at the time of the first Passover, every firstborn male of man and beast became consecrated to God (13:2; 34:19); the beasts were sacrificed, while the men were redeemed (13:13, 15; 34:20; cf. Lev 27:6; cf. Luke 2:27). At Sinai the Levites were substituted for the Israelite firstborn (Num 3:12, 41, 46; 8:13-19).

Among the Israelites the first-born son possessed special privileges. He succeeded his father as the head of the house and received as his share of the inheritance a double portion. Israel was the Lord's firstborn (Exod 4:22) and was thus entitled to special privileges, as compared with other peoples. Jesus is described as the firstborn (Rom 8:29; Col 1:15; Heb 1:6; cf. Ps 89:27).

FIRSTFRUITS (Heb. *rē'shîth, bikkûrîm*, Gr. *aparchē*). In acknowledgment of the fact that all the products of the land came from God, and to show thankfulness for his goodness, Israelites brought as an offering a portion of the fruits that ripened first. These were looked on as a pledge of the coming harvest. Such an offering was made both on behalf of the nation (Lev 23:10, 17) and by individuals (Exod 23:19; Deut 26:1-11). These firstfruits went for the support of the priesthood.

Jesus is the firstfruits of all who die in faith (1 Cor 15:20). Believers, in turn, are "a kind of firstfruits" of all that God created (James 1:18); creation will share in the redemption of the children of God (Rom 8:19-21).

FISH (See ANIMALS)

FISH GATE An ancient gate on the east side of the wall of Jerusalem, where fish and various wares were sold on the Sabbath by men of Tyre during Nehemiah's time (2 Chron 33:14; Neh 13:16; cf. Jer 39:3).

FISHHOOK Not only the means of catching fish, but also of keeping them, at least for a time (Job 41:1-2; Amos 4:2; Matt 17:27).

FISHING (See OCCUPATIONS AND PROFESSIONS)

FITCH (See PLANTS)

FLAG (See PLANTS)

FLAX (See PLANTS)

FLEA (See ANIMALS)

FLEECE The shorn wool of a sheep. The first of the shearing was to be given to the priesthood, as a part of their means of support (Deut 18:4). Gideon's experience (Judg 6:37-40) has given rise to the custom of "putting out a fleece" in seeking God's guidance.

FLESH (Heb. *bāsār, shē'er*, Gr. *sarx*). 1. Literally, the soft part of the bodies of people and animals. 2. All animals (Gen 6:19). 3. Mankind in general, (Num 16:22). 4. Our ordinary human constitution as opposed to our mental and moral qualities (Matt 26:41 KJV). 5. Human nature deprived of the Spirit of God and dominated by sin (Col 2:13; 1 John 2:16 KJV). The believer's "sinful nature" (NIV), which is opposed to the life of the Spirit (Rom 8:12-17; Gal 5:16-23).

FLIES (See ANIMALS)

FLINT (See MINERALS)

FLOCK A collection of sheep under the care of a shepherd, sometimes including goats also (Gen 27:9). The larger animals such as cattle, camels, asses, etc. were counted as herds, not flocks. A man's flocks made up most of his wealth, providing clothing, food, milk, and animals for sacrifice. Figuratively, Israel and the

---

Tabulated Chronology of the Flood

1. The making of the ark (Gen 6:14)	
2. Collection of the animals (Gen 7:9)	seven days before the rain started
3. Springs of the great deep burst forth and the floodgates of heaven were opened (Gen 7:11)	Second month, seventeenth day in Noah's 600th year
4. Rain (Gen 7:12)	forty days and forty nights
5. All the high hills covered (Gen 7:19)	
6. Water flooded the earth (Gen 7:24)	150 days
7. Water receded from off the earth (Gen 8:3)	150 days
8. Ark rested on the mountains of Ararat (Gen 8:4)	Seventh month, seventeenth day
9. Waters decreased (Gen 8:4)	
10. Tops of mountains seen (Gen 8:5)	Tenth month, first day
11. Noah waited (Gen 8:6)	forty days
12. Noah sent out a raven and a dove; dove returned (Gen 8:7–9)	
13. Noah waited (Gen 8:10)	seven days
14. Noah sent forth dove again (Gen 8:10); dove returned with olive branch (Gen 8:11)	seven days
15. Noah waited (Gen 8:12)	seven days
16. Noah sent out a dove, which did not return (Gen 8:12)	seven days
17. Noah removed covering; face of the ground was dry (Gen 8:13)	first month, first day, Noah's 601st year
18. Earth dried; Noah left ark (Gen 8:14)	second month, twenty-seventh day

church are counted as flocks, and God is the Good Shepherd (Isa 40:11; Matt 26:31; Luke 12:32; 1 Peter 5:2–3).

FLOG (See SCOURGE; STRIPES)

FLOOD, THE The Deluge, or world-wide destruction of man and beast, except for Noah, his family, and the animals in the ark. The Noahic flood has been a subject for discussion among scientists and theologians for many centuries. The reality of the Flood can hardly be questioned, because of the many references to it in both the OT and NT (Gen 6–8; 9:11, 28; 10:1, 32; Matt 24:38–39; Luke 17:27; 2 Peter 2:5).

An important aspect of the Deluge is that God preserved some men, for Noah and his family were saved from destruction by going into an ark that Noah made according to God's specifications, and in which he gathered animals and birds preserved to replenish the earth.

The Flood was brought on the earth as a judgment on the sins of the people (Gen 6:5–7; 2 Peter 2:5–6). The Bible refers to the Flood in connection with the judgment at the second coming of the Lord (Matt 24:39) and with the destruction of Sodom and Gomorrah (Luke 17:27–29; 2 Peter 2:5–6). The Flood is compared with the creation of the world and is a miracle of the same order (2 Peter 3:5–6). The final destruction of the world is given the same miraculous explanation as the Noahic flood (3:7–10). The source of the water is explained by

"all the springs of the great deep burst forth, and the floodgates of the heavens were opened" (Gen 7:11). This could mean that water rose from the ocean or from fresh water springs on the earth or both. From the time the rain started (Gen 7:11) to the time Noah left the ark (8:14) was between 371 and 376 days.

Traditions regarding a disastrous flood that occurred long ago are handed down by many peoples—including tribes in all parts of the world. The Hebrews, Assyrians, and Babylonians all had traditions of a great flood. These narratives stated the purpose of the Flood to be punishment because the world was full of violence, but the Hebrew account remained simple and credible, whereas the other accounts became complex and fanciful. Only the biblical account retained a monotheistic viewpoint.

One of the great differences of opinion in describing the Flood concerns its extent. Traditionally, most biblical interpreters considered the submergence to be universal; that is, it covered the entire globe including the highest mountains. They point to the universal terms found in the Genesis account (Gen 7:19, 21). If the Flood were local, God could have directed Noah to move to an area that was not to be submerged.

The fact that many civilizations have flood traditions has been cited as an evidence for a universal flood. The same evidence could be used to argue for a local flood because the accounts of floods in other parts of the world are less like the Hebrew tradition than those of the Assyrians and Babylonians, who lived in the same area as the Hebrews.

Today many conservative scholars defend a local flood. The crux of their argument seems to center in the covenant relation of God to man. He deals with certain groups, such as the children of Israel. The reasoning in regard to Noah is that Noah was not a preacher of righteousness to peoples of other areas but was concerned with the culture from which Abraham eventually came. Physical arguments have also been raised against a universal flood.

FLOUR Fine-crushed and sifted grain, generally wheat or rye or barley (Judg 7:13). Eastern flour was not quite as fine or as white as ours, and thus the bread was more wholesome. The "meat" (it should be "meal") offerings were of flour (Lev 6:15 KJV).

FLOWER (See PLANTS)

FLUTE (See MUSIC AND MUSICAL INSTRUMENTS)

FLY (See ANIMALS)

FOAL (See ANIMALS)

FODDER The mixed food of cattle, generally from several kinds of grain sown together (Job 6:5; 24:6; Isa 30:24).

FOOD Before sin had entered into human history, God apparently prescribed a vegetarian diet, both for man and beast (Gen 1:29–30), but one must not build too much on silence here as regarding the content of diet. By the time that Noah built the ark, there was a distinction between clean and unclean beasts (7:2–3); when God made his covenant with Noah after the Flood (9:3–4), flesh was permitted as food. Blood was forbidden, and it seems that the reason for this prohibition was as much theological as sanitary (cf. Lev 17:11). In the time of Moses, fat was also prohibited as food (3:16–17) and again, the reason given is religious, not hygienic.

The animals most frequently mentioned in the Bible are the domestic herbivorous animals, and these are divided sharply into two classes: the clean and the unclean (see Lev 11). The clean animals were used for food and for sacrifice, and the four-footed ones were distinguished by their hoofs and by whether they chewed the cud. Many of the distinctions between "clean" and "unclean" foods were clearly based on sanitary reasons.

In Palestine and Syria, fresh fruit can be obtained throughout the year. Food is also used as a figure of spiritual sustenance (1 Cor 3:1–2; 1 Peter 2:2).

FOOLISHNESS, FOLLY The opposite of wisdom, with which the OT often contrasts it (Eccl 2:13). The fool exhibits many characteristics ranging from simple stupidity (Prov 7:7, 22) and a hot temper (14:17) to wickedness (Gen 34:7), atheism (Ps 14:1), and rejection of God (Job 2:9–10). In the NT it can mean thoughtlessness (Gal 3:3) or lack of intelligence (Rom 1:21). The Lord called the scribes and Pharisees fools, not implying intellectual stupidity but spiritual blindness (Matt 23:17; cf. 1 Cor 1:18).

FOOT The foot of man, because it comes in contact with the earth, is thought to be less honorable than the hand or the head. But in the Christian church "the foot" (i.e., the lowest member) should not suffer a feeling of inferiority or of envy (1 Cor 12:15), nor should the more prominent directing member ("the head") say to the foot, "I don't need you!" (12:21). In the East shoes are ordinarily removed when entering a house, and the lowest servant is detailed to wash the feet of the visitor. The priests, before entering the tabernacle in divine service, washed their feet as well as their hands at the laver, just outside, so that no trace of defilement would accompany their service (cf. John 13:10; Heb 10:22). To completely humiliate an enemy, one sometimes put his foot on the captives' necks as Joshua's captains did (Josh 10:24).

FOOTMAN 1. A member of the infantry as distinguished from the cavalry—horsemen and charioteers. The bulk of ancient armies consisted of footmen. **2.** A runner, one of the king's bodyguard (1 Sam 22:17 KJV).

FOOTSTOOL (Heb. *keves*, Gr. *hypopodion*). A word used in Scripture both literally (2 Chron 9:18) and figuratively: of the earth (Isa 66:1; Matt 5:35); of the temple (Lam 2:1); of the ark (Ps 99:5); and of subjection, especially of heathen enemies by the messianic King (Ps 110:1; Luke 20:43; Acts 2:35).

FORD (Heb. *ma'avar, mavarah*). A shallow place in a stream where men and animals can cross on foot. In the small streams of Palestine and Syria, fording places are quite frequent and can easily be found simply by following the main roads (probably Gen 32:22; Isa 16:2). When Israel crossed the Jordan, God miraculously stopped the waters upstream by a landslide. John the Baptist baptized at Bethabara (John 1:28; NIV "Bethany"), the name indicating that a ford was there. Joshua's spies (Josh 2:7) evidently forded the Jordan, and Ehud (Judg 3:28) took the same place to prevent Moabites from crossing there. Jephthah (12:5–6) made his famous "Shibboleth test" at a ford of the Jordan.

FOREHEAD A prominent part of the face whose appearance often determines our opinion of the person. It may reveal shamelessness (Jer 3:3), courage (Ezek 3:9), and godliness (Rev 7:3). The forehead is also the place for the front of a crown or mitre (Exod 28:38), where the emblem of holiness on Aaron's forehead would make the gifts of the people acceptable before the Lord. A mark was put on the foreheads of the men of Jerusalem who mourned for its wickedness, and they were spared in a time of terrible judgment (Ezek 9:4). In the ages of glory that are to come, the name of God will be marked on the foreheads of his own people (Rev 22:4).

FOREIGNER (See STRANGER)

FOREKNOWLEDGE; FOREORDINATION (See ELECTION AND PREDESTINATION)

FORESKIN (Heb. *'orlâh*, Gr. *akrobystia*). The fold of skin that is cut off in the operation of circumcision. Just as the American Indians used scalps of enemies as signs of their prowess, so David presented 200 foreskins of the Philistines (1 Sam 18:25–27). The word is used figuratively, meaning submission to God's law (Deut 10:16). It also refers to the indecent exhibitionism of a drunken man (Hab 2:16).

FOREST (Heb. *ya'ar, sevakh, āvîm*). A piece of land covered with trees naturally planted, as distinguished from a park where man's hand is more evident. In ancient times, most of the highlands of Canaan and Syria except the tops of the high mountains were covered with forests (e.g., 2 Sam 18:8; 1 Kings 5:8–10; 7:2).

FORGIVENESS (Heb. *kāphar, nāsā', sālach*, Gr. *apoluein, charizesthai, aphēsis, parēsis*). In the OT, *pardon*, and in the NT, *remission*, are often used as the equivalents of *forgiveness*. It means giving up resentment or claim to requital on account of an offense. The offense may be a deprivation of a person's property, rights, or honor; or it may be a violation of moral law.

The normal conditions of forgiveness are repentance and the willingness to make reparation or atonement; and the effect of forgiveness is the restoration of both parties to the former state of relationship. Forgiveness is a duty, and no limit should be set to the extent of forgiveness (Luke 17:4). An unforgiving spirit is one of the most serious of sins (Matt 18:34–35; Luke 15:28–30). God forgives man's sins because of the atoning death of Christ. God's forgiveness of humans is closely related to human forgiveness of others (Matt 5:23–24; 6:12; Col 1:14; 3:13). Those forgiven by God before the Incarnation were forgiven because of Christ, whose death was foreordained from eternity (Heb 11:40). The deity of Christ includes the power to forgive sins (Mark 2:7; Luke 5:21; 7:49).

FORNICATION (Heb. *zānâh*, Gr. *porneia*). Used in the KJV for unlawful sexual intercourse of an unwed person (e.g., 1 Cor 6:9, 18; Eph 5:3–4). It is to be distinguished from adultery, which has to do with unfaithfulness on the part of a married person, and from rape, which is a crime of violence and without the consent of the person sinned against. When these sins are mentioned in the Bible, they are often figurative of disloyalty (Jer 2:20–36; Ezek 16; Hos 1–3).

Herodium, a fortress built by Herod the Great in the first century B.C., located 4 miles southeast of Bethlehem. The fortress consists of a citadel with four round towers and retaining walls, inside of which stood Herod's palace. Courtesy Seffie Ben-Yoseph

FORT, FORTRESS Every major city in ancient times was fortified by a wall and its citadel. The KJV often speaks of such cities as "fenced," the NIV as "fortified." Even before the Israelites entered Canaan, they were terrified by the reports of cities "fortified and very large" (Num 13; Deut 1:28). Jerusalem was so well fortified that it was not until the time of David that the city was captured from the

Jebusites. Many times there was both an inner and an outer wall. The wails were built of brick and stone and were many feet thick. After the Israelites entered the land they too built fortified cities (Deut 28:52; 2 Sam 20:6).

FORUM APPII (See APPIUS, FORUM OF)

FOUNDATION (Heb. *yāsadh, to found,* Gr. *katabolē, themelios*). The word is used of the foundation of the earth (Job 38:4; Ps 78:69; Isa 24:18), the righteous (Prov 10:25 KJV), and as the basis of a person's life (Luke 6:48), Christ (1 Cor 3:11), the apostles and prophets (Eph 2:20), the proper use of wealth (1 Tim 6:17–19), and God's truth (2 Tim 2:19).

FOUNTAIN A spring of water issuing from the earth. Many towns and other locations are named for the springs at their sites (e.g., Gen 38:21; Josh 15:62). The break up of "the fountains of the great deep" (Gen 7:11 KJV), with the rain, caused the Flood. The word is used both literally and figuratively, both pleasantly and unpleasantly. Figuratively, it refers in the KJV to the source of hemorrhages (Lev 20:18; Mark 5:29). In the bridegroom's praise of his pure bride (Song of Songs 4:15) she is "a garden fountain." David speaks (Ps 36:9) of "the fountain of life," as being with the Lord. Jesus told the woman at the well of "a spring of water welling up to eternal life"(John 4:14). Among the delights of heaven will be "the spring of the water of life" (Rev 21:6).

FOUNTAIN GATE The gate at the SE corner of the walls of ancient Jerusalem (Neh 2:14; 3:15; 12:37).

FOWL (See BIRDS)

FOWLER (Heb. *yōkēsh*). A bird-catcher. Because fowlers caught their prey by trickery, "fowler" describes those who try to ensnare the unwary and bring them to ruin (Pss 91:3; 124:7).

FOX (See ANIMALS)

FRANKINCENSE (See PLANTS)

FREEDMAN, FREE WOMAN A slave who has received his freedom (1 Cor 7:22), and a free person as opposed to a slave (Gal 4:22–23, 30; Rev 6:15).

FREEDOM (See LIBERTY)

FRET (Heb. *hārâh, mā'ar*). To be vexed, chafed, irritated, angry. The godly man is not to fret (Ps 37:1, 7–8) but is to have his mind stayed on the Lord (Isa 26:3).

FRINGE (See TASSEL)

FROG (See ANIMALS)

FRONTLET (See DRESS)

FROST (Heb. *kephōr, hănāmāl*). Usual in winter on the hills and high plains in Bible lands. The manna in the wilderness is compared to frost (Exod 16:14). Frost is an evidence of God's power (Job 38:29).

FRUIT (Heb. *perî*, Gr. *karpos*). The fruits most often mentioned in Scripture are the grape, pomegranate, fig, olive, and apple. The word "fruit" is often used metaphorically (Deut 7:13; Prov 1:31; Gal 5:22–23).

FUEL (Heb. *'ōkhlâh,* or *ma'ăkhōleth, food*). In ancient times, wood, charcoal, various kinds of thorn bushes, dried grass, and the dung of camels and cattle were used as fuel (Isa 9:5, 19; Ezek 4:12; 15:4, 6; 21:32).

FULLER (See OCCUPATIONS AND PROFESSIONS)

FULLER'S FIELD (Heb. *sedhēh khôvēs*). A field just outside of Jerusalem where fullers, or washermen, washed the cloth material they were processing (2 Kings 18:17; Isa 7:3; 36:2; NIV "Washerman's Field").

FULLER'S SOAP An alkali prepared from the ashes of certain plants and used for cleansing and fulling new cloth. The word is used figuratively (Mal 3:2 NIV "launderer's soap").

FUNERAL The word does not occur in the KJV, and in NIV is found only twice, both times as an adjective (Jer 16:5; 34:5). Funeral rites differed with the place, the religion, and the times; except for royal burials in Egypt, the elaborate ceremonies we use today were not held.

Generally in Palestine there was no embalmment and the body was buried a few hours after death, sometimes in a tomb but more often in a cave. Coffins were unknown. The body was washed and often anointed with aromatic spices (John 12:7; 19:39). The procession of mourners, made up of relatives and friends of the deceased, was led by professional mourning women, whose shrieks and lamentations pierced the air. It was an insult to a man's reputation to be refused proper burial (Jer 22:19). (See page 210.)

FURLONG (See WEIGHTS AND MEASURES)

FURNACE (Heb. *kivshān, kûr, attûn, 'ălîl, tannûr,* Gr. *kaminos*). Furnaces for central heating are not mentioned in the Bible, nor are they much used today in Bible lands. The burning fiery furnace

Funeral procession showing men (dressed in short pleated skirts) carrying the deceased, his personal belongings (e.g., bed, chair, shoes), and offerings, on wall painting from the tomb of Ramose at Thebes, 12th Dynasty. Courtesy Egyptian Expedition, The Metropolitan Museum of Art (30.4.37)

(Dan 3) was probably a smelting furnace and was used only incidentally for human punishment. Furnaces were used for melting—Proverbs 17:3 (gold), Ezekiel 22:22 (silver), 22:18 (copper, tin, iron, and lead)—and for baking bread (Neh 3:11 JB, KJV, MLB, NASB; "ovens" in NIV, RSV). The word "furnace" is sometimes used figuratively—e.g., to refer to Egypt (Deut 4:20) and to the punishment of the wicked at the end of the world (Matt 13:42, 50).

FURNISHINGS (Heb. *hār, kēlîm,* Gr. *skevē*). In the Bible the principal reference to furnishings is in the articles in and about the tabernacle and the temple. The main items were the large altar and the laver, outside; then the table of the bread of the Presence, the lampstand or "candlestick," and the altar of incense in the Holy Place; then in the Most Holy Place the ark of the covenant (Exod 25–40). Royalty had beds (Deut 3:11) and tables (Judg 1:7; Mark 7:28).

FUTURE LIFE (See ESCHATOLOGY)

—G—

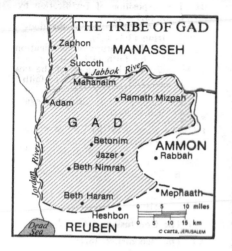

THE TRIBE OF GAD

GAAL (gā'ăl, Heb. *ga'al, loathing*). A son of Ebed (Judg 9:26–41), who led an unsuccessful rebellion against Abimelech (9:42–45). Abimelech had murdered all but one of his 70 brothers in order to become king of Shechem (9:1–5). After gaining the confidence of the men of Shechem, Gaal boasted under intoxication that he could overcome Abimelech if made leader of the Shechemites. Zebul, the governor of Shechem, was jealous of Gaal and secretly relayed this information to Abimelech who set up an ambush by night with four companies against Shechem. In the morning when Gaal stood in the gate of the city, Abimelech and his army chased Gaal and his company into the city, but Zebul turned them out. Abimelech fought against the rebels, killed them, destroyed their city, and sowed it with salt (9:42–45). Nothing more is known of Gaal, but clearly his weakness was boasting.

GAASH (gā'ăsh, Heb. *ga'ash, quaking*). A hill near Mt. Ephraim. On its north side was Timnath Serah, the city given to Joshua (Josh 19:49–50), where he was buried (Judg 2:9). The "ravines of Gaash" were Hiddai's native place (2 Sam 23:30).

GABA (See GEBA)

GABBATHA (găb'à-thà, Aram *gabbetha', height, ridge*). The place called "the Stone Pavement" (John 19:13). Here Pilate sat on the Bema, or judgment seat, and sentenced Jesus before the people. An early pavement has been excavated near here, perhaps the pavement where Jesus was brought from the judgment hall for sentencing.

GABRIEL (gā'brĭ-ĕl, Heb. *gavrî 'ēl, man of God*, Gr. *Gabriēl*). An angel mentioned four times in Scripture, each time bringing a momentous message: twice to Daniel (Dan 8:16–17; 9:21–22); to Zechariah, father of John the Baptist (Luke 1:11–20); and to Mary, the mother of Jesus (1:26–38). The Bible does not define his status as an angel, but he appears in the Book of Enoch (chs. 9, 20, 40) as an archangel.

GAD (Heb. *gādh, fortune*). **1.** Jacob's seventh son, firstborn of Zilpah, Leah's handmaid (Gen 30:9–11). He had seven sons at the time of the descent into Egypt (46:16). The Gadites numbered 45,650 adult males at the census at Sinai (Num 1:24–25), but at the second census their number had fallen to 40,500 (26:18). Their position on the march was south of the tabernacle, next to Reuben. These two tribes and the half-tribe of Manasseh remained shepherds like their forefathers, and because of their "very large herds and flocks" (32:1) they requested of Moses the rich pasture lands east of Jordan for their possession. This was granted (Josh 18:7). The warriors of these two and a half tribes took the lead in the conquest of western Palestine (1:12–18; 4:12) and returned to their families with Joshua's blessing (22:1–9).

Genesis 49:19 seems to describe the military prowess of the Gadites. They were known for their bravery and their faith (Deut 33:20; 2 Sam 17:27; 19:31–40; 1 Chron 5:16–22; 12:8). The land of Gad was along the battlefield between Syria and Israel (2 Kings 10:33). Gad finally was carried captive by Assyria (15:29; 1 Chron 5:26), and Ammon seized their land and cities (Jer 49:1).

2. The seer or prophet of King David (1 Sam 22:5; 2 Sam 24:11–18; 1 Chron 21:9–17). Gad assisted in arranging the musical services of the temple (2 Chron 29:25) and recorded the acts of David in a book (1 Chron 29:29).

3. A Canaanite god of fortune, seen in compound names such as Baal Gad (Josh 11:17; 12:7; 13:5) and Migdal Gad (15:37).

GADARA, GADARENES (găd'à-rà, găd-à-rĕnz', Gr. *Gadarēnoi, Gadara*). Gadara was a member of the Decapolis and is associated with "the country of the

Gadarenes" in the Gospels (Matt 8:28; Mark 5:1; Luke 8:26, 37), SE of the Sea of Galilee.

GADFLY (See ANIMALS)

GAIUS (gā'yŭs, Gr. *Gaios*). **1.** A Macedonian who traveled with Paul (Acts 19:29). **2.** A man of Derbe who accompanied Paul from Macedonia to Asia (Acts 20:4). **3.** A Corinthian whom Paul baptized (1 Cor 1:14), perhaps the Gaius who was his host (Rom 16:23). **4.** The addressee of 3 John (3 John 1, 5–8).

GALAL (gā'lăl). The name of two Levites (1 Chronicles 9:15, 16; Neh 11:17).

GALATIA (gà-lā'shǐ-à). The designation in NT times of a territory in north-central Asia Minor, also a Roman province in central Asia Minor (1 Cor 16:1; Gal 1:2; 2 Tim 4:10; 1 Peter 1:1). Antioch, Iconium, Lystra, and Derbe were in the province of Galatia. Both Peter (1 Peter 1:1) and Paul (Gal 1:1; 1 Cor 16:1) seem to use the term to refer to the province as a whole.

GALATIANS, LETTER TO THE A short but very important letter of Paul, containing his passionate polemic against the perversion or contamination of the gospel of God's grace. It has aptly been described as "the Magna Carta of spiritual emancipation."

It is the only letter by Paul that is specifically addressed to a group of churches. They were all founded by Paul (Gal 1:8, 11; 4:19–20), were all the fruit of a single mission (3:1–3; 4:13–14), and were all affected by the same disturbance (1:6–7; 5:7–9).

The startling information received by Paul that a sudden and drastic change in attitude toward him and his gospel was taking place in the Galatian churches caused the writing of the letter. Certain Jewish teachers were obscuring the simplicity of the gospel of free grace with their propaganda, insisting believers be circumcised and obey the Mosaic Law (2:16; 3:2–3; 4:10, 21; 5:2–4; 6:12). The letter may be outlined as follows:

I. The Introduction (1:1–10).
  A. The salutation (1:1–5).
  B. The rebuke (1:6–10).

II. The Vindication of His Apostolic Authority (1:11–2:21).
  A. The reception of his gospel by revelation (1:11–24).
  B. The confirmation of his gospel by the apostles at Jerusalem (2:1–10).
  C. The illustration of his independence (2:11–21).

III. The Exposition of Justification by Faith (3:1–4:31).
  A. The elaboration of the doctrine (3:1–4:7).
    1. The nature of justification by faith (3:1–14).
    2. The limitations of the law and its relations to faith (3:15–4:7).
  B. The appeal to drop all legalism (4:8–31).

IV. The Nature of the Life of Christian Liberty (5:1–6:10).
  A. The call to maintain their liberty (5:1).
  B. The peril of Christian liberty (5:2–12).
  C. The life of liberty (5:13–6:10).

V. The Conclusion (6:11–17).

VI. The Benediction (6:18).

GALBANUM (See PLANTS)

GALILEAN (găl'ǐ-lē'ăn). A native or resident of Galilee (Matt 26:69; John 4:45; Acts 1:11; 5:37), often detected as such by his dialect (Mark 14:70).

GALILEE (găl'ǐ-lē, Heb. *hā-gālîl, the ring or circuit*, Gr. *Galilaia*). The most northerly of the three provinces of Palestine (Galilee, Samaria, Judea). Measuring approximately 50 miles (83 km.) north to south and 30 miles (50 km.) east to west, it was bounded on the west by the plain of Akka to the foot of Mt. Carmel.

The land was luxurious and productive, a rugged mountainous country of oaks and terebinths interrupted by fertile plains. It was said that Asher in the west would eat fat for bread and yield royal dainties and dip his feet in oil (Gen 49:20; Deut 33:24–25). Important caravan trade routes carried their busy traffic through Galilee from Egypt and southern Palestine to Damascus in the NE as well as east and west from the Mediterranean to the Far East.

The northern part of Naphtali was inhabited by a mixed race of Jews and pagans (Judg 1:33). Its Israelite population was carried away captive to Assyria and was replaced by a colony of pagan immigrants (2 Kings 15:29; 17:24), hence called "Galilee of the nations" or "Gentiles" (Isa 9:1; Matt 4:15–16). During and after the captivity, the predominant mixture of Gentile races impoverished the worship of Judaism. For the same reason the Galilean accent and dialect were noticeably peculiar (26:73). The southern Jews of purer blood and more orthodox tradition despised them (John 1:46; 7:52; cf. Isa 42:6; Matt 15:24). Jesus preached his first public sermon in the synagogue at Nazareth in Lower Galilee, where he had been brought up (Luke 4:16-30). His disciples came from Galilee (Matt 4:18; John 1:43-44; Acts 1:11; 2:7); in Cana of Galilee he performed his first miracle (John 2:11). Capernaum in Galilee, the home of his manhood (Matt 4:13; 9:1), is where the first three Gospels present his major ministry. Galilee's debasement made some of its people feel their need of the Savior. This and its comparative freedom from priestly and pharisaical prejudice may have been additional reasons for its receiving the larger share of the Lord's ministry.

GALILEE, SEA OF So called from its location east of Galilee, it is also called "the Lake of Gennesaret" (Luke 5:1), since the fertile Plain of Gennesaret lies on the NW (Matt 14:34). The OT calls it "the Sea of Kinnereth" (Heb. "harp-shaped," Num 34:11; Deut 3:17; Josh 13:27), from the town so named on its shore (19:35), of which Gennesaret is probably the corruption. "The Sea of Tiberias" is another designation (John 6:1; 21:1); associated with Tiberias, the capital of Herod Antipas.
Located some 60 miles (100 km.) north of Jerusalem, its bed is but a lower depression of the Jordan Valley. As the Jordan River plunges southward on its course from Mt. Hermon to the Dead Sea, it enters the Sea of Galilee at its northern end and flows out of its southern end, a distance of 13 miles (22 km.). The greatest width of the sea is 8 miles (13 km.), at Magdala. The Sea of Galilee is noted for its sudden and violent storms (Mark 4:39; cf. Matt 14:22-34; Mark 6:45-53; John 6:15-21).

GALL (See PLANTS)

GALLERY Three terraced passageways or balconies running around the chambers in/ the temple of Ezekiel's vision (Ezek 41:15-16; 42:3, 5-6). The upper two stories were shorter because of the absence of supporting pillars.

GALLEY (See SHIPS)

GALLIM (găl'lĭm, Heb. gallîm, heaps). A town of Benjamin named with Laish and Anathoth (Isa 10:30). "Daughter of Gallim" refers to its inhabitants. It was the home of Phalti, the son of Laish (1 Sam 25:44).

GALLIO (găl'ĭ-ō, Gr. Galliōn). Roman proconsul of Achaia of whom the Roman philosopher Seneca had said, "No mortal was ever so sweet to one as Gallio was to all." The Jews brought Paul before him, hoping to show that Paul was guilty of an offense against a lawful religion, and hence against the Roman government itself (Acts 18:12-17). Gallio rejected their argument. His action amounted to an authoritative decision that Paul's preaching was not subversive against Rome, giving the apostle the protection he needed. Gallio did not become a Christian; he died by committing suicide.

GALLON (See WEIGHTS AND MEASURES)

GALLOWS A pole for executing and exhibiting a victim by impalement. Made 75 feet (23 m.) high by Haman for Mordecai (Esth 5:14; 6:4).

GAMALIEL (gà-mā'lĭ-ĕl, Heb. gamlî'ēl, reward of God, Gr. Gamaliēl). 1. Son of Pedahzur and chief of the tribe of Manasseh (Num 1:10; 2:20; 7:54, 59; 10:23). He assisted Moses in numbering the people. 2. A Pharisee and eminent doctor of the law; grandson of Hillel and first of only seven rabbis to be given the title of Rabban. Paul was one of his pupils (Acts 22:3). When the enraged Sanhedrin sought to kill the apostles, Gamaliel urged judicious caution on the ground that if the new doctrine was of God they could not overthrow it, and if it was of man it would fail (5:34-39). God used his counsel to give a needed respite to the infant church.

GAMES Not much is known about the amusements of the ancient Israelites (Zech 8:5). In the NT the only children's game mentioned is that of mimicking the wedding dance and the funeral wail to the music of the flute (Matt 11:16-17; Luke 7:32). Condemned criminals were thrown to lions in the arena as punishment and for sport (1 Cor 4:9; 15:32; 2 Tim 4:17).
The Isthmian games, celebrated every two years on the Isthmus of Corinth, are vividly alluded to (1 Cor 9:24-27). Held in honor of the Greek gods, they were events of patriotic pride, a passion rather than a pastime, and thus made a suitable image of earnestness in the Christian race. The NT alludes to the competition (Acts 20:24; Eph 6:12; Phil 3:12-14; 1 Tim 6:12; 2 Tim 4:7; Heb 12:1-2) and the crown, or prize (Col 3:15; 2 Tim 2:5; James 1:12; Rev 2:10).

GARDEN (Heb. gan, gannâh, a covered or hidden place; Gr. kēpos). A cultivated piece of ground, usually in the suburbs, planted with flowers, vegetables, shrubs, or trees, fenced with a mud or stone wall (Prov 24:31) or thorny hedges (Isa 5:5), and guarded (whence "garden") by a watchman in a lodge (1:8) or tower (Mark 12:1) to drive away wild beasts and robbers.

The Hebrews used gardens as burial places (Gen 23:17; 2 Kings 21:18, 26). The Garden of Gethsemane was a favorite retreat of Jesus for meditation and prayer (Matt 26:36; John 18:1–2). In idolatrous periods gardens were the scenes of superstition and image worship, the awful counterpart of the primitive Eden (Isa 1:29; 65:3; 66:17). The new paradise regained by the people of God (Rev 22:1–5) suggests in a fuller way the old paradise planted by God but lost through sin (Gen 2:8).

The believer is a garden watered by the Holy Spirit (Isa 1:30; 58:11; Jer 2:13; 17:7–8; 31:12; John 4:13–14; 7:37–39).

GARDENER (See OCCUPATIONS AND PROFESSIONS: *Farmer*)

GAREB (gā'rĕb, Heb. *gārēv, scabby*). **1.** An Ithrite, a member of one of the families of Kiriath Jearim (1 Chron 2:53) and one of David's mighty men (2 Sam 23:38; 1 Chron 11:40). **2.** A hill near Jerusalem to which the city would expand (Jer 31:39).

GARLIC (See PLANTS)

GARMENTS (See DRESS)

GARNER (See STOREHOUSE)

GARRISON (Heb. *matstsāv, netsîv*). A military post for the occupation of a conquered country (1 Sam 10:5; 13:3; 14:1, 6; 2 Sam 8:6, 14; 1 Chron 11:16; 18:13; 2 Chron 17:2).

GASHMU (See GESHEM)

GATAM (gā'tăm, Heb. *ga'tām*). Grandson of Esau; an Edomite chief (Gen 36:11, 16; 1 Chron 1:36).

GATE (Heb. usually *sha'ar, opening,* Gr. *pylē*). The entrance to enclosed buildings, grounds, or cities. It was at the gates of a city that the people of the Middle East went for legal business, conversation, bargaining, and news (Ps 69:12). The usual gateway consisted of double doors plated with metal (Ps 107:16; Isa 45:2). Wooden doors without iron plating were easily set on fire (Judg 9:52; Neh 2:3, 17). Some gates were made of brass (Acts 3:2); others were of solid stone (Isa 54:12; Rev 21:21).

As the weakest points in a city's walls, the gates were often the object of enemy

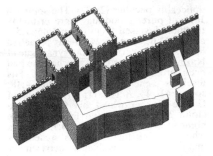

Reconstruction of the Israelite gate at Beer-sheba based on archaeological evidence. Tenth century B.C. Courtesy Carta, Jerusalem

attack (Judg 5:8; 1 Sam 23:7; Ezek 21:15, 22) and therefore were flanked by towers (2 Sam 18:24, 33; 2 Chron 14:7; 26:9). To "possess the gates" was to possess the city (Gen 24:60). Gates were shut at night and opened again in the morning (Deut 3:5; Josh 2:5, 7).

Markets were held at the gate, and the main item sold there often gave its name to the gate ("Sheep Gate," Neh 3:1; "Fish Gate," Neh 3:3; "Horse Gate," Neh 3:28). The gate was the place where people met to hear an important announcement (2 Chron 32:6; Jer 7:2; 17:19–27) or the reading of the law (Neh 8:1, 3) or where the elders transacted legal business (Deut 16:18; 21:18–20; Josh 20:4; Ruth 4:1–2, 11). The gate was also the king's or chief's place of audience (2 Sam 19:8; 1 Kings 22:10; Dan 2:48–49 KJV; NIV "royal court").

Figuratively, gates refer to the glory of a city (Isa 3:26; 14:31) or to the city itself (Pss 87:2; 122:2).

GATH (găth, Heb. *gath, winepress*). One of the five great Philistine cities (Ashdod, Gaza, Ashkelon, Gath, and Ekron [Josh 13:3; 1 Sam 5:8–9; 6:17]). Its people were the Gittites, including Goliath and other giants (2 Sam 21:19–22). In harmony with this fact is the record of the Anakites' presence in Gath after Joshua had destroyed the neighboring territory (Josh 11:22). David fled from Saul to Gath, where he feigned madness to save his life (1 Sam 21:10–15; cf. 27:2–29:11; 2 Sam 15:18–21). Although David conquered it (1 Chron 18:1), Gath retained its own king (1 Kings 2:39). Rehoboam rebuilt and fortified the town (2 Chron 11:8). Later, Hazael, king of Syria, captured Gath from Jehoash (2 Kings 12:17), but Uzziah won it back (2 Chron 26:6). In a

reference to the fall of this walled city
Amos sounds a warning to those at ease
in Zion (Amos 6:2). The omission of Gath
from the later lists of the five cities (Amos
1:6, 8; Zeph 2:4–5; Zech 9:5–6) indicates
it had lost its place among them by that
time.

GATH HEPHER (găth hē'fêr, Heb. *gath
ha-hēpher, winepress of the well*). A
town on Zebulun's border (Josh 19:12–
13). Birthplace of Jonah the prophet
(2 Kings 14:25). Now El Meshed, where
his supposed tomb is still shown, on a hill
two miles (three km.) from Nazareth in
Galilee.

GATH RIMMON (găth rĭm'ŭn, Heb. *gath
rimmôn, winepress of Rimmon or pomegranates*). **1.** A city of Dan on the Philistine plain, given to the Levites (Josh
19:45; 21:24; 1 Chron 6:69). **2.** A town of
Manasseh, west of the Jordan, assigned
to the Levites (Josh 21:25). It may also be
called Bileam (1 Chron 6:70).

GAULANITIS (See GOLAN)

GAZA (gā'zà, Heb. *'azzâh, strong*, Gr.
Gaza). One of the five chief Philistine
cities and the most southwesterly toward
Egypt. Its position and *strength* (the
meaning of its name) made it the key of
this line of communications. It is called
by its Hebrew name *Azzah* in the KJV
(Deut 2:23; 1 Kings 4:24; Jer 25:20).
Originally a Canaanite city (Gen 10:19),
Gaza had been occupied by Anakites
(Josh 11:22; 13:3) but was assigned to
(15:47) and occupied by Judah (Judg
1:18). The Philistines soon recovered it
(13:1); Samson perished there while destroying his captors (16:1, 21). Solomon
ruled over it (1 Kings 4:24), but it was
Hezekiah who gave the decisive blow to
the Philistines (2 Kings 18:8). God's
threatened destruction by fire (Amos 1:6)
was fulfilled by Egypt (Jer 47:1). The
predictions that Gaza would be forsaken
(Zeph 2:4) and that its king would perish
(Zech 9:5) were fulfilled by Alexander the
Great (332 B.C.).
Philip met the Ethiopian eunuch on the
road to Gaza (Acts 8:26).

GAZELLE (See ANIMALS)

GAZER (See GEZER)

GAZEZ (gā'zĕz). **1.** Son of Ephah and
2. Grandson of Ephah, Caleb's concubine
(1 Chron 2:46).

GEBA (gē'bà, Heb. *geva', hill*). A town
in the territory of Benjamin (Josh 18:24;
KJV "Gaba"), assigned to the Levites
(21:17; 1 Chron 6:60; 8:6). There Jonathan defeated the Philistines (1 Sam

Sarcophagus of King Ahiram of Byblos
(Gebal, between Beirut and Tripoli), thirteenth century B.C. The king is seated on a
throne before a table of offerings approached by seven attendants. On the
edge of the lid is a dedication inscription
written in Phoenician, one of the earliest
examples of Phoenician script to be found.
Courtesy Studium Biblicum Franciscanum, Jerusalem. Photo Manoug

13:3); he and Saul remained there (13:16;
KJV "Gibeah"). In the time of Hezekiah,
Geba was the northernmost city of Judah,
as Beersheba was its southernmost
(2 Kings 23:8; 2 Chron 16:6).

GEBAL (gē'băl, Heb. *geval, border*, Gr.
Byblos, Biblos). **1.** A seaport of Phoenicia, between Sidon and Tripolis, 25 miles
(42 km.) north of Beirut. It was called
Byblos, from the manufacture of papyrus
there. It was also noted for expert stone-
masonry and shipbuilding (cf. 1 Kings
5:17–18; Ezek 27:9). The land of the
Giblites or Gebalites (at the foot of Mt.
Hermon) was part of the land God gave
to Israel (Josh 13:5–6). **2.** A land between the Dead Sea and Petra; modern
Jibal in NE Edom. It was allied with
Israel's enemies (Ps 83:6–8).

GEBER (gē'bêr). **1.** One of Solomon's 12
purveyors for southern Gilead (1 Kings
4:13; NIV "Ben Geber"). **2.** The son of
Uri. He was over great pasture lands east
of the Jordan (1 Kings 4:19). Perhaps the
same as #1.

GECKO (See ANIMALS)

GEDALIAH (gĕd'à-lī'à, Heb. *gedha-
lyâh*). **1.** A son of Shaphan, King Josiah's
secretary and governor of Mizpah
(2 Kings 25:22–25; Jer 39:14; 40:5–16;
41:1–18; 43:6). This Judean of high rank
shared Jeremiah's views and protected
him from the anti-Chaldeans. He was
assassinated two months after Nebuchadnezzar made him governor. **2.** Grandfather of the prophet Zephaniah (Zeph

1:1). **3.** One of the six sons of Jeduthun, a harpist and head of the second of 24 companies (1 Chron 25:8–9). **4.** A son of Pashhur and the prince who caused Jeremiah to be imprisoned (Jer 38:1–6). **5.** A priest who had taken a foreign wife during the Exile (Ezra 10:18).

GEDOR (gē'dôr, Heb. *gedhôr, wall*). **1.** A city in the hill country of Judah (Josh 15:58). **2.** The town where Jeroham lived, whose sons were among the Benjamites who came to David at Ziklag (1 Chron 12:7). **3.** A descendant of Benjamin who lived at Gibeon (8:31; 9:37). **4.** Among the descendants of Judah, Penuel (4:4) and Jered (4:18) are both named as the "father" of Gedor. The genealogical tables are different, indicating two persons named Gedor. **5.** In the time of Hezekiah, princes of Simeon went to Gedor and found good pasture there. Then they drove out the inhabitants and settled there (4:38–41).

GEHAZI (gē-hā'zī, Heb. *gêhăzî, valley of vision*). The servant of Elisha (2 Kings 4:8–37; 5:1–27; 8:4–6) who contracted leprosy after the healing of Naaman because of his greed. Gehazi was an efficient servant but weak enough to yield to greed. He lacked his master's clear moral insight and stamina, and he had no such relation with Elisha as Elisha had with Elijah.

GEHENNA (gē-hĕn'à, Gr. *geenna*, a transliteration of the Aramaic form of Heb. *gê-ben-hinnôm, valley of the son of Hinnom*). The Valley of Ben Hinnom (NIV) or the valley of the son of Hinnom (KJV, RSV, ASV). A valley west and SW of Jerusalem that formed part of the border between Judah and Benjamin (Josh 15:8; cf. 18:16; Neh 11:30–31). Here Ahaz (2 Kings 16:3; 2 Chron 28:3) and Manasseh (2 Kings 21:6; 2 Chron 33:6) sacrificed their sons to Molech (Jer 32:35; cf. 7:31–32; 19:1–13). For this reason Josiah defiled the place (2 Kings 23:10). After the OT period, Jewish apocalyptic writers began to call the Valley of Hinnom the entrance to hell, later hell itself. The NT distinguishes sharply between Hades, the intermediate, bodiless state, and Gehenna, the state of final punishment after the resurrection of the body. Gehenna existed before the judgment (Matt 25:41). The word is used 12 times in the NT (11 times by Jesus), always translated "hell." Terms parallel to Gehenna include "fiery furnace" (Matt 13:42, 50), "fiery lake" (Rev 19:20; 20:14–15), "lake of burning sulfur" (20:10), "eternal fire" (Jude 7), and

"hell" (2 Peter 2:4). Its use by Jesus warns us of the destiny that even the love of God does not avert from those who finally refuse his forgiveness. See also HADES; HELL.

GEM (See MINERALS)

GEMARIAH (gĕm'à-rī'à, *Jehovah has fulfilled*, or, *accomplishment of the Lord*). **1.** A prince, son of Shaphan the scribe and friend of Jeremiah (Jer 36:10–25). He tried to prevent the burning of the roll Baruch had written at Jeremiah's dictation. **2.** A son of Hilkiah, sent by King Zedekiah as ambassador to Nebuchadnezzar (29:3).

GENEALOGY (jĕn'ē-ăl'ŏ-jē, Heb. *yachas*, Gr. *genealogia*). A list of ancestors or descendants, descent from an ancestor, or the study of lines of descent. Genealogies are compiled to show biological descent, the right of inheritance, succession to an office, or ethnological and geographical relationships. The word occurs several times in Scripture (1 Chron 4:33; 5:1, 7; 7:5, 7, 9, 40; 9:22; 2 Chron 12:15; 31:16–19; Ezra 2:62; 8:1; Neh 7:5, 64; 1 Tim 1:4; Titus 3:9).

The earliest genealogy (Gen 4:1–2, 17–22) by its emphasis on occupations shows when new features of the culture were introduced. A few genealogies span long periods of Bible history (5:1–32; 11:10–22; 1 Chron 1–9; Matt 1:1–17; Luke 3:23–38). The genealogy in Luke 3 includes Jesus' ancestors back to Adam. Ezra 2:1–63; 8:1–20; and Nehemiah 7:7–63 name by families those who returned with Zerubbabel from Babylonian captivity. The NT shows far less concern for genealogies than does the OT. In the OT, God was bringing together a chosen people devoted to preserving his revelation until he sent his Son, who would draw to himself a new people, united not by genealogical descent but by a new and spiritual birth.

GENEALOGY OF JESUS CHRIST Two genealogies of Jesus are given in the NT (Matt 1:1–17; Luke 3:23–38). Matthew traces the descent of Jesus from Abraham and David and divides it into three sets of fourteen generations each. Matthew omits three generations after Joram—Ahaziah, Joash, and Amaziah (1 Chron 3:11–12). Contrary to Hebrew practice, he mentions five women: Tamar, Rahab, Ruth, Bathsheba, and Mary. Matthew carefully excludes the physical paternity of Joseph by saying "Joseph, the husband of Mary, of whom was born Jesus" (1:16; the word "whom" is feminine singular in Greek).

Luke's genealogy moves from Jesus to Adam. Between Abraham and Adam it has the same names as three OT genealogies (Gen 5:1–32; 11:10–22; 1 Chron 1:1–7, 24–28), and from David to Abraham, Luke agrees with OT genealogies and with Matthew. Between Jesus and David, Luke's list differs from Matthew's, and there is no OT list to compare with Luke's.

Matthew gives the legal descent of heirship to the throne of David, through Joseph, while Luke gives the physical descent of Jesus through Mary. Matthew is concerned with the kingship of Jesus, Luke with his humanity.

GENERATION In the OT the translation of two Hebrew words: (1) *tôledhôth,* from a root *yalad,* to beget, used always in the plural, refers to lines of descent from an ancestor and occurs in the phrase "these are the generations of" in Genesis (introducing each of 11 sections) and elsewhere. (2) *Dôr,* a period of time (e.g., Deut 32:7, past; Exod 3:15, future; Ps 102:24, both). It can signify also all the people living in a given period (e.g., Gen 7:1; Judg 3:2), a class of people characterized by a certain quality (e.g., Deut 32:5; Ps 14:5), and a dwelling place or habitation (Isa 58:12; Ps 49:19).

In the NT "generation" translates four Greek words: (1) *Genea* signifying the lines of descent from an ancestor (e.g., Matt 1:17), all the people living in a given period (e.g., 11:16); or a class of people characterized by a certain quality (e.g., 12:39), or a period of time (Acts 13:36; Col 1:26). (2) *Genesis* (Matt 1:1, in a heading to vv 2–17), meaning "genealogy." (3) *Gennēma,* in the phrase "brood of vipers" (3:7; 12:34; 23:33; Luke 3:7; KJV "generation," ASV "offspring"). (4) *Genos,* meaning "race" (1 Peter 2:9; KJV "generation," RSV "race," NIV "people"). "This generation" (*genea* — Matt 24:34; Mark 13:30; Luke 21:32) may refer to (1) the people then living, (2) the Second Coming, or (3) the Jewish nation.

GENESIS (jĕn'ĕ-sĭs). The first book of the Bible. In the Jewish tradition the book is named from its first word *berēshîth* ("in the beginning"). The name Genesis, which means "beginning," derives from the LXX and is found also in the Latin tradition (*Liber Genesis*). Much of the book is concerned with origins. Tradition ascribes the book to Moses. Many historical accounts in Genesis predate Moses by great expanses of time. There is no reason why he could not have arranged these ancient accounts into the literary structure of the book.

Genesis may be divided roughly into three parts: (1) Creation to the death of Terah, the father of Abraham (1–11), (2) a history of the patriarchs Abraham, Isaac, and Jacob (12–36), and (3) the account of Joseph (37–50)

The first section begins with the account of creation, and records the fall of the human race, the Flood, and the Tower of Babel. The patriarchal accounts record the first formal statement of the promise to Abraham. The promise, which later was put into the form of a covenant (15:12–21), guaranteed an inheritance to the people of God in all ages. Jacob is the progenitor of the twelve tribes of Israel (Gen 35:23–26). Jacob and his sons came into Egypt as a result of a widespread famine. Joseph was then reunited with his family and settled them in the land of Egypt (Gen 47:11–12). The narratives concerning Joseph provide the historical background for the Book of Exodus, which records the bondage of the Israelites in Egypt and their subsequent exodus from that land. These narratives also look back to the period of Egyptian bondage mentioned in the Abrahamic covenant (Gen 15:13–14).

GENNESARET (gĕ-nĕs'à-rĕt). 1. A plain stretching about 3 miles (5 km.) along the NW shore of the Sea of Galilee, the only easily tillable land bordering the Sea of Galilee (Matt 14:34; Mark 6:53). 2. "The Lake of Gennesaret" (Luke 5:1), elsewhere in Luke simply "the lake"; the same as the Sea of Galilee (Matt 4:18; 15:29; Mark 1:16; 7:31; John 6:1) or the

The fertile Plain of Gennesaret along the northwest shore of the Sea of Galilee. The forbidding promontory to the left is Mount Arbel, associated with Beth Arbel (Hos 10:14). Courtesy Israel Government Press Office

OT "Sea of Kinnereth" (Num 34:11; Josh 12:3).

GENTILES (Heb. *gôy*, plural *gôyîm*, *nation*, *people*). The KJV translates the Hebrew word as "Gentiles" 30 times, "people" 11 times, "heathen" 142 times, and "nation" 373 times (this being the usual translation also in ASV, RSV, NIV). Sometimes *gôy* refers to Israel (Gen 12:2; Deut 32:28; Josh 3:17; 4:1; 10:13; 2 Sam 7:23; Isa 1:4; Zeph 2:9; translated "nation" or "people" in KJV as well as in other versions). In the NT, Greek *ethnos* ("Gentiles" in the NT) is a translation of *gôy*, while *laos* corresponds to Hebrew *'âm*. *Hellēnes* is translated "Gentiles" in KJV, "Greeks" in ASV, RSV (John 7:35; Rom 2:9–10; 3:9; 1 Cor 10:32; 12:13), and both ways in the NIV.

In times of peace, considerate treatment was accorded Gentiles under OT law (e.g., Num 35:15; Deut 10:19; 24:14–15; Ezek 47:22). Men of Israel often married Gentile women, of whom Rahab, Ruth, and Bathsheba are notable examples, but the practice was frowned on after the return from exile (Ezra 9:12; 10:2–44; Neh 10:30; 13:23–31). Separation between Jew and Gentile became more strict, until in the NT period the hostility was complete. The intensity of this feeling varied and gave way before unusual kindness (Luke 7:4–5).

While Jesus' teachings ultimately united Jews and Gentiles (e.g., Rom 1:16; 1 Cor 1:24; Gal 3:28; Eph 2:14; Col 3:11), Jesus limited his ministry to Jews, with rare exceptions (Matt 15:21–28; Mark 7:24–30; John 4:1–42; 12:20–36). He instructed his twelve disciples not to go to Gentiles or Samaritans (Matt 10:5). Jesus' mission was first to Israel, "his own" (John 1:11), the chosen people of God.

In Acts, from the appointment of Paul as the apostle to the Gentiles (9:15), the Gentiles become increasingly prominent. Even the letters addressed particularly to Jewish Christians (Rom 9–11; Hebrews; James; 1 Peter) are relevant to Gentiles also.

GENTLENESS (Gr. *epieikeia* and *prautēs*). The adjective *epieikēs* occurs five times (Phil 4:5; 1 Tim 3:3; Titus 3:2; James 3:17; 1 Peter 2:18), and the noun *epieikeia* twice (Acts 24:4; 2 Cor 10:1). The basic idea involves not standing on one's rights—being conciliatory and showing forbearance.

The noun *prautēs* (2 Cor 10:1) and adjective *praus* (Matt 11:29; 21:5) are both used of Jesus. The noun is also used to describe one aspect of the fruit of the Spirit (Gal 5:23; cf. 1 Cor 4:21; Gal 6:1; Eph 4:2; Col 3:12; 2 Tim 2:25; James 1:21; 3:13; 1 Peter 3:15). KJV always translates this word as "meek" and "meekness." The basic idea is that of real strength under control. Thus, it derives from the character of God, whom KJV describes as "gentle" (2 Sam 22:36; Ps 18:35). See also MEEKNESS.

GERA (gē'rà, Heb. *gērā'*, *grain*). A name common in the tribe of Benjamin: **1.** A son of Benjamin (Gen 46:21). **2.** A son of Bela and grandson of Benjamin (1 Chron 8:3, 5). **3.** The father of Ehud (Judg 3:15). **4.** A son of Ehud (1 Chron 8:7). **5.** The father of Shimei (2 Sam 16:5; 19:16, 18; 1 Kings 2:8).

GERAH (See WEIGHTS AND MEASURES)

GERAR (gē'ràr, Heb. *gerār*, *circle, region*). A town in the Negev on a protected inland caravan route from Palestine to Egypt (Gen 10:19). Here Abraham stayed with its king, Abimelech (20:1–2); and later Isaac (26:1–33) had similar and more extended experiences with the king and people of the region.

GERASA (gē-rà'sà). A city east of Jordan midway between the Sea of Galilee and the Dead Sea. The name does not occur in the Bible, but the adjective Gerasenes does (Mark 5:1 and in some versions of Matt 8:28 and Luke 8:26, 37). The MSS vary between Gadarenes, Gerasenes, and Gergesenes; the place where the gospel incident occurred may have been referred to sometimes as the country (1) of the Gergesenes, a purely local name; or (2) of the Gadarenes, from the nearest city; or (3) of the Gerasenes, from the most important city of the district. See also GADARENES.

GERGESA (See GERASA)

GERIZIM (gĕ-rī'zĭm, gĕr'ĭ-zĭm), A mountain of Samaria, Jebel et-Tôr, 2,849 feet (890 m.) high, SW of Mt. Ebal. Moses commanded that when the Israelites came into the Promised Land, the blessing for keeping the law should be spoken from Mt. Gerizim and the curse for not obeying it from Mt. Ebal (Deut 11:29; 27:4–26), six tribes standing on the slopes of each peak (27:11–14).

From the top of Mt. Gerizim, Jotham shouted his parable of the trees to the men of Shechem (Judg 9:7–21). After the Israelites, returning from Babylonian exile, refused to let the mixed races of Samaria help rebuild Jerusalem (Ezra 4:1–4; Neh 2:19–20; 13:28), the Samaritans built themselves a temple on Mt. Gerizim (John 4:20–21); they worshiped in the open after their temple was destroyed by the Maccabees. Samaritan tradition maintains that Abraham attempted to sacrifice Isaac on this mountain (Gen 22:1–19), that at a nearby Salem he met Melchizedek (14:17–20), and that Jacob's dream (28:10–17) occurred at Khirbet Lanzah on Mt. Gerizim.

GERSHOM (gûr'shŏm, from Heb. *gārash, to cast out,* but in popular etymology explained as from *gēr, stranger,* Exod 2:22; 18:3). **1.** The firstborn son of Moses and Zipporah (2:22; 4:21–28; 18:3; 1 Chron 23:15–16; 26:24). **2.** The eldest son of Levi (6:16–17, 20, 43, 62, 71; 15:7). Elsewhere called Gershon. **3.** One of the family of Phinehas who returned with Ezra from Babylon (Ezra 8:2). **4.** Father of Jonathan, the Levite who became priest to the Danites who settled in Laish (Judg 18:30). KJV and NASB call him "son of Manasseh," but ASV, RSV, NIV have "son of Moses."

GERSHON (See GERSHOM)

GERZITES, GIZRITES, GERIZZITES (See GIRZITES)

GESHEM (gē'shĕm). The Arabian who, along with Sanballat and Tobiah, sought to oppose the building of the wall of Jerusalem by Nehemiah (Neh 2:19; 6:1–2). The same as Gashmu (6:6 KJV).

GESHUR (gē'shûr, Heb. *geshûr, bridge).* **1.** A country in Syria (2 Sam 15:8) on the western border of Og's kingdom of Bashan east of the Jordan (Josh 12:5; 13:11, 13; Deut 3:14). David made an alliance with Talmai, king of Geshur, by marrying his daughter Maacah (2 Sam 3:3; 1 Chron 3:2). Her son Absalom, after murdering Ammon, sought refuge with her father (2 Sam 13:37–38). **2.** A district between southern Palestine and Sinai, near Philistine territory (Josh 13:2; 1 Sam 27:8).

GETHSEMANE (gĕth-sĕm'à-nē, probably from the Aramaic for "oil-press"). The place of Jesus' agony and arrest (Matt 26:36–56; Mark 14:32–52; Luke 22:39–54; John 18:1–12). A favorite place of Jesus on the Mount of Olives, a garden across the Kidron Valley from Jerusalem.

GEZER (gē'zêr, Heb. *gezer, portion).* A fortified place, Tell-Jezer, 18 miles (30 km.) NW of Jerusalem. When Israel entered the land, Horam king of Gezer came to help Lachish, whose king had been killed in the battle of the day on which the sun stood still (Josh 10:1–34). Horam and his army were completely destroyed, but Gezer was not taken. The

Gethsemane, the place of Jesus' agony (Matt 26:36), lying at the foot of the Mount of Olives outside the east wall of Jerusalem. Some of the present olive trees alongside the Church of All Nations (foreground) are believed to date back to the time of Jesus. Courtesy Zev Radovan

king of Gezer is listed (12:12) among those whom Joshua defeated, but the inhabitants of Gezer were not driven out (16:10; Judg 1:29) and later became slave labor. Gezer was given to the Kohathite Levites (Josh 21:21; 1 Chron 6:67). Solomon reduced the people of Gezer to forced labor and rebuilt the city, which the pharaoh of Egypt had taken and burned and later given to Solomon as a dowry with his daughter (1 Kings 9:15–17).

GHOST The human spirit as distinguished from the body. To "give up the ghost" (KJV, ASV) means to die (Gen 25:8; 35:29; 49:33; Job 11:20; Matt 27:50; John 19:30). "Holy Ghost" in KJV is usually " Holy Spirit" in other versions. See HOLY SPIRIT.

GIANTS The first mention of giants in the Bible is in Genesis 6:4 (ASV, RSV, NIV all have *Nephilim,* a Hebrew word of uncertain etymology). Nephilim were found in Canaan when the spies went through the land (Num 13:33; KJV giants). The Israelites met giants when they tried to enter

Canaan through Moab (Deut 2:11, 20), called Rephaim in ASV, RSV, and Rephaites in NIV. The last of this race was Og, king of Bashan, whose famous iron bedstead was nine cubits long (2:11; Josh 12:4; 13:12). The land of the giants (Rephaites) is referred to later (15:8; 17:15; 18:16; 2 Sam 5:18, 22; 23:13; 1 Chron 11:15; 14:9; Isa 17:5). David's mighty men met descendants of the giant Rapha (2 Sam 21:15–22). The best-known giant of all, Goliath of Gath, whom young David killed (1 Sam 17), is not called a giant but is described as huge of stature, possessing great strength. It was not necessary to name the obvious. Thus giants terrorized the Israelites from their entry into Canaan until the time of David.

GIBBETHON (gĭb'ē-thŏn). Tell el-Melât, west of Gezer in the territory of Dan (Josh 19:44), allotted to the Kohathite Levites (21:23). Baasha killed King Nadab at Gibbethon while Israel was besieging the city (1 Kings 15:27). A quarter century later, Israel again besieged Gibbethon, and Omri was made king there (16:15–17).

GIBEAH (gĭb'ē-à). 1. A city in the hill country of Judah (Josh 15:57). 2. A city of Benjamin (18:28) about 3 miles (5 km.) north of Jerusalem, also called Gibeah of Saul, where excavation has uncovered the rustic but strong fortress-palace from which Saul ruled Israel. A Levite's concubine being raped and abused brought war between Benjamin and the rest of Israel (Judg 19–20). Other events occurred at Gibeah, including the hanging of seven of Saul's descendants (1 Sam 7:1; 10:26; 11:4; 13:2, 15–16; 14:2; 14:16; 15:34; 22:6; 23:19; 26:1; 2 Sam 6:3; 21:6; 23:29; 1 Chron 11:31; Isa 10:29; Hos 5:8; 9:9; 10:9).

GIBEON (gĭb'ē-ŏn, Heb. *giv'ôn, pertaining to a hill*). A city of Benjamin (Josh 18:25) NW of Jerusalem, given to the priests (21:17). At the time of the Conquest, Joshua, without consulting the Lord, made a treaty with Gibeon, made its people woodcutters and water carriers, and then defended them (chs 9–10). No other city made peace with Israel (11:19). Gibeon was the chief of four Hivite cities (9:17). Here Abner met Joab (2 Sam 2:8–28; 3:30), Joab murdered Amasa (20:8–10), Zadok the priest ministered at the high place (1 Chron 16:39–40; 21:29), and Solomon sacrificed and received messages from God (1 Kings 3:3–15; 9:1–9; 2 Chron 1:2–13).

GIBEONITES (gĭb'ē-ŏn-īts). The inhabitants of Gibeon; Hivites (Josh 9:3, 7), Hurrians, or Horites (Gen 36:20; Deut 2:12) who had formerly lived in Edom. Joshua made them slave laborers for menial tasks (Josh 9). They were the peasants of the Mittannian Empire, which in 1500 B.C. reached from Media to the Mediterranean. The Gibeonites and their allies, at the time of the conquest by Joshua, controlled a tetrapolis—Berroth, Chephirah, Kiriath Baal, and Gibeon. David turned over seven descendants of Saul to the Gibeonites for vengeance (2 Sam 21:1–9). A Gibeonite was leader of David's 30 mighty men (1 Chron 12:4). Gibeonites helped repair the walls of Jerusalem (Neh 3:7).

GIBLITES (See GEBAL)

GIDDEL (gĭd'ĕl). 1. A member of the family of temple servants (KJV "Nethinims") who returned from exile with Zerubbabel (Ezra 2:47; Neh 7:49). 2. A servant of Solomon (Ezra 2:56; Neh 7:58).

GIDEON (gĭd'ē-ŏn, Heb. *Gidh'ôn, feller* or *hewer*). The son of Joash, an Abiezrite (Judg 6:11) who lived in Ophrah not far from Mt. Gerizim. The record about Gideon is found in Judges 6:1–9:6. A supernatural fire that consumed Gideon's sacrifice (6:17–23) attested to the fact that the messenger who called Gideon to lead Israel was from God.

Gideon responded to the call and, with some friends, overthrew the altar of Baal and cut down the sacred grove around it. He erected instead a new altar, naming it Jahveh-Shalom, "The LORD is Peace" (Judg 6:24). The followers of Baal wanted to kill him, but his father intervened. Instead of death he was given a new name, Jerub-Baal, or "contender with Baal" (6:28–32). Later the name was changed to Jerubbosheth, "contender with the Idol," evidently to eliminate any recognition of Baal (2 Sam 11:21). Gideon then issued a call to adjoining tribesmen to war against the Midianites. Having gathered a formidable host, he sought confirmation of his task and so put forth the famous test of the fleece (Judg 6:36–40; cf. 7:9–14). To prevent human boasting, God reduced Gideon's force from 32,000 to 300 men (7:1–8).

Gideon's night attack in 3 groups of 100 each surprised the sleeping Midianites, who killed one another in their mad flight (Judg 7:15–22). The country was delivered all the way to the Jordan (7:22–23; 8:1–21). When his people wanted to make him king, Gideon refused. He served 40 years as judge (8:28) and had 71 sons (8:30). One, Abimelech, by a concu-

Gideon's Battles

bine of Shechem (8:31), destroyed 69 of them; Jotham escaped by hiding (9:1–6).

GIER EAGLE (See BIRDS)

GIFTS, SPIRITUAL (Gr. *charismata*). A theological term meaning any endowment that comes through the grace of God (Rom 1:11). Spiritual gifts were given for special tasks in and through the churches (12:6–8; 1 Cor 12–14; 2 Cor 1:11; 1 Peter 4:10). They include the ability to speak an unlearned tongue (1 Cor 14:1–33), the interpretation of tongues (1 Cor 12:30; 14:27–28), power to drive out evil spirits (Matt 8:16; Acts 13:7–12), special ability in healing the sick (1 Cor 12:9), prophecy (Rom 12:6), keenness of wisdom (1 Cor 12:8), and special knowledge (1 Cor 12:8). Paul told the Corinthians to diligently seek these gifts (12:31), but he pointed out that "the most excellent way" was love (12:31; 13:13).

Everyone is accountable for any gift given to him or her by the Holy Spirit (1 Cor 4:7; Heb 2:4; 1 Peter 4:10). Claims of having such gifts are to be tested by doctrine (1 Cor 12:2–3) and on moral grounds (Matt 7:15; Rom 8:9).

GIHON (gī'hŏn, Heb. *gîhôn, burst forth*). 1. One of the four rivers in Eden (Gen

2:8–14). The name indicates that it arose either from some large spring or from a cataract. Since it wound through "the whole land of Ethiopia" (KJV), it is thought to be the Nile, although it is possible that Gihon was a small stream in the Tigris-Euphrates region. 2. A noted spring near Jerusalem (2 Sam 5:6; 1 Kings 1:32–40) that provided a good water supply (2 Chron 32:27–30; Isa 8:6).

GILBOA (gĭl-bō'à, Heb. *gilbō'a, bubbling*). A range of barren hills on the eastern side of the Plain of Esdraelon, where Saul gathered his forces to await an attack by the Philistines. Fear drove him to consult the witch of Endor (1 Sam 28:4–7). During the battle he was wounded, his forces were routed, and he committed suicide (1 Chron 10:1–8).

GILEAD (gĭl'ē-ăd, Heb. *gil'ādh, rugged*). Israel's possession east of the Jordan River, extending from the end of the Sea of Galilee to the northern end of the Dead Sea. Jacob camped there when fleeing from Laban (Gen 31:22–25, 47) and had his reconciliation with Esau (32:22–33:15). When Canaan was allocated to the Israelites, Gilead fell to the Reubenites, Gadites, and to half the tribe of Manasseh (Deut 3:13). Jair, a Gileadite, served for 20 years as judge in Israel (Judg 10:3). Jephthah, a greatgrandson of Manasseh, was also a judge (11:1–3; cf. 12:1–7). Absalom gathered his forces in Gilead when he rebelled against David (2 Sam 15:13–23). The Gileadites finally fell into gross idolatry (Hos 6:8; 12:11), were overcome by Hazael (2 Kings 10:32–34), and were led into captivity by Tiglath-Pileser (15:27–29).

Gilead became famous because of some of its products. Balm was exported to Tyre (Ezek 27:17); Jeremiah knew of its curative power (Jer 8:22; 46:11; 51:8). The Ishmaelites who bought Joseph carried balm to Egypt (Gen 37:25).

GILGAL (gĭl'găl, Heb. *Gilgāl, circle of stones*). The first camp of Israel after they had crossed the Jordan (Josh 4:19–20). There Joshua restored the Hebrew rite of circumcision (5:2–9). The memorial altar of stones erected there became a pagan shrine of later years against which Hosea (4:15) and Amos (4:4) warned the people.

Samuel sent Saul to Gilgal to be confirmed as king over Israel (1 Sam 11:15). There Saul later grew restless because of Samuel's delay in coming and offended the Lord by presuming to act as priest and make his own sacrifice (13:1–10). Judah gathered at Gilgal to meet

A limestone relief of a wheat field, from Tell-el Amarna, c. 1350 B.C. Courtesy Israel Museum, Jerusalem

David when he returned from defeating the rebels under Absalom (2 Sam 19).

Gilgal is not mentioned in the NT, and its location is not known. The town from which Elijah ascended to heaven was not this Gilgal (2 Kings 2:1). Gilgal furnished singers who had part in the dedication of the wall of Jerusalem (Neh 12:27–43).

GILOH (gī'lō). Home of Ahithophel, one of David's counselors who rebelled with Absalom (2 Sam 15:12); also a town of Judah (Josh 15:51).

GIN (See SNARE)

GIRDLE (See DRESS; ARMS AND ARMOR)

GIRGASHITES (gûr'gà-shītes). One of seven Canaanite tribes conquered by Joshua (Josh 7:1). They were descendants of Ham (Gen 10:15–16). Their land was promised to Abram (15:21) and to Israel (Josh 3:10). Tradition says they fled to Africa.

GIRZITES (gûr'zīts). Variously called Gerzites, Gizrites, or Gerizzites. Listed along with the Geshurites and the Amalekites as the ancient inhabitants of the land south of Judah (1 Sam 27:8).

GITTAIM (gĭt'ā-īm, Heb. *gittayim*, perhaps *two wine presses*). A town of Benjamin (Neh 11:31, 33) to which the Beerothites fled, probably at the time of Saul's cruelty (2 Sam 4:3), and lived as protected strangers.

GITTITES (gĭt'īt, *of Gath*). Natives of Gath, unconquered at the time of Joshua's death (Josh 13:1–3). The ark was kept in a Gittite home (2 Sam 6:8–11). David's guard included 600 men of Gath (15:18). Goliath was a Gittite (21:19).

GITTITH (gĭt'ĭth, Heb. *gittîth*). A word found in the titles of Psalms 8, 81, 84. Its meaning is uncertain. It may denote some musical instrument made in Gath, or a melody or march that was popular in Gath.

GLASS (See MINERALS)

GLEAN (Heb. lāqat, *'ālal*). The Hebrew custom of allowing the poor to follow the reapers and gather the remaining grain or grapes (Judg 8:2; Ruth 2:2, 16; Isa 17:6), backed by one of the laws of Moses (Lev 19:9; 23:22; Deut 24:19–21). The word is also used figuratively to describe the utter destruction of Israel (Jer 6:9).

GLEDE (See BIRDS)

GLORY The Hebrew word so translated, *kābôd,* means the "weight" and therefore the "worth" of something—as we speak of someone whose word "carries weight." The glory of God is the worthiness of God—the presence of God in the fullness of his attributes in some place or everywhere (Exod 16:10; 29:43; 33:19–34:8; Isa 6:3). The indwelling presence of

God was later defined as the shekinah (or "indwelling").

NT references to the shekinah glory are seen in John 1:14 and Romans 9:4. Glory is both physical and spiritual, as is seen in Luke 2:9 ("the glory of the Lord shone around them") and John 17:22, where it refers to the glory of the Father that Jesus gave to his disciples. As for the saints, glory culminates in the changing of their bodies to the likeness of their glorified Lord (Phil 3:21).

GNASH (Heb. *hāraq,* Gr. *brygmos*). In the OT the expression "to gnash with the teeth" most often represents rage, anger, or hatred (Job 16:9; Pss 35:16; 37:12; 112:10). In the NT it expresses disappointment and agony of spirit rather than anger (Matt 8:12; 13:42, 50; 22:13; 24:51; 25:30; Luke 13:28).

GNAT (See ANIMALS)

GNOSTICISM (Gr. *gnōsis, knowledge*). Though sometimes used of false teaching within the period when the NT was written, the word more accurately describes systems of knowledge in opposition to orthodox Christianity in the second and third centuries. It linked aspects of traditional Christianity with attractive ideas taken from Greek philosophy and Eastern religion, magic, and astrology. Its main themes were as follows: The true God is pure spirit and dwells in the realm of pure light, totally separated from this dark world. This world is evil, for it is made of matter, and matter is evil. The true God will have nothing to do with it, for it was created by a lesser god and was a mistake. People in this world are normally made of body and mind, but in a few there is a spark of pure spirit. Such "spiritual" people need to be rescued from this evil world; thus there is need for a Savior. Jesus, who is pure spirit even though he appears to be body and mind, is the Savior who comes from the true God in light to bring knowledge (*gnōsis*) of the spiritual realm of light. Therefore those who have the spark of spirit can receive the knowledge and be reunited with the true God.

Within the NT there are references to claims to knowledge and wisdom (e.g., 1 Cor 1:17ff.; 8:1; 13:8) that could be the roots of the growth that led to developed Gnosticism. There was a heresy in the church of Colosse (Col 2:8–23) and false teaching in the churches Timothy knew (1 Tim 1:4ff.; 4:3ff.; 2 Tim 2:18; 3:5–7) that may be termed a false *gnōsis* (1 Tim 6:20). Then in the Epistles of John there are references to false teaching about the reality of the humanity of Jesus (1 John 4:3; 2 John 7). But there is certainly nothing in the NT of the developed kind of false doctrines that the teachers of the church had to face a century or so later.

GOAD (gōd, Heb. *dōrevān, malmādh,* Gr. *kentron*). An 8-foot (2 1/2 m.) wooden pole, having at one end a spade for removing mud from the plow and at the other a sharp point for prodding oxen. It was a formidable weapon in the hands of Shamgar (Judg 3:31). For oxen to "kick against the goads" (cf. Acts 26:14) pictures useless resistance to a greater power.

GOD (Heb. *'ĕlōhîm, ēl, 'elyôn, shaddāy, yahweh,* Gr. *theos*). The Bible does not contain a formal definition of the word "God," yet God's being and attributes are displayed on every page. The greatest definition of the word in the history of Christendom, that is, in the culture in which the Bible has been a prevailing influence, is the one found in the Westminster Shorter Catechism (Q.4): "God is a Spirit, infinite, eternal, and unchangeable, in his being, wisdom, power, holiness, justice, goodness, and truth."

God is a nonmaterial personal being, self-conscious and self-determining. He is everywhere; everything everywhere is immediately in his presence. His omniscience is all-inclusive—he eternally knows what he has known in the past and what he will know in the future. His omnipotence is the ability to do with power all that power can do, controlling all the power that is or can be.

Holiness is God's central ethical attribute. Basic ethical principles are revealed by the will of God and derived from and based on the character of God. He possesses all logic and rationality. The axioms of logic and mathematics are not laws apart from God to which God must be subject. They are attributes of his own character.

God is eternal—without temporal beginning or ending. In a figurative sense "eternal" may designate (as in the words "eternal life") a quality of being suitable for eternity.

Unchangeable, in Bible language, points to the perfect self-consistency of God's character throughout all eternity and in all his relations with his creatures. That God brings to pass, in time, the events of his redemptive program is not contradictory. The notion that God's immutability is static immobility (as in Thomism) is like the notion of timelessness and is contrary to the biblical view.

God is known supremely through his Son (Heb 1:1ff.). Further, his "invisible" being, that is, his "eternal power and divine character" (*theiotēs* as distinguished from *theotēs*") are known through his creation (Rom 1:20). "The heavens declare the glory of God" (Ps 19; Rom 10:18). It is customary to distinguish between "natural revelation," all that God has made, and "special revelation," the Bible.

God is known by faith, beyond the mere cognitive sense, in fellowship with his people. Moses, leading his people in the Exodus, was assured, "My Presence will go with you, and I will give you rest." And Moses replied, "If your Presence does not go with us, do not send us up from here" (Exod 33:13–14). The Bible abounds in invitations to seek and find fellowship with God. See Psalm 27, Isaiah 55, and many similar gracious invitations.

Other gods are referred to in the Bible as false gods (Judg 6:31; 1 Kings 18:27; 1 Cor 8:4–6) or as demonic (10:19–22).

GODLINESS (Gr. *eusebeia, theosebeia*). The piety toward God and the proper conduct that springs from a right relationship with him. It is the sum total of religious character and actions, and it produces both a present and future state of happiness. It is not right action that is done from a sense of duty, but is the spontaneous virtue that comes from the indwelling Christ and reflects him.

GOG AND MAGOG (See MAGOG)

GOIIM (gŏy'ĭm). The territory, perhaps of a "mixed population," ruled by an otherwise unknown king named Tidal (Gen 14:1, 9), who was part of the confederacy defeated by Abraham when he rescued Lot. Also the name of the territory of an unnamed king defeated by Joshua (Josh 12:23, "Goyim"). See also HAROSHETH HAGGOYIM; HEATHEN, PAGAN.

GOLAN (gō'lăn, Heb. *gôlān*). A city of refuge in Manasseh east of the Jordan (Deut 4:43). Probably an important city in its day, it was destroyed by Alexander Janneus after his army had been ambushed there.

GOLD (See MINERALS)

GOLDSMITH (See OCCUPATIONS AND PROFESSIONS)

GOLGOTHA (gŏl'gō-thà, Gr. *Golgotha*, from Aram. *gulgaltā'*, *skull*). The place of our Lord's crucifixion. From the Hebrew *gulgoleth*, which implies a bald, round, skull-like mound or hillock. The Latin name, *Calvarius* ("bald skull"), has been retained in the form *Calvary* (Luke 23:33). In NIV, following RSV, it is simply, "The Skull." Two explanations of the name are found: (1) It was a place of execution and therefore abounded in skulls; (2) the place had the appearance of a skull when viewed from a short distance. Both Matthew (27:33) and Mark (15:22) locate it outside the city, but close to it (John 19:20) on the public highway, the type of location usually chosen by the Romans for executions. Tradition locates it within the present city.

GOLIATH (gō-lī'ăth, Heb. *golyāth*). A gigantic warrior of the Philistine army, probably one of the Anakites (Num 13:33; Josh 11:22). Goliath's size was extraordinary. If a cubit is 21 inches (54 cm.), he was over 11 feet (3½ m.) in height; if about 18 inches (46 cm.), he was over 9 feet (almost 3 m.). The only mention made of Goliath is his appearance as a champion of the Philistines (1 Sam 17). The Philistines had taken a firm position on the slope of a hill, with Israel camped on the opposite hill. Goliath made daily challenges to personal combat, but went unanswered until David went to face Goliath, armed only with a sling and five stones. David killed the giant, and the Philistines fled, pursued by Israel. The Goliath of 2 Samuel 21:19 was probably the son of the giant whom David killed. He was killed by Elhanan, one of David's men.

GOMER (gō'mĕr, Heb. *gōmer,* possibly meaning God *accomplishes it* or *completion*). 1. Gomer was the oldest son of Japheth (Gen 10:2–3; 1 Chron 1:5–6) and the father ancestor of a people (Ezek 38:6), probably to be equated with the Indo-European tribes, the Cimmerians (Gimirrai) of classical history who settled in Cappadocia. 2. Gomer was the unfaithful wife of the prophet Hosea, who bore Jezreel, Lo-Ruhamah, and Lo-Ammi. Her unfaithfulness was used by God to illustrate the unfaithfulness of Israel in their covenant relationship to himself. See also HOSEA, BOOK OF.

GOMORRAH (gō-mŏr'rà, Heb. *'ămō-râh*, Gr. *Gomorra, submersion*). One of the five "cities of the plain" located in the Vale of Siddim at the south end of the Dead Sea, destroyed by fire from heaven in the time of Abraham and Lot. Today traces of the punitive catastrophe abound—great quantities of salt, with

The land of Goshen, a rich and fertile land where Joseph settled his family (Gen 47:11), with an irrigation canal in the foreground and the pyramids of Giza in the distance.
Courtesy Seffie Ben-Yoseph

deposits of bitumen, sulphur, and niter on the shores of the Dead Sea.

GOOD, GOODNESS (Heb. *tôbh*, Gr. *agathos, kalos*). The nonmoral (and nonreligious) use of "good" is common in the Bible (e.g., Matt 7:19; 13:23–24). Apart from this general use the word "good" is used preeminently of God himself (Father, Son [Jesus], and Holy Spirit), who alone is truly good (Ps 136:1; Matt 19:17; Mark 10:18; Luke 18:19; John 10:11, 14, 32 KJV; Heb. 9:11).

The Lord revealed his goodness in his relation to, and treatment of, Israel (1 Chron 16:34; Pss 106:1; 107:1; 118:1). The whole universe, the work of God's creative power, is good (Gen 1:4, 10, 12, 18, 31; 1 Tim 4:4). God's self-revelation of his character and will, his word, and his law are good (Ps 119:39; Isa 61:1; Rom 7:12; Heb 10:1). The gospel is good tidings and good news. Further, the way God establishes and maintains relationships with people is good, as well as the gifts he gives to them and the providential care he exercises over them (Ps 145:9; Matt 7:11; Acts 14:17; Rom 8:28; James 1:17).

Although in themselves, because of their sin, human beings have no goodness that is acceptable in God's sight, they can receive and become channels of the goodness of God. When they respond positively to the grace, love, gifts, and providence of God, then what they do (Gal 6:10; Eph 2:10; 1 Thess 5:15), enjoy (1 Tim 1:5, 19; Heb 13:18), and become (Acts 11:24) may be described as good.

"Good" also describes behavior that is acceptable or commendable as a citizen (Rom 13:3–4).

GOPHER WOOD (See PLANTS)

GOSHEN (gō'shĕn, Heb. *gōshen*, probably *mound of earth*). **1.** The NE section of the Nile delta region, where Israel settled in the time of Joseph (Gen 46). Because of irrigation it is some of the best land for agriculture and pasture in Egypt. The district had two principal cities, both built for the pharaohs by the Hebrews. In a building at Pithom (Exod 5:7–13) three types of bricks are found. At its foundation straw was used. After Pharaoh refused to supply straw any longer, the Hebrews desperately gathered all bits of straw and stubble they could find, and such bricks are found higher in the building. It was completed with bricks devoid of straw, as the uppermost bricks indicate. **2.** A district of south Palestine, lying between Gaza and Gibeon (Josh 10:41). **3.** A town mentioned with Debir, Socoh, and others, in the SW part of the mountains of Judah (15:51).

GOSPEL (Gr. *euangelion, good news*). The English word *gospel* is derived from the Anglo-Saxon *godspell*, which meant "good tidings" and, later, the "story concerning God." As now used, the word describes the message of Christianity and the books in which the record of Christ's life and teaching is found. This message is the Good News that God has provided a way of redemption through his Son Jesus Christ. Through the gospel, the Holy

Spirit works for the salvation of human beings (Rom 1:15–16). In the NT the word never means a book (one of the four Gospels), but the good tidings that Christ and the apostles announced.

GOSPEL: THE FOUR GOSPELS The gospel was originally proclaimed in oral form, but has been transmitted through the writings called the "Gospels." Although Matthew, Mark, Luke, and John differ considerably in detail, they agree on the general outline of Jesus' career, on the supernatural character of his life, and on the high quality of his moral precepts. From the earliest period of the church they have been accepted as authoritative accounts of his life and teachings.

Reduced to writing, the gospel message constitutes a new type of literature. Although it is framed in history, it is not pure history, for the allusions to contemporary events are incidental, and the Gospels do not attempt to develop them. They contain biographical material, but they cannot be called biography in the modern sense of the word, since they do not present a complete summary of the life of Jesus. The chief purpose of the Gospels is to create faith in Christ.

Of the numerous accounts and fragments that were composed to perpetuate the ministry and teaching of Jesus, only four are accorded a place in the NT: Matthew, written by Jesus' disciple Matthew Levi, the tax-gatherer; Mark, from the pen of John Mark, an inhabitant of Jerusalem and a companion of Barnabas and Paul; Luke, the first half of a history of Christianity in two volumes (Luke and Acts) by an associate of Paul; and John, a collection of select memoirs by John, the son of Zebedee.

Luke derived his facts from those who "from the first were eyewitnesses and servants of the word" (Luke 1:2). Not only had his informants shared in the events of which they spoke, but also they had been so affected that they became propagandists of the new faith. Luke had been a contemporary of these witnesses and had investigated personally the truth of their claims, so that he might produce an orderly and accurate record of the work of Christ (1:1–4).

John also committed his Gospel to writing so that he might influence others to faith in Christ as the Son of God (John 20:30–31). He did not profess to give an exhaustive account of Jesus' activities, but took for granted that many of them would be familiar to his readers. The selective process that he used was deter-mined by his evangelistic purpose and theological viewpoint.

The introduction of Matthew (Matt 1:1) duplicates the phraseology of Genesis (Gen 5:1) to convey the impression that, like Genesis, it is giving a significant chapter in the history of God's dealing with the human race. Mark's terse opening line (Mark 1:1) is a title, labeling the following text as a summary of current preaching.

All the Gospels were composed for use in the growing movement of the church; they were not written solely for literary effect. Matthew obviously wished to identify Jesus with the Messiah of the OT by pointing out that he was the fulfillment of prophecy and that he was intimately related to the manifestation of the kingdom. Mark, by his terse descriptive paragraphs, depicted the Son of God in action among men. Luke used a smoother literary style and a larger stock of parables to interest a cultured and perhaps humanistic audience. John selected episodes and discourses that others had not used in order to promote belief in Jesus as the Son of God.

Where and when these documents were first given to the public is uncertain. The earliest quotations from the gospel material appear in the letters of Ignatius, the *Epistle of Barnabas,* the *Teaching of the Twelve Apostles,* and the *Epistle of Polycarp.* All of these are related to Antioch of Syria, and their quotations or allusions bear a stronger resemblance to the text of Matthew than to that of any other gospel. If, as Papias said, Matthew was first written for the Hebrew or Aramaic church in Jerusalem, it may have been the basis for a Greek edition issued from Antioch during the development of the Gentile church in that city. It would, therefore, have been put into circulation some time after A.D. 50 and before the destruction of Jerusalem in 70.

Irenaeus (c. 100), Clement's contemporary, affirmed that Mark handed down Peter's preaching in writing after his death. If Mark's Gospel represents the memoirs of Peter, it is possible that its content did not become fixed in literary form until A.D. 65 or later.

Luke can hardly have been written later than A.D. 62, since it must have preceded Acts, which was written about the end of Paul's first imprisonment.

The last chapter of John's Gospel tries to correct a rumor that John would never die. It is possible that it can be dated before A.D. 50, but most conservative scholars place it about 85. Traditionally it has been ascribed to the apostle John.

Matthew, Mark, and Luke are called *synoptic* from the Greek word *synoptikos,* which means "to see the whole together, to take a comprehensive view." They present similar views of the career and teaching of Christ and resemble each other closely in content and in phraseology.

Almost the entire content of Mark can be found in both Matthew and Luke, while much material not found in Mark is common to the two other Gospels. On the other hand, each Gospel has a different emphasis and organization.

All three Gospels are dealing with the life of the same Person, whose deeds and utterances were being preached continually as a public message. Constant repetition and frequent contact between the preachers tended toward fixing the content of the message. As the church expanded, the written accounts were created to meet the demand for instruction, and they reproduced the phraseology and content of the oral teaching. Each Gospel, however, was shaped to its own purpose and audience, so that the variations in wording reflected the differences of interest and environment. Matthew was written for Christians with a Jewish background; Mark, for active Gentiles, probably Romans; Luke, for a cultured and literary Greek. All three, however, bear united witness to the supernatural character and saving purpose of Jesus Christ.

The Gospels were among the first writings to be quoted as sacred and authoritative. Matthew, Mark, Luke, and John were already the chief sources of information concerning the life and works of Jesus in the first half of the second century. Growing intercommunication between the churches and the need for strengthening their defenses against heresy and the attacks of pagan critics promoted the interest of the churches in a canon of the Gospels. By 170 the four Gospels were securely established as the sole authorities. See also CANONICITY; JOHN, GOSPEL OF; LUKE, GOSPEL OF; MARK, GOSPEL OF; MATTHEW, GOSPEL OF.

GOURD (See PLANTS)

GOVERNOR One who governs a land for a supreme ruler to whom he is subordinate—e.g., Joseph in Egypt (Gen 42:6) and Gedaliah in Judah (Jer 41:2). In the NT the term occurs chiefly in reference to the Roman procurators of Judea—Pilate, Felix, and Festus. In the first century A.D., Roman provinces were of two kinds: imperial and senatorial. The first

were ruled by procurators appointed by the emperor; the second, by proconsuls appointed by the senate. Judea was an imperial province. Pontius Pilate was the fifth governor of Judea; Felix, the eleventh; and Festus, the twelfth. Procurators were directly responsible to the emperor for their actions and ruled for as long as he willed.

GOYIM (See GOIIM)

GOZAN (gō'zăn, Heb. *gôzān*). A city located in NE Mesopotamia, on the Habor River. Here the Israelites were deported by the Assyrians following the fall of Samaria, the capital of the northern kingdom (2 Kings 17:6; 18:11; 19:12; 1 Chron 5:26).

GRACE (Heb. *hēn*, Gr. *charis*). A term used by the biblical writers with a considerable variety of meaning: (1) Properly speaking, that which affords joy, pleasure, delight, charm, sweetness, loveliness; (2) good will, loving-kindness, mercy, etc.; (3) the kindness of a master toward a slave. Thus by analogy, grace has come to signify the kindness of God to man (Luke 1:30). The NT writers, at the end of their various letters, frequently invoke God's gracious favor on their readers (Rom 16:20; Phil 4:23; Col 1:19; 1 Thess 5:28). In addition, the word "grace" is often used to express the concept of kindness given to someone who doesn't deserve it: hence, undeserved favor, especially that kind or degree of favor bestowed on sinners through Jesus Christ (Eph 2:4–5). Grace, therefore, is that unmerited favor of God toward fallen man whereby, for the sake of Christ—the only begotten of the Father, full of grace and truth (John 1:14)—he has provided for man's redemption. He has from all eternity determined to extend favor toward all who have faith in Christ as Lord and Savior.

The relationship between law and grace is one of the major themes of Paul's writings (Rom 5:2, 15–17; 8:1–2; Gal 5:4–5; Eph 2:8–9). Grace is the medium or instrument through which God has effected the salvation of all believers (Titus 2:11). Grace is also the sustaining influence enabling the believer to persevere in the Christian life (Acts 11:23; 20:32; 2 Cor 9:14). It is also used as a token or proof of salvation (1:5). A special gift of grace is imparted to the humble (James 4:6; 1 Peter 5:5). Grace can also refer to the capacity for the reception of divine life (1:10). It may also mean a gift of knowledge (1 Cor 1:4) and thanksgiving or gratitude expressed for favor (10:30; 1 Tim 1:1–2).

GRAFT A horticultural process by which the branches of the wild olive tree are cut back so that branches from a cultivated olive may be inserted and grafting take place. Paul makes use of this practice in reverse (Rom 11:17–24) where the opposite process is envisioned; i.e., the wild branches, the Gentiles, are thought of as "grafted in" to the good stock of the parent tree, the children of Israel.

GRAIN (See PLANTS)

GRANARY (Heb. *māzû*, Gr. *apothēkē*). Derived from a Hebrew word meaning "to gather" (Ps 144:13) or Hebrew *ôtzār*, meaning "storehouse" (Joel 1:17; cf. Gen 41:56). In the NT the term is sometimes rendered "barn," and sometimes "garner" (Matt 3:12; Luke 3:17 KJV).

GRAPE (See PLANTS)

GRASSHOPPER (See ANIMALS)

GRATING, GRATE (Heb. *resheth*). A copper network, moved by a copper ring at each corner and placed under the top of the great altar (Exod 27:4; 35:16; 38:4–5)—to help the burning of the sacrifices, and to allow the ashes to fall.

GRAVE (Heb. *qěvěr, she'ôl,* Gr. *mnēmeion*). A place for the interment of the dead; a tomb, a sepulcher. Graves were mere holes in the earth (Gen 35:8; 1 Sam 31:13), natural caves or grottoes, or artificial tombs hewn out of the rock (Luke 7:12; John 11:30). Flat stones were placed on the graves as markers to warn passers-by that they should not contract ceremonial defilement by unwittingly trespassing. These stones were white-washed annually, which provided the underlying figure for Jesus' denunciation of the Pharisees (Matt 23:27).

GRAVE CLOTHES (Gr. *keiria, winding sheet*). Before burial the body was washed, perhaps anointed with spices, wrapped in a linen winding sheet, with hands and feet bound with grave-bands, and the face covered with a napkin (John 11:44; 19:40).

GRAVEN IMAGE An image of wood, stone, or metal, shaped with a sharp cutting instrument as distinguished from one cast in a mold (Isa 30:22; 44:16–17; 45:20 KJV; NIV "idols"). Images were, however, sometimes cast and then finished by the graver (40:19). Such images were used by the Canaanites (Deut 7:5), the Babylonians, and others (Jer 50:38; 51:47, 52), but were forbidden to Israel (Exod 20:4).

GREAT LIZARD (See ANIMALS)

GREAT OWL (See BIRDS)

GREAVES (See ARMS AND ARMOR)

GRECIA, GRECIANS Grecia is Greece, the home of the Hellenes. Greeks are generally those of Hellenic race (e.g., Acts 16:1; 18:4; and probably John 12:20), but the word may be used to indicate non-Jews, foreigners, and aliens (Rom 1:16). Grecians were Greek-speaking Jews, people of the Dispersion, from areas predominantly Greek (Acts 6:1).

Greece and its associated island groups form the SE end of southern Europe's mountain system, a rugged peninsula and archipelago, not rich in fertile or arable land. The southward movement of the Indo-European-speaking tribes, who became the Greek people, ended here. These tribes, or their predecessors, had established ordered life in the peninsula and islands by the twelfth century before Christ. Their civilization vanished before 1000 B.C., in a dark age of destruction and invasion occasioned by further waves of wandering tribes. Out of four centuries of chaos emerged the complex of peoples on island and mainland who are called the Greeks. Their own generic name was Hellenes, but Grecia was a portion of the land that, lying in the NW, naturally came first to the attention of Rome. After the common fashion of popular nomenclature (see also PALESTINE), the name of the part that first became known was extended to include the whole. Mediated through Rome, the term Greece was applied to all Hellas, and all Hellenes were called Greeks by Western Europe.

As early as the eighth century before Christ, Greek ports and trading posts were scattered from Crimea to Cadiz, and the first flowering of Greek thought and poetry began. The fifth-century of Athens was one of the great golden ages of man, making immortal contributions to literature, art, philosophy and political thought. Hellenism was shaped by Athens in the short years of its spiritual supremacy.

The Greek language, Greek thought, and Greek culture, in the wake of Alexander the Great (d. 323 B.C.), provided a unifying element in all the Middle East. Without the vast flow of the Greek tide eastward, the NT could not have been born. Greece provided its language and fashion of thought. Hellenism was a stimulus to the human mind. To reason, question, and speculate, was a habit with the Greeks. Paul of Tarsus (along with

Stephen and Philip) was heir of both Hellenism and Judaism.

GREECE (See GRECIA)

GREEK LANGUAGE A major branch of the Indo-European language that is the presumed parent of all the languages of Europe except Basque, Finnish, and Hungarian, and of Sanskrit and the languages that derive from the Sanskrit stock in India. From Ireland to Pakistan this linguistic kinship can be demonstrated from vocabulary, morphology, and syntax. No monuments of the original Indo-European language exist, but the wide diffusion of demonstrably related tongues is strong argument for some form of early unity. Attic Greek was one of the major achievements of the human mind. The richness and subtlety of its syntax, its flexibility, the delicacy of its particles—these and other linguistic features make Attic the most expressive medium ever developed for human thought. The dialects passed with the passing of the city states and with the unification of Greece, and were followed by a basic Greek that developed in the form of a simplified Attic. This, spread by Alexander's conquests throughout the eastern end of the Mediterranean, was called the *Koinē* or Common Dialect. It was the speech of the LXX and the NT, and the major influence in bringing the contributions of Palestine, Greece, and Rome into the partnership that determined the form and shape of the NT, the

global gospel of Paul of Tarsus, the Christian church, and modern Europe.

GREEK VERSIONS 1. The first and most famous of the Greek versions of the OT, and the only one to survive in its entirety, is the Septuagint (the LXX), the version most frequently quoted in the NT. It became the Bible of the Hellenistic Jews, as the Vulgate became the Bible of the Latin world. The Vulgate was, in fact, in direct succession, being a translation of the Septuagint. The LXX was published in the time of Ptolemy II Philadelphus (295–247 B.C.), the golden age of Greek Alexandria. The production of the Greek version of the Scriptures was probably a nationalistic gesture, designed to demonstrate the worth of Jewish literature. The LXX is written in the common dialect, but tinged by Hebraisms. The quality of the language and style varies, but on the whole the Greek is odd and undistinguished.

2. The acceptance of the Septuagint as the Bible of Greek-speaking Christianity prompted orthodox Jewry to produce its own version, that of Aquila of Hadrian's day (A.D. 117–38), of which only fragments exist.

3. Theodotian, an Ephesian of the second century and an Ebionite Christian, produced a revision of the Septuagint. It found favor with the Christian community. Symmachus produced, perhaps at the end of the second century, a Greek version that appears to have been

THE HELLENISTIC WORLD, C. 275 B.C.

Seleucid Empire
Ptolemaic Empire
Macedonian Empire

the best of all the translations, a rendering into idiomatic Greek.

GREYHOUND (See ANIMALS)

GRIND (Heb. *tāhan*, Gr. *alēthō, grind with a hand mill*). The grinding of grain into flour between two heavy stones was a domestic art usually performed by women (Matt 24:41; Luke 17:35).

GROVE (Heb. *ăshērâh*, Gr. *alsos*, translated "grove" in the KJV following the LXX and the Vulgate). The equipment for iniquitous worship, probably Phoenician in origin, was the "high place" (Heb. *bāmôth*). It was crowned by the altar, the standing pillars, and the images of the Asherah. The worship, interwoven with the concept of the fertility of the land, became a fertility cult. The chosen symbol of the cult was the trunk of a tree. This explains the prohibition against the planting of trees by the altar of the Lord (Deut 16:21; Judg 6:25, 28, 31). The goddess of the cult was Asherah, who also appears as mistress of the sea. The prophets of Israel roundly condemned the worship of Asherah and congratulated those kings who destroyed her shrines (1 Kings 15:13–14; 2 Kings 17:10; 21:3; 23:4).

GUARD The translation of a number of Hebrew and Greek words. (1) *Tabbāh* ("slaughterer") is used in the title "captain of the guard," which was applied 6 times to Potiphar (Gen 37–41), 19 times to Nebuzaradan (2 Kings 23; Jer 39–41, 43, 52), and once to Arioch (Dan 2:14). (2) *Rûts* ("runner") occurs 14 times in the OT and refers to the trusted foot soldiers of a king (1 Kings 14; 2 Kings 10–11; 2 Chron 12). (3) *Mishmār* ("watch") is a general term for one who guards (Neh 4:22, 23; Ezek 38:7). (4) *Mishma'ath* ("guard") is used twice of David's guard (2 Sam 23:23; 1 Chron 11:25). (5) *Spekoulatōr* ("guard, a spy, executioner") is used only to identify the one who beheaded John the Baptist (Mark 6:27). (6) *Koustōdia* ("watch") is used only of those assigned to guard Jesus' grave (Matt 27:65–66; 28:11). (7) *Stratopedarchō* ("captain of the guard") is used of the one to whom Paul and other prisoners were discharged in Rome (Acts 28:16 in some versions).

GUEST CHAMBER (Heb. *lishkâh*, Gr. *kataluma*). The *lishkâh* occurs 47 times in the OT and is usually translated "hall" in NIV and "chamber" in KJV, perhaps at times meaning a room in which sacrificial feasts were held. The Greek word occurs three times in the NT; once it means

A view inside the tunnel built by King Hezekiah in the eighth century B.C., known as Hezekiah's Tunnel, or the Gutter (2 Kings 20:20). Courtesy Israel Department of Antiquities and Museums

"inn" (Luke 2:7), and twice it is used to refer to the room in which the Last Supper took place (Mark 14:14; Luke 22:11).

GUILT The deserving of punishment because of the violation of a law or a breach of conduct. In the OT, the concept of guilt is largely ritualistic and legalistic. A person could be guiltless before both God and the nation (Num 32:22); on the other hand, one could be guilty because of unwitting sin (Lev 5:17), Israel, moreover, was viewed as an organic whole: what one does affects all. There is collective responsibility for sin; when Achan sinned, all Israel suffered. The prophets stressed the ethical and personal aspects of sin and of guilt. God is less interested in ritual correctness than in moral obedience.

In the NT, Jesus stressed the importance of right heart attitude over against outwardly correct acts and taught that there are degrees of guilt, depending on a person's knowledge and motive (Luke 11:29–32; 12:47–48; 23:34). Paul likewise recognized differences of degree in guilt (Acts 17:30; Eph 4:18), though also stating that the law makes everyone guilty before God (Rom 3:19).

GUILT OFFERING (See SACRIFICE AND OFFERING)

GULL (See DIRDS)

GUNI (gū'nī). 1. A family clan of the tribe of Naphtali (Gen 46:24; Num 26:48; 1 Chron 7:13). 2. The head of a Gadite family (5:15).

GUTTER (Heb. *tsinnôr, pipe, spout, conduit*). The channel or tunnel (RSV, NIV "water shaft") through which David's soldiers are inferred to have marched to win the city of Jerusalem from Jebusite rule (2 Sam 5:8), at the fountain of Gihon, site of the later tunnel Hezekiah built (2 Kings 20:20) to connect the spring at Gihon with the pool of Siloam. It was 1,800 feet (563 m.) long and 6 feet (2 m.) high. It was dug out as a farsighted measure so that the city's water supply would not be in danger during the impending siege at the hands of Sennacherib of Assyria.

-H-

HABAIAH (See HOBAIAH)

HABAKKUK (hà-băk'ŭk, Heb. *hăvaqqûq, embrace*). The name of a prophet and of the eighth book of the Minor Prophets (Hab 1:1). Nothing is known of Habakkuk outside of the book that bears his name.

Most traditional scholars believe the book to be a unity, the work of one author, Habakkuk, produced in Judah during the Chaldean period. The temple still stands (Hab 2:20) and the rise of the Chaldean power is predicted (1:5–6). The argument here depends on the Hebrew word *kasdîm*, translated "Chaldeans." Some recent scholars emend the word to *kittîm*, meaning Cyprots, and understand it to refer to the Macedonian Greeks under Alexander the Great. They therefore date the book to this much later period. There is no good reason to make this emendation. *Kasdîm* clearly means Chaldeans.

The Neo-Babylonian, or Chaldean, empire first came to prominence when the Babylonian king Nebuchadnezzar defeated the Egyptians at the battle of Carchemish in 605 B.C. and reestablished Babylon as the seat of world power. The prophecy of Habakkuk could hardly have been given before 605. Jerusalem fell to Nebuchadnezzar in 587. The book must be placed somewhere between these dates, probably during the reign of the Judean king Jehoiakim. Some date the book earlier, believing that the Chaldeans were known to Judah before Carchemish and emphasizing the unexpectedness of the attack mentioned by Habakkuk (Hab 1:5).

The first two chapters set forth Habakkuk's prophetic oracle, or burden. Twice the prophet is perplexed and asks for divine enlightenment; twice he is answered. First he is concerned over the violence and sin of his people. Why are they not punished (Hab 1:2–4)? The answer is that God is about to send the Babylonians (Chaldeans) to judge Judah (1:5–11). This plunges Habakkuk into a greater perplexity: How can a righteous God use the wicked Babylonians to punish Judah, which, though apostate, is still better than the Babylonians (1:12–17)? God's answer is that the proud conquerors will themselves be punished (2:2–20). That the righteous will live by faithfulness (2:4) becomes important to the NT writers (Rom 1:17; Gal 3:11; Heb 10:38).

Habakkuk 3 is called "a prayer of Habakkuk the prophet" (3:1). In a moving lyric poem the prophet describes the divine revelation in terms of a story theophany (3:2–15) but concludes that no matter what comes he will trust in God (3:16–19).

HABERGEON (hăb' êr-jŭn, Heb. *tahărā'*). A jacket of mail to protect the breast and neck (2 Chron 26:14; Neh 4:16; NIV has "coat of armor" or simply "armor"). It also translates a different Hebrew word of uncertain meaning (Exod 28:32; 39:23 KJV).

HABIRU (hà-bī'rū). The name of a people first mentioned in the Amarna Tablets (15th century B.C.) as among those who were intruders into Palestine. The name has also appeared in Babylonian texts and documents from Mari (18th century), the Hittite records from Boghaz-keui, and the Hurrian texts from Nuzi (14th century). The same name appears in Egyptian records as *Apiru* as late as the 12th century. Abraham is the first person in the Bible to bear the name Hebrew, *'Ibri* (Gen 14:13). Some scholars equate the names Habiru and 'Ibri. The meaning of Habiru seems to be "wanderers." It is not an ethnic designation, for the Habiru of these various texts were of mixed racial origin, including both Semites and non-Semites. The name Habiru describes more than the Hebrews, therefore, but it came to be associated with them particularly.

HABOR (hā'bôr, Heb. *hāvôr*). A river of Gozan, the region in the northern part of Mesopotamia to which Shalmanezer, king of Assyria, banished the northern tribes of Israel (2 Kings 17:6; 18:11). Tiglath-Pileser had carried the tribes east of Jordan to this same region (1 Chron 5:26).

HACHILAH (See HAKILAH)

HACMONI (hăk'mō-nī, Heb. *hakhmônî, wise*). The father of Jehiel, an associate of David's sons (1 Chron 27:32) and of Jashobeam, one of David's mighty men (11:11). "Tahkemonite" in 2 Samuel 23:8 is probably a variant of Hacmonite, but the text here is obscure.

HADAD (hā'dăd, *sharpness, fierceness*). **1.** A grandson of Abraham through Ishmael (Gen 25:15; 1 Chron 1:30). **2.** An early king of Edom, whose capital was at Pau or Pai (1 Chron 1:50). **3.** An earlier king of Edom who defeated Midian in the

Drawing from basalt stele, from Arslan Tash, c. 744–727 B.C., of Hadad, the Syrian storm god, standing on a bull and holding in each hand a double three-pronged fork that represents lightning.
Courtesy Carta, Jerusalem

country of Moab (Gen 36:35; 1 Chron 1:46). **4.** An Edomite of royal descent whose life had been saved in his early childhood by flight from David's devastating attacks. Hadad went to Egypt, where Pharaoh received him and his men, gave him a house, and highly favored him. Hadad became brother-in-law to Tahpenes, queen of Egypt, and later became an adversary to Solomon (1 Kings 11:14–25). **5.** The supreme god of Syria, whose name is found in proper names like Ben-Hadad and Hadadezer.

HADADEZER, HADAREZER (hăd'ăd-ē'zêr, hăd'ăr-ē'zêr, *Hadad is a help*). A

king of Zobah (NE of Damascus), twice defeated in battle by David (2 Sam 8:3ff.; 10:15–19; 1 Chron 18:3ff.).

HADAD RIMMON (hā'dăd rĭm'ŏn, *Hadad and Rimmon*, [two Syrian divinities]). A place in the Valley of Megiddo where Josiah, the last good king of Judah, was fatally wounded (2 Kings 23:29–30), and where later there was a memorable mourning for him (Zech 12:11).

HADAR (hā'dàr). **1.** A son of Ishmael (Gen 25:15 KJV; NIV and ASV have Hadad, supported by 1 Chron 1:30). **2.** The last of the ancient kings of Edom (Gen 36:39; NIV and 1 Chron 1:50–51 have Hadad).

HADATTAH (See HAZOR)

HADES (hā'dēz, Gr. *Hadēs, haidēs, not to be seen*). The place or state of the dead, as contrasted with the final punishment of the wicked. In Greek mythology *Hades* was the god of the lower regions. Although the word was taken from pagan myths, the concept is from the OT word *Sheol*. *Sheol* occurs 65 times in the Hebrew OT and is rendered in KJV as "hell" 31 times, "the grave" 31 times, and "the pit" 3 times; but in ASV it is uniformly transliterated *Sheol*, even as *Hades* in the ASV is a transliteration rather than an attempt to translate the Greek. The word "hell" in English always has an unpleasant connotation and is properly thought of as the final destiny of the wicked when it translates *gehenna*, which occurs 12 times and is always rendered "hell."

The NT generally does not give definite light on Hades. It is a place of torment (Luke 16:19–31). Capernaum will go down into Hades (Matt 11:23; cf. Luke 10:15). The preposition "down" points to the OT teaching that Sheol is inside the earth (Ps 139:8; Amos 9:2); the day of judgment for both Sodom and Capernaum is later than the stay in Hades (Matt 11:24). Our Lord arose from the dead and was not left in Hades (Ps 16:8–11; Acts 2:25–31). In Revelation, death and Hades are four times associated (1:18; 6:8; 20:13–14), being treated as almost synonymous terms. See also GEHENNA.

HADID (hā'dĭd, Heb. *hādhîdh, sharp*). A village in Benjamin named with Lod and Ono (Ezra 2:33; Neh 7:37; 11:34). It was located about 3 miles (5 km.) east of Lydda.

HADORAM (hà-dō'răm, Heb. *hădhō-răm*). **1.** A son of Joktan (Gen 10:27; 1 Chron 1:21). **2.** Son of the king of Hamath sent to congratulate David on his victory over Hadadezer (18:9–11; Joram in 2 Sam 8:10). **3.** Rehoboam's superintendent of the men under forced labor (2 Chron 10:18; NIV "Adoniram," see footnote). Perhaps the same as Adoniram of 1 Kings 4:6.

HAELEPH (See ELEPH)

HAGAR (hā′gàr, Heb. *hāghār, emigration, flight*). An Egyptian handmaid who, following the marital customs of the times, was given by Sarai to Abram (Gen 16:1–16). When Hagar saw that she had conceived, she despised her mistress, causing trouble in the household. Hagar was driven out, but the angel of the Lord appeared and sent her back to her mistress (16:7–14). At a great feast held in connection with Isaac's weaning, Ishmael scoffed at the proceedings (21:9), so Sarah insisted that Hagar and her son be cast out, and Abraham unwillingly complied. God told Abraham that Ishmael's descendants would become a nation. Hagar is last seen taking a wife for her son out of Egypt, her own land (21:1–21). Paul made Hagar's experience an allegory of the difference between law and grace (Gal 4:21–5:1).

HAGARENES, HAGARITES (See HAGRITES)

HAGGAI (hăg′ā-ī, Heb. *haggay, festal*). Prophet of the Lord to the Jews in 520 B.C. Little is known of his personal history. He lived soon after the Captivity and was a contemporary of Zechariah (cf. Hag 1:1 with Zech 1:1).

After the return from the Captivity, the Israelites set up the altar on its base, established daily worship, and laid the foundation for the second temple; then they were compelled to cease building for some years. However, during his reign, Darius Hystaspes (Ezra 4–6; Haggai; Zech 1–6) helped and encouraged the Jews to go ahead and allowed no opposition. In the second year of Darius (520) Haggai fulfilled his brilliant mission of rebuking and encouraging the Jews. The five short messages that make up his book are all dated, occupying only 3 months and 23 days; and in those few weeks the whole situation changed from defeat and discouragement to victory. Zechariah assisted Haggai in the last month of his recorded ministry (Zech 1:1–6).

HAGGERI (See HAGRITES)

HAGGI (hăg′ī, *festal*). A son of Gad and grandson of Jacob (Gen 46:16); patriarch of the Haggites (Num 26:15).

HAGGITH (hăg′ĭth, *festal*). Wife of David (2 Sam 3:4) and mother of Adonijah (1 Kings 1:5–31).

HAGIOGRAPHA (hăg′ĭ-ŏg′rà-fä, *holy writings*). A name applied to the third division of the OT by the Jews, the other two being the Law and the Prophets. Sometimes called the "Writings," the books involved are in the following order: Psalms, Proverbs, Job, Song of Songs, Ruth, Lamentations, Ecclesiastes, Esther, Daniel, Ezra, Nehemiah, 1 and 2 Chronicles.

HAGRITES (hăg′rīts). An Arab people with whom, in the days of King Saul, the tribe of Reuben made war (1 Chron 5:19–20). The Hagrites were so strong that Reuben won the victory only by crying to God in the battle (cf. Ps 83).

HAI (See AI)

HAIL 1. Hailstorms sometimes take place in the Near East in the spring and summer and do considerable damage to crops, sometimes even injuring property and endangering life. Plagues of hail are also mentioned (Exod 9:23–24; Josh 10:11). Hail was a means of punishing the wicked (Isa 28:2; Ezek 38:22; Rev 8:7; 11:19). **2.** An interjection found only in the Gospels (Matt 27:29; Mark 15:18; John 19:3) as a translation of *chairē*, used as a greeting similar to one in modern Greece.

HAIR Hair was a mark of beauty and sometimes of pride. Absalom's hair (2 Sam 14:26; 18:9) caused his death. Samson's uncut hair was a symbol of his Naziritic dedication; and when he lost his hair, his strength went with it (Judg 13:7; 16:17–20). In NT times the length of the hair was one mark of distinction between the sexes, and Paul said that this distinction should continue, pointing out that even nature teaches that long hair is a shame for a man but a glory for a woman (1 Cor 11:14–16). The men of Israel were not to clip off the edges of the beard (Lev 19:27), thus the "prayer-locks" in front of the ears of Orthodox Jewish men today. The word "hair" is also used figuratively (e.g., Judg 20:16; 1 Sam 14:45; Ps 40:12).

HAKILAH (hà-kī′là). A hill in the wilderness SE of Hebron, near Siph and Maon (1 Sam 23:19; 26:1, 3). Here David hid from Saul but was discovered, and here Saul camped when he was seeking David.

HAKKOZ (hăk′ŏz, *the nimble;* KJV sometimes has Koz, once Coz). **1.** A descendant of Aaron whose descendants returned with Zerubbabel from the Captivity

(1 Chron 24:10; Ezra 2:61; Neh 3:4, 21).
2. A man of Judah (1 Chron 4:8 ASV; KOZ
in NIV, RSV, KJV).

HALAH (hā'là). A district in Media to
which many of the captive Israelites were
taken by Shalmanezer and by
Tiglath-Pileser (2 Kings 17:6; 18:11;
1 Chron 5:26).

HALL In the KJV this denotes (1) the
court of the high priest's palace (Luke
22:55) and (2) the official residence of a
Roman provincial governor. It was called
the praetorium (Matt 27:27; Mark 15:16).

HALLEL (hă-lāl, *praise*). Psalms 113–
118, which were read on Passover Day,
were called the "Egyptian Hallel"; Psalm
136 is an antiphonal psalm of praise and is
sometimes called "The Hallel." Psalms
120–136 are often called "The Great
Hallel."

HALLELUJAH (hăl'-lē-lū'yà, Heb. *halel-
lû-yâh*, Gr. *allēlouia, praise ye Jehovah*).
A word of praise found in most of the
languages into which the Bible has been
translated. The word is often translated
"Praise the Lord" (Pss 104:35; 105:45;
106:1, 48; 111:1; 112:1; 113:1, 9; 115:18;
116:19; 117:2; 135:1, 21; first and last
verses of Pss 146 to 150). The term in
Revelation 19:1, 3, 4, 6 is borrowed from
these psalms.

HALLOHESH (hăl-lō'hĕsh, *the whisper-
er*). In Nehemiah 3:12 father of Shallum,
a ruler, and in 10:24 one of the covenanters with Nehemiah; perhaps the
same man.

HALLOW (hăl´ō. *to render or treat
as holy*). The setting apart of a person
or thing for sacred use; to reverence as
holy.

HAM (Heb. *hām*, perhaps *hot*). **1.**
The youngest son of Noah, born probably
about 96 years before the Flood, and
one of the eight persons to live through the
Flood. He became the progenitor of
the Egyptians, Ethiopians, Libyans,
and Canaanites (Gen 10:6–20). His inde-
cency when his father lay drunk brought
a curse on Canaan (Gen 9:20–27). **2.** The
descendants of Ham (Pss 78:51; 105:
23; 106:22). In these passages "Ham" is
used as another name for Egypt as representing Ham's principal descendants. **3.** A
city of the Zuzites, east of the Jordan (Gen
14:5).

HAMAN (hā'măn, Heb. *hāmān*). The
great enemy of the Jews in the days of
Esther. Because Mordecai, the noble
Jew, refused to bow down to him, Haman
plotted to destroy the Jewish race, but

God intervened. Esther foiled his plot
(Esth 7) and Haman died on the gallows
he had made for Mordecai.

HAMATH (hā'măth, Heb. *hămāth,
fortification*). One of the most ancient
surviving cities on earth, located in upper
Syria. The "entrance to Hamath" (Num
34:8; NIV "Lebo Hamath") was to be the
northern limit of Israel, but God left some
of the Hivites in that neighborhood to be
a test of the faithfulness of Israel (Judg
3:3–4). In the days of David, Hamath
had a king of its own (2 Sam 8:9). Jeroboam II (2 Kings 14:23–28) recovered
Hamath for Israel. Later it was under the
power of Assyria (18:34) and Babylonia
(Jer 39:5), and Antiochus Epiphanes of
Syria (c. 175–164 B.C.) renamed it Epiphaneia after himself.

HAMMATH (hăm'ăth, *hot spring*). **1.**
One of the fortified cities assigned to
Naphtali (Josh 19:35). It may have been
the same as the Hammoth Dor (21:32)
and Hammon (1 Chron 6:76). **2.** The
founder of the house of Recab (2:55; KJV
Hemath).

HAMMER The OT uses two chief words
here: *patfish*, a tool for smoothing metals
and for breaking rocks (Isa 41:7; Jer
23:29); and *maqqeveth*, a mallet to drive
tent-pins into the ground (Judg 4:21;
1 Kings 6:7), for building, and for making
idols (Isa 44:12; Jer 10:4). The word is
also used figuratively for any crushing
power, such as Babylon (Jer 50:23) or
God's Word (23:29).

HAMMON (hăm'ŏn, *hot springs*). **1.** A
place in Asher about 10 miles (17 km.)
south of Tyre (Josh 19:28). **2.** A city of
Naphtali (1 Chron 6:76). Hammath (Josh
19:35) may be the same place.

HAMMURABI (hàm'ū-rà'bē). The king
of the city of Babylon who brought that
city to its century-and-a-half rule over
southern Mesopotamia, known as the Old
Babylonian Kingdom. He was an Amorite, the name given to a Semitic group
that invaded the Fertile Crescent about
2000 B.C., destroying its civilization and
establishing their own Semitic culture.
Many recent scholars favor 1728–1686
B.C. as the time of his reign.

Hammurabi made Babylon one of the
great cities of the ancient world. Archaeologists have discovered that in his
city the streets were laid out in straight
lines that intersect approximately at right
angles, an innovation that bears witness
to city planning and strong central government, both little known in Babylon
before this time. Marduk, the god of

Detail of upper part of the Hammurabi code, showing Hammurabi receiving the command to inscribe the laws from the sun-god Shamash. Diorite stele from Susa, 1728–1686 B.C. Courtesy Réunion des Musées Nationaux

Babylon, now became the head of the pantheon, and his temple, Etemenanki, became one of the wonders of the ancient world.

Hammurabi began the first golden age of Babylon—the second being that of Nebuchadnezzar, over 1,000 years later. He systematically unified all of the old world of Sumer and Akkad (southern Mesopotamia) under his strongly centralized government. By far Hammurabi's most famous claim to fame is his law code.

It is now known that Hammurabi's was not the first attempt to systematize the laws of Babylonia. Fragments of several previous law codes have been found. But Hammurabi's code is the most complete expression of early Babylonian law and undoubtedly incorporated many earlier laws and customs.

The law code itself included nearly 300 paragraphs of legal provisions concerning commercial, social, domestic, and moral life. There are regulations governing such matters as liability for (and exemption from) military service, control of trade in alcoholic drinks, banking and usury, and the responsibility of a man toward his wife and children, including the liability

of a husband for the payment of his wife's debts. Hammurabi's code was harsher for upper-class offenders than on a commoner committing the same offense. Death was the penalty not only for homicide but also for theft, adultery, and bearing false witness in cases involving the accused's life.

A neglected wife could obtain a divorce. A concubine who had become a mother was entitled to the restitution of whatever she had brought with her or a pecuniary indemnity appropriate to her social position.

Both Hammurabi's code and Mosaic legislation say that a false witness is to be punished with the penalty he had thought to bring on the other person. Kidnapping, adultery, and breaking into another person's house were capital offenses in both. The principle of retaliation, on which a number of Hammurabi's laws were based, is vividly stated in Exodus 21:23–25.

HAMON GOG, VALLEY OF (hā'mŏn gŏg, *multitude of Gog*). A place east of the Dead Sea that will be set apart for the burial of the "multitude of Gog" (Ezek 39:11–15), after God's destruction of the northern host that will invade Israel in "the latter years" (38:8 KJV).

HAMOR (hā'môr, Heb. *hămôr, an ass*). Father of the Shechem who criminally assaulted Dinah, a daughter of Jacob, as a result of which both father and son were killed in revenge by her brothers Simeon and Levi (Gen 34:1–31).

HAMSTRING (Hebrew '*āqar, to hamstring an animal*). God commanded Joshua to hamstring (KJV, ASV "hough") the horses of the Canaanites (Josh 11:6, 9). David hamstrung the horses of Hadadezer, king of Zobah (2 Sam 8:4; 1 Chron 18:4). This was a cruel practice, justified only by extreme military necessity.

HAMUTAL (hà-mū'tàl, *father-in-law is dew*). Mother of two kings of Judah, Jehoahaz (2 Kings 23:31) and Zedekiah (24:18).

HANAMEL, HANAMEEL (hăn'à-měl). Mentioned only in Jeremiah 32:7–12, he was a cousin of Jeremiah the prophet. While in prison Jeremiah bought a field from Hanamel when real estate values were low because of the Chaldean invasion. His purpose was to encourage the Jews to believe that the captivity would not be permanent and that restoration was certain.

HANAN (hā'năn, Heb. *hānān, gracious*). 1. A Benjamite of Jerusalem (1 Chron

8:33), **2.** A son of Azel, a descendant of Jonathan (9:44). **3.** One of David's mighty men, son of Maacah (11:43). **4.** One of the Nethinim (KJV) or temple servants who returned with Zerubbabel (Ezra 2:46; Neh 7:49). **5.** An interpreter of the Law (8:7). **6.** Three covenanters with Nehemiah (10:10, 22, 26). **7.** An influential Jew in Jerusalem (Jer 35:4).

HANANEL, HANANEEL (hà-năn'ĕl, hà-năn'ē-ĕl, Heb. *hănan'ēl, God is gracious*). A tower in the wall of Jerusalem (Jer 31:38; Zech 14:10) on the north side between the Sheep Gate and the Fish Gate (Neh 3:1; 12:39).

HANANI (hà-nā'nī, Heb. *hănānî, gracious*). **1.** A son of Heman, David's seer who served in music (1 Chron 25:4, 25). **2.** A seer who rebuked Asa and was imprisoned (2 Chron 16:7–10). **3.** A priest who had married a foreigner (Ezra 10:20). **4.** Brother of the great Nehemiah (Neh 1:2; 7:2) who told him about Jerusalem's sad state. He was later given authority over Jerusalem. **5.** One of the musical priests whom Nehemiah appointed for the celebration at the dedication of the wall of Jerusalem (12:36).

HANANIAH (hăn'à-nī'à, Heb. *hănanyâh, Jehovah is gracious*). **1.** A son of Heman, David's seer (1 Chron 25:4, 23) who headed the sixteenth course of musical Levites. **2.** A captain of Uzziah's army (2 Chron 26:11). **3.** Father of Zedekiah, who was one of Jehoiakim's princes (Jer 36:12). **4.** The grandfather of Irijah, who arrested Jeremiah for alleged treason (37:13). **5.** Father of a Benjamite household who lived in Jerusalem (1 Chron 8:24). **6.** The Hebrew name of Shadrach, one of the three who survived the furnace of fire (Dan 1:6–7). **7.** A son of Zerubbabel (1 Chron 3:19, 21). **8.** A priest who had married a foreign woman (Ezra 10:28). **9.** A perfumer who repaired a section of the wall of Jerusalem in the time of Nehemiah (Neh 3:8). **10.** Another repairer of the wall of Jerusalem (3:30). **11.** A governor of the castle in Jerusalem, a faithful man who feared God (7:2). **12.** One of the chief covenanters, perhaps the same as no. 11 (10:23). **13.** Head of a priestly house in the days of the high priest Joiakim (12:12, 41). **14.** A false prophet of Gibeon in the tribe of Benjamin in the days of Zedekiah, the last king of Judah (Jer 28).

HAND One of the most frequently used words in Scripture, occurring over 1,600 times. Besides its literal use, it figuratively stands for power (e.g., Gen 9:2). To put one's hand under another's thigh (24:2, 9; 47:29) meant to take a solemn oath, evidently related to covenant obligations; to put one's hand on the head meant blessing (48:14), and signified ordination (1 Tim 4:14; 2 Tim 1:6).

The hand is also the symbol of personal agency (e.g., 1 Sam 5:11; 26:23; John 10:29; Acts 4:30). "To consecrate" is "to fill the hand" (e.g., Exod 29:9 KJV; see footnote).

To be placed at the right hand of royalty is a high honor and, of course, at "the right hand" of God is incomparably higher (Ps 110:1; Matt 25:31–46). In a trial the accuser stood at the right hand of the accused (Zech 3:1); but our Advocate stands also at our right hand to defend us (Pss 16:8; 109:31).

HANDKERCHIEF The Gr. *soudarion* is a transliteration of the Latin word *sudarium*, which was a cloth intended to wipe sweat from the face. Handkerchiefs were brought from Paul's body for healing purposes (Acts 19:12); the wicked servant (Luke 19:20–23) kept his lord's money "in a piece of cloth"; the face of dead Lazarus and that of Jesus were enclosed in a cloth (John 11:44; 20:7).

HANDLE The noun is found only in Song of Songs 5:5, referring to the doorknob. The Hebrew word has over a dozen meanings.

HANDMAID, HANDMAIDEN In the KJV a female slave or servant. When used of oneself, it indicates humility, as in the case of Ruth (Ruth 3:9), Hannah (1 Sam 1:11, 16), and Mary (Luke 1:38, 48).

HANDS, IMPOSITION OF (See LAYING ON OF HANDS)

HANGING Death by strangulation was not a form of capital punishment used in Bible times. Where the word is found in Scripture, except in the two cases of suicide by hanging (Ahithophel, 2 Sam 17:23; Judas, Matt 27:5), it refers to the suspension of a body from a tree or post after the criminal had been put to death. This was practiced by the Egyptians (Gen 40:19, 22), the Israelites (Deut 21:22), and the Persians. Hanging added to the disgrace. The body was buried before nightfall (Deut 21:23; Josh 8:29; cf. 1 Sam 31:8–13).

HANGINGS (Heb. *kelā'îm, māsākh*). The "curtains" (NIV) of the tabernacle and its court that preserved the privacy and the sacredness of what was within. Some were more or less permanent, but others could be removed to permit passage of a person. Of the first class were

Part of relief from central palace of Tiglath-Pileser III (744–727 B.C.) at Calah depicting three prisoners of war impaled on gallows. Reproduced by courtesy of the Trustees of the British Museum

the "hangings" (KJV) of finely twined linen that enclosed the court (Exod 27:9–19) and the curtains of the tent itself (26:1–14); of the second class were the screen of the court (27:14–16), the curtain at the door of the tent (26:36), and the veil that did not allow anyone but the high priest to look into the Most Holy Place (26:31–35). This veil was the curtain that God tore from top to bottom when Jesus died (Matt 27:51; Heb 9:8; 10:19–20).

HANIEL (See HANNIEL)

HANNAH (Heb. *hannâh, grace, favor*). One of the two wives of Elkanah, a Levite who lived at Ramah (1 Sam 1:19). Although Hannah was his favored wife (1:5), she was barren. Hannah, a godly woman, prayed for a son and vowed to give him to the Lord as a perpetual Nazirite (1:11). Eli saw Hannah's lips moving in silent prayer and rebuked her for what he thought was drunkenness. She replied very humbly and Eli apologized. The family returned home; Hannah conceived and became the mother of Samuel, the great prophet of Israel and the last of the judges. Hannah's praise (2:1–10) shows that she was a deeply spiritual woman (cf. Ps 113:7–9; Luke 1:46–55).

HANNIEL (han'ĭ-ĕl, Heb. *hannî'ēl, the favor of God*). 1. Son of Ephod, the

prince of the tribe of Manasseh, who was appointed by Moses to help in dividing the land (Num 34:23). 2. Son of Ulla, and a descendant of Asher (1 Chron 7:39).

HANOCH (hā'nŏk, Heb. *hănôkh, initiation*). 1. A grandson of Abraham and Keturah through their son Midian (Gen 25:4; 1 Chron 1:33; KJV Henoch). 2. Eldest son of Reuben (Gen 46:9; Exod 6:14; 1 Chron 5:3), he was the head of the family of the Hanochites (Num 26:5).

HANUKKAH (See FEASTS)

HANUN (hā'nŭn, Heb. *hănûn, favored*). 1. King of Ammon who, having mistaken David's friendly servants for spies, mistreated them, thus bringing on a war in which the Ammonites lost their independence (2 Sam 10; 1 Chron 19). 2. A man who helped build the Valley Gate of Jerusalem (Neh 3:13). 3. Son of Zalaph who helped repair the wall of Jerusalem (3:30).

HARAN (hā'răn, Heb. *hārān, mountaineer*). 1. The youngest brother of Abram, and father of Lot, Abram's nephew. He died in Ur before his father Terah took his family from that city (Gen 11:27–28). 2. A son of Caleb by his concubine Ephah who had a son named Gazez (1 Chron 2:46). 3. A Gershonite Levite who lived in the time of David (23:9).

HARAN, CHARRAN (hā'răn, chă'răn, Heb. *hārān*, Gr. *charran*). A city located in northern Mesopotamia to which Abram's father Terah emigrated with his family (Gen 11:31). Abram's brother Nahor remained there. Abraham later sent his servant there to find a wife for his son Isaac among his relatives (24:4). Afterward Jacob, at the request of his father Isaac, came to this same area in search of a wife (29:4–5). Haran and other cities in the same area were conquered by Assyria (2 Kings 19:12; Isa 37:12). Haran carried on trade with Tyre (Ezek 27:23).

HARARITE (hā'rà-rīte, Heb. *hărārî, mountain dweller*). An area in the hill country of either Judah or Ephraim. This term occurs only in the catalog of David's mighty men: Shammah (2 Sam 23:11, 33), Jonathan (1 Chron 11:34), and Ahiam (11:35).

HARE (See ANIMALS)

HARIM (hā'rĭm, Heb. *hārim, consecrated or slit-nosed*). 1. A priest assigned to the third division for temple service in David's time (1 Chron 24:8). 2. A family who returned from Babylon with Zerubbabel (Ezra 2:32; Neh 7:35). 3. A family of priests who returned from exile with

Threshing with a crude wooden sledge pulled over grain by a horse in the Holy Land today. Courtesy Zev Radovan

Zerubbabel (Ezra 2:39; Neh 7:42; 12:15). Members of this family married foreign wives (Ezra 10:21). **4.** Another family who married foreign wives (10:31). **5.** Father of Malkijah, a worker on the wall of Jerusalem (Neh 3:11). Perhaps the same as he who entered into a covenant with the Lord under Nehemiah (10:5). **6.** Another man who covenanted with the Lord under Nehemiah (10:27).

HARIPH (hā′rĭf, Heb. *harîph, autumn*). A family who returned to Judah from Babylon with Zerubbabel (Neh 7:24; Ezra 2:18 has Jorah). A man of this name was among those who signed the covenant with God (Neh 10:19).

HARLOT (See Prostitute)

HAROSHETH HAGGOYIM (hā-rō′shĕth hă-gōyĭm). A town in northern Palestine that was the home of Sisera, the captain of the army of Jabin (Judg 4:2, 13, 16). The significance of the phrase "of the Gentiles" (see KJV) is unknown but suggests that mixed races lived there.

HARP (See Music and Musical Instruments)

HARROW (Heb. *sādhādh*). The Hebrew word occurs three times, always as a

verb. In Job 39:10 it is translated "till" (KJV "harrow"). It is also translated by "breaking up and harrowing the ground" (Isa 28:24) and by "break up the ground" (Hos 10:11). From the root of the word it seems to mean dragging or leveling off a field.

HART (See Animals)

HARVEST (hàr-vĕst, Heb. *qātsîr*, Gr. *therismos*). Because the economy of the Israelites was strictly agricultural, harvest time was a very significant event. They had three each year. The barley reaping (Ruth 1:22) came in April–May; the wheat harvest (Gen 30:14) was about six weeks later, in June–July; and the ingathering of the fruits of tree or vine took place in the months of September and October.

Grain crops were reaped with sickles, and the cut stalks were laid in bunches that were carried to the threshing floor. Some laws governed these simple harvest operations. The corners of the fields were not to be reaped, and the scatterings of the cut grain were not to be picked up. The part of the crop thus left was for the poor people to use (Lev 23:22). The owner was required each year to present the firstfruits of the crop as an offering to God before he could take any of it for his own use (23:10, 14). Stalks of grain that grew up without being sown were not to be harvested (25:5). With a new orchard or vineyard the fruit was not to be gathered for three years, and the fourth year's crop had to be given entirely to the Lord. So the owner had to wait until the fifth year to get any fruit for himself (19:23–25).

The Lord fitted the three main religious feasts that he prescribed for the people into this agricultural economy. The Passover came in the season of the barley harvest (Exod 23:16). At the time of the wheat harvest the Feast of Pentecost occurred (34:22). The Feast of Tabernacles was observed in the period of the fruit harvest (34:22).

In the NT, most of the time the term "harvest" is used figuratively for the gathering in of the redeemed saints at the end of the age (Matt 13:39).

HASENUAH (See HASSENUAH)

HASHABIAH (hăsh-à-bī'à, Heb. *hăshavyâh, whom Jehovah esteems*). **1.** An ancestor of Ethan, a Levite and temple singer in David's time (1 Chron 6:45). **2.** An ancestor of Shemaiah, a Levite who returned from Babylon (9:14) and lived in Jerusalem (Neh 11:15). **3.** A son of Jeduthun, a musician in David's time (1 Chron 25:3). **4.** A civil official in David's time (26:30). **5.** Overseer of the tribe of Levi in David's time (27:17). **6.** A chief of the Levites in Josiah's time (2 Chron 35:9). **7.** A Levite teacher whom Ezra brought with him (Ezra 8:19). **8.** A chief priest in Ezra's company (8:24). **9.** Ruler of half of the district of Keilah, a worker on the wall (Neh 3:17). **10.** A priest, head of the family of Hilkiah (12:21). **11.** An ancestor of Uzzi, the overseer of the Levites at Jerusalem in Nehemiah's time (11:22). **12.** A chief of the Levites who sealed the covenant (3:17) and was appointed to praise God (12:24).

HASHABNEIAH (hăsh'ăb-nē-īà, Heb. *hăshavneyâh*). **1.** The father of Hattush, a worker on the wall (Neh 3:10). **2.** One of the Levites who prayed at the confession of sin after Ezra had read from the "Book of the Law of God" (8:18–9:5).

HASHUB (See HASSHUB)

HASHUM (hā'shŭm, Heb. *hāshum*). **1.** A family that returned from exile under Zerubbabel (Ezra 2:19; 10:33; Neh 7:22). **2.** A priest who stood at the left of Ezra as he read the Law to the people (8:4). **3.** A chief of the people who sealed the

covenant (10:18). Perhaps the same as no. 2.

HASMONEANS (See MACCABEES)

HASSENUAH (hăs-ė-nū'à, Heb. *hassenūâh*, the word is *senuah*, with the definite article prefixed, meaning *the hated one*). **1.** An ancestor of Sallu, a Benjamite who returned from exile (1 Chron 9:7). **2.** The father of Judah, the assistant overseer of Jerusalem in Nehemiah's time (Neh 11:9; KJV Senuah).

HASSHUB (hăsh'ŭb, Heb. *hashshûv, considerate*). **1.** The father of Shemaiah, a Levite who returned from exile (1 Chron 9:14). He lived in Jerusalem (Neh 11:15; KJV Hashub). **2.** A worker on the wall of Jerusalem (3:11). **3.** Another such worker (3:23). **4.** One who sealed the covenant (10:23). Perhaps identical with no. 2 or 3.

HASSOPHERETH (See SOPHERETH)

HASUPHA (Hă-sū'fà). A family who returned from exile under Zerubbabel (Ezra 2:43; Neh 7:46).

HAT (See DRESS)

HATTUSH (hăt'ŭsh, Heb. *hattûsh*, meaning unknown). **1.** A descendant in the royal line of Judah in the fifth generation from Zerubbabel (1 Chron 3:22). **2.** A descendant of David who returned from Babylon with Ezra (Ezra 8:2). **3.** A worker on the wall of Jerusalem (Neh 3:10); perhaps the same as no. 2. **4.** One of those who sealed the covenant (10:4); perhaps the same as no. 2 or 3. **5.** A priest who returned with Zerubbabel (12:2).

HAURAN (hà'ū-ràn, Heb. *hawrān*, probably *black* or *black land*). The modern name of a great plain situated on a plateau 2,000 feet (625 m.) high east of the Jordan River and north of the land of Gilead. In ancient times it was called Bashan. Its soil is of volcanic origin and is very rich, making the region famous for its wheat crops. The name Hauran is mentioned only by Ezekiel in his description of the boundaries of the land of Israel in the millennial age (Ezek 47:16, 18). The Israelites never had a very great hold on this area.

HAVILAH (hăv'-ĭ-là, Heb. *hăwîlâh, sand land*). **1.** A son of Cush, a descendant of Ham (Gen 10:7; 1 Chron 1:9). **2.** A son of Joktan, a descendant of Shem (Gen 10:29; 1 Chron 1:23). **3.** A land through which the Pishon River flowed from a source in the Garden of Eden (Gen 2:11–12). **4.** A land mentioned as one of the boundaries of the dwelling of the Ishmaelites (25:18; 1 Sam 15:7). This Havilah is probably the name as the one mentioned in no. 2 above.

HAVVOTH JAIR (hā-vŏth jā'îr, Heb. *hawwŏth-yā'îr, villages of Jair*). A group of 30 villages in Gilead that Jair, son of Manasseh, took (Num 32:41; Judg 10:4; 1 Chron 2:22–23). Jair captured Bashan as well, which evidently contained 30 more towns (Deut 3:14; Josh 13:30; 1 Kings 4:13; 1 Chron 2:23).

HAWK (See BIRDS)

HAZAEL (hăz'-ā-ĕl, Heb. *hăzā'ēl, God sees*). A high official of Ben-Hadad, king of Syria, who was sent to inquire of Elisha when the king was sick. Elisha told Hazael to tell the king that he would certainly recover, but he would in fact die (2 Kings 8:7–15). Previously God had instructed Elijah to anoint Hazael king of Syria (1 Kings 19:15). Hazael pretended to be surprised by Elisha's statement that he would become king. He returned, suffocated Ben-Hadad, and seized the throne during the period 844–841 (2 Kings 8:7–15). He reigned at least until 798 (13:22). He died shortly afterward (13:24). Hazael greatly punished Israel (8:29; 10:32; 12:17–18; 13:3, 22), as Elisha had foreseen (8:12).

HAZAR SHUAL (hā'zàr shū'ăl, *village of the jackal*). A town in southern Judah (Josh 15:28) later given to Simeon (19:3). After the Captivity it was held by Simeon (1 Chron 4:28) and Judah (Neh 11:27).

HAZEL (See PLANTS)

HAZEROTH (hà-zē'rŏth, *courts* or *villages*). A station on Israel's journeys in the wilderness, about 42 (70 km.) miles from Mt. Sinai where the people stayed after the terrible plague at Kibroth Hattaavah (Num 11:35). Aaron and Miriam rebelled against Moses there (ch. 12).

HAZEZON TAMAR (See HAZAZON TAMAR)

HAZOR (hā'zôr, Heb. *hātsôr, an enclosed place*). **1.** An important town in northern Palestine, ruled in the days of Joshua by Jabin (Josh 11:1, 10). Jabin led them against Joshua, who almost annihilated them. Nearly two centuries later, another Jabin (Judg 4) reigning at Hazor was reckoned as king of Canaan, but God used Deborah and Barak to subdue and destroy him. Hazor was fortified by Solomon (1 Kings 9:15). Its Israelite inhabitants were carried away into captivity (2 Kings 15:29) in Assyria. **2.** A town in the extreme south of Judah (Josh 15:23). **3.** Another town in the south of Judah (15:25). **4.** A town

". . . He took the coverlet and dipped it in water and spread it over his face, till he died. And Hazael became king in his stead" (2 Kings 8:15). Ivory figure thought to represent Hazael, king of Damascus, from Arslan Tash, ninth century B.C. Courtesy Réunion des Musées Nationaux

north of Jerusalem, inhabited by Benjamites in the restoration (Neh 11:33). **5.** A region in southern Arabia against which Jeremiah pronounced a "doom" (Jer 49:28–33).

HAZOR HADATTAH (See HAZOR)

HE (hā). The fifth letter of the Hebrew alphabet, pronounced like the English *h*. It was also used for the number 5.

HEAD (Heb. *rō'sh,* Gr. *kephalē*). The OT uses *rō'sh* 592 times, translated "chief," "leader," "top," "company," "beginning," "captain," and "hair" but most often "head," sometimes used figuratively (e.g., Exod 18:25; Josh 2:19; 1 Sam 28:2; 2 Sam 3:8; Job 10:15; 20:6).

Almost all the NT uses of *kephalē* refer to the upper part of the body, but eight verses use it figuratively for the God-ordained order of authority—(1) the husband as head of the wife (1 Cor 11:3; Eph 5:23), (2) Christ as head of the church (Eph 4:15; 5:22, 23; Col 1:18; 2:19), (3) Christ as head over all people and power (1 Cor 11:3; Col 2:10; 1 Peter 2:7), and (4) God the Father as head of Christ (1 Cor 11:3).

HEADBAND, HEADDRESS (See DRESS)

HEADSTONE (See CORNERSTONE)

HEART (Heb. *lēv, lēvāv,* Gr. *kardia*). Scripture uses the word *heart* more than 900 times, almost never literally; the principal exception is in Exodus 28:29–30, which speaks of the breastplate of decision over the heart of Aaron. The heart is regarded (as in the modern usage) as the seat of the affections (e.g., Gen 18:5; Ps 62:10) but also as the seat of the intellect (e.g., Gen 6:5) and of the will (e.g., Ps 119:2). Often it signifies the innermost being (e.g., Gen 6:6).

HEARTH In ancient times homes were heated very differently from today. In the houses of the poorer people the hearth consisted of a depression in the floor of a room in which a fire was kindled for cooking or for warmth. Chimneys were unknown; smoke escaped from the house as it could, or through a latticed opening for the purpose. The better houses were heated by means of a brazier of burning coals. The brazier was a wide, shallow pan that could also be used for cooking. (See Gen 18:6; Ps 102:3; Isa 30:14; Jer 36:22–23; Hos 13:3; Zech 12:6.)

HEATHEN, PAGAN (Heb. *gôy,* pl. *gôyim,* Gr. *ethnos, people, nation*). In the OT *gôy* is rendered "Gentiles," "heathen," and "nation," but it is usually used for a non-Israelitish people, and thus has the meaning of "Gentiles." Sometimes, however, it refers to the Israelites (e.g., Gen 12:2; Deut 32:28), but the word ordinarily used for them is *'ām*. In the NT *ethnos* is the equivalent of OT *gôy,* while *laos* corresponds to *'ām*. Sometimes in the KJV the Greek *Hellenes* is translated "Gentiles" (John 7:35; Rom 2:9–10).

The differentiation between Israelites and Gentiles was more sharply accentuated in NT times than in OT times, because the Jews had suffered so much from Gentile hands. Gentiles were looked on with aversion and hatred (John 18:28; Acts 10:28; 11:3).

God's interest in and concern for the heathen is seen in the OT, especially in the Book of Jonah. In the NT Jesus commanded the apostles to preach the gospel to all the world; and we find them proclaiming it to Gentile nations throughout the Mediterranean world.

HEAVEN (Heb. *shāmayim,* Gr. *ouranos*). 1. Cosmologically, one of two great divisions of the universe, the earth and the heavens (Gen 1:1; 14:19); or one of three—heaven, earth, and the waters under the earth (Exod 20:4). In the visible heavens are the stars and planets (Gen 1:14–17; Ezek 32:7–8). The term "heaven of heavens" (Deut 10:14; 1 Kings 8:27; Ps 148:4) is "highest heavens" in NIV. 2. The abode of God (Gen 28:17; Ps 80:14; Isa 66:1; Matt 5:12; 2 Cor 12:2) and of the good angels (Matt 24:36). It is the place where the redeemed will someday be (5:12; 6:20; Eph 3:15), where the Redeemer has gone and intercedes for the saints, and from where he will someday come for his own (1 Thess 4:16). 3. The inhabitants of heaven (Luke 15:18; Rev 18:20).

HEBER (hē'bēr, *associate*). 1. A great-grandson of Jacob through Asher and Beriah (Gen 46:17). 2. The Kenite whose wife Jael killed Sisera (Judg 4:11–21). 3. A son of Ezrah (KJV "Ezra") of the tribe of Judah and probably of the family of Caleb (1 Chron 4:18). 4. A man of the tribe of Benjamin, and son of Elpaal (8:17). 5. The head of a family in the tribe of Gad (5:13 KJV; NIV "Eber"). 6. A Benjamite, son of Shashak (8:22 KJV; NIV "Eber"). 7. One mentioned in Christ's genealogy (Luke 3:35 KJV), father of Peleg and Joktan, properly called Eber in NIV and other versions (Gen 10:24–25; 11:14–17).

HEBREW, HEBREWS These are traditionally considered designations for Abraham and his descendants, especially through Jacob, the equivalent of Israelite(s); 1 Samuel 14:21 may suggest that the terms are to be equated. Jews quite uniformly have used "Israel" and "the children of Israel" (later "Jews") in referring to themselves, finding in such terminology treasured religious and national associations. Foreigners thought of them as "Hebrews" (Exod 1:16; 2:6), and they so identified themselves in speaking to non-Jews (Gen 40:15; Exod 10:3; Jonah 1:9). The term appears involving contrasts between Israelites and people of other nations (Gen 43:32; Exod 1:15; 2:11; 1 Sam 13:3; 14:21).

NT "Hebrews" references contrast people (Acts 6:1) and language (John 5:2; 19:13, 17, 20; 20:16) to differentiate between the Greeks and Hellenistic culture on the one hand and Jews and their traditional life and speech on the other. What is called "Hebrew language" may in John's Gospel refer to Aramaic, but in the Apocalypse to Hebrew proper (Rev 9:11; 16:16).

Etymologically, it has been debated whether "Hebrew" is to be traced to Eber, the father of Peleg and Joktan (Gen 10:24–25; 11:12–16) or is derived from the Hebrew root "to pass over" and has reference to "a land on the other side," as the dweller east of the Euphrates might think of Canaan. However, the possible equating of the Hebrews and the Habiru might suggest that the Hebrews were "those who crossed over" in the sense of trespassing, i.e., "trespassers."

HEBREW LANGUAGE With the exception of Aramaic (Ezra 4:8–6:18; 7:12–26; Dan 2:4–7:28; Jer 10:11), Hebrew is the language of the OT. The term "Hebrew" was first used as a designation for individuals or a people and only later denoted a language. The OT refers to the language not as "Hebrew" but as "the language of Canaan" (Isa 19:18) or "the Jews' language" (2 Kings 18:26, 28 KJV and parallel passages; also Neh 13:24). Josephus, Ecclesiasticus, and the NT (Rev 9:11; 16:16), however, speak of it as "Hebrew." With close affinity to Ugaritic, Phoenician, Moabitic, and the Canaanite dialects, Hebrew represents the northwest branch of the Semitic language family. Its sister languages include Arabic, Akkadian, and Aramaic. With few exceptions, extant texts of ancient Hebrew are those of the OT and certain of the apocryphal and pseudepigraphic works. Inscriptions employing the language include the Siloam Inscription from the 8th century B.C. and the Gezer Calendar from the 10th century.

Though Aramaic is itself a very ancient language and the presence of "Aramaisms" in the OT often indicates an early rather than a late date for the passages in which they occur, from the time of the Exile onward Hebrew was spoken less and less and correspondingly the use of Aramaic flourished. Some of the Dead Sea Scrolls were written in Hebrew. Hebrew was also the vehicle for the writing of such Jewish religious literature as the Mishna and the Midrashim in the early part of the Christian era and in medieval times for biblical commentaries and philosophical and literary works. In modern Israel, Hebrew has again become a living tongue.

The historical origins of the language are somewhat obscure but go back beyond 2000 B.C. The OT literature, written over a period of more than a 1,000 years, reveals a minimum of stylistic changes, though loan words and new ways of expression became more or less noticeable with the passing of years, especially after the Exile. It is also true that at a given time dialectical differences existed, a fact attested by the narrative in Judges 12, in which Ephraimites were unable to pronounce the "sh" of their neighbors to the south.

With its short sentences and simple coordinating conjunctions, ancient Hebrew lent itself well to the vivid expression of events. These features, together with parallelism and rhythm and special meanings and constructions, made Hebrew poetry, as found in the Psalms and to a large extent in the Prophets, most expressive and strikingly effective. (See page 244.)

HEBREW OF HEBREWS When Paul in Philippians 3:5 so described himself, he meant that he was a pure-blooded Hebrew who had retained the language and customs of his fathers, in contrast to other Jews who had adopted Greek language and customs.

HEBREWS, LETTER TO THE The writer of Hebrews does not attach his name to his letter. First John is the only other letter in the NT to which a name is not attached. Many Christians have considered Paul to be the author of Hebrews, but others have thought it was Apollos, Barnabas, or someone else.

The letter was first known in Rome and the West. Its first readers were Jewish Christians who spoke and wrote Greek. The brief statement "Those from Italy send you their greetings" (Heb 13:24) certainly favors the readers' being located in Italy. The writer knows the readers well. He refers to their spiritual dullness (5:11–14), their faithful ministering to the saints (6:9–10), and their experiences after their conversion (10:32–36). The term used for their spiritual leaders or rulers is *hoi hēgoumenoi* (13:7, 17, 24), a

Ancient Semitic Alphabets

(With modern Hebrew, in column at right, for comparison)

Inscr. of Dibon 9th cent.B.C. Gram. ¶2,2. ¶5,1.	Phoenician Coins and Inscript.	New Punic	Old Hebr. Coins and Gems	Sama- ritan	Aram.- Egyptian 5th-1st cent. B.C.	Palmyra Inscript. 1st cent. B.C. -4th cent. A.D.	Heb. Inscr. Christ's Time	Square Char.	Raschi	Modern Hebrew	
✝✝	⟊⟊⟊	Ж	⟊⟊ғ⟊Ж	⟊⟊	✝✝⟊⟊	α א	∧ℵ	א	ƒ	א	'
ᵹᵹ	ᵹᵹᵹ	9,'	ᵹᵹᵺ	ᵹ	4ᵹ5'	ᵹᵹ	בב	ב	ȝ	ב	b,bh
⟊ʅ	∧∧∧	⅄∧	∧⟊ʅ	⟙	∧∧	⅄⅄		ȝ	ȝ	ג	g,gh
◁△	△9△	9,ı	494ᴛ	⅁	44⅄	⅄⅄	ᴛᴛ	ד	ʔ	ד	d,dh
Ⰸ⟊	ⰈⰈⰈᴙ	ᴙ	ⰈⰈᴛⰈ	Ж	ᴙᴙⰈᴙ	Жᴙ	הה	ה	ƀ	ה	h
⅄⅄	ᴙᴙ⅂	⅄	Ⰸᴙᴙ⟊ⅈ	ᴙᴙ	⅁⅁⅁	⅄ᴙᴙ	ıı⅃	ו	ı	ו	w
ⲍ	⟊Ⲍⲏ	ʅⅈ	ⲍⲍ(⅁)	ᴙⅈ	ⅈⅈ	ıı	ıⅇ	ז	ᴦ	ז	z
ⲎⲎⲎ	ⲎⲎⲎ	ⅈⲭⲭ	ⲎⲎⲎⲎⲎ	Ⲏⲭ	ⲎⲎⲎⲎ	Жж	Ⲏⲏ	ח	ⲏ	ח	ch
ⲟⲟⲟ	ⲟⲟⲟ	ⲟⲟ	ⲟⲟⲟ	ⲟⲟⲟ	ⲟⲟⲟⲟ	ƀƀ		ט	ⲩ	ט	ţ
ⲍⲍⲍⲭ	⅍ⲭⲭⲭ	ⲍⲍ	ⲍⲭⲍⲍ	ⲭⲭ	ⲍⲍⅎⲭⲭⲭ	ᴧⲍⲍ	ıı	'	'	'	y
⅄⅄	⅄⅄⅄⅄	⅄⅄	⅄⅄⅄	⅄⅄	⅄⅄⅄⅄	⅄⅄⅄	בⲭⲃ	ⲃⲭ	ⲭⲦ	כך	k,kh
⅃⅃	⅃⅃⅃⅃	⅃∽	⅃⅃⅃⅃	Ⲭ⅃	⅃⅃⅃ⅈ	⅃⅃	⅃⅃	⅃	⅃	ל	l
⅄⅄	⅄⅄⅄	ⲭⲭⲭ⅄⅄	ⲃⲃⲃ	ⲭⲭⲭⲭ	ⲭⲭⲭ	⅄⅄⅄	ⲭⲟ	ⲃⲟ	ⲃⲟⲭ	מם	m
ⅉⅉ	ⅉⅉⅉ	ⅈ⅃	ⲭⅉⅉⅉ	ⲃⲃⲃ	ⅉⅉⅉ⅂	ⅉ⅄	⅃	ⲃⅉ	ⅉⅉ	נן	n
ⲭⲭ	ⲭⲭⲭⲭ	Ⲭ⅄	ⲭⲭ	ᵹ	ⅉ⅄ⅉⲭ	ⲃ⅄	ⲟⲟ	ⲟ	ⲟ	ס	s
ⲟ	ⲟⲟⲟⲟ	ⲟⲟⲟⲟⲟ	ⲟ⟊⟊	ⲟⲟ	ⲟⲃ⅄⅄	⅄	⅄⅄	⅄	⅄	ע	'
ⅉⅉ	ⅉⅉⅉ	ⅉ�ⅉⅉ	ᵹ	ⅉⅉⅉ	ⅉⅉⅉ	ⅉⅉ	ⅉⅉ	ⅉ⅁	ⅉƀ	פף	p,ph
ⲭⲭⲭ	ⲭⲭⲭⲭ	Ⲭⲭⲭⲭ	ⅈⲭⲭⅈⅎ	ⲭⲭ	ⲭⲭⲭ	Ⲭⅎ	Ⲭ	ⲭⲭ	ⅈⅉ	צץ	ş
ⲭⲭⲭⲭ	ⲭⲭⅈⲭ	ⅈⲭ	ⅈⲭⲭ	ⲟⲭ	ⅈⲭⅈⲭ	ⲭⲃ	ⲭ	ⲭ	⅄	ק	q
ⅉⅉⅉ	ⅉⅉⅉ	ⅉ,ı	ⅉⅉⅉ	ⅉⅉ	ⅉⅉⅉ	⅄ⅉⅉ	⅂⅂	⅂	⅂	ר	r
ⲱⲱ	ⲱⲱⲱⲱ	ⲱⲱ	ⲱⲱⲱⲱ	ⲱⲱ	Ⅴ⅄Ⅴ	Ⅴ⅄	⅄⅄	ⱳⱳ	ⲧ	ש	sh
ⲭ	ƀƀⲭⲭ	ƀⅈ	ⅈⅈⅈ	ⲭⲭ	ⅎⅎ ƀ ⅎ	ⅉⅉⅉ	ⅉⅉ	ת	ת	ת	t

From Davies-Mitchell, *Student's Hebrew Lexicon*. See also article on WRITING.

technical term not found elsewhere in the NT; but other writings coming from Rome and the West have this same term (cf. 1 Clement 1:3; 21:6; Shepherd of Hermas 2, 2:6; 9:7 [proēgoumenoi]). Their first leaders seem to have died (13:7), while their present leaders are continually engaged in the task of watching over the flock (13:17). To these the writer sends greetings (13:24).

An outline shows the centrality of Jesus Christ in the Book of Hebrews.

I. **Prologue: Course and Climax of Divine Revelation (1:1-3)**

II. **Preeminence of Christ (1:4-4:13)**
   A. Superiority of Christ to angels (1:4-14)
   B. Warning: Peril of indifference to these truths (2:1-4)
   C. Reason Christ became human (2:5-18)
   D. Superiority of Christ's position to that of Moses (3:1-6)
   E. Warning: Unbelief's temporal and eternal effects (3:7-4:13)

III. **Priesthood of Christ (4:14-10:18)**
   A. Importance of his priesthood for a believer's conduct (4:14-16)
   B. Qualifications of a high priest (5:1-10)
   C. Warning: Conquering immaturity and apostasy only by faith, longsuffering, and hope (5:11-6:20a)
   D. Melchizedek's eternal successor (6:20b-7:28)
   E. Heavenly sanctuary and new covenant (8:1-13)
   F. Priestly service under the old covenant and the new (9:1-28)
   G. Inadequacy of the sacrifices under the law contrasted with the efficacy and finality of Christ's sacrifice (10:1-18)

IV. **Perseverance of Christians (10:19-12:29)**
   A. Attitudes to be sought and attitudes to be shunned (10:19-39)
   B. Faith in action—illustrious examples from the past (11:1-40)
   C. Incentives for action in the present scene and in the future goal (12:1-29)

V. **Postscript: Exhortations, Personal Concerns, Benediction (13:1-25)**

This letter has much to say about Christ. He is fully God and fully man. He is active in creation. The atonement of Christ, as both priest and sacrificial victim, is developed in detail. In the role of a priest, he is a leader and guide. He also is the revealer of God. Great depth is achieved in all of these teachings about Christ's person and work.

The old and new covenants are compared and reasons for the superiority of the new or eternal covenant are given.

The doctrine of sin in Hebrews focuses attention on unbelief and the failure to go on with God to the eternal city.

Shadow and reality are carefully contrasted. Heaven is the scene of reality. Earth is concerned with both shadow and reality. Christ is the bridge between the temporary and the eternal.

The people of God are looked on as migrating from a transitory setting to an abiding city. This migration involves God's Word; the matter of testing, discipline, or punishment; faithfulness; and God's activity in sanctifying or making holy. The Christian life is developed in the framework of this heavenly pilgrimage.

HEBRON (hē'brŏn, Heb. *hevrôn, league, confederacy*). 1. One of the oldest cities of the world, and one that has had several names at different times. Located 19 miles (32 km.) SW of Jerusalem on the main road to Beersheba, it has one of the longest records of continuous occupation. Hebron's original name was Kiriath Arba, i.e., "fourfold city" (Josh 14:15; 15:13).

Hebron is replete with historical interest. It was a camping place for Abram (Gen 13:18). The only land that Abram owned, though God had promised him Canaan (15:18-21), was the field of Machpelah near Mamre, which he purchased from the Hittites as a burial place for Sarah (23:17-20; Heb 11:8-10). In this cave Sarah and Abraham, later Isaac and Rebekah, then Jacob and Leah, were buried. Hebron and its environs were given to Caleb to conquer (Josh 14:6-15), and he did so (15:14-19); but later the city itself was given to the Kohathite Levites (1 Chron 6:55-56), though Caleb's descendants kept the suburban fields and villages. When David was king over Judah, but not yet over all Israel, his capital city was Hebron for seven and a half years. There the elders of Israel anointed him king over all Israel (2 Sam 5:3-5). Later he moved the capital to Jerusalem. When Absalom rebelled against his father, he made Hebron his headquarters and there prepared his coup d'etat (15:7-12).

General view of Hebron. The mosque in the center is built over the Cave of Machpelah, traditional burial place of Abraham and Sarah. Courtesy Ecole Biblique et Archéologique Française, Jerusalem

2. Third son of Kohath, and so an uncle of Moses, Aaron, and Miriam (Exod 6:18). His descendants, 1,700 men of valor in the days of David, had the responsibility for the Lord's business and for the service of the king west of the Jordan (1 Chron 26:30).
3. A town in Asher (Josh 19:28 KJV). ASV, NASB, and RSV, as well as most Hebrew MSS, have "Ebron," but "Abdon" (21:30, copied in 1 Chron 6:74) is found in JB and NIV.
4. A descendant of Caleb, son of Hezron, son of Perez, son of Judah (1 Chron 2:42–43), not to be confused with Caleb, the good spy, who was a distant cousin.

HEDGE Loose stone walls without mortar, or cut thorn branches or thorny bushes, common as "hedges" and "fences" in Palestine. The word can be translated "fence," "wall," or "hedge." The use of a hedge about a vine or tree was mainly for its protection (Ps 80:12). Figuratively, prophets should make up a hedge for the people's protection (Ezek 13:5), and God is pictured as doing so for his people (Mark 12:1). The very poor live in highways and hedges (Luke 14:23).

HEGAI, HEGE (hĕg'ā-ī, hē'gē). The eunuch employed by Xerxes (KJV Ahasuerus) as keeper of the women in the king's harem (Esth 2:3, 8, 15). Some think that "hegai" is not a proper name but means "eunuch."

HEIFER (See ANIMALS)

HEIFER, RED (See ANIMALS)

HEIR (See INHERITANCE)

HELDAI (hĕl'dā-ī). **1.** An army captain over 24,000 men under David (1 Chron 27:15). Probably the same as Heled (11:30) and as Heleb (2 Sam 23:29). **2.** One of three noble Jews who brought gold and silver from Babylon to make a crown for the high priest (Zech 6:9–15). The name is Helem in 6:14 in KJV (cf. NIV footnote).

HELEM (hē'lĕm, *health*). **1.** A man of the tribe of Asher (1 Chron 7:35), called Hotham in verse 32. **2.** An ambassador, mentioned only in Zechariah 6:14, but also certainly the same person as Heldai in Zechariah 6:10 (so NIV).

HELEZ (hē'lĕz). **1.** A man of Judah, of the family of Hezron, but also of Egyptian descent (1 Chron 2:39). **2.** One of David's mighty leaders, called a Paltite (2 Sam 23:26) and a Pelonite (1 Chron 11:27); an Ephraimite (27:10).

HELI (hē'lī, Heb. *'ēlî*). Either (1) the father of Joseph, the husband of Mary, or (2) the father of Mary, the mother of Jesus (Luke 3:23). See also GENEALOGY OF JESUS CHRIST.

HELIOPOLIS (hē-lĭ-ŏp'ō-lĭs, Heb. 'ôn, Gr. *Heliopolis, city of the sun*). A city near the south end of the Nile delta, the site of a temple to the sun built by Amenophis I. It is called "On" in most modern versions of Scripture. It was a very old and holy city, with a learned school of priests. Joseph's father-in-law belonged to the priests of the sun temple (Gen 41:45; 46:20). See also ON.

HELKATH (hěl'kăth, Heb. *helqath, a field*). A town on the southern border of the tribe of Asher (Josh 19:25) that was given to the Gershonite Levites (21:31). It was later called Hukok (1 Chron 6:75).

HELL The real existence of hell is irrefutably taught in Scripture as both a *place* of the wicked dead and a *condition* of retribution for the unredeemed (e.g., Ezek 3:18; Dan 12:2). Sheol, which is in one sense the undifferentiated place of all the dead (cf. Job 3:13–22), is in another sense the special doom of the wicked (Ps 49:14). It is necessary to follow the NIV footnotes in such references, for if KJV was inaccurate in translating Sheol as "hell" (e.g., Ps 9:17), NIV is equally inaccurate in formalizing it as "the grave."

The *nature* of hell is indicated by the repeated reference to eternal punishment (Matt 25:46), eternal fire (18:8, Jude 7), everlasting chains (Jude 6), the pit of the Abyss (Rev 9:2, 11), outer darkness (Matt 8:12), the wrath of God (Rom 2:5), second death (Rev 21:8), eternal destruction from the face of God (2 Thess 1:9), and eternal sin (Mark 3:29).

The *duration* is explicitly indicated in the NT. The word "eternal" (*aiōnios*) is derived from the verb *aiōn*, signifying an "age" or "duration." Scripture speaks of two *aeons*, or ages: the present age and the age to come (Matt 12:32; Mark 10:30; Luke 18:30; Eph 1:21). The present age—this world—is always contrasted with the age to come as temporal, while the future age will be endless. As the everlasting life of the believer is to be endless, just so the retributive aspect of hell refers to the future infinite age. In every reference in which *aiōnios* applies to the future punishment of the wicked, it indisputably denotes endless duration (Matt 18:8; 25:41, 46; Mark 3:29; 2 Thess 1:9; Heb 6:2; Jude 7).

Three basic ideas are associated with the concept of hell: absence of righteousness (Mark 3:29), separation from God (John 3:36), and judgment (Matt 8:12; 25:31–46).

HELLENISTS (See GRECIA, GRECIANS)

HELMET (See ARMS AND ARMOR)

HELPMEET Now often used as one word, meaning a helper (so NIV), generally a wife; but in Genesis 2:18 (KJV) it is two words. "I will make him a help meet for him," i.e., a helper suitable for or complementing him.

HELPS The NT lists "gifts" that God has given to his church (Rom 12:6–8; 1 Cor 12:7–11, 28–31; Eph 4:11–12). "Helps" are mentioned only once (1 Cor 12:28), and the Greek word *antilēmpseis* occurs only there. It means protector or assistant and probably refers to the ability to perform helpful works in a gracious manner.

HEMAM (See HOMAM)

HEMAN (hē'măn, Heb. *hêmān, faithful*). 1. A grandson of Judah through Zerah (1 Chron 2:6) and listed as one of the most notable wise men. 2. The first of three Levites David appointed to lead music (6:33). His fourteen sons and three daughters were in the choir (25:5–6). 3. Psalm 88 is attributed to Heman the Ezrahite, and if this means "Zerahite," as many think, he may be the same as no. 1 above.

HEMATH (See HAMATH; HAMMATH)

HEMLOCK (See PLANTS)

HEM OF A GARMENT Fringes or tassels, with a blue thread in each, on the borders of the Jewish outer garment (Num 15:38–39; Matt 9:20–21; 14:36). The word "hem" (Exod 28:33–34; 39:24–26) is translated "skirt" in ASV.

HEN (Heb. *hēn, favor*). 1. A son of Zephaniah (Zech 6:14). 2. See BIRDS.

HENA (hēn'à, Heb. *hēna'*). A city on the south bank of the Euphrates, about 180 miles (300 km.) NW of ancient Babylon. It was mentioned by Rabshakeh, along with four other cities whose gods could not save them from destruction by Sennacherib, as a proof that the Lord could not save Jerusalem (2 Kings 18:34; 19:13; Isa 37:13).

HENADAD (hěn'à-dăd, *favor of Hadad*). Head of a family of Levites who helped Zerubbabel (Ezra 3:9) and who in the next century helped Nehemiah in rebuilding the wall of Jerusalem (Neh 3:18, 24).

HENNA (See PLANTS)

HENOCH (See HANOCH)

HEPHER (hē'fēr, *pit, well*). 1. Head of the family of the Hepherites (Num 26:32). His son Zelophehad had five daughters who were commanded to marry within their tribe so as not to cause any of the tribal property of Manasseh to be deeded to another tribe (27:1–8; 36:1–9). **2.** A son of Ashhur, the "father" of Tekoa (1 Chron 4:5–6). **3.** One of David's mighty men (11:36). **4.** A royal city in Canaan that Joshua conquered (Josh 12:17). The land of Hepher (1 Kings 4:10) was SW of Jerusalem.

HEPHZIBAH (hĕf'zĭ-bà, Heb. *hephtsî-vâh, my delight is in her*). **1.** Wife of King Hezekiah (2 Kings 21:1) and mother of Manasseh. **2.** A symbolical name given to Zion (Isa 62:4).

HERB (See PLANTS)

HERD The herds consisted of the larger animals, as contrasted with the flocks of sheep, goats, etc. The cattle were used in plowing and threshing and for sacrifice but were not commonly fattened for food (though in contrast, see Ezek 39:18).

HERDSMAN (See OCCUPATIONS AND PROFESSIONS)

HERES (hē'rēz, *sun*). **1.** A district around Aijalon from which the Amorites were not expelled (Judg 1:35). **2.** A place east of the Jordan from which Gideon returned after his defeat of Zebah and Zalmunna (8:13). **3.** An Egyptian city (Isa 19:18).

HERESY (hâr'ĕ-sē, Gr. *hairēsis, sect, heretical group or opinion*, from *haireō, to choose*). A doctrine or group considered contrary to correct doctrine—from the Jewish (Acts 24:14; cf. 28:22) or Christian (2 Peter 2:1) perspective.

HERMES (hûr'mēz, Gr. *Hermēs*). **1.** One of the Greek mythological gods, a messenger of the gods (Acts 14:12); the Romans called him "Mercury" (as in ASV, KJV, and NEB). **2.** One to whom Paul sends greetings (Rom 16:14).

HERMON (Heb. *hermôn, sacred mountain*). The mountain that marks the southern terminus of the Anti-Lebanon range. A line drawn from Damascus to Tyre will pass through Mt. Hermon at its middle point and will practically coincide with the northern boundary of Palestine. The ridge of Hermon is about 20 miles (33 km.) long. It has three peaks, two of them rising over 9,000 feet (2,813 m.). Hermon has had several names: the ancient Amorites called it "Shenir" or "Senir" (Deut 3:9; cf. Ps 29:6; Ezek 27:5, where it is called a source of fir trees for Tyre); the Sidonians called it "Sirion" (Deut 3:9, though Ps 29:6 would apparently separate them); and the Arabs call it "Jebel-esh-Sheikh" or "Mountain of the Old Man,"

perhaps because of its white head, but more likely because of its dignity.

The Lord's transfiguration almost certainly occurred on its slopes, for he was at Caesarea Philippi, just south of the mountain, only a week before. Hermon is once called "Sion" (Deut 4:48; NIV "Siyon").

The three Herodian towers, north of Herod's palace (from left to right—Phasael, Hippicus, and Mariamne), as seen in the scale model of Jerusalem in A.D. 66–70, located at the Holyland Hotel, Jerusalem.
Courtesy Zev Radovan

HEROD (hĕr'ŭd). **1.** Herod the Great. When the Roman ruler Pompey organized the East in 63 B.C., he appointed Hyrcanus, the second person of that name, to be the high-priestly ruler over Galilee, Samaria, Judea, and Perea. Antipater, an Idumean, was Hyrcanus' senior officer. Gabinius modified Pompey's arrangement in 57 by reducing Hyrcanus' authority and dividing the ethnarchy into autonomous communities. Notable services rendered at Alexandria to Julius Caesar in 48 led to the restoration of Hyrcanus' authority and the appointment (in 47) of Antipater to the procuratorship of Judea. Antipater persuaded the now-aged Hyrcanus to appoint Phasael, Antipater's eldest son, to the prefecture of Jerusalem, and Herod, his second son, to the governorship of Galilee.

When Antipater was murdered in 43 B.C., his two sons succeeded to his position in Hyrcanus' court—the year after Julius Caesar's assassination. The Parthians penetrated Palestine, carried off Hyrcanus, and drove Phasael, also a captive, to suicide. Herod eluded both military action and Parthian treachery. He won the support of Octavian and Antony—by charm, daring, political acumen, and consummate diplomacy.

Two years of tireless activity (39–37 B.C.) made him, by age 36, the master of his inheritance. He was a ruthless fighter, a cunning negotiator, a subtle diplomat, and an opportunist. For 34 years he governed subjects who hated him.

In 30 B.C. Herod succeeded in retaining the favor of Octavian, shared though that favor had been with the defeated rival Antony. He was confirmed in his kingdom, and for the rest of his life he never departed from the policy of supporting the emperor and in all ways promoting his honor. The restored town of Samaria was called Sebaste, the Greek rendering of Augustus; Caesarea was built to form a harbor on the difficult open coast of Palestine, providing Rome a base on the edge of a turbulent province and forming a center of Caesar-worship in the land of the nationalistic and monotheistic Jews.

Herod followed a policy of Hellenization, establishing games at Jerusalem and adorning many of the Hellenistic cities of his domain. At the same time he sought to reconcile the Jews, who hated his pro-Roman and Hellenizing policies and who never forgave him for his Edomite blood. During the great famine of 25 B.C. in Judea and Samaria, Herod spared no trouble or private expense to import Egyptian corn. In the 18th year of his reign (20) he began to build the great Jerusalem temple, which was 46 years under construction (John 2:20). He was married to Mariamne, the heiress of the Hasmonean house. He built up a nobility of service, drawing on both Jews and Greeks. He encouraged the political party of the Herodians (Mark 3:6; 12:13), whose policy seems to have been the support of the royal house and a Hellenized society.

The king's sister Salome and his son Antipater by Doris, his first consort, seem to have been in league against Mariamne, his favorite wife. Mariamne was put to death in 29 B.C. and her two sons, Alexander and Aristobulus, in 7 B.C. . Antipater himself was put to death by Herod in the last days of Herod's reign. Herod died in 4 B.C., but not before the murder of the innocent babies of Bethlehem (Matt 2:16-18).

2. Archelaus. Herod's will divided the kingdom. Archelaus, son of Malthace, a Samaritan woman, took Judea and Idumea—by far the choicest share. Herod Antipas, of the same mother, received Galilee and Perea; and Philip, son of a Jewess named Cleopatra, took Iturea, Trachonitis, and associated districts in the northeast. Archelaus, who inherited his father's vices without his ability, took the title of king and violently put down

the disorders that broke out in Jerusalem (cf. Matt 2:22-23).

Archelaus went to Rome to secure from Augustus confirmation of his position before the situation in Palestine could be presented in too lurid a light by his enemies. Archelaus' petition was opposed in person by Herod Antipas and by a Jewish embassy. Somewhat surprisingly, Augustus declared in favor of Archelaus, though he denied him the royal title, providing the background for the Parable of the Pounds (Luke 19:11-27).

3. Herod Antipas (the word is an abbreviation for Antipater). "That fox" (Luke 13:32) has reference to his cunning, his subtle diplomacy, and his astute management of a difficult situation—qualities that enabled Antipas to retain his puppet position and petty royal power until A.D. 39. His half-brother Philip (not the tetrarch of Iturea) was the son of an unnamed wife of Herod I. As the daughter of Aristobulus, son of Herod I and Mariamne, Herodias was Philip's niece as well as his wife. They lived quietly in Rome, and it was here that Antipas met Herodias.

Herod came home to find a troublesome frontier war on his lands. He celebrated his birthday and had John the Baptist executed (Mark 6:14-29) at the stronghold of Machaerus. The crime so dramatically contrived was the final turning point in Herod's life. Until then there had been some faint aspiration for good (6:20). Emperor Caligula deposed Antipas on suspicion of treason, a charge leveled by Antipas' nephew, Herod Agrippa I.

4. Philip, tetrarch of Iturea. Salome—Herodias' daughter, the dancer of the Machaerus feast—married her uncle Philip, tetrarch of Iturea, about 30. Philip seems to have been the best of Herod's three surviving sons. He beautified the town of Caesarea Philippi and marked his continuation of the Herodian pro-Roman policy by changing the name of the northern Bethsaida to Julias, after Augustus' unfortunate daughter.

5. Herod Agrippa I. The grandson of Herod I, son of Aristobulus and brother of Herodias, he had been brought up in Rome under the protection of Tiberius' favorite son, Drusus. He had all the Herodian charm and diplomatic subtlety, and in A.D. 37, on Caligula's succession as emperor, Herod Agrippa was granted Philip's realm. Galilee and Perea were added when Antipas and Herodias were exiled. The malicious word in Rome had paid rich dividends. When Caligula was assassinated in 41, Agrippa remained in

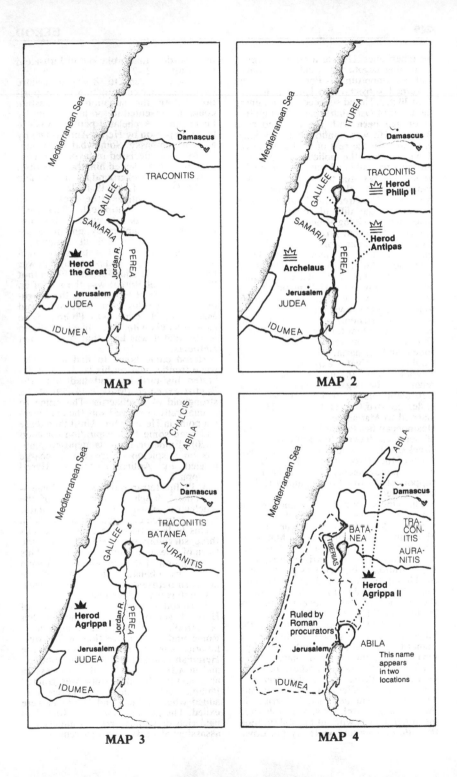

MAP 1

MAP 2

MAP 3

MAP 4

House of Herod

2nd Generation (Map 2)

1st Generation (Map 1)

♔ **Herod the Great** — King of Judea, Galilee, Iturea, Traconitis (37–4 B.C.) Birth of Jesus (Mt 2:1–19; Lk 1:5)

♕ **Herod Philip II** *(MOTHER: CLEOPATRA)* Tetrarch of Iturea and Traconitis (4 B.C.–A.D. 34) (Lk 3:1)

♕ **Archelaus** *(MOTHER: MALTHACE)* Governor of Judea, Idumea and Samaria (4 B.C.–A.D. 6) When Mary and Joseph left Egypt, they avoided Judea and settled in Nazareth (Mt 2:19–23)

Aristobulus *(MOTHER: MARIAMNE)* (d. 10 B.C.) Not mentioned in the Bible.

♕ **Herod Antipas** *(MOTHER: MALTHACE)* Tetrarch of Galilee and Perea (4 B.C.–A.D. 39) (Lk 3:1) Second husband of Herodias. He put John the Baptist to death (Mt 14:1–12; Mk 6:14–29); Pilate sent Jesus to him (Lk 23:7–12)

Herod Philip I *(MOTHER: MARIAMNE)* He did not rule. First husband of Herodias (Mt 14:3; Mk 6:17) (d.c. A.D. 34)

Antipater *(MOTHER: DORIS)*

3rd Generation (Map 3)

Herod of Chalcis

♔ **Herod Agrippa I** King of Judea (A.D. 37–44) Killed James; put Peter into prison. Struck down by an angel (Ac 12:1–24)

HERODIAS Married her uncle Herod Philip I, and then a second uncle, Herod Antipas (Mt 14:3; Mk 6:17)

4th Generation (Map 4)

Felix (Governor of Judea)

DRUSILLA Married Felix, governor of Judea A.D. 52–59; Felix tried Paul (Ac 24:24)

♔ **Herod Agrippa II** King of Judea; Paul made a legal defense before him (Ac 25:13–26:32)

BERNICE With her brother at the time of Paul's defense (Ac 25:13)

SALOME Daughter of Herodias and Herod Philip I. Danced for the head of John the Baptist (Mt 14:1–12; Mk 6:14–29)

KEY:

♔ King

♕ Tetrarch

BERNICE denotes women

Antipater bloodline of Herod the Great

Felix non-bloodline

- - - Denotes Herodias's marriage to Herod Antipas

········ Denotes Herodias's marriage to Herod Philip I and daughter of that marriage

the favor of Claudius, who turned over to Agrippa's control the whole area of his grandfather's kingdom. He succeeded to such power, moreover, with the consent and the favor of the Jews. Agrippa died in 44 (Acts 12:20–23).

6. Herod Agrippa II. Agrippa left a teen-age son, whom Claudius made king of Chalcis in A.D. 48. In 53 the territory of Philip the tetrarch and Lysanias were added to this realm, together with an area on the western side of Galilee, including Tiberias. The appointment carried the title of king, so in 53 Agrippa became Agrippa II, last of the Herodian line. As Festus' guest, he heard the defense of Paul (Acts 25). After the fashion of Eastern monarchies, Agrippa was married to his sister Bernice. Another sister was the wife of Antonius Felix, the procurator of Judea, whom Festus had succeeded.

Agrippa lived on in the garrison town of Caesarea to see the vast ruin and destruction of his country in the Great Revolt of 66 to 70. So ended the Herods, an astonishingly able family, whose pro-Roman policy went far to postpone the inevitable clash between Rome and the Jews, and played, in consequence, an unwitting but significant part in holding the peace during the formative years of the Christian church in Palestine.

HERODIANS (hĕ-rō'dĭ-ănz, Gr. *Hērōdianoi*). A party (Matt 22:16; Mark 3:6; 12:13) who joined with the Pharisees to oppose Jesus. It appears that they were neither a religious sect nor a political party, but Jews who supported the dynasty of Herod and therefore the rule of Rome.

HERODIAS (hĕ-rō'dĭ-ăs, Gr. *Hērōdias*). A wicked granddaughter of Herod the Great who married her uncle Philip; but his brother Antipas saw her at Rome, desired her, and married her. When John the Baptist rebuked Herod Antipas (Luke 3:19–20), John was imprisoned (Matt 14:3–12; Mark 6:14–29). This did not satisfy Herodias, so by a sordid scheme she secured his death. Later Antipas was banished to Spain. Herodias accompanied him and died there.

HERON (See BIRDS)

HESHBON (hĕsh'bŏn, Heb. *heshbôn*, *reckoning*). An ancient city of the Moabites lying nearly 20 miles (33 km.) west of the Jordan. Sihon, king of the Amorites in the days of Moses, took this and the surrounding country from the Moabites, and Israel in turn took it from Sihon (Num 21:21–31). The tribe of Reuben asked Moses for this land because it was suitable for cattle, and Moses granted their request; so, 300 years later (1260 B.C.), when the Ammonites made war against Israel, Jephthah taunted them (Judg 11:12–28) with the fact that their god Chemosh was not able to stand against Israel for all those centuries. Heshbon and its suburbs were given to the Levites (1 Chron 6:81) but later were retaken by Moab (Isa 15:4; 16:8–9). When Jeremiah, a century later, pronounced his dooms, Heshbon was still standing, though soon to be judged by the Lord (Jer 48:2–35; 49:3).

HETH (Heb. *hēth*). Great-grandson of Noah through Ham and Canaan (Gen 10:15) and progenitor of the great Hittite people, sometimes called "sons" and "daughters" of Heth (23:3; 27:46). See also HITTITES.

HEXATEUCH (hĕk'sà-tūk). "The six-volumed book," a term invented to include the Book of Joshua with the Pentateuch in a literary unit, on the assumption that its component parts were combined by a common editor.

HEZEKIAH (hĕz'ē-kī'à, Heb. *hizqîyâh*, *Jehovah has strengthened*). **1.** King of Judah from c. 724 to 695 B.C. The record of his life is found in 2 Kings 18–20, 2 Chronicles 29–32, and Isaiah 36–39. He lived in one of the great periods of human history. The first Olympiad from which the Greeks dated their history occurred in 776; Rome was reputed to have been founded in 753; Assyria, though approaching its end, was still a mighty power; and Egypt, though weak, was still strong enough to oppose Assyria.

For a while Hezekiah was associated in the government with his father, but because of his father's incapacitation he was made active ruler. He began his reign, at the age of 25, in troubled and threatening times. Some counseled him to side with Egypt against Assyria; others favored surrender to Assyria to save themselves from Egypt. Isaiah warned against trusting in foreign alliances. One of the first acts of Hezekiah was the cleansing and reopening of the temple, which his father had left closed and desecrated. After this was accomplished, the Passover feast was celebrated (2 Chron 30). The idolatrous altars and high places were destroyed.

From the fourth to the sixth year of Hezekiah's reign the northern kingdom was in trouble. Sargon finally destroyed

Samaria and deported the people to Assyria. Hezekiah became ill, probably from a carbuncle, and almost died; but God granted him a 15-year extension of life (2 Kings 20:1–11). After Hezekiah's recovery, Merodach-Baladan of Babylon sent an embassy supposedly to congratulate him but actually to persuade him to join a secret confederacy against the Assyrian power. The Lord had pledged he would deliver Jerusalem from the Assyrians (Isa 38:6–7). Instead of trusting in God's promise Hezekiah listened to the ambassadors' proposal of a military alliance. When Isaiah learned that Hezekiah had entertained the ambassadors and their suggestion, he knew that all was over for Judah and immediately (39:5–7) predicted the Babylonian captivity. Hezekiah paid a high price for dabbling in rebellion. Assyria compelled Judah to pay heavy tribute but later decided to destroy Jerusalem. But God saved the city by sending a sudden plague that in one night killed 185,000 soldiers. After Hezekiah's death, his son Manasseh succeeded him (2 Kings 20:21).
2. One of the covenanters with Nehemiah (Neh 10:17; KJV Hizkijah).

HEZIR (hē'zir, *swine*). 1. A priest in the 17th course of Aaronic priests (1 Chron 24:15). 2. One of the covenanters with Nehemiah (Neh 10:20).

HEZRON (hĕz'rŏn, *enclosure*). 1. A grandson of Judah through Perez (Gen 46:12). 2. A son of Reuben (46:9). 3. A place on the southern border of Judah (Josh 15:3). See also HAZOR (no. 3), which is the same place.

HIDDAI (hĭd'ā-ī). One of David's heroes (2 Sam 23:30), the same as Hurai (1 Chron 11:32).

HIDDEKEL (See TIGRIS)

HIEL (hī'ĕl, Heb. *hî 'ēl*, probably, *God liveth*). A man of Bethel during the reign of Ahab who rebuilt Jericho, bringing on himself and his sons the curse that Joshua had pronounced 650 years earlier (1 Kings 16:34; cf. Josh 6:26).

HIERAPOLIS (hī'ĕr-ăp'ō-lĭs, Gr. *Hierapolis, sacred city*). A city in the territory of ancient Phrygia, later a part of the Roman province of Asia (Col 4:13). It was the seat of worship of important deities. Tradition connects the apostle Philip with the church; and Papias, notable disciple of John the beloved, was born there.

HIEROGLYPHICS (See WRITING)

The tunnel constructed by King Hezekiah (2 Kings 20:20) that connected the Gihon Spring with the pool of Siloam, so that Jerusalem's water supply would not be imperiled by the impending siege by Sennacherib's army. Courtesy Zev Radovan

HIGGAION (hĭ-gā'yŏn, Heb. *higgāyôn*). A musical term in Psalm 9:16, probably referring to the "solemn sound" (so 92:3 KJV) of harp music that was to be played at that point.

HIGH PLACES (Heb. *bāmâh, rāmâh, elevation*). From earliest times people have tended to choose high places for their worship, whether of the true God or of the false gods that man has invented. The worshipers chose an exposed site where the "god" was likely to see what they were doing and to perform there some act comparable to what they wished their god to do for them (see also BAAL). In Canaan the high places had become the scenes of orgies and human sacrifice connected with the idolatrous worship of these imaginary gods; and so when Israel entered the Promised Land they were told to destroy all high places (Num 33:52). Israel's failure to destroy them resulted in idolatry.
Before Solomon built the temple, there was a mixed condition of worship. The

The "Great High Place" at Petra in Transjordan. The site is marked by two altars and a rectangular court, all hewn out of solid rock. It probably dates to the Nabatean period (second century B.C. to second century A.D.) and is built on an earlier Edomite site. Courtesy Garo Nalbandian

Tent of Meeting (i.e., the tabernacle) with most of its furniture was at the high place at Gibeon though David had brought the ark to Jerusalem. Solomon offered sacrifices there and God heard his prayer, granting him surpassing wisdom (2 Chron 1:1–13). Later some godly kings, including Hezekiah (31:1), destroyed the high places, but others, including Manasseh, relapsed and rebuilt them (33:3). Through the godliness of Josiah, especially after he had heard the Law read (2 Kings 22:8–20), the judgment was delayed until after his death. God's attitude toward the godly kings depended largely on their attitude toward the high places.

HIGH PRIEST (See PRIEST)

HILEN (hī′lĕn). A city of Judah assigned to the Levites (1 Chron 6:58). It is also spelled Holon (Josh 15:51; 21:15).

HILKIAH (hĭl-kī′à, Heb. *hilqîyâh, the portion of Jehovah*). 1. The father of Eliakim who was manager of Hezekiah's household (2 Kings 18:18). 2. A Merarite Levite (1 Chron 6:45). 3. Another Merarite, doorkeeper in David's time (26:11). 4. The high priest who found the Book of the Law (perhaps Deuteronomy) while cleaning the temple and sent it to Josiah (2 Kings 22; 2 Chron 34). 5. A priest who returned to Jerusalem with Zerubbabel, 536 B.C. (Neh 12:7). 6. The father of Jeremiah. He lived at Anathoth (Jer 1:1). 7. The father of Gemariah (29:3), a priest who stood with Ezra at the Bible reading (Neh 8:4).

HILL COUNTRY (Heb. *giv′âh, har, ʿōphel*). A term applied to any region of

hills and valleys that could not quite be called mountainous. In Scripture it generally applies to the higher part of Judea (Luke 1:39, 65) and in the OT to the southern part of Lebanon east of Sidon (Josh 13:6; NIV "mountain region").

HIN (See WEIGHTS AND MEASURES)

HIND (See ANIMALS)

HINGE A contrivance that enables a movable part such as a door or window to swing in its place, often used figuratively for something of prime importance. Ancient heavy doors swung on "ball and socket" joints. KJV, MLB, MOF, and NASB have "hinges" in 1 Kings 7:50; NIV and RSV have "sockets"; and NEB has "panels."

HINNOM, VALLEY OF More properly, "the valley of the son of Hinnom," running southward from the Jaffa Gate at the west side of Jerusalem, then turning eastward and running south of the city until it joined the valley of the Kidron. It was a part of the boundary between Judah on the south (Josh 15:8) and Benjamin on the north (18:16). It seems to have been a dumping ground and a place for burning. Topheth was here (2 Kings 23:10), where human sacrifices had been offered to Molech, and so it was later to be called "the Valley of Slaughter" (Jer 19:6). The Hebrew name, transliterated into Greek as *geenna* (or *gehenna*), becomes the word for "hell." Jesus uses it in referring to the final destination of the wicked; and probably "the fiery lake of burning sulfur" (Rev 19:20; 20:10, 14–15; 21:8) is a description of the same terrible place. See also GEHENNA.

HIP AND THIGH Used only in Judges 15:8 (KJV, MLB, NEB, RSV) of Samson's thoroughness in killing Philistines (NIV "viciously").

HIPPOPOTAMUS (See ANIMALS)

HIRAM (hī′răm, Heb. *hîrām,* sometimes also *hûrām* and *hîrôm*). 1. King of Tyre in the reigns of David and Solomon, with both of whom he was on friendly terms. His father was Abibaal. Hiram, almost at the beginning of his reign, sent messengers to David with cedar logs, carpenters, and masons who built David a house (2 Sam 5:11).

Hiram, an admirer of David, sent an embassy to Solomon after David's death (1 Kings 5:1); and Solomon promptly took advantage of the situation and arranged for Hiram to send him cedar and fir timber from Lebanon. Solomon not only supplied Hiram with vast quantities of wheat and olive oil annually for food

(3:11), but he surrendered to Hiram 20 "towns" of Galilee (9:10–13). Hiram and Solomon built a navy and made expeditions from Ezion Geber at the head of the Gulf of Aqabah southward to Ophir, bringing back gold (9:28). They also had a "navy of Tarshish" (see NIV footnote) on the Mediterranean; this navy brought "gold, silver and ivory, and apes and baboons" (10:22). Hiram had a daughter who became one of Solomon's "seven hundred wives" (11:1, 3).
2. A worker in brass whom Solomon brought from Tyre to help build the temple (1 Kings 7:13–14, 40–45 JB, KJV, MLB, MOF, NASB, RSV; "Huram" in 2 Chron 2:13–14; 4:11–16). See also HURAM.

HIRELING A laborer who works for his wages. He was ordinarily to be paid at once (Deut 24:15; cf. Matt 20:1–6). But service might be for a longer time, as when Jacob worked seven years for each of his wives and six years for his flocks and herds (Gen 29:15–20, 27–28; 30:28–36). A hireling from outside Israel could not eat the Passover (Exod 12:45).

HITTITES (hĭt'ĭts, Heb. *hittîm*). With the Mesopotamians and Egyptians (2 Kings 7:6), they were one of the three great powers confronting early Israel. The biblical portrayals of Hittite dominance, once held to be unreliable, were first substantiated by discoveries at Carchemish on the Euphrates in 1871 and then by excavations at Khattusa (Boghaz-köy) in Turkey, 1906–7. Ten thousand tablets from this ancient Hittite capital served to confirm Joshua's description of the entire western Fertile Crescent as "all the Hittite country" (Josh 1:4).

The original Hittites, or "Hattians," sprang from Ham, through Canaan's second son Heth (Gen 10:15; 1 Chron 1:13). Scripture regularly lists "Hittites" among the peoples of Canaan (Gen 15:20; Exod 3:8, 17; Deut 7:1; 20:17). They were "the people of the land" (Gen 23:7), especially in the central hills (Num 13:29; Josh 11:3). At Hebron in 2029 B.C. Abraham purchased Machpelah from the Hittites (Gen 23:3–20; 49:29–32; 50:13); 60 years later, Esau married Hittite (or Hurrian-Hivite) wives (26:34; 36:2), to the distress of Rebekah (27:46). During the early 15th century, Egypt swept north to the Euphrates; and on Egyptian withdrawal, the conquering Hebrews under Joshua overwhelmed the Palestinian Hittites (1406–1400; Josh 9:1; 11:3). With Israel's conquest of Canaan, despite the Mosaic ban (Deut 20:17), Hittite unions became common (Judg 3:5–6); and from Solomon

to Ezra (1 Kings 11:1; Ezra 9:1) such intermarriage continued. Ezekiel thus condemned his people's morals and race by exclaiming, "Your mother was a Hittite and your father an Amorite" (Ezek 16:3, 45).

King Toi of Hamath, 1000 B.C., supported David (2 Sam 8:9–10); and Hittite warriors served among his heroes (1 Sam 26:6; 2 Sam 11:3; 23:39). Solomon reduced the Palestinian Hittites to bond service (1 Kings 9:20), but one of Ahab's major allies against Assyria at the battle of Qarqar in 853 was Irkhuleni of Hamath. The Hittite stronghold of Carchemish fell to the Assyrians only in 717 (cf. 2 Kings 19:13).

In the service of their depraved mother-goddess of fertility, "Artemis of the Ephesians" (Acts 19:24–35), the Hittites corrupted Israel (Ezek 16:44–45).

HIVITES (hī'vīts, Heb. *hiwwî*). One of the seven nations of the land of Canaan that the Lord delivered into the hand of Joshua (Josh 24:11). They are listed with the Canaanite descendants of Ham, Noah's youngest son (Gen 10). They seem to have been located in diverse places (34:2; Josh 9:1, 7; 11:3; 2 Chron 8:7) and to have been a peaceable, commercial people (Gen 34:21), though with Canaanite morals. Perhaps they were the same as the Horites.

HIZKIAH, HIZKIJAH (hĭz-kī'à, hĭz-kī'jà). 1. The great-great-grandfather of Zephaniah (Zeph 1:1). The spelling should be Hezekiah, as in NIV. 2. One of the covenants with Nehemiah (Neh 10:17). The spelling here also should be Hezekiah, as in NIV. 3. A son of Neariah, a member of the royal line after the Exile (1 Chron 3:23).

HOBAB (hō'băb, Heb. *hōvāv, beloved*). A person who is named only twice in the Bible. In Numbers 10:29 he is called "son of Reuel the Midianite, Moses' father-in-law"; this would seem to make him a brother of Moses' wife Zipporah (Exod 18:2) and thus Moses' brother-in-law. In Judges 4:11, most versions—e.g., KJV, JB, MLB, MOF, NASB, and RSV—speak of Hobab as the "father-in-law of Moses," while ASV, NEB, and NIV refer to him as "Moses' brother-in-law." The Hebrew word generally refers to one who gives his daughter in marriage. In any case, Moses pleaded with Hobab to accompany Israel; after refusing at first, evidently he finally consented (Num 10:29; Judg 1:16; 4:11).

HOBAIAH (hō-bā'yà, *Jehovah has hidden*). Ancestor of some priests in Zerubbabel's time (NIV, Ezra 2:61; Neh 7:63; "Habaiah" in other versions).

HODAVIAH, HODAIAH (hō'dà-vī'à, hōdā'yà). **1.** A son of Elioenai, a descendant of the royal line of Judah (1 Chron 3:24). **2.** A chief of the half-tribe of Manasseh, east of the Jordan (5:24). **3.** The son of Hassenuah, a Benjamite (9:7). **4.** A Levite, founder of the "line of Hodaviah" (Ezra 2:40). KJV, MLB, NASB, and RSV have "Hodevah" in Nehemiah 7:43 and "Judah" in Ezra 3:9 (NIV has "Hodaviah" in both).

HODEVAH (See HODAVIAH)

HODIAH (hō-dī'à). **1.** Either the sister of Naham (KJV, NEB) or the husband of the sister of Naham (ASV, NIV, RSV); in any case, a member of the tribe of Judah (1 Chron 4:19). **2.** A Levite of the time of Ezra and Nehemiah (Neh 8:7; 9:5; 10:10, 13). **3.** A chief of the people under Nehemiah (10:18).

HOGLAH (hŏg'là). One of the five daughters of Zelophehad, a Manassite. Their father had no sons, so a new law was made that permitted daughters to inherit, provided they did not marry outside the tribe (Num 26:33; 27:1–11; 36:1–12; Josh 17:3–4).

HOLINESS, HOLY Usually translations of words derived from a Hebrew root *qadash* and Greek *hag-*. The basic meaning of *qadash* is "separateness, withdrawal." Greek *hag-* is an equivalent of *qadash*, and its history is similar.

The words "holiness" and "holy" do not occur in Genesis, (but see Gen 28:16–17), but from Exodus 3:5 on, holiness is constantly stressed. God is "majestic in holiness" (Exod 15:11); holiness characterizes God's actions (Isa 52:10), his words and promises (Ps 105:42; Jer 23:9), his name (Lev 20:3; 1 Chron 29:16), and Spirit (Ps 51:11; Isa 63:10–11; see HOLY SPIRIT). Places are made holy by God's special presence: his dwelling in heaven (Deut 26:15), his manifestation on earth (Exod 3:5; Josh 5:15), the tabernacle (Exod 40:9), the temple (2 Chron 29:5, 7), Jerusalem (Isa 48:2), and Zion (Obad 17). Anything set apart for sacred uses was holy: the altars and other furniture of the tabernacle (Exod 29:37; 30:10, 29), animal sacrifices (Num 18:17), food (Lev 21:22), the tithe (27:30), firstfruits (19:24; 23:20), anything consecrated (Exod 28:38), and the anointing oil and incense (30:23–25, 34–38). Persons connected with holy places and holy services were holy: priests (Lev 21:1–6) and their garments (Exod 28:2, 4), Israel as a nation (Jer 2:3), Israel individually (Deut 33:3), and many things connected with Israel (1 Chron 16:29). Times given to worship were holy (Exod 12:16; 16:23; 20:8; Isa 58:13).

What in Isaiah 6:3 was a personal revelation to the prophet is proclaimed to all from heaven in Revelation 4:8, with power and glory. God is holy and true (Rev 6:10). In one of his prayers, Jesus addressed God in this way: "Holy Father" (John 17:11). God is holy and his people are to be holy (1 Peter 1:15, quoting Lev 19:2). Jesus' disciples are to pray that the name of God may be treated as holy (Matt 6:9; Luke 11:2). The holiness of Jesus Christ is specifically stressed (Mark 1:24; Luke 1:35; 4:34; John 10:36; Acts 3:14; 4:27, 30; cf. Isa 42:1–4 quoted in Matt 12:16–21; Heb 2:11; Rev 3:7).

The holiness of the church is developed in the NT. As in the OT, Jerusalem is holy (Matt 4:5; 27:53; Rev 11:2), so is the temple (Matt 24:15; Acts 6:13) and the new temple, the church, collectively (Eph 2:21–22) and individually (1 Cor 3:16–17). Stephen refers to Mt. Sinai as "holy ground" (Acts 7:33) and Peter to the Mt. of Transfiguration as "the holy mount" (2 Peter 1:18 KJV; NIV "sacred mountain"). The Scriptures are holy (Rom 1:2; 2 Tim 3:15). The law is holy (Rom 7:12). Since the earthly holy place, priests, cult apparatus, sacrifices, and services were holy, much more are the heavenly (Heb 8:5). The church is a holy nation (1 Peter 2:9). The argument of Romans 11:11–32 rests the holiness of Gentile Christians on their growing out of the root (11:16) of Jesse (15:12). Christ died for the church to make it holy (1 Cor 1:2; 6:11; Eph 5:26). The church as a whole, the local churches, and individual Christians are holy, "called . . . saints" (Rom 1:7; 1 Cor 1:2; 2 Cor 1:1; Eph 1:1; Phil 1:1; Col 1:2; "saints" being a translation of *hagioi*, holy). The life of the individual Christian is to be a living, holy sacrifice (Rom 12:1), not only through death (Phil 2:17), but through life itself (1:21–26). Holiness is equated with purity (Matt 5:8; 23:26; 1 Tim 1:5; 2 Tim 2:22; Titus 1:15; James 1:27), a purity that in Acts 18:6 and 20:26 is innocence. The means of purification is the truth of the Word of God (John 17:17). The "holy kiss," in the early churches, was a seal of holy fellowship (1 Cor 16:20; 2 Cor 13:12; 1 Thess 5:26). Holiness is prominent in Revelation from 3:7 to 22:11.

HOLON (hō'lŏn). **1.** A city in the hill country of Judah (Josh 15:51; 21:15) assigned to the Levites (called Hilen in 1 Chron 6:58); Khirbet Alin. **2.** A town probably in the Plain of Moab near Medeba (Jer 48:21).

HOLY GHOST (See HOLY SPIRIT)

HOLY OF HOLIES (See TABERNACLE)

HOLY PLACE (See TABERNACLE)

HOLY SPIRIT (Gr. *pneuma hagion;* in KJV of NT, Holy Ghost). The third person of the triune Godhead (Matt 28:19; 2 Cor 13:14).

There is a rich revelation of the Spirit of the Lord in the OT that is preparatory to the NT. The Spirit was active in creating the world (e.g., Gen 1:2; Pss 33:6; 104:30), animals (Isa 34:16), and man (Job 27:3; cf. Isa 42:5). Second, the Spirit is the agent in the providential work of God in the moral sphere, the areas of history and ethical relationships (Gen 6:3; 1 Sam 16:14; Ps 51:11; cf. Isa 4:4; 30:1; 63:14; Ezek 1:12, 20). Third, the Spirit is known in the OT as a personal endowment. He indwells the people of God as a whole (Hag 2:5), just as he was among them at the Exodus (Isa 63:11). He endowed certain people for special purposes (e.g., Bezalel, Exod 31:3; some judges, Judg 3:10; 6:34; 11:29; David, 1 Sam 16:13). There is also the constant endowment of individuals (Num 11:17, 29; 27:18; 1 Sam 16:13), especially those individuals who stood directly in the great messianic line (Isa 11:2; 42:1; 48:16; 61:1). The OT, indeed, looks forward to the messianic day as a time of special enjoyment of the Spirit of God (Isa 32:15; 44:3; 59:21; Ezek 36:27; 39:29; Joel 2:28-29), pointing to an unknown abundance. Fourth, the Spirit inspired the prophets (Num 11:29; 24:2; 1 Sam 10:6, 10; 2 Sam 23:2; 1 Kings 22:24; Neh 9:30; Hos 9:7; Joel 2:28-29; Mic 3:8; Zech 7:12).

The Spirit is wise (Isa 40:13; cf. 11:2; Dan 4:8-9, 18), vexed by sin and rebellion (Isa 63:10), and at rest when sin has been dealt with (Zech 6:8). He is holy (Ps 51:11; Isa 63:10) and good (Neh 9:20; Ps 143:10). The Spirit is the very presence of God himself in all the world (Ps 139:7; Isa 63:10, 14). The ascription of holiness (e.g., Ps 51:11) accords to the Spirit the character and personality of God.

His personal nature is shown by the things the Spirit does: he dwells with us (John 14:17), teaches and brings to remembrance (14:26), bears witness (15:26), convinces of sin (16:8), guides, speaks, declares (16:13, 15), inspires the Scriptures (Acts 1:16; 2 Peter 1:21), speaks to his servants (Acts 8:29), calls ministers (13:2), sends out workers (13:4), forbids certain actions (16:6-7), and intercedes (Rom 8:26). He has the attributes of personality: love (Rom 15:30), will (1 Cor 12:11), mind (Rom 8:27), thought, knowledge, words (1 Cor 2:10-13). The Holy Spirit can be treated as one may treat a human person: he can be lied to and tempted (Acts 5:3-4, 9), resisted (7:51), grieved (Eph 4:30), outraged (Heb 10:29 RSV), blasphemed against (Matt 12:31). The Holy Spirit is God, equated with the Father and the Son (Matt 28:19; 2 Cor 13:14). Jesus speaks of him as of his other self (John 14:16-17), whose presence with the disciples will be of greater advantage than his own (16:7). To have the Spirit of God is to have Christ (Rom 8:9-12). God is spirit (John 4:24) in essential nature, and the Father sends the Holy Spirit to live and work in people (14:26; 16:7).

The Hebrew and Greek words that are translated "spirit" are *rûach* and *pneuma,* both meaning literally "wind, breath." Both came to be used for the unseen reality of living beings, especially God and man. Therefore, breath and wind are symbols of the Holy Spirit (Gen 2:7; Job 32:8; 33:4; Ezek 37:9-10; John 20:22). Other symbols are the dove (Matt 3:16; Mark 1:10; Luke 3:22; John 1:32), oil (Luke 4:18; Acts 10:38; 1 John 2:20), fire for purification (Matt 3:11; Luke 3:16; Acts 2:3-4), living water (Isa 44:3; John 4:14; 7:37-39) and earnest or guarantee of all that God has in store for us (2 Cor 1:22; Eph 1:13-14).

In the Gospels, as in the OT, the Holy Spirit comes upon certain persons for special reasons: John the Baptist and his parents (Luke 1:15, 41, 67), Simeon (2:25-27), and Jesus as a man (Matt 1:18, 20; 3:16; 4:1; Mark 1:8, 10; Luke 1:35; 3:16, 22; 4:1, 14, 18; John 1:32-33). Jesus promises the Holy Spirit in a new way to those who believe in him (7:37-39; cf. 4:10-15; Luke 24:49; Acts 1:1-8). Jesus taught about the nature and work of the Holy Spirit (John 14:16, 26; 15:26; 16:7-15). Jesus "breathed on" the disciples (Thomas being absent) and said, "Receive the Holy Spirit" (John 20:22). This was not the complete endowment of the Holy Spirit that Jesus had taught and promised and that occurred at Pentecost, but it was provisional and enabled the disciples to persevere in prayer until the promised day.

At Pentecost a new phase of the revelation of God to people began (Acts 2). The Holy Spirit indwells believers (Rom 8:1-27; 1 Cor 6:19), gives gifts (12:4), and produces "the fruit of the Spirit" (Gal

5:22–23). Being "filled with the Spirit" (Eph 5:18) means that one experiences Christ living within (Rom 8:9–10). Teaching concerning the Holy Spirit has been both neglected and distorted, but the subject deserves careful attention as one reads the NT.

HOMAM (hō′măm). Seir's grandson (1 Chron 1:39). Genesis 36:22 has Hemam (JB, KJV, NASB, NEB), Heman (ASV, RSV), Homam (NIV).

HOMER (See WEIGHTS AND MEASURES)

HONEY (Heb. *devash*, Gr. *meli*, *honey*). Early regarded as among "the best products of the land" (Gen 43:11), it was found in clefts of the rocks (Deut 32:13; Ps 81:16) in the comb on the ground (1 Sam 14:25–43), and in a lion's carcass (Judg 14:8–18). Job 20:17 speaks of brooks of honey and butter, indicating abundance due to the domestication of bees. Canaan was "a land flowing with milk and honey" (Exod 3:8; Ezek 20:15), Assyria "a land of olive trees and honey" (2 Kings 18:32). Honey was a product of Palestine (Jer 41:8; Ezek 27:17) and became a common food (2 Sam 17:29) even in times of scarcity (Isa 7:15, 22). It was never part of a sacrifice, but it was a firstfruits offering (Lev 2:11; 2 Chron 31:5). Strained honey was kept in a jar or cruse (1 Kings 14:3). Honey is a recommended food, but in moderation (Prov 24:13; 25:16, 27; 27:7; Ezek 16:13, 19). Honey is a standard of comparison for pleasant things, good or bad (Prov 16:24; 5:3; Song of Songs 4:11; 5:1; Ezek 3:3; Rev 10:9). John the Baptist ate honey (Matt 3:4; Mark 1:6).

HOOD (See DRESS)

HOOK The translation of several Hebrew words: **1.** *'aghmôn*, "reed" (Job 41:2, KJV where a rope of rushes is meant; NIV "cord"). **2.** *Wāw*, "hook" or "peg" of gold or silver, used to support the hangings of the tabernacle (Exod 26:32, 37; 27:10, 17; 36:36, 38; 38:10–19, 28). **3.** *Ḥaḥ*, "hook, ring, fetter" (2 Kings 19:28; Isa 37:29; Ezek 29:4; 38:4). **4.** *Hakkâh*, "angle, hook, fishhook" (Job 41:1 RSV, NIV). **5.** *Tsinnâh*, "thorn, hook" (Amos 4:2). **6.** *Shephattayim*, "hook-shaped pegs, double hooks" (Ezek 40:43). **7.** *Fleshhook*, *mazlēgh*, probably a small pitchfork with two or three tines (Exod 27:3; RSV "forks," NIV "meat forks"). **8.** "Pruning hook," *mazemērôth*, a sickle-shaped knife for pruning vines. **9.** *Hôah*, "hook" (Job 41:2b RSV, NIV; KJV "thorn"). **10.** The Greek word, occurring only once in the NT, is *ankis-*

tron, "fishing hook" (Matt 17:27 KJV; NIV "line").

HOOPOE (See BIRDS)

HOPE A gift of the Holy Spirit that, with faith and love, is an essential characteristic of the Christian when prophecies, tongues, and knowledge pass away (1 Cor 13:8, 13). The Greek noun *elpis* and its related verb *elpizo*, usually rendered "hope," occur 54 and 31 times respectively in the NT. The biblical concept of hope is not mere expectation and desire, as in Greek literature, but includes confidence (Rom 15:13). Christ in you is the hope of glory (Col 1:27; cf. 1 Tim 1:1). All creation hopes for redemption (Rom 8:19–25 RSV). Christians have a "blessed hope—the glorious appearing of . . . Jesus Christ" (Titus 1:2; 2:13), which motivates purity (1 John 3:3). Hope is linked with faith (Heb 11:1). It depends on Jesus' resurrection (1 Cor 15:19). Hope is little spoken of in the Gospels, while Jesus was on earth, or in Revelation. The hope that animated Paul (Acts 26:6–8) was "the hope of Israel" (28:20). NT hope has deep roots in the OT, where KJV "hope" translates a variety of Hebrew words, which mean "confidence," "trust," "safety," etc., sometimes so rendered in more modern versions.

HOPHNI (hŏf′nī, Heb. *hophnî*). A son of Eli, the high priest and judge who proved unworthy of his sacred offices (1 Sam 1:3; 2:34; 4:4, 17). Hophni is always associated with his brother Phinehas. The two were partners in evil practices and brought a curse on their heads (2:34; 3:14). Both were killed at the battle of Aphek, and their death, coupled with the loss of the ark, caused the death of Eli (4:17–18). Both sons disgraced their priestly office by claiming and appropriating more than their share of the sacrifices (2:13–17) and by their immoral actions in the tabernacle (1 Sam 2:22; Amos 2:6–8).

HOPHRA (See PHARAOH)

HOPPER (See ANIMALS)

HOPPING LOCUST (See ANIMALS)

HOR (hôr, Heb. *hôr*, *mountain*). **1.** A conspicuous mountain, probably a day's march north or NE of Kadesh Barnea, where Aaron died and was buried (Num 20:22–29; 33:37–41; Deut 32:50). Israel marched south from here toward the Red Sea (Num 21:4). **2.** A mountain on the northern border of the land given to the Israelites, between the Great Sea (Mediterranean) and the entrance of Hamath (34:7–8).

HOR HAGGIDGAD (hôr'hă-gĭd'găd, *hollow* or *cavern of Gilgad*). An Israelite camp in the wilderness, between Bene Jaakan and Jotbathah (Num 33:32–33), also called Gudgodah (Deut 10:7). See also GUDGODAH.

HOREB (hō'rĕb, *drought, desert*). The mountain where Moses received his commission (Exod 3:1); where he brought water out of the rock (17:6); and where the people stripped off their ornaments in token of repentance (33:6). It was 11 days' journey from Kadesh Barnea (Deut 1:2; cf. 1:6, 19; 4:10, 15; 5:2; 9:8; 18:16; 1 Kings 8:9; 2 Chron 5:10; Ps 106:19; Mal 4:4). Elijah fled here (1 Kings 19:8). It is geographically indistinguishable from Sinai.

HORI (hō'rī, *cave-dweller*). **1.** A son of Seir, a Horite, and founder of the Horites (Gen 36:22, 29–30; 1 Chron 1:39). **2.** A Simeonite whose son Shaphat was one of the 12 spies whom Joshua sent to investigate the land of Canaan (Num 13:5).

HORITE, HORIM (hō'rīt, hō'rĭm). A people found in Mt. Seir as early as the time of Abraham and conquered by Kedorlaomer and his allies (Gen 14:6)—the early inhabitants, before the Edomites dispossessed them and intermarried with them (36:20–30; Deut 2:12, 22). Esau married the daughter of one of their chieftains, also called a Hivite (Gen 36:2). The Hivites are thought to be identical with, or else confused with, the Horites (34:2; Josh 9:7). The Horites are now commonly thought to be Hurrians, from the highlands of Media, who before the middle of the second millennium B.C. overspread the region from Media to the Mediterranean, forming, or being merged in, the kingdom of Mitanni, subsequently destroyed by the Hittites.

HORMAH (hôr'mà, Heb. *hormâh, a devoted place*). Here the disobedient Israelites were defeated by Amalekites and Canaanites (Num 14:45; Deut 1:44). In the war with the king of Arad the place was taken by the Israelites and given the name Hormah, meaning "devoted," because it was devoted to destruction (Num 21:1–3). In the list of kings conquered by Joshua it appears with Arad (Josh 12:14). Hormah was originally given to Judah (15:30), but shortly after was allotted to Simeon (19:4) because Judah's portion was too large for them. Judah and Simeon subdued Zephath and renamed it Hormah (Judg 1:17). David sent part of the spoil of Ziklag to Hormah, as one of the cities of Judah (1 Sam 30:26–30), but Hormah was reckoned among the cities of Simeon

"until the reign of David" (1 Chron 4:30–31).

Horned incense altar from Megiddo, tenth-ninth century B.C. Courtesy Israel Department of Antiquities and Museums

HORN (Heb. and Aram. *qeren*, Gr. *keras, an animal horn*). Inkhorn (Ezek 9:2–3, 11) is Hebrew *qeseth*, translated "writing case" in RSV, "writing kit" in NIV. In Joshua 6, Hebrew *yôvēl*, from a root meaning "ram," appears to refer to the rams' horns that were blown on solemn occasions, and whose use gave rise to the term "Jubilee" for the 50th year of release, "the year of the ram's [horn]." *Qeren* referred to the horn on the animal (Gen 22:13), the horn used as a musical instrument (Josh 6:5; 1 Chron 25:5, but RSV and NIV have "to exalt him"), or a vessel to hold liquids (1 Sam 16:1, 13; 1 Kings 1:39). Tusks are meant in Ezekiel 27:15 (so RSV, NIV).

The "horns of the altar" were of one piece with the frame of the altar of burnt offering, made of acacia wood overlaid with bronze (Exod 27:2; cf. Ezek 43:15) —likewise the altar of incense (Exod 30:2; 37:26; cf. Rev 9:13), but overlaid with gold. Blood of sacrificial animals was put on the horns of both altars on certain occasions (Exod 30:10; Lev 4:7, 18, 25, 30, 34; 16:18; cf. Ezek 43:20). To cut off its horns rendered an altar useless for religious purposes (Amos 3:14). A person seeking sanctuary might catch hold of the horns of the altar in the temple, but this did not save Adonijah (1 Kings 1:50–51; 2:28–34). Jeremiah felt that the sin of Judah was engraved on the horns of their altars (Jer 17:1). For Psalm 118:27, NIV has: "Bind the festal sacrifice with ropes, and take it up to the horns of the altar" (contra JB, KJV, MLB, NASB, NEB, RSV).

Horns represent aggressive force (1 Kings 22:11; 2 Chron 18:10; Dan 8:7, symbolically; Deut 33:17; Pss 22:21; 92:10; Zech 1:18–21; Luke 1:69, figuratively). Horns in Habakkuk 3:4 are translated "rays" in ASV, RSV, NIV, because of the context (light). Multiple horns on one animal denote successive nations or rulers (Dan 7:7–24; 8:3–22; Rev 13:1; 17:3–16); "seven" with "horns" (Rev 5:6; 12:3) indicates perfection of power, good or evil. The beast with two horns like a lamb, which spoke like a dragon (Rev 13:11), suggests outward lamblikeness and inward wickedness.

HORNED OWL (See BIRDS)

HORNET (See ANIMALS)

HORONAIM (hôr-ŏ-nā'ĭm, *two hollows, caves* or *ravines*). A place in Moab, location uncertain (Isa 15:5; Jer 48:3, 5, 34).

HORONITE (hôr'ō-nīt). A designation of Sanballat (Neh 2:10, 19; 13:28), probably indicating Moabite origin (from Beth Horon or Horonaim).

HORSE (See ANIMALS)

HORSE GATE One of the gates of Jerusalem, between the Water Gate and the Sheep Gate; probably near the SE corner of the city (Neh 3:28–32; Jer 31:38–40). Here Athaliah was killed by order of Jehoiada the priest (2 Kings 11:16; 2 Chron 23:15).

HORSE LEECH (See ANIMALS)

HOSAH (hō'sà, Heb. *hōsâh, refuge*). 1. A town on the northern border of Asher, near Tyre (Josh 19:29). 2. A Levite porter selected by David to be one of the first doorkeepers to the ark after its return (1 Chron 16:38; 26:10–11, 16).

HOSANNA (hō-zăn'à, Heb. *hôsa'-nā', Gr. *hōsanna, save now*). Originally a prayer, "Save now, pray" (Ps 118:25), lost its primary meaning and became an exclamation of praise (Matt 21:9, 15; Mark 11:9–10; John 12:13). Not that the Hebrew word no longer had any connection with salvation: the context, which is a reminiscence of Psalm 118:25–26, if not a direct quotation from or allusion to it, shows that in its application to God the

Father and to Jesus, hosanna was concerned with the messianic salvation.

HOSEA (Heb. *hôshēa', salvation*). Hosea is the only OT book from the northern kingdom of Israel. This notable eighth-century B.C. prophet lived during a period of great national anxiety. He was born during the reign of Jeroboam II (c. 786–746), and exercised his prophetic ministry in Israel when Uzziah (c. 783–743), Jotham (c. 742–735), Ahaz (c. 735–715), and Hezekiah (c. 715–686) reigned in Judah.

The time of Hosea was marked by great material prosperity. Under Jeroboam II the northern kingdom experienced a degree of economic and commercial development unknown since the early days of the united kingdom.

While there is no reference to the occupation of Beeri, father of Hosea, he may well have been a middle-class merchant, perhaps a baker. Hosea himself was an educated person and probably came from a town in Ephraim or Manasseh. A man of profound spiritual vision, he was gifted with intellectual qualities that enabled him to comprehend the significance of those unhappy events that marked his domestic life and interpret them as a timely reminder of divine love toward a wayward, sinful Israel.

The cultic rites were celebrated several times each year and were marked by drunkenness, ritual prostitution, acts of violence, and indulgence in pagan forms

First century B.C. Dead Sea Scroll of Hosea 2:8-9, 10–14 with commentary (4Qp Hosª), found in Qumran Cave 4. Courtesy Israel Museum, Jerusalem

of worship at the shrines. The widespread prevalence of cultic prostitution is evident from the fact that in Jeremiah's day, a century after the time of Hosea, prostitution flourished in the temple precincts (2 Kings 23:7).

Israel's worship was the exact opposite of what God desired of his people. The Sinaitic covenant emphasized the exclusive worship of the Lord by a nation holy to him. However, the religious life of the covenant people had degenerated to the point of becoming identified with the shameless immoral worship of the pagan Canaanite deities. The emphasis on unbridled sexual activity coupled with excessive indulgence in alcohol was sapping the vitality not only of the Canaanites but also of Israel. All this, carried out against a background of magic and pagan mythology, was vastly removed from the purity of worship contemplated in the Sinai covenant.

The catalyst of Hosea's prophetic message is his marriage to a woman named Gomer. There are two major views of this relationship. The proleptic view holds that Gomer was pure when she married Hosea but later proved unfaithful. Another major view holds that she was a harlot when the prophet married her. Either way, the shock effect of Hosea's marital difficulties would have had telling impact on the people of his community. The children born of this marriage were given symbolic names indicating divine displeasure with Israel. After Gomer had pursued her paramours, she was to be brought back and with patient love readmitted to Hosea's home, there to await in penitence and grief the time of restoration to full favor. This was a clear picture of wayward Israel in its relationship with God and showed the unending faithfulness of the Almighty.

Hosea may be outlined thus:

1-3 Hosea's unhappy marriage and its results.
4 The priests condone immorality.
5 Israel's sin will be punished unless she repents.
6 Israel's sin is thoroughgoing; her repentance half-hearted.
7 Inner depravity and outward decay.
8 The nearness of judgment.
9 The impending calamity.
10 Israel's guilt and punishment.
11 God pursues Israel with love.
12-14 An exhortation to repentance, with promised restoration.

HOSHAIAH (hō-shā'yà, Heb. *hôsha 'yâh, Jehovah has saved*). **1.** The man who led half the princes of Judah and walked behind the chorus at the dedication of the wall of the city of Jerusalem (Neh 12:32). **2.** The father of Jezaniah (Jer 42:1) or Azariah (43:2), who opposed Jeremiah after the fall of Jerusalem (42:1-43:7). If Jaazaniah of 2 Kings 25:23 and Jeremiah 40:8 is the same Jezaniah, this Hoshaiah was a Maacathite.

HOSHEA (hō-shē'à, Heb. *hôshēa', salvation*). **1.** Joshua's earlier name, changed by Moses (Num 13:8, 16 ASV, RSV, NIV; Deut 32:44 KJV). **2.** The son of Azaziah and prince of Ephraim in David's reign (1 Chron 27:20). **3.** A son of Elah; the last king of the northern kingdom (2 Kings 15:30; 17:1-6; 18:1-10). **4.** A chief ruler under Nehemiah who signed the covenant (Neh 10:23).

HOSPITALITY (Gr. *philoxenia, loving strangers*). Although the word occurs only a few times in the Bible (e.g., Rom 12:13; 16:23; 1 Tim 3:2; 5:10; Titus 1:8; 1 Peter 4:9; 3 John 8), the idea appears as early as Abraham (Gen 14:17-19). One might be entertaining angels unawares (Heb 13:2) as Abraham did (Gen 18). Lot entertained the same angels (ch. 19), vv. 4-9 illustrating the extreme to which protection of a stranger might be carried. Rebekah showed kindness to Abraham's servant, giving him and his camels water and receiving various gold ornaments as a reward (24:15-28). Laban seconded her hospitality (24:29-31). Jacob fared well in the same household (29:1-14). Joseph's hospitality to his brothers had a purpose (43:15-34). As a refugee, Moses found welcome with Reuel, after helping his daughters water their flocks (Exod 2:15-22). Manoah entertained an angel (Judg 13:2-23), combining hospitality with a burnt offering. The plight of a stranger in a city where only one old man showed the ancient virtue of hospitality is told in Judges 19:11-28. Solomon entertained lavishly (1 Kings 4:22), as did Xerxes (Esth 1:2-8) and Vashti (1:9). Esther's dinners were private and purposeful (5:4-8; 7:1-10). Jezebel fed 850 false prophets (1 Kings 18:19). The common people continued to be hospitable (1 Sam 28:21-25; 2 Kings 4:8-10). Nehemiah regularly entertained 150 (Neh 5:17). The Law enjoined love and kindness to aliens (Lev 19:33-34). Jesus exercised hospitality when he fed 5,000 (Matt 14:15-21; Mark 6:35-44; Luke 9:12-17; John 6:4-13), 4,000 (Matt 15:32-38; Mark 8:1-9), and, after the

Resurrection, his disciples (John 21:4–13). He received hospitality from grudging Pharisees (Luke 7:36–50; 14:1–14) and loving hospitality in a home at Bethany (Matt 21:17; 26:6–13; Mark 14:3–9; Luke 10:38–42; John 12:1–8). Jesus invited himself to Zacchaeus' house and was shown hospitality there (Luke 19:5–10). The disciples at Emmaus were hospitable to Jesus, even when they did not recognize him (Luke 24:29–32). Jesus taught hospitality (10:30–37) and told his disciples where they would and would not find it (Matt 10:11–15; Luke 10:5–12). The NT exhibits and exhorts hospitality (Acts, Philemon, 2 John; 3 John).

HOST In the OT: **1.** Most often Hebrew *tāvā'*, "army" (Gen 21:22, RSV "army," NIV "forces"); *angels* (Josh 5:14, RSV and NIV "army"; Dan 8:11); *heavenly bodies* (Deut 4:19, NIV "heavenly array"); *creation* (Gen 2:1); *God of hosts* (1 Sam 17:45, NIV "armies"). **2.** Hebrew *hayil*, "army" (Exod 14:4). **3.** Twice Hebrew *hêl* (2 Kings 18:17, "army" in ASV, RSV, NIV; Obadiah 20, "army" in RSV and NIV). **4.** Hebrew *mahanĕh*, more often translated "camp" (Exod 14:24; 32:27, RSV, NIV "army"). In the NT: **1.** Greek *stratia*, "army" (Luke 2:13, "heavenly host"; Acts 7:42, "heavenly bodies" as objects of worship). **2.** Greek *xenos*, "guest," also "host" (Rom 16:23). **3.** Greek *pandocheus*, "one who receives all comers" (Luke 10:35, RSV and NIV "innkeeper").

HOSTAGE (Heb. *ben-ta'ărûvôth, son of pledges*). Jehoash (Joash), king of Israel, took hostages after his victory over Judah, to ensure that King Amaziah would keep the peace (2 Chron 25:24).

HOTHAM, IIOTHAN (hō'thăm, hō'-thăn). **1.** A son of Heber, of the family of Beriah. He was an Asherite (1 Chron 7:32), also called "Helem" (7:35). **2.** An Aroerite, whose two sons Shama and Jeiel were among David's heroes (11:44).

HOUGH (See HAMSTRING)

HOUR The word is found in the KJV OT only in Daniel as the translation of Aramaic *she'ā'*, "a brief time, a moment" (Dan 3:6, 15; 4:33; 5:5, where RSV, NIV have "immediately," except in 5:5, which has "suddenly"). In 4:19 ASV has "a while," NIV "a time," RSV "a long time." The day was divided into "degrees" (KJV, 2 Kings 20:9–11; Isa 38:8; "steps" in ASV, RSV, NIV) on the stairway of Ahaz. "Hour" is found in Ecclesiastes 9:12, a translation of Hebrew *'ēth*, "time."

In the NT, Greek *hōra*, "hour," is often used of a point of time (e.g., Matt 8:13). The day had 12 hours (John 11:9). The parable of the vineyard (Matt 20:1–16) names the third, sixth, ninth, and eleventh hours. As these are working hours, they obviously begin in the morning; this is the Palestinian mode of reckoning. References in Revelation—8:1 ("half an hour"); 9:15 ("this very hour"); 17:12; 18:10, 17, 19 ("one hour")—emphasize the brevity of a period of time.

HOUSE In the OT it is most often Hebrew and Aramaic *bayith* ("a dwelling place"). It is used to refer to a "household," or "family" (Exod 2:1), the tabernacle (23:19; 34:26) or temple (1 Kings 5:3–7:1) as the house of God, and a temple of heathen gods (Judg 16:23–30; 1 Sam 31:9–10). It might be a nomad tent (Gen 14:13–14; cf. 18:1; 27:15) or a building (Gen 19:2–11) in a city. God contrasts tent with house in 2 Samuel 7:6. Jacob called a place outdoors marked by a stone "the house of God" (Gen 28:17–22). In the NT, Greek *oikia* ("house") usually indicates a building; sometimes it refers to the inhabitants of a house (Matt 12:25; Mark 3:25; John 4:53; 1 Cor 16:15; Phil 4:22) or even to the human body (2 Cor 5:1). In 2 Corinthians 5:1 the first house (RSV, NIV "tent"; Greek "tent-house") is the physical body, the second house the resurrection body. The related Greek *oikos* also refers to a building (Matt 9:6–7, RSV, NIV "home"), but often to its inhabitants (Luke 19:9; Acts 11:14, RSV, NIV "household") or to descendants (Matt 10:6; Luke 1:33) or to the temple (Matt 12:4; 21:13; Mark 2:26; 11:17; Luke 6:4; 11:51; 19:46; John 2:16, 17; Acts 2:46).

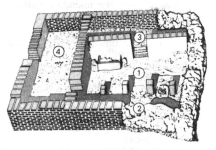

Reconstruction of a typical Israelite house, based on the excavations of Tell Qasila near Tel Aviv: (1) central open courtyard, (2) and (3) kitchen and storerooms, and (4) living and sleeping rooms. Courtesy Carta, Jerusalem

We read of no shelters in Eden, for probably none were needed in its mild climate; but Cain built a city (Gen 4:17). When Lot separated from Abraham, he first moved his tent to Sodom (13:12) but later lived in a house (19:2–11). Finally Lot took refuge in a cave (19:30). The law made provision in advance of the settlement in Canaan for the cleansing of a stone house in which there was leprosy (Lev 14:33–55).

After the conquest under Joshua, the Israelites came increasingly to live in houses in the cities and towns of Canaan; though some, like the Recabites (Jer 35:7, 10), continued to live in tents, and some took refuge in caves in times of uncertainty (1 Kings 19:9). House walls were often of rough stone as much as three feet (one m.) thick and often of unburned clay brick (Job 4:19), sometimes protected with a casing of stone slabs. In larger buildings the stones were squared, smoothed, and pointed. To enter the ordinary small house, from the street one first entered a forecourt, with a covered portion on one side. From the forecourt, doors opened into a living room, with two small bedchambers beyond. When sons married, additions were made as space permitted by using the court, complicating the design. Especially on a hilly site, a large boulder would be built into the corner to support the walls, the most necessary stone being called the cornerstone (Isa 28:16). The importance of dedicating a new house (in earliest times by sacrifices) was recognized by excusing a man from military duty until he had done so (Deut 20:5). The floor might be a leveled surface of stone, more often beaten clay. The rich often had a stone slab floor. Solomon's temple had a floor of cypress boards (1 Kings 6:15). For doors there were square openings in the wall with a stone or wood lintel, doorposts (Exod 12:22–23; 1 Kings 6:31), and a stone threshold. Doors might be of textiles, leather, or rushes, but wooden doors fastened by a bar were used early. Stone sill and head-sockets indicate pivot hinges, requiring sturdier construction of the door. A key is referred to as early as Judges 3:25. Locks (Song of Songs 5:5) may have been bolts. Hearths were provided, but no chimney, the smoke escaping through doors and windows. Braziers or firepots were also used (Jer 36:22). Windows were high, small openings with covers like the doors for protection; some had lattices.

Roofs had beams with transverse rafters covered with brushwood and overlaid with mud mixed with chopped straw. They were flat and were beaten and rolled. The roof was used for worship (2 Kings 23:12; Jer 19:13; 32:29; Acts 10:9). Absalom pitched his tent on the roof for publicity (2 Sam 16:22). Three thousand Philistines used the roof of their temple as a grandstand (Judg 16:27), illustrating its strength, while its weakness was demonstrated when Samson pushed apart the middle pillars on which the structure depended. There were outside stairs leading to the roof of a house and its "upper chamber." In some cases the "upper room" may have been inside the house. In the living room a raised brick platform ran across one side of the room (in the Hellenistic period at least), sometimes with ducts to heat it, and on this the family spread their bedding by night or sat by day. In cold weather the cattle might be admitted to the lower part of the living room of a poor family.

Palaces were much more elaborate (1 Kings 7:1–12). There is a sharp contrast between the humble homes of the common people and the luxurious dwellings of kings and the very rich in Egypt, Mesopotamia, Palestine under the Hebrew monarchy and after, and in Greece and Rome of the Hellenistic period. A Christian community, many of whose members were slaves, would be familiar with the lavish contents of large houses (2 Tim 2:20). While Christians at first continued to worship in temple and synagogue, from the beginning they met also in private homes (Acts 1:13; 2:2, 46). Worship in homes was a well-established pattern in Paul's ministry (Rom 16:5; 1 Cor 16:19; Col 4:15; Philem 2). Special buildings for Christian churches do not appear in the NT. The family had been the religious unit from the beginning of creation; worship centered in the house, from tent to palace. Tabernacle and temple were "the house of God." In the NT the house where a Christian family lived was open to other Christian brothers and sisters to worship together; and when the temple was destroyed and the synagogue was closed to Christians, the church in the home became the sole refuge of the believer, until special buildings were erected. Thus the sanctifying influences of corporate worship were added to the human associations that made a house a home.

HUKOK (See HELKATH)

HULDAH (hŭl'dà, Heb. *huldâh, weasel*). A prophetess in the reign of Josiah (2 Kings 22:14–20; 2 Chron 34:22–28), and the wife of Shallum. When Hilkiah

Ancient tomb on the Mount of Olives in Jerusalem, thought to be the tomb of Huldah, the prophetess from days of King Josiah (2 Kings 22:1–23:30). Courtesy Zev Radovan

found the Book of the Law in the temple, Josiah sent messengers to Huldah. She attested the genuineness of the book and prophesied ruin because of desertion of the Law. Her message greatly influenced the reforms carried out by Josiah.

HUMILITY (Heb. *'ănāwâh*, Gr. *tapein-ophrosynē*). Humility and the related substantive and verb *humble*, translate several OT Hebrew words and the NT Greek *tapeinoō* family. The meaning shades off in various directions, but the central thought is freedom from pride — lowliness, meekness, modesty, mildness. There is a "false humility" (Col 2:18, 23) called "self-abasement" in RSV. God humbles people to bring them to obedience (Deut 8:2). To humble ourselves is a condition of God's favor (2 Chron 7:14) and his supreme requirement (Mic 6:8). God dwells with the humble (Isa 57:15). Humility is encouraged (Prov 15:33; 18:12; 22:4). To the Greeks, humility was weak and despicable, but Jesus made it the cornerstone of character (Matt 5:3, 5; 18:4; 23:12; Luke 14:11; 18:14). Jesus by his humility drew people to himself (Matt 11:28–30; John 13:1–20; Rev 3:20). Paul emphasized the humility of Jesus (2 Cor 8:9; Phil 2:1–11), commanded us to be humble toward one another (Rom 12:10; 1 Cor 13:4–6; Phil 2:3–4), and spoke of himself as an example (Acts 20:19). Peter exhorted humility before the brethren and before God (1 Peter 5:5–6). Humility is an effect of the action of God, circumstances, other people, ourselves, or of any or all of these on our lives.

HUNTER (See OCCUPATIONS AND PROFESSIONS)

HUPHAM (hū'făm). A son of Benjamin and founder of a tribal family known as the Huphamites (Num 26:39). Probably the same as Huppim (Gen 46:21) and Huppites (1 Chron 7:12), and Huram (8:5).

HUPPIM, HUPPITES (hŭp'ĭm, hŭp'ĭts, Heb. *huppîm, coast people*). Probably the same as Hupham (Gen 46:21; 1 Chron 7:12, 15).

HUR (hûr, Heb. *hûr, whiteness*). **1.** One who, with Aaron, held up Moses' hands during a battle against Amalek, bringing victory to Israel (Exod 17:10, 12). He was appointed magistrate while Moses was on the mountain (24:14). **2.** Grandfather of Bezalel of the tribe of Judah, chief workman in the tabernacle (31:2; 35:30; 38:22; 2 Chron 1:5). Jewish tradition identifies nos. 1 and 2 as the same person and calls him the husband of Miriam, Moses' sister. **3.** One of five Midianite kings killed with Balaam (Num 31:1–8). He was a leader of Midian and a prince of Sihon, the Amorite king (Josh 13:21). **4.** In KJV the father of one of 12 officers who supplied food for Solomon's household (1 Kings 4:8). **5.** Father of Rephaiah, who helped Nehemiah build the wall; ruler of half of Jerusalem (Neh 3:9).

HURAI (hū'rā-ī, hū'rī). One of David's heroes from the brooks of Gaash (1 Chron 11:32). He is also called Hiddai (2 Sam 23:30).

HURAM (hū'răm, Heb. *hûrām, noble-born*). **1.** A Benjamite, son of Bela (1 Chron 8:5). See also HUPHAM. **2.** The king of Tyre who aided Solomon (2 Chron 2:3, 11–12 in most versions), usually called Hiram (so NIV). **3.** A Tyrian artificer sent to Solomon by Hiram king of Tyre (no. 2) (2:13–14; 4:11–16; called "Hiram" in most versions in 1 Kings 7:13–14, 40–45). His mother was a woman from the tribe of Dan who had married first into the tribe of Naphtali and then later a Tyrian man.

HURRIANS (See HORITE)

HUSBAND (See FAMILY; MARRIAGE)

HUSBANDMAN (See OCCUPATIONS AND PROFESSIONS)

HUSHAI (hū'shī, hū'shā-ī). One of David's two leading men, an Arkite (Josh 16:2, 7; 2 Sam 15:32, 37; 16:16–18; 17:5–15; 1 Chron 27:33) — the friend and counselor of David who overthrew the counsels of Ahithophel.

HUSHATHITE (hū'shăth-īt). The family name of Sibbecai, one of David's thirty heroes (2 Sam 21:18; 1 Chron 11:29; 20:4; 27:11), also called Mebunnai (2 Sam 23:27).

HUSHIM, HUSHITES (hū'shĭm, hū'shīts). **1.** The sons of Dan (Gen 46:23), called Shuham (Num 26:42). **2.** The sons of Aher, a Benjamite (1 Chron 7:12). **3.** One of the two wives of Shaharaim (8:8, 11).

HUSKS (See PLANTS)

HUZ (See UZ)

HUZZAB (hŭz'ăb, Heb. *hûtstsav*). It is disputed whether the word in Nahum 2:7 is to be taken as a noun or a verb. If a noun (KJV, RSV), it may be an epithet of Nineveh or of its queen. If a verb, it may be translated "it is decreed," as in ASV and NIV. Moffatt and the Jewish version have "the queen." Knox has "the warriors of Nineve(h)."

HYACINTH (hī'à-sĭnth, Gr. *hyakinthos*). The name of a color in ASV (Rev 9:17; RSV "sapphire," NIV "dark blue," KJV "jacinth").

HYENA (See ANIMALS)

HYMENAEUS (hī'mĕ-nē'ŭs, Gr. *Hymenaios, pertaining to Hymen*, the god of marriage). A professed Christian who had fallen into heresies, tried to shipwreck the faith of true believers, and was excommunicated by Paul (1 Tim 1:19–20; 2 Tim 2:16–18).

HYMN (See MUSIC AND MUSICAL INSTRUMENTS)

HYPOCRISY (hĭ-pŏk'rĭ-sē). From a Hebrew root *hnph*, "pollute," correctly translated "profane," "godless," "ungodly" in ASV, RSV, NIV (Job 8:13; 13:16; Ps 35:16; Prov 22:9; Isa 9:17; 10:6; 32:6; 33:14). The LXX used Greek *hypokrinomai*, "act a part in a play"; *hypokrisis*, "hypocrisy"; *hypokritēs*, "hypocrite," which occur in the NT and are taken over in English (Matt 6:2, 5, 16; 7:5; 23:27–28; Mark 7:6; 12:15; Luke 12:1, 56; 13:15; cf. 20:20; Matt 6:1–18; 23:13–36; 2 Tim 3:5). The Greek word *anypokritos*, "without hypocrisy" (Rom 12:9; 2 Cor 6:6; 1 Tim 1:5; 2 Tim 1:5; 1 Peter 1:22), is usually rendered "sincere," "genuine" in RSV and NIV.

HYSSOP (See PLANTS)

IBEX (See ANIMALS)

IBIS (See BIRDS)

IBLEAM (ĭb′lē-ăm, Heb. *yivie′ām*). A town in the territory of Issachar, given to the tribe of Manasseh (Josh 17:11). The inhabitants, however, were not driven out and continued to live in the land (Judg 1:27). Ahaziah, king of Judah, was killed near there when he fled from Jehu (2 Kings 9:27). Zechariah, king of Israel, was killed there (15:10, see NIV footnote). It is generally identified with Bileam, a town of Manasseh given to the Levites (1 Chron 6:70).

IBZAN (ĭb′zăn, Heb. *'ivtsān*). The tenth judge of Israel, who ruled for seven years. He was a native of Bethlehem (whether of Judah or Zebulun is not stated). He had 30 sons and 30 daughters (Judg 12:8–10).

ICHABOD (ĭk′ă-bŏd, Heb. *'îkhāvôdh, inglorious*). Son of Phinehas, Eli's son who was killed by the Philistines at the battle of Aphek when the ark was taken. Ichabod was born after his father's death and was given this name by his mother on her deathbed because, she said, "The glory has departed from Israel" (1 Sam 4:19–22). His nephew Ahijah was one of those who remained with Saul and his men at Gibeah just before Jonathan attacked the Philistines (14:2ff.).

ICONIUM (ī-cō′nĭ-ŭm, Gr. *Ikonion*). A city of Asia Minor that Paul and Barnabas visited on Paul's first missionary journey and revisited on their return journey to Antioch (Acts 13:51ff.). Paul with Silas stopped off at Iconium to read the letter sent out by the Jerusalem Council on the Judaizing question (16:1–5). Paul alludes to persecutions he endured at Antioch, Iconium, and Lystra (2 Tim 3:11). In the first century it was one of the chief cities in the southern part of the Roman province of Galatia.

IDDO (ĭd′ō). 1. Hebrew *yiddô*. (a) Son of Zechariah and a captain under David in Manasseh (1 Chron 27:21). (b) One who had taken a foreign wife at the time of Ezra (Ezra 10:43 ASV; NIV "Jaddai"). 2. Hebrew ʾ *iddô*. The head of a community of temple servants (KJV Nethinim) at Casiphia (Ezra 8:17). 3. Hebrew *yiddô, ye′dô, ye′dî*. (a) A Levite descended from Gershom (1 Chron 6:21). (b) A seer and prophet who wrote a book that was the chronicler's source for the reigns of Solomon and Jeroboam (2 Chron 9:29);

he also wrote books about the deeds of Rehoboam (12:15) and Abijah (13:22). (c) Father of Ahinadab, a district governor of Solomon at Mahanaim in Gilead (1 Kings 4:14). (d) Grandfather of Zechariah (Zech 1:1, 7; Ezra 5:1; 6:14).

IDOLATRY (ī-dŏl′à-trē, Gr. *eidōlolatria*). Idolatry in ancient times included two forms of departure from the true religion: the worship of false gods (whether by means of images or otherwise); and the worship of the Lord by means of images. All the nations surrounding ancient Israel were idolatrous. The early Semites of Mesopotamia worshiped mountains, springs, trees, and blocks of stone. A typical example of such wooden representations is the sacred pole or Asherah pole, such as the idol of Gideon's clan that he later destroyed (Judg 6:25–32).

The religion of the Egyptians centered mostly about the veneration of the sun and of the Nile as sources of life. They also had a number of sacred animals: the bull, cow, cat, baboon, crocodile, etc. Some of the deities were represented with human bodies and animal heads. Among the Canaanites, religion took on a very barbarous character. The chief gods were personifications of life and fertility. The gods had no moral character whatsoever, and worship of them carried with it demoralizing practices, including child sacrifice, prostitution, and snake worship. Human and animal images of the deities were worshiped. When the Israelites conquered the land they were commanded to destroy these idols (Exod 23:24; 34:13; Num 33:52; Deut 7:5).

The word "idolatry" has no exact Hebrew equivalent. There are, however, a number of Hebrew words that are translated "idol." They all give expression to the loathing, contempt, and dread excited in godly men by idolatry. The terms are as follows: (1) *Aven*, "emptiness, nothingness"; that is, a vain, false, wicked thing (Isa 66:3). (2) *Emah*, "an object of horror or terror," referring either to the hideousness of the idols or the shameful character of their worship (Jer 50:38). (3) *El*, the name of the supreme god of Canaan; used also as a neutral expression for any divinity (Isa 57:5). (4) *Elil*, "a thing of naught, a nonentity," resembling *aven* in meaning (Lev 19:4; 26:1; 1 Chron 16:26). (5) *Miphletseth*, "a fright, a horror" (1 Kings 15:12; 2 Chron 15:16). (6) *Sem-*

el, "a likeness, semblance" (33:7, 15). (7) *Atsabh ,* "a cause of grief" (1 Sam 31:9; 1 Chron 10:9). (8) *Etseb* "a cause of grief" (Jer 22:28 KJV). (9) *Otseb* "a cause of grief" (Isa 48:5). (10) *Tsir,* "a form," and hence an idol (45:16). Besides the above words there are a number of others that are not translated "idol" but refer to it, expressing the degradation associated with idolatry: *bosheth,* "shameful thing," applied to Baal and referring to the obscenity of his worship (Jer 11:13; Hos 9:10); *gillulim,* a term of contempt meaning "shapeless, dungy things" (Zeph 1:17); and *shikkuts,* "filth," referring especially to the obscene rites associated with idolatry (Ezek 37:23; Nah 3:6). Theologically, idolaters thought of their gods as spiritual beings (or forces) of cosmic significance and, theoretically, to them the idol was as a focal point for worship. The OT insists, however, that the heathen worship idols and nothing more (cf. Ps 115:2–8; Isa 44:6–20).

The first clear case of idolatry in the Bible is the account of Rachel stealing her father's teraphim, which were images of household gods (Gen 31:19) used in Babylonia. During their long sojourn in Egypt, the Israelites defiled themselves with the idols of the land (Josh 24:14; Ezek 20:7). Moses defied these gods by attacking their symbols in the plagues of Egypt (Num 33:4). At Sinai Israel persuaded Aaron to make them a golden calf, an emblem of the productive power of nature with which they had become familiar in Egypt. The second commandment was directed against idolatry (Exod 20:4–5; Deut 5:8–9).

Judges tells of successive apostasies, judgments, and repentances. The narrative concerning Micah (Judg 17–18) illustrates how idolatry was often combined with outward worship of God; this involved Jonathan, a Levite and a grandson of Moses, the first of a line of priests to officiate at the shrine of the stolen idols all the time that the tabernacle was at Shiloh.

The prophet Samuel persuaded the people to repent of their sin and to renounce idolatry; but in Solomon's reign the king himself made compromises that affected disastrously the whole future of the kingdom. Solomon's wives brought their own heathen gods with them and openly worshiped them. Rehoboam, Solomon's son by an Ammonite mother, continued the worst features of his father's idolatry (1 Kings 14:22–24). Jeroboam, first king of the northern kingdom, effected a great and permanent schism in the religion of Israel when he erected golden calves at Bethel and at Dan and had his people worship there instead of in Jerusalem. Ahab, to please his Zidonian queen Jezebel, built a temple and an altar to Baal in Samaria (16:31–33), while she put to death as many prophets of the Lord as she could find (18:4–13). Baal worship came to be identified with the kingdom of Israel, and no king ever rose up against it.

Hezekiah restored the temple services, but the change was only outward (2 Chron 28–29; Isa 29:13). Not long before the destruction of Jerusalem by Babylonia, Josiah made a final effort to bring about a purer worship, but it did not last (2 Chron 34). Ezra found that many Jews had married foreign wives and that the land was filled with abominations (Ezra 9:11). More than 200 years later, when Antiochus Epiphanes tried to eradicate Judaism and Hellenize the Jews, many of them obeyed his command to offer sacrifices to idols, although his action led to the Maccabean war.

In the ritual of idol worship the chief elements were: offering burnt sacrifices (2 Kings 5:17), burning incense in honor of the idol (1 Kings 11:8), pouring out libations (Isa 57:6), presenting tithes and the firstfruits of the land (Hos 2:8), kissing the idol (1 Kings 19:18), stretching out the hands to it in adoration, prostrat-

Bronze stand (c. 10 cm. high) found at Megiddo and dating from Iron Age I (c. 1200–1000 B.C.), with square base and round top. On each side a figure is shown presenting a gift to, or standing in adoration before, a seated deity. *Courtesy* Israel Department of Antiquities and Museums

ing oneself before it, and sometimes even cutting oneself with knives (18:26, 28).

For an Israelite, idolatry was the most heinous of crimes. In the OT the relation between God and his covenant people is often represented as a marriage bond (Isa 54:5; Jer 3:14), and the worship of false gods was regarded as religious harlotry. The penalty was death (Exod 22:20). To attempt to seduce others to false worship was a crime of equal enormity (Deut 13:6–10). The God of Israel was a jealous God who tolerated no rivals.

NT references to idolatry are understandably few. The Maccabean war resulted in the Jews becoming fanatically opposed to the crass idolatry of OT times. Jesus warned that to make possessions central in life is idolatry (Matt 6:24). Idolatry is the result of deliberate religious apostasy (Rom 1:18–25). Christians in apostolic times, many of whom were converted from heathenism, are repeatedly warned in the letters of the NT to be on their guard against idolatry (e.g., 1 Cor 5:10; Gal 5:20). The OT conception of idolatry is widened to include anything that leads to the dethronement of God from the heart—e.g., covetousness (Eph 5:5; Col 3:5).

A special problem arose for Christians in connection with meat offered to idols (Acts 15:29; 1 Cor 8–10). There will be a time of idolatrous apostasy in the last days, when the Beast and his image will be accorded divine honors (Rev 9:20; 13:14).

IDUMEA (ĭd'ū-mēā, Gr. *pertaining to Edom*). The name used by the Greeks and Romans for the country of Edom (Mark 3:8). See also EDOM.

IEZER (See ABIEZER)

IGAL (ī'găl, Heb. *yigh'āl, God redeems*). **1.** One of the 12 spies sent by Moses to search out the land of Canaan (Num 13:7). **2.** One of David's heroes, the son of Nathan (2 Sam 23:36). **3.** A son of Shemaiah, a descendant of King Jehoiachin (1 Chron 3:22).

IIM (See IYIM)

IJON (ī'jŏn, Heb. *'îyôn, a ruin*). A town in the territory of Naphtali captured by Ben-Hadad, king of Syria, at the instigation of Asa (1 Kings 15:20; 2 Chron 16:4) and depopulated by Tiglath-Pileser (2 Kings 15:29).

ILAI (ī'lā-ī, Heb. *'îlay*). One of David's mighty men (1 Chron 11:29); also called Zalmon (2 Sam 23:28).

ILLYRICUM (ĭl-ĭr'ĭ-kŭm, Gr. *Illyrikon*). A province of the Roman Empire on the east coast of the Adriatic Sea where Paul preached (Rom 15:19), probably on his third missionary journey.

IMAGE, IMAGE WORSHIP (See IDOLATRY)

IMAGE OF GOD Two fundamental truths about man taught in Scripture are that he is created by God and that God made him in his own image (Gen 1:26–27; 5:1, 3; 9:6; Ps 8; Acts 17:22–31; 1 Cor 11:7; Eph 4:24; Col 3:10; James 3:9). The Scriptures do not define precisely the nature of the image of God in man. The words "image" and "likeness" in the OT usually refer to outward, visible form (e.g., 1 Sam 6:5; 2 Kings 16:10), an actual copy.

The image of God in man seems to include personality, rationality, morality and spirituality—all giving a basis for dominion over the earth (Gen 1:27–28).

IMLAH (ĭm'là, Heb. *yimlâh, fullness*). The father of Micaiah, a prophet of the Lord in the days of Ahab (1 Kings 22:8–9; 2 Chron 18:7–8).

IMMANUEL (ĭ-măn'ū-ĕl, Heb. *'immānû' ēl, God is with us*). The name of a child (Isa 7:14; 8:8; Matt 1:23) whose birth was foretold by Isaiah and who was to be a sign to Ahaz during the Syro-Ephraimitic war (Isa 7). At this time, 735 B.C., Judah was threatened by the allied forces of Syria and Israel. They were trying to compel Judah to form an alliance with them against Assyria, whose king, Tiglath-Pileser, was attempting to bring the whole of Western Asia under his sway.

Isaiah's words have led to much controversy and have been variously interpreted, chiefly because of the indefinite terms of the prediction and the fact that there is no record of their fulfillment in any contemporary event.

1. The traditional Christian interpretation emphasizes the virgin birth of our Immanuel, Jesus Christ (Matt 1:22–23). See VIRGIN BIRTH. 2. Another explanation is that the event of the birth of the child is intended as a sign to Ahaz and nothing more. At the time of Judah's deliverance from Syria and Ephraim, some young mothers who give birth to sons will spontaneously name them "Immanuel"—a sign to Ahaz of the truth of Isaiah's words. 3. A third view, somewhat similar to the preceding one, is that Isaiah has a certain child in mind, the *almah* being his own wife or one of Ahaz's wives or perhaps someone else.

Before the child has emerged from infancy, Syria and Ephraim will be no more (Isa 7:16); and later in his life Judah will be a country fit only for the pastoral life (7:15). 4. Some apply the prophecy to a child of Isaiah's time and also to Jesus Christ. 5. Perhaps the most widely held view among Evangelicals is that Isaiah has in mind Israel's Messiah. In the coming of Immanuel people will recognize the truth of the prophet's words. He would be Israel's deliverer, and the government would rest on his shoulders (Isa 9:6).

IMMER (ĭm'ēr, Heb. *'immēr*). **1.** The ancestral head of the 16th course of priests in David's time (1 Chron 24:14; Ezra 2:37; 10:20; Nehemiah 3:29; 7:40; 11:13. **2.** A priest in Jeremiah's time; he was the father of Pashhur (Jer 20:1). It is possible that he was a descendant of the Immer mentioned in no. 1. **3.** The Babylonian home of a priestly family (Ezra 2:59)

IMMORTALITY (See ESCHATOLOGY)

IMMUTABILITY (i-mū-tà-bĭl'ĭ-tē). The perfection of God by which he is devoid of all change in essence, attributes, consciousness, will, and promises. No change is possible in God, because all change must be to better or worse, and God is absolute perfection. No cause for change in God exists, either in himself or outside of him. The immutability of God (Ps 102:26; Mal 3:6; James 1:17) must not be confused with immobility. God's repenting (e.g., Jonah 3:10) is only an anthropomorphism.

IMNAH (ĭm'nà, Heb. *yimnâh, right hand*, or, *good fortune*). **1.** Son of Asher and founder of a tribal family (Gen 46:17; Num 26:44; 1 Chron 7:30). **2.** A Levite, father of Kore, in the reign of Hezekiah (2 Chron 31:14).

IMPRECATORY PSALMS A number of OT psalms (especially 2, 37, 69, 79, 109, 139, and 143) contain expressions of an apparent vengeful attitude toward enemies. We must note, however: (1) Imprecations are not confined to the OT (cf. Luke 11:37–52; Gal 1:8ff.; Rev 6:10; 18:20; 19:1–6). (2) Many if not all of the imprecatory psalms contain (as well as the imprecation) theological and moral sentiments that we should wish to attain (e.g., Ps 139). (3) In fact, OT morality stoutly opposed a hostile and vindictive response to opponents (e.g., Lev 19:14–18). (4) All the imprecatory psalms except Psalm 137 are prayers, addressed to God about opponents. (5) The imprecatory

psalms are full of longing for the vindication of the Lord's good name, not personal relief (e.g., Pss 58:11; 83:16–18). (6) Many of the actual imprecations do no more than ask God to do what he has already said that he will do in such situations (e.g., 5:10; 54:5; 79:6–7). (7) The Bible teaches that there is a "pure anger." The fact that we do not feel it and cannot express it does not mean that God's people have never risen to such heights of holiness. (8) The one imprecation that is not contained in a prayer is Psalm 137:8, and here the Bible translators continue to choose English renderings that in fact themselves create the problem (cf. NIV "happy"). The word concerned (*ashre*) can mean any of three things: (a) "blessed," i.e., under God's approval and blessing; (b) "happy," i.e., personally fulfilled and enjoying well-being; and (c) "right," i.e., matching exactly the moral norms that operate in such a situation. Psalm 137:8 would better read, "How right he is . . . ." The psalmist himself does not rejoice in it but bows before its justice.

IMPUTE (Heb. *hāshav*, Gr. *logizomai*). A word meaning to attribute something to another person, to reckon something to another's account. This sometimes takes place in a judicial manner, so that the thing imputed becomes grounds for reward or punishment. In some versions the Hebrew and Greek words are also translated "to account, to count, to esteem, to reckon, to think." Imputation is mentioned throughout Scripture (Lev 7:18; 17:4; 2 Sam 19:19; Ps 32:2; Rom 4:3–25; 5:13; 2 Cor 5:19; Gal 3:6; James 2:23), underlying the doctrines of original sin, atonement, and justification.

Adam's sin not only affected but was imputed to his posterity (Rom 5:12–21). By Adam's sin death and sin entered the world and passed to all men. All men were condemned and made sinners in Adam.

Christ bore our sins and died in our place (Isa 53; 2 Cor 5:21; 1 Peter 2:24). This truth is basic to the doctrine of the atonement.

Justification (Rom 3:24; 5:15; Gal 5:4; Titus 3:7) involves the merits of Christ's suffering and obedience being imputed to the sinner, and from then on he is viewed as just in God's sight.

IMRI (ĭm'rī, Heb. *'imrî*, contraction of *Amariah*). **1.** A man of Judah, son of Bani (1 Chron 9:4). **2.** The father of Zaccur, who helped in the rebuilding of the wall of Jerusalem after the Captivity (Neh 3:2).

INCARNATION The doctrine of the Incarnation is taught or assumed throughout the Bible (e.g., John 1:14; Rom 8:3; Phil 2:5–11; 1 Tim 3:16). "Incarnation" is from the Latin meaning "becoming flesh," that is, "becoming human." The doctrine of the Incarnation teaches that the eternal Son of God (see TRINITY) became human without in any manner or degree diminishing his divine nature.

In the process of ordinary birth, a new personality begins. The Virgin Birth was a miracle, wrought by the Holy Spirit, whereby the eternal Son of God "became flesh," i.e., took a genuine human nature in addition to his eternal divine nature. It was a *virgin* birth, a miracle. The Holy Spirit has never been thought of as the father of Jesus. Jesus was fully God, the Second Person of the Trinity (Col 2:9), and genuinely human (1 John 4:2–3).

The council of Chalcedon, A.D. 451 declared that Christ is "to be acknowledged in two natures, inconfusedly, unchangeably, indivisibly, inseparably . . . the property of each nature being preserved, and concurring in one Person. . . ." The Westminster Shorter Catechism, Question 21 states: "The only Redeemer of God's elect is the Lord Jesus Christ, who, being the eternal Son of God, became man, and so was, and continueth to be, God and man, in two distinct natures and one Person for ever."

The person who was God and with God "in the beginning" before the created universe is the same person who sat wearily at the well of Sychar, the same person who said, "Father, forgive them," on the cross. The distinction of his natures means, and has always meant to the church, that Jesus is just as truly God as the Father and the Spirit are God, and at the same time, without confusion or contradiction, he is just as truly human as we are human.

INCENSE The KJV translation of two Hebrew words that were distinct in meaning at first, although later the second came to have virtually the same meaning as the first: *levônâh,* "frankincense," and *qetôrâh,* "incense." Incense was an aromatic substance made of gums and spices to be burned, especially in religious worship. It was compounded according to a definite prescription of gum resin, onycha, galbanum, and pure frankincense in equal proportions, and was tempered with salt (Exod 30:34–35). It could not be made for ordinary purposes (30:34–38; Lev 10:1–7). Incense not properly com-

Vessel composed of a bowl, decorated with knobs, surmounting a stand. The stand has four windows and is decorated with a frieze portraying human heads, each molded separately and then attached. It was probably used for incense, and it is thought to originate in the Hebron hills. Late Israelite (Iron) period, c. 1000–586 B.C. Courtesy Reuben and Edith Hecht Museum, University of Haifa

pounded was rejected as "strange incense" (Exod 30:9 KJV).

The altar of incense was overlaid with pure gold and was set in the Holy Place. Originally the high priest burned incense each morning when he dressed the lamps (Exod 30:1–9). On the Day of Atonement he brought the incense within the veil and burned it in a censer in the Most Holy Place (Lev 16:12–13). The Korahites were punished with death for presuming to take on themselves the right to burn incense (Num 16); the sons of Aaron died for offering it improperly (Lev 10; cf. 16:13). By the time of Christ, incense was offered by ordinary priests, from among whom one was chosen by lot each morning and evening (Luke 1:9).

The offering of incense was common in the religious ceremonies of nearly all ancient nations (Egyptians, Babylonians, Assyrians, Phoenicians, etc.) and was extensively used in the ritual of Israel.

Incense was symbolic of the ascending prayer of the officiating high priest (Ps 141:2; Rev 8:3-5).

INDIA (Heb. *hôddû*). The name occurs only twice in the Bible (Esth 1:1; 8:9). This country marked the eastern limit of the territory of Xerxes (KJV Ahasuerus). The Hebrew word comes from the name of the Indus, *Hondu*, and refers not to the peninsula of Hindustan, but to the country adjoining the Indus, i.e., the Punjab, and perhaps also Scinde. Some have thought that this country is the Havilah of Genesis 2:11 and that the Indus is the Pishon.

INERRANCY (See INSPIRATION)

INFLAMMATION (See DISEASES)

INHERITANCE The English word in the OT means something inherited, an estate, a portion. A fundamental principle of Hebrew society was that real, as distinguished from personal, property belonged to the family rather than to the individual. This came from the idea that the land was given by God to his people and must remain in the family. Only the sons of a legal wife had the right of inheritance. The firstborn son possessed the birthright, i.e., the right to a double portion of the father's possession; and to him belonged the duty of maintaining the females of the family (Deut 21:15-17). The other sons received equal shares. If there were no sons, the property went to the daughters (Num 27:8), on the condition that they not marry outside of their own tribe (36:6ff.). If the widow was left without children, the nearest of kin on her husband's side had the right to marry her; and if he refused, the next of kin (Ruth 3:12-13). If no one married her, the inheritance remained with her until her death, and then reverted to the next of kin (Num 27:9-11). An estate could not pass from one tribe to another. Thus, testamentary dispositions or wills were not needed and family genealogies were carefully preserved.

"Inheritance" in the OT at first refers to the inheritance promised by God to Abraham and his descendants—the land of Canaan (1 Kings 8:36; cf. Num 34:2; Deut 4:21, 38; 12:9-10; 15:4; Pss 47:4; 105:9-11).

Israelites came to learn that the Lord himself was the inheritance of his people (Jer 10:16) and of the individual believer (Pss 16:5-6; 73:26; 142:5), and that his inheritance is his elect (Deut 4:20; cf. 32:9), later broadened to include the Gentiles (Ps 2:8; Isa 19:25; 47:6; 63:17).

In the NT, Christ is the heir by virtue of being the Son (Mark 12:7; Heb 1:2). Through Christ's redemptive work believers are sons of God by adoption and fellow-heirs with Christ (Rom 8:17; Gal 4:7). As a guarantee of "the promised eternal inheritance" (Heb 9:15), Christ has given to them the Holy Spirit (Eph 1:14). In the New Covenant there is a better inheritance for all true believers, including Gentiles (Heb 3:6). The inheritance is the kingdom of God with all its blessings (Matt 25:34; 1 Cor 6:9; Gal 5:21), both present and eschatological (Rom 8:17-23; 1 Cor 15:50; Heb 11:13; 1 Peter 1:3-4). It is wholly the gift of God's sovereign grace.

INK (Heb. *deyô*, from a root meaning *slowly flowing*, Gr. *melan, black*). Any liquid used with pen or brush to form written characters. Mentioned once in the OT (Jer 36:18), Hebrew ink was probably lampblack and gum (Exod 32:33; cf. Num 5:23); but it is possible that in the course of Jewish history various inks were used. The word occurs three times in the NT (2 Cor 3:3; 2 John 12; 3 John 13).

INN (Heb. *mālôn*, Gr. *pandocheion, katalyma*). The Hebrew word means a "night resting-place" and can apply to any place where there is encampment for the night, whether by caravans, individuals, or even armies (Jer 9:2). The presence of a building is not implied. Inns in the modern sense were not very necessary in primitive times, since travelers found hospitality the rule (Exod 2:20; Judg 19:15-21; 2 Kings 4:8; Acts 28:7; Heb 13:2). An inn of the Middle East bore little resemblance to a modern hotel. It was a mere shelter for man and beast, a large quadrangular court into which admission was gained by a strong gateway. The more elaborate ones were almost as strong as a fortress. In the center of the court there was a well, and around the sides there were rooms and stalls. An upper story was reached by stairways. Travelers usually brought food for themselves and their animals.

Innkeepers in ancient times had a very bad reputation; and this, together with the Semitic spirit of hospitality, led Jews and Christians to recommend hospitality for the entertainment of strangers. One of the best-known inns in Palestine was halfway between Jerusalem and Jericho (Luke 10:34). The Upper Room, where the Last Supper was held (Mark 14:14) and the place in Bethlehem that turned away Joseph and Mary (Luke 2:7) were probably rooms in private houses rather than in public inns.

INNOCENTS, SLAUGHTER OF (Matt 2:16). The murder by Herod the Great of all the male children in Bethlehem two years old and under, when the wise men failed to return and tell him where they found the infant Jesus.

I.N.R.I The initials of the Latin superscription that Pilate had placed above the cross of Jesus in three languages (Greek, Hebrew, Latin). The Latin reads: *IESUS NAZARENUS, REX IUDAERUM*, "Jesus of Nazareth, King of the Jews" (Matt 27:37; Mark 15:26; Luke 23:38; John 19:19).

INSECTS (See ANIMALS)

INSPIRATION The word *inspiration* is used twice in the KJV (Job 32:8, NIV "breath"; 2 Tim 3:16). The written documents, called Holy Scripture, are a divine product.

In both 2 Timothy 3:16 and 2 Peter 1:19–21 the fact of the divine productivity (spiration rather than *in*spiration) of the "Holy Writings" is explicitly asserted. The authors of Scripture wrote in or by the Spirit (Mark 12:36). What the Scripture states is really what God has said (Acts 4:25; Heb 3:7; see 1:5ff.). This is true whether or not in the particular passage cited the words are ascribed to God or are the statements of the human author. Jesus attributed directly to God the authorship of Scripture (Matt 19:4–5).

Because of the character of the God of Truth who "inspired" (or produced) the Holy Scriptures, the result of "inspiration" is to constitute the Bible as fully trustworthy and authoritative (Pss 19:7–14; 119:89, 97, 113, 160; Zech 7:12; Matt 5:17–19; Luke 16:17; John 10:34–35; 1 Thess 2:13). Besides those passages directly teaching the authority of Scripture, such phrases as "It is written" (Matt 21:13; Luke 4:4, 8, 10), "it [or he] says" (Rom 9:15; Gal 3:16), and "Scripture says" (Rom 9:17; Gal 3:8) all clearly imply an absolute authority for the OT Scriptures. Since the authority and trustworthiness of Scripture are complete, inspiration itself also extends to all of Scripture (Matt 5:17–19; Luke 16:17; 24:25; John 10:34–35).

Inerrancy and *infallibility* as applied to the inspiration of Scripture, though not exactly synonymous terms, are nevertheless both correctly applied to Scripture in order to indicate that inspiration and authority are complete. The word *inerrant* suggests that the Scriptures do not wander from the truth. *Infallible* is stronger, suggesting an incapability of wandering from the truth.

By God's sovereign preparation and control, men could and freely did write just what God desired—his divinely authoritative message to his people. Biblical inspiration may be defined as the work of the Holy Spirit by which, through the instrumentality of the personality and literary talents of its human authors, he constituted the words of the Bible in all of its several parts as his written word to the human race and, therefore, of divine authority and without error.

INTEREST The OT forbade lending at interest to a fellow Israelite (Exod 22:25) but permitted charging interest to a foreigner (Deut 23:20). A needy Israelite might sell himself as a servant (Lev 25:39; 2 Kings 4:1). The prophets condemn the taking of interest as a heinous sin (Jer 15:10; Ezek 18:8, 13, 17). In the NT the receiving of interest (Matt 25:27; Luke 19:23) is distinctly encouraged.

INTERMEDIATE STATE (See ESCHATOLOGY)

IR (Ir, Heb. *'îr*, *watcher*). The ancestral head of a clan of Benjamin (1 Chron 7:12). It is the same as Iri (7:7).

IR SHEMESH (Ir shĕ'mĕsh, Heb. *'îr shemesh, city of the sun*). A city of Dan (Josh 19:41), the same as Beth Shemesh.

IRA (ī'rà, Heb. *'îr'a*). 1. A chief minister or priest in the time of David (2 Sam 20:26). 2. A son of Ikkesh, a Tekoite, one of David's mighty men (23:26; 1 Chron 11:28). 3. An Ithrite, one of David's heroes (2 Sam 23:38; 1 Chron 11:40).

IRI (ī'rī, Heb. *îrî*). A Benjamite of the family of Bela (1 Chron 7:7). It is the same as Ir (7:12).

IRON (See MINERALS)

IRRIGATION A word for which there is no Hebrew or Greek equivalent in the Bible, though the use of irrigation for watering plants and trees is frequently implied (Eccl 2:5–6; Isa 58:11).

ISAAC (ī'zàk, Heb. *yitshāk*, Gr. *Isaak, one laughs*). The only son of Abraham by Sarah, and the second of the three Hebrew patriarchs. He was born in the south country, probably Beersheba (Gen 21:14, 31), when Abraham was 100 and Sarah 90 years old (17:17; 21:5). He was named Isaac because both Abraham and Sarah had laughed incredulously at the thought of having a child at their age (17:17–19; 18:9–15; 21:6). His birth must be regarded as a miracle. Twenty-five years after God had promised the childless Abraham and Sarah a son, the promise was fulfilled. He is thus rightly called

The sacrifice of Isaac (Gen 22:2ff.), as depicted at Bet Alfa, a sixth-century synagogue found in Kibbutz Heftzi Bah in the Jezreel Valley. Courtesy Zev Radovan

the child of promise. When Isaac was eight days old, he was circumcised (21:4). Fearing future jealousy and strife between the two boys when she observed Ishmael mocking Isaac, Sarah tried to persuade Abraham to cast out Hagar and Ishmael. Abraham was loath to do this because he loved the boy and did so only when he received explicit direction from God, who said to him that his seed would be reckoned through Isaac, but he would also make a nation of Ishmael (21:9-13).

God commanded Abraham to offer Isaac as a sacrifice on a mountain in the land of Moriah (Gen 22). Isaac's unquestioning submission and obedience to his father stand out almost as remarkably as his father's faith. Bound on the altar and about to die, his life was spared when an angel of the Lord interposed and substituted for him a ram, which was offered up in his place.

Sarah died at Hebron when Isaac was 36 years old (Gen 23:1). At the age of 40 Isaac married Rebekah, a kinswoman from Mesopotamia (ch. 24); but he and his wife were childless until, in answer to prayer, twin sons, Esau and Jacob, were born to them when he was 60 (25:20, 26). At a time of famine, God admonished him not to go down into Egypt, as he had thought of doing, but to remain in the Promised Land; and he pledged his word to be with him. He went to the Philistine city of Gerar, and there, fearing for his own life, he passed his wife off as his sister, as Abraham had done with Sarah. He was justly rebuked by Abimelech the king for his duplicity (26:10), but later, after trouble over some wells, the two men formally entered into a covenant (26:26-31).

The last prominent event in the life of Isaac is the blessing of his sons (Gen 27). He wished to bestow his last blessing on his elder son; but through Rebekah's cunning and guile Jacob the younger supplanted his brother, and the blessing of the birthright was given to him. Isaac is mentioned only once more—20 years later, when Jacob returned from his sojourn in Mesopotamia, having married into Laban's family. Isaac died at 180 years of age, and his two sons, Esau and Jacob, buried him (Gen 35:27-29).

The NT refers to Abraham's sacrifice of Isaac (Heb 11:17-18; James 2:21). Isaac is contrasted with Ishmael, as the child of promise (Rom 9:7, 10; Gal 4:28; Heb 11:18). Isaac, although dead in human terms, is still living to God (Luke 20:37) and will be present in the future in the kingdom of heaven (Matt 8:11).

Of the three patriarchs, Isaac was the least conspicuous, traveled the least, had the fewest extraordinary adventures, but lived the longest. He was free from violent passions; quiet, gentle, dutiful; less a man of action than of thought and suffering. His name is always joined in equal honor with Abraham and Jacob.

ISAIAH His name Isaiah (*Salvation of Jehovah*) is almost identical in meaning with Joshua (*Jehovah is Salvation*), which appears in the NT as Jesus, the name of the Messiah whom Isaiah heralded. Isaiah was married and had two children to whom he gave significant names (Isa 7:3; 8:3).

Isaiah prophesied during four reigns of kings of Judah, from Uzziah to Hezekiah (Isa 1:1). The first date given is the year of Uzziah's death (6:1), which probably occurred about 740 B.C. The last historical event referred to is the death of Sennacherib (37:38), which occurred in 681. The most important events are the Syro-Ephraimitic war in the days of Ahaz (7:1-9), which Isaiah treated, despite its devastation (2 Chron 28:5-15), as almost insignificant compared with the far greater scourge from Assyria, which was so soon to follow (Isa 7:17-25). Assyria is the great enemy that much of chapters 7-39 deal with; and beyond it looms an even mightier foe, Babylon, whose downfall is foretold already in chapters 13-14 and who is the great theme of chapters 40-48. Over against these terrible instruments of divine judgment Isaiah pictures the messianic hope, first in counseling unbelieving Ahaz, and repeatedly thereafter.

The structure of Isaiah may be briefly analyzed as follows:

Isaiah 1-5, Introduction. Chapter 1 contains the "great arraignment." Like so many of Isaiah's utterances, it combines dire threatenings with urgent calls

Part of the oldest surviving complete scroll of Isaiah in Hebrew found in Cave 1 at Qumran near the Dead Sea, dated c. 125–100 B.C. The entire scroll measures 24 feet (7 m.) in length. Courtesy The Shrine of the Book, D. Samuel and Jeane H. Gottesman, Center for Biblical Manuscripts, Israel Museum, Jerusalem

to repentance and gracious offers of forgiveness and blessing. It is followed by the promise of world redemption (2:1–5). Then comes a series of threatening passages, including a detailed description of the finery of the women of Jerusalem as illustrating the sinful frivolity of the people as a whole. The land is likened to an unfruitful vineyard, which will soon become desolate.

Isaiah 6, The Temple Vision. This chapter is a vision of the "Holy One of Israel," one of Isaiah's favorite titles for God.

Isaiah 7–12, The Book of Immanuel. This group of chapters belongs to the period of the Syro-Ephraimitic war (2 Kings 16:1–20; 2 Chron 28). In the midst of this time of peril, Isaiah utters the great prophecies regarding Immanuel (Isa 7:14–16; 9:6–7; 11:1–10).

Isaiah 13–23, Prophecies Against the Nations. These are ten "oracles" against nations that either were or would be a menace to God's people: Babylon (Isa 13–14:27), Philistia (14:28–32), Moab (15–16), Damascus (17–18), Egypt (19–20), Babylon (21:1–10), Dumah (21:11–12), Arabia (21:13–17), Jerusalem (22), Tyre (23). Here prophecies regarding the near future (16:14; 21:16; cf. 22:20 with 37:2) appear along with others that refer to a more distant (23:17) or a quite remote time.

Isaiah 24–35. Isaiah 24 looks far into the future. It is world-embracing and may be called an *apocalypse.* The world judgment will be followed by songs of thanksgiving for divine blessing (25–26). A prophecy against Egypt follows (27). Then there are again six woes (28–34), the last being a frightful curse on Edom. This group also closes with a beautiful prophetic picture of future blessedness (35).

Isaiah 36–39, Historical (cf. parallel passages in Kings and Chronicles). These chapters describe the blasphemous threats of Sennacherib against Jerusalem, Hezekiah's appeal to Isaiah, who ridicules the invader, and the flight and death of the blasphemer (36–37)—one of the most thrilling episodes in the whole Bible. Probably Hezekiah's illness and the envoy of Merodach-Baladan (38–39) took place during the reign of Sargon, king of Assyria and father of Sennacherib. If so, the arrangement is topical and intended to prepare for the prophecies of consolation that follow.

Isaiah 40–66. These chapters have been called the Book of Consolation. They fall into three parts as is suggested by the refrain-like words, " 'There is no peace,' says the LORD, 'for the wicked' " (48:22; cf. 57:21), which have their terrible echo in Isaiah's final words (66:24).

Isaiah is preeminently the prophet of redemption. The greatness and majesty of God, his holiness and hatred of sin and the folly of idolatry, his grace and mercy and love, and the blessed rewards of obedience are constantly recurring themes. *Redeemer* and *savior* (save, salvation) are among Isaiah's favorite words. The words that describe the character of the promised Messiah (9:6) are frequently on his lips: Wonderful (25:1; 28:29; 29:14), Counselor (19:17; 25:1; 28:29; 40:13–14, 16–17), Mighty God (30:29; 33:13; 40:26–28; 49:20–26; 60:16), Everlasting Father (26:4; 40:28; 45:17; 55:3; 57:15; 60:19–20; 63:16; 64:8), Prince of Peace (26:12; 45:7; 52:7; 53:5; 55:12; 57:19; 66:12). Isaiah had a deep appreciation of beauty and wonder of the world of nature (e.g., ch. 35). A striking figure that he upon repeatedly is the "highway" (11:16; 19:23; 33:8; 35:8; 36:2; 40:3; 49:11; 57:14; 62:10). All the barriers that separate nation from nation and delay the coming of the King to his kingdom will be removed (Isa 40:5).

Isaiah is quoted by name 21 times, slightly more than all the other writing prophets taken together; and there are many more allusions and quotations where his name is not given. He has been called the evangelist of the OT, and his book has many of the most precious verses in the Bible. Jesus began his public ministry at Nazareth by reading from Isaiah 61.

A new theory regarding prophecy widely prevalent today minimizes or denies prediction, declaring that the OT prophet spoke only to the people of his own time and not to future generations. This theory is refuted by the fact that the NT frequently quotes the words of the prophets, notably Isaiah, as fulfilled in Jesus' earthly life. John 12:38–40 brings together two quotations from Isaiah, the one from 53:1, the other from 6:9–10; and as if to make it quite clear that they have one and the same source, the evangelist adds: "Isaiah said this because he saw Jesus' glory and spoke about him."

The main argument for a second Isaiah is that Cyrus is referred to as one who has already entered on his career of conquest (e.g., Isa 41:1–2, 25); and it is claimed that the writer of all or part of chapters 40–66 must have lived at the close of the Babylonian captivity. We must note, therefore, that the prophets, notably Isaiah, often spoke as if they were eyewitnesses of the future events they described. The viewpoint or situation of the one who penned chapter 53 is Calvary. He describes the sufferings of the Servant as ended and depicts in glowing colors the glory that will follow, yet the prophet cannot have lived at that time. He must have lived many years, even centuries, before the advent of the One whose death he vividly portrays. Consequently, one must hold that the prophet, neither in chapters 7–12 nor in chapter 53, predicted the coming and work of the Messiah; or one must hold that he could and did speak of future events, of the coming of Cyrus, of One greater than Cyrus, as if he were living in the glorious days of which he spoke.

ISCARIOT (See JUDAS ISCARIOT)

ISH-BOSHETH (ĭsh'-bōshĕth, Heb. *'ĭsh-bōsheth, man of shame*). The fourth son of Saul (2 Sam 2:8), originally called Eshbaal, "man of Baal," but for some reason his name was subsequently changed. After the death of Saul and his three elder sons at the battle of Gilboa, he was proclaimed king over Israel by Abner, the captain of Saul's army, at Mahanaim (2:8ff.), while Judah proclaimed David its king. Ish-Bosheth was then about 40 years old and reigned two years (2:8–10). He was not successful in the war he waged with David to rule over all 12 tribes, but the war did not come to a close until Abner transferred his allegiance to David because of a serious charge made against him by Ish-Bosheth (3:6ff.). Abner fulfilled David's condition to return to him Michal, his wife, before peace could be made. It was not, however, until Abner was murdered at Hebron that Ish-Bosheth lost heart and gave up hope of retaining his power (2 Sam 4). Soon after, Ish-Bosheth was murdered by his own captains, but David had the assassins put to death and buried Ish-Bosheth in the grave of Abner at Hebron. Ish-Bosheth's death ended the dynasty of Saul.

ISHI (ĭsh'ī, Heb. *'îshî, my husband*). A symbolic term that expresses the ideal relation between the Lord and Israel (Hos 2:16 KJV, NASB), also rendered "my husband" (NIV, RSV).

ISHI (Heb. *yish'î, salutary*). 1. A man of Judah (1 Chron 2:31). 2. Another man of Judah (4:20). 3. A descendant of Simeon (4:42). 4. The head of a family of Manasseh (5:24).

ISHIAH (See ISSHIAH)

ISHMAEL (ĭsh'mā-ĕl, Heb. *yishmā'ēl, God hears,* Gr. *Ismaēl*). 1. The son of Abraham by Hagar, the Egyptian maid of his wife Sarah. Sarah was barren (Gen 16:1); and in accordance with the custom of the age she gave to Abraham her handmaid Hagar as his concubine, hoping that he might obtain a family by her. When Hagar saw that she had conceived, she began to despise her mistress. Sarah made things so difficult for Hagar that she fled, and somewhere on the road to Egypt the angel of the Lord met her and told her to return to her mistress and submit herself to her. He encouraged her with a promise of many descendants. Ishmael was circumcised when he was 13 (17:25). Abraham loved him (17:18).

After the weaning of Isaac, Sarah urged Abraham to get rid of Ishmael and his slave mother. Sent away with bread and a bottle of water, Ishmael and his mother wandered about in the wilderness of Beersheba. The angel of the Lord appeared to her, directed her to some water, and renewed his former promise of Ishmael's future greatness (Gen 21:19–20). Ishmael grew up and became famous as an archer in the wilderness of Paran. His mother gave him in marriage to an Egyptian wife. When Abraham died, Ishmael returned from exile to help Isaac bury their father (25:9). He became the father of 12 sons and a daughter, whom Esau took for his wife. He died at the age of 137 (25:17). In Galatians 4:21–31 Paul uses the lives of Ishmael and Isaac allegorically. **2.** A descendant of Jonathan (1 Chron 8:38; 9:44). **3.** The father of Zebadiah, a ruler in the house of Judah in the reign of Jehoshaphat (2 Chron 19:11). **4.** The son of Jehohanan. He helped Jehoiada to restore Jehoash to the throne of Judah (23:1). **5.** The son of Nethaniah, a member of the royal house of David. About two months after the destruction of Jerusalem, Gedaliah and others with him were murdered at a banquet held in honor of Ishmael, who then succeeded in escaping to the king of Ammon (2 Kings 25:25; Jer 40:7–41:18).

ISHMAELITE (ĭsh'mā-ĕl-īt, Heb. *yishme'ēlîm*). A descendant of Ishmael, the son of Abraham and Hagar (Gen 21:14–21). The 12 sons of Ishmael and his Egyptian wife became princes and progenitors of many tribes. They lived in camps in the desert of northern Arabia, though occasionally some of them, such as the Nabateans, settled down (cf. 16:12). The word is apparently used in the OT in a wider sense, referring to the nomadic tribes of northern Arabia generally (37:28, 36; Judg 8:24; cf. Gen 37:25–28). All Arabs, following Muhammad's example, claim descent from Ishmael.

ISHMAIAH (ĭsh-mā'yà, Heb. *yishma'yâh*, *Jehovah hears*). **1.** A Gibeonite who joined David at Ziklag (1 Chron 12:4). **2.** Chief of the Zebulunites in David's reign (27:19).

ISHOD (See ISHHOD)

ISHTOB (See TOB)

ISHUI, ISHUAI (See ISHVI)

ISHVI (ĭsh'vī, Heb. *yishwi*, *level*). **1.** The third son of Asher, and founder of a tribal family (Gen 46:17, KJV "Isui"; Num 26:44, KJV "Jesui"; 1 Chron 7:30, KJV "Ishuai"). **2.** A son of Saul (1 Sam 14:49; KJV Ishui).

ISLAND, ISLE The Hebrew word has a much wider significance than the English words. Its root meaning is supposed to be "habitable land." **1.** Dry land, as opposed to water (Isa 42:15).

2. An island as usually understood (Jer 2:10). **3.** A coastland, whether belonging to continents or islands (Gen 10:5; Isa 20:6). **4.** The farthest regions of the earth (41:5; Zeph 2:11).

ISMAIAH (See ISHMAIAH)

ISPAH (See ISHPAH)

ISRAEL (ĭz'rā-ĕl). Used in Scripture to designate: (1) an individual man, the son of Isaac (see JACOB); or (2) his descendants, the twelve tribes of the Hebrews; or (3) the ten northern tribes, led by the tribe of Ephraim, as opposed to the southern, under the tribe of Judah.

Before the year 2100 B.C., the God who directs all history chose the patriarch Abraham and called him out of Ur of the Chaldees (Gen 11:31; Neh 9:7). The Lord's redemptive purpose was to bring Abraham and his descendants into a saving (covenant) relationship with himself (Gen 17:7) and also to make of Abraham's seed a nation in Palestine (17:8) and through them to some day bring salvation to the entire world (12:3; 22:18). God accordingly blessed Abraham's grandson Jacob with many children. Furthermore, when Jacob returned to Palestine in 1909 B.C., God "wrestled" with him and brought him to a point of total submission (32:25; Hos 12:4). By yielding his life to God's purpose, Jacob achieved victory; and God changed his name to Israel, Hebrew *Yisrā'ēl*, which means, "He strives with God and prevails" (Gen 32:28; 35:10). Jacob's 12 sons were, literally, the children of "Israel" (42:5; 45:21). Israel, however, was aware that God would build each of them into a large tribe (49:7, 16). The term "children of Israel" came to signify the whole body of God's chosen people (32:32; 34:7).

I. Mosaic Period. God increased Israel from a clan of several hundred (Gen 14:14; 46:27) to a nation of almost 3 million souls (Exod 12:37; Num 1:46), equipped with all the material and cultural advantages of Egypt (Exod 2:10; 12:36; Acts 7:22). Israel was enslaved and compelled to erect certain Hyksos store-cities in the region of the eastern delta (Exod 1:11; cf. Gen 15:13) and was threatened with total national destruction under the anti-Semitic policy of the empire (Exod 1:16). Moses (born 1527 B.C.) was befriended by an Egyptian princess, perhaps the one who was to become the famous queen, Hatshepsut; but even he was forced to flee Egypt during the reign of the great conqueror and oppressor Thothmes III (1501–1447 B.C.).

God, however, still remembered his

covenant promises with Abraham (Exod 2:24–25). At the death of the great Pharaoh (2:23) God appeared to Moses in a burning bush at Mt. Sinai and commissioned him to deliver the enslaved people (3:10). Only after a series of ten miraculous plagues, climaxing in the death of all the first-born of Egypt (see PASSOVER), was the hardhearted Pharaoh compelled to yield to the Lord (12:31).

The Exodus took place in the spring of 1446 B.C. (Exod 12:37–40). This date has been reduced by a number of critical scholars to about 1290 B.C. Scripture, however, is explicit in placing the Exodus in the 480th year before the beginning of Solomon's temple in 966 (1 Kings 6:1); and the 15th-century date is then confirmed by other scriptural testimonies (cf. Judg 11:26; Acts 13:19 ASV). Israel marched eastward from Goshen toward the Red Sea. But when the perfidious Pharaoh pursued after the seemingly entrapped Hebrews (Exod 14:3), the Lord sent a strong east wind that blew back the waters of the sea (14:21). Israel crossed, and then the Lord caused the waters to return so that the Egyptians were destroyed to the last man (14:28; excepting Pharaoh, who is not mentioned after v. 10).

Israel reached Mt. Sinai at the beginning of summer, 1446 B.C. (Exod 19:1). Here God extended the covenant offer of reconciliation that he had made with Abraham and Jacob (Gen 12:1–3; 28:13–15) so as to embrace the whole nation of the sons of Israel. In May 1445 B.C. Israel broke up camp (Num 10:11) and marched northeast to Kadesh on the southern border of Canaan. But after taking 40 days to spy out the land, all the tribal representatives except Caleb and Joshua reported unfavorably on attempting any conquest of Canaan (13:28). Impetuous Israel then refused to advance into the Promised Land and prayed for a return to Egypt (14:4). Moses' intercession did save them from immediate divine wrath; but the Lord still condemned them to wander for 40 years in the wilderness, one year for each day of spying, until that entire generation died away (14:32–34).

During the last month of Moses' life, God's great servant conducted a "numbering" or census of the people, which indicated a figure of over 600,000 fighting men, only slightly less than had taken part in the Exodus 40 years before (Num 26:51; cf. 1:46). Moses then granted the request of the tribes of Reuben, Gad, and half of Manasseh to settle in the conquered lands of Transjordan (ch. 32); and he provided for the division of western

The Merneptah Stele, c. 1234–1222 B.C., found in Merneptah's mortuary temple west of Thebes. It contains the only mention of the name "Israel" in all ancient Egyptian writing. Courtesy Encyclopaedia Judaica Photo Archive, Jerusalem

Canaan among the remaining tribes (chs. 33–34). At this time Balaam, who had been employed by the Moabites to curse Israel, uttered his famous blessings, predicting the future messianic king (24:17). Moses then anointed Joshua as his successor (27:23), spoke the final two addresses that constitute most of the Book of Deuteronomy (chs. 1–4 and 5–30), and ascended Mt. Pisgah to view the Promised Land. There Moses died and was buried by God's own hand (Deut 34:5–6).

II. The Conquest. In the spring of 1406 B.C. the Jordan River was in its annual flood stage (Josh 3:15). But a miracle of divine intervention (3:13, 16) allowed

Israel to march across the dry riverbed, led by the ark of God's testament (3:13).

Joshua's war of conquest developed in three major campaigns: in central, southern, and northern Canaan. His first objective was the city of Jericho. Within six years of the fall of Jericho (cf. 14:10) all Canaan had come to lie at Joshua's feet (11:16). "So the LORD gave Israel all the land he had sworn to give their forefathers . . . every [promise] was fulfilled" (21:43, 45). The Canaanites had not yet lost their potential for resistance; and indeed, what the Lord had sworn to Israel had been a gradual occupation of the land (Exod 23:28–30; Deut 7:22). Much still remained to be possessed (Josh 13:1), but at this point Joshua was compelled by advancing age to divide the land among the 12 Hebrew tribes (Josh 13–22).

III. Judges. Moses had ordered the "devotion" (extermination) of the Canaanites (Deut 7:2), both because of their longstanding immoralities (9:5; cf. Gen 9:22, 25; 15:16) and because of their debasing religious influence on God's people (Deut 7:4; 12:31). In the years immediately following Joshua's death, Judah accordingly accomplished an initial capture of Jerusalem (Judg 1:8; though the city was not held, 1:21); Ephraim and western Manasseh killed the men of Bethel (1:25) because the city had begun to reassert itself. But then came failure: Israel ceased to eradicate the Canaanites, no more cities were taken (1:27–34), and the tribe of Dan actually suffered eviction themselves (1:34). Israel's tolerance of evil had to be rectified by national chastening (2:3).

The next 350 years were used of God to impress on his people three major lessons: (1) The Lord's wrath because of sin (Judg 2:14). (2) God's mercy when people repented (2:18). (3) Man's total depravity (2:19). The period of the 14 judges (12 in Judges, plus Eli and Samuel in 1 Samuel) demonstrates a repeated cycle of human sin, of servitude or supplication, and then of salvation.

From about 1400 to 1250 B.C. the chief external forces that God employed for the execution of his providential dealings were the rival empires of the Hittites north of Palestine and of the Egyptians to the south. Neither of these powers was conscious of the way God was using them; but still, the years in which either succeeded in maintaining Palestinian law and order proved to be just the period that God had chosen for granting "rest" to Israel.

IV. The United Kingdom of Israel was precipitated by the demand of the people themselves. Despite God's directive that they be holy and separate (Lev 20:26), they still wished to be like "all the other nations" (1 Sam 8:5). Saul's accession proceeded in three steps. He was first privately anointed by Samuel (10:1) and filled with God's Spirit (10:10), then publicly selected at Mizpah (10:24), and at last popularly confirmed at Gilgal (ch. 11). The primary concern of his 40-year reign (1050–1010 B.C., cf. Acts 13:21) was the Philistines. Saul terminated their oppression but, by his failure to submit to Samuel (1 Sam 13:8–9), suffered the rejection of his dynasty from the throne of Israel (13:14).

From his capital in Gibeah of Benjamin, Saul "fought valiantly" and pushed back the enemies of Israel on every hand (1 Sam 14:47–48). In about 1025 B.C., however, having been ordered to destroy Israel's implacable enemies the Amalekites (15:1–3; cf. Exod 17:14), Saul disobeyed and spared both the king and the best of the spoils, under pretext of making offerings to God (1 Sam 15:15). Samuel stated that "to obey is better than sacrifice" (15:22) and declared Saul's personal deposition from the kingship (15:23, 28).

Samuel then privately anointed David, a son of Jesse of Judah, as king over Israel (16:13). David was about 15 at the time (cf. 2 Sam 5:4); but by God's providence, he gained rapid promotion at court, first as a minstrel (1 Sam 16:21–23) and then by his victory over the Philistine champion Goliath (ch. 17). Even Saul's growing jealousy, which removed David from court to the dangers of battle, augmented the latter's popularity (18:27–30). Saul's overt hostility finally drove David and his followers into exile, first as outlaws in Judah (1 Sam 20–26) and then as vassals to the Philistine king of Gath (1 Sam 27–30). But while Saul was diverting his resources in the futile pursuit of David, the Philistines prepared for a third, all-out attack on Israel in 1010. David barely escaped engaging in war against his own people (29:4; cf. v. 8); and Saul, routed at Mt. Gilboa, committed suicide rather than suffering capture (31:4). Israel's sinful demand for a king had brought about their own punishment.

Having learned of the death of Saul, David moved to Hebron and was there proclaimed king over his own tribe of Judah (2 Sam 2:4). But despite David's diplomacy, the supporters of Saul set up his son Ish-Bosheth over the northern and eastern tribes (2:8–9). Civil war followed, but David increasingly gained the upper hand (3:1). Finally, after the death of Ish-Bosheth, the tribal representatives assembled to Hebron and there anointed David as king over all Israel (5:3; 1003 B.C.). The Philistines now realized that their future depended on prompt action. David, however, after an initial flight to his former outlaw retreat (5:17), rallied his devoted forces (cf. 23:13–17) and, by two brilliant victories in the vicinity of Jerusalem (5:9–25), he not only terminated the last Philistine oppression but eventually incorporated Gath into his own territory and subdued the remaining Philistine states (1 Chron 18:1).

The time was ripe for the rise of a Hebrew empire. The Hittites had succumbed to barbarian invasion; the 21st Dynasty of Egypt stagnated under the alternating rule of priests and merchants (1100 B.C. on); and Assyria, after having weakened others, was itself restrained by inactive kings. With Philistia broken, Israel remained free from foreign threat for 150 years. David's first strategic move was to capture Jerusalem from the Canaanites. Militarily, Mt. Zion constituted a splendid fortress (2 Sam 5:6, 9); politically, the city afforded David a neutral capital between the recently hostile areas of Judah and northern Israel; and religiously, Zion's possession of the ark of God's testament (6:17) centered the people's spiritual hopes within its walls (Ps 87). From about 1002 to 995 David extended his power on every side, from the Euphrates River on the north (2 Sam 8:3) to the Red Sea on the south (8:14).

In his later life David became involved in sins of adultery and murder (2 Sam 11) and of failure to control his sons (chs. 13–14), and for this he received corresponding punishments (chs. 15–16; cf. 12:10–12). The revolt of Absalom served also to intensify the antagonism between northern Israel and southern Judah (19:41–43). But at his death in 970 B.C. David was able to commit to his son Solomon an empire that marked the peak of Israel's power.

Solomon, after a bloody accession (1 Kings 2:25, 34, 36), reigned in peace, culture, and luxury, experiencing only one military campaign in 40 years (2 Chron 8:3). King Solomon is most famous for his unexcelled wisdom (1 Kings 4:31). His greatest undertaking was the building of the Jerusalem temple, erected from 966 to 959 B.C. (1 Kings 6) out of materials lavishly provided by David (1 Chron 22). Like the tabernacle before it, the temple symbolized the abiding presence of God with his people (1 Kings 8:11).

But Solomon also engaged in a number of luxurious building projects of his own (1 Kings 7:1–12), so that despite his great commercial revenues (9:26–28; 10:14–15) indebtedness forced him to surrender territory (9:11–12) and to engage in excessive taxation and labor conscription. Unrest grew throughout the empire; and, while the tribute continued during his lifetime (4:21), surrounding subject countries, such as Edom and Damascus, became increasingly independent (11:14, 23). More serious was Solomon's spiritual failure, induced by wanton polygamy (11:1–8). "The LORD became angry with Solomon because his heart had turned away from the LORD . . . . So the LORD said to Solomon 'Since this is your attitude and you have not kept my covenant, . . . I will most certainly tear the kingdom away from you and give it to one of your subordinates . . . . Yet I will not tear the whole kingdom from [your son], but will give him one tribe for the sake of David my servant and for the sake of Jerusalem, which I have chosen' " (11:9–12).

V. The Divided Kingdom. Early in 930 B.C. Solomon died, and his son Rehoboam went to Shechem to be confirmed as king. The people, however, were led by Jeroboam of Ephraim to demand relief from Solomon's tyranny (1 Kings 12:4), and when Rehoboam spurned their pleas, the ten northern tribes seceded to form an

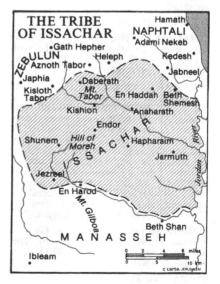

THE TRIBE OF ISSACHAR

independent kingdom of Israel (or Ephraim).

ISSACHAR (ĭs′à-kàr, Heb. *yissākhār,* meaning uncertain). **1.** The ninth son of Jacob and the fifth of Leah (Gen 30:17–18; 35:23). He had four sons, who went with him into Egypt (46:13; Exod 1:3). There he died and was buried. His descendants formed a tribe, consisting of five great tribal families (Num 26:23–24). **2.** A Korahite doorkeeper in the reign of David (1 Chron 26:5). (See page 279.)

ISSHIAH (ĭs′shī′à, Heb. *yishshîyāhû, Jehovah exists*). **1.** A man of Issachar (NIV 1 Chron 7:3; Izrachiah in JB, KJV, MLB, NASB, NEB, RSV). **2.** One of those who came to David at Ziklag (12:6, Jesiah in KJV). **3.** A Levite of the house of Rehabiah (24:21). **4.** A Levite of the house of Uzziel (23:20; 24:25).

ISUAH (See ISHVAH)

ISUI (See ISHVI)

ITALIAN REGIMENT A cohort of volunteer Roman soldiers recruited in Italy and stationed in Caesarea when Peter preached the gospel to Cornelius, who was a centurion in it (Acts 10:1). It consisted mostly of Italians who could not find service in the Praetorian Guard.

ITALY (Gr. *Italia*). The geographical term for the country of which Rome was the capital. It is referred to four times in the NT (Acts 10:1; 18:2; 27:1; Heb 13:24). Christianity was introduced early into Italy, but the time and circumstances are uncertain.

ITCH (See DISEASES)

ITHAI (îth′à-ī, Heb. *'îthay*). A Benjamite, one of David's chief men (1 Chron 11:31); Ittai in 2 Samuel 23:29 (JB, KJV, MLB, NASB, NEB, RSV).

ITHAMAR (ĭth′à-mär, Heb. *'îthāmār*). The youngest of the four sons of Aaron, the others being Eleazar, Nadab, and Abihu. Aaron and his sons were consecrated to the priesthood (Exod 28:1). During the wilderness wanderings Ithamar was the treasurer of the offerings for the tabernacle (Exod 38:21) and superintendent of the Gershonites and Merarites (Num 4:28, 33). He founded the priestly family to which Eli and his descendants belonged, and this continued after the Captivity (1 Chron 24:4–6; Ezra 8:2).

ITHIEL (ĭth′ĭ-ĕl, Heb. *'îthî'ēl, God is*). **1.** One of two persons to whom Agur addressed his sayings (Prov 30:1). **2.** A Benjamite (Neh 11:7).

ITHRA (See JETHER)

ITHRAN (ĭth′răn, Heb. *yithrān, excellent*). **1.** A Horite, son of Dishon (Gen 36:26; 1 Chron 1:41). **2.** A son of Zophah of the tribe of Asher (7:37).

ITHRITE (ĭth′rīt, Heb. *yithrî, excellence*). A family that lived at Kiriath Jearim (1 Chron 2:53). Two of David's heroes belonged to this family: Ira and Gareb (2 Sam 23:28; 1 Chron 11:40).

ITTAI (ĭt′à-ī, Heb. *'ittay*). **1.** A son of Ribai, a Benjamite, one of David's 30 mighty men (2 Sam 23:29 JB, KJV, MLB, NASB, NEB, RSV; but NIV has "Ithai," as in 1 Chron 11:31).
2. A native of Gath who left his Philistine city, joined David's army, and was loyal to David through all the ups and downs of his reign (2 Sam 15:18–22; 18:2, 5).

ITUREA (ĭt′û-rē′à, Gr. *Itouraia, pertaining to Jetur*). This word is found only once in Scripture, in the description of Philip's territory: "of Iturea and Traconitis" (Luke 3:1). It was a region NE of Palestine, beyond the Jordan, and cannot now be exactly located. The Itureans were descended from Ishmael (Gen 25:15), who had a son named Jetur, from whom the name Iturea is derived. The Itureans were seminomads and famous archers, a lawless and predatory people.

IVORY (Heb. *shēn,* Gr. *elephantinos*). Ivory was brought to Palestine by both ship and caravan and came from India. Solomon's throne was made of ivory

Ivory carvings (c. 1350–1300 B.C.) from Megiddo, found in a treasury beneath the Canaanite Palace. Courtesy Israel Department of Antiquities and Museums

(1 Kings 10:18), and he imported large
quantities of it. Amos denounced Israel
for its luxuries, among them the use of
ivory (Amos 3:15; 6:4). Palaces were
inlaid and decorated with ivory (1 Kings
22:39; Ps 45:8).

IVVAH, IVAH (ĭ'và, Heb. *'iwwâh*). A
city, probably in Syria, captured by the
Assyrians, according to the boast of
Sennacherib's representative (2 Kings
18:34; 19:13; Isa 37:13)

IYIM (ĭ'ĭm, Heb. *'îyîm, heaps, ruins*). 1.
A town in Judah near Edom (Josh 15:29;

NIV Iim). 2. A town east of the Jordan
River (Num 33:45).

IZHAR (ĭz'hàr, Heb. *yitshãr, the shining
one*). 1. A Levite, son of Kohath, whose
descendants formed a tribal family (Exod
6:18–19; Num 3:19; 1 Chron 6:18, 38). 2.
In ASV and RSV a descendant of Judah,
whose mother was Helah (4:7). NIV has
"Zohar"; KJV and NEB have "Jezoar."

IZRI (ĭz'-rī, Heb. *yitsrî, creator, former*).
A man of the sons of Jeduthun, chief of
one of the Levitical choirs (1 Chron
25:11). Called Zeri in 25:3.

– J –

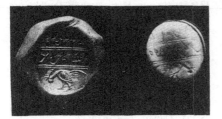

The seal of Jaazaniah (right) and its impression from Mizpah (Tell en-Nasbeh), late seventh century B.C. Inscription reads, "(Belonging) to Jaazaniah, servant of the king." Courtesy Palestine Institute of Pacific School of Religion, Berkeley, California

JAAKAN (jā'à-kăn, Heb.*ya'ăqān*). A descendant of Esau (1 Chron 1:35–42; NIV "Akan"; KJV "Jakan"). He was the son of Ezer, who was a Horite (Gen 36:20–27, "Akan"). Israel rested in the land of the Jaakanites, where there were wells, and Aaron was buried there (Deut 10:6–7). In the report of Israel's wanderings the camp is called *Bene* (sons of) *Jaakan* (Num 33:31–32).

JAALAM (See JALAM)

JAANAI (See JANAI; JANNAI)

JAARESHIAH (jā'à-rē-sī'à). A son of Jerohan (1 Chron 8:27), of the tribe of Benjamin.

JAAZANIAH (jā-ăz'à-nī'à, Heb. *ya'ăzanyāhû, ya'ăzanyah, Jehovah hears*). 1. A soldier from Maacah whose land east of the Jordan was given to the tribe of Manasseh (Josh 13:7–11). He was captain under Gedaliah (2 Kings 25:23). Jeremiah calls him Jezaniah (Jer 42:1), Azariah (43:2), as well as Jaazaniah (40:8). He joined a group who killed Gedaliah and then, contrary to advice from Jeremiah, led a band of refugees into Egypt (43:1–7). 2. The son of a Recabite named Jeremiah. He was among a group of refugees who refused to drink wine offered by Jeremiah the prophet (35:1–11). 3. A leader in idolatrous worship that Ezekiel saw in a vision (Ezek 8:11–12). 4. The son of Azzur, one of a band of 25 men who led in wickedness and idolatry in Israel (11:1–3).

JAAZER (See JAZER)

JABAL (jā'băl, Heb. *yāvāl*, meaning uncertain). A son of Lamech, who was the great-grandson of Cain (Gen 4:19–20). He and his brothers, Jubal and Tubal-Cain, are credited with the origin of civilized society (4:21–22).

JABBOK (jăb'ŏk, Heb. *yabbōq, flowing*). An important river east of the Jordan about halfway between the Dead Sea and the Sea of Galilee. It formed the northern border of the Amorite king Sihon (Josh 12:2) and was captured by the Hebrews after Sihon refused to let them cross his land (Num 21:21–25). It was also the southern border of the kingdom of Og (Josh 12:5). At a ford on the Jabbok, Jacob had his encounter with the angel — the encounter that resulted in his being given a new name (Gen 32:22–30). The word for "wrestle" is *abbaq* and may have given the Hebrew name to the stream.

JABESH (jā'běsh, Heb. *yavēsh, dry*). 1. Father of Shallum, who murdered Zachariah and reigned over Israel for a month (2 Kings 15:8–13). 2. A short term for Jabesh Gilead (1 Chron 10:12). See also JABESH GILEAD.

JABESH GILEAD (jā'běsh gĭl'ē-ăd, Heb. *yavēsh gil'ādh, dry*). The metropolis of the Gileadites (*Antiq.* 6.5.1). It lay a night's journey across the Jordan from Beth Shan (1 Sam 31:11–12). It was in Manasseh's territory (Num 32:33). When the citizens refused to attend the sacred assembly at Mizpah, an army was sent to destroy them (Judg 21:8–15). The city was not destroyed and grew again in power and wealth. During Saul's reign, Nahash, king of Ammon, besieged the city. Saul's army defeated Nahash; the city was saved and the nation reunited (1 Sam 11:1–15). One of the purposes behind this military aid was to secure wives for the Benjamites, since Israel had sworn never to allow Benjamites to marry their daughters (Judg 21:1). Later, when Saul's forces had been routed by the Philistines and he and his sons had been killed, men of Jabesh Gilead rescued their bodies, cremated them, and buried the remains in Jabesh (1 Sam 31:1–13). After becoming king, David sent thanks for the act (2 Sam 2:4–6) and had the remains of Saul and Jonathan exhumed and interred in the tomb of Kish in the land of Benjamin (21:12–14).

JABEZ (jā'běz, Heb. *ya'bēts, to grieve*). 1. The head of a family in Judah (1 Chron 4:9) whose offspring are listed as scribes and as Kenites (2:55). He was more

Woodcut from the Bishops' Bible, 1568, that illustrates Jacob's Ladder Dream (Gen 28:10–15). Courtesy The British Library

honorable than his brothers (4:9). He made an earnest appeal for a blessing and it was granted (4:10). Zobebah (4:8) is probably another title for him. **2.** Jabez was also an unidentified town in Judah where scribes carried on their trade (2:55).

JABIN (jā′bĭn, Heb. *yāvîn, able to discern*). **1.** A king of Hazor, the leading city in northern Palestine (Josh 11:1). Joshua and his forces engaged in battle with Jabin and the alliance he had formed and defeated them (Josh 11:1–10). Hazor was captured, and Jabin was killed (11:10). **2.** Another king of Hazor who enslaved Israel. He was defeated by Barak (Judg 4; cf. 1 Sam 12:9; Ps 83:9).

JABNEEL (jăb′nē-ĕl, Heb. *yavne'ēl, God causes to build*). A town on the northern border of Judah, just south of Joppa (Josh 15:11), also called Jabneh (2 Chron 26:6). It belonged to the tribe of Dan.

JABNEH (See JABNEEL)

JACHIN (See JAKIN)

JACINTH (See MINERALS)

JACKAL (See ANIMALS)

JACOB (jā′kŭb, Heb. *ya' ăqōv, supplanter*). At the age of 40, Isaac married Rebekah, a sister of his uncle Laban (Gen 25:20). In answer to his prayer on behalf of his barren wife, she conceived twins (25:21). An unusual prenatal incident caused her to consult the Lord, who revealed to her that her children would become the founders of two great nations (25:23). An ominous rivalry, begun in the womb, became visible during the birth of the children. Esau came first; Jacob followed at once, holding Esau by the heel, giving Jacob the name "tripper" or "supplanter" (25:25–26). Rebekah was partial to Jacob (25:28), while Isaac favored the older son. Jacob's cunning was revealed in the way he induced Esau to sell his birthright (25:27–34).

After cheating Esau out of Isaac's blessing (Gen 27), Jacob, while fleeing to Haran, had a dream of a ladder, with angels ascending and descending (28:1–22). God promised Jacob that he would inherit the land and have numerous children (Gen 28:10–15). He named the place

Bethel, "House of God" (28:16–19), and made a vow to tithe all his further possessions (28:20–22). In Haran Jacob entered the home of his uncle Laban (29:1–14) and served him for 20 years for his daughters Leah and Rachel (29:1–30).

The conflict between Jacob and Esau had its counterpart in the conflict between Leah and Rachel, who, with their handmaids (Zilpah and Bilhah) gave Jacob 11 sons and a daughter (chs. 29–31). With his family and many possessions he fled from Laban (ch. 31).

While returning home Jacob heard that his brother Esau was approaching with a formidable force. He wrestled with the angel of the Lord and secured a new name, Israel, or "Prince of God" (Gen 32:24–32). The meeting with Esau was emotion-packed (33:1–17). Jacob then journeyed to Shechem, where Dinah was raped; then Simeon and Levi killed the men of the city and pillaged their town (34:1–31). Jacob fled to Bethel. The 12th son, Benjamin, *son of my right hand*, was born, and Rachel died in giving him birth (35:1–20). Jacob went to Egypt after a famine where his son Joseph had become Pharoah's chief ruler (chs. 42–46). Jacob later died there (ch. 49).

JACOB'S WELL Modern *Bir Ya'kub* is doubtless the well mentioned in John 4:6 as the well of Jacob. For more than 23 centuries Samaritans and Jews have believed that this is true. The ground had been purchased by Jacob (Gen 33:19). The area was later wrested by force from the Amorites (48:22). The well is near the base of Mt. Gerizim, whose bluffs may have been meant in Jesus' phrase "this mountain" (John 4:21). The depth of the well has not been determined.

JADAH (jā'dà, *honeycomb*). A descendant of Saul (1 Chron 9:42, KJV Jarah; called Jehoaddah in 8:36).

JADDUA (jā-dū'à, Heb. *yaddûa'*, *known*). 1. An Israelite prince who participated in making the covenant after the return from Babylon (Neh 10:21). 2. A priest who returned with Zerubbabel from Babylon (12:11, 22).

JAEL (jā'ĕl, Heb. *yā'ĕl, wild goat*). The wife of Heber the Kenite (Judg 4:17). Sisera fled to Heber's tent when defeated by Barak (4:15, 17). Jael killed him with a tent peg and was praised for her deed (4:21, 5:24).

JAH (Heb. *yāh*). A contraction of *Jahweh*. It is found in poetry (e.g., Pss 68:4; 118:14, RSV mg), and is seen in such compound words as Isaiah, *Jah is savior* and Abijah, *Jah is father*.

JAHATH (jā'hăth, Heb. *yahath*, perhaps *God will snatch up*). 1. A grandson of Judah (1 Chron 4:1–2). 2. A great-grandson of Levi (6:20, 43; NIV "Jeheth" in v. 20). 3. A chief among the Gershonite Levites (23:10–11). 4. Another Levite of the Izharite clan (24:22). 5. An overseer of construction during the restoration of the temple under Josiah (2 Chron 34:8–12).

JAHAZ (jā'hăz). A city in Reuben's heritage (Josh 13:18) in the land given to the Merarites (21:34–36). Israel captured the city, conquered King Sihon, and took the region (Num 21:21–25). It was once a stronghold north of the Arnon River. Isaiah (15:4) and Jeremiah (48:20–21) call it a city of Moab.

JAHAZIAH (See JAHZEIAH)

JAHAZIEL (jà-hā'zĭ-ĕl, Heb. *yahăzî'ēl*, *God sees*). 1. One of a band of ambidextrous warriors who aided David at Ziklag (1 Chron 12:1–4). 2. A priest who sounded the trumpet before the ark (16:6). 3. A son of Hebron and one of a host called by David to help build the temple (23:2–20). 4. A descendant of Asaph who announced a victory when defeat seemed certain (2 Chron 20:14ff.). Psalm 83 may have been written by him to commemorate the victory. 5. An ancestor of one of the families of the restoration (Ezra 8:5).

JAHWEH (See GOD; YHWH)

JAHZAH (jà'zà). A town given to Reuben (1 Chron 6:78; Jer 48:21). It is the same as Jahaz; see also JAHAZ.

JAHZEEL (See JAHZIEL)

JAHZEIAH (jà-zĭ'à, Heb. *yahzeyâh, God sees*). One of four who opposed Ezra's plan to rid Israel of alien wives married during the Captivity (Ezra 10:15).

JAHZIEL, JAHZEEL (jà'zĭ-ĕl, jà'zē-ĕl). A son of Naphtali (Gen 46:24; 1 Chron 7:13), founder of the Jahzeelite clan (Num 26:48).

JAIR (jā'ēr, Heb. *yā'îr, he enlightens*). 1. A son of Manasseh and a leading warrior in the conquest of Gilead by Moses (Num 32:40–41). 2. One of the judges, a Gileadite who served 20 years (Judg 10:3–5). 3. A Bethlehemite and the father of Elhanan (1 Chron 20:5). The name is given as Jaare-Oregim in 2 Samuel 21:19 (NIV). 4. The father of Mordecai (Esth 2:5).

JAIRUS (ja'ĭ-rŭs, Gr. *Iaeiros*). A synagogue ruler whose child Jesus raised from death (Mark 5:22; Luke 8:41).

JAKAN (See JAAKAN)

JAKEH (jā'kĕ, Heb. *yāqeh, very religious*). The father of Agur, a writer of proverbs (Prov 30:1-27).

JAKIM (jā'kĭm, Heb. *yākîm, God lifts*). 1. A son of Elpaal, a Benjamite (1 Chron 8:12, 19). 2. The head of the 12th course of priests (24:12).

JAKIN (jā'kĭn, Heb. *yākhîn, he will set up*). 1. Son of Simeon (Gen 46:10; Jarib in 1 Chron 4:24). Founder of the clan of Jakinites (Num 26:12). 2. One of the priests in Jerusalem during the Captivity (Neh 11:10). 3. During David's reign a leader of the 21st course of priests (1 Chron 24:17).

JAKIN AND BOAZ (jā'kĭn, bō'ăz, Heb. *yākhîn, he will set up; bō'az, fleetness, strength*). The names of two symbolic pillars in the porch of Solomon's temple, Jakin on the south, Boaz on the north, designed by Huram of Tyre (1 Kings 7:13-22).

JAMES (Gr. *Iakōbos*). The English form of Jacob. The name occurs 38 times in the NT, mostly in the Synoptic Gospels. Some scholars argue for only two or three different men.
1. James, the son of Zebedee, was a

Reconstruction of the palace entrance at Tell Ta'yinat in Syria. The two pillars are reminiscent of Jakin and Boaz, the two symbolic pillars in the porch of Solomon's temple (2 Chron 3:17). Courtesy Carta, Jerusalem

Galilean fisherman who was called to be one of the 12 apostles at the same time as his brother John (Matt 4:21; Mark 1:19-20). James, John, and Simon (Peter)—a trio that attained in some sense a place of primacy among the disciples—are often found at the center of events; e.g., when Jairus' daughter was raised (Mark 5:37; Luke 8:51), at the Transfiguration (Matt 17:1; Mark 9:2; Luke 9:28), on the Mt. of Olives (Mark 13:3), and in the Garden of Gethsemane (Matt 26:37; Mark 14:33). James and John had earlier accompanied Jesus to the home of Simon and Andrew (Mark 1:29).

James and John were given by Jesus the name "Boanerges" ("Sons of Thunder," Mark 3:17). They evidenced presumption and ill-considered thinking (Mark 9:38; 10:35ff.; Luke 9:49-50, 54; cf. Matt 20:20ff.). James' name is nowhere mentioned in the Fourth Gospel.

James was executed by Herod Agrippa I about A.D. 44 (Acts 12:2), and was the first of the Twelve whose martyrdom was referred to in the NT.

2. James, the son of Alphaeus. Another of the apostles (Matt 10:3; Mark 3:18; Luke 6:15; Acts 1:13). Since Levi or Matthew is also described as "the son of Alphaeus" (Mark 2:14), he and James may have been brothers.

3. James "the younger," the son of a Mary (Matt 27:56; Mark 15:40; Luke 24:10) who might have been the wife (or the daughter) of Clopas.

4. James, the brother of Jesus. The only two references to him in the Gospels mention him with his brothers Joses, Simon, and Judas (Matt 13:55; Mark 6:3). He saw the risen Christ (1 Cor 15:7), became head of the Jewish Christian church at Jerusalem (Acts 12:17; 15:19ff.; 21:18; Gal 2:9), was regarded as an apostle (1:19), and is regarded as the author of the NT epistle that bears his name (James 1:1).

According to Hegesippus (c. A.D. 180), James' faithful adherence to the Jewish law and his austere lifestyle led to the designation "the just." It seems clear that he suffered martyrdom; Josephus places his death in the year 61 when there was a Jewish uprising after the death of Festus the procurator and before his successor had been appointed.

5. James, a relative of the apostle Judas. This Judas (not Judas Iscariot, John 14:22) is called Thaddaeus in Matthew and Mark. The elliptical text in two passages ("Judas of James"—Luke 6:16; Acts 1:13) has been interpreted in two ways: Judas was the brother (KJV) or the son (most other versions) of James.

JAMES, LETTER OF This letter is among the last to become firmly established in the NT canon. In the East the church accepted it from a very early period, but in the West it was not received into the canon until the end of the fourth century.

The NT mentions five who bore the name of James. See JAMES. Tradition attributes the authorship of the letter to James the brother of the Lord. All the characteristics of the letter support this view. The author speaks with the authority of one who knew he did not need to justify or defend his position. There is no more Jewish book in the NT than this letter; and this is to be expected from a man whom both tradition and the rest of the NT show was distinguished by a greater attachment to the law of Moses than Paul had.

The letter is addressed to "the twelve tribes scattered among the nations," an ambiguous expression interpreted in a number of ways: (1) The Jews of the Diaspora in general, who were living throughout the Mediterranean world outside Palestine. This meaning is impossible, for the writer is addressing Christians (James 1:18, 25; 2:1, 12; 5:7–9). (2) The Jewish Christians of the Diaspora. (3) The Christian church as the new people of God living far from their heavenly homeland—the true Israel (Gal 6:16), the true circumcision (Phil 3:3), and the seed of Abraham (Rom 4:16; Gal 3:29).

There is no doubt, however, that the letter is intended for Jewish Christians, although its message is applicable to all Christians. Those to whom the author writes worship in synagogues (James 2:2), and the faults he attacks were characteristic of Jews: misuse of the tongue (3:2–12; 4:2, 11), unkind judgments of one's neighbors (3:14; 4:11), the making of rash oaths (5:12), undue regard for wealth (2:1–13), etc. On the other hand, there is no mention of specifically pagan vices—e.g., idolatry, drunkenness, and impurity—against which Paul so often warns Gentile Christians.

After the address (James 1:1), James first admonishes his readers on having a right attitude toward tribulations and temptations (1:2–18) and exhorts them to be doers and not merely hearers of the Word of God (1:19–25). He forbids them to slight the poor and favor the rich (2:1–13) and shows them the insufficiency of faith without works (2:14–26). He then warns them against the misuse of the tongue (3:1–12) and sets forth the nature of true and false wisdom (3:13–18). He rebukes them for their greed and lust (4:1–12) and for making foolhardy plans for the future in business (4:13–17). The letter closes with a warning to the godless rich (5:1–6), an exhortation to patience in suffering (5:7–12), a reminder of the power of prayer in every need (5:13–18), and a declaration of the joy of Christian service (5:19–20).

JAMIN (jā'mĭn, Heb. *yāmîn, right hand*). 1. A son of Simeon (Gen 46:10; 1 Chron 4:24), or a clan of Simeon (Num 26:12). 2. A son of Ram of the tribe of Judah (1 Chron 2:27). 3. A teacher of the law under Ezra (Neh 8:7).

JANNES AND JAMBRES (jăn'ēz, jăm'brēz). Two magicians who withstood Moses and Aaron by duplicating some of their miracles. Paul, who was familiar with rabbinical traditions, named them as types of evil men of the last days (2 Tim 3:8).

JANOAH (jȧ-nō'ȧ). 1. A town of Naphtali captured by Assyria (2 Kings 15:29). 2. A town on the boundary of Ephraim (Josh 16:6–7).

JAPHETH (jā'fĕth, Heb. *yepheth, God will enlarge,* Gen 9:27). A son of Noah who was older than Shem (Gen 10:21), but comes third in some lists of the three sons (6:10; 9:18). Shem is usually named first (5:32; 11:10). Japheth and his wife were saved in the ark (7:7). Japheth aided Shem in covering the naked body of their drunken father (9:20–27). He is the progenitor of the more remote northern peoples of SE Europe. That he was to occupy the tents of Shem (9:27) is thought to refer to conquests of the Greeks, who were descendants of Japheth. This happened during the days of Assyrian power. He had seven sons whose descendants occupied the isles of the Gentiles, Hellenes or Greeks (10:5), an area including Asia Minor and upper Greece.

JAPHIA (jȧ-fī'ȧ, Heb. *yāphîa', tall* or *may God make bright*). 1. A ruler of Lachish who joined a coalition against Joshua and was defeated and executed (Josh 10:1–27). 2. A son of David born in Jerusalem (2 Sam 5:15; 1 Chron 3:7). 3. A small city on the eastern border of Zebulun (Josh 19:12).

JAR (See PITCHER)

JARAH (See JADAH)

JARESIAH (See JAARESHIAH)

JARHA (jär'hä). An Egyptian slave of Sheshan, a Jerahmeelite (1 Chron 2:34–35). Since Sheshan had no son, he gave Jarha his freedom so he could marry one of Sheshan's daughters. Jewish sources claim him as a proselyte.

JARIB (jär'ĭb, *he strives*). **1.** A son of Simeon (1 Chron 4:24), also called Jakin (Gen 46:10). **2.** A chief of returning captives, sent by Ezra to secure Levites to carry on the temple worship (Ezra 8:15–20). **3.** One of the priests who was ordered to put away his alien wives (10:18).

JARMUTH (jär'mŭth, Heb. *yarmûth, height*). **1.** One of the numerous places included in the heritage of Judah (Josh 15:35), 16 miles (27 km.) WSW from Jerusalem. **2.** A city given to the Gershonite Levites from the heritage of Issachar (21:27–29), also called Remeth (19:21) and Ramoth (1 Chron 6:73).

JASHAR, BOOK OF (jā'shàr). Quoted in Joshua 10:13; 2 Samuel 1:18; and in LXX of 1 Kings 8:53, this ancient book is thought to have been a collection of poetry, probably odes and psalms in praise of Israel's heroes and exploits. KJV spells the name "Jasher."

JASHEN (jā'shĕn, *brilliant*). Father of some of David's heroes (2 Sam 23:32). Confusion arises from the fact that 1 Chronicles 11:33–34 calls him Hashem, the Gizonite (evidently another spelling); the LXX there has "the Gunite."

JASHER, BOOK OF (See JASHAR, BOOK OF)

JASHOBEAM (jà-shō'bē-ăm, Heb. *yāshôv'ām, the people return*). **1.** One of the heroic men who went to Ziklag to aid David in his struggle against Saul (1 Chron 12:6). **2.** One of David's chieftains who was a ruler of captains. He killed 300 during one battle (11:11; or 800, 2 Sam 23:8–perhaps a scribal error). The LXX usually gives the name as Ishbaal. He is also called Josheb-Basshebeth (23:8; but cf. footnote; KJV Adino). Jashobeam is supposed to have been one of the three who brought David water from the well of Bethlehem (1 Chron 11:15–19). **3.** One who commanded a division of 24,000 men of Israel (27:2–3). This man may be the same as no. 2; if so, Hacmonite was an official title.

JASHUB, JASHUBITE (jā'shŭb, jā'shŭb-īt, Heb. *yāshûv, he returns*). **1.** A son of Issachar (Num 26:24). Based on MT, Genesis 46:13 has "Job" (KJV, MLB) or "Iob" (NASB, NEB, RSV); LXX has "Ja-shub" (NIV). **2.** One of those who had married foreign wives (Ezra 10:29).

JASIEL (See JAASIEL)

JASON (Gr. *Iason, to heal*). A believer who sheltered Paul and Silas in Thessalonica (Acts 17:5–9). He was among those who sent greetings from Corinth to Rome (Rom 16:21).

JASPER (See MINERALS)

JATTIR (jä'têr). A large town in the hills of Judah (Josh 15:20, 48), given to the Levites (1 Chron 6:57). It was an important center (1 Sam 30:27).

JAVAN (jā'văn, Heb. *yāwān, Ionian*). **1.** A son of Japheth (Gen 10:2, 4; 1 Chron 1:5, 7). **2.** A region (perhaps settled by Javan), seen by Ezekiel (Ezek 27:13, 19; cf. Isa 66:19) as an important trade center. Javan (Gr. *Iōnia*) came to be the name the Hebrews gave to Greece. From 700 to 630 B.C., the Ionians carried on extensive trade in the Near East; hence all people of Greece were called Javan.

JAVELIN (See ARMS, ARMOR)

JAZER (jā'zêr). A city, with dependent villages, in Gilead east of the Jordan (Num 21:31–32). Built by Gadites (32:34–35), it later became a Levitical city (Josh 21:34–39). David found mighty men among her citizens (1 Chron 26:31).

JEALOUSY, WATER OF The name given holy water used to determine the guilt or innocence of a wife accused by her husband of unfaithfulness (Num 5:11–28).

JEBUS (jē'bŭs, Heb. *yevûs*). The name by which Jerusalem was known while occupied by the Jebusites (Josh 15:63; Judg 19:10; 1 Chron 11:4). It was taken by David and made his capital (2 Sam 5:1–9).

JEBUSITES (jĕb'ū-zīts, Heb. *yebûsi*). A Canaanite tribe, descended from Canaan (Gen 10), and dwelling in the land before the Israelite conquest (10:15–16; Exod 3:8, 17; Deut 7:1; 20:17; Josh 3:10; 10:1–5; Judg 1:8). They were not dislodged until David sent Joab and his men into the city (2 Sam 5:6–7; cf. 24:18ff.). (See page 288.)

JECAMIAH (See JEKAMIAH)

JECONIAH (jĕk'ō-nī'à, Gr. *Iechonias*). A variant of Jehoiachin (Matt 1:11–12), sometimes contracted to Coniah (Jer 22:24, 28; 37:1 JB, KJV, MLB, NASB, NEB; Koniah MOF; Jehoiachin NIV). A son of Jehoiakim and grandson of Josiah (1 Chron 3:15–17), he began to reign at

Eastern slope of Mt. Ophel, looking south, showing the site of the Jebusite citadel called "Zion" and the terracing believed to be the *millo* ("filling") referred to in 1 Kings 9:15, 24. Courtesy Encyclopaedia Judaica Photo Archive, Jerusalem. Photo David Eisenberg

age 18, but Nebuchadnezzar took him captive after only three months (Esth 2:6; Jer 24:1; 27:20; 28:4; 29:2).

JEDAIAH (jĕ-dā'yà, Heb. *yedha'yâh, Jehovah knows*). **1.** A descendant of Simeon and the father of a prince (1 Chron 4:37–38). **2.** A priest who returned with Zerubbabel and aided in rebuilding the walls of Jerusalem (Neh 3:10; 12:6, 19). **3.** A priest whose name appeared in the genealogy of the Hebrew captives in Babylon (1 Chron 9:1–10) and received the second lot in the temple service (24:7). Ancestor of a very large family (Ezra 2:1, 36; Neh 7:39).

JEDIAEL (jĕ-dī'ā-ĕl, Heb. *yedhî'ā'ĕl, known of God*). **1.** A son of Benjamin who became head of a mighty clan (1 Chron 7:6, 11), perhaps the same as Ashbel (8:1) and as the Jediael who joined David (1 Chron 12:20). **2.** Another valiant man in David's band (11:45), probably the same as no. 1. **3.** A temple doorkeeper, a descendant of Kore (26:1–2).

JEDUTHUN (jĕ-dū'thŭn, Heb. *yedhûthûn, praise*). A Levite whom, with Heman and others, David set over the

service of praise in the tabernacle (1 Chron 25:1–3). Psalm 39 by David is dedicated to Jeduthun and Psalms 62 and 77 are "after the manner of Jeduthun."

JEEZER (See ABIEZER)

JEHALLELEL (jĕ-hăl'ē-lĕl). **1.** A descendant of Judah (1 Chron 4:16). **2.** A Merarite Levite, father of one of the leaders in cleansing the temple in the days of Hezekiah (29:12).

JEHATH (See JAHATH)

JEHDEIAH (jĕ-dē'yà, *Jehovah will be glad*). **1.** A descendant of Moses and contemporary of David (1 Chron 24:20). **2.** A man of the tribe of Zebulun whom David appointed to have charge of the donkeys that belonged to the king (27:30).

JEHIEL (jĕ-hī'ĕl, *God lives*). **1.** One of the players on psalteries in David's time (1 Chron 15:18, 20; 16:5). **2.** A Gershonite Levite treasurer for the Lord's house (23:8; 29:8). **3.** A son of Hacmoni "the wise," who was with David's sons, probably as tutor (27:32). **4.** A son of Jehoshaphat (2 Chron 21:2). **5.** A descendant of Heman the singer in Hezekiah's time (29:14; ASV, RSV, Jehuel). **6.** One of the overseers of the offerings brought to the temple under Hezekiah (31:13). **7.** One of the rulers of the house of God in Josiah's time (35:8). **8.** Father of Obadiah who came from captivity with 218 men in Ezra's day (Ezra 8:9). **9.** Father of Shecaniah who confessed to having married a foreign wife and who proposed a covenant with God to put away these foreign wives and their children (10:2). **10.** One of the priests who confessed to having married a foreign woman (10:21).

JEHOADDAH (jē-hō'à-dà). A descendant of King Saul through Jonathan (1 Chron 8:36). In 1 Chronicles 9:42 he is called Jadah (NIV) or Jarah (JB, KJV, MLB, NASB, NEB, RSV).

JEHOAHAZ (jē-hō'à-hăz, Heb. *yehô-'āhāz, Jehovah has grasped*). **1.** The eleventh king of Israel, c. 815–800 B.C. (2 Kings 10:35; 13:1). Like his father Jehu, he maintained the calf worship begun by Jeroboam; and as a result of his apostasy God permitted the Syrians to inflict heavy defeats on his armed forces, until he had almost none left. In desperation he called on the Lord for help. God answered his prayers after his death in the persons of his two successors, Jehoash and Jeroboam II, through whom Israel's ancient boundaries were restored. The life of Elisha extended through his reign. **2.** King of Judah, 608 B.C. The third son of Josiah, he reigned only three months and was then deposed and taken in chains into Egypt by Pharaoh Neco, who had defeated Josiah in battle. He is also called Shallum (1 Chron 3:15; Jer 22:10–12). **3.** A variant form of the name of Ahaziah (2 Chron 21:17; cf. 22:1). **4.** The full name of Ahaz, king of Judah, according to an inscription of Tiglath-Pileser III.

JEHOASH, JOASH (jē-hō′ăsh, Heb. *yehô'āsh;* jō′ăsh, Heb. *yô'āsh*). A word of uncertain meaning, perhaps *Jehovah supports* or *whom Jehovah gave.* **1.** A son of Beker and grandson of Benjamin, probably born soon after the descent into Egypt (1 Chron 7:8). **2.** An early descendant of Judah through Shelah, who with his brother Saraph ruled in Moab (4:22). **3.** A descendant of Abiezer son of Manasseh (Josh 17:2; Judg 6:11). Evidently his family had become insignificant (Judg 6:15), but his son Gideon could call on ten of his servants for help (6:27). Joash had succumbed to the polytheism around him and built an altar to Baal. However he defended his son Gideon when he destroyed this altar (6:30–32). **4.** The keeper of David's cellars of oil (1 Chron 27:28). **5.** A relative of King Saul who sided with David and became one of the commanders of his forces (12:3). **6.** A son of King Ahab who was ordered to imprison Micaiah the prophet (1 Kings 22:26; 2 Chron 18:25–26). **7.** King of Judah from 884 to 848 B.C. (2 Kings 11–13; 2 Chron 24–25), who was rescued from Athaliah's massacre as an infant (22:8–9). He lived a godly and useful life all the time that his uncle instructed him (2 Kings 12; 2 Chron 24). **8.** The king of Israel from 848 to 832 B.C. (2 Kings 13:10–13; 14:8–16; 2 Chron 25:17–24).

JEHOHANAN (jē′hō-hā′năn, Heb. *yehôhānān, Jehovah is gracious*). **1.** One of six brothers, doorkeepers of the tabernacle in David's time (1 Chron 26:3). **2.** A military leader in Jehoshaphat's time (2 Chron 17:15). **3.** The father of Ishmael, who assisted Jehoiada (23:1). **4.** One who had married a foreigner in Ezra's time (Ezra 10:28). **5.** A priest and head of a priestly family in the days of Joiakim the high priest (Neh 12:13). **6.** A priestly singer at the dedication of the new wall of Jerusalem, rebuilt by Nehemiah (12:42). **7.** An Ephraimite chief (NIV 2 Chron 28:12; JB, KJV, MLB, NEB, NASB, RSV Johanan). **8.** One who married a foreign woman in Nehemiah's time (Neh 6:18; KJV Johanan). **9.** Ezra used his room to fast or mourn for those who had taken foreign wives (Ezra 10:6; KJV Johanan).

Jehohanan, or Johanan, is the origin of the name John.

JEHOIACHIN (jē-hoi′ă-kĭn, Heb. *yehôyākhîn, Jehovah establishes*). Next to the last king of Judah, reigning at Jerusalem three months and ten days (2 Chron 36:9) in 597 B.C. He is called Coniah three times (Jer 22:24, 28; 37:1 JB, KJV, MLB, NASB, NEB; Jehoiachin NIV), Jeconiah seven times, and Jechonias (the Hellenized name) once (Matt 1:11–12 lit., KJV).

Jehoiachin was 18 (2 Kings 24:8) when he came to the throne. Because of his short reign, Jehoiachin had virtually no chance of developing an independent policy, though he endorsed the religious and social attitudes of his father (2 Kings 24:9). He is characterized as "a strong lion. He learned to tear the prey and he devoured men" (Ezek 19:5–9). In his three months of power "he did evil in the eyes of the LORD, just as his father had done" (2 Kings 24:9). Nebuchadnezzar took him captive to Babylon (2 Chron 36:10), and his son Evil-Merodach took Jehoiachin from prison after 37 years of captivity (2 Kings 25:27–30).

JEHOIADA (jē-hoi′ă-dà, Heb. *yehôyādhā', Jehovah knows*). **1.** Father of Benaiah, one of David's most faithful officers. He is mentioned 20 times, but only as the father of his more notable son, who was over the mercenary troops of David (2 Sam 20:23; 23:20; 1 Kings 1:38). **2.** Grandson of no. 1 (1 Chron 27:34). This Jehoiada was second counselor of David, immediately after Ahithophel, who later became a traitor. **3.** A powerful descendant of Aaron who with 3,700 men came to David at Ziklag (12:27). **4.** Brother of Amariah whom he succeeded as high priest. Jehoiada was a high priest; a statesman; a man of God; by marriage a member of the royal family of Judah (2 Chron 22:11); and, humanly speaking, the preserver of the messianic line. He lived 130 years (24:15). He married Jehosheba (2 Kings 11:2), also called Jehoshebeath (2 Chron 22:11 KJV, MLB, MOF, NASB, RSV), and she bore him that Zechariah (24:20–22; Luke 11:51) who so denounced the wickedness of the people that they stoned him at Joash's command. He and his wife hid the child Joash from his evil grandmother (2 Kings 11). When Joash was seven years old, Jehoiada prepared his coup d'etat. During the early years of Joash's reign, when he was under the instruction and guidance of the godly Jehoiada, the temple was repaired and Judah began again to prosper. Jehoiada was buried among the kings (2 Chron 24:16).

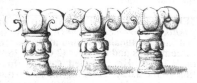

Drawing of a stone window railing from palace of Jehoiakim, king of Judah (607–597 B.C.), at Ramat Rahel near Jerusalem.
Courtesy Carta, Jerusalem

JEHOIAKIM (jē-hoi'à-kĭm, Heb. *yehô-yāqîm, Jehovah sets up*). Second son of the godly Josiah, king of Judah. He was originally named "Eliakim" (*whom God sets up*). Pharaoh Neco of Egypt marched northward to fight the king of Assyria, but was intercepted by Josiah, who was mortally wounded. The people of Judah passed by Eliakim and made his youngest brother, Shallum, or Jehoahaz, king after Josiah (1 Chron 3:15; 2 Chron 36:1). Jehoahaz reigned for three months in Jerusalem, when Neco in displeasure deported him to Egypt, where he died (2 Kings 23:33–34). The king of Egypt next took Eliakim, elder half-brother of Jehoahaz, changed his name to Jehoiakim, put the land under heavy tribute, and made Jehoiakim king over Jerusalem, where he reigned from 607–597. Jehoiakim was an oppressive and thoroughly godless king (23:36–24:7; 2 Chron 36:4–8; cf. Jer 22–36). Jehoiakim died in disgrace and had "the burial of a donkey" (22:19).

JEHOIARIB, JOIARIB (jē-hoi'à-rĭb, joi'à-rĭb, Heb. *yehôyārîv, Jehovah will contend*). 1. A priest in David's time who drew first place in the divine service (1 Chron 24:7). 2. One of the first priests to return from exile with Zerubbabel (9:10). 3. A man Ezra sent back to Babylon to obtain Levites to assist the priests (Ezra 8:16–17). 4. The son of Zechariah, son of a man of Shiloh but of the tribe of Judah (Neh 11:5). 5. A priest who returned with Zerubbabel (11:10; 12:6).

JEHONADAB (jē-hŏn'à-dăb, Heb. *yehônādhāv, Jehovah is liberal*). Also appears as *Jonadab*. 1. Son of David's brother Shimeah (2 Sam 13:3; NIV "Jonadab"). 2. Son of Recab, of the Kenite clan, who assisted Jehu in abolishing Baal worship in Samaria (2 Kings 10). He is called the forefather of the Recabites (Jer 35).

JEHONATHAN (jē-hŏn'à-thăn, Heb. *yehônāthān, Jehovah gave*). Variant form of *Jonathan*. 1. An administrator of David's property (1 Chron 27:25). 2. One of the teaching Levites appointed by Jehoshaphat (2 Chron 17:8). 3. A priest in the days of Joiakim the high priest (Neh 12:18).

JEHORAM (jē-hō'răm, Heb. *yehôrām, Jehovah is exalted*). Often contracted to *Joram*. 1. Jehoram was associated with his father in the kingship for the last four or five years of Jehoshaphat's reign. When Jehoram became the sole ruler, he murdered his six brothers with the sword. Jehoshaphat had been a godly man, but he had made one terrible error: political association with Ahab (1 Kings 22; 2 Chron 18). Through this league, Jehoram had married the wicked Athaliah. As soon as his father died (900) Jehoram began to slip into the idolatrous ways of the northern kingdom. God did not take away his kingdom but did cause him to have real troubles. Edom and Libnah revolted (2 Kings 8:22). Meanwhile, the great prophet Elijah sent Jehoram a letter of denunciation for his wickedness. God sent a plague on Judah, especially on the family of Jehoram. He suffered and died unlamented from a horrible disease (2 Chron 21:18–20). The Arabs or their associated forces killed all of Jehoram's sons (21:17) except Ahaziah, the youngest, who succeeded his father at his death.

2. Second son of Ahab and Jezebel, he succeeded his brother Ahaziah, who died childless, as king of Israel (853–840 B.C.). Mesha, king of Moab, who had been paying tribute to Israel (2 Kings 3:4) rebelled after the death of Ahab, and Jehoram made war against him—with the aid of Jehoshaphat (3:7). Jehoram came to his end, with all his family, at the hand of Jehu (ch. 9).

3. A priest whom Jehoshaphat sent with a group of learned Levites to go through Judah and to teach the people the law of the Lord (2 Chron 17:8).

JEHOSHABEATH (jē'hō-shăb'ē-ăth, Heb. *yehôshav'ath, the oath of Jehovah*). The name of Jehosheba as it is found in 2 Chronicles 22:11 (ASV, KJV, MLB, MOF, NASB, RSV).

JEHOSHAPHAT (jē-hŏsh'à-făt, Heb. *yehôshāphat, Jehovah is judge*; shortened to *Joshaphat* in 1 Chron 15:24; Gr. *Jōsaphat* [Matt 1:8, KJV Josaphat]). 1. A priest who blew a trumpet before the ark of the Lord (1 Chron 15:24, NIV Joshaphat). 2. Recorder or chronicler in the time of David (2 Sam 8:16; 20:24). **3.** Officer of the commissariat over the tribe of Issachar (1 Kings 4:17). **4.** Son and successor of King Asa on the throne of Judah (c. 871-850 B.C., 1 Kings 22; 2 Chron 17–20). Jehoshaphat was the second of the five kings of Judah who were outstanding for godliness, the later ones being Joash, Hezekiah, and Josiah. He took away the high places and Asherah poles from Judah (17:6), though he apparently was not able to keep the people from using certain high places in worshiping the Lord (1 Kings 22:43). He sent out princes, priests, and Levites to teach the people the law of the Lord (2 Chron 17:7–9). Because of Jehoshaphat's godliness, "the fear of the LORD" fell on the surrounding nations, and even the Philistines and the Arabs brought him tribute. He made the great and almost fatal mistake of associating with the wicked King Ahab; so much so that his son Jehoram married Athaliah, who was almost as wicked as her mother Jezebel. **5.** The son of Nimshi, and father of Jehu who destroyed the house of Ahab (2 Kings 9:2, 14).

JEHOSHAPHAT, VALLEY OF (jē-hŏsh'à-făt, Heb. *yehôshāphāt, Jehovah judges*). The scene where all nations will be gathered by the Lord for judgment (Joel 3:2, 12). Since the fourth century the Kidron Valley has been named the Valley of Jehoshaphat, although there is no reason to suppose this is the location referred to by Joel.

JEHOSHEBA (jē-hŏsh'ē-bà, Heb. *yehôsheva', Jehovah is an oath*). Sister of Ahaziah (2 Kings 11:2), daughter of Jehoram and his wicked consort Athaliah (Jezebel's daughter), and wife of the high priest Jehoiada. When Athaliah usurped the throne and killed the royal line, Jehosheba (called Jehoshabeath in 2 Chron 22:11 ASV, KJV, MLB, MOF, NASB, RSV) rescued the baby Joash, hid him with his nurse in a bedchamber in the temple, and preserved the messianic line.

JEHOSHUA, JEHOSHUAH (See JOSHUA)

JEHOVAH English rendering of the Hebrew consonants YHWH, which make up the divine name. At a late date it became a matter of binding scruple not to pronounce the divine name, and Jews (in reading the Scriptures) customarily substituted the noun *adhonai*, which means "Lord." LXX followed this lead, using the Greek *kyrios*, "Lord," to stand for the divine name—a significant thing in the light of the usual NT designation of

Jesus as *kyrios*. But the formulation "Jehovah" arose by inserting the vowels of *adhonai* into the consonants YHWH.

According to Exodus 6:2–3, the name YHWH had not been used prior to Moses as a meaningful understanding of the divine nature. The name is related to the Hebrew verb "to be," "to be actually present." "I am who I am" means either "I am actively present as and when I choose" or "I bring to pass whatever I choose." Yahweh is a God who speaks before he is a God who acts (chs. 3–4; 6:1–8). Moses is informed about events before they happen, so that the occurrence of the events serves to confirm God's revelation. Yahweh is fundamentally the covenant-Redeemer, the God who brought his people out of Egypt (Exod 20:1ff.).

JEHOVAH-JIREH (jē-hō'vá-jī'rĕ, *Jehovah will provide*). The name Abraham gave to the place where God provided a ram in place of his son Isaac (Gen 22:14 KJV, MLB, MOF, NEB).

JEHOVAH-NISSI (jē-hō'vá-nĭs'ī, *Jehovah is my banner*). The name Moses gave to an altar he built as a memorial of Israel's victory over the Amalekites at Rephidim (Exod 17:15 JB, KJV, NEB).

JEHOVAH-SHALOM (jē-hō'vá-shā'lŏm, *Jehovah is peace*). The name Gideon gave to an altar he built at Ophra to commemorate the word spoken to him by the Lord, "The Lord is Peace" (Judg 6:24 KJV).

JEHOVAH-SHAMMAH (jē-hō'vá-shā'mà, *Jehovah is there*). The name of the heavenly Jerusalem (Ezek 48:35 KJV, marginal note).

JEHOVAH-TSIDKENU (jē-hō'vá-tsĭd-kē'nū, *Jehovah is our righteousness*). The symbolic name given to the king who is to rule over restored Israel (Jer 23:6) and to the state or capital (33:16).

JEHOZABAD (jē-hŏz'á-băd, Heb. *yehôzāvādh, Jehovah has bestowed*). **1.** Son of Obed-Edom, a doorkeeper of the tabernacle (1 Chron 26:4). He is not to be confused with the Obed-Edom of 2 Samuel 6:10–12. **2.** A Benjamite in the days of King Jehoshaphat (2 Chron 17:18). He was commander of 180,000 soldiers prepared for war. **3.** A son of Shimrith, a Moabitess. He conspired against King Joash (24:26).

JEHOZADAK (jē-hŏz'á-dăk, Heb. *yehôtsādhāk, Jehovah is righteous*). The high priest of Israel through most of the Babylonian captivity (1 Chron 6:14–15). His

Detail of the Black Obelisk of Shalmaneser III of Assyria, set up at Nimrud (858–824 B.C.), which shows Jehu, king of Israel, bowing before the king. Behind him are porters bringing in tribute. Reproduced by courtesy of the Trustees of the British Museum

father, Seraiah, was killed by the Babylonians (2 Kings 25:18–21), and Jehozadak was taken into captivity. In Haggai and Zechariah, where he is six times referred to as father of Joshua, the high priest at the first return, KJV spells his name "Josedech"; and in Ezra and Nehemiah, KJV and ASV, referring to him in the same way five times, call him "Jozadak," a shortened form of Jehozadak.

JEHU (jē'hū, Heb. *yēhû'*, probably *Jehovah is he*). **1.** Son of Obed and father of Azariah (1 Chron 2:38). **2.** A Simeonite (4:35). **3.** A Benjamite of Anathoth who joined David at Ziklag (12:3). **4.** Son of Hanani, and a prophet of Israel who cursed Baasha in almost the same words used against Jeroboam (cf. 1 Kings 14:11; 16:4). Later he denounced Jehoshaphat (2 Chron 19:1–3; cf. 20:34). **5.** Tenth king of Israel (c. 842–814 B.C.) and founder of its fourth dynasty. Jehu was commissioned by Elijah to conquer the house of Ahab. He denounced Joram, killed him, and had his body thrown into the field of Naboth (2 Kings 9:24–26); then he caused Ahaziah, king of Judah, to be killed as well as Jezebel. He executed God's judgments on the house of Ahab and thoroughly exterminated the worship of Baal. Because of his zeal for the Lord in the matter of Ahab's house, God allowed him to set up a dynasty that lasted just over 100 years (Jehu, Jehoahaz, Joram, and Jeroboam II).

JEHUSH (See JEUSH)

JEIEL (jē-ī'ĕl, Heb. *ye'î'ēl*, probably *God has gathered*). **1.** A Reubenite (1 Chron 5:7). **2.** A Benjamite of Gibeon (9:35). **3.** Son of Hotham of Aroer. He was one of David's mighty men (11:44). **4.** A harpist in the days of King David who also acted as gatekeeper of the tabernacle (15:18, 21). **5.** A Levite of the sons of Asaph (2 Chron 20:14). **6.** A scribe who acted as recorder of the military forces under Uzziah (26:11). **7.** A Levite who took part in the reformation under Hezekiah (29:13). **8.** A chief of the Levites in the days of Josiah (35:9). **9.** A husband of a foreign wife in Ezra's time (Ezra 10:43).

JEKAMIAH (jĕk'à-mī'à, Heb. *yekamyâh, may Jehovah establish*). **1.** A man from Judah, son of Shallum (1 Chron 2:41). **2.** A son of King Jeconiah (Jehoiachin); in KJV Jecamiah (3:18).

JEMUEL (jē-mū'ĕl, Heb. *yemû'ēl*, meaning unknown). A son of Simeon (Gen

46:10; Exod 6:15). He is also called "Nemuel" (Num 26:12; 1 Chron 4:24).

JEPHTHAH (jěf'thà, Heb. *yiphtâh, opened* or *opener*). Eighth judge of Israel (Judg 10:6–12:7; 1 Sam 12:11; Heb 11:32). The son of a harlot, his brothers drove him from the paternal home. He made a name for himself by his prowess and gathered about him a band of men without employment, like David's men (1 Sam 22:2). He was a God-fearing man, with a high sense of justice and of the sacredness of vows made to God. At the time of his expulsion by his brothers, Israel had been for many years under bondage to the Ammonites. The elders in desperation went to Jephthah and urged him to become a captain of Israel's army. Endued with the Spirit of the Lord, Jephthah prepared for war. Before going out to battle, he made a vow that if he was victorious he would offer to God as a burnt offering whatever first came to him out of his house. He defeated his enemies with a very great slaughter, recovered 20 cities from them, and then killed the Ephraimites who had refused to help fight the Ammonites. His daughter was the first to meet him when he turned home. Although he "did to her as he had vowed. And she was a virgin" (Judg 11:39), there is some debate among scholars as to whether she was actually sacrificed, or redeemed with money and given to the service of the Lord as a perpetual virgin.

JEPHUNNEH (jē-fŭn'ĕ, Heb. *yephunneh, it will be prepared*). **1.** The father of Caleb, one of the 12 spies (Num 13:6). **2.** A son of Jether, an Asherite (1 Chron 7:38).

JERAHMEEL (jē-rà'mē-ĕl, Heb. *yerahme'ēl, may God have compassion,* or *God pities*). **1.** A descendant of Judah through Perez and Hezron (1 Chron 2:9, 25–27, 33, 42). **2.** A Merarite Levite, son of Kish, not Saul's father (24:29). **3.** One of the three officers sent by King Jehoiakim to arrest Jeremiah and Baruch (Jer 36:26).

JERASH (See GERASA)

JERED (jē'rĕd, Heb. *yeredh, descent*). **1.** Son of Mahalaleel (1 Chron 1:2 KJV; NIV "Jared"). **2.** A Judahite and father of the inhabitants of Gedor (4:18).

JEREMIAH (jěr'ĕ-mī'à, Heb. *yirmeyâhû, Jehovah founds,* or perhaps, *exalts*), in KJV of NT "Jeremy" and "Jeremias" (Matt 2:17; 16:14). Jeremiah was one of the greatest Hebrew prophets, born into a priestly family of Anathoth, a Benjamite town

two and a half miles (four km.) NE of Jerusalem. Because of the autobiographical nature of his book, it is possible to understand his life, character, and times better than those of any other Hebrew prophet. Jeremiah was called to prophesy in the 13th year of King Josiah (626 B.C.), five years after the last great revival before Judah's captivity (2 Kings 23). This was a time of decision, a time filled with both hope and foreboding, the time of the revival of the Babylonian Empire. Jeremiah's ministry continued through the reigns of five successive Judean kings; Jeremiah saw the final destruction of Jerusalem in 587 and died in Egypt, probably a few years later.

Jeremiah's call is described in Jeremiah 1. The young priest pleads his youth (1:6), but God assures him that he will be given strength for his task. Undoubtedly Jeremiah supported Josiah's reform (Jer 11:1–8; 17:19–27), but as time went on he realized its inadequacy to stave off national disaster (3:10). After Josiah's unhappy death (609 B.C.) Jeremiah mourned Judah's last good king (2 Chron 35:25), and life became more difficult for him. Jehoahaz, son of Josiah, reigned only three months before he was deported to Egypt. Jehoiakim, the brother of Jehoahaz, succeeded him and reigned 11 years. A strong ruler and a very wicked man, he tried to do away with the prophet and, failing that, to silence him. In Jehoiakim's fourth year Jeremiah dictated the first edition of his prophecies to Baruch, but the king promptly destroyed it (ch. 36). During this reign Jeremiah preached the great temple discourse (chs. 7–10) that led to a plot to kill him; he was saved only by the intervention of friendly nobles who were a remnant of Josiah's administration (ch. 26). Judah was brought into the Babylonian orbit when Jerusalem fell to Nebuchadnezzar in 605 and a few Hebrews (Daniel among them) were deported to Babylon. Jehoiakim later rebelled against Babylon. Jeremiah opposed the strong-willed Jehoiakim all his reign and predicted a violent death for him (22:13–19).

For the events in Judah after the destruction of Jerusalem we are dependent almost exclusively on Jeremiah 40–45. The captors treated Jeremiah with kindness, giving him the choice of going to Babylon or remaining in Judah. He chose to stay behind with some of the common people who had been left in Judah when most of the Jews were deported. Gedaliah was made puppet governor over this little group. After civil unrest, in which Gedaliah was assassinat-

The village of Anathoth, birthplace of Jeremiah, northeast of Jerusalem. Courtesy Ecole Biblique et Archéologique Française, Jerusalem

ed, the Jews fled to Egypt, forcing Jeremiah to accompany them.

Jeremiah was regarded as a meddler and a traitor; and leaders, nobles, and kings tried to put him to death. Although he needed the love, sympathy, and encouragement of a wife, he was not permitted to marry; and in this prohibition he became a sign that normal life was soon to cease for Jerusalem (Jer 16:1–4). Because his book is full of autobiographical sections—Jeremiah's "Confessions"—Jeremiah's personality can be understood more clearly than that of any other prophet. These outpourings of the human spirit are some of the most poignant and pathetic statements of the tension of a man under divine imperative to be found anywhere in Scripture. The most important are listed below.

10:23–24	17:9–11, 14–18
11:18–12:6	18:18–23
15:10–21	20:7–18

Jeremiah's penetrating understanding of the religious condition of his people is seen in his emphasis on the inner spiritual character of true religion. The external theocratic state will go, as will the temple and its ritual. Even Josiah's reform ap-

pears to have been a thing of the outward appearance—almost engineered by the king, an upsurge of nationalism more than a religious revival (Jer 3:10). The old covenant had failed; a new and better one will take its place, and then God's law will be written on men's hearts (31:31–34). God will give his renewed people a heart to know him (24:7). In this doctrine of the "new heart" Jeremiah unfolds the depth of human sin and predicts the intervention of divine grace (Heb. 8:1–9:28).

Six other Jeremiahs are briefly mentioned in the OT: a Benjamite and two Gadites who joined David at Ziklag (1 Chron 12:4, 10, 13); the head of a family in Manasseh (5:24); a native of Libnah and the father of Hamutal, wife of King Josiah and mother of Jehoahaz (2 Kings 23:30–31); and the son of Habazziniah, a Recabite (Jer 35:3).

JEREMIAH, BOOK OF Jeremiah is a book of prophetic oracles or sermons, together with much autobiographical and historical material that gives the background of these oracles. The material contained in Jeremiah's book is not arranged in chronological order. The out-

line given below indicates what seems to
have been the purpose of the book.

I. **Jeremiah's Oracles Against the
   Theocracy, 1:1–25:38.**
   A. The prophet's call, 1:1–19.
   B. Reproofs and admonitions,
      mostly from the time of Josi-
      ah, 2:1–20:18.
   C. Later prophecies, 21:1–25:38.

II. **Events in the Life of Jeremiah,
    26:1–45:5.**
   A. The temple sermon and Jere-
      miah's arrest, 26:1–24.
   B. The yoke of Babylon, 27:1–
      29:32.
   C. The book of consolation,
      30:1–33:26.
   D. Some of Jeremiah's experi-
      ences before Jerusalem fell,
      34:1–36:32.
   E. Jeremiah during the siege and
      destruction of Jerusalem,
      37:1–39:18.
   F. The last years of Jeremiah,
      40:1–45:5.

III. **Jeremiah's Oracles Against For-
     eign Nations, 46:1–51:64.**
   A. Against Egypt, 46:1–28.
   B. Against the Philistines,
      47:1–7.
   C. Against Moab, 48:1–47.
   D. Against the Ammonites,
      49:1–6.
   E. Against Edom, 49:7–22.
   F. Against Damascus, 49:23–27.
   G. Against Kedar and Hazor,
      49:28–33.
   H. Against Elam, 49:34–39.
   I. Against Babylon, 50:1–51:64.

IV. **Appendix: The Fall of Jerusalem
    and Related Events, 52:1–34.**

In spite of the fact that the book is not
at all in chronological order, it is possible
to date many of its sections because they
contain chronological notations. These
sections are here listed with their dates.
1. In the Reign of Josiah.
   In the thirteenth year, ch. 1.
   Later in this reign, chs. 2–6.
   Possibly much of chs. 7–20 (ex-
      cept material specifically listed
      below) is to be dated to Josi-
      ah's reign.
2. In the Reign of Jehoahaz.
   None.
3. In the Reign of Jehoiakim.
   Early in this reign, ch. 26 and
      probably 7:1–8:3; 22:1–23.
   In the fourth year, chs. 25; 36;
      45; 46:1–12.

After the fourth year, ch. 35.
4. In the Reign of Jehoiachin.
   22:24–30; possibly ch. 14.
5. In the Reign of Zedekiah.
   In the beginning, chs. 24; 49:34–
      39.
   In the fourth year, chs. 27–28;
      51:59–64.
   In unnoted years, chs. 21; 29.
   During the early part of the
      siege, ch. 34.
   During the interruption of the
      siege, ch. 37.
   During the resumption of the
      siege, chs. 32; 33; 38; 39:15–
      18.
6. In Judah After the Fall of Jerusa-
   lem. 39:1–4; 40:1–43:7.
   In Egypt After Jeremiah Was
      Taken There. 43:8–44:30.

JEREMOTH (jĕr'ĕ-mŏth, Heb. *yerē-
moth, swollen, thick*). **1.** A Benjamite of
the family of Beker (1 Chron 7:8). **2.**
Another Benjamite (8:14). **3.** A Levite,
family of Merari, house of Mushi (23:23).
His name also appears as Jerimoth
(24:30). **4.** Three men by this name who
consented to put away their foreign wives
in the time of Ezra (Ezra 10:26–27, 29).

JERIAH (jē-rī'à, Heb. *yerîyāhû, Jehovah
sees*). Head of a Levitical house, the
house of Hebron (1 Chron 23:19; 24:23;
26:31).

JERICHO (jĕr'ĭ-kō, Heb. *yerēhô, yerîhô,*
Gr. *Ierichō, moon city*). Jericho, also
called the City of Palms (Deut 34:3), is
located 5 miles (8 km.) west of the Jordan
and 7 miles (12 km.) north of the Dead
Sea, some 800 feet (250 m.) below sea
level. Its climate is tropical, with great
heat during the summer.

There are three Jerichos. The OT city
was situated on a mound a mile NW of
the modern town. NT Jericho is on a
higher elevation nearby. Modern Jericho
has a population of about 10,000 people
of very mixed racial descent. Jericho is
probably the oldest city in the world. Its
strategic site by a ford of the Jordan
controlled the ancient trade routes from
the East. Jericho controlled the access to
the hill country of Palestine from Transjordan.

Jericho first entered the biblical record
when it was visited by two spies and
captured by Joshua (Josh 6). The city's
location made its capture the key to the
invasion of the central hill country. The
city was devoted to God, totally destroyed and burned except for metal
objects found in it (6:17–19). Only Rahab

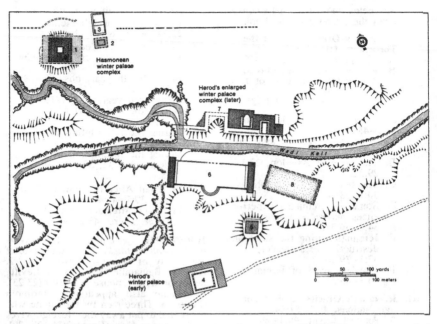

The general plan of ancient Jericho: (1) main palace, (2) pavilion(?), (3) pool surrounded by court, (4) palace (gymnasium), now covered over, (5) southern mound, (6) sunken garden, with the "Grand Façade" south of it, (7) northern wing, (8) pool, and (9) villa(?) built over Hasmonean palace. These ruins are located just west of the modern town and south of Tell es-Sultan. Courtesy Carta, Jerusalem

and her family, who had cared for the spies, were saved (6:22–23, 25). Joshua placed a curse on the place, that it might not be rebuilt (6:26).

Jericho was rebuilt by Hiel the Bethelite in the days of Ahab (c. 850 B.C.; 1 Kings 16:34). Evidently it again became an important place during the divided kingdom era. It is mentioned in connection with Elisha's ministry (2 Kings 2:5, 18; 25:5; 2 Chron 28:15; Ezra 2:34; Neh 3:2; 7:36; Jer 39:5).

In the time of Christ, Jericho was an important place yielding a large revenue to the royal family. Since the road from the fords of the Jordan to Jerusalem passed through it, it became a stopping place for Galilean pilgrims to Jerusalem, who came south through Perea to avoid defilement by contact with Samaritans. Thus Jesus passed through it on a number of occasions. Nearby are the supposed sites of his baptism (in the Jordan) and his temptation (the hill Quarantania, west of the city). Near the city Jesus healed Bartimaeus (Mark 10:46–52) and one or two other blind men (Matt 20:29–34).

The conversion of Zacchaeus occurred here (Luke 19:1–10), one of the most graphic of the Gospel narratives. In the parable of the Good Samaritan (10:29–37) the traveler was attacked as he was going down from Jerusalem to Jericho.

JERIMOTH (jĕr′ĭ-mŏth, Heb. *yerēmôth, thick, swollen*). **1.** A Benjamite (1 Chron 7:7). **2.** A Benjamite who joined David at Ziklag (12:5). **3.** A son of David and the father of Mahalath, the wife of Rehoboam (2 Chron 11:18). **4.** A Levite, an overseer of the temple in the reign of Hezekiah (31:13). **5.** A Levite musician in David's time (1 Chron 25:4; in 25:22 Jerimoth in NIV, Jeremoth in JB, MLB, KJV, NASB, NEB, RSV). **6.** A son of Mushi, a Merarite (24:30); also called Jeremoth (23:23). **7.** A prince of the tribe of Naphtali during David's reign (27:19).

JEROBOAM I (jĕr′ō-bō′ăm, Heb. *yārov′ām, the people contend*, or *the people become numerous*). Son of Nebat, of the tribe of Ephraim, and of Zeruah, a widow (1 Kings 11:26–40). He founded the kingdom of Israel when the nation was

split following the death of Solomon.
Previously he had been the overseer of
public works under Solomon (1 Kings
11:28); later he was told by Ahijah the
prophet the he would become the head of
ten tribes. Solomon tried to kill him but
he escaped to Egypt. After Solomon's
death and his son Rehoboam rejected the
people's demands, the ten tribes revolted
from the house of David and made Jeroboam their king (12:1–16).

Fearing the loyalty of the people if they
journeyed to Jerusalem to worship each
year, he decided to establish centers of
worship at the two extremities of his
kingdom—Dan in the north and Bethel in
the south (1 Kings 12:26–33; 16:26). To
establish his throne firmly, he led the
people into the immoralities of heathenism, which led eventually to the
destruction of the nation. The successive
kings, with possibly one exception
(Jehu), supported this idolatrous worship
until Israel fell.

God gave him a solemn warning to give
heed to his evil ways through an unnamed
prophet who came to Bethel from Judah
(1 Kings 13:1–6). In spite of this terrible
warning from God, Jeroboam continued
in his evil way. Jeroboam reigned for 22
years and was succeeded to the throne by
his son Nadab (2 Kings 14:20). For the
people of Israel, the reign of Jeroboam
was a supreme political and religious
calamity. The warfare between the two
kingdoms inevitably brought weakness to
both, leaving them open to outside attack.

JEROBOAM II (jĕr-ō-bō'ăm, Heb. *yăr-
ov'ām, the people contend,* or *the people
become numerous*). The son and successor of Jehoash, king of Israel; fourth son
of the dynasty of Jehu. He became king
in Samaria c. 785 B.C. and reigned 41
years. He followed the example of Jeroboam I in keeping up the idolatrous
worship of the golden calves (2 Kings
14:23). He continued and brought to a
successful conclusion the wars that his
father had undertaken against Syria, restoring territory to Israel (14:25; Amos
6:14). Moab and Ammon, probably paying tribute to Syria, were reconquered
(1:13; 2:1–3).

All these successful wars brought
much tribute to Jeroboam and his nobles.
The wealthy had both winter and summer
homes (Amos 6:4–6). But side by side
with this luxury there was much poverty
in the land. Twice the prophet says that
the needy were sold for a pair of shoes
(2:6; 8:6). Worship went on not only at
Dan and Bethel, but also at subsidiary

Cast of the "Seal of Shema, Servant of
Jeroboam" (probably Jeroboam II), from
Megiddo. Courtesy Israel Department of Antiq-
uities and Museums

temples and altars at Gilgal and Beersheba (4:4; 5:5; 8:14). During the reign of
Jeroboam the prophets Hosea, Joel, Jonah, and Amos ministered. Jeroboam
was succeeded on his death by his son
Zechariah (2 Kings 14:29), a weak king
with whom the dynasty ended.

JEROHAM (jĕ-rō'hăm, Heb. *jerōhăm,
may he be compassionate,* or *be pitied
[by God]*). **1.** A Levite, the father of
Elkanah and grandfather of Samuel
(1 Sam 1:1; 1 Chron 6:27, 34). **2.** A Benjamite whose sons were chief men in
Jerusalem (8:27). Probably identical with
no.3. **3.** A Benjamite, father of Ibneiah
(9;8), **4.** An ancestor of a priest in Jerusalem (9:12; Neh 11:12). **5.** A Benjamite of
Gedor, father of two of David's recruits
at Ziklag (1 Chron 12:7). **6.** The father of
Azarel, chief of the tribe of Dan (27:22).
7. The father of Azariah, one of the
captains who supported Jehoiada in over-
throwing Queen Athaliah and putting
Joash on the throne of Judah (2 Chron
23:1).

JERUB-BAAL (See GIDEON)

JERUB-BESHETH (See GIDEON)

JERUSALEM The most important city on
earth in the history of God's acts by
which redemption has been accomplished. It was the royal city, the capital
of the only kingdom God has (thus far)
established on earth. Here the temple
was erected, and here, during the kingdom age, sacrifices were legitimately offered. This was the city of the prophets,
as well as the kings of David's line. Here
occurred the death, resurrection, and
ascension of Jesus Christ, David's greatest Son. The Holy Spirit descended at
Pentecost on an assembled group in this
city, giving birth to the Christian church;

The gates of Jerusalem: (1) Jaffa Gate in the west, (2) Golden Gate in the east, (3) St. Stephen's Gate, or Lions' Gate, in the northeast, and (4) Zion Gate in the southwest. Most of the gates to be found today in the Old City wall were built after the Turkish conquest, c. 450 years ago. The gates shown here, a notable exception being the Zion Gate, were rebuilt on the foundations of the gates from Roman times. The Zion Gate was altered to facilitate the approach to Mount Zion and the Tomb of David. Courtesy Israel Government Press Office

and here the first great church council was held. Rightly did the chronicler refer to Jerusalem as "the city the LORD had chosen out of all the tribes of Israel in which to put his Name" (1 Kings 14:21). Even the first-century Roman historian Pliny referred to Jerusalem as "by far the most famous city of the ancient Orient." This city has been the preeminent objective of the pilgrimages of devout men and women for over 2,000 years, and it was in an attempt to recover the Church of the Holy Sepulchre in Jerusalem that the Crusades were organized.

No site in all Scripture receives such constant and exalted praise as Jerusalem. Concerning no place in the world have such promises been made of ultimate glory and permanent peace.

While the word *Jerusalem* is Semitic, it apparently was not a name given to the city for the first time by the Hebrew people. Far back in the time of the Amarna Letters (1400 B.C.), it was called *U-ru-sa-lim*, that is, a city of Salim, generally taken to mean "city of peace." In the Hebrew Bible the word first appears in Joshua 10:1. The rabbis say there are 60 different names for Jerusalem in the Bible, a characteristic exaggeration, but there truly are a great number. The name Jerusalem itself occurs about 600 times in the OT.

Jerusalem appears in the NT after the close of the Book of Acts rather infrequently, four times near the conclusion of the Letter to the Romans (15:19, 25, 26, 31), once at the end of the First Letter to the Corinthians, and again in Galatians (1:17–18; 2:1). The name most often used for this city, apart from Jerusalem itself, is *Zion*, which occurs over 100 times in the OT. Jerusalem is often called "the city of David" (2 Sam 5:7, 9; 6:10–16; Neh 3:15; 12:37; Isa 22:9). This title is later applied to Bethlehem (Luke 2:4, 11).

Unlike most cities that have witnessed great historical events over many centuries, Jerusalem has always remained on the same site. It is situated 33 miles (55 km.) east of the Mediterranean and 14 miles (23 km.) west of the Dead Sea, at an elevation of 2,550 feet (797 m.) above sea level. The city rests on three hills. The SE hill, the original city of the Jebusites, the city that David seized, later to be called Zion, occupied about eight to ten acres. The area of the fortress city of Megiddo in contrast was 30 acres. The northern hill was the one on which Solomon built the great temple and his own palace, called Ophel. On the east of these two hills was a deep valley known as the Kidron. To the south of the city was another deep valley called the Hinnom. On the far side of the western hill was the Valley of Gehenna, a continuation of Hinnom. These valleys today give no idea of their original depth, for debris has filled them up in some places to a depth of 50 to 60 feet (16 to 19 m.). The city never occupied a large area. Even in the time of Herod the Great, the area within the walls was not more than a mile (about one and one-half km.) in length, nor more than five-eighths of a mile (about one km.) in width. The city was off the beaten path of the great caravan routes and was not, as most larger world capitals, on a navigable river or on a large body of water. Its site, therefore, had an exclusiveness about it. On the other hand, being 19 miles (32 km.) north of Hebron and 30 miles (50 km.) south of Samaria, it was centrally located to serve as the capital of the kingdom of Israel.

There is a reference to the Jebusites, who inhabited Jerusalem (Gen 10:15–19). Actually, the first reference to Jerusalem as such is found in the account of Abraham's interview with Melchizedek, king of *Salem* (14:17–24). Many believe, and

tradition is unanimous here, that the place where Abraham offered up Isaac at Mt. Moriah (22:2; 2 Chron 3:1) is the exact site on which, centuries later, the temple of Solomon was built.

The actual name Jerusalem occurs for the first time in Joshua 10:5, where the king of the city confederated with four other kings in a futile attempt to defeat Joshua. In the same book it is frankly confessed that the Israelites were unable to drive out the Jebusites (15:8, 63; 18:28). For a brief space the Israelites held part of this city but were not able to keep it (Judg 1:7, 21). Nothing is known of the history of Jerusalem either from biblical or nonbiblical writings from the time of Joshua's death until the capture of this city by David (2 Sam 5:6–10).

With the death of Solomon, the glory of Israel and so also the glory of Jerusalem began to dim. In the fifth year of Rehoboam, 917 B.C., Shishak king of Egypt, without any struggle, came up to Jerusalem and "carried off the treasures of the temple of the LORD and the treasures of the royal palace. He took everything, including all the gold shields Solomon had made" (1 Kings 14:26; 2 Chron 12:9). This is the first of eight different plunderings of the Jerusalem temple, occurring within a little more than 300 years.

In 701 B.C. an event occurred that was given more space and greater detail in the OT than even the destruction of Jerusalem by Nebuchadnezzar. Sennacherib threatened the city (704–681), casting one insult after another in the face of King Hezekiah (715–687), reminding him that he, Sennacherib, had already captured practically every city of Judah, and how could the king think Jerusalem would escape? But by divine intervention, with God's assurance that the king would this time be kept from invasion, Sennacherib's army suffered a mysterious destruction, and he returned to Assyria without fulfilling his threat (2 Kings 18–19; 2 Chron 32; Isa 36).

Jesus made four principal statements about the city, all of them with a note of sadness (Matt 23:37; 24:2; Luke 13:33; 19:42; cf. Mark 13:2; Luke 21:24). The Book of Acts opens with a group of the followers of Jesus meeting together in an upper room in Jerusalem. The church was born in Jerusalem on the Day of Pentecost (Acts 2). The early persecutions occurred in that city. In this city the first great crisis of the church was successfully faced in the first Council, deciding forever the fact that salvation is wholly by grace, apart from works (ch.

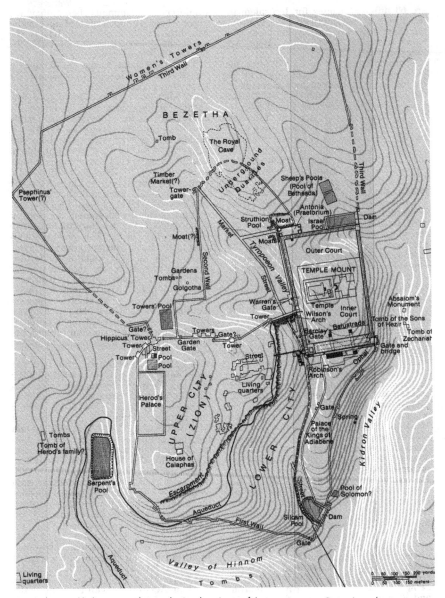

Jerusalem and the second temple in the time of Jesus. Courtesy Carta, Jerusalem

15). Years later in this same city, the apostle Paul was arrested, mobbed in the temple, and falsely accused (chs. 21–22).

The destruction of the city after a siege of 143 days by Roman armies under the leadership of Titus, though predicted in the Gospels, is not actually recorded anywhere in the NT. Before this dreadful event concluded, 600,000 Jews were killed and thousands more were led away into captivity. One futile and tragic attempt of the Jews to win freedom from

Silver tetradrachma struck in the second year of the Bar-Kokhba War in A.D 133. It depicts a temple façade symbolizing the temple of Jerusalem, which Bar-Kokhba wished to restore. The reverse depicts the four species of the Feast of Tabernacles. Hebrew inscriptions: obverse—"Year 2 of the freedom of Israel"; reverse—"Jerusalem." Courtesy Reuben and Edith Hecht Museum, University of Haifa

the Romans was concentrated in the rebellion of A.D. 134, led by the false messiah Bar Kochba. This rebellion was overwhelmingly crushed, and what was left of the city was leveled to the ground, and even the foundations were plowed up. Two years later the Romans began rebuilding the city, now to be called Aelia Capitolina. All Jews were strictly excluded from this new city for two centuries, until the reign of Constantine. In the early part of the fourth century, due to the fervent devotion of Helena, the mother of the emperor, the great Church of the Holy Sepulchre, called Anastasis (the Greek word for resurrection), was built. From then on, Jerusalem became increasingly the object of pilgrimages and of rich gifts.

In A.D. 614 a Persian general under King Chosroes II seized the city and slaughtered 60,000 Christians, taking 35,000 more into slavery. In 688 the first Dome of the Rock was erected.

Muhammad, more or less acquainted with both the OT and NT, felt it was necessary to be in some way identified with this city, holy to both Jews and Christians; and Islam soon interpreted a passage in the Koran as implying that Muhammad was miraculously carried to Jerusalem and was divinely consecrated there, but there is no real evidence for this journey. In 1009 the Caliph Hakim, son of a Christian mother, began his devastating work in Jerusalem by ordering the destruction of the Church of the Holy Sepulchre. By 1014 some 30,000 churches in Palestine had been burned or pillaged.

On July 14, A.D. 1099, the Christian army of the First Crusade seized Jerusalem, and the awful slaughter pursued by these so-called Christian knights was something that the Muslim world has never forgotten nor forgiven. Saladin, after his overwhelming victory in his battle with the Crusaders at the Horns of Hattin, camped before the city on September 20, 1187. He entered it on October 2, enforcing strict orders that no violence or orgy of conquest should be engaged in by his soldiers such as the Christian Crusaders had participated in almost a century before. In 1229, it was regained by Frederick II, through negotiations. In 1244 it fell before the Kharezmian Tartars. In 1247 it was seized again by the Egyptians. In 1260 it was recaptured by the Tartars. In 1517 it was taken by the Ottoman Turks. On December 9, 1917, the British General Allenby entered the city on foot; on October 31, 1918, the armistice was signed, and 400 years of Turkish misrule came to an end.

On April 24, A.D. 1920, the mandate for Palestine and Transjordan was assigned to Great Britain, and for nearly 30 years she suffered one reverse after another in attempting to rule the country. On May 14, 1948, the British mandate terminated, and the National Council at Tel-Aviv proclaimed the State of Israel. There followed the bitter, often brutal war for Palestine, as a result of which nearly a million Arabs were driven from their homes. By the spring of 1949, Israel was recognized by 45 governments. The struggle with the Arab bloc of nations has unhappily continued. One round of hostilities ended in 1967 with the end of Arab administration in the Old City and the assumption of Israeli control over the whole city of Jerusalem. The city had been proclaimed the country's capital in 1950, but this was not recognized by the United Nations. The city's population (after a low of 350,000 in 1785) had grown to 448,200 by 1980; by 1987 it had declined to 400,000.

Here is a bare summary of prophecies pertaining to Jerusalem.

1. In Deuteronomy 12, though no name is mentioned, there are six references to the future place of the sanctuary, "the place the LORD your God will choose" (see also 1 Kings 8:29, 48).

2. The promise that Sennacherib's attempt to capture the city would fail (2 Kings 19:32–34; Isa 29:7; 30:19; 31:4–5).

3. The destruction of the city by Nebuchadnezzar (2 Kings 22:16–17; 2 Chron 34:24–25; Isa 4:3–5; 10:11–12; 22:9–11; Ezek 24:1ff.).

At the entrance to the Citadel (Tower of David) inside the Jaffa Gate, the reading of General Allenby's address, ending four hundred years of Turkish rule, December 11, 1917. Courtesy Imperial War Museum

4. The desecration of the city by Antiochus Epiphanes (Dan 8:11–14; 11:30–32).

5. The destruction of the city by the Romans under Titus (Dan 9:26; Matt 24:2; Mark 13:2; Luke 13:33–35; 19:41–44; 21:6, 20, 24).

6. A prophecy concerning this city during the present age (Dan 9:26; Zech 12:3; Luke 21:24).

7. The Jewish people at the end of this age will return to Palestine; sometimes Jerusalem is specifically designated (Joel 3:1). The erection of some kind of temple in the Holy City is also prophesied (Isa 55:11; 60:1–3; Jer 31:8–9; Dan 9:27; 12:11; Matt 24:15; Mark 13:14; 2 Thess 2:3–4).

8. The episode of the two witnesses to be martyred in this city (Rev 11).

9. A final assault on this city by the nations of the earth (Isa 29:1–7; 31–34; Joel 3:9–12; Zech 14:1–3).

10. A cleansing of the city of its spiritual uncleanness (Isa 1:25–26; 4:3–4; Joel 3:17; Zech 14:1–3).

11. A city that will ultimately and permanently know the presence of the glory of God (Isa 62:2; Ezek 43:1–2);

peace (Ps 122:6–9; Isa 60:17; 66:12); and joy (Ps 53:6).

12. The city to which the nations of the earth will come for instruction and blessing (Ps 102:21–22; Isa 2:2–4).

JERUSALEM, NEW A name found twice in the Bible (Rev 3:12; 21:2) where Jerusalem is described as coming down out of heaven from God. It is also called "the Holy City" (Rev 21:2) and "the Holy City, Jerusalem" (21:10). In Revelation 21:10–22:5 there is a description of the city.

JERUSHA, JERUSHAH (jē-rū'shà, Heb. *yerûsha', possessed,* i.e., *married*). The wife of Uzziah, king of Judah, and mother of Jotham, his successor (2 Kings 15:33; 2 Chron 27:1). Her father's name was Zadok (1 Chron 6:12).

JESARELAH (jĕ'sà-rē'là, Heb. *yesar-'ēlâh,* meaning doubtful). The ancestral head of the seventh course of musicians (1 Chron 25:14).

JESHAIAH, JESAIAH (jē-shā'yà, jē-sā'yà, Heb. *yesha'yâhû, yesha'yâh, Jehovah saves*). **1.** A son of Jeduthun, and a musician in David's reign; he became the ancestral head of one of the courses of musicians (1 Chron 25:3, 15). **2.** A Levite, son of Rehabiah and ancestor of Shelomith, one of David's treasurers (26:25). **3.** A son of Hananiah, and grandson of Zerubbabel (3:21). **4.** A son of Athaliah and descendant of Elam. He returned from Babylon with Ezra (Ezra 8:7). **5.** A descendant of Merari who returned with Ezra from Babylon (8:19). **6.** A Benjamite, the father of Ithiel (Neh 11:7).

JESHARELAH (See JESARELAH)

JESHIMON (jē-shī'mŏn, Heb. *hay-eshîmōn, a waste, a desert*). The word is often used as a common noun to refer to the desert of Sinai (e.g., Deut 32:10; Pss 78:40; 106:14; Isa 43:19) and is usually translated "desert." Sometimes it is used as a geographical term and probably refers to two different districts:

1. The "desert" in the Jordan Valley, NE of the Dead Sea, seen from the top of Pisgah (Num 21:20; 23:28 KJV; NIV "wasteland"). This is a bare, salty land without any vegetation.

2. The sterile plateau to which David went in fleeing from Saul—the eastern section of the Judean hills, which stretch toward the Dead Sea (1 Sam 23:19, 24; 26:1, 3).

JESHUA, JESHUAH (jĕsh'ū-à, Heb. *yēshūa',* another form of Joshua, *Jehovah is salvation*). **1.** A name used once for Joshua, the son of Nun (Neh 8:17 KJV;

NIV retains "Joshua"). **3.** The head of the ninth of the 24 courses of priests (1 Chron 24:11). **3.** The name of a family of Pahath-Moab, who returned with Zerubbabel to Jerusalem (Ezra 2:6; Neh 7:11). **4.** A Levite in charge of the distribution of tithes in Hezekiah's time (2 Chron 31:15). **5.** The high priest who returned with Zerubbabel (Ezra 2:2; Neh 7:7; called "Joshua" in Hag 1:1 and in Zech 3:1ff.). He helped to rebuild the altar (Ezra 3:2, 8) and the house of God (4:3; 5:2). **6.** A Levite who supervised the workmen in the temple after the Exile (2:40; 3:9; Neh 7:43). He also assisted in explaining the law to the people (8:7), in leading in worship (9:4), and in sealing the covenant (10:9). **7.** A postexilic town in southern Judah (11:26). It is identified with Tell es-Sa'weh and may be the same as the Shema of Joshua 15:26.

JESHURUN (jĕsh'ū-rŭn, Heb. *yeshûrûn, upright one*). A poetical or ideal title of Israel (Deut 32:15; 33:5, 26; Isa 44:2).

JESIAH (See ISSHIAH)

JESSE (jĕs'ē, Heb. *yishay*, meaning uncertain). Descendant of Nahshon (chief of the tribe of Judah in the days of Moses) and the grandson of Boaz (Ruth 4:18–22). He had eight sons, of whom the youngest was David (1 Sam 17:12–14), and two daughters, the latter being by a different wife from David's mother (1 Chron 2:16; cf. 2 Sam 17:25). Jesse lived at Bethlehem. When Samuel went to Jesse to anoint a king from among his sons, neither of them at first discerned God's choice (1 Sam 16:11). His small beginnings are contrasted with future glory (Isa 11:1, 10; Mic 5:2).

JESUI (See ISHVI)

JESUS, JESUS CHRIST (See CHRIST, JESUS)

JETHER (jē'thêr, Heb. *yether, abundance, excellence*). **1.** Another name for Jethro, father-in-law of Moses (Exod 4:18; see KJV marginal note). **2.** Gideon's oldest son (Judg 8:20–21), who shrank from killing the captives, Zebah and Zalmunna. **3.** The father of Amasa, Absalom's commander-in-chief (1 Kings 2:5). He was an Ishmaelite (1 Chron 2:17). **4.** A descendant of Judah through Jerahmeel (2:32). **5.** A Judahite, the son of Ezrah (4:17). **6.** A man of Asher, apparently the same as Ithran, son of Zophah (7:37; cf. v. 38).

JETHLAH (See ITHLAH)

JETHRO (jĕth'rō, Heb. *yithrô, excellence*). A priest of Midian and father-in-law of Moses (Exod 3:1). It seems that

The Valley of Jethro, or Jethro's Pass, looking northwest. In the center is the monastery of St. Catherine, built at the foot of Mt. Sinai in the mid-sixth century by the emperor Justinian. It was here that Codex Sinaiticus, the famous fourth-century Greek Bible manuscript, was discovered. The library, containing about 3,000 old manuscripts, historical documents, etc., is considered one of the most precious in the world. Courtesy Ecole Biblique et Archéologique Française, Jerusalem

Reuel, which means "friend of God," was his personal name (2:18; 3:1) and Jethro was his honorary title. When Moses fled from Egypt to Midian, he was welcomed into the household of Jethro because of his kindness to the priest's seven daughters, whom he helped water their flocks. Moses married Zipporah and kept his father-in-law's flocks for about 40 years (3:1–2). After the Lord commanded Moses to return to Egypt to deliver the enslaved Israelites, Jethro gave him permission to depart. Moses took with him his wife Zipporah and their two sons (4:18–20), but later he sent the three back to stay with Jethro temporarily. After the deliverance from Egypt, before the Israelites reached Sinai, Jethro came to see Moses, bringing back to him his daughter and her two sons (18:1–7). Jethro suggested the appointment of judges of various grades to help Moses decide cases of minor importance (18:17–27).

JETUR (jē'têr, Heb. *yetûr*, meaning uncertain). A people descended from Ishmael (Gen 25:15; 1 Chron 1:31). Reuben, Gad, and the half-tribe of Manasseh warred against this clan (5:18–19). They are the Itureans of NT times.

JEUEL (jē-ū'ĕl, Heb. *ye'û'ēl*, meaning unknown). **1.** A man of Judah who with 690 of his clan lived at Jerusalem (1 Chron 9:6). **2.** A leader of Ezra's company (Ezra 8:13, JB, KJV, NEB Jeiel).

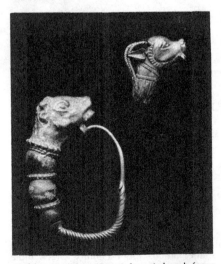

Gold earrings in shape of ram's head, from Ashdod (fourth century B.C.). Courtesy Israel Museum, Jerusalem. Photo David Harris

JEUSH (jē'ŭsh, Heb. *ye'ûsh, he comes to help*). **1.** A son of Esau by his wife Oholibamah (Gen 36:5). **2.** A Benjamite, son of Bilhan (1 Chron 7:10). **3.** A Gershonite Levite (23:10–11). **4.** A descendant of Jonathan (8:39; Jehush KJV).

JEW (Heb. *yehûdî*, Gr. *Ioudaios*, Lat. *Judaeus*). This word does not occur before the period of Jeremiah in OT literature. Originally it denoted one belonging to the tribe of Judah or to the two tribes of the southern kingdom (2 Kings 16:6; 25:25). Later it was applied to anyone of the Hebrew race who returned from the Captivity. As most of the exiles came from Judah, and as they were the main historical representatives of ancient Israel, the term *Jew* came finally to comprehend all of the Hebrew race throughout the world (Esth 2:5; Matt 2:2). As early as the days of Hezekiah the language of Judah was called Jewish (NIV Hebrew). In the OT the adjective applies only to the Jews' language or speech (2 Kings 18:26, 28; Neh 13:24; Isa 36:11, 13). In the Gospels, *Jews* (always plural, except for John 4:9; 18:35) is the usual term for Israelites; and in the NT, Jews (Israelites) and Gentiles are sometimes contrasted (Mark 7:3; John 2:6; Act 10:28). Paul warns against Jewish myths (Titus 1:14) and speaks of the Jews' religion (Gal 1:13–14, lit., KJV; Judaism NIV, RSV).

JEWEL, JEWELRY Among the articles of jewelry in OT times were diadems, bracelets, necklaces, anklets, rings for the fingers, gold nets for the hair, pendants, gems for head attire, amulets and pendants with magical meanings, jeweled perfume and ointment boxes, and crescents for camels.

The servant of Abraham gave Rebekah and others in the family precious things (Gen 24:22, 30, 53). When the Israelites left Egypt with Moses, they took articles of silver and gold from the Egyptians (Exod 12:35). Later they took their golden earrings and gave them to Aaron to make a golden calf (32:2–4). As evidence of their repentance, they were commanded by Moses to strip themselves of their ornaments (33:4–6). For the building of the first tabernacle, the people contributed, at Moses' request, bracelets, earrings, rings, tablets, and jewels of gold (35:22).

Exodus 39 gives a description of the official garments of the Jewish high priest, worn when discharging his peculiar duties. They were gorgeous in their jeweled splendor. Later Gideon used the jewelry captured from the Midianites to

Late Bronze Age (1550–1200 B.C.) jewelry, made of carnelian and gold, apparently found in the anthropoid coffins from Deir el-Balah. Courtesy Edith and Reuben Hecht Museum, University of Haifa. Photo E. Lessing

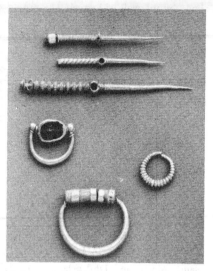

Gold jewelry from Tell el-Ajjul (Beth Eglaim), c. 1500–1400 B.C. Three togglepins, a mounted scarab, a ribbed earring, and a ring with a bar of lapis lazuli beads. Courtesy Israel Department of Antiquities and Museums. Photo David Harris

make an ephod, that was later regarded idolatrously (Judg 8:24–27).

David accumulated a large mass of jewels, mostly won in conquests against Syrians, Moabites, Ammonites, Amalekites, and Philistines. All these he dedicated to the Lord (2 Sam 8:7–8) and passed on to Solomon for the building of the temple in Jerusalem. When his nobles saw what he was donating, they brought for the same purpose gold, silver, brass, and iron; and the common people added what they could (1 Chron 29). OT prophets warned the Israelites that apostasy would be punished with the loss of their gems (Ezek 23:26).

Not a great deal is said about jewelry in the NT, and what is said is mostly condemnatory. Jesus twice mentioned jewels (Matt. 7:6; 13:45–46). Paul exhorts Christian women not to rely on them for adornment (1 Tim 2:9) and James warns not to give preference to those who possess fine jewels (James 2:2). The new Jerusalem is described in terms of many precious stones (Rev 21) reminiscent of those found in the breastpiece of the high priest. See also MINERALS.

JEZANIAH (jěz-à-nī′à, Heb. *yezanyāhû*, probably *Jehovah hears*). An army officer, son of Hoshaiah, a Maacathite. He lived at the time of the fall of Jerusalem (Jer 42:1; "Jaazaniah" in 2 Kings 25:23; Jer 40:7–8).

JEZEBEL (jěz′à-běl, Heb. *'îzevel*, meaning uncertain, perhaps *unexalted, unhusbanded*). **1.** Daughter of Ethbaal, king of the Zidonians, and queen of Ahab, king of Israel (c. 874–853 B.C.). She had been brought up a zealous worshiper of Baal, and as the wife of Ahab she not only continued her ancestral religion but tried to impose it on the people of Israel. To please her, Ahab built a temple and an altar to Baal in Samaria (1 Kings 16:32), and 450 prophets of Baal ate at her table (18:19). She killed all the prophets of the Lord on whom she could lay her hands (18:4–13). When she was told of the slaughter of the prophets of Baal by Elijah, she threatened Elijah's life, and he was obliged to flee. The killing of Ahab's family was a punishment for the persecution of the prophets of the Lord by Jezebel (2 Kings 9:7). Later she secured Naboth's vineyard for Ahab by having its owner unjustly executed (1 Kings 21). When Elijah heard of this crime, he told Ahab that God's vengeance would fall on him and that dogs would eat Jezebel's body by the wall of Jezreel. The prophecy was fulfilled (2 Kings 9:7, 30–37). **2.** In Revelation 2:20, in the letter to Thyatira, we read of "that woman Jezebel, who calls herself a prophetess"; she led some members of the Christian church there to commit spiritual fornication. This may be a symbolic name, given because of the resemblance between her and the idolatrous wife of Ahab.

JEZER (jē'zēr, Heb. *yetser, form, purpose*). A son of Naphtali and founder of a tribal family (Gen 46:24; Num 26:49; 1 Chron 7:13).

JEZOAR (See ZOHAR)

JEZREEL (jĕz'rē-ĕl, jĕz'rēl, Heb. *yizre'e'l, God sows*). **1.** A city on the border of the territory of Issachar (Josh 19:18), not far from Mt. Gilboa. The Israelites made their camp near it before the battle of Gilboa (1 Sam 29:1), its people remaining faithful to the house of Saul. Abner set Ish-Bosheth over it among other places (2 Sam 2:9). Ahab built a palace there (1 Kings 21:2), and his son Joram also lived there (2 Kings 8:29). Naboth was a Jezreelite, and he was stoned outside the city for refusing to give up his vineyard to Ahab (1 Kings 21). Jehu ordered that the heads of Ahab's 70 sons be placed in heaps at the gate of Jezreel (2 Kings 10:1–11). Jezebel met her death by being thrown from a window of the palace in Jezreel, and it was there that her body was eaten by dogs (9:30–35). Jezreel was the scene of the meetings between Elijah and Ahab (1 Kings 21:17ff.). **2.** A town in the hill country of Judah from which David obtained his wife Ahinoam the Jezreelitess (1 Sam 25:43; 27:3). **3.** A descendant of Judah (1 Chron 4:3). **4.** A son of the prophet Hosea, so called because God had declared that he would avenge the blood of Jezreel on the house of Jehu (Hos 1:4–5).

JIMNA (See IMNAH)

JOAB (jō'ăb, Heb. *yô'āv, Jehovah is father*). **1.** The second of the three sons of Zeruiah, the half-sister of David, the two others being Abishai and Asahel (2 Sam 8:16; 1 Chron 2:16). After Saul's death, he was David's captain of the army, while Abner led the forces of Ish-Bosheth. When the two armies met, a tournament took place between 12 men from each side, followed by a general engagement in which, after Joab's men were routed, Asahel was killed in his pursuit of Abner (2 Sam 2:12–32). When Abner transferred his allegiance to David, Joab treacherously killed him, with the connivance of Abishai, for killing Asahel at the battle of Gibeon, though Abner had done so in self-defense.

Joab was made the commander of all David's armies as a reward for being the first to enter the fortress on Mt. Zion when that stronghold was assaulted. In the war against the Ammonites, Joab achieved a great victory, utterly routing the enemy (2 Sam 10:1–14; 1 Chron 19:1–15). He called for David to storm the town of Rabbah, which he himself had successfully besieged, in order that David might get credit for the victory (2 Sam 11:1; 12:26–29). It was during this war that David got Joab to put Uriah in the forefront of the battle so that he might be killed and David be free to marry Bathsheba (11:6–27).

Joab got David to receive his son Absalom back into the royal home after his banishment for the murder of his brother Ammon (2 Sam 14:1–33). When Absalom rebelled, he made Amasa, another nephew of David, general instead of Joab (17:24–25). Joab remained loyal to David, and when the king fled, pursued by Absalom, he led one of the three divisions of the royal forces and defeated the rebels. Informed that Absalom was caught in a tree by his hair, he first scolded his informer for not having killed him and then himself killed the prince by thrusting three javelins through his heart. When David gave vent to extravagant grief at the death of his rebel son, Joab sternly rebuked him (19:1–8).

When David returned to Jerusalem, he replaced Joab as captain of his forces with Amasa. Shortly after this, Sheba, a Benjamite, led a revolt against David; and when Amasa took more time than was thought necessary to prepare to quell it, David asked Abishai to take the field. Joab seems to have gone with him. The two met Amasa at Gibeon, and there Joab, on pretense of kissing his rival, killed him. He then assumed command of Amasa's men, besieged Sheba in Abel Beth Maacah, and arranged with a woman of the city to deliver to him the head of Sheba. Thus ended the revolt (2 Sam 20:1–22).

Joab was opposed to David's suggestion of a census but eventually carried it out, though he intentionally did the work imperfectly (2 Sam 24:1–9; 1 Chron 21:1–6). He supported Adonijah in his claim to the throne, but deserted him on hearing that Solomon had been proclaimed king (1 Kings 1:7, 28–49). David on his deathbed made known that Joab should be brought to justice for the murders of Abner and of Amasa (2:5). At the order of Solomon, Joab was killed as he clung to the horns of the altar in the court of the tabernacle. His executioner was Benaiah, chief of the bodyguard, who became his successor as head of the army. He was buried in his own house in the wilderness (2:5–6, 28–34). **2.** Son of Seraiah and father of Ge Harashim (1 Chron 4:14). **3.** Founder of a family of returned exiles (Ezra 2:6; 8:9; Neh 7:11). **4.** A village, apparently in Judah (1 Chron 2:54 RV).

JOAH (jō'à, Heb. *yô'āh, Jehovah is brother*). **1.** A son of Obed-Edom (1 Chron 26:4). **2.** A Levite (6:21) who may have helped in the religious reformation under King Hezekiah (2 Chron 29:12). **3.** Son of Asaph and recorder under King Hezekiah (2 Kings 18:18, 26; Isa 36:3, 11, 22). He was one of the three men sent by Hezekiah to speak to the Assyrian envoys at the siege of Jerusalem. **4.** Son of Joahaz and recorder under King Josiah (2 Chron 34:8).

JOANNA (Gr. *Iōana or Iōanna*). The wife of Cuza, Herod's steward. Along with other women whom Jesus healed, she traveled with him and financially supported his ministry (Luke 8:2–3). After preparing spices and ointments to embalm Jesus' body, she and other women went to the tomb and heard about the Resurrection (23:55–56; 24:10).

JOASH (See JEHOASH)

JOATHAM (See JOTHAM)

JOB (jōb, Heb. *'íyôv*, meaning uncertain). **1.** The main character of the Book of Job (see JOB, BOOK OF; see also Ezek 14:14, 20; James 5:11). **2.** A son of Issachar (Gen 46:13).

JOB, BOOK OF This OT Wisdom book applied foundational Mosaic revelation to the problems of human existence and conduct. Even an approximate date for the anonymous author is uncertain. The events he narrates belong to the early patriarchal period.

   I. Desolation: The Trial of Job's Wisdom (1:1–2:10)

   II. Complaint: The Way of Wisdom Lost (2:11–3:26)

   III. Judgment: The Way of Wisdom Darkened and Illuminated (4:1–41:34)

   A. The verdicts of men (4:1–37:24)
      1. First cycle of debate (4:1–14:22)
      2. Second cycle of debate (15:1–21:34)
      3. Third cycle of debate (22:1–31:40)
      4. Ministry of Elihu (32:1–37:24)
   B. The voice of God (38:1–41:34)

   IV. Confession: The Way of Wisdom Regained (42:1–6)

   V. Restoration: The Triumph of Job's Wisdom (42:7–17)

Job proclaims the fundamental stipulation of the covenant, a call for perfect consecration to our covenant head, the Lord. By proving under fierce temptation the genuineness of his devotion to God, Job vindicates the truthfulness of God's redemptive promise and proves his sovereignty in putting enmity between his people and Satan. Prostrated by total grief, he still turns and cries to no one but God. By following the covenant way, Job shows himself ready by God's grace, and contrary to Satan's insinuations, to serve his Lord "for nothing."

Although no comprehensive answer is given to the problem of suffering, considerable light is shed. Elihu traces the mystery to the principle of divine grace: sufferings are a sovereign gift, calling to repentance and life. Moreover, impressive assurance is given that God, as a just and omnipotent covenant Lord, will ultimately visit both the curses and blessings of the covenant on his subjects according to righteousness. Especially significant are the insights Job himself attains into the role God will play as his heavenly vindicator, redeeming his name from all slander and his life from the king of terrors. Job utters in raw faith what is later revealed in the doctrines of eschatological theophany: resurrection of the dead and the final judgment. This vision does not reveal the why of the particular sufferings of Job or any other believer, but it does present the servants of God with a framework for hope.

JOBAB (jō'bāb, Heb. *yôvāv, to call loudly, howl*). **1.** An Arabian tribe descended from Joktan (Gen 10:29; 1 Chron 1:23). **2.** The second king of Edom. He was the son of Zerah of Bozrah (Gen 36:33; 1 Chron 1:44–45). **3.** A king of Madon who joined the northern confederacy against Joshua, but was thoroughly defeated (Josh 11:1; 12:19). **4.** A Benjamite (1 Chron 8:9). **5.** A Benjamite (8:18).

JOCHEBED (jŏk'ĕ-bĕd, Heb. *yôkhevedh, Jehovah is glory*). Daughter of Levi, wife of Amram and mother of Moses (Exod 6:20; Num 26:59). She was a sister of Kohtah, Amram's father (Exod 6:20).

JODA (jō'dà). An ancestor of Jesus (Luke 3:26; KJV "Juda").

JOEL (jō'ĕl, Heb. *yô'ēl, Jehovah is God*). **1.** The prophet, son of Pethuel and author of the second book of the Minor Prophets. **2.** Samuel's firstborn son (1 Sam 8:2; 1 Chron 6:33). **3.** A Simeonite prince (4:35). **4.** A Reubenite chief (5:4, 8). **5.** A Gadite chief (5:12). **6.** An ancestor of Samuel, of the tribe of Levi (6:36). **7.** A chief of Issachar (7:3). **8.** One of David's mighty men (11:38). **9.** A Levite (15:7, 11, 17), probably also mentioned in 1 Chronicles 23:8; 26:22. **10.** David's officer over half of Manasseh (27:20). **11.** A Levite of Hezekiah's time (2 Chron 29:12). **12.** A Jew who had married a foreign wife (Ezra 10:43). **13.** A Benjamite overseer (Neh 11:9).

JOEL, BOOK OF (jō'ĕl, Heb. *yô'ēl, Jehovah is God*). The Book of Joel is without the customary dating formula used by the prophets (Hos 1:1; Amos 1:1), and nowhere indicates the date either of the ministry of the prophet Joel or of the writing of the book.

Scholars who follow the traditional viewpoint believe the book to be preexilic, written perhaps during the reign of the boy king Joash (837–800 B.C.), for the following reasons: (1) The enemies of Judah that are mentioned—the Philistines and Phoenicians (Joel 3:4), Egypt and Edom (3:19)—are those of the preexilic period (2 Kings 8:20–22; 2 Chron 21:16–17) rather than the Assyrians and Babylonians, who later troubled Judah. (2) Amos, a prophet during this time, seems to have been acquainted with Joel's prophecies (3:16; cf. Amos 1:2; 3:18; cf. 9:13). (3) The fact that the elders and priests are mentioned rather than the king would seem to point to the time of Joash's minority (2 Kings 11:21). (4) The location of the book between two early prophets and its style, quite different from that of the postexilic prophets, also argue for a preexilic date.

The occasion of the book was a devastating locust plague. The prophet, after describing the plague and its resulting chaos, urges the nation to repent of its

sins and then goes on to predict a worse visitation, the future Day of the Lord.

I. The Locust Plague and Its Removal (1:1–2:27).
  A. The plague of locusts (1:1–20).
  B. The people urged to repent (2:1–17).
  C. God pities and promises relief (2:18–27).

II. The Future Day of the Lord (2:28–3:21).
  A. The Spirit of God to be poured out (2:28–32).
  B. The judgment of the nations (3:1–17).
  C. Blessing on Israel following judgment (3:18–21).

Joel's greatest contribution to Christian thought is his teaching about the outpouring of the Holy Spirit "on all people" (Joel 2:28), quoted by Peter in his Pentecostal sermon (Acts 2:14–21). In a special way the new age was to be one of the Spirit (Isa 32:15; Zech 12:10; John 7:39). All of God's people would now be priests and prophets, for the ideal stated when the law was given but never achieved would now become a reality (Exod 19:5–6; 1 Peter 2:9–10).

JOHA (jō'hà, Heb. *yôhā'*, meaning unknown). **1.** A Benjamite, son of Beriah (1 Chron 8:16). **2.** A Tizite, son of Shimri, and one of David's mighty men (11:45).

JOHANAN (jō-hā'năn, Heb. *yôhānān, Jehovah has been gracious*). **1.** Son of Kareah, a captain who with his men submitted to Gedaliah, appointed by Nebuchadnezzar as governor over Judah (2 Kings 25:22–23; Jer 40:8–9). He warned Gedaliah of Ishmael's plot to murder him (40:13–14); and when the governor paid no heed and was assassinated, he tried to avenge his death (41:11–15). Against the advice of Jeremiah, he and other Jewish leaders led the remnant down into Egypt, taking Jeremiah with them. **2.** The eldest son of King Josiah (1 Chron 3:15). **3.** A son of Elioenai (3:24). **4.** The father of the Azariah who was priest in Solomon's time (6:9–10). **5.** A Benjamite recruit of David at Ziklag (12:4). **6.** A Gadite recruit of David at Ziklag who was made captain in David's army (12:12, 14). **7.** An Ephraimite chief (2 Chron 28:12 KJV, MLB, NASB, RSV; Jehohanan NEB, NIV). **8.** A son of Hakkatan, of the clan of Azgad. He accompanied Ezra from Babylon (Ezra 8:12). **9.** A son of Tobiah the Ammonite who married a Jewess in the days of

Nehemiah (Neh 6:18 KJV; NIV "Jehohanan"). **10.** A son of Eliashib. Ezra used his chamber to mourn for the sin of those who had contracted foreign marriages (Ezra 10:6). **11.** A high priest, grandson of Eliashib (Neh 12:22). The Jews at Elephantine appealed to him for help when their temple was destroyed in 411 B.C. (Elephantine Papyri). Josephus says that he killed his brother Jesus in the temple because he feared he might be superseded as high priest (*Antiq.* 11.7.1).

JOHN (Gr. *Iōannēs*, from Heb. *Yôhānān, Jehovah has been gracious*). **1.** Father of Simon Peter (John 1:42; 21:15, 17, called Jonas in KJV). **2.** A relative of Annas the high priest who took part in calling Peter and John to account for their preaching about Jesus (Acts 4:6). See also JOHN, THE APOSTLE; JOHN THE BAPTIST; JOHN MARK.

JOHN, THE APOSTLE The son of Zebedee, and brother of James the apostle, who was put to death by Herod Agrippa I about A.D. 44 (Matt 4:21; Acts 12:1–2). It may be reasonably inferred that his mother was Salome (cf. Matt 27:56 with Mark 15:40) and that she was the sister of Mary the mother of Jesus. Jesus and John would then have been cousins. The family lived in Galilee, probably at Bethsaida. The father and the two sons were fishermen on the Sea of Galilee (Mark 1:19–20).

John, first introduced as a disciple of John the Baptist (John 1:35), later became Jesus' disciple (1:35–39). Jesus called him to become a fisher of men (Matt 4:18–22; Mark 1:16–20; Luke 5:1–11). Later, he was chosen to the apostolate (Matt 10:2–4; Mark 3:13–19; Luke 6:12–19). Jesus surnamed James and John "Boanerges," that is, Sons of Thunder, evidently because of the impetuosity of their temperament (Mark 3:17).

John was one of the three apostles who were closest to Jesus, the other two being Peter and James, John's brother. With the other two in the inner circle of the apostles, he was admitted to witness the raising of Jairus' daughter (Mark 5:37; Luke 8:51), the Transfiguration (Matt 17:1; Mark 9:2; Luke 9:28), and his agony in Gethsemane (Matt 26:37; Mark 14:33). It was John who told Jesus that they had seen someone casting out devils in his name and that they had forbidden him because he was not of their company (Mark 9:38; Luke 9:49). The two brothers, James and John, gave evidence of their impetuosity when a Samaritan village refused to allow them to pass through on their way to Jerusalem (Luke 9:54). They showed tactlessness and presumptuous ambition when they went to Jesus with their mother and requested that in the coming kingdom they be given places of honor above the others (Mark 10:35). John was among those who asked Jesus when his prediction about the destruction of the temple would be fulfilled (13:3). He and Peter were sent by Jesus to make preparations for the Passover (Luke 22:8), and at the Passover feast John lay close to the breast of Jesus and asked who his betrayer would be (John 13:25). When Jesus was arrested, John fled, as did the other apostles (Matt 26:56), but he recovered enough courage to be present at the trial of Jesus. Through his acquaintance with the high priest, he was able to have Peter come in too (John 18:16). He stood near the cross on which Jesus was nailed and there received Jesus' commission to look after his mother (19:26). On the morning of the Resurrection, when he and Peter were told by Mary Magdalene about the empty grave, they went together to see for themselves (20:2–3). In the account of the appearance of the risen Lord in Galilee the sons of Zebedee received special mention, and it is John who first recognized Jesus (21:1–7). In the scene that follows, the impression is corrected that John should not die before the Lord's return. At the end of the chapter the truthfulness of the gospel record is confirmed (21:20–24).

John and Peter healed a man who had been lame from his birth, were arrested, and were warned not to preach about Jesus (Acts 4:1–22). Later, they prayed and laid hands on new converts in Samaria that they might receive the Holy Spirit (8:14–15). John's name is once mentioned in Paul's letters (Gal 2:9) and in Revelation 1:1, 4, 9, where the authorship of the book is ascribed to him.

Five books of the NT are attributed to him—the Fourth Gospel, three letters, and Revelation. The only one in which his name actually appears is the last. According to tradition, he spent his last years in Ephesus and died about the end of the century.

John is described as the disciple whom Jesus loved. The defects of character with which he began his career as an apostle—an undue vehemence, intolerance, and selfish ambition—were in the course of time brought under control, until he became especially known for his gentleness and kindly love.

JOHN, GOSPEL OF Never was there a book written that made higher claim for

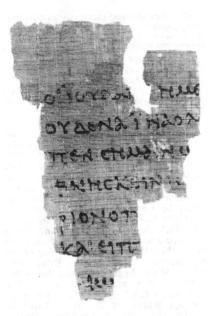

Papyrus fragment of John 18:31–33, the earliest extant copy of New Testament book dated C. A.D. 150. Found in Egypt. Courtesy John Rylands Library, Manchester, England

its "hero." To the Jesus of history its author gives the most exalted titles. In fact, in the very opening verse he calls him *God*. Tradition holds the apostle John to be this author and that the date and place of authorship was sometime toward the close of the first century A.D., Asia Minor.

Internal evidence, moreover, is in line with tradition. The author was evidently a Jew, as his style (showing acquaintance with the OT) and intimate knowledge of Jewish religious beliefs and customs indicate (John 2:13, 17, 23; 4:9, 25; 5:1; 6:4, 15; 7:2, 27, 37–38, 42; 10:22–23, 34–35; 11:38, 44, 49; 12:40). He was probably a Palestinian Jew, for he has a detailed knowledge of Palestinian topography (1:28; 2:1, 12; 3:23; 4:11, 20; 11:1, 54; 12:21), particularly of Jerusalem and its immediate vicinity (5:2; 9:7; 11:18; 18:1; 19:17) and of the temple (2:14, 20; 8:2, 20; 10:22–23; 18:1, 20). Having been an eyewitness, he remembered the time and place where the events occurred (1:29, 35, 39; 2:1; 3:24; 4:6, 40, 52–53; 6:22; 7:14; 11:6; 12:1; 13:1–2; 19:14, 31; 20:1, 19, 26). He knew that Jesus was weary

when he sat down by the well (4:6), remembered the very words spoken by the neighbors of the man born blind (9:8–10), saw the blood and water issuing from Jesus' pierced side (19:33–35), knew the servant of the high priest by name (18:10), and was acquainted with the high priest (18:15). So intimate and full is his knowledge of the actions, words, and feelings of the other disciples that he must have been one of the Twelve (1:35–42; 2:17, 22; 4:27; 6:19; 11:16; 13:22–28; 18:15–16; 20:2; 21:20–23). Though he does not mention himself by name but calls himself "the disciple whom Jesus loved," he distinguishes himself from others whom he does mention by name (Simon Peter, 1:40, 41–42, 44; Andrew 1:40, 44; 6:8; 12:22; Philip 1:43–46; Nathanael, 1:45–49; 21:2; Thomas, 11:16; 14:5; 20:24–29; 21:2; Judas [not Iscariot], 14:22; and Judas the Traitor, 6:71; 12:4; 13:2, 26, 29; 18:2–3, 5). Matthew's name can be eliminated for it is associated with another Gospel. So also the names of obscure disciples like James the Less and Simon the Zealot can be eliminated. This leaves only the sons of Zebedee: James and John. But James died an early death (Acts 12), while this Gospel's author survived even Peter (who survived James). It is clearly evident from 21:19–24 that John was still alive and bearing witness when the Fourth Gospel first appeared (note present tense in 21:24), though Peter had already gained the martyr's crown (21:19). The reasonable conclusion would surely seem to be that the apostle John wrote the Fourth Gospel.

John states that his purpose for writing is that the readers might believe that Jesus is the Christ, the Son of God, and thus receive life (John 20:30–31). It is not the kingdom (as in the other Gospels) but the King himself on whom the emphasis falls. This also accounts for the seven "I Ams" (John 6:35; 8:12; 10:9, 11; 11:25; 14:6; 15:5). This Gospel, far more than the others, records Christ's work in Judea. It also abounds in nonparabolic teaching and dwells at great length on the events and discourses that belong to a period of less than 24 hours (chs. 13–19). It records with special emphasis the promise of the coming and work of the Holy Spirit (John 14:16–17, 26; 15:26; 16:13–14).

The Book of John shows that Jesus Christ is the Son of God:

I. During His Public Ministry

A. Revealing himself to ever-widening circles, *rejected* (chs. 1–6).

B. Making his tender appeal to sinners, *bitterly resisted* (chs. 7–10).

C. Manifesting himself as the Messiah by two mighty deeds, *repulsed* (chs. 11–12).

II. **During His Private Ministry**

A. Issuing and illustrating his new commandment (ch. 13).

B. Tenderly instructing his disciples and committing them to the Father's care (chs. 14–17).

C. Dying as a substitute for his people (chs. 18–19).

D. Triumphing gloriously (chs. 20–21).

JOHN, LETTERS OF

The First Letter of John is evidently written by the author of the Fourth Gospel. The author does not give his name in the letter or the gospel, but the early church attributed both works to the apostle John, which is supported by internal evidence.

The purpose of the author is to warn the readers against false teachers (Gnostics) who are trying to mislead them, and to exhort them to hold fast to the Christian faith they have received and to fulfill conscientiously the duties, especially brotherly love, that flow from it.

Although 1 John does not have the usual characteristics of ancient Graeco-Roman letters — salutation, final greetings, messages to individuals, etc. — there is no doubt that it is a genuine letter. Most likely it is a pastoral or circular letter addressed to the churches in the province of Asia, where the church was in danger of the errors that are warned against.

The Second Letter of John and 3 John are similar in words, style, ideas, and character to 1 John, and must have been written by the same author, who refers to himself simply as "the elder" (2 John 1; 3 John 1). Both are very brief, containing just the number of words that could conveniently be written on one sheet of papyrus. "The chosen lady and her children" (2 John 1) may refer to a church and its spiritual children or to a particular individual named Kyria (Gr. for *lady*).

The Third Letter of John is addressed to Gaius, "my dear friend" (3 John 1), who is eulogized for walking in the truth and being hospitable to evangelists. The

The traditional birthplace of John the Baptist, Ein Karem, today within the southwest municipal boundary of Jerusalem. Courtesy Duby Tal

author then censures another member of the church, the talkative, overbearing Diotrephes.

JOHN THE BAPTIST The immediate forerunner of Jesus, sent by God to prepare the way for the coming of the Messiah. John was of priestly descent on the side of both his parents (Luke 1:5–25, 56–58). He lived as a Nazirite in the desert and was filled with the Holy Spirit even from birth (1:15).

His first public appearance is carefully dated by Luke (3:1–2), somewhere about A.D. 26 or 27. His early ministry took place in the wilderness of Judea and in the Jordan Valley. The main theme of his preaching was the near approach of the messianic age and the need for adequate spiritual preparation to be ready for it. His mission was to prepare the people for the advent of the Messiah. The baptism by water that he administered signified a break with and cleansing from sin. His baptism prepared for a new condition; the Jews baptized only Gentiles, but he called on Jews themselves to be baptized; and his baptism was a baptism of water only in preparation for the messianic baptism of the Spirit anticipated by the prophets.

Although Jesus and John were cousins, it appears that John did not know that Jesus was the Messiah until he saw the Holy Spirit descend on him at his baptism (John 1:32–34). John's training of his disciples included forms of prayer (Luke 11:1) and frequent fastings (Matt 9:14), but he must also have taught them much concerning the Messiah and his work. Their loyalty to him is shown in their concern about Jesus' overshadowing popularity, their refusal to abandon him in his imprisonment, the reverent care they gave his body after his death, and the fact that 20 years later there were disciples of his, including Apollos, the learned Alexandrian Jew, in faraway Ephesus (Acts 19:1–7). Jesus expressed the frankest appreciation of John, declaring him to be more than a prophet, and that he was indeed God's messenger sent to prepare the way for him (Matt 11:10–19).

The Gospels tell that John met his death through the vindictiveness of Herodias, whom John had denounced for her sin of living in adultery with Herod.

JOHN MARK (See MARK, JOHN)

JOIADA (joi'à-dà, Heb. *yôyādhā'*, *Jehovah knows*). **1.** A son of Paseah, one of those who repaired the walls of Jerusalem (Neh 3:6, KJV Jehoiada). **2.** A son of

Eliashib the high priest. One of his sons married the daughter of Sanballat, the governor of Samaria, and was therefore expelled from the priesthood by Nehemiah (12:10; 13:28).

JOIARIB (See JEHOIARIB)

JOKTAN (jŏk'tăn, Heb. *yoqtān*, meaning unknown). A tribe descended from Shem through Eber and from whom 13 tribes of Arabia subsequently descended (Gen 10:25–26, 29; 1 Chron 1:19–20, 23).

JOKTHEEL (jŏk'thē-ĕl, Heb. *yoqe-the'ēl*). **1.** A town in the lowland of Judah (Josh 15:38). **2.** A name given to a place in Edom (2 Kings 14:7), usually identified with Petra, the capital of Edom.

JONA (See JONAS)

JONADAB (jŏn'à-dăb, Heb. *yehônādhāv*, *Jehovah is bounteous*). **1.** Son of David's brother Shimeah (2 Sam 13:3). He planned for Amnon the sin against Tamar. **2.** The son of Recab (2 Kings 10:15–16; NIV Jehonadab). After becoming head of his tribe, he taught them to live in tents, to live a nomadic life, and to refrain from wine. They kept these rules, so that their behavior became characteristic of the Recabites. He helped Jehu abolish Baal worship in Samaria.

JONAH (Heb. *yônâh, dove*). A prophet of Israel. He was the son of Amittai and came from the town of Gath Hepher in the tribe of Zebulun (2 Kings 14:25). He predicted the restoration of the land of Israel to its ancient boundaries through the efforts of Jeroboam II (790–750 B.C.) who became the most powerful of all the monarchs who ever sat on the throne of Samaria. He captured Hamath and Damascus and restored to Israel all the territory it used to have from Hamath to the Dead Sea.

The identity of the prophet with the prophet of the Book of Jonah cannot reasonably be doubted. It is extremely unlikely that there were two prophets with the same name.

The spirit and teaching of the Book of Jonah rank with the highest of the OT prophetical books. Not as much can be said for the prophet himself, who ranks low in the catalog of OT prophets. He was a proud, self-centered egotist: willful, pouting, jealous, bloodthirsty; a good patriot and lover of Israel, without proper respect for God or love for his enemies.

JONAH, BOOK OF While the Minor Prophets for the most part contain prophetic discourses, with a minimum of narrative material, the Book of Jonah is mainly occupied with a narrative, and the

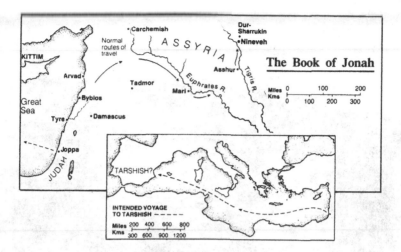

The Book of Jonah

Normal routes of travel

INTENDED VOYAGE TO TARSHISH — — — —

prophetic message in it is almost incidental. The chapter divisions mark the natural divisions of the book: chapter 1, Jonah's disobedience; chapter 2, Jonah's prayer; chapter 3, Jonah's preaching to the Ninevites; chapter 4, Jonah's complaints.

The purpose of the book is primarily to teach that God's gracious purposes are not limited to Israel but extend to the Gentile world. The author wishes to enlarge the sympathies of Israel, so that as God's missionaries they will lead the Gentiles to repentance and to God. The ready response of the Ninevites shows that the heathen are capable of genuine repentance. The Book of Jonah may be regarded as a great work on foreign missions. It anticipates the universality of Jesus' gospel, and is the OT counterpart of John 3:16, "For God so loved the world."

The traditional view, that Jonah is the author and the narrative is historically true, is supported by a number of considerations. (1) The book was written as a simple narrative, and it was so regarded by both Jews and Christians until about a century ago. (2) There seems no doubt that Jesus thought of the narrative as history and taught it as such. Some critics, taking refuge in the doctrine of the Kenosis (that Christ was somehow limited by his human nature; see Phil 2:5–8), set aside the teaching of Jesus on this point as erroneous; others, holding to a doctrine of accommodation, think that Jesus did not consider it worthwhile to correct the wrong views of his contemporaries. Neither of these explanations har-monizes with a biblical view of the person of Christ.

Most modern critical scholars in the last hundred years have regarded the book as a work of the imagination. Some call it a myth; others, an allegory; others, a parable; others, a didactic story, and so on. This interpretation avoids the miraculous elements in the narrative, which the critics find impossible to accept; but it does not do justice to the fact that our Lord very evidently held to the historicity of the book.

JONAS, JONA (jō'nås, jō'nà, Gr. *Iōnas, Iōna*). **1.** The literal rendering, given in the KJV, of the Greek name of the prophet Jonah (Matt 12:39–41; 16:4; Luke 11:29, 30, 32).**2.** The name given (John 21:15–17, KJV) to the father of the apostle Peter (Jona in John 1:42; Bar-jona in Matt 16:17).

JONATHAN (jŏn'à-thăn, Heb. *yehônāthān, yônāthān, Jehovah has given*). **1.** A Levite (Judg 18:30) in Bethlehem-Judah, who became the priest of Micah in Ephraim. At Laish he founded a priesthood that officiated at the shrine of the stolen idols (18:30). **2.** Son of King Saul (see separate article below). **3.** Son of the high priest Abiathar. He helped David during Absalom's rebellion (2 Sam 15:27, 36; 17:17, 20; 1 Kings 1:42–43). **4.** A son of Shimeah, a nephew of David (2 Sam 21:21). **5.** One of David's mighty men (23:32). **6.** A Jerahmeelite (1 Chron 2:32–33). **7.** A son of Uzziah, one of David's treasurers (27:25; Jehonathan, lit., KJV). **8.** David's "uncle," a wise man and a scribe (27:32). He may be the same as no.

The modern city of Jaffa, ancient Joppa, on the Mediterranean coast. Courtesy Duby Tal.

4 above. **9.** The father of Ebed, a returned exile (Ezra 8:6). **10.** A son of Asahel who opposed Ezra in the matter of foreign marriages (10:15). **11.** A priest, a son of Joiada, descended from Jeshua (Neh 12:11). **12.** A priest in the days of the high priest Joiakim (12:14). **13.** A Levite of the lineage of Asaph (12:35). **14.** A scribe in whose house Jeremiah was imprisoned (Jer 37:15, 20). **15.** A son of Kareah, probably the same as no. 14 above (40:8).

JONATHAN The oldest son of Saul, the first king of Israel (1 Sam 14:49). He gained an important victory over the Ammonites, who had been harassing the Israelites. Saul's army numbered 3,000 men (13:2), a third of whom he placed under the command of Jonathan at Gibeah. Jonathan, assisted only by his armor-bearer, surprised the Philistine outpost at Geba and killed 20 men (14:1–14). The resulting panic spread to the main camp, and soon the whole Philistine army was in headlong flight.

Jonathan is best remembered as the friend of David. He exemplified all that is noblest in friendship—warmth of affection, unselfishness, helpfulness, and loyalty. His love for David began the day the two first met after the killing of Goliath (1 Sam 18:1–4), and it remained steadfast despite Saul's suggestion that David would someday be king in their stead (20:31). When Jonathan first realized his father's animosity toward David, he interceded for his friend (19:1–7); and later, more than once, he risked his life for him. Once Saul, angered by what he regarded as unfilial conduct, threw a javelin at him, as he had done several times at David. The last meeting of the two friends took place in the desert of Ziph, where Jonathan "helped his friend find strength in God" (23:16). He would not take part in the proceedings of his father against David. There was one temporary estrangement between Saul and Jonathan, provoked when Saul impugned the honor of Jonathan's mother (20:30). Jonathan died with Saul and his brothers on Mt. Gilboa in battle against the Philistines (31:2). Their bodies were hung on the walls of Bethshan, but under cover of night the men of Jabesh Gilead, out of gratitude for what Saul had done for them, removed them and gave them honorable burial (31:11–13). One son, Mephibosheth, survived (1 Chron 8:34; 9:40ff.).

JOPPA (jŏp'pȧ, Heb. *yāphô*, Gr. *Ioppē*). Once in KJV Japho (Josh 19:46), an ancient walled town on the coast of Palestine, about 35 miles (58 km.) from

A view of the Jordan, looking downstream, at the traditional site where John the Baptist preached and baptized. Courtesy Duby Tal

Jerusalem. Mentioned in the Amarna Letters, it was the seaport for Jerusalem. Timber from the forests of Lebanon was floated from Tyre to Joppa for the building (2 Chron 2:16) and rebuilding of the temple (Ezra 3:7). Jonah boarded a ship there when he fled from the presence of the Lord (Jonah 1:3). In NT times Peter raised Dorcas to life there (Acts 9:36–37), and on the roof of Simon the tanner's house he received the famous vision that taught him the gospel was intended for Jew and Gentile alike (10:1ff.; 11:5ff.).

JORAM (jō'răm, Heb. *yôrām, Jehovah is exalted*). **1.** A son of Tou, king of Hamath, who congratulated David on his victory over Hadadezer (2 Sam 8:10). **2.** A Levite (1 Chron 26:25). **3.** Son of Ahab king of Israel. He succeeded his brother Ahaziah on the throne. The name is the same as Jehoram (2 Kings 8:29). **4.** Same as Jehoram king of Judah (8:21–24; 11:2; 1 Chron 3:11; Matt 1:8).

JORDAN RIVER The only large flowing body of water in Palestine, it played a significant part in the history of Israel, as well as in the earlier days of our Lord's ministry. The word *Jordan* derives from a Hebrew word, *hayyardēn,* meaning "flowing downward," or "the descender." Four rivers in Syria are the source of what later becomes the Jordan River proper. They join and pour into Lake Huleh, the surface of which is 7 feet (2 m.) above sea level. The Jordan then descends to the Sea of Galilee and enters the Dead Sea, 1,292 feet (404 m.) below sea level. The river itself varies from 90 to 100 feet (28 to 31 m.) in width, and from 3 to 10 feet (1 to 3 m.) in depth.

Though the largest river of Palestine, the Jordan differs from other great national rivers in that, because it has 27 rapids between the Sea of Galilee and the Dead Sea, it carries no traffic; and because of the swampy condition of part of this valley, the terrific heat in many places, and the presence of many wild

An aerial view showing the winding course of the Jordan River, looking northward. This picture, which was taken near Jericho, just north of the Dead Sea, covers approximately 3 miles (5 km.). Courtesy Carta, Jerusalem

animals, especially during Israel's history, no large city was ever built directly on the banks of the Jordan.

Although the Jordan is never called by any other name in the Bible, it is once referred to as "the river of the wilderness" (Amos 6:14 KJV) and "the pride of the Jordan" (Jer 12:5; 49:19; 50:44; Zech 11:3, KJV).

By far the most significant single event relating to the Jordan River in the entire history of Israel is the crossing on the part of the Israelites (Josh 3–4), when they occupied the land flowing with milk and honey (Num 35:10; Deut 3:20; 11:31; 31:13; Josh 1:2). In the NT, John the Baptist carried on his ministry here (Matt 3:6; Mark 1:5; John 1:28; 3:26), and in this river Jesus himself was baptized (Matt 3:13; Mark 1:9; Luke 4:1).

JOSABAD (See JOZABAD)

JOSAPHAT (See JEHOSHAPHAT)

JOSEPH (jō'zĕf, Heb. *yôsēph, may God add*). **1.** The 11th of Jacob's 12 sons, and the firstborn son of Rachel (Gen 30:22–24). He became the ancestor of the two northern tribes, Manasseh and Ephraim.

The account of the rest of his life is found in Genesis 37–50.

He was born in Paddan Aram when his father was 90 years old; he was his father's favorite child because he was Rachel's child and the son of his old age. The father's favoritism was shown in Joseph's coat of many colors, probably a token of rank indicating that it was his intention to make Joseph the head of the tribe. This favoritism naturally aroused the envy of Joseph's older brothers. Their ill will was increased when he somewhat imprudently told them two dreams he had that were suggestive of his future greatness and their subservience to him.

When he was 17 years old, his father sent him to see how his brothers were doing. They sold Joseph and then took his coat of many colors, smeared it with the blood of a goat they had killed, and took it to Jacob with the story that they had found the coat and assumed that their brother was dead, torn to pieces by some wild beast. Jacob mourned the loss of his son for many days.

In the meantime, Joseph was taken to Egypt by the Ishmaelites and sold in the slave market to an officer of Pharaoh, an Egyptian named Potiphar. The young slave proved himself to be so intelligent and trustworthy that his master soon entrusted to him all the affairs of his household, which prospered under Joseph's administration. But on the false accusations of Potiphar's wife, whose improper advances Joseph had rejected, he was cast into prison, where he remained for years. God was with him, however, and the providence that had previously saved his life now brought him to the favorable attention of the pharaoh. The prison keeper, finding he could put implicit confidence in Joseph, committed to his charge the other prisoners. Among these were two of the pharaoh's officers, his chief butler and chief baker, who had been imprisoned for offending the king. Joseph interpreted for them two dreams they had had; and three days later, on the king's birthday, as Joseph had foretold, the chief baker was hanged and the chief butler restored to his office (Gen 40:5–23).

After two years, Pharaoh had two dreams that no one could interpret. The chief butler now remembered Joseph and told the king of Joseph's skill in interpreting dreams. Joseph told Pharaoh that each dream had the same meaning: Seven years of plenty would be followed by seven years of famine. He then suggested that preparation be made for the years of famine by storing up the surplus produce during the seven years of plenty. Pharaoh immediately made Joseph head of the royal granaries and invested him with the authority necessary to carry out his proposals. As the head of the department of state, Joseph became one of the officials next in rank to the pharaoh (Gen 41:39–44), and as a further mark of royal favor, he was given an Egyptian name and was married to the daughter of the priest of the great national temple of On. Joseph was now 30 years old. His wife bore him two sons, Manasseh and Ephraim.

During the famine, all the known world came to Egypt to buy corn, including Joseph's brothers. They did not recognize him, but he knew them; and when they prostrated themselves before him, he saw the fulfillment of the dreams that had aroused their intense jealousy years before. Joseph, after testing their character in various ways, made himself known to them, told them that he bore no ill will for the wrong they had done him, and persuaded them and their father to settle in Egypt. The pharaohs reigning in Egypt during that era were probably members of the Hyksos dynasty and were Semites, like Joseph; and the present pharaoh consequently cordially welcomed Jacob and his family to Egypt.

In the years that followed, Joseph brought about a permanent change in the Egyptian system of land tenure because of the famine and the consequent poverty of the people, so that almost all the land became the property of the pharaoh, and the previous owners became his tenants. Jacob lived with Joseph in Egypt for 17 years. Before he died, he adopted Joseph's two sons, putting them on the same level as his own sons in the division of the inheritance. Joseph lived to the age of 110. Shortly before he died he expressed his confidence that God would some day bring the children of Israel back to Canaan and solemnly directed that his bones be buried there. His wishes were carried out (Josh 24:32). He became the ancestor of the two tribes Manasseh and Ephraim, the latter being the most powerful and important in northern Israel. Joseph presents a noble ideal of character, remarkable for his gentleness, faithfulness to duty, magnanimity, and forgiving spirit, so that he is often regarded as an OT type of Christ.

2. The father of Igal of Issachar, one of the 12 spies (Num 13:7). **3.** A son of Asaph and head of a course of musicians in the reign of David (1 Chron 25:2, 9). **4.** A son of Bani who had married a foreign wife but later put her away (Ezra 10:42).

5. A priest of the family of Shecaniah in the days of the high priest Joiakim (Neh 12:14). **6.** The name of three ancestors of Jesus, according to the KJV (Luke 3:24, 26, 30); the NIV reads "Josech" in 3:26.

7. The husband of Mary, the mother of Jesus (Matt 1:16; Luke 3:23). He was a carpenter (Matt 13:55) living in Nazareth (Luke 2:4). He was of Davidic descent (Matt 1:20; Luke 2:4), the son of Heli (3:23) or Jacob (Matt 1:16), and thought by many of that day to be the father of Jesus (13:55; Luke 3:23; 4:22; John 1:45; 6:42). After learning that Mary was pregnant before marriage, he had in mind to divorce her quietly, but an angel assured him in a dream that the child to be born had been conceived by the Holy Spirit, so he made her his wife (Matt 1:18–25). Joseph and Mary went to Bethlehem to enroll in the census, and there Jesus was born. The shepherds came to do homage to Jesus (Luke 2:8–20), and 40 days later Jesus was presented in the temple. Warned by the Lord in a dream that Herod was plotting the murder of the child, he fled with Mary and Jesus to Egypt (Matt 2:13–19), returning to Nazareth after the death of Herod. Every year Joseph attended the Passover Feast in Jerusalem (Luke 2:41); and when Jesus was 12, he too went with Joseph and Mary. Joseph undoubtedly taught Jesus the carpenter trade (Mark 6:3). It is likely that he was alive after the ministry of Jesus had well begun (Matt 13:55), but as we do not hear of him in connection with the Crucifixion, and as Jesus commended Mary to John at the Crucifixion (John 19:26–27), it may be inferred that he had died prior to that event.

8. One of the brothers of Jesus (Matt 13:55). KJV has "Joses." **9.** A Jew of Arimathea, a rich man, a member of the Sanhedrin (27:57; Mark 15:43), and a righteous man looking for the kingdom of God (15:43; Luke 23:50). A secret disciple of Jesus because of his fear of the Jews (John 19:38), he did not take part in the resolution of the Sanhedrin to put Jesus to death. After the Crucifixion he secured permission from Pilate to remove the body of Jesus from the cross, and he laid it in his own new tomb (Matt 27:57–60; Luke 23:50–53; John 19:38). **10.** A Christian called Barsabbas, or son of Sabas, and surnamed Justus (Acts 1:23). He was one of those who had accompanied Jesus and the apostles from the time of Jesus' baptism and was one of the two candidates considered to replace Judas Iscariot (1:21). **11.** The personal name of Barnabas (4:36; KJV Joses).

JOSES (jō'sĕz, Gr. *Iōsēs,* Gr. form of *Joseph*). **1.** One of Jesus' brothers (Mark 6:3 KJV). NIV and some MSS have *Joseph* in Matthew 13:55. **2.** A name of Barnabas, for a time a co-worker of Paul (Acts 4:36 KJV). Here, too, NIV and some Greek MSS have *Joseph.*

JOSHAPHAT (jŏsh'à-făt, Heb. *yôshā-phāt, Jehovah had judged*). **1.** One of David's mighty men (1 Chron 11:43). **2.** A priest and trumpeter in David's time (15:24; KJV Jehoshaphat).

JOSHIBIAH (jŏsh'ĭ-bī'à). A Simeonite mentioned only in 1 Chronicles 4:35.

JOSHUA (jŏsh'ū-à). A son of Nun, an Ephraimite (1 Chron 7:22–27). Although born in Egyptian bondage c. 1500 B.C., he was named Hoshea (Oshea), "salvation" (Num 13:8; Deut 32:44). Two months after Israel's exodus, he was appointed Moses' commander and successfully repulsed an Amalekite attack (Exod 17:9). Moses changed Hoshea's name to Jehoshua, *yehôshûa',* "Jehovah is salvation" (Num 13:16; 1 Chron 7:27), or Joshua, later forms of which are Jeshua (*yēshûa',* Neh 8:17) and, in Greek, Jesus (*Iēsous,* Acts 7:45; Heb. 4:8; cf. Matt 1:21). Joshua attended Moses on Sinai (Exod 24:13; 32:17) and guarded both his tent (33:11) and position (Num 11:28). Later he represented Ephraim in spying out Canaan. Joshua opposed the majority report, insisting that Israel, if faithful to God, could conquer Canaan. He almost suffered stoning for his trust in God (14:7–10). For having "followed the LORD wholeheartedly" (32:12), he not only escaped destruction (14:38) but also received assurance, unique to himself and Caleb (13:30; 14:24), of entering the Promised Land (14:30; 26:65).

About 40 years later God designated Joshua as Moses' successor (Num 27:18). After Moses' death, Joshua's actions include making preparations for war (Josh 1:10–18), sending spies against Jericho (2:1, 23–24), and then ordering Israel's advance across Jordan (3:1). The appearance of "the commander of the army of the LORD" (5:13–15) served as a visible confirmation of Joshua's divine call. Joshua then executed the God-directed siege (Josh 6:2–6). He destroyed Jericho (6:17), pronounced a curse on its rebuilding (6:26; 1 Kings 16:34), and achieved widespread recognition (Josh 6:27).

It was really the Lord who gave Israel her victories. In six years (Josh 14:10) Joshua took the whole land (11:15, 23). Moses had anticipated a gradual occupa-

tion (Exod 23:28–30). God had left in Canaan many nations, subdued but still powerful, to test his people (Josh 13:2–6; Judg 2:21–3:4); so Joshua could not achieve Israel's final "rest" (Heb 4:8). Thus, because of his advanced age, he divided Canaan among the tribes (Josh 13:6–7; 14:1; 19:51).

JOSHUA, BOOK OF This book describes how Moses' successor conquered Canaan (Josh 1:1; 24:31; see JOSHUA). But while Joshua is the first of "the historical books" in English (and Greek), it introduces "the prophets" in the original Hebrew canon of Law, Prophets, and Writings. These prophetic books include the "former prophets"—Joshua, Judges, Samuel, and Kings.

Joshua's prophetic author is not named; but his statements about the death of Joshua and his colleagues (Josh 24:29–31), plus his allusions to Othniel, the migration of the Danites (15:17; 19:47), and the name Hormah (12:14; 15:30; 19:4) indicate that he lived after the rise of Israel's judges, c. 1380 B.C. (Judg 1:12–13, 17). At the same time, his designation of Jerusalem as Jebusite (Josh 15:8, 63; 18:16, 28) and his writing before its choice as the site of God's temple (9:27), indicate that he wrote before the time of David, 1000 (1 Chron 11:4–6; 22:1). His references, moreover, to Sidon rather than to Tyre as Phoenicia's leading city (Josh 11:8; 13:4–6; 19:28) suggest a date prior to 1200. Indeed, the writer must have been an eyewitness of the events he describes (5:1, 6; 6:25; 15:4; cf. 2:3–22; 7:16–26; 15:9, 49, 54). Someone, then, composed the Book of Joshua about 1375 B.C.

The Book of Joshua has two parts: conquest (Josh 1–12) and settlement (chs. 13–24).

JOSIAH (jō-zī'à, Heb. *yō'shîyāhû, Jehovah supports him*). Son of Amon and Jedidah and the grandson of Manasseh, the son of Hezekiah (2 Kings 22:1). Josiah's reign on the Davidic throne for 31 years was the last surge of political independence and religious revival before the disintegration of the southern kingdom that ended with the destruction of Jerusalem in 586 B.C.

When palace officials murdered King Amon in 642 B.C. (2 Kings 21:23) the eight-year-old Josiah was crowned king of Judah. In the eighth year of his reign (c. 632) he began to seek after God and four years later initiated reforms. Images, altars, and all manner of idolatrous practices were destroyed not only in Jerusalem and Judah but in the cities of Manasseh, Ephraim, Simeon, and as far north as Naphtali. At the same time offerings and contributions were collected throughout the nation for the restoration of the temple in Jerusalem, which had been neglected for such a long period.

In the course of renovating the temple (622 B.C.) the Book of the Law was recovered. The reformation movement was now stimulated anew by its reading (2 Chron 34:15). Stirred by these developments Josiah led his nation in the observance of the Passover in a manner unprecedented in Judah's history. With the king himself leading the reformation movement, changes in personnel occurred. Priests serving by royal appointment of former kings and dedicated to idol worship were removed from office. In 609 B.C. Josiah's leadership was abruptly ended. In an effort to interfere with Pharaoh Neco's plans to aid the Assyrians, Josiah was fatally wounded at Megiddo (2 Chron 35:20–24). National and religious hopes vanished with the funeral of this 39-year-old king so that all Judah had reason to join Jeremiah in lamenting for Josiah (35:25).

JOSIBIAH (See JOSHIBIAH)

JOT A corruption of *iote,* an English transliteration of *iota,* the ninth letter of the Greek alphabet and the nearest equivalent to Hebrew *yodh,* the smallest letter in the Hebrew alphabet and almost identical with our apostrophe sign ('). Used figuratively, the jot signifies something of apparently small moment (Matt 5:17–18).

JOTBAH (jŏt′bȧ, Heb. *yotbâh, pleasantness*). A Levitical city in Judah, just south of Hebron, called Juttah in Joshua 15:55; 21:16. The home of the father-in-law of Jotham, king of Judah (2 Kings 21:19).

JOTHAM (jō′thăm, Heb. *yôthām, Jehovah is perfect*). 1. The youngest of the 70 sons of Gideon, and the speaker of the first Bible parable (Judg 9:5–57). After the death of Gideon, Abimelech, an illegitimate son desired to make himself a king over Israel. He murdered all his half-brothers, except for Jotham. 2. A man of the tribe of Judah (1 Chron 2:47). 3. King of Judah, son of Uzziah. Jotham began to reign just about the time Isaiah began his great ministry (Isa 6:1) and was probably influenced by that godly man, and perhaps by Hosea and Micah also. He had victory over the Ammonites, who were forced to pay him heavy tribute, and he was a great builder (2 Kings 15:32–38; 2 Chron 27).

JOY In the OT, joy is commonly a group expression, often associated with dancing (Ps 96:11) or the blessings of prosperity (Isa 60:15). Feasting or offering sacrifice (Deut 12:12; Isa 56:7), celebration of harvest or victory (1 Sam 18:6; Joel 1:16), and enjoying prosperity or personal triumph (Ps 31:7; Isa 61:3ff.) are all occasions of joy.

In the NT, the word is often found in connection with salvation (1 Peter 1:6), or with eating, drinking, and feasting (Luke 12:19; Acts 7:41). The NT applies joy to suffering as well as to salvation (Matt 5:11–12). Joy comes from the Holy Spirit (Gal 5:22).

JOZABAD (jŏz′ȧ-băd, Heb. *yôzāvādh, Jehovah endows*). 1. A man from Gederah in Judah who joined David at Ziklag (1 Chron 12:4; "Josabad" in KJV). 2. Two men of the tribe of Manasseh who also joined David (12:20). 3. One of the Levites appointed to be overseers in the house of God (2 Chron 31:13). 4. A chief Levite in the time of Josiah who gave large offerings of cattle to the Levites for Passover offerings (35:9). 5. A Levite who assisted in the weighing of the gold and silver for the house of God (Ezra 8:33). 6. A priest who had married a woman outside of Israel in the days of Ezra, and who gave his promise to put her away (10:22). 7. A Levite who had committed the same offense (10:23). 8. When the law was read during Nehemiah's reformation this Levite translated it from the Hebrew into the Aramaic so that the common people could understand (Neh 8:7). 9. A chief Levite in

Drawing of an impression of a seal ring believed to be that of Jotham, king of Judah. The seal, from Ezion Geber, depicts a ram; Hebrew inscription reads, "[Belonging] to Jotham." Jotham is described as one "who did right in the eyes of the LORD" (2 Kings 15–22ff.; see also Isa 1:1). Courtesy Carta, Jerusalem

Nehemiah's time who helped oversee the "outside work" of the temple (11:16).

JOZACHAR (See ZABAD)

JOZADAK (jŏz'à-dăk, Heb. *yehôtsādhāq, Jehovah is righteous*). Father of Jeshua the priest who returned with Zerubbabel (Ezra 3:2, 8; 5:2; 10:18). He is called Josedech in Haggai and Zechariah.

JUBILEE (Heb. *yôvēl, ram's horn, trumpet*). Every 50th year in Israel (Lev 25). Three essential features characterized this year. First, liberty was proclaimed to all Israelites who were in bondage to any of their countrymen. The law provided that the price of slaves was to vary according to the proximity of the Jubilee Year. Second, there was to be a return of ancestral possessions to those who had been compelled to sell them because of poverty. This, of course, excluded the possibility of selling a piece of land permanently. This law applied to lands and houses outside of the walled cities and also to the houses owned by Levites, whether in walled cities or not. As in the case of the price of slaves, the law made provision that the price of real property was to vary according to the proximity of the Jubilee Year. The third feature of this year was that it was to be a year of rest for the land. The land was to remain fallow, even though it had been so in the previous sabbatical year. The people were to live simply, on what the fields had produced in the sixth year and whatever grew spontaneously. It is impossible to say whether the Jewish people ever really observed the Jubilee Year.

JUBILEES, BOOK OF A Jewish apocalyptic book written in the intertestamental period. It gives a history of the world from the creation to the giving of the law, and defends Pharisaical views against liberal Hellenistic tendencies. See also APOCALYPTIC LITERATURE.

JUDA (See JODA)

JUDAEA (See JUDEA)

JUDAH (jū'dà, Heb. *yehûdhâh, praised*).
1. The fourth son of Jacob; his mother was Leah (Gen 29:35). He saved Joseph's life by persuading his brothers to sell him to the Midianites at Dothan (37:26–28). His disgraceful actions are recorded as well (Gen 38). He gradually appears to have achieved leadership among his brothers (43:3; 46:28; 49:8–12), and during his own lifetime there arose among them the rivalry that was much later to give rise to the division of the kingdom. Through his son Perez, Judah became an ancestor of David (Ruth 4:18–22) and of

Jesus Christ (Matt 1:3–16). The blessing of dying Jacob to Judah (Gen 49:9–10) is usually understood as being a messianic prophecy.
2. The Hebrew tribe descended from the man Judah described above. Caleb was a member of this tribe (Num 13:6; 34:19). After Joshua's death, this tribe seems to have been first in occupying its allotted territory in the southern hill country of Canaan, even to occupying temporarily the city of Jerusalem (Judg 1:1–20).

During the period of the rule of the judges, Judah tended to be separated from the rest of the Hebrew tribes, which were to the north, by the pagan people who lived between them (Gibeonites, Josh 9; Jebusites, Judg 19:10–13), and also by rough and wild land, with deep east-west valleys. The Simeonites, who lived in southern Judean cities, tended to become assimilated into Judah and thus to lose their tribal identity.

Othniel, the judge who delivered the people from the domination of Mesopotamia, was a Judean (Judg 3:8–11). The Philistine threat must have been especially troublesome to this tribe, for the Philistine plain was actually Judah's coastal plain land. The account of Ruth and Boaz occurred during the time of the judges and first brought the country town of Bethlehem into prominence in Hebrew history. Saul, whose reign brought the period of the judges to an end, ruled from Judah; and it was the Judeans who first anointed their fellow tribesman, David, king at Hebron (2 Sam 2:1–4).
3. Judah is also the name of five individuals who are mentioned in Ezra and Nehemiah. Three were Levites (Ezra 3:9 KJV; 10:23; Neh 12:8), one a Benjamite (11:9), and the fifth probably a prince of Judah (12:34). NIV has "Hodaviah" in Ezra 3:9 (cf. footnote). A Judah other than the son of Jacob is also named in Luke 3:30 as an ancestor of Jesus (KJV "Juda").

JUDAH, KINGDOM OF When Solomon died, the Davidic dynasty continued to rule at Jerusalem over a small remnant of the nation, the kingdom of Judah. The boundary between Judah and Israel must have run a few miles north of Jerusalem. All of southern Palestine (much of it desert) was held by Rehoboam—not more than half the size of the northern kingdom, less than one-fourth the arable land. The northern kingdom had the best farm land and was favored with more rainfall. Judah's history from the death of Solomon to the fall of Jerusalem to the

The Judean hills west of Jerusalem. Historically, this region was the heart of the kingdom of Judah. Courtesy Zev Radovan

Babylonians may be divided into three periods:

1. From the death of Solomon to the mid-eighth century (922–742 B.C.) Judah and Israel lived side by side.

2. During the period of the Assyrian Ascendancy (742–687 B.C.) Israel was destroyed by Assyria (722), and Judah was severely damaged.

3. The last century of the kingdom of Judah (687–587 B.C.) saw intermittent warfare and finally her fall to the last Semitic world empire—Babylon. Archaeologists have found that all of the cities of Judah were completely destroyed at this time. Although the other nations conquered by the Assyrians and Babylonians ceased to exist, the prophets proclaimed a better hope for the chosen people. A purged remnant would return and become the basis for a new Israel.

JUDAISM The religious system held by the Jews. Its teachings come from the OT, especially from the law of Moses as found from Exodus 20 through Deuteronomy; but also from the traditions of the elders (Mark 7:3–13), some of which our Lord condemned. The principal elements of Judaism include circumcision, a strict

monotheism, an abhorrence of idolatry, and Sabbath-keeping.

JUDAS, JUDA (Heb. *yehûdhâh, praised,* Gr. *Ioudas*). **1.** An ancestor of our Lord (Luke 3:30 KJV; NIV "Judah"). **2.** A Galilean insurrectionist (Acts 5:37). According to Gamaliel, this Judas perished and his followers were scattered. **3.** One of the brothers of Jesus (Matt 13:55). This Judas is almost certainly the "Jude" who wrote the letter by that name. See also JUDE. **4.** An apostle of Jesus called "Judas of James" (Luke 6:16), different versions rendering it either "brother of James" or "son of James." **5.** One who apparently had a guest-house or hostel in the street called Straight in the city of Damascus and with whom Paul lodged (Acts 9:11). **6.** One of the leading brethren at the Council of Jerusalem (15:6–35). His surname Barsabbas, i.e., "son of Saba," hints that he may have been a brother of Joseph Barsabbas (1:23), who was so highly regarded by the brethren before Pentecost that he was suggested as a replacement for Judas Iscariot. Judas Barsabbas was a preacher ("prophet," 15:32) and with Silas was entrusted with

The Judean desert, composed of hilly escarpments stretching from the eastern edge of the Judean hills to the Dead Sea. Courtesy Zev Radovan

the decrees of the council for safe delivery to the Christians at Antioch.

JUDAS ISCARIOT The archtraitor, who betrayed the Lord. He and his father Simon were both surnamed "Iscariot" (John 6:71), a word thought to be from the Hebrew *Ish Kerioth,* i.e., "a man of Kerioth." Kerioth is almost certainly in southern Judah (Josh 15:25). He was appointed treasurer for the disciples (John 12:6; 13:29), but after his hopes for a high place in an earthly kingdom of Jesus were dashed (6:66), he became a thief. His indignation when Jesus was anointed at Bethany was hypocritical (12:6), though the disciples of Jesus apparently trusted him to the end (13:21–30). Jesus, however, was not deceived (6:64) but knew from the beginning who would betray him. It was only at the Last Supper that Jesus revealed that one of them would betray him (6:71). Then Satan entered into Judas. Jesus dismissed him and Judas went out to do what he had already planned (Mark 14:10). He sold the Lord for 30 pieces of silver and betrayed him with a kiss. Then in remorse he threw down the money before the chief priests and elders (Matt 27:3–

10) and went out and committed suicide (Matt 27:5; Acts 1:18). He is always mentioned last among the apostles.

JUDE (Gr. *Ioudas*). Writer of the last of the letters in the NT. Both James and Jude in the opening of their letters show their Christian humility and their faith in the deity of Jesus by referring to themselves as servants of Jesus Christ, rather than as his brothers in the flesh. Beyond this we only know that, like his brothers, he did not believe in Jesus during his earthly ministry (John 7:5) but became his follower after the Resurrection (Acts 1:14).

JUDE, LETTER OF One of the General Epistles included in the earliest-known list (probably second century A.D.) of NT writings, although not otherwise cited or even mentioned by any of the early church fathers until Clement of Alexandria (c. 150–c. 215).

The author may be the same person as "Judas," brother of James and Jesus (Matt 13:55; Mark 6:3; see BROTHERS OF THE LORD). The problems he discusses were common during the last quarter of the first century when heresy was increasing (Jude 3).

Jude reminds Christians of the inevitability of opposition, of the need for compassion toward sinners, and of the ineffable attributes of God. He denounces those who would undermine the true faith (Jude 4-16). Jude reminds his readers of God's punishment in the OT (Gen 6:1-4; 19:24; Num 14:29, 37) against people, angels, and cities that should have known better, and he leaves them in no doubt that God still punishes sin. Jude 17-25 exhorts to continued perseverance. There is a reminder that the apostles had foretold the coming of the "scoffers" (cf. 2 Peter 3:3) who love worldly things and sow dissension among believers.

JUDEA, JUDAEA (jū-dē'à, Heb. *yehû-dhâh*, Gr. *Ioudaia*). A geographical term that first appears in the Bible in Ezra 5:8 (KJV, NIV "district of Judah"), where it designates a province of the Persian Empire. The land of Judea is also mentioned in the apocryphal books 1 Esdras (1:30) and 1 Maccabees (5:45; 7:10). Since most of the exiles who returned from the Babylonian exile belonged to the tribe of Judah, they came to be called Jews, and their land Judea.

Under the Persian Empire, Judea was a district administered by a governor who was usually a Jew (Hag 1:14; 2:2). Under Rome, with the banishment of Herod's son Archelaus, Judea became annexed to the Roman province of Syria; but its governors were procurators appointed by the Roman emperor. Their immediate superior was the proconsul of Syria, who ruled from Antioch (Luke 3:1). The official residence of the procurators was Caesarea. Judea was about 55 miles (92 km.) north to south and the same distance east to west, extending from the Mediterranean to the Dead Sea, with its northern boundary at Joppa and its southern boundary a few miles south of Gaza and the southern portion of the Dead Sea. Its exact boundary was, however, never fixed.

JUDGE (See OCCUPATIONS AND PROFESSIONS)

JUDGES, BOOK OF The seventh book of the OT takes its name from the title of the men who ruled Israel during the period from Joshua to Samuel. They are called judges (*shōphetîm*, Judg 2:16), their principal function being that of military deliverers to the oppressed Hebrews.

The Book of Judges bridges the historical gap between the death of Joshua and the inauguration of the monarchy and shows the moral and political degradation of a people who neglected their religious heritage and compromised their faith with the surrounding paganism, as well as showing the need of the people for the unity and leadership by a strong central government in the person of a king.

In its structure the book falls into three easily recognizable parts: (1) Introduction: the state of things at the death of Joshua (Judg 1:1-2:10), (2) Main body: the judges' cycles (2:11-16:31), (3) Appendix: life in Israel in the days of the judges (chs. 17-21).

The judges and the part of Israel that they served (when that can be known) are listed here:

1. Othniel (3:7-11).
2. Ehud (3:12-30): Central Palestine and Transjordan.
3. Shamgar (3:31): Philistine plain.
4. Deborah and Barak (chs. 4-5): Central Palestine and Galilee.
5. Gideon (chs. 6-8): Central Palestine and Transjordan.
6. Abimelech (ch. 9): Central Palestine. Abimelech is considered by many as merely an outlaw and not a judge.
7. Tola (10:1-2): Central Palestine.
8. Jair (10:3-5): Transjordan.
9. Jephthah (10:6-12:7): Transjordan.
10. Ibzan (12:8-10): Southern Palestine.
11. Elon (12:11-12): Northern Palestine.
12. Abdon (12:13-15): Central Palestine.
13. Samson (chs. 13-16): Philistine plain.

The events recorded in Judges 17-21 seem to have occurred, not after the judges mentioned in the main part of the book, but during their judgeships. These narratives describe life during this turbulent near-pagan period and give a frank and unvarnished description of the brutality and paganism that Israel was contaminated with because of her close association with her pagan Canaanite neighbors. The writer is not approving of everything he records but gives a history of God's judgment on a people who failed to keep their heritage of true religious faith by assimilating far too much of their surrounding culture.

JUDGES, THE
In patriarchal times Hebrew life was organized around the family and the clan. Heads of families ("patriarchs") and elders of the tribes were the judges (Gen 38:24).

After the Exodus from Egypt, Moses (on the advice of Jethro; Exod 18:13-26), organized the nation into groups of thousands, hundreds, fifties, and tens, within each tribe. Over each unit a qualified man was placed as judge, and only the most important cases were brought before Moses (Deut 1:12–18; 21:2). After entering Canaan, a similar plan of local government was followed (16:18–20; 17:2–13; 19:15–20; Josh 8:33; 23:2; 24:1; 1 Sam 8:1).

When the monarchy was instituted, the king himself tried important cases (2 Sam 15:2; 1 Kings 3:9, 28; 7:7; Prov 20:8). David assigned Levites to the judicial office and appointed 6,000 men as officers and judges (1 Chron 23:4; 26:29). Jehoshaphat enlarged the judicial system of Judah with a kind of supreme court at Jerusalem, made up of Levites, priests, and heads of fathers' houses (2 Chron 19:5–8).

The prophets often complained bitterly that justice was corrupted by bribery and false witness (Isa 1:23; 5:23; 10:1; Amos 5:12; 6:12; Mic 3:11; 7:3). Kings were often unjust (1 Kings 22:26; 2 Kings 21:16; Jer 36:26). The case of Ahab's seizure of Naboth's vineyard (1 Kings 21:1–13) shows how far a king could go in getting his own way, in flagrant contradiction of law and custom, at least in the northern kingdom of Israel.

In OT times the judges' activities were not limited to what today would be considered judicial functions. Our present division of powers among the legislative, executive, and judicial branches is a modern innovation. The word *judge* is often parallel to *king* (Pss 2:10; 148:11; Isa 33:22; 40:23; Amos 2:3). In several Semitic languages the term used in the Hebrew Bible for judge (*shōphēt*) is used for rulers of various kinds. This breadth of meaning attached to the term judge in ancient times leads to its extended use in the Book of Judges.

From the time of the death of Joshua to the reign of Saul, Israel's first king, the principal leaders of the people were called judges. These men and their times are described in the Book of Judges and in 1 Samuel 1–7. They were charismatic leaders; that is, they were raised up to be Israel's "saviors" by a special endowment of the Spirit of God. They were principally military deliverers, raised up to save the people of Israel from oppressing foreign powers. See JUDGES, BOOK OF.

The period was cruel, barbarous, and bloody. The tribes, scattered in the hill country of Canaan, were divided into many separate enclaves. Even the tabernacle at Shiloh, which should have pro-vided a religious unity, seems to have been generally neglected in favor of the local high places. Only an unusual crisis, such as the crime that brought on the Benjamite war (Judg 19:1–30; 20:1), could bring the tribes to united action. It appears that Judah in the south was unusually isolated from the other tribes.

The first judge mentioned in detail is Ehud, son of Gera (Judg 3:12–30). A Benjamite, he was lefthanded, a serious defect in those superstitious times. Few if any of the judges are pictured as ideal individuals. The occasion of God's raising up Ehud was the oppression by Eglon, king of Moab, who with the Ammonites and Amalekites (all Transjordanian herdsmen or nomads), occupied the region of Jericho ("the City of Palms," 3:13). After 18 years of oppression, Ehud, when he presented the tribute, led a revolt by killing Eglon. With Ephraimite help Eglon took the fords of the Jordan and killed the Moabites as they sought to flee homeward. An 80-year period of peace followed.

In the second detailed deliverance narrative (Judg 4–5), the scene shifts from the lower Jordan Valley to the Valley of Jezreel and the Galilee hill country in northern Palestine. The oppressor is Jabin, king of Canaan, who reigned in Hazor and whose 900 chariots of iron must have struck terror into the Hebrew tribes, for they had no such machines of war (1 Sam 13:19–22). The recent excavation of Hazor by Israeli scholars has underscored the importance of this Canaanite stronghold, probably the largest city in ancient Palestine. The deliverers were Deborah, "a prophetess" (Judg 4:4), and Barak, son of Abinoam, a fearful man (4:8) who led the Hebrew army at Deborah's urging. Evidently a cloudburst upstream caused the Kishon to overflow onto the plains through which it flows, thus immobilizing the chariots on which the Canaanites depended (4:15; 5:20–22). When the army of Jabin was defeated, his general Sisera fled, only to be killed by the woman Jael (4:17–22). Deborah's warlike song of praise (ch. 5) is believed to be one of the oldest poems of the Bible and is noted for its rough, primitive vigor. A 40-year rest followed this deliverance.

The third great judge was Gideon (Judg 6–8). The oppressing Midianites, desert Bedouin from the Transjordan region, had crossed the Jordan and were raiding in Palestine proper. Gideon is commonly remembered for his doubt and reluctance to take action (6:15, 17, 36–40; 7:10), but once he assumed command he proved a steady and effective soldier (6:25–27; 7:15–24), and he ruled for 40 years. He and 300 companions frightened the Bedouin into full retreat across the Jordan. Gideon promptly called the Ephraimites to take the Jordan fords and thereby they destroyed the Midianites.

Gideon's son Abimelech had a violent rule over the Shechem area (Judg 9). He died as he lived—his skull was cracked by a millstone, and he was finally killed by his armorbearer.

Jephthah, a Transjordanian chieftain, appears (Judg 11–12) as the deliverer of Gilead and Manasseh (northern Transjordan) from the oppression of the Ammonites. He is chiefly remembered for his thoughtless vow (11:30–39).

The last of the great judges was Samson (Judg 13–16), with whom the scene shifts to a different part of Palestine—the Philistine plain. It is likely that Samson lived late in the judges period, at the time when a large invasion of the Palestinian seacoast was occurring. The invaders, sea peoples from the Aegean area, had been repulsed in their attempt to enter Egypt (by Rameses III). Samson was dedicated to a life of Nazirite obedience before his birth. Hardly a very religious person, Samson was known for his great strength. His failure to discipline his sensuous nature led him into three liaisons with Philistine women.

He made single-handed exploits in Philistine territory, a number of which are described (Judg 14:19; 15:4–5, 8, 15; 16:3). The account of Samson's being subdued at the hand of Delilah is well-known. Killing in his death more Philistines than he killed in his life (16:30), he became at the last a tragic figure. He judged Israel 20 years.

Eli (1 Sam 1–4) and Samuel (2:12) are also called judges. They did some of the work of the judges described above, but also served as priest and prophet respectively—transitional figures preparing the way for the monarchy.

JUDGMENT (Heb. *dhîn, mishpāt,* Gr. *krima, krisis*). Sometimes it refers to the pronouncing of a formal opinion or decision by human beings, but more often it indicates either a calamity regarded as sent by God for punishment or a sentence of God as the Judge of all. Important judgments of God prior to the Exodus are those on Adam, Eve, and the serpent after the Fall (Gen 3), the Flood (6:5), Sodom and Gomorrah (18:20), and the confusion of tongues (11:1–9).

In the OT, the relationship between the Lord and Israel is thought of as a covenant. Of his own will, the Lord brought first Noah (Gen 6:18), then Abraham and his sons (15:18; 17:1ff.), into a close relationship with himself. He bound himself to them by covenant and looked in return for their responsive devotion. Similarly, with Israel in the time of Moses, grace reached out to redeem and restore (Exod 6:4) and looked for responsive, loving obedience (20:1ff.). Within the covenant, the Lord pledged blessing on obedience and judgment on disobedience (e.g., Deut 27:1–26; 28:1–68; cf. Lev 26:3–13ff.). The history of Israel, beginning with the Exodus, is the record of a succession of judgments on the enemies of God's people and on his covenant nation when they flouted his will. The "day of the LORD" becomes a day of punishment for all the unjust (Isa 2:12; Hos 5:8; Amos 5:18). The purpose of the judgment is purification. A remnant will survive, the nucleus of the new Israel (Amos 5:15). The later prophets expressed the hope of an ultimate victory of the divine Judge, of his intervention in history at the end of time.

In the NT the idea of judgment appears in both human and divine contexts. Jesus warns against uncharitable judgments (Matt 7:1). Paul says that the spiritual man cannot be judged by unbelievers (1 Cor 2:15), and he warns against judging those who are "weak" in the faith (Rom 14; 1 Cor 8–10).

In the NT judgment is one of the aspects of the coming of the kingdom of God. God's judgment will fall on those who do not make ready the way of the Lord (Luke 3:9). Jesus will come to judge both the living and the dead (Matt 25:31ff.).

In the NT, as in the OT, judgment is an aspect of the deliverance of believers (Luke 18:1–8; 2 Thess 1:5–10; Rev 6:10). God is long-suffering in meting out judgment so that people may be able to come to repentance (Luke 13:6–9; Rom 2:4; 2 Peter 3:9). Judgment, when God will overthrow every resistance, both among evil spiritual powers (1 Cor 6:2–3) and also among people (Matt 25:31–46), will affect all people, because all are responsible to God according to the grace that has been granted them (Matt 11:20–24; Luke 12:17ff.; Rom 2:12–16). This present world will be shaken and destroyed (Matt 24:29, 35), and a new world will replace the present one (2 Peter 3:13; Rev 21:1). God will entrust the administration of this final judgment to his son at his appearance in glory (Matt 3:11–12; John 5:22; Rom 2:16).

See also ESCHATOLOGY.

JUDGMENT HALL (Gr. *praitōrion*). Originally the tent or building where the general or governor held council, it (or "hall of judgment") appears five times in KJV (John 18:28, 33; 19:9; Acts 23:35). The Greek term is used of (1) Pontius Pilate's palace in Jerusalem (Matt 27:27; Mark 15:16; John 18:28, 33; 19:9), (2) Herod's palace at Caesarea, used also as the official residence by the governors Felix and Festus (Acts 23:35), and (3) the imperial palace in Rome (Phil 1:13).

JUDGMENT SEAT (Gr. *bēma, a raised place, platform, tribune*). The bench or seat where a judge sits to hear arguments and pleas and to deliver sentence. Although the word is used principally in the NT in connection with the trials of Christ (Matt 27:19; John 19:13) and of Paul (Acts 18:12), its main association is with the judgment seat of Christ, before which all believers will stand (Rom 14:10; 2 Cor 5:10).

JUDGMENT SEAT OF CHRIST (See ESCHATOLOGY)

JUDGMENT, THE LAST (See ESCHATOLOGY)

JUDITH, BOOK OF (See APOCRYPHA)

JULIUS (Gr. *Ioulios*). A Roman centurion of the Imperial Regiment (KJV "Augustan band") in whose care Paul was placed for the journey to Rome (Acts 27:1, 3). He trusted Paul to go to his friends at Sidon, and he and his soldiers saved Paul's life and their own lives by frustrating the sailors' plot near Malta.

JUNIPER (See PLANTS)

JUPITER (See ZEUS)

JUSTICE (See RIGHTEOUSNESS)

JUSTIFICATION (Heb. *tsedheq, tsādhēq*; Gr. *dikaioō, to make valid, to absolve, to vindicate, to set right*). Justification may be defined as "that judicial act of God by which, on the basis of the meritorious work of Christ, imputed to the sinner and received through faith, God declares the sinner absolved from sin, released from its penalty, and restored as righteous." It is being placed by God in a right relationship with himself (see RIGHTEOUSNESS). The doctrine is found in Paul's letters, chiefly those to Galatia and Rome.

As a reversal of God's attitude toward the sinner because of the sinner's new relation in Christ, justification is: (1) a *declarative* act by which the sinner is declared to be free from guilt and the consequences of sin (Rom 4:6–8; 5:18–19; 8:33–34; 2 Cor 5:19–21); (2) a *judicial*

act in which the idea of judgment and salvation are combined to represent Christ fulfilling the law on behalf of the sinner (Matt 10:41; Rom 3:26; 8:3; 2 Cor 5:21; Gal 3:13; 1 Tim 1:9; 1 Peter 3:18); (3) a *remissive* act in which God actually remits sin in complete forgiveness (Rom 4:5; 6:7); and (4) a *restorative* act by which the forgiven sinner is restored to favor through the imputation of Christ's righteousness (Rom 5:11; 1 Cor 1:30; Gal 3:6).

Four basic essentials in the act of justification are taught by Scripture. Justification involves:

A. **Remission of punishment,** in which the justified believer is declared to be free of the demands of the law since they have been satisfied in Christ (Rom 4:5) and is no longer exposed to the penalty of the law (6:7).

B. **Restoration to favor,** in which the justified believer is declared to be personally righteous in Christ. Mere acquittal or remission would leave the sinner in the position of a discharged criminal. Justification implies that God's treatment of the sinner is as if that one had never sinned. The sinner is now regarded as being personally righteous in Christ (Gal 3:6). There is not only acquittal but also approval, not only pardon, but also promotion.

C. **Imputed righteousness of God,** which is granted the justified believer through Christ's presence. Salvation in Christ imparts the quality and character of Christ's righteousness to the believer (Rom 3:22–26; Phil 3:9). Christ is made the Justifier through whom a new life is inaugurated in the believer (1 Cor 1:30).

D. **New legal standing before God** in which, instead of being under the condemnation of sin, the justified believer stands before God in Christ. Christ takes the place of the sinner, the place of curse (Gal 3:15), being made sin (2 Cor 5:21) and being judged for sin; the believer now stands in Christ's righteousness (Rom 3:25) and is viewed as a son (Gal 4:5).

The ground on which justification rests is the redeeming work of Christ's death. The inherent righteousness of Christ is the sole basis on which God can justify the sinner (Rom 3:24; 5:19; 8:1; 10:4; 1 Cor 1:8; 6:11; Phil 3:9; Titus 3:7).

The instrumental cause of justification is faith, as the response of the soul to God's redeeming grace (Rom 3:28). Faith is the condition of justification not in that it is considered meritorious, but only as the condition by which the meritorious work of Christ is accepted by the sinner. The final ground of justification is the completed, finished, sufficient work of Christ atoning for the sinner in his redeeming work on the cross.

JUSTUS (Gr. *Ioustos, just*). **1.** The surname of Joseph Barsabbas, one of the two whom the "brethren" appointed as candidates for Judas' place among the Twelve (Acts 1:23–26). **2.** The surname of Titius of Corinth, with whom Paul lodged for a time (18:7). **3.** The surname of Jesus, an early Hebrew Christian at Rome, evidently known to the Christians at Colosse (Col 4:11).

–K–

General view of the oasis at Kadesh Barnea, the most important place in the desert wanderings of the Israelites. It was also the departure point of the twelve spies (Deut 1:19–23). Courtesy Zev Radovan

KAB (See CAB; WEIGHTS AND MEASURES)

KADESH, KADESH BARNEA (kā'dĕsh bár'nē-à, Heb. *qādhēsh*, from *qādhôsh, be holy*). Also possibly Kedesh (Josh 15:23) and En Mishpat (Gen 14:7; cf. 20:1), probably about 50 miles (83 km.) south of Beersheba. The first biblical reference to Kadesh is Genesis 14:7, where it is equated with En Mishpat. The primary relationship of the Israelites to Kadesh centers in the period of time that they spent there during the Exodus (cf. Deut 1:46; Num 33:37–38; Deut 2:14). From Horeb (Sinai), via Seir, it was an 11-day journey to Kadesh (Deut 1:2). Kadesh is described as being in the wilderness of Paran (Num 13:26); it is also said to be in the wilderness of Zin (33:36; cf. 20:1); Psalm 29:8 mentions "the Desert of Kadesh." When the Israelites reached this place, Moses sent the 12 spies to scout southern Canaan (Num 13:1, 17, 26; 32:8; Deut 1:19–25; Josh 14:6–7). Encouraged by the Lord to invade the land at that time, the people rebelled (Deut 9:23) and were sentenced to the delay in possessing the land (Num 14:34). At Kadesh, Miriam died and was buried (20:1). It was in this area also that the waters of Meribah ("quarreling") were located (Num 20:2–13, 24; Meribath-Kadesh, Num 27:14; Deut 32:51). It was from Kadesh that Moses sent emissaries to the king of Edom to request permission for Israel to pass through Edomite territory (Num 20:14–16, 22; cf. Judg 11:16–17). The conquest of the southern section of Palestine by Joshua refers to an area from Kadesh to Gaza (Josh 10:41). Kadesh also is named as marking the southern border of Judah (15:3, 23) and therefore the southern boundary of the land possessed by the Israelites (Num 34:4; Ezek 47:19; 48:28).

KADMIEL (kăd'mĭ-ĕl, Heb. *kadmî'ēl, God is in front*). Head of a family of Levites who returned with Zerubbabel (Ezra 2:40; Neh 7:43). He helped in the rebuilding of the temple (Ezra 3:9). One of his family sealed the covenant (Neh 10:9).

KAIN (kān, Heb. *kāyin, smith*). **1.** A town in Judah, in KJV spelled Cain (Josh 15:57). **2.** In ASV and RSV a tribal name; NIV has "the Kenite" (Num 24:22; Judg 4:11). See also KENITES.

KANAH (kā'nà, Heb. *qānâh, reeds*). **1.** A brook running from south of Shechem westward to the Mediterranean Sea (Josh 16:8; 17:9). **2.** A city near the boundary of the tribes of Asher (19:28).

KATYDID (See ANIMALS)

KEBAR (kē'bàr). A river or canal beside which Ezekiel saw visions (Ezek 1:1; 3:23; 10:15, 20, 22; 43:3); in Babylonia (1:3), at Tel Aviv (3:15).

KEDAR (kē'dêr, Heb. *kēdhār*, probably either *mighty* or *dark*). **1.** One of the 12 sons of Ishmael, son of Abraham by Hagar (Gen 25:13). These sons were called "tribal rulers." They helped originate the Arab peoples. **2.** The tribe that descended from Kedar (Jer 49:28–33) and their territory. They were nomads for the most part (Ps 120:5; Song of Songs 1:5), raising sheep (Isa 60:7) but sometimes intruding into villages (42:11). Their territory was in the northern part of the Arabian Desert.

KEDEMOTH (kĕd'ē-mŏth, Heb. *qedhē-môth, eastern parts*). A place east of the Jordan from which Moses sent a message to Sihon king of Heshbon asking for safe passage through his land (Deut 2:26). It was given to the tribe of Reuben (Josh 13:18) but was later set apart, with its suburbs, for Merarite Levites (21:37).

KEDESH (kē'dĕsh, Heb. *qedesh, sacred place*). **1.** A city of the Canaanites conquered by Joshua in his northern campaign (Josh 12:22), later given to the tribe of Naphtali (19:37), appointed as a city of refuge (20:7; 21:32), and given to the Gershonite Levites. Here Barak and Deborah assembled the armies of Israel to fight against Sisera of the Canaanites (Judg 4:6–10); 600 years later Tiglath-Pileser conquered Naphtali, including Kedesh, and took their people to Assyria (2 Kings 15:29). **2.** A city in the tribe of Issachar, given to the Gershonite Levites (1 Chron 6:72). **3.** A city in the very southern part of Judah near the border of Edom (Josh 15:23). Perhaps it is the same as Kadesh Barnea.

KEDORLAOMER (kĕd'ŏr-lā-ō'mûr). King of Elam (Gen 14), which was south of Media and east of Babylonia. He and his allies met the king of Sodom and his allies on the same battleground (the Valley of Siddim, or the Salt Sea) where Kedorlaomer had defeated them 14 years

earlier. The bitumen or tar pits of the region were the undoing of the local defenders. But Abram the Hebrew in a swift night raid with 318 retainers, recovered the spoil of Sodom and pursued the invaders to a point near Damascus.

KEDRON (See KIDRON)

KEILAH (kē-ī'là, Heb. *ke'îlâh*). **1.** A city in the foothills of Judah (Josh 15:44) threatened by the Philistines, but rescued by David (1 Sam 23:1–13). **2.** A man of Judah, descended from Caleb, son of Jephunneh (1 Chron 4:19).

KELAIAH (kē-lā'yà, Heb. *kēlāyâh*). Also Kelita, a Levite who had taken a foreign wife in the days of Ezra and gave her up (Ezra 10:23).

KELITA (See KELAIAH)

KELUB (ke'lŭb, Heb. *kelûv*, another form of *Caleb*). **1.** A brother of Shuhah, a Judahite (1 Chron 4:11). **2.** Father of Ezri, and superintendent of the field workers who farmed the land in David's time (27:26).

KEMUEL (kĕm'ū-ĕl, Heb. *kemû'ēl*). **1.** The son of Nahor and brother of Bethuel, therefore uncle of Laban and Rebekah (Gen 22:21). **2.** A prince of the tribe of Ephraim appointed by Moses to help divide the land of Canaan (Num 34:24). **3.** The father of Hashabiah, a leading Levite in the days of David (1 Chron 27:17).

KENAANAH (kē-nā'à-nà). **1.** The father of the false prophet Zedekiah, who slapped Micaiah (1 Kings 22:11, 24; 2 Chron 18:10, 23). **2.** Son of Bilham of the tribe of Benjamin (1 Chron 7:10).

KENAN (kē'nàn). A great-grandson of Adam (1 Chron 1:2), also translated "Cainan" (Gen 5:9–14; Luke 3:36).

KENANIAH (kĕn'à-nī'à). **1.** A chief Levite when David brought up the ark from the house of Obed-Edom (1 Chron 15:22, 27). **2.** An Izharite, an officer of David's (26:29). Some identify the two as one.

KENATH (kē'nàth, Heb. *qenāth, possession*). A city of the Amorites in the region of Bashan in the kingdom of Og. In the last days of Moses, Nobah took it with its outlying villages and named it after himself (Num 32:42). Later the two little kingdoms of Geshur and Aram, near Mt. Hermon, took Kenath along with Havvoth-Jair and the surrounding 60 cities in the land of Gilead (1 Chron 2:22–23).

KENAZ (kē'nàz, *qenaz, hunting*). **1.** A grandson of Esau through Eliphaz (Gen 36:11, 15). **2.** Father of Othniel (Josh

15:17; Judg 1:13; 3:9–11). **3.** A grandson of Caleb through his son Elah (1 Chron 4:15).

KENEZITE (See KENIZZITE)

KENITES (kē'nīts, Heb. *ha-qênī, smith*). **1.** One of the ten tribes of Canaan in the time of Abraham (Gen 15:19), perhaps the same as those doomed by the prophecy of Balaam (Num 24:21–22). **2.** The descendants of Hobab, the brother-in-law of Moses (Judg 4:11). They were friendly with Israel; they went with Judah from Jericho (1:16) and amalgamated with the tribe of Judah. Later, Heber the Kenite (4:11) separated from the others, moved northward to Kedesh near the Sea of Galilee, and made peace with Jabin king of Hazor. Heber's wife Jael killed Sisera, the Canaanite general (4:17–22). Later Saul, sent to destroy the Amalekites, gave friendly warning to the Kenites (1 Sam 15:6) to depart and save themselves, because of the kindness they had shown to Israel more than 500 years before.

KENIZZITE (kē'nĭz-īt, Heb. *qenizzî*). A family name derived from Kenaz. One of the ten tribes of Canaan in the days of Abram (Gen 15:19). Some think that the Edomite tribe descended from Kenaz, grandson of Esau (36:11, 15), united at least in part with Israel because Caleb of the tribe of Judah (Josh 14:6, 14) is called the "son" of Jephunneh the Kenizzite.

KEPHIRAH (kē-fī'rà). A Hivite town that, with Gibeon, gained the protection of the Israelites by deceit (Josh 9:17). It was in the territory of Benjamin (18:26). Some of its citizens returned after the Exile (Ezra 2:25; Neh 7:29).

KERETHITES (kĕr'ĕ-thīts). A Philistine tribe in southern Palestine (1 Sam 30:14; Ezek 25:16; Zeph 2:5), from whom David drew his bodyguard, commanded by Benaiah (2 Sam 8:18; 15:18; 20:7, 23; 1 Kings 1:38, 44; 1 Chron 18:17). Twice LXX translates "Cretans" (Ezek 25:16; Zeph 2:5), since the Philistines originated in Crete. Elsewhere the LXX has *Cheleththi* or *Cherethi* (except 1 Sam 30:14, *Cholthi*).

KERIOTH (kēr'ĭ-ŏth, Heb. *qerîyôth, cities*). **1.** Kerioth Hezron ("Kerioth and Hezron" KJV), a city in the south of Judah (Josh 15:25), elsewhere called "Hazor." **2.** A city of Moab and, judging from Amos 2:1–3, probably its capital in the eighth century B.C. In "the judgment of Moab" (Jer 48), Moab is pictured as ruined because of its idolatry (48:13) and

its pride (48:29), and Kerioth is pictured as under judgment from God (48:24, 41).

KERITH (kē'rĭth). The brook where God directed Elijah to hide during the first part of the famine he had predicted (1 Kings 17:1–5). Its location is uncertain–perhaps it was as obscure in Elijah's day and therefore a secure hiding place.

KETTLE (Heb. *dûdh, a cooking vessel*). Mentioned with pan, pot, and caldron, and elsewhere translated by all these terms. Also a basket for carrying clay or bricks (1 Sam 2:14).

KETURAH (kĕ-tū'rà). Abraham's second wife (Gen 25:1), probably taken after the death of Sarah and the marriage of Isaac (24:67), but she was called his concubine (1 Chron 1:32; cf. Gen 25:6). She was the mother of six sons, ancestors of Arabian tribes (Gen 25:2–6; 1 Chron 1:33).

KEY (Heb. *maphtēah, opener*). An Oriental key was made of wood, with nails or wooden pegs to fit corresponding holes in the bolt holding the door fast (Judg 3:25). Figuratively, a symbol of authority, carried on the shoulder (Isa 22:20–22). Greek *kleis,* "something that shuts" (Luke 11:52); symbolic of the authority given to Peter (Matt 16:19), but which Jesus still retains (Rev 1:18; 3:7); the key that keeps destructive forces (9:1) and Satan (20:1) in the bottomless pit.

KIBROTH HATTAAVAH (kĭb'rŏth hă-tā'à-và, *the graves of lust or greed*). The first encampment of the Israelites after they left the wilderness of Sinai. Here they longed for meat and gorged themselves on the quails God sent, dying of the resulting sickness. This explains the name (Num 11:34–35; 33:16–17; Deut 9:22).

KID (See ANIMALS)

KIDNEY (Heb. always in the pl. *kelāyôth,* Gr. *nephroi*). This organ, being surrounded by pure fat, was adapted to burning in sacrifice when the whole animal was not burned (Exod 29:13, 22; Lev 3:4, 10, 15; 4:9; 7:4; 8:16, 25; 9:10, 19). Slaughter in a war that was a judgment of God was a sacrifice in which the kidneys figured (Isa 34:6). From their inaccessible location in the body, the kidneys were regarded as the seat of the emotions; KJV, ASV marginal note, "reins"; usually "heart" in ASV, RSV, NIV (Job 19:27; Ps 7:9; Jer 11:20).

KIDRON (kĭd'rŏn, kī'drŏn, Heb. *qidh-rôn,* Gr. *Kedrōn*). The valley along the east side of Jerusalem, where the Pool of

Section of the Kidron Valley in Jerusalem, facing northeast. The tombs shown are from left to right: the Pillar of Absalom, the tomb of the priestly family of Hezir, and the tomb of Zechariah. All were built during the second temple period. Courtesy Zev Radovan

Gihon is located, whose water was brought by an aqueduct into the Pools of Siloam within the walls. South of the city the Kidron joins the Valley of Hinnom near the Pool of En Rogel, and the united valley, Wadi en-Nar, runs down to the Dead Sea. David's crossing of the Kidron (2 Sam 15:23) in his escape from his rebellious son Absalom marked the decisive abandonment of his throne. When Solomon spared Shimei, he warned him that to cross the Kidron would bring him death (1 Kings 2:37). Asa burned idols at the brook (15:13; 2 Chron 15:16), as did Josiah (2 Kings 23:4, 6, 12) and Hezekiah (2 Chron 29:16; 30:14). It is called "the stream" (32:4) that Hezekiah stopped, to deny the attacking Assyrians a water supply. Nehemiah went up it by night to view the state of the walls of Jerusalem (Neh 2:15 KJV, ASV "brook," RSV, NIV "valley"). Jeremiah mentions it in prophesying the permanent rebuilding of Jerusalem (Jer 31:38–40). After the Last Supper, Jesus and his disciples crossed it on their way out of the city to reach the Garden of Gethsemane (John 18:1, KJV Cedron). Jesus must often have looked across this valley from the Mt. of Olives (e.g., Matt 24:3; Mark 13:3), and he must have crossed it on his triumphal entry into the city of Jerusalem (Matt 21:1–11; Mark 11:1–10; Luke 19:28–44; John 12:12–19).

KILEAB (kĭl'ē-ăb). The second son of David (the first by Abigail) born at Hebron (2 Sam 3:3). Called Daniel in 1 Chronicles 3:1.

KILION (kĭl'ĭ-ŏn). One of the two sons of Elimelech and Naomi, who married Orpah in Moab and died there (Ruth 1:2–5; 4:9–10).

KIMHAM (See GERUTH KIMHAM)

KIN (See KINSMAN)

KING A male ruler, usually hereditary, of a city, tribe, or nation. Hebrew *melekh* may mean "possessor," stressing physical strength, or "counselor, decider," stressing intellectual superiority. Greek *basileus* always denoted a ruler and leader of a people, city, or state. Kings often had priestly functions in the maintenance of the religion of the group. In the Orient kings came to be regarded as divine beings. This was true of Egypt from the beginning. The idea was taken over by the Greek empire of Alexander and his successors, later by the Romans, after their empire came to include most of the East.

The earliest king mentioned in the Bible is Nimrod (Gen 10:8–12), whose Mesopotamian kingdom was extensive. From this region the kings who warred with kings of Canaan came and were driven off by Abraham (ch. 14). God promised Abraham (17:6) and Jacob (35:11) that kings would be among their descendants. There were city-kings such as Abimelech (20:2), called king of the Philistines (26:1, 8), and kings in Edom (36:31; 1 Chron 1:43) before Israel had kings. Kings of Egypt, the pharaohs, figure in the Egyptian period of Israelite history (Gen 39–Exod 14; Deut 7:8, 11:3); they also appear later when Egyptian influence was strong in Judah. Israel contacted many kings in their wanderings (Num 20:14–33:40; Deut 1:4–4:47; 7:24; 29:7; 31:4) and in Canaan (Josh 2:2–24:12; Judg 1:7–11:25; 1 Sam 14:47; 15:8, 20, 32; 21:10, 12; 22:4). These varied in power from headmen of towns to rulers of large areas.

In the time of the judges there was no king in Israel (Judg 17:6; 18:1; 19:1; 21:25); everyone did what was right in his own eyes. Moses had foreseen that the people would demand a king as a strong human ruler (Deut 17:14–15; 28:36), not content with a theocracy, the direct rule of God as king over them (33:5). Hannah looked forward to a time when there would be a king of Israel who was appointed and anointed by God (1 Sam 2:10). Toward the end of Samuel's judgeship Israel was unwilling to wait for a messianic king and demanded one "such as all the other nations have" (1 Sam 8:5, 22; 10:19, 24; 12:1–25; cf. Hos 13:10). Samuel duly warned the people what to expect of a king, then selected Saul, whose choice they ratified. The reigns of Israelite kings are recorded as follows: Saul (1 Sam 12–31; 1 Chron 10); David (2 Sam; 1 Kings 1; 1 Chron 11–29); Solomon (1 Kings 1–11; 1 Chron 28–2 Chron 9); later kings of Israel ar.d Judah (1 Kings 12–2 Kings 25; 2 Chron 10–36). Ezra, Nehemiah, and Esther deal with kings of Persia.

The prophets (especially Isa 1–31; 36:1–39:7; Jer; Lam; Ezek; Dan) refer to kings of Judah and other nations. Job reflects that in death all are equal with kings (Job 3:14); that God debases kings (12:18); Eliphaz observes that trouble and anguish overwhelm a man like a king prepared for attack (15:24). Psalm 2 contrasts the messianic king (2:6) with kings of the earth (2:2, 10). Some references in Psalms are to human kings (Pss 20:9; 21:1, 7; 33:16; 63:11; 68:12, 14, 29; 72:10–11; 76:12; 89:27; 102:15; 105:14, 20, 30; 110:5; 119:46; 135:10–11; 136:17–20; 138:4; 144:10; 148:11; 149:8), some to God as king (5:2; 10:16; 18:50; 145:1; 149:2). Psalm 24 acclaims the Lord as king of glory. Proverbs contains maxims for a king's conduct (e.g., Prov 31:1–9). Isaiah develops the concept of a messianic king (Isa 32:1; 33:17) identified with the Lord (33:22; 41:21; 43:15; 44:6). Jeremiah refers to God as king (Jer 8:19; 10:7, 10; 46:18; 48:15; 51:57) and to the messianic king (23:5). Ezekiel 37:22, 24 refers to the Davidic king of restored Israel whom the context shows to be messianic. The messianic king enters Jerusalem riding on a colt (Zech 9:9), and God is king (14:9, 16–17; Mal 1:14). Nebuchadnezzar praises the king of heaven (Dan 4:37).

The Gospels speak of kings in general (Matt 10:18; 11:8; 17:25; 18:23; 22:2, 7, 11, 13; Mark 13:9; Luke 10:24; 14:31; 21:12; 22:25) and in particular: Herod the Great (Matt 2:1, 3, 9; Luke 1:5); Herod Antipas (Matt 14:9; Mark 6:14, 22–27); David (Matt 1:6); the messianic king of the Jews (Matt 2:2; 21:5; 25:34, 40, 27:11, 29, 37, 42; Mark 15:2, 9, 12, 18, 26, 32; Luke 19:38; 23:2–3, 37–38; John 1:49; 6:15; 12:13, 15; 18:37, 39; 19:3–21); and God (Matt 5:35). References in Acts are to earthly kings except 17:7, which refers to Jesus. A few references in the epistles are to earthly kings; one is to God (1 Tim 1:17; cf. 6:15). In Revelation, besides earthly kings, Jesus Christ is introduced as prince (ruler) of the kings of the earth (1:5), who made us kings (1:6; 5:10 KJV; ASV, NIV "a kingdom"; cf. 1 Peter 2:9). The king of the apocalyptic locusts (Rev 9:11) is the angel of the bottomless pit. God is king (15:3) and the Lamb is king of kings (17:14).

A king sits on a throne, holds a scepter (Ps 45:6), wears a crown (2 Kings 11:12), lives in a palace (1 Chron 29:1), and rides in a royal chariot (1 Sam 8:11). From a few military and civil officers for city-kings and for Saul, the royal bureaucracy rapidly expanded (8:10–18) to the dimensions of David's (2 Sam 23:8–39; 1 Chron 11:10–47) and Solomon's (1 Kings 9:22; 4:1–28; 2 Chron 8:9–10) establishments. Yet Solomon judged comparatively trivial cases (1 Kings 3:16–28); Ahab shared the personal oversight of his cattle (18:5–6). The Persian monarchy was a vast empire (Esth 1:1). Kings frequently met death by assassination. Jesus is sovereign until at the resurrection he delivers the kingdom to his Father (1 Cor 15:24–28).

KINGDOM OF GOD (Gr. *basileia tou theou*). The word *kingdom* is capable of three different meanings: (1) the realm over which a monarch reigns, (2) the people over whom he or she reigns, and (3) the actual reign or rule itself. In English the third use of the word is archaic and so is not always given its rightful place in discussion of the term; but in Greek and Hebrew, this is the primary meaning. All three meanings are found in the NT.

1. The kingdom of God is sometimes the people of the kingdom (Rev 1:6; 5:10).

2. The kingdom of God is the realm in which God's reign is experienced. This realm is sometimes something present, sometimes future. It is a realm introduced after the ministry of John the Baptist; people enter it with violent determination (Luke 16:16). John did not stand within this new realm but only on its threshold; but so great are the blessings of God's kingdom that the least in it is greater than John (Matt 11:11). Jesus offered the kingdom to Israel, for they were its proper heirs (8:12); but the religious leaders, followed by most of the people, not only refused to enter its blessings but tried to prevent others from entering (23:13). Nevertheless, many tax collectors and prostitutes did enter the kingdom (21:31; cf. Col 1:13).

Elsewhere the kingdom is a future realm inaugurated by the return of Christ. The righteous will inherit this kingdom (Matt 25:34) and will shine like the sun in God's kingdom (13:43). Entrance into this future kingdom is synonymous with entering the eternal life of the age to come (19:16, 23–30; Mark 10:30).

3. The kingdom is also God's reign or rule. *Basileia* is used of kings who have not received "royal power" (RSV) or authority to rule as kings (Rev 17:12). Later, these kings give their "kingdoms," i.e., their authority, to the beast (17:17). A nobleman went into a distant country to receive the crown (*basileia*) that he might be king over his country (Luke 19:12; cf. Matt 6:33; Mark 10:15). God's kingdom is, however, not merely an abstract rule. The kingdom is God's rule *dynamically* defeating evil and redeeming sinners. Christ must reign as King until he has destroyed (*katargeō*) all enemies, the last of which is death; then he will deliver the kingdom to the Father (1 Cor 15:24–26).

The kingdom of God—his redemptive rule—has come into history in the person of Christ to break the power of death and Satan; it will come in power and glory with the return of Christ to complete the destruction of these enemies. Because of this present victory of God's kingdom, we may enter the realm of its blessings in the present, yet look forward to greater blessings when Christ comes again.

We may now define the kingdom of God as the sovereign rule of God manifested in Christ to defeat his enemies, creating a people over whom he reigns and issuing in a realm or realms in which the power of his reign is experienced.

KINGDOM OF HEAVEN (See KINGDOM OF GOD)

KING JAMES VERSION (See BIBLE, ENGLISH VERSIONS)

KINGS, 1 AND 2, BOOKS OF These are named in English, as in Hebrew, by subject matter: They cover four centuries of Israelite kings, from David (his death in 930 B.C.) to Jehoiachin (in Babylon, after 561). The LXX actually entitles 1 and 2 Samuel "Books A and B of the Kingdoms" (Latin Vulgate and KJV subtitle: "I and II Books of the Kings"), so that 1 and 2 Kings become, correspondingly, "III and IV King(dom)s." Like Samuel, Kings was written as a unit but was divided in two at the time of the LXX translation, about 200 B.C. In the original Hebrew canon (the Law, Prophets, and Writings), Kings preceded Isaiah-Malachi as the concluding volume of the "former prophets," following Joshua, Judges, and Samuel. For though listed among the "historical books" in English (and Greek), these four works possess an essentially prophetic character (contrast the priestly volumes of Chronicles), employing the events of past history as a vehicle for contemporary preaching (cf. Dan 9:6).

A key to the theological aims of Kings appears in David's opening admonition: ". . . observe what the Lord your God requires . . . as written in the Law of Moses, so that you may prosper in all you do . . ." (1 Kings 2:3; cf. 3:14; 2 Sam 7:14). Divine retribution is traced through the history of Solomon (1 Kings 1–11), the divided kingdoms, treated synchronously, (1 Kings 12–2 Kings 17), and the history of surviving Judah (2 Kings 18–25). Accordingly, punishment is meted out to sinful Israel (2 Kings 17:7–23) and Judah (23:26–27; 24:1–4), but rewards are also given the righteous in both the northern (1 Kings 21:29) and southern (2 Kings 22:19–20) kingdoms. Hope is even extended into the Exile (25:27–30).

KINNERETH (kĭn'ē-rĕth). **1.** A fortified city on the NW shore of the Sea of Galilee (Josh 19:35). Kinnereth means "harp," and the hill on which it stood is harp-shaped. **2.** A district in Galilee (1 Kings 15:20). **3.** The sea later known as Gennesaret or Galilee (Num 34:11; Deut 3:17; Josh 11:2; 12:3; 13:27). The sea also is harp-shaped.

KINSMAN (Heb. *gō'ēl, one who has the right to redeem*). Boaz exercised the right of redemption by marrying Ruth and purchasing the property of her first husband's father, a near relative (Ruth 2:20–4:14). In Ruth 2:1 the Hebrew *môdha'*, "acquaintance," is used, the feminine form of which can also be used figuratively (Prov 7:4, RSV "intimate friend"). In Psalm 38:11 the Hebrew *qārôv*, is translated "neighbor." Hebrew *she'ēr* (its feminine form means "flesh") is used of an incestuous relationship (Lev 18:12–13, 17; also translated "kin" or "close relative" in 18:6; 20:19; 21:2). Once it is used of a relative who can inherit (Num 27:11). Once *gō'ēl* refers to one who can receive restitution for a wrong done to a dead relative (5:8). In the NT, Greek *syngenēs*, "of the same race," is usually translated "relative" (Mark 6:4; Luke 14:12; John 18:26; Acts 10:24; Rom 9:3; 16:7, 11, 21). The NT meaning is always the broad one of undefined relationship. In the OT, kinsman translates Hebrew words with three distinct ideas: one who has a right to redeem or avenge; one too closely related for marriage; a neighbor, friend, or acquaintance. See also AVENGER.

KIR (kûr, kĭr, Heb. *qîr, enclosure, wall*). A place to which the Assyrians carried captive the inhabitants of Damascus (2 Kings 16:9; Amos 1:5) and from which they were to be restored to Syria (9:7). In Isaiah 22:6 soldiers from Kir are associated with others from Elam.

KIR HARESETH (kĭr hăr'ĕ-sĕth). El-Kerak, east of the southern part of the Dead Sea. The name appears in various forms. It was the capital of Moab when Joram king of Israel made war on Mesha king of Moab (2 Kings 3:4–25) and devastated the country except for this city, which he besieged. When Mesha offered his son as a sacrifice on the wall, the siege was raised (3:26–27). Its later destruction is a subject for serious lamentation (Isa 15:1; 16:7, 11; Jer 48:31, 36).

KIRIATH, KIRJATH (kĭr'ĭ-ăth, kĭr'jăth, Heb. *qiryath, a city*). The word occurs alone (Josh 18:28) where Kiriath Jearim (so RSV) is meant, and as part of other names identified with the same (e.g., Gen 23:2; Num 22:39; Josh 15:60; Ezra 2:25).

KIRIATHAIM (kĭr'ĭ-à-thā'ĭm, Heb. means *double city*). **1.** A city in the uplands of Moab, given to Reuben, who fortified it (Num 32:37; Josh 13:19). Later Israel lost it, and it became a Moabite town again (Jer 48:1, 23; Ezek 25:9). Around it were plains, Shaveh Kiriathaim (Gen 14:5). **2.** A city of the Gershonite Levites in Naphtali (1 Chron 6:76); Kartan in Joshua 21:32.

KIRIATH JEARIM (kĭr'ĭ-ăth jē'à-rĭm, *city of woods*). With Gibeon, Kephirah, and Beeroth, one of four Gibeonite towns (Josh 9:17), same as Baalah (15:9) and Kiriath Baal (15:60); a Canaanite high place and center of Baal worship, first assigned to Judah (15:60); at the SW corner of the boundary with Benjamin, to which it was later assigned (18:14–15, 28). Men of Dan, seeking a new home, encamped west of it in Judah at Mahaneh Dan (Judg 18:12). Here the men of Beth Shemesh brought the ark when it was returned by the Philistines (1 Sam 6:21; 7:1–2); it remained here 20 years until David brought it up to Jerusalem (1 Chron 13:5–6; 2 Chron 1:4; it is called Baalah of Judah in 2 Sam 6:2). Men from Kiriath Jearim were among the returning exiles (Neh 7:29; Ezra 2:25); some were

El Kerak, identified with Kir Hareseth, situated on a high rocky plateau east of the Dead Sea and south of the Amon River. Today the hill is crowned by a medieval castle. Courtesy Studium Biblicum Franciscanum, Jerusalem

listed in the genealogies (1 Chron 2:50–53). The prophet Uriah came from Kiriath Jearim (Jer 26:20).

KISH (kĭsh, Heb. *qîsh, bow, power*). **1.** A Benjamite, a son of Abiel and father of Saul, Israel's first king (1 Sam 9:1, 3; 10:11, 21). Called Cis in KJV of Acts 13:21. **2.** A son of Abi Gibeon, a Benjamite (1 Chron 8:30; 9:36). **3.** A Levite of the family of Merari (23:21–22; 24:29). **4.** A Levite and a Merarite who assisted in the cleansing of the temple in Hezekiah's time (2 Chron 29:12). **5.** A Benjamite, an ancestor of Mordecai, the cousin of Queen Esther (Esth 2:5).

KISHION (kĭsh'ĭ-ŏn, kĭsh'yŏn). A city in the tribe of Issachar, given to the Gershonite Levites (Josh 19:20; 21:28 KJV Kishon; in 1 Chron 6:72 called Kedesh).

KISHON (kī'shŏn, kĭsh'ŏn, Heb. *qîshôn, curving*). A stream that flows from sources on Mt. Tabor and Mt. Gilboa westward through the Plain of Esdraelon (Valley of Jezreel), and enters the Bay of Acre north of Mt. Carmel. In winter it becomes a raging torrent. Along the banks of the River Kishon, Deborah the prophetess and Barak led Israel to victory over the Canaanite hosts of Jabin, under their commander Sisera (Judg 4–5). The heavily armed soldiers and chariots that were not cut down by the pursuing Israelites were swept away by the raging Kishon (5:21; Ps 83:9, KJV Kison). After his contest with the priests of Baal on Mt. Carmel, Elijah had the priests brought down to the brook Kishon and killed there (1 Kings 18:40).

KISLEV (kĭz'lĕv, KJV Chisleu). The ninth month of the Hebrew ritual year (Zech 7:1).

KISS (Heb. *nāshaq*, Gr. *phileō, philēma, kataphileō*). A common greeting among male relatives (Gen 29:13; 33:4; 45:15; Exod 4:27; 18:7; 2 Sam 14:33), male and female relatives (Gen 29:11; 31:28), in farewell (31:55; Ruth 1:9, 14), and before death (Gen 50:1). The kiss had a more formal character in connection with a blessing (27:26–27; 48:10) or the anointing of a king (1 Sam 10:1). Friends kissed (20:41; 2 Sam 19:39). The act might be a pretense (15:5; 20:9; Prov 27:6). Kissing was an act of worship toward heathen gods (1 Kings 19:18, 20; Job 31:27; Hos 13:2). Righteousness and peace will "kiss" each other; i.e., will unite to bless restored Israel (Ps 85:10). Kisses may be a lure to illicit love (Prov 7:13). The kiss in Psalm 2:12 is one of homage to the king's son. The kiss was generally given

on the cheek, forehead, or beard, though a kiss on the lips is sometimes indicated (Prov 24:26) and is probable (in Song of Songs 1:2; 8:1). In the NT the Greek verb *phileō* is usually translated "love," but when associated with the strengthened form *kataphileō*, "kiss repeatedly, effusively," it is translated "kiss," and the noun *philēma* is always so translated. Once Jesus' host did not give him this customary greeting, but a sinful woman kissed his feet (Luke 7:38, 45). The father kissed the returning prodigal (15:20). Judas kissed Jesus as a sign to the temple police (Matt 26:48–49; Mark 14:44–45; Luke 22:47–48). The Ephesian elders kissed Paul in farewell (Acts 20:37). The kiss was adopted as a formal greeting among believers, the holy kiss (Rom 16:16; 1 Cor 16:20; 2 Cor 13:12; 1 Thess 5:26) or kiss of charity or love (1 Peter 5:14), given by men to men and by women to women.

KITE (See BIRDS)

KITTIM (kĭt'ĭm, Heb. *kittîm*). **1.** Descendants of Javan (Gen 10:4; 1 Chron 1:7). **2.** The island of Cyprus is probably meant in three verses (Isa 23:1, 12; Ezek 27:6; KJV "Chittim"). The word can characterize ships of Grecian pattern (Num 24:24), which roamed the Mediterranean very early (cf. Dan 11:30).

Clay figurine that shows the kneading of dough in a trough, from cemetery at Aczib (mentioned in Josh 19:29–31), ninth–early sixth century B.C. Courtesy Israel Department of Antiquities and Museums

KNEADING TROUGH A dish in which dough was prepared to be made into bread. The plague of frogs infested them in Egypt (Exod 8:3). The Israelites bound their kneading troughs, dough and all, in the bundles of clothing on their backs, when they escaped from Egypt (12:34). They are called "kneading bowls" in RSV. KJV has "store" for the same Hebrew word where ASV and NIV have "kneading trough" (Deut 28:5, 17).

KNEE (Heb. *berekh*, Gr. *gonu*). The first references are to taking on the knees in token of adoption (Gen 30:3 KJV; 48:12; 50:23). The knees are equivalent to the lap (Judg 16:19; 2 Kings 4:20; Job 3:12). Their strength or weakness is commented on (Job 4:4; Ps 109:24; Heb 12:12). Gideon rejected men who knelt to drink (Judg 7:5-6). Diseased knees follow disobedience (Deut 28:35). Knees knock and give way in fear (Dan 5:6; Nah 2:10). Daniel was set trembling on hands and knees (Dan 10:10). To bow the knee to Baal identified one as his worshiper (1 Kings 19:18; Rom 11:4). Kneeling expressed homage or worship (2 Kings 1:13, to Elisha; Matt 17:14; Mark 1:40; 10:17; Luke 5:8, to Jesus; 1 Kings 8:54; 2 Chron 6:13; Ezra 9:5; Rom 14:11 quoting Isa 45:23; Acts 7:60; 9:40; 20:36; 21:5; Eph 3:14; Phil 2:10, to God in prayer; notably Luke 22:41; Dan 6:10). Kneeling in mockery is related in Mark 15:19.

KNIFE 1. Hebrew *herev*, usually "sword," occasionally some other tool with a cutting edge. The "flint knives" used in circumcision (Josh 5:2-3) were kept for religious purposes long after bronze and iron were introduced; the priests of Baal cut themselves with "swords" (RSV, NIV) in their contest with Elijah (1 Kings 18:28). "A sharp sword" (ASV, RSV, NIV) was sometimes used as a razor (Ezek 5:1-2). 2. Hebrew *ma'ăkheleth*, a knife used to carve sacrifices (Gen 22:6, 10; Judg 19:29; figuratively, Prov 30:14). 3. Hebrew *sukkîn*, knife (Prov 23:2). 4. Hebrew *mahălāph* (Ezra 1:9); named among temple vessels taken from Jerusalem as spoils, and returned after the Exile, were 29 knives (KJV, ASV), which RSV calls "censers" and NIV "silver pans." A "scribe's knife" (Jer 36:23) was used to sharpen reed pens. Knives were not used for eating. Meat was cut into small pieces before serving, and bread was broken at the table. The Philistines had metal knives long before they came into general use in Israel (see 1 Sam 13:19, 22).

KOHATH, KOHATHITE (kō'hăth, -ĭt). Second son of Levi (Gen 46:11), ancestor of Moses (Exod 6:16-20; Num 3:17, 19; 1 Chron 6:1-3). His descendants, the Kohathites, one of three divisions of the Levites, comprised four families (Num 3:17-20, 27-31). They camped south of the tabernacle. Numbering 8,600, on duty they cared for the ark, table, lampstand, altars, and vessels of the sanctuary. These they carried on foot, no wagons being assigned them (7:8-9). Joshua allotted them 23 cities (Josh 21:4-5). Under the monarchy they were prominent (1 Chron 23:13-20; 24:20-25), especially Heman in the service of song (6:33ff.; 16:41ff.; 25:1ff.). They took part in the religious service the day before Jehoshaphat's victory over his allied enemies (2 Chron 20:19); and they assisted in Hezekiah's cleansing of the temple (29:12-19).

KOLAIAH (kō-lā'yà, Heb. *qôlāyâh, voice of Jehovah*). 1. A Benjamite who settled in Jerusalem after the Captivity (Neh 11:7). 2. The father of the false prophet Ahab (Jer 29:21).

KORAH, KORAHITE (kō'rà, -ĭt, Heb. *qōrah*). 1. A son of Esau (Gen 36:5, 14, 18; 1 Chron 1:35). 2. A grandson of Esau, nephew of no. 1 (Gen 36:16). 3. A descendant of Caleb (1 Chron 2:43). 4. A son of Izhar, the son of Kohath, the son of Levi (Exod 6:21, 24; 1 Chron 6:37; 9:19). He led a rebellion, with two companions, resisting the civil authority of Moses (Num 16; 26:9-11; 27:3; Jude 11, KJV Core). Korah, Dathan, Abiram and their followers were swallowed up by the earth, but the children of Korah were spared (Num 26:11). From him descended the Korahites, who were doorkeepers and musicians in the tabernacle and temple (Exod 6:24; 1 Chron 6:22). The Korahites (KJV also Korhites, Korathites) are mentioned in several passages (Exod 6:24; Num 26:58; 1 Chron 9:19, 31, 12:6, 26:1; 2 Chron 20:19). The sons of Korah are named in the titles of Psalms 42, 44-49, 84, 85, 87, and 88.

KORAZIN (kō-rā'zĭn). About 2 miles (3 km.) north of Capernaum, Korazin is mentioned only in the woes Christ pronounced on it (Matt. 11:21; Luke 10:13).

KORE (kō'rē). 1. A Korahite whose son, Shallum, was a tabernacle gatekeeper (1 Chron 9:19; 26:1, 19). 2. A Levite, son of Imnah, set over the freewill offerings in Hezekiah's time (2 Chron 31:14).

LAADAN (See LADAN)

LABAN (lā'băn, Heb. *lāvān, white*).
1. The nephew of Abraham who lived in Haran (Gen 24:29–60). In ancient Semitic custom, the brother was the guardian of the sister, and thus Laban takes a prominent place in the account of Rebekah's leaving for Canaan to be Isaac's bride.

When Jacob fled from the anger of his brother Esau, he settled in his uncle Laban's house in Haran and stayed there 20 years. Even in the circumstances surrounding the marriage of Jacob to Laban's daughters Rachel and Leah (Gen 29), competition is evident. After Jacob had served fourteen years for his brides, there followed six more years in Haran during which, according to Jacob's testimony, Laban changed his wages ten times (31:41), including the famous contract involving the speckled and spotted sheep (30:31–43).

Jacob quietly stole away from Laban, taking his now-large family with him to Canaan (Gen 31). Laban overtook him in Gilead. After mutual protestations and incriminations, uncle and nephew parted, after erecting a "witness heap"—a kind of dividing line—between them.
2. An unidentified place in the Plains of Moab, or perhaps in the Sinai peninsula (Deut 1:1).

LABOR The noun is today confined to the abstract use—the act of laboring (Gen 31:42; Rom 16:6). Formerly it expressed also the fruit of labor (Exod 23:16; John 4:38) and the labor in childbirth (Gen 35:16 KJV). The conscription of freemen for labor on government building projects was practiced by Solomon (1 Kings 5:13–17) and Asa (15:22).

LACHISH (lā'kĭsh, Heb. *lākhîsh*, perhaps meaning *rough*). The name of a Canaanite royal city and Judean border fortress that occupied a strategic valley 25 miles (42 km.) SW of Jerusalem.

Its king, Japhia, joined with Adoni-Zedek of Jerusalem in a confederacy against Joshua in 1406 (Josh 10:3), only to be defeated and executed (10:23–26; 12:11). In Joshua's subsequent sweep through the southwest, Israel captured Lachish (reinforced by Gezer) and annihilated its inhabitants, in accordance with Moses' ban (Deut 7:2; Josh 10:31–33). Scripture contains no record, however, of its destruction (cf. 11:13).

Lachish was fortified by Rehoboam shortly after the division of the Hebrew kingdom in 930 B.C. (2 Chron 11:9); and it was there that King Amaziah was murdered in 767 (25:27). The prophet Micah condemned Lachish's chariots (Mic 1:13; cf. Deut 17:16; 1 Kings 10:28–29). Lachish was successfully besieged by Sennacherib in 701 (2 Chron 32:9); Hezekiah sent a message of submission there (2 Kings 18:14); and from it Sennacherib's troops marched against Jerusalem (18:17; 19:8). Lachish and Azekah were the last cities, before Jerusalem, to fall to Nebuchadnezzar (Jer 34:7). In Nehemiah's day it was resettled (Neh 11:30).

LADAN (lā'dăn). **1.** An Ephraimite, an ancestor of Joshua (1 Chron 7:26). **2.** A Levite of the family of Gershon (23:7–9; 26:21), also called Libni (6:17).

LADDER (See STAIRS, STAIRWAY)

LAISH (lā'ĭsh, Heb. *layish*). **1.** A city captured by the Danites and renamed Dan (Judg 18:7, 14, 27, 29). It is called Leshem in Joshua 19:47. Laish in the KJV and NEB of Isaiah 10:30 is Laishah in other versions (e.g., NASB, NIV). **2.** The father of Phalti or Phaltiel, a Benjamite, to whom Michal, David's wife, was given by Saul (1 Sam 25:44; 2 Sam 3:15).

LAISHAH (See LAISH)

LAMB A translation of several Hebrew words in the English Bible, most of them referring to the young of the sheep. One, however (*sheh*, used in Exod 12:3–6), refers to the young of either sheep or goats (cf. 12:5) and seems to include adult specimens at times. The meat of lambs was considered a delicacy among the ancient Hebrews (Deut 32:14; 2 Sam 12:3–6; Amos 6:4). Meat was scarce among them, and the killing of a lamb would mark an important occasion. Lambs were used for sacrifices from the earliest times (Gen 4:4; 22:7).

The lamb was a staple in the Mosaic sacrificial system. A lamb was offered for the continual burnt offering each morning and evening (Exod 29:38–42), and on the Sabbath the number was doubled (Num 28:9). On the first day of each month (28:11), during the seven days of the Passover (28:16, 19), at the Feast of Weeks (28:26–27) and the Feast of Trumpets (29:1–2), on the Day of Atonement (29:7–8), and on the Feast of Tabernacles (29:13–36) lambs were offered. The lamb was one of the sacrifices accepted for the ceremonial cleansing of a woman after

Stone statue of a man carrying a sacrificial lamb, from Susa, middle of third millennium B.C. Courtesy Réunion des Musées Nationaux

childbirth (Lev 12:6) or for the cleansing of a recovered leper (14:10–18). See also ANIMALS.

LAMB OF GOD Jesus was called the Lamb of God by John the Baptist (John 1:29, 36), emphasizing the redemptive character of the work of Christ. More than a score of times in the Book of Revelation the lamb is used as a symbol of Christ. The Passover lamb (Exod 12:3–6) became in time a picture of redemption from sin (1 Cor 5:7). The substitutionary use of the unblemished lamb in sacrifice led to the idea of the Suffering Servant, who as a lamb died in the place of sinners (Isa 53:4–7).

LAME (See DISEASES)

LAMECH (lā'mĕk, Heb. *lemekh,* meaning undetermined). **1.** A son of Methushael (Gen 4:18–24) and a descendant of Cain, who had two wives, Adah and Zillah. His sons founded the nomadic life and the musical arts, and invented metalcrafts and instruments of war. Lamech's song (4:23–24) expresses every feature of

Hebrew poetry (alliteration, parallelism, poetic diction, etc.). **2.** The son of Methuselah (5:28–31). This man, a descendant of Seth, became the father of Noah. His faith is attested by the name he gave his son, Noah (meaning "rest"), and by the hope of "comfort" (5:29) that he anticipated in his son's life.

LAMENTATIONS The book comprises five poems lamenting the desolation that had overtaken the Holy City in 586 B.C. The first four compositions consist of acrostics based on the Hebrew alphabet. Each verse of chapters 1 and 2 commences with a word whose initial consonant is successively one of the 22 letters of the Hebrew alphabet. A slight variation of the regular order occurs in 2:16–17; 3:47–48; and 4:16–17. The third chapter is peculiar in that a triple alphabetical arrangement is followed, so that all three lines in each stanza commence with the same letter. The fifth chapter is not an acrostic, although like the others it contains 22 stanzas, and is a prayer rather than an elegy. Alphabetical forms of this kind probably served as a useful stimulus to memory at a time when manuscripts were rare and costly.

Although in the Hebrew no name was attached to the book, the authorship was uniformly ascribed by ancient authorities to Jeremiah.

The book bewails the siege and destruction of Jerusalem and sorrows over the sufferings of the inhabitants during this time. It makes poignant confession of sin on behalf of the people and their leaders, acknowledges complete submission to the divine will, and prays that God will once again favor and restore his people.

Analysis:
1. The fallen city admits its sin and the justice of divine judgment (chs. 1–2).
2. Lamentation; reassertion of divine mercy and judgment; prayer for divine intervention (chs. 3–4).
3. Further confession and prayers for mercy (ch. 5).

LAMP Archaeology has recovered many specimens in a great variety of forms, from the early simple, shallow, saucerlike bowl (with one side slightly pointed for the lighted wick) to the later closed bowl (with only a hole on top to pour in the oil, a spout for the wick, and a handle to carry it). Lamps for domestic use were generally of terra-cotta or of bronze. KJV often has "candle" and "candlestick" and NEB has "standing lamp" where NIV has "lamp" and "lampstand."

The use of lamps is mentioned in

Two pottery lamps from the Hasmonean and Herodian period, c. 332 B.C.–A.D. 70. Courtesy Reuben and Edith Hecht Museum, University of Haifa

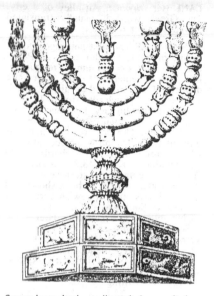

Seven-branched candlestick from relief on the Arch of Titus in Rome. Courtesy Carta, Jerusalem

Seventeen-branched oil lamp discovered in excavations near Jericho, dating from the Roman period. Courtesy Zev Radovan

connection with the golden lamps in the tabernacle and the ten golden lamps in the temple (Exod 25:37; 1 Kings 7:49; 2 Chron 4:20; 13:11; Zech 4:2). The common NT mention of lamps is in connection with their household usage (Matt 5:15; Mark 4:21; Luke 8:16; 11:33; 15:8). Such lamps were generally placed on a "lampstand," usually a niche built into the wall. It appears that the Hebrews were accustomed to burning lamps overnight in their chambers, perhaps because of a dread of darkness, more likely to keep away prowlers. Oil-fed lamps in a marriage procession (Matt 25:1) contained only a few spoonfuls of oil, so a reserve supply would be a necessity. The lighted lamp is also mentioned metaphori-

cally to symbolize (1) God's Word (Ps 119:105), (2) God's guidance (2 Sam 22:29; Ps 18:28), (3) God's salvation (Isa 62:1 KJV), (4) the human spirit (Prov 20:27), (5) outward prosperity (Prov 13:9), and (6) a son as successor (1 Kings 11:36; 15:4).

LAMPSTAND The Hebrew word *menô-râh*, always rendered "candlestick" in KJV, occurs 43 times in the OT. In the tabernacle the lampstand (Exod 25:31–40) with its seven branches holding seven lamps of gold, stood at the left as the priest entered the Holy Place. In the temple that Solomon built, there were ten lampstands of gold (2 Chron 4:7), but they were placed in front of the Most Holy Place (1 Kings 7:49; 2 Chron 4:7).

LANCE (See ARMS AND ARMOR)

LANDMARK (Heb. *gevûl*). An object used to mark the boundary of a field. Landmarks were often such movable objects as a stone or a post. Removal of landmarks was prohibited by the Mosaic Law (Deut 19:14; 27:17). Hebrew piety denounced the act (Prov 22:28; 23:10), and it was considered equal to theft (Job 24:2).

LANE (Gr. *rhymē*). An alley of a city. The Greek word is usually translated "street" (Matt 6:2; Acts 9:11).

LANGUAGES The first language spoken by the invading Israelite tribes in Palestine was Hebrew, a Semitic tongue related to Phoenician, to the Canaanite dialects of the tribes they dispossessed, and to the speech of Moab. Hebrew remained the literary language permanently. In colloquial use it was replaced by Aramaic. The date of this change is difficult to determine with precision. Eliakim's request to Sennacherib's field commander (2 Kings 18:26) to speak in Aramaic (a common eastern language of diplomacy) and not in Hebrew shows that the latter was still the Jewish vernacular in 713 B.C. Such was still the case as late as Nehemiah, two centuries later.

Some NT phrases in the Palestinian vernacular (e.g., Matt 27:46; Mark 5:41) are undoubtedly Aramaic. The other colloquial dialect of NT times was Greek, which also provided the literary language for the NT writings.

LAODICEA (lā-ŏd'ĭ-sē'à, Gr. *Laodikia*). A wealthy city in Asia Minor founded by Antiochus II (261–246 B.C.), and head of the "circuit" of "the seven churches in the province of Asia" (Rev 1:4). The city lay on one of the great Asian trade routes, and this insured its commercial prosperity. Laodicea was a leading banking center. She was "rich and increased with goods" and had "need of nothing" (3:17 KJV). The Lycus Valley produced a glossy black wool, the source of black cloaks and carpets, for which the city was famous. Laodicea was also the home of a medical school and the manufacture of collyrium, a famous eye salve. The imagery of the letter to Laodicea reflects these activities, as well as the emetic qualities of the soda-laden warm water from nearby Hierapolis, the source of Laodicea's water supply.

LAODICEANS, LETTER TO Mentioned by Paul in Colossians 4:16 in urging the Colossians to exchange letters with the Laodiceans. A letter written by the Laodiceans to Paul is ruled out by the context: "from" (*ek*) here denotes present locality, not origin. There are three views of its identity: (1) The spurious "Letter to the Laodiceans" found among Paul's letters in some Latin MSS from the sixth to the fifteenth centuries. Its 20 verses, being phrases strung together from Philippians and Galatians, are a forgery with no heretical motive. (2) A Pauline letter to the Laodiceans now lost.

(3) Our Ephesians. This view is very probable if Ephesians is accepted as being encyclical, and it accounts for Marcion's title of Ephesians as "the epistle to the Laodiceans."

LAPIS LAZULI (See MINERALS)

LAPWING (See BIRDS)

LASH (See SCOURGE, STRIPES)

LAST JUDGMENT (See ESCHATOLOGY)

LATIN The language of the Romans and, in Palestine, used primarily by the Romans. The official superscription on the cross was written in Hebrew, Greek, and Latin (John 19:20). The NT contains about 25 administrative and military Latin words translated into Greek.

LATTICE Latticework, made by crossing laths or other materials across an opening, served a threefold purpose: (1) privacy, so that one might look out without being seen, (2) ventilation, so that a breeze might flow in and the sun's hot rays kept out, and (3) decoration, so that a house or public building might be architecturally more attractive (Judg 5:28; 2 Kings 1:2; Prov 7:6; Song of Songs 2:9).

LAUGHTER 1. Laughter's limitations: it cannot satisfy (Prov 14:13; Eccl 2:2; 7:3, 6; 10:19). **2.** God's laughter: he laughs at his enemies (Pss 2:4; 37:13; 59:8). **3.** The believers' laughter: they sometimes laugh incredulously (Gen 17:17; 18:12–15; 21:6), but they can laugh for real joy (Ps 126:2; Luke 6:21) and in derision of the wicked (Job 22:19; Ps 52:6; Isa 37:22). **4.** The unbelievers' laughter: they laugh at Christ (Ps 22:7; Matt 9:24), at believers (Neh 2:19; Job 12:4; Ps 80:6), and at God's ordinances (2 Chron 30:10); but their laughter will vanish (Prov 1:26; Luke 6:25; James 4:9).

LAUNDERER'S SOAP (See FULLER'S SOAP)

LAW I. The Terms of Scripture. Of Hebrew words, the one most often used, *tôrāh*, may refer to human instruction (Prov 1:8), to divine instruction (Isa 1:10), to a regulation (Lev 7:7), to the law of Moses (1 Kings 2:3), or to custom (2 Sam 7:19). Other words that may be so translated include *dâth, hôq, mitswâh, and mishpat*. The common Greek word *nomos* is occasionally used of law(s) in the most general sense (Rom 3:27) of a principle that governs one's actions (7:23), of the Pentateuch (Gal 3:10), and of the other portions of Holy Scripture (as John 10:34; 1 Cor 14:21), but most often for the Mosaic Law (Acts 15:5).

Fragment of a leather scroll (first century B.C.) found at Qumran containing Deuteronomy 5, the Ten Commandments being shown in third column from the right. Courtesy Israel Department of Antiquities and Museums

English synonyms include *command-ment, direction, judgment, ordinance, precept, statute,* and *testimony.*

II. The Moral Law. It is plain from the Decalogue (Exod 20:3–17; Deut 5:7–21) that morality is not to be derived from human standards and the verdict of society but from God. The Ten Commandments declare the broad principles of God's moral law.

Rather than setting aside the moral law, the NT reiterates its commands, develops more fully the germinal truths contained in it, and focuses attention on the spirit of the law as over against merely the letter. The NT also emphasizes the law of love (Rom 13:8–10; Gal 5:14; James 2:8) and selflessness and humility as representative of the mind of Christ (Phil 2:3–8).

The law made humans aware of their sinfulness (Rom 7:7, 13), condemned them as unrighteous (7:9–11; Gal 3:13; James 2:9), and, having removed any hope of salvation through their own righteousness, brought them to the place where they would cast themselves on the grace of God and trust only in the righteousness and merit of the atoning Savior, Jesus Christ (Gal 3:24). Christians are under obligation to keep the moral law (cf. Matt 5:19ff.; Eph 4:28; 5:3; 6:2; Col 3:9; 1 Peter 4:15) and this because of love for the One who redeemed them (Rom 13:8–10; 1 John 5:2–3).

III. Social Legislation. OT laws of judicial, civil, or political nature are to be found in the block of legislative material known as the Book of the Covenant (Exod 20:23–23:33), in the so-called Holiness Code (Lev 17–26), and here and there throughout most of the Book of Deuteronomy, especially chapters 21–25.

The family was governed by various regulations to preserve it from corruption and dissolution. There were many prescriptions regarding marriage itself (Exod 21–22, 34; Lev 18, 21; Num 5, 25; Deut 7, 21–22, 24–25, 27). Within the family, children were to honor and obey their parents (Exod 20:12; Deut 5:16; 21:18–21; 27:16). And since the family circle might include servants, slaves, and strangers, there were laws pertaining to them also (Exod 12, 21–22; Lev 19, 22, 24–25; Num 9, 15, 35; Deut 1, 12, 14–16, 23–24, 27).

Crimes against society were to be punished according to law. These might be (1) of a moral nature, such as sexual violations or perversions (Exod 20–22; Lev 18–20; Num 5; Deut 5:22–25, 27), (2) against individuals, either their persons (Gen 9; Exod 20–23; Lev 19, 24; Num 35; Deut 5, 19, 21–22, 24, 27) or their property (Exod 20, 22; Lev 6, 19; Deut 5, 19, 23, 25, 27), or (3) against the state (Exod 20, 23; Lev 19; Deut 5, 16, 19, 27). Other regulations governed property (Exod 21–23; Lev 6, 24–25; Num 27, 36; Deut 21–22, 25).

Certain aspects of political organization were outlined (Exod 22; Num 1, 3–4, 26, 33; Deut 17, 23). Specifications were made regarding the army (Num 1–2, 10, 26, 31; Deut 7, 11, 20–21, 23–24). Judicial prescriptions were set forth (Exod 18, 20–21, 23; Lev 5, 19; Num 35; Deut 1, 4–5, 16–17, 19, 25, 27), and provision was made for bringing to the people a knowledge of the law (Deut 6, 11, 27, 31; Josh 8).

Many Israelite laws were laws of kindness. Even the treatment of animals was subject to regulation (Exod 23, 34; Lev 22, 25; Deut 22, 25). The general commandment of love, whether for friends or strangers, was invoked (Exod 23; Lev 19; Deut 10). The poor, unfortunate, lowly, defenseless, and needy were to be treated humanely (Exod 21–23; Lev 19, 23, 25; Deut 14–16, 21–27).

Basic principles of worship are outlined in the Decalogue (Exod 20:3–11). Other so-called gods were not to be worshiped (Exod 22–23, 34; Deut 5–6, 8, 11, 17, 30), apostasy was a sin (Deut 4:25–31; 31:16; cf. Lev 19, 26; Deut 27), and such occult arts as witchcraft, sorcery, and divination were not to be practiced (Exod 22; Lev 18–20; Deut 18). So also, blasphemy was not to be tolerated (Exod 22; Lev 18–19, 24), and God's Sabbath Day was to be kept inviolate (Exod 23, 31, 34–35; Lev 19, 26; Num 15).

Since the Lord is the only true God, Israel was not only to study and keep his law (Lev 18–20, 25; Num 15; Deut 4–8, 10–11, 22, 26–27, 30), but his people were to separate themselves from the heathen and their religious practices (Exod 22–23, 34; Lev 18–20; Deut 6–7, 12, 14, 18). They were to be a holy nation (Exod 19, 22; Lev 19, 26; Deut 7, 14, 18, 26, 28), and give to God the allegiance, love, gratitude, and obedient service due him (Exod 23, 34; Lev 19, 25; Deut 4–6, 8, 10–11, 13–14, 17, 30–31).

Mosaic legislation prescribes the kinds of sacrifices and the details governing them: the whole burnt offering (Exod 20; Lev 1, 6; Deut 12:27), the sin offering (Lev 4–6, 8–10; Num 15), the guilt offering (Lev 5–7, 19; Num 5), and the peace offering (Lev 3, 7, 19, 22). Also the law had much to say about other offerings and sacrificial dues (Exod 10, 13, 18, 22–23, 29–30, 34; Lev 2–3, 6, 14, 19, 22–23, 27; Num 3, 5–6, 8, 15, 18–19, 28, 30–31; Deut 12, 14–18, 23, 26).

Many passages contain laws pertaining to the priesthood (Exod 28–30, 39–40; Lev 2:5–8, 10, 16; 21–24, 27; Num 3–6, 15, 18, 31). The law codes regulated ceremonial cleanliness not only for the priests but also in reference to food (Exod 12, 22–23, 34; Lev 3, 7, 11, 17, 19–20, 22; Deut 12, 14–15) and purification (Lev 5:11–15:22; Num 6, 19, 31; Deut 21, 24).

Christ spoke negatively regarding the traditions of the Jews but not of the ceremonial law as set forth in the OT. Yet he indicated that the time was coming when the ritual of the law would give place to spiritual worship (John 4:24).

In the transitional period after the Cross, the Resurrection, and the Ascension, conditions in each case determined whether the stipulations of the law should be observed. Paul might circumcise Timothy (Acts 16:3) but not Titus (Gal 2:3–4). He could assure the Corinthians that circumcision in the flesh was not essential for salvation (1 Cor 7:18–19); and, in writing to the Galatians, he could argue strongly against the contentions of the Judaizers (Gal 2:4ff.; 5:1ff.) in line with

the decisions of the Jerusalem Council (Acts 15:4ff.). The argument of the Book of Hebrews is that the types and shadows of the ceremonial law have passed away with the coming of Christ, the perfect High Priest, who as the Lamb of God offered himself on Golgotha that he might satisfy every demand of the law and purchase salvation for his people.

By means of the ceremonial law, God spoke in picture language of the salvation he was to effect through the life and death of the Incarnate Son. Therefore, it was necessarily imperfect and temporary. The social legislation governing Israel was designed for a particular culture at a given period of history, and so it, too, was only for a time; yet its principles are timeless and applicable to all generations. God's moral law is in force everywhere and at all times, for it is a reflection of his very being. It has never been annulled, nor indeed can be.

LAWGIVER (Heb. *mehōqēq*, Gen 49:10; Num 21:18; Deut 33:21; Pss 60:7; 108:8; Isa 33:22; Gr. *nomothetēs*, James 4:12). God is the only absolute lawgiver. Instrumentally, Moses bears this description (John 1:17; 7:19).

LAWYER (See Occupations and Professions)

LAYING ON OF HANDS In the OT the act symbolizes (1) the parental bestowal of inheritance rights (Gen 48:14–20), (2) the gifts and rights of an office (Num 27:18, 23; Deut 34:9), and (3) substitution, of an animal for one's guilt (Exod 29:10, 15, 19; Lev 1:4; 3:2, 8, 13; 4:4, 15, 24, 29, 33; 8:14, 18, 22; 16:21; cf. Gen 22:9–13), of the Levites for the firstborn of the other tribes (Num 8:10–19), and of one's innocence for another's guilt (Lev 24:13–16; Deut 13:9; 17:7). In the NT the act symbolizes (1) the bestowal of blessings and benediction (Matt 19:13, 15; cf. Luke 24:50), (2) the restoration of health (Matt 9:18; Acts 9:12, 17), (3) the reception of the Holy Spirit in baptism (8:17, 19; 19:6), and (4) the gifts and rights of an office (6:6; 13:3; 1 Tim 4:14; 2 Tim 1:6).

LAZARUS (lăz′á-rŭs, Lat. from Gr., for Heb. *Eleazar*). **1.** Lazarus, the brother of Martha and Mary, who lived in Bethany. During Christ's absence Lazarus became sick and died; after some delay Christ returned and raised him from death (John 11:1–12:19). The following factors enhance the importance of this miracle: (1) the number of days (four) between death and resurrection (11:39), (2) the number of witnesses involved (11:45; 12:17–18),

The traditional tomb of Lazarus at Bethany. "Then Jesus . . . came to the tomb; it was a cave, and a stone lay upon it" (John 11:38). Courtesy Studium Biblicum Franciscanum, Jerusalem

(3) the evident health of Lazarus after the event (12:1, 2, 9), and (4) the significance of the event among the Jews (11:53; 12:10–11). 2. Lazarus, a beggar who died and went to Abraham's bosom (Luke 16:19–31). The passage illustrates these truths: (1) destiny is settled at death; (2) no purgatory awaits the righteous; and (3) man has sufficient warning now.

LEAD (See MINERALS)

LEAF 1. The leaf of a tree (Ezek 17:6; Dan 4:12, 14, 21) is connected with (1) the insufficiency of man's righteousness (Gen 3:7), (2) the fruitfulness of the restored earth (8:11), (3) the sign of a distressed and nervous spirit (Lev 26:36; Job 13:25), (4) the spiritual productivity of the righteous (Ps 1:3; Prov 11:28; Jer 17:8), (5) the spiritual unproductivity of the wicked (Isa 1:30), (6) the completeness of God's judgment (Isa 34:4; Jer 8:13), (7) the frailty and transiency of humans (Isa 64:6), (8) the blessings of messianic times (Ezek 47:12), (9) the unfruitfulness of Israel (17:9 KJV; Matt 21:19; Mark 11:13), (10) the nearness of the eschatological judgment (Matt 24:32; Mark 13:28), (11) the glory of an earthly kingdom (Dan 4:12, 14, 21), and (12) the glory and fruitfulness of the heavenly kingdom (Rev 22:2). **2.** The leaf of a door (1 Kings 6:34; Ezek 41:24). **3.** The leaf of a book (Jer 36:23).

LEAH (lē'à, Heb. *lē'āh*, meaning uncertain). Laban's daughter and Jacob's first wife (Gen 29:21–30); mother of Reuben, Simeon, Levi, Judah, Issachar, Zebulun, and Dinah (29:31–35; 30:17–21). Loyal to Jacob (31:14–16), she returned with him to Canaan, where, at her death, she was buried in Machpelah (49:31). Two of her sons (Levi and Judah) became progenitors of prominent tribes in Israel, and through Judah, Jesus Christ came (49:10; Mic 5:2; Matt 2:6; Heb 7:14; Rev 5:5; cf. Ruth 4:11).

LEATHER (Heb. *'ôr, skin*, Gr. *dermatinos, made of skin*). The skin of certain animals after it has been specially treated. Those who performed this work as a trade were called tanners (Acts 10:32). Leather was an article of clothing (Lev 13:48; Heb 11:37). However, John the Baptist (Matt 3:4) and his prototype, Elijah (2 Kings 1:8), are the only ones specifically mentioned as wearing "a leather belt." Leather was used also for armor, shoes, containers, and writing material.

LEAVEN (lĕv'ĕn, Heb. *se'ōr, hāmēts*, Gr. *zymē*). Leaven was rigorously excluded from meal offerings (Exod 29:2, 23, 32; Lev 2:1–16; 6:14–23; 7:9–10; 8:2, 26, 31; 10:12; Num 15:1–9, 17–21; 18:9, cf. Exod 23:18; 34:15). It represented corruption and therefore symbolized evil. It was permitted in certain other offerings (Exod 23:15; 34:22–23; Lev 2:11; 7:13–14; 23:17–18; Num 15:20), perhaps indicating that leaven, a part of the daily food, symbolizes the evil that is still inherent in the worshiper. Leaven was excluded from the Passover (Exod 12:14–20; 23:15; 34:18; Deut 16:2–4) due to Israel's haste in leaving Egypt (Exod 12:11, 29; Deut 16:3) and the fact that the Passover was a type of Christ, who was wholly free of corruption (cf. 1 Cor 5:7–8). The degenerate northern kingdom (Amos 4:5) mixed the permitted (Lev 7:13; 23:17) with the forbidden (Exod 23:18; 34:25; Lev 2:11). In the NT, leaven symbolizes either Jewish legalism (Matt 16:6, 12; Gal 5:9) or moral corruption (1 Cor 5:6ff.).

LEBANON (lĕb'à-nŏn, Heb. *levānôn, white*). Lebanon's southern slopes grade into the foothills of Galilee, and the gorge of the Litany marks out a natural NW boundary for Israel (Deut 11:24; 2 Kings 19:23). Strictly speaking, Lebanon lies outside Palestine and, though included in God's promise, it was never totally occupied (Josh 13:5; though cf. its eschatological possession, Ezek 47:15–16). Its isolated crags, however, supported watchtowers (Song of Songs 7:4) and refuge points (Jer 22:20, 23) and came to symbolize the exalted status of Judah's royal house (22:6; Ezek 17:3).

Coastal Lebanon was early inhabited by Phoenicians (Josh 13:5–6), skilled in the employment of its cedars for civil and

The great cedars of Lebanon, used in biblical times in the construction of palaces and other major buildings. Felled intensively during many generations, only a few large trees remain. "The righteous . . . grow like a cedar in Lebanon" (Ps 92:12). Courtesy Biblicum Franciscanum, Jerusalem. Photo Manoug

marine construction (Ezek 27:4–5), while its sparser inland population was Hivite (Josh 11:3; Judg 3:3). The name Lebanon appears in ancient Ugaritic, Hittite, Egyptian, and Babylonian, its first biblical mention being Mosaic, 1406 B.C. (Deut 1:7). It was cited in Jotham's fable against Shechem, c. 1130 (Judg 9.15, cf. the reference to fire hazard), as well as in Jehoash's fable against Amaziah over 300 years later (2 Kings 14:9; 2 Chron 25:18). King Solomon contracted with Hiram of Tyre for the use of Lebanon's cedars in the Jerusalem temple, 966–959 (1 Kings 5:6–18; cf. Ezra 3:7, concerning the second temple also), 10,000 workers per month hewing the timbers and floating them in great rafts along the Mediterranean coast. Solomon likewise erected government buildings and palaces in his capital, including a hall and armory called "the Palace of the Forest of Lebanon" from its rows of cedar pillars and paneling (1 Kings 7:2–7; 10:17, 21; Isa 22:8). The king's Lebanese building projects (cf. 1 Kings 10:27) led him to construction work in Lebanon itself, at least portions of which came within his widespread

domains (9:19; Song of Songs 4:8). Subsequent advances by the pagan empires of antiquity furthered both the conquest and ruthless exploitation of Lebanon's resources (Isa 33:9). Egyptians, Assyrians, and Greeks left their successive inscriptions at the mouth of the Dog River (Nahr el-Kelb); and Ezekiel compares the destruction of Assyria's king with the felling of cedars of Lebanon (Ezek 31:3, 15–16; cf. Zech 11:1). Habakkuk bewails the violence also done by Babylon in cutting down these forest giants (Hab 2:17; cf. Isa 14:8).

LEBAOTH (lĕ-bā'ōthe, Heb. *levā'ōthe, lionesses*). A town in the southern part of Judah (Josh 15:32), also called Beth Lebaoth (19:6) and (probably) Beth Biri (1 Chron 4:31).

LEBBAEUS (See THADDAEUS)

LEBO HAMATH (See HAMATH)

LEECH (See ANIMALS)

LEEKS (See PLANTS)

LEES (Heb. *shemārîm*, pl. from *shemer, something preserved*). A word in the

KJV that describes that undisturbed and thick portion of wine that naturally falls to the bottom of the vat. The word is used figuratively throughout to express (1) the blessings of messianic times (Isa 25:6; cf. 55:1), (2) the spiritual lethargy and decadence of Moab (Jer 48:11), (3) the indifference of Israelites to spiritual realities (Zeph 1:12), and (4) the bitterness and inevitability of God's wrath on the wicked (Ps 75:8, "dregs"). Usually translated "dregs" in NIV.

LEGION (Gr. *legiōn*, or *legeōn*, Lat. *legio*). The largest single unit in the Roman army, including infantry and cavalry. A division of infantry at full strength consisted of about 6,000 Roman soldiers. Each division was divided into ten cohorts, and each cohort was further divided into six centuries. The term "legion" in the NT represents a vast number (Matt 26:53; Mark 5:9, 15; Luke 8:30).

LEHABITES, LEHABIM (lē'hà-bīts, lē-hăb'ĭm, Heb. *lehāvîm*, meaning uncertain). The descendants of the third son of Mizraim (Gen 10:13; 1 Chron 1:11). It is now generally believed that Libyans and Lehabites represent the same ethnic group (2 Chron 12:3; 16:8; Isa 66:19; Ezek 30:5; 38:5; Dan 11:43; Nah 3:9; Acts 2:10). Descendants of Ham, they occupied the north coast of Africa west of Egypt.

LEMUEL (lĕm'ū-ĕl, Heb. *lemû' ēl*, devoted to God). A king, otherwise unknown, to whom his mother taught maxims in Proverbs 31:2–9. Though many identities have been proposed, the name undoubtedly describes Solomon (Prov 31:1).

LENTIL (See PLANTS)

LEOPARD (See ANIMALS)

LEPROSY, LEPER (See DISEASES)

LETHEK (See WEIGHTS AND MEASURES)

LETTER This designates generally (1) an alphabetical symbol (Gal 6:11), (2) rudimentary education (John 7:15 KJV), (3) a written communication (see below), (4) the external (Rom 2:27, 29 KJV), or (5) Jewish legalism (2 Cor 3:6).

A letter is a means of communication for (1) information and instruction (2 Sam 11:14–15; Esth 1:22; 3:13, NIV "dispatches"; 9:20–30; Jer 29:1ff.), (2) a credential of authority (Ezra 7:11–28; Neh 2:7–9; Esth 8:5, 10ff., NIV "dispatches"; Acts 9:1ff.; 1 Cor 16:3; 2 Cor 3:1), (3) propaganda and strife (1 Kings 21:8–11; Ezra 4:7–24; Jer 29:24–32), (4) forged counterinstruction (1 Kings 21:8–

11; 2 Thess 2:2), and (5) invitation (2 Chron 30:1–6). A letter could be a cause of misunderstanding (2 Kings 5:5–7; 2 Cor 10:9–11) and a cause for concern (2 Kings 19:14ff.).

LEVI (lē'vī, Heb. *lēwî, joined*). 1. Jacob's third son by Leah (Gen 29:34; 35:23). He joined his brothers in sinister plots against Joseph (37:4, 28); and, with them, eventually bowed before Joseph (42:6). A predicted famine caused Jacob's entire family to migrate to Egypt, where Levi died at age 137 (Exod 6:16). His three sons—Gershon, Kohath, and Merari (Gen 46:11)—later became heads of families. Three things deserve special attention. (1) His mother named him "Levi," hoping that Jacob, his father, would now be "attached" to her (29:34). (2) His part in the massacre of the Shechemites because of Shechem's raping of Dinah, his sister, showed two facets of his character: duplicity and righteous indignation (34:25–31). (3) Jacob, facing death, pronounced a curse on Simeon and Levi because of their iniquitous deed at Shechem (cf. 34:25–31 with 49:5–7); but because of holy zeal manifested at Sinai (Exod 32:25–29) and in his descendant Phinehas (Num 25:6–13), Levi's curse was turned into a blessing (Deut 33:8–11) for his descendants. See also LEVITES.

2. and 3. Ancestors of Jesus (Luke 3:24, 29). 4. See MATTHEW.

LEVIATHAN (See ANIMALS)

LEVIRATE MARRIAGE (lĕv'ĭ-rāt, lē'vĭ-rāt, from Lat. *levir, a husband's brother*). An ancient custom, sanctioned by practice (Gen 38:8ff.) and by law (Deut 25:5–10, which does not contradict Lev 18:16; 20:21, where the participants are all alive), whereby a deceased man's brother or nearest male kin was required to marry his brother's widow and raise up seed in his brother's name. To repudiate this obligation meant public infamy (Gen 38:8–10). Ruth's marriage to Boaz recognized this law (Ruth 4:1–17). It also underlies the argument of the Sadducees in Matthew 22:23–33.

LEVITES (lē'vīts). The name given to the descendants of Levi. Several discernible factors undoubtedly influenced the selection of Levi's descendants for their special place in Israel's religion. (1) The divine selection of Moses and Aaron, who were descendants of Kohath, one of Levi's three sons (Exod 2:1–10; 6:14–27; Num 26:59), obviously conferred on the Levites an honor that was recognized by the other tribes. (2) However, an event of transcending importance at Mt. Sinai (Exod 32:25–29) gave to the Levites as a tribe their place of privilege and responsibility in God's plan. This event transformed the curse of Jacob's prophecy (Gen 49:5–7) into the blessing of Moses' prophecy (Deut 33:8–11). (3) Moreover, this choice was undoubtedly confirmed by a very similar event when an individual Levite, Phinehas, stayed the plague that was about to decimate the Israelites (Num 25:1–13). Thus the true record of history shows how the curse on Levi the ancestor became, by the wonders of God's providence, a blessing to his descendants.

Let us consider here some of the purposes served in the divine plan by the selection of the Levites for their special ministry in the worship of God's ancient people. (1) Their selection and appointment were rewards for their faithfulness to the Lord in a time of moral deterioration (Exod 32:25–29). (2) The doctrine of substitution was illustrated by the selection of this tribe, for, although God claimed the firstborn males of all the tribes on the basis of the death of the firstborn among the Egyptians (13:11–16), God graciously allowed the Levites to become substitutes for their fellow tribesmen (Num 3:9, 11–13, 40–41, 45–51; 8:14–19). (3) The simplification of service would surely result from the selection of one tribe, for one such tribe closely knit by blood and by ancestral prestige, would be more manageable than uncertain detachments from many tribes. (4) The law of the tithe enhanced the selection of the Levites, for, in a sense, this tribe was a tithe of all the tribes; and it was to this tribe that the tithe was paid (Num 18:20–21; Deut 18:1–8; Neh 10:37 39; Heb 7:5, 9) (5) Israel's separation from the nations was further intensified by the selection of one tribe that was separated from all the other tribes and purified to the Lord (Num 8:5–22). (6) Life as a sojourner without an inheritance here is illustrated by the fact that the Levites had no inheritance in Israel; the Lord alone was their inheritance (Num 18:20–24; 26:62; Deut 10:9; 12:12; 14:27). Nevertheless it is clear (Exod 19:4–5) that humanly speaking the appointment of Levi as the priestly tribe to act on behalf of the whole people was an expedient arising from the fact that the people of God in their entirety could not yet attain to their privilege as priests of the Lord. This, however, has now been secured for us by Christ (cf. 1 Peter 2:9).

A threefold organization is discernible: (1) Aaron and his sons were priests in the restricted sense, part of the family of Kohath. (2) The middle echelon included all the other Kohathites, who had certain privileges in carrying the most sacred parts of the tabernacle (Num 3:27–32; 4:4–15; 7:9). (3) The bottom echelon comprised the families of Gershon and Merari, who had lesser duties (3:21–26, 33–37). Only the priest had the right to minister at the altar and to enter the sanctuary (Exod 28:1; 29:9; Num 3:10, 38; 4:15, 19–20; 18:1–7; 25:10–13). Certain Levites, particularly Asaph, became musicians and probably wrote some of the Psalms (1 Chron 6:39, 43; 15:16ff.; 16:4ff.; 25:1–9; Pss 50, 73–83).

In the disruption of the united kingdom many Levites from the northern kingdom sought political and religious asylum in Judah (2 Chron 11:13–16; 13:9–12; 15:9); but some Levites were evidently involved in the apostasy of the northern kingdom (Ezek 44:10–15). The Levites during this period were still considered teachers (2 Chron 17:8ff.; 19:8; cf. Deut 33:10).

In the postexilic period Levites did not return from Babylon in the same proportion as the priests (Ezra 2:36–42; Neh 7:39–45). Later, a special effort was required to get the Levites to return (Ezra 8:15–19). They were still considered to be teachers (8:15ff.) and musicians (2:40–41; 3:10ff.; Neh 7:43–44).

Only a few references to the Levites are found in the NT (Luke 10:32; John 1:19; Acts 4:36; Heb 7:11). Levi, through his ancestor Abraham, paid tithes to Melchizedek (Gen 14:17–20), thus proving the superiority of Melchizedek's (i.e., Christ's) priesthood to Aaron's (Heb 7:4–10). Since the Levitical priesthood could not bring perfection, it was required that another priest, from a different tribe and a different order, arise (Heb 7:11–17; cf. Gen 49:10; Ps 110).

LEVITICAL CITIES The plan (set out in Num 35:1–8, fulfilled in Josh 21) gave the Levites 48 cities. Because they were "scattered" in Israel, fulfilling Jacob's dying prophecy (Gen 49:7), they could carry out their teaching ministry better (Deut 33:10). Since six of their cities were to be "cities of refuge" (Num 35:6), they would thereby become more accessible to those seeking legal protection (Deut 19:1–3, 7–10, 17ff.).

LEVITICUS (lĕ-vĭt'ĭ-kŭs, Gr. *Levitikon*, *relating to the Levites*). The designation in the English Bible of the third book of the Pentateuch, derived from the Latin rendering (*Liber Leviticus*) of the Greek

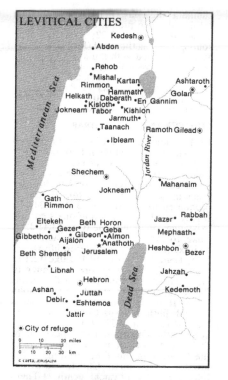

LEVITICAL CITIES

Kedesh⊙
• Abdon

• Rehob
• Mishal Kartan
Rimmon
Hammath   Ashtaroth
Helkath Daberath   Golan⊙
•Kisloth• •En Gannim
Jokneam Tabor •Kishion
Jarmuth•
•Taanach   Ramoth Gilead⊙
• Ibleam

Shechem⊙
•Mahanaim
Jokneam•
•Gath
Rimmon

Eltekeh   Beth Horon   Jazer• Rabbah
•Gezer• Gibeon•Geba
Gibbethon Aijalon •Almon   Mephaath•
• ★Anathoth
Beth Shemesh Jerusalem   Heshbon ⊙ Bezer

•Libnah   Jahzah•

⊙Hebron

Ashan•   •Juttah   Kedemoth
Debir• •Eshtemoa
•Jattir

⊙ City of refuge

0   10   20 miles
0   10   20   30 km
C CARTA, JERUSALEM

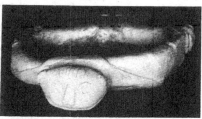

Stone libation tray decorated with a carved lion's head, from Tell Beit Mirsim (Debir), c. 1400–1200 B.C. Courtesy Israel Department of Antiquities and Museums

title *Levitikon*. The book is closely associated with Exodus and Numbers in historical continuity, but differs from them in that the purely historical element is subordinate to legal and ritual considerations. Although the emphasis in Leviticus is more on priests than on Levites, the English title is not inappropriate, since the Jewish priesthood was essentially Levitical (cf. Heb 7:11).

The first seven chapters of Leviticus give the detailed sacrificial procedures for the various kinds of burnt offerings, the meal offering, the sin and guilt offerings, and other sacrifices for the removal of sin and defilement under the covenant. A subsequent liturgical section (8:1–10:20) describes the consecration of Aaron and the priesthood, followed by the designation of clean and unclean beasts and certain rules of hygiene (11:1–15:33). The ritual of the Day of Atonement occurs in chapter 16, followed by a section (17:1–20:27) treating sacrificial blood, ethical laws, and penalties for transgressors. The theme of 21:1–24:23 is priestly holiness and the consecration of seasons, while the following chapter deals with the legislation surrounding the sabbatical and jubilee years. A concluding chapter outlines promises and threats (26:1–46), and an appendix (27:1–34) covers vows. Man as sinner, substitutionary atonement, and divine holiness are prominent throughout Leviticus.

LEVY (lĕv′ē, Heb. *mas, tribute*). A tax or tribute, often to be rendered in service. It is used of the 30,000 free Israelites conscripted by Solomon for four months' service a year in Lebanon (1 Kings 5:13–14 KJV), of the tribute labor imposed on the surviving Canaanites (9:21 KJV), and of the tribute of gold and silver imposed by Pharaoh Neco on Judah (NIV—2 Kings 23:33; 2 Chron 36:3).

LIBATION Usually referred to as a "drink offering"; the pouring out of liquids, such as wine, water, oil, etc., but generally wine, as an offering to a deity. Libations were common among the heathen nations (Deut 32:38). Drink offerings accompanied many OT sacrifices (Exod 29:40–41; Lev 23:13, 18, 37; Num 15:4–10, 24; 28:7–10). Paul pictures his death as a drink offering (Phil 2:17; 2 Tim 4:6). See also SACRIFICE AND OFFERINGS.

LIBERTINES (Gr. *Libertinoi*). Probably originally captive Jews brought to Rome by Pompey in 63 B.C., subsequently freed and returned to Palestine, where, presumably, they built a synagogue still occupied by their descendants a century after Pompey's Palestinian campaign (Acts 6:9).

LIBERTY Freedom, the opposite of servitude or bondage, whether physical, moral, or spiritual. The term is used of slaves or captives being set free from physical servitude or imprisonment (Lev 25:10; Jer 34:8, 15–17; Ezek 46:17; Acts 26:23; Heb 13:23), or the granting of certain privileges while imprisoned (Acts 24:23; 27:3). Freedom from the ceremonial law (Gal 5:1; 2:4) must be valued and guarded. The essence of Christian liberty lies not in external freedom but in deliverance from the bondage of sin and its consequent inner corruption (John 8:34–36; Rom 6:20–22).

Spiritual liberty is the result of the Spirit's regenerating work, for his presence and work within produces liberty (2 Cor 3:17), giving a sense of freedom through a filial relation with God (Rom 8:15–16). Godly men of the OT knew a measure of this spiritual liberty (Ps 119:45), but the gospel reveals and offers it in its fullness. Believers are warned against abuse of liberty in sinful indulgence (Gal 5:13; 1 Peter 2:16; 2 Peter 2:19); and speech and conduct are to be judged by "the law of liberty" (James 2:12), which has taken the place of the ancient law.

LIBNAH (lĭb'nà, Heb. *livnâh, whiteness*). **1.** A desert camp of Israel, the fifth station after leaving Sinai (Num 33:20–21), perhaps the same as Laban (Deut 1:1). **2.** A Canaanite city, near Lachish, captured by Joshua (Josh 10:29–32; 12:15) and named at the head of a group of nine cities in the lowland (15:42–44). It was designated a Levitical city in Judah (21:13; 1 Chron 6:57). Simultaneously with Edom it revolted from Jehoram (2 Kings 8:22; 2 Chron 21:10). As a strong fortified center it sustained the siege of Sennacherib for some time (2 Kings 19:8; Isa 37:8).

LIBNI (lĭb'nī, Heb. *livnî, white*). **1.** The first-named of the two sons of Gershon, the son of Levi (Exod 6:17; Num 3:18; 1 Chron 6:17, 20). He is also called Ladan (23:7; 26:21). His descendants are called Libnites (Num 3:21; 26:58). **2.** A Levite, son of Mahli, son of Merari (1 Chron 6:29).

LIBYA (lĭb'ĭ-à). The ancient Greek name for northern Africa west of Egypt. The Hebrew is *Put* (Jer 46:9; Ezek 30:5; 38:5; Dan 11:43), and is so rendered by ASV and NIV, except Daniel 11:43. It was the country of the Lubim, descendants of Ham (Gen 10:13). Cyrene was one of its cities (Acts 2:10).

LICE (See ANIMALS)

LIE, LYING (Heb. *seqer,* Gr. *pseudos*). Although God cannot lie, humans do (Num 23:19). There are laws against bearing false witness (Exod 20:16) and perjury (Lev 19:12), and there is the general command, "Do not lie" (19:11). People of the world prefer a lie to truth (Rom 1:25—exchanging the truth about God for a lie). Some make God a liar by claiming they are not sinners (1 John 1:10) and some preach a lie—that Jesus is not the Christ (2:22; Rev 2:2). The source of lies is the devil (John 8:44; Acts 5:3). Connected with the idea of a lie are those who live a lie or convey a lie—a false brother (2 Cor 11:26), a false apostle (11:13), a false teacher (2 Peter 2:1), a false witness (Matt 26:60), a false prophet (7:15), and a false Christ (24:24).

LIEUTENANT (See SATRAP)

LIFE It may denote *physical* or natural life, whether animal (Gen 1:20; 6:17; Rev 8:9) or human (Lev 17:14; Matt 2:20; Luke 12:22). It is the vital principle God imparted to man (Gen 2:7). This life is a precious gift, and the taking of life is prohibited (9:5; Exod 20:13; Lev 24:17). It may signify the period of one's earthly existence, one's lifetime (Gen 23:1; 25:7; Luke 16:25), or the relations, activities, and experiences that make up life (Exod 1:14; Deut 32:47; Job 10:1; Luke 12:15). Occasionally it means one's manner of life (1 Tim 2:2; 1 John 2:16) or the means for sustaining life (Deut 24:6; 1 John 3:17). It is the gift of God, mediated through faith in Jesus Christ (John 3:36; 5:24; Rom 5:10; 6:23; 1 John 5:12). Involving the impartation of a new nature (2 Peter 1:3–4), it is communicated to the believer in this life, resulting in fellowship with God in Christ, and is not interrupted by physical death (1 Thess 5:10). It will find its perfection and full reality of blessedness with God in the life to come (Rom 2:7; 2 Cor 5:4). As "the living God" (Deut 5:26; Ps 42:2; 1 Thess 1:9; 1 Tim 3:15), the eternal and self-existent One, God has *absolute* life in himself (John 5:26) and is the source of all life (Ps 36:9; John 1:4; 17:3; 1 John 1:1–2; 5:21).

LIFE, THE BOOK OF God's record of those who inherit eternal life (Phil 4:3; Rev 3:5; 21:27). From man's point of view individuals may be blotted out of that book (Ps 69:28; Matt 25:29); but from God's point of view it contains only the names of the elect, which will not be blotted out (Rev 3:5; 13:8; 17:8; 20:15).

LIGHT The first recorded utterance of God is "Let there be light" (Gen 1:3). God is the creator of both light and darkness (Isa 45:6–7; 1 John 1:5) and watches over their orderly succession (Ps 104:20; Amos 4:13), yet light is superior (Eccl 2:13). Light is above all the source of life (11:7). The word is often used in synonyms for being alive (Job 3:20), being born (3:16), the pleasures of life (Ps 97:11), good days for the righteous

(112:4), or an essential in man's happiness (36:9). Light and truth are coupled biblically (Ps 43:3; cf. Ps 19; Prov 6:23; Isa 51:4). Truth and law give knowledge (Pss 19:8; 139:11–12) and guidance (Deut 28:29; Job 22:28; Prov 4:18; cf. Mic 7:8). The recipient of light becomes a light, shining outwardly (Ps 34:5; Eccl 8:1) and inwardly (Prov 20:27; Dan 5:11). The manifestations of light are the work of "the Father of the heavenly lights" (James 1:17), he who dwells in light (Exod 13:21; Ps 104:2; 1 Tim 6:16) and who imparts light as a divine gift. Scripture is a lamp or a light (2 Peter 1:19). Conversion is spoken of as illumination (Heb 6:4; 10:32). Believers are "people of the light" (Luke 16:8; 1 Thess 5:5) and the "light of the world" (Matt 5:14). Because the gift may be lost through inactivity (John 5:35; 1 Thess 5:5–6), the heavenly light must be used as armor or a weapon (Rom 13:12; Eph 6:12) in the fight against darkness. The light is permanently present in Christ (John 1:7–9; Heb 1:3) and in the gospel (Acts 26:23; 2 Cor 4:4). In the new age there will be no more night (Rev 21:23). See also DARKNESS.

LIGHTNING (Heb. *bārāq*, Gr. *astrapē*). A visible electric discharge between rain clouds or between a rain cloud and the earth, producing a thunderclap. In Palestine and Syria lightning is common during the heavy fall and spring rains. Lightning is generally accompanied by heavy rain and at times by hail (Exod 9:23–24). Lightning is a manifestation of God's power (Job 28:26; 38:35; Ps 135:7; Zech 10:1), his instrument in bringing about the destruction of his opponents (Ps 18:14; 144:6; Zech 9:14–15). Lightning is a symbol of speed (Ezek 1:14; Nah 2:4; Zech 9:14) and of dazzling brightness (Dan 10:6; Matt 28:3).

LILY (See PLANTS)

LINE Usually the meaning is *a measuring line* (Jer 31:39; Ezek 47:3; Zech 1:16; 2:1) or a cord or thread (Josh 2:18, 21; Ezek 40:3). In Isaiah 44:13 it means either "pencil" (ASV) or a cutting instrument (NIV, however, retains "line"). In Psalm 16:6 it means "portion" as fixed by measurement (NIV "boundary lines"); in 19:4 it signifies the sound made by a musical chord (cf. Rom 10:18).

LINEN Thread or cloth prepared from the fiber of flax. Flax was cultivated in Mesopotamia, Assyria, and Egypt, and linen was well known in the ancient biblical world. Flax was being cultivated in the tropical climate around Jericho at the time of the conquest (Josh 2:6). Having

learned the art in Egypt (Exod 35:25), Hebrew women practiced the spinning and weaving of flax (Prov 31:13, 19). The clans of Beth Ashbea attained eminence as workers in linen (1 Chron 4:21). Israelites were forbidden to wear a garment made of two sorts of thread, linen and woolen (Lev 19:19; Deut 22:11).

The Hebrew *sādhîn* denotes an undergarment of linen worn next to the body (Prov 31:24; Isa 3:23; "sheet" in Judg 14:12–13 KJV) and is synonymous with the Greek *sindon*, the term for the linen sheet in which the body of Jesus was wrapped (Matt 27:59; Mark 15:46; Luke 23:53). "Linen clothes" (Luke 24:12; John 19:40; 20:5ff.; NIV "strips of linen") is *othonion*, linen bands, linen cloth torn into strips.

Its use is frequently mentioned in connection with the garments of the Aaronic priests (Exod 28:42; Lev 6:10; 1 Sam 22:18), their tunics, undergarments, and headdresses being exclusively of linen, and the girdle largely of it (Exod 28:39; 39:27–29). It was worn by the child Samuel (1 Sam 2:18), by the Levitical singers in the temple (2 Chron 5:12), and even by royal personages (2 Sam 6:14; 1 Chron 15:27). Angels wear it (Ezek 9:2; 10:2; Dan 10:5; 12:6), as do the host of the redeemed returning with Christ from heaven (Rev 19:14). It is used figuratively of the moral purity of the saints (19:8). Linen was used also for garments of distinction (Gen 41:42; Esth 8:15). Apparently linen garments of a coarser material were worn by men (Judg 14:12–13) and women (Prov 31:22). But the use of fine linen for ordinary purposes was apparently a sign of luxury and extravagance (Isa 3:23; Ezek 16:10; Luke 16:19; Rev 18:12, 16). Linen was used also for nets (Isa 19:9), measuring lines (Ezek 40:3), girdles (Jer 13:1), and for fine hangings (Esth 1:6).

LION (See ANIMALS)

LITTLE OWL (See BIRDS)

LIVER (Heb. *kāvēdh, heavy*). The heaviest of the viscera, both in weight and importance, mentioned 14 times in the OT. Usually the reference is to the bodily organ in connection with sacrificial instructions (e.g., Exod 29:13, 22; Lev 3:4, 10, 15; 4:9; 7:4). Its use for purposes of divination was common among heathen nations (Ezek 21:21). It is mentioned in depicting profound sorrow (Lam 2:11 KJV), and piercing it was fatal (Prov 7:22–23). (See page 350.)

LIVING CREATURES A term (often "beasts" in KJV) that apparently some-

Clay liver model inscribed with omens and magical formulae for the use of diviners from Babylonia, c. 1830–1530 B.C. Reproduced by courtesy of the Trustees of the British Museum

times indicates the cherubim (Ezek 1:5–22; 3:13; 10:15–20; Rev 4:6–9). In the Creation account "living creatures" designates aquatic animals (Gen 1:21), mammals (1:24), or any animals (2:19).

LIZARD (See ANIMALS)

LO-AMMI (lō-ăm'ī, Heb. *lō'-'ammî, not my people*). The symbolic name given to Hosea's third child; it is transliterated "Lo-Ammi" in Hoses 1:9a, but translated "not my people" in Hosea 1:9b–10; 2:23. Originally applied to express the rejection of the northern kingdom in contrast to the election of Judah (1:6–7), the name prophetically and paradoxically (1:11; 2:23) becomes the designation of the rejected Gentiles who are now, during Israel's present blindness (Rom 11:25–26), incorporated into the true Israel of God (9:24–26; cf. Deut 32:21; Isa 65:1; Rom 2:28–29; 9:6ff.; 10:19–20; 1 Peter 2:9–10).

LOCK, LOCKS 1. A mechanical device for fastening a city gate or a door. The primitive locks used to fasten city gates consisted simply of heavy beams of wood, the ends of which were dropped into slots cut into the masonry of the gate (Neh 3:3–15; cf. Deut 3:5; 1 Sam 23:7). Used figuratively, their strengthening spoke of divine protection (Ps 147:13), their burning of a country's invasion (Jer 51:30; Nah 3:13). To strengthen them, iron bars were used (1 Kings 4:13; Isa

45:2). When used to lock house doors (Judg 3:23–24) they were smaller and were flat bolts. **2.** The term indicates the unshorn and disheveled locks of the Nazirite (Num 6:5), the braided locks of the Nazirite Samson (Judg 16:13, 19), a forelock of the prophet's hair (Ezek 8:3), and the luxuriant locks of the Hebrew youth (Song of Songs 5:2, 11).

LOCUST (See ANIMALS)

LODGE A temporary shelter erected in a garden for a watchman guarding the ripening fruit (Isa 1:8, KJV; NIV "hut"), more temporary than a watchtower, or a temporary place of sojourn for strangers (Acts 28:23; Philem 22 KJV).

LOGIA The Greek word for "sententious sayings" or "epigrams," employed in reference to the nonbiblical sayings of Christ, the latest collection of which is the so-called Gospel of Thomas discovered in A.D. 1945 and first made public in 1959. The church has always been aware of sayings of Christ not included in the Gospels. Paul speaks of "the words the Lord Jesus himself said: 'It is more blessed to give than to receive' " (Acts 20:35).

LOGOS (Gr. *logos*). A philosophical and theological term and concept; a dynamic principle of reason operating in the world and forming a medium of communion between God and man. The latter function becomes prominent in Philo, with whom the Logos is at once the Stoics' active, intelligent, world-principle, the thought in the divine mind, which was identical with sum-total of Plato's "Forms" or "Ideas," and a mediator between God and the matter of his creation. For Philo and his predecessors the Logos is neither personal nor impersonal. It was vaguely equated with God's utterance (Gen 1:3; Ps 33:9), his "word" in such passages as Psalms 107:20; 147:15, 18, and such expressions as "the angel of the covenant," and with "wisdom" in such personifications as those of Proverbs 8 and Wisdom of Solomon 10. It is possible that the Qumran community fused the same Hebrew and Hellenistic concepts into their doctrine of the spirit of truth, which, like the spirit of error, was a creature of God.

In the New Testament the Logos appears principally in John's writings (John 1:1ff.; 1 John 1:1; Rev 19:13; cf. 1 Cor 8:6; Col 1:15–17; Heb 1:2–3). Logos is imperfectly translated "Word," and it is not easy to comprehend the full context of the idea in its Judeo-Hellenistic context.

LOIN Used in the KJV to describe the part of the body between the ribs and the hip bones. It is the place where the girdle was worn (Exod 12:11; 2 Kings 1:8; Jer 13:1; Matt 3:4) and the sword was fastened (2 Sam 20:8). Pain and terror were reflected in weakness and shaking of the loins (Pss 38:7; 66:11; 69:23; Jer 30:6). Girding the loins with sackcloth was a sign of mourning (1 Kings 20:32; Isa 32:11; Jer 48:37). As the place of the reproductive organs the loins are used for the generative function (Gen 35:11; 1 Kings 8:19; Acts 2:30; Heb 7:5). Since Oriental garments were worn ungirded about the house, to gird up the loins signified preparation for vigorous action (Exod 12:11; 1 Kings 18:46; Job 38:3; Prov 31:17; Luke 12:35; 1 Peter 1:13). To have the loins girded with truth signified strength in attachment to truth (Eph 6:14; cf. Isa 11:5).

LOIS (lō′ĭs, Gr. *Lōis*). The maternal grandmother of Timothy. Commended by Paul for her faith (2 Tim 1:5), she apparently was associated with Eunice in the religious training of Timothy.

LONGSUFFERING (Heb. *'erekh, 'appayim, slow to anger*, Gr. *makrothymia*). The noun preferred by KJV (other versions use "forbearance") to account for the delay of the Lord in inflicting punishment or exercising his anger wrath (Exod 34:6; Num 14:18; Ps 86:15; Jer 15:15; Rom 2:4; 2 Peter 3:9; cf. 1 Tim 1:16; 2 Peter 3:15).

KJV also uses the noun to describe human beings (other versions use "patience" and "forbearance"). As so used, it refers to being patient, especially when being faced with evil (Matt 18:21–35, esp. vv. 26, 29; Gal 5:22; 2 Tim 2:24).

LORD It is applied to both men and God and expresses varied degrees of honor, dignity, and majesty. In the KJV, *'ădhōnay* is given as "Lord," and Jehovah (Heb. *Yahweh*, "the self-existent One") is printed "LORD." The Jews (due to their interpretation of Lev 24:16) read *'ădhōnay* to avoid pronouncing *Yahweh* (the supreme name of God alone). In the ASV it is given as "Jehovah," which the KJV has only four times (Exod 6:3; Ps 83:18; Isa 12:2; 26:4) and the NIV never.

It is frequently used of God (Matt 1:22; Mark 5:19; Acts 7:33) as well as of Jesus as Messiah, who by his resurrection and ascension was exalted to lordship (2:36; Rom 1:4; 14:8; Phil 2:9–11). At times it is difficult to determine whether by "the Lord" the Father or the Son is meant

(Acts 1:24; 9:31; 16:14; Rom 14:11; 1 Cor 4:19; 2 Thess 3:16).

LORD'S DAY The day especially associated with the Lord Jesus Christ. The expression occurs in the NT only in Revelation 1:10. The adjective *kyriakos*, translated "the Lord's," is a possessive and means "belonging to the Lord" — to Christ. It denotes a day consecrated to the Lord (cf. the parallel expression "the Lord's Supper," 1 Cor 11:20). Some would equate it with the OT prophetic "day of the Lord" but clearly John is not speaking of that prophetic day. The form of his expression marks a distinction between the prophetic "day of the Lord" (1 Cor 5:5; 2 Cor 1:14; 1 Thess 5:2) and the first day of the week, on which Christ arose. The gospel emphasis on "the first day of the week" as the day of resurrection stresses its distinctiveness. On that day the risen Christ repeatedly appeared to his disciples (Luke 24:13–49; John 20:1–25), and again a week later (20:26). Sunday is a Christian institution and must be sharply distinguished from the Sabbath. Nor were the OT Sabbath regulations transferred to the Lord's Day as a "Christian Sabbath." The Sabbath related to the old creation (Exod 20:8–11; 31:12–17; Heb 4:4), whereas the Lord's Day commemorates the new creation in Christ Jesus. No "Sabbath" observance was stipulated in the demands on Gentile Christians (Acts 15:28–29). Some Jewish Christians continued to observe the Sabbath and Jewish festivals, while some members of the primitive church made no distinction between days (Rom 14:5–6), but it was held to be a matter of liberty (14:1, 5), as long as the observance of a special day was not regarded as necessary for salvation (Gal 4:10; Col 2:16–17).

LORD'S PRAYER Properly, "the Disciples' Prayer," since it was not prayed with but taught to them by Jesus (Matt 6:9–13; Luke 11:2–4). In Luke, Jesus, at the request of a disciple, gave a modified form of his earlier spontaneous presentation in the Sermon on the Mount. The earlier form is fuller and is commonly used. As a pattern prayer it is unsurpassed for conciseness and fullness, showing the proper approach and order in prayer.

LORD'S SUPPER (Gr. *kyriakon deipnon*). This expression occurs once in the NT (1 Cor 11:20), but there is a related expression, "Lord's table" (10:21). Its institution (Matt 26:26–29; Mark 14:22–25; Luke 22:15–20; 1 Cor 11:23–25) was

Traditional room of the Last Supper, or Coenaculum, on Mount Zion in Jerusalem. The Basilica of Zion built over the Cenacle, is believed to have been the first Christian church. Courtesy Zev Radovan

on the night before the Crucifixion. Jesus told the disciples that the cup of red wine represented his own blood, shed to inaugurate a new covenant between God and "the many" (Isa 52:15; 53:12). He also pointed toward the full realization and consummation of the kingdom of God at the end of the age, when the meal would be resumed in the "messianic banquet." Thus, it may be said that the Lord's Supper is eaten in remembrance of his atoning death and in expectation of the arrival of the kingdom of God in its fullness.

Acts 2:42 refers to the table fellowship as "breaking of bread" (cf. Acts 20:7). At first the Supper was a part of a larger meal (1 Cor 11:17ff.). It became the second half of the Sunday worship of the local church, the first part being the ministry of the Word, prayers, singing of psalms, and intercessions.

Nowhere in the NT is the Lord's Supper called a sacrifice. While the Supper is the memorial of a sacrifice, and is a sacrifice of praise offered to God, it is neither a repetition of the sacrifice of Christ made at Calvary nor a participation in the self-offering that Christ is perpetually making to the Father in heaven as the heavenly Priest. It is a proclamation of the Lord's death sacramentally until he returns to earth.

LO-RUHAMAH (lō-rū-hà'mà, Heb. *lô'-rūhāmâh, not pitied*). The symbolic name given to Hosea's daughter—transliter-

ated "Lo-Ruhamah" in Hoses 1:6, 8, but translated "not my loved one" in Hosea 2:23. It would seem to be a lesser description of the people described in Hosea as Lo-Ammi.

LOT 1. A means of deciding an issue or of determining the divine will in a matter. The practice of casting lots was common among the nations of antiquity (Esth 3:7; Jonah 1:7; Matt 27:35; cf. Joel 3:3; Nahum 3:10; Obad 11). Its use among the Jews, generally with religious intent, is mentioned in determining the scapegoat (Lev 16:8), assigning the land of Palestine among the tribes (Num 26:55; Josh 18:10; Acts 13:19), selecting men for an expedition (Judg 1:1–3; 20:9), detecting a guilty person (Josh 7:14; 1 Sam 14:40–42), selecting the first king (10:20–21), dividing the returned priests into 24 divisions (1 Chron 24:3–19), and determining the service of the priests in the temple worship (Luke 1:5–9). In none of these instances is there a direct statement of the method or methods used in casting lots (but cf. Prov 16:33). It was held in religious esteem by the covenant people, and its use to determine God's will was usually accompanied by prayer (Judg 1:1–3; Acts 1:24–26). Many scholars think that Urim and Thummim were used as lots. Only in the choice of a successor to Judas (1:26) is the use of lots by Christ's followers mentioned. **2.** That which is assigned by lot, as a *portion, share,* or *inheritance* (Deut 32:9; Josh 15:1; Pss 105:11; 125:3; Isa 17:14; Acts 8:21).

LOT (Heb. *lôt, envelope, covering*). Haran's son and Abraham's nephew (Gen 11:31; 12:5). His life may be summarized under the following heads: (1) *Departure and dependence.* Lot's father died and left him his possessions; Lot now was willing to follow Abraham from Mesopotamia to Canaan, to Egypt, and back to Canaan (11:27–32; 12:5, 10; 13:1). (2) *Decision and destiny.* Because of a conflict between their herdsmen, Lot chose the environs of Sodom, a city that had already become notorious because of its wickedness (13:5–13). (3) *Devastation and deportation.* Lot, then in Sodom, was taken captive when Kedorlaomer and his confederates conquered the king of Sodom and his four allies (14:1–12). Abraham pursued the enemies and rescued his nephew (14:13–16). (4) *Depravity and degeneration.* Angels visited Lot in Sodom to hasten his departure from the imminent doom decreed on the wicked city. Although originally only a sojourner (19:9), Lot acted like a citizen;

he had imbibed their mores and standards. Look at his willingness to sacrifice his daughters' chastity (19:8), his utter ineffectiveness in dealing with his sons-in-law (19:14), his hesitation in leaving the doomed city (19:15–16), and his unwillingness to leave the comforts of a city (19:17–22). Yet Lot was "a righteous man" (2 Peter 2:7–8); and, furthermore, his righteous soul was daily vexed with the lawless deeds (2:8) of Sodom's inhabitants. By implication, it seems that the term "godly" is also applied to Lot (2:9). (5) *Dénouement and disgrace.* Lot, because of fear, left Zoar and lived in a cave with his two daughters (Gen 19:30), his wife already having become, because of unbelief, "a pillar of salt" (19:17, 26; Luke 17:29). Made drunk by his daughters, Lot became the unwitting father of their sons, Moab and Ben-Ammi, the progenitors of the Moabites and the Ammonites (Gen 19:31–38; Deut 2:9, 19; Ps 83:8). Ruth was a Moabitess, the great-grandmother of David and thus a member of the messianic line (Ruth 1:16–18; 4:13–21).

Lot's life illustrates spiritual truths: (1) The degenerating influence of a selfish choice (Gen 13:11–12); (2) the effect of a wicked environment on one's family (Gen 19); (3) retribution in one's children (19:8, 31ff.); (4) God as the only true judge of a man's real state (2 Peter 2:7ff.).

Pillars of salt on the western shore of the Dead Sea, reminiscent of the fate of Lot's wife (Gen 19:26). Courtesy Seffie Ben-Yoseph

LOTAN (lō'tăn, Heb. *lôtăn, a wrapping up*). Son of Seir and father of Hori and Homam (1 Chron 1:38–39; in Gen 36:20, 22, 29 NIV has Homam; JB, KJV, MLB, MOF, NASB, NEB have Hemam).

LOVE (Heb. *'ahăvâh,* Gr. *agapē*). This is the very nature of God (1 John 4:8, 16) and the greatest of the Christian virtues (1 Cor 13:13), essential to man's relations to God and man (Matt 22:37–40; Mark 12:28–31; John 13:34–35). On it hang all the law and the prophets (Matt 22:40). It is the fulfillment of the law (Rom 13:8–10). Love found its supreme expression in the self-sacrifice on Calvary (1 John 4:10).

The Bible makes the unique revelation that God in his very nature and essence is love (1 John 4:8, 16). God not only loves, he *is* love. In this supreme attribute all the other attributes are harmonized. His own Son, Jesus Christ, is the unique object of this eternal love (Isa 42:1; Matt 3:17; 17:5; John 17:24). God loves the world as a whole (John 3:16), individuals (Gal 2:20), creatures (Acts 14:17), sinners (Rom 5:8; 1 John 4:9–10), and especially believers in Christ (John 16:27; 17:23).

Love is created in the believer by the Holy Spirit (Rom 5:5; Gal 5:22), and is the chief test of Christian discipleship (Luke 14:26; John 13:35; 1 John 3:14). Love is vitally related to faith; faith is basic (John 6:29; Heb 11:6), but a faith that does not manifest itself in love both toward God and man is dead and worthless (Gal 5:6, 13; James 2:17–26). The Christian must love his enemy as well as his brother (Matt 5:43–48; Rom 12:19–20; 1 John 3:14), without hypocrisy (Rom 12:9). See also LOVING-KINDNESS.

LOVE FEAST (Gr. *agapē*). A common meal eaten by early Christians in connection with the Lord's Supper to express and deepen brotherly love. Although often mentioned in postcanonical literature, these feasts are spoken of in the NT only in Jude 12 and the dubious footnote to 2 Peter 2:13. But the situation in 1 Corinthians 11:20–22, 33–34 makes it clear that they were observed in the early Jerusalem church (Acts 2:42–47; 4:35; 6:1). As implied by the situation in 1 Corinthians 11, these love feasts were observed before, but in connection with, the Lord's Supper (perhaps after the close relation between the first Lord's Supper and the Passover). Because of abuses, which already appeared in apostolic churches (1 Cor 11:23–29; Jude 12), they were separated from the Lord's Supper. They subsequently fell into disfavor and were ultimately forbidden to be held in churches, largely due to the growth of the sacerdotal view of the Eucharist—a view that regarded the union of the two as sacrilegious. A few smaller Christian groups today observe them.

LOVING-KINDNESS The Hebrew word *hesedh* is one of the most important in the OT and lies at the center of the Lord's self-revelation of his attitude toward his people. His *hesedh* is rooted in his grace (Gen 19:19; it combines the ideas of love, commitment, duty, and care). It is explicitly linked with "truth"—i.e., being true to oneself, truthfulness, reliability—and so there is a stress on the loyalty with which love acts (32:10; Exod 34:6).

LUBIM (See LIBYA)

LUCIFER (See DEVIL; SATAN)

LUCIUS (lū'shĭ-ŭs, Gr. *Loukios*). **1.** A Christian from Cyrene ministering in the church at Antioch (Acts 13:1). **2.** A kinsman of Paul who evidently was with him in Corinth when he wrote his letter to Rome (Rom 16:21).

LUD, LUDITES (lŭd, lŭ'dīts, Heb. *lûdh, lûdhîm*). Either one or two nations of antiquity. Lud was the son of Shem (Gen 10:22; 1 Chron 1:17). It is generally agreed that Lud was the kingdom of Lydia in Asia Minor. Ludites were the sons of Mizraim (Egypt) (Gen 10:13; 1 Chron 1:11), indicating an African country. Other references suggest its location to be the Mediterranean area (Isa 66:19) or Africa (Jer 46:9; Ezek 27:10; 30:5).

LUKE (Gr. *Loukas*). The writer of the Third Gospel and the Acts of the Apostles. From the latter book his association with Paul is established (16:10–17; 20:5–15; 21:1–18; 27:1–28:16). Apart from this he is mentioned three times in the NT (Col 4:14; Philem 24; 2 Tim 4:11). Luke was a physician (Col 4:14) and was with Paul some time after he disappears from view at the end of the Acts of the Apostles (2 Tim 4:11). The context of the Colossians reference also suggests that Luke was a Gentile and a proselyte.

It appears from Luke's own writings that he was a man of education and culture. He is an accurate and able historian and has left some of the most powerful descriptive writing in the NT. His medical knowledge and his interest in seafaring are apparent from his writings. Eusebius and Jerome say that Luke was a Syrian of Antioch. A bare tradition states that he suffered martyrdom in Greece.

LUKE, GOSPEL OF Third book of the NT, written by Luke—definitely before he wrote Acts (Acts 1:1), presumably before A.D. 70, perhaps during Paul's

imprisonment in Caesarea (conjecturally 58–59).

Many incidents and much teaching are found only in Luke's Gospel: the Nativity section (Luke 1–2), the human genealogy (3:23–38) of Christ, the childhood of Jesus (2:41–52), some of Jesus' discourses and sayings (e.g., much of chs. 7, 9–10, 14:25–35; 17:1–10; 19:1–11), some parables and illustrative anecdotes that only Luke records (7:41–43; 10:30–37; 11:5–8; 12:16–21; 13:6–9; 15:3–32; 16:1–12, 19–31; 18:2–14; 19:13–27), certain miracles (5:1–11; 7:11–14; 13:11–13; 14:2–6; 17:12–19; 22:51), the prayer on the cross (23:34), the penitent thief (23:39–43), the walk to Emmaus (24:13–35), and much of the Ascension narrative. Luke emphasizes women, the poor, and prayer.

LUNATIC (See DISEASES)

LUTE (See MUSICAL INSTRUMENTS)

LUZ (lŭz, Heb. *lûz, turning aside*). **1.** A town on the northern boundary of Benjamin (Josh 16:2; 18:13). Jacob came here when fleeing from home. He slept here, and God appeared to him in a dream. To commemorate the occasion Jacob changed the name of the town to Bethel ("house of God," Gen 28:19). **2.** A town in the land of the Hittites built by a man from Luz in Canaan (Judg 1:26).

LYCAONIA (lĭk'á-ō'nĭ-à, Gr. *Lykaonia*). A district in the central plain of Asia north of the Taurus range. Iconium was the administrative capital (Acts 14:6).

LYCIA (lĭsh'ĭ-à, Gr. *Lykia*). A district on the coast of the southern bulge of western Asia Minor, forming the western shore of the Gulf of Adalia (1 Macc 15:23; Acts 27:5).

LYDDA (lĭd'à, Heb. *lôdh*, Gr. *Lydda*). Lydda, or Lod, lies some 30 miles (50 km.) NW of Jerusalem at the head of an old highway called the Valley of the Smiths in recollection of ancient Philistine supremacy in iron (1 Sam 13:19). After the Exile, the returning Jews reached this point before meeting the resistance of the occupants of the plain (Ezra 2:33; Neh 7:37, "Lod"). The incident of Peter and Aeneas took place at Lydda (Acts 9:32–38).

LYDIA (lĭd'ĭ-à, Gr. *Lydia*). Paul's first convert in Europe. She resided in Philippi as a seller of the purple garments for which Thyatira, her native city, was famous. She was evidently well-to-do, as she owned her house and had servants. She was "a worshiper of God," meaning a proselyte, and came into contact with the gospel when Paul and his company came to the river where she and others gathered for worship. She became a believer, and after she and her household had been baptized, she invited the group to come to her home to stay, and they did so (Acts 16:14–15). Her home thus became the first church in Philippi (16:40).

LYING (See LIE, LYING)

LYRE (See MUSIC AND MUSICAL INSTRUMENTS)

LYSANIAS (lī-sā'nĭ-ăs, Gr. *Lysanias*). Tetrarch of Abilene mentioned by Luke (3:1). The tetrarchy is a small region in Lebanon.

LYSIAS (lĭs'ĭ-ăs, Gr. *Lysias*). Claudius Lysias, of the Jerusalem garrison, tribune by rank, was a Greek whose first name was assumed when he secured Roman citizenship at "a big price" (Acts 22:28), no doubt by bribing one of the freedmen of the court. Paul was fortunate in encountering this officer, who was a vigorous and capable soldier.

LYSTRA (lĭs'trà, Gr. *Lystra*). A Roman colony founded by Augustus with an aristocratic core of citizens with franchise, a group likely to honor the similar status of Paul. At Isauria, not far away, an inscription has been found to "Zeus before the gate," hence it was probably the location of the proposed ceremony mentioned in Acts 14:13. Timothy was a native of Lystra (Acts 16:1).

MAACAH, MAACHAH (mā'à-kà, Heb. *ma'ăkhâh, oppression*). **1.** Son of Nahor, brother of Abraham (Gen 22:24). **2.** A wife of David and the mother of Absalom (2 Sam 3:3; 1 Chron 3:2). **3.** The father of Achish, king of Gath (1 Kings 2:39). **4.** The favorite wife of Rehoboam, and the mother of Abijam (2 Chron 11:20–22). She outlived Abijam and was queen during the reign of her grandson Asa, until he deposed her for making an idol (1 Kings 15:10, 13; 2 Chron 15:16). **5.** A concubine of Caleb (1 Chron 2:48). **6.** Wife of Machir, the son of Manasseh (7:14–16). **7.** The wife of Jeiel, the founder of Gibeon (8:29; 9:35). **8.** The father of Hanan, one of David's mighty men (11:43). **9.** The father of Shephatiah (27:16). **10.** A small country on the edge of the Syrian desert north of Gilead. In fighting against David, the Ammonites and their helpers from Maacah were put to rout and the Arameans fled (2 Sam 10:6–14; Aram Maacah in 1 Chron 19:6). David defeated them and they became subservient to him (2 Sam 10:18–19).

MAACATHITES (mā-ăk'à-thīts, Heb. *ma'ăkhāthî*). The people of the nation of Maacah, residing near the Geshurites in the region of Bashan. They were in the area taken by Jair, the son of Manasseh (Deut 3:14), situated on the border of the kingdom of Og king of Bashan (Josh 12:5). The Israelites did not drive out the Maacathites or Geshurites but lived with them (13:13). The grandfather of Eliphelet, one of David's mighty men, and others were Maacathites (2 Sam 23:34; 2 Kings 25:23; Jer 40:8; 1 Chron 4:19).

MAADIAH (mā-à-dī'à, Heb. *ma'adhyâh, the LORD is ornament*). One of the chiefs of the priests who returned from exile with Zerubbabel (Neh 12:5).

MAALEH-ACRABBIM (See AKRABIM)

MAASEIAH (mā'à-sē'yà, Heb. *ma'ăsēyāhû, work of the LORD*). **1.** One of the Levites appointed to play a psaltery in praise of God while the ark was brought up to Jerusalem (1 Chron 15:18, 20). **2.** One of the captains of hundreds. Jehoiada made a covenant with him to resist the usurpation by Athaliah (2 Chron 23:1). **3.** An officer of Uzziah king of Judah (26:11). **4.** A son of Ahaz who was killed by Zicri (28:7). **5.** The governor of Jerusalem in Josiah's reign (34:8). **6.** One of the priests who had married a foreign woman (Ezra 10:18). **7.** A priest of the family of Harim who

took a foreign wife (10:21). **8.** A priest of the family of Pashhur who took a foreign wife (10:22). **9.** A man of the family of Pahath-Moab who took a foreign wife (10:30). **10.** The father of Azariah (Neh 3:23). **11.** One of the men who stood on the right side of Ezra as he read the Law to the people (8:4). **12.** One of the men who explained the Law to the people (8:7). **13.** One of the chiefs of the people who sealed the covenant with Nehemiah (10:25). May be the same as no. 12. **14.** One of the descendants of the son of Baruch in Jerusalem (11:5). **15.** A Benjamite whose descendants lived in Jerusalem (11:7). **16.** A priest who blew a trumpet at the dedication of the wall of Jerusalem (12:41). **17.** Another priest who took part in the dedication of the wall (12:42). **18.** A priest, father of Zephaniah (Jer 21:1; 37:3). **19.** The father of Zedekiah, a false prophet whom Jeremiah condemned (29:21). **20.** The doorkeeper of the temple in Jeremiah's time (35:4). **21.** An ancestor of Baruch (32:12; ASV, NIV Mahseiah).

MAAZIAH (mā-à-zī'à, Heb. *ma'azyâhû, consolation of the LORD*). **1.** A priest of the 24 sons of Eleazar and Ithamar (1 Chron 24:18). **2.** A priest who sealed the covenant with Nehemiah (Neh 10:8).

MACBANNAI (măk'bà-nī, Heb. *makhbannay, clad with a cloak*). A Gadite who joined David's forces at Ziklag (1 Chron 12:13).

MACBENAH (măk-bē'nà, Heb. *makhbēnâh, bond*). The name of a place in Judah that occurs in the genealogical list of Caleb. It is from the same root as Cabban (1 Chron 2:49).

MACCABEES (măk'à-bēs, Gr. *Makkabaioi*). The name given to a Jewish family who initiated the Jewish revolt against Antiochus Epiphanes, the Seleucid Syrian king who was forcing his Hellenizing policies on Palestine.

The revolt began in 168 B.C. when Mattathias, an aged priest, struck down a royal commissioner and an apostate Jew who were about to offer a pagan sacrifice. After a few months of guerrilla warfare, the old priest died and his sons, Eleazar and John were killed. The remaining three sons—Judas, Jonathan, and Simon—each in turn led the insurrection; and all left a deep mark on Jewish history.

Judas won the name of Maccabee, or "the Hammerer," and he was the only

THE MACCABEAN KINGDOM, 76 B.C.

member of the family to whom the term was applied in the Apocrypha. Later history used it as a surname for all three brothers. Judas was a fine soldier and patriot, with a clear policy of Jewish independence and religious reconstruction. After defeating several military expeditions, he formally cleansed the temple of Syrian pollution and celebrated the occasion with a great festival. This festival became a permanent fixture, falling on December 25 and lasting eight days (1 Macc 4:52–59; 2 Macc 10:6; John 10:22). Judas was later defeated and killed at Elasa (1 Macc 3–9:22).

Jonathan succeeded his brother in 161 B.C., and the Maccabean revolt reverted to the guerrilla warfare with which it had begun. Alexander Balas, supported by Pergamum and Egypt, aspired to the Syrian throne; and both Demetrius (the ruler of Syria) and Alexander tried to gain Jonathan's support. Demetrius offered the control of all military forces in Palestine and the governorship of Jerusalem. Alexander added an offer of the high priesthood. Jonathan chose Alexander and thus became the founder of the Hasmonean priesthood.

Simon, the third brother, was an able diplomat, who carried on his brother's policy of profiting with some success by Syria's internal troubles. In 143 and 142 B.C. he succeeded in establishing the virtual political independence of Judea. In 141, at a great assembly of princes, priests, and elders of the land, Simon was elected to be high priest, military com-

mander, and civil governor of the Jews, "for ever until there should arise a faithful prophet." The high priesthood was thus rendered hereditary in the family of Simon. His son, the celebrated John Hyrcanus, succeeded him and held the inherited authority for 30 years before passing it on to his son Aristobulus, who assumed the royal title. The Hasmoneans continued their dynasty until 34, when Herod and the Romans put down Antigonus, the last of Mattathias' line; but the Maccabees proper ended with Simon in 134.

The story as above outlined is told in two independent narratives written by authors of different emphases and abilities, the First and Second Books of the Maccabees. The first book is an honest piece of historical writing, detailing without adornment the events of a stirring struggle for freedom. The second book covers much of the same material but slants the account in the direction of religious instruction and admonition.

MACCABEES, 1 and 2 (See APOCRYPHA)

MACEDONIA (măs'ĕ-dō'nĭ-à, Gr. *Makedŏnia*). Lying geographically between the Balkan highlands and the Greek peninsula, Macedonia was both a Greek kingdom and a Roman province, and was the first part of Europe to receive Christianity (Acts 16:9ff.; Phil 4:15). Paul was more than once in the province (Acts 19:21; 20:1–3; 1 Cor 16:5; 2 Cor 1:16). Macedonians were close to the apostle; for example, Gaius and Aristarchus, Secundus, Sopater, and Epaphroditus (Acts 17:11; 20:4; Phil 4:10–19; 1 Thess 2:8, 17–20; 3:10).

MACHAERUS (mă-kē'rŭs, Gr. *Machairous*). Herod's southernmost stronghold east of the Dead Sea on the border of Perea, the tetrarchy of Herod Antipas. Herod's wife escaped from Machaerus to her father in the Arnon Valley when Herod tried to replace her with Herodias. In the subsequent troubles Herod occupied Machaerus with Herodias and Salome, and here John the Baptist died (Matt 14:3ff). In the Great Rebellion Jewish zealots were starved out of Machaerus by the Romans and the fort was razed.

MACHBANAI (See MACBANNAI)

MACHBENAH (See MACBENAH)

MACHI (See MAKI)

MACHIR (See MAKIR)

MACHPELAH (măk-pē'là, Heb. *makhpēlâh, a doubling*). A field near Hebron that Abraham purchased from Ephron the Hittite in order to use a cave there as a burial place for Sarah (Gen 23:19–20). Abraham, Isaac, Rebekah, Leah, and Jacob were also buried there (25:9; 49:31; 50:13).

MADMANNAH (măd-măn'nà, Heb. *madhmannâh, dunghill*). **1.** A town in southern Judah located about 8 miles (13 km.) south of Kiriath Sepher (Josh 15:31). **2.** A grandson of Caleb (1 Chron 2:48–49).

MAGADAN (See MAGDALA)

MAGDALA (măg'dà-là, Gr. *Magdala*). A town on the NW shore of the Sea of Galilee (Matt 15:39; ASV and NIV have Magadan; Mark 8:10, Dalmanutha). The town was the home or birthplace of Mary Magdalene (Matt 27:56, 61; 28:1; Mark 15:40, 47; 16:1, 9; Luke 8:2; 24:10; John 19:25; 20:1, 18).

MAGDALENE (See MAGDALA; MARY)

MAGGOT (See ANIMALS)

MAGI (mā'jī, Gr. *magoi*). Originally a religious caste among the Persians. Their devotion to astrology, divination, and the interpretation of dreams led to an extension in the meaning of the word, and by the first century B.C. the terms "magi" and "Chaldean" were applied generally to fortune tellers and the exponents of esoteric religious cults throughout the Mediterranean world. Magus or "sorcerer" is the name given to Simon (Acts 8:9), Bar-Jesus (13:6), and Elymas (13:8). The "wise men from the East" (Matt 2) are often referred to as "the Magi." Nothing is known of their land of origin, but it is a likely theory that they came from Arabia Felix (Southern Arabia). Astrology was practiced there, and a tradition of Israelite messianic expectation may have survived in the region since the days of the Queen of Sheba. Early legend connects Southern Arabia with Solomon's Israel, but the legend of "the Three Kings" is late and medieval.

MAGIC Originally the word meant the science or art of the Magi, the Persian priestly caste, who, like the Levites, were devoted to the practice of religion. With the wide extension of the term "magus," the word magic, too, acquired broader significance. It came to mean all occult rituals or processes designed to influence or control the course of nature; to dominate men or circumstances by the alliance, aid, or use of supernatural powers; and generally to tap and to employ the forces of an unseen world. Divination, the art of forecasting the future with

a view to avoiding its perils and pitfalls, might be included under the same classification. Its methods were frequently "magic." The Bible gives stern prohibitions against all forms of "wizardry" and "sorcery" (Exod 22:18; Lev 19:26; 20:27; Deut 18:10–11), causing security precautions like those surrounding the royal visit to "the witch of Endor" (1 Sam 28). Contact with magic and its practitioners was strictly forbidden (e.g., Deut 18:9–14).

Magic is man's attempt to make the future secure, whether by trying to find out about it in advance or by casting spells so as to make things happen in a predetermined and favorable way. The Lord's desire for his people is that they should recognize that his sovereignty has planned the future already, and that their part is, therefore, to walk trustfully into it. Furthermore, the voice of prophecy brings them all the immediate guidance and future knowledge that God thinks they need, and their task is to trust his trustworthiness.

Magic was widely practiced in Egypt (Exod 7:11; 8:7, 18–19; 9:11) and in Babylon (Dan 1:20; 2:2). The intrusion of such unhealthy beliefs may be detected in Hebrew history (Gen 30:14; and perhaps 30:37). Jacob believed his knowledge of animal genetics was determining the breeding trend, but God revealed to him in a dream that it was the Lord, not his own manipulations, that caused the favorable results (30:10–12). Jacob's family was remote from the lofty monotheism of Abraham, and the Euphrates Valley towns were devoted to magic, hence the "teraphim," or "household gods," later in the account (Gen 31:19; see also Judg 17:5; 1 Sam 19:13; Ezek 21:21–26; Zech 10:2). These were household deities, crudely carved, like the Roman Lares and Penates. Similar in concept was the cult of the "baals" of the fields, whose corrupt worship in fertility rituals and sympathetic magic was fiercely condemned by the prophets. In every revival of pure worship the teraphim were swept away with other forms of vicious paganism (e.g., 2 Kings 23:24).

In the NT the reference to the pagans' "vain repetitions" (Matt 6:7 KJV; e.g., see 1 Kings 18:26 and Acts 19:28) may allude to the belief in the magic repetition of set formulas such as the Tibetan's meaningless *"om mani padme hum"* ("Hail to the jewel in the lotus flower"). Simon (Acts 8:9) and Elymas (13:8) are spoken of as practicing "sorcery." There is evidence that this tribe of charlatans was widespread and often Jewish in ori-

to burn. The estimated price was "fifty thousand drachmas." The reference is probably to a silver coin, one of which was the standard wage for a day's labor in the Palestine of the Gospels. The early church in general did not dismiss magic as a delusion, but attributed its results to the work of malign and evil beings who were without power against a Christian. The Council of Ancyra (A.D. 315) first legislated against magic.

MAGISTRATE (măg'ĭs-trăt, Heb. *shephat, judge,* Gr. *archōn, ruler, stratēgos, commander*). Rulers (Ezra 7:25; Luke 12:58; Acts 16:20, 22, 35, 36, 38), especially of a Roman colony.

MAGNIFICAT (măg-nĭf'ĭ-kăt). The song of praise by Mary recorded in Luke 1:46–55. This name comes from its first word in the Vulgate version, *Magnificat mea anima* ("My soul doth magnify"). The song resembles closely the poetry of the OT, with striking similarity to Hannah's prayer (1 Sam 2:1–10).

MAGOG (mā'gŏg, Heb. *māghôgh, land of God?*). A son of Japheth (Gen 10:2; 1 Chron 1:5). Josephus and Greek writers generally applied this name to the Scythians. Some modern Christian writers indicate the Tartars of Russia and southern Europe. The names of King Gog, "prince of Rosh, Meshech and Tubal" (Ezek 38:2; cf, Rev 20:8) resemble the modern Russia, Moscow, and Tobolsk.

MAGUS, SIMON (See SIMON)

MAHALAH (See MAHLAH)

MAHALALEL (mȧ-hā'lȧ-lĕl, Heb. *mahălal'ēl, praise of God*). The son of Kenan and the father of Jared, He lived 895 years (Gen 5:12–13, 15–17; 1 Chron 1:2; Luke 3:37). In Luke 3:37 NIV has "Mahalaleel."

MAHALATH (mā'hȧ-lăth, Heb. *mahălath, sickness*). 1. A daughter of Ishmael whom Esau took for his third wife (Gen 28:9). 2. The first wife of Rehoboam (2 Chron 11:18). 3. A musical term in the heading of Psalms 53 and 88.

MAHALI (See MAHLI)

MAHANAIM (mā'hȧ-nā'ĭm, Heb. *mahă- nayim, two hosts*). A town so named by Jacob when he was met there by angels as he was returning from Paddan Aram to Canaan (Gen 32:2). This town was appointed a city of refuge and was assigned to the Levites (Josh 21:38; 1 Chron 6:80). It was situated in Gilead east of the Jordan, on the boundary between Gad and Manasseh (Josh 13:26, 30). After the death of Saul, Mahanaim

Clay figurine of bound prisoner, inscribed with magical formulae (execration text) intended to place a curse upon the enemies of Egypt. Saqqara, c. eighteenth century B.C. Courtesy Carta, Jerusalem

gin (e.g., "the Sons of Sceva" in Ephesus, Acts 19:14). The record of the first Christian impact on the city of Ephesus reveals the tremendous influence of magic among the populace at large. With the spread of Christian doctrine, those who practiced "curious arts" brought their books of incantations of magic formulas

was made the capital of Israel for a short time (2 Sam 2:8). David, fleeing from Absalom, came to this place (19:32). Solomon's officer Abinadab was stationed in this city (1 Kings 4:14).

Mahanaim is mentioned in an Egyptian inscription as one of the cities conquered by Sheshonk I (Shishak of the Bible). This occurred on his raid into Palestine (1 Kings 14:25–26; 2 Chron 12:2–3). It is also the name of a dance (Song of Songs 6:13).

MAHANEH DAN (mā'hȧ-nĕ dăn, Heb. *mahănēh-dhān, camp of Dan*). **1.** A place where Samson grew up and was first moved by the Spirit of the Lord (Judg 13:25). **2.** A place where 600 men of Dan encamped on their way to conquer Laish (Judg 18:12). This may be the same place as no. 1.

MAHARAI (mȧ-hăr'ā-ī, Heb. *mahăray, impetuous*). One of David's mighty men (2 Sam 23:28; 1 Chron 11:30) who was the captain over 24,000. He was a Zerahite living in Netoph (27:13).

MAHATH (mā'hăth, Heb. *mahath, seizing*). **1.** A Kohathite, an ancestor of Heman the singer (1 Chron 6:35). **2.** One of the Levites who cleansed the temple in Hezekiah's reign (2 Chron 29:12). He was appointed one of the overseers of the dedicated things (31:13).

MAHER-SHALAL-HASH-BAZ (mā'hēr-shăl'ăl-hăsh'băz, Heb. *the spoil speeds, the prey hastens*). Phrase written by Isaiah and given to his second son as a sign that Samaria would be carried away before the child would be old enough to talk (Isa 8:1, 3).

MAHLAH (mä'lȧ, Heb. *mahlâh, disease*). **1.** Oldest daughter of Zelophehad of the tribe of Manasseh. This man had no sons but seven daughters, who obtained permission to inherit land as if they were sons, provided they married within the tribe (Num 26:33; 27:1ff.; 36:1ff.; Josh 17:3ff.). **2.** Daughter of Hammoleketh, the sister of Makir, son of Manasseh (1 Chron 7:18).

MAHLI (mȧh'lī, Heb. *mahlî, sick*). **1.** Son of Merari, son of Levi, ancestor of the Mahlites (Exod 6:19; Num 3:20; Ezra 8:18). **2.** Son of Mushi (1 Chron 6:47; 23:23; 24:30).

MAHLITE (mȧh'līt, Heb. *mahlî*). A descendant of Mahli, son of Merari (Num 3:33; 26:58). There was one case among them of a family of daughters who married cousins (1 Chron 23:22).

MAHLON (mȧ'lŏn, Heb. *mahlôn, sick*). Son of Elimelech. He married Ruth in Moab, leaving her a widow about ten years later (Ruth 1:2, 5; 4:9–10).

MAHSEIAH (See MAASEIAH)

MAID, MAIDEN 1. Hebrew '*āmâh, handmaiden, or female slave*, the property of her owners (Exod 2:5; 21:20, 26) and often a bondmaid (Lev 25:44). **2.** Hebrew *bethûlâh, virgin*, a girl secluded and separated from intercourse with men (Exod 22:16; Judg 19:24; Pss 78:63; 148:12). **3.** Hebrew *har'ărâh, girl, maiden* (Exod 2:5; Ruth 2:8, 22–23; 3:2). **4.** Hebrew '*almâh, a girl of marriageable age*, occurs only seven times (Gen 24:43; Exod 2:8; Ps 68:25; Prov 30:19; Song of Songs 1:3; 6:8; Isa 7:14). **5.** Hebrew *shiphhâh, maid servant*, a synonym of *amah, maid* (Gen 16:2–3, 5–6, 8; 29:24, 29; 30:9ff.), *bondmaid* (Lev 19:20), *bond woman* (Deut 28:68; 2 Chron 28:10; Esth 7:4), *handmaid* (Gen 16:1; 25:12; 29:24, 29), *maidservant* (12:16; 24:35; 30:43).

MAIL, COAT OF (See ARMS AND ARMOR)

MAIMED (See DISEASES)

MAKI (mā'kī, Heb. *mākhî*). The father of Geuel, who was appointed from the tribe of Gad to be one of those who spied out the Promised Land (Num 13:15).

MAKIR (mā'kīr, Heb. *mākhîr, sold*). **1.** The oldest son of Manasseh, son of Joseph. He married and had a family before the Israelites left Egypt (Gen 50:23). His descendants, the Makirites, conquered Gilead and settled there (Num 32:39–40), except the family of Hepher, who settled in Canaan (Josh 17:3). So Makir is called the father of Gilead several times, and he is even said to have begotten Gilead (Num 26:29). In Judges 5:14 Makir stands for Manasseh. **2.** The son of Ammiel. David took Mephibosheth out of his house (2 Sam 9:4–5). This Makir was one of the men who brought refreshments to David as he fled from Absalom (17:27).

MALACHI (măl'ȧ-kī, Heb. *mal'ākhî, messenger of the LORD* or *my messenger*). The last book of the OT and the prophet whose oracles the book contains (Mal 1:1). *Malachi* is the Hebrew expression meaning "my messenger" (3:1; cf. Ezek 3:8–9). The Book of Malachi is clearly postexilic. The temple had been completed, and sacrifices were being offered (Mal 1:7–10; 3:8). A Persian governor (1:8) was ruling in Jerusalem. This indicates a date later than that of Haggai and Zechariah.

It is also clear that the early zeal for the rebuilding of the temple had died out, and a situation of moral and religious deterioration had set in. The mixed marriages (Mal 2:10–12), failure to pay tithes (3:8–10), and offering of blemished sacrifices (1:6–14) are conditions not unlike those referred to in the times of Ezra and Nehemiah (Ezra 7–Neh 13); and it would seem that Malachi's prophecy was given at about that time, or possibly shortly thereafter—about the middle or end of the fifth century B.C.

There are two principal themes in the book: (1) The sin and apostasy of the people of Israel (esp. chs. 1–2), and (2) the judgment that will come on the faithless and the blessing in store for those who repent (esp. chs. 3–4). A more detailed analysis follows:

I. Contents
1. Title, 1:1.
2. An argument for the love of God toward Israel as shown in the contrasted experiences of Edom and Israel, 1:2–5.
3. A protest against the negligence of the priests in worship, 1:6–2:9.
4. A condemnation of those who divorce their wives and marry foreign women, 2:10–16.
5. An answer to those who complain that God is indifferent to injustice: a day of judgment is at hand, 2:17–3:5.
6. A rebuke for the neglect of tithes and offerings, 3:6–12.
7. A reply to doubters and a promise to the faithful, 3:13–4:3.
8. A recall to the law and prophecy of the coming of Elijah, 4:4–6.

II. Unique Features
1. The use of the rhetorical question and answer as a method of communication. This device begins most of the eight sections referred to above.
2. Malachi contains prophetic and priestly interests. It has been called "prophecy within the law." Generally the prophets exhibit little interest in sacrifices and ceremonial laws, preferring to stress the more inward aspects of religious life. Malachi, however, sees the people's apostasy manifested by their carelessness in the sacrificial offerings (Mal 1:6–14), the priests' neglect of their duties (2:1–9), and the failure of the people to pay their tithes and other offerings (3:7–12). This book disproves the view commonly held today that the prophets did not believe in the necessity of the ritual law.
3. The growing OT messianic expectation is witnessed to in the announcement of God's "messenger of the covenant," by whose coming Israel will be purified

and judged (Mal 3:1–5; cf. Matt 11:10), and of the prophet Elijah who will announce the Day of the Lord (Mal 4:5–6; cf. Matt 17:9–13).

MALCHAM, MALCAM (See MOLECH)

MALCHIAH (See MALKIJAH)

MALCHIEL (See MALKIEL)

MALCHIJAH (See MALKIJAH)

MALCHIRAM (See MALKIRAM)

MALCHI-SHUA (See MALKI-SHUA)

MALELEEL (See MAHALALEL)

MALICE (Gr. *kakia*). An evil desire to do harm to or act wickedly toward someone. KJV translates *kakia* as "malice" (Rom 1:29; 1 Cor 5:8; 14:20; Eph 4:31; Col 3:8; Titus 3:3; 1 Peter 2:1, 16), and in most cases so do RSV and NIV. It is an internal attitude that Christians must put away (Eph 4:31; 1 Peter 2:1), for it is wholly opposed to their new life. See also EVIL.

MALKIEL (măl'kĭ-ĕl, Heb. *malkî'ēl, God is my king*). Son of Beriah, son of Asher (Gen 46:17; Num 26:45; 1 Chron 7:31).

MALKIJAH, MALCHIAH (măl-kī'jà, măl-kī'à, Heb. *malkîyâh, malkîâ, my king is the LORD*). 1. A Gershonite, the ancestor of Asaph, the singer in David's time (1 Chron 6:40). 2. An ancestor of the priest Adaiah who returned from exile and lived in Jerusalem (9:12; Neh 11:12). 3. A priest in David's time (1 Chron 24:9). 4. An Israelite who had married a foreign woman (Ezra 10:25). 5. Another in the same family who did the same (10:25). 6. Another man who did this (10:31). 7. A son of Harim who worked on the wall (Neh 3:11), possibly the same as no. 6. 8. The son of Recab who repaired the Dung Gate of the wall (3:14). 9. A goldsmith who worked on the wall (3:31). 10. One of the men who stood on the left side of Ezra as he read the law to the people (8:4). 11. One of those who sealed the covenant with Nehemiah (10:3). 12. A priest who took part in the dedication of the wall (12:42). Perhaps the same as no. 11. 13. Father of Pashhur (Jer 21:1). Pashhur helped arrest the prophet (38:1). 14. The son of King Zedekiah and the owner of the dungeon into which Jeremiah was put (38:6).

MALKIRAM (măl-kī'răm, Heb. *malkî-răm, my king is high*). Son of Jehoiachin (1 Chron 3:18).

MALKI-SHUA (măl-kĭ-shū'à, Heb. *mal-kîshûa', king of aid*). Third son of King

Saul (1 Sam 14:49; 31:2; 1 Chron 8:33; 9:39). He was killed by the Philistines (1 Sam 31:2; 1 Chron 10:2).

MALLOW (See PLANTS)

MALLUCH (măl'ŭk, Heb. *mallûkh, counselor*). **1.** Ancestor of Ethan, a Levite, son of Merari (1 Chron 6:44). **2.** A son of Bani. He married a foreign woman (Ezra 10:29). **3.** A son of Harim who did the same thing (10:32). **4.** A priest who sealed the covenant (Neh 10:4). He had come from Babylon under Zerubbabel (12:2). **5.** A chief of the people who sealed the covenant (10:27).

MALTA (Gr. *Melitē*). An island situated in a strategically important position some 60 miles (100 km.) south of Sicily. Rome acquired the island in 218 B.C., but the Carthaginian language continued to be spoken, accounting for Luke's phrase "the barbarous people" (Acts 28:2 KJV), where "barbarous" is used in the Greek sense of "foreign-speaking." Malta was the scene of Paul's shipwreck (27:27ff.).

MAMMON (Gr. *mamōnas, riches*). The Aramaic word for "riches," that Christ used for a life goal opposed to God (Matt 6:24; Luke 16:13 KJV; NIV "Money"). Jesus also used the word in the phrase "mammon of unrighteousness" (Luke 16:11, 13 KJV).

View of Herodian ruins at Mamre (Ramat el-Khalil), near Hebron. Courtesy Duby Tal

MAMRE (măm'rē, Heb. *mamrē', strength*). **1.** An Amorite allied with Abram (Gen 14:13, 24). **2.** A place a few miles north of Hebron where oak trees grew (13:18; 18:1). This place apparently derived its name from the Amorite above who lived there. The burial cave in the field of Machpelah is described as located before Mamre (23:17, 19; 25:9; 35:27; 49:30; 50:13).

MAN (Heb. *'ādhām, 'îsh,* Gr. *anthrōpos*). The human species and the male

member. Thus the doctrine of man is the teaching concerning human beings in their relation to God and his creation. God made the human species, first the male and then the female (Gen 1–2), as a single species (Acts 17:26) separate from the animal world. God made man in the image and likeness of himself (Gen 1:26–27; Ps 8:5). Man is separated from the animals in terms of his moral conscience, self-knowledge, and capacity for a spiritual communion with his Creator. This capacity has been seriously restricted, misdirected, and abused because of sin. Adam and Eve, the first pair of human beings, freely chose to disobey the divine command, resulting in loss of communion with God. This disobedience also affected their lives and relationships, as well as their children and their children's children (Gen 3; Rom 6:12ff.). Human beings show signs both of being God's special creation and of being sinful creatures (7:14–25). The eternal Son of God became Man in order to provide salvation from sin and a new, permanent relationship with God (5:12ff.). As such, Jesus Christ is called the "last Adam" (1 Cor 15:45). Thus in Christ human beings are restored to their right and proper relationship both with their Creator and with his created order (Col 1:15–20). Either as unbeliever or believer, each human being is held by God to be a responsible creature, and so each person will be judged at the Last Judgment (Rom 2:16). See also ADAM; WOMAN.

MAN, SON OF (See SON OF MAN)

MANAHATH (măn'à-hăth, Heb. *mānahath, resting place*). **1.** An Edomite, the son of Shobal (Gen 36:23; 1 Chron 1:40). **2.** A town in Edom (8:6).

MANAHATHITES (mà-nā'hăth-īts, Heb. *mānahtî*). **1.** Half of the Manahathites were descendants of Shobal, son of Caleb (1 Chron 2:52). **2.** Another group, "half the Manahathites," descended from Salma (2:54).

MANASSEH (mă-năs'sĕ, Heb. *menashsheh, one who forgets*). **1.** The older son of Joseph, born in Egypt (Gen 41:51). Jacob claimed him and his younger brother Ephraim for his own sons, and when he blessed them he predicted Ephraim would be greater than Manasseh (48:5, 19).

2. King of Judah and son of Hezekiah. He was only 12 years old when he came to the throne in 687 B.C. He became a fanatical idolater, bringing a whole host of heathen practices into his realm. He also put a heathen altar in the temple and later moved the Asherah pole into this building (2 Kings 21:1-7). He also had horses and chariots dedicated to the sun (23:11).

Manasseh made his son pass through the fire, practiced soothsaying, used enchantments, indulged in sorcery, and sponsored ghosts and familiar spirits (2 Kings 21:6; 2 Chron 33:6). He persecuted the pious people who were faithful to the Lord (2 Kings 21:6). Jewish tradition says he sawed the prophet Isaiah in two. The subsequent reformation of Josiah could not bring the people back to true worship. Manasseh brought his country to ruin (Jer 15:4).

He was taken captive to Babylon. After a time he repented of his sins and was returned to his throne in Jerusalem, where he tried to undo his evil work (2 Chron 33:10-13, 15-17).

3. A priest of an idol at Dan (Judg 18:30 KJV, NASB; NIV and RSV read "Moses"). **4.** One of those who married a foreign woman (Ezra 10:30). **5.** Another who did this (10:33).

MANASSEH, PRAYER OF (See APOCRYPHA)

MANASSEH, TRIBE OF The descendants of Manasseh. This tribe contained 32,200 men of war, those over 20 years old (Num 1:34), before the Israelites marched from Sinai, increasing to 52,700 40 years later (26:34). Before the Israelites crossed over the Jordan River into Canaan, half the tribe of Manasseh along with the tribes of Reuben and Gad chose land east of the river, and Moses assigned it to them (32:33). The rest of the tribe was given ten parts of land in Canaan (Josh 17:1-10). Gideon, Jair, and Jephthah came from Manasseh (Judg 6:15; 10:3; 11:1). This half-tribe, with Reuben and Gad, fell into idolatry and was later carried away into captivity by Assyria (1 Chron 5:25-26) during Pekah's reign over Israel (2 Kings 15:29). Men of Manasseh joined David while he was a fugitive from Saul (1 Chron 12:19-22).

MANASSITES (mà-năs'ĭts, Heb. *menashshî, forgetting*). Descendants of the oldest son of Joseph (Gen 41:51). This was a tribe of noble standing, which Gilead, under Jephthah, delivered from the Ephraimites by the password "Shibboleth" (Judg 12:4-6). Moses gave them a city of refuge in Bashan (Deut 4:41-

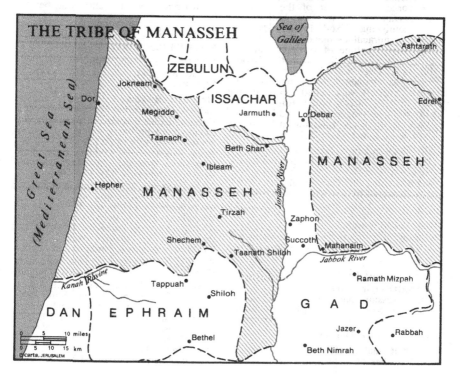

THE TRIBE OF MANASSEH

43). Because of evil under Jehu, God caused the Manassites to be cut off (2 Kings 10:31–33).

MANDRAKE (See PLANTS)

MANEH (See WEIGHTS AND MEASURES)

MANGER (Gr. *phatnē, a stall*). The LXX used *phatnē* for the Hebrew, which is given in 2 Chronicles 32:28 as "stalls" and in the KJV of Job 39:9 as "crib" (see Prov 14:4; Isa 1:3). Luke also gives *phatnē* as the birthplace of Jesus. Justin Martyr wrote about A.D. 100 that the stall was in a cave adjoining an inn. It is more probable that the stalls were arranged around a courtyard of an inn with guest rooms and balcony above.

MANNA (Heb. *mān*, Gr. *manna*). A special food provided for the Hebrews during the exodus from Egypt. The Hebrew *mān* is a question and prefixed to *hu* would be "What is it?" On the other hand, it may be an adaptation of the Egyptian *mennu*, food. Josephus and other ancient writers attribute the name to the question "Is it food?" which is in keeping with the wilderness setting. It came at night (Num 11:9). It was white, of delicious flavor, and resembled seed of the coriander, a plant of the eastern Mediterranean area that was both tasty and nourishing (Exod 16:31). That it came by miraculous means is shown by its nature, its time of coming, and its preservation over the Sabbath (Exod 16:20–26; Deut 8:3). As soon as other food was available, the manna ceased (Josh 5:12). It was called "corn from heaven" (Ps 78:24), bread from heaven (105:40), and "angels' bread" (2 Esd 2:1; Wisd 16:20). Jesus, referring to himself, used it as a metaphor (John 6:31–58).

MANOAH (mà-nō'à, Heb. *mānôah, rest*). The father of Samson, of the tribe of Dan. He was a good Hebrew who desired a son and heir (Judg 13). The appeal of his wife was answered by a visiting angel, whose promise of a son was confirmed by a miracle during a sacrifice. He was a trustworthy parent, rearing Samson according to instructions. But he failed to teach him that marrying a pagan woman was abhorrent (Judg 14:1–11).

MAN OF SIN (See ANTICHRIST)

MANSION (Gr. *monē, an abiding place*). An expression that occurs only in John 14:2 (KJV; NIV "rooms"), where the plural is used.

MANTLE (See DRESS)

MAOCH (mā'ŏk, Heb. *mā'ôkh, a poor one*). Father of Achish, a king of Gath

(1 Sam 27:2). He protected David and his troop from Saul (29:1–11).

MAON (mā'ŏn, Heb. *mā'ôn, habitation*). **1.** A descendant of Caleb (1 Chron 2:42–45). **2.** A town on an elevated plain south of Hebron, the hill was called Rock of Separation (1 Sam 23:24–28 mg; NIV "Sela Hammahlekoth," "rock of parting"). It was the home of Nabal and Abigail (25:1–3).

MAONITES (mā'ŏn-īts). They are named with others who were defeated by the Lord (Judg 10:11–12). They were called Mehunim and may have been from Arabia. Their descendants were among the temple servants of Ezra's day (Ezra 2:50).

MARAH (mā'rà, Heb. *mārâh, bitterness*). A place about three days' journey from the Red Sea crossing, where the Hebrews found bitter water. When they complained, God showed Moses a plant whose foliage sweetened the water (Exod 15:23–26).

MARANATHA (mār'à-năth'à, Aramaic, *mārānā' 'āthāh, our Lord comes!*). An expression meaning "Our Lord comes" (1 Cor 16:22). Paul put this word over against *anathema*, the curse that befalls idolaters.

MARBLE (See MINERALS)

MARCUS (See MARK, JOHN)

MARDUK (màr'dūk, Heb. *merōdhākh*, Akkad. *Marduk*). A Babylonian god (Jer 50:2; KJV "Merodach").

MARESHAH (mà-rē'shà, Heb. *mārēshâh, a possession*). **1.** The father of Hebron (1 Chron 2:42). **2.** A grandson of Judah, more probably a town (4:21). **3.** An important city of Judah, SW of Jerusalem (Josh 15:44), which Rehoboam considered strategic and which he fortified (2 Chron 11:5–12). King Asa met a big Ethiopian army at Mareshah in the Valley of Zephathah and with divine aid overwhelmed it (14:9–15). Eliezer, a native of Mareshah, delivered a warning from God to wicked King Jehoshaphat for an unholy alliance with Ahaziah (20:35–37). It was a good city in Micah's day and he promised its people an heir (Mic 1:15).

MARK (1) *'Ôth*, a special sign or brand (Gen 4:15). The marks Paul bore were scars (*stigmata*) caused by the beatings he had suffered (Gal 6:17). (2) *Tāu'*, a seal or sign of ownership (Ezek 9:4, 6; Rev 7:2–8). (3) *Mattārā'*, a target (1 Sam 20:20; Job 16:12; Lam 3:12). (4) *Qa'aqa'*, a form of tattooing banned by the Lord

Marduk, chief god in the Babylonian pantheon, as depicted on a cylinder seal from Babylon, mid-ninth century B.C.
"Babylon will be captured;
Bel will be put to shame,
Marduk filled with terror" (Jer 50:2)
Courtesy Carta, Jerusalem

(Lev 19:28). (5) *Skopos*, a goal or end to be attained (Phil 3:14). (6) *Charagma*, a particular brand or characteristic, denoting the nature and rank of people (Rev 13:16).

MARK, GOSPEL OF The shortest of the four Gospels. In comparison with Matthew and Luke, it contains relatively little of the teachings of Jesus and nothing at all about his birth and childhood.

On two points the tradition of the early church is unanimous: the Second Gospel was written by Mark and presents the preaching of Peter. Most scholars today place the writing of Mark between A.D. 65 and 70, shortly before the destruction of Jerusalem in the latter year. Conservatives commonly hold to a date in the 50s.

From the early church—with the exception of Chrysostom—to the present it has been held that Mark's Gospel was written at Rome. Several distinctive features point in this direction. Mark uses ten Latin words, some of which do not occur elsewhere in the NT. He explains Jewish customs because he is writing to Gentiles. To his Roman readers he presents Jesus as the mighty conqueror and the suffering servant of the Lord. Because of this purpose no genealogy nor infancy narratives are given.

In addition to those just mentioned, there are three main characteristics of this Gospel. The first is *rapidity of action*. The narrative moves quickly from one event to the next. This probably reflects the impulsive personality of Peter. More than 40 times we find the Greek word *euthys*, translated (KJV) "immediately," "straightway," "forthwith." The second characteristic is *vividness of detail*. Mark often includes details omitted by the other Synoptics that make the narrative more alive. He gives special attention to the looks and gestures of Jesus. The third characteristic is *picturesqueness of description*. Mark's is preeminently the pictorial Gospel. He describes, for instance, the 5,000 sitting on the green grass in "groups" (literally, "flower beds"). Peter evidently was impressed with the striking scene of the groups of people in brightly colored Oriental garments of red and yellow sitting on the green hillside, and Mark has preserved the picture for us.

Mark's is the Gospel of action. Only one long message of Jesus is recorded, the Olivet Discourse (Mark 13). Mark includes 18 miracles of Jesus, about the same number as Matthew or Luke. In contrast he has only 4 of the parables, compared with 18 in Matthew and 19 in Luke.

The period of preparation (Mark 1:1–13) for Jesus' public ministry is described very briefly. It consists of three items: the ministry of John the Baptist (1:1–8), the baptism of Jesus (1:9–11), and the temptation of Jesus (1:12–13). After an introduction of only 13 verses—in contrast to 76 in Matthew and 183 in Luke—Mark plunges immediately into the public ministry of the Master.

First comes the great Galilean ministry (Mark 1:14–9:50). This is commonly thought to have lasted about a year and a half. It may be divided into three sections. The first period (1:4–3:12) was a time of immense popularity. Jesus called four fishermen to follow him—and later Levi—and engaged in a vigorous healing ministry. This was the time when large crowds thronged about him.

In the second period (Mark 3:13–7:23) he appointed the 12 apostles, and opposition began to show itself. The Pharisees clashed with Jesus over questions about Sabbath observance and ceremonial cleansing. He healed the Gerasene demoniac and the woman with the issue of blood and raised Jairus' daughter. He sent out the Twelve and fed the 5,000.

In the third period (Mark 7:24–9:50) Jesus gave more attention to his disciples. Three times he is described as withdrawing from the crowd to teach the disciples. After Peter's confession at Caesarea Philippi he began a new phase of teaching: predicting his passion.

The great Galilean ministry was followed by the briefer Perean ministry (Mark 10:1–52), and then by Passion Week (11:1–15:47) and the Resurrection (ch. 16).

MARK, JOHN (Gr. *Markos*, from Lat. *Marcus, a large hammer*, Gr. *Iōannēs*, from Heb. *Yôhānān, the LORD is gracious*). Mentioned by name ten times in the NT. John was his Jewish name, Mark (Marcus) his Roman. In Acts he is twice (13:5, 13) referred to simply as John, once (15:37) as Mark, and three times (12:12, 25; 15:37) as "John, also called Mark." In the Epistles he is uniformly (four times) called simply Mark (KJV calling him Marcus three times).

The first allusion to John Mark may be in Mark 14:51–52. The first definite reference to John Mark is Acts 12:12. When Barnabas and Saul returned to Antioch from their famine visit at Jerusalem (11:27–30), they took along John Mark (12:25). This opened the opportunity for him to accompany them on their missionary journey as "their helper" (13:5).

The missionaries first evangelized the island of Cyprus. When they reached Perga in Pamphylia, John returned home to Jerusalem. Whatever his motive, Paul distrusted him and refused to take him on the second journey (15:37–38). Two missionary parties were formed. Barnabas took Mark and revisited Cyprus, while Paul chose a new associate, Silas, and went overland to Asia Minor.

Mark next appears in Rome, where he is a fellow worker with Paul (Philem 24). Paul recommended him to the church at Colosse (Col 4:10). Here he was called "the cousin of Barnabas." That John Mark had fully reinstated himself with Paul is shown by the latter's statement in 2 Timothy 4:11. Peter refers to him as "my son Mark" (1 Peter 5:13). This may be a mere expression of affection, or it may indicate that Mark was converted under Peter's ministry.

MARKET (Heb. *ma'ărāv, a place for trade*). The term also means things traded ("market" of Ezek 27:13, 17, 19 is "merchandise" in NIV). The NT word is *agora*, the civic center where people gathered for recreation (Matt 11:16–17),

View of the Roman ruins at Palmyra, ancient Tadmor, a city about 120 miles (193 km.) northeast of Damascus. The agora, or market place, is shown in foreground. Courtesy Studium Biblicum Franciscanum, Jerusalem

where the unemployed loafed (20:3, 6), and where the proud paraded (Mark 12:38; Luke 11:43). It was a courtroom (Acts 16:19) and also a forum (17:17).

MARRIAGE The formalization and sanctification of the union of man and woman for the procreation of children. The common Hebrew term *lāqah*,"to take in marriage," should be seen in association with the verb *bā'al*, "to be master, rule, or possess in marriage," as well as with the noun *ba'al*, "master, lord, husband."

The father was responsible for finding a suitable bride for his son, and the wishes and feelings of the young people were largely irrelevant to this decision. Isaac's marriage was arranged between his father's servant and his future wife's brother. She was then consulted (Gen 24:33–53, 57–58), though perhaps only because her father was no longer living. On rare occasions, parental advice was either ignored, rejected, or not sought (26:34–35), and, in a most unusual initiative, Michal, daughter of Saul, expressed her love for David (1Sam 18:20).

Marriage to a foreigner was generally discouraged, though some Hebrews took wives from among those women captured in war. Samson received permission from his parents to marry a Philistine woman (Judg 14:2–3). Concern was always expressed that marriage with a non-Israelite would dilute the covenantal faith by the introduction of ideas and practices concerning strange gods (1 Kings 11:4).

Because marriages with close relatives were common, limits of consanguinity are recorded for the Israelites to follow (Lev 18:6–18). Formerly, a man could

Marriage contract between Ananiah ben Haggai and Yehoyishma on Aramaic papyrus from Elephantine, Egypt, c. 450 B.C. Courtesy The Brooklyn Museum, Bequest of Miss Theodora Wilbour

marry his half-sister on his father's side (Gen 20:12;cf. 2 Sam 13:13), though this is forbidden in Leviticus 20:17. Cousins — such as Isaac and Rebekah, as well as Jacob, Rachel, and Leah — frequently married, though a simultaneous marriage with two sisters was specifically forbidden (Lev 18:18). The union between an aunt and her nephew produced Moses (Exod 6:20; Num 26:59), though a marriage between such relatives was subsequently forbidden by the Mosaic Law.

Jacob, already married to the two sisters Rachel and Leah, was also provided with the maid of each of his wives (Gen 30:3–9), while his brother Esau had three wives (26:34; 28:9; 36:1–5). Gideon is described as having "many wives" (Judg 8:30–31), and Solomon had 700 wives and 300 concubines (1 Kings 11:1–3).

Despite these examples of polygamy, the most general and acceptable form of marriage was monogamy, which received the sanction of the Mosaic Law (cf. Exod 20:17; 21:5; Deut 5:21, et al.). The teaching of Jesus on marriage stressed the lifetime nature of the commitment, and while recognizing that Moses had regularized an already existing practice of divorce "because of the hardness of your hearts" (Mark 10:4–5), he taught the traditional Hebrew monogamy and added that the remarriage of a divorced person while the spouse was still alive constituted adultery (10:11–12).

Levirate marriage helped maintain and protect the family name and property. Where a man died without issue, it was the responsibility of the closest male relative, usually his brother, to marry the widow. The first baby born of this union would then be regarded as the child of the dead man and would be entitled to his name and the entire rights of his property. Even if the widow already had children, the male relative would still be expected to marry and support her.

Before marriage, a woman was a member of her father's household, and as such she was subject to his authority. At marriage, her husband became her protector, and on his death, through her levirate marriage, she found her new "redeemer." Like many other Hebrew traditions, the levirate marriage was also known to the Canaanites, Assyrians, and Hittites. The best-known levirate marriage in the Old Testament is that of Ruth the Moabitess, who married Boaz after the next of kin refused to undertake the responsibility (Deut 25:5–10; Ruth 4:1–12). See also KINSMAN.

The betrothal (Deut 28:30; 2 Sam 3:14) had a particular legal status attached to it that made it almost identical to marriage. The law required that a man committing adultery with a betrothed virgin should be stoned for violating his neighbor's wife (Deut 22:23–24). A one-year betrothal was considered normal, and it constituted a part of the permanent marriage relationship (Matt 1:18; Luke 1:27; 2:5). For one year after being married the groom was exempt from military service (Deut 24:5) so that the marriage might be established on a proper footing. The bride's father already used the term "son-in-law" from the time of the betrothal (Gen 19:14), a custom that enhanced the concept of family solidarity. In the pre-Christian period, divorce was an option that was always available to the husband and sometimes also to the wife. After the return from exile, wholesale divorce was required of those Hebrews who had married foreign wives to prevent the influence of idolatry on God's people. Normally, however, there was a distinct tendency in Jewish tradition to discourage divorce and, following Egyptian custom, a substantial fine of "divorce money" was levied as a deterrent. The status of the wife was not very high, however, and the bill of divorce could take the form of a simple repudiation by the husband in some such expression as, "She is not my wife, and I am not her husband" (Hos 2:2). In the early Christian period, divorce could be considered only when there was a mixed marriage (between a Christian and a pagan), and even then the Christian was not permitted to remarry while the spouse was alive. It was even thought that the early church was exercising leniency when it first permitted widows to remarry.

MARROW The soft tissue in the cavities of bones (Job 21:24; Heb 4:12). It is used figuratively of richness (Ps 63:5 KJV) and good things (Isa 25:6 KJV).

MARS HILL (Gr. *Areios pagos, Hill of Ares*). A barren hill, 370 feet (116 m.) high, NW of the famous Acropolis in Athens. It was dedicated to Ares, the god of war. The elevated place became the seat of the Greek council, the Areopagus. Because of the Athenians' sudden interest in his message, Paul was taken there to clarify his mysterious teachings (Acts 17:16-34).

MARSH Swamplands near the mouths of some rivers and at various places along the banks of the Jordan and of the Dead Sea (cf. Ezek 47:11).

MARTHA (Aram. *lady, mistress*) Sister of Lazarus and Mary of Bethany. Luke mentions a visit of Jesus to the home of Martha at a certain village (Luke 10:38). It is inferred from this that the beloved friends of Jesus had resided in Galilee before going to Bethany. The sisters knew of Jesus' ability to work miracles (John 11:3, 5). He, no doubt, was a guest in their home during the last days before Calvary (Matt 21:17; Mark 11:1, 11). Martha was a careful hostess and was familiar enough with Jesus to complain to him about her sister's conduct (Luke 10:38-42) and about his delay in coming when Lazarus was ill (John 11:1-3, 21). She gave the Master an occasion for presenting the great statement about the resurrection (11:25).

MARTYR (Gr. *martys, martyr, witness*). Because of its use in connection with

Stephen (Acts 22:20) and others who died for Christ, the word came to mean one who paid the extreme price for fidelity to Christ. Antipas was a faithful witness (Rev 2:13). The harlot, Babylon, was drunk with the blood of martyrs (17:6).

MARY (Gr. *Maria, Mariam,* from Heb. *miryām*). **1.** Mary of Rome. A diligent worker in the church (Rom 16:6). **2.** The mother of John Mark who lived in Jerusalem, where she had a house in which Christians met for prayer (Acts 12:1-16). She may have been a woman of some means, as she had at least one servant, a girl named Rhoda (12:13). Some scholars think the Upper Room in which Jesus observed the Lord's Supper was in her home, but there is no proof of this. **3.** Mary of Bethany, the sister of Lazarus and Martha (John 11:1). Jesus commended her for being more interested in hearing him than in providing a bounteous dinner (Luke 10:42). She joined with Martha in saying to Jesus after the death of Lazarus, "Lord, . . . if you had been here, my brother would not have died" (John 11:21). Afterward, a week before the last Passover, when Jesus was a guest in the house of Simon the Leper (Mark 14:3), she showed her devotion to Jesus by anointing his head and feet with costly ointment and wiping his feet with her hair (John 12:3). Her act would always be remembered (Matt 26:6-13; Mark 14:3-9), an act of love and a preparation for his coming death (John 12:7-8). **4.** Mary the mother of James and Joses. There is reason for thinking that she (Matt 27:56), the "other Mary" (27:61), and Mary the wife of Clopas (John 19:25) were the same person. She was at the cross when Jesus died (Matt 27:56; Mark 15:40). She witnessed the burial of her Lord (15:47), came to the tomb to anoint his body (16:1), and fled when told by the angel that Jesus was not in the tomb (16:8). The mother of James and Joses was also the wife of Clopas (Matt 28:1; Mark 16:1; Luke 24:10). That Clopas (Cleopas, 24:18) and Alphaeus (Matt 10:3) were the same has not been proved.

5. Mary Magdalene. Her name probably indicates that she came from Magdala, on the SW coast of the Sea of Galilee. After Jesus cast seven demons out of her (Mark 16:9; Luke 8:2), she became one of his devoted followers. She followed the body of Jesus to the grave (Matt 27:61) and was the first to learn of the Resurrection (28:1-8; Mark 16:9; Luke 24:1, 10).

MARY, THE MOTHER OF JESUS She was descended from David (Rom 1:3; Acts 2:30; 2 Tim 2:8). The source of the

Majdal, a ruin on the northwest shore of the Sea of Galilee, identified with Magdala, birthplace of Mary Magdalene. The domed structure in foreground is the tomb of the Moslem Sheikh Mohammed Raslan.
Courtesy Zev Radovan

infancy narratives (Matt 1–2; Luke 1–2) is not known, but it is more than likely that they came from Mary herself. She lived into the apostolic period, whereas Joseph seems to have died before the crucifixion of Jesus, for there is no mention of him after the incident of Jesus in the temple when he was 12. Mary could very well have told this to the early leaders of the church, including Luke. She was a relative of Elizabeth, the mother of John the Baptist (Luke 1:36). Luke writes of her maidenly fears (1:26–27), her humble submission to the will of God (1:38), and her hymn of praise to God for the favor accorded her in being the mother of the Messiah (1:39–55). Neither she nor Joseph fully understood her Son (2:50). At Cana in Galilee (John 2:1–11), Mary seems to have some intimation that Jesus had more than natural powers, but she needed some correction regarding her notion about the use of these powers.

In one episode (Matt 12:46; Mark 3:21, 31ff.; Luke 8:19–21) Jesus teaches that physical relationship to him conveys no special privilege, no right of interference with him — the same lesson he taught on a later occasion (11:27). Mary was at the Cross (John 19:25ff.) and in the Upper Room (Acts 1:14) after the resurrection and ascension of Jesus.

After Mary's death, many legends grew up around her name, but none of them are trustworthy. Augustine was among the earliest of the church fathers who thought it possible that she had never committed actual sins, though he agreed that she shared the common corruption of humanity. This led eventually to the promulgation by the pope of the dogma of the Immaculate Conception of Mary (A.D. 1854). In 1950 Pope Pius XII declared the dogma of the Assumption of Mary; that is, that Mary's body did not decompose in the grave but was reunited by God to her soul soon after she died. Roman Catholic theologians now openly refer to Mary as the "Co-creator" and the "Co-redemptrix" of the human race. None of these postapostolic developments has any support in Scripture.

MASH (Heb. *mash*). A son of Aram and grandson of Shem (Gen 10:22–23 JB, KJV, MLB, MOF, NASB, NEB, RSV; NIV has Meshech). He is also called Meshech (1 Chron 1:17).

MASHAL (mā'shăl). A village of the tribe of Asher (1 Chron 6:74), assigned to the Gershonite Levites. It is also called "Mishal" (KJV "Misheal"; Josh 19:26; 21:30).

MASKIL, MASCHIL (màs'kĭl, Heb. *maskîl, attentive, intelligent*). A Hebrew word found in the titles of Psalms 32, 42, 44, 45, 52–55, 74, 78, 88, 89, and 142; usually taken to mean an instructive or meditative ode.

MASON (See OCCUPATIONS AND PROFESSIONS)

MASREKAH (măs'rē-kà, Heb. *masrēqâh*, perhaps, *vineyard*). The royal city of Samlah, son of Hadad (Gen 36:31, 36; 1 Chron 1:47).

MASSAH (măs'à, *strife*). The site of the rock in Horeb from which Moses drew water for the rebellious Hebrews (Exod 17:1–17; Deut 6:16; 9:22; 33:8).

MASTER A term used for five Hebrew and seven Greek words in the Bible: (1) *'ādhôn*, "lord, master, ruler," often denoting the master of a servant or slave (Gen 24:9; 39:2); (2) *sar*, "captain, chief, prince, ruler" (1 Chron 15:27); (3) *ba'al*, "husband, owner" (Exod 22:8; Isa 1:3); (4) *'ûr*, "to awake, stir up" (Mal 2:12); (5) *rav*, "elder, great, mighty" (Dan 1:3; Jonah 1:6); (6) *didaskalos*, "teacher" (Matt 8:19; 9:11); (7) *despotēs*, "sovereign master" (1 Tim 6:1); (8) *epistatēs*, "overseer" (Luke 5:5; 8:24); (9) *kathēgētēs*, "guide, leader" (Matt 23:10); (10) *kyrios*, "lord" (1:20, 24); (11) *kybernētēs*, "steersman, shipmaster" (Acts 27:11); (12) *rhabbi*, "teacher" (Matt 26:25, 49).

MATRED (mā'trĕd, Heb. *matredh, expulsion*). The mother of Mehetabel, wife of King Hadar (Gen 36:39, KJV, MLB, MOF, NASB, RSV; Hadad JB, NIV) or Hadad (1 Chron 1:50) of Edom.

MATTAN (măt'ăn, Heb. *mattān, a gift*). **1.** A priest of Baal killed during Jehoiada's purge (2 Kings 11:1–18). **2.** One of the conspirators who cast Jeremiah into a filthy dungeon (Jer 38:1–28).

MATTANIAH (măt'à-nī'à, Heb. *mattanyāhû, gift from the LORD*). **1.** A brother of Jehoiachin's father whom Nebuchadnezzar set up in Jehoiachin's place as king, changing his name to Zedekiah (2 Kings 24:17). **2.** A descendant of Asaph and chief choir leader (Neh 11:17; 12:8) and a watchman over the storehouse (12:25). **3.** A musician whom David appointed (1 Chron 25:4–5, 7, 16). **4.** A Levite (2 Chron 20:14). **5.** A descendant of Asaph and one who helped Hezekiah restore the temple worship (29:13). **6.** Son of Elam who put away his foreign wife (Ezra 10:26). **7.** A son of Zattu who divorced his foreign wife (10:27). **8.** A son of Pahath-Moab who did the same (10:30). **9.** A son of Bani. He also put away his alien wife (10:37). **10.** A grandfather of Hanan (Neh 13:10–13).

MATTENAI (măt'ē-nā'ī, Heb. *mattenay, a gift from the LORD*). **1.** A priest of the Restoration who was among a special class called "heads of the priestly families" (Neh 12:12–19). **2.** Two priests under Ezra who were among the many who put away alien wives (Ezra 10:33, 37).

MATTHEW (Gr. *Maththaios*). Son of Alphaeus (Mark 2:14), a tax collector (*telōnēs*), also called Levi (2:14; Luke 5:27), whom Jesus met at the tax office and called to be one of his disciples (Matt 9:9; Mark 2:14; Luke 5:27).

Matthew's background and talents would be of great value to Jesus. As a tax collector he was skilled at writing and keeping records. He invited his former colleagues to a dinner at his own house (5:29–32) with Jesus as the honored guest. No doubt his purpose was to win these men to Christ. Apart from the mention of Matthew in the lists of the apostles (Matt 10:3; Mark 3:18; Acts 1:13), no further notices of him are found in the NT.

MATTHEW, GOSPEL OF Matthew is by far the most often quoted Gospel in the Christian literature before A.D. 180. The church, from the early second century until the rise of modern critical studies, unanimously ascribed it to Matthew. Matthew's occupation as a tax collector qualified him to be the official recorder of the words and works of Jesus. There is a good historical tradition that Matthew actually wrote Gospel material. This comes from Papias of Hierapolis as quoted by the church historian Eusebius.

We do not know precisely when Matthew was written. Its dependence on Mark and its failure to mention the destruction of Jerusalem (especially in connection with Jesus' prediction of that event in ch. 24) suggest a date shortly before A.D. 70. Antioch is the most likely place of origin. Early in the second century Ignatius of that city refers to Matthew as "the Gospel." Also, the Gentile-Jewish character of the Antioch church accords well with the contents of the book.

Characteristics: 1. Matthew is the teaching Gospel par excellence. **2.** Matthew is the Gospel of the church, the only Gospel to use the word "church" at all (Matt 16:18; 18:17). **3.** Matthew is the Gospel of fulfillment, showing that Christianity is the fulfillment of the OT revelation. **4.** Matthew is the Gospel of the King. The genealogy of chapter 1 traces Jesus' lineage back to David: at his birth the Magi come asking, "Where is the one who has been born king of the Jews?" (2:2); eight times the regal title "Son of David" is ascribed to Christ (1:1; 9:27; 12:23; 15:22; 20:30–31; 21:9, 15); the Triumphal Entry clearly has kingly significance (21:1–11); in the Olivet Discourse Jesus prophesied his future kingly reign (25:31); to Pilate's question "Are you the king of the Jews?" Jesus gave the tacit assent, "Yes, it is as you say" (27:11); and over the cross were written these words: "This is Jesus the king of the Jews" (27:37). The climax comes at the very end of the Gospel, where Jesus in the Great Commission declared: "All authority in heaven and on earth has been given to me" (28:18).

The whole of the Gospel is woven around five great discourses: (Matt 5–7; 10; 13; 18; 24–25), each of which concludes with the refrain, "And it came to pass when Jesus ended these sayings . . . . ''

Outline:
    1. Prologue: The birth of the King (1–2).
    2. Narrative: The preparation of the King (3–4).
    3. First discourse: The law of the kingdom (5–7).
    4. Narrative: The power of the King (8–9).

Cross section of an Assyrian officer's tent where a meal and couch are being prepared for him. In the adjoining tent a butcher prepares a carcass. Relief from Nineveh. Courtesy Bildarchiv Foto, Marburg

5. Second discourse: The proclamation of the kingdom (10).
6. Narrative: The rejection of the King (11–12).
7. Third discourse: The growth of the kingdom (13).
8. Narrative: The mission of the King (14–17).
9. Fourth discourse: The fellowship of the kingdom (18).
10. Narrative: The King goes to Jerusalem (19–23).
11. Fifth discourse: The consummation of the kingdom (24–25).
12. Narrative: The death and resurrection of the King (26:1–28:15).
13. Epilogue: The great challenge of the Kingdom (28:16–20).

MATTHIAS (mă-thī′ăs, Gr. *Matthias* or *Maththias, gift of the LORD*). The one chosen by lot after the death of Judas Iscariot to take his place among the 12 apostles (Acts 1:15–26).

MATTITHIAH (măt′ĭ-thī′à, Heb. *mattithyâh, gift of the LORD*). **1.** A Korahite Levite put in charge of the baked offerings of the temple after the Exile (1 Chron 9:31). **2.** A Levite appointed by David to minister before the ark in music and thanksgiving (15:18, 21; 16:5; 25:3, 21). **3.** One of the sons of Nebo who after the Exile put away his Gentile wife (Ezra 10:43). **4.** One who stood at Ezra's right

hand as he read the Law to the people (Neh 8:4). Possibly same as no. 1.

MATTOCK (Heb. *mahărēshâh* in 1 Sam 13:20–21; *herob* in 2 Chron 34:6 RV mg; *ma′dēr* in Isa 7:25). A single-headed pickax with a point on one side and a broad edge on the other for digging and cutting.

MAUL (Heb. *mēphîts, a breaker*). Originally a hammer such as used by coppersmiths. Today it refers to any smashing weapon like those carried by shepherds (Prov 25:18 KJV; NIV "club").

MEADOW (Heb. *′āhû* in Gen 41:2, 18; *ma′arēh* in Judg 20:33). A place where reeds grow; a portion of land without trees.

MEAL (Heb. *qemah* in Gen 18:6; *sōleth* in Lev 2:1; Gr. *aleuron* in Matt 13:33). The ground grain used for both food and sacrificial offerings. It typified Christ in his perfect humanity. It has a remote figurative use in such passages as Isaiah 47:2 and Hosea 8:7. NIV generally reads "flour."

MEAL OFFERING (See SACRIFICE AND OFFERINGS)

MEALS In Bible times, the first meal of the day could be served at any time from early morning until noon (Prov 31:15; John 21:12, 15). The noon meal came after the work of the morning was completed (Mark 7:4) or when the noonday heat made work too difficult (Ruth 2:14). The evening meal was usually the principal meal of the Hebrews (3:7), whereas the Egyptians served their main meal at noon (Gen 43:16). Jesus fed the multitudes at the end of the day (Matt 14:15; Mark 6:35; Luke 9:12).

The food of the Eastern peoples generally may be classified into four groups: grains, vegetables, fruits, and animal foods. Grain was often picked in the field, rubbed in the hands to separate it from the chaff, and eaten raw (Luke 6:1). Sometimes it was crushed with mortar and pestle and made into a porridge or cakes (Num 11:8; Prov 27:22), usually by women (Matt 24:41) or by servants (Exod 11:5; Judg 16:21).

Fruits grew in great abundance in Palestine and consisted of grapes, figs, olives, mulberries, pomegranates, oranges, lemons, melons, dates, almonds, and walnuts. Grapes were eaten as fresh food and dried as raisins. They were the chief source of the wines, which were used both sweet and fermented. Olives were eaten as food as well as used to make olive oil. There were two kinds of figs, early (Isa 28:4) and late (Jer 8:13). The late figs were dried and pressed into cakes. Dates were used both raw and dried.

The bulk of the meat came from sheep, lambs, kids, and fatted calves. Pork was eaten, but not by the Hebrews. Some eggs were used for food (Isa 10:14). Locusts and fish were also eaten. The Hebrews used milk from cattle and goats for drinking. From this they made cheese and butter.

Knives, forks, and spoons were not used in eating. The hands were usually washed and a prayer was offered before the meal. Meat was cooked and placed with its gravy in a large dish on the table. The contents were taken either with the fingers or placed on bread and carried to the mouth. The Egyptians sat at a small round table for their meals. The early Hebrews sat, knelt, or squatted as they ate, but later they evidently reclined at meals. Three generally lay on one couch, thus the head of one was on the bosom of another (John 13:23–25). They reclined at the three sides of a rectangular table leaving the fourth side free for the servants to use in serving.

Food was cooked in a variety of ways over a fire made from charcoal (Prov 26:21), sticks (1 Kings 17:10), thorns (Isa 33:12), or grass (Luke 12:28).

MEASURES (See WEIGHTS AND MEASURES)

MEAT (See FOOD)

MEAT OFFERING (See SACRIFICE AND OFFERINGS)

MEBUNNAI (mē-bŭn'ī, Heb. *mevunnay, well-built*). One of David's bodyguards (2 Sam 23:27) who killed a Philistine giant (21:18, Sibbecai).

MECHERATHITE (See MEKERATHITE)

MEDAD (mē'dăd, Heb. *mēdhādh, affectionate*). One of the 70 elders appointed to assist Moses in the government of the people (Num 11:24–30). He, together with Eldad, empowered by the Spirit, remained in the camp and prophesied. Joshua attempted to hinder them, but they were defended by Moses.

MEDEBA (mĕd'ē-bà, Heb. *mêdhevā', uncertain*). A city lying high in the grazing section of Moab east of the Jordan (Num 21:30), assigned to the tribe of Reuben (Josh 13:9). The city was constantly changing hands (1 Chron 19:7; Isa 15:2).

MEDES, MEDIA (mēdz, mē'dĭ-à, Heb. *mādhî, mādhay*). The inhabitants of the land of Media, west and south of the Caspian Sea. The people of Media were warlike and skilled in their use of the bow; for a long period they were a strong power. The Scriptures refer to their cities (2 Kings 17:6; 18:11), the binding character of their laws (Esth 1:19), their power against Babylon (Isa 13:17; Dan 5:28), and their representatives in Jerusalem at the time of Pentecost (Acts 2:9).

MEDIATOR (Gr. *mesitēs, a middle man*). One who brings about friendly relations between two or more estranged people. He corresponds to the "umpire" ("daysman" KJV) of Job 9:33. The NT uses *mesitēs* twice in connection with Moses as the mediator of the law (Gal 3:19–20) and four times regarding Jesus (1 Tim 2:5; Heb 8:6; 9:15; 12:24).

In the Old Testament, Jonathan was intercessor for David before Saul (1 Sam 19:4). Abraham made intercession on behalf of Abimelech (Gen 20) and Sodom (18:23–33). Moses was mediator on behalf of Pharaoh (Exod 8:8–13; 9:28–33) and for Israel (33:12–17). Samuel was middleman when Israel was given a king (1 Sam 9:15–27) and when she became wicked (12:19).

Angels acted as media through whom God's will was made known to man (Gen 22:15; 24:40; 32:1; Judg 6:11). At times God appeared in human form (Gen 12:7;

Relief (cf. 521–465 B.C.) on stairway from Persepolis, that shows the head of a Mede. He wears a high rounded cap with neck flap, and earring that protrudes from elaborately curled hair and beard. Courtesy Oriental Institute, University of Chicago

17:1; 35:7, 9; Dan 8:17). In some cases the "angel of the Lord" seems to have been a manifestation of God, perhaps a temporary appearance of Messiah (Gen 16:7–13). Later, the priestly class acted as mediators between man and God (Lev 1–7).

MEDITERRANEAN SEA Because this body of water was the largest known to the Hebrews, it became known as *The Sea* (Deut 11:24; 34:2; Josh 1:4). It was known also as the Sea of the Philistines (Exod 23:31).

MEEKNESS (Heb. *'ănāwâh, suffering,* Gr. *praütēs*). The meek (oppressed) are assured of divine help and ultimate victory (Pss 22:26; 25:9; 37:11). Jesus was sent to minister to them (45:4; Isa 11:4; 29:19; Zeph 2:3). Meekness is a fruit of the Spirit (Gal 5:23) and characteristic of Jesus (Matt 11:29; 2 Cor 10:1). Believers are commanded to be meek and to show a lowly spirit to one another (Eph 4:2; Col 3:12; Titus 3:2) and to unbelievers (1 Peter 3:15). A teacher should be meek (2 Tim 2:25). Meekness is a mark of true

discipleship and does not imply a weak or vacillating nature.

MEGIDDO, MEGIDDON (mĕ-gĭd′ō, Heb. *meghiddô, meghiddôn*). A city situated on the Great Road, which linked Gaza and Damascus. It controlled the principal pass through the Carmel Range, connecting the coastal plain and the Plain of Esdraelon. The road was the channel for the flow of peaceful commerce and also the route by which the armies of antiquity marched. Megiddo was in the territory of Manasseh (Josh 12:21; 17:11; Judg 1:27).

Israelite forces under Deborah and Barak annihilated the army of Sisera in a battle by Megiddo (Judg 5:19). Ahaziah died there (2 Kings 9:27). In the Plain of Megiddo, Josiah was hit by Egyptian archers and soon died (23:29–30; 2 Chron 35:20–27). Armageddon, the last great battle, will occur at the "hill of Megiddo" (Rev 16:16). (See p. 374.)

MEHETABEL (mĕ-hĕt′à-bĕl, *God benefits*). 1. A daughter of Matred. She was wife of King Hadad (Gen 36:39). 2. One who sought to betray Nehemiah (Neh 6:10–13).

MEKERATHITE (mē-kē′răth-īt, Heb. *mekhērāthî, dweller in Mekarah*). A description of Hepher, one of David's mighty men (1 Chron 11:36). Perhaps the name should read Maacathite (2 Sam 23:34).

MELCHI (See MELKI)

MELCHIAH (See MALKIJAH)

MELCHI-SHUA (See MALKI-SHUA)

MELCHIZEDEK, MELCHISEDEK (mĕl-kĭz′ĕ-dĕk, Heb. *malkî-tsedhek, king of righteousness*). A priest and king of Salem, a city identified with Jerusalem.

Melchizedek went out to meet Abram after his return from the slaughter of Kedorlaomer and the kings who were with him. He presented Abram with bread and wine and blessed him in the name of "God Most High, Creator of heaven and earth." Abram gave him "a tenth of everything." The Hebrew word for God in this instance is the same as in such phrases as "God Almighty" (Gen 17:1), "the Eternal God" (21:33), and "God of Bethel" (35:7) and is the oldest Semitic designation for God. Melchizedek was thus a monotheist and worshiped essentially the same God as Abram, who recognized him as a priest.

He appears next in Psalm 110:4: "You are a priest forever, in the order of Melchizedek." This psalm is of special interest because Jesus referred to it (Matt

22:44; Mark 12:35–36; Luke 20:41–42), and it is regarded as one of the messianic psalms. The ideal ruler of the Hebrew nation would be one who combined in his person the role of both priest and king. The author of the Letter to the Hebrews uses Melchizedek (Heb 5–7) in his great argument showing Jesus Christ as the final and perfect revelation of God. The ideal priest must belong to "the order of Melchizedek," and Christ was the fulfillment of this prophecy, for he came out of Judah, a tribe with no connection to the Levitical priesthood.

MELICU (See MALLUCH)

MELITA (See MALTA)

MELKI (mĕl'kī, Gr. *Melchi*). The name of two ancestors of Jesus through Mary, according to Luke's genealogy: **1.** The son of Addi and the father of Neri (Luke 3:28). **2.** The son of Janna and the father of Levi, fourth from Mary (3:24).

MELON (See PLANTS)

MEMBER (Heb. *yātsur*, Gr. *melos*). A word usually denoting any feature or part of the body (Job 17:7; James 3:5 KJV, MOF, NEB, RSV), "the members" meaning

"the body" (Ps 139:16). The word is used for members of the body of Christ (1 Cor 6:15; 12:12–27; Eph 4:25; 5:30).

MEMPHIS (mĕm'fĭs, Heb. *nōph, mōph,* Copt. *menphe, memphi,* Gr. *Memphis*). The first capital of united Egypt (c. 3200 B.C.), situated on the west bank of the Nile, about 20 miles (33 km.) south of modern Cairo. Hosea foretold a return of Israelites to Egypt and refers to Memphis (Hos 9:6). After the murder of Gedaliah, a number of Jews fled from Palestine to Egypt (cf. Jer 41:16–18), and Memphis is mentioned as a place of their residence (44:1). Both Isaiah and Jeremiah had seen the results of an Egyptian-Judean alliance and refer to Memphis (Isa 19:13; Jer 2:16). Jeremiah prophesied that Memphis would become a ruin (cf. 46:14, 19; cf. Ezek 30:13, 16).

MENAHEM (mĕn'à-hĕm, Heb. *menahēm, comforted*). Son of Gadi and king of Israel (2 Kings 15:13–22). His evil reign of ten years began by his killing his predecessor Shallum.

MENAN (See MENNA)

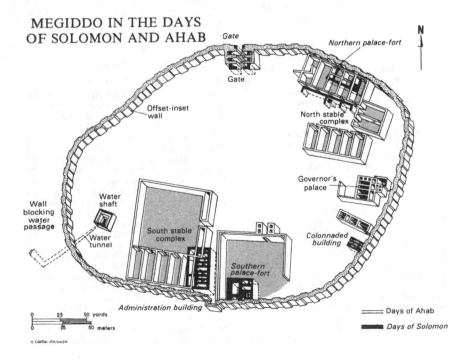

MEGIDDO IN THE DAYS OF SOLOMON AND AHAB

N

Gate
Gate
Northern palace-fort
Offset-inset wall
North stable complex
Governor's palace
Wall blocking water passage
Water shaft
Water tunnel
South stable complex
Southern palace-fort
Colonnaded building
Administration building

0 25 50 yards
0 25 50 meters

═══ Days of Ahab
▬▬▬ Days of Solomon

© Carta, JERUSALEM

The famous alabaster sphinx. "The word . . . concerning all the Jews . . . in . . . Memphis . . ." (Jer 44:1). This is what they could see every day. Courtesy Seffie Ben-Yoseph

MENE, MENE, TEKEL, PARSIN (mē'nē, mē'nē, tē'kĕl, ū-pàr'sĭn). Four Aramaic words that suddenly appeared on the wall of Belshazzar's banquet hall (Dan 5:1). The words seem to refer to three weights in common use: the "mina," the "shekel," and the "half-mina." Or they may be terms used in Mesopotamian counting houses: "numbered, numbered, weighed, and divisions." *Upharsin* (KJV, MLB, NASB, NEB; *parsin* NIV, RSV) in the inscription (Dan 5:25) is *peres* in the interpretation (5:28). The *u* is the connecting participle "and"; *pharsin* is the plural of *peres*, a word that naturally suggests the Persians. Daniel interpreted the message as "God had numbered" the days of the kingdom; the king had "been weighed on the scales and found wanting"; his "kingdom is divided and given to the Medes and Persians." There was not much time between interpretation and fulfillment, for "that very night Belshazzar, king of the Babylonians, was slain."

MEPHIBOSHETH (mē-fĭb'ō-shĕth, Heb. *mephîvōsheth*). **1.** A son of King Saul and his concubine Rizpah. Together with his brother and other men, Mephibosheth was delivered to the Gibeonites to be hanged, with David's consent (2 Sam 21:8). **2.** A son of Jonathan and grandson of Saul. His name also appears as Merib-Baal (1 Chron 8:34; 9:40). After the disaster at Mt. Gilboa (2 Sam 1:4; 1 Chron 10:1–8), Mephibosheth as a child of five was carried by his nurse east of the Jordan (2 Sam 9:4). On David's accession to the throne, Mephibosheth was called back to Jerusalem, given his father's inheritance, and allowed to eat at the king's table for the rest of his life. Ziba represented Mephibosheth as a traitor (16:1–4), but David received him in a friendly manner (19:24–30).

MERAB (mē'răb, Heb. *mĕrav*, perhaps *increase*). The older daughter of King Saul. Saul sought to have David killed by the Philistines and so promised him Merab as wife if he would fight valiantly; however, he then gave Merab to another man.

MERAIOTH (mē-rā'yŏth, Heb. *merā-yôth, rebellious*). **1.** A high priest of Israel (1 Chron 6:6–7). **2.** Another in the priestly line and ancestor of the great Hilkiah (9:11). **3.** Ancestor of Helkai (Neh 12:15 KJV, MLB, MOF, NASB, NEB, RSV). The NIV has "Meremoth" (as in Neh 12:3).

MERARI (mē-ra'rī, Heb. *merārî, bitter*). The youngest son of Levi. The Merarites had the responsibility for the wood framing of the tabernacle in its journeys (Num 3:17, 33–37). Later they had 12 cities in Reuben, Gad, and Zebulun (Josh 21:7, 34–40).

MERCURY, MERCURIUS (See HERMES)

MERCY (Heb. *hesedh, kindness; raham, bowels; hānan, gracious; Gr. eleos, kindness; oiktirmos, compassion*). **1.** Forbearance from inflicting punishment on an adversary or a lawbreaker. **2.** The compassion that causes one to help the weak, the sick, or the poor—a cardinal virtue of a true Christian (James 2:1–13) and a "fruit of the Spirit" (Gal 5:22–23). God's mercy was shown in giving his beloved Son to die in the place of sinful man; Christ's mercy enabled him to willingly make the awful sacrifice (Rom 5:8). The Hebrew word *raham* is the most emotional of the terms used to describe the Lord's love for his people (Ps 103:13), rightly meriting the translation "compassion."

MERCY SEAT (See TABERNACLE)

MEREMOTH (mĕr'ē-mŏth, Heb. *merē-môth, elevations*). **1.** A priest who returned from Babylon with Zerubbabel (Neh 12:3). **2.** One who returned with Ezra and weighed silver and gold (Ezra

8:33). He helped Nehemiah to rebuild the wall (Neh 3:4, 21). (This may possibly be two persons.) **3.** One who had taken a foreign wife (Ezra 10:36). **4.** A priest who signed the covenant with Nehemiah (Neh 10:5).

MERIBAH (mĕr'ĭ-bà, Heb. *merîbâh, contention*). **1.** A place near and to the NW of Sinai where Moses, at the Lord's command, struck the rock and water gushed out for the refreshment of the people (Exod 17:1–7). Moses named the place "Massah," i.e., "tempting," and "Meribah," because of the quarreling of the children of Israel and because they tempted the Lord. **2.** A place near Kadesh Barnea where the people again thirsted and where the Lord commanded Moses to speak to the rock, but instead Moses struck it (Num 20:1–13). As a result of his disobedience, he was forbidden to enter the Promised Land.

MERIBAH KADESH (See MERIBAH)

MERODACH (See MARDUK)

MERODACH-BALADAN (mĕ-rō'dăk-băl'à-dän, *Marduk has given a son*). A king of Babylon (2 Kings 20:12) who was by far the most successful rebel against the then dominant power of Assyria. He sent a special delegation to Hezekiah (Isa 39) to encourage diversionary rebellions in western Palestine. Isaiah's prophecy prevented Hezekiah's revolt.

MEROM (mĕ'rŏm, Heb. *mĕrôm, a high place*). A district near the headwaters of the Jordan River. Its only mention in Scripture is (Josh 11:5, 7) as the site of the great battle of Joshua's northern campaign in which he defeated Jabin king of Hazor and his Canaanite allies. The men of the tribe of Dan (Judg 18) passed through this region and described it as "very good" and said that "the land is large."

MERONOTHITE (mĕ-rŏn'à-thīt). An inhabitant of Meronoth, a region in Galilee that was given to the tribe of Naphtali. Its principal town was Shimron Meron, which Joshua conquered (Josh 11:1; 12:20). For two Meronothites see 1 Chronicles 27:30; Nehemiah 3:7.

MEROZ (mĕ'roz, Heb. *mĕrôz*). A place in Galilee not far from Nazareth. It is infamous because its inhabitants "did not come to help the Lord" when Deborah and Barak needed help against Jabin, king of Canaan. Judges 5:23 attributes its being cursed to the angel of the Lord.

MESECH (See MESHECH)

Below the emblems of four deities of Babylonia, Merodach-Baladan investing an official with a grant of patronage and land. Black marble, seventh century B.C. Courtesy Bildarchiv Foto, Marburg

MESHA (mĕ'shà, Heb. *mēshā', mē-shā'*). **1.** A place in southern Arabia (Gen 10:30). **2.** A Benjamite (1 Chron 8:9). Nos. 1 and 2 seem to have the root meaning "retreat," whereas nos. 3 and 4 are spelled differently in Hebrew and mean "welfare." **3.** A descendant of Judah through Perez, Hezron, and Caleb (2:42). **4.** A king of Moab (2 Kings 3:4). When he rebelled against Ahaziah, Jehoram,, with the help of Jehoshaphat of Judah, attacked and defeated him (3:4–27). Mesha in desperation sacrificed his own son.

MESHACH (mĕ'shăk, Heb. *mēshakh*). A pagan name given to Mishael, one of the four princes of Judah taken by Nebuchadnezzar to be trained in his palace as counselors to the king. These four had Hebrew names containing the syllable "el" for "God" or "iah" for "the LORD," but the names were changed to honor gods of Babylon (Dan 1:3–7).

MESHECH (mĕ'shĕk, Heb. *meshekh, tall*). **1.** A son of Japheth (Gen 10:2) associated with Magog and Tubal and thought by many to have been progenitors of Russians and other Slavic peoples. **2.** A grandson of Shem (1 Chron 1:17); called Mash in Genesis 10:23 (except NIV). **3.** The people descended from the preceding, noted for their trade with Tyre in slaves and bronze (Ezek 27:13), and mentioned in prophecy (Ezek 38–39). **4.** A tribe mentioned in Psalm 120:5 with (or probably contrasted with) the tents of Kedar. Probably the same as no. 3 above.

MESHELEMIAH (mē-shĕl′ē-mī′à). Father of Zechariah, leading gatekeeper of the tent of meeting. He had seven sons (1 Chron 9:21; 26:1–2, 9). This man is also called "Shelemiah" (26:14).

MESHEZABEL (mē-shĕz′à-bēl, *God delivers*). **1.** Ancestor of Meshullam (Neh 3:4). **2.** A covenanter with Nehemiah (10:21). **3.** A descendant of Judah through Zerah (11:24).

MESHILLEMITH, MESHILLEMOTH (mē-shĭl′ē-mĭth, mē-shĭl′ē-mŏth, *recompense*). **1.** Father of Berekiah (2 Chron 28:12). **2.** Priestly ancestor of Amashsai (Neh 11:13). Meshillemith (1 Chron 9:12) is another spelling of the same name.

MESHULLAM (mē-shŭl′ăm, Heb. *meshullām, reconciled*). **1.** A grandfather of Shaphan, trusted scribe of King Josiah (2 Kings 22:3). **2.** A son of Zerubbabel in the Jewish royal family (1 Chron 3:19). **3.** A leading Gadite in the days of Jeroboam II (5:13). **4.** A chief Benjamite in Jerusalem (8:17). **5.** The father of Sallu, a Benjamite of Jerusalem after the Captivity (9:7). **6.** Another Benjamite of Jerusalem (9:8). **7.** A priest in the high-priestly lines (9:11; Neh 11:11). **8.** An ancestor of another priest (1 Chron 9:12). **9.** A Kohathite, overseer of repairing the temple in the days of Josiah (2 Chron 34:12). **10.** A chief man who returned with Ezra in 457 B.C. (Ezra 8:16). **11.** One appointed by Ezra in the matter of doing away with foreign marriages (10:15). **12.** One of the offenders in this matter (10:29). **13.** One who rebuilt two portions of the wall but was connected by marriage with Tobiah, who hindered the rebuilding (Neh 3:4, 30; 6:18). **14.** Another repairer (3:6). **15.** One who stood with Ezra in the revival (8:4). **16.** A priest who signed the covenant with Nehemiah (10:7). **17.** Another covenanter (10:20). **18.** A man of Benjamin (11:7). **19.** A priest c. 470 B.C. (12:13). **20.** Possibly the same man as no. 19 (12:33). **21.** Another priest c. 470 B.C. (12:16). **22.** A Levite gatekeeper at the same time (12:25).

MESOPOTAMIA (mĕs′ō-pō-tā′mĭ-à, from Gr. *mesos, middle*, and *potamos,*

river). The name applied in particular to the area between the Tigris and Euphrates rivers, a region that in Hebrew is called Aram, Aram Naharaim, or Paddan Aram—practically coextensive with modern Iraq. There are indications of the latter usage in the NT, such as Acts 7:2 and possibly Acts 2:9. Balaam came from Pethor "in Aram Naharaim" (Deut 23:4; cf. Num 22:5). In Judges 3:8, 10 the oppressor of the Israelites, Cushan-Rishathaim, is called "king of Aram Naharaim."

Aram (Gen 10:22–23; 1 Chron 1:17) was the progenitor of the Arameans, or Syrians. Bethuel and Laban are called Arameans in NIV, Syrians in KJV (Gen 25:20; 31:20), and even Jacob is referred to as "a wandering Aramean" (Deut 26:5) from his stay in Paddan Aram (which the LXX gives as Mesopotamia or Mesopotamia-Syria).

Mesopotamia is one of the regions from which the Jews of the Diaspora had come to Jerusalem (Acts 2:9). Stephen recalls the fact that the call of God came to Abraham while he was in Mesopotamia (7:2), in the city of Ur (Gen 11:31). The southern part of Mesopotamia, including Ur and a number of other city-states, was known as Sumer; the central section was called Akkad and later was named Babylonia, after the city of Babylon gained the ascendancy; the northern division along the Tigris was Assyria, the land of Asshur.

MESSIAH A word that represents the Hebrew *māshîah*, the Aramaic *meshîhā'*, and the Greek *Messias*. "Messias" (John 1:41, 4:25 KJV) is a transcription of the Greek word. The basic meaning of the word is "anointed one." "Christ" is the English form of the Greek *Christos*, which means "anointed." The Septuagint uses *Christos* 40 times to translate the Hebrew *māshîah*. In ancient Israel both persons and things consecrated to sacred purposes were anointed by having oil poured over them. In the OT the primary significance of the expression "the Lord's anointed" refers to the earthly king who is reigning over the Lord's people. The Israelites did not think of crowning a king but of anointing him when he was enthroned. The fact that he was anointed was the essential characteristic of the ruler.

Isaiah uses the term only of Cyrus (Isa 45:1). Later the expression "Son of David" was a synonym for "Messiah" (Matt 21:9; Mark 10:47–48). Except for

Daniel 9:25–26 the title "Messiah" as a reference to Israel's eschatological king does not occur in the OT. It appears in this sense later in the NT and in the literature of Judaism. In the NT the Messiah is "the Christ," the Greek equivalent of the Hebrew *māshîah*.

Closely related to the eschatological character of the Messiah is his political significance. He will destroy the world powers in an act of judgment, deliver Israel from her enemies, and restore her as a nation. The Messiah is the king of this future kingdom to whose political and religious domination the other nations will yield. His mission is the redemption of Israel and his dominion is universal. This is the clear picture of the Messiah in practically all of the OT passages that refer to him. The Messiah will put an end to war, for he is the Prince of Peace, and he will rule righteously over his people. He himself is righteous and is called the righteous Messiah or the Messiah of righteousness (Jer 23:6). Through the Messiah the kingdom of the end time will be established, the kingdom of God on earth, the restoration of Israel. As the Messiah was present from the first in the creation so he is also present as the central figure of the last events. He is declared to be the firstborn of creation and also the end and goal of creation (John 1:1; Col 1:15–17; Rev 3:14).

The essential features of the OT picture of the Messiah are in the person of Jesus. The suffering, dying, and glorified Servant of the Lord of the OT is that same NT Son of Man who will return on the clouds of heaven. The Messiah, as the Son of Man, will suffer, die, and rise again on the third day, "according to the Scriptures." But even though Jesus was victorious over death in his resurrection and ascension, he did not yet reign in his full messiahship in his righteous kingdom. His ultimate victory is revealed to be in the future, and consequently he must come again in power to establish his messianic throne and kingdom.

The Messiah as the Son of Man is a preexistent heavenly being. Long before Abraham, Jesus said, the Son of Man *was* (John 8:58; cf. 17:5; Col 1:17). The origin of creation is linked with the Messiah Jesus in various Scriptures (1 Cor 8:6; 2 Cor 8:9; Col 1:15–17). It is also as preexistent that Jesus is called "elect" (1 Peter 2:6; NIV "chosen"). The Messiah is the Son of Man in a unique sense (John 1:1; Rom 1:4). Jesus was asked to declare if he was "the Messiah, the Son of God" (Matt 26:63–64; Mark 14:61; Luke 22:67–70), and his claim is clear.

METALS (See MINERALS)

METHUSELAH (mē-thū'zĕ-là, Heb. *methûshelah, man of the javelin*). A descendant of Seth before the Flood. He died at 969 years of age, in the very year of the Flood (Gen 5:22–27). He was the son of Enoch and the father of Lamech (5:21, 25).

MEUNIM, MEUNITES (mē-ū'nĭm, mē-ū'nīts, Heb. *me'ûnîm, the people of Maon*). The people of an Arab city still existing south of the Dead Sea not far from the more famous Petra. They are listed among the tribes that Uzziah of Judah conquered. Ezra 2:50, repeated in Nehemiah 7:52, speaks of their descendants. The Masoretes say that the word rendered by some versions as "habitations" (1 Chron 4:41) should read "Meunim." Ezra counts them among the Nethinim (temple servants) at the return from exile (Ezra 2:50, KJV Mehunim; in 2 Chron 26:7, KJV Mehunims).

MIAMIN (See MIJAMIN)

MIBSAM (mĭb'săm, Heb. *mivsām, sweet odor*, related to *balsam*). 1. One of the 12 Ishmaelite patriarchs, corresponding to the 12 sons of Jacob (Gen 25:13). 2. A grandson or great-grandson of Simeon (1 Chron 4:25).

MICA, MICHA (mī'kà, Heb. *mîkhā'*, evidently, like Micah, an abbrev. of Micaiah, *Who is like Jehovah?*). 1. A grandson of Jonathan (2 Sam 9:12). 2. A Levite covenanter (Neh 10:11). 3. Another Levite (11:17). 4. Another Levite (1 Chron 9:15; Neh 11:22).

MICAH (mī'kà, Heb. *mîkkâh*). Short form of the name *Micaiah* (or Michael), meaning "Who is like God?" 1. An Ephraimite (Judg 17–18). 2. A Reubenite (1 Chron 5:5). 3. A grandson of Jonathan (8:34; 9:40). 4. A Levite (23:20). 5. The father of Abdon (2 Chron 34:20); called "Acbor son of Micaiah" in 2 Kings 22:12. 6. The canonical prophet Micah from Moresheth (Mic 1:1; Jer 26:18).

MICAH, BOOK OF The fifth of the Minor Prophets, dating from the late 700s B.C. The book predicts the fall of Samaria, which occurred in 722, but concerns more especially the sins and dangers of Jerusalem in the days of Hezekiah around 700. As the following outline shows, the message varies between condemnation for the present sins and God's purpose of ultimate blessing for his people:

I. Predicted Desolation of Samaria and Jerusalem (1:1–3:12)

II. Eventual Blessings for Zion (4:1–8)

III. Invasion and Deliverance by Davidic Ruler (4:9–5:15)

IV. Condemnations for Sins (6:1–7:6)

V. Eventual Help From God (7:7–20)

In the opening portion of the book (1:1–3:12), God's judgment is first announced on Samaria for her idolatry. Micah's interest seems to lie chiefly in Jerusalem, however, whose desolation is announced in 3:12 in very similar terms. Chapters 2 and 3 are a catalogue of Judah's sins. Oppression of the poor was one characteristic, but another was the refusal to hear God's prophets. As in Jeremiah's day, they preferred prophets who predicted peace (cf. 3:5 with Jer 8:10–11; Ezek 13:10). It is not improbable that Jeremiah and Ezekiel took their texts on this subject from Micah. At least Micah's warnings of 3:12 were well known in Jeremiah's day (Jer 26:18).

The second section (4:1–8) includes a passage that is practically identical with Isaiah 2:1–4. Isaiah 2:1 calls this passage the word of Isaiah. Micah evidently uses Isaiah's promise and skillfully weaves it into his own composition.

The third section (4:9–5:15) comes against the background of the wars of Hezekiah's day. The Assyrians carried captive 40 cities of Judah and received tribute from Hezekiah (cf. 2 Kings 18:13–16).

The condemnations of the fourth section (6:1–7:6) include several references to the Pentateuch and other historical books (6:4–5, 16; cf. also 5:6 with Gen 10:8–9). The response of Micah 6:8 is famous. Some have argued that it teaches salvation apart from sacrifice. Actually, it alludes to Deuteronomy 10:12 and involves Israel's duty to obey *all* the Mosaic injunctions. Christ probably refers to this verse in his condemnation of the formalistic Pharisees (Matt 23:23). The book closes with the prophet's declaration of faith in the ultimate fulfillment of God's covenant of blessing for Abraham.

MICAIAH (mī-kā'yà, Heb. *mîkhāyāhû, Who is like Jehovah?*). 1. A true prophet of God, residing at Samaria, the capital of the northern tribes of Israel c. 900 B.C., who predicted the death of Ahab (1 Kings 22:8; 2 Chron 18). 2. Father of Acbor (2 Kings 22:12–14; "Abdon son of Micah," 2 Chron 34:20). 3. A daughter of Uriel (13:2, JB, KJV, MLB, NASB, RSV; Maacah NEB, NIV). She was the wife of

King Rehoboam (Maacah in 1 Kings 15:2). 4. A prince of Judah whom Jehoshaphat sent to teach the people (2 Chron 17:7). 5. An ancestor of a priest in Nehemiah's time (Neh 12:35). 6. A priest in Nehemiah's time (12:41). 7. Grandson of Shaphan the scribe (Jer 36:11–13).

MICHA (See MICA, MICHA)

MICHAEL (mī'kĕl, Heb. *mîkhā'ēl, Who is like God?*). 1. Father of Sethur, a spy from the tribe of Asher (Num 13:13). 2. Two Gadites who lived in Bashan (1 Chron 5:13–14). 3. A Gershonite of the eleventh generation, great-grandfather of Asaph, the singer (6:40). 4. A chief man of Issachar (7:3). 5. A Benjamite (8:16). 6. A captain of Manasseh who joined David in Ziklag (12:20). 7. The father of Omri of Issachar, one of David's mighty men (27:18). 8. A prince of Judah, son of Jehoshaphat and brother of Jehoram, kings of Judah (2 Chron 21:2). 9. Father of Zebadiah, a chief Jew who returned with Ezra (Ezra 8:8). 10. The archangel whose chief responsibility seems to have been the care of the Jewish people (Dan 12:1). Michael had a dispute with Satan himself (Jude 9).

MICHAIAH (See MICAIAH)

MICHAL (mī'kăl, Heb. *mîkhāl,* a contraction of *mîkhā'ēl, Michael*). The younger daughter of King Saul (1 Sam 14:49). Saul offered David his elder daughter Merab for his service against the Philistines, but changed his mind and gave her to another; then he learned that Michal loved David, so he offered her to David if he would give evidence of having killed 100 Philistines. David killed 200 and married Michal; but Saul hated him all the more. Once, when Saul sent some men to kill David, Michal helped him to escape (19:11–17). Though Michal truly loved David, she could not understand him, and so mocked him for rejoicing before the Lord (2 Sam 6:16–23). As a result, she never had a child.

MICMASH, MICHMASH (mĭk'măsh, Heb. *mĭk'hmash, a hidden place*). A place in the ancient tribe of Benjamin about 8 miles (13 km.) NE of Jerusalem. A notable battle occurred here between Israel and the Philistines in the reign of Saul (1 Sam 13–14). In the return from the Captivity under Zerubbabel (Ezra 2:27; Neh 7:31) 122 men of this place are mentioned, indicating that it was a fair-sized community at the time.

MIDIAN, MIDIANITES (mĭd'ĭ-ăn, -īts, Heb. *midhyān, midhānîm*). 1. A son of Abraham by Keturah (Gen 25:1–6). 2.

Midian's descendants and the land they claimed, lying mostly east of the Jordan and the Dead Sea, then southward through the Arabah and (in the time of Moses) including the southern and eastern parts of the Sinai peninsula. Traders in a caravan are called "Ishmaelites" (Gen 37:25), then "Midianites" (37:36), the former referring to their descent from Ishmael (25:12–18) and the latter to their abode in the land of Midian. When Moses fled from Egypt 40 years before the Exodus (Exod 2:15–21), he helped the daughters of Reuel (or Jethro) the priest of Midian. He was invited to their encampment, and later married Zipporah, the priest's daughter. Jethro, though priest of Midian, acknowledged the God of Israel as supreme (18:11); but neither he nor his son Hobab, though very friendly to Moses, joined Israel (Num 10:29).

Toward the end of Moses' life, Midian had apparently become confederate with Moab (Num 22:4). Through the counsel of Balaam, the Midianite women and girls caused much harm in Israel, and God commanded Moses to conquer the nation (25:16–18). Later God delivered Israel into the hand of Midian for seven years (Judg 6:1–6). Gideon defeated them and killed their two kings Zebah and Zalmunna (8:21).

Though the Midianites were nomads, they had great wealth in the time of Moses. They had not only 675,000 sheep, 72,000 oxen, and 61,000 donkeys, but also gold, silver, brass, iron, tin, and lead; all of which are mentioned in the booty taken by the men of Israel (Num 31:22, 32–34). The Midianites have long since disappeared from the earth.

MIGDAL EDER (mĭg'dăl ē'dêr). A place between Bethlehem and Hebron where Jacob stayed after Rachel's death and Reuben lay with his father's concubine (NEB, NIV Gen 35:21–22; tower of Edar [Eder] KJV, MLB, NASB, RSV).

MIGDOL (mĭg'dŏl, Heb. *mighdôl*). 1. A place just west of the former shallow bay at the north end of the Gulf of Suez, the westward arm of the Red Sea (Exod 14:2; Num 33:7). 2. A place in northern Egypt where many Jews went in the days of Jeremiah (Jer 44:1–14; 46:14).

MIGRON (mĭg'rŏn, Heb. mighrôn, *precipice*). A locality near Gibeah of Saul about 7 miles (12 km.) NE of Jerusalem, in the tribe of Benjamin. Saul made this place his headquarters for a small troop (1 Sam 14:2). In Isaiah 10:28 the prophet pictures the Assyrians passing Migron as they approached to attack Jerusalem.

MIJAMIN (mĭj'à-mĭn, Heb. *mîyāmîn, from the right hand*). 1. A priest in David's time (1 Chron 24:9). 2. A priest who covenanted with Nehemiah (Neh 10:7). 3. A priest who returned with Zerubbabel from Babylon (12:5). 4. A man who put away his foreign wife (Ezra 10:25).

MIKLOTH (mĭk'lŏth, Heb. *miqlôth, rods*). 1. A Benjamite in Jerusalem after the Exile (1 Chron 8:32; 9:37–38). 2. A ruler of 24,000 men in the time of David (27:4).

MILCAH (mĭl'kà, Heb. *milkâh, counsel*). 1. A daughter of Haran, Abram's youngest brother. She married her uncle Nahor and bore him eight children, of whom one was Bethuel, father of Rebekah and Laban (Gen 11:27–29; 22:20–23; 24:24). 2. One of the five daughters of Zelophehad, the Manassite. They had to marry within their tribe (Num 36).

MILCOM (See MOLECH)

MILDEW A pale fungus growth that discolors and spoils grains and fruits in warm, damp weather. In Scripture it is always associated with "blight" (Deut 28:22; 1 Kings 8:37; Amos 4:9; Hag 2:17). Leviticus contains many laws regarding contamination by mildew in clothing and houses (e.g., Lev 13:47, 55–56; 14:35, 39, 44). It is called leprosy in the KJV.

MILE (See WEIGHTS AND MEASURES)

MILETUS (mĭ-lē'tŭs, Gr. *Milētos*). In KJV once Miletum (2 Tim 4:20), southernmost of the Greek cities of Asia Minor. A silting harbor, the common problem of that coast, ended her sea power and sea-borne commerce. At the time of Paul's visit (Acts 20:15, 17) Miletus was a city of no great standing in the Roman province of Asia.

MILK (See FOOD)

MILL (Heb. *rêheh*, Gr. *mylos, mylōn*). An apparatus used to grind any edible grain—wheat, barley, oats, rye, etc.—into flour. It consists of two circular stones, the lower one having a slightly convex upper surface to help the drifting of the broken grain toward the outer edge from which it drops (Exod 11:5; Num 11:7–8).

It was forbidden to take a millstone in pledge (Deut 24:6). In Jeremiah 25:10 "the sound of millstones" is mentioned as a sign of happy prosperous life, but in Isaiah 47:2 the prophet taunted the proud and delicate women of Babylon with the thought that they would have to become

The ancient harbor at Miletus, now silted up and deserted, with remains of the city's bathhouse and theater in the background. Miletus was visited by Paul on his third missionary journey, and here he said farewell to the Ephesian elders (Acts 20:15–17). Courtesy Dan Bahat

slaves and labor at the mill. When the Philistines blinded Samson (Judg 16:21), he had to grind in the prison, and this mill was probably a large one ordinarily turned by a blinded ox or donkey. Abimelech, usurping "king" of Israel, was killed by a woman who dropped a millstone on his head (9:53). Our Lord prophesied that at his coming "two women will be grinding with a hand mill; one will be taken and the other left" (Matt 24:41). A millstone cast into the sea is a symbol of absolute destruction (Rev 18:21).

MILLENNIUM (See KINGDOM OF GOD)

MILLET (See PLANTS)

MILLO (mĭl'ō, Heb. *millô', fullness*). A mound or rampart built up and filled in with earth and stones to raise the level. **1.** An ancient fortification in or near Shechem (Judg 9:6, 20). **2.** A place just north of Mt. Zion and outside the city of David, though inside Jerusalem from Hezekiah's time onward (2 Sam 5:9). When David had taken Zion (5:7–9), he began to fill up Millo and to build inward toward Zion. Solomon later strengthened Millo (1 Kings 9:15, 24; 11:27), as did Hezekiah, this time against the Assyrians (2 Chron 32:5). The "Beth Millo" where the godly Joash, king of Judah, was killed by his own officials was probably this same fortification (2 Kings 12:20–21).

MINA (See WEIGHTS AND MEASURES)

MIND A word for the Hebrew *lebh*, "heart"; *nephesh*, "soul"; and the Greek *nous* and *dianoia*, the former denoting the faculty of reflective consciousness, of moral thinking and knowing, while the latter means "meditation, reflection." None of these words is used with any precision of meaning. In the NT the word "mind" frequently occurs in an ethical sense (e.g., Rom 7:25; Col 2:18).

MINERALS The present science of mineralogy with its names and exact terminology is a young science and certainly did not exist at the time the Bible was written. It is impossible to be certain in all cases that when a mineral is named in the Bible it is the same mineral designated by that name in modern mineralogy, especially in the case of gemstones or precious stones.

The minerals will be grouped as follows:

    I. Precious stones.

    II. Metals.

    III. Common minerals such as salt, sulfur, and water.

    I. Precious Stones. There are four principal lists of minerals recorded in Scripture. (1) The 12 precious stones of Aaron's breastplate. Each stone represented one of the tribes of Israel (Exod 28:17–20; 39:10–13). (2) The wisdom of Job (Job 28:16–19). Listed are onyx, sapphire, crystal, coral, jaspar, ruby, and topaz. (3) The gems of the king of Tyre (Ezek 28:13). Listed are ruby, topaz, emerald, chrysolite, onyx, jaspar, sapphire, turquoise, and beryl. (4) The precious stones of the Holy City (Rev 21:18–21). There is a precious stone for each of 12 foundations.

The precious stones of the Bible are as follows:

A. **Agate** (ăg'àt) (Exod 28:19; 39:12; see Chalcedony).

B. **Amethyst** (ăm'ė-thĭst) (Exod 28:19; 39:12; Rev 21:20). A purple to blue-violet form of quartz.

C. **Beryl** (bĕr'yl) (Exod 28:17; 39:10; Ezek 28:13; Rev 21:20). A beryllium aluminum silicate. Gem varieties include yellow or golden beryl; emerald, which is a highly prized translucent to transparent sea-green stone; aquamarine, which is blue; and morganite, which is a rose-red variety.

D. **Carnelian** (kàr-nēl'yàn) (Rev 4:3; 21:20; see under Chalcedony.) Carnelian is also known as sard or sardius.

E. **Chalcedony** (kăl-sĕd'ō-nĭ) (Rev 21:19). Any crystalline character that the various forms of chalcedony have is of microscopic size. The lighter colored varieties are named chalcedony in contrast to such names as carnelian and jaspar.

The following are some of the varieties of chalcedony.

1. **Agate**. Agate is chalcedony with colors unevenly distributed, often banded, with the bands curved. Petrified wood is often a form of agate in which the silicon dioxide has replaced the original wood. Agates are very common and many varieties exist. They have become one of the most popular minerals for cutting and polishing.

2. **Carnelian, sard, or sardius.** Carnelian is chalcedony with colors usually clear red to brownish red. Iron oxide imparts the color.

3. **Chrysoprase.** This is an apple-green variety of chalcedony, sometimes called green jaspar.

4. **Flint.** This is usually a dull gray to black form, not prized or classified as a precious stone, but highly prized for arrowheads, spear points, skinning knives, etc.

5. **Jaspar.** Jaspar is hard, opaque, and takes a beautiful polish.

6. **Onyx.** Onyx is similar to banded agates, except that the bands are flat.

7. **Sardonyx.** Sardonyx is merely onyx that includes layers of carnelian or sard.

F. **Chrysolite** (krĭs'ō-līt) (Exod 28:20; 39:13; Song of Songs 5:14; Ezek 1:16; 10:9; 28:13; Dan 10:6; Rev 21:20). Chrysolite is a yellow to greenish-yellow form of olivine. A green olivine is known as peridot. The mineral is a silicate of magnesium and iron.

G. **Chrysoprase** (krĭs'ō-prāz) (Rev 21:20). (See under Chalcedony.)

H. **Coral** (Job 28:18; Ezek 27:16). Factors that contributed to the value of coral in the ancient world probably included its beauty, its use in the production of jewelry (creating an economic demand for it), and its workability.

I. **Crystal** (Job 28:17; Rev 4:6; 21:11; 22:1). It is generally understood to refer to glass or clear quartz. This type of quartz is remarkably brilliant and beautifully shaped, even as it is found in nature.

J. **Emerald** (Exod 28:18; 39:11; Ezek 28:13; Rev 4:3; 21:19). The emerald is a transparent to translucent deep green form of beryl (beryllium aluminum silicate).

K. **Flint** (Exod 4:25; Josh 5:2–3; Isa 5:28; 50:7; Jer 17:1; Ezek 3:9; Zech 7:12). (See under Chalcedony.) In all its occurrences in the Bible the emphasis is on its hardness and its ability to hold a sharp edge.

L. **Jacinth** (jā'sĭnth) (Exod 28:19; 39:12; Rev 21:20). In the Greek the word connotes a dark blue stone. It is possible that it is the sapphire; if so, the NIV renderings of "sapphire" may represent lapis lazuli (see Sapphire).

M. **Jaspar** (Exod 28:20; 39:13; Job 28:18; Ezek 28:13; Rev 4:3; 21:11, 18–19). (See under Chalcedony.)

N. **Lapis lazuli** (lăp'ĭs lăz'ū-lĭ). (NIV margin for sapphire in OT.) The lapis lazuli is a gem of deep azure-blue. It is a soft stone composed of sodium aluminum silicate. It was fashioned by the ancients into various types of ornaments (see Sapphire).

O. **Onyx** (ŏn'ĭks) (Gen 2:12; Exod 25:7; 28:9, 20; 35:9, 27; 39:6, 13; 1 Chron 29:2; Job 28:16; Ezek 28:13). (See under Chalcedony.)

P. **Pearl** (Gen 2:12 mg.; Matt 7:6; 13:45; 1 Tim 2:9; Rev 17:4; 18:12, 16; 21:21). Pearls, like coral, develop in the sea by the abstraction of calcium carbonate from sea water. The pearl develops around a bit of foreign matter within the shell of oysters or mussels. They are not much harder than a fingernail.

Q. **Ruby** (Exod 28:17; 39:10; Job 28:18; Prov 3:15; 8:11; 20:15; 31:10; Isa 54:12; Lam 4:7; Ezek 27:16; 28:13). Corundum

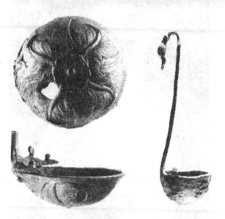

A second-century B.C. bronze bowl (bottom and full view) and ladle found at Tell Anafa, an ancient mound in the Upper Galilee region. Courtesy Museum of Art and Archaeology, University of Missouri

Gold dagger and sheath found attached to a belt in a grave at Ur, twenty-fifth century B.C. Ur, Abraham's city of origin, had one of the most advanced cultures of the world. Courtesy The University Museum, University of Pennsylvania

as a mineral usually occurs as a dull, unattractive but hard form of aluminum oxide, often crystallized in hexagonal forms. Corundum of a rich, clear, red variety is the ruby, whereas the other colors of gem-quality corundum account for the sapphires.

R. **Sapphire** (săf'īr) (Exod 24:10; 28:18; 39:11; Job 28:6, 16; Song of Songs 5:14; Isa 54:11; Lam 4:7; Ezek 1:26; 10:1; 28:13; Rev 21:19). Sapphires, like rubies, belong to the corundum or aluminum-oxide family, with a hardness of 9, or next to diamond. True sapphires are blue; others are colorless, yellow, or pink.

S. **Sardonyx** (sär-dŏn'ĭks) (Rev 21:20). The sardonyx is an onyx layered with red sard or carnelian.

T. **Topaz** (tō'păz) (Exod 28:17; 39:10; Job 28:19; Ezek 28:13; Rev 21:20). The most highly prized is the yellow topaz; but colorless, pink, blue, and green varieties occur as well.

U. **Turquoise** (tûr'koiz) (Exod 28:18; 39:11; 1 Chron 29:2; Isa 54:11; Ezek 27:16; 28:13). A blue to bluish-green mineral which is a hydrous phosphate of aluminum and copper.

II. Metals. Of the 103 elements now known to man, 78 are metals. Of these only gold, silver, iron, copper, lead, tin, and mercury were known to the ancients. A metal is an element with a metallic luster; it is usually a good conductor of heat and electricity. Metals such as gold, silver, and copper may occur in nature as the free recognizable metal, or as is true of most metals, they may occur in compound form, chemically united with other elements in such a way that the ore appears dull and nonmetallic. The earliest reference to a man skilled in iron and bronze work is to Tubal-Cain (Gen 4:22).

A. **Bronze.** A metal alloy composed of varying amounts of copper and tin. Bronze was used in ornamental construction (Exod 25:3; 26:11; 27:2) and the manufacture of such utilitarian objects as pots (Lev 6:28) and mirrors (Job 37:18). Cymbals of bronze were used in the temple for worship (1 Chron 15:19). Bronze weaponry was used in the armament of Goliath (1 Sam 17:5–38) and shields (2 Chron 12:10). Job 20:24 speaks of arrows tipped with bronze.

B. **Copper.** Copper is a heavy, reddish-yellow metal. Pliny claimed that copper was found first on the island of Cyprus and indicated that it was sometimes alloyed with silver and gold. The Bible refers to the presence of copper ore in Canaan as one of the benefits (Deut 8:9), the process of smelting copper (Job 28:2; Ezek 22:18, 20; 24:11), and the use of copper in coinage (Matt 10:9; Mark 12:42; Luke 21:2).

C. **Gold.** Gold was used freely and

skillfully in the oldest of civilizations (Gen 2:11–12). We are told that in the land of Havilah, in the vicinity of the Garden of Eden, there was gold. Why has man valued gold so highly? Why is gold good? Perhaps because it is warmly beautiful, enduring, never rusts or dissolves away, and retains its beauty.

D. **Iron.** The first reference to iron in the Bible is found in Genesis 4:22 where Tubal-Cain is cited as a worker of iron. The Hebrews were familiar with furnaces for the making of iron (Deut 4:20; 1 Kings 8:51; Jer 11:4). There is evidence that as slaves in Egypt they had to work at these furnaces. The smith and his forge were well known to Isaiah (44:12 and 54:16). The Israelites were forced to go to the Philistines to sharpen their plowshares, mattocks, axes, and sickles (1 Sam 13:19–20; cf. Deut 3:11; Josh 17:16, 18; 1 Sam 17:7; Pss 2:9; 107:10; Jer 28:13–14).

E. **Lead.** Lead is listed with copper, tin, and iron as metals melted in a furnace (Ezek 22:18, 20) and again with silver, iron, and tin as metals used for monetary exchange (27:12; cf. Exod 15:10; Num 31:22; Job 19:24; Jer 6:29; Zech 5:7–8).

F. **Silver.** Silver is ten times as abundant in the crust of the earth as is gold, and much of it was mined by the ancients. Many objects made of silver are referred to in the Scriptures. The cup that Joseph had hidden in Benjamin's sack was a silver cup (Gen 44:2). Demetrius, the silversmith of Ephesus, made silver shrines for Diana (Acts 19:24).

III. The Common Minerals.

A. **Alabaster** (Matt 26:7; Mark 14:3; Luke 7:37). These passages refer to an alabaster box or jar used to contain a precious ointment.

B. **Glass** (Rev 4:6; 15:2; 21:18, 21). Glass is a product of the fusion of silicates, borates, or phosphates.

C. **Marble** (1 Chron 29:2; Esth 1:6; Song of Songs 5:15; Rev 18:12). Marble is recrystallized limestone, capable of receiving a high polish.

D. **Salt.** The evaporation of one cubic mile of sea water would leave approximately 140 million tons of salts, most of which would be sodium chloride, or common salt.

E. **Soda** (Job 9:30; Prov 25:20; Jer 2:22). In the Bible it probably refers only to sodium carbonate.

F. **Sulphur** (Gen 19:24; Deut 29:23; Job 18:15; Ps 11:6; Isa 30:33; 34:9; Ezek 38:22; Luke 17:29; Rev 9:17–18; 14:10; 19:20; 20:10; 21:8). In the Bible sulphur is nearly always associated with fire and metaphorically with punishment or dev-

Alabaster bottle shaped like a flower. Found in Israel but originates in Egypt. Middle Bronze II (c. 1800–1500 B.C.). Courtesy Reuben and Edith Hecht Museum, University of Haifa

astation. The flame of burning sulphur is very hot, and the sulfur dioxide gas has a suffocating stench.

G. **Water.** This is the most marvelous and exciting mineral of the Bible. There are more references to this mineral in the Bible than to any other.

MINES, MINING An occupation of man that is very ancient, for we read in the description of Eden and its surroundings before the Flood of the "land of Havilah, where there is gold" (Gen 2:11–12; cf. 4:22). Mines are mentioned in Job 28:1–11; very ancient copper mines existed in Sinai; the remains of Solomon's blast furnaces for copper are found at Elath. The great development of metalworking in Israel must have come between the time of Saul and the time of Solomon.

One of the ancient copper mines popularly known as "King Solomon's Mines," in the Arabah, north of Elath. The abandoned mine is filled with water from a flood. Archaeological finds indicate that the mines operated chiefly in the Late Bronze and Iron Age. Courtesy Duby Tal

Compare 1 Samuel 13:19–22, where the Philistines are in the Iron Age, which the Israelites had not yet reached, with the accomplishments of Solomon's time (1 Kings 7:13–50) only about a century later.

MINGLED PEOPLE (Heb. *'ērev,* from *'ārav, to mix*). Non-Israelite people who left Egypt with the Israelites (Exod 12:38; cf. Neh 13:3). An expression of contempt for the mixed blood of certain of Israel's enemies (Jer 25:20; cf. Num 11:4).

MINIAMIN (mĭn'yà-mĭn, *from the right hand*). **1.** A Levite in Hezekiah's time (2 Chron 31:15). **2.** Head of a family of priests in Nehemiah's time (Neh 12:17). **3.** A priest in the time of Nehemiah (12:41).

MINISTER (Heb. *shārath, shārēth,* Gr. *diakonos, leitourgos, hypēretēs*). Originally a servant, though distinguished from a slave who may work against his will, and a hireling, who works for wages (Exod 24:13 KJV; NIV "aide"; cf. Num 13:8). The word *hypēretēs,* which originally meant "an under-rower," is also used for "minister" (Luke 4:20 KJV). The same word is used of John Mark (Acts 13:5). God himself has his ministers, the angels (Pss 103:21; 104:4 KJV; NIV "his servants"). The priests of Israel are also God's ministers (Jer 33:21–22). The NT word *diakonos,* i.e., "deacon," means "minister" and indicates the duty as well as the privilege of the office. "Deacon" should not be confused with "elder" or "presbyter."

MINNITH (mĭn'ĭth, Heb. *minnĭth*). A city of the Ammonites that Jephthah defeated while overcoming this nation (Judg 11:33). It was a source of wheat for the markets of Tyre (Ezek 27:17).

MINT (See PLANTS)

MIRACLES The word "miracle" (Latin *miraculum*) literally means a marvelous event or an event that causes wonder. Some of the more important biblical words designating miracles are *thauma,* "wonder"; *pele'* and *teras,* "portent"; *gêvhurâh* and *dynamis,* "display of power"; *'ôth* and *sēmeion,* "sign."

The use of "miracle" in Christian theology includes, but goes beyond, the meanings of the ancient words. A miracle is (1) an extraordinary event, inexplicable in terms of ordinary natural forces, (2) an event that causes the observers to postulate a superhuman personal cause, or (3) an event that constitutes evidence (a "sign") of implications much wider than the event itself.

1. Miracles should be distinguished from works of providence. In the biblical events strictly regarded as miracles, the adversaries of faith acknowledged the supernatural character of what took place (Acts 3:1–4:22; 14:8–23).

2. Miracles are further to be distinguished from the type of answers to prayer that do not constitute "signs" or demonstrative evidence for unbelievers.

3. Miracles of God should also be distinguished from works of magic. In magic the wonder-worker himself possesses a formula that causes the result. The alleged supernatural power is controlled by the performer (Exod 7:11; 8:7). In miracles of God the results depend wholly on the divine will, and the one who works the miracle is simply God's agent.

4. Miracles of God must be distinguished from miracles of Satanic or demonic origin (Matt 24:24; 2 Thess 2:9; cf. Rev 13:14; 16:14; 19:20).

5. Miracles must also be distinguished from mere exotic occurrences, evidences of nothing but oddity. Genuine miracles are always "signs" that teach a lesson. Every miracle of God is a part of God's great integrated system of revealed truth.

The majority of the miracles recorded in the Bible fall into three great epochs (1) the Exodus and Conquest, (2) Elijah and Elisha, and (3) Christ and the apostolic age.

The greatest epoch of miracles in all recorded history occurred in the ministry of Christ and his apostles. About 40 demonstrative "sign" miracles wrought

Miracles of Jesus

	MATT.	MARK	LUKE	JOHN
Healing				
Man with leprosy	8:2−4	1:40−42	5:12−13	
Roman centurion's servant	8:5−13		7:1−10	
Peter's mother-in-law	8:14−15	1:30−31	4:38−39	
Two men from Gadara	8:28−34	5:1−15	8:27−35	
Paralyzed man	9:2−7	2:3−12	5:18−25	
Woman with bleeding	9:20−22	5:25−29	8:43−48	
Two blind men	9:27−31			
Man mute and possessed	9:32−33			
Man with a shriveled hand	12:10−13	3:1−5	6:6−10	
Man blind, mute, and possessed	12:22		11:14	
Canaanite woman's daughter	15:21−28	7:24−30		
Boy with a demon	17:14−18	9:17−29	9:38−43	
Two blind men (one named)	20:29−34	10:46−52	18:35−43	
Deaf mute		7:31−37		
Man possessed, synagogue		1:23−26	4:33−35	
Blind man at Bethsaida		8:22−26		
Crippled woman			13:11−13	
Man with dropsy			14:1−4	
Ten men with leprosy			17:11−19	
The high priest's servant			22:50−51	
Official's son at Capernaum				4:46−54
Sick man, pool of Bethesda				5:1−9
Man born blind				9:1−7
Command over the forces of nature				
Calming the storm	8:23−27	4:37−41	8:22−25	
Walking on the water	14:25	6:48−51		6:19−21
5,000 people fed	14:15−21	6:35−44	9:12−17	6:5−13
4,000 people fed	15:32−38	8:1−9		
Coin in the fish's mouth	17:24−27			
Fig tree withered	21:18−22	11:12−14, 20−25		
Catch of fish			5:4−1	
Water turned into wine				2:1−11
Another catch of fish				21:1−11
Bringing the dead back to life				
Jairus's daughter	9:18−19, 23−25	5:22−24, 38−42	8:41−42, 49−56	
Widow's son at Nain			7:11−15	
Lazarus				11:1−44

by Christ are recorded in the Gospels, selected by the writers from among a much larger number (John 20:30).

The ministry of the apostles after Christ's ascension began with the miracle of "languages" on the Day of Pentecost. This miracle recurred until the church organization for this age was well established, and probably until the NT books were all put into circulation. There were numerous other demonstrative miracles (Heb 2:3−4).

The purpose of miracles is revelation and edification (John 20:31). Christ rebuffed those who had only a desire to see the spectacular but followed his rebuke with a powerful reference to Jonah as a type of his own resurrection (Matt 12:39−40; cf. also Luke 23:8). To seek to see miracles is better than merely to seek free food (John 6:26). His miracles were evidence of the genuineness of his message (5:36). He preferred that people would accept his message for its intrinsic worth, but to believe him because of his miracles was not wrong (10:37–38).

The Bible does not specifically say that God cannot or will not work demonstrative "sign" miracles in our day, but God generally ceased to work through "sign" miracles when the NT was finished, and that the "miracle of grace," the witness of the Spirit, answered prayer, and, supremely, the written Word shall be the chief sources of knowledge of himself for his people during this age.

Miracles are an absolutely essential element in Christianity. If Jesus Christ is not God manifest in the flesh, our faith is a silly myth. If he did not arise from the dead in bodily form, the grave being empty and his appearance being recognizable, then "we are yet in our sins and of all people most miserable." If the miracle of grace is not verifiable in the transformation of the life of the one who puts his faith in Jesus as his Lord and Savior, then our Christian gospel is nothing more than a fraud.

MIRIAM (mĭr′ĭ-ăm, Heb. *miryām*, various suggested meanings). The daughter of Amram and Jochebed and the sister of Moses and Aaron (Exod 15:20; Num 26:59; 1 Chron 6:3; Mic 6:4). She showed concern and wisdom in behalf of her infant brother Moses when he was discovered in the Nile by the Egyptian princess (Exod 2:4, 7–8). After passing through the Red Sea, she led the Israelite women in dancing and instrumental accompaniment while she sang the song of praise and victory (15:20–21). Miriam and Aaron criticized Moses for his marriage to a Cushite woman; because of this criticism, Miriam was punished by the Lord with leprosy (Num 12:1, 9; Deut 24:9), but on the protest of Aaron and the prayer of Moses (Num 12:11, 13) she was restored after a period of seven days, during which she was isolated from the camp and the march was delayed. Miriam died at Kadesh and was buried there (20:1).

MIRROR The mirrors of the serving women were made of brass (Exod 38:8; Job 37:18). Of the inadequacy of these ancient mirrors Paul says (1 Cor 13:12) that "now we see but a poor reflection." James compares a hearer of the word who is not also a doer to "a man who looks at his face in a mirror" (James 1:23–24) and then forgets what he looks like. "Mirror" is a better translation than

"glass" or "looking glass," because the material was metal, not glass.

Bronze mirror from Egypt, New Kingdom, c. 1550–1350 B.C. Courtesy The University Museum, University of Pennsylvania

MISHAEL (mĭsh′ā-ĕl, Heb. *mîshā'ēl, Who is what God is?*). 1. A cousin of Moses and Aaron (Exod 6:22; Lev 10:4) who helped dispose of the bodies of Nadab and Abihu. 2. A man who stood with Ezra at the reading of the Law (Neh 8:4). 3. A prince of Judah, taken captive by Nebuchadnezzar. A chief official of Babylon changed his name to Meshach. Mishael and his companions, Hananiah and Azariah, were thrown into a blazing furnace (Dan 3:19–30) but came out unharmed.

MISHAL (mī′shăl, Heb. *mish'āl*). A Levitical city (Gershonite) in the tribe of Asher (Josh 21:30), called also "Misheal" (19:26 KJV) and "Mashal" (1 Chron 6:74).

MISHEAL (See MISHAL)

MISHMA (mĭsh'mà, Heb. *mishmā'*). **1.** A son of Ishmael and a prince of the Ishmaelites (Gen 25:14; 1 Chron 1:30). **2.** Progenitor of a large family of Simeonites through his descendant Shimei (4:25ff.).

MISREPHOTH MAIM (mĭs'rē-fŏth mā'ĭm, *hot springs*). A town or a region near Sidon to which Joshua chased the kings of the north who had joined against him (Josh 11:8; 13:6). Perhaps the same as Zarephath where Elijah lodged (1 Kings 17:9–10; Luke 4:26). It is on the coast between Sidon and Tyre.

MIST 1. Steamy vapor rising from warm, damp ground into a humid atmosphere (Gen 2:6 KJV; NIV "streams"). **2.** A blinding dimness of vision like that caused by cataracts (Acts 13:11). **3.** A part of the description of false teachers (2 Peter 2:17).

MITE (See MONEY)

MITHRAISM The cult of Mithras, a Persian sun god, the worship of which reached Rome in or about A.D. 69. Based on the trials, sufferings, and exploits of Mithras, the cult appealed to soldiers. December 25 was the chief feast of Mithras, and in fixing on that date for Christmas, the early church sought to overlay both the Mithraic festival and the Saturnalia. Christianity triumphed over Mithraism because of its written records of a historic Christ, and its associated body of doctrine adapted for preaching, evangelism, and the needs of every day. Christianity, too, was universal, excluding neither woman, child, nor slave. It preached salvation by faith and demanded no stern ordeals.

MITHREDATH (mĭth'rē-dăth, Heb. *mithredhāth, given by Mithras*, i.e., by the sun). The Persian name of two men. **1.** The treasurer of Cyrus, king of Persia (Ezra 1:8). **2.** An enemy of the Jews in the days of Artaxerxes, the son of Cyrus (4:7).

MITRE (See DRESS; PRIEST, PRIESTHOOD)

MITYLENE (mĭt-ĭ-lē'nē, Gr. *Mitylēnē*). The name is more properly spelled Mytilene. It was the chief city of Lesbos, a splendid port with a double harbor (Acts 20:14), and a center of Greek culture.

MIXED MULTITUDE (See MINGLED PEOPLE)

MIZPAH (mĭz'pà, Heb. *mitspâh, mitspēh, watchtower, lookout-post*). A common noun meaning "watchtower, guardpost" (2 Chron 20:24; Isa 21:8). As a proper noun, it is used of the following: **1.** An unidentified town in the territory of Judah (Josh 15:38). **2.** An unknown city in Moab (1 Sam 22:3). **3.** An unidentified region or valley (Josh 11:3 *mitspâh*; 11:8). **4.** A town in Gilead (Judg 11:29; cf. Ramath Mizpah, Josh 13:26). **5.** A town in Benjamin (18:26).

Mizpah is: (1) A town in Gilead (see no. 4 above; Gen 31:49; Josh 10:17; Judg 11:34). (2) Most frequently Mizpah refers to the town of Benjamin (no. 5 above).

At Mizpah the Israelites gathered to consider the steps to be taken against Gibeah in the case of the atrocity related in Judges 19 (cf. Judg 20:1, 3; 21:1, 5, 8). Mizpah was one of the cities closely associated with Samuel (1 Sam 7:5–16). The Ebenezer memorial was set up between "between Mizpah and Shen" to celebrate Israel's victory over the Philistines. After the destruction of Jerusalem by Nebuchadnezzar in 587/6 B.C., Gedaliah, who was appointed governor of Judah, located his headquarters at Mizpah (2 Kings 25:22–23; Jer 40:5–12). He was later killed there along with other Jews and Babylonian soldiers (2 Kings 25:25; Jer 41:1–3). Mizpah also appears in the lists of rebuilders of the walls of Jerusalem (Neh 3:7, 15, 19) and is mentioned by Hosea (5:1) in his rebuke of Israel.

MIZPEH (See MIZPAH)

MIZRAIM (mĭz'rā-ĭm, Heb. *mitsrayim*, form and derivation uncertain). **1.** The second son of Ham (Gen 10:6; 1 Chron 1:8) is associated with NE Africa, possibly along with his brothers, Cush and Put. Some of the descendants of Mizraim (Gen 10:13–14; 1 Chron 1:11–12) probably are also to be linked with this area. **2.** The usual Hebrew word for "Egypt" and always so translated in the RSV.

MOAB (mō'ăb, Heb. *mô'āv, seed*). **1.** Grandson of Lot by incest with his elder daughter (Gen 19:30–38). **2.** The nation or people descended from Moab. They settled first at Ar, just east of the southern part of the Dead Sea. The Lord commanded Moses not to vex them when Israel passed through their vicinity on their way to the Promised Land. However, their king Balak hired Balaam to come and curse Israel (Num 22–24). After God prevented him from cursing the Israelites, Balaam suggested other tactics. The Moabite girls entered the camp of Israel (Num 31:16) and seduced the men (25:1–9). As a result God sent a plague that killed 24,000 men.

It was on Mt. Pisgah in the land of Moab that Moses died.

Nearly a century after the conquest of Canaan, Israel was subject to Moab for 18 years (Judg 3:12–14). God raised up Ehud, who killed their king Eglon and so subdued Moab (3:30). Ruth the Moabitess was an ancestress of David. David, when in difficulty with King Saul, took his father and mother to the king of Moab for their protection (1 Sam 22:3–4). Later Mesha king of Moab paid heavy tribute to Ahab king of Israel (2 Kings 3:4). After the death of Ahab, he rebelled, but Joram king of Israel with Jehoshaphat of Judah thoroughly defeated him and, so far as poss ible, ruined his land. From that time on, Moab gradually declined in accordance with the word of the Lord through his prophets (Isaiah 15–16; Jer 48; Ezek 25:8–11; Amos 2:1–3; Zeph 2:8–11).

3. The land of the Moabites. Moab was bounded on the west by the Dead Sea, on the east by the desert, on the north by the Arnon, and on the south by Edom.

MOABITE STONE, THE An inscribed stone found in Moab and recording Moabite history. The writing consisted of 34 lines, in the Moabite language (practically a dialect of the Hebrew) by Mesha, king of the Moabites in the time of Ahaziah and Joram, the sons of Ahab. It gives his side of the account found in 2 Kings 3.

MOADIAH (See MAADIAH)

MOLADAH (mŏl'à-dà, Heb. *môlādhâh, birth*). One of the cities mentioned in Joshua 15 and 19 in the lists both of Judah and of Simeon, lying about 10 miles (17 km.) east of Beersheba. At the Restoration, Judah occupied it (Neh 11:26).

MOLE (See ANIMALS)

MOLECH, MOLOCH (mō'lĕk, mō'lŏk, Heb. *ha-mōlekh*). A heathen god, especially of the Ammonites, who was worshiped with gruesome orgies in which children were sacrificed. At least in some places an image of the god was heated and the bodies of children who had just been slain were placed in its arms. The worship of Molech was known to Israel before they entered Canaan, for Moses very sternly forbade its worship (Lev 18:21; 20:1–5). In spite of this prohibition, King Solomon, to please his numerous heathen wives, set up high places for Chemosh and for Molech on Mt. Olivet (1 Kings 11:7), though Molech's principal place of worship in and after Manasseh's time was the valley of Ben Hinnom (2 Chron 33:6), a place of such ill repute that Gehenna ("the valley of Hinnom")

became a type for hell (Matt 5:29–30). The words *Malcham* (Zeph 1:5 KJV), *Milcom* (1 Kings 11:5 KJV), *Molech*, and *Moloch* are all variants of Hebrew words meaning "the reigning one." Later Jews, after making sacrifices to Molech, often went to worship in the house of the Lord (Ezek 23:37–39); this was particularly offensive to God (Jer 7:9–11; 19:4–13). Because of this heathen worship God allowed the enemies of Israel to rule over them for many years (Ps 106:35–42).

MOLTEN SEA (See TABERNACLE)

MONEY Money in the sense of stamped coins did not exist in Israel, so far as is known, until after the Exile. Before this time exchange of values took place by bartering. Wealth is first mentioned in the Bible in connection with Abraham (Gen 12:5; cf. 12:16, 20), who possessed the three main items of wealth in the ancient world: livestock, silver and gold (Gen 13:2). Among the Romans the word for money was *pecunia*, which is derived from *pecus*, the Latin word for cow or cattle. Perfumes and ointments also had great value.

The first metal exchange was crude, often shapeless, and heavy so as to approximate the value of the item purchased in actual weight. The buyer usually weighed his "money" to the seller. The Jewish shekel was such a weight (*shekel* means "weight"). Among the Jews the shekel was used for the temple tax, the poll tax, and redemption from the priesthood (Exod 30:11–16; 13:13; Num 3:44–51). Since Jesus was a firstborn son not of the tribe of Levi, his parents redeemed him from the priesthood (Luke 2:21ff.) by payment of a shekel, worth about a day's wages at the time. Other weights mentioned in the Bible are: *talent* (circle), *māneh* (part), *gērâh* (grain), and *beqa'* (half shekel). It required 3,000 shekels to equal one talent of silver, which reveals that the 10,000 talents the unmerciful servant owed his master (Matt 18:23–25) was an overwhelming debt. The *pound* (Luke 19:13) is a translation of the old weight *mina* or *māneh* (Greek: *mna*). Since a talent was 60 minas, a mina equaled 50 shekels in Attic weight and 100 shekels in OT weight, which means that in the parable the gift of the Lord to his people is a most precious gift, namely, the gospel.

Most historians believe that the earliest money pieces were struck about 700 B.C. in the small kingdom of Lydia in Asia Minor. These early Lydian "coins" were simply crude pieces of metal cut into small lumps of a standard weight and

A hoard of ancient Tyrian and Jewish shekels and the vessel in which they were found, dated A.D. 68. On loan from the Reifenberg family. Courtesy Israel Museum, Jerusalem

stamped with official marks to guarantee the value.

Animals, natural objects, and the Greek gods were used as symbols on Greek coins. Each coin was made individually with hammer, punch, and die. The Greeks called these coins drachmas (*drachma* means "handful"). Later the terms *drachma* and *shekel* were used more or less interchangeably. The "lost coin" (Luke 15:8) was a silver drachma equivalent to a Roman denarius, a day's wages. The temple or half-shekel tax (Matt 17:24) was a didrachma.

The coin Peter found in the fish's mouth was the Greek stater (Matt 17:27). Since the temple tax was a half-shekel, the stater would pay for two. It is believed that the 30 pieces of silver (Matt 26:15; 27:3–5) that bought the greatest betrayal in history were tetradrachmas; 30 shekels was the price of a slave (Exod 21:32).

The Greek assarion is mentioned twice in the NT (Matt 10:29; Luke 12:6), as a coin small in both size and value. The lepton, a tiny bronze or copper coin was the "widow's mite" (Mark 12:42; Luke 21:2). *Lepton* was translated "mite" in

the KJV because it was the coin of least value among coins (12:59).

The most interesting coin of the Bible is the Roman denarius (Gr. *denarion*), known by collectors as the "penny" of the Bible because of this translation in KJV. This silver coin, which looks like our dime, was the most common Roman coin during the days of Jesus and the apostles. The true value of the denarius may be seen in our Lord's parable of the laborers in the vineyard (Matt 20:2, 10; cf. Luke 10:35; John 6:7). The generous act of Mary was "worth a year's wages" (12:3–5; cf. Rev 6:6). The denarius was also the "tribute money" imposed by the Romans on the Jewish people. The "image" on the denarius handed our Lord in Matthew 22:19 was the head of either Caesar Augustus (43 B.C. to A.D. 14) or that of Tiberius Caesar (A.D. 14–39).

MONEYCHANGER (See CHANGERS OF MONEY)

MONOTHEISM (mŏn'ō-thē-ĭzm, from Gr. *monos, one, theos, god*). The doctrine or belief that there is but one God. Atheism is the belief that there is no god; polytheism, that there is more than one god; monolatry, the worship of one god as supreme, without denying there are other gods; and henotheism, belief in one god, though not to the exclusion of belief in others. There are three great monotheistic religions: Judaism, Christianity, and Islam, the latter two having their origin in the first. According to the Bible, man was originally a monotheist.

MONSTERS (See ANIMALS)

MONTII (See CALENDAR; TIME)

MOON (See ASTRONOMY)

MORASTHITE (See MORESHETH GATH)

MORDECAI (môr'dē-kī, Heb. *mordekhay*, from *Marduk*, chief god of Babylon).
1. A leader of the people of Judah during the return of Zerubbabel from exile (Ezra 2:2; Neh 7:7).
2. The deliverer of the Jews in the Book of Esther. He was a Benjamite who had been deported during the reign of Jehoiachin (Esth 2:5–6). He lived in Susa (KJV "Shushan"), the Persian capital, and brought up his cousin Esther, whose parents were dead (2:7). When Esther was taken into the royal harem, Mordecai forbade her to reveal her nationality (2:20); yet he remained in close connection with her. Mordecai discovered at the palace gate a plot against the king. By informing Esther of the plot, he secured the execution of the two eunuchs responsible (2:19–23). When Haman was made

chief minister, Mordecai aroused his wrath by refusing to bow before him. To avenge the slight, Haman procured from the king a decree to destroy the Jews (ch. 3). Mordecai then sent Esther to the king to seek protection for her people (ch. 4). Haman meanwhile prepared a high gallows on which he planned to hang Mordecai (ch. 5). By a singular, highly dramatic series of events, Haman fell from favor and was hanged on the gallows he had prepared for Mordecai (ch. 7). Mordecai succeeded him as chief minister of the king (ch. 8). The Book of Esther ends with an account of the fame and dignity of Mordecai (ch. 10).

MOREH, TREE OF (NIV tree; NASB, RSV oak; KJV plain). A place near Shechem where Abraham camped and erected an altar to the Lord (Gen 12:6). It was probably the tree under which Jacob later buried the amulets and idols his family had brought from Haran (Gen 35:4). In Deuteronomy 11:30 there is mention of "the great trees of Moreh" as a landmark near Ebal and Gerizim.

MORESHETH GATH (mō'rĕsh-ĕth găth, Heb. *possession of Gath*). A town mentioned only in Micah 1:14 in a group of places in the Judah-Philistine border area. Micah calls himself an inhabitant of Moresheth (Mic 1:1; Jer 26:18)—probably the same place. Gath may have been added to the name to indicate that this was the Moresheth that is near Gath. It may be identified with Tell ej-Judeideh, about five miles (eight km.) west of Gath in the Shephelah.

MORIAH (mō-rī'à, Heb. *mōrîyâh*). A land or district where Abraham was told to offer up Isaac (Gen 22:2). Jewish tradition has identified it with Jerusalem; Samaritan tradition identifies it with Mt. Gerizim. According to 2 Chronicles 3:1, Solomon built the temple on Mt. Moriah, where God had appeared to David (1 Chron 21:15–22:1). Whether this is the same Mt. Moriah mentioned in the account of Abraham is not certain.

MORNING SACRIFICE (See OFFERINGS)

MORNING STAR (See DAYSTAR)

MORTAL, MORTALITY In the OT (only in Job 4:17) this represents the Hebrew *'ĕnôsh* (lit. "man"), translated "mortal man." In the NT it is the translation of *thnētos*—subject to death (Rom 8:11; 1 Cor 15:53–54). "Mortality" occurs only in 2 Corinthians 5:4 and is a translation of the same Greek word.

MORTAR 1. A bowl-shaped vessel of stone or basalt rock in which grain, spices, etc., were crushed with the use of a pestle (Num 11:8; cf. Prov 27:22). **2.** A substance used to bind bricks or stones together in a wall. Mud or clay was often used (Nah 3:14); for better houses, mortar made of sand and lime was used.

MOSES (Heb. *mōseheh*, Egyp. *mēs, drawn out, born*). The national hero who delivered the Israelites from Egyptian slavery, established them as an independent nation, and prepared them for entrance into Canaan. On the basis of an early date for the Exodus, c. 1440 B.C., Moses was born about 1520 of Israelite parents in the land of Egypt (Exod 2:1–10). Hidden among the reeds near the river's bank, Moses was discovered by Pharaoh's daughter. She requested Moses' mother to nurse him until he was old enough to be taken to the royal court, where he spent the first 40 years of his life.

Stephen in his address to the Sanhedrin (Acts 7:22) asserts that Moses was not only instructed in the science and learning of the Egyptians but also was endowed with oratorical ability and distinctive leadership qualities.

Moses' first valiant attempt to aid his own people ended in failure. He killed an Egyptian and fled to Midian, where he spent a 40-year period in seclusion. In the land of Midian Moses found favor in the home of a priest named Jethro. He married Jethro's daughter Zipporah and became the shepherd of his father-in-law's flocks. Confronted with a bush afire, he was given a revelation from God, who commissioned him to deliver his people Israel from Egyptian bondage (Exod 3). Two miraculous signs—Moses' staff changed to a serpent and his hand became leprous and later was healed—were provided as evidence for the verification of divine authority (Exod 4:1–17).

In a series of ten plagues Moses and Aaron countered Pharaoh's attempt to retain Israel in bondage (Exod 7–11). As a whole these plagues were directed against the gods of Egypt, demonstrating God's power to the Egyptians as well as to the Israelites.

On the eve of Israel's departure the Passover Feast was initially observed (Exod 12). Each family unit that followed the simple instructions of killing a year-old male lamb or goat and applying the blood to the doorposts and lintel of their home was passed by in the execution of divine judgment.

Drawing of Moses and the burning bush, from a wall painting in the synagogue at Dura-Europos, Syria, third century. Courtesy Carta, Jerusalem

The exact route by which Moses led the Israelites, who numbered some 600,000 men, plus women and children, is difficult to ascertain. The Israelites safely crossed the Red Sea through God's intervention, and the Egyptian forces were drowned. At Rephidim Moses was commanded to strike the rock, which brought forth a gushing water supply for his people (Exod 17:1–7). Confronted by an Amalekite attack, Moses prevailed in intercessory prayer with the support of Aaron and Hur, while Joshua led the armies of Israel in a victorious battle (17:8–16). In his administrative duties Moses appointed 70 elders to serve under him in accordance with Jethro's advice. In less than a three months' journey from Egypt the Israelites settled in the environs of Mt. Sinai (Horeb), where they remained for approximately one year (Exod 18–19).

As a representative for his people Moses received the law from God. This law constituted God's covenant with his newly delivered nation. In turn the congregation ratified this covenant (Exod 20–24), which included the Ten Commandments. To enable the Israelites to worship their God properly Moses was given detailed instructions for the building and erection of the tabernacle, which were carefully executed under Moses' supervision. At the same time the Aaronic family, supported by the Levites, was designated for their priestly service and carefully equipped for their ministry (Exod 25–40). Moses also supervised the military census and organization of the Israelites during this encampment in the Sinaitic peninsula.

Moses not only encountered the murmurings of the multitude but was also severely criticized by Miriam and Aaron (Num 11–12). The grumbling crowds who hungered for meat they had eaten in Egypt were filled to the point of sickness when quails were supplied in excessive abundance. Aaron and Miriam were humiliated when she was temporarily subjected to leprosy.

While at Kadesh, Moses sent out twelve representatives to spy out the land of Canaan (Num 13–14). The majority report, given by ten spies, influenced the Israelites to demonstrate their unbelief. Only Joshua and Caleb recommended that they should conquer and occupy the land promised to them. When God proposed to destroy the rebellious Israelites, Moses interceded in behalf of his people.

Not only was the political leadership of Moses challenged by Dathan and Abiram, but Korah and his supporters contested the ecclesiastical position of Aaron and his family. In the course of these rebellions 14,000 people perished in divine judgment.

Moses forfeited entrance into the Promised Land when he struck the rock that he should have commanded to supply water for his people (Num 20). When a scourge of serpents caused many murmuring Israelites to die, Moses erected a bronze snake, which offered healing to all who turned to it in obedience (21:4–9; cf. John 3:14–16).

Anticipating Israel's successful occupation of the land of Canaan, Moses admonished them to destroy the idolatrous inhabitants. He appointed 12 tribal leaders to divide the land among the tribes and instructed them to provide 48 cities throughout Canaan for the Levites with adequate pasture area adjoining each city. Six of these Levitical cities were to be designed as cities of refuge where people might flee for safety in case of accidental bloodshed (Num 34–35). Moses also provided solutions to inheritance problems when daughters inherited the family possessions (Num 36).

The greatness of Moses' character is clearly set forth in his farewell speeches to his beloved people. Even though he himself was denied participation in the conquest and occupation of the land, he coveted the best for the Israelites as they entered Canaan. His admonition to them is summed up in his addresses as given in the Book of Deuteronomy. He reviewed the journey, beginning from Mt. Horeb, where God had made a covenant with Israel. He pointed out especially the places where the Israelites had murmured, reminding them of their disobedience. With that as the background Moses warned them to be obedient. The recent victories God had given them over the Amorites provided a reasonable basis for the hope of victory under the leadership of Joshua as they actually entered the land of Canaan (Deut 1:1–4:43).

In his second speech (Deut 4:44–28:68) Moses emphasized that love as well as obedience is essential for a wholesome relationship with God. The Decalogue at Mt. Sinai was repeated. Wholehearted love for God in daily life represented the basis for maintaining this covenant relationship in such a way that they could enjoy God's blessing. Consequently each generation was responsible for teaching the fear of the Lord their God to the next generation by precept and obedience.

At the close of Moses' career, Joshua, who had already been designated as Israel's leader, was ordained as successor to Moses. In a song (Deut 32) Moses expressed his praise to God, recounting how God had delivered Israel and provided for them through the wilderness journey. Then, with the pronouncement of the blessing on each tribe, Moses departed for Mt. Nebo, where he was privileged to view the Promised Land before he died.

MOSES, ASSUMPTION OF
(See APOCALYPTIC LITERATURE)

MOST HIGH A name applied to God. It represents the Hebrew word *el-elyon* (Gen 14:18, 20, 22; Ps 7:17), which is translated "God Most High." The expression comes into the Greek of the NT as a part of the Semitic background inherited from the OT (Mark 5:7; Acts 7:48).

MOST HOLY PLACE
(See TABERNACLE)

MOTE A particle of dust or chaff, or a splinter of wood that might enter the eye. Rendered as "speck" by NIV, the word is used by Jesus (Matt 7:3–5; Luke 6:41–42) in contrast with "beam" (KJV), "log"

(RSV), or "plank" (NIV) to rebuke self-righteousness in correcting small faults in others, while cherishing greater ones of our own.

MOTH (See ANIMALS)

MOTHER (See FAMILY; MARRIAGE)

MOUNT, MOUNTAIN *Hill, mount,* and *mountain* are terms roughly synonymous in the English Bible. Much of Palestine is hilly or mountainous. These elevations are not dramatically high but are old worn-down hills. A central hill country stretches from north to south in Palestine, attaining its greatest elevations in Galilee (nearly 4,000 feet [1,250 m.] above sea level) and finally ending in the Negev in the south. Much of Transjordan is high plateau land, although in Syria north of Palestine this section reaches a great height in Mt. Hermon (c. 9,000 feet [2,813 m.] above sea level), which is snow-covered throughout the year.

Many ancient peoples considered mountains holy places. Mt. Sinai (Deut 33:2; Judg 5:4–5) and Mt. Zion (Ps 68:16) were specially honored by the Hebrews as the places of God's revelation and abode. Mountains in Scripture are symbolic of eternity (Gen 49:26), strength, and stability, but God is infinitely strong and stable (Pss 97:5; 121:1–2 RSV; Isa 40:12). They also portray the difficult obstacles of life, but God will overcome these mountains for his people (Isa 49:11; Matt 21:21).

"Mount" in several places in the KJV refers to the mounds raised against the wall of a besieged city by an attacking army (Jer 6:6; Ezek 26:8).

MOUNT OF BEATITUDES The site of the Sermon on the Mount (Matt 5–7; Luke 6:20–49), which contains the Beatitudes, is not identified in the Gospels. Although tradition has identified it with Karn Hattin, near Capernaum, its exact location is unknown.

MOURN, MOURNING The ancient Hebrews placed a much greater emphasis on external symbolic acts than do modern Western people; people in the East today still carry on this respect for symbolic actions. Ceremonies for expressing grief at the death of a relative or on any unhappy occasion are referred to frequently in the Bible; they were a natural valid manifestation of grief in that culture.

The OT contains warnings against pagan mourning rites (Lev 19:27–28; Deut 14:1–2). Israelite priests were not allowed to take part in any mourning or

Painting from the tomb of Ramose at Thebes, 12th Dynasty. Women and girls stand with raised hands mourning for the deceased. One small girl is shown nude; others wear long, flowing garments that extend to the feet. Indication of tears can be seen on the faces. Courtesy Egyptian Expedition, The Metropolitan Museum of Art (30.4.37)

other funeral ceremonies (Lev 21:1-4, 10-11).

When bad news was received or when sudden calamity came, it was customary to tear the clothes (2 Sam 1:2) and to sprinkle earth or ashes on the head (Josh 7:6). Hair cloth ("sackcloth") was adopted as clothing in times of grief (Isa 22:12). We read of covering the head in mourning (Jer 14:3), and also the lower part of the face (Ezek 24:17, 22). Among those who habitually wore some covering on the head it was a sign of mourning to let the hair go loose (Lev 10:6), which normally (like that of a Greek Orthodox priest in the Near East) would be coiled up.

Professional mourners were often called in for a funeral (Jer 9:17-22; Amos 5:16; Matt 9:23). Jeremiah, the weeping prophet, made many references to mourning. He taught the mourning women their dirge (Jer 9:17-22), heard the land lament because of the destruction by the Babylonians (9:10; 12:4, 11; 14:2; 23:10), and mentioned Rachel's mourning (31:15-16). He urged Israel to mourn for its sins (4:8; 6:26; 7:29) and secretly mourned for the nation himself (9:1; 13:17).

MOUSE (See ANIMALS)

MOUTH The principal Hebrew words are *peh*, translated "mouth," but also "language," "corner," "edge," "skirt," and any opening, such as of a well (Gen 29:2), of a sack (Gen 42:27), of a cave (Josh 10:22), or of a grave (Ps 141:7); and *hēkh*, translated "mouth" and "roof of the mouth" (Job 29:10). In the NT *stōma* is translated "mouth" except in the idiomatic "face to face" (lit., "mouth to mouth," 2 John 12; 3 John 14), and "edge [lit., mouth] of the sword" (Heb 11:34).

The way in which the Bible constantly uses the organ of speech in the sense of "language" is a good example of the employment of the concrete for the abstract. Silence is the laying of the hand on the mouth (Job 40:4), freedom of speech is the enlarged mouth (Eph 6:19). So to receive a message is to have words put into the mouth (Jer 1:9). Humiliation is the mouth laid in the dust (Lam 3:29).

Finally, the mouth is personified; it is an independent agent. It brings freewill offerings (Ps 119:108). God sets a watch before it (141:3); it selects food (Prov 15:14), uses a rod (14:3), and has a sword (Rev 19:15). This personification helped to contribute to the Jewish idea of the Angel of the Lord and the voice of the Lord and prepared the way for the "word made flesh" (John 1:14).

MOZA (mō'zà, Heb. *môtsâh, sunrise*). 1. A man of Judah, of the family of Hezron, the house of Caleb (1 Chron 2:46). 2. A descendant of Jonathan (8:36-37).

MUFFLER (See DRESS)

MULBERRY TREE (See PLANTS)

MULE (See ANIMALS)

MUPPIM (mŭp'ĭm, Heb. *muppîm*). A son or descendant of Benjamin (Gen 46:21). He is also called Shupham (Num 26:39) and Shuppim (1 Chron 7:12, 15). Possibly the same as Shephuphan (8:5).

MURDER From the days of Noah the biblical penalty for murder was death (Gen 9:6). Throughout the OT times, the ancient Semitic custom of the avenger of blood was followed: a murdered man's nearest relative (the *goel*) had the duty to pursue and kill the murderer (Num 35:19). Since in the practice of avenging blood in this fashion men failed to distinguish between murder and manslaughter, and vicious blood feuds would frequently arise, the Mosaic Law provided for cities of refuge (Num 35). It appears likely that the advent of the monarchy began a trend away from the ancient *goel* custom, for we find the king putting a murderer to

Wall painting from Theban tomb of Djeserkaraseneb, time of Thutmose IV (c. 1421–1413 B.C.). Egyptian musicians with (left to right) harp, lute, double-pipe, and lyre. In center, a small girl dances with clenched fists. Courtesy Egyptian Expedition, The Metropolitan Museum of Art (30.4.9)

death (1 Kings 2:34) and pardoning another (2 Sam 14:6–8).

In a murder trial, the agreeing testimony of at least two persons was necessary for conviction (Num 35:30; Deut 17:6). An animal known to be vicious had to be confined, and if it caused the death of anyone, it was destroyed and the owner held guilty of murder (Exod 21:29, 31).

The right of asylum in a holy place was not granted a murderer; he was dragged away even from the horns of the altar (Exod 21:14; 1 Kings 2:28–34). No ransom could be accepted for a murderer (Num 35:21). When a murder had been committed and the killer could not be found, the people of the community nearest the place where the corpse was found were reckoned guilty. To clear them of guilt, the elders of that community would kill a heifer, wash their hands over it, state their innocence, and thus be judged clean (Deut 21:1–9).

MUSHI, MUSHITES (mū'shī, mū'shīts). A Levite, son of Merari, and the founder of the tribal family or "house" called the Mushites (Exod 6:19; Num 3:20; 26:58; 1 Chron 6:19, 47; 23:21, 23; 24:26, 30).

MUSIC AND MUSICAL INSTRUMENTS
I. Musical Instruments.

The high priest's robe was to have gold bells in the hem (Exod 28:33–35).

The only permanent percussive instrument in the temple orchestra was the cymbal. In the Bible, the use of cymbals is solely confined to religious ceremonies—bringing back the ark from Kiriath Jearim (1 Chron 15:16, 19, 28), the dedication of Solomon's temple (2 Chron 5:13), the restoration of worship by Hezekiah (29:25), the laying of the foundation of the second temple (Ezra 3:10), and the dedication of the wall of Jerusalem (Neh 12:27).

In Psalm 150 two types of cymbals are mentioned. The larger clashing cymbals were played with two hands. The resounding cymbals were much smaller and were played by one hand—the cymbals being attached to the thumb and the middle finger. The chief singer of David, Asaph, was a cymbal player (1 Chron 16:5).

According to Josephus, the harp was played with the fingers and had twelve strings, in contrast to ten strings of the lyre, which was played with a plectrum. These two instruments were the most important ones in the temple orchestra, essential for any public religious ceremony. The harp seems to have been a vertical, angular instrument, larger in

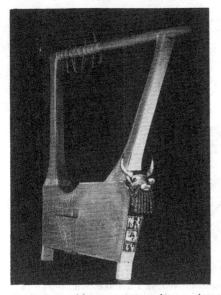

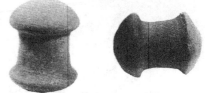

Cylinder shaped rattles made of clay, with small stones inside. Iron Age (c. 1200–1000 B.C.). Courtesy Reuben and Edith Hecht Museum, University of Haifa. Photo Hanna Ophir-Rosenstein

Reconstructed lyre consisting of a wooden sound-box with a gold head of a bearded bull at its end, from the graves at Ur, c. 2500 B.C. Courtesy University Museum, University of Pennsylvania

size, louder, and lower in pitch than the lyre. The harp is mentioned frequently in the Book of Psalms (33:2; 57:8; 71:22; 81:2; 92:3; 108:2; 144:9; 150:3). Erroneously called "King David's harp," the lyre (1 Sam 16:23; 1 Kings 10:12; 1 Chron 25:3) was a stringed instrument, but it had no resonant body like the harp.

The pipe (chālîl) was a double-reed instrument and is the biblical equivalent of the modern oboe (1 Kings 1:40). It was probably also a double-pipe instrument, whose pipes could be blown individually as well as simultaneously.

The shepherd's pipe (NASB, NEB, RSV), flute (MLB, NIV), or organ (KJV) is the other musical instrument mentioned in Genesis 4:21. There are only three other OT references to 'ûgabh (Job 21:12; 30:31; Ps 150:4).

The psaltery is mentioned twice in the Psalms in connection with the harp (Pss 33:2; 144:9) and with both harp and lyre (kinnôr) in Psalm 92:3. It is generally accepted that this was a ten-stringed, rectangular zither. To the early church fathers this psaltery was symbolical: the ten strings, the Ten Commandments; and the four sides, the Gospels.

The most disputed musical term in

Hebrew has been translated many times as triangles, triangular harps, three-stringed instruments, and three-stringed lutes (even three-stringed fiddles and a kind of pipe). Of its 21 OT occurrences, only once is it perhaps a musical term (1 Sam 18:6).

Another term occurs only in 2 Samuel 6:5, where NIV translates it "sistrum" (cornets KJV; castanets JB, NASB, NEB, RSV). This seems to refer to an instrument that is to be shaken, perhaps the sistrum, a rattle of Sumerian origin, which consisted of a handle and a frame with jingling crossbars.

The tambourine was a small drum made of a wooden hoop and probably two skins, without any jingling contrivance like the modern tambourine. It was a rhythm-indicator and was used for dances and joyous occasions as well as religious celebrations (Exod 15:20; Judg 11:34; 1 Sam 18:6; 2 Sam 6:5; Pss 81:2; 149:3; 150:4).

The only temple instrument still being used today in the synagogue is the shôphār or qeren. Originally, it was a ram's horn without a mouthpiece. It was used chiefly as a signal instrument in religious as well as in secular ceremonies (Josh 6:20; Judg 7:16–22; Zech 9:14–15). During the latter part of the period of the second temple, two types of shôphār were in use: the curved ram's horn and the straight (female) mountain goat's horn.

The trumpet (Num 10:1–2, 9–10) and the shôphār were blown by the priests and not by the Levites, who were the professional musicians of the temple. Both these instruments served the same function of signaling. Jewish historian Josephus has described the trumpet as a straight tube, "a little less than a cubit long," its mouthpiece wide and its body expanding into a bell-like ending.

The orchestral instruments of Nebuchadnezzar king of Babylon, included a horn or trumpet, a pipe or a whistle, a kind of harp, and a psaltery, a stringed instrument that was used to accompany psalms (Dan 3:5).

II. Music.

The history of Hebrew music, as well as the history of Israel's higher civilization in general and the organization of the musical service in the temple, began with King David's reign. To King David has been ascribed not only the creation and singing of the psalms, but also the invention of musical instruments (1 Chron 15:16; 23:5; 2 Chron 7:6).

During Solomon's reign, the number of Levites who were instructed in the songs of the Lord was 288, divided into 24 classes (1 Chron 25:6–7; cf. 2 Chron 5:12–14). In Solomon's temple the choir formed a distinct body. They were furnished homes and were on salary. Ezekiel says they had chambers between the walls and windows with southern views (Ezek 40:44). The choir numbered 2,000 singers and was divided into two choirs.

The orchestra and the choir personnel were greatly reduced in the second temple. The orchestra consisted of a minimum of two harps and a maximum of six; a minimum of nine lyres, maximum limitless; a minimum of two oboes and a

Zither player seated on a folding stool. On terracotta relief from Tell Asmar, early second millennium B.C. Courtesy Réunion des Musées Nationaux

maximum of twelve; and one cymbal. The second temple choir consisted of a minimum of twelve adult singers, maximum limitless. The singers, all male, were between 30 and 50 years of age. Five years of musical training was a prerequisite to membership in the second temple choir. In addition to the male adults, sons of the Levites were permitted to participate in the choir.

The order of the Psalms in the daily service of the temple was as follows: on the first day of the week, Psalm 24; on the second day Psalm 48; on the third day, Psalm 82; on the fourth day, Psalm 94; on the fifth day, Psalm 81; on the sixth day, Psalm 93; on the seventh day, Psalm 92.

With the singing of the daily psalm, the morning sacrifice came to a close. The evening sacrifice was identical to the morning sacrifice, with the exception that the incense offering followed the evening sacrifice, at sunset. Thus they began and ended the day with prayer and praise, of which the burning of incense was symbolical.

Dance was considered an integral part of the religious ceremonies in ancient Israel (Exod 15:20; Judg 11:34; 2 Sam 6:14). Religious dancing fell into disuse in the Jerusalem temple, and it is mentioned only twice in Psalms (149:3; 150:4). On the Feast of Tabernacles, at the celebration of "water libation," prominent men would dance, displaying their artistic skill in throwing and catching burning torches. The custom, however, of a procession around the sanctuary or around the altar on the Feast of Tabernacles was retained in the temple, accompanied with singing.

MUSTARD (See PLANTS)

MUTE (See DISEASES)

MUTHLABBEN (mŭth'lăb'ĕn). An expression of uncertain meaning, occurring only in the title of Psalm 9 (KJV, MLB, NASB, RSV). Probably it indicates the name of the tune (NIV; cf. Christian hymnals) or the instruments of accompaniment (JB) to which the psalm was sung.

MUZZLE The Mosaic Law forbade the muzzling of oxen when they were treading out the grain, i.e., threshing (Deut 25:4). This was a simple, humane command, in accordance with the kindly spirit of much of the law. Paul makes use of this injunction (1 Cor 9:9; 1 Tim 5:18).

MYRA (mī'rà, Gr. *Myra*). Now Dembre, one of the southernmost ports of Asia Minor, and once the chief haven of Lycia. Paul came here on a ship from

Adramyttium (Acts 27:2, 5), the seaport on the Aegean opposite Lesbos.

MYRRH (See PLANTS)

MYRTLE (See PLANTS)

MYSIA (mĭsh'ĭ-à, Gr. *Mysia*). A district occupying the NW end of Asia Minor bounded (proceeding clockwise from the west) by the Aegean, the Hellespont (i.e., the Dardanelles), the Propontis (i.e., the Sea of Marmora), Bithynia, Phrygia, and Lydia.

From 280 B.C. Mysia formed part of the kingdom of Pergamum and fell to the Romans in 133 by the will and testament of Attalus III. It thereafter formed part of the province of Asia. The area was traversed by Paul on his second missionary journey (Acts 16:7-8), but no work was done. There is, however, evidence of very early church foundations.

MYSTERY (Gr. *mystērion*). The Greek word occurs 28 times in the NT. Neither the word nor the idea is found in the OT. Among the Greeks, *mystery* meant not something obscure or incomprehensible, but a secret imparted only to the initiated, what is unknown until it is revealed. This word is connected with the mystery religions of Hellenistic times (see separate article). The mysteries appealed to the emotions rather than the intellect and offered to their devotees a mystical union with the deity, through death to life, thus securing for them a blessed immortality. Great symbolism characterized their secret ritual, climaxing in the initiation into the full secret of the cult.

The chief use of mystery in the NT is by Paul. He, as an educated man of his day, knew well the thought world of the pagans and accepted this term to indicate the fact that "his gospel" had been revealed to him by the risen Christ. This fact could best be made clear to his contemporaries by adopting the pagan term they all understood, pouring into it a special Christian meaning.

In a few passages the term refers to a symbol, allegory, or parable, which conceals its meaning from those who look only at the literal sense, but is the medium of revelation to those who have the key to its interpretation (Rev 1:20; 17:5, 7; Mark 4:11; Eph 5:32).

The more common meaning of mystery in the NT, Paul's usual use of the word, is that of a divine truth once hidden but now revealed in the gospel (Rom 16:25-26; cf.

Col 1:26; Eph 3:3-6). A mystery is thus *now* a revelation: Christian mysteries are revealed doctrines (Rom 16:26; Eph 1:9; 3:3, 5, 10; 6:19; Col 4:3-4; 1 Tim 3:16). Christianity, therefore, has no secret doctrines, as did the ancient mystery religions. To the worldly wise and prudent the gospel is foolishness (Matt 11:25; 1 Cor 2:6-9); it is communicated to them, but they do not have the capacity to understand it (2 Cor 4:2-4). The Christian mystery, then, is God's world-embracing purpose of redemption through Christ (Rom 16:25).

MYSTERY RELIGIONS A term applied in the Greek, the Hellenistic, and the Roman world to the cult of certain deities that involved a private initiation ceremony and a reserved and secret ritual. They were probably vestiges of earlier religions, maintaining themselves as secret societies after the introduction of the Olympian and other Indo-European deities, and ending after what seems a common social pattern, by winning their way with the conquering people. The deities with whose worship the Greek "mysteries" were principally connected were Demeter, whose cult was organized into the ceremonials of Eleusis, and Dionysus, a predominantly female cult. The worship of Demeter and Dionysus appears to have been in origin a nature worship, with a ritual symbolizing death and resurrection in a seasonal sequence, and a spiritual reference of this natural pattern to the experience of the soul.

Little is known about the rites of worship and initiation, for the initiates seem to have been faithful in the keeping of their vows of secrecy; but it is fairly certain that the worship had to do with notions of sin, ritual uncleanness, purification, regeneration, and spiritual preparation for another life. It is probable that their influence was widespread, and, on the whole, promoted tranquility of spirit and upright conduct. Besides the worship of the goddess and the god already named in connection with Greece, there were other ancient deities whose cults can be properly named "mystery religions," for example, the worship of Orpheus, Adonis or Tammuz, Isis, and especially Mithras. Paul adapted some of the vocabulary of the mystery cults to a Christian purpose, and his use of the word "mystery" for a truth revealed but comprehended only by the "initiated," is a clear reference to them.

NAAMAH (nā'à-mà, Heb. *na'ămâh, pleasant*). **1.** A daughter of Lamech and Zillah (Gen 4:22) and sister of Tubal-Cain. **2.** A woman of Ammon, wife of Solomon, and mother of Rehoboam (1 Kings 14:21, 31). **3.** A town in Judah (Josh 15:41) situated in the lowland, probably near Makkedah. **4.** Possibly a town in north Arabia. In Job 2:11 Zophar is called the Naamathite and may have been from this town.

NAAMAN (nā'à-măn, Heb. *na'ămân, pleasant*). **1.** A son of Bela and grandson of Benjamin (Gen 46:21), and the head of the clan called the Naamites (Num 26:40). **2.** The "commander of the army of the king of Aram" (2 Kings 5:1). He was a courageous and successful general, but he had leprosy. This was a most dreadful disease at the time and meant ostracism and an untimely death. A young girl, who had been taken captive from Israel, served Naaman's wife. One day she told her mistress about the prophet in Samaria who could cure him (2 Kings 5:3). Naaman went to the prophet Elisha and was told to wash seven times in the River Jordan; his servants urged him to follow the prophet's instructions, and as a result he was healed (5:5–19). Jesus referred to this incident when he spoke in the synagogue at Nazareth (Luke 4:27).

NAAMATHITE (nā'à-mà-thīt, Heb. *na'ămāthî, a dweller in Naamah*). A gentilic noun with an article, applied to Zophar, one of Job's friends (Job 2:11; 11:1; 20:1; 42:9). The place was probably in north Arabia. See NAAMAH.

NAARAH (nā'à-rà, Heb. *na'ărâh, girl*). **1.** One of the wives of Ashhur, the father of Tekoa (1 Chron 4:5–6). **2.** A place on the border of Ephraim (Josh 16:7).

NAASHON, NAASSON (See NAHSHON).

NABAL (nā'băl, Heb. *nāvāl, fool*). A rich sheepmaster of Maon in the southern highland of Judah (1 Sam 25:1–42) who insulted David when he asked for food for his men, although David had protected Nabal's men and flocks. His wife Abigail averted David's vengeance by her gifts and wise words and so won David's esteem. Abigail returned home to find Nabal feasting like a king. After he sobered she told him, and his heart died within him, and he became as a stone, dying ten days later. Then David sought and won Abigail as his wife.

Khaznet Far'un (treasury) at the Nabatean capital city of Petra. The most magnificent monument at Petra, this columned façade probably dates from the second century A.D. Courtesy Ecole Biblique et Archéologique Française, Jerusalem

NABATEA, NABATEANS (năb'à-tē'ăn, Gr. *Nabataioi*). An Arabian tribe named in the Apocrypha but not in the Bible, they were important to Bible history. Between the sixth and fourth centuries B.C. they moved to Edom and Moab (as alluded to in Obad 1–7; Mal 1:1–7). By NT times their territory stretched from the Mediterranean Sea south of Gaza and the Red Sea, to the Euphrates, including Damascus. They lost Damascus when the Romans came to the aid of the Jews against them, but later recovered it so that their king, Aretas IV, controlled it when Paul was there (2 Cor 11:32). Nabatea was absorbed into the Roman province of Arabia in A.D. 106. The architecture of Petra is remarkable; its religious high places, pillars, and figures carved out of sandstone cliffs of a canyon, are accessible only on foot or muleback.

NABOPOLASSAR (năb'ō-pō-lăs'âr). First ruler of the Neo-Babylonian Empire, 626–605 B.C. Allied with Medes and Scythians, he overthrew the Assyrian

Empire, destroying Nineveh in 612 (prophesied in Nah 2:1–3:9; Zeph 2:13–15). When Pharaoh Neco came to aid the Assyrians, Josiah (king of Judah) opposed him and was killed at Megiddo (2 Kings 23:29; 2 Chron 35:20–27). Nabopolassar died in Babylon about the time his son Nebuchadnezzar II was engaged in the battle of Carchemish.

NABOTH (nā'bŏth, Heb. *nāvôth*). The Israelite who owned a vineyard beside the palace of King Ahab in Jezreel. The king coveted this land for a garden, but Naboth's refusal to sell his inheritance made Ahab angry and sullen (1 Kings 21:1–4). His wife Jezebel obtained it for him by having Naboth falsely accused of blasphemy and stoned to death (21:7–14). Punishment fell on Ahab (22:24–40) and on his son Joram and wife Jezebel (2 Kings 9:25–37).

NACHOR (See NAHOR)

NACON, NACHON (nā'kŏn, Heb. *nākhôn*). A Benjamite at whose threshing floor Uzzah was struck dead for touching the ark (2 Sam 6:6). He is also called Kidon (1 Chron 13:9).

NADAB (nā'dăb, Heb. *nādhāv*). 1. Firstborn son of Aaron and Elisheba (Exod 6:23; Num 3:2; 26:60; 1 Chron 6:3; 24:1). He accompanied Moses, Aaron, the 70 elders, and his brother Abihu up Mt. Sinai, where they saw the God of Israel (Exod 24:1–2, 9–15). He and his father and brothers were appointed priests (28:1). Nadab and Abihu offered unauthorized (NIV; unholy RSV; strange KJV, NASB) fire in burning incense before the Lord. Fire from the Lord devoured them; they were buried, and mourning was forbidden (Lev 10:1–7; Num 3:4; 26:61). 2. A great-grandson of Jerahmeel (1 Chron 2:26, 28, 30). 3. A son of Jeiel the "father" of Gibeon (8:30; 9:36). 4. A son of Jeroboam I and king of Israel for two years (1 Kings 14:20; 15:25–31). His evil reign was ended by his assassination at the hands of Baasha, ending the dynasty of Jeroboam and fulfilling Ahijah's prophecy (14:1–20).

NAHALAL, NAHALOL (nā'hȧ-lăl, nā'hȧ-lŏl). A town in Zeubulun whose inhabitants were not driven out but were subjected to forced labor. In Joshua 19:15 KJV has Nahallal and (with other versions) Nahalal in Joshua 21:35, Nahalol in Judges 1:30.

NAHASH (nā'hăsh, Heb. *nāhāsh*, probably from a root meaning *serpent* rather than from one meaning *oracle* or one meaning *copper*). 1. An Ammonite king whose harsh demands on the men of Jabesh Gilead led Saul to rally the Israelites against him and to defeat him. This victory proved decisive in making Saul king (1 Sam 11:1–2; 12:12). 2. An Ammonite king whose son Hanun David befriended (2 Sam 10; 1 Chron 19). His son Shobi brought provisions to David during his flight from Absalom (2 Sam 17:27–29). 3. A parent of Abigail and Zeruiah (17:25). First Chronicles 2:16 calls Jesse father of Abigail and Zeruiah.

NAHATH (nā'hăth, Heb. *nahath*). 1. A son of Reuel, son of Esau (Gen 36:13, 17; 1 Chron 1:37). 2. A descendant of Levi, ancestor of Samuel (6:26); perhaps the same as Toah (6:34) and Tohu (1 Sam 1:1). 3. A Levite, overseer of offerings in the days of Hezekiah (2 Chron 31:13).

NAHOR (nā'hôr, Heb. *nāhôr*). 1. Grandfather of Abraham (Gen 11:22–26; 1 Chron 1:26–27). 2. Son of Terah and brother of Abraham (Gen 11:26–29; 22:20–23; 24:15, 24, 47; 29:5; Josh 24:2). The city of Nahor is in Mesopotamia (Gen 24:10). Nahor's God is the same God as Abraham's God (31:53). KJV has Nachor (lit. translation) in Joshua 24:2 and Luke 3:34.

NAHSHON (nȧ'shŏn, Heb. *nahshôn*). The son of Amminadab (1 Chron 2:10–11); ancestor of David (Ruth 4:20); leader of the tribe of Judah on the march through the wilderness (Num 1:7; 2:3; 10:14) and in presenting offerings at the dedication of the tabernacle (7:12, 17). His sister Elisheba married Aaron (Exod 6:23, KJV Naashon). He is named Naasson in Jesus' genealogies (lit. translation, KJV in each—Matt 1:4; Luke 3:32).

NAHUM (nā'hŭm, Heb. *nahûm, compassionate*). The name is a shortened form of Nehemiah. 1. Nahum the Elkoshite, a prophet (Nah 1:1). See NAHUM, BOOK OF. 2. One of the ancestors of Christ mentioned in Luke 3:25 (KJV "Naum").

NAHUM, BOOK OF The short Book of Nahum is largely a poem, a literary masterpiece, predicting the downfall of Nineveh, the capital of Assyria. Nineveh was conquered by the Babylonians, Medes, and Scythians in 612 B.C. Nahum declared that Nineveh would fall as did Thebes, which the Assyrians themselves had conquered in 663. The book therefore was written between 663 and 612—in turbulent times. Zephaniah also predicted in Josiah's time the overthrow of Nineveh (Zeph 1:1; 2:13).

The Book of Nahum is in two parts: a poem concerning the greatness of God

(Nah 1:2–15), then a longer poem detailing the overthrow of Nineveh (2:1–3:19). The cruelty of the Assyrians is almost beyond belief. Their policy seems to have been one of calculated terror. Their own pictures show captives staked to the ground and being skinned alive. No wonder Nahum exulted at the overthrow of the proud, rich, cruel empire of Assyria. If it was wrong for Nahum to rejoice at Nineveh's fall, what shall be said of the heavenly throng of Revelation 19:1–6 (cf. Neh 2:3; 4:4–5)?

NAIN (nā'ĭn, Gr. *Nain*). Near its gates Jesus raised a widow's son from death (Luke 7:11–17). It is situated on the NW slope of the Hill of Moreh. Eastward are ancient rock-hewn tombs.

NAIOTH (nā'ŏth, ŏth, Heb. *nāyôth*). A place in or near Ramah of Benjamin where David stayed with Samuel during an early flight from Saul (1 Sam 19:18–20:1); it was also the home of a band of prophets.

NAME (Heb. *shem*, Gr. *onoma*). In Bible times the notion of "name" had a significance it does not have today, when it is usually a label without special meaning. A name was given only by a person in a position of authority (Gen 2:19; 2 Kings 23:34) and signified that the person named was appointed to a particular position, function, or relationship (Gen 35:18; 2 Sam 12:25). The name given was often determined by some circumstance at the time of birth (Gen 19:22); sometimes the name expressed a hope or a prophecy (Isa 8:1–4; Hos 1:4). When a person gave his own name to another, it signified the joining of the two in very close unity, as when God gave his name to Israel (Deut 28:9–10). To be baptized into someone's name therefore meant to pass into new ownership (Matt 28:19; Acts 8:16; 1 Cor 1:13, 15). In the Scriptures there is the closest possible relationship between a person and his name, the two being practically equivalent, so that to remove the name was to extinguish the person (Num 27:4; Deut 7:24). To forget God's name is to depart from him (Jer 23:27). The name, moreover, was the person as he had been revealed; for example, the "name of the LORD" signified the Lord in the attributes he had manifested—holiness, power, love, etc. Often in the Bible the name signified the presence of the person in the character revealed (1 Kings 18:24). To be sent or to speak in someone's name meant to carry that person's authority (Jer 11:21; 2 Cor 5:20). In later Jewish usage the name *Jehovah* was not pronounced in reading the Scriptures (cf. Wisdom 14:21), the name *Adhonai* ("my Lord") being substituted for it. To pray in the name of Jesus is to pray as his representatives on earth—in his Spirit and with his aim—and implies the closest union with Christ.

NAMES When God named what he had made, he described for man the essence of the thing (Gen 1:5, 8, 10; 2:11–14). By allowing Adam to give names, God enabled him to express relationships to his fellow creatures: Adam named the beasts (2:19–20) and woman (2:23). Eve's personal name is from her function as mother of all living (human) beings (3:20). Cain's name is a play on two Hebrew words (4:1). Seth is a reminder that God "appointed" him instead of Abel (4:25). God changed the name of Abram to Abraham in view of his destiny (17:5). People were named for animals (Caleb, dog; Tabitha and Dorcas, gazelle), plants (Tamar, palm tree), precious things (Peninnah, coral or pearl), qualities (Hannah, grace; Ikkesh, perverse; Ira, watchful), historical circumstances (Ichabod, inglorious), or relatives (Absalom named a daughter after his sister Tamar).

The significance of the names of the tribes of Israel is brought out in Genesis 48–49. Men were distinguished as sons (ben, bar), women as daughters (bath) of their fathers (Benzoheth, Simon bar-Jona, Bathsheba). Names compounded with El (God), or with Jeho- or -iah (Jehovah) became common. Jacob (Gen 32:24–32) received the name Israel, prince of God, for Jacob, supplanter, and recognized God without learning his secret name. Prophets gave their children symbolic names (Isa 8:1–4; Hos 1:4–11). The Messiah was given significant names: Immanuel, God with us; Jesus, Savior (Isa 7:14; Matt 1:21, 23; Luke 1:31). In Jesus' name (Acts 3:16) miracles were performed, just as he had promised (John 14:13–14). When we act in Jesus' name, we represent him (Matt 10:42). Place-names are for natural features (Lebanon, white, because it is snow-capped; Bethsaida and Sidon from their fishing; Tirzah, pleasantness, for its beauty). By NT times both personal and family names were common (Simon bar-Jona) or descriptive phrases were added, as for the several Marys. Hybrid or duplicate names occur in a bilingual culture: Bar (Heb.), -timeus (Gr.); Saul (Heb.) = Paul (Gr.); John (Heb.), Mark (Rom.). Patriarchal times saw names as indicators of character, function, or destiny. Soon names began to be given more hopefully than discriminatingly, until finally we are not sure whether the name tells us anything about the nature: Was Philip a "lover of horses," or could Archippus ride them?

NAOMI (nā'ō-mī, nā-ō'mĭ, Heb. *nā'ŏmî*). Wife of Elimelech of Bethlehem. Left without husband or sons, she returned from a stay in Moab with her Moabite daughter-in-law Ruth. In her depression she said she should no longer be called Naomi, "pleasantness," but now more appropriately Mara, "bitterness." She advised Ruth in the steps that led to Ruth's marriage to Boaz (Ruth 3:1-6), and she nursed Ruth's child (4:16-17).

NAPHISH (nā'fĭsh, Heb. *nāphîsh*). A son of Ishmael (Gen 25:15; 1 Chron 1:31; 5:19). His descendants, temple servants (KJV Nethinim), returned with Zerubbabel from exile (Ezra 2:50; Neh 7:52; NIV Nephussim).

NAPHOTH DOR (See DOR)

NAPHTALI (năf'tà-lī, Heb. *naphtālî*). **1.** A son of Jacob; the second son of Bilhah, Rachel's handmaid. He had four sons (Gen 46:24).
2. The tribe of Naphtali. Naphtali appears in the lists of Numbers as a tribe of moderate size. It furnished 53,400 soldiers at Kadesh Barnea (Num 1:43) and 45,000 at the mustering of the troops across from Jericho (26:50). Naphtali received the next to the last lot in the final division of the land (Josh 19:32-39), but in many ways its inheritance was the best.

Kadesh Naphtali was the home of Barak, and Naphtali figured largely in Deborah's conquest of Hazor (Judg 5:18). Men from this tribe also assisted Gideon (7:23).

NAPKIN (See HANDKERCHIEF)

NARD (See PLANTS)

NATHAN (nā'thăn, Heb. *nāthān, God has given*). **1.** The prophet at the royal court in Jerusalem during the reign of David and the early years of Solomon. David consulted him regarding the building of the temple (2 Sam 7; 1 Chron 17). Later Nathan rebuked David for adultery with Bathsheba (2 Sam 12:1-25). When Adonijah sought to supplant his aged father David as king, Nathan intervened through Bathsheba to secure the succession for her son Solomon (1 Kings 1:8-53). Nathan wrote chronicles of the reign of David (1 Chron 29:29) and shared in writing the history of the reign of Solomon (2 Chron 9:29). He was associated

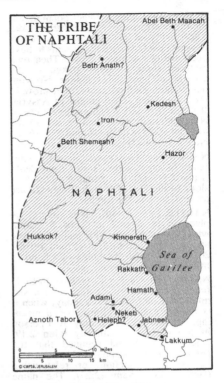

THE TRIBE OF NAPHTALI

with David and Gad the seer in arranging the musical services for the house of God (29:25).
2. A son of David (2 Sam 5:14; 1 Chron 14:4) named in the genealogy of Jesus Christ (Luke 3:31). **3.** Nathan of Zobah (2 Sam 23:36). He may be the same as Nathan the brother of Joel (1 Chron 11:38). **4.** The two Nathans mentioned in 1 Kings 4:5 as fathers of Azariah and Zabud may be the same man, and identified with no. 1, the prophet. If Zabad (1 Chron 2:36) is the same as Zabud, his father Nathan may also be the prophet. In that case we know that the prophet's father was Attai, a descendant of Jerahmeel (2:25). **5.** A leading man who returned from exile (Ezra 8:16) **6.** A returning exile who had married a foreign wife (10:39).

NATHANAEL (nà-thăn'ă-ĕl, Heb. *nethan'ĕl, God has given*). One of the apostles introduced to Christ by Philip (John 1:45ff.; 21:2). Christ praised his integrity at their initial encounter; his knowledge of Scripture was evidenced in his discussion with Jesus (1:47-51). Nathanael is commonly identified as Bartholomew.

Panoramic view of Nazareth, looking east. The Plain of Esdraelon is pictured in the background: the hills of Gilboa (right), the Hill of Moreh (center), and the area of Gilead (left). Courtesy Garo Nalbandian

The two names are used interchangeably by the church fathers.

NATHAN-MELECH (nā'thăn-mē'lek, Heb. *nethan melekh, king's gift*). An officer to whom King Josiah remanded the horses "dedicated to the sun" after burning the chariots in the fire (2 Kings 23:11). The LXX identifies him as "Nathan, the king's eunuch."

NATIONS (See GENTILES; HEATHEN)

NATURAL 1. The word is used once (Deut 34:7) for Moses' physical ability (natural force KJV, RSV; strength NIV). **2.** In the NT the word translates four Greek words: *physis*, "nature" (Rom 11:21, 24 natural branches; 2 Peter 2:12 natural brute beasts [NIV brute beasts, creatures of instinct]), *physikos*, "belonging to nature" (Rom 1:26-27 natural relations [KJV natural use]), *psychikos*, "animal, sensuous" (1 Cor 2:14, natural man [NIV man without the Spirit]; 1 Cor 15:44, natural body), and *genesis*, "origin, birth" (James 1:23, natural face [NIV face]).

NATURE A word that in KJV is found only in the NT, where it is a translation of *genesis* once (James 3:6, course of nature; RSV cycle of nature; NIV course of . . . life) and *physis* ten times—the inherent character of a person or thing (Rom 1:26; 2:14; 11:24; 1 Cor 11:14; Gal 4:8), birth (Rom 2:27; Gal 2:15; Eph 2:3), or disposition (2 Peter 1:4).

NAUM (See NAHUM)

NAVEL (nā'vĕl, Heb. *shōr*). The umbilical cord (Job 40:16; Prov 3:8; Song of Songs 7:2; Ezek 16:4).

NAZARENE (năz'à-rēn, Gr. *Nazarēnos, Nazōraios*). **1.** A word derived from Nazareth, the hometown of Christ. Jesus was often called a Nazarene. Used by his friends, it had a friendly meaning (Acts 2:22; 3:6; 10:38). Used by his enemies, it was a title of scorn (Matt 26:71; Mark 14:67). It is usually thought that Matthew (Matt 2:23) refers to Isaiah 11:1, where the Messiah is called *netser*, or shoot out of the roots of Jesse. The name Nazareth was probably derived from the same root. **2.** In Acts 24:5 adherents of Christianity are called Nazarenes.

NAZARETH (năz'à-rĕth, Gr. *Nazaret* and other forms). A town in lower Galilee, the hometown of Mary and Joseph, the human parents of Jesus (Luke 1:26; 2:4; cf. Matt 2:23).

In the synagogue of Nazareth it seems as if there were two rejections of Christ (cf. Luke 4:16-30 with Mark 6:1-6 and Matt 13:54-58.) The people of Nazareth had established a rather poor reputation in morals and religion, as seen in Nathaniel's question: "Nazareth! Can anything good come from there?" (John 1:46).

NAZARETH DECREE An inscription cut on a slab of white marble, dating A.D. 40 to 50, written by Claudius Caesar and found in Nazareth, decreeing capital punishment for anyone disturbing graves and tombs.

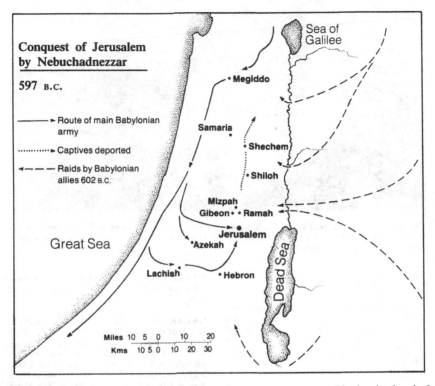

Conquest of Jerusalem by Nebuchadnezzar

597 B.C.

──── ► Route of main Babylonian army

··········► Captives deported

◄── ── Raids by Babylonian allies 602 B.C.

Great Sea

Sea of Galilee

• Megiddo

Samaria
•

• Shechem

• Shiloh

Mizpah
•
Gibeon • • Ramah

Jerusalem
•Azekah

Lachish•

• Hebron

Dead Sea

Miles 10 5 0   10   20

Kms   10 5 0   10   20   30

NAZIRITE, NAZARITE (năz'ĭ-rīt, năz'à-rīt, Heb. *nāzîr;* connected with *nadhar, to vow,* hence, *people of the vow,* i.e., *dedicated* or *consecrated*). An Israelite who consecrated himself or herself and took a vow of separation and self-imposed abstinence for the purpose of some special service (Num 6:1–23). There were two different types of Naziritism, the temporary and the perpetual. We know of only three of the latter class: Samson, Samuel, and John the Baptist.

The three principal marks that distinguished the Nazirite were (1) a renunciation of wine and all products of the vine, including grapes, (2) prohibition of the use of the razor, and (3) avoidance of contact with a dead body.

John the Baptist, the forerunner of Christ, was a Nazirite from birth (Luke 1:15). Although it cannot be established that Paul assumed such a vow, it is certain that he did assume the expenses of those who did (Acts 21:23f.).

The reasons for taking a Nazirite vow were numerous. A vow might be assumed by a parent before the birth of a child, by one in some sort of distress or trouble, or by a woman suspected by her husband of unfaithfulness in their marriage relationship until the suspicion could be removed. Women and slaves could take vows only if sanctioned by their husbands or masters.

The period of time for the Nazirite vow was anywhere from 30 days to a whole lifetime. During the Maccabean days, a number of Jews became Nazirites as a matter of protest against the Hellenistic practices and demands of Antiochus Epiphanes. There is only one clear-cut mention of the Nazirites by the prophets (Amos 2:11–12).

NEAPOLIS (nē-ăp'ō-lĭs, Gr. *Neapolis*). A town on the north shore of the Aegean Sea: the seaport of Philippi where Paul and his party sailed after seeing the "Man of Macedonia" at Troas (Acts 16:11–12). Paul may have revisited Neapolis on his return trip to Jerusalem (20:3–5).

NEARIAH (nē'à-rī'à). **1.** A descendant of David (1 Chron 3:22). **2.** A descendant of Simeon (4:42).

NEBAIOTH, NEBAJOTH (nē-bā'yŏth, nē-bā'jŏth, Heb. *nevāyôth*). **1.** The

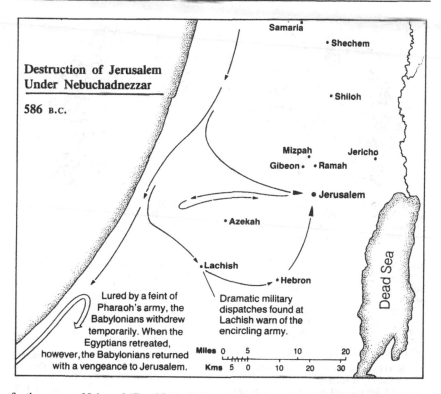

Destruction of Jerusalem Under Nebuchadnezzar

586 B.C.

Samaria
• Shechem
• Shiloh
Mizpah   Jericho
Gibeon • • Ramah
• Jerusalem
• Azekah
•Lachish
• Hebron

Lured by a feint of Pharaoh's army, the Babylonians withdrew temporarily. When the Egyptians retreated, however, the Babylonians returned with a vengeance to Jerusalem.

Dramatic military dispatches found at Lachish warn of the encircling army.

Dead Sea

Miles 0   5   10   20
Kms 5 0   10   20   30

firstborn son of Ishmael (Gen 25:13; 28:9; 36:3; 1 Chron 1:29). **2.** A tribe (Isa 60:7), perhaps identical with the Nabateans.

NEBO (nē'bō, Heb. *nevô*, Assyr. *Nabu*). **1.** A god of Babylonian mythology (Isa 46:1) who was the god of science and learning. **2.** The mountain (Pisgah) from which Moses viewed the Promised Land (Deut 34:1ff.). **3.** A Moabite town near or on Mt. Nebo (Num 32:3). **4.** A town mentioned immediately after Bethel and Ai (Ezra 2:29; Neh 7:33).

NEBUCHADNEZZAR, NEBUCHADREZZAR (nĕb'ū-kăd-nĕz'êr, nĕb'ū-kăd-rĕz'êr). The great king of the Neo-Babylonian Empire (605 to 562 B.C.). It was he who carried away Judah in the 70-year Babylonian captivity. He figures prominently in the books of Jeremiah, Ezekiel, Daniel, and the later chapters of Kings and Chronicles.

In 605 he decisively defeated the Egyptians at Carchemish. Jehoiakim, king of Judah, did homage to Babylon but later revolted (2 Kings 24:1). In 597 Jehoiakim rebelled again, and Nebuchadnezzar called out his troops for another western expedition. Jehoiakim died (Jer 22:18–19), and his son Jehoiachin ascended the throne for three months; he was taken as a hostage to Babylon, where he lived and finally was given relative freedom (2 Kings 25:27–30). Ezekiel was among the captives of this expedition. Nebuchadnezzar's chronicle agrees with the biblical account. This discovery gives about the best authenticated date in the OT.

There is no extra-biblical account of the madness of Nebuchadnezzar (Dan 4), although more than one king suffered from illness and from mental distress (Ashurbanipal and Cambyses). Much of Nebuchadnezzar's reign is a historical blank. Nebuchadnezzar was succeeded by his son Evil-Merodach, but with the passing of the brilliant Nebuchadnezzar, the Neo-Babylonian Empire soon fell prey to the Persians under Cyrus.

NEBUZARADAN (nĕb'ū-zàr-ā'dăn, Akkad. *Nebo has given seed*). Nebuchadnezzar's general when the Babylonians besieged Jerusalem (2 Kings 25:8, 11–12, 20; Jer 52:12ff.). Jeremiah was made his special responsibility (Jer 39:11–14).

Reconstruction of the palace of Nebuchadnezzar II at Babylon: (1) Ishtar Gate, (2) Nebuchadnezzar's throne room, perhaps the scene of Belshazzar's feast, and (3) the temple dedicated to Ninmah, located to the east of Ishtar Gate and the Processional Way. After Koldewey. Courtesy Carta, Jerusalem

After the fall of Jerusalem in 586–85 B.C., Nebuzaradan conducted the captives to Babylon. Before the appointment of Gedaliah (40:5) Nebuzaradan was provisional governor of Palestine for the Babylonians. Nebuzaradan presented the option to Jeremiah to travel with him to Babylon or to remain in his own land (40:1–6). The prophet chose to remain.

NECK (Heb. *tsawwār, tsawwā'râh*, Gr. *nōtos, back*). A term often used in Scripture with literal and figurative meanings. The bowed neck is often used as a symbol of submission, while the unbowed or "stiff neck" represents insubordination and disobedience (Exod 32:9; Deut 9:13; Ps 75:5; Acts 7:51). It was a military custom for the conqueror to place his foot on the neck of the vanquished (Josh 10:24; Ps 110:1; Rom 16:20). "To fall upon the neck" of (NIV to embrace, or throw one's arms around) a person is a common mode of salutation in the East and sometimes portrays great emotional stress (Gen 46:29; Luke 15:20; Acts 20:37).

NECKLACE (Heb. *ravidh*). A chain worn as an ornament around the neck, and to which might be attached pendants (Isa 3:18) or rings (Gen 38:25). The word is not found in the KJV but is used in the NIV, and such ornaments were very popular in ancient times.

NECO, NECHO, NECHOH (*nē'kō*, Heb. *par'ōh nekhōh* or *nechoh*). Ruler of Egypt (609–595 B.C.). After Josiah's defeat by Neco at the battle of Megiddo (2 Kings 23:29; 2 Chron 35:20ff.), Jehoahaz was made king, but Neco dethroned

him and set up in his stead Jehoahaz's brother Jehoiakim (2 Kings 23:29–34; 2 Chron 35:20–36:4). In 605 Neco was badly defeated by Nebuchadnezzar at the battle of Carchemish and lost all of his Asiatic possessions (2 Kings 24:7).

NECROMANCER, NECROMANCY (*nĕk'rō-măn-sēr, nĕk'rō-măn-sē*). Necromancy was a form of witchcraft and was considered one of the "black" or diabolical arts. Etymologically, the term signifies conversing with the dead for purposes of consultation or divination. The Mosaic Law sternly forbade such a practice (Deut 18:10–11). The most familiar case in the Bible is that of King Saul and the witch of Endor (1 Sam 28:7–25). Perhaps the most feasible view of this difficult passage is that God for his own purpose allowed Saul to converse with the deceased Samuel (cf. v. 12).

NEEDLE'S EYE (Gr. *raphis*). By this expression (Matt 19:24; Mark 10:25; Luke 18:25) Jesus probably intended to teach that it is utterly absurd for a man bound up in his riches to expect to enter the kingdom of God.

NEEDLEWORK (See EMBROIDERY)

NEGEV, NEGEB (*nĕg'ĕv, nĕg'ĕb*, Heb. *neghev, dry*). The desert region lying to the south of Judea, the term also has the meaning of the "south" (usually so rendered in the KJV), because of its direction from Judah, and the "desert," because of its aridity.

The Negev has rolling hills that abruptly terminate in the desert region and is bounded on the east by the Dead Sea and on the west by the Mediterranean Sea. In this territory Hagar encountered the angel when she fled from Sarah (Gen 16:7, 14). Here both Isaac and Jacob lived (24:62; 37:1). This territory was part of the original land of the Amalekites (Num 13:29). The Negev was allotted to the tribe of Simeon (Josh 19:1–9), or to Judah (15:20–31). Many of David's exploits during the reign of Saul happened in the Negev, centering around Ziklag (1 Sam 27:5ff.).

NEHEMIAH (nē'hĕ-mī'à, Heb. *nehem-yâh, Jehovah has comforted*). 1. One of the leaders of the returning exiles under Zerubbabel (Ezra 2:2; Neh 7:7). 2. The son of Azbuk (3:16). 3. The governor of the Persian province of Judah after 444 B.C. Nehemiah was a "cupbearer" to King Artaxerxes (Neh 1:11; 2:1), who ruled from 465 to 423 B.C.

When Nehemiah arrived at Jerusalem, he first privately surveyed the scene of rubble (Neh 2:1–16). Then he organized the community to carry out the effort of rebuilding the broken-down wall. Nehemiah cooperated with Ezra in numerous reforms and especially in the public instruction in the law (Neh 8). However, he left for Persia, probably on official business, in 431 B.C. (13:6). Later he returned to Jerusalem.

NEHEMIAH, BOOK OF The Book of Nehemiah closes the history of the biblical period. Closely allied to the Book of Ezra, it was attached to it in the old Jewish reckoning. It gives the history and reforms of Nehemiah the governor from 444 to about 420 B.C.

Outline:

I. Nehemiah Returns to Jerusalem (1:1–2:20).

II. Building Despite Opposition (3:1–7:4).

III. Genealogy of the First Returning Exiles (7:5–73 [= Ezra 2:2–70]).

IV. The Revival and Covenant Sealing (8:1–10:39).

V. Dwellers at Jerusalem and Genealogies (11:1–12:26).

VI. Final Reforms (13:1–31).

Nehemiah's great work of restoring the wall of Jerusalem depended on securing permission from the king. Earlier Ezra had returned to Jerusalem, but had been hindered in his work by adverse royal decrees secured by his enemies. In God's providence Nehemiah secured the restoration of royal favor. The actual building

of the wall was parceled out among different leaders. Although Nehemiah encountered opposition from Sanballat, the wall was successfully completed.

Nehemiah's reform involved the teaching of Moses' Law by Ezra and others at the Feast of Tabernacles (commanded in Deut 31:10). This led to the great prayer of confession of Nehemiah 9. A covenant was solemnly sealed to walk in the Law of the Lord as given by Moses (10:29).

NEHUSHTA (nē-hŭsh'tà, Heb. *nehush-tā'*). The mother of King Jehoiachin of Judah (2 Kings 24:8) who was exiled with her son to Babylon (24:12; Jer 29:2).

NEHUSHTAN (nĕ-hŭsh'tăn, Heb. *nehushtān, perhaps brass serpent*). The name given to the brass serpent of Moses that was later destroyed by Hezekiah because the Israelites had made it an object of worship (2 Kings 18:4).

NEIGHBOR (Heb. *rēa', 'āmîth, friend, qārôv, shākhēn*, Gr. *plēsion, nearby, geitōn, inhabitant*). The tenth commandment is directed toward the protection of the neighbor's property (Exod 20:17); the ninth, toward the protection of a neighbor's reputation (20:16). Cities of refuge were appointed for one who killed his neighbor accidentally (Deut 19:4). Proverbs is full of admonitions concerning one's neighbor (Prov 14:21). Due regard for one's neighbor is expressed in the great OT and NT precept, "Love your neighbor as yourself" (Lev 19:18; Matt 19:19). The parable of the Good Samaritan (Luke 10:30–37) was given in answer to the question, "And who is my neighbor?" (10:29).

NEKODA (nē-kō'dà). The head of a family of temple servants (KJV Nethinim) who could not prove their Israelite descent at the return from Babylon (Ezra 2:48, 60; Neh 7:50, 62).

NEMUEL (nĕm'ū-ĕl, Heb. *nemû'ēl*). 1. A Reubenite, brother of Dathan and Abiram (Num 26:9). 2. A son of Simeon (26:12; 1 Chron 4:24), also called Jemuel (Gen 46:10).

NEPHEG (nē'fĕg, Heb. *nephegh, sprout, shoot*). 1. Son of Izhar (Exod 6:21). 2. A son of David (2 Sam 5:15; 1 Chron 3:7; 14:6).

NEPHEW (Heb. *nekēdh*, Gr. *ekgonon*). A term found in the KJV four times, meaning grandson (Judg 12:14), descendant (Job 18:19; Isa 14:22), grandchild (1 Tim 5:4). NIV uses it three times, all with today's common meaning of the son of one's sister or brother (Gen 12:5; 14:12; Ezra 8:19).

NEPHILIM (See GIANTS)

NEPHISH (See NAPHISH)

NEPHTHALIM (See NAPHTALI)

NER (nûr, Heb. *nēr, a lamp*). 1. Father of Abner (1 Sam 14:50; 26:14). 2. The grandfather of King Saul (1 Chron 8:33; cf. 1 Kings 2:5, 32).

NERGAL (nûr'gàl, Heb. *nereghal*). A Babylonian deity of destruction and disaster, associated with the planet Mars (2 Kings 17:30).

NERGAL-SHAREZER (nûr'gǎl-shà-rē'-zêr, Assyr. *nerghal sar-usar, may Nergal protect the prince*). The son-in-law of Nebuchadnezzar, also called Neriglissar. Evil-Merodach (Amil-Marduk), who succeeded Nebuchadnezzar as king, was assassinated by Nergal-Sharezer, who then became king (Jer 39:3–13).

NERIAH (nē-rī'à, Heb. *nērîyâh, whose lamp is Jehovah*). The father of Seraiah and Baruch, the latter being the scribe of Jeremiah (Jer 32:12, 16; 36:4; 43:3).

NERIGLISSAR (See NERGAL-SHAREZER)

NERO (nē'rō, Gr. *Nērōn*). The fifth Roman emperor, born A.D. 37, commenced reign 54, died June 9, 68. Nero's father was Enaeus Domitus Ahenobarbus, a man given to viciousness and vice. His mother was Agrippina, who cared little for her son's morals but was interested only in his temporal advancement.

The first years of Nero's reign were peaceful. Nero himself could boast that not a single person had been unjustly executed throughout his extensive empire. During these "rational years" of Nero's administration, the apostle Paul, in compliance with his own expressed appeal (Acts 25:10–11), was brought before Nero as the reigning Caesar (c. A.D. 63). We may infer that Paul was freed of all charges to continue his labors of evangelization.

Nero's marriage to Poppaea opened the second period of his reign. He killed his mother, his chief advisers Seneca and Burrus, and many of the nobility to secure their fortunes.

In A.D. 64 a large part of Rome was destroyed by fire. Whether or not Nero actually ordered the burning of the city is very controversial. A scapegoat was provided in the Christians. Even the Roman historian Tacitus reported the severity of the sufferings inflicted on them.

The Roman emperor Nero (A.D. 54–68). Courtesy Carta, Jerusalem

Nero's private life was a scandal; he indulged himself in the most evil forms of pleasure. Conspiracies and plots dogged his latter years. Advised to destroy himself, he could not find the courage to do so. Learning that the Senate had decreed his death, Nero's last cruel act was to put many of the Senate members to death. He finally died by his own hand in the summer of A.D. 68, the last of the line of Julius Caesar. Both Paul and Peter suffered martyrdom under Nero.

NEST (Heb. *qēn*, Gr. *nossia* or *katuskēnōsis*). The nests of birds differ from species to species (Ps 104:17; Jer 48:28; Ezek 31:6). Many nests are built high (Job 39:27; Jer 49:16; Obad 4; Hab 2:9). Mosaic law forbade one who found a bird's nest with the mother and her brood from harming the mother bird (Deut 22:6). Isaiah compares the despoiling of Israel by the Assyrians to the robbing of a bird's nest (Isa 10:14). Jesus contrasts birds having nests with his having no home (Matt 8:20; Luke 9:58).

NETHANEL, NETHANEEL (nē-thăn'ĕl, nē-thăn'ē-ĕl, Heb. *nethan'ēl, God has given*). 1. A prince of Issachar (Num 1:8; 2:5). 2. Son of Jesse (1 Chron 2:14). 3. One of the priests who played trumpets before the ark (15:24). 4. A Levitical scribe (24:6). 5. Fifth son of Obed-Edom (26:4). 6. A prince of Judah whom Jehoshaphat appointed to teach in Israel

(2 Chron 17:7). **7.** A wealthy Levite in Josiah's time (35:9). **8.** A priest in Ezra's time who had taken a foreign wife (Ezra 10:22). **9.** A priest and head of a household (Neh 12:21). **10.** A priestly musician in the days of Nehemiah (12:36).

Nathanael of Cana of Galilee in the days of Jesus (John 1:45–49) had the same name, though in the Greek it is slightly changed.

NETHANIAH (nĕth'à-nī'a, Heb. *nethanyāhû, whom Jehovah gave*). **1.** Father of Ishmael the assassin of Gedaliah (Jer 40:8–41:18). **2.** A chief singer (1 Chron 25:2, 12). **3.** A teaching Levite (2 Chron 17:8). **4.** Father of Jehudi (Jer 36:14).

NETHINIM (nĕth'ĭ-nĭm, Heb. *nethînîm, given ones*). A large group of temple servants, mentioned only in the later books of the OT. In a sense, all the Levites were Nethinim (Num 8:19), for they were given by the Lord as a gift to Aaron and his sons for the divine service. At the conquest of Midian (ch. 31) the plunder was divided between the warriors and the congregation, and a fixed proportion was "given" for the Lord's service (31:40, 42, 47), of which 32 were "nethinim" to the priests and 320 to the Levites in general. Later, when the men of Gibeon deceived Israel by claiming to have come a great distance (Josh 9), they were allowed to live but were made "hewers of wood and drawers of water." The 392 descendants of these two groups, called Nethinim 18 times in the KJV (1 Chron 9:2; Ezra; Neh), came back with Israel after the Babylonian captivity (Ezra 2:43–58). At Ezra's return he lists 220 Nethinim (8:20) and explains that David had appointed these for the service of the Levites.

NETOPHAH, NETOPHATHITES (nĕtō'fà, nĕ-tŏ'fa-thīts). A village of Judah and its inhabitants. The "villages of the Netophathites" (1 Chron 9:16; Neh 12:28) were apparently given to, or inhabited by, Levites, although Netophah is not mentioned in the earlier books. Several of David's men are named as from this place (2 Sam 23:28–29; 1 Chron 2:54).

NETTLE (See PLANTS)

NETWORK 1. Networks (Isa 19:9 KJV; white cloth JB, NASB; white cotton RSV; fine linen NIV). **2.** An ornamental carving or bas-relief on the pillars of Solomon's temple (1 Kings 7:18–42). **3.** A network of brass that served as a grate for the great altar of burnt offering at the tabernacle (Exod 27:4; 38:4).

NEW BIRTH (See REGENERATION)

NEW MOON (See CALENDAR; FEASTS)

NEW TESTAMENT A collection of 27 documents, the second part of the sacred Scriptures of the Christian church, the first part being called by contrast the "Old Testament." In the name "New Testament," apparently first given to the collection in the latter half of the second century, the word "testament" represents Greek *diathēkē*, variously translated "testament," "settlement," "covenant" (the last of these being on the whole the most satisfactory equivalent). The new covenant is the new order or dispensation inaugurated by the death of Jesus (Luke 22:20; 1 Cor 11:25), fulfilling God's promise (Jer 31:31–34; cf. Heb 8:6–12). The earlier covenant established by God with Israel in Moses' day came to be known as the "old covenant" (cf. 2 Cor 3:14; Heb 8:13).

The order in which the 27 documents appear in our NT today is an order of subject-matter rather than a chronological order. First come the four Gospels— narrating Jesus' ministry, death, and resurrection. These are followed by the Acts of the Apostles, which begins by mentioning Jesus' appearances to the disciples following the Resurrection; from then on we are told how, over the next 30 years, Christianity spread along the road from Jerusalem to Rome. This book was originally written as the continuation of the Gospel of Luke. These five constitute the narrative section of the NT.

The next 21 documents take the form of letters written to communities or individuals; 13 of these bear the name of Paul as writer, one the name of James, two of Peter, and one of Jude (Judas). The others are anonymous.

The 'ast book of the NT bears some featui of the epistolary style in that it is introduced by seven covering letters addressed to churches in the Roman province of Asia; but for the most part it belongs to the class of literature to which it has given its own name ("apocalyptic," from "Apocalypse" or "Revelation"). In apocalyptic literature the out-working of God's purpose on earth is given in the form of symbolical visions.

Jesus himself wrote no book, but he gave his teaching to his disciples in forms that could be easily memorized and taught to others. There is good reason to believe that one of the earliest Christian writings was a compilation of his teaching, arranged according to the chief subjects he treated, though this document has not been preserved in its original

The last three verses of Luke and the beginning of John (1:1–16) from the Bodmer XIV–XV papyrus (early third century A.D.) found in Upper Egypt. Courtesy Foundation Martin Bodmer

form but has been incorporated into some of the existing NT books. Paul and the other writers were conscious of the fact that they expressed the mind of Christ, under the guidance of his Spirit. Their letters are therefore full of teaching, imparted to the first readers by apostolic authority, which retains its validity to the present day, and have by divine providence been preserved for our instruction.

The Gospels began to appear about the end of the first generation following the death and resurrection of Jesus. By that time the eyewitnesses were being removed by death, one by one, and before long none of them would be left. It was desirable, therefore, that their testimony should be placed on permanent record, so that those who came after would not be at a disadvantage as compared with Christians of the first generation.

For some time these four evangelic records circulated independently and locally, being valued, no doubt, by those for whom they were primarily written. But by the early years of the second century they were gathered together and began to circulate as a fourfold record throughout the Christian world. When this happened, Acts was detached from Luke's Gospel, to which it originally formed the sequel, and set out on a new, but not insignificant, career of its own.

Paul's letters were preserved at first by those to whom they were sent. At least, all that have come down to us were so preserved, for here and there in his surviving correspondence we find reference to a letter that may have been lost at a very early date (cf. 1 Cor 5:9; Col 4:16). But by the last decade of the first century there is evidence of a move to bring his available letters together and circulate them as a collection among the churches.

From the second half of the second century, the church came to acknowledge a NT of the same general dimensions as ours. For a considerable time there was some questioning about a few of the books at the end of our NT, and arguments were occasionally put forward for the recognition of books that did not ultimately maintain their place within the collection. But after some generations of debate about the few "disputed" books in relation to the majority of "acknowledged" books, we find the 27 books that make up our NT today listed by Athanasius of Alexandria in A.D. 367, and not long after by Jerome and Augustine in the West. These leaders did not impose decisions of their own but published what was generally recognized. When first a church council did make a pronouncement on this subject (A.D. 393), it did no more than record the consensus of the church in East and West.

The authority of the NT is not based on archaeological evidence or on any other line of comparative study, but on the authority of Christ, whether exercised in his own person or delegated to his apostles. The NT documents are the written deposit of the apostles' witness to Christ and of the teaching they imparted in his name. The NT canon serves as the church's rule of faith and life. It continues to call Christians back to the ways of apostolic purity.

In all this the place of the OT as an integral part of the Christian Scriptures is not ignored. The two Testaments are so organically interwoven that the authority of the one carries with it the authority of the other. If the OT records the divine promise, the New records its fulfillment; if the OT tells how preparation was made over many centuries for the coming of Christ, the New tells how he came and what his coming brought about. If even the OT writings are able to make the readers "wise for salvation through faith in Christ Jesus" and equip them thoroughly for the service of God (2 Tim 3:15–17), how much more is this true of the NT writings! Our Lord's statement of the highest function of the earlier Scriptures applies with at least equal force to those of the NT: "These are the Scriptures that testify about me" (John 5:39).

NEW YEAR (See Feasts)

NICODEMUS (nĭk'ō-dē'mŭs, Gr. *Nikodēmos, victor over the people*). A leading Pharisee, "a ruler of the Jews," and a member of the Sanhedrin. He came to Jesus by night (John 3:1–14). Jesus made him aware of his need for a new birth. Later, at the Feast of Tabernacles (7:25–44), when the Jewish leaders were planning to kill Jesus, Nicodemus spoke up, though timidly, in the Sanhedrin, suggesting their injustice in condemning a man without a fair trial. After the death of Jesus, however, Nicodemus came boldly with Joseph of Arimathea (19:38–42), provided a rich store of spices for the embalmment, and assisted in the burial of the body.

NICOLAITANS (nĭk'ō-lā'ĭ-tănz, Gr. *Nikolaitai*). A group of persons whose works both the church at Ephesus and our Lord hated (Rev 2:6) and whose doctrine was held by some in the Pergamum church (2:15). Their doctrine was similar to that of Balaam, through whose influence the Israelites ate things sacrificed to idols and committed fornication (2:14–15). A sect of Nicolaitans existed among the Gnostics in the third century.

NIGHT (See Time)

NIGHT HAWK (See Birds)

NILE (nīl, Gr. *Neilos,* meaning not certainly known). The main river, not only of Egypt, but of Africa as well, ranking sixth among the river systems of the world. The word *Nile* does not appear in the Hebrew OT or in the KJV. When we find in Scripture the words *the River*, we can generally judge by the context whether the Nile (e.g., Gen 41:1) or the Euphrates (e.g., 31:21) is intended.

About the beginning of July the lifegiving inundation begins so that the delta region overflows and the stream deposits the rich sediment brought down from the mountains. If the inundation is unusually deep, many houses are destroyed and

The Nile River, with the typical sailboat, the felucca. Courtesy Seffie Ben-Yoseph

loss ensues, while if it is much below the average level, famine follows. A failure of this inundation for seven successive years (Gen 41) was used by God to work a great but peaceful revolution in Egypt in which Joseph bought up for the pharaoh practically all private property except that of the priests and brought the Israelites into Egypt for a stay of several hundred years.

From the days of Abraham, who as Abram went down into Egypt (Gen 12:10), until the infancy of our Lord Jesus Christ (Matt 2:14), Egypt and the Nile were well known by Israel and exerted a strong effect on the civilization of Israel (cf. Deut 11:10–12). We find various references to the rivers of Egypt in the prophets (e.g., Isa 7:18; 19:5, 7).

NIMRAH (nĭm'rà, Heb. *nimrâh, limpid* or *flowing water*). A city in Gilead, assigned by Moses to the tribe of Gad (Num 32:3; cf. 32:36, where it is called "Beth Nimrah," i.e., "house of limpid water"). It lies about 10 miles (17 km.) NE of Jericho. In Joshua 13:27 it is described as being "in the valley" and a part of the former kingdom of Sihon, king of the Amorites.

NIMROD (nĭm'rŏd, Heb. *nimrōdh*). In the "Table of the Nations" (Gen 10) Nimrod stands out as an individual man and a very interesting character. The beginning of his kingdom was in Babylonia; later he founded Nineveh and other cities in or near Assyria. He became distinguished as a hunter, ruler, and builder. Some have associated Nimrod with the building of the Tower of Babel (11:1–9).

NINEVEH, NINEVE (nĭn'ĕ-vĕ, Heb. *nîneweh*). One of the most ancient cities of the world, founded by Nimrod (Gen 10:11–12), a great-grandson of Noah, and enduring till 612 B.C. Nineveh lay on the banks of the Tigris and was the capital of the great Assyrian Empire. From David's time to that of Hezekiah and Manasseh, Nineveh and its kings were paramount. God sent Jonah to warn the people of Nineveh of the coming judgment (Jonah 3:4), but God gave Nineveh a respite for nearly 200 years. About 623 Cyaxares, king of the Medes, made his first attack on Nineveh, and this was probably the occasion of Nahum's prophecy. His book is undated, but 3:8 speaks of Thebes (Heb., *No Amon*) in the past tense (it was destroyed in 663) and of Nineveh's destruction as future, so it must have been written about this time.

Nineveh was excavated (largely by Botta and Layard from A.D. 1843–45), and among its buried ruins the great palace of Sargon, with its wonderful library of cuneiform inscriptions and its still-striking wall ornamentation, has been uncovered. Because the name Sargon was omitted in some of the ancient lists of kings, some of the scholars scoffed (around 1840) at Isaiah 20:1, "sent by Sargon king of Assyria." It is said that when Botta sent to Berlin some ancient bricks with the name Sargon baked into them, the "scholars" claimed that he forged the bricks!

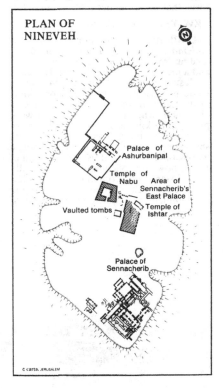

PLAN OF NINEVEH

Palace of Ashurbanipal

Temple of Nabu   Area of Sennacherib's East Palace

Vaulted tombs   Temple of Ishtar

Palace of Sennacherib

© Carta, JERUSALEM

NISAN (See CALENDAR)

NISROCH (nĭs'rŏk, Heb. *nisrōkh*). A god who was worshiped at Nineveh. In the temple of this god Sennacherib was killed by his two sons Adrammelech and Sharezer after his return from his disastrous experience near Jerusalem (Isa 37:36–38; 2 Kings 19:35–37).

NITER (nī'tẽr, Heb. *nether*). Not the same as our present niter, but an impure mixture of washing and baking sodas found in deposits around the alkali lakes of Egypt. The references in Scripture are to its fizzing with vinegar and its use in cleansing (Prov 25:20; Jer 2:22; "soda" in NIV, "nitre" in KJV).

NO (Heb. *nō'* *'āmôn, the city of the god Amon*). The great city and capital of Upper Egypt, lying on both sides of the Nile about 400 miles (667 km.) south of Cairo. Egypt's capital as early as the eleventh century, its tremendous ruins at Luxor and Karnak are among the world's wonders. Its fuller name was No Amon (Amon from a local god). KJV translates *Nō'* *'āmôn* in Jeremiah 46:25 as "multitude of No," but NIV has "Amon god of Thebes"; in 46:25 KJV again translates *'āmôn* by "multitude," but NIV has "craftsmen." In Nahum 3:8, however, KJV translates *Nō'* *'āmôn* as "populace No"; NIV has simply "Thebes," the name known to the classical writers.

NOADIAH (nō'à-dī'à, Heb. *nô'adhyâh, with whom Jehovah meets*). **1.** One of the Levites (Ezra 8:33). **2.** A false prophetess who tried to terrorize Nehemiah (Neh 6:14).

NOAH (nō'à, Heb. *nōah, rest*). **1.** The son of Lamech and tenth in descent from Adam in the line of Seth (Gen 5:28–29). He received this name because Lamech foresaw that through him God would comfort (Heb. *nāham,* same root as "Noah") the race and partially alleviate the effects of the Edenic curse. Noah was uniquely righteous (6:1–13). When he was 480 years old, 120 years before the Flood (6:3), God warned him that the world would be destroyed by water (Heb 11:7). He was then given exact instructions for building the ark (Gen 6:14–16). While engaged in this colossal task, he warned men of the coming catastrophe (2 Peter 2:5), while God in longsuffering waited for men to repent (1 Peter 3:20). Noah's three sons—Shem, Ham, and Japheth—were not born until he was 500 years old (Gen 5:32). One week before the Flood God led Noah and his family into the ark and supernaturally directed the animals also to enter. When all were safely inside, God shut the door (7:16). The Flood came in Noah's 600th year, increased steadily for 40 days, maintained its mountain-covering depth for 110 more days, and then subsided sufficiently for Noah to disembark in the mountains of Ararat after another 221 days (see FLOOD). To determine whether it was safe to disembark, Noah sent forth first a raven, and then a dove at regular intervals (8:6–10). The olive leaf proved to him that such sturdy plants had already

begun to grow on the mountain heights. God commanded him to disembark, and Noah built an altar and offered clean beasts as burnt offerings to God. The Lord then promised never to send another universal flood, confirming it with the rainbow sign (8:21–22; 9:9–17). God blessed Noah and his family and commanded them to multiply and fill the earth (9:1). From now on animals would fear man, and they were given to him as food, except the blood (9:2–4). Human government was instituted by the provision of capital punishment for murderers (9:5–6).

Noah planted a vineyard, drank himself into a drunken stupor, and shamefully exposed himself in his tent (9:20–21). Ham, presumably led by his son Canaan, made fun of Noah. For this foul deed, Canaan was cursed and Ham received no blessing (9:25–27). On the other hand, Shem and Japheth showed due respect to their father (9:23) and received rich blessings for their descendants. Noah lived 350 years after the Flood, dying at the age of 950 (9:29).

2. One of the five daughters of Zelophehad, of the tribe of Manasseh (Num 26:33; 27:1; 36:11; Josh 17:3), who received an inheritance in the land in their father's name, in spite of having no brothers.

NOB (nōb, Heb. *nōv*). A town of the priests in the tribe of Benjamin just north of the city of Jerusalem. The language of Isaiah 10:32 indicates that it was within sight of Jerusalem. In the time of King Saul the tabernacle stood here for a time, and David's visit to Ahimelech the priest (1 Sam 21) was the cause or at least the occasion for the complete destruction of the city by Saul (22:19).

NOBAH (nō'bà, Heb. *nōvâh, barking*). **1.** A man of Manasseh in the days of Moses, who in the conquest of the land of Bashan took the city of Kenath from the Amorites (Num 32:42). **2.** A town in the neighborhood of which Gideon finally defeated the Midianites and took their kings (Judg 8:11).

NOBAI (See NEBAI)

NOBLEMAN One belonging to a king, *basilikos,* as in John 4:46–53 (NIV "royal official"), or one well-born, *eugenēs,* as in the parable of the pounds (Luke 19:12–27).

NOE (See NOAH)

NON (See NUN)

NOON (See TIME)

NOPH (nŏf, Heb. *nōph*). Better known as Memphis, a city on the west side of the Nile south of Cairo (Isa 19:13; Jer 2:16; 46:19).

NORTH The word often occurs merely as a point of the compass, but there are many passages, especially in the prophets, where it refers to a particular country, usually Assyria or Babylonia (Jer 3:18; 46:6; Ezek 26:7; Zeph 2:13). Although Nineveh and Babylon were east of Jerusalem, they are usually referred to as "the north" because armies from there could not come across the desert, but had first to go north to Syria and then south.

NOSE, NOSTRILS (Heb. *'aph, nehî-rayim*). Because the nostrils quiver in anger, the word for nostril is rendered "anger," almost like "snorting" in 171 places; and this is used not only of Jacob (Gen 27:45) but also of Moses (Exod 32:19) and even of the Lord (Num 11:1, 10). A stormy wind is described as "the blast of your nostrils" (Exod 15:8; 2 Sam 22:16), referring to God. A long nose was counted an element of beauty (Song of Songs 7:4), and the nose was often decorated with a ring (Ezek 16:12 NIV, cf. Isa 3:21). A hook in the nose however was a means of subjection (37:29).

NOSE JEWEL (See DRESS)

NOVICE (nŏv'ĭs, Gr. *neophytos, newly planted*). Used only in 1 Timothy 3:6 (KJV; MLB, NASB new convert; NIV recent convert) concerning the requirements for being a bishop. This is the Greek term from which we get *neophyte*.

NUMBERS The Hebrews in ancient times used the common decimal system as a method of counting. There is no evidence that they used figures to denote numbers. Before the Exile they spelled the numbers out in full, as is seen in the present text of the Hebrew Scriptures. After the Exile some of the Jews employed such signs as were used among the Egyptians, the Arameans, and the Phoenicians—an upright line for 1, two such lines for 2, three for 3, etc., and special signs for 10, 20, 100. At least as far back as the reign of Simon Maccabeus (143–135 B.C.), they numbered the chapters and verses of the Hebrew Bible and expressed dates by using the consonants of the Hebrew alphabet: aleph for 1, beth for 2, etc. The letters of the Greek alphabet were used in the same way.

Numbers were used conventionally and symbolically. Certain numbers and their multiples had sacred or symbolic significance: 3, 4, 7, 10, 12, 40, 70. For example, three expressed emphasis, as in "A ruin! A ruin! I will make it a ruin!" (Ezek 21:27). From early times seven was a sacred number among the Semites (Gen 2:2; 4:24; 21:28); ten was regarded as a complete number.

The later rabbis developed the theory that all numbers have secret meanings and that all objects have their fundamental numbers, and elaborate mathematical rules were devised to carry out these concepts. The system came to be known as gematria (a corruption of geometria). Some Bible students think that an example of this is found in Revelation 13:18, where the number of the Beast is 666.

NUMBERS, BOOK OF The fourth book of the Pentateuch, called *In the Wilderness* by the Jews after its first significant word. The Hebrew title is more meaningful than the English, for the book picks up the account of the wilderness wandering after the arrival at Sinai (Exod 19) and records the Bedouinlike travels of Israel through all the 40 years of wandering.

The name *Numbers* comes from the Greek translation. Both at the beginning (1:2–46) and near the end (26:2–51) the number of the Israelites is given—a little over 600,000 males 20 years of age and older. This was a count of the fighting forces, given twice because the army was called up twice for battle—first at the abortive attempt to invade the land at Kadesh Barnea, and second at the end of the 40 years of wandering just before the conquest of Canaan.

The body of Numbers up to 10:11 gives additional legislation and the organization of the host. From 10:11 to 12:16 the march from Sinai to Kadesh Barnea is recorded. Then comes the debacle at Kadesh recorded in chapters 13 and 14. The three leaders of this occasion—Joshua and Caleb, the believing spies, and Moses the intercessor—are forever memorialized as among God's great men. Chapters 15 to 21:11 record the repeated faithlessness on the part of the people. Apparently during much of the 40 years (Amos 5:25–26; Josh 5:2ff.), the people wandered far away from God, and even their national unity may have lapsed temporarily.

From Numbers 21:11 on, the accounts of the conquest of Transjordan and the preparations to enter the land are given. Sihon and Og of the northern territory were conquered in swift moves detailed more extensively in Deuteronomy. Then Numbers portrays the very interesting activity of Balaam, the hireling prophet who was supernaturally restrained from cursing Israel (chs. 22–24). Final material includes Joshua's installation (ch. 27), the summary of the journeys (ch. 33), and the provision of cities of refuge (ch. 35).

NUN (nŭn, Heb. *nûn*). A man of Ephraim and the father of Joshua (Exod 33:11; Neh 8:17). His descent is given in 1 Chronicles 7:25–27.

NURSE (See Occupations and Professions)

NUT (See Plants)

–O–

OAK (See PLANTS)

OATH (ōth, Heb. *shevû'âh, 'ālâh,* Gr. *horkos*). An appeal to God to witness the truth of a statement or of the binding character of a promise (Gen 21:23; 31:53; Gal 1:20; Heb 6:16). Two varieties of the oath are found in the OT—a simple one for common use and a more solemn one. Oaths played a very important part not only in legal and state affairs but in the dealings of everyday life. A number of formulas were used in taking an oath, such as "the LORD is witness between you and me forever" (1 Sam 20:23) and "as the LORD who rescues Israel lives" (14:39). Certain ceremonies were observed in taking an oath—in ordinary cases the raising of the hand toward heaven (Gen 14:22; Deut 32:40), in exceptional cases the putting of the hand under the thigh of the one to whom the oath was made (Gen 24:2; 47:29). Sometimes one taking an oath killed an animal, divided it into two parts, and passed between the pieces (15:8–18). Swearing was done by the life of the person addressed (1 Sam 1:26), by the life of the king (17:55), by one's own head (Matt 5:36), by the angels, by the temple (23:16), by Jerusalem (5:35), and by God. It was forbidden to swear by a false god (Josh 23:7). By the time of Christ the OT law regarding oaths (Exod 22:11) was much perverted by the scribes, and Jesus therefore condemned indiscriminate and light taking of oaths. The lawfulness of oaths is recognized by the apostles, who called on God to witness to the truth of what they said (2 Cor 11:31; Gal 1:20).

OBADIAH (ō'bà-dī'à, Heb. *'ōvadhyâh, servant of Jehovah*). 1. The governor of Ahab's household (1 Kings 18:3–16). 2. The head of a household of David's descendants (1 Chron 3:21). 3. A chief man of Issachar (7:3). 4. One of the six sons of Azel, a Benjamite (8:38 copied in 9:44). 5. A Levite who returned early from captivity (9:16); also called "Abda" (Neh 11:17). 6. One of the martial Gadites who joined David in the wilderness (1 Chron 12:9). 7. Father of Ishmaiah (27:19). 8. One of five princes of Judah whom Jehoshaphat sent out to teach the people of Judah the Law of the Lord (2 Chron 17:7). 9. A Levite and overseer of repairing the temple (34:12). 10. A Jew who led back 218 men in Ezra's return from captivity (Ezra 8:9). 11. A priestly covenanter with Nehemiah (Neh 10:5).

12. A gatekeeper of Jerusalem (12:25). 13. The prophet who wrote the Book of Obadiah.

OBADIAH, BOOK OF The subject of the book is the destruction of Edom (Obad 1). The book is undated.

Obadiah 1–9 pronounces punishment on Edom (cf. Jer 49:7–22). Perhaps either Jeremiah or Obadiah made use of the other, or both made use of a common source that is no longer available.

In Obadiah 10–14 Edom is charged for its guilt in standing with the enemies of Israel in the time when Judah and Jerusalem were in deep distress. In verses 12–14 the prophet exhorts Edom to quit its evil association with the enemies of Jerusalem. In verses 15–16 "the day of the LORD," i.e., a time of awful judgment, is proclaimed as being "near for all nations," and national annihilation is predicted for those peoples who fight against the Lord—they will "be as if they had never been." Israel will greatly enlarge its borders (vv. 19–21). The principal message of Obadiah to the peoples of today seems to be the proclamation, not only of the danger of fighting against God, but also of the peril of fighting his people.

OBAL (ō'băl). An early Arab, son of Joktan (Gen 10:28), called Ebal in the Hebrew and most versions of 1 Chronicles 1:22 (JB, KJV, MLB, MOF, NASB, NEB, RSV; NIV Obal).

OBED (ō'běd, Heb. *'ōvēdh,* worshiper). 1. Grandfather of David (Ruth 4:21–22; 1 Chron 2:12; Matt 1:5; Luke 3:32). 2. An early man of Judah (1 Chron 2:37–38). 3. One of the mighty men of David's army (11:47). 4. A Levitical gatekeeper of the tabernacle (26:7). 5. The father of a captain whom Jehoiada chose to help make Joash king (2 Chron 23:1).

OBED-EDOM (ō'běd-ē'dŏm, Heb. *'ōvēdh-'ědhôm, one who serves Edom*). 1. A man of Gath into whose house David had the ark of God carried (2 Sam 6:10–12; 1 Chron 13:9–13). He probably is the same Obed-Edom as the one who had 8 sons and 72 early descendants (26:4–8). 2. One of the musical Levites (15:18–24) who played a harp. 3. A son of Jeduthun who was a gatekeeper of the tabernacle (16:38). 4. Perhaps the same as no. 3, appointed with his sons over the treasury (26:15). 5. A descendant of no. 4 who kept the treasury in Amaziah's time (2 Chron 25:24).

Baking bread in a *taboon*, a clay-lined oven in which the dough, spread very thin, is placed on a layer of heated pebbles and almost immediately taken out, baked. Courtesy Zev Radovan

OBEDIENCE (Heb. *shāma'*, Gr. *hypakoē*). The Bible, by exhortation and commandment, requires submission and obedience to six principal authorities: (1) parents (Eph 6:1; Col 3:20), (2) teachers (Prov 5:12–13), (3) husbands (Eph 5:21-22, 24; Col 3:18; Titus 2:5; 1 Peter 3:1, 5, 6), (4) masters—today, employers—(Eph 6:5; Col 3:22; Titus 2:9; 1 Peter 2:18), (5) government (Rom 13:1–2, 5; Titus 3:1; 1 Peter 2:13), and (6) God (Gen 26:5; Eph 5:24; Heb 5:9; 12:9; James 4:7). When there is a clear conflict regarding obedience to authority, Christians are to obey God, not human beings (Acts 5:29). The supreme test of faith in God is obedience (1 Sam 28:18); the Bible often links obedience to faith (Gen 22:18; Rom 1:5; 1 Peter 1:14). Jesus' obedience to the Father (Phil 2:8) is the supreme example for Christians, who are to be "obedient children" (1 Peter 1:14).

OBEISANCE (ō-bā′săns, Heb. *shāhâh*). The act of bowing low or of prostrating oneself—before (1) God (Mic 6:6), (2) a god (2 Kings 5:18), (3) an earthly ruler (Gen 42:6), or (4) one's equals in a

gesture of courtesy (23:12). Courteous obeisance is a mark of culture; worshipful obeisance is a dreadful sin if directed to any other than the true God (Exod 20:4–6).

OBLATION (See SACRIFICE AND OFFERINGS)

OCCUPATIONS AND PROFESSIONS
   Apothecary. See *Perfumer*.
   Artificer. See *Craftsman*.
   Author. The composer of a literary production; an authority on a statement or fact (Prov 30:1; 31:1).
   Baker. A trade that occupied a special street in Jerusalem (Jer 37:21; 1 Sam 8:13). In addition to the home baker and the public baker, there was the royal baker, who baked for the king (Gen 40:1–22; 41:10).
   Barber. One whose trade possibly originated in connection with the shaving of the head as part of a vow (Num 6:18–19). The word *barber* occurs only once in Scripture (Ezek 5:1).
   Beggar. The beggar as a professional class was unknown during Mosaic times.

Limestone relief of Ur-nanshe, king of Lagash, seated on a throne with a goblet in his hand and being served by a cupbearer who stands behind him. From Tello, first half of third millennium B.C. Courtesy Réunion des Musées Nationaux

The law of Moses made ample provision for the poor of the land. In imprecatory fashion, Psalm 109:10 sets forth begging as the fate and punishment of the children of the wicked. As cities developed, begging became more prevalent. In the NT beggars appear with some frequency: the blind beggar (John 9:8–9); blind Bartimaeus (Mark 10:46–52); the beggar by the "Beautiful" gate of the temple (Acts 3:1–11); and perhaps most famous of all, Lazarus, the godly beggar who is presented in opposition to the ungodly rich man (Luke 16:19–31).

Butler. See *Cupbearer.*

Carpenter. A worker in wood; a builder. Joseph, the legal or foster father of Jesus, was a carpenter (Matt 13:55); so was Jesus (Mark 6:3). The work of carpenters is often mentioned in the Bible (Gen 6:14; Exod 37; Isa 44:13). David employed Phoenician carpenters in building his palace (2 Sam 5:11; 1 Chron 14:1). Some of the tools used by the ancient Egyptians were the adze, saw, square, awl, hammer, and glue-pot (Exod 21:6; Jer 10:4).

Chamberlain. An officer employed to look after the personal affairs of a sovereign (Gen 39:1). A chamberlain was introduced into the court by Solomon and was sometimes referred to as "steward" (1 Kings 4:6; 16:9; 18:3) or "governor." His duties seem to have been to superintend the palace and attend to royal etiquette. This post later became one of

special influence, including the right of introduction to the king. He thus became the chief minister (Rom 16:23).

Clerk. The clerk (Acts 19:35) was probably the city recorder. This term originally signified a temple servant whose business it was to sweep out and decorate the temple.

Confectioner. A perfumer or apothecary. When the orange trees, violets, and roses were in bloom, the women, who performed this function in the OT, made scented waters that they kept in large, tightly sealed bottles for use in the summer as cooling syrup drinks (1 Sam 8:13).

Coppersmith. A worker in any kind of metal (2 Tim 4:14). Smelters were located so as to face the wind currents, thus using the natural winds to fan their fires sufficiently for smelting.

Counselor. An adviser in any matter, particularly as the king's state adviser (2 Sam 15:12; 1 Chron 27:33). His position usually ranked him among the chief men of the government (Ezra 4:5; Job 3:14; 12:17; Isa 19:11). In the NT the name probably refers to a member of the Sanhedrin (Mark 15:43; Luke 23:50).

Craftsman. A fabricator of any material, as carpenter, smith, engraver, etc. (Gen 4:22; Isa 3:3). Also called artisans and artificers (KJV), these workers were skilled in metals, carving wood and plating it with gold, setting precious stones, and designing embroideries (2 Kings 24:14, 16; Jer 24:1; Acts 19:24). Solomon procured many craftsmen from Hiram, king of Tyre, when building the temple (1 Chron 29:5; 2 Chron 34:11).

Cupbearer. An officer of considerable responsibility who attended Eastern monarchs. The cupbearer (sometimes called the butler in KJV) was required to taste the foods and wines before serving them, as a pledge that they were not poisoned (Gen 40:1; Neh 1:11). The butlers enjoyed the esteem and confidence of their royal masters (1 Kings 10:5; 2 Chron 9:4).

Diviner. One who obtains or seems to obtain secret knowledge, particularly of the future. He stands in contrast to the prophet of the Lord, since he was believed to be inspired by demon power, while the Lord's prophet was inspired by the Spirit of God (Zech 10:2). Balaam was a heathen diviner but temporarily rose to the status of a bona-fide prophet of the Lord. He later advised Balak on a plan to destroy Israel (Num 22–25; 31:15–16). Though the diviner is classed with the prophet, this does not mean an endorsement of divination (1 Sam 6:2; Jer 27:9; Dan 4:7).

Dyer. The dyer obtained his dye from various sources. The crimson was obtained from a worm or grub that fed on the oak or other plants. Indigo was made from the rind of the pomegranate. Purple was made from the murex shellfish found on the beach at the city of Acre. It was also found along the Phoenician coast north of Acre. Lydia was a dealer in purple cloth (Acts 16:14). Excavations have revealed that "a guild of dyers" existed in the vicinity of Thyatira.

Elder. Men of Israel who formed one of the three classes represented in the Sanhedrin. The scribes and priests made up the two other classes (Acts 5:21). The elders were considered chief men or magistrates (Ps 105:22; cf. Num 11:16–30; Mark 14:43).

Engraver. Signet rings, engraved with a man's seal or sign, were common (Gen 38:18; Esth 3:12: Jer 22:24). Each of the two onyx stones on the high priest's shoulders was engraved with the names of six tribes, and his breastplate bore 12 stones, each engraved with the name of a tribe (Exod 28:9–21). Bezaleel and Aholiab were craftsmen in gold, silver, brass, stones, and wood (31:1–9; 35:30–35; 38:22–23).

Farmer. Cain tilled the soil, and Abel was a livestock farmer, perhaps a shepherd (Gen 4). When Israel entered the land of Canaan, farming took on a new aspect. Every seventh year, the farmers allowed the ground to remain idle. Whatever grew of itself was left to the poor, the stranger, and the beasts of the field (Lev 25:1–7). Farming was practiced by Cain, Noah, Elisha, David, Uzziah, and Solomon. Farmers were also called husbandmen, tillers of the ground, and laborers, and they were subject to certain laws (Isa 28:24; Jer 14:4; Matt 13:3; Mark 12:1; James 5:7).

Fisher. The frequent allusions to the art of fishing in Scripture are in connection with the Sea of Galilee (Matt 4:18; 13:48; Mark 1:16; Luke 5:2). Several methods of fishing were practiced. (1) The casting net was a common method used. (2) The dragnet was used in herring and salmon fishing, with floats marking the location of the submerged nets. (3) Hooks or angles were occasionally used. Fish were speared on the Mediterranean coast, being attracted to the surface by a moving torch. Night fishing was very common, especially on the Sea of Galilee. Schools of fish are sometimes seen on the Sea of Galilee from the shore when the fishermen in the boat cannot see them (John 21:4–6).

Fuller. One who washes or bleaches clothing. The cleansing was done by treading or stamping the garments with the feet or with rods or sticks in containers of water. The fuller's shop was usually located outside the city because of the offensive odors of the materials used in the bleaching process (alkali, soap, putrid urine, fumes of sulphur, etc.). In Jerusalem the "fuller's field" or the "washerman's field" was located near the conduit of the upper pool (2 Kings 18:17; Isa 7:3; 36:2).

Gatekeeper. Often translated "porter" in KJV. The biblical porter was a gatekeeper and not a burden-bearer (2 Sam 18:26; 1 Chron 9:22). The Levites who had charge of the various entrances to the temple were called gatekeepers (9:17; 15:18; 2 Chron 23:19). In some versions the word used is "doorkeeper" (1 Chron 15:23–24). A gatekeeper was stationed at the city gates and among the shepherds, where he was responsible for guarding the doors of the sheepfold. In David's time, the gatekeepers of the temple, who were also guards, numbered 4,000 (23:5).

Goldsmith. An artisan who works in gold. The furnishings of the tabernacle and the temple that were constructed of gold or overlaid with gold required skilled workmen (e.g., Exod 25). Goldsmiths were not above helping out in the reconstruction of the wall of Jerusalem after the Exile (Neh 3:8, 31–32). Most often the word "goldsmith" in the NIV is used of those who craft idols from gold (Isa 40:19; 41:7; 46:6; Jer 10:9 et al.).

Herdsman. A tender of oxen, sheep, goats, and camels. The patriarchs were great herdsmen. David's herdsmen were among his chief officers of state. In general, however, the herdsman was seldom the owner of the flock or herd that he tended (Gen 13:7; 26:20; 1 Sam 21:7; Amos 1:1; 7:14). The herdsmen's duty was to protect the herd from wild beasts, to keep them from straying, and to lead them to suitable pasture.

Hunter. The work of hunter or fowler was one of the earliest occupations. Originally a means of support, it later became a source of recreation. It was held in very high repute and was engaged in by all classes, mostly by royalty (Gen 10:9; 27:3, 5; 1 Sam 26:20; Job 38:39; Prov 6:5). Three principal methods of hunting are mentioned in the Bible: (1) shooting with bow and arrows (Gen 27:3), (2) snaring by spring net and cage, especially for birds such as quail, partridge, and duck (Jer 5:27; Amos 3:5), and (3) pits covered with a net and brushwood for deer, foxes, wolves, bears, lions, etc. (Ps 35:7; Isa 24:18; 42:22).

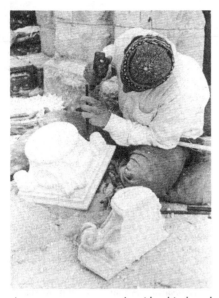

A stone mason at work with chisel and hammer. Courtesy Zev Radovan

Husbandman. See *Farmer.*

Judge. There were to be judges over 1000s and 100s and 50s (Exod 18:19–26; Deut 1:16). After coming into Canaan, judges sat at the gates of the cities (16:18).

Lawyer. One who is knowledgeable about the law. There were court lawyers and synagogue lawyers (Matt 22:35; Luke 7:30; 10:25; 11:45–46, 52; 14:3; Titus 3:13). The scribe functioned in the capacity of a lawyer in the pronouncement of legal decisions. (See *Teacher of the Law.*)

Magician. One who practices superstitious ceremonies to hurt or to benefit mankind. The Hebrews were forbidden to consult magicians (Gen 41:8; Exod 7:11, 22; Dan 1:20; 2:2; 5:11; Acts 13:6, 8). Magic is of two kinds: (1) natural, or scientific, and (2) supernatural, or spiritual. The first attributes its power to a deep, practical acquaintance with the power of nature. The second attributes its power to an acquaintance with celestial or infernal agencies.

Mason. A worker in stone. His equipment consisted of the plumb line, the measuring reed, the leveling line, the hammer with the toothed edge for shaping stones, and a small basket for carrying off earth (2 Kings 12:12; 22:6; 1 Chron 22:15; 2 Chron 24:12; Ezra 3:7).

Merchant. A dealer in merchandise.

Sometimes merchants are spoken of appreciatively (2 Chron 9:13–14; Song of Songs 3:6), but sometimes they were dishonest (Hos 12:7), and sometimes they are condemned for seeking only material gain (Rev 18:3, 11, 15, 23).

Musician. Hebrew music was primarily vocal, yet many of the psalms have signs indicating that they were to be accompanied by musical instruments (1 Kings 10:12; 2 Chron 9:11; Rev 18:22). The "chief musician" occurs in the titles of 54 psalms. Asaph and his brothers were apparently the first to hold this position, and the office was probably hereditary in the family (1 Chron 15:19; 2 Chron 35:15). Among the instruments used by the Hebrews were the cymbal, harp, organ, pipe, psaltery, and trumpet. See separate article MUSIC AND MUSICAL INSTRUMENTS.

Nurse. One who looks after, tutors, or guides another, as in a period of inexperience or sickness. In ancient times the nurse had an honored position in a home, often as a nursemaid, or nanny (2 Sam 4:4; 2 Kings 11:2). Rebekah's nurse went with her to Canaan and was buried with great mourning (Gen 24:59; 35:8). Foster fathers or mothers were sometimes referred to as nurses (Ruth 4:16; Isa 49:23).

Perfumer. A compounder of drugs, oils, and perfumes. KJV translates the word as "apothecary." All large oriental towns had their perfumers' street. Their stock included anything fragrant in the form of loose powder, compressed cake, or essences in spirit, oil, or fat, as well as seeds, leaves, and bark.

Perfumes were used in connection with the holy oil and incense of the tabernacle (Exod 30:25, 33, 35; 37:29; 2 Chron 16:14; Neh 3:8). The ritual of Baal-worshipers (Isa 57:9) and the embalming of the dead and rites of burial (2 Chron 16:14; Mark 16:1; Luke 23:56) all used perfume. The apothecary compounded and sold these sweet spices and anointing oils (Eccl 10:1).

The frequent references in the OT to physicians and perfumers indicate the high esteem in which the professions were held (Gen 50:2; Jer 8:22; Luke 4:23).

Physician. One who understands and practices medicine in the art of healing. The priests and prophets were expected to have some knowledge of medicine. In the days of Moses there were midwives and regular physicians who attended the Israelites (Exod 1:19). In Egypt the physicians also aided in embalming (Gen 50:2). See also DISEASES.

Plowman. The terms *husbandmen* and *plowmen* were used synonymously in the

Scriptures. The plowman was a farmer in general.

Porter. See *Gatekeeper*.

Potter. In antiquity, potters lived in settlements in the lower city of Jerusalem (Jer 18:2–4), in the neighborhood of Hebron and Beit Jibrin, where clay was plentiful and where the royal potteries probably were situated (1 Chron 4:23).

The maker of earthenware was one of the first manufacturers. The potter found the right kind of clay, prepared it by removing stones and other rough substances, shaped and made it into the vessel desired, baked it, and marketed it. If the vessel became marred in the shaping process, it was made over again into another vessel. When one broke after baking, it was discarded and thrown into the "potter's field" (Matt 27:7, 10). The Hebrew potter, sitting at his work, turned the clay, which had first been kneaded with his feet, into various kinds of vessels on his potting wheels, which were generally made of wood (Lam 4:2). See also POTTERY.

Preacher. One who heralds or proclaims, usually by delivering a discourse on a text of Scripture. Noah is referred to as "a preacher of righteousness" (2 Peter 2:5). Since the completion of the Bible, preaching has come to mean the exposition of the Word of God to believers or the declaration of the gospel message to unbelievers.

Priest. See separate article PRIEST, PRIESTHOOD.

Publican. See *Tax Collector*.

Rabbi. A title given by the Jews to the teachers of their law. It was also applied to Christ by his disciples and others (Matt 23:7–8; John 1:38, 49). The term *rabbi* means "master" or "teacher" (20:16).

Recorder. An officer of high rank in the Jewish state, exercising the functions not simply of an annalist, but of chancellor or president of the privy council (Isa 36:3, 22). He was not only the grand custodian of the public records, but he also kept the responsible registry of the current transactions of government (2 Sam 8:16; 20:24; 2 Kings 18:18). In David's court, the recorder appears among the high officers of his household (2 Sam 8:16; 20:24). In Solomon's court, the recorder is associated with the three secretaries (1 Kings 4:3).

Robber. One who engages in theft and plunder. Ishmael became a robber (Gen 16:12). Among the nomad tribes of the East, it was considered a most worthy profession. Hosea compares the apostate priests to robbers, bandits, and marauders (Hos 6:9, 7:1). Robbery is often

mentioned in the Bible, but it is never commended (Isa 61:8; Ezek 22:29; John 10:8).

Ruler. One who governs or assists in carrying on government. Daniel was made a ruler in Babylonia (Dan 2:10, 38; 5:7, 16, 29). There was the ruler of the synagogue, the ruler of the treasures, or the chief treasurer, and the high priest who was considered the "ruler of the house of God" (1 Chron 9:11; Mic 3:1, 9; Luke 8:49).

Sailor. One whose occupation is navigation, or the operation of ships, particularly one who manipulates a ship with sails (1 Kings 9:27; Rev 18:17).

Saleswoman. A woman who sells merchandise (e.g., Lydia, Acts 16:14–15, 40).

Schoolmaster. One who exercises careful supervision over scholars, educating them, forming their manners, etc. (Gal 3:24 KJV).

Scribe. A person employed to handle correspondence and to keep accounts, given a high place alongside the high priest (Prov 25:1). The scribe became known as a student and an interpreter of the law (Neh 8:1–13; Jer 36:26). In the time of Christ, the scribes had attained great influence and power as a class and were regarded with much respect (Matt 23:5; Luke 14:7).

Painted limestone statue of an Egyptian scribe holding a partly opened roll of papyrus. The eyes are inlaid with quartz, crystal, and ebony wood. From Saqqara, 5th Dynasty (2500–2350 B.C.). Courtesy Réunion des Musées Nationaux

Shepherdess tending her flocks alongside a Bedouin camp in the Negev. Courtesy Zev Radovan

Seer. One who is considered able to foresee things or events; a prophet (1 Sam 9:9, 11, 19). Often kings and rulers had their own personal seers to assist them in decision making, especially when the future seemed unclear (2 Sam 24:11; 2 Chron 29:25; 35:15).

Senator. See *Elder.*

Sergeant. A Roman lictor or officer who attended the chief magistrates when they appeared in public (Acts 16:35, 38 KJV; NIV "officers").

Servant. Anyone under the authority of another, sometimes meaning "young man" or "minister." It is applied to the relation of men to others occupying high position, as Eliezer, whose place in the household of Abraham compared with that of a prime minister (Gen 15:2; 24:2; Prov 14:35).

Sheepmaster. One who is both a shepherd and the owner of the sheep (2 Kings 3:4 KJV, MOF; NIV raised sheep).

Sheepshearer. When the wool of the sheep is long and ready to "harvest," a sheep-shearing time is announced, and it is a great time of rejoicing (Gen 38:12; 2 Sam 13:23–24). This festival is usually marked by revelry and merry-making (Gen 31:19).

Shepherd. One employed in tending, feeding, and guarding the sheep (e.g., Abel, Rachel, David). The shepherd's equipment consisted of a bag made of goat's skin with legs tied, in which food and other articles were placed; a sling for protection against wild animals; a rod (stick) about 30 inches (77 cm.) in length with a knob on one end; a staff, usually with a crook on one end; a flute made of reeds for entertainment and for calming the sheep; and a cloak to use as bedding at night. Sheep would learn to recognize the voice of their master (Gen 46:32; 1 Sam 17:20; John 10:3–4). Metaphorically, God is pictured as the shepherd of his flock (Gen 48:15; John 10; Rev 7:17).

Silversmith. A worker in silver, the most famous example of which was Demetrius (Judg 17:4; Prov 25:4; Acts 19:24).

Singer. A trained or professional vocalist. Hebrew music was primarily vocal (2 Sam 19:35). Solomon was a composer of songs (1 Kings 4:32). David's trained choir numbered 288 members (1 Chron 25:7).

Slave. A person held in bondage to another. Jewish slaves were of two classes—Hebrew and non-Hebrew—and both were protected by law. Hebrew became slaves through poverty, debt, inability to repay, or sale as maidservants. The slavery of Hebrews was the mildest form of bondservice (Exod 21:20–32; Deut 21:14; Jer 34:8–16).

At the time of Christ, slavery was established throughout the world and was considered even by the wisest people as a normal state of society. Christianity instructed believers how to live under slavery (1 Cor 12:13; Gal 3:28; Col 3:11; Rev 19:18).

Slave Driver. One whose duty is to assign tasks; an overseer or bond master. Pharaoh appointed slave drivers over the Hebrews to make their work hard and tiring. He hoped such oppression would break down their physical strength and reduce their numerical growth as well as crushing their hope of ever gaining their liberty (Exod 1:11; 3:7; 5:6, 10, 13–14).

Smith. A workman in stone, wood, or metal. The first smith mentioned in Scripture is Tubal-Cain (Gen 4:22). So necessary was the trade of the smith in ancient warfare that conquerors removed the smiths from a vanquished nation to more certainly disable it (Isa 44:12; 54:16; Jer 24:1).

Soldier. One who engages in military service and receives pay for it. In earlier times, every man above the age of 20 was a soldier (Num 1:3); and each tribe formed a regiment, with its own banner and its own leader (2:2; 10:14). Up until the time of David, the army consisted entirely of infantry (1 Sam 4:10; 15:4), since the use of horses was restrained by divine command (Deut 17:16). The Jews eventually attached much importance to chariots (1 Kings 22; 2 Kings 9; 1 Chron 19:6–7).

Soothsayer. See *Magician*.

Sorcerer. One who practices the arts of the magicians and astrologers, pretending to foretell events with the assistance of evil spirits (Isa 47:9, 12; Acts 8:9, 11). In its broader sense, a sorcerer is one who practices in the whole field of the occult (Exod 7:11: 22:18; Jer 27:9).

Spinner. A person who uses the distaff and the spindle in the making of thread from wool, flax, or cotton (Prov 31:19; Matt 6:28).

Steward. One to whose care is committed the management of the household (Gen 43:19; Luke 16:1). The term is also applied to ministers (1 Cor 4:1 KJV) and to Christians (1 Peter 4:10 KJV). The meaning of the word is different in Genesis 15:2, where NIV has "the one who will inherit my estate."

Tanner. One who is skilled in dressing and preserving hides or skins of animals.

Among the ancient Jews, ceremonial uncleanness was attached to the occupation of the tanner, and hence he was obliged to do his work outside the town. The tanneries of Joppa are now on the shore south of the city, where possibly the "house of Simon" was located (Acts 9:43; 10:6, 32).

Taskmaster. See *Slave Driver*.

Tax Collector. A collector of Roman revenue—either (1) the "chief tax collector" (Luke 19:2), or (2) the ordinary publican (Matt 9:11). Tax collectors were noted for imposing more taxes than were required so that they might grow rich more quickly. The publicans of the NT were regarded as traitors and apostates, defiled by their frequent contacts with pagans, and willing tools of the oppressor (Matt 9:11; 21:31; Mark 2:16; Luke 5:27–30).

Teacher. One who imparts instruction, and communicates knowledge of religious truth or other matters. Teachers are mentioned among the those having divine gifts (Eph 4:11).

Teacher of the Law. Gamaliel (Acts 5:34), as a teacher of the law, kept and handed down the sacred laws as received from Mt. Sinai. He was the 35th receiver of the traditions.

Tentmaker. One skilled in making tents from hair, wool, or skins. Paul, a tentmaker, practiced his trade with Aquila at Corinth (Acts 18:1–3).

Tetrarch. A ruler over a fourth part of a kingdom or province in the Roman Empire. Locally, his authority was similar to that of a king, and the title of king was often given to him (Matt 14:1; Luke 3:1; Acts 13:1).

Tiller. See *Farmer; Plowman*.

Treasurer. An important officer in Middle East courts, probably having charge of the receipts and disbursements of the public treasury (Ezra 1:8; 7:21; Isa 22:15; Dan 3:2–3). This title was given to the officer of state, was considered superior to all others, and was sometimes filled by the heir to the throne (2 Chron 26:21).

Watchman. One who stood in the tower on the walls or at the gates of the city and patrolled the streets. Besides protecting the city and its inhabitants from violence, he was required to call out the hours of the night (2 Sam 18:24–27; Song of Songs 5:7; Isa 21:11–12). God's prophets were also his "watchmen" to warn his people (Isa 21:6 KJV; NIV "lookout").

Weaver. One who is skilled in the making of cloth or rugs from spun thread or string. The fibrous materials woven were usually linen, flax, and wool (Exod

35:35; Lev 13:48; 1 Chron 11:23; Isa 38:12).

Witch. A "knowing or wise one." Witch was the name given to the woman and wizard the name given to the man who practiced "witchcraft." There was an apparent communication with demons and a pretended conversation with the spirits of the dead by means of which future events were revealed, diseases cured, and evil spirits driven away. The woman of Endor to whom Saul went for help is called a medium in NIV (1 Sam 28). Witchcraft was severely denounced (Lev 20:6; 2 Kings 9:22; Gal 5:20). See also *Sorcerer*.

Writer. The knowledge of writing was possessed by the Hebrews at a very early period. They wrote on various kinds of materials: tables of stone, metal, plaster, skins, paper made from bulrushes, and fine parchment. The pens were also different, to correspond with the writing material (Judg 5:14; Ps 45:1; Ezek 9:2). The prophets were often told by the Lord to write (Rev 1:11; 21:5).

ODED (ō′dĕd, Heb. *'ôdhĕdh, he was restored*, or *prophet*). **1.** The father of Azariah the prophet (2 Chron 15:1). **2.** A prophet in Samaria in the days of Ahaz (2 Chron 28:9–15).

ODOR (ō′dêr, Heb. *besem*, Gr. *osmē*). That which affects the sense of smell. The Levitical offerings that did not deal with sin were called offerings of sweet savor; and the incense also (Mal 1:11) with its perfumed odor was acceptable to the Lord. The prayers of the saints (figuratively) are offerings of a sweet savor to the Lord (Rev 5:8). Hypocrisy stinks (Amos 5:21).

OFFAL (See DUNG)

OFFENSE (ŏ-fĕns′, Heb. *'āsham, hātā'*, Gr. *skandalon*). Injury, hurt, damage, occasion of sin, a stumbling block, an infraction of law, sin, transgression, state of being offended; in the NT often a stumbling block (Matt 5:30; 11:6; 18:6; 1 Cor 8:13).

OFFERINGS (See SACRIFICE AND OFFERINGS)

OFFICER A holder of an official position: (1) one who has been set up over others (1 Kings 4:27); (2) a eunuch (Esth 1:10); (3) a writer or clerk (Deut 20:9); (4) a police officer or bailiff (Luke 12:58); (5) originally an assistant or underruler (Matt 5:25).

OFFSCOURING (Heb. *sehî, refuse*, Gr. *peripsēma, dirt*). A contemptuous word

in the KJV for sweepings, scrapings, filth, dung (Lam 3:45; 1 Cor 4:13).

OG (ŏg, Heb. *'ôgh*). Amorite king of Bashan (Deut 31:4; Josh 2:10; 13:12; 1 Kings 4:19). He was a man of gigantic stature, a physical characteristic of which there is strong evidence among the Canaanite tribes. He held sway over 60 separate communities. Og's defeat before the invading Hebrews (Deut 3:1–13) became proverbial, for it dispelled a legend of invincibility based on the daunting appearance of some of the Canaanite giants (1:28). The tradition was long-lived (Pss 135:11; 136:20). The "bed . . . of iron" was preserved as a museum piece at Rabbah among the Amorites (Deut 3:11).

OHOLAH, OHOLIBAH (ō-hō′là, ō-hŏl′ï-bà, Heb. *'ohŏlâh, 'ohŏlîvâh, tent-woman, my tent is in her*). A woman is mentioned in Ezekiel 23 who represents Samaria, capital of the northern kingdom, whose worship was self-devised (John 4:9, 20–22). Her sister Oholibah is a symbol of Jerusalem (Ezek 23:4), capital of Judah, whose worship was appointed by God. These "women" had been unfaithful to the Lord, their true husband (Isa 54:5). Later, Oholah (Israel) was spiritually adulterous by her coalition with Egypt and Assyria. For these whoredoms God punished her with captivity by the very agent of her sin (Ezek 23:9–10). Oholibah (Judah) yielded to Babylonian culture (23:11–22), for which God promised her a similar captivity by the very agent of her sin (23:22–49).

OHOLIBAMAH (ō-hŏl′ï-bă′mà, Heb. *'ohŏlîvamâh, tent of the high place*). **1.** One of Esau's three wives (Gen 36:2, 14, 18), also called Judith, perhaps her personal name (26:34), Oholibamah being her married name. **2.** A chief descended from Esau (36:41; 1 Chron 1:52).

OIL (Heb. *shemen*, Gr. *elaion*). In the Bible almost always olive oil, perhaps the only exception being Esther 2:12, where it is oil of myrrh. The olives were sometimes beaten (Lev 24:2), sometimes trodden (Mic 6:15), but generally crushed in a mill designed for that purpose. The upper stone, instead of rubbing against the lower as in a flour mill, rolled on it and so pressed out the oil. The wheel usually was turned by ox-power or donkey-power, the animal being blindfolded. Olive oil was not only a prime article of food, bread being dipped in it, but it was also used for cooking, for anointing, and for lighting. Oil was one of the principal ingredients in making soap (Jer 2:22).

An ancient oil press found among the ruins at Capernaum. There were three stages in producing oil. First, the hard olives were crushed into a soft paste. This was then squeezed, the crude oil flowing out, as a result of the pressure, into the vat shown here. Finally, the crude oil was stored in vessels or vats for some time, in which the sediments and water from the olives settled and the pure oil rose to the surface. The oil was then collected for storage or use.
Courtesy Zev Radovan

Anointing with oil was for three diverse purposes: wounded animals were anointed for the soothing and curative effects of the oil (Ps 23:5); people anointed themselves with oil for its cosmetic value (104:15); but most notably men were anointed as an official inauguration into high office. Priests (Exod 28:41; 29:7), prophets, and kings (1 Kings 19:15–16) were anointed and were called "messiahs," i.e., "anointed ones" (Lev 4:3, 5, 16; 1 Sam 2:10; 1 Chron 16:22). Anointing the head of a guest with oil was a mark of high courtesy (Luke 7:46).

OIL TREE (See PLANTS)

OINTMENTS AND PERFUMES The use of perfume in the form of ointment or impregnated oil was a Middle Eastern practice long before it spread to the Mediterranean world. In all probability it was originally used for ceremonial purposes, first religious then secular, and became a personal habit with the growing sophistication of society and the need for deodorants in hot lands (Esth 2:12; Prov 7:17; 27:9; Isa 57:9). So universal was the practice that its suspension was an accepted sign of mourning (Deut 28:40; Ruth 3:3; 2 Sam 14:2; Dan 10:3; Amos 6:6; Mic 6:15). The skin as well as the hair was perfumed and anointed (Ps 104:15); and, especially on high occa-

A cosmetic flask (1500–1200 B.C.), found at Lachish and made from an ivory tusk. In lands where water was very scarce, ointments and perfumes were often used in lieu of bathing and for self-enhancement.
Courtesy Israel Department of Antiquities and Museums

sions, perfume was used with profusion (133:2). Anointing an honored guest was a courtesy a host performed (Luke 7:46). Among the directions listed for the service of the tabernacle are two prescribed "recipes," possibly Egyptian in form (Exod 30:23–25, 34–36). One recipe prescribes 750 ounces of solids in six quarts of oil. The process of manufacture is not clear (Exod 30:25, 35; Neh 3:8; Eccl 10:1). In its later trade form perfume was sometimes packed in alabaster boxes or flasks (Luke 7:37). Such ointment was heavily scented (John 12:3) and costly (12:5).

OLD TESTAMENT The OT is composed of 39 books—5 of law, 12 of history, 5 of poetry, 5 of major prophets, and 12 of minor prophets. The classification of the present Hebrew Bible is different—5 of law, 8 of prophets, and 11 of miscella-

Panoramic view of the Mount of Olives in Jerusalem, facing east. Note the Basilica of the Agony at the foot of the mount. The onion-shaped domes of the Russian Church of Mary Magdalene are in the center. Courtesy Israel Government Press Office

neous writings. These 24 in various combinations contain all of our 39 books. Neither of these classifications exhibits the fact that much of the Pentateuch is history, nor do they show the chronological relation of the books. A logical survey of the OT literature may approach the subject chronologically.

Outline:
I. Before Abraham (Gen 1–11).
II. The Flood (Gen 6–8).
III. Early Genealogies (11:10–26).
IV. Abraham and the Patriarchs (chs. 12-50).
V. Bondage and Exodus (Exodus 1–19).
VI. Israel's Law (Exod 20–Num 10).
VII. The Wilderness (Num 11–36).
VIII. Deuteronomy.
IX. Job
X. The Conquest (Josh 1–12).
XI. The Judges and Ruth.
XII. The Early Monarchy.
XIII. The Golden Age.
XIV. Divided Monarchy to Ahab.
XV. The Kingdoms to Hezekiah.
XVI. Isaiah and His Contemporaries.
XVII. Judah's Fall.
XVIII. The Exile.
XIX. Postexilic Times.

Malachi, the final book of the OT, was written around 400. It reveals the problems of the day caused by insincerity among some of the priests themselves. But it also, like so many of the other prophets, pointed forward to messianic times. The OT closes with the annunciation of the rise of a new and greater prophet in the spirit and power of Elijah who would precede the Messiah of Israel.

OLIVE (See PLANTS)

OLIVES, MOUNT OF (called Olivet twice in the KJV—2 Sam 15:30; Acts 1:12). The Mt. of Olives is a flattened, rounded ridge with four identifiable summits. Its name is derived from the olive groves that covered it in ancient times. Near the foot of the Mt. of Olives, on the western slope above the Kidron, is the likely site of the Garden of Gethsemane.

In NT times the whole area seems to have been a place of resort for those who sought relief from the heat of the crowded city streets.

The ridge, besides being a tactical vantage point in war, was a peacetime highway into Jerusalem. It was the route of David's flight from Absalom in the time of the palace rebellion (2 Sam 15:30; 16:1, 13) and, significantly, was the route of Christ's approach for the triumphal entry on Palm Sunday. Christ's first sight of the city was from the summit of the Mount of Olives (Luke 19:41), and his visits to the home of Mary, Martha, and Lazarus in Bethany must have frequently taken him that way (21:37). The barren fig tree of his striking object lesson on fruitless profession was probably on the slopes (Matt 21:19). The mount was also the scene of his apocalyptic utterance, inspired no doubt by the prospect of doomed Jerusalem from the mountainside (chs. 24–25).

OMEGA (ō-mē'gà). Literally, large "O," the last letter of the Greek alphabet, long "o." In three contexts (Rev 1:8; 21:6; 22:13) it is used as a symbol of inclusiveness.

OMER (See WEIGHTS AND MEASURES)

OMNIPOTENCE (ŏm-nĭp'ō-tĕns). The attribute of God that describes his ability to do whatever he wills. God's will is limited by his nature, and he therefore cannot do anything contrary to his nature as God, such as to ignore sin, to sin, or to do something absurd or self-contradictory. God is not controlled by his power but has complete control over it: otherwise he would not be a free being (Job 42:2; Jer 32:17; Matt 19:26; Luke 1:37; Rev 19:6).

OMNIPRESENCE (ŏm'nĭ-prĕz'ĕns). The attribute of God by virtue of which he fills the universe in all its parts and is present everywhere at once. Not a part, but the whole of God is present in every place. The Bible teaches the omnipresence of God (Ps 139:7–12; Jer 23:23–24; Acts 17:27–28). This is true of all three members of the Trinity. They are so closely related that where one is the others can be said to be also (John 14:9–11).

OMNISCIENCE (ŏm-nĭsh'ĕns). The attribute by which God perfectly and eternally knows all things that can be known— past, present, and future. God knows how best to attain his desired ends. God's omniscience is clearly taught in Scripture (Ps 147:5; Prov 15:11; Isa 46:10).

OMRI (ŏm'rē, Heb. 'ŏmrî). 1. The sixth king of Israel (886 to 874 B.C.). Omri, an able if unscrupulous soldier and founder of a dynasty, is the first Hebrew monarch to be mentioned in nonbiblical records: Mesha included Omri's name in the inscription of the Moabite Stone (847).

Omri is dismissed by the Hebrew historian as an evil influence (1 Kings 16:25–26). Indeed, the marriage of his son Ahab to Jezebel, princess of Tyre, probably to cement a trade alliance, had the most disastrous consequences, even though it was a continuation of Solomon and David's Tyrian policy. The calf worship of Jeroboam (1 Kings 12:32) was continued at Bethel throughout Omri's reign; and 140 years after Omri's death, Micah is found denouncing "the statutes of Omri" (Mic 6:16). The palace of Omri has been excavated at Samaria, a series of open courts with rooms arranged around them. 2. A Benjamite, family of Beker (1 Chron 7:8). 3. A man of Judah, family of Perez (9:4). 4. A prince of the tribe of Issachar in David's reign (27:18).

ON (ŏn, Heb. 'ôn). 1. A delta city of Egypt, called by the Greeks Heliopolis (City of the Sun) and so translated in the Septuagint (Gen 41:45, 50; 46:20; cf. Jer 43:13; Ezek 30:17, both NIV). On is an Egyptian word signifying "light" or "sun." It was a center of communication and commerce in northern Egypt. The priest of On, whose daughter Asenath became Joseph's wife, was thus a person of considerable importance. The worship of the sun god, which was centered there, had peculiar features that suggest Syrian influence. Ra was identified with Baal by Semites and with Apollo by the Greeks. On is named as the place of sojourn of the holy family after the flight into Egypt. 2. A Reubenite chief who took part in the rebellion of Korah (Num 16:1).

ONAM (ō'năm, Heb. 'ônām, strong). 1. Fifth son of Shobal (Gen 36:23). 2. Great-great-grandson of Judah (1 Chron 2:26, 28).

ONAN (ō'năn, Heb. 'ônān, strong). Second son of Judah by a Canaanite wife who was a daughter of Shua. He refused to consummate a levirate marriage with Tamar, widow of his elder brother Er, who had been wicked, and so the Lord put him to death also, leaving Tamar twice a widow (Gen 38:4–10).

ONESIMUS (ō-nĕs'ĭ-mŭs, Gr. Onesimos, profitable). Probably a common nickname for a slave. Paul plays on the word onesimos (Philem 11, 20). Onesimus was a slave of Philemon of Colosse. He robbed his master and made his way to Rome, the frequent goal of such fugitives. Some Ephesian or Colossian person in Rome, perhaps Aristarchus (Acts 27:2; Col 4:10–14; Philem 24), or Epaphras (Col 1:7; 4:12–13; Philem 23) seems to have recognized the man and brought him to Paul in his captivity. Onesimus became a Christian and was persuaded to return to his master. From that incident came the exquisite letter of Paul to Philemon. It appears that Onesimus left Rome in company with Tychicus, carrying the letter to Philemon and also Paul's letters to the Ephesian and Colossian churches.

ONESIPHORUS (ŏn'ĕ-sĭf'ō-rŭs, Gr. *Onēsiphoros, profit-bringer*). An Ephesian who ministered fearlessly to Paul at the time of the apostle's second captivity in Rome (2 Tim 1:16–18; 4:19). Paul's warm gratitude and, in the midst of his own distress, his thoughtfulness in greeting the Ephesian family, shed light on his generous character and give further evidence of his capacity for commanding devotion.

ONION (See PLANTS)

ONLY-BEGOTTEN A title that appears six times in the KJV of the NT, five times of Jesus (John 1:14, 18; 3:16, 18; 1 John 4:9; cf. NIV footnotes), connected with the doctrine of the "eternal generation of the Son of God" (cf. Ps 2:7 with Acts 13:33; Heb 1:5; 5:5), and once to Isaac (Heb 11:17).

ONO (ō'nō, Heb. *'ônô, strong*). A town ascribed to Benjamin (1 Chron 8:12) because it was built by Shemed, a Benjamite, though it was in the territory originally assigned to the tribe of Dan. It lay in the plain, near the Valley of the Craftsmen (Neh 11:35) and was about 6 miles (10 km.) SE of Joppa. Many of its men returned from captivity with Zerubbabel (Ezra 2:33), and the town was later inhabited by men of Benjamin (Neh 11:35). Nehemiah refused an invitation to go there (6:2).

ONYCHA (See PLANTS)

ONYX (See MINERALS)

OPHEL (ō'fĕl, Heb. *ha-'ōphel, hill*). Properly a hill, but when used with the definite article in Hebrew, it is translated "Ophel" and refers to a part of Jerusalem. In 2 Kings 5:24 the word is translated "tower" in the KJV and "hill" in the NIV, but no one knows the exact location. In Micah 4:8 it is translated "stronghold" in the KJV and NIV, but the ASV has "the hill of the daughter of Zion," and probably refers to *the* Ophel of Jerusalem. In Isaiah 32:14, the KJV has "forts," and the NIV "citadel," but the ASV, more accurately, reads "hill," probably referring to Ophel. Ophel lies outside the wall of modern Jerusalem. Jotham, king of Judah, built much on the wall of Ophel (2 Chron 27:3), and his great-grandson Manasseh further improved it (33:14), so that from then on it was inside the ancient city. In the restoration period it was principally a place of residence for the temple servants (KJV Nethinim; Neh 11:21).

OPHIR (ō'fêr, Heb. *'ôphîr*). **1.** A son of Joktan, son of Eber (Gen 10:29). The names in "the table of nations" (Gen 10) often place locations, and Ophir is placed between Sheba and Havilah, both in southern Arabia. **2.** The land occupied by the descendants of Ophir. In 1 Kings 9:28 it is mentioned as the source of much gold (cf. Gen 2:11–12, where Ophir's neighbor Havilah is cited for its good gold). Ophir in Arabia was not only the source of gold, but it may have been a way-station for the "ships of Tarshish" coming westward from India—that is, if the apes, ivory, and baboons (1 Kings 10:22), as well as the almugwood (10:11–12), had to come from India. Ophir was famous for its gold from very early days (Job 22:24; 28:16).

OPHRAH (ŏf'rà, Heb. *'ophrâh, hind*). **1.** A town in Benjamin (Josh 18:23). It lies on a conical hill about 3 miles (5 km.) NE of Bethel and probably is the "Ephraim" (John 11:54) to which our Lord retired when under persecution. **2.** A town in the tribe of Manasseh (Judg 6:24) where the angel of God appeared to Gideon, commissioning him to deliver Israel from the Midianites. Gideon placed in Ophrah the ephod that the children of Israel worshiped (8:27). **3.** A son of Meonothai, an early member of the tribe of Judah (1 Chron 4:14).

ORACLE (ŏr'à-k'l, Heb. *dâvar*, Gr. *logion*). **1.** An utterance supposedly coming from a deity and generally through an inspired medium (cf. "Sibylline Oracles"). **2.** In the Bible, an utterance from God (2 Sam 16:23). **3.** The OT (Acts 7:38; Heb 5:12; 1 Peter 4:11).

ORATOR 1. In Isaiah 3:3, KJV has "eloquent orator," but other versions more accurately have "soothsayer" (JB), "clever enchanter" (NIV), or "expert in charms" (RSV). **2.** A public speaker, especially an advocate (Acts 24:1).

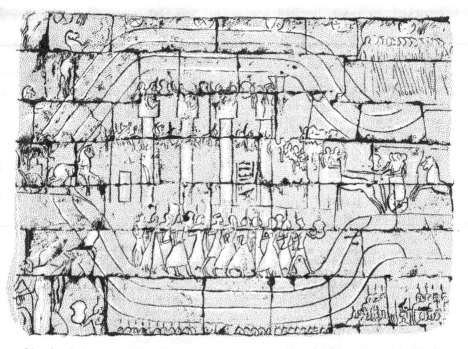

The fortified town of Kadesh on the Orontes, surrounded by a moat, scene of the culminating battle of Rameses II against the Hittites in 1288 B.C. Drawing from relief on east tower at Luxor. Courtesy Carta, Jerusalem

ORCHARD (See GARDEN)

ORDAIN, ORDINATION In the KJV *ordain* is the translation of about 35 different Hebrew and Greek words. The word has many shades of meaning, chiefly four: (1) set in order, arrange (Ps 132:17; Isa 30:33); (2) bring into being (Num 28:6; 1 Kings 12:32; Ps 8:2–3); (3) decree (Esth 9:27; Acts 16:4; Rom 7:10); (4) set apart for an office or duty (Jer 1:5; Mark 3:14; John 15:16; Acts 14:23; 1 Tim 2:7; Titus 1:5; Heb 5:1; 8:3).

Ordination in the sense of setting aside officers of the church for a certain work by the laying on of hands was practiced in apostolic times (1 Tim 4:14; 2 Tim 1:6).

OREB AND ZEEB (ō'rĕb, zē'ĕb, Heb. *'ōrēv, se'ēv, raven* and *wolf*). Two princes of the Midianites in the days of Gideon. Oreb died at the rock of Oreb and Zeeb at the winepress of Zeeb (Judg 7:24–25). Asaph, hundreds of years later, recalls these events in Psalm 83:11.

OREB, ROCK OF (See OREB AND ZEEB)

ORGAN (See MUSIC AND MUSICAL INSTRUMENTS: *Pipe*)

ORION (See ASTRONOMY)

ORNAMENT (See DRESS)

ORNAN (See ARAUNAH)

ORONTES (ō-rŏn'tēz). The chief river in Aram (Syria), almost 400 miles (640 km.) long, begins in the Anti-Lebanon range, at the height of almost 4,000 feet (1,250 m.), and flows north for the major portion of its course.

ORPAH (ôr'pà, Heb. *'orpâh, neck,* i.e. *stubbornness*). A Moabite woman whom Kilion, son of Elimelech and Naomi, married. She loved her mother-in-law, but kissed her good-by and remained in Moab, while Ruth, Naomi's other daughter-in-law, stayed with her (Ruth 1:4, 14; 4:9–10).

OSNAPPER (See ASHURBANIPAL)

OSPREY (See BIRDS)

OSSIFRAGE (See BIRDS)

OSTRACA (ŏs'trȧ-kȧ). Inscribed fragments of pottery (sing., *ostracon*). In the ancient world handy writing material was rare, but potsherds, or broken pieces of earthenware, were abundant, hence the habit of writing brief memoranda or communications on such ready material. The surface holds the inscription well and some important ancient documents have come down to us in this form (e.g., the Lachish Letters). In ancient Athens the use of potsherds, or straka, for voting tablets in the peculiar Athenian process of relegation, led to the term "ostracize." The verb originally meant the writing on an ostracon of the name of the person the voter wished thus to exile.

OSTRICH (See BIRDS)

OTHNIEL (ŏth'nĭ-ĕl, Heb. *'othnî'ēl*). A son of Kenaz, brother of Caleb. Caleb, in his old age at the division of the land, offered his daughter to any one who would take Debir. His nephew Othniel took Debir and so acquired Acsah as wife (Josh 15:13–19; Judg 1:11–15). Within 15 years after the death of Joshua, Israel fell into apostasy, and God delivered them into the hand of Cushan-Rishathaim (3:8–11), king of Mesopotamia. In their distress they prayed to the Lord, who raised up Othniel to deliver them, the first of the seven judges. He so restored Israel that a period of 40 years of peace set in. His son was Hathath (1 Chron 4:13).

OUCHES (ouch'ĕz, Heb. *mishbetsôth*). Settings for precious stones on the high priest's ephod (Exod 28:11 KJV). NIV reads "filigree settings."

OUTPOST (See GARRISON)

OVEN A chamber that is heated so as to roast or to bake the food materials placed inside. There were three principal types. In Egypt there was in nearly every house a structure of clay built on the house floor. In this, or on it, baking was done. In Palestine and Syria, a barrel-shaped hole in the ground was coated with clay and a quick hot fire of brambles or dry dung mixed with straw heated it. The dough, beaten very thin, was spread on the inside and almost immediately taken out, fully baked. In some places, a curved plate of iron was put over the sunken oven; but in cities the oven was a chamber of stone, from which the fire is raked when the oven is very hot and into which the unbaked loaves are then placed (Hos 7:4–7). See also BREAD; OCCUPATIONS AND PROFESSIONS: *Baker*.

OVERSEER The translation of several Hebrew and Greek words, each with its distinctive meaning: Heb. *pāqadh*, "inspector, overseer" (Gen 39:4–5; 2 Chron 34:12, 17); *menatstsehîm*, "foreman" (2:18; 34:13); *shōtēr*, almost always "officer"; Greek *episkopos*, "bishop, overseer" (Acts 20:28).

OWL (See BIRDS)

OX (See ANIMALS)

OXGOAD (See GOAD)

OZEM (ō'zĕm, Heb. *'ōtsem*). **1.** The sixth son of Jesse (1 Chron 2:15). **2.** A son of Jerahmeel (2:25).

OZIAS (See UZZIAH)

– P –

PAARAI (pā'à-rī, Heb. *pa'ăray, devotee of Peor*). One of David's mighty men called "the Arbite" (2 Sam 23:35). He is also called Naarai (1 Chron 11:37).

PADDAN ARAM (pā'dăn-ā'răm, *plain of Aram*). The home of Jacob's exile (Gen 31:18), the home of Laban. It is almost certainly to be identified with Haran of the upper Euphrates Valley. It is also sometimes translated simply as "Mesopotamia." In Genesis 48:7 it is given as Paddan only.

PAHATH-MOAB (pā'hăth-mō'ăb, Heb. *pahath-mô'ăv, governor of Moab*). A head of one of the chief houses of Judah. Part of the descendants of this man returned from Babylon with Zerubbabel (Ezra 2:6; Neh 7:11) and another part returned with Ezra (Ezra 8:4). A son of Pahath-Moab, Hasshub, aided in repairing both the wall and the Tower of the Ovens (Neh 3:11). He is one of the lay princes who signed the covenant with Nehemiah (9:38; 10:14). His place (second) in this list speaks of his importance. Eight of the sons of this man put away their foreign wives (Ezra 10:30).

PAI (See PAU)

PALACE (Heb. *'armôn, bîrâh, hēkhāl*, Gr. *aulē*). The dwelling place of an important official. At Gezer the remains of a palace belonging to the period of Joshua's conquest have been found. It is thought to be the palace of Horam, king of Gezer, whom Joshua conquered (Josh 10:33).

David had two palaces at different times in his reign. The first was a simple one located at Hebron, but the second one was much more elaborate, built of cedar trees furnished by Hiram of Tyre and erected by workmen that Hiram supplied (2 Sam 5:11). Solomon's palace, which was built later, was a much more lavish structure, judging from its description (1 Kings 7). It was about 150 feet (47 m.) by 75 feet (23 m.) in size, constructed mostly of cedar in the interior and of hand-hewn stones for the exterior. Some of the foundation stones were 15 feet (4.6 m.) long. Solomon's wealth and the skill of the Phoenician craftsmen must have produced a magnificent building. Nothing remains of this building today.

An ivory palace belonging to Ahab (1 Kings 22:39) was a large edifice 300 feet (94 m.) long from north to south. Many of its walls were faced with white marble. Wall paneling, plaques, and fur-

Model of Herod's Palace. Courtesy Israel Government Press Office.

niture made of or adorned with ivory have been uncovered.

Probably the most famous palace in the NT period was the one belonging to Herod the Great. Josephus informs us that this structure was built in Jerusalem. Its rooms were of a very great height and were adorned with all kinds of costly furniture.

PALESTINE (păl'ĕs-tīn, Heb. *pelesheth*). The term *Palestine* is not used in the NIV; it occurs four times in the KJV (Exod 15:14; Isa 14:29, 31; Joel 3:4). In all four contexts it refers to Philistia (so NIV), the SE coastal strip of the Mediterranean. *Philistia* derives from the Hebrew term for the region, *eres Pelistim* ("the land of the Philistines"), and *Philistine* was a native term of unknown origin and significance. Herodotus, the fifth-century Greek historian, first used the term to cover a wider area (2.104; 3.5; 91.7.89). The name Palestine is therefore another example of the common phenomenon whereby a land or a people is named after the part or the division with which first contact is made. A Philistine settlement had existed there since patriarchal times (Gen 26). The older Semitic name was Canaan, a word of doubtful origin.

The limits of Palestine in ancient times lack precise definition, except in the case of the second-century Roman province of that name, whose boundaries may be fairly certainly drawn—"from Dan to Beersheba" (Judg 20:1). Dan was Laish, 30 miles (50 km.) due east of Tyre on the sources of the Jordan. Beersheba lay 150 miles (250 km.) to the south, just where Palestine merges into the desert of the Negev. The "Promised Land" of Joshua 1:4 is geographically much more inclusive. The seacoast formed a definite enough western boundary, though alien powers, from ancient Philistine to modern Egyptian, have always disputed the possession of these fertile lowlands behind the coast. The deepening desert made a firm, though changing boundary line to the east. West of a line drawn down the Jordan Valley, Palestine measures 6,000 square miles (15,385 sq. km.). If areas east of the Jordan, from time to time counted part of Palestine, are also included, the total area is nearer 10,000 square miles (25,640 sq. km.). It is thus a little larger than the state of Vermont. Again, the distance from Dan to Beersheba is 150 miles (250 km.). From west to east the distances are smaller still. In the north, from Acco to the Sea of Galilee, the distance is 28 miles (47 km.). From Gaza to the Dead Sea in the south the distance is 54 miles (90 km.).

In spite of its narrow limits, the varied configuration of Palestine produces a great variety of climates. The coastal plain is temperate, with an average annual temperature of 57 degrees at Joppa. Inland 34 miles (57 km.), Jerusalem, because of its height of 2,600 feet (813 m.) registers an annual average of 63 degrees, though with wider variations. At Jericho, 15 miles (25 km.) away, and 3,300 feet (1,031 m.) below Jerusalem or 700 feet (219 m.) below sea level, a tropical climate prevails with intense summer heat. A similar contrast marks the temperate climate around the Sea of Galilee and the tropical heat around the Dead Sea. Prevailing winds are west or SW and precipitate their moisture on the western slopes of the high country in a rainy season extending roughly from October to April. An occasional sirocco, or east wind, brings burning air from the great deserts (Job 1:19; Jer 18:17; Ezek 17:10; 27:26). The southern desert, south of Beersheba, is a parched wilderness. The "former rain" of the biblical phrase (Jer 5:24; Joel 2:23 KJV; NIV "autumn rain") was the early part of the rainy season. The period is commonly followed by a time of heavy falls alternating with fine clear weather, until March or April, when the "latter rain" (NIV "spring rain") falls with immense advantage to the maturing crops

before the dry season, the ripening, and the harvest.

PALLU, PALLUITE (păl'ū, păl'ū-īt, Heb. *pallû', distinguished, a descendant of Pallu*). Reuben's second son (Gen 46:9; see also Exod 6:14; Num 26:5, 8; 1 Chron 5:3). He was the founder of the Palluites (Num 26:5).

PALMER WORM (See ANIMALS)

PALM TREE (See PLANTS)

PALMYRA (See TADMOR)

PALSY (See DISEASES)

PALTIEL (păl'tĭ-ĕl, Heb. *paltî'ēl, God delivers*). **1.** The son of Azzan who helped in the division of the Promised Land (Num 34:26). **2.** The man to whom Saul gave Michal, David's wife (KJV has lit., Phalti, in 1 Sam 25:44 and lit., Phaltiel, in 2 Sam 3:15).

PALTITE (păl'tīt, Heb. *paltî, delivered*). The Gentile name of Helez, one of David's valiant men. Called the Pelonite (1 Chron 11:27; 27:10).

PAMPHYLIA (păm-fĭl'ĭ-à, Gr. *Pamphylia*). At the time of Paul, Pamphylia was a small Roman province of southern Asia Minor, extending 75 miles (125 km.) along the Mediterranean coast and 30 miles (50 km.) inland to the Taurus Mountains. It was surrounded by Pisidia on the north, Cilicia to the east, and Lycia to the SW.

The tiny country is first mentioned in the NT in Acts 2:10. Paul visited the territory on his first missionary journey when he preached at Perga, its chief city (Acts 13:13; 14:24). It was at this point that John Mark left the party and returned to Jerusalem (13:13; 15:38). Later, when Paul as a prisoner sailed near Pamphylia (27:5), he evidently crossed the Pamphylian Gulf.

PANNAG (See PLANTS)

PAP (Heb. *shadh*, Gr. *mastos, bulging*). An English word, now obsolete, that has been replaced by the word "breast," e.g., in RSV (Luke 11:27; Rev 1:13, NIV "chest").

PAPER (See PAPYRUS; WRITING)

PAPHOS (pā'fŏs, Gr. *Paphos*). A Roman city rebuilt by Augustus on western Cyprus. There Paul and Barnabas encountered the wiles of the Jewish sorcerer Elymas in the court of Sergius Paulus, the Roman governor. Paul's miracle of blinding the magician led to the conversion of Paulus (Acts 13:6–13).

An Aramaic papyrus letter, rolled and tied with a cord from Elephantine. Under the Persian Empire, a mercenary garrison including Aramaic-writing Jews was posted on the island. Courtesy The Brooklyn Museum, Bequest of Miss Theodora Wilbour.

PAPYRUS (pà-pī'rŭs, Gr. *papyros*). A plantlike reed or rush that grows in swamps and along rivers or lakes, often to the height of 12 feet (almost 4 m.) with beautiful flowers at the top. In ancient times it was found mainly along the Nile in Egypt but was also known in Palestine. For commercial use the stalk was cut into sections about one foot (one-third m.) long, and these pieces were then sliced lengthwise into thin strips, which were shaped and squared and laid edge to edge to form a larger piece. Other strips were laid horizontally over these strips and both were pressed together, dried in the sun, scraped, and rubbed until there emerged a smooth yellowish sheet much like our heavy wrapping paper, only thicker and heavier. The juice of the pith served as the glue, but sometimes other paste was added.

The manufacture of papyrus was a flourishing business in Egypt, where baskets, sandals, boats, and other articles were made of it. It was not unknown among the Hebrews (Job 8:11), and some believe that the ark that held baby Moses was made of papyrus (Exod 2:3). But the most common use of the product was for writing material, so much so that *papyrus* became the name for writing paper. The art of making papyrus goes back to 2000 B.C., and it was the common writing material in the Greek and Roman worlds from 500 B.C. until A.D. 400, when vellum largely replaced it. There is little doubt that the NT books were written on papyrus (pl. *papyri*). The material was also called *chartēs* in Greek, and John no doubt wrote his second letter on such paper (2 John 12). For long books (rolls or scrolls) many pieces of papyrus were glued together and rolled up. Such a roll was called *biblos* or *biblion*, from which our word *Bible* is derived (cf. Ezek 2:9–10; 2 Tim 4:13; Rev 10:2, 8, 9–10). The width of the roll varied from 3 to 12 inches (8 to 31 cm.), and sometimes the roll got to be as long as 25 feet (8 m.).

Luke's Gospel is estimated to have been 30 feet (9 1/2 m.) long, 2 Thessalonians may have been only 18 inches (46 cm.) long, and short letters like Jude or Philemon were perhaps written on a single small sheet. The writer wrote in columns evenly spaced along the length of the roll, and the reader read one column at a time, unrolling with one hand and rolling up with the other.

Papyrus, however, becomes brittle with age and easily decays, especially when damp. This is why the autographs of the NT writings have perished. They may also have been literally read to pieces or during persecution deliberately destroyed. But thousands of ancient papyri have been found in the dry sands of Egypt and elsewhere. Our libraries contain large collections of both biblical and secular papyri—Bible texts, legal documents, marriage contracts, letters, etc. Many of the NT papyri antedate all other codices. Examples are the Rylands Papyrus, the famous Chester Beatty Papyri, and the more recent Bodmer Papyrus of the Gospel of John. They have added much to our knowledge of the Greek language and the text of the NT.

PARABLE (Gr. *parabolē, likeness*). Derived from the Greek verb *paraballō*, composed of the preposition *para* meaning "beside" and the verb *ballō*, "to cast." A parable is thus a comparison of two objects for the purpose of teaching, usually in the form of a story.

Although the word properly belongs to the NT and is used frequently there, it does occur several times in the OT. There it is the translation of the Hebrew *māshāl*, used in the OT in several senses. It is seen more as a prophetic figurative discourse (Num 23:7, 18 KJV). Ezekiel uses the word much as one would today with the idea of similitude or parable (Ezek 17:2; 24:3). A writer in Psalms treats the word as a poem (Ps 78:2). Finally it is associated with the riddle or "dark saying" (49:4; Ezek 17:2; 20:49). Five times the NT uses the Greek word *paroimia* for parable. This may be synonymous with *parabolē* or it may refer to a didactic, symbolic, or figurative utterance (John 10:6 KJV). Because of varied definitions of a parable, scholars have counted 79, 71, 59, 39, 37, and 33 parables in the NT.

In comparing the parable with the similar figures of speech, one must bear in mind that often the parable contains elements of these other figures. For instance, there are often elements in the parable that must be treated as allegorical interpretation.

While Christ did not invent the parable, it is significant that he is the only one who used it in the NT. At one time in his ministry it was his only method of speaking to the masses (Matt 13:34). It is interesting to note when Christ began to use this methodology. So abrupt was the change in his form of teaching that his disciples asked him why he did this (13:10). It was an effective method of revealing truth to the spiritual and ready mind and at the same time of concealing it from others (13:11). Christ came as Israel's King, and only after they had rejected him did he employ this form of imparting spiritual truth (13:11).

The following classification of parables is adapted from A. B. Bruce, *The Parabolic Teaching of Christ,* pp. 8ff.:

I. Didactic Parables
 A. Nature and Development of the Kingdom
  1. The Sower (Matt 13:3–8; Mark 4:4–8; Luke 8:5–8)
  2. The Tares (Matt 13:24–30)
  3. The Mustard Seed (Matt 13:31–32; Mark 4:30–32; Luke 13:18–19)
  4. The Leaven (Matt 13:33; Luke 13:20–21)
  5. The Hidden Treasure (Matt 13:44)
  6. The Pearl of Great Price (Matt 13:45–46)
  7. The Drag Net (Matt 13:47–50)
  8. The Blade, the Ear, and the Full Corn (Mark 4:26–29)
 B. Service and Rewards
  1. The Laborers in the Vineyard (Matt 20:1–16)
  2. The Talents (Matt 25:14–30)
  3. The Pounds (Luke 19:11–27)
  4. The Unprofitable Servants (Luke 17:7–10)
 C. Prayer
  1. The Friend at Midnight (Luke 11:5–8)
  2. The Unjust Judge (Luke 18:1–8)
 D. Love for Neighbor: The Good Samaritan (Luke 10:30–37)
 E. Humility
  1. The Lowest Seat at the Feast (Luke 14:7–11)
  2. The Pharisee and the Publican (Luke 18:9–14)
 F. Worldly Wealth
  1. The Unjust Steward (Luke 16:1–9)
  2. The Rich Fool (Luke 12:16–21)
  3. The Great Supper (Luke 14:15–24)

II. Evangelic Parables
 A. God's Love for the Lost
  1. The Lost Sheep (Matt 18:12–14; Luke 15:3–7)
  2. The Lost Coin (Luke 15:8–10)
  3. The Lost Son (Luke 15:11–32)
 B. Gratitude of the Redeemed: The Two Debtors (Luke 7:41–43)

III. Prophetic and Judicial Parables
 A. Watchfulness for Christ's Return
  1. The Ten Virgins (Matt 25:1–13)
  2. The Faithful and Unfaithful Servants (Matt 24:45–51; Luke 12:42–48)
  3. The Watchful Porter (Mark 13:34–37)
 B. Judgment on Israel and Within the Kingdom
  1. The Two Sons (Matt 21:28–32)
  2. The Wicked Husbandmen (Matt 21:33–44; Mark 12:1–12; Luke 20:9–18)
  3. The Barren Fig Tree (Luke 13:6–9)
  4. The Marriage Feast of the King's Son (Matt 22:1–14)
  5. The Unforgiving Servant (Matt 18:23–35)

PARACLETE (See HOLY SPIRIT)

PARADISE (Gr. *paradeisos, park*). A word of Persian origin, found only three times in Scripture (Luke 23:43; 2 Cor 12:4; Rev 2:7), referring in each case to heaven. There was a similar word in the Hebrew OT, *pardēs,* translated "forest" or "orchard" or "park" (Neh 2:8; Eccl 2:5; Song of Songs 4:13).

The LXX uses the Greek word 46 times, applying it to quite a wide category of places. It is used of the Adamic Eden (Gen 2:15; 3:23) and of the well-watered plains of the Jordan that Lot viewed (13:10).

The exact location of paradise is uncertain. Paul uses it in 2 Corinthians 12:4, identifying it with the third heaven. Ecclesiasticus 44:16 identifies paradise with heaven into which Enoch was translated.

PARALYSIS, PARALYTIC (See DIS-EASES)

PARAMOUR (păr'à-mūr, Heb. *pileghesh, a concubine*). KJV (Ezek 23:20, NIV lovers; elsewhere [36 times] KJV, NIV concubine) for a Hebrew term that only here means "male lover."

PARAN (pā'răn, Heb. *pā'rān, ornamental*). A wilderness area first referred to as "El Paran" (Gen 14:6). Its boundaries seem uncertain. It lies in the central area of the Sinaitic Peninsula. The four eastern kings passed through this region in trying to suppress the rebellion of their subjects (14:6). It was the area in which Ishmael lived (21:21). Twice after the Israelites left Mt. Sinai they camped in this wilderness (Num 10:12; 12:16). When Moses commanded the spies to search the land of Canaan as God had ordered, they went up from the wilderness of Paran (13:3) and later returned to it (13:26). When David was grieved at the loss of Samuel, he resorted to Paran (1 Sam 25:1). One of the main trade routes of that day ran through Paran, so that Hadad after revolting from Solomon traversed it in his flight to Egypt. Twice in the Scriptures (Deut 33:2; Hab 3:3) Mt. Paran is mentioned. Two mountains are suggested as being identified as Mt. Paran, but the rugged range of mountains west of the Gulf of Aqabah seems to be the most logical site.

PARCHMENT (See WRITING)

PARDON (See FORGIVENESS)

PARENT (Gr. *goneus*). A distinctly NT word, occurring only in the plural (*goneis, parents*). Children were to honor their parents (Exod 20:12) and obey and reverence them (Lev 19:3; Deut 5:16). Failure here on the child's part could be punished by death (21:18–21). The same high regard for parents is expected of children in the NT (Eph 6:1; Col 3:20). Parents were expected to love their children, care and provide for them, and not to provoke them to wrath (2 Cor 12:14; Eph 6:4; Col 3:21).

PAROSH (pā'rŏsh, Heb. *par'ŏsh, a flea*). One whose descendants returned to Babylon under Zerubbabel (Ezra 2:3; Neh 7:8) and under Ezra (Ezra 8:3, *Pharosh* in KJV). One of their number, Pedaiah, helped rebuild the walls (Neh 3:25).

PAROUSIA (See ESCHATOLOGY)

PARTHIANS (pàr'thĭ-ănz, Gr. *Parthoi*). Luke's geographical list of the people

An oasis in Wadi Faran in the central Sinai Peninsula, thought to be the wilderness area of Paran. This is the region settled by Ishmael (Gen 21:21) and crossed by the Israelites at the Exodus (Num 10:12; 12:16). Courtesy Israel Government Press Office

who were in Jerusalem on the Day of Pentecost (Acts 2:9) is headed by "Parthians and Medes." By "Parthians" Luke no doubt meant all the Jews and proselytes who lived in the old Parthian Empire to the east, known today as Iran.

PARTITION, MIDDLE WALL OF In Ephesians 2:14 (KJV) Paul asserts that Christ has broken down the "middle wall of partition" (NIV "dividing wall of hostility") that divided Jews and Gentiles, and has made of the two one new people. Paul probably has in mind a literal wall as a tangible symbol of the division between Jews and Gentiles—the wall in the temple area in Jerusalem separating the court of the Gentiles from the courts into which only Jews might enter. On this wall was a notice in Greek and Latin, warning Gentiles to keep out on pain of death. In A.D. 1871 archaeologists who were excavating the site of the temple found a pillar with this inscription, "No man of another nation is to enter within the fence and enclosure around the temple, and whoever is caught will have himself to blame that his death ensues." Paul himself almost lost his life in the temple enclosure when at the end of his third missionary journey his Jewish enemies accused him of bringing Trophimus the Ephesian past this barrier in the temple (Acts 21:29).

PARTRIDGE (See BIRDS)

PAS DAMMIM (pās'dăm'ĭm, Heb. *pas-damîm, place of bloodshed*). A place of encounter between David and the Philistines in Judah (1 Chron 11:13; also in 2 Sam 23:9 in NIV). It is called also Ephes Dammim (1 Sam 17:1).

PASEAH (pà-sē'à, Heb. *pāsēah, lame*). **1.** A son of Eshton (1 Chron 4:12). **2.** The head of a family of temple servants (KJV Nethinim) (Ezra 2:49; Neh 7:51), one of whose descendants helped in the restoration of one of the gates of Jerusalem (3:6).

PASHHUR (păsh'hêr, Heb. *pashhûr*). **1.** A priest, the son of Immer (Jer 20:1), the "chief officer" in the Lord's house. Angered by Jeremiah's prophecies, he placed him in stocks located near the house of the Lord. When released, Jeremiah told him that the Lord had changed his name to Magor-Missabib, meaning "terror on every side." **2.** The priestly son of Malkijah (Jer 21:1) who sought to have Jeremiah put to death. Probably he is the same person referred to elsewhere (1 Chron 9:12; Ezra 2:38; Neh 7:41; 10:3; 11:12). **3.** The father of Gedaliah (Jer 38:1).

PASSION OF CHRIST (See CHRIST, JESUS)

PASSOVER, FEAST OF (See FEASTS)

PASTORAL LETTERS
  I. Authorship. The term "Pastoral Letters," as a common title for 1 and 2 Timothy and Titus, dates from the early part of the 18th century. It is not exact. Though these letters do furnish worthwhile directions for pastors, the addressees were not pastors in the usual, present-day sense of that term. Rather, they were Paul's special envoys sent by him on specific missions and entrusted with concrete assignments according to the need of the hour.
  Paul's authorship has been disputed on the basis of chronology, ecclesiastical organization, style, theology, and vocabulary. The differences, however, between the Pastorals and Paul's other epistles can be explained on the basis of a change of destination, purpose, subject matter, and time—these epistles being written to Paul's special co-workers with special problems after Paul's missionary trips recorded in Acts.
  Released from his first Roman imprisonment, Paul, perhaps while on his way to Asia Minor, left Titus on the island of Crete to bring to completion the organization of its church(es) (Titus 1:5). At Ephesus Paul was joined by Timothy (back from Philippi? cf. Phil 2:19–23). On leaving for Macedonia, Paul instructed Timothy to remain in Ephesus, which was sorely in need of his ministry (1 Tim 1:3–4). From Macedonia Paul wrote a letter to Timothy in Ephesus (1 Tim) and one to Titus in Crete (Titus).
  Emperor Nero, blamed for Rome's fearful conflagration (July, A.D. 64), in turn blamed Christians, who suffered frightful persecution. Paul was imprisoned (second Roman imprisonment). He faced death (2 Tim 1:16–17; 2:9); Luke alone was with him. Others had left him, either on legitimate missions (Crescens, Titus) or because they had become enamored of the present world (Demas; 4:6–11). Meanwhile, soul-destroying error continued in Timothy's Ephesus (1:8; 2:3, 12, 14–18, 23; 3:8–13).

  II. Contents.

  1 Timothy. Theme: The apostle Paul, writing to Timothy, gives directions for the administration of the church.

  Chapter 1. Paul salutes Timothy and repeats his order that Timothy remain at Ephesus to combat the error of those who refuse to see their own sinful condition in the light of God's holy law, while pretending to be law experts. By contrast, Paul thanks God for having made him, who regards himself as "chief of sinners," a minister of the gospel.

  Chapter 2. Paul gives directions with respect to public worship. Prayers must be made in behalf of all men. Both the men and the women must come spiritually prepared.

  Chapter 3. The apostle gives directions with respect to the offices and functions in the church.

  Chapter 4. He warns against apostasy and instructs Timothy how to deal with it.

  Chapters 5 and 6. He gives directions with respect to certain definite groups and individuals: old(er) men, young(er) men, old(er) women, young(er) women, etc.

  2 Timothy. Theme: Sound Doctrine.

  Chapter 1. *Hold on to it,* as did Lois and Eunice, as I (Paul) do, and as did Onesiphorus.

  Chapter 2. *Teach it.* This brings great reward, for the gospel is glorious in its contents. Vain disputes serve no useful purpose.

Chapter 3. *Abide in it,* knowing that enemies will arise, and that it is based on the sacred writings.

Chapter 4. *Preach it,* in season, out of season. Remain faithful in view of the fact that I, Paul, am about to set sail.

Titus. Theme: The apostle Paul, writing to Titus, gives directions for the promotion of the spirit of sanctification.

Chapter 1. *In congregational life.* Well-qualified elders must be appointed in every town. Reason: Crete is not lacking in disreputable people who must be sternly rebuked.

Chapter 2. *In family and individual life.* All classes of individuals who compose the home-circle must conduct themselves so that by their life they adorn their doctrine. Reason: the grace of God has appeared to all for sanctification and joyful expectation of the coming of "our great God and Savior, Jesus Christ."

Chapter 3. *In social (i.e., public) life.* Believers should be obedient to the authorities and kind to all people. Foolish questions should be shunned and persistently factious people should be rejected. Concluding directions are given with respect to kingdom travelers and believers in general.

PATHROS (păth′rŏs, Heb. *pathrôs*). Mentioned twice in the OT (Ezek 29:14; 30:14) in connection with the return of Jewish remnants to Israel. The KJV also uses the name in Isaiah 11:11 and Jeremiah 44:1, 15 where NIV has "Upper Egypt." Pathros was Upper Egypt, the Egyptian "Pteres" or "Southland," extending from south of Memphis to the first cataract. The "Pathrusites" of Genesis 10:14 seem to have been the inhabitants of this territory.

PATHRUSITES, PATHRUSIM (Heb. *pathrûsî, an inhabitant of Pathros*). Egyptians who, it is believed, came from Pathros, Egypt (see PATHROS). They are descended from Mizraim (Gen 10:13–14; 1 Chron 1:11–12).

PATIENCE (Gr. *hypomonē* and *makrothymia*). Both of these Greek words are translated by our English word *patience,* but they are not exactly synonymous in meaning. *Hypomonē* is the quality of endurance under trials. Those possessing this virtue are free from cowardice or discouragement. It is mainly an attitude of heart with respect to things. *Makrothymia* ("longsuffering") is an attitude with respect to people. Patience is a fruit of the Spirit (Gal 5:22, KJV longsuffering); it

is a virtue that God prizes highly in human beings and seems to be best developed under trials (Rom 5:3–4; James 1:3–4; 5:11 KJV; NIV perseverance). Both terms are used of God (Rom 2:4; 1 Peter 3:20), apparently always in relation to persons. See also LONGSUFFERING.

PATMOS (Gr. *Patmos*). A tiny windswept island lying off the coast of Asia Minor in the Aegean Sea. It is only 10 miles (17 km.) long and 6 miles (10 km.) wide at the broadest point, and its coastline is so irregular that it is only 25 square miles (64 sq. km.) in area. Being of volcanic origin, it is rocky and almost treeless. It was one of the many isolated places to which the Romans banished their exiles, and tradition identifies the Emperor Domitian as the one who banished the apostle John to this lonely place from Ephesus in A.D. 95 (Rev 1:9). During the estimated 18 months spent there, he received the visions of the Lord now recorded in the Book of Revelation.

PATRIARCH (Gr. *patriarchēs, the father of a family, tribe,* or *race*). A title given in the NT to those who founded the Hebrew race and nation—Abraham (Heb 7:4), the sons of Jacob (Acts 7:8–9), and David (2:29). See also ABRAHAM; ISAAC; JACOB; JOSEPH.

PAU (pā′ū, Heb. *pā′û, bleating*). The capital city of King Hadar of Edom (Gen 36:39). Also called Pai (1 Chron 1:50 most versions; Pau NIV), it remains unidentified.

PAUL (Gr. *Paulos,* from Latin *Paulis, little*). The great apostle to the Gentiles. Many events in his checkered and stirring career are unrecorded (cf. 2 Cor 11:24–28).

His Hebrew name was Saul (Gr. *Saulos*), and this name is always used in Acts until his clash with Bar-Jesus at Paphos (Acts 13:9). Thereafter in Acts he is always called Paul.

Providentially, three elements of the world's life of that day—Greek culture, Roman citizenship, and Hebrew religion—met in the apostle to the Gentiles. Paul was born near the beginning of the first century in the busy Greco-Roman city of Tarsus. A noted trading center, it was known for its manufacture of goats' hair cloth, and here the young Saul learned his trade of tentmaking (Acts 18:3). He had the further privilege of being born a Roman citizen (22:28). Paul knew how to use that citizenship as a shield against injustice from local magistrates and to enhance the status of the

Timeline of Paul's Life

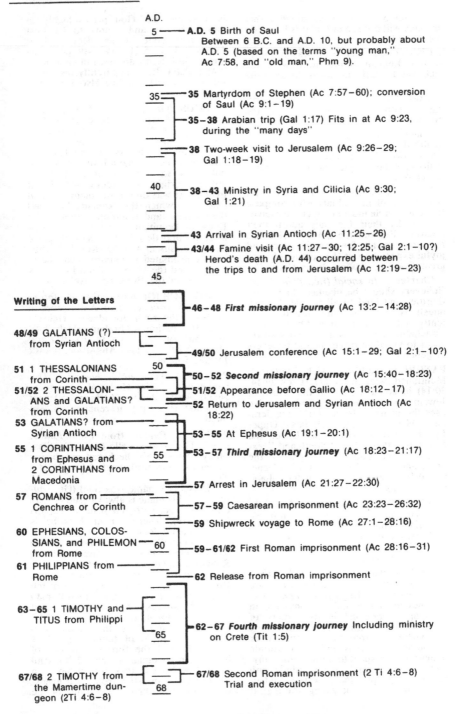

A.D.

A.D. 5 Birth of Saul
Between 6 B.C. and A.D. 10, but probably about A.D. 5 (based on the terms "young man," Ac 7:58, and "old man," Phm 9).

35 Martyrdom of Stephen (Ac 7:57–60); conversion of Saul (Ac 9:1–19)

35–38 Arabian trip (Gal 1:17) Fits in at Ac 9:23, during the "many days"

38 Two-week visit to Jerusalem (Ac 9:26–29; Gal 1:18–19)

38–43 Ministry in Syria and Cilicia (Ac 9:30; Gal 1:21)

43 Arrival in Syrian Antioch (Ac 11:25–26)

43/44 Famine visit (Ac 11:27–30; 12:25; Gal 2:1–10?) Herod's death (A.D. 44) occurred between the trips to and from Jerusalem (Ac 12:19–23)

Writing of the Letters

46–48 *First missionary journey* (Ac 13:2–14:28)

48/49 GALATIANS (?) from Syrian Antioch

49/50 Jerusalem conference (Ac 15:1–29; Gal 2:1–10?)

51 1 THESSALONIANS from Corinth

50–52 *Second missionary journey* (Ac 15:40–18:23)

51/52 2 THESSALONI-ANS and GALATIANS? from Corinth

51/52 Appearance before Gallio (Ac 18:12–17)

52 Return to Jerusalem and Syrian Antioch (Ac 18:22)

53 GALATIANS? from Syrian Antioch

53–55 At Ephesus (Ac 19:1–20:1)

55 1 CORINTHIANS from Ephesus and 2 CORINTHIANS from Macedonia

53–57 *Third missionary journey* (Ac 18:23–21:17)

57 Arrest in Jerusalem (Ac 21:27–22:30)

57 ROMANS from Cenchrea or Corinth

57–59 Caesarean imprisonment (Ac 23:23–26:32)

59 Shipwreck voyage to Rome (Ac 27:1–28:16)

60 EPHESIANS, COLOS-SIANS, and PHILEMON from Rome

59–61/62 First Roman imprisonment (Ac 28:16–31)

61 PHILIPPIANS from Rome

62 Release from Roman imprisonment

63–65 1 TIMOTHY and TITUS from Philippi

62–67 *Fourth missionary journey* Including ministry on Crete (Tit 1:5)

67/68 2 TIMOTHY from the Mamertime dungeon (2Ti 4:6–8)

67/68 Second Roman imprisonment (2 Ti 4:6–8) Trial and execution

The theater at Ephesus, magnificent memorial of Ephesus' greatness and locale for Acts 19 ("they rushed together into the theater," v. 29), overlooking the Arcadian Way, which led to the harbor. Courtesy Duby Tal

Christian faith. His Gentile connections greatly aided him in bridging the chasm between the Gentile and the Jew. But of central significance was his strong Jewish heritage, which was fundamental to all he was and became. He was never ashamed to acknowledge himself a Jew (21:39; 22:3), was justly proud of his Jewish background (2 Cor 11:22), and retained a deep and abiding love for his brethren according to the flesh (Rom 9:1–2; 10:1). Becoming a Christian meant no conscious departure on his part from the religious hopes of his people as embodied in the OT Scriptures (Acts 24:14–16; 26:6–7). This racial affinity with the Jews enabled Paul with great profit to begin his missionary labors in each city in the synagogue, for there he had the best-prepared audience.

Born of purest Jewish blood (Phil 3:5), the son of a Pharisee (Acts 23:6), Saul was cradled in orthodox Judaism. At the proper age, perhaps 13, he was sent to Jerusalem and completed his studies under the famous Gamaliel (22:3; 26:4–5) as a superior, zealous student (Gal 1:14).

In his first appearance in Acts (Acts 7:58), when he was probably at least 30 years old, Paul was already an acknowledged leader in Judaism. His active opposition to Christianity marked him as the natural leader of the persecution that arose after the death of Stephen (7:58–8:3; 9:1–2). The persecutions described in 26:10–11 indicate his fanatical devotion to Judaism. He was convinced that Christians were heretics and that the honor of the Lord demanded their extermination (26:9). He acted in confirmed unbelief (1 Tim 1:13).

As he approached Damascus, armed with authority from the high priest, the transforming crisis in his life occurred. Only an acknowledgment of divine intervention can explain it (1 Cor 9:16–17; 15:10; Gal 1:15–16; Eph 3:7–9; 1 Tim 1:12–16). Luke's own account (Acts 9) is historical, relating the event objectively, while the two accounts by Paul (Acts 22, 26) stress those aspects appropriate to his immediate endeavor. Later in reviewing his former life Paul clearly recognized how God had been preparing him for his future work (Gal 1:15–16).

The new convert at once proclaimed the deity and messiahship of Jesus in the Jewish synagogues of Damascus, truths

General view of the ancient port city of Myra, looking westward. It was here that Paul boarded an Alexandrian ship sailing for Italy (Acts 27:5–6). Courtesy Duby Tal

that had seized his soul (Acts 9:20–22). Since the purpose of his coming was no secret, this action caused consternation among the Jews. Paul's visit to Arabia, mentioned in Galatians 1:17, seems best placed between Acts 9:22 and 23.

After returning to Damascus, his aggressive preaching forced him to flee the murderous fury of the Jews (Acts 9:23–25; Gal 1:17; 2 Cor 11:32–33). Three years after his conversion Saul returned to Jerusalem with the intention of becoming acquainted with Peter (Gal 1:18). The Jerusalem believers regarded him with cold suspicion, but with the help of Barnabas he became accepted among them (Acts 9:26–28). His bold witness to the Hellenistic Jews aroused bitter hostility and cut the visit to 15 days (Gal 1:18). Instructed by the Lord in a vision to leave (Acts 22:17–21), he agreed to be sent home to Tarsus (9:30), where he remained in obscurity for some years. Galatians 1:21–23 implies that he did some evangelistic work there, but we have no further details. Some think that many of the events of 2 Corinthians 11:24–26 must be placed here.

After the opening of the door of the gospel to the Gentiles in the house of Cornelius, a Gentile church was soon established in Syrian Antioch. Barnabas, who had been sent to superintend the revival, saw the need for assistance, remembered Saul's commission to the Gentiles, and brought him to Antioch. An aggressive year-long teaching ministry produced a profound impact on the city, resulting in the designation of the disciples as "Christians" (Acts 11:20–26).

Informed by visiting prophets of an impending famine, the Antioch church raised a collection and sent it to the Jerusalem elders by Barnabas and Saul (11:27–30), marking Saul's second visit to Jerusalem since his conversion. Some scholars equate this visit with that of Galatians 2:1–10, but Acts 11–12 reveals no traces as yet of such a serious conflict in the church about circumcision.

The work of Gentile foreign missions was inaugurated by the church at Antioch under the direction of the Holy Spirit in the sending forth of Barnabas and Saul (Acts 13:1–3).

The first missionary journey, begun apparently in the spring of A.D. 48, started with work among the Jews on Cyprus. Efforts at Paphos to gain the attention of the proconsul Sergius Paulus encountered the determined opposition of the sorcerer Elymas. Saul publicly exposed Elymas' diabolical character, and the swift judgment that fell on Elymas caused the amazed proconsul to believe (13:4–12).

After the events at Paphos, Paul emerged as the recognized leader of the missionary party. Steps to carry the gospel to new regions were taken when the party sailed to Perga in Pamphylia on the southern shores of Asia Minor. Here their attendant, John Mark, cousin of Barnabas (Col 4:10), deserted them and returned to Jerusalem, an act that Paul regarded as unjustified. Arriving at Pisidian Antioch, located in the province of Galatia, the missionaries found a ready opening in the Jewish synagogue. Paul's address to an audience composed of Jews and God-fearing Gentiles, his first recorded address in Acts, is reported at length by Luke as representative of his synagogue ministry (Acts 13:16–41). The message made a deep impression, and the people requested that he preach again the next Sabbath. The large crowd, mainly of Gentiles, who flocked to the synagogue the following Sabbath aroused the jealousy and fierce opposition of the Jewish leaders. In consequence Paul announced a turning to the Gentiles with their message. Gentiles formed the core of the church established in Pisidian Antioch (13:42–52).

Jewish-inspired opposition forced the missionaries to depart for Iconium, SE of Antioch, where the results were duplicated and a flourishing church begun. Compelled to flee a threatened stoning at Iconium, the missionaries crossed into the territory of Lycaonia, still within the province of Galatia, and began work at Lystra, which was apparently without a synagogue. The healing of a congenital cripple caused a pagan attempt to offer sacrifices to the missionaries as gods in human form. Paul's horrified protest (14:15–17), arresting the attempt, reveals his dealings with pagans who did not have the OT revelation. Timothy apparently was converted at this time. Fanatical agitators from Antioch and Iconium turned the disillusioned pagans against the missionaries, and in the uproar Paul was stoned. Dragged out of the city, the unconscious apostle was left for dead, but as the disciples stood around him, he regained consciousness, and reentered the city. The next day he was able to go on to neighboring Derbe. After a fruitful and unmolested ministry there, the missionaries retraced their steps to instruct their converts and organize them into churches with responsible leaders (14:1–23). They returned to Syrian Antioch and reported how God "had opened the door of faith to the Gentiles" (14:27).

For the second missionary journey Paul and Barnabas separated because of their "sharp disagreement" concerning John Mark. Barnabas sailed to Cyprus with Mark, while Paul chose Silas and revisited the churches in Galatia (Acts 15:36–41). At Lystra Paul added young Timothy to the missionary party, having circumcised him to make him acceptable for work among the Jews. Negative leadings closed the door to missionary work in Asia and Bithynia, but at Troas Paul received the positive call to Macedonia (16:1–9).

An expository ministry in the synagogue at Thessalonica ended with the synagogue closed to Paul; he apparently carried on a successful Gentile ministry there. A Jewish-instigated riot forced the missionaries to flee to Berea, where a fruitful ministry resulted. When the work there was interrupted by agitators from Thessalonica, Silas and Timothy remained, but Paul was brought to Athens by some brothers (Acts 17:1–15).

Distressed by the Athenian idolatry, Paul preached in the synagogue and daily in the marketplace. Drawing the attention of the Athenian philosophers, he was requested to give a formal exposition of his teaching. His appearance at the Areopagus was not a formal trial. His memorable speech before the pagan philosophers (Acts 17:22–31) is a masterpiece of tact, insight, and condensation. A few converts were made, but Paul regarded the mission at cultured, philosophical, sophisticated Athens with keen disappointment.

By contrast, the work at Corinth—a city of commerce, wealth, squalor, and gross immorality—proved to be a definite success, lasting 18 months (Acts 18:1–17). A successful work among the Gentiles resulted in the formation of a large church, the majority of the members being from the lower levels of society (1 Cor 1:26).

When he left Corinth, Paul took Aquila and Priscilla with him as far as Ephesus and then hurried to Judea. He apparently visited Jerusalem and then spent some time at Antioch (Acts 18:18–22).

Paul's departure from Antioch traditionally marks the beginning of the third missionary journey. It is convenient to retain the traditional designation, but we should remember that with the second journey Antioch ceased to be the center for Paul's activities.

Having strengthened the disciples in "the region of Galatia and Phrygia," Paul commenced a fruitful ministry at Ephesus that lasted nearly three years (Acts 19:1–41; 20:31). His work at Ephesus, one of the most influential cities of the east, placed Paul at the heart of Greco-Roman civilization. After three months of work in the synagogue, Paul launched an independent Gentile work, centering his daily preaching in the school of Tyrannus for a two-year period. The Ephesian ministry was marked by systematic teaching (20:18–21), extraordinary miracles (19:11–12), a signal victory over the magical arts (19:13–19), and devastating inroads on the worship of Diana (19:23–27). Streams of people came to Ephesus for purposes of commerce, religion, or pleasure. Many of them came into con-

Remains of the Forum of Augustus at Rome, first inaugurated in 2 B.C. Courtesy Gerald Nowotny

tact with the gospel, were converted, and spread the message throughout the province (19:10). But the work was marked by constant and fierce opposition (20:19; 1 Cor 15:32). The financially prompted riot led by Demetrius brought the work of Paul at Ephesus to a close (Acts 19:23–20:1).

At Ephesus Paul had inaugurated a collection among the Gentile churches for the saints in Judea (1 Cor 16:1–4). Since its delivery was to mark the close of his work in the east, Paul was making plans to visit Rome (Acts 19:21), intending to go from there to Spain (Rom 15:22–29).

Paul went to Jerusalem by way of Macedonia (Acts 20:3–6). At Troas he spent a busy and eventful night (20:7–12). Paul called the Ephesian elders to meet him at Miletus (20:17–35). The journey to Jerusalem was marked by repeated warnings to Paul of what awaited him there (21:1–16).

Although cordially received at Jerusalem by James and the elders, Paul's presence created tension in the church because of reports that he taught Jews in the Dispersion to forsake Moses. To neutralize these reports, the elders suggested to Paul a plan to prove that he had no aversion to a voluntary keeping of the law (Acts 21:17–25). The act of conciliation apparently satisfied the Judean believers, but it caused Paul's arrest. Paul secured permission to address the Jews from the steps of the barracks (21:37–22:29). Informed of a plot to murder Paul, the commander sent Paul to Caesarea under a large protective guard (23:17–35).

The trial before Felix at Caesarea made it clear to the governor that the charges against Paul were false, but, unwilling to antagonize the Jews, he simply postponed a decision. Felix dismissed the preacher but later sent for him frequently, hoping Paul would try to use bribery to secure his release. After two years Felix was summoned to Rome and left Paul an uncondemned prisoner (Acts 24:1–27).

With the coming of the new governor, Festus, the Jewish leaders renewed their efforts to have Paul condemned. When it became clear to Paul that he could not expect justice from the new governor, he appealed his case to Caesar (Acts 25:1–12). When Herod Agrippa II and his sister Bernice came to visit the new governor, Festus discussed Paul's case with Agrippa, an acknowledged expert in Jewish affairs. The next day before his royal audience Paul delivered a masterly exposition of his position and used the occasion to seek to win Agrippa to Christ. Uncomfortable under Paul's efforts, Agrippa terminated the meeting but frankly declared Paul's innocence to the governor (25:13–26:32).

Paul was sent to Rome, perhaps in the autumn of A.D. 60, under the escort of a centurion named Julius. Paul's treatment in Rome was lenient; he lived in his own hired house with a soldier guarding him. Permitted to receive all who came, he was able to exercise an important ministry in Rome (Acts 27-28). The Prison Letters—Colossians, Philemon, Ephesians, and Philippians—are lasting fruit of this period.

There is strong evidence for believing that he was released at the end of two years. The amicable attitude of the Roman government in Acts favors it, the Prison Letters expect it, the Pastoral Letters demand it, and tradition asserts it. After his release, perhaps in the spring of A.D. 63, Paul went east, visited Ephesus, stationing Timothy there when he left for Macedonia (1 Tim 1:3). He left Titus to complete the missionary work on Crete and in writing to him mentions plans to spend the winter at Nicopolis (Titus 1:5; 3:12). From Nicopolis he may have made the traditional visit to Spain, working there at the outbreak of the persecution by Nero in the autumn of 64.

Paul again became a prisoner in Rome, kept in close confinement as a malefactor (2 Timothy 1:16–17; 2:9). At his first appearance before the court he escaped immediate condemnation (4:16–18), but to Timothy he writes of no hope for release (4:6–8). He was executed at Rome in late 66 or early 67. Tradition says he was beheaded on the Ostian Way.

Paul's labors firmly planted churches in the strategic centers. His foresight led him to select and train strong young workers to carry on the work after him. Paul was supremely the interpreter of the gospel of Jesus Christ, interpreted to the Gentile world through his labors and letters. His letters to various churches are vital to Christian theology and practice.

Physically, Paul did not present an imposing appearance (2 Cor 10:10). He underwent hardships and sufferings (11:23–27) and was especially afflicted by "a thorn in [his] flesh" (12:7). The exact nature of the affliction can only be conjectured; his feelings of weakness made him constantly dependent on God's power (2 Cor 12:10; Phil 4:12–13).

He was characterized by native zeal and ardor, giving himself wholly to his work. He was warm-hearted and affectionate, longing for and making strong friendships. He was humble, sincere, and sympathetic. He was by nature a religious man, and, already as a Jew but much more as a Christian, his faith dominated his life and activities. The secret of his unique career lay in his fervent nature as possessed and empowered by the living Christ.

PAULUS, SERGIUS (pô'lŭs, sûr'jĭ-ŭs, Gr. *Paulos Sergios*). The Roman proconsul on Cyprus (Acts 13:6–12), who became a Christian through Paul's preaching and the miracle of blindness that struck his court magician, Elymas.

PAVEMENT (See GABBATHA)

PAVILION (pà-vĭl'yŭn, Heb. *sōkh* in Ps 27:5, *sukkâh* in 31:20, *booth, tent*). Used in KJV to refer to a covered place in which a person may be kept hidden. NIV usually has "dwelling." It is used chiefly to symbolize God's favor and protection provided for his children (18:11). It grows out of the fact that no one has access to the eastern king's inner court or pavilion except those to whom he gives permission.

PEACE (Heb. *shālôm, peace*, Gr. *eirēnē, concord*). "Completeness," "soundness," neighborliness (Ps 28:3 KJV), well-being and security (Eccl 3:8), or the reward of a mind stayed on God (Isa 26:3). It is linked with honest dealing and true justice (Zech 8:16 KJV), and is a prominent feature of the coming Messiah (Isa 9:6).

Peace results from God's forgiveness (Phil 4:7) and is the ideal relation with one's brother (2 Cor 13:11; cf. Matt 5:23–24). Peace, a mark of serenity (John 14:27) to be sought after (Heb 12:14), summarizes the gospel message (Acts 10:36). It is a fruit of the Spirit (Gal 5:22), will benefit those who practice it both now (James 3:18) and at the Second Coming (Rom 2:10), and is the opposite of disorder or confusion (1 Cor 14:33). Peace is the presence of God, not the absence of conflict. Christ brought, preached, and is our peace (Eph 2:14ff.).

PEACE OFFERING (See SACRIFICE AND OFFERINGS)

PEACOCK (See ANIMALS; BIRDS)

PEARL (See MINERALS)

PEDAIAH (pē-dā'yà, Heb. *pedhāyāhû, Jehovah redeems*). 1. One from Rumah, father of Zebidah (2 Kings 23:36). 2. Father of Zerubbabel, son of Jeconiah

(1 Chron 3:18). **3.** The father of Joel and ruler of western Manasseh under David (27:20). **4.** One from the family of Parosh who aided in repairing the wall of Jerusalem (Neh 3:25). **5.** A Benjamite, father of Joed (11:7). **6.** A Levite and a treasurer over the Lord's house (13:13).

PEG (See PIN)

PEKAH (pē'kà, Heb. *peqah, to open*). The son of Remaliah, he usurped the throne by murdering Pekahiah and reigned 20 years (2 Kings 15:27). He formed a league with the Gileadites to resist the advances of Assyria and allied himself with Rezin of Damascus against Jotham king of Judah (15:37–38; 16; 2 Chron 28). Pekah became subject to the Assyrians (2 Kings 15:29) and a short time later was murdered by Hoshea (15:30).

PEKAHIAH (pĕk'à-hī'à, Heb. *peqahyâh, Jehovah has opened*). Israel's 17th king was a wicked king, following the practices of idolatry formulated by Jeroboam (2 Kings 15:24). After a brief reign of only two years, he was brutally murdered.

PELAIAH (pē-lā'yà, Heb. *pelā'yâh, Jehovah is wonderful*). **1.** Elioenai's son from Judah's royal house (1 Chron 3:24). **2.** The Levite who aided Ezra in explaining the law (Neh 8:7) and later sealed the covenant with Nehemiah (10:10).

PELATIAH (pĕl'à-tī'à, Heb. *pelatyâh, Jehovah has delivered*). **1.** Hananiah's son (1 Chron 3:21). **2.** Ishi's son who headed a Simeonite group that helped rid the area of the Amalekites (4:42) in Hezekiah's reign. **3.** One of those who sealed the covenant with Nehemiah (Neh 10:22). **4.** Son of Benaiah (Ezek 11:1). He plotted evil and gave wicked advice in Jerusalem (11:2). Ezekiel was instructed to prophesy against them, and while he was doing so Pelatiah fell dead (11:13).

PELEG (pē'lĕg, Heb. *pelegh, division*). One of the sons of Eber (Gen 10:25; 11:16–19; 1 Chron 1:25). The reason for his being named Peleg is that "in his time the earth was divided." This probably refers to the confounding of the language and the consequent scattering of the descendants of Noah (Gen 11:1–9).

PELET (pē'lĕt, Heb. *pelet, deliverance*). **1.** Jahdai's son (1 Chron 2:47). **2.** One of Azmaveth's sons who joined David at Ziklag while David hid from Saul (12:3).

PELETH (pē'lĕth, Heb. *peleth, swiftness*). **1.** The father of On, who became a part of the conspiracy against Moses and

Aaron (Num 16:1). **2.** A descendant of Jerahmeel (1 Chron 2:33).

PELETHITES (pĕl'ē-thīts, Heb. *pelēthî, courier*). A group who along with the Kerethites formed David's bodyguard (2 Sam 8:18; 20:7; 1 Kings 1:38, 44; 1 Chron 18:17). Perhaps they were the ones who conveyed the king's messages to distant places.

PELICAN (See BIRDS)

PEN (See WRITING)

PENCE (See MONEY)

PENDANT (See DRESS)

PENIEL (pē-nī'ĕl, Heb. *penî'ēl, face of God*). The place where Jacob wrestled with the angel of God (Gen 32:24–32). The exact location is not known, though it was not far from Succoth and east of the Jordan.

PENNY (See MONEY)

PENTATEUCH, THE (pĕn'tà-tūk, Heb. *tôrâh, law or teaching*). The first five books of the Bible: Genesis, Exodus, Leviticus, Numbers, and Deuteronomy. The Pentateuch covers the period of time from the creation to the end of the Mosaic era.

Genesis begins with an account of creation but soon narrows its interest to the human race. Adam and Eve were entrusted with the responsibility of caring for the world about them, but forfeited their privilege through disobedience and sin. In subsequent generations all mankind became so wicked that the entire human race, except Noah and his family, was destroyed. When the new civilization degenerated, God chose to fulfill his promises of redemption through Abraham.

The patriarchal era (Gen 12–50) narrates the events of approximately four generations—namely, those of Abraham, Isaac, Jacob, and Joseph. After the opening verses of Exodus the rest of the Pentateuch is chronologically confined to the lifetime of Moses. Consequently the deliverance of Israel from Egypt and their preparation for entrance into the land of Canaan is the prevailing theme. The historical core of these books is briefly outlined as follows:

Exodus 1–19, from Egypt to Mt. Sinai.

Exodus 19–Numbers 10, encampment at Mt. Sinai (approximately one year).

Numbers 10–21, wilderness wanderings (approximately 38 years).

Numbers 22–Deuteronomy 34, encampment before Canaan (approximately one year).

The Mosaic Law was given at Mt. Sinai. As God's covenant people the Israelites were not to conform to the idolatrous practices of the Egyptians nor to the customs of the Canaanites whose land they were to conquer and possess. Israel's religion was a revealed religion. The entrance into Canaan was delayed for almost 40 years because of the unbelief of the Israelites.

For study purposes the Pentateuch lends itself to the following analysis:

I. **The Era of Beginnings (Gen 1:1–11:32)**
   A. The account of creation (1:1–2:25)
   B. Man's fall and its consequences (3:1–6:10)
   C. The Flood: God's judgment on man (6:11–8:19)
   D. Man's new beginning (8:20–11:32)

II. **The Patriarchal Period (Gen 12:1–50:26)**
   A. The life of Abraham (12:1–25:18)
   B. Isaac and Jacob (25:19–36:43)
   C. Joseph (37:1–50:26)

III. **Emancipation of Israel (Exod 1:1–19:2)**
   A. Israel freed from slavery (1:1–13:19)
   B. From Egypt to Mt. Sinai (13:20–19:2)

IV. **The Religion of Israel (Exod 19:3–Lev 27:34)**
   A. God's covenant with Israel (Exod 19:3–24:8)
   B. The place of worship (24:9–40:38)
   C. Instructions for holy living (Lev 1:1–27:34)
      1. The offerings (1:1–7:38)
      2. The priesthood (8:1–10:20)
      3. Laws of purification (11:1–15:33)
      4. Day of atonement (16:1–34)
      5. Heathen customs forbidden (17:1–18:30)
      6. Laws of holiness (19:1–22:33)
      7. Feasts and seasons (23:1–25:55)
      8. Conditions of God's blessings (26:1–27:34)

V. **Organization of Israel (Num 1:1–12:10)**
   A. The numbering of Israel (1:1–4:49)

B. Camp regulations (5:1–6:21)
C. Religious life of Israel (6:22–9:14)
D. Provisions for guidance (9:15–10:10)

VI. **Wilderness Wanderings (Num 10:11–22:1)**
   A. From Mt. Sinai to Kadesh (10:11–12:16)
   B. The Kadesh crisis (13:1–14:45)
   C. The years of wandering (15:1–19:22)
   D. From Kadesh to the Plains of Moab (20:1–22:1)

VII. **Instructions for Entering Canaan (Num 22:2–36:13)**
   A. Preservation of God's chosen people (22:2–25:18)
   B. Preparation for conquest (26:1–33:49)
   C. Anticipation of occupation (33:50–36:13)

VIII. **Retrospect and Prospect (Deut 1:1–34:12)**
   A. History and its significance (1:1–4:43)
   B. The law and its significance (4:44–28:68)
   C. Final preparation and farewell (29:1–34:12)

PENTECOST (pĕn'tĕ-kŏst, Gr. *pentēcostē*). The word derives from the Greek for "the 50th day." It was the Jewish Feast of Weeks (Exod 34:22; Deut 16:9–11), variously called the Feast of Harvest (Exod 23:16) or the Day of Firstfruits (Num 28:26), which fell on the 50th day after the Feast of the Passover.

Leviticus 23 prescribes the sacred nature of the holiday and lists the appropriate sacrifices. The events of Acts 2 transformed the Jewish festival into a Christian one. Some have seen a symbolic connection between this ancient festival and the firstfruits of the Christian dispensation. "Whitsunday" is the 50th day after Easter Sunday. The name derives from the wearing of white garments by those seeking baptism at this festival.

PENUEL (pē-nū'ĕl, Heb. *penî'ēl, face of God*). **1.** Hur's son, the father of Gedor (1 Chron 4:4). **2.** One of Shashak's sons (8:25).

PEOR (pē'ôr, Heb. *pe'ôr, opening*). **1.** The name given to the mountain in Moab where King Balak led Balaam that he might see and curse Israel (Num 23:28), a high peak near the town of Beth Peor (Deut 3:29). **2.** In Numbers 25:18, 31:16, and Joshua 22:17, Peor is used four times as a contraction for Baal Peor. 3. The god of Baal Peor (Num 25:18; 31:16).

PERAEA (See PEREA)

PERATH The Hebrew name for the Euphrates River (a Greek word). Used in Jeremiah 13:4–7 to refer to the place where Jeremiah was instructed to hide a linen belt. See also EUPHRATES.

PERDITION (pêr-dĭ'shun, Gr. *apōleia, perishing, destruction*). The idea of a loss or destruction predominates in the use of this word. Each of the eight uses of perdition in the KJV (John 17:12; Phil 1:28; 2 Thess 2:3; 1 Tim 6:9; Heb 10:39; 2 Peter 3:7; Rev 17:8, 11; NIV destruction, destroyed; RSV perdition, destruction [each four times]) refers to the final state of the wicked.

PERDITION, SON OF (Gr. *huios tēs apōleias*). A phrase used to designate two men in the NT: Judas Iscariot (John 17:12 KJV, NASB, RSV; NIV one doomed to destruction) and the "man of lawlessness" (the Antichrist; 2 Thess 2:3). The phrase comes from the Hebrew custom of noting a certain trait or characteristic in a person and then referring to him as the son of that trait.

PEREA (pĕ-rē'à, Gr. *Peraia, Peraios, Peraites*). A word that does not occur in the Bible but was used by Josephus and others to designate the small territory on the east side of the Jordan opposite old Judea and Samaria; known in the Gospels as the land "beyond the Jordan" (cf. Matt 4:15, 25; 19:1; Mark 3:7–8). John baptized in Bethabara "on the other side of Jordan," or in Perea (John 1:28). Jesus did much of his teaching in Perea (Mark 10:1–33) and made his final journey to Jerusalem from there (John 10:40; 11:54).

PEREZ (pē'rĕz, Heb. *perets, pherets, breach*; Gr. *phares*). Twin son of Judah (Gen 38:29), often called *Pherez* (e.g., 1 Chron 2:4, 5; *Pharez* KJV 10 of 13 times), three times called *Phares* (KJV Matt 1:3; Luke 3:33).

PERFECTION, PERFECT (Heb. *shālēm, tāmîm*, Gr. *teleios, teleiotēs*). God alone, who lacks nothing in terms of goodness or excellence, is truly perfect. Everything he is, thinks, and does has the character of perfection (Deut 32:4; 2 Sam 22:31; Job 37:16; Pss 18:30; 19:7; Matt 5:48). When human beings are called perfect in the OT, it means that they are "upright" or "blameless" (Gen 6:9; Job 1:1; Ps 37:37). Sacrificial animals were deemed perfect if they were without spot or blemish and thus wholesome or sound (Lev 3:1, 6; 4:3; 14:10).

The Greek *teleios* conveys the idea of reaching the point of full growth or maturity (1 Cor 2:6; 14:20; Eph 4:13; Phil 3:15; Col 1:28; 4:12; Heb 5:14).

PERFUME (See OINTMENTS AND PERFUMES)

PERFUMER (See OCCUPATIONS AND PROFESSIONS)

PERGA (pûr'gà, Gr. *pergē*). The chief city of old Pamphylia of Asia Minor. Paul and Barnabas passed through the city twice on the first missionary journey, both going and returning (Acts 13:13–14; 14:24–25). Here John Mark left the party and returned to Jerusalem.

PERGAMUM, PERGAMOS (pûr'gà-mŭm, Gr. *Pergamos*). A city of Mysia, in KJV, Pergamos (Rev 1:11; 2:12), the chief town of the province of Asia. It was the site of the first temple of the Caesar cult, and a second shrine was later dedicated to Trajan. On the crag above Pergamum was a thronelike altar to Zeus (cf. Rev. 2:13). It is natural that "Nicolaitanism" should flourish in a place where politics and paganism were so closely allied (2:15), and where pressure on Christians to compromise must have been heavy.

PERIZZITE (pâr'ĭ-zīt, Heb. *perizzî*). A pre-Israelite tribe or racial group of Palestine (Gen 13:7; 34:30; Exod 3:8, 17; 23:23; 33:2; 34:11; Deut 20:17; Josh 3:10; 24:11; Judg 1:4) mentioned only in the Bible.

PERJURY A word rarely found in our English Bible (but see Mal 3:5; Jer 7:9; 1 Tim 1:10). Oaths were considered to be binding promises, so that to break an oath or to use falsehood under oath was perjury (Lev 19:12; Ezek 16:59).

PERSECUTION A particular course or period of systematic infliction of punishment or penalty for adherence to a particular religious belief. Oppression is to be distinguished from it. Pharaoh oppressed the Hebrews; so did Nebuchadnezzar. Daniel and Jeremiah were persecuted. Systematic persecution began with the Roman imperial government. Notably tolerant toward alien religious beliefs in general, the Romans clashed with the Christians over the formalities of Caesar worship. Nero must be regarded as the first persecutor. In 64 (Tactitus, *Annals* 15:38–44) this emperor used the small Christian community as a scapegoat for a disastrous fire in Rome, placing on the Christians the charge of arson that was popularly leveled against him.

Ancient Pergamum, situated on a hill 1,000 feet high, looking north over the Caicus valley. Most extant remains date from the third to second centuries B.C. Shown here are the city walls, the theater in foreground, and the temple of Dionysus at lower left. "I know where you live—where Satan has his throne" (Rev 2:12–13). Courtesy Dan Bahat

PERSEVERANCE (Gr. *proskarterēsis*). This word occurs only once in the NT (Eph 6:18 KJV, RSV) and means there persistence and steadfastness in prayer. The word, however, has become an "umbrella term," especially in the expression "the perseverance of the saints." It is used to cover the biblical theme that, because God's gift of salvation is an eternal gift, believers are to persist in their Christian commitment and life, whatever their circumstances, knowing that God is on their side (Rom 8:31; cf. 1 Cor 15:10; Phil 1:6; 2:12–13; 2 Thess 3:3; 1 Peter 1:5).

PERSIA (pûr'zhà, Heb. *pāras*, Gr. *Persis*). As a geographical term Persia may be taken to mean the Iranian plateau, bounded by the Tigris Valley on the west and south, the Indus Valley on the east, and by the Armenian ranges and the Caspian Sea to the north, comprising in all something near one million square miles (2.5 million sq. km.). The imperial Persia of the OT rose on the ruins of Babylon and is seen in the life of Esther. It also formed the background of the events described in the books of Ezra and Nehemiah.

Cyrus established the Persians as the dominant tribe in 549 B.C. He then moved west to defeat the Lydian Empire of Croesus in 545, and south to defeat Nabonidus of Babylon in 538. The conquest of Lydia gave Cyrus Asia Minor; the overthrow of Babylon made him master of the Euphrates River plain, Assyria, Syria, and Palestine. It was the first of the world's great imperial organizations, foreshadowing Rome; it was humane when compared with the Assyrian Empire. The conflict between Samaria and Jerusalem, depicted in the life of Nehemiah, is an illustration of the problems of such a large empire. Nehemiah was working by royal decree and yet found his work hampered by armed interference. Ezra's fear (Ezra 8:22) suggests similar pockets of anarchy. The four books of the OT in which Persia forms a background (Ezra, Esther, Ezekiel, and Daniel) all illustrate the royal tendency to delegate special authority to individuals for specific tasks.

It will be useful to list the Persian kings whose reigns have significance in OT history:

1. Cyrus, 538–529 B.C. (2 Chron

The ruins of Persepolis, royal seat of the Achaemenid kings of Persia. Construction was begun by Darius I in 518 B.C. and completed in 460 B.C. Courtesy B. Brandl

36:22–23; Ezra 1–5 passim; Isa 44:28; 45:1; Dan 1:21; 6:28; 10:1).

2. Cambyses, 529–522 B.C. Some have suggested that Cambyses is the mysterious Darius the Mede (Dan 5:31; 6:9, 25; 9:1; 11:1). Others think this obscure person was Gobryas, governor of Media, who exercised authority for Cyrus in Babylon.

3. Gaumata, a usurper, who held brief royal authority until put down by Darius, 522–521 B.C.

4. Darius I (Hystaspis), 521–486 B.C., the great imperialist, whose seaborne attack on Greece was defeated at Marathon in 490. This is the Darius (mentioned by Ezra) under whose protection permission was given for the temple to be built.

5. Xerxes I (Ahasuerus), 486–465 B.C. (Esth 1:1–2; 2:16). This mad king in a mighty combined operation sought to avenge Marathon and was defeated by the Greeks at Salamis (480) and Plataea (479).

6. Artaxerxes I (Longimanus), 464–424 B.C. It was this monarch who permitted Ezra to go to Jerusalem to restore the affairs of the Jewish community (Ezra 7–8), and who promoted the mission of his cupbearer Nehemiah, 13 years later. Darius the Persian (Neh 12:22) is Codomannus, the last king of Persia, overthrown by Alexander in 330.

PERUDA (See PERIDA)

PESHITTA (pĕ-shēt'tà). Often called "simple" version, it is the common name for the ancient Syriac (Aramaic) transla-

tion of the Bible. The OT was translated before the Christian era, probably by Jews who spoke Aramaic. Syriac Christians translated the NT during the early centuries of the church.

PEST (See ANIMALS)

PESTILENCE (pĕs'tĭlĕns, Heb. *dever*, Gr. *loimos*). In the OT (KJV 47 vv.; NIV 4 vv.), any fatal epidemic, often the result of divine judgment (Exod 5:3 KJV, MLB, MOF, NASB, NEB, RSV; plague(s) JB, NIV); NT usage is only by Jesus (Matt 24:7; Luke 21:11).

PESTLE (pĕs''l, Heb. *'ĕlî*, *lifted*). An instrument either of wood or of stone, rounded at the ends and used to grind material in a mortar (Prov 27:22).

PETER (pētêr, Gr. *Petros*, *rock*). The most prominent of the 12 apostles in the Gospels and an outstanding leader in the early days of the Christian church. His original name was Simon, a common Greek name, or more properly Symeon (Acts 15:14), a popular Hebrew name.

He was a native of Bethsaida (John 1:44), the son of a certain John (1:42; 21:15–17), apparently an abbreviation for Jonah (Matt 16:17). As a native of "Galilee of the Gentiles" he was able to converse in Greek, while his native Aramaic was marked with provincialisms of pronunciation and diction (26:73). He and his brother Andrew followed the hardy occupation of fishermen on the Sea of Galilee, being partners with Zebedee's sons, James and John (Luke 5:7). He was a married man (Mark 1:30; 1 Cor 9:5) and at the time of Christ's Galilean ministry lived in Capernaum (Mark 1:21, 29).

He was personally introduced to Jesus by his brother Andrew (John 1:42). After a period of companionship with Jesus during his early Judean ministry (1:42–4:43), Peter resumed his ordinary occupation.

With the commencement of Christ's Galilean ministry, Peter and Andrew, with James and John, were called by Jesus to full-time association with him to be trained as "fishers of men" (Mark 1:16–20; Luke 5:1–11). With the growth of the work, Jesus selected 12 of his followers to be his nearest companions for special training (Mark 3:13–19; Luke 6:12–16). In the lists of these 12 designated apostles (Luke 6:13), Peter is always named first (Matt 10:2–4; Mark 3:16–19; Luke 6:14–16; Acts 1:13–14).

The development of an inner circle among the disciples is first seen when Jesus took Peter, James, and John with him into the house of Jairus (Mark 5:37; Luke 8:51). The three were further privileged to witness the Transfiguration (Matt 17:1; Mark 9:2; Luke 9:28) and the agony in the Garden (Matt 26:37; Mark 14:33).

Peter was the natural spokesman of the 12 (Matt 16:16, 18; 22:41–46; John 6:66–69). By his believing confession Peter has identified himself with Christ the true Rock (Isa 28:16; 1 Cor 3:11; 1 Peter 2:4–5), thus fulfilling Christ's prediction concerning him (John 1:42). He has thus become a rock (*petros*); and on "this rock" (*petra*), composed of Peter and the other apostles, joined by faith in Christ the chief cornerstone (Eph 2:20), Jesus will build his triumphant church.

The account in Acts historically interprets Peter's use of the keys in opening the doors of Christian opportunity at Pentecost (Acts 2), in Samaria (ch. 8), and to the Gentiles (ch. 10). The power of binding and loosing was not limited to Peter (Matt 18:18; John 20:3). But Peter was also the spokesman in attempting to dissuade Jesus from his announced path of suffering, thus proving himself a "stumbling block" (Matt 16:23; Mark 8:33).

Peter came into prominence in the Gospels also in connection with the matter of the payment of the temple tax (Matt 17:24–27), his inquiry as to the limits on forgiveness (18:21), and his reminder to Jesus that they had left all to follow him (19:27; Mark 10:28). During Passion Week his activities were prominent. He called Jesus' attention to the withered fig tree (Mark 11:21), and with three others

he asked Jesus concerning his prediction about the temple (13:3). With John he was commissioned to prepare for the Passover (Luke 22:8). Peter objected to the Lord's washing his feet in the Upper Room, but impulsively swung to the opposite extreme when informed of the implications of his denial (John 13:1–11). He beckoned to John to ask the identity of the betrayer (13:23–24) and stoutly contradicted Jesus when warned of his impending denials (Matt 26:33–35; Mark 14:29–31; Luke 22:31–34; John 13:37–38). In the Garden of Gethsemene, when chosen with James and John to watch with Jesus, he slept (Matt 26:37–46; Mark 14:33–42). In fleshly zeal he sought to defend Jesus, and Jesus rebuked him for it (John 18:10–11). He fled with the other disciples when Jesus was bound; but, anxious to see the end, he followed afar, was admitted (through John's action) into the court of the high priest, and there shamefully denied his Lord three times (Matt 26:58, 69–75; Mark 14:66–72; Luke 22:54–62; John 18:15–18, 25–27). The look of Jesus broke his heart, and he went out and wept bitterly (Luke 22:61–62). That Peter witnessed the Crucifixion is not stated (but cf. 1 Peter 5:1).

On the Resurrection morning he and John ran to the tomb of Jesus to investigate the report of Mary Magdalene (John 20:1–10). Somewhere during that day the risen Lord appeared to Peter (1 Cor 15:5). At his postresurrection manifestation to seven at the Sea of Galilee, John was the first to recognize the Lord; but, typically, Peter was the first to act. Following the group breakfast, Christ tested Peter's love and formally restored him by the threefold commission to feed his sheep (John 21:1–23).

The third period in Peter's life began with the ascension of Jesus. In the early days of the church (Acts 1–12), Peter appeared as the spokesman of the apostolic group, but there is no hint that he assumed any authority not also exercised by the other apostles. He suggested the choice of another to fill the place of Judas (1:15–26), preached the Spirit-empowered sermon on Pentecost (2:14–40), and with John healed the lame man, the first apostolic miracle to arouse persecution (3:1–4:21). He was used to expose the sin of Ananias and Sapphira (5:1–12), was held in high esteem by the people during the miracle ministry in the church that followed (5:12–16), and spoke for the Twelve when arraigned before the Sanhedrin (5:27–41). With John he was sent to

One of Israel's most recent and exciting discoveries—the first ancient boat to be found in the Sea of Galilee, dated from the first century B.C. to second century A.D. and thus popularly called "the boat of Jesus." Courtesy The Israel Department of Antiquities and Museums

Samaria, where, through the laying on of hands, the Holy Spirit fell on the Samaritan believers and Peter exposed the unworthy motives of Simon (8:14–24). While on a tour through Judea, Peter healed Aeneas and raised Dorcas from the dead (9:32–43). Through a divinely given vision at Joppa, Peter was prepared and commissioned to preach the gospel to Cornelius at Caesarea, thus opening the door to the Gentiles (10:1–48). This brought on him the criticism of the circumcision party in Jerusalem (11:1–18). During the persecution of the church by Agrippa I in A.D. 44, Peter escaped death by a miraculous deliverance from prison (12:1–19).

In the Acts narrative Peter is last mentioned in connection with the Jerusalem conference, where he championed the liberty of the Gentiles (15:6–11, 14). The remaining NT references to Peter are scanty. Galatians 2:11–21 records a visit to Syrian Antioch, where his inconsistent conduct resulted in a public rebuke from Paul. From 1 Corinthians 9:5 it appears that Peter traveled widely, taking his wife with him, doubtless in Jewish evangelism (Gal 2:9).

Nothing further is heard of Peter until the writing of the two letters that bear his name, apparently written from Rome. A final NT reference to the closing years of Peter's life is found in John 21:18–19. John's interpretation of Christ's prediction makes it clear that the reference is to Peter's violent death. Beyond this the NT is silent about him.

Tradition uniformily asserts that Peter went to Rome, that he labored there, and there in his old age suffered martyrdom under Nero. The embellished tradition that he was bishop of Rome for 25 years is contrary to all NT evidence. He apparently came to Rome shortly after Paul's release from his first imprisonment there.

The character of Peter is one of the most vividly drawn and charming in the NT. His sheer humanness has made him one of the most beloved and winsome members of the apostolic band. He was eager, impulsive, energetic, self-confident, aggressive, and daring, but also unstable, fickle, weak, and cowardly. He was guided more by quick impulse than logical reasoning, and he readily swayed from one extreme to the other. He was preeminently a man of action. His life exhibits the defects of his character as well as his tremendous capacities for good. He was forward and often rash, liable to instability and inconsistency, but his love for and associations with Christ molded him into a man of stability, humility, and courageous service for God. In the power of the Holy Spirit he became one of the noble pillars (Gal 2:9) of the church.

PETER, FIRST LETTER OF The keynote of the First Letter of Peter is suffering and the Christian method of meeting it. It was unanimously accepted as a letter of Peter by all of the church fathers, who mention it by name, beginning with Irenaeus (c. 170). There are some remarkable agreements between the vocabulary of 1 Peter and the speeches of Peter in Acts—1 Peter 1:17, Acts 10:34; 1 Peter 1:21, Acts 2:32, 10:40–41; 1 Peter 2:7–8, Acts 4:10–11).

The letter was directed to members of the Dispersion located in the northern Roman provinces of Asia Minor. The place of writing is closely connected with the date. "Babylon" (1 Peter 5:13) may refer to the ancient city on the Euphrates, where there was a large Jewish settlement in Peter's day, or to a town in Egypt near Alexandria, where Mark traditionally ministered, or figuratively to Rome as the center of the pagan world (Rev 17:5; 18:10). The second alternative need not be considered seriously, for the Egyptian Babylon was only a border fort. Opinion among commentators is divided between the other two opinions. In the absence of any strong tradition that Peter ever visited in the literal Babylon, it seems more likely that he wrote this letter from Rome shortly before his martyrdom. He would have had opportunity to find some of Paul's writings there and to have met Silas and Mark, both of whom were familiar to Paul.

In general arrangement 1 Peter closely resembles the letters of Paul, with a salutation, body, and conclusion. Its main subject is the Christian's behavior under the pressure of suffering. Its key is the salvation that is to be revealed at the last time (1 Peter 1:5). The letter may be outlined as follows:

I. Introduction (1:1–2)

II. The Nature of Salvation (1:3–12)

III. The Experience of Salvation (1:13–25)

IV. The Obligations of Salvation (2:1–10)

V. The Ethics of Salvation (2:11–3:12)

VI. The Confidence of Salvation (3:13–4:11)

VII. The Behavior of the Saved Under Suffering (4:12–5:11)

VIII. Concluding Salutations (5:12–14)

PETER, SECOND LETTER OF A general treatise, written to warn its readers of threatening apostasy. It claims to have been written by Simon Peter and contains a definite allusion to a preceding letter (2 Peter 3:1).

Second Peter has the poorest external attestation of any book in the canon of the NT. It is not quoted directly by any of the church fathers before Origen (c. A.D. 250). Its literary style and vocabulary differ from that of 1 Peter, and it closely resembles the Book of Jude.

On the other hand, the internal evidence favors authorship by Peter. If a forger knew 1 Peter, it seems he could have been more careful to follow its style exactly. The allusions to Peter's career agree with the existing records and can best be explained as the testimony of an eyewitness. They include the Transfiguration (2 Peter 1:17–18; cf. Matt 17:1–18) and the Lord's prediction of his death (2 Peter 1:14; John 21:18–19). The Greek of the second letter is more labored than that of the first, but if Peter did not have the aid of Silas in this work, as he did in the first letter (1 Peter 5:12), he may have been forced to rely on his own writing. Doubtlessly he knew Greek, as most Galileans did, but he may not have been able to write it easily.

Second Peter must have been written subsequent to the publication of at least some of Paul's letters, if not of the entire collection (2 Peter 3:15). It cannot, therefore, have been written before A.D. 60; but if Paul was living and was still well known to the existing generation, it could not have been later than 70. Probably 67 is as satisfactory a date as can be established. The writer was anticipating a speedy death (2 Peter 1:14), and this may mean that the letter was sent from Rome during the tense days of the persecution under Nero.

The reference to a previous letter sent to the same group (2 Peter 3:1) connects the document with 1 Peter, which was written to the Christians of northern Asia Minor. Whereas the first letter was an attempt to encourage a church threatened with official persecution and repression, the second letter dealt with the peril of apostasy, which was an even greater threat.

The key to this letter is the word "know" or "knowledge," which occurs frequently in the three chapters, often referring to the knowledge of Christ. This knowledge is not primarily academic, but spiritual, arising from a growing experience of Christ (2 Peter 3:18). It produces peace and grace (1:2) and fruitfulness (1:8), is the secret of freedom from defilement (2:20), and is the sphere of Christian growth (3:18).

Second Peter definitely teaches the inspiration of Scripture (2 Peter 1:19–21) and stresses the doctrine of the personal return of Christ, which was ridiculed by the false teachers (3:1–7). It concludes with an appeal for holy living and with the promise of the new heavens and the new earth.

The following is a brief outline of the Epistle:

I. **Salutation (1:1)**

II. **The Character of Spiritual Knowledge (1:2–21)**

III. **The Nature and Perils of Apostasy (2:1–22)**

IV. **The Doom of the Ungodly (3:1–7)**

V. **The Hope of Believers (3:8–13)**

VI. **Concluding Exhortation (3:14–18)**

PETHAHIAH (pĕth'à-hī'à, Heb. *pethah-yâh, Jehovah opens up*). **1.** The head priest of the 19th course (1 Chron 24:16). **2.** A disobedient Levite who, in Ezra's time, married a foreign woman (Ezra 10:23). Most scholars identify him with the one named in Nehemiah 9:5. **3.** Meshezabel's son who was the counselor for King Artaxerxes (Neh 11:24).

PETRA (pē'trà). Translates *sela'*, meaning *rock, cliff*, or *crag*, and, as a proper noun, seems to refer to one or two places in the OT (Judg 1:36; 2 Kings 14:7; Isa 16:1; NIV "Sela"). The second reference may be to the capital city of the Nabateans from the close of the fourth century B.C. until A.D. 105, when it became part of the Roman Empire. It is famous for its rock-hewn temples and tombs in the surrounding cliffs.

The tomb of ed-Deir at Petra. Elaborately carved in the mountainside, the façade measures 132 feet (40 m.) in height and 154 feet (47m.) in width, being the largest surviving monument of the Nabatean site. Courtesy Garo Nalbandian

PHALEC (See PELEG)

PHALLU (See PALLU)

PHALTI (See PALTIEL)

PHALTIEL (See PALTIEL)

PHARAOH (fâr'ō, Heb. *par'ōh*). The government of Egypt, and ultimately the supreme monarch in whom all its powers were vested, was known as the "Great House," in Egyptian "Per-o," whence comes the term *pharaoh*. The recorded rulers of Egypt, 26 separate dynasties, extend from Menes, 3400 B.C. to Psamtik III, deposed at the Persian conquest in 525.

Pharaohs of Egypt are mentioned in the following OT contexts: **1.** Genesis 12:10–20. The date of Abram's descent into Egypt must be in the early years of the second millennium B.C. Amenemhet I, according to Breasted's dating, was Pharaoh from 2000 to 1970. **2.** Genesis 39 to 50 passim. It is reasonable to place the period of Joseph's (and Israel's) favor in Egypt in the times of the Hyksos invaders, who were driven out in 1580 B.C. **3.** Exodus 1 to 15 passim. The Pharaoh of the Oppression and the Hebrew exodus.

Two of four colossal seated statues of Pharaoh Ramses II, part of the façade of the great temple at Abu Simbel. The temple is located between the first and second cataracts of the Nile. Courtesy Seffie Ben-Yoseph

4. First Chronicles 4:18. A Pharoah whose daughter married Mered. **5.** First Kings 3:1; 9:16, 24; 11:1. Solomon's reign may be reliably dated 961 to 922 B.C., a period that corresponds with the reign of Pharaoh Sheshonk I (945 to 924). **6.** Second Kings 18:21 and Isaiah 36:6. The Pharaoh of Sennacherib's day. **7.** Second Kings 23:20–35. Pharaoh Neco was the last Pharaoh to endeavor to reestablish Egyptian authority in the northern approaches (609–593 B.C.). On the Plain of Megiddo, where Egypt had won control of the land 900 years before, Neco routed and killed Josiah. He deposed Jehoahaz and sent him to die in Egypt; he placed Jehoiakim on the throne of Judah and fixed a tribute for the conquered land. Two years later Neco's new empire fell before the attack of Babylon. Jeremiah refers to the event (Jer 37:7; 46:2). **8.** Ezekiel 29:1. The date is 587 B.C., and the Pharaoh referred to must therefore be Hophra, or Apries, in the first year of his rule. He reigned from 588 to 569. This was the Pharaoh whose troops failed to relieve Jerusalem in 586 and whose weak action against Nebuchadnezzar's Babylon brilliantly vindicated the advice of Jeremiah. Jeremiah (44:30, the sole biblical reference to Hophra by name) prophesied his end. See EGYPT.

PHARISEES (fâr′ĭ-sēz, Heb. *perûshûn*, Gr. *Pharisaioi*). Of the three prominent parties of Judaism at the time of Christ— Pharisees, Sadducees, and Essenes—the Pharisees were by far the most influential.

The name "Pharisee," which in its Semitic form means "the separated ones, separatists," first appears during the reign of John Hyrcanus (135 B.C.). Generally, the term is in the plural rather than in the singular. They were also known as *chasidim*, meaning "loved of God" or "loyal to God." According to Josephus, their number at the height of their popularity was more than 6,000.

Three facets, or characteristics, of the Jewish nation contributed to the development of the Pharisees, or, paradoxically, it may be said that the Pharisees made these contributions to Judaism, so that ultimately Pharisaism and Judaism became almost synonymous. The first of these is Jewish legalism, which began in earnest after the Babylonian captivity. Temple worship and sacrifices had ceased, and Judaism began to center its activities in Jewish Law and the synagogue. The rise of the Jewish scribes, who were closely associated with the Pharisees, also gave great impetus to Jewish legalism. The Pharisees—more of a fraternal order or religious society than a sect—were the organized followers of these experts in interpreting the Scriptures; they formalized the religion of the scribes and put it into practice. This is why the NT mentions the scribes and Pharisees together 19 times, all in the Gospels (e.g, Matt 5:20; 15:1; 23:2, 13, 14, 15, 23, 25, 27, 29; Luke 11:39, 42, 43, 44, 53). The Pharisees were the religious leaders of the Jews, not the practical politicians (like the more liberal Sadducees).

A second characteristic was Jewish nationalism. Continued persecution and isolation crystallized this spirit. During the Captivity the Jews were a small minority in a strange nation. The fierce persecution of Antiochus Epiphanes (175–164 B.C.), who made a bold attempt to Hellenize and assimilate the Jews, only drew the Jewish people closer together. The Pharisees took the occasion to cultivate a national and religious consciousness that has hardly been equaled.

A third contributing factor to Pharisaism was the development and organization of the Jewish religion itself after the Captivity and the revolt. Formulation and adaptation of Mosaic Law by scribe and rabbi, increased tradition, and a more extreme separatism resulted in an almost new religion, vehemently opposing all secularization of Judaism by the pagan Greek thought that penetrated Jewish life after the Alexandrian conquest. The Pharisees became a closely organized group, very loyal to the society and to each other, but separate from others, even their own people. They pledged themselves to obey all facets of the traditions to the minutest detail and were sticklers for ceremonial purity.

The doctrines of the Pharisees included predestination, the immortality of the soul, and belief in spirit life—teachings the Sadducees denied (Acts 23:6–9). They believed in a final reward for good works and that the souls of the wicked were detained forever under the earth, while those of the virtuous rose again and even migrated into other bodies (Josephus, *Antiq.* 18.1.3; Acts 23:8). They accepted the OT Scriptures and fostered the usual Jewish messianic hope, which they gave a material and nationalistic twist.

It was inevitable, in view of these factors, that the Pharisees bitterly opposed Jesus and his teachings (John 9:16,

22). Clashes between Jesus and the Pharisees were frequent and bitter (Matt 3:7; 5:20; 9:12, 34; 12:2, 14; 19:3; Mark 12:17; Luke 5:21; 7:30; 16:14; 12:1). Jesus' longest rebuke of the Pharisees is found in Matthew 23.

The picture of the Pharisees painted by the NT is almost entirely negative. Jesus condemned especially the Pharisees' ostentation, their hypocrisy, their salvation by works, their impenitence and lovelessness, but not always Pharisees as such. Some of the Pharisees were members of the Christian movement in the beginning (Acts 6:7). Some of the great men of the NT were Pharisees—Nicodemus (John 3:1), Gamaliel (Acts 5:34), and Paul (26:5; Phil 3:5). When Paul says he was a Pharisee (Phil 3:5), he did not think of himself as a hypocrite but claimed the highest degree of faithfulness to the law.

PHAROSH (See PAROSH)

PHARZITE (See PEREZ)

PHASEAH (See PASEAH)

PHEBE (See PHOEBE)

PHICOL (fī'kŏl, Heb. *pîkhōl*). The army captain belonging to Abimelech, who was the Philistine king of Gerah (Gen 21:22, 32; 26:26).

PHILADELPHIA (Gr. *Philadelphia, brotherly love*). One of the seven churches addressed in Revelation (3:7–13), a Lydian city founded by Attalus II Philadelphus (159–138 B.C.). The king was so named from his devotion to his brother Eumenes, and the city perpetuated his title.

PHILEMON, LETTER TO (fī-lēmŏn, Gr. Philēmŏn, *loving*). Paul's letter to Philemon dates, in all probability, from the period of his Roman imprisonment. Paul's authorship is not seriously disputed. The letter is addressed to Philemon, Apphia (Philemon's wife), and Archippus (probably his son, cf. Col 4:17). The Christian community was organized around a home.

The occasion of the letter was the return of the runaway slave Onesimus to his master. Paul writes with exquisite tact and words of praise before referring to obligation. He reminds Philemon that, in respect to bondage, his own position did not vary from that of the man for whom he pleaded. Onesimus was a fellow bondsman and a son. "Onesimus" means "useful," and the writer makes a play on the word in verse 11, proceeding immediately to point to the sacrifice he himself was making.

PHILETUS (fĭ-lē'tŭs, Gr. *Philētos, worthy of love*). Paul refers to him as a false teacher in the church of Ephesus who, together with Hymenaeus, held that "the resurrection has already taken place" (2 Tim 2:18); that is, he did not radically deny a doctrine of the resurrection but allegorized it into a spiritual awakening or conversion and not a bodily resurrection as Paul taught (1 Cor 15).

PHILIP (See HEROD)

The Valley of Bethsaida, at the northeastern edge of the Sea of Galilee, possible site of the feeding of the 5000 (Luke 9:10). Courtesy Duby Tal

PHILIP THE APOSTLE (Gr. *Philippos, lover of horses*). The fifth in the lists of the apostles (Matt 10:3). His hometown was Bethsaida of Galilee, the town of Andrew and Peter (John 1:44). He brought Nathanael to Jesus (1:43), but was reluctant to believe wholeheartedly in the kingdom, and at times he seems to have had difficulty in grasping its meaning (14:8–14). This no doubt is why Jesus asked him the unusual question to arouse and test his faith before feeding the 5,000 (6:5–6). He is known for bringing Gentiles to Jesus (12:20–23). The last information regarding Philip in the NT is found in Acts 1:13 where we are told that he was among the number of disciples in the upper chamber before Pentecost. The best tradition says he did mission work in Asia Minor.

PHILIP THE EVANGELIST (Gr. *Philippos, lover of horses*). One of the famous seven deacons (Acts 6:5). Since he was a Hellenist (a Greek-speaking Jew), as a deacon he was to serve under the apostles (6:6) by taking care of the neglected Hellenist widows and the poor in general in the Jerusalem church. He was an evangelist and performed signs and wonders among the people (8:39; 8:6). Philip preached in Samaria with great success, cast out devils, and healed the paralytics and the lame just as the apostles did (ch. 8). Some of his converts were Simon the sorcerer of Samaria (8:9–13) and the Ethiopian eunuch (8:26–40). Thus perhaps Philip was instrumental in introducing Christianity into Africa. Paul stayed at his home (21:8–9). Philip was a forerunner of Paul in preaching to the Gentiles. He had four unmarried daughters who were prophets (ch. 21).

PHILIPPI (fĭ-lĭp'ī, Gr. *Philippoi*). A Macedonian town that became the center for the battle of 42 B.C., in which Antony defeated Brutus and Cassius. "The leading city of that district" (Acts 16:12), it was the first European city to hear a Christian missionary, as far as the records go. Paul's choice of the locality throws light on the strategy of his evangelism.

PHILIPPIANS, LETTER TO THE (fĭ-lĭp'ī-ănz). One of the most personal of all Paul's letters. It was written to "all the saints in Christ Jesus at Philippi" (Phil 1:1).

The church at Philippi in ancient Macedonia was the first European church founded by Paul (Acts 16:9–40) and thus represents the first major penetration of the gospel into Gentile territory (cf. Phil 4:14–15). Paul's first convert there was a merchant woman named Lydia, a seller of purple. Her whole household was baptized and became the nucleus of the new church (Acts 16:15). The remarkable conversion of the jailer with its accompanying miraculous events also took place in Philippi (16:25–34). This church, though poor, on several occasions collected funds for Paul and also aided him while he was in prison (Phil 4:10–16). He has no rebuke for it in this letter. The members are his "joy and crown" (4:1).

The letter was occasioned by the gift of funds and clothing that Epaphroditus brought to Paul in prison (either at Caesarea, Ephesus, or Rome). Paul took the opportunity to thank the Philippians for this and other favors. In doing so, as was his custom, Paul added practical Christian admonition to humility, joy, and steadfastness. The main emphasis is joy; the concept "rejoice" appears no fewer than 16 times in the letter. The doctrines of the person and work of Christ, justification by faith, and the second coming of Christ are found among the practical admonitions.

General outline of contents of Philippians:

The great battle of Ramses III against the Sea Peoples (Philistines), as depicted on a relief from temple of Ramses III at Medinet Habu, Thebes, c. 1182–1151 B.C. Courtesy Seffie Ben-Yoseph

PHILISTINES (fĭ-lĭs'tēnz, Heb. *pelishtîm*). The name given to the people who inhabited the Philistine plain of Palestine during the greater part of OT times. The five cities of the Philistines were Ashdod, Gaza, Ashkelon, Gath, and Ekron (Josh 13:3; 1 Sam 6:17). They were situated in the broad coastal plain of southern Palestine, except for Gath, which is in the Shephelah (or hill country). Our word "Palestine" is derived from the term "Philistine."

The Philistines are said to have come from Caphtor (Jer 47:4; Amos 9:7), which is believed to be a name for Crete, or perhaps for the island world of the Aegean area.

The Philistines had a unique political organization. Their five city-states were ruled by five "lords of the Philistines" (Josh 13:3; Judg 16:5 KJV). It is clear that the Philistines were more wealthy and more advanced in technology than their Hebrew neighbors. According to 1 Samuel 13:19–22 they had the knowledge of metallurgy, whereas the Hebrews did not. The Philistines jealously guarded this monopoly, forcing the Hebrews to come

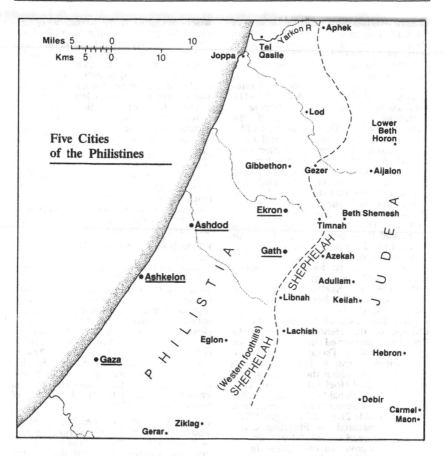

Five Cities of the Philistines

Miles 5 0 10
Kms 5 0 10

Aphek

Yarkon R

Joppa
Tel Qasile

Lod

Lower Beth Horon

Gibbethon• Gezer •Aijalon

Ekron• Beth Shemesh

•Ashdod Timnah

Gath• •Azekah

SHEPHELAH

•Ashkelon Adullam•

•Libnah Keilah•

PHILISTIA

Eglon• •Lachish

SHEPHELAH (Western foothills)

Hebron•

•Gaza

•Debir

Carmel•
Maon•

Ziklag•
Gerar•

JUDEA

to them even for agricultural implements, which they repaired at exorbitant cost (13:21). This superiority (the Philistines even had chariots, 13:5) is the reason for the their military domination of the Hebrews so evident toward the end of the period of the judges and in Saul's reign.

The Philistines worshiped the Semitic gods Dagon (Judg 16:23; 1 Sam 5:1–7), Ashtoreth (31:10), and Baal-Zebub (2 Kings 1:2, 6, 16). On the other hand, their non-Semitic origin is recalled in the epithet "uncircumcised" (Judg 14:3), so frequently used of them in the Bible.

The Book of Judges names the Philistines as a major contender against the Hebrews for the possession of Palestine. No doubt the tribes of Judah, Simeon, and Dan felt the pressure most, for their lands were adjacent to the Philistines. The judge Shamgar fought them (Judg 3:31). A Philistine oppression is briefly

mentioned in Judges 10:6–7. The life of Samson, the last of the deliverers mentioned in Judges, is set in a violent struggle with the Philistines (chs. 13–16; note 14:4c; 15:11). Samson, a man of great strength but little self-discipline, was finally snared by a Philistine spy, Delilah (16:4–21). No doubt the Danite migration (ch. 18) was occasioned by the Philistine pressure that kept the Danites from occupying the territory assigned them. The Book of 1 Samuel opens with the theme of Philistine oppression with which Judges closes. Eli's judgeship seems to have been characterized by Philistine domination (1 Sam 4–6). Samuel was able to see a measure of victory when he defeated them at the battle of Mizpah and forced them to return certain cities they had taken from Israel (7:7–14). Saul's reign ended in complete defeat for the Hebrews; and the Philistines seem to have overrun most of Palestine west of the Jordan, even occupying Beth Shan at the eastern end of the Valley of Jezreel (13:5; 14:1-52; 17:1-58; 31:1-13).

During the latter part of the reign of Saul, David, the contender for the throne, fled for safety to the Philistines (1 Sam 21:10-15; 27:1-28:2; 29:1-11), who gladly protected him, hoping to contribute to the weakness of the Hebrews. Perhaps David remained a Philistine vassal during the seven and a half years he reigned at Hebron (2 Sam 2:1-4). When at the end of this time he asserted his independence and united all Israel under his rule, he was immediately opposed by the Philistines, but he decisively defeated them in two battles (5:17-25). In later campaigns (21:15-22; 23:9-17) David consistently defeated them, and it seems clear that from this time on the Philistines were confined to their own territory and were no longer a threat. David must have had peaceful relations with them at times, for his bodyguards, the Kerethites and Pelethites, appear to have been recruited from them (8:18; 15:18).

After the death of Solomon and the division of the Hebrew kingdom, the Philistines reasserted the independence they had lost to David and Solomon. Their cities appear to have engaged in commerce, for which their location certainly was ideal (Joel 3:4-8; Amos 1:6-8). Some of them paid tribute to Jehoshaphat, after whose death they raided Judah (2 Chron 17:11; 21:16-17). Sargon (722-705 B.C.) captured the Philistine cities, deported some of the inhabitants, and set an Assyrian governor over them. In the days of Hezekiah the Philistines played a great part in the revolt against Sennacherib.

Esarhaddon and Ashurbanipal name Philistine tributaries as well as the Judean king Manasseh. The later struggles between Egypt and Assyria were the cause of great suffering to the Philistine cities, and practically close their history as strictly Philistinian. The cities did continue as predominantly non-Jewish centers, becoming Hellenistic cities in the Greek period.

PHILO JUDAEUS (fī'lō jū-dē'ŭs). Jewish scholar and philosopher, born in Alexandria about 20 B.C. Alexandria had an old tradition of Jewish scholarship, and Philo came from a rich and priestly family. Few details are known of his life, except that in A.D. 39 he took part in an embassy to Rome to plead the case of the Jews whose religious privileges, previously wisely recognized by Rome, were menaced by the mad Caligula. Philo lived until 50 and was a prolific author. His writings include philosophical works, commentaries on the Pentateuch, and historical and apologetic works. He sought to synthesize his own Hellenistic and Jewish traditions. Clement and Origen used his works; and the Latin fathers, generally following his methods of allegorical interpretation, established a tradition of exegesis that some still favor.

PHILOSOPHY The word with its cognate terms is usually found in a derogatory sense in the Bible (e.g., 1 Cor 1:18-2:16; 3:18-21; Col 2:8). Paul emphasized the inadequacy of worldly wisdom and proclaimed a wisdom based on revelation. For the "philosophers" of Acts 17:18, see EPICUREANS and STOICS.

PHINEHAS (fĭn'ē-ăs, Heb. *pînehās, mouth of brass*). **1.** A son of Eleazar and grandson of Aaron (Exod 6:25; 1 Chron 6:4, 50; 9:20; Ezra 7:5; 8:2). He killed Zimri and Cozbi at God's command (Num 25:6-15; Ps 106:30). He conducted a successful embassy to the Transjordan tribes regarding the altar they had built (Josh 22:13-34). **2.** A son of Eli, unfaithful in his ministration of the priest's office (1 Sam 1:3; 2:12-17, 22-25, 27-36; 3:11-13). He and his brother Hophni brought the ark into the camp of Israel, but the ark was taken and Hophni and Phinehas killed (ch. 4). **3.** Father of Eleazar (Ezra 8:33).

PHOEBE (fē'bē, Gr. *Phoibē, pure*). A woman mentioned in the Scriptures only in Romans 16:1-2. She was one of the first deaconesses (if not the first) of the Christian church and was highly recommended by Paul. She served in the church at Cenchrea, port of Corinth.

PHOENICIA, PHENICIA (fē-nĭsh'ĭ-à, Gr. *Phoinikē*). A strip of coastal territory between the Lebanon range, the uplands of Galilee, and the Mediterranean Sea. The Phoenicians were Semites and were the most notable sailors of the ancient world; their colonization spread their trading posts around the African coast from Carthage westward and established them in Spain and Sicily.

Sidon was the most powerful and influential of the Phoenician cities. "The gods of Sidon," Baal and Ashtaroth (Judg 10:6), were the gods of the Phoenicians generally (cf. 18:7; 1 Kings 5:6; 11:5, 33; 16:31; 2 Kings 23:13). The reference to "Jezebel daughter of Ethbaal king of the Sidonians" (1 Kings 16:31) is at first sight strange, for Ethbaal was king of

The god Shadrafa standing on a lion above mountains and swinging a small lion in his hand. Limestone stele from Amrit in Phoenicia, c. 550 B.C. Courtesy Réunion des Musées Nationaux

Tyre, but "Sidonian" had become a generic term for "Phoenician."

Phoenicia first appears in recorded history in the Egyptian account of the northern campaigns of Thutmose III. In his campaign against the Hittites of 1471 B.C., the pharaoh found it necessary to secure the Phoenician coastal strip as an essential avenue of communications. Ramses XII (1118–1090 B.C.) sent the priest Wen-Amon to buy cedar for his funeral barge. A century later Hiram, king of Tyre, allied with David, a partnership that developed into a trade alliance in the days of Solomon. Solomon's fleet of "ships of Tarshish" at Ezion Geber on the Gulf of Aqabah seems to have been part of a combined trading venture whereby the Phoenicians used Solomon's port and piloted Solomon's ships to southern Arabia and India (1 Kings 10:22; 2 Chron 9:21).

With the division of Israel, Phoenicia became the neighbor and partner of the northern kingdom, while Judah lay along the communication route with the Gulf of Aqabah and the Red Sea. Hence Ahab's alliance with Jezebel, the prosperity of the north (Ahab's "Ivory House"), and the sequence of events that led to Elijah's protest and the contest on Carmel.

All the Phoenician cities submitted to Alexander after Issus (333), except Tyre, which Alexander took after a vigorous siege of seven months. Under the successors, the power of the Ptolemies of Egypt first extended far up the Phoenician coast, but after 197 the Seleucids of Syria controlled the land, until the whole area passed into Roman hands in 65. The reference to a woman "born in Syrian Phoenicia" in Mark 7:26 reflects the century and a half of Syrian rule.

The Phoenician stock must by this time have been heavily diluted by immigrant blood, principally Greek. The whole area figured largely in the early evangelism of the church (Acts 11:19; 15:3; 21:2). Phoenicia's achievement was principally in the realm of trade and in her simplification and diffusion of the alphabet, as a tool and means, no doubt, of commerce. Ezekiel 27 and 28 give some notion of the extent and variety of Phoenician trade, but the Phoenicians did nothing to spread or communicate the knowledge, geographical and social, that their voyaging won. Tyre's colony at Carthage blockaded the Straits of Gibraltar for many generations in an attempt to guard the western and Atlantic trade routes, and this secrecy was a Phoenician principle. The land made no contribution to art and literature, and its religious influence, heavily infected with the cruder fertility cults, was destructive.

PHRYGIA (frĭj'ĭ-à, Gr. *Phrygia*). In Bible times an inland province of SW Asia Minor. Paul and his co-workers visited the fertile territory during all three missionary journeys. If Phrygia is understood in its broader sense, Paul and Barnabas introduced Christianity into the province during the first journey (Acts 13:13; 14:24). Acts 16:6 briefly describes the visit of Paul and Silas on the second journey. On his third journey Paul quickly revisited the province on his way to Ephesus and Corinth (18:23). Although a great deal of Christian activity took place in ancient Phrygia, with this reference it passes from the biblical record.

PHURAH (See PURAH)

PHUT (See PUT)

PHUVAH (See PUAH)

PHYGELUS, PHYGELLUS (fĭ-jĕl'ŭs, Gr. *Phygelos*). In his second letter to Timothy (1:15) Paul mentions Phygelus and Hermogenes by name as being among those Christians of Asia (western province of Asia Minor) who had turned away from the apostle. From the context

Early photograph of the Ecce Homo Arch in Jerusalem. This is the traditional site of Pilate's famous declaration "Behold the man!" Courtesy University Library, Istanbul

(2 Tim 1:13–14) it may be assumed that the apostasy included the repudiation of Paul's doctrine. If we connect Phygelus with 2 Timothy 4:16, we may infer that he, being in Rome, forsook Paul's personal cause in the Roman courts at a crucial time when his testimony could have meant much for the future of the church. Some scholars feel that Phygelus may also have been one of the leaders of a group of wayward Christians in Rome (Phil 1:15–16).

PHYLACTERY (See DRESS)

PHYSICIAN (See OCCUPATIONS AND PROFESSIONS)

PI BESETH (See BUBASTIS)

PICTURES The word occurs three times in the KJV. In Numbers 33:52, ASV and RSV have "figured stones," NIV "carved images." In Proverbs 25:11, ASV has "network," RSV and NIV "setting," an apparent reference to pleasing inlaid work in gold and silver. In Isaiah 2:16 another word from the same Hebrew root is translated "imagery" in ASV. RSV has "beautiful craft." NIV reads "stately vessel."

PIETY The word occurs only once in KJV and ASV (1 Tim 5:4): "Let them learn first to show piety at home." RSV uses "religious duty," NIV "put their religion into practice." NIV has "piety" three times in Job (4:6; 15:4; 22:4), where other versions use "fear" (of God) or (once in RSV) "integrity."

PIG (See ANIMALS)

PIGEON (See BIRDS)

PI HAHIROTH (pī hà-hī'rŏth, Heb. *pî-ha-hîrôth*). The place in NE Egypt where the Israelites last camped before crossing the Red Sea. Here the Egyptian army overtook them (Exod 14:2, 9; Num 33:7).

PILATE (pī'làt, Gr. *Pilatos*). The fifth procurator, or governmental representative, of imperial Rome in Palestine (A.D. 26 to 36), the only Roman official named in the Apostles' Creed. The four Gospels relate Jesus' trial and crucifixion fully, especially the Gospel of John. Pilate is also mentioned in Acts (3:13; 4:27; 13:28) and in 1 Timothy 6:13.

The Romans had many such governors throughout the provinces, which was part of their success in local government. Judea had a succession of these smaller rulers before and after Pilate. Generally they were in charge of tax and financial matters, but governing Palestine was so difficult that the procurator there was directly responsible to the emperor and also had supreme judicial authority such as Pilate used regarding Christ. His territory included Judea, Samaria, and old Idumea.

Pilate never really understood the Jews, as his frequent rash and foolish acts reveal. The Jewish historian Josephus tells us that he immediately offended the Jews by bringing the "outrageous" Roman standards into the Holy City. At another time he hung golden shields inscribed with the names and images of Roman deities in the temple itself. Once he even appropriated some of the temple tax to build an aqueduct. To this must be added the horrible incident mentioned in Luke 13:1 about "the Galileans whose blood Pilate had mixed with their sacrifices," meaning no doubt that Roman soldiers killed these men while they were sacrificing in the Holy Place. These fearful events seem to disagree with the role Pilate played in the trial of Jesus, where he was as clay in the hands of the Jews, but this may be explained by the fact that his fear of the Jews increased because of their frequent complaints to Rome.

According to his custom, Pilate was in Jerusalem to keep order during the Passover Feast. His usual headquarters were in Caesarea. After the Jews had condemned Jesus in their own courts, they brought him early in the morning to Pilate, who was no doubt residing in Herod's palace near the temple. It is surprising he gave them a hearing so early in the day (John 18:28). From the beginning of the hearing he was torn between offending the Jews and condemning an innocent person, and, apart from simply acquitting him, he tried every device to set Jesus free.

According to Josephus, his political career came to an end six years later when he sent soldiers to Samaria to suppress a small harmless religious rebellion, and in that suppression innocent men were killed. The Samaritans complained to Vitellius, legate of Syria, who sent Pilate to Rome. His friend Tiberius the emperor died while Pilate was on his way to Rome, and Pilate's name disappears from the official history of Rome. The historian Eusebius says that soon afterward, "wearied with misfortunes," he took his own life.

PILEHA (See PILHA)

PILGRIM (Gr. *parepidēmos, a sojourner in a strange place*). Hebrews 11:13–16 (KJV) shows that the faithful sought a heavenly city and did not consider themselves permanently attached to earth. First Peter 2:11 exhorts Christians to purity because of this status. Pilgrims might be exiles (RSV) or voluntary sojourners in a foreign country. NIV uses the terms "aliens" and "strangers."

PILGRIMAGE (Heb. *māghôr, a place of sojourning*, or *the act of sojourning;* see Exod 6:4, NIV "lived as aliens;" Ps 119:54). In Genesis 47:9 a lifetime is meant. The Hebrew root *ghûr* means "to dwell as a foreigner, newly come into a land in which he has no citizens' rights, such as the original inhabitants possess." The biblical usage, whether the word is translated "pilgrimage" or otherwise, began with the wanderings of Abraham and his descendants, and later was applied to the status of a believer in the one true God, living on an earth unfriendly to God and to his people.

PILHA (Heb. *pilhā'*). One of those who, with Nehemiah, sealed the covenant (Neh 10:24).

PILLAR There is a religious element in the purpose and use of pillars: stones were set erect as memorials of a divine appearance in connection with the worship of the one true God (Gen 28:18–22; 31:13; 35:14; Exod 24:4; Isa 19:19; Hos 3:4; 10:1–2). Lot's wife became a pillar of salt (Gen 19:26). People also set up stone pillars to signify an agreement with religious conditions between them (31:43–52), or to mark graves (35:20).

Standing stones used in idolatrous worship are referred to (Deut 12:3) and are usually called images in KJV (NIV "sacred stones"), where ASV and RSV read "pillars" (Exod 23:24; 34:13; Lev 26:1; Deut 7:5; 12:3; 16:22; 1 Kings 14:23; 2 Kings 17:10; 18:4; 23:14; 2 Chron 14:3; 31:1; Mic 5:13). In Ezekiel 26:11 KJV reads "garrisons," ASV, NIV, RSV "pillars."

Another common Hebrew word for pillar, *amudh*, from a root "to stand," refers to (1) the pillar of cloud and fire (see next article) that guided Israel in the wilderness, (2) tabernacle pillars either of shittim wood (KJV; acacia ASV, RSV, NIV) or of bronze or material not named (Exod 26:32, 37; 27:10–17; 36:36, 38; 38:10–17, 28; 39:33, 40; 40:18; Num 3:36–37; 4:31–32), (3) the pillars of Solomon's temple (1 Kings 7:2–42; 2 Kings 25:13–17; 1 Chron 18:8; 2 Chron 3:15, 17; 4:12–13; Jer 27:19; 52:17–22), (4) the pillars of Ezekiel's new temple (Ezek 40:49; 42:6), (5) the supporting pillars that Samson pushed apart in the Philistine temple (Judg 16:25–29), (6) the marble pillars of the Persian king's palace (Esth 1:6), and (7) the pillars (KJV, MLB; posts NIV, RSV)

A Canaanite shrine with a series of a basalt stelae representing sacred pillars, ranged round an offering table, at Hazor, thirteenth century B.C. Courtesy Israel Department of Antiquities and Museums

of silver of Solomon's litter or carriage (Song of Songs 3:10).

The word is also used figuratively (Song of Songs 3:6; 5:15; Jer 1:18; Joel 2:30). The four NT uses of *stylos* ("pillar") are figurative: a victorious Christian (Rev 3:12), the church (1 Tim 3:15), apostles (Gal 2:9), and an angel (Rev 10:1).

PILLAR OF CLOUD AND FIRE God guided Israel out of Egypt and through the wilderness by a pillar of cloud by day. This became a pillar of fire by night that they might escape from the Egyptian army (Exod 13:21–22). When the Egyptians overtook the Israelites, the angel of the Lord removed this cloudy, fiery pillar from before them and placed it behind them as an effective barrier (14:19–20, 24). The pillar of cloud stood over the tent of meeting outside the camp whenever the Lord met Moses there (33:7–11). The Lord came down for judgment in the cloud (Num 12; 14:13–35). No natural phenomenon fits the biblical description. The cloud and fire were divine manifestations, in a form sufficiently well-defined to be called a pillar.

PILLOW In Genesis 28:11, 18, Heb. *mera'ăshôth*, "at the head," refers to the stones Jacob set up, either under his head (ASV, RSV, NIV) or at his head when

sleeping outdoors. The same Hebrew word is translated "bolster" (1 Sam 19:13, 16, KJV) in connection with *kevîr*, a "quilt" (ASV footnote). NIV prefers to say simply "at the head." In Ezekiel 13:18, 20 the Hebrew word is *kesãthôth*, "fillet, arm-band," from a root "to bind, take captive." In modern Hebrew it means "pillow, bolster, cushion." Only in Mark 4:38, Greek *proskephalaion*, "cushion for the head," or any cushion (ASV, RSV, NIV), do we have an approach to the modern meaning. This is probably the pad on which a rower sat.

PIM (See WEIGHTS AND MEASURES)

PIN (Heb. *yāthēdh*). A tent peg, usually of wood, sharpened at one end, shaped at the other for attaching the tent cord (Judg 4:20, 21; 5:26 nail KJV, tent pin ASV, tent peg NIV, RSV). The tent pins or pegs of the tabernacle (Exod 35:18; 38:31; 39:40; Num 3:37; 4:32) were of bronze (Exod 27:19; 38:20). The pin of Judges 16:14 was a stick used for beating up the woof in the loom. The tent peg, like the cornerstone, assures support (Zech 10:4). The crisping pins (Heb. *hărîtîm* KJV, satchels ASV, handbags RSV, purses NIV) of Isaiah 3:22 were probably bags or purses.

PINE (See PLANTS)

PINNACLE (pĭn'à-k'l, pĭn'ĭ-k'l, Gr. *pterygion*). Anything shaped like a wing; a turret, battlement, pointed roof, or peak of a building. The temple pinnacle (Matt 4:5; Luke 4:9 KJV, MOF, NASB, RSV; highest point NIV) is the spot to which Satan brought Jesus, tempting him to jump off.

PIPES (See MUSIC AND MUSICAL INSTRUMENTS)

PIRATHON (pĭr'à-thŏn, Heb. *pir'āthôn*). A town of Ephraim in the hill country of the Amalekites, where Abdon, one of the judges, lived and was buried (Judg 12:13–15). Benaiah was from Pirathon (2 Sam 23:30; 1 Chron 11:31; 27:14).

PISGAH (pĭz'gà, Heb. *ha-pisgâh*). A mountain on the NE shore of the Dead Sea; Ras es-Siaghah, slightly NW of Mt. Nebo. First mentioned in Numbers 21:20 as a peak in Moab looking down on Jeshimon (KJV) or the desert (ASV, RSV; NIV "the wasteland"), or the route of the Israelites toward the Promised Land. Balak brought Balaam into the field of Zophim, to the top of Pisgah, where he built seven altars and tried to persuade Balaam to curse Israel (Num 23:14). Ashdoth Pisgah (KJV) or the slopes of Pisgah (ASV, RSV, NIV) helps define the territory of the tribes settled east of the Jordan (Deut 3:17). The springs of Pisgah are named in bounding the same territory, as taken from the kings of the Amorites (4:49). From the top of Mt. Pisgah Moses viewed the Land of Promise, which he was not permitted to enter (3:27; 34:1). The latter verse either identifies or closely associates Mt. Pisgah with Mt. Nebo.

PISHON, PISON (pī'shŏn, Heb. *pîshôn*). First of the four rivers of Eden, flowing around the whole land of Havilah (Gen 2:11). Numerous rivers of SW Asia have been suggested, including the Persian Gulf and the Nile.

PISIDIA (pĭ-sĭd'ĭ-à, Gr. *Pisidia*). One of the small Roman provinces in southern Asia Minor, just north of Pamphylia and lying along the coast. It was mountainous but more densely populated than the rough coastal areas, especially because it contained the important city of Antioch. Because of this, Paul visited the city twice (Acts 13:14–50; 14:21–24).

PISTACHIO (See PLANTS)

PIT This represents several Hebrew and two Greek words whose usages are not sharply distinguished. A pit may be a bitumen deposit (Gen 14:10, so RSV; NIV "tar pit"); a deep place, natural or manmade (Gen 37:20–29; Exod 21:33–34; 2 Sam 17:9; Matt 12:11); often a well (Luke 14:5) or cistern (Isa 30:14; Jer 14:3; Lev 11:33 ASV, "earthen vessel," NIV "clay pot"). "Pit" also stands for death, the grave, or Sheol (Num 16:30, 33; Job 33:18; Isa 14:15; Rev 9:1–2).

PITCH (Heb. *zepheth, kōpher, pitch*). 1. Either bitumen or a viscous, inflammable liquid associated with it. It was found in Mesopotamia and around the Dead Sea (Gen 14:10; RSV; NIV "tar") and was used to make vessels watertight (Gen 6:14 [*kōpher* and cognate verb]; Exod 2:3 [*zepheth*]). Also used as a destructive agent (Isa 34:9; cf. Gen 19:24). 2. "Pitch" is a translation of several Hebrew words also translated "encamp, set up" and refers to placing tents or the tabernacle (12:8; 31:25; Exod 17:1; Num 1:51; Josh 8:11) or other objects (Josh 4:20).

PITCHER (Heb. *kadh*). An earthenware jar with one or two handles, ordinarily borne on the head or shoulder for carrying water (Gen 24:14–20, 43–46 KJV; jar ASV, NIV, RSV). Pitchers empty of water once held lamps (Judg 7:16–20 KJV; jars NIV, RSV). To break one was so serious as to be a figure for death (Eccl 12:6). The NT uses *keramion* ("earthenware vessel") twice (Mark 14:13; Luke 22:10).

PITHOM (pī'thŏm, Heb. *pithōm*). A city in Egypt in the valley between the Nile and Lake Timsah built by the slave labor of the Israelites (Exod 1:11), probably in the reign of Seti I or Ramses II (1319–1234 B.C.). Recent excavations at Tell Mashkutah near Succoth have uncovered bricks made without straw in the upper layers; made with stubble and weeds pulled up by the roots on the middle level; and made with good, clean straw at the bottom of the walls. An inscription at Rameses relates that it was built with Semitic slave labor from Asia.

PITY A tender, considerate feeling for others, ranging from judicial clemency (Deut 7:16) through kindness (Job 6:14; Prov 19:17; 28:8) and mercy (Matt 18:33) to compassion (Lam 4:10). Pity may be mere concern for a thing (Jonah 4:10) or for a thing deeply desired (Ezek 24:21). It may also be the concern of God for his holy name (36:21). Pity for one's children is of the essence of fatherhood, human or divine (Ps 103:13 KJV), inherent in the redemptive activity of God (72:13). In the NT the word *esplangnizō* is used to express pity (Luke 10:33). Three Greek words occur once each: *eleeō*, "have mercy" (Matt 18:33); *eusplangchnos*, "sympathetic" (1 Peter 3:8); *polysplang-*

chnos, "full of compassion" (James 5:11 KJV), referring to God.

PLAGUE (See DISEASES)

PLAGUES OF EGYPT Ten in number, these were the means by which God induced Pharaoh to let the Israelites leave Egypt. A series chiefly of natural phenomena, they were unusual (1) in their severity, (2) in that all occurred within one year, (3) in their accurate timing, (4) in that Goshen and its people were spared some of them, and (5) in the evidence of God's control over them. The plagues overcame the opposition of Pharaoh, discredited the gods of Egypt, and defiled their temples.

1. **Water Became Blood** (Exod 7:14–25). When the Nile is at its lowest, in May, the water is sometimes red, not fit to drink, and fish die. The Egyptians had to dig wells, into which river water would filter through sand. God directed Moses to lift up his rod at the right time. Once the time was disclosed, the Egyptian magicians could do likewise.

2. **Frogs** (Exod 8:1–15). When the flood waters recede, frogs spawn in the marshes and invade the dry land. God directed Moses to lift up his rod at such a time. This sign the Egyptian magicians also claimed to produce.

3. **Lice** (Exod 8:16–19). What insect is meant is uncertain; RSV and NIV have "gnats"; ASV footnote, "sand flies or fleas." So many biting, stinging pests abound in Egypt that people might not be discriminating in naming them. The magicians failed, by their own admission, to reproduce this plague and recognized in it "the finger of God"; but Pharaoh would not listen to them.

4. **Flies** (Exod 8:20–31). Swarms of flies came over Egypt in unusual density to feed on dead frogs. God directed Moses as to the time. The magicians no longer competed with Moses. Now there was a differentiation between Goshen and the rest of Egypt. Pharaoh offered to let the people sacrifice only in the land of Egypt (8:25). Moses insisted that they must go three days' journey into the wilderness. Pharaoh agreed and the plague was stayed at Moses' request. When the plague was removed, Pharaoh again refused to let Israel go.

5. **The plague** (RSV, NIV) **of murrain** (KJV) **on cattle** (Exod 9:1–7). This was announced with a set time (tomorrow) for its occurrence. There is no record of its removal. Presumably it wore itself out. The Israelite cattle were spared, evidence of God's favor and power.

6. **Boils** (KJV, NIV), **blains** (ASV), **or sores** (RSV) **on man and beast** (Exod 9:8–12). Moses was told to take soot (KJV "ashes") from a furnace and sprinkle it in the air. The air over Egypt was filled with dust, and it became boils breaking out on man and beast. The magicians, still watching Moses, could not stand because of the boils. We may infer that the Israelites were not attacked. This plague was not recalled.

7. **Hail** (Exod 9:13–35). God directed Moses to stretch forth his hand, and hail (which rarely occurs in Egypt) descended in unusual violence. Egyptians who feared the word of the Lord brought their cattle in out of the coming storm. Those who did not lost them to the violent hail. Only in Goshen was there no hail.

8. **Locusts** (Exod 10:1–20). After seven plagues, even a frequently recurring one such as locusts, was so dreaded that Pharaoh's servants used bold language in advising that the Israelites be let go (10:7). Goshen was not spared the locusts' visitation. Still Pharaoh refused.

9. **Darkness** (Exod 10:21–29). A sandstorm, accentuated by the dust-bowl condition of the land and borne on the west wind that drove off the locusts, brought a choking darkness. The patience of God was at an end: Pharaoh would see the face of Moses no more. The darkness lasted three days, but the children of Israel had light where they lived.

10. **Death of the firstborn** (Exod 11:1–12:36). This final and convincing demonstration of God's power broke down the resistance of Pharaoh long enough for the Israelites to escape. The Israelites were directed to protect their firstborn with the blood of the Passover lamb, that they might not be killed along with the firstborn of the Egyptians. They "borrowed" valuables of the Egyptians and, amid the lamentations of the latter, were allowed to leave. Egypt had had enough.

The memory of the plagues was cultivated as a warning to Israel for generations to come (Pss 78:43–51; 105:26–36; 135:8–9; Acts 7:36; 13:17; Heb 11:28).

PLAIN 1. Hebrew '*āvēl*, "meadow" (Judg 11:33 KJV; rendered by NIV as a place name: see ABEL KERAMIN). **2.** Hebrew '*ēlôn*, "terebinth" (Gen 13:18 KJV; ASV "oaks," NIV "great trees"). **3.** Hebrew *biq'âh*, "broad valley, plain" (11:2; Ezek 3:22). **4.** Hebrew *kikkār*, "a round thing"; the Plain of Jordan (Gen 13:10–12; RSV "valley"); the Valley of Jericho (Deut 34:3); the plain around Jerusalem (Neh 12:28 KJV; RSV "circuit," NIV "region"). **5.** Hebrew *mîshôr*, "a level place, the tableland" east of Jordan

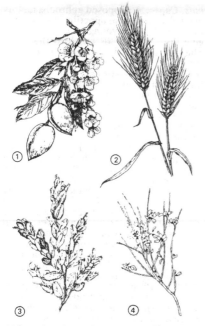

"When the almond tree blossoms and the grasshopper drags himself along . . . then man goes to his eternal home" (Eccl 12:5). (1) Almond branch in bloom; (2) barley; (3) box tree branch; (4) broom tree branch.
Courtesy Carta, Jerusalem

(Deut 3:10 KJV; NIV "plateau"); a plain as opposed to the hills (1 Kings 20:23); tableland as distinguished from the low country or Shephelah (2 Chron 26:10); a plain path (Ps 27:11 KJV; RSV "level," NIV, "straight"). **6.** Hebrew *'ǎrābāh*, "desert-plain, steppe"; of Moab (Num 22:1); of Jordan near Jericho (31:12); the Arabah, the deep valley from the upper Jordan to the Persian Gulf (Deut 1:1). **7.** Hebrew *shephēlâh*, "lowland"; usually the strip west of the mountains of Judea (1 Chron 27:28 KJV; NIV "western foothills"). **8.** Greek *topos pedinos*, "a level, flat place" (Luke 6:17), which may have been on a mountain (Matt 5:1) or elsewhere. **9.** An adjective and adverb: Hebrew *nākôah* (Prov 8:9 KJV; RSV "straight," NIV "right"). Hebrew *tam* (Gen 25:27 KJV; NIV "quiet"); Greek *orthos*, "straight, correct" (Mark 7:35 KJV; RSV and NIV "plainly"). **10.** As verb, Hebrew *bā'ar* (Hab 2:2); Hebrew *shavâh* (Isa 28:25 KJV; NIV "leveled"); Hebrew *sālal* (Prov 15:19, KJV; NIV "highway," RSV "level highway").

PLAITING (See DRESS)

PLANE TREE (See PLANTS)

PLANK (See BEAM)

PLANTS The following plants are mentioned in the Bible. With more accurate botantical analyses, most of the names of plants growing in Palestine during Bible times present little difficulty for the translator, although the origins of some are lost in antiquity.

Acacia. Gnarled, rough-barked, thorny tree (Isa 41:19). The acacia or shittim wood was durable, close-grained wood, used to construct the tabernacle and the ark of the covenant (Exod 25–27, 35–38; Deut 10:3). **Algum Tree.** Solomon used algumwood in the construction of the temple (2 Chron 2:8; 9:10–11). Taking a high polish, this sweet-scented timber has strength, beauty, and long life (1 Kings 10:11–12). **Almond.** Under normal conditions its blossoms will appear before its leaves. In antiquity, the almond nut was used as a confectionary, a source of almond oil, and for food (Gen 43:11; cf. Num 17:8; Eccl 12:5; Jer 1:11). The Israelites adopted the buds and blossoms of the almond flower (Exod 25:33–36; 37:19–20) for the ornamentation of the cups of the golden lampstand. **Almug Tree.** See *Algum Tree.* **Aloe.** The OT references to aloes (Num 24:6 lign aloes KJV; Ps 45:8; Prov 7:17; Song of Songs 4:14) are more likely referring to a large and spreading tree known as the eaglewood. When decaying, the inner wood gives off a fragrant resin used in making perfumes. John 19:39 is probably the only biblical reference to true aloe, a shrubby succulent plant containing juices that were used by the ancients for embalming and as a purgative. **Anise.** See *Dill.* **Apple.** See *Apricot.* **Apricot.** Traditionally this fruit has been translated "apple" (Song of Songs 2:3, 5; 7:8; 8:5; Joel 1:12; Zech 2:8).

Balm of Gilead. See *Balsam.* **Balsam.** An aromatic resinous substance flowing from a plant, used as a healing ointment, and rendered "balm" in most translations (Jer 8:22; 46:11; 51:8; cf. Ezek 27:17). **Barley.** The main staple bread plant of the Hebrews (Deut 8:8), the main food of the poor (Ruth 1:22; 2 Kings 4:42; John 6:9, 13), and bedding and feed for livestock. **Bay Tree.** The Hebrew term for bay, meaning "native," is found only in Psalm 37:35, where it describes a tree symbolic of wealth and wickedness. **Bean.** A staple article of diet for the poor of Palestine (2 Sam 17:28), the dried ground beans were mixed in with grain flour to make bread (Ezek 4:9). **Bitter Herb.** See *Herb*. **Bramble.** A fast-growing rough, prickly shrub of the rose family, usually associated with thorns or nettles (Isa 34:13; Luke 6:44 KJV; NIV "thorns") or representing the rabble of society (Judg 9:14–15 KJV; NIV "thornbush"). **Brier, Briar.** A plant with a woody or prickly stem (Judg 8:7, 16; Ezek 28:24). **Broom.** The white broom's scant foliage provides little relief from the desert sun (1 Kings 19:4); its burning quality makes good firewood (Ps 120:4); and its mildly poisonous roots supply little gratification to hungry people (Job 30:4). **Bulrush.** A tall, slender reedlike plant that was prevalent along the banks of the Nile (Exod 2:3). Papyrus provided the earliest known material for the making of paper, which receives its name from the plant (Exod 2:3; Job 8:11; Isa 18:2). **Bush, Burning Bush.** See *Acacia*.

Calamus. Its bruised leaves give off a strong, spicy, aromatic scent and their pungent taste is like ginger. The sweet calamus is a valuable import item in Palestine (Song of Songs 4:14; Jer 6:20; Ezek 27:19). Cane (KJV "calamus") was an ingredient mixed in the sacred ointment used in the tabernacle (Exod 30:23). **Camphire.** See *Henna*. **Cane.** See *Cala-*

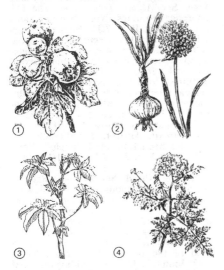

"See! The winter is past, the rains are over and gone. Flowers appear on the earth . . . the fig tree forms its early fruit. The blossoming vines spread their fragrance" (S of Songs 2:11–13). (1) Fig branch; (2) garlic; (3) gourd; (4) hemlock. Courtesy Carta, Jerusalem

mus. **Caper.** A supposed aphrodisiac, this plant also acts as an appetite stimulant for the aged. It is the young pickled buds that give the "desire" or relish to the food. The fruit is inedible. Translated "desire" (NIV, KJV, RSV) or "caperberry" (NASB) (Eccl 12:5). **Caraway.** See *Dill*. **Carob.** Called "St. John's bread" from a belief that carob pods rather than insects were the locusts that John the Baptist ate (Matt 3:4; Mark 1:6). Doubtless the pods of the carob tree were the "pods" (KJV "husks") eaten by the prodigal son in Jesus' parable (Luke 15:16). **Cassia.** Cassia was mixed into the holy anointing oil of the tabernacle (Exod 30:24) and was a valuable trade product (Ezek 27:19). **Cedar.** The cedar of Lebanon, frequently referred to in the OT (1 Kings 6:9; Job 40:17; Ps 92:12; Ezek 27:5), was once abundant in the Mediterranean region but now is scarce. **Cinnamon.** The sweet, light brown aromatic spice was as precious as gold to the ancients. It was used for embalming and witchcraft in Egypt, the anointing oil of the tabernacle (Exod 30:23), perfume (Prov 7:17), spice (Song of Songs 4:14), and trade merchandise (Rev 18:13). **Citron, Citrus Tree.** The fruit is used in the Jewish Feast of Tabernacles. The Greek word occurs once in the NT (Rev 18:12). This wood is commonly said to be "worth its weight in gold." **Cockle.** An annual sturdy noxious weed (Job 31:40 KJV, MLB; stinkweed NASB; weed NIV, RSV). **Coriander.** The coriander seed is used for culinary and medicinal purposes. In the OT it was comparable in color and size to manna (Exod 16:31; Num 11:7). **Corn.** See *Grain*. **Cotton.** It was imported into Palestine from Persia shortly after the Captivity. The Egyptians spun cotton into a fabric in which they wrapped their mummies. The RSV translation of "cotton" in Esther 1:6 and Isaiah 19:9 is perhaps more accurately "linen" (so NIV)—the material made from cotton fibers. **Cucumber.** The refreshing fruit of the cucumber vine was one delicacy the children of Israel longed for in the hot wilderness after leaving Egypt (Num 11:5). **Cummin.** The strong-smelling, warm-tasting cummin seeds were used as culinary spices and served medicinal functions (Matt 23:23). **Cypress.** A tall, pyramidal-shaped tree with hard, durable, reddish-hued wood (Isa 41:19; 60:13; box JB, KJV, NEB). NIV says cypress was used in the ark (Gen 6:14; gopher wood KJV, NASB, RSV). KJV has *cypress* once, the one OT use of *tirzah* (Isa 44:14).

Date Palm. See *Palm*. **Desire.** See *Caper*. **Dill.** Used as a culinary seasoning

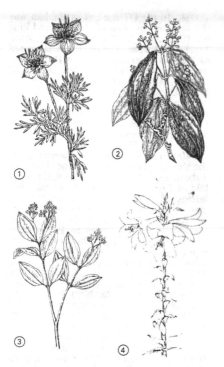

"And why do you worry about clothes? See how the lilies of the field grow" (Matt 6:28). (1) Caraway; (2) cassia; (3) cinnamon branch; (4) lily. Courtesy Carta, Jerusalem

and for medicinal purposes, this plant was cultivated for its aromatic seeds, which were subject to tithe (Matt 23:23 KJV anise).

Fig. A versatile, bushlike tree producing pear-shaped fruit, excellent for eating (1 Sam 25:18; Matt 21; Mark 11). Because of its natural abundance in most Mediterranean countries and its good food qualities, it has become known as "the poor man's food." The first plant mentioned in the Bible (Gen 3:7), it represented peace and prosperity (1 Kings 4:25; Mic 4:4; Zech 3:10). **Fir Tree.** An emblem of nobility and great stature (Isa 41:19; 60:13). The Hebrew word has been variously translated as pine, juniper, cypress, and fir. **Fitch.** See *Dill*. **Flag.** See *Bulrush*. **Flax.** Cultivated to make linen and linseed oil, the fibers from the stem of the plant are the most ancient of the textile fibers (Exod 9:31; Josh 2:6), manufactured into various grades of linen for clothing and other articles where material

requiring strength and resistance to moisture is necessary (Prov 31:13; Isa 19:9). **Frankincense.** A clear yellow resin obtained from certain trees native to northern India and Arabia. It is used in perfumes, as a medicine, and as incense in religious rites (Exod 30:34–38; Lev 2:1, 15–16).

Galbanum. A brownish yellow aromatic, bitter gum that has a disagreeable odor, but when mixed with other ingredients in incense the fragrance was increased and lasted longer (See Exod 30:34). Galbanum also functions as an antispasmodic. **Gall.** Orange-colored fruit used as a cathartic (Deut 29:18; Jer 8:14; 9:15 KJV; NIV "poison, poisoned"). The other Hebrew word means "bitter" and refers to human gall (Job 16:13; 20:25) and to the venom of the serpent (KJV). The Greek word, found in Matthew 27:34 (cf. Ps 69:21) correlates with the myrrh of Mark 15:23. It was a bitter resin added to the analgesic potion given to criminals before crucifixion to deaden their pain. **Garlic.** It grew in great abundance in Egypt, and Israel longed for the garlic of Egypt while they were traveling through the wilderness (Num 11:5). **Goodly Tree.** See *Citron, Citrus Tree*. **Gopher Wood.** See *Cypress*. **Gourd.** Better described as the castor-oil plant, its oil was used as fuel for lamps and oil for ceremonial rites (Jonah 4:5–7 KJV; NIV "vine"). **Grain.** The most common kinds of grain were barley, millet, spelt, and wheat. The KJV uses "corn" for grain (Gen 27:28, 37; Deut 7:13; and Josh 5:11–12; Luke 6:1; 1 Tim 5:18). **Grape.** Grapes may be eaten fresh or dried as raisins or drunk as grape juice or wine. The grapevine is the first plant to be recorded as cultivated in biblical history (Gen 9:20). The grape was a symbol of fruitfulness, and the grape harvest was a time of joyous festivity (40:9–11; Deut 8:8; Ps 105:33; Zech 3:10). **Grass.** Grass is used figuratively to portray the brevity of life (Ps 103:15–16; Matt 6:30; Luke 12:28), to represent abundance (Job 5:25; Ps 72:16), and as a barometer for OT Israel's spiritual condition (Jer 12:4).

Hemlock. The KJV translation of a poisonous substance alluded to in Hosea 10:4 and Amos 6:12. The substance probably comes from the colocynth (see *Gall*) or wormwood. **Henna.** Rendered "camphire" in KJV, this is a small thorny shrub with fragrant white flowers. Its leaves were made into a yellow paste for staining the hair and beard (cf. Deut 21:11–14). King Solomon praised its fragrance (Song of Songs 1:14; 4:13). **Herb.** Bitter herbs were gathered fresh and eaten as a salad at the time of the Passover (Exod 12:8; Num 9:11). **Hyssop.** Because itts hairy stem holds water well, it was a suitable instrument for sprinkling blood during the Passover rites (Exod 12:22; Lev 14; Heb 9:19).

Incense. A combination of gums and spices used to emit a fragrant odor when burned. The incense of the Levitical practice was composed of equal amounts of gum resin (KJV "stacte"), onycha, galbanum, and pure frankincense (Exod 30:34–35; Num 7; Heb 9:4).

Juniper. A shrub that shades and whose poisonous roots make excellent charcoal. KJV mentions it (Heb. rōthem; broom NIV) four times (1 Kings 19:4–5; Job 30:4; Ps 120:4). See *Broom.*

Leek. Used in seasoning along with onions and garlic (Num 11:5). **Lentil.** When soaked and cooked, its seeds make a nourishing meal known as "pottage" (Gen 25:30–34; 2 Sam 17:28; Ezek 4:9). **Lily.** The lily flower served as a pattern in ornamental design for Solomon's temple (1 Kings 7:19–26; 2 Chron 4:5). It was also a symbol of loveliness (Song of Songs 2:16; 4:5; 6:3).

Mallow. Mallows (Job 30:4 JB, KJV, MLB, NASB, RSV; salt herbs NIV ; saltwort NEB) are food of the poor. **Mandrake.** Called the "love apple," it was believed to possess magical powers. Although a tasteless and slightly poisonous narcotic, it was used for medicinal purposes, and, as a charm against the evil spirits, and, as indicated by the account of Rachel and Leah, it was credited with aphrodisiac qualities (Gen 30:14–16; Song of Songs 7:13). **Millet.** The common people ate a mixture of wheat, barley, beans, lentils, and millet moistened with camel's milk and oil (Ezek 4:9). **Mint.** Mint was a tithable herb according to Jewish tradition (Matt 23:23; Luke 11:42) and one of the bitter herbs used in the Passover meal. **Mulberry Tree.** The black mulberry or sycamine tree was cultivated throughout Palestine for its delectable fruit (Luke 17:6). **Mustard.** Its seeds were either powdered or made into paste for medicinal and culinary purposes. The mustard tree and seed were used by Jesus to illustrate and explain faith (Matt 13:31; 17:20; Mark 4:31; Luke 13:19; 17:6). **Myrrh.** A spice, medicine, or cosmetic (Song of Songs 5; Matt 2:11; Mark 15:23; John 19:39). **Myrtle.** A symbol of peace and prosperity (Isa 55:13) and used in constructing the booths for the Feast of Tabernacles (Neh 8:15; Zech 1:7–8). **Nettle.** A low, scrubby plant that thrives in neglected areas (Job 30:7; Prov 24:31; Isa 34:13; Hos 9:6; Zeph 2:9).

Oak. In the OT the oak of Bashan was the religious symbol of strength and long life (Gen 35:8; Isa 2:13; Ezek 27:6; Zech 11:2). **Olive Tree.** The olive tree is named or alluded to nearly 80 times throughout the Bible in reference to the tree itself (Isa 24:13; Rom 11), its wood (1 Kings 6:23–33), its oil (Exod 30:24; Rev 18:13), or to a geographical location named for its olive groves (Matt 24:3; John 8:1). **Onycha.** Onycha was added to the sacred mixture for incense used in the tabernacle (Exod 30:34–36).

Palm Tree. Palm branches were used in the Jewish celebration of the Feast of Tabernacles (Lev 23:40; Neh 8:15); were laid at Jesus' feet on his triumphal entry into Jerusalem (John 12:13); and came to signify victory (Rev 7:9). **Pistachio.** Considered a good product of the land, it was carried by Jacob's sons to Egypt (Gen 43:11). **Pomegranate.** The fruit of the pomegranate was used as a decorative model in building (1 Kings 7:18, 20, 42) and as an ornament on the robe of the Levitical high priest (Exod 28:33–34).

Reed. Found in the Near East by the sides of rivers and in standing waters (Job 40:21; Matt 11:7), it metaphorically represents Israel as weak and overcome with sin (1 Kings 14:15). **Rue.** It was used as a culinary spice and for medicinal reasons. It was a customary tithable garden plant (Luke 11:42). **Rush.** A cylindrical, hollow-stalked plant growing in and along the water courses of Palestine (Job 8:11; 41:20; Isa 19:6; 35:7).

Saffron. A purple-flowered, bulbous plant used for food flavoring and coloring, and as a dye (Song of Songs 4:14). **Spelt.** Spelt, sometimes translated "rye" (KJV), was grown in Egypt (Exod 9:32) and in Palestine (Isa 28:25) and was made into bread (Ezek 4:9). **Spice.** Spices were used in the tabernacle (Exod 25:6; 30:23–25; 35:8); they were a precious trade commodity (1 Kings 10; Rev 18:13), part of the palace treasury (2 Kings 20:13; Isa 39:2), valued for their aromatic fragrance (Song of Songs 4:10, 14), and used in preparing Jesus' body for burial (Luke 23:56; John 19:40). **Spikenard.** The rose-red fragrance ointment was a favorite perfume of the ancients (Song of Songs 1:12; 4:13–14 KJV; NIV "perfume, nard"; Mark 14:3; John 12:3). **Sycamore.** The Egyptians made their mummy cases of this wood (1 Kings 10:27; Amos 7:14; Luke 19:4).

Tare. At harvest time the grain is fanned and put through a sieve. The smaller darnel seeds left after fanning pass through the sieve, leaving behind the desired fruit. The darnel is host to an

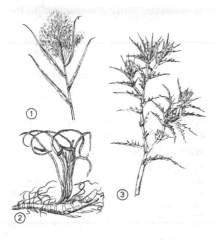

"Finally all the trees said to the thorn bush, 'Come and be our king' " (Judg 9:14). (1) Reed; (2) sweet cane; (3) thorn branch. Courtesy Carta, Jerusalem

ergot-like smut fungus, which infects the seeds and is poisonous to man and herbivorous animals but not to poultry (Matt 13:24–30, 36–43). **Thistle.** Translated bramble, brier, thistle, and thorn (2 Kings 14:9; 2 Chron 25:18; Hos 10:8; Matt 7:16; 13:7; Heb 6:8). **Thorn.** Small, spiny shrubs and vines planted as hedges and used as firewood (Judg 9:14–15; Prov 26:9; Isa 55:13; Matt 7:16; Luke 6:44). **Wheat.** Egypt, Babylonia, Syria, and Palestine were renowned for their quality wheat. Certain varieties of wheat still yield 60 to 100 grains per head as they did in Jesus' day (Matt 13:3–8). Heads roasted over fire constituted the "parched corn" (KJV) of the OT (Lev 23:14; Ruth 2:14; 1 Sam 17:17; 25:18). Straw and stubble are the dried stalks and remnants of wheat and other cereal grains (Exod 5:12; 1 Cor 3:12). **Wormwood.** A bitter, aromatic herb. Related to our sagebrush, the wormwood is the source of an essential oil obtained from the dried leaves and the tops of the plant. The plant was a symbol of bitterness, embodying the hardships and evils of life (Prov 5:4; Lam 3:15, 19; Amos 5:7 KJV; NIV "gall, bitterness"; Rev 8:11).

PLASTER The Egyptians plastered their stone buildings, even the finest granite, inside and out, to make a smooth surface for decoration. The poor used a mixture of clay and straw. On better buildings the first coat was gypsum and red clay or ashes, the finish coat slaked lime and white sand, sometimes including chopped straw. In Palestine and Syria, an outside clay coating had to be renewed after the rainy reason. Mortar was usually made with limestone, the process of its manufacture otherwise similar to that in Egypt.

PLATTER (See CHARGER)

PLEDGE Personal property of a debtor held to secure a payment (Gen 38:17–18, 20). Mosaic Law protected the poor. An outer garment, taken as a pledge, had to be restored at sunset for a bed covering (Exod 22:26–27; Deut 24:12–13). The creditor was forbidden to enter his neighbor's house to take the pledge (24:10–11). A handmill or its upper millstone might not be taken (24:6), nor a widow's clothing (24:17–18). Abuses of the pledge were censured (Job 22:6; 24:3, 9; Amos 2:8; Hab 2:6). In two passages (2 Kings 18:23; Isa 36:8) a wager (JB, RSV; bargain NIV) seems to be meant. The garment of a person who puts up security for strangers ought to be taken in pledge (Prov 20:16; 27:13).

PLEIADES (See ASTRONOMY)

PLOWMAN (See OCCUPATIONS AND PROFESSIONS)

PLOW, PLOUGH An ancient plow scratched the surface but did not turn over the soil. It consisted of a branched stick that was hitched to animals, usually a yoke of oxen (Job 1:14; Amos 6:12). Plowing with an ox and an ass yoked together was forbidden (Deut 22:10), but this prohibition is not observed today. Plowing may indicate destruction (Jer 26:18; Mic 3:12). Hosea 10:11–13 contrasts plowing for righteous and for evil ends (Job 4:8; Ps 129:3).

PLOWSHARE (Heb. *'ēth, the blade of a plow*). To beat swords into plowshares was symbolic of an age of peace (Isa 2:4; Mic 4:3); to beat plowshares into swords indicated coming war (Joel 3:10).

PLUMB LINE (Heb. *'anāk*). A cord with a stone or metal weight, the plummet, tied to one end; used by builders to keep a wall perpendicular. Plumb line and plummet are used figuratively of God's action in testing the uprightness of his people (2 Kings 21:13; Isa 28:17; Amos 7:7–9).

POCHERETH (See POKERETH-HAZZEBAIM)

PODS (See PLANTS)

POET (Gr. *poiētēs, a maker*). In Acts 17:28 Paul quotes from *Phaenomena*, 5, by the Greek poet Aratus (c. 270 B.C.) of Soli in Cilicia. A similar phrase occurs in the *Hymn to Zeus* by the Stoic philosopher Cleanthes (300–220 B.C.), who taught at Athens. First Corinthians 15:32 may contain a quotation from Menander; Titus 1:12, from Epimenides.

POETRY In OT poetry everything is subservient to meaning. The most familiar feature of Hebrew poetry arises from the balance between successive lines (parallelism). The three principal varieties of poetry are *synonymous*, in which the meaning of both members is similar (1 Sam 18:7; Pss 15:1; 24:1–3); *antithetic*, in which the meanings of the members are opposed (Ps 37:9; Prov 10:1; 11:3); and *synthetic*, in which noun corresponds to noun, verb to verb, and member to member, and each member adds something new (Ps 19:8–9). Quite a number of poems are alphabetical acrostics—the successive lines of the poem begin with the successive letters of the Hebrew alphabet (e.g., Pss 34, 37; Lam 1–4). In Psalm 119 each group of eight verses begins with the same letter. The alphabetical acrostic implies a total coverage of the chosen theme. Thus in Psalm 119 we have a total statement about the Word of God.

Short poems (usually so printed in NIV) are embedded in the historical books (cf. Gen 2:23; Exod 15:1–18). In the NT, easily recognizable poems are all in Luke: The Magnificat of Mary (1:46b–55); the prophecy of Zechariah (Luke 1:68–79); the angels' Gloria in Excelsis (2:14); and the Nunc Dimittis of Simeon (2:29–32). Snatches of Christian hymns are thought to be found in some of the letters (Eph 5:14; 1 Tim 1:17; 3:16; 6:16; 2 Tim 4:18)

POISON (Heb. *hēmâh, rō'sh,* Gr. *thymos, ios*). The venom of reptiles (Deut 32:24, 33; Job 20:16; Ps 58:4; Rom 3:13). Vegetable poisons also were known (Hos 10:4; KJV hemlock; RSV and NIV poisonous weeds; 2 Kings 4:39–40, gourds). The "deadly thing" of Mark 16:18 was a poisoned drink (cf. NIV).

POKERETH-HAZZEBAIM (pŏk'ē-rĕth-hăz'à-bā'Ĭm). The head of a postexilic family; a servant of Solomon (Ezra 2:57; Neh 7:59). KJV has "Pochereth of Zebaim."

POLLUTION (Heb. *gā'al,* Gr. *alisgēma*). This may be regarded as from menstruation (Ezek 22:10 KJV; NIV "ceremonially unclean"), from food sacrificed to idols (Acts 15:20, 29), or from the evil in the world (2 Peter 2:20 KJV; RSV "defilements," NIV "corruption"). Imperfect offerings, brought with a wrong motive, were polluted (Mal 1:7–9 KJV; NIV "defiled"). An altar was to be of unhewn stone: to cut the stone was to pollute it (Exod 20:25 KJV; RSV "profane," NIV "defile"). Several Hebrew and Greek words translated "pollute" refer to ceremonial or moral defilement, profanation, and uncleanness.

POLLUX (See CASTOR AND POLLUX)

POLYGAMY (See MARRIAGE)

POMEGRANATE (See PLANTS)

PONTIUS PILATE (See PILATE)

PONTUS (Gr. *Pontos, sea*). A large province of northern Asia Minor that lay along the Black Sea (Pontus Euxinius). There were many Jews in the province (cf. Acts 2:9; 18:2). So far as we know, Pontus and the other northern provinces were not evangelized by Paul. The Holy Spirit did not permit him to preach in Bithynia (16:7). There is a tradition that Peter preached in northern Asia Minor rather than in Rome after Pentecost (cf. 1 Peter 1:1).

POOL A pocket of water, natural or artificial. Pools tell of a restored wilderness (Pss 107:35; 114:8; Isa 35:7; 41:18). Dried-up pools speak of judgment (42:15). We read of the following pools: of Gibeon (2 Sam 2:13), of Hebron (4:12), of Samaria (1 Kings 22:38), of Heshbon (Song of Songs 7:4), of Siloah or Siloam (Neh 3:15; John 9:7, 11), of Bethesda (5:2, 4, 7), the Upper Pool (2 Kings 18:17; Isa 7:3; 36:2), the pool Hezekiah made (2 Kings 20:20), the Lower Pool (Isa 22:9), the Old Pool (22:11), the King's Pool (Neh 2:14), and the artificial pool (3:16).

POOR (Heb. *'evyôn, dal, 'ānî, rûsh,* Gr. *ptochos*). God's love and care for the poor are central to his providence (Pss 34:6; 68:10; Eccl 5:8). He encourages us to do the same (Exod 22:22–23). The Mosaic Law has specific provisions for the benefit of the poor (22:25–27; 23:11; Lev 19:9–10, 13, 15; 25:6, 25–30; Deut 14:28–29; 15:12–13; 16:11–14; Ruth 2:1–7; Neh 8:10). Israel as a nation was born out of deep poverty (Exod 1:8–14; 2:7–10) and was never allowed to forget it (e.g., 1 Kings 8:50–53). If Israel met the conditions of God's covenant, there would be no poor among them; but God knew this would never be realized (Deut 15:4–11). Willful neglect leading to poverty is not condoned (Prov 13:4–18). National disasters caused the poor to become almost synonymous with the

The "pool of Gibeon" (2 Sam 2:13), with its spiral staircase of seventy-nine steps and measuring 36 feet (11 m.) in diameter and 30 feet (9 m.) in depth. Courtesy Zev Radovan

pious (e.g., Ps 68:10; Isa 41:17). The wrongs done to the poor concerned the prophets (e.g., Isa 1:23; 10:1–2; Ezek 34; Amos 2:6; 5:7; 8:6; Mic 2:1–2; Hab 3:14; Mal 3:5).

At the outset of his ministry, Jesus, taking for his text Isaiah 61:1–2, presents as his first aim, "to preach good news to the poor." Physical poverty is meant (Luke 6:20–26). In Matthew 5:3 Jesus commends the poor in spirit, the humble ones. Jesus moved among the poor and humble. He associated himself with them in his manner of living and his freedom from the cares of property ownership (8:20). He understood and appreciated the sacrificial giving of a poor widow (Mark 12:41–44). The early church moved among the poor, who were not too poor to be concerned for one another's welfare (2 Cor 8:2–5, 9–15), drawing inspiration from Christ's leaving heavenly riches for earthly poverty. The origin of the diaconate is linked with a special need (Acts 6:1–6). Those with property contributed to the common fund (2:45; 4:32–37). The Jerusalem Council asked Paul and Barnabas to remember the poor (Gal 2:10). James has some sharp words about the relations of rich and poor (James 1:9–11; 2:1–13; 5:1–6).

POPLAR (See PLANTS)

PORCH (Heb. *'êlām, 'ūlām, porch*). In Solomon's temple (1 Kings 6:3); in Solomon's palace (7:6ff.); in Ezekiel's new temple (Ezek 40:7ff.); at the pool of Bethesda (John 10:23; Acts 3:11; 5:12; RSV "portico," NIV "colonnade"). In every case an area with a roof supported by columns appears to be meant.

PORCIUS (See FESTUS)

PORPHYRY (See MINERALS)

PORTER (See OCCUPATIONS AND PROFESSIONS)

PORTION A part—that is, less than the whole; a share (Num 31:30, 47 KJV), of food served to one person (Neh 8:10, 12; Dan 1:5–16; 11:26 KJV; NIV "amount, provision"; Deut 18:8 KJV) or of property acquired by gift (1 Sam 1:4–5) or by inheritance (Gen 31:14 KJV; Josh 17:14). It can also refer to a plot of ground (2 Kings 9:10, 36–37 KJV) or one's destiny (Job 20:29 KJV; Ps 142:5; Lam 3:24).

POST (Heb. *mezûzâh, doorpost; rûts, to run; 'ayil, strength*). The first word represented the parts to the doorway of a building (1 Kings 6:33 KJV; NIV "jams"). The last word is a post also, but has a wider meaning as well; that is, anything strong (Ezek 40:14, 16 KJV). One of the most common uses of the word *post* is its designation of anyone who conveyed a message speedily. These were very early means of communication (Job 9:25 KJV; NIV "runner"). The first went by foot and later by horses. Royal messages were conveyed in this way (2 Chron 30:6, 10 KJV; NIV "couriers").

POT The translation of more than a dozen Hebrew and Greek words. Most of them referred to utensils for holding liquids and solid substances such as grain or ashes. Some were made of metal, others of clay, and they came in a great variety of sizes and shapes. Their chief NT use was for water or wine (Mark 7:4; John 2:6 KJV; NIV "pitchers, jars").

POTENTATE (pō'tĕn-tāt, Gr. *dynastēs, mighty one*). Used in Luke 1:52 (NIV "rulers") and Acts 8:27 (NIV "important official").

POTIPHAR (pŏt'ĭ-fêr, Heb. *pôtîphara', whom Re has given*). One of the pharaoh's officers. He purchased Joseph from the Midianites and made him head overseer over his house. When Joseph was falsely accused by the wife of Potiphar, he threw Joseph into prison (Gen 39:1–20).

POTIPHERA, POTIPHERAH (pō-tĭf'-êr-à, Heb. *potiphera, the one given by the sun-god*). The Egyptian priest of On whose daughter Asenath was given to Joseph for a wife (Gen 41:45, 50; 46:20).

POTSHERD (pot'shûrd, Heb. *heres*). A piece of earthenware (Job 2:8; Ps 22:15; Isa 45:9). Many inscribed potsherds known as "ostraca" furnish valuable data for the archaeologist. See OSTRACA.

POTTAGE (Heb. *nāzîdh, boiled*). A kind of thick broth made with vegetables and meat or suet (Gen 25:29–30, 34; 2 Kings 4:38–39).

POTTER (See OCCUPATIONS AND PROFESSIONS: *Pottery*)

POTTER'S FIELD (See AKELDAMA)

POTTERY Pottery making is one of the oldest crafts in Bible lands. References, both literal and figurative, to the potter and his products occur throughout the Scriptures. In addition to his workshop the potter needed a field (Matt 27:7) for weathering the clay, mixing it with water, and treading it by foot into potter's clay. For cooking vessels, sand or crushed stone was added to temper the clay. The potter kneaded the clay for several hours to remove all air bubbles. Pottery was made on a wheel as well as freehand. Impurities in the clay or insufficient treading could mar the vessel on the

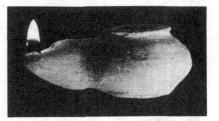

The common slipper-type earthenware oil lamp of biblical times. ". . . keep your lamps burning" (Luke 12:35). Courtesy Zev Radovan

wheel. The potter would then reshape the clay into a ball and make a less elegant object (Jer 18:3–4). After drying the vessel was replaced on the wheel for cutting off excess clay. Then the potter could coat the pot with "slip," clay of the consistency of cream, often with a mineral color added. Next he might burnish or rub the surface with a smooth stone to produce a sheen, or he might paint on a design. Finally, the jar was "fired" by heating it, usually between 700 and 1,050 degrees Celsius in an open fire or in a kiln.

God, who formed (*yātsar*) Adam from the dust ('*āphār*, Gen 2:7), is likened to our Potter, who fashions us according to his will (Job 10:8–9; 33:6; Isa 29:16; 45:9; 64:8; Lam 4:2; Rom 9:20–23; 2 Tim 2:20–21). He will conquer the wicked as one smashes a piece of pottery (Ps 2:9; Jer 19:10–11; Rev 2:27).

Ceramic vessels have been changing in fashion down through the centuries of human existence. Egyptologist Flinders Petrie in A.D. 1890 catalogued the sequence of broken pottery according to the varying shapes and decorations at Tell el-Hesi in SW Palestine. He succeeded in assigning dates to several of his pottery periods by identifying certain wares with wares previously discovered in datable Egyptian tombs. Today when an archaeologist uncovers no more precise evidence (e.g., inscriptions on clay tablets, monuments, or coins), he depends on dominant pottery styles from an occupation level of an ancient city to furnish the clue to the date. In 1953 the Wheaton Archaeological Expedition verified that Dothan was settled in Joseph's time (Gen 37:17) by unearthing orange and black burnished juglets and a double-handled juglet, of the same style as the Hyksos-Age juglets found in the 1930s at Megiddo.

Depending on the accuracy of dating

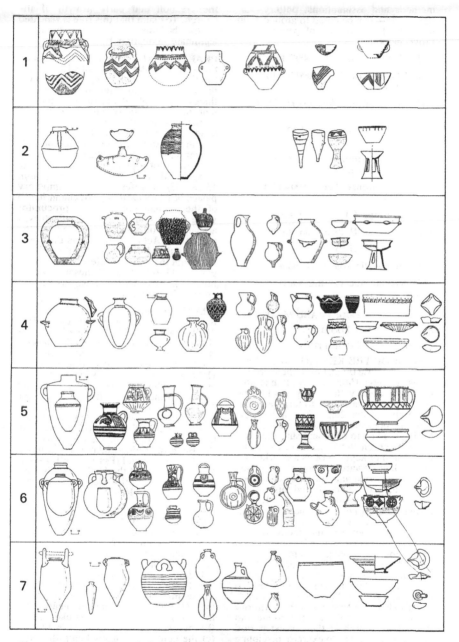

Chart showing profiles of characteristic pottery types from the principal archaeological periods in Palestine. (1) Neolithic Age (5500–4000 B.C.); (2) Chalcolithic Age (4000–3000 B.C.); (3) Early Bronze Age (3000–2000 B.C.); (4) Middle Bronze Age (2000–1500 B.C.); (5) Late Bronze Age (1500–1200 B.C.); (6) Iron Age (1200–600 B.C.); (7) Persian period (586–332 B.C.). Courtesy Carta, Jerusalem methods and assumptions, pottery—all handmade—can be dated to around 4500 B.C. The following list of periods may prove helpful.

I. Neolithic Age (?–4000? B.C.).

II. Chalcolithic Age (4000?–3100 B.C.).

III. Early Bronze Age (3100–2100 B.C.).

IV. Middle Bronze Age I (2100–1900 B.C.).

V. Middle Bronze Age II (1900–1550 1480 B.C.).

VI. Late Bronze Age (1500–1230 B.C.).

VII. Iron Age I (1230–925 B.C.).

VIII. Iron Age II (925–586 B.C.).

IX. Iron Age II (538–333 B.C.).

X. Hellenistic Age (333–63 B.C.).

XI. Roman Age (63 B.C.–A.D. 325).

POULTRY (See BIRDS)

POUND (See WEIGHTS AND MEASURES)

POVERTY (See POOR)

POWER (See AUTHORITY)

POWER OF THE KEYS (Gr. *kleis*, *key*). A phrase whose origin lies in the words of Jesus to Peter (Matt 16:19). It has also been connected with binding and loosing (18:18) and the authority to forgive or not to forgive (John 20:22–23). Moreover, Jesus is presented in Revelation 3:7 as having the key to open and shut the door into the church and kingdom of God. The possession of keys—not as a doorkeeper but as chief steward in a household—was a symbol of rule and authority conferred by the master. God conferred this authority on the Messiah, and the Messiah conferred it on Peter and the other apostles. They had authority to preach the gospel and perform its deeds of the gospel, and in so doing to admit into God's household those who responded in repentance and faith. They were not to be like the Pharisees whose word and example actually shut the kingdom of heaven (Matt 23:13). The "power of the keys" has also been understood as the authority to make binding rules for the young and developing church in the earliest period and or as the power to exercise discipline within the church through the use of the power of excommunication. Further, the words of Jesus to Peter (16:17–19) seem to establish a particular role for Peter in

the creation and early growth of the church. To claim that this role is repeated in the bishops of Rome is hardly a legitimate deduction from the text.

PRAETORIUM (prē-tō′rĭ-ŭm). Sometimes spelled Pretorium, the Latin term for the Greek *praitōrion*, which among the Romans could refer to a number of things. Originally it meant the general's tent in the camp of an army station. Sometimes it referred to the military headquarters in Rome itself or in the provincial capitals. It also meant the staff of men in such an establishment or even the session of a planning council. In the Gospels (Matt 27:27; Mark 15:16; John 18:28, 33) it refers to the temporary palace or headquarters ("judgment hall") of the Roman governor or procurator while he was in Jerusalem, which was actually Herod's palace adjacent to the temple (cf. Acts 23:35). It was the scene of the trial of Jesus before Pontius Pilate. No doubt the debated reference in Philippians 1:13 (cf. 4:22, "Caesar's household") means the headquarters of the emperor's bodyguard.

PRAISE A general term for words or deeds that exalt or honor men (Prov 27:21), women (31:30), heathen gods (Judg 16:24), or God, especially in song (Exod 15:11 KJV, NASB, NEB; glorious deeds RSV; glory NIV). Some of the Hebrew and Greek words mean "thanksgiving," "blessing," or "glory," and are often so translated (2 Chron 7:3, 6; Luke 1:64; John 9:24). *Aretē* ("virtue") is translated "praises," or "excellencies," in 1 Peter 2:9. We are to be the praise of God's glory (Eph 1:6, 12, 14). Praise fills the Book of Psalms, increasing in intensity toward the end (Pss 145–50). Psalms 113 18 are called the Hallel, the praises. Praise for redemption dominates the NT (Luke 2:13–14; Rev 19:5–7).

PRAYER The spiritual response (spoken and unspoken) to God. Prayer covers a wide spectrum of addressing and hearing God, interceding with and waiting for the Lord, and contemplating and petitioning our Father in heaven.

I. **Jesus at Prayer.** In the Gospels there are 17 references to Jesus at prayer. These may be divided into four groupings. (1) Prayers at critical moments in his life: (a) his baptism (Luke 3:21), (b) the choice of the apostles (6:12–13), (c) the confession of his being the Messiah (9:18), (d) his Transfiguration (9:29), (e) before the cross in Gethsemane (22:39–40), and (f) on the cross (23:46). (2) Prayers during his ministry: (a) before

A votive statue of a man from Mari with hands clasped and wearing a long fleece-like woolen skirt. White stone. Mid-third millennium B.C. Courtesy Studium Biblicum Franciscanum, Jerusalem

the conflict with the Jewish leaders (5:16), (b) before providing the "Lord's Prayer" (11:1), (c) when Greeks came to him (John 12:7–8), and (d) after feeding the 5,000 (Mark 6:46). (3) Prayers at his miracles: (a) healing the multitudes (1:35), (b) before feeding the 5,000 (6:41), (c) healing a deaf-mute (7:34), and (d) raising Lazarus from death (John 11:41). (4) Prayers for others: (a) for the Eleven (17:6–19), (b) for the whole church (17:20–26), (c) for those who nailed him to the cross (Luke 23:34), and (d) for Peter (22:32). We are to understand these as pointing to a rich prayer life rather than the only times when Jesus prayed (Heb 5:7).

II. Jesus' Teaching on Prayer. It was seeing the prayer life of Jesus (so different from the usual way of prayer in Judaism) that led the disciples to say, "Lord, teach us to pray" (Luke 11:1). In response, Jesus provided them with what we now call the Lord's Prayer (11:2–4; Matt 6:9–13). This prayer has three parts: (1) Invocation: "Our Father, who art in heaven." (2) Petition: there are six requests—for God's name to be hallowed, for God's kingdom to come, for God's will to be done, for daily bread to be provided, for forgiveness of our debts (sins), and for deliverance from temptation (testing) and evil (the evil one). (3) Doxology: "Thine is the kingdom, the power and the glory. . . ."

From the rest of the teaching of Jesus we note that he taught that prayer may be characterized by (1) importunity (Luke 11:5–8)—a laying hold of God's willingness to bless; (2) tenacity (18:1–8)—a persistence and certainty in praying; (3) humility (18:10–14)—penitence and a sense of unworthiness; (4) compassion (Matt 18:21–35); (5) simplicity (6:5–6; Mark 12:38–40); (6) intensity and watchfulness (Mark 13:33; 14:38); (7) unity of heart and mind in the community of prayer (Matt 18:19ff.); and (8) expectancy (Mark 11:24).

Jesus also indicated some of the themes for intercession in prayer. (1) The casting out of evil forces from the hearts of those in darkness and despair (Mark 9:14–29). (2) The extension of the kingdom of God in the hearts and minds of people everywhere (Matt 9:35ff.; Luke 10:2). (3) The true good of enemies (Matt 5:44; Luke 6:28).

A major new departure in the method of prayer introduced by Jesus was that disciples should ask the Father in the name of Jesus (John 14:13; 16:23–24)—not a magic formula but rather the new ground on which the worshiper stands, a new plea for the success of his petitions, and a new mind within which the prayer is conceived. Thus the aim of prayer is not to make God change his will but to enable disciples of Jesus to change their minds and dispositions as they are molded by his Spirit.

III. The Apostles' Teaching on Prayer. The letters of Paul are filled with references to prayer ranging from praise to petition. Conscious at all times that the exalted Jesus is making intercession for his church (Rom 8:34), Paul saw prayer as arising through the presence and activity of the Spirit (sent from Christ) within the body of Christ and within the individual believer (8:15–16), and being offered to the Father in and through the Lord Jesus.

A variety of verbs are used to cover the spectrum of prayer; e.g., (1) *doxazō*, to glorify God the Father (Rom 15:6, 9); (2) *exomologeuomai*, to praise God the Father (Eph 1:6, 12, 14); (3) *eulogeomai*, to bless (or give thanks to) God (1 Cor 14:16; 2 Cor 1:3); (4) *proskyneō*, to worship God the Father (John 4:20–24; 1 Cor 14:25); (5) *eucharisteō*, to offer thanksgiving to God the Father (Phil 1:3; Col 1:3); (6) *deomai* and *proseuchomai*, to ask God for personal things (Rom 1:10; 1 Cor 14:13; 2 Cor 12:8); (7) *hyperentynchanō*, to ask God on behalf of others (Gal 1:3; 6:16; 1 Thess 3:10–13; 5:23). James also saw the Christian life as a life of prayer (James 5:13–16).

IV. Examples of Prayers and Ways to Pray. Most of the recorded prayers of leaders of Israel are intercessions; see the prayers of Moses (Exod 32:11–13, 31–32; 33:12–16; Num 11:11–15; 14:13–19; Deut 9:18–21), Aaron (Num 6:22–27), Samuel (1 Sam 7:5–13), Solomon (1 Kings 8:22–53), and Hezekiah (2 Kings 19:14–19). God always answered the prayers of his people, but sometimes his answer was no (Exod 32:30–35). Once Jeremiah was commanded not to intercede (Jer 7:16; 11:14; 14:11). We are to assume that the prophets were constantly engaged in prayer in order to be the recipients of the word of the Lord (see Isa 6; Dan 9:20ff.; Hab 2:1–3).

The Psalter contains communal hymns (Pss 33, 145–150), communal laments (44, 74, 79), royal psalms (2, 18, 20, 21), laments of the individual Israelite (3, 5–7, 13), thanksgivings of the individual Israelite (30, 32, 138), songs for pilgrimage (84, 122), thanksgivings of the community (67, 124), wisdom poems (1, 37, 73, 112), and liturgies (15, 24, 60, 75). Obviously the emphasis in the whole

Bible is not on the right posture or the correct position, but on the right attitude in prayer. Thus people pray kneeling (1 Kings 8:54; Ezra 9:5; Dan 6:10; Acts 20:36), standing (Jer 18:20), sitting (2 Sam 7:18), or even lying prostrate (Matt 26:39). They pray sometimes with hands uplifted (1 Kings 8:22; Pss 28:2; 134:2; 1 Tim 2:8). They pray silently (1 Sam 1:13) and aloud (Ezek 11:13); they pray alone (Matt 6:6; Mark 1:35) and together (Ps 35:18; Matt 18:19; Acts 4:31); they pray at fixed times (Ps 55:17; Dan 6:10) or at any time (Luke 18:1). They pray everywhere (1 Tim 2:8)—in bed (Ps 63:6), in an open field (Gen 24:11–12), in the temple (2 Kings 19:14), at the riverside (Acts 16:13), on the seashore (21:5), on the battlefield (1 Sam 7:5). They pray spontaneously (Matt 6:7); they pray liturgically (Pss 120–126); they pray quite literally for everything (Gen 24:12–14; Phil 4:6; 1 Tim 2:1–4). See also WORSHIP.

PREACHER, PREACHING (See OCCUPATIONS AND PROFESSIONS)

PRECIOUS STONES (See MINERALS)

PREDESTINATION (See ELECTION)

PREFECT (prē'fĕct). A person appointed to a position of responsibility in the Babylonian government (Dan 3:2–3, 27; 6:7; KJV has "governor").

PRESBYTERY (prĕz'bĭ-têr-ē, Gr. *presbyterion*). The Christian elders who formally recognized Timothy's spiritual gift (1 Tim 4:14 KJV, NASB; JB, NIV body of elders). The same word occurs in Luke 22:66 (elders KJV, MLB, NEB; council of the elders NIV) and Acts 22:5 for the organized body of Jewish elders in Jerusalem.

PRESIDENTS (Heb. *sārekhîn, chief*). Administrative officers whose duties are not clearly defined. Three were placed by Darius over the 120 satraps in his kingdom, and Daniel was one of the three (Dan 6:2–7). NIV translates this word as "administrators."

PRESS (for oil or wine). A rendering of several Hebrew and Greek words that refer to a device used for extracting liquids from certain fruits from which wines and oils were made. Some of these were small handmills while others were made of two large stones. One turned on the other by horses or mules so that the fruit was crushed between them.

PRIDE One of the worst forms of sin, regarded, indeed, by many as the basis of all sin. The various Hebrew words reflect the deep-seated and far-reaching nature of pride, for they are associated with terms such as presumption, vanity, vain boasting, haughtiness, and arrogance. Pride makes impossible a right perspective toward both God and man. It deceives the heart (Jer 49:16) and hardens it (Dan 5:20). It brings contention (Prov 13:10; 28:25) and destruction (16:18). It was a fundamental fault of the wandering Israelites that brought a stern warning from God (Lev 26:19) and was associated with the punishment on King Uzziah (2 Chron 26:16ff.), Moab (Isa 25:11), Judah and Jerusalem (Jer 13:9), Jacob (Amos 6:8), and Edom (Obad 3), among others. The Greek words used also convey the idea of empty display, glorying, and arrogance. James quotes Proverbs 3:34 in pointing out God's opposition to the proud (James 4:6). Paul made it clear that no one has any grounds for boasting in God's sight, but he does also speak of "pride" as a legitimate attribute (e.g., 2 Cor 5:12; 7:4).

PRIEST, PRIESTHOOD The formal priesthood in Israel began with the time of the Exodus. In the patriarchal times the heads of families offered sacrifices and intercessory prayers and performed general religious functions, but there seems to have been no separate priestly office, as there was among the Egyptians (Gen 47:22, 26) and in the instance of Melchizedek (14:18–20).

The appointment of Aaron and his sons as priests (Exod 28–29; Lev 8) precedes the events at Sinai (Exod 32) that led to the special appointment of the tribe of Levi to officiate before the Lord, and to do so instead of the firstborn (Num 8:16). The tribe of Levi was chosen to serve as assistants to the Aaronic priests (Num 3; cf. Exod 32:26–29; Num 8:16ff.).

After the establishment of the Aaronic priesthood, it was considered an offense in Israel for anyone not officially consecrated as a priest to offer formal ritual sacrifices. The rebellion of Korah (Num 16) involved intrusion into the priesthood, even though he and his associates were Levites (16:8–9). King Saul was most severely rebuked for a similar intrusion (1 Sam 13:8ff.), and King Uzziah was struck with leprosy for this offense (2 Chron 26:16ff.).

The offices of prophet and priest might be combined in one person (John 11:49–52). Jeremiah was a member of a priestly family (Jer 1:1). The offices of king and prophet might also be combined (Acts 2:29–31), but the kingly line of David was of the nonpriestly tribe of Judah, and

The ephod, as worn by the high priest, carefully reconstructed according to Exod 28:31–35 and 39:22-26. From *The Tabernacle,* courtesy M. Levine, "Melechet Hamishkan."

therefore no king of David's line could have been also a priest according to the Levitical law.

The NT writers made much of the fact that Jesus belonged to the house and line of David (Luke 2:4–5; cf. Matt 21:9; Mark 11:10). How then could he be also a priest? The author of the Letter to the

Hebrews finds the scriptural answer in the priestly order of Melchizedek (Heb 6:20–7:17), who was Abraham's superior and both king and priest. This amplifies Zechariah's prophecy (6:13; cf. Isa 4:2; Jer 23:5–6).

The atonement of Christ was just as effective before the event as afterward. The high priestly office of Christ did not begin at his incarnation; it was a fact known to David (Ps 110:4) along with his sovereign lordship (110:1). The Bible presents Christ as our Prophet, Priest, and King.

The priestly ministry of Christ is introduced in Hebrews 1:3, a reference to his death on the cross regarded as an atoning sacrifice. But this act of sacrifice was not a mere symbol, as were all of the Aaronic priestly acts; it was of infinite intrinsic worth (2:9).

Christ's priesthood was in no sense contrary to the Aaronic order, but fulfilled the redemptive significance of it. But the priesthood of Christ furnished the *substance* of which the Aaronic priesthood was only the shadow (Col 2:17; Heb 8:5) and symbol.

The tabernacle of which Christ is the High Priest is the entire cosmic scene of the redemption of God's elect. This was the "pattern" that Moses saw (Heb 8:5)—God's plan of salvation. It includes all the spiritual and temporal furniture of heaven and earth. The cross of Christ was the altar of sacrifice on which he offered himself. When he gave up his life on the cross, the atonement was "finished" (John 19:30) once and for all (Heb 7:27; 9:26) with absolutely nothing more for God or man to add to it.

On the Day of Atonement in Levitical ritual (Lev 16) the high priest had to go in and out past the curtain that separated the Most Holy Place from the Holy Place. By this symbolism the Holy Spirit (Heb 9:8–9) signified that "the way into the Most Holy Place had not yet been disclosed" while the Levitical mode of worship still had its proper standing. But when Jesus' body was broken on the cross, this symbolized the tearing of the curtain (10:19–22) and the clear revealing of the way into the very presence of God (Matt 27:51; Mark 15:38; Luke 23:45).

The curtain is once spoken of as though it still cuts off our view (Heb 6:18–20; see also 4:14), but this is a different metaphor. It is not the "mercy seat" that is hidden in Hebrews 6:18–20, but the "hope offered to us," the "kingdom that cannot be shaken" (9:28; 12:14–29).

The comparisons of different priesthoods in the Letter to the Hebrews are between the *outward form* of Judaism and the *reality* in Christ. Every argument against Judaism could be turned with equal logic against the outward forms of the church, if Christ is not the center of it all.

The nation of Israel was called "a kingdom of priests" (Exod 19:6), and the church (1 Peter 2:5, 9 priesthood KJV; Rev 1:6; 5:10) and all who have part in the first resurrection (Rev 20:6) are called priests. Paul uses symbols of priestly ritual with reference to his own ministry (Rom 15:16; Phil 2:17; and 2 Tim 4:6). Neither the apostles (Matt 19:28; Luke 22:18, 28–30) nor believers in general (Rev 20:6; cf. 1 Cor 4:8) reign with Christ—i.e., are "kings"—until he comes to reign. The priestly function of believers continues through the millennial reign of Christ (Rev 20:6) but is not mentioned as being part of the perfection of the new heavens and new earth, when mortality will have ended, and sin will have been completely eliminated. There will be no need for the priesthood of believers after the Great White Throne judgment; "today" is the day of salvation (Heb 3:13).

PRINCE, PRINCESS A prince is a leader, an exalted person clothed with authority. A princess is the daughter or wife of a chief or king. There were princes of various nations (Matt 20:25), of (part of) the land of Canaan (Gen 34:2), of Ishmael's descendants (17:20; 25:16), of the Hittites (23:6), of Egypt (12:15), of the Philistines (1 Sam 18:30), of Persia (Esth 1:3; called "satraps" in Dan 3:2), of Babylon (Jer 39:13), of Tyre (Ezek 32:30), and of Meshech and Tubal (38:2). There were merchant princes in Tyre (Isa 23:8). The heads of the tribes or of the congregation of Israel were princes (Num 1:16; Josh 9:15). Jeroboam is called "leader" or "prince" (1 Kings 14:7), and David called Abner a prince (2 Sam 3:38). The enemies of Jesus called him Beelzebub, prince of the demons (Mark 3:22). The devil is the prince of this world (John 12:31). The personal spiritual powers of evil are princes (1 Cor 2:6; Eph 2:2). Messiah is the Prince (Dan 9:25): of Peace (Isa 9:6), of Life (Acts 3:15), of the kings of the earth (Rev 1:5). Bethlehem is called one of the princes of Judah (Matt 2:6) because the Davidic dynasty had its origin there.

Of princesses far less is said. Solomon had 700 princesses or women "of royal birth" as wives, in contrast with 300 concubines (1 Kings 11:3). Jerusalem is called a princess or queen (Lam 1:1). A king's daughter (Ps 45:9-13), a prince's daughter (Song of Songs 7:1), and daughter of a leader of Midian (Num 25:18) are mentioned. The new name of Abraham's wife, Sarah, means "princess" (Gen 17:15).

PRINCIPALITIES (Heb. *mera'ä-shôth, headparts,* Gr. *archē, first*). The Hebrew word is found only in Jeremiah 13:18. The KJV uses the word with reference to powerful angels and demons (e.g., Rom 8:38; Eph 6:12; Col 2:15).

PRISCILLA, PRISCA (prĭ-sĭl'à, prĭs'kà, Gr. *Priskilla, Priska*). Priscilla (diminutive of *Prisca,* Rom 16:3, see NIV footnote) was the wife of the Jewish Christian, Aquila, with whom she is always mentioned in the NT. They were tentmakers whom Paul met in Corinth (Acts 18:2); they instructed Apollos in Ephesus (18:24-26); Paul sent them greetings in Rome (Rom 16:3); they had a church in their house (1 Cor 16:19). In Romans 16:3-4 Paul praised not only their service but also their courage, and plainly stated that all the churches owed them a debt of gratitude.

PRISON A place where persons suspected, accused, or convicted of crime are kept. Joseph was thrown into a pit, while his brothers decided how to dispose of him (Gen 37:22-28), and into the Egyptian king's prison, in the house of the captain of the guard (39:20-40:7). Samson was confined in a Philistine prison at Gaza (Judg 16:21, 25). Prisoners taken in war were usually killed or enslaved (Num 21:1; Isa 20:4). Micaiah the prophet was put into prison (1 Kings 22:27; 2 Chron 18:26), and Jeremiah was subjected to long imprisonment (Jer 32:2; 33:1; 38:2-28). Kings were imprisoned by conquerors (2 Kings 17:4; 25:27, 29; Eccl 4:14; Jer 52:11, 33).

The pitiable state of those in prison is spoken of (Ps 79:11; Isa 14:17; 42:22; Lam 3:34; Zech 9:11), and sometimes their hope in God is declared (Pss 69:33; 102:20; 142:7; 146:7; Isa 42:7). John the Baptist was imprisoned for criticizing a king's marriage (Matt 4:12; 11:2; 14:3, 10); Peter and John were imprisoned for preaching about Jesus (Acts 4:3; 5:18-25); Peter was delivered by an angel (12:3-19). Paul led Christians to prison (8:3; 22:4; 26:10) and was himself often in prison (2 Cor 11:23): with Silas at Philippi (Acts 16:23-40), in Jerusalem (23:18), in Caesarea (25:27), and on shipboard (27:1, 42). He was under house arrest in his own rented dwelling (28:16-17, 30). He refers to his imprisonment as for the Lord (Eph

3:1; 4:1; Phil 1:14; 17; 2 Tim 1:8; Philem 9), and he mentions his fellow prisoners (Rom 16:7; Col 4:10). Barabbas was released from prison in place of Jesus (Matt 27:15-16). Jesus refers to imprisonment for debt (Matt 5:25; 18:30; Luke 12:58) and to visiting those in prison (Matt 25:36, 39, 43-44). He predicts that his followers will be put in prison during persecution (Luke 21:12; Rev 2:10). Peter expresses willingness to go to prison with Jesus (Luke 22:33). Disobedient spirits are now in prison (1 Peter 3:19-20); Satan will be imprisoned during the Millennium (Rev 20:1-7).

PROCONSUL (prō'kŏn-sŭl, Gr. *anthypatos*). A Roman official, generally of praetorian or consular rank, who served as deputy consul in the Roman provinces. The term of office was one year, though it could be longer in special instances, but the powers of the proconsul were unlimited in both the military and civil areas. Both Sergius Paulus, Paul's famous convert (Acts 13:7), and Gallio (18:12) were such officials. They are often called "deputy" in the English Bible.

PROCURATOR (prŏ'kŭ-rā'têr). The Latin term for the Greek *hēgemōn,* translated "governor" in KJV. Pilate, Felix, and Festus were such governors in Palestine with headquarters in Caesarea. Generally the procurators were appointed directly by the emperor to govern the Roman provinces and were often subject to the imperial legate of a large political area. Quirinius (Luke 2:2) was really not a procurator but an imperial legate of the larger province of Syria.

PROFANE (Heb. *hālal, to open* and Gr. *bebēloō, to desecrate*). The basic idea seems to be to desecrate or defile. For one to do what he was not allowed to do in connection with holy things or places was to profane them. Such things as the altar, the Sabbath, the sanctuary, and God's name could all be profaned. Esau was called a profane person (Heb 12:16; cf. 1 Tim 1:9).

PROFESSIONS (See OCCUPATIONS AND PROFESSIONS)

PROMISE (Heb. *dāvār, speaking, speech; dāvar, to speak; 'amar, to say; 'ōmer, speech;* Gr. *epaggelia, promise*). In the OT there is no Hebrew word corresponding to "promise"; the words "word," "speak," and "say" are used instead. In the NT, however, the word "promise" is often used, usually in the technical sense of God's design to visit his people redemptively in the person of his Son. This promise was first given in the *proto-evangelium* (Gen 3:15) and was repeated to Abraham (12:2, 7). It was given also to David when God declared that his house would continue on his throne (2 Sam 7:12–13, 28). It is found repeatedly in the OT (Isa 2:2–5; 4:2; 55:5). In the NT all these promises are regarded as having their fulfillment in Christ and his disciples (2 Cor 1:20; Eph 3:6). Jesus' promise of the Spirit was fulfilled at Pentecost. Paul makes clear that God's promises to Abraham's seed were meant not only for the circumcision but for all who have Abraham's faith (Rom 4:13–16). In the NT there are many promises of blessing to believers, among them the kingdom (James 2:5), eternal life (1 Tim 4:8), and Christ's coming (2 Peter 3:9).

PROPHETESS (Heb. *nevî'âh*, Gr. *prophētis*). A woman who exercised the prophetic gift in ancient Israel or in the early church. There are at least five women bearing this designation in the OT: (1) Miriam, sister of Moses (Exod 15:20); (2) Deborah (Judg 4:4); (3) Huldah (2 Kings 22:14); (4) Noadiah (Neh 6:14); and (5) the unnamed wife of Isaiah, whose children were given prophetic names by Isaiah (Isa 8:3). In the NT there was Anna (Luke 2:36), and Philip the evangelist's four daughters (Acts 21:8–9). After Pentecost the differentiation between sexes regarding prophetic gifts was removed (Acts 2:19; cf. Joel 2:28). See also PROPHETS.

PROPHETS One who is spokesman for God (Exod 4:15–16; 7:1), whether by vision or otherwise, and is given insight into the mind of God, and declares what he has "seen" as a message to the people. It is not the mysterious mode of reception of the prophetic revelation that is emphasized, but rather the deliverance of the message itself for God.

The biblical prophet must be distinguished from the *prophētēs* of the Greeks. The latter really acted as an *interpreter* for the muses and the oracles of the gods. The prophets, however, were not interpreters. They uttered the actual words that God had given to them, without any modification or interpretation on their part (Deut 18:18).

When Israel entered Canaan, it would find a people that sought to learn the future and the will of the gods by the practice of various superstitions, which the Bible calls "abominations" or "detestable ways" (Deut 18:9). To offset this danger the Lord declared that he would raise up the prophets and that the Israel-

ites were to listen to the prophets and to obey them (18:15). In this passage, Scripture points both to a great individual prophet, one who would be as significant and central to the people as was Moses at Sinai, and also to what we would call the successive line of prophets. Note that in verses 21–22 a test was given to distinguish the true prophet from the false. Just as later the people would wonder if the next Davidic king in line would be the promised Greater David, so also from the time of Moses onward there was expectation of the coming Mosaic prophet (cf. Deut 34:10), and each prophet who arose would be scrutinized (cf. John 1:21) to see if he were the one Moses predicted. By the order of prophets, the Lord enabled his people to walk into the unknown future with faith and obedience, trusting in the sovereign God, not, as the pagan, trying to secure and control the future by magic rites. See also MAGIC.

In ancient Greece we have the god, the oracle, the prophet, and the people. The same seems to have been the case in the Mesopotamian countries. In Israel, however, there was only one intermediary between God and the people, namely, the prophet. This arrangement was truly unique.

It is sometimes said that the prophets were forth-tellers and not foretellers. Such a separation, however, is not warranted. The prophets were both forth-tellers, speaking forth the message of the Lord, as well as announcing the future.

In the arrangement of the books of the Hebrew OT there are three parts—the Law, the Prophets, and the Writings. The division known as the Prophets is further subdivided into the former and the latter prophets. Under the first heading are included Joshua, Judges, 1–2 Samuel, and 1–2 Kings. These books are anonymous, their authors are not known. These books are rightly classified as "former prophets" because the history they contain conforms to the biblical definition of prophecy as a declaration of the wonderful works of God (Acts 2:11, 18). This does not mean they are less than true history, but that the process of selection of things to record was performed to show how God was at work in and for his people and how the moral principles of divine providence worked out over the centuries.

The latter prophets are also called writing prophets. They are the prophets who exercised so great a ministry in Israel—Isaiah, Jeremiah, Ezekiel, and the Twelve. The designation "latter" does not necessarily have reference to

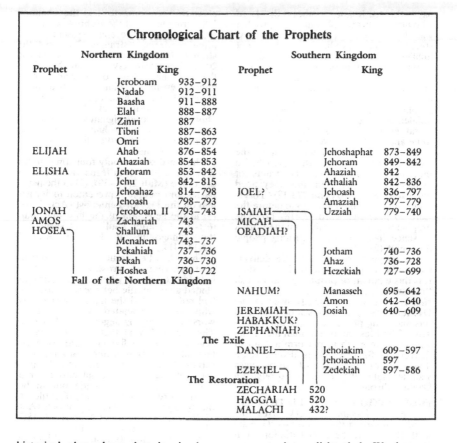

Chronological Chart of the Prophets

Northern Kingdom			Southern Kingdom		
Prophet	King		Prophet	King	
	Jeroboam	933–912			
	Nadab	912–911			
	Baasha	911–888			
	Elah	888–887			
	Zimri	887			
	Tibni	887–863			
	Omri	887–877			
ELIJAH	Ahab	876–854		Jehoshaphat	873–849
	Ahaziah	854–853		Jehoram	849–842
ELISHA	Jehoram	853–842		Ahaziah	842
	Jehu	842–815		Athaliah	842–836
	Jehoahaz	814–798	JOEL?	Jehoash	836–797
	Jehoash	798–793		Amaziah	797–779
JONAH	Jeroboam II	793–743	ISAIAH——┐	Uzziah	779–740
AMOS	Zachariah	743	MICAH——┐		
HOSEA┐	Shallum	743	OBADIAH?		
	Menahem	743–737		Jotham	740–736
	Pekahiah	737–736		Ahaz	736–728
	Pekah	736–730		Hezekiah	727–699
	Hoshea	730–722			
Fall of the Northern Kingdom			NAHUM?	Manasseh	695–642
				Amon	642–640
			JEREMIAH——┐	Josiah	640–609
			HABAKKUK?		
			ZEPHANIAH?		
The Exile			DANIEL——┐	Jehoiakim	609–597
				Jehoiachin	597
			EZEKIEL┐	Zedekiah	597–586
The Restoration			ZECHARIAH	520	
			HAGGAI	520	
			MALACHI	432?	

historical chronology, but is simply a designation of those prophetical books that follow the "former" prophets in the Hebrew arrangement of the OT. The "writing" prophets were not anonymous. The reason for this is that they were entrusted by God with the task and responsibility of addressing prophetical messages not only to the people of their own day but also to posterity; they must be accredited to their audience as genuine prophets.

The former and the latter prophets complemented one another. The "former" prophets set forth the history of a particular period in Israel's life; the "latter" prophets interpreted particular phases of that history. The one is necessary for the proper understanding of the other.

Schools of the prophets were raised up and served under Samuel. Following Samuel's death these prophetical bodies seem to have disbanded. We hear no more of them until the times of Elijah and Elisha. In Elijah's day they appear only in the northern kingdom. The designation "sons of the prophets" reveals the close and intimate association in which these men stood to the great prophets Elijah and Elisha. After this period, however, they seem to die out, and we hear no more of them.

Alongside the faithful and true prophets of the Lord there were others, men who had not received a revelation from God. Jeremiah refused to have anything to do with these men. They were not true prophets, but men who deceived.

In the OT there were three tests the people could apply in order to discern between the true and the false prophet. First, the theological test (Deut 13). Even if the prophet performed some sign to give validation to what he was saying, if his message contradicted Mosaic theology—the truth known about the Lord who brought his people out—the prophet was false. Second, the practical test (18:20ff.). The prediction that is not fulfilled has not come from the Lord. We ought to notice that this is a negative test. It does not say that fulfillment is proof that the Lord has spoken, for that might in fact be the evidence offered by a false prophet to validate his word. What is not fulfilled is not from the Lord. Third, the moral test (Jer 23:9ff.). This is a test first to be applied to the lives of the prophets themselves (23:13-14) and then to the tendency of the message they preach. Do they in fact strengthen the hands of evildoers, assuring them that they need not fear judgment to come (23:17)? This is a sure sign they have not stood before the Lord to hear his word (23:18-19). The prophet who comes fresh from the Lord's presence has a message turning people from evil (23:22).

The prophets spoke of future deliverance to be accomplished by the Messiah. It is this element of prophecy that we call "messianic prophecy." The word *Messiah* is itself not frequently used in the OT. It means "one who is anointed," and this anointing possesses an abiding character. The Messiah is a human individual who came to earth to perform a work of deliverance for God. He is also himself a divine person, as appears from passages such as Isaiah 9:5-6. He is to reign on David's throne.

PROPITIATION AND EXPIATION (Gr. *hilastērion, hilasmos*). KJV uses the word *propitiation* three times—"God set forth [Christ] to be a propitiation" (*hilastērion*, Rom 3:25); "[Christ] is the propitiation for our sins" (*hilasmos*, 1 John 2:2); "God . . . sent his Son to be the propitiation for our sins" (*hilasmos*, 4:10)—and NASB uses it a fourth time— "[Christ became a man] to make propitiation for the sins of the people" (*hilaskomai*, Heb 2:17)—in all of which RSV and NEB use *expiation* and NIV has either *sacrifice of atonement* or *atoning sacrifice*.

Propitiation and *expiation* are not synonyms; they are very different in meaning. Propitiation is something done to a person: Christ propitiated God in the sense that he turned God's wrath away from guilty sinners by enduring that wrath himself in the isolation of Calvary. Expiation is what is done to crimes or sins or evil deeds: Jesus provided the means to cancel, or cleanse, them.

PROSELYTE (prŏs′ĕ-līt). The Greek word *prosēlytos* (from the verb *proser-*

chomai, "to come to") is the common LXX translation of the Hebrew word *gēr*, which means a "foreign resident." It is often rendered "stranger," as in "thy stranger that is within thy gates" (Exod 20:10; Deut 5:14 KJV). Before NT times the word had come to apply to a more limited group religiously and a more extended group geographically. In the NT and the writings of Philo and Josephus the word designates a person of Gentile origin who had accepted the Jewish religion, whether living in Palestine or elsewhere.

The word occurs only four times in the KJV of the NT: (1) in Jesus' denunciatory discourse (Matt 23:1-39); (2) in the list of places and people represented in Jerusalem on the Day of Pentecost (Acts 2:10); (3) in the selection of the first diaconate (6:1-6); (4) after Paul's great sermon in the synagogue at Pisidian Antioch (13:14-41).

There has been much scholarly debate over whether all proselytes were fully initiated Jews or whether the term included also Gentile believers in God who had not accepted the initiatory rites, but who were associated with synagogue worship in varying degrees of fellowship. The probability is that the first-century Jews had no very fixed or rigid use of the term and that they differed among themselves. Judaism up to the time of Christ was not the narrow racial national religion it is sometimes made out to be. There were evidently many Gentiles in the synagogue at Pisidian Antioch (Acts 13:16, 26, 43, 50; cf. 10:2, 7; 16:14; 18:7; Matt 8:5-13; Luke 7:1-10).

Among the non-Israelite worshipers of the true God in the OT are Melchizedek, Job, Ruth, Rahab, Naaman, Uriah the Hittite, the Ninevites at the time of Jonah's preaching, and the converts at the time of Esther (Esth 8:17). The magi (Matt 2:1) are in the same category.

The following passages (Ps 15; Isa 2:2-4; 44:5; Jer 3:17; 4:2; 12:16; Zeph 3:9-10; Zech 8:20-23) are only a few of the OT passages indicating an evangelistic attitude toward the Gentiles.

PROSTITUTE A word that, along with "whore" and "harlot," is designated by four terms in the OT: (1) *zonah*, the most frequently used; (2) *qedēshâh*, a religious harlot, a priestess of a heathen religion in which fornication was part of worship (Gen 38:21-22; Deut 23:17); (3) *ishshah zarah*, or *zarah* alone, a "strange woman" (so KJV; NIV usually "wayward wife" or "adulteress"), a term found only in Proverbs; (4) *nokhriyah*, "stranger," "foreigner," a word also used in Proverbs, evidently also meaning "harlot." The NT word is *pornē* ("one sold," "fornicator").

Legal measures were in force concerning prostitutes. Parents were not to force their daughters into the practice (Lev 19:29), priests were not to marry harlots (21:7, 14), and the wages of prostitution were not to be brought into the temple to pay a vow (Deut 23:18).

The actual punishment of prostitutes was severe when enforced. In Genesis 38:24 Judah ordered Tamar to be burned for being a prostitute (until he came to see his own sin as worse than hers, v. 26). Leviticus 21:9 commanded burning for a priest's daughter who became a harlot. Deuteronomy 22:21 ordered stoning for a bride who was found not to be a virgin.

Such a common sin needed to be guarded against. The Book of Proverbs, which mentions every term for harlot except *qedēshâh*, teaches about and warns against prostitutes by admonition and illustrations. The situation in the Corinthian church was such that Paul had to give the Christians there special warnings against fornication with prostitutes (1 Cor 6:15–16).

The words harlot or prostitute, harlotry or prostitution, are used very often, especially in the prophetic books, to describe idolatry. This figurative use was evidently based on the idea that the Lord was the husband of the nation of Israel (Jer 3:20).

PROVERB A pithy saying, comparison, or question; in the OT usually Heb. *māshāl*, from a root meaning "represent," or "be like"; notably of Solomon's proverbs (1 Kings 4:32; Prov 1:1, 6; 10:1; 25:1; Eccl 12:9) and others (1 Sam 10:12; 24:13; Ezek 12:22–23; 16:44; 18:2–3). A person or a nation might become a proverb or a byword (Deut 28:37; 1 Kings 9:7; 2 Chron 7:20). In the NT, Greek *parabolē*, whose basic meaning is "comparison, placing side by side," is once translated "proverb" (Luke 4:23). Usually it is translated "parable"; a few times "comparison or figure." Greek *paroimia*, also equivalent to Hebrew *māshāl* and to *mîdhâh*, means a saying of popular origin, ancient and widely known, accepted as obviously true (2 Peter 2:22). A proverb is thought of as a short saying, a parable as a somewhat longer saying, but the distinction is relative and is not always observed by Bible writers. Comparison, using the concrete facts of life to represent its abstract principles, is the essential char-

acteristic of both. A proverb may be a snatch of poetry with parallel structure, a sharp question, a pithy sentence, or a very brief story.

PROVERBS, BOOK OF The best representative of the so-called Wisdom Literature of ancient Israel, the Book of Proverbs comprises 31 chapters of pithy statements on moral matters. Its text is "The fear of the LORD is the beginning of knowledge" (Prov 1:7).

The headings in Proverbs 1:1 and 10:1 claim a Solomonic authorship for the bulk of the book; and this claim has no objective evidence against it. The book is a survey of moral instruction, dealing with sin and holiness. And the vehicle of instruction is a favorite Semitic device—teaching by contrast.

Outline:

I. **Introduction (1:1–9)**

II. **Sin and Righteousness Personified and Contrasted (1:10–9:18)**

III. **Single-Verse Contrasts of Sin and Righteousness (10:1–22:16)**

IV. **Miscellaneous and Longer Contrasts (22:17–29:27)**

V. **Righteousness in Poems of Climax (30:1–33:31)**

The first section of the book begins (Prov 1:7) and ends (9:10) with the statement that "the fear of the LORD is the beginning of knowledge" and "wisdom." Thus the wisdom extolled in Proverbs is not just a high degree of intelligence but a moral virtue. This is made plain in the first section by the contrasts involved. Wisdom is personified as a righteous woman (8:1). This is natural because *wisdom* is a feminine noun in Hebrew. The foolish woman is depicted as using words similar to those of wisdom, to invite men into her house (9:4, 16), but she invites them to sin. The harlot, who is given prominence in this section, represents all sin. Murder and theft are the opposite of wisdom in chapter 1, but usually the harlot (also called the strange woman, the simple woman, or the foolish woman) is held up as the opposite of personified righteousness. Some find Christ personified in the wisdom cited in Proverbs 8:22.

In the major section (10:1–22:16), the same contrast appears in single-verse aphorisms. Here the personification of sin and righteousness does not appear, but the same synonyms for virtue and vice are repeatedly used and should be understood as such. "Folly" here does not mean stupidity, just as "the woman of folly" (9:13) does not refer to an ignoramus. Both terms refer to sin. Through this whole section the terms *wisdom, understanding, integrity,* and *knowledge* are synonymous terms referring to holiness. Their opposites, *fool, folly, simple, mocker, quarrelsome,* etc., refer to wickedness. In short, a "foolish son" is not a dullard, but a scoundrel. A "mocker" is not just proud, but is a rebel against wisdom. But occasionally a verse is partially repeated elsewhere, where the variant form clarifies the meaning (cf. 27:15 with 21:19).

Section IV (22:19–29:27) is more general but uses the same vocabulary of morality.

The last section (30:1–31:31) includes several climactic proverbs that apparently emphasize the fourth point (cf. 6:16–19, where among seven things the seventh is the climax). Here also is the famous final poem—an alphabetical poem—extolling the wife of noble character.

PROVIDENCE The universal providence of God is the basic assumption of all Scripture. The meaning is "prearrangement." As used historically the theological term "providence" means nothing short of "the universal sovereign rule of God."

The definition of the answer to Question 11 of the Westminster Shorter Catechism expresses the view of all Bible-believing Christians: "God's works of providence are his most holy, wise and powerful preserving and governing all his creatures, and all their actions." Divine providence is the outworking of the divine decrees, which are "the plan of him who works out everything in conformity with the purpose of his will" (Eph 1:11).

The biblical doctrine of divine providence does not imply a mechanistic or fatalistic view of the processes of the world or of human life. This may best be summed up by a quote from The Westminster Confession. "Although, in relation to the foreknowledge and decree of God, the first cause, all things come to pass immutably and infallibly, yet, by the same providence, he ordereth them to fall out according to the nature of second causes, either necessarily, freely, or contingently.

"God's providence includes the permission of all . . . sins of angels and men, and that not a bare permission, but such permission as hath joined with it a most wise and powerful bounding, and other-

wise ordering and governing of them, in a manifold dispensation, to his holy ends; yet so as the sinfulness thereof proceedeth only from the creature, and not from God; who, being most holy and righteous, neither is nor can be the author or approver of sin" (Westminster Confession, ch. V., paragraphs II and IV).

"Second causes" are the ordinary forces and events of nature that God usually employs to accomplish his purposes. That God's providence includes his decree to permit sin should not seem strange or paradoxical (Gen 50:20).

It is customary to distinguish *special* providence from *general* providence. The former term refers to God's particular care over the life and activity of the believer (Ps 37:23; Rom 8:28; Phil 1:28). The entire Book of Job is devoted to the temporal sufferings of a godly man under divine providence. Hebrews 11:40 tells us that providence, for men of faith, includes something far better than experiences of this life. General providence includes the government of the entire universe, but especially of the affairs of men (Deut 10:14; 32:8; cf. Neh 9:6; Dan 4:35).

Although God's grace is always offered to all people (Acts 10:34–35), yet the *main stream* of historical revelation and blessing for the world, through the instrumentality of Israel and the church, is a principal line of all Scripture (7:1–60; 13:16–43; Rom 3:1–2; 9:3–6; 11:1; 1 Tim 3:15; cf. Heb 11:38a). To this end God sometimes moves in unrecognized events and processes (Isa 40:1–5; 44:28–45:4).

Not only is the general course of nature sustained by God's providence, but the moral order and its logical consequences are as well (Gal 6:7–8). Divine providence sustaining the moral order is the principal theme of the Book of Proverbs.

The distinction between God's immanent or natural action and his transcendent or supernatural action is of supreme importance in the understanding of the doctrine of providence. See MIRACLES. The case of Christianity depends entirely on the miracles of the incarnation and the resurrection of Christ. Nevertheless, as the article on miracles shows, godly faith has always existed in a world in which there are long periods of time, even in Bible history, in which God does not choose to give "signs" or display miracles as evidences. It is imperative that we learn to see the glory of God in the regular works of providence as well as in the miraculous.

PROVINCE The sphere of duty of a magistrate. The "roads and forest of Italy" for example, were a *province*, supervised by the appropriate commissioner. With the empire's gradual acquisition of new lands, spheres of magisterial duty signified increasingly the defense, organization, and government of distant territories; and the word *province* acquired the geographical significance that became its prime Latin meaning and its exclusive derived meaning. All provinces were divided into two categories. First there were the imperial provinces, those that required a frontier army and that, in consequence, were kept under the control of the emperor, who was commander-in-chief of all armed forces. Second there were the senatorial provinces, those that presented no major problems of military occupation or defense and that were left in the control of the Senate. Imperial provinces were governed by the emperor's *legati* or, in the case of smaller units like Judea or Thrace, by procurators. The senatorial provinces were under a "proconsul" (NIV) or "deputy" (KJV); see Acts 13:7.

PROVOCATION (prŏv'ō-kā'shŭn, Heb. *ka' as, mārâh*, Gr. *parazeloō, parorgizō*). Any cause of God's anger at sin; the deeds of evil kings (1 Kings 15:30; 21:22; 2 Kings 23:26), of Israel (Ezek 20:28), or mockers (Job 17:2). In their prayer of repentance the returned exiles mentioned the disobedience, rebellion, and idolatry of Israel and pleaded for mercy (Neh 9:18, 26, 36–37). In Psalm 95:8 ASV, RSV, and NIV transliterate instead of translating Hebrew *Meribah*, the geographical location named for the provocation when the Israelites demanded water, which Moses brought out of the rock (Exod 17:1–7; Num 20:13, 24; 27:14; Deut 32:51; 33:8; Ps 81:7), the waters of Meribah. The one NT passage in which (in KJV) *provocation* occurs (Heb 3:8, 15–16 NIV "rebellion") relates to this incident. The verb *provoke* occasionally has a good sense, "to stir up" (Heb 10:24).

PRUNING HOOK (Heb. *mazmerôth*). An agricultural tool used in the cultivation of the vine, with a sharp knifelike end for pruning (Isa 2:4; Joel 3:10; Mic 4:3).

PSALMS, BOOK OF The longest book in the Bible follows "the Law" and "the Prophets" in the Hebrew OT (Luke 24:44) and begins the final division of the OT, called "the Writings" (see CANON). The majority of its chapters, moreover, are preceded in time only by Genesis–

Ruth. But the basic reason why Psalms is more often quoted by the NT and more revered by Christians than any other OT book is found in its inspiring subject matter. Both for public worship—"the hymnbook of Solomon's temple"—and for individual devotional guidance, its 150 poems constitute the height of God-given literature.

The Hebrew designation of Psalms is *Tehillîm*, meaning "praises," a term that reflects much of the book's content (cf. Ps 145, title). Its name in Latin and English Bibles, however, comes from the Greek, *Psalmoi*, which means "twangings [of harp strings]," and then, as a result, songs sung to the accompaniment of harps. Its alternate title, *Psalterion*, means "psaltery," a collection of harp songs, from which comes the English term "Psalter."

Many psalms prefix explanatory titles in prose, indicating their authorship and occasion for writing, often giving poetic and musical direction as well. The phrase, Psalm of Moses (David, etc.), appears most commonly. The Hebrew preposition rendered by the word "of" expresses authorship (cf. Hab 3:1) or

A page of Psalms, beginning with the 23rd, from the King James Version, 1611. Courtesy The British Library

dedication (e.g., Ps 4, "For the director of music"). The Book of Psalms assigns 73 of its chapters to David, two to Solomon (Pss 72, 127), one each to the wise men Heman and Ethan (Pss 88, 89; cf. 1 Kings 4:31), one to Moses (Ps 90), and 23 to Levitical singing clans of Asaph (Pss 50, 73–83) and Korah (Pss 42–49, 84–85, 87–88). Forty-nine remain anonymous.

The NT repeatedly authenticates ascriptions to David: Psalms 16 (Acts 2:25), 32 (Rom 4:6), 69 (Acts 1:16; Rom 11:9), 110 (Luke 20:42; Acts 2:34). Some of the anonymously titled psalms are also recognized as of Davidic composition: Psalms 2 (Acts 4:25), 95 (Heb 4:7), 96, 105, 106 (underlying David's words in 1 Chron 16:8–36, though cf. HDB, IV:148). But it is significant that no psalm that claims *other* authorship, or contains later historical allusions (as Ps 137, exilic) is ever attributed in Scripture to him.

The titles of 14 of the Davidic psalms designate specific occasions of composition and contribute to a historical understanding of Scripture as follows (chronologically):

Psalm 59 (= 1 Sam 19:11) sheds light on David's envious associates (59:12).

Psalm 56 (1 Sam 21:11) shows how David's fear at Gath led to faith (56:3).

Psalm 34 (1 Sam 21:13) illuminates God's subsequent goodness (34:6–8).

Psalm 142 (1 Sam 22:1) depicts David at Adullam, persecuted (142:6).

Psalm 52 (1 Sam 22:9) emphasizes Saul's wickedness (52:1).

Psalm 54 (1 Sam 23:19) judges the Ziphites (54:3).

Psalm 57 (1 Sam 24:3) concerns En Gedi, when Saul was caught in his own trap (57:6).

Psalm 7 (1 Sam 24:9) introduces slanderous Cush (7:3, 8 correspond to 1 Sam 24:11–12).

Psalm 18 (2 Sam 7:1) is repeated in 2 Samuel 22.

Psalm 60 (2 Sam 8:13–14) illumines the dangerous Edomitic campaign (60:10; 1 Kings 11:15).

Psalm 51 (2 Sam 12:13–14) elaborates on David's guilt with Bathsheba.

Psalm 3 (2 Sam 15:16) depicts David's faith versus Absalom's treachery (3:5).

Psalm 63 (2 Sam 16:2) illumines the king's eastward flight (63:11).

Psalm 30 (2 Sam 24:25; cf. 1 Chron 22:1) reviews David's sin prior to his dedication of the temple area (30:5–6).

Among the remaining psalms that ascribe authorship, the 23 composed by Israel's singers exhibit widely separated backgrounds, since these Levitical clans continued active in postexilic times (Ezra 2:41). Most of them concern the Davidic or Solomonic periods. Psalm 83, however, suits the ministry of the Asaphite Jahaziel in 852 B.C. (cf. 83:5–8 with 2 Chron 20:1–2, 14), while Psalms 74, 79, and the concluding strophe of Psalms 88, 89 were produced by Asaphites and Korahites who survived the destruction of Jerusalem in 586 (74:3, 8–9; 79:1; 89:44). A few anonymous psalms stem from the Exile (Ps 137), from the return to Judah in 537 (107:2–3; 126:1), or from Nehemiah's rebuilding of Jerusalem's walls in 444 (147:13). Yet others that depict tragedy could as easily relate to the disorders of Absalom's revolt or to similar Davidic calamities (cf. 102:13–22; 106:41–47). Liberal scholars once spoke confidently of numerous Maccabean psalms (second century B.C.); but the discovery of the Dead Sea Scrolls, which date from this very period and contain manuscripts of both the canonical psalms and secondary psalmodic compositions, establishes the Persian era as the latest possible point for inspired psalmody. It reinforces the evangelical hypothesis of Ezra as the writer of 1–2 Chronicles (the last book in the Hebrew Bible) and as compiler of the entire Jewish canon, shortly after 424 (Darius II, mentioned in Neh 12:22).

Psalms is organized into five books: 1–41, 42–72, 73–89, 90–106, and 107–150; and, since the same psalm appears in more than one collection—e.g., Pss 14 and part of 40 (Book I) as 53 and 70 (Book II), and the latter halves of 57 and 60 (Book II) as 108 (Book V)—it seems likely that each compilation originally experienced independent existence. Furthermore, since the last psalm of each collection was composed with terminal ascriptions that were designed for the book as a whole (41:13; 72:18–20; 89:52; 106:48; and the entire 150th Psalm for Book V), it appears that the origins of these five concluding psalms provide clues for the compilation of their respective books.

Each of the 150 psalms exhibits the formal character of Hebrew poetry. This consists, not primarily in rhyme, or even rhythmic balance, but rather in a parallelism of thought, whereby succeeding phrases either repeat or in some way elaborate the previous line. The poems vary in content.

Particularly significant are the 17 specifically messianic psalms, in the whole or in parts of which Christ either is referred to in the third person (8:4–8; 72:6–17; 89:3–4, 28–29, 34–36; 109:6–19; 118:22; 132:11–12), is addressed in

the second person (45:6-7; 68:18;
102:25-27; 110), or speaks himself in the
first person (2; 16:10; 22; 40:6-8; 41:9;
69:4, 21, 25; 78:2).

Psalm titles in Books I-III contain a
number of musical terms in Hebrew.
Some of these designate ancient melo-
dies, to which the poems may have been
sung: "The Doe of the Morning" (Ps 22);
"Do Not Destroy," probably a vintage
song (Pss 57-59, 75; cf. Isa 65:8); "A
Dove on Distant Oaks" (Ps 56); "The
Death of the Son" (Ps 9); "Lilies" (Pss
45, 69); and "The Lily of the Covenant"
(Pss 60, 80). Others preserve musical
instructions, much of the significance of
which is now uncertain: *alamoth*,
"maidens, treble" (?) (Ps 46), perhaps
contrasted with *sheminith*, "[lower] octave" (Pss 6, 12); *gittith*, "the instrument
from Gath"(?) (Pss 8, 81, 84); *mahalath*
(*leannoth*), "grief" (for afflicting) (Pss 53,
88); *neginoth*, "stringed instruments"
(seven times, plus Hab 3:19); *nehiloth*,
"for flutes" (Ps 5); and Selah (71 times,
not in titles but at the end of strophes; cf.
3:2, 4, 8), perhaps indicating a dramatic
pause for musical effects (cf. *Higgaion*,
Selah, "meditation pause" (?) in 9:16). A
number of Israel's psalms had specific
liturgical usage. The "songs of ascents"
(Pss 120-134) may have been chanted by
pilgrims ascending to Jerusalem (cf.
121:1; 122:4). Psalm 92 was composed for
Sabbath use. The "Hallel" ("praise")
psalms (113-118) accompanied the Passover (cf. Matt 26:30), and the psalms that
begin, "The Lord reigns" (Pss 93-100)
constitute a liturgical series magnifying
God's sovereignty.

While certain poems exhibit group expression (particularly among the pilgrim
songs, 124, 126, even when using "I,"
129), others manifest distinctly individualistic consciousness (Pss 1, 21, 112,
127). The compilation embraces not simply the congregational hymnbook of Solomon's temple, but also the devotional
heartbeat of men like David (1 Sam 30:6).
The richest blessings of the Psalms flow
from their affirmations of personal faith
(Ps 23:1).

PSALMODY, PSALTER, PSALTERY
(See MUSIC AND MUSICAL INSTRUMENTS;
PSALMS, BOOK OF)

PSEUDEPIGRAPHA (sū'dē-pĭg'rà-fà).
Intertestamental books not in the Hebrew
canon or the Apocrypha, ascribed to
earlier authors. They include The Ascension of Isaiah, Assumption of Moses,
Book of Enoch, Book of Jubilees, Greek
Apocalypse of Baruch, Letters of Aristeas, 3 and 4 Maccabees, Psalms of

Solomon, Secrets of Enoch, Sibylline
Oracles, Syriac Apocalypse of Baruch,
Epistle of Baruch, and Testament of the
Twelve Patriarchs. They are important
for their disclosure of Jewish ideas in the
intertestamental period.

PTOLEMAIS (See ACCO)

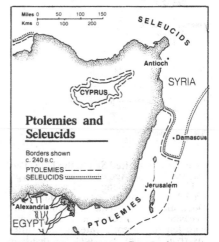

PTOLEMY (tŏl'ĕ-mē, Gr. *Ptolemaios*).
The common name of the 15 Macedonian
kings of Egypt whose dynasty extended
from the death of Alexander the Great in
323 B.C. to the murder of the young
Caesarion, son of Julius Caesar and Cleopatra, at Octavian's orders in 30. The first
Ptolemy, surnamed Soter, 367 to 282,
was a distinguished officer of Alexander.
He became satrap of Egypt in 323, but
converted his command into a kingdom in
305. As a successor of the pharaohs,
Ptolemy I took over the ancient administration of Egypt, and especially the ownership of the land. His vast and highly
centralized bureaucracy, which became a
permanent feature of Ptolemaic rule, prepared the way for the Roman imperial
administration of Egypt and contrasted
with the Hellenistic policies of the rival
Seleucid regime in Syria.

In the reign of Ptolemy II there first
erupted the long rivalry with the Seleucids of Syria over the Palestinian frontier.
Ptolemy II also instituted the cult of the
divine ruler, a preparation for Caesar
worship. The great city of Alexandria
grew during this reign. Ptolemy II built
the amazing Pharos lighthouse outside
the twin harbors, and the Museum, the
most notable center of culture and literature in the ancient world. He established
the famous library of Alexandria and cut

Ptolemies and Seleucids

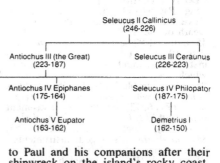

Ptolemy I Lagi Soter
(323-285 B.C.)

Ptolemy II Philadelphus
(285-246)

Ptolemy III Euergetes I
(246-221)

Ptolemy IV Philopator
(221-203)

Ptolemy V Epiphanes ◄·····[m.] Cleopatra I
(203-181)

Ptolemy VI Philometor
(181-146)

Seleucus I Nicator
(311-280 B.C.)

Antiochus I Soter
(280-261)

Berenice [m.]·····► Antiochus II Theos ◄·····[m.] Laodice
(261-246)

Seleucus II Callinicus
(246-226)

Antiochus III (the Great)   Seleucus III Ceraunus
(223-187)   (226-223)

Antiochus IV Epiphanes   Seleucus IV Philopator
(175-164)   (187-175)

Antiochus V Eupator   Demetrius I
(163-162)   (162-150)

a canal from the Red Sea to the Nile. This was the Golden Age of Ptolemaic Egypt.

The wife of Ptolemy XIII was Cleopatra VII, the famous bearer of the name. Domestic, and consequently political and dynastic, strife between husband and wife led to Caesar's intervention, after his rival Pompey had met his death in Egypt. Ptolemy XIV was an insignificant brother of Cleopatra, and Ptolemy XV was her ill-fated son by Caesar.

The great achievement of the Ptolemies was Alexandria, with all that its immense cultural institutions signified in the ancient world. Alexandria was creative and conservative. It preserved much of the literature of Greece and would have preserved more if Islam had not engulfed the land. It produced great writers and scientists and fathered the Septuagint. It created "Alexandrianism," which means much in the literature of Rome. Alexandria always stood apart from Egypt. It was a Greek city, and its peculiar contribution to Hellenism was the gift to history and civilization of the first Ptolemies.

PUAH (pū'à, Heb. *pû'âh*). **1.** A member of the clan of Tola, of the tribe of Issachar (Num 26:23; Judg 10:1). **2.** One of the Hebrew midwives who refused to obey the edict of Pharaoh to destroy the infant sons born of Hebrew women (Exod 1:15–20).

PUBLICAN (See OCCUPATIONS AND PROFESSIONS)

PUBLIUS (pŭb'lĭ-ŭs, Gr. *Poplios*). The chief person on the island of Malta in the Mediterranean. He gave lodging and food

to Paul and his companions after their shipwreck on the island's rocky coast. Paul healed the man's father and many others (Acts 27:27–44; 28:7–10).

PUHITES (See PUTHITES)

PUITES (pū'īts, Heb. *pûnî*). Descendants of Puah, of the tribe of Issachar (Gen 46:13; Num 26:23; 1 Chron 7:1). KJV "Punites."

PUL (pŭl, pūl). **1.** A king of Assyria, Tiglath-Pileser III, who invaded Israel in the days of Menahem and was bribed to depart (2 Kings 15:19), though he carried off captives (1 Chron 5:26). **2.** A tribe or place in Africa, named between Tarshish and Lud (Isa 66:19 KJV).

PUNISHMENT Death was the punishment for the following sins: striking or even reviling a parent (Exod 21:15–17), blasphemy (Lev 24:14, 16, 23), Sabbath-breaking (Num 15:32–36), witchcraft (Exod 22:18), adultery (Lev 20:10), rape (Deut 22:25), incestuous or unnatural connection (Lev 20:11, 14, 16), kidnapping (Exod 21:16), and idolatry (Lev 20:2). Being cut off from the people meant excommunication or outlawry; it meant forfeiture of the privileges of the covenant people (18:29). The hand of God executed the sentence in some cases (Lev 23:30; 20:3; Num 4:15, 18, 20). Capital punishment was by stoning (Deut 22:24), burning (Lev 20:14), the sword (Exod 32:27), hanging (the hanged were accounted accursed, so were buried at evening, as the hanging body defiled the land [2 Sam 21:6, 9; Gal 3:13]), and strangulation (not in Scripture, but in rabbinical writings). Other cruel treatment, including torturous methods of killing, were sawing people in two (Heb 11:37); consigning to hard labor (2 Sam 12:31); throwing people from a cliff (2 Chron 25:12; Luke 4:29); flogging (only 40 lashes were allowed [Deut 25:2–3], therefore, to be safe, only 39 were given [2 Cor 11:24]). The convict who was to be flogged was stripped to the waist and was then given lashes from a three-thonged whip while either lying on the ground (Deut 25:2) or tied to a pillar in a bent position. If the one flogging exceeded the allowed or prescribed number of lashes, he was punished. People who committed crimes against others were often punished in kind (*lex talionis*—Exod 21:23–25), including also the recompense of time or restitution of an article or its equivalent (21:19, 30). Slander of a wife's honor was punished by a fine and flogging (Deut 22:18–19). Crucifixion was not practiced until Roman times. Punishment for sin is widely recognized in the Bible and is in the hands of God (directly, Gen 4:1–16; Lam 3:37–39; 4:6; Zech 14:19; indirectly, 1 Peter 2:14; in everlasting punishment, Matt 25:46).

PUNISHMENT, EVERLASTING (See ESCHATOLOGY)

PUNITES (See PUITES)

PUR (See PURIM)

PURAH (pū'rà, Heb. *purâh, branch*). A servant of Gideon who went down with him to spy on the army of Midian (Judg 7:10–11).

PURE (See CLEAN)

PURIFICATION The attitude to purification of the Jews as a whole, and of the Pharisees as a class, is expressed in Mark 7:3–4. Religious purity was both ceremonial and ethical. Under the Mosaic Law, ceremonial purification was required for four acts: (1) the birth of a child, removed through circumcision (if male) and through the isolation of the mother for a varying period (Lev 12:2ff.); (2) contact with a corpse, the offering of a red heifer being prescribed for sacrifice of purification (Num 19:1–10); (3) certain diseases, such as leprosy (Lev 13:8); and (4) uncleanness due to a running sore (Lev 15). Family purity was guarded through strict regulations concerning sex (Lev 20:1–21; Deut 22:20–21). In the NT, though the emphasis shifts from the outward to the inner, the basic requirements for purity itself remain unchanged (Matt 5:27–28; 19:3–9; Mark 10:2–11; 1 Cor 5:9–13; 6:18–20; 7:8ff.).

PURIM (pūr'ĭm, Heb. *pûrîm, lots*). A Jewish festival celebrated on the 14th and 15th of the month Adar (Feb.–March), commemorating the deliverance of the Hebrews from the murderous plans of the wicked Haman in the postexilic period (Esth 3:7; 9:26). This festival is named from the casting of the lot to determine the most favorable time for the mass murder of the Jews.

PURITY (See CLEAN; PURIFICATION)

PURPLE (Heb. *'argāmān*, Gr. *porphyra*). (Exod 25:4; 26:36; 28:15; Judg 8:26; 2 Chron 2:14; 3:14; Esth 1:6; 8:15; Song of Songs 3:10; Mark 15:17–20; Luke 16:19; Acts 16:14.) Purple was a costly dye extracted from a small gland of a marine mollusk. The Book of Exodus lists extensive use of purple in the tabernacle and for the priests' garments. Because of its costliness, purple robes were normally worn by royalty. In very ancient times the common people of Sumerian civilization were forbidden on pain of punishment to wear purple. Jesus was dressed in mockery at his trial in a robe of purple (Mark 15:17). Lydia, Paul's first European convert, was a seller of purple (Acts 16:14), i.e., the purple dye.

PURSE (Gr. *ballantion*). A rather finely finished leather pouch or bag that served as a "purse" in ancient times. The term translated "purse" in Matthew 10:9 KJV (NIV "belts") is the Greek word *zōnē* and refers to the Middle Eastern girdle made of crude leather or woven camel's hair worn around the waist. Sometimes these "girdles" were finely tooled and contained "slots" in which gold and silver coins could be kept. If the "girdle" was made of cloth, then the money was placed within the folds themselves (cf. Luke 10:4; 12:34).

PUT (pŭt, Heb. *pût*). The third son of Ham (Gen 10:6; 1 Chron 1:8). His descendants are not named. A comparison of translations of Hebrew *pût* in KJV, ASV, RSV, and NIV reveals the difficulty of locating Put (Isa 66:19; Jer 46:9; Ezek 27:10; 30:5; 38:5; Nah 3:9). The question is partly textual, whether there is confusion between Put and Pul (Isa 66:19), between Ludim and Lubim; partly etymological, whether the word is of Egyptian origin; partly involved in the location of lands with which Put is associated. Some locate Put west of Egypt on the North African coast; some in Nubia; others east of Somaliland, on both sides of the Red Sea, in both Africa and Asia. Genesis 10:6, which names Put between two African lands, Cush (Ethiopia) and

Mizraim (Egypt), and Asian Canaan, suggests the ambiguity, and no other reference removes it. The men of Put were valued mercenary soldiers of Tyre (Ezek 27:10) and Egypt (Jer 46:9). They used shield (Jer 46:9) and helmet (Ezek 38:5), probably also the bow (Isa 66:19). Possibly there were settlements of them in widely scattered places. Certainly they traveled far to fight. See also PUL.

PUTEOLI (pū-tē′ō-lē, Gr. *Potioloi, little wells* or *springs*). A well-known seaport of Italy located in the Bay of Naples; it was the nearest harbor to Rome. It was the natural landing place for travelers from the East to Rome. In Acts 28:13–14 Luke reports that Paul landed there with the other prisoners when he was taken to Rome for trial. Paul and Luke and their party found Christian brothers there and enjoyed their hospitality for seven days before going on to Rome. The old ruins may still be seen in the northern part of the bay, including part of a pier Paul is supposed to have used.

PUTHITES (pū′thits, Heb. *pûthî, simple*). A family descended from Caleb, residing in Kiriath Jearim (1 Chron 2:50, 53).

PUVAH (See PUAH)

PYGARG (See ANIMALS)

PYTHON (See ANIMALS)

QUAIL (See Birds)

QUARRIES (Heb. *pesîlîm, graven images*). The "quarries" are mentioned in a doubtful passage (Judg 3:19, 26 KJV). The marginal readings in KJV and ASV suggest "graven images," a rendering supported by the authority of LXX and Vulgate. RSV has "sculptured stones," NIV "idols." Perhaps the place was a dump for discarded and roughly broken idols. Perhaps the reference is to Joshua's stones of commemoration by Jordan. The word "quarry" occurs in another disputed passage at 1 Kings 6:7. RSV and NIV say that the stones or blocks were dressed "at the quarry." NIV uses the English word in a less doubtful context elsewhere (e.g., Eccl 10:9; Isa 51:1).

QUATERNION (kwȧ-tĕr′nĭ-ŭn, Gr. *tetradion*). A detachment of four men (Acts 12:4). The "four quaternions" (KJV; NIV "four squads of four soldiers each"), to whom the prisoner was committed, were the four patrols who took the four watches of the night. Two, no doubt, watched inside and two outside the guardhouse.

QUEEN Dowager queens, or mothers of the monarch, are those who appear in the most influential roles in the biblical records: (1) Jezebel, princess of Tyre who, during the 22 years of her husband Ahab's reign and during the 13 years of the reigns of her sons Ahaziah and Joram, exercised a strong influence in favor of Phoenician pagan cults (1 Kings 16:28– 2 Kings 9:37, passim). (2) Athaliah, the daughter of Jezebel and of similar character, was the wife of Jehoram of Judah, son of Jehoshaphat. On the accession of her son Ahaziah (not to be confused with Ahaziah of Israel, his uncle), Athaliah exercised a dominant authority and after Ahaziah's assassination held the throne alone, securing her position by dynastic massacre (2 Kings 11). (3) Bathsheba, mother of Solomon, widow of David and Uriah, demonstrated her decisive character as her husband David lay dying (1 Kings 1).

The foreign queens mentioned in the OT are (1) Vashti, the queen that Xerxes (KJV Ahasuerus) of Persia deposed (Esth 1), (2) Esther, the Jewess, Vashti's successor, a brave woman whose situation, nonetheless, violated the tenets of the law and demonstrated the compromised position of those who took no part in the

Elaborate headdress and other twenty-fifth century B.C. jewelry of Queen Shub-ad on a model's head. The jewels, among the oldest discovered, were found with the crushed skull of the queen at Ur. The pieces include four gold diadems, nine yards of gold band, seven-pointed gold comb, lunate earrings, and a necklace of small gold and lapis beads with rosette-shaped pendant. Courtesy University Museum, University of Pennsylvania

movements of restoration headed by Ezra and Nehemiah, (3) Balkis, legendary name of the Queen of Sheba (1 Kings 10), and (4) unnamed queens referred to in Nehemiah 2:6 and Daniel 5:10.

In the NT are (1) Bernice, or Berenice, sister of Agrippa II and wife of her uncle, Herod, king of Chalcis (Acts 25–26), and (2) Drusilla, wife of Azizus, king of Emesa, whom she deserted to become the third wife of Felix, procurator of Judea (Acts 24).

QUEEN OF HEAVEN (Heb. *melekheth ha-shāmayim*). Perhaps the female deity to whom, with their families' aid and connivance, Hebrew women made offerings (Jer 7:18; 44:17–25). The most likely identification is with Ashtoreth, goddess of love and fertility, synonymous with the Assyrian and Babylonian Ishtar and the Roman Venus. The "mourning for Tammuz" was associated with her cult (Ezek

8:14). Its ritual was the license and obscenity characteristic of the eastern fertility cults, ever a temptation to the Hebrews and the chief objective of the prophets' attack on paganism.

QUICKSANDS (See SYRTIS)

QUIET, QUIETNESS. Followers of Christ are encouraged to live (1 Thess 4:11) and work quietly (2 Thess 3:12), those who speak in tongues should remain silent if there is no interpreter present (1 Cor 14:28), a prophet speaking in church is to stop speaking if another prophet gets a revelation (1 Cor 14:30), and women are to have a quiet spirit (1 Peter 3:4) and to remain silent in church (1 Cor 14:34; 1 Tim 2:11, 12).

QUIRINIUS (kwĭ-rĭn'ĭ-ŭs, Gr. *Kyrēnios*). Quirinius (Luke 2:2) was governor of Syria A.D. 6–9. Judea was incorporated at the time and a census was taken that caused the rebellion of Judas (Acts 5:37). Evidence from Egypt has established the 14-year cycle of the census in that province, and fixes A.D. 20 as a census year. This fixes Quirinius' census in A.D. 6 and demands 9 or 8 B.C. for an earlier occasion, or at least 7 or 6 B.C. The difficulty then arises that Sentius Saturninus, and not Quirinius, was governing Syria from 9 to 7 B.C., and Quinctilius Varus from 6 to 4 B.C. A clue to a solution lies in an inscription that states that P. Sulpicius Quirinius governed Syria twice. W. M. Ramsay offers the best solution to this puzzle. He suggests that Quirinius was in control of the foreign relations of Syria during the war with the Cilician hill tribe of the Homonadenses in 6 B.C. An enrollment in Herod's kingdom would thus be supervised by him. The enrollment could have taken place in the autumn of 5 B.C., postponed by the dying Herod's procrastination.

QUIVER (Heb. *'ashpāh, telî*). As a case for carrying arrows, a quiver was used by soldiers (Job 39:23; Isa 22:6; Jer 5:16; Lam 3:13) and by hunters (Gen 27:3). The man who has many children is like the quiver that is full of arrows (Ps 127:4–5), and the servant of Jehovah says that he has been hidden in Jehovah's quiver (Isa 49:2).

QUMRAN (See DEAD SEA SCROLLS)

RA (See EGYPT)

RAAMAH (rā'à-mà, Heb. *ra'mā'*). A son of Cush and grandson of Ham (1 Chron 1:9); the father of Sheba and Dedan (Gen 10:7; cf. 1 Chron 1:9). The prophet Ezekiel identifies Raamah as one of the merchant tribes that traded in spices, gold, and precious stones with Tyre (Ezek 27:22).

RAAMSES (See RAMESES)

RABBAH, RABBATH (răb'à, Heb. *rabbâh*; in KJV twice "Rabbath" [Deut 3:11; Ezek 21:20]). The full name is *rabbath benê 'ammôn*, "Rabbah of the children of Ammon." It was the only city of the Ammonites to receive mention in Scripture. Rabbath lay east of the Jordan and was not assigned to the tribe of Gad at the time of the division of the land (Josh 13:2–5). Its Ammonite monarch grossly insulted the messengers of David (2 Sam 10:1–6). The next spring Rabbah was besieged by the army of David. The city capitulated when Joab captured its water supply. Jeremiah utters imprecatory judgment against Molech, the chief Ammonite deity (Jer 49:2–3). Ezekiel pictures Nebuchadnezzar as pausing at Rabbah to decide his further course of action (Ezek 21:20–21; cf. Amos 1:14). Subsequently, Rabbah was captured by Ptolemy Philadelphus (285–247 B.C.), who changed its name to Philadelphia. It later became the seat of Christian bishops. It is now known as Amman, the capital of the kingdom of Jordan.

RABBI (See OCCUPATIONS AND PROFESSIONS)

RABBIT (See ANIMALS)

RABBONI (răb-bō'nī). A variant of *Rabbi*, the Hebrew word for "Teacher." The title Mary Magdalene used for Jesus on resurrection morning (John 20:16). See OCCUPATIONS AND PROFESSIONS: *Rabbi*.

RABSARIS (răb'sà-rĭs, Heb. *rav-sārîs*). The title of an Assyrian and Babylonian official usually taken to be "chief eunuch," though Assyriologists have produced evidence for the reading "chief of the 'heads' [leaders, leading men]." The title appears in the Bible only in 2 Kings 18:17 (KJV; NIV "chief officer").

RABSHAKEH (răb'shà-kĕ, Heb. *rav-shāqēh*). The title of an Assyrian official, with the meaning "chief cup-bearer" or "chief of the officers[?]" (2 Kings 18:17, 19, 26–28, 37; 19:4, 8, and parallel; Isa

Stone statue of a king, from Amman, c. eighth century B.C. He wears a heavy crown and long garment with short sleeves. A shawl around his waist and over his shoulder ends in a tassel. Courtesy Studium Biblicum Franciscanum, Jerusalem

36:2, 4, 11–13, 22; 37:4, 8). While Sennacherib was besieging Lachish, he sent his Rabshakeh (KJV; NIV "field commander") to Jerusalem to deliver an ultimatum to that city. When representatives of Hezekiah protested that he should speak in Aramaic so that the people on the wall could not understand, he deliberately addressed his challenge to those onlookers and then left to join the Assyrian forces at Libnah.

RACA (rà'kà, Gr. *rhaka, empty, vain,* or *worthless fellow*). A term of contempt, signifying a derogatory estimate of someone's intellectual ability (Matt 5:22).

RACE (Heb. *ōrah, mĕrôts,* Gr. *agōn, stadion,* most frequently, *a foot race*). The clearest uses of these words are in 1 Corinthians 9:24; 2 Timothy 4:7; and Hebrews 12:1. Other passages may well allude to it (Rom 9:16; Gal 5:7; Phil 2:16). The Greek race was one of a series of highly competitive games. It consisted of (1) the goal, a square pillar opposite the entrance to the course, marking the end of the track; (2) the herald, whose duty it was to announce the name and the country of each competitor, as well as the name and family of the victor; (3) the prize, the crown or wreath that was awarded the winner (cf. 1 Cor 9:25; 2 Tim 2:5); and (4) the judges (2 Tim 4:8).

RACHEL (rā'chĕl, Heb. *rāhēl, ewe,* Gr. *Rhachēl*). The wife of Jacob, the mother of Joseph and Benjamin (Gen 29:6, 16, 18, 31; 30:1–9; cf. Jer 31:15; Matt 2:18). Rachel was the younger daughter of Laban, the Aramean (ASV "Syrian"), the brother of Rebekah, Jacob's mother (Gen 28:2); thus Jacob and Rachel were full cousins. Rebekah suggested that Jacob leave home for a time and go to the house of her brother Laban in Haran (Paddan Aram) (27:43–45). On his arrival, Jacob was struck by Rachel's beauty and immediately fell in love with her (29:17–18). He signed a contract with Laban for seven years of labor (the usual period of indentured servants); at the end of this time Rachel was to be his wife. Laban adopted Jacob as his son, giving him both Leah and her sister Rachel as his wives. After becoming prosperous, Jacob took his departure from the house of Laban (31:21). Rachel concealed Laban's household gods in the baggage as she and Jacob fled (31:30–31). These household deities, about the size of miniature dolls, were regarded as indisputable evidence of the rights and privileges of family ownership and inheritance (31:30).

For some time, Rachel remained barren but finally she had Joseph (30:22), while still in the house of Laban. Later Benjamin was born but Rachel died in childbirth (35:16–19). Jacob favored the sons of his beloved Rachel above the sons of Leah. Rachel inherited her family's traits of scheming and duplicity (31:34). A believer in monotheism, she still clung to the forms of polytheism.

RAGUEL (See REUEL)

RAHAB (rā'hăb, Heb. *rāhāv, broad,* Gr. *Rhachab*). 1. A woman best known for her prominent role in the capture of Jericho during the days of Joshua (Josh 2:1ff.; Matt 1:5; Heb 11:31; James 2:25). She hid spies sent by Joshua prior to the siege of the city. As a reward she was promised her own safety and the protection of her family (Josh 2:14–20; cf. 6:17). According to Matthew's genealogy, she is not only one of the four women mentioned in the family tree of the Savior, but also the mother of Boaz, the husband of Ruth, and the great-grandmother of King David (Ruth 4:18–21; Matt 1:5).

2. A mythical monster of the deep. In such passages as Job 9:13 and Psalm 89:10 the motif of the slaying of the dragon appears (cf. Isa 51:9).

RAHEL (See RACHEL)

RAIMENT (See DRESS)

RAIN (Heb. *mātār, geshem, heavy rain, yôreh, former rain, malkôsh, latter rain,* Gr. *brechō, hyetos*). The word in the Scriptures is used in both a literal and a figurative sense. The contrast between rainfall in Egypt and Palestine is brought out in Deuteronomy 11:10–12. Since the summer is very dry in Israel, the rainy seasons come in the spring (the "latter rains") and in the fall (the "former rains"). One can be almost certain that from about May 1 to about October 15, no rain will fall (Song of Songs 2:11). Many people thus sleep on the roofs of the houses to escape the heat and to enjoy the cooling night breezes. The greatest amount of rain falls between November and February. The spring rains are considered such a natural blessing that they assume an eschatological significance (Joel 2:23; Zech 10:1). The withholding of the rain at the proper season, particularly in the spring, was regarded as a most severe punishment (Deut 28:23–24; 1 Kings 17:1–16), and conversely, the abundance of rain denoted the rich blessing of the Lord on his people (Deut 28:12). Famine, one of the more tragic effects of the lack of rain, was therefore seen as an indication of divine displeasure (2 Sam 21:1–14). In pagan concepts, Baal was conceived of as the god of rain. Elijah's contest on Carmel was to prove the superiority of the

God of Israel in the realm of the forces of nature.

RAINBOW (Heb. *qesheth, bow*). God's covenant with Noah declared that he would never again send a universal flood to destroy the whole inhabited earth (Gen 9:8–17). The rainbow is the first of the covenant signs and provides the key to understanding all of them, including the signs of baptism and the Lord's Supper in the new covenant. The rainbow is the Lord's promise made visible. Thus covenant signs express covenant promises to covenant people. Ezekiel compares the glory of God to that of a rainbow (Ezek 1:28). John, as a prisoner on Patmos, beheld the throne of God encircled by the rainbow (Rev 4:3).

RAISINS (See FOOD)

RAM (See ANIMALS)

RAMAH, RAMA (rā'mà, Heb. *hārāmâh, height*). **1.** Ramah Arael, a city assigned by lot to the tribe of Naphtali, probably in the mountains of upper Galilee (Josh 19:36). **2.** Rhama-Ramah, a territory mentioned as forming the boundary of Asher (19:29). **3.** Ramah Iamah (or Ramah of Benjamin, and various other orthographic forms), the headquarters of Deborah (Judg 4:5). At the time of the division of the kingdom, Ramah of Benjamin was destroyed, for we read that Baasha of Israel built it again to ward off his rival, Asa king of Judah (1 Kings 15:16–17; cf. Isa 10:28–32). This is probably the Ramah that is referred to in Jeremiah 31:15 and Matthew 2:18. **4.** Ramah Aramathaim, the hometown of Elkanah and Hannah, and the birthplace of the prophet Samuel (1 Sam 1:19; 2:11). Later Samuel made it the center of his circuit (7:16–17). Here Israel demanded a king (8:4), and here Samuel first became acquainted with King Saul (9:6ff.). Samuel retired here after his final break with Saul (15:34). This is the place where David found refuge from the crazed king (19:18) and where Samuel was buried (25:1; 28:3). **5.** Ramah of the South. A city in the southern sector of Judah that was allotted to the tribe of Simeon (Josh 19:8; 1 Sam 30:27).

RAMATH MIZPEH (rā'măth mĭz'pĕ, Heb. *râmath-mitspeh, the heights*, or *the watchtower*). The northern boundary line of the tribe of Gad (Josh 13:26). It is probably the same place that marked the early sanctuary erected by Jacob and Laban as a witness (Gen 31:46–48). It has the triple names of Mizpeh, Galeed, and Jegar Sahadutha. Mizpeh implies the idea of watching, while the other two names convey the thought of a heap of stones set up as a witness between two contending parties. Probably Mizpeh is the same as Ramoth Gilead, so famous in the subsequent history of Israel.

RAMATH OF THE SOUTH (See RAMAH, RAMA, no. 5)

RAMATHAIM (See RAMAH, RAMA)

RAMATHAIM ZOPHIM (See RAMAH, RAMA)

RAMATHITE (See RAMAH, RAMA)

RAMESES, RAAMSES (râ-ăm'sēz). A Hebrew place-name derived from the Egyptian royal name Ramses. In the OT it appears first as the name of the district of the Delta in which Jacob and his sons were settled by Joseph (Gen 47:11). Rameses and Pithom are the names given (Exod 1:11) for the two store cities the Israelites were forced to build for the Pharaoh of the Oppression. From Rameses the Israelites began their exodus from Egypt (12:37; Num 33:3, 5). At present there is fairly general agreement that Rameses is to be identified with Avaris-Tanis-Zoan, in the NE part of the Delta.

RAMOTH (rāmoth, Heb. *râmôth, height*). **1.** One of the cities of refuge in the tribe of Gad, elsewhere called Ramoth Gilead (Josh 20:8; 21:38). It formed one of the administrative districts of Solomon, over which Ben Geber was stationed (1 Kings 4:13). It is perhaps best known as the scene of the last battle of King Ahab (22:1–37). **2.** Ramoth Negev. See RAMAH, RAMA, no.5. **3.** An Israelite who after the Exile divorced his Gentile wife (Ezra 10:29 KJV; NIV "Jeremoth").

RAMSES, RAMESSES (râ-ăm'sēz). The most common royal Egyptian name in the 19th and 20th dynasties. The most illustrious was Ramses II, who was ambitious and imperious. Ramses established his capital at Tanis, in the Delta, but his building and rebuilding activities extended throughout the land and even beyond Egypt proper, including the hall at Karnak, the temple at Abydos, and the forecourt and pylon of the Luxor temple. (See page 496.)

RAMS' HORNS (See MUSIC AND MUSICAL INSTRUMENTS)

RAM SKINS The skins of the sheep tanned with oil used for outer clothing by the shepherds of the Near East. They were also used as the exterior covering for the tabernacle (Exod 25:5).

Colossal statue of Ramses II, part of the rock-cut façade of the great temple at Abu Simbel, measuring about 69 feet (21 m.) high. Courtesy Seffie Ben-Yoseph

RANSOM (răn'sŭm, Heb. *kōpher*, *pi-dhyôn*, *gā' al*, Gr. *lytron*, *antilytron*). The price paid for the redemption of a slave (Lev 19:20); a reparation paid for injury or damages (Exod 22:10–12); a fee, fine, or heavy assessment laid on a person as a substitute for his own life (21:30). There was no ransom provided for the willful murderer (Num 35:31). In the NT the term signifies the redemptive price of-fered by Christ on the cross for the salvation of his people (Mark 10:45; 1 Tim 2:6).

RAPHA (rā'fà, Heb. *rāphā'*). **1.** The last son of Benjamin (1 Chron 8:2). **2.** Four enemy warriors of David are listed as descendants of Rapha, probably to identify them as giants (so KJV) (2 Sam 21:15–22; 1 Chron 20:6, 8).

RAS SHAMRA (ràs shàm'rà, Arab. *Fennel Head*). The modern name of the mound that marks the site of the ancient city of Ugarit, located on the Syrian coast opposite the island of Cyprus. In A.D. 1928 a peasant struck the roof of a buried tomb with his plow and made a discovery that attracted the attention of the authorities. In 1929 the French archaeologist C. F. A. Schaeffer began a series of

excavations that have revealed much of the history of the site. The texts found at Ugarit contain syllabaries and vocabularies, personal and diplomatic correspondence, business, legal, and governmental records, veterinary texts dealing with diagnosis and treatment of ailments of horses, and, most important, religious literature.

The myths and legends of Ugarit have provided valuable primary sources for the knowledge of Canaanite religion. At the head of the Ugaritic pantheon was El, who was also known as Father of Man, Creator of Creators, Bull El. His consort was Asherah, a fertility goddess who was a stumbling block to Israel. Both Ahab (1 Kings 16:33) and Jezebel (18:19) promoted her worship, and Manasseh even put her image in the temple (2 Kings 21:7). Among the many offspring of El and Asherah was Dagon (Judg 16:23; 1 Sam 5), a grain god, whose son Baal was of great prominence. A god of rain and storm, Baal, whose proper name was Hadad (Thunderer), also figured in the fertility cycle. Baal was also called Ali-yan Baal, Dagon's Son, Servant of El, Rider of Clouds, and Baal-Zebub (cf. 2 Kings 1; Matt 12:24). In Israel the priests of Baal lost an important contest with the prophet of God on Mt. Carmel (1 Kings 18). Baal's sister and wife, the virgin Anat, goddess of love and fertility and goddess of war, is known in the OT as Astarte or Ashtoreth. El ordinarily is easygoing and easily influenced, but sometimes is rash and even immoral, as in his seduction and expulsion of two women. Baal mates with his sister and also with a heifer. Anat slaughters people and wades in blood and gore.

Ugaritic practice illuminates the biblical prohibition against boiling a kid in its mother's milk (Exod 23:19; 34:26; Deut 14:21). A veterinary text refers to a poultice that has been cited as a parallel to Isaiah's prescription for King Hezekiah (2 Kings 20:7; Isa 38:21).

RAT (See ANIMALS)

RAVEN (See BIRDS)

RAVENOUS BIRD (See BIRDS)

RAZOR, RASOR (rā'zêr, Heb. *ta' ar*, *môrâh*). Joseph shaved himself before he was liberated from prison to stand before Pharaoh (Gen 41:14), probably in deference to Egyptian custom, as the priests of Egypt shaved daily. The cutting of the beard by a priest of Israel was forbidden, presumably because of its affinity to pagan practices (Lev 21:5). The Nazirite

Statue (24.8 cm. high) from Ras Shamra, nineteenth to seventeenth century B.C., of a seated goddess. She wears a long garment with a rolled edge or cord at the bottom. A similar cord wound about the upper part of the body may represent a serpent. Courtesy Réunion des Musées Nationaux

was also forbidden the use of a razor as long as his vows were valid (Num 6:5).

RE, RA (rā). A masculine deity in the pantheon of the gods of Egypt, identified with the sun-god. Creation is viewed as a procreation on the part of the male and his female. To the ancients, the elemental forces of nature were the deities to whom they assigned personalized names. Re was thought to have engaged in a fierce battle against the dragon of chaos and darkness. The struggle was repeated yearly, sometimes even daily, in the ceremonial liturgy of Egypt. In later times, Re came to be referred to as Amen-Re, Osiris, and other such names. In the mystery religions, he was designated as Soter-Theos, a "savior-god," a deity who rescued his people from death. The center of the worship of Re was Heliopolis, the ancient On. The ninth plague was in reality a judgment on Re, the sun god (Exod 12:21–23). Joseph, after being made food administrator of the land, married the daughter of the priest of On of the cult of Re (Gen 41:45).

REAIAH, REAIA (rē-ā'yà, Heb. re'āyâh, *God has seen*). 1. The name of a Calebite family (1 Chron 4:2). 2. A Reubenite (5:5). 3. The family name of a company of temple servants (KJV Nethinim) (Ezra 2:47; Neh 7:50).

REAPING (Heb. *qātsar*, Gr. *therizō*). Strict laws for reaping were imposed on Israel (Lev 19:9; 23:10; 25:11; Deut 16:9). Samuel mentions that reaping will be a duty that the nation's newly chosen king, Saul, will demand of them (1 Sam 8:12). The figurative usage of the term speaks of deeds that produce their own harvest (Prov 22:8; Hos 8:7; 1 Cor 9:11; Gal 6:7–8).

REBEKAH, REBECCA (rē-běk'à, Heb. *rivqâh*, Gr. *Rhebekka*). The daughter of Bethuel, the sister of Laban, the wife of Isaac, mother of Esau and Jacob.

In Haran, Abraham's servant Eliezer met Rebekah and successfully persuaded her to become Isaac's wife (Gen 24). Rebekah was loved by Isaac (24:67), but she bore him no children for 20 years. It was only after special intercession by Isaac that God gave twins–Esau and Jacob. Jacob became her favorite and this led her to trick the aged and blind Isaac. Disguised as his brother Esau, Jacob obtained the blessing (27:5–17). When it became evident that Jacob and Esau could no longer live under the same roof, at her suggestion, Jacob fled from home to her relatives in Aram (27:42–46). Rebekah never saw her son again.

RECAB (rē'kăb, Heb. *rēkhāv, horseman*). **1.** One of the assassins of Ish-Bosheth, a son of Saul (2 Sam 4:5-11). **2.** An early ancestor of the Kenite clan, which later became identified with the tribe of Judah (1 Chron 2:55). Recab was the founder of the order of the Recabites (2 Kings 10:15ff.). Jeremiah used the example of the Recabites and their obedience to their father to drink no wine as a method of sharply berating the nation for their lack of obedience to God (Jer 35:1-19). The Recabites, though thirsty, had refused to partake of the wine rather than break faith; the Israelites, though partakers of the divine blessings, had indeed broken the covenant (35:12-16).

RECONCILIATION (rĕk'ŏn-sĭl-ĭ-ā'shŭn, Gr. *katallagē*). Reconciliation is a change of relationship between God and man based on the changed status of man through the redemptive work of Christ. Three aspects of this change are suggested in the NT. **1.** A reconciliation of *persons* between whom there has existed a state of enmity; God establishes in Christ's redemptive work the basis of this changed relationship of persons (Rom 5:10; 2 Cor 5:19). God is never said to be reconciled to man, but man to God, since it is man's sinfulness that creates the enmity (Rom 8:7; Col 1:21) and precipitates God's wrath (Eph 2:3, 5). **2.** A reconciliation of *condition* so that all basis of the enmity relationship is removed and a complete basis of fellowship is established (2 Cor 5:18-20; Eph 2:16). **3.** A reconciliation arising out of the change in man *induced by the action of God.* Man is not reconciled merely because his relationship has changed, but because *God* has changed him through Christ so that he can be reconciled (Rom 5:11; 11:15; 2 Cor 5:18; Eph 2:5). Reconciliation arises, therefore, out of God, through Christ, to man, so that not only may the barriers to fellowship existing in sinful people be removed, but the positive basis for fellowship may be established through the righteousness of Christ imputed to man.

Even though the sufficient ground of reconciliation is established in the completed redemptive work of Christ, reconciliation is the basis on which the continued fellowship is established (Rom 5:10).

RECORDER (See OCCUPATIONS AND PROFESSIONS)

RED (Heb. *ādhōm,* Gr. *erythos*). The adjective "red" is applied to the following items: (1) the dyed ram skins that formed the outward covering for the tabernacle (Exod 25:5; 26:14; 35:7), (2) the color of certain animals (Num 19:2; Zech 1:8; 6:2; Rev 6:4; 12:3), (3) the color of the human skin (Gen 25:25; 1 Sam 16:12), (4) redness of eyes (Gen 49:12; Prov 23:29), (5) certain sores (Num 12:10), (6) wine (Prov 23:31; Isa 27:2 AV), (7) water (2 Kings 3:22), (8) pavement (Esth 1:6), (9) the color of sin (Isa 1:18), (10) the shields of the foe advancing against the city of Nineveh (Nah 2:3), and (11) the Red Sea (Acts 7:36; Heb 11:29). See also RED SEA.

REDEEMER (See REDEMPTION)

REDEMPTION (Heb. *ge'ullâh,* Gr. *lytrōsis, apolytrōsis*). A metaphor used in both OT and NT to describe God's merciful and costly action on behalf of his people (sinful human beings). The basic meaning of the word is release or freedom on payment of a price, deliverance by a costly method. When used of God it does not suggest that he paid a price to anyone, but rather that his mercy required his almighty power and involved the greatest possible depth of suffering. Thus God redeemed Israel from Egypt by delivering the people from bondage and placing them in a new land (Exod 6:6; 15:3; Pss 74:2; 77:15ff.; 106:10; Isa 43:1, 3, 14-16; 48:20; 51:10-11; 63:16; Jer 31:11).

The verb *pādhâh,* in its secular use, is entirely given over to express ransom-price (e.g., Lev 27:27; Num 18:15-17; Ps 49:7). When it is used of the Lord's ransoming work, 13 out of the 39 references allude to the Exodus (e.g., Deut 9:26; 2 Sam 7:23; Neh 1:10). Three references speak specifically of the forgiveness of sins (Deut 21:8; Ps 130:8; Isa 1:27).

To appreciate the NT theme of redemption, the position of human beings as slaves of sin must be assumed (John 8:33-34). Thus they must be set free in order to become the liberated servants of the Lord (Mark 10:45). This redemption paid for by the costly sacrifice of the life of Jesus is a completed act as far as God is concerned. But the results of the redemption as far as we are concerned are experienced in part now and in full at the resurrection of the dead (Luke 21:27-28; Rom 8:23; Eph 4:30).

RED HEIFER The ashes of the red heifer were used for the removal of certain types of ceremonial uncleanness, such as purification of the leper, or defilement incurred through contact with the dead (Num 19:2). See also ANIMALS.

View of the Red Sea, just south of Elath, looking west. Courtesy S. Zur Picture Library

RED SEA (Heb. *yam sûph*). Near the city of Rameses-Tanis (in Goshen, where the Israelite slaves lived) there were two bodies of water, the "Waters of Horus," which is the same as Shihor (Isa 23:3; Jer 2:18), and a body of water that the Egyptians themselves referred to as "Suph," called also the "papyrus marsh." This last-mentioned "Sea of Reeds," or Lake Timsah, is beyond reasonable doubt the body of water crossed by the fleeing Israelites, with the Egyptians in hot pursuit. This newer identification does not diminish the miraculous deliverance by God or the awful judgment that overtook Pharaoh's armies.

REED (Heb. *qāneh, 'ăghammîm, 'ādhû*, Gr. *kalamos*). A reed stalk was used as a measuring rod. Among the Israelites a reed came to denote a fixed length of six long cubits (Ezek 40:5; 41:8). In Revelation 11:1; 21:15–16, a reed is used to measure the temple and the Holy City.

REED SEA (See RED SEA)

REFINER (See OCCUPATIONS AND PROFESSIONS; *Coppersmith, Craftsman, Goldsmith, Silversmith*)

REFUGE, CITIES OF (See CITIES OF REFUGE)

REGENERATION (rē-jĕn-êr-ā'shun, Gr. *palingenesia*). Regeneration has as its basic idea "to be born again" or "to be restored." Though the word is actually used only twice in the NT (Matt 19:28; Titus 3:5), many synonymous passages suggest its basic meaning. Related terms are "born again" (John 3:3, 5, 7), "born of God" (1:13; 1 John 3:9), "quickened" (Eph 2:1, 5), and "renewed" (Rom 12:2; Titus 3:5). Regeneration is the spiritual change wrought in people's hearts in which their inherently sinful nature is changed and by which they are enabled to respond to God in faith.

Regeneration is, therefore, an act of God through the immediate agency of the Holy Spirit operative in man (Col 2:13), originating in him a new dimension of moral life, a resurrection to new life in Christ. This new life is not merely a neutral state arising out of forgiveness of sin, but a positive implantation of Christ's righteousness in man, by which he is quickened (John 5:21), begotten (1 John 5:1), made a new creation (2 Cor 5:17), given a new life (Rom 6:4) and the divine nature (2 Peter 1:4).

REHABIAH (rē'hă-bī'à, Heb. *rehavyâh, rehavâhû, God is wide*). Son of Eliezer, and a grandson of Moses (1 Chron 23:17; 24:21; 26:25).

REHOB (rē'hōb, Heb. *rehōv, broad*). 1. The northern limit to which the spies came as they searched out the land (Num 13:21; 2 Sam 10:8). Rehob and Beth Rehob appear to be identical. 2. Two separate towns belonging to the tribe of Asher (Josh 19:28, 30). 3. The father of Hadadezer, king of Aram (2 Sam 8:3, 12). 4. A Levite who was one of the cosigners of the covenant of Nehemiah (Neh 10:11).

REHOBOAM (rē'hō-bō'ăm, Heb. *rehav'ām*). A son of Solomon, and his successor on the throne of Israel. His mother was Naamah, an Ammonitess (1 Kings 14:21). He was born about 975 B.C. and was 41 when he began to reign. Solomon's wild extravagances and his vain ambition to make Israel the world power of his day led him to set up a tremendously expensive capital and a very elaborate harem. The many pagan women in his harem resulted in a spiritual decline in Israel. The luxuries of his palace and the expenses of his diplomatic corps and building program resulted in heavy taxation. The northern tribes turned for leadership to Jeroboam, to whom God had revealed that he was to rule ten of the tribes (11:26–40). Rehoboam, heeding the advice of young men, refused to lower taxes, with the result that Israel rebelled against him. When Adoram was sent to collect the tribute, he was killed, and Rehoboam fled to Jerusalem (12:16–19). Jeroboam was then made king of the ten tribes. Rehoboam raised an army from Judah and Benjamin, but was forbidden by God to attack (12:20–24).

Rehoboam set to work to make his realm strong. Pagan high places were set up and shrines throughout the land allowed abominable practices to be observed among the people (1 Kings 14:22–24). Rehoboam fortified Bethlehem, Gath, Lachish, Hebron, and other cities and gave refuge to priests and Levites whom Jeroboam had driven from Israel (2 Chron 11:5–17). Rehoboam gathered a substantial harem and reared a large family (11:18–23). He had 18 wives and 60 concubines.

REHOBOTH (rē-hō'bŏth, Heb. *rehōvôth, broad places*). 1. A city built in Assyria (Gen 10:11 KJV; NIV "Rehoboth Ir"). The home of Saul (Shaul in 1 Chron 1:48), a king of Edom prior to the coming of a Hebrew monarch (Gen 36:31–37). 2. A well dug by Isaac in the Valley of Gerar (26:9–22).

REHUM (rē'hŭm, Heb. *rehûm, beloved*). 1. A Hebrew who returned from captivity

with Ezra (Ezra 2:2). Called "Nehum" in Nehemiah 7:7. 2. An officer of Artaxerxes' court who accused the Jews of rebellion (Ezra 4:7–24). 3. A son of Bani. He helped repair the walls of Jerusalem (Neh 3:17). 4. One who signed the covenant with God after Israel had returned from captivity (10:25). 5. A priest among those who returned to Palestine (12:3).

REINS (Heb. *kilyâh*, Gr. *nephros*). The inward parts. The reins (kidneys) were thought by the Israelites to be the seat of the emotions (Job 19:27; Pss 7:9; 26:2; Jer 17:10). NIV usually translates this word as "mind." See also KIDNEYS.

REKEM (rē'kĕm, Heb. *reqem, friendship*). 1. A king of Midian who was executed by order of the Lord (Num 31:1–8). He is called a prince in Joshua 13:21. 2. A city belonging to Benjamin (18:27). 3. A son of Hebron, and the father of Shammai (1 Chron 2:42–44).

RELIGION (Gr. *thrēskeia, outward expression of spiritual devotion*). The Latin *religare* means to hold back or restrain. It came to be applied to the services and ritual and rules by which faith in and devotion to deity were expressed. In the OT there is no word for religion. Fear (Ps 2:11; Prov 1:7) and worship (Deut 4:19; 29:26; Pss 5:7; 29:2) of God refer primarily to attitudes of the mind and acts of adoration, rather than to a ritual. *Thrēskeia* in the NT means outward expression of religion and the content of faith. James makes a distinction between the sham and the reality of religious expression (James 1:26–27). Paul was loyal to his Hebrew religion before being converted (Acts 26:1–5). *Religious* in James 1:26 (*thrēskos*) implies superstition.

REMETH (rē'mĕth, Heb. *remeth, height*). A city in the tribe of Issachar (Josh 19:17–21); probably Ramoth (1 Chron 6:73) and Jarmuth (Josh 21:29).

REMMON (See RIMMON)

REMNANT A translation of different Hebrew words: *yether*, "what is left" (Deut 3:11; 28:54); *she'ar*, "the remainder" (Ezra 3:8; Isa 10:20; 11:16); *she'ērîth*, "residue" (2 Kings 19:31; Isa 14:30). It came to mean the spiritual kernel of the nation who would survive God's judgment and become the germ of the new people of God. Thus Micah saw the returning glory of Israel (Mic 2:12; 5:7). Zephaniah saw the triumph of this remnant (Zeph 2:4–7), and so did Zechariah (Zech 8:1–8). Isaiah named a son She'ar-Jashub, which means "a remnant returns" (Isa 7:3).

REMON METHOAR (See RIMMON)

REMPHAN (See REPHAN)

REPENTANCE (Heb. *nāham, sûbh,* Gr. *metanoia*). The process of changing one's mind. God is described as repenting (Exod 32:14; 1 Sam 15:11; Jonah 3:9–10; 4:2—using *nāham*), in the sense that he changed his attitude to a people because of a change within the people. God as perfect Deity does not change in his essential nature but changes his relation and attitude from wrath to mercy and from blessing to judgment, as the occasion requires. Human repentance is a change for the better and is a conscious turning from evil or disobedience or sin or idolatry to the living God (2 Kings 17:13; Isa 19:22; Jer 3:12, 14, 22; Jonah 3:10—using *shûbh*).

In the NT repentance and faith are the two sides of one coin (Acts 20:21). They are a response to grace. Jesus preached the need for the Jews to repent (Matt 4:17), and required his apostles/disciples to preach repentance to Jews and Gentiles (Luke 24:47; Acts 2:38; 17:30). Repentance is a profound change of mind involving the changing of the direction of life. The positive side of repentance is conversion, the actual turning to God or Christ for grace.

REPHAIAH (rē-fā'yà, Heb. *rephayah, Jehovah heals*). **1.** Descendant of David (1 Chron 3:21, "Rhesa" of Luke 3:27). **2.** A son of Ishi. He helped defeat the Amalekites (1 Chron 4:42–43). **3.** A grandson of Issachar (7:2). **4.** A descendant of Jonathan (9:40–43). **5.** Son of Hur, a builder (Neh 3:9).

REPHAIM, VALLEY OF (rĕf'ā-ĭm, *vale of giants*). This was a fertile plain south of Jerusalem, 3 miles (5 km.) from Bethlehem. It was a productive area (Isa 17:4–5); David twice defeated the Philistines in this valley (1 Chron 14:8–16).

REPHAITES, REPHAIM (rĕf'ā-īts, rĕf'ā-ĭm, Heb. *rephā'îm, mighty*). The name of a giant people, called also Rephainer (Gen 14:5; 15:20 KJV), who lived in Canaan even before the time of Abraham. Listed among Canaanites who were to be dispossessed (15:20), they were like the Anakim (Deut 2:11, 20). Og, king of Bashan, was a descendant of the Rephaites (Josh 12:4; 13:12).

REPHAN (rē'făn). A pagan deity worshiped by the Israelites in the wilderness (Acts 7:37–50). It is probably a name for Chiun or Saturn (Amos 5:26; see NIV footnote), a view supported by the LXX.

REPHIDIM (rĕf'ĭ-dĭm, Heb. *rephidhîm, plains*). A camping site of the Hebrews in the wilderness before they reached Sinai. There Moses struck a rock to secure water (Exod 17:1–7; 19:2), and the battle with the Amalekites occurred (17:8–16).

REPROBATE (rĕp'rō-bāt, Gr. *adokimos*). The basic idea in reprobation is that of failing "to stand the test," disapproval or rejection. When applied to humanity's relation to God, it suggests moral corruption, unfitness, disqualification—all arising out of a lack of positive holiness. The KJV uses it of a reprobate [disapproved] mind (Rom 1:28) and of a sinful nature (2 Cor 13:5, 6, 7). Its other NT uses (2 Tim 3:8; Titus 1:16) bear the same disapproval quality.

REPTILE (See ANIMALS)

RESERVOIR (Heb. *miqwâh, a source of water*). Some of the reservoirs and many private cisterns were hewn into solid rock (Neh 9:25; 2 Chron 26:10). Elisha told Israel to provide many special reservoirs (ditches) near Jerusalem (2 Kings 3:12–17). It was considered wise for each home to have its own cistern (18:31). Among the most famous reservoirs of Palestine were the pools of Solomon, 13 miles (22 km.) from the city (Eccl 2:6). Water from these was conveyed to the city by aqueducts, some of which remain today.

RESIN, GUM RESIN (See PLANTS)

REST (Heb. *nûah, menûhâh, peace, quiet,* Gr. *anapausis, katapausis*). A word of frequent occurrence in the Bible, in both Testaments. It is used of God as resting from his work (Gen 2:2), and as having his rest in the temple (1 Chron 28:2). God commanded that the seventh day was to be one of rest (Exod 16:23; 31:15) and that the land was to have its rest every seventh year (Lev 25:4). God promised rest to the Israelites in the land of Canaan (Deut 12:9). The word is sometimes used in the sense of trust and reliance (2 hron 14:11). Christ offers rest of soul (Matt 11:28; Heb 4).

RESURRECTION (Gr. *anastasis, arising, egersis, a raising*). A return to life subsequent to death. To deny the Resurrection is, in biblical thought, to deny any immortality worthy of the character of our faith in God (Matt 22:31–32; Mark 12:26–27; Luke 20:37–38). Between death and resurrection, man in the intermediate state is incomplete and awaits "the redemption of our bodies" (Rom 8:23; cf. 2 Cor 5:3ff.; Rev 6:9–11).

In the OT the most explicit passage on the resurrection is Daniel 12:2. Almost

Entrance to the Garden Tomb enclosure, one of two different sites vying for recognition as the burial place of Jesus. The tomb is located some distance to the right of the bridge. See "The Garden Tomb—Was Jesus Buried Here?" *Biblical Archaeological Review* 12:2 (March/April 1986), pp. 40ff. Courtesy Duby Tal

equally explicit is Isaiah 26:19. In its context, this verse is parallel to verses 11–15 (cf. Job 19:23–27).

The doctrine of resurrection is stated clearly in its simplest form in Paul's words before the Roman law court presided over by Felix (Acts 24:15). The most detailed statement of the doctrine of twofold resurrection is found in Revelation 20:4–15.

In the words of Jesus, the only clear allusion to a twofold resurrection is found in John 5:25, 28–29. Some scholars see in 1 Thessalonians 4:16–17 an implication that the dead who are not "in Christ" will not be raised at the same time as the redeemed. This is possibly also the implication of 1 Corinthians 15:20–28. With 1 Corinthians 15:23 Paul begins an enumeration of three "orders" of resurrection, one of which, the resurrection of Christ, is past. Paul's second and third "orders" of resurrection coincide with John's future "first resurrection" and his resurrection of "the rest of the dead" (Rev 20:4–15).

RESURRECTION OF JESUS CHRIST
(Gr. *anastasis, egeirō, anistēmi*). There

were no witnesses of the resurrection of Jesus of Nazareth. What the disciples witnessed was the appearance of the resurrected Jesus. They saw also the empty tomb. In fact, only disciples were witnesses of the appearances of Jesus; but both disciples and others saw the empty sepulcher. In the NT there are six accounts of what followed the resurrection of Jesus (Matt 28; Mark 16; Luke 24; John 20–21; Acts 1:1–11; 1 Cor 15:1–11).

The evidence for the Resurrection as an event within history may be listed as follows: 1. The tomb of Jesus was found empty. The body was never located or produced by those who allegedly stole it or by anyone else. 2. The disciples saw Jesus when they were fully awake and when they doubted that he was alive. 3. There is no attempt to describe the Resurrection itself, and there is no obvious collusion between the various writers to doctor or adorn their material. 4. Men who were cowards became fearless preachers, preached the gospel, and saw lives changed by that living Lord.

For Jesus, bodily resurrection meant resuscitation with transformation—that

Resurrection Appearances

EVENT	DATE	Matt.	Mark	Luke	John	Acts	1 Cor.
At the empty tomb outside Jerusalem	Early Sunday morning	28:1-10	16:1-8	24:1-12	20:1-9		
To Mary Magadalene at the tomb	Early Sunday morning		16:9-11		20:11-18		
To two travelers on the road to Emmaus	Sunday at midday			24:13-32			
To Peter in Jerusalem	During the day on Sunday			24:34			15:5
To the ten disciples in the Upper Room	Sunday evening		16:14	24:36-43	20:19-25		
To the eleven disciples in the Upper Room	One week later				20:26-31		15:5
To seven disciples fishing on the Sea of Galilee	One day at daybreak				21:1-23		
To the eleven disciples on the mountain in Galilee	Some time later	28:16-20	16:15-18				
To more than 500	Some time later						15:6
To James	Some time later						15:7
At the Ascension on the Mt. of Olives	Forty days after the Resurrection			24:44-49		1:3-8	

is, what was a physical and mortal body became a spiritual and immortal body, transformed by the power of God.

God raised Jesus from the dead and thereby vindicated him as the true Messiah. The manner of Jesus' death gave the impression that God had rejected him, for to hang on a tree was to be under the divine curse (Deut 21:23; Acts 2:36; 4:11; Rom 1:3-4; 4:25; Gal 3:13). God caused the new age to dawn in the Resurrection (1 Cor 15:20, 23). Jesus is the "first-fruits" of the harvest of the age to come.

RETRIBUTION The word is not found in Scripture, but the idea is expressed in reference to the wrath of God, vengeance, punishment, and judgment (Rom 1:18; 2:6). Retribution is the natural outcome of sin (Gal 6:7-8; cf. Matt 3:7; Luke 3:7; 1 Thess 1:10; Rev 6:16).

REUBEN (rū'bĕn, Heb. *re'ûvēn*). The oldest son of Jacob (Gen 29:32). He brought his mother mandrakes, which she used in getting Jacob to give her another son (30:14-15). Reuben committed incest at Eder (35:22). Either because of this sin or out of innate weakness (49:4) his tribe never rose to power. He delivered Joseph from death by warning his brothers against the results of such an act (37:19-22; 42:22) and later offered his sons as surety for Benjamin (42:37). He took four sons into Egypt (46:9). When Israel left Egypt, he had 46,500 descendants (Num 1:21; 2:10). The Reubenites made a covenant with Moses in order to occupy the rich grazing lands of Gilead (32:1-33). That they kept the covenant is

The entrance to the Garden Tomb. The Garden Tomb is one of two different sites vying for recognition as the burial place of Jesus. Courtesy Duby Tal

THE TRIBE OF REUBEN

Mephaath
Heshbon
Beth Peor • Sibmah • Bezer
Beth Jeshimoth ▲ Mt. Pisgah
Kiriathaim
• Medeba
• Beth Baal Meon
Dead Sea
R E U B E N
• Zereth Shahar
• Ataroth • Jahaz
Kerioth • • Kedemoth
• Dibon
• Aroer
Arnon River
0 5 10 miles
0 5 10 15 km
© Carta, JERUSALEM

attested by the monument to Bohan, a descendant of Reuben (Josh 15:6). When the other tribes were settled in Canaan, Reuben, Gad, and half of Manasseh returned to Gilead and set up a great monument as a reminder of the unity of the Israelites (Josh 22). In protecting their flocks against marauding nomads they became a bold and skilled warlike people (1 Chron 5:1–19). Along with Gad and the half-tribe of Manasseh, they sent 120,000 men to support King David (11:42; 12:37).

REUBENITES (rū'bĕn-īts). Descendants of Reuben, son of Jacob. When Moses took the census in Midian, Reuben numbered 43,730 men of military age (Num 26:1–7). They were joint possessors of Gilead and Bashan (Deut 3:12; 29:8), and were praised by Moses for their fidelity (Josh 22:1–6).

REUEL (rū'ĕl, Heb. *re'ū'ēl, God is friend*). **1.** A son of Esau by Basemath (Gen 36:4, 10). **2.** A priest in Midian who gave Moses a daughter as wife (Exod 2:16–22), probably the same as Jethro (3:1). **3.** The father of Eliasaph in the KJV of Numbers 2:14. Called Deuel in Numbers 1:14; 7:42. NIV retains Deuel in Numbers 2:14. **4.** A Benjamite (1 Chron 9:8).

REVELATION To call the Bible the Word of God is to claim that it is the unique and faithful statement of God's self-revelation to mankind (John 10:34–35; 2 Tim 3:15–16; Heb 3:7–11; 2 Peter 1:19–21). God reveals himself in order that his people might know, love, trust, serve, and obey him as Lord. In the past God spoke to the patriarchs and prophets in many and varied ways, but his com-

plete and final word is given in and through Jesus, the Logos (John 1:1; Heb 1:1). The presence, words, deeds, and exaltation of Jesus constitute revelation (Matt 11:27; Luke 2:32; Titus 2:11; 3:4). The apostles refer to the receiving of revelation not only in terms of the central realities of the faith, but also in the form of personal instructions and guidance for their own lives and ministry (e.g., 2 Cor 12:1–10; Gal 2:2). Christ will reveal God when he returns to earth to judge the living and the dead; Christians should look for the glorious appearing of their Savior (2 Thess 2:8; 1 Tim 6:14; 2 Tim 4:1).

REVELATION, BOOK OF THE (Gr. *apokalypsis, an unveiling*). Sometimes called *The Apocalypse*. This is the last book of the Bible and the only book of the NT that is exclusively prophetic in character. Unlike many apocalyptic books that are either anonymous or published under a false name, Revelation is ascribed to John (Rev 1:9).

There are two prevailing views regarding the date of the Apocalypse. The earlier date in the reign of Nero is favored by some because of the allusion to the temple in Revelation 11:1–2. A second view, better substantiated by the early interpreters of the book, places it in the reign of Domitian (A.D. 81–96), almost at the close of the first century. The place of writing was the island of Patmos, where John had been exiled for his faith. Patmos was the site of a penal colony, where political prisoners were condemned to hard labor in the mines.

Revelation was addressed to seven churches of the Roman province of Asia, which occupied the western third of what is now Turkey. The cities where these churches were located were on the main roads running north and south, so that a messenger carrying these letters could move in a direct circuit from one to the other. Revelation was written in order that the evils in the churches might be corrected and that they might be prepared for the events that were about to confront them.

There are four main schools of interpretation. The *preterist* holds that Revelation is simply a picture of the conditions prevalent in the Roman Empire in the late first century, cast in the form of vision and prophecy to conceal its meaning from hostile pagans. The *historical* view contends that the book represents in symbolic form the entire course of church history from the time of its writing to the final consummation, and that the mystical figures and actions described in it can be identified with human events in history. The *futurist*, on the basis of the threefold division given in Revelation 1:19, suggests that "what you have seen" refers to the immediate environment of the seer and the vision of Christ (1:9–19), "what is now" denotes the churches of Asia or the church age they symbolize (2:1–3:22), and "what will take place later" relates to those events that will attend the return of Christ and the establishment of the city of God. The *idealist* or *symbolic* school treats Revelation as purely a dramatic picture of the conflict of good and evil.

Revelation contains four great visions, each of which is introduced by the phrase "in the Spirit" (Rev 1:10; 4:2; 17:3; 21:10). Each of these visions locates the seer in a different place, each contains a distinctive picture of Christ, and each advances the action significantly toward its goal. The first vision (1:9–3:22) pictures Christ as the critic of the churches, who commends their virtues and condemns their vices in the light of his virtues. The second vision (4:1–16:21) deals with the progressive series of seals, trumpets, and bowls, which mark the judgement of God on a world dominated by evil. The third vision (17:1–21:8) depicts the overthrow of evil society, religion, and government in the destruction of Babylon and the defeat of the beast and his armies by this victorious Christ. The last vision (21:9–22:5) is the establishment of the city of God, the eternal destiny of his people.

Outline:

I. **Introduction: The Return of Christ (1:1–8)**

II. **Christ, the Critic of the Churches (1:9–3:22)**

III. **Christ, the Controller of Destiny (4:1–16:21)**

IV. **Christ, the Conqueror of Evil (17:1–21:8)**

V. **Christ, the Consummator of Hope (21:9–22:5)**

VI. **Epilogue: Appeal and Invitation (22:6–21)**

REVELING, REVELINGS (Gr. *kōmos, orgy*). Any extreme intemperance and lustful indulgence, usually accompanying pagan worship (Rom 13:13; Gal 5:21; 1 Peter 4:3; 2 Peter 2:13).

REVILE (Heb. *qālal*, Gr. *antiloidoreō, blasphēmeō, loidoreō, oneidizō*). A word meaning "to address with abusive or insulting language," "to reproach." Israelites were forbidden to revile their parents on pain of death (Exod 21:17 KJV; NIV "curses"). Israel was reviled by Moab and Ammon (Zeph 2:8 KJV; NIV "taunts"). Jesus endured reviling on the cross (Mark 15:32 KJV). Revilers will have no part in the kingdom of God (1 Cor 6:10 KJV; cf. Pss 10:13; 44:16; 74:10, 18).

REVISED VERSIONS (See BIBLE, ENGLISH VERSIONS)

REWARD Something given, whether for a good or a bad act (Gen 15:1; Ps 91:8; Jer 40:5; Mic 7:3; 1 Tim 5:18; Rev 22:12).

REZIA (See RIZIA)

REZIN (rē'zĭn, Heb. *retsîn*). 1. The last king of Syria to reign in Damascus who was used to chasten Judah (2 Kings 15:37). He recaptured Syrian cities from Judah (16:6). The siege that he and Pekah, the king of Israel, undertook against Jerusalem led Isaiah to assure Judah by issuing the prophecy about the virgin birth of the Messiah (Isa 7:4–16). To escape Rezin, Ahaz king of Judah made an alliance with Tiglath-Pileser, who invaded Israel, captured Damascus, killed Rezin, and carried the Syrians into captivity (2 Kings 16:9). 2. The founder of a family of temple servants (KJV Nethinim; Ezra 2:43–48).

REZON (rē'zŏn, Heb. *rezôn, nobleman*). A citizen of Zobah, a small country NW of Damascus. Evidently a rebel, he took advantage of an invasion of Zobah by David and led a band of guerrillas to Damascus where he made himself king (1 Kings 11:23–25). He made an alliance with Hadad of Edom and began to harass Israel, whom he hated (11:25). He is almost certainly the same as Hezion (15:18), though Hezion could have been his son. In either case, he founded a dynasty of strong Syrian rulers, among them the noted Ben-Hadad I and his son Ben-Hadad II.

RHODA (rō'dà, Gr. *Rhodē, rose*). The name of the girl who answered the door in the very human narrative of Acts 12:13. She was a servant, probably a slave of Mary, John Mark's mother.

RHODES (rōdz, Gr. *Rhodos, rose*). A large island off the mainland of Caria. Rhodes controlled a rich carrying trade, and after the opening of the east by Alexander, became the richest of all Greek communities. Later Rome, seeking an excuse to cripple her trade rival, cut off Rhodes' Carian and Lycian depen-

Lindus (Gr. Lindos), on the eastern coast, was one of the three city-states of ancient Rhodes before their union (408 B.C.). Excavated remains include the Doric temple of Athena Lindia on the acropolis and stoa (colonnade) of the fourth century B.C. Rhodes, an island off the SW coast of Asia Minor, is mentioned in Acts 21:2. Courtesy Gerald Nowotny

dents, and the declaration of Delos as a free port ruined the community (166 B.C.). When Paul stopped on his way from Troas to Caesarea (Acts 21:1), Rhodes was only a station on the trade routes, a free city, but little more than a provincial town. Rhodes was the center of a sun cult, the famous colossus being a statue of Helios.

RIBAI (rĭ'bī). A Benjamite of Gibeah, father of Ithai (2 Sam 23:29), a mighty man (1 Chron 11:26, 31).

RIBLAH (rĭb'là, Heb. *rivlâh*). The city at the head waters of the Orontes River was a stronghold for both Egyptians and Assyrians. Copious water ran from its springs; fertile lands, east and west, and timber lands in nearby Lebanon made it a coveted prize of war. When Pharaoh Neco captured Jerusalem about 600 B.C. he put King Jehoahaz in chains at Riblah and led him to Egypt, where he died (2 Kings 23:31–34). A few years later, Nebuchadnezzar, then at war with Egypt, captured Jeremiah and took King Zedekiah to Riblah as a captive. There Zedekiah's sons were killed before him, his eyes were put out, and he was taken in chains to Babylon (25:6–7). Nebu-

chadnezzar then destroyed Jerusalem, and the chief priests and temple guards were led to Riblah where they were executed (25:21), before the Jews were taken into captivity. Riblah was on the east side of Ain, probably near Mt. Hermon (Num 34:11).

RICHES (See WEALTH)

RIDDLE (Heb. *hîdhâh*, from a root meaning *to bend* or *twist*, hence any artifice in speech, *a hidden saying, a proverb*). This form of language has long been used (Judg 14:14, 18; 1 Kings 10:1; 2 Chron 9:1). Solomon became famous as an author of proverbs and riddles (1 Kings 4:32); Ezekiel was told to speak a riddle to Israel (Ezek 17:2). To know dark sayings is a mark of wisdom (Prov 1:6). Riddle also refers to words of indefinite meaning (Num 12:8; Ps 49:4; Dan 5:12). One NT riddle appears in Revelation 13:18.

RIGHTEOUSNESS (Heb. *sadîq, saddîq*, Gr. *dikaiosynē*). The Lord God always acts in righteousness (Ps 89:14; Jer 9:24). That is, he always has a right relationship with people, and his action is to maintain that relationship. As regards Israel, this

Mandrakion Harbor at Rhodes, site of the famous colossal statue of Helios, 100 feet (30 m.) or more in height. The bronze statue, erected c. 290 B.C., was toppled during a severe earthquake and never rebuilt. It has been immortalized as one of the Seven Wonders of the World. Courtesy Gerald Nowotny

involved acting both in judgment (chastisement) and in deliverance (Pss 68; 103:6; Lam 1:18). The latter activity is often therefore equated with salvation (see Isa 46:12–13; 51:5). In passages from the Prophets (e.g., Isa 1:2–9; Jer 2:4–13; Mic 6:1–8) the Lord is presented as the Judge, and Israel as the accused party, with the covenant supplying the terms of reference.

As God acts in righteousness (because he is righteous), so he called Israel to be righteous as his chosen people. They were placed in his covenant, in right relationship with him through faith (Gen 15:6; Hab 2:4), and were expected to live in right relationship with others. The king was called to be in a right relationship with God, his people, and the surrounding nations (Pss 72:1–4; 146:7–9). Righteousness begins as a forensic term but easily becomes an ethical term in the OT. Much the same is found in the NT.

Righteousness means a right relationship with both God and one's fellow human beings (Matt 5:6, 17–20; Luke 18:14). The gospel is effective because, along with the proclamation, a righteousness goes forth (Rom 1:16–17).

RIMMON (rǐm′ŏn, Heb. *rimmôn, pomegranate*). **1.** A city near Edom in the southern part of Judah's heritage (Josh 15:32), also called En Rimmon (Neh 11:29). **2.** A noted rocky fortress not far from Gibeah was named Sela Rimmon, or the rock of Rimmon (Judg 20:45–47). **3.** A Benjamite of the clan of the Beerothites. He had two sons who murdered Ish-Bosheth (2 Sam 4:2–12). **4.** A Syrian god (2 Kings 5:15–19). **5.** A village of Simeon's heritage (1 Chron 4:32). **6.** A city of Zebulun's heritage (6:77 KJV; NIV "Rimmono").

RIMMONO (See RIMMON)

RING (Heb. *tabba′ath, to sink* or *stamp*, Gr. *daktylios, pertaining to a finger*). This article of jewelry derived its name from its use as a signet. It became the symbol of authority (Gen 41:42–43; Esth 3:10; Luke 15:22). The ring early became very valuable, as is shown by Isaiah's lament (Isa 3:18–23). Originally the signet was worn on a chain or wire about the neck, but the need to safeguard it led to its being put on the hand. The seal was an engraved stone, fastened to the ring (Exod 28:11).

RIVER Of the dozen or so words translated "river" in the Bible, only three need be mentioned. **1.** *Nāhār* (Gr. *potamos*) is used of the largest rivers known to the Israelites—the Tigris and Euphrates (Gen 2:14), the Abana and Pharpar (2 Kings 5:12), the Jordan (Mark 1:5), and the rivers of Ethiopia (Zeph 3:10). "The River" or "the Great River" usually refers to the Euphrates (Gen 15:18; 31:21). **2.** *Nahal* usually means a winter torrent, the bed of which is dry in summer, but may refer to a perennial stream like the Jabbok (Deut 2:37). **3.** *Ye'ôr,* "a stream," usually refers to the Nile and its mouths (Gen 41:1; 2 Kings 19:24). Once it denotes the Tigris (Dan 12:5–7).

RIVER OF EGYPT (See EGYPT, RIVER OF)

RIZIA (rĭ-zī'à). A descendant of Asher (1 Chron 7:39).

RIZPAH (rĭz'pà, Heb. *ritspâh, hot stone*). A daughter of Aiah, a Horite (1 Chron 1:40, called Ajah in Gen 36:24). Saul took her as a concubine (2 Sam 3:7). Ish-Bosheth, a son of Saul, accused Abner, a cousin, of committing incest with her (3:7). The accusation enraged Abner, who transferred his allegiance from Saul to David (3:8–21). In his zeal to establish Israel, Saul had killed a host of Gibeonites, and as a result a serious famine had come to Israel. On consulting Gibeonites about restitution for the evil, David learned that only the death of Saul's sons would atone. Among those turned over to Gibeon were two sons by Rizpah (21:1–8). Because of Rizpah's devotion to her sons, David had the bones of her sons and those of Saul and Jonathan buried in the tomb of Saul's father, Kish (21:14).

ROADS In Palestine the chief south-to-north traverse is the road via Pelusium, Rafia, and Gaza, up the Maritime Plain, the ancient invasion route used by Thutmose, Ramses, Sennacherib, Cambyses, Alexander, Pompey, Titus, Saladin, Napoleon, and Allenby. Carmel closes the northern end. Passage was possible by a rough and exposed route on the seaward side, a path used by Richard I of England and by Napoleon on his withdrawal, and known as *Les Detroits* by the Crusaders. On the landward side Esdraelon and Phoenicia were reached by several low passes, chiefly those that run through Megiddo, and the route through the Valley of Dothan (Gen 37:25). The latter route was used by those traveling to Jordan and Damascus.

A more easterly route from Damascus south lay through the arid deserts and mountains east of the Jordan Valley, through the tribal territories of Manasseh, Reuben, and Gad, into Moab, and down the desert valley of the Arabah (Deut 8:15). This was the so-called King's Highway.

ROBBERY Illegal seizure of another's property, a crime forbidden by law (Lev 19:13). In the days of the judges it was unsafe to travel the highways because of robberies by highwaymen (Judg 5:6; 9:25). Houses were built to resist robbers, who were often base enough to seize the money of orphans and widows (Isa 10:2). Honor did not exist among thieves (Ezek 39:10). Companies of priests had turned to pillage in the time of Hosea (Hos 6:9).

David warned against the lust for riches that resulted in robbery (Ps 62:10). Isaiah wrote of God's hatred for this means of getting a burnt offering (Isa 61:8). Among the vices of God's people listed by Ezekiel is robbery (Ezek 22:29). Nahum accused Nineveh of being a center of numerous robberies (Nah 3:1). Withholding tithes and offerings from God's storehouse was a kind of robbery (Mal 3:8; cf. Matt 6:19–20; Luke 10:30–37; John 10:1; 2 Cor 11:26; Phil 2:6).

ROBE (See DRESS)

ROBOAM (See REHOBOAM)

ROCK (Heb. *sela', a cliff* or *mass of stone, tsûr, a crag,* Gr. *petra,* any *stone*). The rock in Horeb that Moses was to strike was *tsûr* (Exod 17:6), the one he was to speak to in Kadesh was *sela'* (Num 20:8). A *sela'* was often a natural fortress, as at Rimmon (Judg 20:45, 47). Sometimes it was a mountain (1 Sam 23:25–26). *Tsûr* in Numbers 23:9 means a craggy height. Both terms are used to refer to God: the Lord is my rock (2 Sam 22:2), my *sela'* and fortress (Pss 18:2; 71:3). In comparing God with other gods, Scripture says their *tsûr* is not like our Rock (Deut 32:31; see also Pss 61:2; 62:2; 95:1). The NT use of *petra* was both literal and figurative. Building on *petra* gave security to a house (Matt 7:24–25). The Lord's burial place had been cut into a *petra* (Mark 15:46). Jesus made a distinction between Simon the *petros* and the basic truth (*petra*) in Peter's confession, the truth on which the *ekklēsia* was to be built (Matt 16:18). Believers are living stones being built into a spiritual house (1 Peter 2:5).

ROCK BADGER (See ANIMALS)

ROD (Heb. *maqqēl, matteh, shēvet,* Gr. *rhabdos*). Originally a name given to a

piece of tree limb used as a support or as
a weapon. There is little difference between the word for rod and that for staff.
The rod had varying uses in ancient
times. Jacob used rods to change, as he
supposed, the color of Laban's goats and
sheep (Gen 30:37–41; cf. 31:10–12).
Rods became symbols of authority (Jer
48:17; cf. Exod 3:16–17; 4:2, 17, 20; 7:9–
20; 9:23; 10:13; 14:16; 17:5–7; Num
17:9–13; 20). To kill a servant with the
rod was illegal (Exod 21:20). The shepherd's rod was used in counting sheep
(Lev 27:32). God's anger was for Job a
rod (Job 9:34). Chastisement was symbolized by the rod (Pss 89:32; 125:3; Prov
13:24; 22:15; 29:15). The coming of Christ
was to be preceded by the rod (Mic 5:1).
Jesus is to win with a rod (scepter, Ps
2:9). Paul would use a rod if forced to do
so (1 Cor 4:21). Aaron's budding rod was
symbolic of Christ's eternal reign (Heb
9:1–28). The victorious believer will rule
with a scepter or rod (Rev 2:27). The
temple of God was measured with a
rodlike reed (11:1).

RODANIM (rŏd'à-nĭm). A tribe descended from Javan, a son of Japheth
(1 Chron 1:7). Both here and in Genesis
10:4, RSV has "Dodanim," but the LXX
gives "Rodanim" or "Rodians," which
rendering is supported by RSV "men of
Rhodes" (Ezek 27:15), a reading followed by NIV. Ezekiel's account of the
trade by Dedan (KJV) would link the city
with Rhodes. Records of trade between
Rhodes and western Mediterranean ports
date back to 700 B.C.

RODENT (See ANIMALS)

ROE, ROEBUCK (See ANIMALS)

ROGELIM (rō'gē-lĭm). A thrifty community near Mahanaim. Its citizens took
supplies to David's army (2 Sam 17:27,
29) and led him across the Jordan (19:31).

ROLL A scroll, a literary work on papyrus or parchment rolled around a core or
spool. The decree of Cyrus to restore the
temple was a roll (Ezra 1:1), and Jeremiah wrote on such a roll (Jer 36:2).
Books with pages did not come into use
until the second century A.D. See also
PAPYRUS; WRITING.

ROMAN EMPIRE The Roman Empire
was the result of a process of expansion
that began in the sixth and seventh centuries before Christ. In 509 B.C., Rome
early began the search for a stable frontier that was to form the guiding motive
of her history. That quest took her step
by step to the subjugation of the Italian

Painted wooden statuette of King Senwos-
ret I (1971–1926 B.C.) holding a staff or
rod in his left hand and wearing the crown
of Lower Egypt. From the tomb of Imhotep,
Lisht, Egypt, 12th Dynasty. Courtesy The
Metropolitan Museum of Art, Museum Excavations, Contribution of Edward S. Harkness

peninsula and the domination of its peoples.
   By the beginning of the Christian era
the Roman Empire was reaching the
limits of its expansion. A major military
disaster in A.D. 9 caused Augustus to
choose the Rhine as a northern frontier.
The Danube formed its logical eastward
continuation. Spain, Gaul, and Britain
formed stable enough buttresses in the
west, while the southern marches rested
on the Sahara, a desert frontier, and

strategically the most stable of all. The east was never totally secured, and some of the imagery of the Apocalypse reflects the fear felt in the Middle East of the archer cavalry from over the Euphrates.

Politically, the term Roman Empire must be distinguished from the Roman Republic. The Empire describes the system of rule and government known as the principate. The year 31 B.C., the date of the Battle of Actium, is arbitrarily chosen as the dividing line, when Republic became Empire. Octavian, Julius Caesar's adoptive nephew, had defeated Antony. Extraordinary commands and special powers prepared the way for the autocracy that emerged full-fledged with Augustus.

The Roman Empire, using the word in the political sense of the term, was the governmental framework of the Roman Peace, that era of centralized government that kept comparative peace in the Mediterranean world for significant centuries. No wonder the Eastern provinces, accustomed since ancient days to the deification of rulers, early established the custom of worshiping the emperor. The notion gained popularity through the writings of poets such as Horace and Vergil, who genuinely believed in the divine call of Augustus and who, without a higher view of deity, saw no incompatibility in ascribing divine attributes to a mere man of destiny. Such were the sinister beginnings of a cult that Rome chose as a cement of empire.

ROMANS, LETTER TO THE The genuineness of the letter has never been seriously questioned by competent critics familiar with first-century history. Although other NT letters have been wrongly attacked as forgeries not written by the alleged authors, this letter stands with Galatians and 1 and 2 Corinthians as one of the unassailable documents of early church history.

There can be no doubt that the author, Paul, formerly Saul of Tarsus (Acts 13:9), was a highly intellectual, rabbinically educated Jew (Acts 22:3; Gal 1:14) who had been intensely hostile to the Christian movement and had sought to destroy it (Acts 8:1–3; 9:1–2; 1 Cor 15:9; Gal 1:13). Even the critics who reject the supernatural cannot deny the extraordinary nature of the fact that this able enemy became the greatest exponent of the Christian faith and wrote the most powerful statements of Christian doctrine.

This is a letter, not a treatise. It was not intended to be a formal literary product. In the midst of greetings from friends who were with the author as he wrote (Rom 16:21–23), Tertius, the scribe to whom the letter was dictated, puts in his own personal greeting (16:22).

The letter clearly places itself in the three-month period (Acts 20:3) that Paul spent in Corinth just before going to Jerusalem (about December A.D. 56 to February 57).

There was a church already existing at Rome, probably founded by local people who had heard the gospel in their travels. It was Paul's peculiar policy to preach in hitherto unevangelized areas (Rom 15:17–24; cf. also 2 Cor 10:14–16). His proposed visit to Rome was not inconsistent, however, for (1) he had a contribution to make to their spiritual welfare (Rom 1:11–13) and (2) he planned to visit Rome on his way to evangelize Spain (15:24). He was asking the church in Rome to help him in this project. The structure of the letter is built around Paul's travel plans.

It has been said that if Galatians is the "Magna Charta" of the gospel, Romans is the "Constitution." The theological substance of this letter had to be presented to the NT church, whether addressed to Rome or not, but there were circumstances in Rome that made it appropriate for Paul, with time for fuller elaboration, and without having become personally involved in local affairs, as he had in Galatia, to expand the central doctrine of the Letter to the Galatians. Thus he explained his purpose in coming to Rome and the main purpose of his life ministry and message. There was friction and misunderstanding between Jewish and Gentile Christians in the Roman church. We know from the personal greetings at the end that it was a mixed church. The problem is reflected in almost every section of the letter, but especially in chapters 3, 4, 9, 10, and 11. Both sides were stubborn. There was a moment, probably brief, even after Paul had reached Rome, when Mark and a certain Jesus Justus were the only Christian Jews in Rome who would cooperate with Paul (Col 4:10–11). A clarification of the gospel and its implications was needed.

The following very simple outline is suggested. (The great doctrinal themes are discussed in articles on doctrinal topics.)

I. The Apostle Paul to the Christians in Rome.

I am entrusted with a message that I must deliver to

you, i.e., the gospel in all its implications (1:1-17).

II. The World Is Lost
   A. The Gentile world is wretchedly lost (1:18-32) in spite of God's justice for attempted morality (2:1-16).
   B. The Jewish world is equally lost, in spite of all their privileges (2:17-3:20).

III. Justification by Faith Is My Great Message (3:21-5:21). There is no space for the wealth of subtopics.

IV. Holy Living in Principle (6:1-8:39).

V. God Has Not Forgotten the Jews (9:1-11:36).

VI. Details of Christian Conduct (12:1-15:13).

VII. Miscellaneous Notes
   A. Travel plans (15:14-33).
   B. Personal to people in Rome (16:1-20).
   C. Personal from people in Corinth (16:21-23).
   D. Doxology (16:24-27).

ROME In population the city of Rome probably passed the million mark at the beginning of the Christian era, and during the first century may have risen somewhat above this figure.

It is possible to estimate roughly the proportion of Christians over the imperial centuries. In the Catacombs, ten generations of Christians are buried. The most conservative estimate from the evidence of the Catacomb burials is that at least one-fifth of the population were Christians, and that probably the proportion was much larger.

Rome, like Babylon, became a symbol of organized paganism and opposition to Christianity in the Bible (Revelation 17-18). The climax is bitter, as John pictures Rome under the smoke of her burning, the voice of gladness stilled.

The city appears several times in a historical context, the most notable being Paul's enforced stay there. Paul landed at Puteoli; and alerted by the little church there (Acts 28:14-15), members of Rome's Christian community met Paul at two stopping-places. On the evidence of the Nazareth Decree, it appears that a group of believers had been established in Rome since the principate of Claudius in the late 40s of the first century. Paul probably entered Rome by the Capena

Exterior and interior view of the Colosseum, or Amphitheatrum Flarium, in Rome, built by Vespasian and Titus and completed A.D. 82. The scene of gladiator fights and other contests, the structure measures 620 by 513 feet (190 by 155 m.) overall and seats c. 50,000 spectators.
Courtesy Gerald Nowotny

Gate. His "rented house" (28:30) would be in some block of flats, an "insula."

ROOM 1. A chamber in a house (Acts 1:13). 2. In KJV the word also always translates *prōtoklisia*, place of honor at a dinner (Matt 23:6; Mark 12:39; Luke 14:7-8; 20:46).

ROOSTER (See BIRDS)

ROOT (Heb. *shōresh*, Gr. *rhiza*). Usually used in a figurative sense. Judah was promised new roots after the Captivity (2 Kings 19:30; Isa 37:31; see Rom 15:12). The roots of the wicked shall not endure (Isa 5:24). Jesus was the Root of David (11:1, 10). The Messiah was to come from an unexpected root (53:2). Daniel used the word in writing about Nebuchadnezzar, whose roots (the remnant of his kingdom) would remain during his period of suffering for sin (Dan 4:8-23). In the parable of the sower, the roots did not develop on or among stones (Matt 13:20). The fig tree and its roots died (Mark 11:20). The source of spiritual life is in the roots (Rom 11:17-18), even as the love of money is a root of all kinds of evil (1 Tim 6:10).

ROPE (Heb. *hevel, line* or *cord, 'ăvōth, a woven band,* Gr. *schoinion, a cable*). Hushai counseled Absalom to have Israel bring *hevel* (strong cables) with which to pull into the river the city where David might take refuge (2 Sam 17:7-13). Sackcloth on the body and a *hevel* about the head (a woven band) were symbols of deep servility (1 Kings 20:31-32). In 2 Samuel 8:2, *hevel* is a cord, a small linear measure. Rahab used a *hevel* (rope) to let the spies over the wall of Jericho (Josh 2:1-16). *'Avōth* was used for binding Samson (Judg 16:11-12). Isaiah used it in deriding Israel's efforts to pile up iniquity (Isa 5:18-19). Small ropes or cords were used to fasten the sacrificial animal to the altar (Ps 118:27 KJV; see NIV footnote). In the NT *schoinion* means either a rope made of bulrushes (Acts 27:32) or small cords used to lead or drive cattle (John 2:15).

ROSE, ROSE OF SHARON (See PLANTS)

ROSETTA STONE A damaged inscribed basalt slab, found accidentally at Fort St. Julien on the Rosetta branch of the Nile, near the city of Rosetta, by a French army work crew in A.D. 1799. Terms of the French surrender to the British gave the French finds to the victors, and the Rosetta Stone was placed in the British Museum. The monument was originally set up in 196 B.C. as a formal decree of the Egyptian priesthood in honor of Ptolemy V (Epiphanes) with an identical text in three parts: hieroglyphic, demotic, and Greek. The parallel texts furnished the key for the decipherment of the Egyptian, with the proper names providing the basic clues for the achievement. Decipherment of the hieroglyphs was accomplished by Jean François Champollion in A.D. 1822.

ROSH (rŏsh, Heb. *rō'sh, head*). **1.** A son of Benjamin who went to Egypt with Jacob and his sons (Gen 46:21). **2.** In ASV (cf. NIV footnote) head of three nations that are to invade Israel during the latter days (Ezek 38:2, 8). Gog is chief of Magog, Meshech, and Tubal. These tribes were from the far north, hence Rosh could possibly be Russia.

ROW, ROWERS (See SHIPS)

RUBY (See MINERALS)

RUDIMENTS (rū'di-mĕnts, Gr. *stoicheia, the first principles or elements of anything*). Stoicheia is found in the NT seven times, and KJV translates it in

The Rosetta Stone, which takes its name from the Egyptian village 30 miles (48 km.) from Alexandria, is one of the most important archaeological finds in history, with a trilingual inscription in hieroglyphic, demotic, and Greek scripts. Reproduced by courtesy of the Trustees of the British Museum

three different ways: "elements" (Gal 4:3, 9; 2 Peter 3:10, 12), "rudiments" (Col 2:8, 20), and "first principles" (Heb 5:12). NIV also translates it three ways. In 2 Peter it probably means the physical "elements" of the world. NIV has "elementary truths" in Hebrews 5:12; NEB imaginatively reads "the ABC." The other four verses refer to rudimentary religious teachings, in this instance the ceremonial precepts of the worship of the Jews—RSV "elemental spirits," NIV "basic principles."

RUE (See PLANTS)

RUFUS (rū'fŭs, Gr. *Rhouphos*). The brother of Alexander and the son of Simon of Cyrene who bore the cross (Mark 15:21). A Rufus is also greeted by Paul in Romans 16:13. If the two references are to one man, it may be conjectured that Simon or Simon's widow became a Christian and emigrated from Cyrene to Rome, this being the reason for Mark's cryptic reference. Mark was probably writing in Rome.

RUHAMAH (See LO-RUHAMAH)

RULER (See OCCUPATIONS AND PROFESSIONS: *Prince, Princess*)

RUSH (See PLANTS)

RUTH, BOOK OF The author of this book is unknown. The historical setting is the period of the judges (Ruth 1:1), but there are certain indications that it was composed, or at least worked into its final form, at a much later time. For example, the opening words, "In the days when the judges ruled" looks back to that period; the "gloss" in 4:7 explains an ancient custom for later readers; and 4:22 mentions David. Thus the final editorial process could not have ended before the time of David. It is best to place its final shaping in, or immediately following, the reign of David.

The book records the circumstances that led to the marriage of Ruth, a Moabitess, to Boaz, an Israelite. A famine forced Naomi and her husband to move to Moab, where her sons married Moabite women, one of whom was Ruth. Naomi and her daughter-in-law became widows, and Ruth and Naomi settled in Bethlehem. In the course of providing food for herself and her mother-in-law, Ruth met Boaz, a prosperous farmer and a relative of Naomi. With Naomi's encouragement, Ruth tenderly reminded Boaz of the levirate obligation (Ruth 3:1-9), a Deuteronomic law that required a man to marry his brother's widow if she was childless, the purpose being that the dead man have an heir (Deut 25:5-10). However, Boaz was not the nearest of kin. When the closest relative learned that there was a levirate obligation attached to the redemption of Naomi's land, he rejected it (Ruth 4:1-6), and Boaz was free to marry Ruth.

The Book of Ruth demonstrates the providence of God at work in the life of an individual, and it exalts family loyalty. It shows how a Gentile became part of the Davidic ancestry (Ruth 4:17-21); thus Ruth is cited in the genealogy of Christ in Matthew 1:5.

RYE (See PLANTS)

- S -

SABAEANS (See SABEANS)

SABACHTHANI (See ELOI, ELOI, LAMA SABACHTHANI)

SABAOTH, LORD OF (săb'ă-ŏth, Gr. *sabaoth, hosts*). The "Lord of Sabaoth" is the same as "Lord of hosts." The phrase is used in the KJV of Romans 9:29 and James 5:4, where NIV has "Lord Almighty." The "Lord of hosts" is often found in the OT. All created agencies and forces are under the command and leadership of the Lord.

SABBATH (săb'ăth, Heb. *shabbāth*, Gr. *Sabbaton, to desist, cease, rest*). The weekly day of rest and worship of the Jews. The Sabbath was instituted at creation. The record of creation (Gen 1:1–2:3) closes with an account of God's hallowing of the seventh day, because on it he rested from his creative labors (2:3). There is no distinct mention of the Sabbath in Genesis, but a seven-day period is mentioned several times in connection with the Flood (7:4, 10; 8:10, 12) and once in connection with Jacob's years at Haran (29:27–28), showing that the division of time into sevens must have been known then.

There is no express mention of the Sabbath before Exodus 16:21–30. Shortly afterward the Ten Commandments were given by the Lord at Sinai (20:1–17; 34:1–5). The fourth commandment enjoined Israel to observe the seventh day as a holy day on which no work should be done by man or beast. Everyone, including strangers, was to desist from all work and to keep the day holy. The Sabbath, frequently mentioned in the Levitical legislation, was to be kept holy for the worship of the Lord (Lev 23:3) and was to remind the Israelites that God had sanctified them (Exod 31:13; cf. Deut 5:15). Among the Hebrews the Sabbath was associated with the idea of rest, worship, and divine favor, not certain taboos.

The sanctity of the Sabbath is shown by the offering on it of two lambs, in addition to the regular burnt offering (Num 28:9–10). The 12 loaves of showbread were also presented on that day (Lev 24:5–9; 1 Chron 9:32).

With the development of the synagogue during the Exile, the Sabbath became a day for worship and the study of the Law, as well as a day of rest. During the period between Ezra and the Christian era the scribes formulated innumer-

Ruins of the ancient synagogue at Capernaum, with a row of Corinthian capitals shown in foreground. Below, a reconstruction of the synagogue façade. Courtesy Zev Radovan (photo) and Carta, Jerusalem (drawing)

able legal restrictions for the conduct of life under the law. Two whole treatises in the Talmud are devoted to the details of Sabbath observance.

Jesus was critical of these restrictions (Luke 11:46). He came into conflict with the religious leaders of the Jews especially on two points: His claim to be the Messiah, and on the matter of Sabbath observance. The rabbis regarded the Sabbath as an end in itself, whereas Jesus taught that the Sabbath was made for man's benefit, and that man's needs must take precedence over the law of the Sabbath (Matt 12:1–14; Mark 2:23–3:6; Luke 6:1–11; John 5:1–18). He himself regularly attended worship in the synagogue on the Sabbath (Luke 4:16).

The early Christians, most of whom were Jews, kept the seventh day as a Sabbath, but since the resurrection of

Jesus was so crucial to their faith, they began very early also to meet for worship on the first day of the week (Acts 2:1) and designated it as the Lord's Day. Paul directed the Corinthian Christians to bring their weekly offering to the charities of the church on the first day of the week (1 Cor 16:1–2). As the split between the Jews and Christians widened, the Christians came gradually to meet for worship only on the Lord's Day and gave up the observance of the seventh day.

SABBATH DAY'S WALK Used only in Acts 1:12 (KJV "sabbath day's journey"), where it designates the distance between Mt. Olivet and Jerusalem. A Sabbath day's walk was a journey of limited extent that the scribes thought a Jew might travel on the Sabbath without breaking the law (cf. Josh 3:4).

SABBATICAL YEAR (See FEASTS)

SABEANS (să-bē'ănz, Heb. *sevā'îm*). Seba was a son of Cush (Gen 10:7; 1 Chron 1:9). In Isaiah 43:3 the name is coupled with Ethiopia, and in Psalm 72:10 with Sheba (cf. Isa 45:14; Ezek 23:42). Saba was situated between the Nile and the Atbara and was known to the Hebrews as Cush. Another Sabean race (Gen 10:28; 25:3) was located in Arabia. They built a unique civilization and great empire. The queen of Sheba, who made a visit of state to the court of Solomon, came from there.

SACAR (să'kàr, Heb. *sākhār, wages*). 1. Father of Ahiam, a follower of David. He was a Hararite (1 Chron 11:35). In 2 Samuel 23:33 the name is spelled "Sharar." 2. A son of Obed-Edom (1 Chron 26:4).

SACKCLOTH The English word is derived from the Hebrew *sak,* a coarse cloth, dark in color, usually made of goat's hair. It was worn by mourners (2 Sam 3:31; 2 Kings 19:1–2), prophets (Isa 20:2; Rev 11:3), and captives (1 Kings 20:31). It was usually worn over another garment, but sometimes next to the skin (21:27; 2 Kings 6:30; Job 16:15; Isa 32:11; Jonah 3:6).

SACRAMENT (săk'rà-mĕnt). The word *sacramentum* was used with a distinctively Christian meaning for the first time in the Old Latin Bible and in Tertullian (end of the second century). In the Old Latin and in the Vulgate it was employed to translate the Greek *mystērion,* "mystery" (e.g., Eph 5:32; 1 Tim 3:16; Rev 1:20; 17:7). For a long time it was used not only to refer to religious rites but to doctrines and facts.

Sabean grave stele from South Arabia. In upper register is a figure seated before an offering table with attendants standing alongside. In lower register are two camels and a rider. The Sabeans were known for the extent of their trade (Job 6:19; Isa 60:6; Jer 6:20). Second or third century A.D. Courtesy Réunion des Musées Nationaux

Because of the absence of any defined sacramental concept in the early history of the church, the number of sacraments was not regarded as fixed. Baptism and the Lord's Supper were the chief. In the 12th century Hugo of St. Victor listed 30 sacraments that had been recognized by the church, while Gregory of Bergamo and Peter Lombard listed only seven: baptism, confirmation, the Eucharist, penance, extreme unction, orders, and matrimony—a list adopted by Thomas Aquinas and later by the Council of Trent.

Baptism and the Lord's Supper were regarded as ritual acts of faith and obedience toward God (Matt 28:19–20; Acts 2:38; Rom 6:3–5; 1 Cor 11:23–27; Col 2:11–12). They are symbolic rites setting forth the central truths of the Christian faith: death and resurrection with Christ and participation in the redemptive benefits of Christ's mediatorial death. They are visible enactments of the gospel message that Christ lived, died, was raised from the dead, ascended to heaven, and will some day return, and that all this is for man's salvation. See also BAPTISM; LORD'S SUPPER; MYSTERY.

SACRIFICE AND OFFERINGS (Heb. *zevah*, Gr. *thysia*). A religious act belonging to worship in which offering is made to God of some material object belonging to the offerer. Sacrifices have been classified in a variety of ways, chiefly the following: (1) Those on behalf of the whole congregation and those on behalf of the individual. (2) Animal or bleeding sacrifices and bloodless offerings. (3) Sacrifices assuming an undisturbed covenant relationship and those intended to restore a relationship that has been disturbed. (4) Animal sacrifices, vegetable sacrifices, liquid and incense offerings. (5) Sacrifices made without the help of a priest, those made by a priest alone, and those made by a layman with the help of a priest. (6) Sacrifices that express homage to God, those designed to make atonement for sin, and peace offerings (to express or promote peaceful relations with God). (7) Self-dedicatory sacrifices, eucharistic sacrifices, and expiatory sacrifices. (8) Sacrifices in which the offering was wholly devoted to God, and sacrifices in which God received a portion and the worshiper feasted on the remainder.

The sacrifices of Cain and Abel (Gen 4:4–5) show that the rite goes back almost to the beginnings of the human race. The sacrifice of Noah after the Flood (8:20–21) is called a burnt offering and is closely connected with the covenant of God (9:8–17). In his sacrifices, Abraham (12:7–8; 13:4, 18; 15:4ff.) expressed his adoration of God. The establishment of the covenant between Israel and the Lord was accompanied by solemn sacrifices. The foundation principle of this covenant was *obedience,* not sacrifices (Exod 19:4–8). Sacrifices were incidental—aids to obedience but valueless without it.

Every offering had to be the honestly acquired property of the offerer (2 Sam 24:24). The only animals allowed for sacrifice were oxen, sheep, goats, and pigeons. The produce of the field allowed for offerings was wine, oil, grain, either in the ear or in the form of meal, dough, or cakes. Sacrifices were of two kinds:

Offering plaque (19 cm. high), 2500–1500 B.C., from Nippur, the chief religious center of Sumer. In the upper register is a duplicate scene: a nude priest is offering libations to a seated god. The bottom register shows a sheep and a goat driven by two figures, one bearing a container on his head, the other carrying a stick. Courtesy Istanbul Museum. Photo: B. Brandl

animal (with the shedding of blood) and vegetable or bloodless.

Animal Sacrifices. 1. The Sin Offering (Lev 4:1–35; 6:24–30). This was for sins unconsciously or unintentionally committed; sins committed intentionally, but with mitigating circumstances (5:2–3; 12:6–8); certain kinds of ceremonial defilements (5:2–3; 12:6–8); and sins deliberately committed but afterwards voluntarily confessed. **2.** The Guilt Offering (Lev 5:14–6:7). (In the KJV the "trespass offering.") This was a special kind of sin offering and was offered for transgressions where restitution or other legal satisfaction could be made, or was made. **3.** The Burnt Offering (Lev 1). It was wholly consumed on the altar, while in other animal sacrifices only the fat portions were burned. The purpose of the offering was propitiation and the entire consecration of the worshiper to the Lord. **4.** The Fellowship Offering (Lev 3). (In the KJV the "peace offering.") These were called fellowship offerings because they were offered by those who were at peace with God, to express gratitude and obligation to God, and fellowship with him.

Vegetable or Bloodless Sacrifices. These were of two kinds, and were offered on the altar of the forecourt. **1.** The Grain Offerings (Lev 2:1–16; 6:14–18) were offerings of fine flour or of unleavened bread, cakes, wafers, or of ears of grain

Middle Kingdom (twentieth to nineteenth century B.C.) wooden statue of Egyptian woman bearing offerings for the dead. In her hand is a vessel for water and, on her head, a chest surmounted by a leg of beef.
Courtesy Réunion des Musées Nationaux

toasted, always with salt and, except in the sin offering, with olive oil (2:1, 4, 13–14; 5:11). **2.** The Drink Offerings were not independent offerings under the law but were made only in connection with the grain offering that accompanied all burnt offerings and all fellowship offerings that were Nazirite, votive, or freewill (Num 6:17; 15:1–2).

Besides the above, three offerings were regularly made in the Holy Place: the 12 loaves of showbread, renewed every Sabbath; the oil for the seven-branched lampstand, which was filled every morning; and the incense for the altar of incense, which was renewed every morning and evening.

SACRILEGE (săk'rĭ-lĕj). The expression *commit sacrilege*, used once (Rom 2:22 KJV, MLB), translates *hierosyleō* in the NT; *hierosylos*, a related term, may generally mean one who commits irreverent acts against a holy place.

SADDLE (Heb. *mercāv, a riding seat*). The verb *habhash*, "to bind on," is used of getting a beast (always a donkey) ready for riding (Gen 22:3; Num 22:21; Judg 19:10; 2 Sam 16:1; 17:23; 19:26; 1 Kings 2:40; 2 Kings 4:24). Donkeys were not ridden with saddles. A donkey carrying a heavy burden had a thick cushion on its back to relieve the pressure.

SADDUCEES (săd'yū-sēz, Gr. *Saddoukaioi*). One of the religious parties that existed among the Jews in the days of Christ and the early church, but exercised comparatively little influence among the people. They resisted the truth of the gospel. The root of the word means "to be righteous." Probably the name is derived from someone named Zadok.

The Sadducees were the political party of the Jewish aristocratic priesthood from the time of the Maccabees to the final fall of the Jewish state. They became leaders in the Hellenizing movement that began with Alexander the Great. Because of their sympathy with the policy of Antiochus Epiphanes, they took no part in the Maccabean struggle, which was supported mainly by the Pharisees. The Sadducees under the Romans become the party favorable to the government. Since they were satisfied with the present, they did not look forward to a future messianic age.

The Sadducees had a number of distinctive beliefs, contrasting strongly with those of the Pharisees: **1.** They held only to the written law and rejected the traditions of the Pharisees. In other words, the Sadducees believed that the Word of God alone was the seat of religious authority. The Pharisees, on the contrary, believed that just as binding as the Law itself was the supposed oral tradition of the teachings of Moses and the rulings on the law made by the scribes over the years. **2.** A second distinctive belief of the Sadducees was their denial of the resurrection of the body, personal immortality, and retribution in a future life (Matt 22:23; Mark 12:18; Luke 20:27; Acts 23:8; cf. Acts 4:1–2). **3.** The Sadducees denied the existence of angels and spirits (Acts 23:8). A number of factors may have been responsible for this: Their general indifference to religion, their rationalistic temper, and the wild extravagances of the angelology and demonology of the Pharisees. **4.** The Sadducees differed from both the Pharisees and the Essenes on the matter of divine predestination and the freedom of the human will. They threw aside all ideas of divine interposition in the government of the world.

The Sadducees are mentioned by name in the NT only about a dozen times (Matt 3:7; 16:1, 6, 11–12; 22:23, 34; Mark 12:18; Luke 20:27; Acts 4:1; 5:17; 23:6–8); but it must be remembered that when mention is made of the chief priests, practically the same persons are referred to.

After the Day of Pentecost the Sadducees were very active against the infant church. They arrested Peter and John and put them in prison. A little later they arrested all the apostles and made plans to kill them (Acts 5:17, 33). There is no record of a Sadducee being admitted into the Christian church. According to Josephus (*Antiq.* 20.9.1), they were responsible for the death of James, the brother of the Lord. With the destruction of Jerusalem in A.D. 70, the Sadducean party disappeared.

SAFFRON (See PLANTS)

SAIL (See SHIPS)

SAILOR (See OCCUPATIONS AND PROFESSIONS)

SAINT In a religious sense it means that which is separated or dedicated to God, and therefore removed from secular use. The word is applied to people, places, and things (e.g., the temple, vessels, garments, the city of Jerusalem, priests). In a personal sense it means holy. In the NT the word *hagioi* is applied to OT (Matt 27:52) and NT believers (e.g., Acts 26:10; Rom 8:27; 12:13; 16:2; 2 Cor 1:1; Eph 1:1; 1 Thess 3:13; Jude 3; Rev 13:7, 10). The church is made up of people called out of the world (Rom 1:7;

1 Cor 1:2) by God's electing grace to be his own people. All who are in covenant relation with him through repentance and faith in his Son are regarded as saints. Objectively, the saints are God's chosen and peculiar people, belonging exclusively to him. Subjectively, they are separated from all defilement and sin and partake of God's holiness. Saints are urged to live lives befitting their position (Eph 4:1, 12; 5:3; Col 1:10; cf. 2 Cor 8:4).

SAKIA (sà-kī'à, Heb. *sakheyah,* probably *Jehovah has hedged about*). Son of Shaharaim, a Benjamite (1 Chron 8:10).

SALA, SALAH (See SHELAH)

SALAMIS (săl'à-mĭs Gr. *Salamis*). A town on the east coast of Cyprus, possessing a good harbor; it was a populous and flourishing town in the Hellenic and Roman periods. Paul and Barnabas preached the gospel there in the synagogues of the Jews (Acts 13:5). Paul did not return to Salamis, but Barnabas doubtless did on his second missionary journey (15:39). According to tradition he was martyred there in the reign of Nero.

SALATHIEL (See SHEALTIEL)

SALECAH, SALCAH (Heb. *salekhâh*). A city on the extreme NE boundary of the kingdom of Bashan, near Edrei (Deut 3:10; Josh 12:5; 13:11). Og, king of Bashan, once ruled it. Later it became the northern limit of the Gadites (1 Chron 5:11).

SALEM (sā'lĕm, Heb. *shālēm, peace*). The name of the city of which Melchizedek was king (Gen 14:18; Heb 7:1–2). Josephus says that Jewish writers generally regarded it as a synonym of Jerusalem (e.g., Ps 76:2).

SALIM (sā'lĭm, Gr. *Saleim*). A place referred to in John 3:23 as near Aenon, where John was baptizing. It must have been west of the Jordan (John 1:28; 3:26; 10:40).

SALLU (săl'ū, Heb. *Sallay*). **1.** The head of a family of Benjamin who settled in Jerusalem after the Exile (1 Chron 9:7; Neh 11:7). **2.** The head of a family of priests who returned with Zerubbabel (12:7, 20; KJV has "Sallai" in 12:20).

SALMON (săl'mŏn, Heb. *salmôn, clothing*). The father of Boaz (Ruth 4:20–21; 1 Chron 2:11; Matt 1:4–5; Luke 3:32).

SALOME (sà-lō'mē, Gr. *Salōmē,* fem. of Solomon). **1.** The wife of Zebedee, and mother of James and John (cf. Matt 27:56 with Mark 15:40–41; 16:1). **2.** The daughter of Herodias, and the grandniece of

Herod Antipas. As a reward for her dancing she was given the head of John the Baptist (Matt 14:3–11; Mark 6:17–28). Her name is not given in the Gospels (but see Josephus, *Antiq.* 17.5.4).

SALT (See MINERALS)

SALT, COVENANT OF A covenant of permanent and perpetual obligation. When covenants were made, they were usually confirmed with sacrificial meals, and salt was always present (Num 18:19).

SALT SEA (See DEAD SEA)

SALT, VALLEY OF A valley in which great victories were won over the Edomites (2 Sam 8:13; 2 Kings 14:7; 2 Chron 25:11). It was between Jerusalem and Edom.

SALUTATION (săl-ū-tā′shŭn, Gr. *aspasmos*). A greeting given either orally (Luke 1:29, 41, 44) or in writing (1 Cor 16:21; Col 4:18; 2 Thess 3:17). Greetings in the Bible sometimes included acts as well as words: a profound obeisance or prostration, a kissing of the hand, kneeling, falling on the neck of another, or embracing. Among the more common salutations on meetings were the following: "God be gracious to you" (Gen 43:29); "The LORD be with you" (Ruth 2:4); "Peace be with you" (Luke 24:36); "Greetings" (Matt 26:49). Monarchs were saluted with the words "May the king live forever" (Neh 2:3; 1 Kings 1:31). The Pharisees especially liked salutations in public places (Matt 23:7; Mark 12:38). Because salutations were usually time-consuming, when Jesus sent out the Seventy, he forbade salutations by the way (Luke 10:4). Salutations were given at partings as well as at meetings. "Go in peace," or "Farewell" (1 Sam 1:17; 20:42; 2 Sam 15:9; Mark 5:34).

SALVATION (Heb. *yeshû′âh*, Gr. *sōtēria*). God is called "Savior" (Hos 13:4; Luke 1:47) and portrayed as the "God of salvation" (Ps 68:19–20; Luke 3:6; Acts 28:28).

In the OT, salvation refers both to everyday, regular types of deliverance—as from enemies, disease, and danger (see 1 Sam 10:24; Ps 72:4)—and to those major deliverances that are specifically interpreted as being a definite part of God's unique and special involvement in human history as well as special revelations of his character and will. The supreme example of the latter is the Exodus (Exod 14:13, 30–31; 15:1–2, 13; 18:8), which involved deliverance from the bondage of Egypt, safe travel to the Land of Promise, and settlement there as a new

people in a new relationship with God (Deut 6:21–23; 26:2–10; 33:29).

There are two further aspects to salvation in the OT. First, salvation refers to the future action of God when he will deliver Israel from all her enemies and ills and create a new order of existence (see Isa 49:5–13; 65:17ff.; 66:22–23; Hag 2:4–9; Zech 2:7–13). Second is the hope of the Messiah, who will deliver his people from their sins (Isa 43:11; 52:13; 53:12).

Further, in the OT when God acts to deliver Israel, he acts in righteousness, and his act is also one of salvation (Isa 45:21; 46:12–13). God's future salvation involves a new creation, the remaking and renewing of the old created order (9:2–7; 11:1–9; 65:17ff.).

In the NT, Jesus is portrayed as the Savior of sinners (Luke 2:11; John 4:42; Acts 5:31; 13:23; Phil 3:20; 2 Peter 1:1, 11; 1 John 4:14). The title reserved for God in the OT is transferred to Jesus. When a person repented and believed, that person received salvation (Mark 2:5; Luke 7:50; 19:9–10).

Because of the life, death, and exaltation of Jesus, salvation is a present reality. It is deliverance from the dominion of sin and Satan; it is freedom to love and serve God now (Acts 4:12; 2 Cor 6:2; Heb 2:3). Salvation is also, however, a future hope (Rom 5:9; 1 Peter 1:5; Rev 19:1). See also JUSTIFICATION; KINGDOM OF GOD; RECONCILIATION; REDEMPTION.

SALVE (See EYESALVE)

SAMARIA (sȧ-mâr′ĭ-ȧ, Heb. *shōmerôn*, Gr. *Samareia*). The country of Samaria occupied a rough square of some 40 miles (67 km.) north and south by 35 miles (58 km.) east and west. It was the territory occupied by the ten tribes led by Jeroboam, extending roughly from Bethel to Dan and from the Mediterranean to Syria and Ammon. The earliest name for this section of the Palestinian uplands was Mt. Ephraim (Josh 17:15; 19:50; Judg 3:27; 4:5). For further details on Samaria, see BETHEL; SHECHEM; SHILOH; SYCHAR.

SAMARITANS (sȧ-măr′ĭ-tăns, Heb. *shōmerōnîm*, Gr. *Samareitai*). The word may signify, according to context, (1) the inhabitants of Samaria (the region rather than the town; e.g., 2 Kings 17:26; Matt 10:5; Luke 9:52; 10:33; 17:16; John 4:9, 30, 40; Acts 8:25); (2) the sect that derived its name from Samaria, a term of contempt with the Jews (John 8:48); (3) since the 17th century A.D., "a good

Samaritans congregating in prayer during a Samaritan Passover feast on Mount Gerizim.
Courtesy S. Zur Picture Library

Samaritan" (Luke 10:33) has signified a generous and self-forgetful person.

In 721 B.C. Sargon of Assyria destroyed Samaria. Newcomers from the north intermarried with the Israelite remnant, and ultimately the population took the general name of Samaritans. The completeness of the devastation left by the Assyrian invasion is evident from the infestation by wild beasts of which the immigrants complained (2 Kings 17). A mixed religion developed (17:33). After the return from Captivity, hatred developed between the Samaritans and the Jewish remnant of Ezra and Nehemiah. On the strength of their worship of the LORD "since the time of Esarhaddon" (Ezra 4:2), the Samaritans sought a share in the rebuilding of the temple in Jerusalem, but were firmly refused. Sanballat of Samaria was a serious hindrance to Nehemiah's work (Neh 2:10, 19; 4:6–7). Sanballat's son-in-law was Manasseh, grandson of the Jewish high priest; and Nehemiah's drive for racial purity led to the expulsion of this young man from Jerusalem. By his emigration with a large band of dissident Jews to Samaria, the rift between the peoples, politically and religiously, was made permanent. Manasseh persuaded the Samaritans, according to tradition, to abandon many of their idolatrous practices; and with Sanballat's building on Mt. Gerizim of a schismatic temple for his son-in-law, the sect of the Samaritans was established. It was from this time too that Samaria became a refuge for malcontent Jews, with the consequent use of "Samaritan" as a term of abuse for a dissident rebel (John 4:20–21; 8:48).

Founded as it was before the rise of the great prophetic tradition, the religion of the Samaritans was based on the Pentateuch alone. At one Passover, some Samaritans had intruded and polluted the Holy Place by scattering human bones in the porches. Samaritans were thereafter excluded from the services (Josephus, *Antiq.* 18.2.2). The whole situation narrated in John 4 is therefore remarkable — the buying of food in Sychar, the conver-

A Samaritan priest with an ancient scroll, traditionally dating from the thirteenth year of the Israelite settlement in Canaan. "Samaritan" in the NT refers to an Israelite sect whose central sanctuary was on Mount Gerizim (John 4:19). Courtesy Encyclopaedia Judaica Photo Archive, Jerusalem. Photo David Harris

sation at Jacob's Well, and the subsequent evangelization of the area (cf. Acts 8:5–25.) It illustrates the freedom from prejudice Christianity could bring.

SAMOS (să'mŏs, Gr. *Samos, height*). An island off western Asia Minor. Paul touched at Samos on his last voyage to Jerusalem (Acts 20:15).

SAMOTHRACE (săm'ō-thrās, Gr. *Samothrakē, Samos of Thrake*). An island in the NE Aegean and the home of the mystery cult of the Cabiri, popular during the Hellenistic age. Paul called here on his first voyage to Europe (Acts 16:11).

SAMSON (săm'sŭn, Heb. *shimshôn,* probably *little sun,* Gr. *Sampsōn,* Lat. and Eng. *Samson*). One of the judges of Israel (Judg 13–16). He was an Israelite of the tribe of Dan, the son of Manoah. Zorah, where he was born, was about halfway between Jerusalem and the Mediterranean, along the coast of which the Philistines lived. His birth was announced by the angel of the Lord beforehand to his mother, who was barren. The angel told her that this son should be a Nazirite from his birth, and that the Lord would begin to use him to deliver Israel

out of the hand of the Philistines. The unusual strength that Samson exhibited at various times in his career was not his because he was a natural giant, but because the Spirit of the Lord came on him to accomplish great deeds.

Almost from the beginning of his career Samson showed one conspicuous weakness, which was ultimately to wreck him: he was a slave to passion. He insisted, against the objections of his parents, on marrying a Philistine woman. At the wedding feast he challenged the guests with a riddle, and when he was tricked, he killed 30 Philistines to fulfill his wager. He went home without his wife. When he returned later, he found that her father had given her in marriage to someone else, and he was offered her sister in her stead. In revenge Samson sent 300 foxes with burning torches tied between their tails through the Philistine grain fields. The Philistines retaliated by burning his wife and her father to death.

This act of vengeance only provoked an even greater vengeance from Samson. He "attacked them viciously and slaughtered many of them." The Philistines invaded Judah and demanded the surrender of their archenemy. Samson agreed to allow the Israelites to deliver him into the hands of the Philistines; but on the way he broke the cords that bound him and, seizing the jawbone of a donkey, killed 1,000 men with it. With this great feat Samson clearly established his title to the position of a judge in Israel (Judg 15:20).

Samson later loved a Philistine woman named Delilah. The Philistine leaders bribed her to betray him into their hands. By their direction she begged him to tell her the secret of his great strength. After three deceitful answers, he revealed that if only his hair were cut he would be like other men. As he slept, his hair was cut, and when he awoke he found that not merely his strength but also God had departed from him. Now at the mercy of his enemies, he was bound with chains, his eyes were put out, and he was sent to grind in the prison of Gaza.

On the occasion of a great feast to the god Dagon, his captors resolved to make fun of him. Meanwhile, his hair had grown again, and with his returning strength he longed for revenge on his enemies for his two blinded eyes (Judg 16:28). Taking hold of the two pillars on which the temple rested, he prayed that God would help him once more; and with a mighty effort he moved the pillars from their position and brought down the roof, burying with himself a large number of

Philistines in its ruins. In dying he killed more than he had killed in his life.

With all of his failings he is listed with the heroes of faith in Hebrews 11:32. By faith in God's gift and calling, he received strength to do the wonders he performed. He was without real self-control, and accordingly he wrought no permanent deliverance for Israel.

SAMUEL (săm'ū-ĕl, Heb. *shemû'ēl, name of God,* or *his name is El;* some grammarians prefer a derivation from *yishma'' El, God hears;* others associate the name with *sha'al, to ask,* on the basis of 1 Sam 1:20). Samuel is often called the last of the judges (cf. 1 Sam 7:6, 15--17) and the first of the prophets (3:20; Acts 3:24; 13:20). He was the son of Elkanah, a Zuphite, and Hannah, of Ramathaim in the hill country of Ephraim. The events associated with the birth of Samuel indicate that his parents were a devoted and devout couple (1 Sam 1:1–2:10). Hannah's prayer for a child was answered. After Samuel was weaned, she took him to the Lord's house at Shiloh.

The Lord called to Samuel in the night and revealed to him the impending doom of Eli's house. The Lord blessed Samuel and "let none of his words fall to the ground" (1 Sam 3:19), so that all Israel knew that Samuel was a prophet of the Lord. Eli died when he received the news of the death of his sons and the capture of the ark of the covenant in a Philistine victory over Israel. Some time after the return of the ark to Israel, Samuel challenged the people to put away foreign gods and to serve the Lord only (7:3). When the Philistines threatened the Israelite gathering at Mizpah, Samuel interceded for Israel and the Lord answered with thunder against the enemy. The Philistines were routed and Samuel set up a memorial stone, which he called Ebenezer ("stone of help," 7:12).

Samuel, judge and priest, made his home at Ramah, where he administered justice and also built an altar. He went on circuit to Bethel, Gilgal, and Mizpah (1 Sam 7:15). In his old age he appointed his sons, Joel and Abijah (cf. 1 Chron 6:28), as judges in Beersheba, but the people protested that his sons did not walk in his ways but took bribes and perverted justice. The people requested a king to rule them (1 Sam 8:5–6). God revealed to Samuel that Saul was to come to see him, and at the conclusion of this first meeting, Samuel secretly anointed Saul as king (10:1) and foretold some confirmatory signs, which came to pass as predicted (10:1–13). Samuel then

called an assembly of Israel at Mizpah, and the choice of Saul was confirmed by lot.

Saul engaged in a victorious battle with the Philistines. After Saul's success, Samuel commissioned him to annihilate the Amalekites (1 Sam 15). In this expedition Saul showed incomplete obedience; Samuel reminded him of the necessity of absolute obedience and told him God had rejected him as king (15:35).

The Lord sent Samuel to Bethlehem to anoint the young shepherd David as Saul's successor (cf. 1 Chron 11:3). Later, in flight from Saul, David took refuge on one occasion with Samuel in Naioth of Ramah (1 Sam 19:18), where Samuel was head of a group of prophets. When Saul came after David, the Spirit of God came on Saul, and he prophesied before Samuel (19:23–24). Samuel was diligent in the Lord's service and kept the Passover faithfully (2 Chron 35:18); he was also a writer (cf. 1 Sam 10:25; 1 Chron 29:29). Samuel died while Saul was still king; he was buried by solemn assembly of the people at Ramah (1 Sam 25:1).

SAMUEL, BOOKS OF The books are named after Samuel, the outstanding figure of the early section. Originally there was only one book of Samuel, but the LXX divided it into two.

I. Authorship and Date. There is little external or internal evidence about the authorship of Samuel. Jewish tradition ascribes the work to the prophet Samuel. All of the events of 1 Samuel 25–31 and 2 Samuel occurred after Samuel's death. The statement of 1 Samuel 27:6 is taken by some to refer to a date in the divided kingdom; others insist that this need not be later than the end of the reign of David. Samuel was a writer, and certainly his writing was used in the composition of these books (1 Chron 29:29).

II. Content. (Outline after Pfeiffer)
    A. Shiloh and Samuel (1 Sam 1:1–7:1)
    B. Samuel and Saul (1 Sam 7:2–15:35)
    C. Saul and David (1 Sam 16–31; 2 Sam 1)
    D. David as King of Judah (2 Sam 2–4)
    E. David as King of All Israel (2 Sam 5–24)

The books of Samuel present the establishment of the kingship in Israel. In preserving the account of Samuel, the judge and prophet, the books mark the transition from judgeship to monarchy, since Samuel filled the prophetic office and administered the divine induction into office of Israel's first two kings.

SANBALLAT (săn-băl'ăt, Heb. *sanvallat*, Assyr, *Sin-uballit, the god Sin has given life*). A Horite, that is, a man of Beth Horon. He was a very influential Samaritan who tried unsuccessfully to defeat Nehemiah's plans for rebuilding the walls of Jerusalem (Neh 4:1ff.). He then plotted with others to invite Nehemiah to a conference at Ono in order to assassinate him, but Nehemiah saw through his plan and refused to come. When this device failed, he tried vainly to intimidate the Jewish governor (6:5–14). Sanballat's daughter married into the family of Eliashib, the high priest at the time of the annulment of the mixed marriages forbidden by the law (13:28); but her husband refused to forsake her and went with her to Shechem, where he became the high priest of a new temple built by his father-in-law on Mt. Gerizim.

SANCTIFICATION (Gr. *hagiasmos* from the verb *hagiazō*). The process or result of being made holy. Holiness when applied to things, places, and people means that they are consecrated and set apart for the use of God. When used of people, it can have a moral dimension. Thus in the NT, believers are described as already (objectively) sanctified in Christ (1 Cor 1:2, 30). Believers are called to show that consecration in their lives (1 Thess 4:3; 5:23; Heb 2:11; 9:13; 10:10, 14, 29; 13:12). They are to be holy in practice in the power of the Holy Spirit. See also HOLINESS; HOLY SPIRIT.

SANCTUARY (Heb. *miqdāsh*, Gr. *hagion, holy place*). This refers almost exclusively to the tabernacle or temple. God's sanctuary was his established earthly abode, the place where he chose to dwell among his people (Ps 114:2). God himself is a sanctuary for his people (Isa 8:14; Ezek 11:19). The word is used particularly of the Most Holy Place, whether of the tabernacle or of the temple. When it is used in the plural, it usually denotes idolatrous shrines, or high places, which Israelites who compromised with heathenism sometimes built (Amos 7:9). A sanctuary was also a place of asylum, the horns of the altar especially being regarded as inviolable (cf. 1 Kings 2:28–29). In Hebrews (8:2; 9:1–2; 13:11) the author makes clear that the earthly sanctuary was only a type of the true sanctuary, which is in heaven, of which Christ is the High Priest and in which he offers himself as a sacrifice (10:1–18).

SAND (Heb. *hôl*, Gr. *ammos*). A symbol of (1) numberlessness, vastness, (2) weight, (3) instability. The descendants of Abraham were numberless (Gen 22:17; Jer 33:22; Rom 9:27; Heb 11:12); as were the enemies of Israel (Josh 11:4; Judg 7:12; 1 Sam 13:5). Joseph accumulated grain as measureless as the sand of the sea (Gen 41:49). God gave to Solomon understanding and largeness of heart as the sand on the seashore (1 Kings 4:29). The thoughts of God (Ps 139:18) and Job's grief (Job 6:3) are compared to the sand of the sea. A house built on sand symbolizes a life not built on hearing the teachings of Jesus (Matt 7:26).

SAND LIZARD (See ANIMALS)

SAND REPTILE (See ANIMALS)

SANDAL (See DRESS)

SANHEDRIN (săn'hē-drĭn, Talmudic Heb. transcription of the Gr. *synedrion, a council*). The highest Jewish tribunal during the Greek and Roman periods (KJV "council"). During the reign of the Hellenistic kings Palestine was practically under home rule and was governed by an aristocratic council of elders, which was presided over by the hereditary high priest. The council was called *gerousia,* which always signifies an aristocratic body. This later developed into the Sanhedrin. During most of the Roman period the internal government of the country was practically in its hands, and its influence was recognized even in the Diaspora (Acts 9:2; 22:5; 26:12). After the death of Herod the Great, however, during the reign of Archelaus and the Roman procurators, the civil authority of the Sanhedrin was probably restricted to Judea, and this is very likely the reason why it had no judicial authority over Jesus so long as he remained in Galilee. The Sanhedrin was abolished after the destruction of Jerusalem (A.D. 70).

The members of the Sanhedrin were drawn from the three classes named in Matthew 16:21; 27:41; Mark 8:31; 11:27; 14:43, 53; 15:1; Luke 9:22; 22:66: "the elders, the chief priests and the teachers of the law." By the chief priests is meant the acting high priest, those who had been high priests, and members of the privileged families from which the high priests were taken. The priestly aristocracy comprised the leading persons in the community, and they were the chief members of the Sanhedrin. The teachers of the law (KJV scribes) formed the Pharisaic element in the Sanhedrin, though not all Pharisees were professional scribes. The elders were the tribal and family

Top view showing the entrance to the tombs of the Sanhedrin in north. Jerusalem and below, the interior. The caves were cut during the second temple period and are believed to be the tombs of the Sanhedrin court of judges. At least three of the members of the Sanhedrin—Nicodemus (John 3:1), Joseph of Arimathea (John 19:38), and Gamaliel (Acts 5:34)—are mentioned in the New Testament. Courtesy Zev Radovan

heads of the people and priesthood, mostly the secular nobility of Jerusalem. The president bore the honorable title of "prince." Besides the president, there were subordinate officials (Matt 5:25; 26:51; Mark 14:47; John 18:10). According to Josephus, in the time of Christ the Sanhedrin was formally led by the Sadducean high priests, but practically ruled by the Pharisees, who were immensely popular with the people (*Antiq.* 18.1.4).

In the time of Christ the Sanhedrin exercised not only civil jurisdiction, according to Jewish law, but also criminal. It could deal with all those judicial matters of an administrative character that could not be competently handled by lower courts, or that the Roman procurator had not specially reserved for himself. It was the final court of appeal for all questions connected with the Mosaic Law. It could order arrests by its own officers of justice (Matt 26:47; Mark 14:43; Acts 4:3; 5:17-18; 9:2). It was also the final court of appeal from all inferior courts. It had the right of capital punishment until about 40 years before the destruction of Jerusalem. After that it could still pass, but not execute, a sentence of death without the confirmation of the Roman procurator. That is why Jesus had to be tried not only before the Sanhedrin but also before Pilate (John 18:31-32). But for this, he would have been put to death in some other way than by crucifixion, for crucifixion was not a Jewish mode of punishment. The Roman authority was, however, always absolute, and the procurator or the tribune of the garrison could direct the Sanhedrin to investigate some matter and could remove a prisoner from its jurisdiction, as was done in the case of Paul (Acts 22:30; 23:23-24).

SANSANNAH (săn-săn'à, Heb. *sansan-nâh, a palm branch*). A town in the south of Judah (Josh 15:31), identical with Hazar Susah, a town of Simeon (19:5), and almost certainly the same as Hazar Susim (1 Chron 4:31).

SAPH (Heb. *saph, a basin, threshold*). A Philistine giant, one of the four champions of the race of Rapha who was killed by one of David's heroes (2 Sam 21:18; "Sippai" in 1 Chron 20:4).

SAPHIR (See SHAPHIR)

SAPPHIRA (să-fî'rà, Aramaic *shappîrā', beautiful*). The wife of Ananias who with her husband was struck dead because they lied to God (Acts 5:1-10).

SAPPHIRE (See MINERALS)

SARAH, SARA, SARAI (sâ'rà, Heb. *sârâh, sāray,* Gr. *Sara.* Sarah means *princess;* the meaning of Sarai is doubtful). She was ten years younger than Abraham and was married to him in Ur of the Chaldees (Gen 11:29-31). She was Abraham's half-sister (20:12). Her name was originally Sarai. She was about 65 years old when Abraham left Ur for Haran. Later she accompanied Abraham into Egypt and was there passed off by him as his sister because he feared the Egyptians might kill him if they knew she was his wife. Years later Abraham did the same thing at Gerar (20:1-18). God's intervention protected Sarah and Abraham was rebuked by the pagan rulers. Still childless at the age of 75, Sarah induced Abraham to take her handmaid Hagar as a concubine. A son born of this woman would be regarded as the son and heir of Abraham and Sarah. When Hagar conceived, she treated her mistress with such insolence that Sarah drove her from the house. Hagar, however, returned at God's direction, submitted herself to her mistress, and gave birth to Ishmael. Afterward, when Sarah was about 90, God promised her a son; her name was changed; and a year later Isaac, the child of promise, was born (17:15–27; 21:1–3). A few years later, at a great feast celebrating the weaning of Isaac, Sarah observed Ishmael mocking her son, and demanded the expulsion of Hagar and Ishmael (ch. 21). Abraham reluctantly acceded, after God had instructed him to do so. Sarah died at Kiriath Arba (Hebron) at the age of 127 and was buried in the cave of Machpelah, which Abraham purchased as a family sepulcher (23:1–2). Sarah is mentioned again in the OT only in Isaiah 51:2, as the mother of the chosen race. She is mentioned several times in the NT (Rom 4:19; 9:9; Gal 4:21–5:1; Heb 11:11; 1 Peter 3:6).

SARDINE (See MINERALS)

SARDIS (sàr'dĭs, Gr. *Sardeis*). The chief city of Lydia. Capital of Lydia under Croesus, Sardis was famous for arts and crafts and was the first center to mint gold and silver coins. The capture of the great citadel by surprise attack by Cyrus and his Persians in 549 B.C., and three centuries later by the Romans, may have provided the imagery for John's warning in Revelation 3:3. The great earthquake of A.D. 17 ruined Sardis physically and financially.

SARDITE (See SEREDITE)

SARDONYX, SARDIUS (See MINERALS)

SAREPTA (See ZAREPHATH)

SARGON (sàr'gŏn, Heb. *sargôn, the constituted king*). **1.** Sargon I was a famous king of early Babylon who founded an empire that extended to the Mediterranean (2400 B.C.).

2. Sargon II (722–705 B.C.) was an Assyrian king (Isa 20:1) who claimed to have captured Samaria, and a certain ambiguity in 2 Kings 17:6 allows for a new, although unnamed, Assyrian monarch there. Soon after Sargon came to the throne, the Babylonians, assisted by the Elamites, revolted against him and were subdued with difficulty. According to Sargon's inscriptions the remnant of the Israelites at Samaria, who had been put under an Assyrian governor, revolted, along with other Syrian and Palestinian provinces (720 B.C.). This revolt Sargon quickly suppressed. At this time he also defeated the Egyptian ruler So, who had

Relief portrait of Sargon II, King of Assyria (722–705 B.C.), from palace at Khorsabad. Sargon is mentioned in Isaiah 20:1. Reproduced by courtesy of the Trustees of the British Museum

come to the aid of rebelling Gaza (2 Kings 17:4).

Later Sargon captured Carchemish, the great Hittite city (717 B.C.), thus precipitating the fall of the Hittite Empire. Evidently Judah became more or less involved in a rebellion against Assyria, led by Ashdod. This Philistine city was captured by the Assyrians and reorganized as an Assyrian province (711; cf. Isa 20:1), and Judah was subdued but not harmed.

SARON (See SHARON)

SARUCH (See SERUG)

SATAN (sā'tăn, Heb. *sātān*, Gr. *Satan* or *Satanas*, *an adversary*). The chief of the fallen spirits, the grand adversary of God and man. Without the article, the Hebrew word is used in a general sense to denote someone who is an opponent, an adversary—e.g., the angel who stood in Balaam's way (Num 22:22), David as a possible opponent in battle (1 Sam 29:4), and a political adversary (1 Kings 11:14). With the definite article prefixed, it is a proper noun (Job 1-2; Zech 3:1-2), designating Satan as a personality. In Psalm 109:6 the article is lacking, and reference may be to a human adversary (cf. NIV "an accuser"), but it is generally conceded that in 1 Chronicles 21:1 the word is a proper name without the article.

In the NT the term *Satan*, transliterated from the Hebrew, always designates the personal Satan (but cf. Matt 16:23; Mark 8:33). He is often called the devil (Gr. *diabolos*), meaning "the slanderer" (Matt 4:1; Luke 4:2; John 8:44; Eph 6:11; Rev 12:12). ("Devils" in KJV and ERV is properly "demons.") Other titles or descriptive designations applied to him are "Abaddon" or "Apollyon" (Rev 9:11); "Accuser of our brothers" (12:10); "enemy," Greek *antidikos* (1 Peter 5:8); "Beelzebub" (Matt 12:24); "Belial" (2 Cor 6:15); the one who "leads the whole world astray" (Rev 12:9); "the evil one" (Matt 13:19, 38; 1 John 2:13; 5:19); "the father of lies" (John 8:44); "the god of this age" (2 Cor 4:4); "a murderer" (John 8:44); "that ancient serpent" (Rev 12:9); "the prince of this world" (John 12:31; 14:30); "the ruler of the kingdom of the air" (Eph 2:2); "the tempter" (Matt 4:5; 1 Thess 3:5).

In the Book of Job he is pictured as mixing with the sons of God (angels) in their appearing before God, though by his moral nature not one of them. Jude 9 pictures him as a formidable foe to Michael the archangel. While clearly very powerful and clever, he is not an independent rival of God but is definitely subordinate, able to go only as far as God permits (Job 1:12; 2:6; Luke 22:31). Christ gives a fundamental description of his moral nature in calling him the evil one (Matt 13:19, 38; cf. John 8:44).

The origin of Satan is not explicitly asserted in Scripture, but the statement that he did not hold to the truth (John 8:44) implies that he is a fallen being, while 1 Timothy 3:6 indicates that he fell under God's condemnation because of ambitious pride. While many theologians refuse to apply the far-reaching prophecies in Isaiah 14:12-14 and Ezekiel 28:12-15 to Satan, contending that these passages are strictly addressed to the kings of Babylon and Tyre, conservative scholars generally hold that they contain a clear revelation of Satan's origin (cf. Dan 10:13; John 12:31; Eph 6:12). These passages picture Satan's prefall splendor as well as his apostasy through pride and self-exaltation against God. A consuming passion of Satan is to be worshiped (Isa 14:14; Matt 4:9; 1 Cor 10:20; Rev 13:4, 15). In his fall Satan drew a vast number of lesser celestial creatures with him (Rev 12:4).

Satan is the ruler of a powerful kingdom standing in opposition to the kingdom of God (Matt 12:26; Luke 11:18). He exercises authority in two different realms. He is the head of a vast, compact organization of spirit-beings, "his angels" (Matt 25:41; Eph 2:2; 6:12). Acts 10:38 makes it clear that the outburst of demonic activities during the ministry of Jesus was Satan-inspired. Satan is not omnipresent, but through his subordinates he makes his influence practically world-wide. He also exercises domination over the world of lost humanity (John 12:31, 14:30, 16:11), the evil world system that he has organized on his own principles (2 Cor 4:3-4; Col 1:13; 1 John 2:15-17; 5:19).

Animated by an unrelenting hatred against God and all goodness, Satan is engaged in a world-wide and age-long struggle against God, ever seeking to defeat the divine plans of grace toward mankind and to seduce people to evil and ruin. His primary method is that of deception—about himself, his purpose, his activities, and his coming defeat (Rev 12:9). Satan was the seducer of Adam and Eve (Gen 3:1-7; 2 Cor 11:3); he insinuated to God that Job served him only for what he got out of it (Job 1:9); and he stood up against Israel (1 Chron 21:1) and God's high priest (Zech 3:1-2). Under divinely imposed limitations he may be instrumental in causing physical affliction or financial loss (Job 1:11-22; 2:4-7; Luke 13:16; 2 Cor 12:7). He snatches away the Word of God sown in the hearts of the unsaved (Matt 3:19), sows his counterfeit Christians among the children of the kingdom (13:25, 38-39), blinds the minds of people to the gospel (2 Cor 4:3-4), and induces them to accept his lie (2 Thess 2:9-10). Often he transforms himself into "an angel of light" by presenting his apostles of falsehood as messengers of truth (2 Cor 11:13-15). He clashes in fierce conflict with the saints (Eph 6:11-18), is ever alert to try to destroy them (1 Peter 5:8), and hinders the work of God's servants (1 Thess

2:18). Certain members of the church who were expelled are said to have been delivered to Satan but with the design to produce their reformation, not their destruction (1 Cor 5:5; 1 Tim 1:20).

Although Satan was judged in the Cross (John 13:31–33), he is still permitted to carry on the conflict, often with startling success. But his revealed doom is sure. He now has a sphere of activities in the heavenly realms (Eph 6:12); he will be cast down to the earth and will cause great woe because of his wrath, which he will exercise through "the dragon" (2 Thess 2:9; Rev 12:7–12; 13:2–8). With Christ's return to earth he will be incarcerated in the bottomless pit for 1,000 years; when released for a season, he will again attempt to deceive the nations but will be cast into "the eternal fire" prepared for him and his angels (Matt 25:41), to suffer eternal doom with those he deceived (Rev 20:1–3, 7–10).

SATRAP (sã'trăp). The official title of the viceroy who in the Persian Empire ruled several small provinces combined as one government. Each province had its own governor. Where NIV has "satrap," KJV consistently has "princes" for the Aramaic term (nine verses) and "lieutenants" for the Hebrew term (four verses).

SATYR (sāt'êr). A word used (Isa 13:21; 34:14; JB, KJV, RSV; goat NIV; he-goat NEB; shaggy goat MLB) to translate the two OT uses of the Hebrew word *sā'ir*, in one passage (13:21) describing the wild animals or demons that would dance among the ruins of Babylon.

SAUL (sôl, Heb. *shā'ûl, asked of God,* Gr. *Saulos*). **1.** A king of Edom (see SHAUL, SHAULITES). **2.** A son of Simeon (see SHAUL, SHAULITES). **3.** An ancestor of Samuel and descendant of Levi (see SHAUL, SHAULITES). **4.** A prominent apostle (see PAUL).

5. The first king of Israel, a son of Kish (Acts 13:21), of the tribe of Benjamin, a handsome man a head taller than his fellow Israelites. He is introduced in 1 Samuel 9, after the people had asked Samuel for a king (1 Sam 8). Saul and Samuel met for the first time when Saul was searching for some lost donkeys of his father. Greeted by Samuel with compliments, Saul replied with becoming humility (9:21; cf. Judg 6:15), but he was diffident and personally insecure more than most, making him both attractively unassuming and also (in later days) pathologically defensive and highly overreactive. Before Saul left, Samuel secretly anointed him as king of Israel, as the

Lord had directed. God gave Saul a changed heart (1 Sam 10:9), and Saul prophesied among a group of prophets who met him on his way home. Saul's new heart corresponds to the blessing of regeneration—Saul became a child of God.

The choice of Saul as king was confirmed by lot at an assembly of Israel convened by Samuel at Mizpah, but the bashful young man was in hiding and had to be brought before the people. He was ridiculed by some riffraff but he kept silent (1 Sam 10:27). His forbearance was supplemented by compassion and decision in his rescue of Jabesh Gilead from the threat of the Ammonites (1 Sam 11).

After the deliverance of the city, Saul showed his generosity by insisting that his earlier detractors should not be punished. A military crisis with the Philistines revealed flaws in the character of Saul. When Samuel delayed in coming to make offering before battle, Saul presumed to present the offering himself. Saul had a command (cf. 1 Sam 10:8), and his sin was that he listened to the voice of his own insecurity rather than to the plain word of God. For this the privilege of founding a dynasty was withdrawn from him (13:13–14).

On the human side we are reminded of the pressure of the situation: the great numerical superiority of the Philistines (1 Sam 13:5), attitude (13:6–7), and equipment (13:19–23). The Philistines were routed in spite of Saul's bad judgment in denying food to the Israelites at a time when they most needed strength. Saul fought valiantly and successfully against all the enemies of Israel (14:47–48); though he was a brave leader he was not a good soldier, for he was not aware of the necessity of absolute obedience. We have no ground for accepting the excuse Saul made for his incomplete obedience (1 Sam 15:21). It is consistent with Saul's deep-seated inner insecurity that popular pressure, coupled with his genuine religious feeling, made him a compromiser in such a situation. Obedience has been sacrificed on the altar of temperament, and this time (15:27–28) the continuance of his own period of reign and indeed the validity of his kingship itself comes under judgment.

David enters the narrative in 1 Samuel 16. Jealousy, hatred, and fear led Saul to both direct and indirect attempts against David's life (18:10–11, 21; 19:1, 11) and resulted in the hide-and-seek chase that twice drove David into Philistine territory (21:10; 27:1ff.). The unsuspecting aid given to David by the priests of Nob moved Saul to slaughter the priests and to annihilate the city (22:17–19). Saul's life was spared by David on two occasions— at En Gedi (24:1–7) and in the wilderness of Ziph (26:6–12).

The eve of what proved to be Saul's final battle brought the king under desperate pressure. He turned to the forces of darkness, those same forces he had earlier banished from the land (1 Sam 28:3). Samuel could give him no earthly comfort, but his message included God's grace: "Tomorrow you and your sons will be with me" (28:19). The next day Saul and his sons died in the battle on Mt. Gilboa. The Philistines decapitated Saul and took his remains to Beth Shan, where they placed his armor in the temple of the Ashtoreths (31:10), his head in the temple of Dagon (1 Chron 10:10), and his body on the city wall. The men of Jabesh Gilead remembered Saul's concern for them; in gratitude they recovered his body and the bodies of his sons from the walls of Beth Shan, gave them honorable burial at Jabesh, and fasted in mourning. David also, when he heard the report, went into mourning and expressed his grief (2 Sam 1:19–27).

SAVIOR (sāv'yôr, Gr. *sōtēr, savior, deliverer, preserver*). One who saves, delivers, or preserves from any evil or danger, whether physical or spiritual, temporal, or eternal. A basic OT concept is that God is the Deliverer of his people; man cannot save himself, and the Lord alone is the Savior (Ps 44:3, 7; Isa 43:11; 45:21; 60:16; Jer 14:8; Hos 13:4). In the OT the term is not applied to the Messiah; he received salvation from God (2 Sam 22:51; Pss 28:8; 144:10); but he came to offer salvation to all (Isa 49:6, 8; Zech 9:9). The term is also applied to people who are used as the instruments of God's deliverance (Judg 3:9, 15 ASV; 2 Kings 13:5; Neh 9:27; Obad 21).

The Greeks applied the title *sōtēr* (Savior) to their gods; it was also used of philosophers (e.g., Epicurus) or rulers (e.g., Ptolemy I, Nero) or men who had brought notable benefits on their country. But in the NT it is a strictly religious term and is never applied to a mere man. It is used of both God the Father and Christ the Son. God the Father is Savior, for he is the author of our salvation, which he provided through Christ (Luke 1:47; 1 Tim 1:1; 2:3; 4:10; Titus 1:3; 2:10; 3:4; Jude 25). Savior is preeminently the title of the Son (2 Tim 1:10; Titus 1:4; 2:13; 3:6; 2 Peter 1:1, 11; 2:20; 3:2, 18; 1 John 4:14). At his birth the angel announced him as a Savior (Luke 2:11). His mission to save his people from their sins was announced before his birth (Matt 1:21) and was stated by Jesus as the aim of his coming (Luke 19:10). The salvation that he wrought is for all mankind (John 4:42; 1 John 4:14). Those who are saved are brought into a spiritual union with Christ as members of his body; hence he is called the Savior of the body (the church) (Eph 5:23). Believers await a future work of Christ as Savior when he will come again to consummate our salvation in the transformation of our bodies (Phil 3:20).

SAVOUR (sā'vôr, Heb. *rēah*, Gr. *osmē*). The KJV translation of words meaning "taste" (Matt 5:13; Luke 14:34) or, more often, "smell." In the latter case it is in the OT usually qualified by the word "sweet" and is used to refer to a sacrifice that pleased God (Gen 8:21; cf. Num 15:3). *Osmē* refers to the scent of Mary's ointment (John 12:3) and (metaphorically) the incense burned in a victor's triumphal procession (2 Cor 2:14), a Christian's influence (2:16), Christ's obedience to God (Eph 5:2), and a Christian's sacrifice of obedience to God (Phil 4:18).

SAW (Heb. *megerah*). Small handsaws were like ours today, but the teeth were shaped in the other direction, so that the worker did not shove but pulled against the wood. Large handsaws were unknown in Bible times.

Stone was sawed as well as wood (1 Kings 7:9). When Scripture says that David put his war captives under saws (2 Sam 12:31 KJV, NASB; cf. 1 Chron 20:3), it probably means that he made them labor with saws (NIV, RSV).

Hebrews 11:37 speaks of martyrs who were sawn asunder (sawn in two NIV). Jewish tradition states that the prophet Isaiah was sawn asunder with a wooden saw by Manasseh.

SCAB (See DISEASES)

SCAFFOLD (Heb. *kiyyôr*). Solomon knelt on a "brazen scaffold" when he dedicated the temple (2 Chron 6:13 KJV; RSV, NIV"a bronze platform").

SCALE 1. Fish having fins and scales were permitted as food (Lev 11:9–12). **2.** The Greek word *lepis* means "rind, husk, flake," and is used to describe Saul's recovery from temporary blindness (Acts 9:18). See also DISEASES. **3.** Scales as an instrument for weighing (Isa 40:12; Prov 16:11, balance, KJV)—a simple balance. The weights used in these scales were obviously handmade and never uniform (20:23).

SCAPEGOAT (Heb. *'ăzā'zēl*). A term that occurs only in Leviticus 16:8, 10, 26 and has been interpreted variously. It is used to refer to the second of two goats for which lots were cast on the Day of Atonement. The first goat was sacrificed as a sin offering (16:9), but the scapegoat (16:26) had the people's sins transferred to it by prayer and the laying on of hands and was then taken into the wilderness.

A parallel to the scapegoat may be seen in the Scriptures. In the ritual for a recovered leper, a living bird was released in the country to carry the evil away, and the leper was declared clean (Lev 14:6).

SCARLET In Daniel 5:7, 16, 29 the Aramaic word for purple has been translated "scarlet" in some older versions (RSV, NIV retain "purple"). The color was probably a bright rich crimson, obtained from the eggs of an insect (see PLANTS: *Scarlet*). Scarlet cloth was used for the hangings of the tabernacle (Exod 25:4; Num 4:8) and for the high priest's garments (Exod 39:1). Scarlet yarn was used for the cleansing of the recovered leper (Lev 14:4) and in other ceremonies of purification (Num 19:6). Royal or expensive apparel was of scarlet (2 Sam 1:24; Prov 31:21; Lam 4:5; Matt 27:28; Rev 17:4). Scarlet thread or rope appears to have been used to mark things (Gen 38:28, 30; Josh 2:18, 21), and the lips of the bride are likened to scarlet ribbon (Song of Songs 4:3). Sins are "like scarlet" (Isa 1:18); this may be the origin of the custom of using the term red or scarlet to denote things sinful.

SCEPTER (sĕp'têr, Heb. *shēvet*, Gr. *rhabdos*). A rod held in the hands of kings as a token of authority. The Hebrew *shēvet* is the word for "rod" or "club," and is used of an ordinary rod (2 Sam 7:14), a shepherd's crook (Ps 23:4), or the staff of a commander (as NIV translates Judg 5:14; KJV "writer") who evidently mustered the troops, as well as of the symbol of authority.

This staff-scepter might be used for protection (2 Sam 23:21; Ps 23:4) or for punishment (Isa 10:24; 30:31). When dying Jacob blessed his son Judah and promised him the royal leadership in words that Christians understand as a messianic prediction, it was the scepter that denoted the royal prerogative (Gen 49:10). Thus, frequently the scepter indicates sovereignty in general, perhaps even conquest (Num 24:17; Isa 14:5;

Sandstone statue (1.02 m. high) from Nimrud, 883–859 B.C., of King Ashurnasirpal II of Assyria holding a royal scepter in his right hand and a mace in his left. Reproduced by courtesy of the Trustees of the British Museum

Amos 1:5, 8; Zech 10:11). God's kingship is also represented thus (Ps 45:6).

The use of the scepter by an oriental monarch is illustrated by the account of King Xerxes (KJV Ahasuerus), who held his scepter out to Esther as a mark of favor (Esth 5:1-2). The scepter of Xerxes was of gold; Ezekiel refers to scepters made from vine branches (Ezek 19:11, 14). When Christ was mocked as a king, a reed or staff was placed in his hand for a scepter (Matt 27:29).

SCEVA (sē'và, Gr. *Skeua*). A Jew, who was a chief priest living in Ephesus, whose seven sons were exorcists (Acts 19:14-17). There were only synagogues in Asia Minor, so he could not have been an officiating high priest.

SCHISM (sĭz'm, Gr. *schisma, a rent or division*). Used once (1 Cor 12:25 KJV; discord RSV; division NIV) to translate *schisma*, referring to dissensions that threaten disruption, not always involving doctrinal heresy (the more modern meaning). *Schisma* is also used of a garment (Matt 9:16; Mark 2:21 rent KJV; tear NIV), of a crowd (John 7:43; 9:16; 10:19 division), and again of divisions among Christians (1 Cor 1:10; 11:18).

SCHOOL The word "school" occurs in the English Bible only in Acts 19:9 (KJV) where the reference is to the lecture hall (so NIV) of Tyrannus, apparently a Greek teacher of rhetoric or philosophy. Mosaic legislation contains no commands requiring the establishment of schools for formal religious instruction. Hebrew education was mainly domestic and continued to be so until after the return from the Babylonian captivity.

God called Abraham as the father of the chosen people and put on him the responsibility to train his children and his household to walk in the ways of the Lord (Gen 18:19; cf. Ps 78:5-7). The varied commands in Deuteronomy to teach the children clearly imply domestic education (Deut 4:9; 6:7-9; 11:19; 32:46). Proverbs 22:6 is an exhortation extolling the importance of parental instruction. The training was imparted primarily through conversation, example, and imitation; it utilized effectively the interest aroused by actual life situations, such as the Passover, the redemption of the firstborn, and family rites (Exod 12:26-27; 13:14-16). Although all teaching was religiously oriented, reading, writing, and elementary arithmetic were taught.

The priests and Levites, supported by the offerings of the people, were to be the religious teachers of the nation, but it seems clear that this aspect of their work was not consistently maintained. The ineffective teaching ministry of a corrupt priesthood was supplemented by the service of the prophets, the first of whom was Samuel. To make his reform permanent and effective, Samuel instituted a school of the prophets at Ramah (1 Sam 19:19-20). Later such schools flourished at Bethel (2 Kings 2:3), Jericho (2:5), Gilgal (4:38), and elsewhere (6:1).

Regular teaching was carried on during the days of Ezra and Nehemiah, the Levites being the teachers of the people (Ezra 7:10; Neh 8:7-9). The synagogue, which has a prominent place in postexile Jewish life, apparently had its origin during the Babylonian captivity from the reading of the Scriptures and prayer (Luke 4:17-21; Acts 13:15-16; 15:21). Even before the days of Jesus, synagogues with schools for the young were to be found in every important Jewish community. The synagogue "attendant" (Luke 4:20) generally served as teacher. Memorization had a prominent place. Students seeking training beyond that given in the synagogue schools turned to eminent scribes for further instruction. The instruction was devoted to the rabbinical interpretation of the law and its applications to life. Such advanced theological training Saul of Tarsus received in Jerusalem "under Gamaliel" (Acts 22:3).

SCHOOLMASTER (See OCCUPATIONS AND PROFESSIONS)

SCIENCE The KJV translation of Hebrew *maddā'* in Daniel 1:4 and Greek *gnōsis* in 1 Timothy 6:20, both meaning "knowledge." Daniel 1:4 is literally "understanding knowledge or thought." In 1 Timothy 6:20 the reference is to that professed knowledge that sets itself up in contradiction to the truth of the gospel.

SCORPION (See ANIMALS)

SCORPION PASS (See AKRABIM)

SCOURGE (skûrj, Heb. generally *shut, to whip, lash, scourge; shôt, a whip, scourge*, Gr. *mastigoō, to whip, flog, scourge; mastix, a whip, lash; phragelloō, to flog, scourge*, as a public punishment of the condemned). The act or the instrument used to inflict severe pain by beating. Scourging, well known in the East, was familiar to the Hebrews from Egypt. The Mosaic Law authorized the beating of a culprit, apparently with a rod, but limited to 40 the strokes given the prostrate victim (Deut 25:3). Leviticus 19:20 does not impose true scourging (*biqqoreth*, translated "due punishment" in NIV, expresses an investigation). First Kings 12:11, 14 apparently refers to true scourging. It was later legalized among the Jews, and a three-thonged whip was used, but the legal limitation was observed (2 Cor 11:24). It was administered by local synagogue authorities (Matt 10:17; Acts 22:19) or by the Sanhedrin (Acts 5:40).

Among the Romans either rods were used (Acts 16:22; 2 Cor 11:25) or whips, the thongs of which were weighted with jagged pieces of bone or metal (Matt 27:26; Mark 15:15; John 19:1). It was used to force confessions and secrets from its victims (Acts 22:24). The number of blows was left to the whim of the commanding officer. Its victims generally fainted and some even died. Scourging of Roman citizens was forbidden (22:25); that punishment was generally reserved for slaves or those condemned to death.

"Scourge" is used figuratively for "affliction" in Job 9:23; Isaiah 28:15, 18. Note the mixed metaphors in Isaiah 28:15.

SCREECH OWL (See BIRDS)

SCRIBE (See OCCUPATIONS AND PROFESSIONS)

SCRIBES, JEWISH A class of learned men who made the systematic study of the law and its exposition their professional occupation (Matt 22:35; Luke 5:17; 7:30; 10:25; 11:45; 14:3; Acts 5:34). They are often associated with the Pharisees (Matt 5:20; 12:38; 15:1; 23:2, 13; Mark 7:5; Luke 5:21, 30; 6:7; 11:53; 15:2; John 8:3). But they are also mentioned alone and were not necessarily Pharisees (Matt 9:3; Mark 2:6; 3:22; 9:14; Luke 20:39). The majority of the scribes belonged to the Pharisee party, which recognized the legal interpretations of the scribes; the Sadducees also had their scribes (Mark 2:16; Luke 5:30; Acts 23:9).

The scribes of preexilic days were public writers, governmental secretaries, and copiers of the law and other documents (2 Sam 8:17; 20:25; 1 Kings 4:3; 2 Kings 12:10; Prov 25:1; Jer 8:8; 36:18). The distinctive nature of the office begins with Ezra, who set himself to the task of teaching the law to the returning exiles (Ezra 7:6, 10–11, 21). At first this naturally fell to the priests (Neh 8), but gradually there arose a separate group of professional students who devoted themselves to the preservation, transcription, and exposition of the law. When during the Hellenistic period the leading priests became largely tainted with paganism, the scribes became the zealous defenders

A Jewish scribe penning a manuscript from the Book of Esther. Courtesy Zev Radovan

of the law and the true teachers of the common people. By NT times they were recognized as the exponents of the law. Proudly they claimed the positions of first rank and dressed in long robes like the nobility (Matt 23:5–7; Mark 12:38–39; Luke 11:43; 20:46).

The scribes developed an extensive and complicated system of teaching intended to safeguard the sanctity of the law. By their practice of making "a fence about the law" they added to its actual requirements (Matt 23:4; Luke 11:46). This vast and complicated mass of scribal teaching, known as "the tradition of the elders" (Matt 15:2–6; Mark 7:1–13), was orally transmitted and required prolonged study to master. All higher instruction was in their hands. They constituted an important element in the membership of the Sanhedrin (Matt 26:57; Mark 14:43; 15:1; Luke 22:66; Acts 4:5). Since the scribes functioned as judges and the law prohibited judges from receiving presents or bribes (Exod 23:8; Deut 16:19), they were obliged to make their living some other way. Most of them, like Paul (Acts 18:3), followed some trade even though their activity as scribe was primary. Christ's denunciation of their greed made it obvious that while they professed to offer instruction without charge they had indirect ways of securing their fees (Mark 12:40; Luke 20:47).

Because Jesus refused to be bound by the scribal additions to the law (Mark 7:1–13; John 5:10–18), the scribes soon fiercely opposed him. Throughout his ministry they were his most determined opponents (Mark 2:16; Luke 5:30; 15:2). Their hypocrisy and unrelenting hatred drew forth Christ's devastating denunciation of them (Matt 23). They played an important part in the death of Jesus (26:57; 27:41; Mark 15:1, 31; Luke 22:66; 23:10) and in the persecution of the early church (Acts 4:5; 6:12). Nicodemus and Gamaliel were scribes.

SCRIP (See DRESS)

SCRIPTS (See WRITING)

SCRIPTURE (See BIBLE; CANON; NEW TESTAMENT; OLD TESTAMENT)

SCROLL The scroll, or roll, was the usual form of a book in Bible times. It had been used in Egypt from very early times, the early ones being made of papyrus, the paperlike tissue taken from the reeds growing along the Nile. Since the burning of skins in an open fire pot would have produced an intolerably bad smell, the roll of a book, mentioned three times in the OT (KJV *megillath-sephēr*, Jer 36:2, 4; Ezek 2:9; scroll for [of] a book NIV; *megillath* ["roll, scroll"] appears by itself another 18 times, 12 in Jer 36 alone), was probably made of papyrus. The papyrus was imported from Egypt. Several sheets, glued together to the desired length, were rolled on rods so that the beginning of the scroll was on the right and the end on the left (the Hebrews wrote from right to left).

A library or royal archives is called a house of rolls (Ezra 6:1 KJV). Ezekiel was commanded to eat a scroll (Ezek 2:9– 3:3), no doubt in a vision.

SCROLLS, DEAD SEA (See DEAD SEA SCROLLS)

SCULPTURE (See ART)

SCUM (See OFFSCOURING)

SCURVY (See DISEASES)

SCYTHIAN (sīth'ē-ăn, Gr. *hoi Skythai*). A term for the savage and uncivilized (Col 3:11). Scythia was the name given by the Greeks to an ill-defined area between the Carpathians and the Don, the western portion of which included the black earth wheatlands of the modern Ukraine.

SEA (Heb. *yām*, Gr. *thalassa*). **1.** The ocean (Gen 1:10; Pss 8:8; 24:2). **2.** Almost

A Samaritan high priest displaying an ancient scroll. Courtesy Zev Radovan

Limestone scarab seal inscribed with hieroglyphs from Lachish, eighteenth century B.C. Courtesy Israel Department of Antiquities and Museums

Cylinder seal and its impression from Mesopotamia, picturing the liberation of the sun-god from between two mountains. Akkadian period, c. 2360–2180 B.C. Reproduced by courtesy of the Trustees of the British Museum

Typical Hebrew royal seal on a jar handle, from Lachish, late seventh century B.C. Inscription reads, "[Belonging] to the king . . . Hebron." Courtesy Israel Department of Antiquities and Museums

any body of water, salt or fresh (Exod 13:18; 14:2; Num 34:11; Deut 3:17; Matt 4:18; Acts 10:6). **3.** Even rivers may be called a sea: the Nile (Isa 18:2; 19:5) and the Euphrates (21:1). **4.** The basin at Solomon's temple (see BRONZE SEA). The ancient Hebrews were not a sea people. The sea in the Bible becomes a symbol of restlessness, instability, and sin (Isa 57:20; Jer 49:23; James 1:6; Jude 13; Rev 13:1).

SEA, BRAZEN (See BRONZE SEA)

SEA MEW (See BIRDS: *Sea Gull*)

SEA OF GLASS In the vision of heaven in the Revelation, a glassy sea is seen before the throne of God (Rev 4:6; 15:2). It is translucent and symbolizes God's purity and holiness.

SEAH (See WEIGHTS AND MEASURES)

SEAL (Heb. *hôthām, seal, signet, tabb'ath, signet ring, hātham, to seal,* Gr. *sphragizō, katasphragizomai, to seal*). **1.** Literal sense. A device bearing a design or a name made so that it can impart an impression in relief on a soft substance like clay or wax. When the clay or wax hardens, it permanently bears the impression of the seal.

Seals were used for various purposes: (1) as a mark of authenticity and authority to letters, royal commands, etc. (1 Kings 21:8; Esth 3:12; 8:8, 10); (2) as a mark of the formal ratification of a transaction or covenant (Neh 9:38; 10:1; Jer 32:11–14); (3) as a means of protecting books and other documents so that they would not be tampered with (32:14; Rev 5:2, 5, 9; 6:1, 3); (4) as a proof of delegated authority and power (Gen 41:42; Esth 3:10; 8:2); (5) as a means of sealing closed doors so as to keep out unauthorized persons (Dan 6:17; Matt 27:66; Rev 20:3)—usually by stretching a cord across them and then sealing the cord; and (6) as an official mark of ownership, as, for example, on jar handles and jar stoppers.

2. Figurative sense. Scripture often uses the term metaphorically to indicate authentication, confirmation, ownership, evidence, or security (Deut 32:34; Job 14:17; Dan 12:4, 9; Rom 4:11; 15:28; 1 Cor 9:2; Eph 1:13; 4:30; Rev 5:1ff.; 7:2–4; 10:4).

SEASONS (See CALENDAR; TIME)

SEAT (Heb. *môshāv, sheveth, kissē', tekhûnâh,* Gr. *kathēdra, thronos*). A place or thing on which one sits, as a chair or stool (Judg 3:20; 1 Sam 20:18).

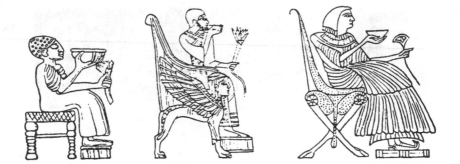

Drawings of Palestinian seats from Megiddo (left, center) and Tell el-Far'ah (right). Courtesy Carta, Jerusalem

Often (especially when it represents the Greek word *thronos*) it means "throne" (Luke 1:52; Rev 2:13; 4:4; 11:16; 13:2; 16:10). It is used also of the exalted position occupied by men of rank or influence (Ps 1:1; Matt 23:2). Jesus reproached some of the men of his day for preferring the chief seats in the synagogue (Matt 23:6; Mark 12:39; Luke 11:43; 20:46). These were special seats set in front of the reader's platform, facing the congregation, reserved for those held in honor.

SEBAM (See SIBMAH)

SEBAT (See CALENDAR)

SECHU (See SECU)

SECOND COMING (See ESCHATOLOGY)

SECT (Gr. *hairesis, sect*). Pertaining to schools of philosophy — Sadducees (Acts 5:17), Pharisees (15:5; 26:5), and Christians (24:5; 28:22). *Hairesis* also refers to heresy (KJV; Acts 24:14 sect NIV; 1 Cor 11:19 differences NIV; Gal 5:20 factions NIV; 2 Peter 2:1 heresies NIV).

SECU (sē'kū, Heb. *sēkhû*). A village near Samuel's town of Ramah (1 Sam 19:22), probably in the direction of Gibeah (19:9). The name is spelled Sechu in KJV.

SEED (Heb. *zera'*, Gr. *sperma, sporos*). 1. *Agricultural*. The farmer held his seed in his upturned garment, casting it out as he walked. Grain was sown in the early winter, after the first rains (Mark 4:1–20; Luke 8:5–15). Land was measured by the amount of seed that could be sown on it (Lev 27:16). 2. *Physiological*. A "man's seed" (KJV) or "emission of semen" (NIV) is a frequent expression in the Hebrew laws of cleanness (Lev 15:16ff.). The NT speaks of Christians as having

been begotten by God (1 Peter 1:23; 1 John 3:9). 3. *Figurative*. Here seed means descendants (Gen 13:16 KJV; cf. Gal 3:16) or genealogy (Ezra 2:59; Neh 7:61 KJV) or a class of people ("seed of evildoers," Isa 1:4 KJV). "The holy seed" (Ezra 9:2; Isa 6:13) symbolizes the people of Israel.

SEEDTIME (See AGRICULTURE)

SEER (See OCCUPATIONS AND PROFESSIONS)

SEGUB (sē'gŭb, Heb. *seghûv*). 1. The younger son of Hiel. He died when his father set up the gates of Jericho (1 Kings 16:34), fulfilling Joshua's curse (Josh 6:26). 2. Son of Hezron by a daughter of Makir (1 Chron 2:21–22).

SEIR (sē'ēr, Heb. *sē'îr*). Seir the Horite (Gen 36:20; 1 Chron 1:38) was the ancestor of the inhabitants of the land of Seir. See next entry.

SEIR, LAND OF; SEIR, MOUNT (sē'ēr, Heb. *sē'îr*). 1. The land of Seir and Mt. Seir are alternate names for the region occupied by the descendants of Edom or Esau. Originally called the land of Seir (Gen 32:3; 36:20–21, 30; Num 24:18), it was later called Edom. It is a mountainous and extremely rugged country, about 100 miles (167 km.) long, extending south from Moab on both sides of the Arabah or the great depression connecting the southern part of the Dead Sea with the Gulf of Aqabah (Gen 14:6; Deut 2:1, 12; Josh 15:1; Judg 11:17–18; 1 Kings 9:26). The summit of Mt. Seir rises about 3,500 feet (1,094 m.) above the adjacent Arabah. The land is very rocky and not nearly so fertile as Palestine (cf. Mal 1:2–4). Sela was the Edomite capital in the days of the Hebrew monarchy; later the place was called Petra. Bozrah and Teman were important places. In the Greek period the name of the land was modified to Idumea.

Esau made his home in Mt. Seir, and his descendants dispossessed the Horites (Deut 2:12; Josh 24:4), the original inhabitants (Gen 14:6). A remnant of the Amalekites took refuge in these mountain strongholds, but they were finally destroyed by the Simeonites (1 Chron 4:42–43). The term Seir is also used collectively for the people who lived in Mt. Seir (Ezek 25:8).

2. Another region, on the border of the territory of Judah west of Kiriath Jearim (Josh 15:10).

SELA (sē'là, Heb. *sela'*, Gr. *petra*). A place in Edom taken by King Ahaziah (2 Kings 14:7). It may also be referred to in three passages (of the 60 OT uses of *sela'*) where the KJV has "rock" (2 Chron 25:12, cliff NIV, RSV; Isa 42:11, Sela NIV, RSV; Obad 3, rock RSV, rocks NIV, Sela NIV footnote). It seems to be the place made famous in Greek times by the name Petra, the Nabateans' capital.

SELAH (sē'là, Heb. *sālal, to lift up*). A term occurring 71 times in the Psalms and also in Habakkuk 3:3, 9, 13. The meaning of selah is unknown. It is generally believed that its usage was that of a musical or liturgical sign. The LXX seems to understand it as a direction to the orchestra—"lift up"; i.e., play the instruments while the singers are silent. The word usually occurs at a place where a very significant statement has been made, making that a good place for a break or pause.

SELEUCIA (sē-lū'shĭ-à, Gr. *Seleukia*). The Seleucia of the NT was founded in 300 B.C. by Seleucus I Nicator, to provide a seaport for Syrian Antioch, 16 miles (27 km.) inland. It lay near the mouth of the Orontes and was a naval base in Roman imperial times. It was the port of departure for Paul and Barnabas on their first journey (Acts 13:4).

SELEUCIDS (sē-lū'sĭds, Gr. *Seleukos*). The Seleucids took their name from Seleucus, a cavalry officer of Alexander. He was one of the Diadochi, or "Successors," the name given to those remarkable military personalities who successfully divided Alexander's empire after his death. By 312 B.C. Seleucus had established himself in command of Babylonia, Susiana, and Media, and from this date his dynasty and era can be conveniently reckoned. By 301 he was master of Syria,

founding Antioch and Seleucia to express the westward expansion of his kingdom and to balance Seleucia on the Tigris, its eastern bastion.

SEM (See SHEM)

SEMITES (sĕm'īts). The term *Semite* is derived from Noah's son Shem (Gen 9:18–19; 10:21–31) and is used to identify a diverse group of ancient peoples whose languages are related.

The world of the Semites was the Fertile Crescent including Mesopotamia, Syria, and Palestine. The great Arabian desert appears to have been the original homeland of the Semites. From earliest times there have been irruptions from this desert into the Fertile Crescent: the Amorites, the Canaanites, the Arameans, the Nabateans, and the Arabs.

The principal Semitic peoples of ancient times were:

I. The Akkadians. The Babylonians and Assyrians who lived in Mesopotamia spoke a common language. From c. 2350 to 538 B.C. these gifted, vigorous people dominated Mesopotamia. Several times they produced empires that ruled the ancient world. Their Akkadian language, written on clay by means of cuneiform signs, was for more than a millennium the

Part of relief showing the figure of a Semite, from the temple of Ramses II at Abu Simbel, on the Nile in Nubia. Courtesy Bildarchiv Foto, Marburg

language of the world of that time. The cities of Ur, Babylon, and Nineveh and rulers such as Sargon I, Shalmaneser III and V, Sennacherib, Hammurabi the law codifier (who though an Amorite ruled the Babylonian Empire), and Ashurbanipal the library builder testify to the greatness of the Akkadian civilization.

II. The Arameans. Principally traders and catalysts of culture rather than its creators, the Aramean-speaking people lived in Syria from c. 1700 B.C. to the time of Christ. Damascus, Aleppo, Hama, and Zobah were their cities. Their language supplanted Akkadian as the world language and was adopted by the Jews after their return from exile. It became the language of much of the Talmud, and half of the Book of Daniel was written in Aramaic. It was through the Aramaic language that the Semitic civilization was given to the Greeks and Romans.

III. The Canaanites. This term is used to designate a number of peoples who lived in southern Syria (including Palestine) in ancient times (Edomites, Ammonites, and Moabites). It appears that the Canaanites invented the alphabet. The Phoenicians were a Canaanite people who took to the sea and became the first people to dominate the Mediterranean and make it their common highway (1200–400 B.C.).

IV. The Arabs. Little is known about the inhabitants of Arabia prior to Muhammad. The great contributions of the Arabs after the coming of Islam lie beyond the scope of this work.

V. The Ethiopians. Across the Red Sea from southern Arabia, the Ethiopians had a flourishing Semitic civilization from 500 B.C. to the time of Mohammed.

SENAAH (sē-nā'à, Heb. *senā'âh*). The descendants of Senaah (sometimes called Hassenaah, with the Hebrew definite article attached). These people were a part of the company returning from captivity under Zerubbabel (Ezra 2:35; Neh 7:38). They rebuilt the Fish Gate of Jerusalem (3:3). The name may also refer to a place (unknown).

SENATE (Gr. *gerousia, a council of elders*). Mentioned in Acts 5:21, in KJV, RSV, NEB (NIV "assembly of the elders"); not a body different from the "council" (Sanhedrin), but a more precise designation indicating its dignity as composed of old men.

SENATOR (See OCCUPATIONS AND PROFESSIONS)

SENIR (sē'nĭr, Heb. *senîr*). The Amorite name of Mt. Hermon (Deut 3:9; Song of Songs 4:8), a source of fir timber (Ezek 27:5). Twice spelled Shenir in KJV.

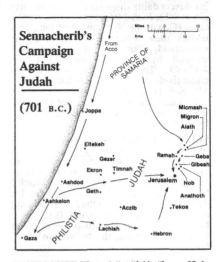

Sennacherib's Campaign Against Judah (701 B.C.)

SENNACHERIB (sĕ-năk'êr-ĭb, Heb. *sanhērîv*, Assyr. *Sin-ahe-irba, Sin* [moongod] *multiplied brothers*). An Assyrian king (705–681 B.C.), the son and successor of Sargon II (722–705). He restored the capital to Nineveh, on the east bank of the Tigris, opposite the present city of Mosul. It is represented today by the mounds Kuyunjik and Nebi Yunus ("prophet Jonah"). Sennacherib constructed palaces, temples, city walls, and a water system. He was an able soldier, and it is in this capacity that he is best remembered. On his succession to the throne he found it necessary to deal with revolts throughout the empire. Exasperated by the repeated intrigues of Babylon and its king, Merodach-Baladan, he finally reduced the city to ruins in 689. In the west there was also rebellion; among the rebels was Hezekiah of Judah. On his third campaign in 701, Sennacherib marched west to settle those difficulties. Sennacherib took Sidon and then moved south, receiving tribute and capturing Ashkelon, Beth Dagon, Joppa, and other Palestinian cities. At Eltekeh (cf. Josh 19:44; 21:23) he defeated a coalition of Palestinians, plus some Egyptian forces. Hezekiah had taken Padi, the king of Ekron, who was allied with Sennacherib, and had made him a captive. Sennacherib now seized Ekron and restored Padi to his throne. He did not take Jerusalem, but he boasted that he shut up Hezekiah

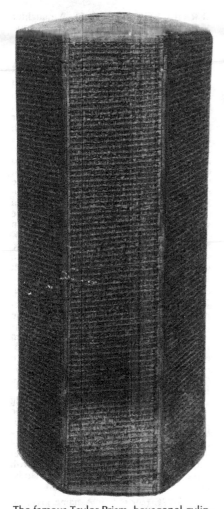

The famous Taylor Prism, hexagonal cylinder bearing an account of Sennacherib's raid into Judah, dated 701 B.C. (cf. 2 Kings 18:13). Reproduced by courtesy of the Trustees of the British Museum

"like a bird in a cage." The OT gives three records of this invasion and its results (2 Kings 18:13–19:17; 2 Chron 32:1–22; Isa 36:1–37:38).

It was in the 14th year of Hezekiah that Sennacherib came against Judah and took all of its fortified cities. Hezekiah offered to pay tribute and had to strip the temple of its treasures to make payment. The Bible relates that Jerusalem was delivered by the Lord, who sent his angel to strike the Assyrian armies and force Sennacherib to retire to his homeland (2 Kings 19:35–36; 2 Chron 32:21; Isa 37:36–37). Back in Nineveh, Sennacherib was assassinated by two of his sons in 681 B.C. (2 Kings 19:37; Isa 37:38) in an effort to upset the succession that he had decreed for Esarhaddon, but Esarhaddon was equal to the situation and gained the throne.

SENSUAL (Gr. *psychikos, pertaining to the soul*). Used twice in the KJV to denote the unspiritual nature and characteristics of the soul, the natural life that human beings have in common with brutes (James 3:15; Jude 19). It is also used twice in the NIV (Col 2:23; 1 Tim 5:11). *Psychikos* is used six times (1 Cor 2:14; 15:44 [twice], 46; James 3:15; Jude 19).

SENUAH (See HASSENUAH)

SEPHARVAIM, SEPHARVITE (sĕf'ȧr-vā'ĭm, sĕ'fär-vĭt). The place from which the Assyrians brought colonists to live in Samaria (2 Kings 17:24, 31). The inhabitants of the place were called Sepharvites. The place is also referred to in the Assyrian commander's threatening speech to Jerusalem (18:34; 19:13) as a place conquered by the Assyrian armies, perhaps the Sibraim of Ezekiel 47:16, a place located in the region of Hamath.

SEPTUAGINT (sĕp'tū-à-jĭnt). The first and most important of a number of ancient translations of the Hebrew OT into Greek. The story of the origin of the Septuagint is told in the *Letter of Aristeas*, a pseudepigraphical book written in the second half of the second century B.C. It states that Ptolemy II (called Philadelphus, the king of Egypt, 285–247) wished to have a translation of the Jewish law for his famous library in Alexandria. At his request the high priest Eleazer of Jerusalem sent 72 men, 6 from each tribe, to Egypt with a scroll of the Law. In 72 days they translated one section each from this scroll and afterward decided on the wording together. So the version was called the Septuagint (the translation of the 70, abbreviated LXX). Later writers elaborated on this story to the effect that the 72 had translated the whole OT (not the Pentateuch only), each independently of the other, in seclusion. The exact agreement of the 72 copies proved the work's inspiration.

It is generally agreed that the Pentateuch was translated from Hebrew into Greek in Egypt around the time of Ptolemy II, ca. 280 B.C. The rest of the OT was done at a later date.

The fact that the LXX was not made all at once is plain by the unevenness of its character. Some parts, e.g., the Pentateuch, are a rather literal and accurate translation of the Hebrew text. Other books, such as 1 and 2 Samuel, differ greatly from the Masoretic Text (our present Hebrew Bible). Recent finds at Qumran ("The Dead Sea Scrolls") include a Hebrew MS of Samuel whose text seems very close to the LXX of this book. The LXX Daniel was such a free paraphrase that it was set aside in favor of a later translation made by Theodotion. The LXX Jeremiah is one-seventh, and the LXX Job is about one-fourth shorter than the Masoretic Text.

The LXX came to have great authority among the non-Palestinian Jews. Its use in the synagogues of the Dispersion made it one of the most important missionary aids. Probably it was the first work of substantial size ever to be translated into another language. When the NT quotes from the OT, as it frequently does, the form of the quotation often follows the LXX.

The early Christian church, built largely on converts from the synagogues of the Greek-speaking world, took over the LXX as their Bible. Their use of it, to prove to the Jews that Jesus was the Messiah, caused a change in the Jews' attitude toward it. Soon after A.D. 100 the Jews completely gave up the LXX, and it became a Christian book. Our oldest copies of the LXX today are from the three great Greek MSS of the Bible from the fourth and fifth centuries A.D.—Sinaiticus, Vaticanus, and Alexandrinus. The textual criticism of the LXX is a difficult task.

The LXX is of use in two ways to biblical studies today: 1. It is a valuable witness to the understanding of the OT in pre-Christian days. 2. The LXX is a very important tool for use in the science of textual criticism—the attempt to bring to light the original text of the Bible. In quite a few cases the Masoretic Text and the LXX do not agree. A person knowing neither of the original languages can sense the difference by comparing Amos 9:11–12 with Acts 15:16–17. James quotes Amos, and his quotation agrees in general with the LXX, which is quite different from the Masoretic Text. Of course, the great majority of the differences between the two are inconsequential.

SEPULCHER (See TOMB)

SERAH (sē'rà, Heb. *serah*). A daughter of Asher (Gen 46:17; Num 26:46; 1 Chron 7:30).

SERAIAH (sē-rā'yà, Heb. *serāyāhû*). **1.** A son of Kenaz (1 Chron 4:13). **2.** A scribe who held office under David (2 Sam 8:17). **3.** A Simeonite, son of Asiel (1 Chron 4:35). **4.** One of the men sent to arrest Jeremiah and Baruch (Jer 36:26). **5.** The high priest when Nebuchadnezzar captured Jerusalem. He was put to death by Nebuchadnezzar at Riblah (2 Kings 25:18–21; Jer 52:24–27). He was the father of Jehozadak, who was taken into captivity, and the grandfather of Jeshua, the high priest under Zerubbabel at the return from exile. He may also be the Seraiah named as an ancestor of Ezra (1 Chron 6:14–15; Ezra 2:2; 7:1). **6.** The son of Neriah (Jer 51:59–64). **7.** The son of Tanhumeth (2 Kings 25:23; Jer 40:8). **8.** A priest, the third in the list of those who returned from Babylon to Jerusalem with Zerubbabel (Ezra 2:2; Neh 7:7; 10:2; 11:11; cf. 1 Chron 9:11).

SERAPHS, SERAPHIM (sĕr'à-fĭm, Heb. *serāphîm*). Called seraphs (JB, NIV), seraphim (MLB, NASB, NEB, RSV, -*im* being the Hebrew plural ending), and seraphims (KJV). They were celestial beings whom Isaiah, when he was called to the prophetic ministry, saw standing before the enthroned Lord (Isa 6:2–3, 6–7). This is the only mention of these creatures in the Bible.

The word *seraphim* means "burning ones." The same word is used to describe the snakes in the wilderness (Num 21:6, 8; cf. Deut 8:15; Isa 14:29; 30:6). They belong to an order of unearthly beings attending the throne of God. Isaiah described them as standing upright with three pairs of wings and human hands, faces, and voices. See also FIRE.

SEREDITE (sĕr'è-dīt). A name given to the descendants of Sered (Gen 46:14; Num 26:26). KJV has "Sardite."

SERGEANT (See OCCUPATIONS AND PROFESSIONS)

SERGIUS PAULUS (See PAULUS, SERGIUS)

SERMON ON THE MOUNT The first of six extended discourses of Jesus given in Matthew (chs. 5–7). The other discourses are (2) the mission of the Twelve (Matt 9:35–11:1), (3) the parables by the sea (13:1–52), (4) humility (ch. 18), (5) denunciation of hypocrisy (ch. 23), and (6) eschatology (chs. 24–25).

Much of the teaching material that Matthew gives in these long discourses is

Six-winged figure on basalt relief from Tell Halaf, reminiscent of the creature Isaiah saw standing before the enthroned Lord (Isa 6:2). The figure, perhaps a woman, wears a long fringed robe and six wings, two springing from her shoulders, two from her hips, and two emerging from her knees. She wears an elaborate crown, perhaps intended to represent horns. Courtesy Carta, Jerusalem

given also by Mark and Luke, with close verbal similarity, but in fragments in other settings than Matthew's. The nature of Jesus' itinerant ministry to shifting crowds was such that he must have repeated similar material a great many times under a great variety of circumstances. Moreover, in any one extended session of his teaching, there were interruptions, questions, arguments, digressions. The "sermon" is a student's (Matthew's) report of a class lecture and discussion and should be studied in that light.

SERPENT (See ANIMALS)

SERUG (sē'rŭg, Heb. serûgh, meaning uncertain). A descendant of Shem (Gen 11:20, 22–23; 1 Chron 1:26). In KJV of Luke 3:35 he is called Saruch (NIV Serug).

SERVANT (See OCCUPATIONS AND PROFESSIONS)

SERVANT OF JEHOVAH A term applied in the KJV of the OT to the patriarchs (Exod 32:13), Moses (Num 12:7–8), Joshua (Judg 2:8), David (2 Sam 7:5–29), the prophets (Zech 1:6), and others. It is chiefly used, however, as a title for the Messiah (Isa 42:1–4; 49:1–6; 50:4–9; 52:13–53:12). NIV generally has "a servant of the LORD" or "my servant."

Earlier in Isaiah (7:14; 9:6–7; 11:1–5) the Servant had been described. He is also identified as "the Branch" (cf. Isa 4:2; 11:1; 53:2 with Jer 23:5–6; 33:15; Zech 3:8; 6:12–13).

The NT applies Isaiah's Servant passages to Christ (Isa 42:1–4 is quoted as fulfilled in Matt 12:18–21; and Isa 52:13–53:12 is quoted in Matt 8:17; Luke 22:37; John 12:38; Acts 8:32–33; Rom 10:16; cf. also John 1:29; Rom 8:34; Heb 9:28; 1 Peter 2:21–25). The Servant's mission is fulfilled only in Christ: election (Isa 42:1; 49:7; 1 Peter 2:4, 6), birth (Isa 49:1; 53:2; Luke 1:31–35), anointing (Isa 42:1; 48:16; 59:21; 61:1; Matt 3:16; Luke 4:18–19), ministry (Isa 49:8–13; Acts 3:13–18), obedience (Isa 50:4–7; Phil 2:7–8), new covenant (Isa 42:6; 49:8; 55:3; Matt 26:26–29), vicarious death (Isa 53:4–12; 1 Peter 2:22–25), resurrection (Isa 53:10–12; Acts 2:24–36), offer of salvation (Isa 49:8; Luke 24:46–49), mission to Gentiles (Isa 42:1, 6–7; 49:6, 12; 60:3, 9; Matt 28:18–20), glorification and intercession (Isa 49:3; 53:12; Acts 2:33–36; Phil 2:6–11; Heb 7:24–25).

SETH (Heb. shēth, "appointed," i.e., "substituted"). Adam's third son (Gen 4:25–26; 5:3–8). His name signifies that he was considered a "substitute" for Abel (4:25). His birth recalled man's tragic loss of the divine image (5:1–2). He became the founder of the line of faith (Gen 4:26; Luke 3:38).

SEVENEH (See ASWAN)

SEVENTY, THE Disciples of our Lord. The mission of the Seventy (mentioned only in Luke 10:1–20 KJV, MLB, MOF, NASB, RSV; 72 JB, NEB, NIV) has parallels—in both the disciples' responsibilities and the conditions they would meet—with the work of the early church: (1) the mission of others than the Twelve (Luke 10:1; Acts 8:1, 4), (2) the inclusion of the Gentiles (Luke 10:8; Acts 10:17), (3) the kingdom of God proclaimed (Luke

10:9, 11; Acts 8:22), (4) the reception (Luke 10:5-9; Acts 2:41-42) and rejection (Luke 10:10ff.; Acts 7:54-60) of the gospel, (5) triumph over demons (Luke 10:17ff.; Acts 16:16ff.), and (6) the joy of discipleship (Luke 10:17; Acts 5:41). Between this mission and Pentecost, however, Jesus radically altered the guidelines for the disciples' equipment (Luke 22:35-39).

SEVENTY WEEKS, THE A name applied to Daniel 9:24-27, a prophecy that presumably, in contrast to the general prophecies in Daniel 2 and 7, pinpoints the exact time within the fourth kingdom when the Messiah will appear. Almost all agree that the "weeks" designate 490 years. The prophecy is (1) divided: the successive periods are described as 7, 62, 1; (2) dated: its *terminus a quo* ("from"—9:25) and its *terminus ad quem* ("until"—9:25); (3) determinative: its purposes regard Israel (9:24), redemption (9:24), the Messiah (9:24, 26-27), the sacrifices (9:27), and Jerusalem (9:25-27); and (4) debated (see below).

Three main views are held. (1) The *critical view* says that the "prophecy" was written by a pseudo-Daniel in 165 B.C. and synchronizes (inaccurately) with the history between 586 B.C. (Jerusalem's fall) and 164 B.C. (Antiochus). (2) The *dispensational view* has the 69th week terminating before the Crucifixion, leaving the 70th (the present age being a "great parenthesis") to be fulfilled in the Great Tribulation. (3) The *conservative*, or *traditional*, *view* says the 70th week was introduced by Christ's baptism and bisected (three and a half years) by his death, thus causing the sacrifices to cease (9:27).

SEVEN WORDS FROM THE CROSS These words of Christ were probably uttered in the following order: (1) Before the darkness (Luke 23:34, 43; John 19:26); (2) During the darkness (Matt 27:46; Mark 15:34); (3) After the darkness (John 19:28, 30; Luke 23:46). Theologically, these words illustrate (1) divine forgiveness, (2) assurance of immortality, (3) good works, (4) the awfulness of Christ's death, (5) the true humanity of Christ, (6) the perfection of Christ's atonement, and (7) the divine complacency.

SHAALBIM (shā-ăl'bĭm, Heb. *sha'albîm*). A town won by the Danites from the Amorites with the help of the Ephraimites (Judg 1:35). In Solomon's time a representative from this town was appointed as commissary officer (1 Kings

4:9). "Eliahba the Shaalbonite" (2 Sam 23:32; 1 Chron 11:33), one of David's special guards, came from this town (Shaalbon = Shaalbim).

SHAALBONITE (See SHAALBIM)

SHAALIM (shā'lĭm, Heb. *sha'alîm, district of foxes*). A region, probably near the northern boundary of Benhamin's territory, traversed by Saul in search of his father's donkeys (1 Sam 9:4).

SHAAPH (shā'ăf, Heb. *sha'aph*, meaning uncertain). 1. The sixth in a list of sons of Jahdai (1 Chron 2:47). 2. A son of Caleb by Maachah, a concubine (2:49; cf. Josh 15:31).

SHAARAIM (shā'à-rā'ĭm, Heb. *sha'ărayim, two gates*, so rendered in LXX of 1 Sam 17:52; KJV [incorrectly] Sharaim in Josh 15:36). 1. A town belonging to Judah (Josh 15:36; 1 Sam 17:52). 2. A town belonging to Simeon (1 Chron 4:31). It is listed as Sharuhen (Josh 19:6) and Shilhim (15:32).

SHABBETHAI (shăb'ē-thī, Heb. *shabbethay, Sabbath-born*). A Levite of Ezra's time who is mentioned as a participant in the foreign-wives controversy (Ezra 10:15), as an interpreter of the Law (Neh 8:7-8), and as a chief Levite over the temple (11:16).

SHACHIA (See SAKIA)

SHACKLES Bonds, chains, or fetters, generally for the feet of prisoners, and made of bronze or of iron (Judg 16:21; Ps 105:18; 149:8). The NT word (Mark 5:4; Luke 8:29) indicates that the shackles were for the feet.

SHADDAI (See EL SHADDAI)

SHADOW Literally, a shadow of a mountain (Judg 9:36), of a tree (Hos 4:13; Mark 4:32), of a dial (2 Kings 20:9-11), of a booth (Jonah 4:5), of a gourd (4:6), of a person (Acts 5:15). Figuratively, it signifies life's shortness (1 Chron 29:15; Job 8:9; Ps 102:11), protection (either good, as in Pss 17:8; 36:7; 91:1; or evil, as in Isa 30:3; Jer 48:45), the Messiah's blessings (Isa 4:6; 32:2; 49:2; 51:16), and death (either physical, as in Job 10:21-22; Ps 23:4; or spiritual as in Isa 9:2; Matt 4:16; Luke 1:79). Theologically it is used (1) of God's unchangeableness (James 1:17); (2) of the typical nature of the OT (Col 2:17; Heb 8:5; 10:1), illustrated in these facts: the OT prefigures in outline the NT substance; the OT represents externally (in rites and ceremonies) what the NT fulfills internally; the OT saints, nevertheless, could by faith comprehend the inner reality of the shadow; the NT, therefore, fulfills and abolishes the OT shadow; the NT saints, however, can still draw spiritual instruction from the shadow; and, finally, even NT saints, with the shadow and the substance, await the full day of spiritual understanding (1 Cor 13:12).

SHADRACH (shā'drăk, Heb. *shadhrakh*, meaning uncertain). The Babylonian name given to Hananiah; Meshach and Abednego are mentioned in all 15 places his name appears (Dan 1:7; 2:49; 3:12–30). They were captives with Daniel.

SHALIM, LAND OF (See SHAALIM)

SHALLUM, SHALLUN (shăl'ŭm, shăl'ŭn, Heb. *shallûm,* or *shallûn, recompense*). A name (*Shallum*) applied to all of the following except the last (*Shallun*). **1.** The youngest son of Naphtali (1 Chron 7:13 KJV; NIV Shillem; cf. Gen 46:24; Num 26:48–49). **2.** The son of Shaul and grandson of Simeon (1 Chron 4:25; cf. Gen 46:10; Exod 6:15; Num 26:12–13). **3.** The son of Sismai and father of Jekamiah (1 Chron 2:40–41).**4.** Son of Kore and chief of the gatekeepers (9:17, 19, 31; Ezra 2:42; 10:24; Neh 7:45; Meshelemiah in 1 Chron 26:1 and Shelemiah in 1 Chron 26:14). **5.** Son of Zadok and father of Hilkiah (6:12–13); ancestor of Ezra (Ezra 7:1–2; Meshullam in 1 Chron 9:11 and Neh 11:11). **6.** A king of Israel who murdered Zechariah and reigned in his place for one month (2 Kings 15:10–15). **7.** The father of Jehizkiah and an Ephraimite chief (2 Chron 28:12). **8.** Son of Tikvah and husband of the prophetess Huldah; custodian of the priests' wardrobe (2 Kings 22:14; 2 Chron 34:22; perhaps also Jer 32:7, Jeremiah's uncle; see No. 10). **9.** A king of Judah, son of Josiah (1 Chron 3:15; Jer 22:11); better known as Jehoahaz II (2 Kings 23:30–31, 34; 2 Chron 36:1). **10.** An uncle of Jeremiah (Jer 32:7; see No. 8). **11.** The father of Maaseiah (35:4; cf. 52:24). **12.** One of the Levitical porters who was compelled to divorce his foreign wife (Ezra 10:24). **13.** A son of Bani who was compelled to divorce his foreign wife (10:42). **14.** The son of Hallohesh; a ruler who, with his daughters, helped to build the walls of Jerusalem (Neh 3:12). **15.** Shallun, son of Col-Hozeh; ruler of the Mizpah district (Neh 3:15 Shallum RSV).

SHALMANESER (shăl'măn-ē'zêr, Heb. *shalman'-eser*, Assyr. *Sulman-asaridu, Sulman [the god] is chief*). The title of five Assyrian kings, only one of whom is directly mentioned in the OT.
   1. Shalmaneser III (859–824 B.C.), son

Stele (2.20 m. high) of Shalmaneser III, King of Assyria (858–824 B.C.). In front of the king are carved the symbols of four of the Assyrian gods. The inscription describes the events of the first six years of his reign. From Kurkh, southeast Turkey, c. 850 B.C. Reproduced by courtesy of the Trustees of the British Museum

of Ashurnasirpal; the first Assyrian king who, as far as the records reveal, had political and military contacts with a king of the northern kingdom of Israel. Although Shalmaneser III is not mentioned as such in the biblical narrative (1 Kings 16:29–22:40; 2 Chron 18:1–34), yet his

Detail from the Black Obelisk of Shalmaneser III showing, in top panels, Jehu bringing tribute. Reproduced by courtesy of the Trustees of the British Museum

Monolith Inscription in the British Museum recounts a coalition composed principally of Syria (Hadadezer = Ben-Hadad) and of Israel ("Ahab, the Israelite"), which he met and presumably defeated at Karkar, north of Hamath in the Orontes Valley, in 853. Ahab, according to this inscription, contributed 2,000 chariots and 10,000 troops in the battle against Shalmaneser.

2. Shalmaneser V (726-722 B.C.), son of Tiglath-Pileser (who died in 727); the only Assyrian king named Shalmaneser in the OT history (unless Shalman, in Hos 10:14, is a contraction of Shalmaneser). There are two references to him (2 Kings 17:3-5; 18:9-11; cf. Hos 5:13; 7:11; 8:9; 10:6; 12:1).

SHAMARIAH (See SHEMARIAH)

SHAMBLES (Gr. *makellon*, from Lat. *macellum, meat market*, which latter meaning is followed by RSV and NIV). The meat market. Meat there had perhaps used in pagan sacrifices, but as food it had not been affected (cf. 1 Tim 4:4). However, Christian liberty to eat it was not to endanger a weaker brother's conscience (1 Cor 10:23-33).

SHAME, SHAMEFACEDNESS (Heb. *bosheth*, Gr. *aischynē*, Gr. *aidos*). This subject has many aspects: subjective (Gen 2:25; 3:7) and objective (Jer 11:13; Hos 9:10); positive (Prov 19:26; 28:7) and negative (10:5; Rom 1:16; 1 John 2:28); literal (Exod 32:25) and figurative (Rev 3:18; 16:15); individual (Gen 38:23) and national (Judg 18:7; Isa 30:3-5); removable (Isa 54:4) and unremovable (Jer 23:40); loved (Hos 4:18 ASV) and hated (Eph 5:12); punitive (Isa 47:3; Ezek 16:51-54; 44:12) and commendatory (1 Sam 20:30-34; 2 Sam 6:20; 13:11-14); now (Heb 6:6) and future (Ezek 32:24-25; Dan 12:2); human (Ps 119:31) and divine (Pss 69:7-9; 89:45; Isa 50:6; Heb 12:2); due to something natural (2 Sam 19:1-5; 1 Cor 11:6, 14) and due to something unnatural (2 Sam 13:11-14; Phil 3:19). "Shamefacedness" in 1 Timothy 2:9 KJV denotes sexual modesty (NIV "decency and propriety").

SHAMED (See SHEMED)

SHAMER (See SHEMER)

SHAMGAR (shăm'gàr, Heb. *shamgar*). A son of Anath; slayer of 600 Philistines (Judg 3:31; cf. 1 Sam 13:19-22). He is listed as a judge between Ehud and Deborah. He prepared the way for the greater deliverance of Israel under Deborah and Barak.

SHAMHUTH (shăm'hŭth, Heb. *shamhûth, desolation*). An Izrahite. He was the fifth divisional commander, for the fifth month of the year, in David's organization of his army (1 Chron 27:8); probably the same person as Shammah the Harodite (2 Sam 23:25) and Shammoth the Harorite (1 Chron 11:27).

SHAMIR (shā'mêr, Heb. *shāmîr, a sharp point*). 1. A town allotted to Judah (Josh

15:48). **2.** A town in Mt. Ephraim (Judg 10:1-2). **3.** A Levite, son of Micah; a temple attendant (1 Chron 24:24).

SHAMMAH (shăm'à, Heb. *shammâ, waste*). **1.** Son of Reuel and grandson of Esau (Gen 36:13, 17; 1 Chron 1:37). **2.** The third son of Jesse and brother of David (1 Sam 16:9; 17:13); also called Shimea (1 Chron 20:7), Shimeah (2 Sam 13:3, 32), and Shimei (21:21). **3.** One of David's three mightiest men, the son of Agee (23:11-17; Shagee in 1 Chron 11:34). **4.** One of David's mighty men (2 Sam 23:33); also called Shammoth (plural of Shammah, 1 Chron 11:27) and Shamhuth (27:8). Perhaps the same as no. 3.

SHAMMAI (shăm'ā-ī, Heb. *shammay*, contraction of *shema'yâ, Jehovah has heard*). The name of three descendants of Judah: **1.** A son of Onam (1 Chron 2:28, 32). **2.** A son of Rekem and father of Maon (2:44-45). **3.** A descendant of Ezrah (4:17-18).

SHAMMOTH (shăm'ŏth, Heb. *shammôth, desolation*). One of David's mighty men of war (1 Chron 11:27); apparently the same as Shammah (2 Sam 23:25) and Shamhuth (1 Chron 27:8).

SHAMMUA, SHAMMUAH (shă-mū'à, Heb. *ashammû'a, heard* or *renowned*). **1.** One of spies sent into Canaan as the representative of the tribe of Reuben (Num 13:4). **2.** A son of David by Bathsheba; brother of Solomon (2 Sam 5:14, KJV has Shammuah; 1 Chron 3:5, KJV has Shimea; 14:4). **3.** A Levite, father of Abda (or Obadiah) (Neh 11:17; Shemaiah in 1 Chron 9:16). **4.** A priest whose father returned with Zerubbabel (Neh 12:1-7, 12, 18).

SHAPHAN (shā'făn, Heb. *shāphān, hyrax* or *rock rabbit*). The faithful scribe during Josiah's reign (2 Kings 22:3-20; 2 Chron 34:8-28). Shaphan's faith is seen in the names he gave his sons: Ahikam (*my brother has risen up*); Gemariah (*the LORD has accomplished*); Elasah (*God has made*); Jaazaniah (*the LORD hearkens*). Shaphan's faith is seen in his sons' lives: Ahikim accompanied his father on the mission to Huldah (34:20ff.) and later became Jeremiah's protector (Jer 26:24); Elasah, with others, transmitted Jeremiah's message to exiles in Babylon (29:1-3); Gemariah resisted destructive attempts against Jeremiah's writings (36:10, 12, 25); but Jaazaniah did not possess his father's faith (Ezek 8:11). Two sons of Ahikam, however, continued their grandfather's faith: Micaiah (Jer 36:11-13) and Gedaliah (39:14; 40:5-12; 43:6).

SHAPHAT (shā'făt, Heb. *shāphāt, he has judged*). **1.** One of the spies sent to Canaan as a representative of the tribe of Simeon (Num 13:5). **2.** The father of Elisha the prophet (1 Kings 19:16, 19; 2 Kings 3:11; 6:31). **3.** A Gadite chief in Bashan (1 Chron 5:12). **4.** A son of Adlai, one of David's herdsmen (27:29). **5.** A descendant of the royal line of David (3:22).

SHAPHER (See SHEPHER)

SHAPHIR (shā'fĕr, Heb. *shāphîr, glittering*). One of a group of towns mentioned in Micah 1:10-15. Because of its association with Gath, Aczib (of Judah), and Mareshah, it seems likely that it was located in SW Palestine.

SHARAIM (See SHAARAIM)

SHAREZER (shà-rē'zêr, Heb. *sar'etser*, Assyr. *Shar-usur, protect the king*). **1.** A son of the Assyrian king Sennacherib who, with his brother Adrammelech, murdered his father (2 Kings 19:37; Isa 37:38). **2.** A contemporary of Zechariah the prophet and member of a delegation sent from Bethel to Jerusalem (Zech 7:2; Sherezer in KJV).

SHARON (shăr'ŭn, Heb. *shārôn, plain*). **1.** The coastal plain between Joppa and Mt. Carmel (1 Chron 27:29; Song of Songs 2:1; Isa 35:2). **2.** The suburban pasturelands of Sharon possessed by the tribe of Gad (1 Chron 5:16). **3.** Figuratively, it may mean (1) a person's state of regeneracy—of fruitfulness and glory (Isa 35:2) or (2) a person's eternal state—of peace forevermore (65:10, 17).

SHARUHEN (shà-rū'hĕn, Heb. *shārûhen*). An ancient town south of Gaza and west of Beersheba, assigned to Simeon within Judah's territory (Josh 19:6; cf. Gen 49:7); apparently the same as Shilhim (Josh 15:32) and Shaaraim (1 Chron 4:31).

SHAUL, SHAULITES (shā'ŭl, shā'ŭ-līts, Heb. *shā'ûl, asked* [of the LORD], *shā'ûlî, of Shaul*). **1.** The sixth in a list of eight kings who ruled over Edom (Gen 36:37-38 [Saul in KJV]; 1 Chron 1:48-49). **2.** A son of Simeon (Gen 46:10; Exod 6:15; Num 26:13; 1 Chron 4:24). **3.** A descendant of Levi, son of Uzziah (6:24). An ancestor of Samuel (6:27).

SHAVING The Hebrew words are used of animals (except in Job 1:20; Jer 7:29; Mic 1:16; Nah 1:12). The Greek word *xyraō* is used only in Acts 21:24 and 1 Corinthians 11:5-6. The priests (Lev

21:5; Ezek 44:20) and the Nazirites (Num 6:5; cf. 1 Sam 1:11) were prohibited from shaving. Shaving expressed (1) contrition (Job 1:20), (2) accommodation to a custom (Gen 41:14), (3) consecration for Levites (Num 6:9; 8:7), (4) cleansing for lepers (Lev 14:8–9; 13:32ff.), (5) completion of a vow (Num 6:18; Acts 18:18; 21:24), (6) commitment to a captive woman (Deut 21:12), (7) conspiracy against a man's Nazirite vow (Judg 16:19), (8) contempt (2 Sam 10:4; 1 Chron 19:4), and (9) cleansing of a corrupt nation (Isa 7:20; cf. 1:16; 6:5; and 2 Kings 18:13ff.).

SHAVSHA (shăv'shà, Heb. *shawshā'*). David's secretary of state (1 Chron 18:16; Shisha in 1 Kings 4:3; Seraiah in 2 Sam 8:17; Sheva in 2 Sam 20:25).

SHEAF (Heb. *'ălummâh*, *'ōmer*, *'āmîr*). The sheaf was a handful of grain left behind the reaper (Jer 9:22 RSV), gathered and bound usually by children or women (Ruth 2:7, 15) in a joyous mood (Pss 126:6; 129:7–8). Thus stacked the sheaves became dry and inflammable (Zech 12:6; cf. Judg 15:1–5 ASV); but they made a beautiful sight (Song of Songs 7:2). A donkey (Neh 13:15) or a heavily loaded cart (Amos 2:13) bore these bundles to the threshing floor (Ruth 3:6–7; Mic 4:12). Some sheaves, however, were left behind for the poor (Deut 24:19; cf. Ruth 2:7, 15; Job 24:10). The sheaf of the firstfruit (Lev 23:10–15; cf. 2 Chron 31:5–10) typically represents (1) Christians, as representatives of a larger harvest (Rom 16:5; 1 Cor 16:15; James 1:18), possessed by the Spirit (Rom 8:23), and dedicated to God (Rev 14:1–5) or (2) Christ, as an evidence of believers' later resurrection (1 Cor 15:20, 23).

SHEALTIEL (shĕ-ăl'tĭel, Gr. *Salathiel, I have asked God;* KJV "Salathiel"). The son of Jeconiah, king of Judah, and father of Zerubbabel, according to the genealogy in Matthew 1:12. In Luke's genealogy he appears as father of Zerubbabel, but as the son of Neri (Luke 3:27). Matthew's genealogy is based on the legal succession, while Luke's is based on the actual succession. If the direct line failed in Jeconiah because he had no son to succeed him, the right of succession went to Shealtiel, a descendant of Nathan and the son of Neri who, as the legal heir of Jeconiah, was reckoned his son by Matthew.

SHEAR-JASHUB (shē'àr-jà'shŭb, Heb. *she'ār yāshûv, a remnant shall return*). The symbolic name of Isaiah's oldest son (Isa 7:3). The symbolism is reflected in the historic return from Babylon and is fulfilled in the spiritual return to the Lord at Messiah's advent (Isa 1:9; 4:3–4; 10:20–23; 65:8–9; Rom 11:5–6, 16–29).

SHEBA (shē'bà, Heb. *shevā', seven, an oath*). 1. A chief of a Gadite family (1 Chron 5:13). 2. A town allotted to Simeon (Josh 19:2; cf. 1 Chron 4:28). 3. A son of Bicri, a Benjamite. He inspired a short-lived insurrection against the kingship of David. 4. A son of Raamah (Gen 10:7; 1 Chron 1:9). 5. A grandson of Eber (Gen 10:28; 1 Chron 1:22). 6. The oldest son of Jokshan, Abraham's son by Keturah (Gen 25:3; 1 Chron 1:32). It is probable that this man's descendants, by intermarriage or otherwise, finally became identified with the descendants of no. 4 and no. 5 (1 Kings 10:1–13; 2 Chron 9:1–12; Job 1:15; Isa 60:6; Jer 6:20; Ezek 27:22; 38:13; Joel 3:8; Matt 12:42).

SHEBAH (shē'bà, Heb. *shiv'âh, seven or oath*). The name of a well that the servants of Isaac dug. The town Beersheba, i.e., "well of the oath," is so called from this well (Gen 26:31–33; but cf. 21:28–31). NIV renders "Shibah."

SHEBAM (See SIBMAH)

SHEBANIAH (shĕb'à-nī'à, Heb. *shevanyâh*, meaning uncertain). 1. A priest appointed to blow a trumpet before the ark when it was brought to Jerusalem (1 Chron 15:24). 2. One of the Levites who led the people in praising God (Neh 9:4–5; 10:10). 3. Another Levite who was among the covenanters (10:12). 4. A priest who was among the covenanters (10:4). 5. The head of a family of priests (12:14 JB, KJV, MLB, NASB, NEB, RSV; Shecaniah NIV).

SHEBAT (See CALENDAR)

SHEBNA (shĕb'nà, Heb. *shevnā'*). 1. Steward of Hezekiah (Isa 22:15–22). 2. A scribe who met the Assyrian field commander (2 Kings 18; Isa 36:3–37:2).

SHEBUEL (See SHUBAEL)

SHECANIAH, SHECHANIAH (shĕk-ă-nī'à, Heb. *shekhanyâh, dweller with the LORD*). 1. Head of the tenth course of priests (1 Chron 24:11). 2. A priest who assisted in distributing the freewill offerings (2 Chron 31:15). 3. A descendant of David (1 Chron 3:21–22). 4. A descendant of Parosh (Ezra 8:3). 5. A son of Jehaziel (8:5). 6. A son of Jehiel (10:2–4). 7. The keeper of the East Gate (Neh 3:29). 8. Father-in-law to Tobiah, the notorious foe of Nehemiah (6:18). 9. A chief of the priests (12:3). 10. Head of a priestly family (12:14 NIV; **Shebaniah** JD, KJV, MLB, MOF, NASB, NEB, RSV).

SHECHEM (shē'kĕm, Heb. *shekhem, shoulder*). A personal name and the name of a district and city (Gen 33-34) in the hill country of Ephraim in north-central Palestine. Here the Lord appeared to Abram and promised the land to his descendants; Abram responded by building an altar (12:6-7). When Jacob returned from Paddan Aram, he settled down at Shechem and purchased land (33:18-19; Josh 24:32). While Jacob was at Shechem the unfortunate incident of Dinah occurred (Gen 34). Later the brothers of Joseph were herding Jacob's flock at Shechem when Joseph was sent to check on the ir welfare (37:12-14). Shechem, in the territory allotted to Ephraim, was one of the cities of refuge (Josh 20:7; 21:21; 1 Chron 6:67). Joshua gave his farewell address here (Josh 24:1) and made a covenant with the people (24:25). Joseph was buried here (24:32). Abimelech conspired with his mother's relatives to kill all the other sons of Gideon and to have himself made king of Shechem (Judg 9:6). Trouble developed between Abimelech and the people of Shechem, so Abimelech took the city and completely destroyed it (9:46-49).

A view of modern Shechem, which lies in a valley between Mount Ebal and Mount Gerizim. Viewed from Mount Gerizim, facing northwest. Courtesy Zev Radovan

Rehoboam went to Shechem to be made king by all Israel (1 Kings 12:1; 2 Chron 10:1). Jeroboam made Shechem his capital (1 Kings 12:25). The city is mentioned in parallel passages in the Psalms (Pss 60:6; 108:7) and is named in a list of prophetic condemnations against Israel (Hos 6:9).

SHECHINAH (See SHEKINAH)

SHEDEUR (shĕd'ē-êr, Heb. *shedhê'ûr, caster forth of light*). A Reubenite, the father of Elizur, prince of Reuben (Num 1:5; 2:10; 7:30; 10:18).

SHEEP (See ANIMALS)

SHEEPCOTE (See SHEEP PEN)

SHEEPMASTER (See OCCUPATIONS AND PROFESSIONS)

SHEEP PEN, SHEEPFOLD (Heb. *gedhērâh, mikhlâh, nāweh*, Gr. *aulē*). An enclosure intended for the protection of sheep and also to keep them from wandering out and getting lost. These folds were simple walled enclosures, usually without roofs, with the walls covered with thorns to keep out robbers. Several flocks would usually pass the night in one fold under the care of a shepherd who guarded the door. Each shepherd knew his own sheep and was known by them (John 10:1-6).

SHEEPSHEARER (See OCCUPATIONS AND PROFESSIONS)

SHEERAH (shē'rà, Heb. *she'ĕrâh*). A daughter or granddaughter of Ephraim and apparently a powerful woman, for she built or fortified three villages (1 Chron 7:24; cf. 2 Chron 8:5).

SHEET A large piece of linen (Acts 10:11; 11:5). In Judges 14:12-13 "sheets" in KJV probably means "linen undergarments," though NIV has merely "linen garments" (cf. Prov 31:24).

SHEKEL (See MONEY)

SHEKINAH (shè-kī'nà, Heb. *shekhînâh, dwelling of God*). A word, though not occurring in the Bible, that is employed by some Jews and by Christians to describe the visible presence of the Lord (cf. Isa 60:2; Rom 9:4). Moses calls this the "cloud" (Exod 13:21; 14:19-20). It later covered Sinai when God spoke with Moses (24:15-18), filled the tabernacle (40:34-35), guided Israel (40:36-38), filled Solomon's temple (2 Chron 7:1), and was frequently seen in connection with Christ's ministry in the NT (Matt 17:5; Acts 1:9).

SHELAH, SHELANITE (shē'là, Heb. *shēlâh*, Gr. *Sala*, Heb. *shē'là-nīt*, *sprout*). **1.** A son of Arphaxad (Gen 10:24 Salah KJV; Luke 3:35 Sala KJV). **2.** The third son of Judah (Gen 38:5–26). The Shelanites were named after him (Num 26:20).

SHELEMIAH (shĕl-ĕ-mī'à, Heb. *shelemyâh, friend of the LORD*). **1.** Doorkeeper of the house of God (1 Chron 26:14). **2.** The son of Cushi (Jer 36:14). **3.** One of the three whom Jehoiakim sent to arrest Baruch and Jeremiah (36:26). **4.** The father of Jehucal or Jucal (37:3; cf. 38:1). **5.** Captain of the ward who arrested Jeremiah on a false charge (37:13). **6.** Two men of the family of Bani who had taken foreign wives and were compelled to give them up (Ezra 10:39, 41). **7.** The father of Hananiah (Neh 3:30). **8.** A priestly treasurer (13:13).

SHELOMITH, SHELOMOTH (shē-lō'mĭth, shēlō'mŏth, Heb. *shelōmîth, shelōmôth, peaceful*). **1.** A woman whose son was executed for blasphemy (Lev 24:10–12, 23). **2.** A chief Kohathite Levite and a cousin of Miriam, Aaron, and Moses (1 Chron 23:18, Shelomith; 24:22, Shelomoth). **3.** A leading Gershonite Levite in David's time (23:9). **4.** A descendant of Moses through his son Eliezer (26:25). **5.** A son or daughter of Rehoboam, king of Judah (2 Chron 11:20). **6.** A daughter of Zerubbabel—not the Zerubbabel who led back the Jews at the request of Cyrus, but his cousin (1 Chron 3:19). **7.** An ancestor of a family of 160 men who returned with Ezra in 457 B.C. (Ezra 8:10).

SHEM (shĕm, Heb. *shēm*, Gr. *Sēm*, *name, fame*). The second son of Noah and progenitor of the Semitic race (Gen 11:10). He lived 600 years, outliving his descendants for nine generations (except for Eber and Abraham). In the racial prophecy that Noah made after the episode of his drunkenness (9:25–27), he mentioned "the LORD, the God of Shem." The three great monotheistic religions—Judaism, Christianity, and Islam—all had Semitic origins. In the "Table of the nations" (Gen 10) Shem had five sons.

SHEMA (shē'mà, Heb. *shemā', fame, rumor*). **1.** A town in the southern part of Judah (Josh 15:26). **2.** A son of Hebron (1 Chron 2:44). **3.** A son of Joel (5:8). He is possibly the same as Shemaiah no. 2 below (5:4). **4.** A Benjamite (8:13). **5.** One who stood at the right hand of Ezra in the revival in Jerusalem (Neh 8:4). **6.** "Shema" is the Hebrew name for Deuteron-

omy 6:4, probably the most often quoted verse in the Bible, as every good Jew repeats it several times every day— "Hear, O Israel: The LORD our God, the LORD is one."

SHEMAIAH (shē-mā'yà, Heb. *shem'- yâh, The LORD has heard*). **1.** A prince of Simeon (1 Chron 4:37). **2.** A Reubenite (5:4), possibly the same as Shema (no. 3) of verse 8. **3.** A chief Levite (15:8, 11). **4.** A Levite scribe (24:6). **5.** The firstborn son of Obed-Edom (26:4, 6–7). **6.** A brave prophet of God who forbade Rehoboam king of Judah to go against the house of Israel in the north (1 Kings 12:22–24). Shemaiah later wrote a biography of Rehoboam, but it has been lost (2 Chron 12:15). **7.** A descendant of David (1 Chron 3:22). **8.** A Merarite Levite (9:14; Neh 12:18). **9.** A Levite who returned from exile (1 Chron 9:16). He is also called "Shammua" (Neh 11:17). **10.** A Levite whom King Jehoshaphat sent to teach in the towns of Judah (2 Chron 17:8). **11.** One of the Levites who cleansed the temple in the days of Hezekiah (29:14). **12.** A Levite who was appointed to assist in the distribution of food (31:15). **13.** A chief Levite who assisted in the great Passover (35:9). **14.** A leader of the Levites who returned with Ezra (Ezra 8:13). **15.** One whom Ezra sent back for additional Levites (8:16), possibly the same as no. 14. **16.** A descendant of the priests who had married a foreign wife (10:21). **17.** Another man who was guilty of marrying a foreign wife (10:31). **18.** One who helped rebuild the wall (Neh 3:29). **19.** One who tried to intimidate Nehemiah (6:10). **20.** A priest who signed the covenant (10:8). **21.** A priest or Levite who returned with Zerubbabel (12:6). **22.** A musical priest (12:36). **23.** A priest who assisted in the celebration of the completing of the wall of Jerusalem, possibly the same as no. 22 (12:42). **24.** The father of Uriah the prophet (Jer 26:20). **25.** A false prophet who fought against Jeremiah to his own hurt and therefore was not to see God's blessing nor to have any offspring (29:24–32). **26.** The father of Delaiah (36:12).

SHEMARIAH (shĕm-à-rī'à, Heb. *shemaryâh, The LORD keeps*). **1.** One of the mighty men of Benjamin who joined David at Ziklag (1 Chron 12:5). **2.** A son of Rehoboam (2 Chron 11:19). KJV has "Shamariah." **3.** One of the family of Harim (Ezra 10:32). **4.** One of the sons of Bani or Binnui (10:41).

SHEMED (shē'mĕd, Heb. *shamedh, destruction;* however, some MSS have *shamer, watcher*). The third-named son of Elpaal. He built Ono and Lod (1 Chron 8:12).

SHEMER (shē'mēr, Heb. *shemer, guard*). Owner of a hill in central Palestine that Omri king of Israel bought, fortified, and named Samaria after its former owner (1 Kings 16:24; 1 Chron 6:46). This man's name is Shamar in KJV of Chronicles.

SHEMIDA, SHEMIDAH (shē-mī'dà, Heb. *shemîdhā'*). An early member of the tribe of Manasseh through Gilead (Num 26:32; Josh 17:2). He had four sons (1 Chron 7:19).

SHEMINITH (shĕm'ĭ-nĭth, *eighth,* i.e., the octave, and meaning the lower octave). A musical term. The harps tuned to the "sheminith" were to be used with men's voices (1 Chron 15:21, titles for Pss 6 and 12).

SHEMIRAMOTH (shē-mīr'à-mŏth, Heb. *shemîrāmôth*). 1. A Levite whom David selected for making music at the return of the ark to Jerusalem (1 Chron 15:18, 20). 2. One of the teaching Levites (2 Chron 17:8).

SHEMUEL (shĕ-mū'ĕl, Heb. *shemû'ēl, name of God*). The same as Samuel in Hebrew. 1. A Simeonite, divider of Canaan under Joshua (Num 34:20). 2. A Kohathite Levite in charge of music in the temple (1 Chron 6:33; Samuel NIV). 3. The head of a house in Issachar (7:2; Samuel NIV).

SHENIR (See SENIR)

SHEOL (shē'ōl, Heb. *she'ôl*). In the OT the place to which all the dead go, immediately upon death. Sometimes KJV translates it "grave," sometimes "hell," depending on whether or not the individuals in the particular passage were viewed as righteous, but this procedure involves importing distinctions into the OT that were not clarified until Jesus' ministry. NIV prefers to translate *she'ôl* as "grave" (in all but eight passages) and place the name itself in a footnote, a procedure that is neither helpful nor justifiable. It seems best—as in ASV, NASB, and (except for Ps 49:14) RSV—to not translate *she'ôl*, because it is a name.

The OT makes three main points about Sheol: (1) All the dead alike go there (e.g., Gen 37:35; Isa 14:9ff.). (2) Sheol is in some unspecified sense the lot of the wicked. References such as Psalms 6:5; 30:3, 9; 88:3-6 (cf. Job 17:13-16; Isa

38:18) are often quoted as allegedly showing that the OT knew of no hope after death, that the dead are cut off from the Lord and he from them. In all these references, however, the speakers believe themselves to be facing death under the wrath of God, estranged from him, without any indication of divine favor. The OT takes the matter no further; there is some undefined sense in which Sheol involves those who die under wrath in separation from God—the God the ir wickedness has offended. (3) On the other hand, there are those who can confidently look forward to glory (Ps 73:23-24), and this is seen as redemption from Sheol (49:14-15). But again we are not aided by further OT revelation on the point. We must wait for the One who brought life and immortality to light in the gospel (2 Tim 1:10).

SHEPHATIAH (shĕf'à-tī'à, Heb. *shephatyâh, the LORD is judge*). 1. The fifth son of David (2 Sam 3:4). 2. A son of Reuel (1 Chron 9:8). 3. One of the mighty men who joined David at Ziklag (12:5). 4. A son of Maacah. He was a Simeonite officer (27:16). 5. One of the seven sons of Jehoshaphat king of Judah (2 Chron 21:2). 6. The founder of a family with 372 descendants who returned with Zerubbabel (Ezra 2:4). 7. One of the children of Solomon's servants (2:57). 8. One whose descendant Zebadiah returned with Ezra (8:8). Perhaps this is the same as no. 7. 9. A son of Mahalalel. (Neh 11:4). 10. One of the men of Zedekiah who desired that Jeremiah be put to death for prophesying (Jer 38:1).

SHEPHELAH, THE (shē-fē'là, Heb. *ha-shephēlâh, low country*). The undulating country between the mountains of Judah and the maritime plain south of the Plain of Sharon. One of the Promised Land's six geographical sections west of Jordan (Josh 12:8; 1 Kings 10:27). Samson's exploits took place there, and David hid there from Saul.

SHEPHER (shā'fĕr, Heb. *shepher*). The name of a mountain between Kehelathah and Haradah where the Israelites encamped in their wilderness wanderings (Num 33:23). It is otherwise unknown and unidentified. KJV has "Shapher."

SHEPHERD (See OCCUPATIONS AND PROFESSIONS)

SHEPHO (shē'fō, *barrenness*). One of the early descendants of Seir (Gen 36:23; 1 Chron 1:40). KJV has "Shephi" in 1 Chronicles.

SHEPHUPHAN (shē-fū'făm, Heb. *shephûphān*). A grandson of Benjamin (1 Chron 8:5). The name appears in Genesis 46:21 as "Muppim"; in 1 Chronicles 7:12, 15 as Shuppites; and in 26:16 as "Shuppim."

SHERAH (See SHEERAH)

SHEREBIAH (shĕr-ē-bī'à, Heb. *sherēvyâh*). 1. One of the chief priests to whom Ezra entrusted treasures for the temple (Ezra 8:18, 24; Neh 8:7; 9:4). 2. A covenanter with Nehemiah (10:12). 3. A Levite who returned with Zerubbabel (12:8). 4. A chief Levite (12:24).

SHEREZER (See SHAREZER)

SHESHACH (shē'shăk, Heb. *shĕshakh*). In the opinion of many, a cryptogram from "Babel" formed by reversing the letters of the alphabet. When the prophet first used this device (Jer 25:26), it was the first year of Nebuchadnezzar, and it would have been folly openly to predict the doom of Babylon. When he later used it (51:41), Israel was in captivity, Jerusalem had long been in ruins, and the use of the word with its explanation as Babylon could do no harm.

SHESHAI (shē'shī, Heb. *shĕshay*). One of the sons of Anak, giants whom the spies feared (Num 13:22) but whom Caleb drove out (Josh 15:14) and Judah destroyed (Judg 1:10).

SHESHAN (shē'shăn, Heb *shē'shān*). An early descendant of Judah (1 Chron 2:31, 34). He gave his daughter as wife to an Egyptian servant, Jarha (2:35–41).

SHESHBAZZAR (shĕsh-băz'êr, Heb. *sheshbatstsar*). A prince of the Jews. He was made governor, was given the sacred vessels of the temple that had been taken at the Captivity, and helped lay the foundation of the temple (Ezra 1:8, 11; 5:14, 16). He may be the same as Zerubbabel.

SHETH (shĕth, Heb. *shēth, compensation*). 1. In the KJV the name of Eve's third son (1 Chron 1:1, lit. trans.), elsewhere called Seth. 2. "The sons of Sheth" (Num 24:17) refers to the Moabites.

SHEVA (shē'và, Heb. *shewā'*). 1. David's scribe or secretary (2 Sam 20:25), perhaps the same as Seraiah in 8:17. 2. A son of Caleb (probably not the famous spy) by his concubine Maacah (1 Chron 2:49).

SHEWBREAD (See TABERNACLE)

SHIBAH (See SHEBAH)

SHIBBOLETH (shĭb'bō-lĕth, Heb. *shibbôleth, an ear of grain* or *a stream*). A word that was pronounced differently on the two sides of the Jordan, and so was used by the men of Gilead under Jephthah as a test to determine whether the speaker was of Ephraim or not (Judg 12:5–6).

SHIBMAH (See SIBMAH)

SHICRON (See SHIKKERON)

SHIELD (See ARMS AND ARMOR)

SHIGGAION (shĭ-gā'yŏn, Heb. *shiggāyôn*). A musical term found in the heading of Psalm 7. It may refer to a dithyramb or rhapsody.

SHIHON (See SHION)

SHIHOR, SIHOR (shī'hôr, Heb. *shîhôr*). At least three views have been held regarding Shihor (usually Sihor in KJV): (1) it refers to the Nile; (2) it refers to a stream that separated Egypt from Palestine; (3) it refers to a canal, with water drawn from the Nile, on the border between Egypt and Palestine (Josh 13:3; 1 Chron 13:5; Isa 23:3; Jer 2:18).

SHIKKERON (shĭk'rŏn, Heb. *shikkerôn*). A town west of Jerusalem on the northern border of Judah (Josh 15:11). KJV has "Shicron."

SHILLEM, SHILLEMITES (shĭl'ĕm, shĭl'ĕm-īts). The fourth son of Naphtali (Gen 46:24); the family descended from him (Num 26:49). He is also called Shallum (1 Chron 7:13 except NIV).

SHILOAH (See SILOAM)

SHILOH (shī'lō, Heb. *shīlôh*). 1. The person referred to in the prophecy of Jacob in Genesis 49:10. The principal interpretations are the following: (a) The passage is messianic. (b) Shiloh was the town in central Palestine where Joshua placed the tabernacle (Josh 18:1). (c) Shiloh is not regarded as a proper name at all. It is thought to be a compound word meaning "whose it is" (cf. Ezek 21:27).

2. A city in the tribe of Ephraim (Judg 21:19). Israel under Joshua set up the tabernacle here, thus making Shiloh the capital city of Canaan under the theocracy. In the days of Samuel the ark was removed in a battle with the Philistines (1 Sam 4:3) and was not returned until shortly before the days of Solomon's temple. From Shiloh the men of Benjamin, by Israel's permission, kidnapped wives after the Benjamite war under the priesthood of Phinehas, the grandson of Aaron (Judg 21). The godly Elkanah and

The site of Shiloh, about 18 1/2 miles (30 km.) north of Jerusalem. The structure viewed here is thought to have been built on Israelite foundations. "Go now to my place that was in Shiloh, where I made my name to dwell at first, and see what I did to it . . ." (Jer 7:12). Courtesy Duby Tal

his wife went to Shiloh before the birth of Samuel (1 Sam 1:3). Here the boy Samuel received his call from God (3:20–21).

During the reign of King Saul and especially during his war with the Philistines, Ahijah, great-grandson of Eli, was high priest of Israel, wearing the sacred ephod at Shiloh (1 Sam 14:3). After the division of the kingdom, though the ark and the temple were at Jerusalem, and though Jeroboam, the apostate king, had set up centers of worship at Dan and at Bethel, another Ahijah, prophet of the Lord, was still at Shiloh, representing God before the true people of God in the northern kingdom. To him Jeroboam sent to inquire about his sick son (1 Kings 14), and here Ahijah pronounced the doom of Jeroboam's house (14:13). In the days of Jeremiah, Shiloh was a ruin (Jer 7:12, 14), though there were some men there after the destruction of Jerusalem (41:5).

SHILONITE, SHILONI (shī'lō-nīt, shī-lō'nī, Heb. *shîlōnî*). **1.** An inhabitant of Shiloh (1 Kings 12:15; 2 Chron 9:29). **2.** An ancestor of Maaseiah (Neh 11:5 KJV; NIV "a descendant of Shelah").

SHIMEA (shĭm'ē-à, Heb. *shim' ā'*). **1.** A brother of David (1 Chron 20:7). **2.** A son of David (3:5 JB, KJV, MLB, MOF, NASB, NEB, RSV; Shammua NIV). **3.** A Merarite Levite (6:30). **4.** A Gershonite Levite, grandfather of Asaph (6:39). No. 1 is probably the same as Shimma (2:13 KJV), Shammah (1 Sam 16:9), Shimeah (2 Sam 21:21), and Shimei (21:21). The name is spelled three ways in Hebrew, five ways in English.

SHIMEAH (shĭm'ē-à, Heb. *shim' ā'*). **1.** A brother of David (2 Sam 13:3). **2.** A son of Mikloth (1 Chron 8:32). In 9:38 his name is Shimeam.

SHIMEAM (See SHIMEAH)

SHIMEI (shĭm'ē-ī, Heb. *shim' î, famous*). **1.** A son of Gershon; spelled Shimi in KJV (Exod 6:17). **2.** A Gershonite Levite and head of one of the courses of Levites (1 Chron 23:7–10). **3.** One of David's mighty men (1 Kings 1:8). **4.** One of Solomon's district governors (4:18). **5.** The grandson of Jehoiachin (1 Chron 3:19). **6.** A Simeonite, father of 22 children (4:26–27). **7.** An early Reubenite (5:4). **8.** An early Merarite Levite (6:29). **9.** The head of a family in Benjamin (8:21), spelled Shimhi in KJV. **10.** The head of one of the 24 courses of musical Levites (25:17). **11.** A man of Ramah, whom David set over the vineyards (27:27). **12.** A Benjamite of the house of Saul who cursed David and threw stones at him when David was fleeing from his son Absalom. David refused to let his cousin Abishai kill him (2 Sam 16:5–14). When David was returning victorious, Shimei prayed for forgiveness, and David pardoned him (19:16–23); but Solomon, upon ascending the throne, first confined him to Jerusalem, then executed him for disobedience (1 Kings 2:36–46). **13.** One of the descendants of Heman (2 Chron 29:14). **14.** A Levite, treasurer over the freewill offerings and tithes (31:12–13). **15.** One of the Levites who had married a foreign woman (Ezra 10:23). **16.** One of the family of Hashum (10:33). **17.** One of the family of Bani (10:38). **18.** Grandfather of Mordecai (Esth 2:5). **19.** A representative of a leading family who will mourn when they look on the One they have pierced (Zech 12:13).

SHIMHI, SHIMI (See SHIMEI)

SHIMMA (See SHIMEA)

SHIMRI (shĭm'rī, Heb. *shimrî*). **1.** A son of Shemaiah (1 Chron 4:37). **2.** The father of two of David's mighty men (11:45). **3.** A son of Hosah; spelled Simri in KJV (26:10). **4.** A Levite who assisted in cleansing the temple (2 Chron 29:13).

SHIMRITH (shĭm'rĭth, Heb. *shimrîth, watchful*). A Moabitess, mother of Jehozabad, who helped to kill Joash (2 Chron 24:26); also called Shomer (2 Kings 12:21).

SHIMRON, SHIMROM (shĭm'rŏn, shĭm'rŏm, Heb. *shimrôn, a guard*). **1.** The fourth son of Issachar, son of Jacob (Gen 46:13; 1 Chron 7:1 where KJV Shimrom). **2.** A town in the northern part of

Reconstructed model of a warship manned by the Sea Peoples (the "foreigners of the sea," among whom were Philistines), from the days of Ramses III (1182–1151 B.C.), based on a temple relief at Medinet Habu, a modern name applied to a group of ruined temples and a later settlement near the south end of west Thebes. Courtesy The Maritime Museum, Haifa

Canaan whose king helped fight against Joshua (Josh 11:1ff.; cf. 19:15); also called Shimron Meron (12:20).

SHINAR (shī'när, Heb. *shin'ār*). The region containing the cities of Babel, Erech (cf. modern Iraq), Akkad, and Calneh (Gen 10:10), the locations of which, except Akkad, are unknown. Shinar, on the alluvial plain of Babylonia, for many centuries was perhaps the most fertile region on earth. The early post-diluvians traveled east and started to build a tower there (11:1–9). Amraphel, king of Shinar, invaded Canaan in the days of Abraham (14:1). Nebuchadnezzar was ruler of the land of Shinar (Dan 1:2 JB, KJV, MLB, MOF, NASB, NEB, RSV; Babylonia NIV), and it is mentioned in two prophecies (Isa 11:11; Zech 5:11).

SHION (shī'ŏn, Heb. *shî'ôn, overturning*). A town in Issachar, perhaps about three miles (five km.) NW of Mount Tabor (Josh 19:19; KJV Shihon).

SHIPS (Heb. *'ŏnîyâh, tsî, sephînâh,* Gr. *ploion, ploiarion, naus, skaphē*). There is a cryptic reference to some experience of ships in the case of two tribes (Asher and Dan, Judg 5:17), but Hebrew seafaring in general was secondhand. The Phoenicians were prompted by geography to exploit the sea and became, in the pro-

cess, the great navigators of the ancient world (Ezek 27:4–11). Solomon's fleet at Ezion Geber (1 Kings 9–10) consisted of Phoenician ships manned by Phoenicians. Jehoshaphat's later attempt to revive the trade ended in shipwreck, due, no doubt, to Hebrews' inexperienced handling of the ships. The ships of Tarshish mentioned in this connection and elsewhere (e.g., Isa 2:16 JB, KJV, MLB, MOF, NASB, NEB, RSV; trading ship NIV) were probably sturdy vessels built at first for commerce with Tartessus in Spain, the term later being applied, like "China clipper" and "East Indiamen," to vessels generally used for long voyages. Solomon's southern fleet, for example, traded to Ophir, and, if the cargoes are an indication, to southern India as well (1 Kings 10:22).

Psalm 107:23–27 speaks of the terrors of a storm at sea, and Psalm 104:26 briefly mentions ships. Isaiah 18:2 speaks of the boats or rafts built of bound bundles of papyrus. Daniel 11:30 refers to warships from the western coastlands or Cyprus (Chittim or Kittim).

The classic passage on ships is Acts 27, which contains Luke's brilliant account of the voyage and wreck of the Alexandrian grain ship. These vessels were of considerable size. There were 276 people aboard the ship on which Paul and Luke

Scale model of Philistine ship (c. 1200 B.C.), based on wall relief from the temple of
Rameses III at Medinet Habu. It depicts his battle against the "Sea Peoples." Collection of
The National Maritime Museum, Haifa. Photo: Richard Cleave. Courtesy, Carta, Jerusalem

traveled (27:37). Josephus states that he
traveled to Rome on a ship with no fewer
than 600 aboard (*Life* 3). Paul's ship may
have been on a northern route because of
the lateness of the season (27:6).

The ship on which Paul continued his
voyage from Malta to the grain port of
Puteoli had the sign of Castor and Pollux
(28:11). In Greek mythology, the Great
Twin Brethren were the patrons of ship-
men and had special charge of storm-
bound ships (Horace, *Odes* 1:12:27–32).
The account in Acts 27 also tells of
soundings for depth (27:28) and the brac-
ing of the ship by a system of compensa-
tory anchors (27:29). This is the purport
of the metaphor in Hebrews 6:19. James
3:4 refers to the rudder paddles.

The boats of the Sea of Galilee, mentioned in the Gospels, were sturdy fishermen's craft or the barges of local lakeside
trade. They comfortably held a dozen
men, but even two of them could not hold
all that Jesus' miracle produced (Luke
5:7).

SHIPWRIGHT (See OCCUPATIONS AND
PROFESSIONS)

SHISHA (shī'shȧ, Heb. *shîshā'*). The
father of two of Solomon's secretaries
(1 Kings 4:3). He is thought by some to
be identical with Seraiah (2 Sam 8:17),

A Roman warship (bireme) with two banks
of oars, as depicted on a relief dating from
c. 30 B.C. Courtesy Photo Sadeh

Sheva (20:25), and Shavsha (1 Chron
18:16).

SHISHAK (shī'shăk, Heb. *shîshaq*,
Egyp. *Sheshonk*). An Egyptian king, the
founder of the 22nd or Libyan Dynasty.
In the fifth year of Rehoboam king of
Judah, c. 926 B.C., he marched on Palestine, reaching as far north as Megiddo
and Beth Shan and east into Transjordan.
Earlier in his reign he had provided
asylum to the Israelite Jeroboam, who

had fled to Egypt to escape the wrath of Solomon (1 Kings 11:40). With Jeroboam on the northern throne, Shishak showed no favoritism but impartially overran both Judah and Israel. Jerusalem was a victim of this campaign, and the temple was looted of its treasures (14:25–26; 2 Chron 12:1–9).

SHITTAH TREE (See PLANTS)

SHITTIM (shĭt'ĭm, Heb. *ha-shittîm*). The last stop of Israel in the wilderness before crossing the Jordan into the Promised Land (Num 25:1; 33:49). There Balaam tried to curse Israel but had to bless instead, and there he told Balak how to seduce the men of Israel (25:1–3; Mic 6:5). From there Joshua sent the two spies to Jericho (Josh 2:1), and Israel departed to cross the Jordan from Shittim (3:1). Used perhaps symbolically for a place that, in the future, the Lord will richly bless (Joel 3:18 KJV; NIV "valley of acacias").

SHITTIM WOOD (See PLANTS: *Acacia*)

SHOBAB (shō'băb, Heb. *shôvāv*). **1.** A grandson of Hezron (1 Chron 2:18). **2.** A son of David born in Jerusalem (3:5).

SHOBACH (shō'băk, Heb. *shôvakh*). The general of the Syrian army under Hadadezer king of Zobah. He was defeated by David (2 Sam 10:16–18); he is also called Shophach (1 Chron 19:16).

SHOBAL (shō'băl, Heb. *shôvāl*). **1.** One of the sons of Seir, a chief of the Horites, and a very early inhabitant of what was later Edom (Gen 36:20, 23, 29). These Horites, or Hurrians, were expelled and destroyed by the Edomites, descendants of Esau (Deut 2:12). **2.** An early Ephrathite (1 Chron 2:50, 52). **3.** A grandson of Judah and father of Reaiah (4:1–2).

SHOCHO (See SOCO)

SHOE (See DRESS)

SHOE LATCHET (See DRESS)

SHOFAR (See MUSIC AND MUSICAL INSTRUMENTS)

SHOMER (shō'mêr, Heb. *shōmēr, keeper, watcher*). **1.** The father of Jehozabad, one of the conspirators against Joash of Judah (2 Kings 12:20–21; 2 Chron 24:25–26). **2.** A great-grandson of Asher (1 Chron 7:32). In verse 34 he is called Shemer (ASV) and Shamer (KJV).

SHOPHACH (shō'făk, Heb. *shôvakh*). A Syrian general whom David killed (1 Chron 19:16, 18). In 2 Samuel 10:16 he is called Shobach.

SHOPHAR (See MUSIC AND MUSICAL INSTRUMENTS)

SHORE The land where it meets the sea, represented by five words in Scripture— three Hebrew and two Greek: **1.** *Hôph*, that which is washed by the sea (Judg 5:17; Jer 47:7). **2.** *Qātseh*, the end or extremity (Josh 15:2), referring to the Dead Sea. **3.** *Sāphâh*, the lip or edge (Gen 22:17), the sand that is on the seashore. **4.** *Cheilos*, the same idea as no. 3 (Heb 11:12). **5.** *Aigialos*, the beach (Matt 13:2; John 21:4; Acts 27:39 KJV).

SHOSHANNIM (shō-shăn'ĭm, *lilies*). Found in the titles of Psalms 45, 69, and 80 and in Psalm 60 in the singular. Perhaps lily-shaped musical instruments, perhaps the name of spring songs. NIV has "To [the tune of] 'Lilies'" (or "To the tune of 'The Lily [or Lilies] of the Covenant'").

SHOULDER (Heb. *shekkem, kathēph, serôa' shôq*, Gr. *ōmos, brachion*). A word often used in both a literal and a figurative sense. When a man of Israel offered an ox or a sheep as a sacrifice, the shoulder went to the officiating priest as a part of his portion (Deut 18:3). The shoulder pieces of the ephod, the sacred garment of the high priest, were to bear onyx stones on which were engraved the names of the tribes (Exod 28:1–12); similarly, a ruler bears on his shoulders the weight of the government (Isa 9:6). Although in traveling, the sections of the tabernacle could be carried in wagons, the priests had to carry the sacred furniture on their shoulders (Num 7:6–9), much as the Lord is pictured as bearing his beloved on his shoulders (Deut 33:12), and as the good shepherd carries the lost sheep when he finds it (Luke 15:5). In much of the East, the maidservants went to wells to draw water, carrying it on their shoulders (Gen 21:14) in large jars; and even well-born maidens carried water in this way (24:15). To "pull away the shoulder" (Zech 7:11 KJV) is to refuse to obey, and to "shove with flank and shoulder" (Ezek 34:21) is insolence.

SHOULDER PIECE (Heb. *kathēph*). **1.** That part of the ephod where the front and the back were joined together (Exod 28:7–8). **2.** The piece of meat that is taken from the shoulder of the animal (Ezek 24:4).

SHOVEL (Heb. *rahath, ya', yāthēdh*). A tool used for clearing out ashes from the altar (Exod 27:3; 2 Chron 4:11), for sanitary purposes (Deut 23:13), or for winnowing (Isa 30:24).

SHOWBREAD (See TABERNACLE)

SHRINE (Gr. *naos*). A dwelling for a god (Acts 19:24), used only once in the English versions; but the same Greek word *naos* is translated "temple" in its other 45 NT occurrences (e.g., Acts 17:24; 1 Cor 3:16).

SHROUD (Heb. *hōresh*). Generally the dress for the dead. Also can refer to a bough or branch in Ezekiel 31:3, where KJV has "a shadowing shroud" and NIV "overshadowing the forest."

SHRUB (See PLANTS)

SHUA (shū'à, Heb. *shua'*, *prosperity*). 1. A Canaanite whose daughter became Judah's wife (Gen 38:2, 12 JB, MLB, NASB, NIV, RSV; Shuah KJV; Bathshua MOF, NEB). 2. The daughter of Heber (1 Chron 7:32).

SHUAH (*shū'ah*, Heb. *shûah, depression*). 1. A son of Abraham by Keturah (Gen 25:2; 1 Chron 1:32). 2. See SHUA. 3. Kelub's (Chelub's) brother (1 Chron 4:11 KJV; NIV Shuhah).

SHUAL (shū'al, Heb. *shû'āl, fox*). 1. One of the 11 sons of Zophah from the tribe of Asher (1 Chron 7:36). 2. One of the places invaded by one of the marauding tribes of Philistines (1 Sam 13:17).

SHUBAEL (shū-bā'ĕl, Heb. *shevū'ĕl*). 1. A chief Levite in the time of David (1 Chron 24:20), placed over the treasuries of the house of God (26:20). He is also called Shebuel (23:16; 26:24 JB, KJV, NASB, MLB, RSV; Shubael MOF, NEB, NIV). 2. One of the sons of Heman, chief musician in David's service of praise (25:20). He is also called Shebuel (25:4 JB, KJV, NASB, MLB, RSV; Shubael MOF, NEB, NIV).

SHUHAH (See SHUAH)

SHUHAM, SHUHAMITE (shū'hăm, shū'hăm-ĭt, Heb. *shûhām*). The son of Dan (Num 26:42), also called "Hushim" (Gen 46:23). Dan's descendants are called "Shuhamites."

SHUHITE (shū'hīt, Heb. *shûhī, a native of Shuah*). A term describing Job's friend Bildad (Job 2:11; 8:1; 18:1; 25:1; 42:9). It is very likely that this term refers to Abraham's son by Keturah named Shuah. From him came a tribe of Arabs that lived near Uz, the birthplace of Job (1:1; 2:11), likely the far northern area west of the Euphrates. If they were near Uz, as Job 2:11 indicates, this would place Uz farther north than is commonly thought.

SHULAMMITE (shū'lăm-ĭt, Heb. *shûlammīth, peaceful*). A title applied to a young woman in the Song of Songs 6:13. It is not unlikely that it is a feminine form of Solomon. If this word is the same word as "Shunammite," as the LXX rendering would imply, then it could be derived from the town of Shunem. See also SHUNAMMITE; SHUNEM.

SHUNAMMITE (shū'năm-ĭt, Heb. *shûnammīth, a native of Shunem*). 1. An unnamed woman whose son the prophet Elisha raised from the dead (2 Kings 4:12). Later God used Elisha to save her from death during a famine (8:1–6). 2. This word is also applied to David's nurse Abishag (1 Kings 1:3; 2:17–22).

SHUNEM (shū'-nĕm, Heb. *shûnēm*). A place belonging to the tribe of Issachar (Josh 19:18; cf. 1 Sam 28:4; 2 Kings 4:8–37). It lies in a very rich section of Palestine a short distance north of Jezreel at the foot of "Little Hermon."

SHUSHAN (See SUSA)

SHUTHELAH, SHUTHELAHITE (shū-thē'là, shū-thē'là-hīt, Heb. *shûthalhî*). 1. One of the three sons of Ephraim (Num 26:35–36; 1 Chron 7:20–21). 2. The sixth person descending from Shuthelah is also called by his name (7:21).

SHUTTLE (shū't'l, Heb. *'eregh*). A word used as a figure of the quick passing of life (Job 7:6). Job says that his days pass as swiftly as the rapidly moving shuttle of the weaver.

SIBBECAI, SIBBECHAI (sĭb'ē-kī, sĭb'ē-kī, Heb. *sibbekhay*). A captain of several thousand men in David's army. He is usually designated as "the Hushathite" (2 Sam 21:18; 1 Chron 11:29; 20:4; 27:11).

SIBBOLETH (See SHIBBOLETH)

SIBMAH (sĭb'mà, Heb. *sevām*). A town east of the Jordan, belonging originally to Moab, and finally taken by the Amorites (Num 21:26). Later it was captured by and given to the tribe of Reuben (Josh 13:19). Most scholars feel it is to be identified with Sebam (Num 32:3) or Shibmah (32:38 KJV). It was famous for its luxurious vines and fruits (Isa 16:8; Jer 48:32).

SIBYLLINE ORACLES (See APOCALYPTIC LITERATURE)

SICHEM (sī'kĕm, Heb. *shekhem*). The same as Shechem.

SICKLE (sĭk'l, Heb. *hermēsh, a reaping hook, maggāl, a reaping hook*, Gr. *drepanon, a tool used for cutting grain*). These were used mostly for cutting grain, but on occasion they were used for pruning. Mark and John use the sickle in a figurative sense as the instrument of God's judgment (Mark 4:29; Rev 14:14–20).

SICKNESS (See DISEASES)

SIDDIM, VALLEY OF (sĭd'ĭm, Heb. *'ēmeq hasiddîm, the valley of the fields*). The battleground where Kedorlaomer and his allies met the kings of Sodom and other nearby cities (Gen 14:3–8); it was chosen by Lot because of its productivity (13:10).

SIDON (sī'dŏn, Heb. *tsîdhôn*, Gr. *Sidōn*). A Phoenician city midway between Berytus (Beirut) and Tyre. Sidon appears in the OT as the chief city of Phoenicia, and the name was applied frequently to the whole nation (Gen 10:15; Judg 10:12). The city seems to have been a center of trade and enterprise. Sidon came into conflict over Dor with the other occupants of coastal Palestine, the Philistines. Israel suffered from the same burst of activity (Judg 1:31; 10:12). Sidon had a bad name in Scripture as a hotbed of Phoenician idolatry (Isa 23; Ezek 28) and of Gentile materialism (Matt 11:21–22). The neighborhood of Sidon, not more than 50 miles (83 km.) from Nazareth, was visited by Christ (Matt 15:21; Mark 7:24–31), and Sidonians came to him (Mark 3:8; Luke 6:17). Sidon was a residence of Christian disciples and one of Paul's ports of call (Acts 27:3).

SIEGE (See WAR)

SIEVE (sĭv, Heb. *kevārâh, netted, nāphâh, a sieve*). A utensil used to sift grains, used in a figurative sense in both passages where it occurs (Isa 30:28; Amos 9:9).

SIGN (Heb. *'ôth, a signal, môphēth, a miracle, omen,* Gr. *sēmeion, an indication*). In Scripture this word generally refers to something addressed to the senses to attest the existence of a divine power. Miracles in the OT were often signs (Exod 4:8; 8:23). Several specific things were given as signs, such as the rainbow (Gen 9:12–13), some of the feasts (Exod 13:9), the Sabbath (31:13), and circumcision (Rom 4:11). Often extraordinary events were given as a sign to insure faith or demonstrate authority (Exod 4:1–8). Sometimes future events were given as signs, as in the case of Ahaz (Isa 7:14). When Christ was born, the place of his birth and his dress were to be signs of his identity to the shepherds. When the scribes and the Pharisees asked Jesus for a sign, no sign was to

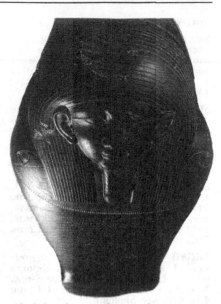

Black basalt sarcophagus of Eshmunazar, king of Sidon, inscribed with a well-preserved Phoenician inscription. Fifth century B.C. Courtesy Réunion des Musées Nationaux

be given them except the sign of Jonah. Revelation tells that before Christ returns there will be signs in the heavens, in the stars, moon, and sun. See also CIRCUMCISION; COVENANT; MIRACLE; RAINBOW.

SIGNET (See SEAL)

SIHON (sī'hŏn, Heb. *sîhôn*). A king of the Amorites who became prominent chiefly because of his opposition to Israel on their journey from Egypt to Palestine. God permitted him to dispossess the Moabites, but when he led the attack against Israel, he was killed and his forces scattered (Num 21:21–24; Deut 1:4, 20; 2:24–30; cf. 3:2; Judg 11:12–13).

SIHOR (See SHIHOR)

SILAS (sī'làs, probably the Aramaic form of Saul, *asked*). A prominent member of the Jerusalem church (Acts 15:22, 32) and a Roman citizen (16:38) who was sent by the church with Paul and Barnabas to deliver the letter which was formulated by the Jerusalem Council to the church at Antioch (15:22–23). He was with Paul at Philippi and shared in both the beating and imprisonment there. When Paul left Berea for Athens, Silas and Timothy were left behind. He, along with Timothy, who had returned to Thessalonica, rejoined Paul at Corinth (18:5). The NT calls him *Silouanos* four times (2 Cor 1:19; 1 Thess 1:1; 2 Thess 1:1; 1 Peter 5:12; Silvanus JB, KJV, MLB, MOF, NASB, NEB, RSV; Silas NIV).

SILENCE (See QUIET, QUIETNESS)

SILK (Heb. *meshî, drawn*, Gr. *sērikon, silken*). The word "silk" is mentioned four times in the KJV of the OT (Prov 31:22; Ezek 16:10, 13). But Revelation 18:12 does refer to actual silk. The Greek word is *sēr*, the Greek name for China, from which silk came.

SILOAM (sĭ-lō'ăm, Gr. *Silōam*). A reservoir located within the city walls of Jerusalem at the southern end of the Tyropoean Valley (2 Kings 20:20; 2 Chron 32:30). The conduit leads from the intermittent Spring of Gihon (Jerusalem's most important water supply) through the rock Ophel to the reservoir called the Pool of Siloam.

In 1880 a native boy wading in the tunnel noticed an inscription which he reported to his teacher, Herr Conrad Schick, who made the information avail-

The Pool of Siloam at the southern end of Hezekiah's Tunnel. The tunnel, discovered in 1880, was cut from both ends through solid rock for 1,700 feet (518 m.). It was built by Hezekiah (c. 715–686) to bring water from the Spring of Gihon into Jerusalem. Referred to in 2 Kings 20:20. Courtesy Israel Government Press Office

able to scholars. The inscription was deciphered by A. H. Sayce, with the help of others. It consists of six lines written in Old Hebrew (Canaanite) with pronglike characters. The Siloam inscription is important both for its fascinating account of the building of the tunnel and for providing a basis for comparison in the dating of other inscriptions. It was to the Pool of Siloam that Jesus sent the blind man (John 9:7). He obeyed and came back seeing.

SILOAM, TOWER IN (sĭ-lō'ăm). A tower that was probably part of the ancient system of fortifications on the walls of the city of Jerusalem near the Pool of Siloam. The collapse of this tower and the resulting death of 18 persons (perhaps workmen employed on the aqueduct that Pilate was building? Cf. Josephus, *War* 2.9.4) is cited by Jesus (Luke 13:4).

SILVANUS (See SILAS)

SILVER (See MINERALS)

SILVERSMITH (See OCCUPATIONS AND PROFESSIONS)

SIMEON (sĭm'ē-ŭn, Heb. *shim' ôn*, Gr. *Symeōn*). 1. The second son of Jacob by Leah (Gen 29:33). He and his brother Levi massacred the Hivites living in Shechem because the Shechem the son of Hamor had raped their sister Dinah (34:24–31). 2. The tribe of which Simeon, the son of Jacob, became the founder. The extreme south of Canaan was assigned to this tribe. Eventually most of the tribe disappeared. 3. An ancestor of Jesus (Luke 3:30). 4. A righteous and devout man to whom the Holy Spirit revealed that he would not die until he had seen the Messiah (2:25, 34). 5. Simon Peter (Acts 15:14). See PETER. 6. One of the Christian leaders in the church of Antioch (Acts 13:1–2).

SIMEONITE A member of the tribe of Simeon; see SIMEON.

SIMON (sĭ'mŭn, Gr. *Simōn, hearing*). 1. The brother of Andrew, a fisherman who became a disciple and apostle of Christ. He was surnamed Peter, "stone," and Cephas, Aramaic for "rock" (Matt 4:18; 16:17–18). See PETER. 2. A disciple of Jesus called the "Canaanite" in the KJV, a member of the party later called "the Zealots" (so NIV, Matt 10:4; Mark 3:18; Luke 6:15; Acts 1:13). 3. A leper of Bethany in whose house Jesus' head was anointed (Matt 26:6; Mark 14:3). 4. A brother of the Lord (Matt 13:55; Mark 6:3). 5. A man from Cyrene, father of Alexander and Rufus, who was compelled to carry the cross of Jesus (Matt

27:32; Mark 15:21; Luke 23:26). **6.** A Pharisee in whose house Jesus' feet were anointed by the sinful woman (7:40, 43-44). **7.** Judas Iscariot's father (John 6:71; 13:2, 26). **8.** Simon Magus, a sorcerer at Samaria and a man of great power and influence among the people (Acts 8:9-13). He "believed" as the result of Philip's preaching and continued with Philip, hoping, no doubt, to learn more of this power. When Simon saw Peter and John bestow the Spirit through the laying on of hands, he wanted to buy this power for himself from the apostles. His request called forth a blistering rebuke by Peter (8:14-24). **9.** A tanner who lived at Joppa. Peter stayed with him for a period of time (Acts 9:43; 10:6, 17, 32).

SIMON MAGUS (See SIMON)

SIMON PETER (See PETER)

SIMPLE (Heb. *pethî, silly*, Gr. *akakos, akeraios, harmless*). The basic idea of the word in the OT is "easily influenced" (Pss 19:7; 119:130; Prov 7:7). The two uses of the word in the KJV of the NT (Rom 16:18-19) are rendered "naïve" and "innocent" in the NIV.

SIMRI (See SHIMRI)

SIN (Heb. *ḥāttā'the, 'awôn, pesha', ra'*, Gr. *adikia, hamartia, hamartēma, parabasis, paraptōma, ponēria*). The biblical writers portray sin in a variety of terms. It is only as they are conscious of God's holiness that they are truly aware of their sin (1 Kings 17:18; Ps 51:4-6; Isa 6).

The first book of the OT reveals how human beings were created by God without sin but chose to act contrary to his revealed will and thereby caused sin to become an endemic feature of human existence (Gen 3; Ps 14:1-3). Sin is revolt against the holiness and sovereign will of God. Therefore, it is both a condition of the heart/mind/will/affections (Isa 29:13; Jer 17:9) and the practical outworking of that condition in thoughts, words, and deeds that offend God and transgress his holy law (Gen 6:5; Isa 59:12-13). For Israel, sin was a failure to keep the conditions of the covenant that the Lord graciously made at Sinai (Exod 19ff.).

There is no person in Israel or the whole world who is not a sinner. However, those who have a right relationship with God, receive his forgiveness, and walk in his ways are sometimes described as righteous (Gen 6:9) and blameless (Job 1:1; Ps 18:20-24). This is not because they are free from sin, but because the true direction of their lives is to serve and please God in the way he requires.

For Israel, the sins of the fathers have repercussions for their children and their children's children (Isa 1:4; Lam 5:7). Yet it is also true that individual Israelites are personally responsible to God for their own sins (Jer 31:19-20; Ezek 18:1ff.; 33:10-20). Sin was punished by God in various ways—e.g., exile from the Promised Land (2 Kings 17:6ff.)—but the final punishment for individual sin and wickedness was death (Gen 2:17; Ps 73:27; Ezek 18:4). This is certainly physical death but is also spiritual death, being cut off from communion with the living God.

The reality of sin and the need for atonement (and confession) are clearly presupposed by the sacrifices offered to God in the temple—e.g., the regular guilt (or trespass) offering and sin offering, as well as the special annual sacrifice of the Day of Atonement (Lev 4; 6:24ff.; 7:1ff.; 16:1ff.)—and in the prophecy of the vicarious suffering of the Servant of the Lord (Isa 53:10, 12).

Jesus was sinless and taught that the root of sin is in the human heart (Mark 7:20-23). The outward life is determined by the inner (Matt 7:15-17), and thus an outward conformity to laws and rules is not in itself a true righteousness if the heart is impure (5:17ff.). But sin is more than failure to keep the law: it is also the rejection of the Messiah and the kingdom he proclaims and personifies (John 16:8-9; 15:22). Further, to live without the light of God from Jesus, the Messiah, is to live in darkness and to be in the grip of evil forces (1:5; 3:19-21; 8:31-34). And to call the light darkness and the Spirit of the Messiah unclean is to commit the unforgivable sin (Matt 12:24, 31).

Sin is revealed by the law of God, but it is only as the Holy Spirit enlightens the mind that a person truly sees what righteousness the law demands of us (Rom 3:20; 5:20; 7:7-20; Gal 3:19-24). Sin begins in the heart (Rom 6:15-23). The origin of sin can be traced back to the first human beings, Adam and Eve, and to their revolt against the Lord (5:12-19; 2 Cor 11:3; 1 Tim 2:14).

SIN, DESERT OF A wilderness through which the Israelites passed on their journey from Elim and Mt. Sinai (Exod 16:1; 17:1; Num 33:11-12). KJV reads "wilderness of Sin."

SINAI (sī'nī, Heb. *sînay*, meaning uncertain). **1.** A peninsula that lay to the south of the Wilderness of Paran between the Gulf of Aqabah on the east and Suez

Mt. Sinai (Jebel Mousa), the traditional site where Moses received the law from God (Exod 19:16–19). Courtesy Israel Government Press Office

on the west. **2.** A wilderness (Exod 19:1) where Israel came in the third month after they left Egypt. **3.** A mountain (Exod 19:20), Horeb. It was there that God met and talked with Moses and gave him the law (19:3). The only later visit to the mount recorded in Scripture is Elijah's when he fled from Jezebel (1 Kings 19:8).

SINEW (sĭ'nū, Heb. *gîdh, sinew*). The tendons and sinews of the body (Job 40:17; Ezek 37:6–9 KJV; NIV "tendons"). The word is used also in a figurative sense (Isa 48:4).

SINGER (See OCCUPATIONS AND PROFESSIONS)

SINGING (See MUSIC AND MUSICAL INSTRUMENTS; SONG)

SINGLE EYE (Gr. *ophthalmos haplous, a healthy eye*). Used in the KJV for an eye that is clear, sound, and healthy, with the connotation "generous" (Matt 6:22; Luke 11:34). NIV has "eyes are good."

SIN OFFERING (See SACRIFICE AND OFFERINGS)

SION, MOUNT (See HERMON)

SISERA (sĭs'ēr-à, Heb. *sîserā'*). **1.** A man employed by Jabin, king of Hazor,

as the captain in his army (Judg 4–5). Sisera oppressed Israel for 20 years, waging war against them with 900 iron chariots (4:2–3). Deborah urged Barak under the direction of God to unite his forces and go against Sisera. These two armies met in battle and the forces of Sisera were killed or scattered, and Sisera fled on foot, taking refuge in the tent of Jael, the wife of Heber the Kenite. Here he was killed by Jael while he slept in her tent. **2.** One of the temple servants (KJV Nethinim) who returned from captivity (Ezra 2:53; Neh 7:55).

SISTER (Heb. *'āhôth,* Gr. *adelphē*). A word used in both Hebrew and Greek with varying ideas. In the OT it is used of females having the same parents, having but one parent in common, a female relative, or a woman of the same country (Gen 20:12; Num 25:18; Lev 18:18; Job 42:11). In the NT it is used of girls belonging to the same family or just to blood relatives (Matt 13:56; Mark 6:3; Luke 10:39). It is also used figuratively (Ezek 16:45; 23:11; Rom 16:1; 2 John 13).

SISTRUMS (See MUSIC AND MUSICAL INSTRUMENTS)

SIVAN (sē-vàn', Heb. *sîwān*). The name given to the third month of the Hebrew sacred year; this is the ninth month of the civil year (Esth 8:9). See also CALENDAR.

SIYON (See HERMON)

SKIN (Heb. *'ôr, naked, geledh, smooth, bāsār, flesh*, Gr. *derma, skin, dermatinos, of a skin*). A very common word in the OT, *'ôr* used of both animal skin (Gen 3:21; 27:16; Jer 13:23) and human skin (Exod 34:35 KJV; Lev 13:2; Job 7:5). *Geledh* is found only once in the Bible (Job 16:15), describing the action of Job putting sackcloth on his body. This was a tight-fitting garment expressive of mourning and perhaps suggesting the sad condition of Job's physical appearance. *Bāsār* is the most common word used for human flesh (Gen 2:21; 2 Kings 4:34; Prov 14:30 KJV; NIV "flesh, body").

Skins of animals were used as bottles both for water and for wine. They formed many useful articles for clothing, including shoes (Ezek 16:10), and protection for the tabernacle in the wilderness.

The word is also used figuratively in several places (Job 2:4; 19:20). The two Greek words are used only three times in the OT (Matt 3:4; Mark 1:6; Heb 11:37) and in each case speak of articles of clothing.

SKINK (See ANIMALS)

SKIRT (See DRESS)

SKULL (See GOLGOTHA)

SKY (Heb. *shahaq, vapor*). A word found only in the plural in the Bible (Ps 18:11; Isa 45:8). The word refers sometimes to the clouds and other times to the firmament. At least once it is used figuratively (Deut 33:26).

SLANDER (Heb. *dibbâh, slander*, Gr. *diabolos, slanderer*). A malicious utterance designed to hurt or defame the person about whom it is uttered. The Scriptures often warn against it (Lev 19:16; Ezek 22:9; Eph 4:31; Col 3:8; James 4:11).

SLAVE, SLAVERY (Heb. *'evedh, servant, slave*, Gr. *doulos, bondslave, servant*). While the Hebrew and Greek words are very common in the Bible, the English word *slave* is found only twice (Jer 2:14; Rev 18:13), and the word *slavery* does not occur at all in KJV, because both the Hebrew and the Greek word involved are more often rendered "servant."

Among the Hebrews, slaves could be acquired in a number of ways: as prisoners of war (Num 31:7–9), by purchase (Lev 25:44), by gift (Gen 29:24), by accepting a person in lieu of a debt (Lev 25:39), by birth from slaves already possessed (Exod 21:4), by arrest if the thief had nothing to pay for the object stolen (22:2–3), and by the voluntary decision of the person wanting to be a slave (21:6). Slaves among the Hebrews were more kindly treated than slaves among other nations, since the Mosaic Law laid down rules governing their treatment. They could gain their freedom in a number of ways (Exod 21:2–27; Lev 25:25ff.; Deut 15:12–23). Slavery continued in NT times, but the love of Christ seemed to weigh against its continued existence (Eph 6:5–9; Gal 3:28).

SLEEP (Heb. *shēnâh, yāshēn, shākhav*, Gr. *hypnos*). A word used in a number of ways in the Bible. Its most natural use is to refer to physical rest (1 Sam 26:7; Jonah 1:5–6). Most cases of physical sleep were natural ones, but some were supernaturally imposed to accomplish a divine purpose (Gen 2:21; 15:12). Believers' rest in sleep is considered a gift from God (Ps 127:2).

Methods of sleep varied usually with the social status of the people. The most common bed was simply a mat (Matt 9:6). No special bed clothes were pr ovided in this case, but those worn during the day were used (Exod 22:26–27). Wealthy people had more elaborate beds variously constructed (Deut 3:11; 1 Sam 19:13).

In the NT, KJV translates *hypnos* "sleep" all six times it occurs, NIV only in John 11:13 and Acts 20:9. Sometimes "sleep" indicates the spiritually indolent (e.g., Rom 13:11, the only figurative use of *hypnos*) or believers who have died (e.g., 1 Cor 11:30; 15:51; 1 Thess 4:13).

SLIME (Heb. *hēmār, boiling up, zepheth, flowing*). Where KJV has *slime* (Gen 11:3; Exod 2:3; slimepits, Gen 14:10), NIV has *tar*. Probably it resembled asphalt, and perhaps it was used most often in waterproofing and as a cement for bricks.

SLING (See ARMS AND ARMOR)

SLOW (Heb. *kāvēdh, heavy, 'erekh, to make long*, Gr. *bradys, dull, argos, inactive*). Moses said he was slow of speech (Exod 4:10); his words did not come readily. "Longsuffering" would almost be a synonym of *'erekh* as seen in many OT passages (Neh 9:17; Pss 103:8; 145:8). It always refers to the passions in the OT. The Greek words are found only three times in the NT (Luke 24:25; Titus 1:12; James 1:19).

SLUG (See ANIMALS)

SMITH (See OCCUPATIONS AND PROFESSIONS)

SMYRNA (smîr'nà, Gr. *Smyrna*). A port on the west coast of Asia Minor. Smyrna petitioned Tiberius to allow the community to build a temple to his deity. The permission was granted, and Smyrna built the second Asian temple to the emperor. The city had worshiped Rome as a spiritual power since 195 B.C., hence Smyrna's historical pride in her Caesar cult. Smyrna was famous for science, medicine, and the majesty of its buildings. Apollonius of Tyana referred to her "crown of porticoes," a circle of beautiful public buildings that ringed the summit of Mt. Pagos like a diadem; hence John's reference (Rev 2:10). Polycarp, Smyrna's martyred bishop of A.D. 155, had been a disciple of John.

SNAIL (See ANIMALS)

SNAKE (See ANIMALS)

SNARE (Heb. *pah, a spring net*, Gr. *pagis, trap, brochos, a noose*). A device for catching both birds (Ps 124:7) and animals. The word is used often in the Bible in a figurative sense, to imply anything that might destroy (Pss 91:3; 141:9) and things God's people should avoid: heathen gods (Deut 7:16), the ephod Gideon made (Judg 8:27), false prophets (Hos 9:8), and riches (1 Tim 6:9 KJV; NIV "trap").

SNOW (Heb. *shelegh, white, telagh, white*, Gr. *chiōn*). Snow is common in the hill country of Palestine. It never gets very deep, and it is not uncommon to have winters without any. The tops of the high mountains are covered with snow most of the year, and this becomes the source of much of the water there.

The Bible often refers to snow figuratively. "Time of snow" (KJV) represents a winter's day (2 Sam 23:20 NIV "snowy day"). Fear of snow is a similar phrase representing cold (Prov 31:21). Snow is a symbol of the highest purity and the condition of the redeemed soul (Ps 51:7; Isa 1:18). It symbolizes whiteness and purity (Matt 28:3; Rev 1:14) and describes the whiteness of the leper (2 Kings 5:27).

SNUFF (Heb. *sha'aph, to inhale, naphah, to blow at*). The first Hebrew word expresses the practice of wild donkeys who pant for wind like jackals because of the heat (Jer 14:6 KJV; NIV "pant"). The second Hebrew word symbolically expresses contempt for God's sacrifices (Mal 1:13 KJV; NIV "sniff").

SO (Heb. *sô'*). King of Egypt (2 Kings 17:4) in the days of Ahaz king of Judah and Hoshea king of Israel. Hoshea made an alliance with So, bringing down the wrath of Assyria on Israel (17:5).

SOAP (Heb. *bôrîth*). Soap in a modern sense was unknown in OT times. Even until recent time it was not used in some parts of Syria. Clothes, cooking utensils, and even the body were cleansed with the ashes of certain plants containing alkali — e.g., soapwort, glasswort, and saltwort (Jer 2:22; Mal 3:2).

SOCKET (See TABERNACLE)

SOCO, SOCOH (sō'kō, Heb. *sōkhōh, branches*). 1. One of the cities given to the tribe of Judah (Josh 15:35). Later, King Rehoboam strengthened this city after the northern tribes had revolted (2 Chron 11:7). From this city Solomon drew his supplies (1 Kings 4:10). 2. About 10 miles (17 km.) SW of Hebron lies another city by this name (Josh 15:48).

SODA (See MINERALS)

SODOM, SODOMA (sŏd'ŭm, sŏ-dō'mà, Heb. *sedhōm*, Gr. *Sodoma*). One of the "Cities of the Plain," along with Admah, Gomorrah, Zeboiim, and Zoar.

An area around the northern end of the Dead Sea is fully within the range of vision from Bethel, from which vantage point Lot made his fatal choice (Gen 13:10–12), and was in Abraham's field of view from a point east of Hebron, from which he looked in the morning toward Sodom and Gomorrah (19:28). Sodom, because of the episode of Genesis 19, became a name for vice, infamy, and judgment (Isa 1:9–10; 3:9; Jer 23:14; Lam 4:6; Ezek 16:46; Amos 4:11; Zeph 2:9; Matt 10:15; Luke 17:29; Rom 9:29; 2 Peter 2:6; Jude 7; Rev 11:8; cf. Sodomites [KJV]—Deut 23:17; 1 Kings 14:24; 15:12; 22:46; 2 Kings 23:7). (See page 560.)

SODOMY (sŏd'ŭm-ĕ, Heb. *qâdhēsh, a male temple prostitute*). A sodomite was one who practiced that unnatural vice for which Sodom became noted (Gen 19:5; cf. Rom 1:27). God strictly forbade this practice (Deut 23:17). Usually the practice was in connection with heathen worship, and its presence was a sign of departure from the Lord (1 Kings 14:24). Both Asa (15:12) and Jehoshaphat took measures against this sin (22:46), but its practice continued, until in the days of Josiah it was being practiced in the Lord's house (2 Kings 23:7).

The southern end of the Dead Sea, now largely dried up with salt deposits, is the area in which Sodom is probably located. Courtesy Duby Tal

SOLDIER (See OCCUPATIONS AND PROFESSIONS; WAR)

SOLOMON (sŏl'ō-mŭn, Heb. *shelōmōh, peaceable*). The third and last king of united Israel. He built the kingdom to its greatest geographical extension and material prosperity. Though a very intelligent man, Solomon in his later years lost his spiritual discernment and for the sake of political advantage and voluptuous living succumbed to apostasy. His policies of oppression and luxury brought the kingdom to the verge of dissolution, and when his son Rehoboam came to the throne the actual split of the kingdom occurred. Solomon was the second son of David and Bathsheba, the former wife of Uriah the Hittite. When he was born, the Lord loved him, so that the child was also called Jedidiah (2 Sam 12:24–25). As David's death drew near, he gave Solomon practical advice as to faithfulness to God, the building of the temple, and the stability of the dynasty. Solomon had to deal harshly with Adonijah and his followers when they continued to plot against him. Adonijah and Joab were put to death, and Abiathar the priest was expelled from the priesthood. David had also told Solomon to kill Shimei, who had cursed David at the time of Absalom's revolt; this was done by Solomon after Shimei violated the probation Solomon had ordered.

Solomon then began a series of marriage alliances that were his eventual undoing. Early in Solomon's reign he loved the Lord. The Lord appeared to him in a dream and told him to request of him whatever he desired. Solomon chose above all else understanding and discernment. God was pleased with this choice, granted his request, and also gave him riches and honor. With taxation and conscription Israel began to see some of the evils of monarchy against which Samuel had warned (1 Sam 8:11ff.), though during the reign of Solomon "Judah and Israel were as numerous as the sand on the seashore; they ate, they drank and they were happy" (1 Kings 4:20). The kingdom extended from the Euphrates in the north to the border of Egypt in the SW.

Solomon was a wise and learned man; it is stated that his wisdom was greater than that of the wise men of the East and of Egypt. Expert in botany and zoology, he was also a writer, credited with 3,000 proverbs and 1,000 songs (1 Kings 4:32) and named the author of two psalms (titles, Pss 72, 127) and of the books of Proverbs (Prov 1:1), Ecclesiastes (Eccl 1:1, 12), and Song of Solomon (Song of Songs 1:1). His fame was widespread, and people came from afar to hear him.

He made an alliance with Hiram king of Tyre, who had been a friend of David. He contracted with Hiram for the supply of cedar and cypress wood and arranged for Phoenician builders to supplement the Israelite conscription of workers. Construction of the temple was begun in the 4th year of Solomon, which was the 480th year after the exodus from Egypt (1 Kings 6:1). David had wanted to build the temple, but the Lord reserved that privilege for Solomon (2 Sam 7:13; 1 Chron 17:4–6, 12; 22:6–11; 28:6); nevertheless, Solomon got the complete plan of the structure from his father (1 Chron 28:11–19). David had also gathered much building material, especially precious metals and other costly commodities, and had taken freewill offerings for the building of the temple (1 Kings 7:51; 1 Chron 22:2–5; 29:1–19). The temple was finished in seven years, and Solomon's palace was thirteen years in building. The altar, the bronze sea, and all sorts of utensils and implements used in the temple service were the responsibility of a

One of the three pools of Solomon, south of Jerusalem. The three pools are on separate levels and connected by conduits. They were part of Jerusalem's water supply in Roman times. Courtesy Seffie Ben-Yoseph.

craftsman, Huram of Tyre (1 Kings 7:14; KJV "Hiram"; cf. 2 Chron 2:13–14). Much of the copper used for these purposes probably came from mines worked by the Israelites.

Solomon had 1,400 chariots and 12,000 horsemen (2 Chron 1:14); he also had 4,000 stalls for horses (9:25). He built cities for his chariots and cavalry. Stables for at least 450 horses were found at Megiddo. Similar stables were excavated at Gezer, Taanach, Tell el Hesi, and Tell el Far'ah. Ophir was a source of gold, almugwood (algumwood), and precious stones. Solomon's ships also went to Tarshish with the Phoenician fleet and brought back all sorts of exotic things. Immense wealth thus came to Solomon by commerce, mining, tribute (1 Kings 4:21), and gifts from visitors (10:25). Among the most distinguished of these visitors was the queen of Sheba.

Women were a serious weakness of Solomon, and he made many political alliances through marriage (1 Kings

11:1–4). God had warned that such marriages would lead to apostasy. The harem of Solomon held a collection of some 700 wives and 300 concubines. He built places of worship for the false gods to satisfy his heathen wives. The Lord was angered at Solomon's failure to keep his explicit commands and announced to him the rift in the kingdom that was to take place in the reign of his son.

The rule of Solomon had been quite peaceful, but trouble was brewing. Hadad the Edomite, who as a child had survived a raid by David and had escaped to Egypt, now returned to plague him. In Syria, Rezon was made king at Damascus and became an enemy of Israel. In Israel a capable young man, Jeroboam the son of Nebat, was informed by the prophet Ahijah that he would become ruler of ten tribes of Israel. Solomon attempted to kill Jeroboam, but Jeroboam took refuge in Egypt until the death of Solomon. A great temporal ruler, possessing every natural advantage, almost inconceivably wealthy

SOLOMON, SONG OF

562

in material splendor, learning, and experience, Solomon was nevertheless a disappointment. Although he began extremely well, the tragedy of his gradual apostasy had more disastrous results than the infamous scandal of his father, who sincerely repented and was a man after the Lord's own heart.

SOLOMON, SONG OF (See SONG OF SONGS)

SOLOMON, WISDOM OF (See APOCRYPHA)

SOLOMON'S COLONNADE A magnificent porch built by Solomon on the east side of the temple area. Christ and the apostles walked in it (John 10:23; Acts 3:11; 5:12).

SOLOMON'S POOLS Three in number, these were located a short distance from Jerusalem and were fed by two chief sources—surface water and springs. Cleverly engineered aqueducts carried water from the desired spring to the pools. From these pools the water was conveyed by the same means to the wells under the temple area (Eccl 2:6).

SOLOMON'S SERVANTS (Heb. *'avedhê shelōmōh*). The descendants of Solomon's servants are named among those returning from Babylon to Jerusalem under Zerubbabel (Ezra 2:55, 58; Neh 7:57, 60; 11:3).

SOLOMON'S PORCH (See SOLOMON'S COLONNADE)

SOLOMON'S TEMPLE (See TEMPLE)

SON (Heb. *bēn*, Gr. *huios*). Genetically the Hebrew word expresses any human offspring regardless of sex (Gen 3:16). In genealogical records the word "son" is often a general term expressing descendants (Dan 5:22). Many times, of course, the word means a person, usually a male, who was the direct child of a given father (Gen 9:19; 16:15).

Another very common biblical use of this word is in combination with another word to express something about the individual or individuals described. Perhaps the most familiar usage of this kind is as a title for our Lord (see SON OF MAN and SON OF GOD). "Son of perdition" is used of Judas. Sometimes groups are thus designated (Gen 6:4; Deut 13:13; 14:1; 1 Thess 5:5; 1 John 3:2). The word sometimes indicates that a person is a member of a guild or of a profession (KJV—2 Kings 2:3, 5; Neh 3:8).

SONG (Heb. *shîr*, *shîrâh*). Singing played a prominent part in the worship and

national life of the Hebrews. The first song in the Bible was sung by Lamech (Gen 4:23–24). It was not uncommon for the Jews to compose a song celebrating some special victory or religious experience (Exod 15). The Psalter has been designated "The Song Book of Israel," and it contains many kinds of songs. Paul urges believers to sing (Eph 5:19; Col 3:16). The Book of Revelation speaks often of heavenly singing (Rev 5:9; 14:3).

SONG OF SONGS, SONG OF SOLOMON (Heb. *shîr ha-shîrîm*). This is unique among biblical books, for it centers in the joys and distresses of the love relationship between a man and a woman. The Hebrew name is taken from 1:1 ("the song of songs which is Solomon's"). There is considerable range of opinion as to the authorship and date of the book. The book ascribes its authorship to Solomon and has affinities with other writings attributed to him. The author's acquaintance with plants and animals is reminiscent of Solomon (1 Kings 4:33).

Though the book is difficult to analyze, the divisions of Delitzsch are often followed: (1) the mutual admiration of the lovers (1:2–2:7); (2) growth in love (2:8–3:5); (3) the marriage (3:6–5:1); (4) longing of the wife for her absent husband (5:2–6:9); (5) the beauty of the Shulammite bride (6:10–8:4); (6) the wonder of love (8:5–8:14).

There is great diversity and much overlapping among interpretations of the Song of Songs. Various views are: (1) allegorical, (2) typical, (3) literal, (4) dramatic, (5) erotic-literary, (6) liturgical, and (7) didactic-moral.

SONG OF THE THREE HOLY CHILDREN (See APOCRYPHA)

SONGS OF DEGREES (See ASCENTS, SONGS OF)

SON OF GOD One of the primary titles of Jesus in the NT. His claim to this title was the principal charge that the Jewish leaders made against him (Matt 26:63–64; Mark 14:61–62; cf. John 5:17–18; 19:7). The confession that Jesus is the Son of God was basic to the teaching of the apostles and the faith of the early church (2 Cor 1:19; Gal 2:20; 1 John 4:15; 5:5, 13). The title is to be understood both as a synonym for Messiah (Ps 2:7; Matt 16:16; 26:63; 27:40) and as implying deity through a unique relation with the Father (John 5:18).

The filial consciousness of Jesus and his unique relationship with the Father are particularly emphasized in John's

Gospel. Jesus is God's only Son (John 1:18), one with the Father (10:30), always doing the Father's will (4:34; 5:30; 6:38), and being in the Father as the Father is in him (10:38). He speaks what he hears from the Father (12:50), has unique knowledge of the Father (10:15; cf. Matt 11:27), and possesses the authority of the Father (John 3:35; 5:22; 13:3; 16:15). Thus, only in and through the Son is God's salvation given (3:36; 5:26; 6:40).

Outside the Gospels, God is called "the God and Father of our Lord Jesus Christ," suggesting a particular intimacy between Father and Son (Rom 15:6; 2 Cor 1:3; Eph 1:3; Col 1:3; 1 Peter 1:3; Rev 1:6). By his resurrection and ascension Jesus is designated Son of God (Rom 1:3) and preached to be so (Acts 8:37; 9:20; 13:33; 2 Cor 1:19). The distinction and difference between Jesus and the great prophets of Israel is that Jesus is the unique Son of God (Heb 1; 3:6). Finally, there is the trinitarian formula in Matthew 28:19. See also SONS OF GOD, CHILDREN OF GOD.

SON OF MAN (Heb. ben 'ādhām, Gr. ho huios tou anthrōpou). An expression found in the OT and used as a self-description of Jesus in the NT. In Hebrew, "son of man" means an individual man, a man from the genus man (Num 23:19; Ps 8:4-5. "Adam" is "mankind"). This phrase was used once by the Lord in addressing Daniel (Dan 8:17) and over 80 times in addressing Ezekiel. Probably the Lord wanted to emphasize to them that they were, after all, only men of the earth, in spite of this privilege of receiving the divine word. In Psalm 80:17 the king of Israel is called "the son of man" whom God has raised up for himself.

Daniel used this phrase to describe a personage whom he saw in a night vision (Dan 7:13-14); it is on the whole entirely in accord with the evidence to see here a messianic figure predictive of the Lord Jesus Christ. In the extrabiblical Similitudes of Enoch the presentation of the Son of Man in the terms found in Daniel's prophecy is continued.

Jesus called himself "Son of Man" (82 times in the Gospels; see also Acts 7:56; Rev 1:13; 14:14). He took it from Daniel's prophecy, which must have been familiar to the Jews. Jesus, in assuming this title, was saying to the Jews, "I am the Son of man in that prophecy."

Jesus certainly used the title in a variety of contexts: (1) As a substitute for "I" (e.g., Matt 11:19; 16:13; Luke 9:58). (2) When making his important declara-

tions and claims (e.g., Matt 20:28; Mark 10:45; Luke 9:56; 11:30; 19:10). (3) Once without the definite article (John 5:27 ASV). Because of his experience as man, living among men, he was qualified to judge man. See also MESSIAH. (4) Concerning his resurrection (Matt 17:9). (5) Concerning the glorious state into which as the exalted Son of Man he would enter (Matt 19:28; 24:30; 26:64; Mark 13:26; 14:62; Luke 17:26, 30; 22:69). (6) Concerning the return to earth in a glorious manner (Matt 24:27, 30, 44; Luke 17:24; 18:8). (7) Concerning his role in judgment (Matt 13:41; 25:31-32; Luke 9:56; 21:36). (8) Most important of all, concerning his passion and violent death (Matt 17:12, 22; 26:2, 24, 45; Mark 9:12, 31; 10:33; 14:21, 41; Luke 9:44; 18:31-32; 22:22, 48). See also ADAM.

SONS OF GOD, CHILDREN OF GOD A description of those who are in a special or intimate relationship with God. In the OT the Lord chose the people Israel and made a holy covenant with them. As a result, the people as a unit (and thus each member) were described as the son(s) of God (Exod 4:22; Deut 14:1). Further, the Davidic king-Messiah was described as the Son of God (see 2 Sam 7:14; Pss 2:7; 89:27-28). This usage is continued in the NT, where the ancient people of Israel are said to possess the "sonship" (Rom 9:4) and be God's children (John 11:52) and the Messiah is seen as God's "Son" (Heb 1:5; citing Ps 2:7 and 2 Sam 7:14).

Building on this OT usage, members of the new covenant are also described as sons/children of God (Rom 8:14ff.; Gal 3:26; 1 John 3:1). Both Paul and John insisted that to be called son or child meant living in a way that reflects this relationship (Rom 8:17, 29; 1 John 3:9). Jesus himself made a similar point (Matt 5:9, 44-45; 12:48-50; cf. Deut 32:6; Isa 1:2; Hos 1:10).

A few passages appear to refer to angels (Job 1:6; 2:1; 38:7; Ps 89:6). Genesis 6:1-2 may likewise involve angels (in this case they are fallen ones) or they may be demon-possessed individuals, but others view these "sons of God" as kings/rulers/princes.

SONS OF THE PROPHETS A title given to members of prophetic guilds or schools. Samuel was the head of a company of prophets at Ramah (1 Sam 7:17; 28:3), and 200 years later Elijah and Elisha were leaders of similar groups. They were men endowed with the prophetic gift (10:10; 19:20-23), who gathered around God's great leader for common worship, united prayer, religious fellowship, and instruction of the people (10:5, 10; 2 Kings 4:38, 40; 6:1–7; 9:1). In the times of Elijah and Elisha they formed a comparatively large company (2:7, 16) and lived together at Bethel, Jericho, and Gilgal (2:3, 5; 4:38).

SOOTHSAYER (See OCCUPATIONS AND PROFESSIONS)

SOP (Gr. *psōmion, a morsel of bread*). The word is used in the KJV and describes a thin wafer used to dip food from a common platter (John 13:26). Using the sop had long been common among the Hebrews (Ruth 2:14; Prov 17:1).

SOPATER (sō'pà-têr, Gr. *Sōpatros*). Son of Pyrrhus who accompanied the apostle Paul on his last journey from Corinth to Jerusalem (Acts 20:4). He was a Christian from the church at Berea and is the same as Sosipater who joined with Timothy, Lucius, and Jason in sending greetings to the church at Rome (Rom 16:21).

SORCERER, SORCERY (See MAGIC; OCCUPATIONS AND PROFESSIONS)

SORE (See DISEASES)

SOREK (sō'rĕk, Heb. *sôrēq, vineyard*). A valley that extends from near Jerusalem to the Mediterranean Sea. It was in this valley that Samson found Delilah (Judg 16:4; cf. 1 Sam 6:10–14; 7:3–14).

SOSIPATER (See SOPATER)

SOSTHENES (sŏs'thĕ-nēz, Gr. *Sōsthenēs*). The apparent successor of Crispus, the ruler of the synagogue at Corinth (Acts 18:17). It is quite possible that he subsequently became a Christian, for a Sosthenes joins Paul in the salutation of 1 Corinthians 1:1. If this is not the Sosthenes of Acts 18, he is otherwise unknown in the NT.

SOUL (Heb. *nephesh*, Gr. *psychē*). The nonmaterial ego of man in its ordinary relationships with earthly and physical things. The "mind" (*nous*) is the self in its rational functions. Again "mind" (*phronēma*) is the self as deeply contemplating. "Heart" (*kardia*) is the self as manifesting a complex of attitudes. "Will" (*thelēsis*) is the self as choosing and deciding. "Spi rit" (*pneuma*) is the self when thought of apart from earthly connections. When the blessed dead in heaven are spoken of as having been put to a martyr's death, they are called "souls" (Rev 6:9). When there is no reference to their former bodily experience, they are called "spirits" (Heb 12:23).

These functional names often overlap. The difference between man and beast is not that man has a soul or spirit (Gen 1:20; 7:15; Eccl 3:21), but that man is created in the image of God, whereas the beast is not.

The above remarks assume dichotomy, that is, that there are only two substantive entities that make up the whole person: (1) the body, which at death returns to dust, awaiting the resurrection, and (2) the nonmaterial self, which if regenerate goes to paradise or heaven; if not, to the abode of the wicked dead. There are many, however, who hold to a trichotomous view, arguing that "soul" and "spirit" are two distinct substantive entities, and the body, a third (1 Cor 15:44; 1 Thess 5:23; Heb 4:12).

SOUTH The translation of various Hebrew words in the KJV. They refer to a compass point, a country, or a general direction. The most common word (*neghev, a dry region*) refers primarily to an indefinite area lying between Palestine and Egypt (Gen 12:9; 13:1; 24:62–67; Deut 1:7; Josh 15:1–47; Judg 1:15; 1 Sam 27:8–12; 30:27; 2 Chron 28:18). The Negev extended from the lower end of the Dead Sea SW to Kadesh Barnea, NW along the River of Egypt to the Mediterranean. In it the Hebrews found Amalekites (Num 13:29), Jerahmeelites (1 Sam 27:10), and other tribes whom they either exterminated or absorbed.

SOVEREIGNTY OF GOD The word "sovereign," although it does not occur in any form in the English Bible, conveys the oft-repeated scriptural thought of the supreme authority of God (2 Cor 6:18; Eph 1:11; 1 Tim 6:15). His sovereignty follows logically from the doctrine that he is God, Creator, and Ruler of the universe.

The sovereignty of God is sometimes presented in the Bible as an unanalyzed ultimate (e.g., Rom 9:20–21; see Isa 45:9; cf. Ps 115:3; Dan 4:35). God is not subject to any power or any abstract rule or law that could be conceived as superior to or other than himself.

The inscrutable sovereignty of God is manifested, not so much in the punishment of the reprobate as in the salvation of his people. In his holy character he must logically punish moral evil (see SIN). But his sovereignty is most marvelously revealed in that he has graciously elected to save a people from their sin and from its consequences.

SOWER, SOWING (See AGRICULTURE)

SPAIN (Gr. *Spania*). The Carthaginians inherited the Phoenician interest in Spain, and New Carthage (Cartagena)

Wooden spindle from Thebes, New Kingdom (c. 1300 B.C.), with a limestone whorl and ancient flaxen thread. An owner's mark is scratched on the underside of the whorl. Reproduced by courtesy of the Trustees of the British Museum

was developed by Hannibal as his base against Italy in the Second Punic War. Trajan, Hadrian, and Theodosius I, among the emperors, were Spaniards; among men of letters the two Senecas,

Lucan, Columella, Quintillian, Martial, and Prudentius came from Spain. Paul's projected visit (Rom 15:24) was clearly in line with his evident policy to capture for the church the principal centers of the empire.

SPAN (See WEIGHTS AND MEASURES)

SPARROW (See BIRDS)

SPEAR (See ARMS AND ARMOR)

SPECKLED (Heb. *nāqōdh, mottled in color*). A word used to denote varied colors of beasts. The most familiar example of its use is in Genesis 30:25–43. It was not Jacob's actions, but God's, that effected the selective breeding (31:10–12).

SPICE (Heb. *besem, bōsem, sammîn, nekhō'th, reqah,* Gr. *arōma, amōmon*). Anything having a pleasant odor, usually herbs. The principal Hebrew word (*besem,* "sweet-scented") refers to any aromatic vegetable compound, such as myrrh, cinnamon, cassia, and so forth (Exod 30:23–24). Spices were often mixed with oil to make them more durable and easily applied (30:25; 35:8). Spices played an important part in worship throughout the Near East (25:1–6). In the temple the Levites were keepers of spices (1 Chron 9:29; cf. a rare spice [*bōsem,* "creating desire"] in the Song of Songs 5:13; 6:2). In Genesis 37:25 and 43:11 spices, or spicery, mean treasure (cf. 2 Kings 20:12–18). Spices were used in preparing the body of Jesus for burial (John 19:40). Some were brought to the tomb after Jesus had risen (Mark 16:1). See also PLANTS: *Spice.*

SPIDER (See ANIMALS)

SPIES (Heb. *rāgal, to travel by foot*). The custom of sending secret agents to discover facts about an enemy is age-old. The Hebrew word for a spy is suggested by the secrecy with which he did his work—he went stealthily (Gen 42; Josh 6:23; 1 Sam 26:1–4; 2 Sam 15:7–10; Luke 20:20).

SPIKENARD (See PLANTS)

SPINDLE (Heb. *kîshôr, shaft*). An implement, 8 to 12 inches (21 to 31 cm.) long, used in spinning. The rope of carded fiber or wool was attached to one end and the spindle rotated by hand. Thus the thread was twisted. In Egypt both men and women did spinning, but among the Hebrews only women did the work (Exod 35:25; Prov 31:19).

SPINNING (See OCCUPATIONS AND PROFESSIONS)

SPIRIT (Heb. *rûach, breath, spirit*, Gr. *pneuma, wind, spirit*). One of the biblical nouns (see the list of such nouns and also the trichotomist view in the article on SOUL) denoting the nonmaterial ego in special relationships. The self is generally called "spirit" in contexts where its bodily, emotional, and intellectual aspects are not prominent, but where the direct relationship of the individual to God is the point of emphasis (e.g., Rom 8:15b–16; cf. Heb 12:22–24; Rev 6:9). The biblical word "spirit" can have an impersonal meaning in both Hebrew and Greek, as it can in English (e.g., Romans 11:8; Isa 29:10 KJV). The same Hebrew and Greek words translated "spirit" can also mean "wind" or "breath" (John 3:8; cf. 4:24).

SPIRIT, HOLY (See HOLY SPIRIT)

SPIRITS IN PRISON The words under consideration occur in 1 Peter 3:18–20, and the same thought is suggested in 1 Peter 4:6. Some use these and other verses to support a doctrine of a *limbus patrum*, or borderland place of confinement of the patriarchs who died before the time of Christ. They see Ephesians 4:8ff. as teaching that, at his ascension, Christ took the patriarchs from this limbus to heaven. Matthew 27:52–53 is sometimes referred to as well, and the phrase "He descended into Hades" in the Apostles' Creed is also brought in.

Another view holds that (1) "made alive by the Spirit" (1 Peter 3:18) refers to Christ's resurrection (Rom 8:11), not to his disembodied state. (2) The time when Christ, in the Spirit, "went and preached" (1 Peter 3:19) was "when God waited patiently in the days of Noah" (3:20; cf. 1:11; 2 Peter 2:5). (3) The "spirits in prison" (1 Peter 3:19–20) are those who, in the days of Noah, refused Noah's message and are now, as Peter writes, in the Tartarus (2 Peter 2:4, see footnote), part of Hades. (4) Thus, 1 Peter 4:6 means "this is why the gospel was preached [of old (cf. Gal 3:8)] to [those who are now] dead, so that they might be judged as men [now] in the flesh [are to be judged], and might live according to God by the Spirit."

Scripture does not warrant the idea that people will hear the gospel after death.

SPIRITUAL GIFTS
(See GIFTS, SPIRITUAL)

SPIT, SPITTLE, SPITTING (Heb. *yāraq, rōq*, Gr. *ptuō*). Spitting in the face indicated gross insult (Num 12:14; Deut

25:9). Allowing spittle to run on the beard made one appear foolish or even "insane" (1 Sam 21:13). Jesus used spittle in curing blind eyes in Bethsaida (Mark 8:23) and put spittle on a mute tongue in the Decapolis (7:33). Jesus was insulted during his trial by being spit on (Matt 26:67; Mark 14:65).

SPOIL (Heb. *bizzâh, meshissâh, shōd, shālāl*, Gr. *harpagē, skylon*). The plunder taken from the enemy in war—pillage, booty, loot. The spoils of war were divided equally between those who went into battle and those who were left behind in camp (Num 31:27; Josh 22:8; 1 Sam 30:24). Parts were given to the Levites and to the Lord (Num 31:28, 30). Under the monarchy, the king received part of the spoils (2 Kings 14:14; 1 Chron 18:7, 11).

SPOKES (Heb. *hishshūrîm*). Rods connecting the rim of a wheel with the hub. In the temple there were ten lavers or basins made of bronze (1 Kings 7:27–33), apparently for the washing of sacrifices. They were set on bases of elaborate design moving on wheels. The spokes were part of these wheels.

SPONGE (See ANIMALS)

SPOT (Heb. *mûm*, Gr. *spilos*). The Hebrew word denotes a blemish or "flaw" on the face (Song of Songs 4:7). It is also rendered "blemish" (Lev 24:19 KJV) and "blot" (Prov 9:7 KJV). The Greek word is used figuratively of a stain of sin (2 Peter 3:14; Jude 23).

SPOUSE (See MARRIAGE)

SPREAD, SPREADING (Heb. *pāras, to disperse*, Gr. *strōnnymi*). To scatter, strew, or disperse, as in "spread abroad" (Isa 21:5; Matt 21:8; Mark 1:28).

SPRING (See FOUNTAIN)

SPRINKLING (Heb. *zāraq, nāzâh*, Gr. *rhantizein*). Sprinkling of blood, water, and oil formed a very important part of the act of sacrifice (Exod 24:6–8). Sprinkling was sometimes done in handfuls, sometimes with the finger, and sometimes with a sprinkler—a bunch of hyssop fastened to a cedar rod.

SPY (See SPIES)

STACTE (See PLANTS)

STADIA (See WEIGHTS AND MEASURES)

STAFF, STAVES (See ROD)

STAG (See ANIMALS)

STAIRS, STAIRWAY, STEPS (Heb. *maălâh, sullam*, Gr. *anabathmos*). The name was given to steps leading to an

Drawing from relief on palace at Nineveh depicting Assyrian army of King Ashurbanipal (668–633 B.C.) using ladders to storm an Egyptian town as prisoners, below, are taken away. Courtesy Carta, Jerusalem

upper chamber (1 Kings 6:8; Acts 9:37). Stairs led up to the city of David (Neh 12:37), to the porch of the temple gate to Jerusalem (Ezek 40:6), and to the altar on its east side (43:17). Since stone steps have not been found among ruins in Palestine, it is supposed that stairs in ancient times were made of wood.

STAKE (Heb. *yāthēdh*). A tent pin or tent peg (Exod 27:19; Isa 33:20; 54:2).

STALL (Heb. *marbēq*, *'āvas*, *'urvâh*, *repheth*, *'ēvūs*, Gr. *phatnē*). A place for the care of livestock (1 Kings 4:26; 2 Chron 9:25). One kind was not enclosed, often being a thatched or tented shelter, at times a fattening place (Amos 6:4 KJV, cf. NIV; Mal 4:2). The stall where Christ was born was a feeding place, usually connected with an inn (Luke 13:15).

STALLION (See ANIMALS)

STANDARD See WEIGHTS AND MEASURES.

STAR (See ASTRONOMY)

STAR OF THE WISE MEN (See ASTRONOMY)

STATURE (Heb. *middâh*, *measure*, and *qômâh*, *standing up*, Gr. *hēlikia*, *greatness*). Used primarily in the KJV, referring to great size, tallness, height (so NIV; Num 13:32–33; 1 Sam 2:26; 2 Sam 21:20; Isa 45:14; Luke 2:52; 19:3). God does not regard stature in size as a primary asset

for leadership (1 Sam 16:7; Isa 10:33; cf. Matt 6:27; Luke 12:25).

STEED (See ANIMALS)

STEEL (See MINERALS)

STEER (See ANIMALS)

STELE (stē'lē, Gr. *stele, an erect block or shaft*). The custom of erecting stone markers, usually upright narrow slabs, prevailed among ancient Egyptians. They were placed in tombs and public buildings where they honored people of high estate. The Hebrews do not seem to have adopted the custom, probably because it was felt they violated the fourth commandment (Exod 20:4).

STEPHANAS (stĕf'à-nās, Gr. *Stephanas, crown*). A Christian at Corinth, whose household were Paul's first converts in Achaia (1 Cor 1:16; 16:15, 17).

STEPHEN (stē'vĕn, Gr. *Stephanos, crown*). One of the seven appointed to look after the daily distribution to the poor in the early church (Acts 6:1–6). He performed great wonders and signs, taught in the synagogue, and there debated with Jews of the Dispersion. Acts 7 records Stephen's remarkable *apologia* before the council. Stephen's exclamation at the close of his speech is particularly important to a proper understanding of it: "Look . . . I see heaven open and the Son of Man standing at the right hand of God" (7:56). This is the only occurrence of the title "Son of Man" in the NT on the lips of anyone other than Jesus himself and reveals Stephen's messianic understanding of the term. Such radical thinking was too much for the listening Sanhedrin. Stephen was stoned to death.

STEPS (See STAIRS)

STEWARD (See OCCUPATIONS AND PROFESSIONS)

STOCK, STOCKS 1. In the KJV the bole of a tree was a stock and was worshiped by apostate Israel (Isa 44:19; Jer 2:27; Hos 4:12). **2.** In the KJV a family (Lev 25:47; Isa 40:24; Acts 13:26; Phil 3:3, 5). **3.** An instrument of punishment. There were various kinds. One was a mechanism by which the body was twisted into an unnatural position and thus made to endure excruciating agony (Jer 20:2–3; cf. 29:26; Acts 16:24).

STOICISM (stō′ĭ-sĭzm). Paul encountered it in Athens (Acts 17:18). Boasting a galaxy of distinguished exponents, both Greek and Roman—e.g., Zeno, Cleanthes, Seneca, Cicero, Epictetus, and Marcus Aurelius—Stoicism was a system of pantheistic monism. It held that fire is the ultimate substance with God, the active principle of the cosmos, permeating everything as a sort of soul. Nature, it taught, is a hierarchical unity controlled by the universal Logos, an impersonal reason at once immanent and divine. As participant in the Logos, man is also participant in deity. Indeed, the true essence of humanity is *nous* or mind, the capacity to understand the rational order veiled by phenomena. As a logos-being, man can perceive and assent to the determinism that makes all events necessary and therefore reduces evil to mere appearance. By assenting to this determinism—indifferently called fate or providence—man is able to live in harmony with nature. Hence the Stoic ethic is egocentrically negative. Nothing lies within man's power except imagination, desire, and emotion; thus by cultivating not only detachment from the world outside him but also mastery over his reactions to the world's impingement on himself, the philosopher achieves freedom, happiness, and self- sufficiency. Stoicism was aristocratic and austere, rigorously excluding pity, denying pardon, and suppressing genuine feeling. Sin was simply an error of judgment, easily rectified by a change of opinion.

STONE (Heb. *'even*, Gr. *lithos*). When entering Canaan, the Hebrews, who had made bricks in Egypt (Exod 5:7), readily turned to the abundant supply of stones, both from quarries and from stream beds.

Large flat slabs were used as covers for wells (Gen 29:2–10), doors for caves (Josh 10:18), and for burial caves (Matt 27:60). Stones were also used as landmarks (2 Sam 20:8), boundary stones (Deut 19:14; 27:17; Josh 15:6; 1 Kings 1:9; Prov 22:28). Great stones were used in the foundation of the temple (1 Kings 6:7).

Stones were used in setting up altars and memorials. These objects were of various kinds: monuments, steles or upright slabs, and circular areas enclosed by rocks (Gen 28:18; 31:45–46; Josh 4:1–9; 8:29; 24:26–28; 1 Sam 7:5–12; 2 Sam 18:17–18).

Stone weapons were frequently used by the Israelites (Exod 21:18; Num 35:17–23; 1 Sam 17; 1 Chron 12:2; 2 Chron 26:14–15). Certain crimes were punished by stoning (Lev 20:2, 27; 24:23). Israel was prone to worship stones. Among other pagan evils Isaiah found libations being offered to river stones (Isa 57:3–7). The law prohibited any such use of stones (Lev 26:1).

Figurative uses of the word *stone* are frequent (Exod 15:5, 16; 1 Sam 25:37; Job 38:30; Ezek 11:19). God has power to change stony hearts into hearts of flesh (Matt 3:9). Jesus gave a new name to Simon (*Petros*, "a little stone") as an indication of the character that this apostle would have in the days ahead (John 1:42). God is the stone of Israel (Gen 49:24; Dan 2:34). The messianic kingdom is a stone that will crush the kingdoms of men (Dan 2:34; Matt 21:44). Jesus Christ is the stone the builders rejected (Ps 118:22; Matt 21:42), the chief cornerstone of the new dispensation (Eph 2:20–22). Believers are living stones in God's temple (1 Peter 2:5–8).

STONES, PRECIOUS (See MINERALS)

STONING The ordinary form of capital punishment prescribed by Hebrew law. Stoning was the penalty for blasphemy (Lev 24:16), idolatry (Deut 13:6–10), desecration of the Sabbath (Num 15:32–36), human sacrifice (Lev 20:2), and occultism (20:27). Achan and his family were stoned because of his treachery to Israel (Josh 7:16–26). Jesus rebuked Jerusalem for stoning prophets (Matt 23:37; Luke 13:34). Stephen was stoned (Acts 7:58–59). Executions by stoning took place outside the city (Lev 24:14; 1 Kings 21:10, 13; Acts 7:58).

STOOL A three- or four-legged seat. The Shunammite woman put one in Elisha's

A well-preserved burial cave in the Adullam region, with a rolling stone at the entrance, second–third century. The city of Adullam figures prominently in the history of Israel from the days of Joshua, when it was a Canaanite royal city-state, to at least the time of Judas Maccabaeus, who retired to the city in 163 B.C. Courtesy Zev Radovan

room (2 Kings 4:10 KJV; NIV "chair"). A stool of peculiar form was used in Egypt for women in childbirth (Exod 1:16).

STORE CITIES Supply depots for provisions and arms (1 Kings 9:15–19; 2 Chron 8:4–6; 16:4; 17:12).

STOREHOUSE A place for keeping treasures, supplies, and equipment. Obedience to the Lord was rewarded with full storehouses (Deut 28:8 KJV; cf. Gen 41:56; 2 Kings 20:13; 1 Chron 26:15–17; Mal 3:10).

STORK (See BIRDS)

STOVE In Palestine the stove was usually made of clay. Some were small portable fireplaces, burning charcoal. Others were built outside the house and were heated with dry sticks, grass, and even dung. The hearth or firepot mentioned in Jeremiah 36:22 was a bronze heater. Only the well-to-do could afford a brazier (Mark 14:67). For cooking, the stove was molded so as to hold the pot or pan above the fire bowl through which air passed from vents at the bottom.

STRAIGHT STREET A name given to any route extending in a straight course across a city. Most streets were narrow and crooked. The avenue that ran through Damascus, 100 feet (31 m.) wide with a walk along each side, was called Straight (Acts 9:11).

STRANGER (Heb. *gēr, sojourner, stranger, tôshāv, sojourner, nokhrî, ben nēkhar, foreigner, zār, stranger*). A *gēr* or *tôshāv* was a foreigner who put himself under the protection of Israel and of Israel's God. He submitted to many requirements of the law of Israel and was therefore given certain privileges not accorded the *nokhrî* and the *zār*, who were also called strangers. The *gēr* was allowed to rest on the Sabbath and was supposed to be treated kindly (Exod 20:10; 22:21; 23:9, 12). He was classed with the Levite, the fatherless, and the widow (Deut 14:21, 29; 16:11; 26:11–13). He offered sacrifices to the Lord and was expected to observe various ceremonial and other requirements (Lev 17:10ff.; 18:26; 20:2; 24:16–22). The *nokhrî* was a foreigner who did not have religious fellowship with Israel, since his allegiance was claimed by another people and another deity. He was forbidden to enter the sanctuary (Ezek 44:7–9), and interest could be exacted from him (Deut 15:3; 23:20). The *zār* was not necessarily a foreigner. It is often used of foreigners as people entirely different from, or even hostile to, Israel (Isa 1:7; Ezek 11:9).

STRANGLE (Heb. *hānaq*, Gr. *pnigō, to choke*). To deprive of life by choking, and so without bloodshed. Israelites were forbidden to eat flesh from strangled animals because it contained the blood of the animals (Lev 17:12). At the Jerusalem Council even Jewish Christians were forbidden to eat such meat (Acts 15:20). The prohibition against eating any meat with the blood still in it is a part of the covenant God made with Noah and has not been invalidated in the New Testament (Gen 9:3–5).

STREAM OF EGYPT (See EGYPT, RIVER OF)

STRINGED INSTRUMENTS (See MUSIC AND MUSICAL INSTRUMENTS)

STRIPES (Heb. *nākâh*, Gr. *plēgē*). Scourging by lashing was a common form of punishment in ancient times. The Jewish law authorized it for certain ecclesiastical offenses (Deut 25:2–3). Among the Jews a scourge consisting of three thongs was used, and the number of stripes varied from a few up to 39 (to make sure that the law's limit of 40 was not exceeded). When scourging took place in the synagogue, it was done by the overseer, but the Sanhedrin also administered such punishment (Acts 5:40). Roman scourges had pieces of metal or bones attached to the lashes. The victim was stripped to the waist and bound in a stooping position. The body was horribly lacerated so that often even the entrails were exposed.

STRONG DRINK (See WINE)

STRONGHOLD A place of refuge, a fortress—literal (Judg 6:2; 1 Sam 24:22) or figurative (Ps 27:1).

STUBBLE (Heb. *qāsh, teven*, Gr. *kalamē*). The stalks of grain, usually about half of the stem, left standing after reaping (Exod 5:10–14). The word became a simile for wayward Israel (Isa 47:14).

STUMBLING BLOCK (Heb. *mikshôl*, Gr. *skandalon*). Anything that causes a person to trip or fall or, figuratively, causes material or spiritual ruin (Jer 18:15; Ezek 14:3–4; Rom 9:32; 14:13; 1 Cor 1:23; 8:9).

SUBMISSION (See OBEDIENCE)

SUBURB (Heb. *migrāsh, open land*). Used in the KJV for lands near cities used for pasturage of animals (e.g, Josh 21:2–42; Ezek 45:2). NIV reads "open land" or "pasturelands."

SUCCOTH (sŭk'ŏth, Heb. *sukkôth, booths* or *huts*). **1.** A place east of the Jordan (Gen 33:17). It was in the Jordan Valley, near Zarethan (1 Kings 7:46), and was assigned to the Gadites (Josh 13:27; Judg 8:5–16). **2.** The first station of the Hebrews on leaving Rameses (Exod 12:37; 13:20; Num 33:5).

SUKKOTH (See FEASTS)

SULFUR, SULPHUR (See BRIMSTONE; MINERALS)

SUN (Heb. *shemesh, server, ôr, luminary, hammâh, hot body, heres, blistering*, Gr. *hēlios, sun*). Sun, moon, and stars determine times and seasons (Gen 1:14; Job 38:33; Jer 31:35). Night and day were "caused" by the sun (Gen 1:5). Mid-morning was when the sun grew hot (1 Sam 11:9); noon was when it was brightest (Gen 43:16); beyond noon the heat waned and it was the cool of the day (3:8). The sun also determined directions. The direction of the rising of the sun became east (Isa 45:6); the direction of its going down (Ps 50:1) became west. The left hand or darker quarter was north, and the right hand or brighter quarter south (Gen 13:14; Job 37:17; Ezek 40:24). The sun also made it possible for man to survive, for it produced fruits (Deut 33:14). The sun is like a bridegroom (Ps 19:4–5), stands in his house (Hab 3:11), is ever watchful (Ps 19:6), dependable (72:5), and tells of God's continuing care (84:11). The problem of astronomy created by the standing sun (Josh 10:13) and the returning sundial (2 Kings 20:11; Isa 38:8) may be answered, at least in part, by scientists' recent discoveries of these extra segments of time in the history of the universe.

SUNDAY The name Sunday is derived from pagan sources. Dividing the calendar into seven-day weeks was the work of Babylonian astrologers. From them the plan went into Egypt, where the days were named for planets, one for the sun. After Christianity had been planted in northern Europe, the Teutonic people substituted the names of their gods for Egyptian titles, so we have Tiwes-day (Tuesday), Woden's Day (Wednesday) and Thor's Day (Thursday). But the first day continued to be called Sun's Day, largely because Emperor Constantine by royal decree In 321 made it *Solis Day*, day of the sun. After the Resurrection (Luke 24:1; John 20:1), Christians met on this day to celebrate the event. Some of Jesus' appearances occurred on the first day of the week (Mark 16:9; John 20:19). The disciples in Troas worshiped on the first day (Acts 20:7; cf. 1 Cor 16:1–2). The term *Lord's Day* occurs only in Revelation 1:10 and is a natural adaptation of a Roman custom of calling the first day of the month "Emperor's Day." By A.D. 150 the designation had been accepted throughout the Christian world. As the stronger Hebrew Christian churches declined in influence, the tendency to observe the Hebrew Sabbath slowly passed.

SUPERSCRIPTION (sū'pêr-skrĭp'shŭn, Gr. *epigraphē, an inscription*—so RSV, NIV). **1.** The wording on coins (Matt 22:20; Mark 12:16; Luke 20:24). **2.** The words inscribed on a board attached to the cross (Matt 27:37; Mark 15:26; Luke 23:38). The Roman custom was to have such a board, naming the crime involved, carried before the condemned person to the place of execution (John 19:19–20).

SUPERSTITIOUS (sū'pêr-stĭsh'ŭs). In Acts 17:22 Paul calls the Athenians *deisidaimonesterous* (extremely [uncommonly] scrupulous JB, NEB; too superstitious KJV; very religious ASV, NIV, RSV). Found only here in the NT, the Greek word is neutral, applying to any religion, good or bad.

SUPH, SUPHAH (sūf, Heb. *sûph*). KJV has "the Red Sea" for both names. Suph (Deut 1:1, ASV, RSV, NIV) is the place in front of which Moses repeated the law to Israel. The sea (*yam sûph*) that the Israelites crossed in their flight from Egypt should be called the Reed Sea rather than the Red Sea. See RED SEA. Suphah (Num 21:14, ASV, RSV, NIV) is also east of Jordan.

SUPPER, LORD'S (See LORD'S SUPPER)

SUPPLICATION (See PRAYER)

SURETY 1. In the phrase "of a surety" meaning "surely," (Gen 15:13; 18:13; 26:9; Acts 12:11, all KJV). **2.** Also in the KJV relating to the giving of a pledge and a promise to give or do something if another fails; signified by "striking hands" (Gen 43:9; Job 17:3; Heb 7:22). Becoming surety for either a foreigner or a neighbor is consistently condemned in Proverbs (6:1–5; 11:15; 17:18; 20:16; 22:26; 27:13) as imperiling the assets and the peace of mind of the surety.

Glazed relief of a winged bull from the palace of King Xerxes at Susa (Shushan), Archemenid period, fourth century B.C. Queen Esther lived in this palace. Courtesy Rëunion des Musées Nationaux

SURFEITING (sûr'fĕt-ĭng, Gr. *kraipalē, a drinking-bout*). Overindulgence in eating or drinking, intoxication, a drunken headache (Luke 21:34 KJV; "dissipation" RSV, NIV).

SUSA (sū'sà, Heb. *shûshan*). A city of the Babylonians, one of the capitals of the Persian Empire (Ezra 4:9; Neh 1:1; Esth 1:2; Dan 8:2). The Hebrews called this place "Shushan" (so KJV).

SUSANNA, THE HISTORY OF (See APOCRYPHA)

SWADDLING BAND (Heb. *hăthullâh,* Gr. *spargana*). Strips of cloth (so NIV) in which a newborn baby was wrapped. The child was placed diagonally on a square piece of cloth, which was folded over the infant's feet and sides. Around this bundle bands of cloth were wound (Luke 2:7, 12 KJV). For a figurative use, see Job 38:9.

SWALLOW (See BIRDS)

SWAN (See BIRDS)

SWARMING THING (See ANIMALS)

SWEAR (See OATH)

SWEAT (Heb. *zē'âh*, Gr. *hidrōs*). After the Fall, God told Adam that he would have to work hard enough to cause sweat in order to get his food (Gen 3:19). Priests in the future temple are not to wear anything that causes them to perspire (Ezek 44:18).

SWEAT, BLOODY A physical manifestation of the agony of Jesus in Gethsemane (Luke 22:44). Ancient and modern medicine has documented cases of blood extravasated from the capillaries mingling

CHORAZIN THE SYNAGOGUE
בית הכנסת   כורזין
© L RITMEYER

Reconstruction of the façade of the third-century synagogue at Korazin (Chorazin). The structure, made of basalt, is similar in style to that found at Capernaum, with the façade characteristically on the side nearest Jerusalem. Courtesy L. Ritmeyer

with and coloring the sweat, under severe stress of emotion. See under DISEASES.

SWIFT (See BIRDS)

SWINE (See ANIMALS)

SWORD (See ARMS AND ARMOR)

SYCAMINE (See PLANTS)

SYCAMORE, SYCOMORE (See PLANTS)

SYCHEM (See SHECHEM)

SYENE (See ASWAN)

SYMBOL That which stands for or represents something else; a visible sign or representation of an idea or quality or of another object. Symbols and their meanings arise out of the culture of the peoples that use them. Those symbols interpreted by the Scriptures are the foundation for all further studies in symbolism (e.g. Rev 5:8; 12:9; 17:15). We should investigate the context thoroughly. By means of a concordance we can check other passages that use the same symbol. Sometimes the nature of the symbol is a clue to its meaning. Not all symbols in the Bible have one and only one meaning; the lion is a symbol both for Christ and the devil (1 Peter 5:8).

It is evident that certain numbers in the Bible have symbolical significance. For instance, seven is probably the most important number in Scripture (it occurs about 600 times), expressing totality or completeness. The Book of Revelation makes frequent use of the number seven. Of special interest is the mysterious number 666 in the Book of Revelation (13:18). This may be an example of Jewish *Gematria*, i.e., the art of attaching values to names according to the combined numerical value of the letters composing them.

Symbolic actions often are prefigurative and are especially associated with the OT prophets (1 Sam 15:27–28; 1 Kings 11:29–30; cf. also 2 Kings 13:14–19; 22:11). Symbolic action is especially frequent in the prophecies of Jeremiah and Ezekiel (e.g., Jer 19; Ezek 2:9–10; 4:1–4).

SYNAGOGUE (Gr. *synagōgē, place of assembly*). A Jewish institution for the reading and exposition of the Holy Scriptures. It originated perhaps as early as the Babylonian exile. By NT times the synagogue was a firmly established institution among the Jews. In the first Christian century synagogues could be found everywhere in the Hellenistic world where there were sufficient Jews to maintain one. In large Jewish centers there might be numbers of them.

The chief purpose of the synagogue was not public worship, but instruction in the Holy Scriptures. How effectively the synagogue, along with the school, fulfilled this purpose is to be seen (1) from the survival of Judaism, especially in the Dispersion despite the pressures of pagan influences; (2) from the thorough Judaistic nature of Galilee in the first century, which in the time of Simon Maccabeus was largely pagan; and (3) from the knowledge of the Scriptures, which the apostle Paul assumes of his hearers in the Hellenistic synagogues.

Although there might be more in some of the larger synagogues, there were always at least two officials. The Ruler of the Synagogue (Heb. *ro'sh ha-keneseth*, Gr. *archisynagōgos*) was responsible for (1) the building and property, (2) the general oversight of the public worship, including the maintenance of order (cf. Luke 13:14), (3) the appointing of persons to read the Scriptures and to pray, and (4) the inviting of strangers to address the congregation (Acts 13:15). Generally there was only one ruler for each synagogue, but some synagogues had more (13:15).

The minister or attendant (Heb. *hazzān*, Gr. *hypēretēs*, cf. Luke 4:20) was a paid officer whose special duty was the care of the synagogue building and its furniture, in particular the rolls of Scripture. During the worship it was the *hazzān* who brought forth the roll from the chest and handed it to the appointed reader. He also returned it to its proper place at the conclusion of the reading (4:20). He had numerous other duties, which included the instruction of children in reading, the administration of scourgings, and the blowing of three blasts on the trumpet from the roof of the synagogue to announce the beginning and end of the Sabbath.

The congregation was separated, the men on one side and the women on the other. The more prominent members took the front seats. The service began with the recitation of the Jewish confession of faith, the *Shema'* (Deut 6:4–5). This was both preceded and followed by thanksgivings, two before and one after the morning *Shema'*, and two both before and after the evening *Shema'*.

After the *Shema'* came the prayer (*Tefillah*). The Ruler of the Synagogue could call on any adult male of the congregation to say this prayer. The person praying usually stood before the chest of the rolls of Scriptures. The oldest form of the *Tefillah* consisted of a series of ascriptions or petitions, each of which ended in the benedictory response: "Blessed art thou, O Lord."

The Scripture lesson that followed the *Tefillah* could be read by any member of the congregation, even children. The only exception was that at the Feast of Purim a minor was not allowed to read the Book of Esther. If priests or Levites were present in the worship service, they were given precedence. The readers usually stood while reading (cf. Luke 4:16).

Prescribed lessons out of the Penta-

teuch for special Sabbaths were established early. For other Sabbaths the reader himself chose the passage, but subsequently all the Pentateuchal readings became fixed. Sections, called *sedarim*, were established to complete the reading of the Pentateuch within a prescribed time. Babylonian Jews divided the Pentateuch into 154 sections and thus completed reading it in three years, whereas Palestinian Jews read it through once every year. A lesson from the Prophets immediately followed the reading from the Pentateuch.

The sermon followed the reading from the Prophets (Matt 4:23; Mark 1:21; 6:2; Luke 4:15; 6:6; 13:10; John 6:59; 18:20; Acts 13:15). The preacher usually sat (Luke 4:20), but the Acts account has Paul standing (Acts 13:16). No single individual was appointed to do the preaching. Any competent worshiper might be invited by the ruler to bring the sermon for the day (Luke 4:16–17; Acts 13:15).

The worship in the synagogue closed with a blessing that had to be pronounced by a priest and to which the congregation responded with an "Amen." If no priest was present, a prayer was substituted for the blessing.

The form of worship of the synagogue was adopted by both the Christian and Muslim religions, and that form in its general outline is to be found today in Jewish places of worship.

SYNOPTICS (See Gospels)

SYNTYCHE (sĭn'tĭ-chē, Gr. *Syntychē*, fortunate). A prominent woman member of the church at Philippi who was having a disagreement with a fellow female Christian, Euodias (Phil 4:2).

SYRACUSE (sĭr'à-kūs, Gr. *Syrakousai*). A town on the east coast of Sicily, Syracuse was the most important and prosperous Greek city on the island. The Alexandrian ship in which Paul sailed from Malta to Puteoli put in at Syracuse for three days (Acts 28:12).

SYRIA (Heb. *'ărām*, Gr. *Syria*). The territory of Syria varied considerably, often had vague boundaries, and really never constituted a political unit. Generally speaking, it included the area south of the Taurus Mountains, north of Galilee and Bashan, west of the Arabian Desert, and east of the Mediterranean—approximately 300 miles (500 km.) north to south and 50 to 150 miles (82 to 250 km.) east to west. The chief cities were Damascus, Antioch, Hama, Biblos, Aleppo, Palmyra, and Carchemish.

Sixteenth to fifteenth century B.C. bronze statuette from Sidon of a Syrian with full beard and wearing a simple kilt held by a broad belt at the waist. Courtesy Réunion des Musées Nationaux

David defeated King Hadadezer in battle along with the Syrians of Damascus who came to Hadadezer's aid (2 Sam 8:3–7). David also subdued Aram Maacah (1 Chron 19:6–19), Aram of Beth Rehob (2 Sam 10:6), and Aram Naharaim (1 Chron 19:6).

Asa king of Judah (911–876 B.C.) appealed to Syria for help against Baasha king of Israel (909–886) (1 Kings 15:16–21). Omri (885–874 B.C.) of Israel formed an alliance with the Phoenicians by the marriage of his son Ahab to Jezebel, daughter of Ethbaal king of the Sidonians (16:31). Twice during Ahab's reign (874–853) the Syrians under Ben-Hadad I tried to invade Israel but were put to flight first at Samaria (20:1–21) and the following year at Aphek (20:26–34). Three years of peace with Syria followed. Then Ahab, in alliance with Jehoshaphat of Judah, made an attempt to recover Ramoth Gilead but was killed on the field of battle.

Jehoram of Israel (852–841 B.C.) allied himself with Ahaziah of Judah (852) to war against Ben-Hadad's successor, Hazael, and was wounded in battle at Ramoth Gilead (2 Kings 8:28–29). During Jehu's reign (841–814 B.C.) Hazael captured the area east of the Jordan (10:32–33), and during the reign of Jehu's son Jehoahaz (814–798) he completely overran Israel and took numbers of its cities. These were retaken by Jehoash (798–782) from Hazael's successor, Ben-Hadad II (13:25). The successes of Jehoash were continued by his son Jeroboam II (782–753), who recovered all of the cities that had been taken by the Syrians from Israel over the years. He even successfully reduced Damascus (14:25–28).

To meet the Assyrian threat, Rezin of Damascus and Pekah of Israel (740–732) formed a military alliance. In 735 or 736 they attacked Jerusalem (2 Kings 16:5; Isa 7:1), either to eliminate Judah as a possible foe or to force her into their coalition. Judah's king, Ahaz (735–715), had just come to the throne. He panicked and, despite the prophet Isaiah's warnings, sent for help from Assyria (Isa 7:1, 25). Tiglath-Pileser III captured the Israelite cities in the territories of Dan and Naphtali (2 Kings 15:29) and took the people captive to Assyria. He then turned his attention to Damascus and in 732 subdued the city and brought an end to the Aramean state.

In subsequent years the Chaldeans and Egyptians fought over Syria and with the rise of the Persians it passed into their hands. The Battle of Issus (331 B.C.) brought Syria under the control of Alexander the Great. At his death it became the most important part of the Seleucid kingdom, which included large areas to the east, including Babylon. By the close of the second century, Syria, with Antioch as its capital, was all that was left of the kingdom of the Seleucids. In 64 the Romans made it a province and increased its area to include all the territory from Egypt to the Taurus Mountains, and from the Mediterranean to the Euphrates.

It was at Antioch that the followers of Jesus were first called Christians (Acts 11:26). Paul was converted in Syria on the road to Damascus (9:1–9) and was commissioned with Barnabas by the Antioch church to take the gospel to the Gentiles.

SYRIAC, SYRIAK The Syrian language. Once in KJV '*ărămîth* is translated Syriak (Dan 2:4; Aramaic NIV), four times Syrian (2 Kings 18:26; Ezra 4:7; Isa 36:11; Aramaic NIV). Syriac is Eastern Aramaic, the literary language of the Christian Syrians.

SYRIAN, SYRIANS (Heb. *'ărăm*, Gr. *Syroi*). 1. The language of Syria (see SYRIAC). 2. The people of Syria (2 Sam 8:5); in earlier times, broadly the Arameans (Gen 25:20; 28:5; Deut 26:5). See also SYRIA.

SYROPHOENICIAN (sī'rō-fē-nĭsh'ăn, Gr. *Syrophoinikissa*). An inhabitant of the region near Tyre and Sidon, modern Lebanon (Mark 7:26; cf. Matt 15:22).

-T-

Elaborately decorated cult stand from Taanach, tenth century B.C., comprised of lion and human faces, with winged leonine bodies in relief along the side panels. On the top register, a calf and a winged sun disk are flanked by columns with voluted decoration. Courtesy Israel Department of Antiquities and Museums. Exhibited and photographed at Israel Museum, Jerusalem

TAANACH (tā'à-năk, Heb. *ta'anak*). A fortified city of Canaan. Its king was defeated by Joshua, but the city was not occupied by the Israelites until later, when it was held by Manasseh (Josh 12:21; 17:11; Judg 1:27; 5:19; 1 Chron 7:29).

TABALIAH (tăb-ă-lī'à, Heb. *tevalyahu*). A son of Hosah, a Merarite Levite, a gatekeeper of the tabernacle under David (1 Chron 26:11).

TABEEL, TABEAL (tā'bē-ĕl, tā'bē-ăl). 1. The father of one of the allied kings whom Rezin of Damascus and Pekah of Israel attempted to make their puppet king of Judah (Isa 7:6). 2. An official in Samaria who complained to Artaxerxes about the activity of the Jews (Ezra 4:7).

TABERAH (tăb'ĕ-rà, Heb. *tav'ērâh, burning*). A place in the wilderness where the fire of the Lord burned some outlying parts of the camp of Israel as punishment for their complaining (Num 11:1-3; Deut 9:22). It was probably three days' journey from Sinai (Num 10:33), but its site is unidentified.

TABERNACLE (Heb. *'ōhel, mô'ēdh, tent of meeting, mishkān, dwelling*, Gr. *skēnē, tent*). A portable sanctuary that embodied all that was necessary for the worship of the Lord under nomadic conditions and also served as a prototype of a subsequent permanent building. At Sinai Moses was given a divine revelation concerning the nature, construction, and furnishings of the tabernacle (Exod 25-40). The work was carried out by Bezaleel, Oholiab, and their workmen; and when the task was accomplished, the tent was covered by a cloud and was filled with the divine glory (40:34).

The tabernacle stood in an outer enclosure or court (Exod 27:9-18; 38:9-20), 150 feet (47 m.) in length and 75 feet (23 m.) in width. The sides were covered with curtains made from finely woven linen. Within this open court the various types of sacrificial offerings were presented and the public acts of worship took place. Near the center the great altar of burnt offering, made from acacia wood overlaid with bronze (Exod 27:1-8), measured nearly 8 feet (2½ m.) square and about 5 feet (1½ m.) in height. Its corner projections were known as the "horns" of the altar. A fire that had been miraculously kindled burned continuously on the altar and was tended by the priests (Lev 6:12; 9:24). Almost in the center of the court was the bronze laver, used by the priests for ritual ablutions (Exod 30:17-21).

To the west end of the enclosure, parallel to the long walls, stood the tabernacle itself. A rectangular structure about 45 feet by 15 feet (14 by 5 m.), it was divided into two parts, a Holy Place and a Most Holy Place. The basic constructional material was acacia wood, easily obtainable in the Sinai Peninsula, fashioned into 48 "boards" some 15 feet (5 m.) in height and a little over 2 feet (1/2 m.) in width, overlaid with gold.

The completed tabernacle was divided into two compartments by a curtain on which cherubim were embroidered in red, purple, and blue, and which was suspended on four acacia supports. The outermost of these two areas was known as the Holy Place and was about 30 feet by 15 feet (9 by 5 m.) in area. The innermost part of the tabernacle, the Holy of Holies or the Most Holy Place,

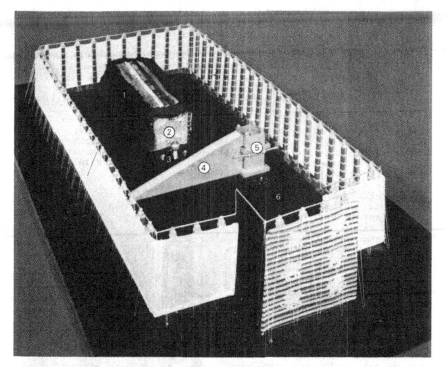

Model of the tabernacle: (1) ram skin covering for the sanctuary, (2) screen, (3) laver, (4) sloped ramp, (5) bronze altar (for burnt offering), (6) and court. Of the 60 pillars of the court, all of acacia wood, 20 stood on the south side, 20 on the north, 10 in the west, and 10 in the east. The pillars were connected to each other by a rod going through the top of the capitals, thus forming a frame. Each pillar was fastened to the ground by ropes stretching from the capital to copper pegs in the ground. Courtesy *The Tabernacle*, M. Levine, "Melechet Hamishkan," Tel Aviv, 1969

was 15 feet (5 m.) square. The entrance to the tabernacle was screened by embroidered curtains supported by 5 acacia pillars overlaid with gold.

The wooden framework of the tabernacle was adorned by 10 linen curtains (Exod 26:1–7) that were embroidered and decorated with figures of cherubim. It measured about 40 feet (12 1/2 m.) in length and 6 feet (2 m.) in width, being joined in groups of 5 to make 2 large curtains. These were then fastened together by means of loops and golden clasps (KJV "taches") to form one long curtain 60 feet (18 m.) long and 42 feet (13 m.) wide.

Exodus 25:10–40 describes the furniture of the sanctuary. The Holy Place, or outer chamber of the tabernacle, contained a table for the bread of the Presence (KJV "shewbread"), a small acacia-wood structure overlaid with gold, measuring 3 feet (1 m.) in length, 18 inches (46 cm.) in breadth and a little over 2 feet (1/2 m.) in height. Twelve cakes were placed on this table along with dishes, incense bowls, and pitchers of gold (Lev 24:5–9). The bread was renewed each week and was placed in two heaps on the table. Nearby stood the elaborately wrought *menorah* or seven-branched lampstand of pure gold. A gold-covered altar of incense, about 18 inches (46 cm.) square and 3 feet (1 m.) in height, had projections on each corner, and like the table of the bread of the Presence, it had golden rings and gold-covered staves to enable it to be moved readily.

The furniture of the innermost shrine, the Most Holy Place, consisted only of the ark of the covenant. This was a small, boxlike structure of acacia wood, whose length was just under 4 feet (1 1/4 m.), while the breadth and height were slightly above 2 feet (1/2 m.). It was covered on the inside and outside with sheet gold and had golden rings and staves like the table of the bread of the Presence and the altar of incense. The lid of the ark, the "mercy seat," was covered with solid gold. On each end was a golden cherub whose wings stretched toward the center of the lid.

The ark was the meeting place of God and his people through Moses, and contained the tablets of the law (Exod 25:16, 22). A pot of manna and Aaron's rod were also placed in the ark (Heb 9:4). An elaborately worked veil separated the Most Holy Place from the outer compartment of the tabernacle, and when the Israelites journeyed from place to place, the sacred ark was secluded from view by being wrapped in this curtain. Consequently the ark normally seen only by the high priest, and that on very special ceremonial occasions.

In the tabernacle all the sacrifices and acts of public worship commanded by the law took place. The tabernacle was set up at Sinai at the beginning of the second year, 14 days before the Passover celebration of the first anniversary of the Exodus (Exod 40:2, 17). When the structure was dismantled during the wanderings, the ark and the two altars were carried by the sons of Kohath, a Levite. The remainder of the tabernacle was transported in six covered wagons drawn by two oxen (Num 7:3ff.).

In Canaan the tabernacle was probably established first at Gilgal (Josh 4:19), then Shiloh (18:1), then Nob (1 Sam 21:1), then Gibeon (1 Chron 16:39; 21:29), and finally Jerusalem (2 Sam 6:17ff.).

TABERNACLES, FEAST OF (See FEASTS)

TABITHA (tăb′ĭ-thà, Aram *Tabeitha*, Gr. *Dorcas*, meaning, in Greece, *a roe;* in Syria and Africa, *a gazelle*). The name of a Christian woman disciple who lived in Joppa and made clothing to give to poor widows. When she died, Peter was summoned, and he raised her from death (Acts 9:36–43).

TABLE (Heb. *lûah,* Gr. *plax, writing tablet*). The law was engraved on stone tablets (Exod 24:12; 2 Cor 3:3; Heb 9:4) and figuratively, on the tablet of the heart (Prov 3:3; 7:3; Jer 17:1). Hebrew *mēsav* (Song of Songs 1:12) and Greek *klinē* (Mark 7:4) mean "couch." Hebrew *shulehan* was originally a leather mat spread on the ground (Pss 23:5; 78:19); the table

of the bread of the Presence (Exod 25:23, et al.; Heb 9:2, Gr. *trapeza*) was made of acacia wood overlaid with gold. Kings, queens, and governors had dining tables (1 Sam 20:29; 1 Kings 18:19; Neh 5:17); sometimes private persons also did (2 Kings 4:10; Job 36:16). Psalm 128:3 is an attractive picture of a family table. Greek *trapeza,* a four-legged table, is used of dining tables (Luke 22:21; Acts 6:2). To eat under the table was for dogs and the despised (Judg 1:7; Matt 15:27; Luke 16:21). Moneychangers used tables (Matt 21:12). Communion is served from the Lord's table (1 Cor 10:21).

Funerary stele from Marash, Hittite period (c. eighth century B.C.) depicting a small table, with bull's feet, laden with offerings for the dead. On each side sits a figure clothed in long garments. The one on the left holds a cup (?) in her upraised hand; the other holds a pomegranate. Courtesy Istanbul Museum. Photo B. Brandl

TABLETS OF THE LAW Stone tablets on which God, with his own finger, engraved the Ten Commandments (Exod 24:3–4, 12; 31:18; 32:15–16, 19; 34:1–4, 27–29; Deut 4:13; 5:22; 9:9–17; 10:1–5). Moses put the two tablets in the ark (Deut 10:5), where they were in the time of Solomon (1 Kings 8:9; 2 Chron 5:10). They are referred to in the NT (2 Cor 3:3; Heb 9:4). See also COMMANDMENTS, TEN.

TABOR (tā′bêr). **1.** A mountain in Galilee where the borders of Issachar, Zebulun, and Naphtali meet (Josh 19:22). On its slopes Barak gathered 10,000 men of Naphtali and Zebulun (Judg 4:6, 12, 14; 5:18), including contingents from some other tribes (5:13–15), to fight against

The magnificent Roman remains of Palmyra, or biblical Tadmor, showing the monumental arch, behind which is the Grand Colonnade. The city of Palmyra was about 120 miles (193 km.) northeast of Damascus. Courtesy Studium Biblicum Franciscanum, Jerusalem

Sisera and the Canaanite army at Megiddo. Here Zebah and Zalmunna, kings of Midian, killed Gideon's brothers (8:18–19). This commanding height was long a sanctuary of idolatrous orgies (Hos 5:1). Ancient tradition places the Transfiguration here. 2. In the KJV the plain of Tabor (ASV, RSV, "oak of Tabor"; NIV "great tree of Tabor," 1 Sam 10:3). 3. A Levite city of the sons of Merari in Zebulun (1 Chron 6:77).

TABRET (See MUSIC AND MUSICAL INSTRUMENTS)

TACHEMONITE (See TAHKEMONITE)

TACHMONITE (See TAHKEMONITE)

TACKLE (Heb. *hevel, rope,* Gr. *skeuē, equipment, ship's tackle*). This refers either to the rigging (Isa 33:23) or furniture (Acts 27:19) of a ship.

TADMOR (tăd'môr, Heb. *tadhmōr*). A city in the desert NE of Damascus. In patriarchal times a much-traveled road ran through it from Damascus north to Haran. Solomon either built a new city close by or rebuilt the old, after his conquest of Hamath Zobah (1 Kings 9:18; 2 Chron 8:4). In NT times Tadmor became Palmyra, city of palm trees, magnificent and wealthy, on the caravan route eastward from Emesa to Babylon and to Dura.

TAHAN, TAHANITE (tā'hăn-īt, Heb. *tahan*). 1. A son of Ephraim, and a founder of a tribal family (Num 26:35). 2. A descendant of the same family in the fourth generation (1 Chron 7:25).

TAHASH (tā'hăsh). A son of Reumah, concubine of Nahor, Abraham's brother (Gen 22:24).

TAHATH (tā'hăth, Heb. *tahath, below*). 1. A Kohathite Levite, son of Assir and father of Uriel (1 Chron 6:24, 37). 2. A son of Bered and descendant of Ephraim (7:20). 3. A grandson of no. 2 (7:20). 4. The 11th station from Sinai (Num 33:26–27).

TAHKEMONITE (tăk'mō-nīt, Heb. *tahkemōnî*). The family of David's chief captain (2 Sam 23:8), who sat in the seat (KJV); his name was Josheb-basshebeth (ASV, NIV, RSV). He is the same as Jashobeam, a Hacmonite (1 Chron 11:11). The text of both verses is difficult.

TAHPANHES, TAHAPANES (tăp'à-nēz, tă-hăp'à-nēz, Heb. *tahpanhēs*). A fortress city at the eastern edge of the Nile Delta. Jews fled here after the fall of Jerusalem (Jer 2:16; 43:1–7), taking Jeremiah with them. Jeremiah prophesied its destruction (43:8–11; 44:1; 46:14); as did Ezekiel (Ezek 30:18).

TAHREA (tá'rē-à, Heb. *tahrēa'*). A grandson of Mephibosheth, son of Micah, and so a descendant of Saul through Jonathan (1 Chron 9:41; called Tarea in 8:35).

TALE The word in KJV renders several Hebrew and Greek words that modern versions translate according to their different meanings. Thus, for example, NIV gives the connotations of a moan (Ps 90:9), a quota (Exod 5:8, 18), a count (1 Chron 9:28), slander (Ezek 22:9), and nonsense (Luke 24:11).

TALEBEARING This is forbidden (Heb. *rākîl*—Lev 19:16 KJV; gossiper MLB; slanderer RSV) and denounced (Heb. *rākîl*—Prov 11:13; 20:19 KJV, MLB; gossip NEB, NIV; Heb. *nirgān*—Prov 18:8; 26:20, 22 JB, KJV; gossip NIV).

TALENT (See MONEY; WEIGHTS AND MEASURES)

TALMAI (tăl'mī, Heb. *talmay*). **1.** A son of Anak and probably the founder of the Anakim, driven from Hebron by Caleb (Num 13:22; Josh 15:14; Judg 1:10). **2.** A king of Geshur, whose daughter Maacah was one of David's wives and Absalom's mother (2 Sam 3:3; 13:37; 1 Chron 3:2).

TALMON (tăl'mŏn, Heb *talmôn*). A Levite porter and founder of a tribal family, members of which returned with Zerubbabel and served as porters in the new temple (1 Chron 9:17; Ezra 2:42; Neh 7:45; 11:19; 12:25).

TALMUD (tăl'mŭd). A collection of Jewish writings of the early Christian centuries. There is a Palestinian Talmud and a later, more authoritative, much longer Babylonian Talmud. Each consists of Mishnah and Gemara.

TAMAH (See TEMAH)

TAMAR (tā'mêr, Heb. *tāmār, palm tree*). **1.** The wife of Er, then the levirate wife of Onan, then (by her father-in-law Judah) mother of twin sons, Perez and Zerah (Gen 38; Ruth 4:12; 1 Chron 2:4; Matt 1:3; KJV Thamar). **2.** A daughter of David and sister of Absalom, whom her half-brother Amon violated (2 Sam 13:1–33). **3.** The daughter of Absalom (14:27). **4.** A place at the SE corner of the future Holy Land (Ezek 47:18–19; 48:28). **5.** A city in Syria, more commonly known as Tadmor, later Palmyra. See TADMOR.

TAMARISK (See PLANTS)

TAMBOURINE (See MUSIC AND MUSICAL INSTRUMENTS)

TAMMUZ (tăm'ŭz, Heb. *tammûz*). A fertility god widely worshiped in Mesopotamia, Syria, and Palestine; equivalent to Osiris in Egypt and Adonis of the Greeks. His consort was the goddess Ishtar (Astarte or Ashtoreth). Their cult involved licentious rites. Tammuz was supposed to have been killed by a wild boar while shepherding his flocks. His wife rescued him from the underworld. His death was taken to represent the onset of winter. The long dry season was broken by spring rains when he came to life again. The fourth month of the Babylonian and later Jewish calendar was named for him (June–July). The only mention of him in the Bible occurs in connection with the custom of women mourning for him (Ezek 8:14). His Greek name, Adonis, is derived from the Phoenician and Hebrew word for "Lord."

TANACH (See TAANACH)

TANIS (See ZOAR)

TANNER, TANNING (See OCCUPATIONS AND PROFESSIONS)

TAPPUAH (tă-pū'à, Heb. *tappûah*). **1.** A city whose king Joshua conquered (Josh 12:17; 15:34). **2.** A town on the boundary of Ephraim (16:8; 17:7, 8). **3.** One of the sons or descendants of Hebron (1 Chron 2:43; cf. Josh 15:53).

TAR (See SLIME)

TARAH (See TERAH)

TARES (See PLANTS)

TARSHISH (tàr'shĭsh, Heb. *tarshîsh*). **1.** A son of Javan, great-grandson of Noah (Gen 10:4). **2.** A place, presumably in the western Mediterranean region, conjecturally identified by many with Tartessus, an ancient city located on the Atlantic coast of Spain (Jonah 1:3). **3.** "Ships of Tarshish" seems to refer to large ships of the kind and size that were used in the Tarshish trade (1 Kings 10:22). **4.** A great-grandson of Benjamin (1 Chron 7:10). **5.** One of the seven princes of Persia and Media who stood in the presence of Xerxes (Esth 1:14).

TARSUS (tàr'sŭs, Gr. *Tarsos*). A city of Cilicia, the capital of the province from A.D. 72, the birthplace and early residence of the apostle Paul (Acts 21:39). Tarsus was an ancient city, the seat of a provincial governor when Persia ruled, and, in the days of the Greek Syrian kings, the center of a lumbering and linen industry. During the first century before

The city of Tarsus, birthplace of Paul, in Asia Minor, showing the "Gate of St. Paul." Courtesy Ecole Biblique et Archéologique Française, Jerusalem

Christ the city was the home of a philosophical school, a university town, where the intellectual atmosphere was colored by Greek thought.

Tarsus stood, like Alexandria, at the confluence of East and West. The wisdom of the Greeks and the world order of Rome, mingled with the good and ill of Oriental mysticism, were deep in its consciousness. A keen-minded Jew, born and bred at Tarsus, would draw the best from more than one world. Paul belonged to a minority of Jews that had Roman citizenship.

TARTAN (tär'tän, Heb. *tartän*). In the KJV a commander-in-chief of the Assyrian army (2 Kings 18:17; Isa 20:1). A title, not a proper name.

TASKMASTERS (See OCCUPATIONS AND PROFESSIONS)

TASSEL (Heb. *tsîtsith, tassel, lock*). The fringe of twisted cords fastened to the outer garments of Israelites to remind them of their obligations to be loyal to the Lord (Num 15:38–39; Deut 22:12). Later they became distinct badges of Judaism (cf. Zech 8:23). They were common in NT times (Matt 23:5).

TATTENAI, TATNAI (tăt'ĕ-nī, tăt'nī, Heb. *tat-tenay*). A Persian governor of the territory west of the Jordan who was ordered to assist the Jews in the rebuilding of the temple (Ezra 5:3, 6; 6:6, 13).

TAVERN (See INN)

TAX COLLECTOR (See OCCUPATIONS AND PROFESSIONS)

TAXES Charges imposed by governments, either political or ecclesiastical, on the persons or the properties of their members or subjects. In the nomadic period taxes were unknown to the Hebrews. Voluntary presents were given to chieftains in return for protection. The conquered Canaanites were forced to render labor (Josh 16:10; 17:13; Judg 1:28–35). Under the theocracy of Israel every man paid a poll tax of a half-shekel for the support of the tabernacle worship (Exod 30:13; 38:25–26), and this was the only fixed tax. It was equal for rich and poor (30:15). Under the kings, as Samuel had warned the people (1 Sam 8:11–18), heavy taxes were imposed (1 Kings 12).

During the days of the divided kingdom Menahem (2 Kings 15:19–20) bribed the Assyrian king with 1,000 talents of silver, which he raised from the rich of his kingdom. Similarly Hoshea (17:3) paid heavy tribute to Assyria, and when he refused to pay further, he lost his kingdom. Later, Pharaoh Neco of Egypt put Judah under heavy tribute, and Jehoiakim oppressively taxed Judah (23:33, 35). Under the Persian domination, "taxes, tribute or duty" (Ezra 4:13) were forms of taxation, though Artaxerxes exempted "priests, Levites," etc. (7:23–24). The Ptolemies, the Seleucids, and later the Romans all adopted the very cruel but efficient method of "farming out the taxes." Each officer extorted more than his share from those under him, adding to the Jewish hatred of the tax collectors. Both Matthew and Zacchaeus were tax collectors who later became converts.

TEACHER, TEACHING (See OCCUPATIONS AND PROFESSIONS; SCHOOL; SYNAGOGUE)

TEACHERS OF THE LAW (See SCRIBES, JEWISH)

TEBAH (tē'bà, Heb. *tevah*). 1. A nephew of Abraham, born to Nahor by his concubine Reumah (Gen 22:24). 2. A city that David captured from Hadadezer. Most versions (JB, KJV, MLB, NASB, NEB, RSV) call it Betah (2 Sam 8:8; Tebah NIV) or Tibhath (1 Chron 18:8; Tebah NIV).

TEBALIAH (See TABALIAH)

TEBETH (See CALENDAR)

TEETH (Heb. *shēn,* Gr. *odous*). Literal teeth (Gen 49:12; Exod 21:24); gnashing with the teeth can be a token of anger (Job 16:9), remorse (Matt 8:12), or contemptuous rage (Lam 2:16; Acts 7:54).

TEIL TREE (See PLANTS)

TEKOA, TEKOAH, TEKOITE (tĕ-kō'à, tĕ-kō'ăīt, Heb. *teqôa', tekô'âh*). A city of Judah, an inhabitant of it. Tekoa, 12 miles (20 km.) south of Jerusalem and the same distance NE of Hebron, was fortified by Rehoboam (2 Chron 11:6; cf. Jer 6:1). Previous to this, Joab, David's cousin and general, had sent to Tekoa for a "wise woman" and plotted with her to persuade David to bring back Absalom. Amos was a shepherd of Tekoa (Amos 1:1; 7:14).

TELAIM (tē-lā'ĭm, Heb. *ha-telā'îm, lambs*). The place where Saul mustered his army against Amalek (1 Sam 15:4); possibly the same as Telem (Josh 15:24) in Judah.

TELEM (tē'lĕm, Heb. *telem*). **1.** A city of Judah near the border of Edom (Josh 15:24). **2.** A porter who put away his foreign wife after the return from captivity (Ezra 10:24).

TELL (Arabic, Heb. *tēl*). A mound or heap of ruins that marks the site of an ancient city and is composed of accumulated occupational debris, usually covering a number of archaeological or historical periods and showing numerous building levels or strata. Ordinarily, city sites were selected in association with certain natural features, such as a spring or other convenient water supply, a hill or similar defense advantage, or trade routes determined by local geography. In the course of the history of a town, many reconstructions would be necessary because of destruction by war, earthquake, fire, neglect, or like causes. In the Bible the fact that a city had become only a mound is often regarded as a result of judgment. Deuteronomy 13:16 prescribes that an apostatizing city should be destroyed and reduced to a tell (Josh 8:28; 11:13; Jer 30:18; 49:2). In addition to these five OT occurrences, the Hebrew term *tel* also appears as an element in place-names of living towns (e.g., Ezra 2:59; Neh 7:61; Ezek 3:15).

TELL EL AMARNA (See AMARNA, TELL EL)

TEMA (tē'mà, Heb. *têmā'*). **1.** One of the 12 sons of Ishmael and progenitor of a tribe (Gen 25:12–16). **2.** A place at the northern edge of the Arabian Desert (Job 6:18–20; Isa 21:14; Jer 25:23).

TEMAH (tē'mà). The children of Temah were temple servants (KJV Nethinim) who returned from exile with Zerubbabel (Ezra 2:53; Neh 7:55).

TEMAN (tē'măn, Heb. *têmān, on the right*, i.e., *toward the south*). **1.** A grandson of Esau (Gen 36:11, 15). **2.** An Edomite chief (36:42). **3.** A city in the NE part of Edom (Jer 49:7).

TEMPERANCE (Gr. *enkrateia, sōphrosynē*). Self-control (Acts 24:25; 1 Cor 9:25; Gal 5:23; 2 Peter 1:6). It is not limited to abstinence from liquor. In Acts 24:25 the reference is to chastity. In 1 Timothy 3:2, 11; Titus 2:2 it is the opposite of "drunken."

TEMPLE (Heb. *hêkhāl, bayith*, Gr. *hieron, naos*). Three temples stood successively on Mt. Moriah (2 Chron 3:1) in Jerusalem. The first was built by Solomon, the second by Zerubbabel, and the third by Herod the Great. Most ancient religions had temples. The Jerusalem temple was distinctive in that it contained no idol in the inner sanctum, but only a box (called the ark) containing the two tablets of the law, with the symbolic worshiping cherubim above.

The central place of the temple in the religious life of ancient Israel is reflected throughout the Bible (e.g., Luke 2:41–51). The Psalms abound in references to it (42:4; 66:13; 84:1–4; 122:1, 9; 132:5, 7–8, 13–17). The temple was the object of religious aspiration (23:6; 27:4–5). Pilgrimage to the temple brought the people of Israel from the ends of the earth (122:1–4; Acts 2:5–11). Jesus exercised some of his ministry there (Matt 26:55; Luke 19:45; John 7:28, 37; 10:23). The early Jerusalem Christians also worshiped there until the break between Israel and the church became final (Acts 3:1; 5:12, 42; 21:26–34).

There are no known remains of Solomon's temple. It was noted for lavish beauty of detail rather than for great size. It was accessible only to the priests; the lay Israelites came to it but never entered it. Completed in seven years, it was dedicated in Solomon's eleventh year, c. 950 B.C. (1 Kings 6:38), and was destroyed when the Babylonians burned Jerusalem in 587 B.C.

The temple consisted of three sections: (1) The *Ulam*, or porch, through which the temple proper was entered. (2) The *Hekhal*, or Holy Place, which was lighted by clerestory windows (1 Kings 6:4). It was 30 feet (9 m.) wide, 60 feet (18 m.) long, and 45 feet (14 m.) high. It was paneled with cedar, with gold inlay to relieve the wooden monotony and to add grandeur. (3) The *Devir*, or Most Holy Place (2 Chron 3:8–13), the inner sanctum, a 30-foot (9-m.) cube, windowless and overlaid with gold. It had a raised floor, and the cubicle was reached by steps from the *Hekhal*. Here God especially manifested his presence by the shekinah glory cloud.

In the courtyard before the temple

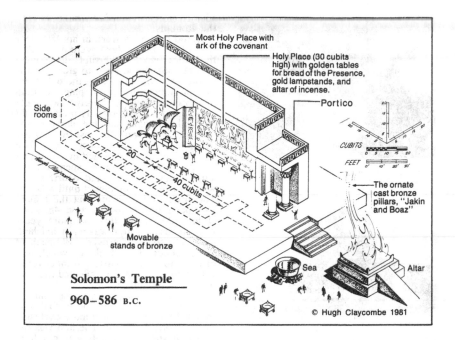

Most Holy Place with ark of the covenant

Holy Place (30 cubits high) with golden tables for bread of the Presence, gold lampstands, and altar of incense.

Side rooms

Portico

CUBITS

FEET

The ornate cast bronze pillars, "Jakin and Boaz"

Movable stands of bronze

Sea

Altar

Solomon's Temple

960–586 B.C.

© Hugh Claycombe 1981

stood two objects intimately connected with the temple worship. The altar of burnt offering was the central object in the sacrificial service. It was made of brass (2 Chron 4:1). South of the altar stood the copper alloy laver, or molten sea (1 Kings 7:22–26; 2 Kings 16:17; 2 Chron 4:2–6). It was 3 1/2 inches (9 cm.) thick, about 15 feet (4 1/2 m.) in diameter and 7 1/2 feet (2 m.) high, and stood on the backs of 12 bulls, three facing in each direction.

Certain changes doubtless took place in the temple during the Hebrew kingdom. Pagan idolatry was occasionally introduced (2 Kings 16:10–18; 21:4–9; Ezek 8:3–18). Pious kings reformed, refurbished, and rededicated the temple (2 Chron 29:3–31:21; 34:8–33). Foreign kings raided it (1 Kings 14:25–26; 2 Kings 12:18; 14:14; 18:15–16). When Jerusalem finally fell to the Babylonians in 587 B.C., the temple along with the rest of the city was destroyed and its valuable contents carried to Babylon (2 Kings 25:8–9, 13–17).

Ezekiel the prophet was also a priest. In the early part of his book he predicts that God will judge his idolatrous people by withdrawing his presence from Jerusalem, leaving it to the Gentiles to desolate. But the latter part of the book predicts the reversal of this. Judah and Israel reunited will be regathered. The climax of this vision is the prophet's description of the restored temple of God, with the living waters proceeding from it and the people of God dwelling around it (Ezek 40–48).

The return from Babylonian exile (in 538 B.C.), made possible by the decree of Cyrus, was a small and unpromising one. The returnees were few in number, and their resources were so meager as to need frequent strengthening from the Jews who remained in Babylon. The temple they built is a good example of this. When the foundation was laid, the old men, who had seen the "first house" (Solomon's temple), wept for sorrow (Hag 2:3), but the young men, who had been born in exile, shouted for joy (Ezra 3:12).

The Holy Place of the new temple seems to have had a curtain at its front. It had one lampstand, a golden altar of incense, and a table for the bread of the Presence. Another curtain separated the *Hekhal* from the Most Holy Place. According to Josephus, the Most Holy Place was empty. Evidently the ark had been destroyed in 587 B.C. and was never replaced. A single slab of stone marked its place. The Babylonian Talmud asserts that five things were lacking in the new temple: the ark, the sacred fire, the

The Rock of Moriah, traditional site of the altar of burnt offering in Solomon's temple, as seen from the dome in the Dome of the Rock mosque, shown below, at the Temple Mount in Jerusalem. Courtesy Ecole Biblique et Archéologique Française, Jerusalem

Shekinah, the Holy Spirit, and the Urim and Thummim.

Antiochus Epiphanes, in 168 B.C., sought to stamp out the Hebrew religion, robbed the temple of its furniture and desecrated it, forcing the high priest to sacrifice a pig on its altar. This action precipitated the Maccabean revolt. In 165 the Jews, led by the Maccabees, recaptured, cleansed, and rededicated the temple. The story of the rededication of the temple and the miraculous supply of oil for the lamps is perpetuated in the Jewish festival of Hanukkah.

Herod the Great (37–4 B.C.) was a tireless builder. Many cities and heathen temples had been rebuilt by him, and it was natural that he should wish to show his own grandeur by replacing the modest restoration temple with a more complex and much more beautiful temple. Other motives probably moved him, especially his desire to ingratiate himself with the more religious Jews, who resented his

Idumean origin and his friendliness with the Romans.

Herod began his work in his 18th year (20–19 B.C.). The Jews were afraid that the work would interrupt the temple service, but Herod went to great lengths to prevent this, rebuilding the old structure piecemeal, never stopping the ritual observances until an entirely new temple came into being. Since only priests could enter the temple and the inner court, 1,000 of them were the masons and the carpenters for that inner area. The "house" itself was finished in a year and a half; eight years were spent on the surrounding buildings and court, which were not finally completed until A.D. 64. The Jews said to Jesus that the temple had been under construction 46 years (John 2:20); more than 30 more years were to pass before it was really finished, then only to be destroyed. All speak of the grandeur of the building, which was of white marble, its eastern front covered with plates of gold that reflected the rays of the rising sun.

Entering the temple area, one came to four successive walled courts that surrounded the temple, each more exclusive than the one outside it. The first was the Court of the Gentiles. It was not holy ground, and non-Jews were permitted there. Here buying and selling went on; it was here that Jesus cleansed the temple (John 2:14–17). Within the Court of the Gentiles were situated the temple and inner courts, built on a platform 22 feet (7 m.) above the floor of the outer court. Stairways led up to this platform. Surrounding it was a stone wall on which were placed stones with inscriptions in Greek and Latin forbidding non-Jews from entering on pain of death. Several of these stones have been found (cf. Acts 21:26–28).

On the platform was the inner court. It was the temple precinct and holy ground. Only the covenant people could enter here. It was surrounded by a high wall, and against the inner side of this wall were built storage chambers and colonnades. Ritual paraphernalia was kept in some of the chambers and the Sanhedrin is believed to have met in one of them. The inner court was divided into two unequal parts by a cross wall running north and south. The eastern and smaller area was the Women's Court. Here women as well as men were permitted and here were located 13 chests like inverted trumpets, into which offerings for the expenses of the temple services were placed. In this place the poor widow was commended by Jesus when she gave her two copper coins (Mark 12:41–44). For reasons of ceremonial purity only men were allowed in the western area, which contained in its center the temple proper. Around the temple was the Court of the Priests, which contained the altar of burnt offering and the laver. Around the Priests' Court was the Court of Israel, accessible to all Jewish males. Here the men gathered when the service was being carried on, to pray and to observe the offering of the sacrifices (Luke 1:10).

In the center of these many courts within courts stood the temple itself, raised 12 steps above the Court of Priests. Perhaps the forbidding inaccessibility of the sanctuary was in Paul's mind when he said that Christ "destroyed the barrier, the dividing wall of hostility" to bring the Gentiles into the fellowship of the people of God (Eph 2:14).

Between the *Hekhal* and the *Devir* or the Most Holy Place hung two curtains, with 18 inches (46 cm.) space between them. On the Day of Atonement the high priest entered the *Devir* with his censer by going to the south side, passing between the curtains to the north side, and thus emerging into the Most Holy Place. The Gospels refer to these as one veil, which was torn in two at the time of Jesus' crucifixion (Matt 27:51; Mark 15:38; Luke 23:45). The *Devir* was empty

and was entered by the high priest only once a year, on the Day of Atonement.

An upper room, 60 feet (19 m.) high, covered the two chambers of the temple. From this room workmen were let down in boxes to effect needed repairs. Probably this was to avoid needless walking through the sacred house. As in Solomon's, so in Herod's temple, there were storerooms along the sides, except for the front or east, where the porch stood. These were used for storage and for the residence of officiating priests. No natural light came into this temple from roof or windows. It depended on the lamps for its light.

In front of the temple, in the Courtyard of the Priests, stood the altar of burnt offering. It is believed that this altar stood on the great rock that is covered today by the building called the Dome of the Rock on the Haram esh-Sherif. It was made of unhewn stones. There was always a fire burning on the altar. At the SW corner was located a drainage channel for the blood to the Kidron Valley. North of the altar were 24 rings affixed to the ground. To these were tied the sacrificial victims, and there they were killed by slitting their throats. Still farther to the north were pillars with iron hooks on which the carcasses were hung for dressing. If this reminds us today of a butcher shop rather

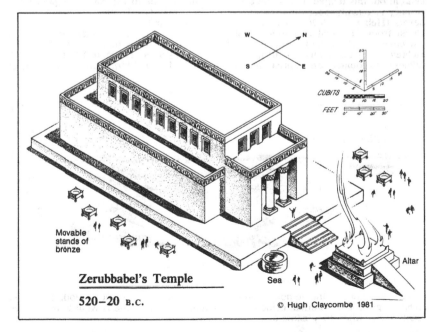

W   N
S   E

CUBITS

FEET

Movable stands of bronze

Zerubbabel's Temple

520–20 B.C.

Sea

Altar

© Hugh Claycombe 1981

than a place of worship, we should remember that this antithesis would have been meaningless in the biblical world. Not only did the priests live by eating many of the sacrificial victims, but any killing of an animal for food anywhere was considered a kind of religious act—a sacrifice—and certain rituals were prescribed.

South of the sacrificial altar was the bronze laver or wash basin, where the priests washed their hands and feet. Water was supplied by pipes from the temple spring.

The temple was burned when Jerusalem fell to the Roman armies in August A.D. 70. Pictures on the Triumphal Arch of Titus in Rome show the soldiers carrying off the temple furniture as loot. This destruction made complete and final the break between the temple and the church and thus helped to establish the church as a religion completely separate from Israel. The early Christians saw in this forced cessation of the Jewish ritual a proof of the validity of Christ's claims to be the Redeemer foreshadowed by the OT ceremonial law.

In the NT the term *temple* is used figuratively in a number of ways. Jesus spoke of the temple of his body (John 2:19, 21). The individual believer is a temple (1 Cor 6:19). So also is the church; but this temple, unlike the earthly one, is equally accessible to all believers (Heb 6:19; 10:20), now freed by Christ from the ritual limitations of the old covenant (Eph 2:14). The Book of Hebrews (especially chs. 7–10) in great fullness expounds on Christ as the

fulfillment of the typology of the temple and its ritual. The culmination of this idea of the "better covenant" is seen in the New Jerusalem where in his vision John "did not see a temple in the city, because the Lord God Almighty and the Lamb are its temple" (Rev 21:22).

TEMPTATION, TESTING (Heb. *massâh*, Gr. *peirasmos*). The idea of putting to the proof–from either a good or bad intention. Jesus, true man, faced both testing from God and temptation from Satan.

The Lord tests individuals—Abraham (Gen 22:1), Job (Job 23:10), Hezekiah (2 Chron 32:31)—and nations (Deut 8:2, 16; 33:8). Sometimes his testing is severe and painful (1 Cor 11:32; Heb 12:4–11; 1 Peter 1:7; 4:8–13), but it originates in holy love.

Until Jesus returns, Satan has freedom to tempt people to sin (1 Chron 21:1). He is called the tempter (Matt 4:3; 1 Thess 3:5) and the adversary of Christians (1 Tim 5:14; 1 Peter 5:8). God sometimes uses this tempting to test believers. Satan afflicted Job within limits God imposed (Job 1:6–22; 2:1–7); he deceived Eve (1 Tim 2:14); Christians are to be constantly watching for temptation (Mark 14:38; Luke 22:40; 2 Cor 2:11; 1 Peter 5:8). They can overcome temptation (1 Cor 10:13). Satan tempted Jesus (Matt 4:1–11). Temptation is not sin: sin is to submit.

To test God is to assert unbelief and lack of trust in him (Exod 17:7; Deut 6:16; Ps 95:8–11; Matt 4:5–6; Acts 5:9; 15:10; 1 Cor 10:9). Before partaking of

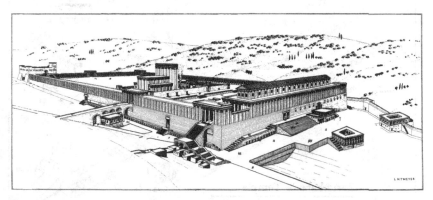

A reconstruction of the temple mount during the second temple period, based on archaeological and historical evidence. Something like this scene is what Jesus and the apostles saw when they came to Jerusalem. Courtesy Carta, Jerusalem

A typical Bedouin tent made of goat's-hair cloth, in the Negev. Courtesy Zev Radovan

the Lord's Supper believers are to test themselves (1 Cor 11:28) to see whether they are spiritually prepared to participate. Such testing should be a regular feature of the Christian life (2 Cor 13:5; Gal 6:4).

TEN COMMANDMENTS (See COMMANDMENTS, TEN)

TENT (Heb. *'ōhel*, Gr. *skēnē*). A temporary dwelling generally made of strong cloth of goat's hair stretched over poles and held in place by cords reaching out to stakes driven into the ground. It is the typical dwelling of nomadic peoples. Tents are of various shapes—round and tapering, flat and oblong. All of a nomadic family's belongings could normally be carried on one pack animal. *Tent* (usually *tabernacle* in KJV) often means any habitation (Gen 9:27; Job 8:22; Ps 84:10) and is often used figuratively (Isa 13:20; 54:2; Jer 10:20).

TENTMAKER (See OCCUPATIONS AND PROFESSIONS)

TENT OF MEETING (See TABERNACLE)

TERAH (tē'rà, Heb. *terah*). 1. Son of Nahor and father of Abram (Gen 11:24–32). He lived at Ur of the Chaldees and was an idolater (Josh 24:2). 2. A stage in Israel's march (Num 33:27–28).

TERAPHIM (tĕr'à-phĕm, Heb. root and meaning dubious). Used in the KJV for a kind of household god and means of divination. Usually rendered "idol" in NIV. The teraphim of Laban, stolen by Rachel (Gen 31:19; cf. Judg 17:5; 18:14–20), were small enough to be concealed in a camel saddle (Gen 31:34–35; cf. 1 Sam

19:13–16). They were a valuable possession, for their ownership involved the inheritance of Laban's property. In the time of the judges, Micah had teraphim among the religious articles of his household shrine (Judg 17:5). In the spiritual revival under King Josiah the teraphim and other "abominations" in Judah and Jerusalem were put away (2 Kings 23:24; cf. Ezek 21:21; Zech 10:2).

TEREBINTH (See PLANTS)

TERROR In ordinary usage this means extreme fear or dread, or sometimes the one who causes such agitation. The word is a translation of about 12 Hebrew and Greek words that are rendered also by "dread," "fear," "horror," "terribleness," "ruin" (e.g., Gen 35:5; Ps 55:4; 2 Cor 5:11).

TERTULLUS, TERTULIUS (têr-tŭl'ŭs, Gr. *Tertyllos*). The professional advocate used by the Jews to state their case against Paul before Felix, procurator of Judea (Acts 24:1).

TESTAMENT A word the KJV uses 13 times to translate the Greek word *diathēkē*, which signifies a testamentary disposition. KJV translates it "covenant" 20 times, as usually the NT uses *diathēkē* in the meaning of its cognate *synthēkē*, which accurately renders the OT *berith*, a binding agreement or contract between one human being and another or between a human being and God (e.g., Luke 22:20; 1 Cor 11:25; cf. Exod 24:8; Heb 9:15–20). Only in Hebrews 9:16–17 does NIV have "will" (testament KJV, MLB, NEB) for *diathēkē* (elsewhere NIV has covenant).

TESTAMENTS OF THE TWELVE PATRIARCHS (See APOCALYPTIC LITERATURE)

TESTIMONY Generally "a solemn affirmation to establish some fact," and commonly among Christians the statement of one's Christian experience. In Scripture it usually refers to that which was placed in the ark of the covenant (Exod 25:21), or to the Word of God (Ps 119:14, 88, 99 KJV; cf. Mark 6:11).

TESTING (See TEMPTATION, TESTING)

TETRARCH (See OCCUPATIONS AND PROFESSIONS)

TEXTS AND VERSIONS (OLD TESTAMENT) The English OT today is identical with the Hebrew Bible but is arranged differently. The customary divisions of the 39 books in the English version are (1) 17 historical books, (2) 5 poetical books, and (3) 17 (major and minor) prophetical books. The Hebrew Bible was divided into (1) Law (*Torah*, i.e., the Pentateuch), (2) Prophets (*Nebhiim*, including Joshua, Judges, Kings, and Later Prophets, Isaiah, Jeremiah, Ezekiel, and the Twelve Minor Prophets), and (3) Writings (*Kethuvim*, composed of the 11 remaining books). The Hebrew OT—combining certain books that are separate in English—numbered only 24 books. Josephus reduced the number to 22 by further combinations.

The final confirmation of the books of the Law, the Prophets, and the Writings as exclusively canonical by Jewish scholars cannot be placed later than 400, 200, and 100 B.C. respectively. However, the writing and adoption by consensus doubtless antedated these dates by centuries. The books of the OT were all inspired writings of men chosen by God, spanning a period of approximately 1,000 years, embraced within the traditional dates of 1450 to 444 B.C.

No autograph texts of any OT writings are known to exist today. Until A.D. 1947, when the Dead Sea Scrolls were discovered, the earliest complete extant manuscripts of the Hebrew Bible were dated about 1000. Writing was known as early as 3000 B.C. among the old civilizations of the Near East (Acts 7:22).

The OT was originally written in Hebrew, with the exception of a few chapters and verses in the later books. These were written in Aramaic, a kindred language (Dan 2:4–7:28; Ezra 4:8–6:18; 7:12–26; Jer 10:11).

The Septuagint was in popular use in Jesus' time and is often quoted by NT writers. It is a translation of Hebrew into Greek by Jewish scholars in Alexandria, Egypt. The Pentateuch was translated about 250 B.C. and the entire OT completed 100 years later. The term *Septuagint* is the Latin word for 70, representing the 72 rabbis who did the translating, probably under orders of Ptolemy Philadelphus. The Greek used was not the classical idiom but rather anticipated that of the NT, the *Koinē*. It was designed to preserve the old religion among the dispersed Jews in a language they commonly used. The oldest extant fragments of the Septuagint today are from a papyrus roll of Deuteronomy, dated about A.D. 150. See also SEPTUAGINT.

Three Greek translations from the Hebrew were made in the second century A.D., but only fragments of them have survived. Aquila, a proselyte Jew, made a very literal translation that became the official Greek version for the Jews. Theodotion, a Christian of Pontus, made a translation between 180 and 192 that seemed to be partially a revision of the Septuagint. It was a free rendering of the idiomatic Greek and became popular in the early Christian churches. In about 200, Symmachus faithfully translated the Hebrew into good, smooth Greek, though it was somewhat a paraphrase. Jerome's commentary on these versions was that "Aquila translates word for word, Symmachus follows the sense, and Theodotion differs slightly from the Septuagint."

The Targums were probably oral translations of the Hebrew Scriptures into Aramaic after the latter replaced the Hebrew as the spoken language of the Jews. The Targums contain religious instructions along with interpretations, which accompanied the reading of Scripture in the synagogues (Luke 4:16–27).

The Peshitta is the Syriac Bible of the OT translated in the second or third century A.D. for the benefit of Christians whose language was Syriac. Many manuscripts survive. The earliest data known on any manuscript of the Bible is found on one containing Genesis, Exodus, Numbers, and Deuteronomy, dating to A.D. 464.

The Old Latin versions probably originated among the Latin-speaking Jews of Carthage and were adopted by the Christians. An entire Bible in "Old Latin" circulated in Carthage by A.D. 250. There were a variety of Latin versions before Jerome's day, representing three types of Old Latin text: African, European, and Italian.

The Vulgate was produced by the scholarly Jerome in a cave in Bethlehem adjacent to what he believed was the Grotto of the Nativity. Jerome translated directly from the Hebrew with references to the Septuagint and Origen's Hexapla. He was commissioned in A.D. 382 by Pope Damasus to make an official revision of the Old Latin Bible. His work was completed in 405. The Vulgate is a creditable work, though not an infallibly accurate translation of the original text. Rather, it was an interpretation of thought put into idiomatic, graceful Latin. It was virtually without a rival for 1,000 years. The Douay Version, translated from the Vulgate, was until recently the only authorized Roman Catholic Bible in English.

The Coptic versions were made for Christians in Egypt in the second or third century A.D. The Ethiopic version was made in the 4th or 5th century. The Gothic version was prepared by Ulfilas about 350. The Armenian version, beautiful and accurate, was made for Christians of eastern Asia Minor about 400. A twin to the latter was the Georgian version of the fifth or sixth century. The Slavonic version of the ninth century is preserved in the oldest manuscript of the whole Bible in existence today. It is dated 1499 and is known as Codex Gennadius, now in Moscow. The Arabic version, necessitated by the Arabic conquests of the seventh and eighth centuries, was begun by Saadya in the tenth century.

For data on English versions, see BIBLE, ENGLISH VERSIONS.

TEXTS AND VERSIONS (NEW TESTAMENT) The NT (with the OT) stands virtually alone in the literature of antiquity as a work that was translated into other languages. In addition to the MSS containing a continuous NT text, many MSS of lectionaries from these centuries have survived. These are MSS that contain NT passages organized for reading on particular days.

From the 1st to the 4th centuries A.D., NT MSS were written in uncial letters on papyrus; from the 4th to the 10th, in uncial letters on vellum; from the 10th to the 14th, in minuscule letters on vellum; from the 14th to the invention of printing in the 15th century, in minuscule letters on paper.

Almost 70 papyrus MSS and fragments are known, about 250 uncial MSS, 2,500 cursive MSS, and 1,600 lectionaries. Papyri are designated by "P" and a superscript number (e.g., P⁶⁶). Uncials are designated by capital letters of the English and Greek alphabets plus א (the Hebrew letter *Aleph*) so far as these

letters permit; but all uncials are also designated by a number with a zero prefixed (e.g., 047). Cursives are designated by a number only (e.g., 565), and lectionaries by a number with a lowercase letter *l* prefixed and sometimes italicized (e.g., *l*299).

If every MS of the NT itself were destroyed, the NT could virtually be reconstructed from another significant source: the thousands of quotations of NT passages in the writings of the ancient church fathers, principally in Greek, Latin, and Syriac. These quotations must be consulted with care, as they were often given from memory or simply as a scriptural allusion and hence not verbally exact. Yet many are textually reliable.

THADDAEUS   (thă-dē'ŭs,   Gr. *Thaddaios*). One of the 12 apostles, mentioned only twice in Scripture (Matt 10:3; Mark 3:18). In Matthew 10:3, KJV has "Lebbaeus, whose surname was Thaddaeus," NEB has "Lebbaeus," and NASB, NIV, and RSV have "Thaddaeus." The other two lists (Luke 6:16; Acts 1:13) insert Judas, son of (or brother of) James instead of this name. Nothing else is certainly known about him, but he may be mentioned in John 14:22. A spurious "Gospel of Thaddaeus" used to exist.

THAHASH (See TAHASH)

THAMAH (See TEMAH)

THAMAR (See TAMAR)

THANK OFFERING (See SACRIFICE AND OFFERINGS)

THARA (See TERAH)

THARSHISH (See TARSHISH)

THEATER Israel produced no drama and thus had no theaters. The word *theater* is from the Greek and is a noun derived from the verb *theaomai*, "to view," or "to look upon." The theater was usually an open-air structure, a semicircle of stone seats built into the side of a hill, and seating perhaps 6,000 people. The seats were cut concentrically, and at the foot of the auditorium a semicircular plane of level pavement provided the "orchestra" or the place where the chorus, an indispensable part of all Greek dramas, and the actors performed. In the more primitive theaters a tent backed the diameter of this semicircle, into which the actors retired to change their masks and, by implication, their roles. (There were only three actors in a Greek tragedy to fill all the roles involved in the play.) On the tent was painted a rough representation

The theater of Dionysus at Athens, first used in the sixth century B.C. Modified in Hellenistic and Roman times, the theater contains 64–78 stone tiers and seats c. 17,500. Courtesy Gerald Nowotny

of trees or a temple or a house, to indicate that the scene of action was town or country and so on. The Greek for "tent" is *skēnē,* hence "scenery" in the dramatic sense. Surviving Greek theaters are acoustically remarkable. Theaters were commonly used for public gatherings, since they were likely to provide the largest places of assembly in the city; hence the use of the only theater mentioned in the NT (Acts 19:29), that of Ephesus. The ruins of this theater, a most imposing structure seating 25,000 people, have been excavated. Roman theaters tended to be more elaborate than those of the Greeks, and, perhaps in conformity with the needs of a severer climate, were at least in part roofed over.

THEBES (See NO)

THEBEZ (thē'bĕz, Heb. *tēvēts*). A city in the tribe of Ephraim about halfway from Beth Shan to Shechem. It is mentioned only in connection with the death of Abimelech, son of Gideon, who wanted to be king (Judg 9:50; 2 Sam 11:21).

Abimelech had taken the city except for a central tower, from the top of which a woman dropped a millstone on him, causing his death.

THEOCRACY (thē-ŏk'rà-sē, Gr. *theokratia*). A government in which God himself is the ruler. The best and perhaps the only illustration among nations is Israel from the time that God redeemed them from the power of the pharaoh by drying the Red Sea (Exod 15:13; 19:5–6) and gave them his law at Mt. Sinai, until the time when Samuel acceded to their demand for a king (1 Sam 8:5). During this period God ruled through Moses (Exod 19–Deut 34), Joshua (Josh 1–24), and "judges." From the human standpoint, the power was largely in the hands of the priests, who acted on the basis of laws passed by God, in which were united all the powers of the state—legislative, executive, and judicial.

THEOPHANY A visible appearance of God, generally in human form. Before man sinned, he walked and talked with God; but after sin entered, Adam and his wife hid when they heard the voice of the Lord God (Gen 3:8). God spoke to Cain (ch. 4), Enoch and Noah "walked with God" (5:24; 6:9), and God gave Noah detailed instructions concerning the ark and the Flood. One of the loveliest and most instructive of the theophanies is found in Genesis 18. From Abraham's time on, theophanies generally occurred when the recipients were asleep, as in Jacob's vision at Bethel (28:10–17), but God addressed Moses "face to face" (Exod 33:11). There is good reason to think that theophanies before the incarnation of Christ were visible manifestations of the preincarnate Son of God. Theophanies ceased with the incarnation of our Lord.

THEOPHILUS (thē-ŏf'ĭ-lŭs, Gr. *Theophilos*). It is reasonable to suppose that Theophilus, to whom Luke dedicated both his gospel (1:3) and the Book of Acts (1:1), was a real person. The title "most excellent" demands this, while the name and title together suggest a person of equestrian rank who became a Christian convert. Nothing is known of the man.

THESSALONIANS, LETTERS TO THE
With the possible exception of Galatians, 1 and 2 Thessalonians are the earliest letters surviving from the correspondence of Paul. They were written to the church in Thessalonica, which was founded by Paul on his second journey en route from Philippi to Achaia. His preaching of Jesus

as the Messiah aroused such violent controversy in the synagogue at Thessalonica that the opposing Jewish faction brought him before the city magistrates, charging him with fomenting insurrection against Caesar (Acts 17:5–9). Paul's friends were placed under bond for his good behavior, and to protect their own security, they sent him away from the city. He proceeded to Berea and after a short stay, interrupted by a fanatical group of Jews from Thessalonica, he went on to Athens, leaving Silas and Timothy to continue the preaching (17:10–14). It is possible that he sent Timothy back again to encourage the Thessalonians while he continued at Athens (1 Thess 3:2). In the meantime Paul moved on to Corinth; and there Timothy found him when he returned with the news of the growth of the Thessalonian church (3:6; Acts 18:5). The first letter was prompted by Timothy's report.

I. 1 Thessalonians

Paul's stay both in Thessalonica and in Athens was brief, and he probably arrived in Corinth about A.D. 50. According to the narrative in Acts, Paul had begun his ministry there while working at the tentmaker's trade with Aquila and Priscilla (Acts 18:1–3). When Silas and Timothy rejoined him after their stay in Macedonia, they brought funds that enabled Paul to stop working and to devote his entire time to evangelism (Acts 18:5; 2 Cor 11:9). Shortly afterward the Jewish opposition to Paul's preaching became so violent that he was forced out of the synagogue. About a year and a half later he was called before the tribunal of Gallio, the Roman proconsul (Acts 18:12). Gallio had taken office only a short time previously, in 51 or 52. The first letter, then, must have been written at Corinth about a year prior to that date, in 50 or 51.

Timothy brought a report concerning the problems of the church, with which Paul dealt in this letter. Some of his Jewish enemies had attacked his character, putting him under obligation to defend himself (1 Thess 2:1–6, 10, 14–16). A few of the converts were still influenced by the lax morality of the paganism from which they had so recently emerged and in which they had to live (4:3–7). Some of the church members had died, causing the rest to worry whether their departed friends would share in the return of Christ (4:13). Still others, anticipating the Second Advent, had given up all regular employment and were idly waiting for the Lord to appear (4:9–12).

Outline and Content, 1 Thessalonians

I. The Conversion of the Thessalonians (1:1–10)

II. The Ministry of Paul (2:1–3:13)
   A. In Founding the Church (2:1–20)
   B. In Concern for the Church (3:1–13)

III. The Problems of the Church (4:1–5:22)
   A. Moral Instruction (4:1–12)
   B. The Lord's Coming (4:13–5:11)
   C. Ethical Duties (5:12–22)

IV. Conclusion (5:23–28)

II. 2 Thessalonians

The genuineness of 2 Thessalonians has been challenged because of its difference from 1 Thessalonians. The warning of signs preceding the Day of the Lord (2 Thess 2:1–3) in contrast to a sudden and unannounced appearing (1 Thess 5:1–3); the teaching on the "man of sin" (2 Thess 2:3–9), unique in Paul's letters; and the generally more somber tone of the whole letter have all been alleged as reasons for rejecting Pauline authorship. None of these is convincing, for the two letters deal with two different aspects of the same general subject, and bear so many resemblances to each other that they are clearly related.

The second letter was probably sent from Corinth in A.D. 51, not more than a few months after the first letter, since Silas and Timothy were still with Paul. Evidently the Thessalonian Christians had been disturbed by the arrival of a letter purporting to come from Paul—a letter he had not authorized (2 Thess 2:2). Some of them were suffering harsh persecution (1:4–5); others were apprehensive that the Last Day was about to arrive (2:2); and there were still a few who were idle and disorderly (3:6–12). The second letter serves to clarify further the problems of the first letter and to confirm the confidence of the readers.

Outline and Content, 2 Thessalonians

I. Salutation (1:1–2)

II. Encouragement in Persecution (1:3–12)

III. The Signs of the Day of Christ (2:1–17)
   A. Warning of false rumors (2:1–2)
   B. The apostasy (2:3)
   C. The revelation of the man of sin (2:4–12)

D. The preservation of God's people (2:13-17)

IV. Spiritual Counsel (3:1-15)

V. Conclusion (3:16-18)

Whereas the first letter heralds the resurrection of the righteous dead and the restoration of the living at the return of Christ, the second letter describes the apostasy preceding the coming of Christ to judgment. Paul stated that the "secret power of lawlessness" was already at work and that its climax would be reached with the removal of the "hinderer" (2 Thess 2:6-7), who has been variously identified with the Holy Spirit, the power of the Roman Empire, and the preaching of Paul himself. With the disappearance of any spiritual restraint, the "man of sin" or "lawlessness" will be revealed, who will (2:3-10) deceive the people and will be energized by the power of Satan himself.

In view of this prospect, Paul exhorted the Thessalonians to retain their faith and to improve their conduct. He spoke even more vehemently to those who persisted in idleness (2 Thess 3:6-12), recommending that the Christians withdraw fellowship from them.

THESSALONICA (thĕs'à-lō-nī'kà, Gr. *Thessalonikē*). A Macedonian town founded by Cassander, Alexander's officer who took control of Greece after Alexander's death in 332 B.C. Its comparatively sheltered harbor made it the chief port of Macedonia. In 147 it became the capital of the Roman province and was Pompey's base a century later in the civil war with Julius Caesar. Prolific coinage suggests a high level of prosperity. The population included a large Roman element and a Jewish colony. Paul visited Thessalonica after Philippi and appears to have worked among a composite group, including the Jews of the synagogue and Greek proselytes.

THIEF, THIEVES (Heb. *gannāv, steal,* Gr. *kleptēs, lestēs, thief*). The word is used for anyone who appropriates someone else's property, including petty thieves and highwaymen (Luke 10:30; John 12:6). Under the law of Moses, thieves who were caught were expected to restore twice the amount stolen. The thieves crucified with Jesus must have been robbers or brigands, judging by the severity of the punishment and the fact that one of them acknowledged that the death penalty imposed on them was just (Luke 23:41).

THIGH (Heb. *yarekh, shôq,* Gr. *mēros*). The upper part of a human leg, or the rear leg of a quadruped. To put one's hand under the thigh of another was to enhance the sacredness of an oath (Gen 24:2, 9; 47:29). To "smite hip and thigh" (Judg 15:8 KJV) implied not only slaughter but slaughter with extreme violence. When the Angel of the Lord wrestled with Jacob so that Jacob might know the weakness of his human strength (Gen 32:24-32), he touched the hollow of Jacob's thigh and threw it out of joint at the hip, altering Jacob's position from struggling to clinging; when he was thus transformed, God changed his name from Jacob ("supplanter") to Israel ("prince with God"). In Oriental feasts the shoulder or the thigh of the meat is often placed before an honored guest (cf. 1 Sam 9:23-24); he has the privilege of sharing it with those near him. The thigh was the place to strap a sword (Judg 3:16; Ps 45:3; Song of Songs 3:8). To smite one's thigh (Jer 31:19; Ezek 21:12 KJV, MLB, NASB, RSV; beat one's breast JB, NEB, NIV) was a sign of amazement or of great shame.

THISTLE (See PLANTS)

THOMAS (tŏm'às, Gr. *Thōmas,* from Aram. *te'oma, twin*). One of the 12 apostles (Matt 10:3). He was called "Didymus" or "the Twin" (cf. John 11:16; 20:24; 21:2). Shortly before the Passion, Thomas asked, "Lord, we don't know where you are going, so how can we know the way?" (14:1-6). Thomas was not with the other apostles when Jesus presented himself to them on the evening of the Resurrection, and he told them later that he could not believe in Jesus' resurrection (20:24-25). Eight days later he was with the apostles when Jesus appeared to them again, and he exclaimed, "My Lord and my God!" (20:26-29). He was with the six other disciples when Jesus appeared to them at the Sea of Galilee (21:1-8) and was with the rest of the apostles in the Upper Room at Jerusalem after the Ascension (Acts 1:13). According to tradition he afterward labored in Parthia, Persia, and India. A place near Madras is called St. Thomas's Mount.

THOMAS, GOSPEL OF This was the major item in a jar of papyri discovered at Nag Hammadi between Cairo and Luxor in A.D. 1945. The Nag Hammadi document is a collection of 114 supposed sayings of Christ in the form of isolated dicta or brief conversations, some known, some entirely new, the whole

work being ascribed to the apostle
Thomas. The collection is dated A.D. 140.

THORN (See PLANTS)

THORN IN THE FLESH Paul's description of a physical ailment that afflicted him and from which he prayed to be relieved (2 Cor 12:7). Some hold that there are hints that it was an inflammation of the eyes. Paul generally dictated his letters, then signed them with his own hand (1 Cor 16:21; 2 Thess 3:17). He wrote the end of Galatians with his own hand, but apologized for the large handwriting (Gal 6:11). His affliction was apparently not only painful but disfiguring. The Galatians did not despise him for it and would have plucked out their own eyes and given them to the apostle, were it possible (4:13–15). He says he was unable to recognize the high priest (Acts 23:5). Some have thought it was a form of recurring malarial fever.

THORNS, CROWN OF (See CROWN)

THOUSAND (Heb. *eleph*, Gr. *chilioi*). Frequently used hyperbolically for a very large but indefinite number, or as the division of a tribe (Num 31:5; Josh 22:14). The word was also used as a tribal subdivision known technically as "a father's house" (Num 1:2, 4, 16; Judg 6:15; 1 Sam 10:19, 21).

THOUSAND YEARS (See KINGDOM OF GOD)

THREE HEBREW CHILDREN, SONG OF (See APOCRYPHA)

THRESHING (Heb. *dûsh, to trample out, hāvat, to beat out or off, dārakh, to tread*, Gr. *aloaō, to tread down*). Threshing was done in one of two ways: (1) by beating the sheaves with a rod or flail or (2) by trampling them under the feet of oxen that pulled a wooden sled around the threshing floor (Isa 28:27). Threshing was done out-of-doors on a hard surface of the ground. The word also had a figurative use (Isa 21:10; 41:15; Mic 4:12–13; 1 Cor 9:10). See also AGRICULTURE; FARMING.

THRESHING FLOOR (Heb. *gōren*, Gr. *halōn*). The place where grain was threshed. Usually clay soil was packed to a hard smooth surface. Sheaves of grain were spread on the floor and trampled by oxen often drawing crude wooden sleds with notched rims (Deut 25:4; Isa 28:27; 1 Cor 9:9). A shovel and fan were used in winnowing the grain (Isa 30:24). Since robbers would visit the floor at threshing time (1 Sam 23:1), the laborers slept there (Ruth 3:4–7). Threshing floors were often

on hills where the night winds could more easily blow away the chaff.

THRONE (Heb. *kissē'*, Gr. *thronos*). A chair of state occupied by one in authority or of high position, such as a high priest, judge, governor, or king (Gen 41:40; 2 Sam 3:10; Neh 3:7; Ps 122:5; Jer 1:15; Matt 19:28). Solomon's throne was an elaborate one (1 Kings 10:18–20; 2 Chron 9:17–19). For ages the throne has been a symbol of authority, exalted position, and majesty (Pss 9:7; 45:6; 94:20; Prov 16:12).

THRUSH (See BIRDS)

THUMB Either the great toe of the foot or the thumb of the hand. The Hebrew word *bōhen*, followed by a modifying term, indicates which is meant (Exod 29:20; Lev 8:23; 14:14). To cut off these members was to handicap a victim and brand him. A son of Reuben was named *Bohan*, "thumb" (Josh 15:6).

THUMMIM (See URIM AND THUMMIM)

THUNDER (Heb. *ra'am, qôl*, Gr. *brontē*). The noise that follows a lightning discharge. In Palestine it was a rare phenomenon during summer months, so if it did occur it was considered a sign of divine displeasure (1 Sam 12:17). A spectacular electrical storm accompanied the plague of hail in Egypt (Exod 9:22–26). Such a display was seen at Sinai (19:16–18). Thunder operates according to natural law (Job 28:26; 38:25). Hebrews considered thunder to be a revelation of God's power (Job 37:2–5; 40:9; Pss 18:13; 29:2–9; Isa 30:30), and it represented God's anger and chastening (1 Sam 2:10).

THUNDER, SONS OF (*huioi brontēs*). The title Jesus gave James and John (Mark 3:17) apparently because of their bold and sometimes rash natures (Matt 20:20–23; Luke 9:54).

THUTMOSE (also Tuthmosis, Thotmes). The word does not appear in the Bible but is a common personal name and one of the great royal names of Egypt. It was given to four kings of the 18th Dynasty. The outstanding Thutmose was Thutmose III, one of the greatest military leaders and administrators of antiquity. Thutmose I made a military expedition beyond the Euphrates and also extended the southern boundary to the Third Cataract. Thutmose II married his half-sister, Hatshepsut, and their daughter became the wife of Thutmose III. Hatshepsut was regent for a period after the death of Thutmose II and even had herself proclaimed "king"; upon her death, Thutmose III burst from obscurity and attempted to eliminate all references to this aunt and mother-in-law. He began his 17 expeditions to Palestine-Syria with a brilliantly strategic victory over an Asiatic coalition at Megiddo. He reached beyond the Euphrates and set up a stele beside that left by his grandfather (Thutmose I). He pushed the southern boundary to Gebel Barkal, just below the Fourth Cataract. The tribute gained from his successes greatly enriched the priesthood of Amon at Thebes, while the influx of foreign products and peoples effected a cosmopolitanism that eventually contributed to the breakdown of the empire that had been built in large measure by the abilities of Thutmose III. For various reasons Thutmose III has been considered the Pharaoh of the Oppression, and his successor, Amenhotep II, the Pharaoh of the Exodus. Thutmose IV, the son of Amenhotep II, is the last of the kings of this name. The Dream Stele, which stills stands between the forelegs of the Sphinx at Giza, relates how he came to the throne.

THYATIRA (thī'à-tī'rà, Gr. *Thyateira*). A city in the province of Asia, on the boundary of Lydia and Mysia. Thyatira has no illustrious history and is scarcely mentioned by ancient writers. Coinage suggests that, lying as it did on a great highway linking two river valleys, Thyatira was a garrison town for many centuries. Its ancient Anatolian deity was a warlike figure armed with a battle-ax and mounted on a charger. An odd coin or two shows a female deity wearing a battlemented crown. The city was a center of commerce, and the records preserve references to more trade guilds than those listed for any other Asian city. Lydia, whom Paul met in Philippi, was a Thyatiran seller of "turkey red," the product of the madder root (Acts 16:14). It is curious to find another woman, nicknamed after the princess who by marriage sealed Ahab's trading partnership with the Phoenicians, leading a party of compromise in the Thyatiran church (Rev 2:20–21). The necessity for membership in a trade guild invited the Christians of Thyatira to compromise and opened the door to many temptations. Thyatira played a significant part in the later history of the church.

TIBERIAS (tī-bē'rĭ-ăs, Gr. *Tiberias*). A city of Herod Antipas, built between the years A.D. 16 and 22 on the western shore of the Sea of Galilee, or the Sea of Tiberias, as John, writing for non-Jewish readers, calls the lake (John 6:1; 21:1). It

was named, of course, after the reigning emperor, Tiberius, reflecting the pro-Roman policy consistently followed by the Herods. Herod built ambitiously. The ruins indicate a wall 3 miles (5 km.) long. He built a palace, a forum, and a great synagogue, for the foundation illustrates strikingly the dual Herodian policy, which sought to combine pro-Roman loyalty with effective patronage of the Jews. Jewish boycott, however, compelled Herod to populate his new town with the lowest elements of the land.

TIBERIAS, SEA OF (See GALILEE, SEA OF)

TIBERIUS (tī-bēr'ĭ-ŭs, Gr. *Tiberios*). Tiberius Julius Caesar Augustus succeeded to the principate on the death of Augustus in A.D. 14, becoming thus the second Roman emperor. Tiberius had great ability and some measure of magnanimity; for, in spite of many unhappy memories, he sought loyally to continue Augustus' policies, foreign and domestic. The rumors of senile debauchery on Capri can be listed with the slanders of earlier years, though there is some evidence of mental disturbance in the later period of the principate. Tiberius died on March 16, A.D. 37. He was the reigning emperor at the time of Christ's death.

TIBHATH (tĭb'hăth, Heb. *tivhath*). In the KJV a city in the kingdom of Zobah, east of the Anti-Lebanon Mountains. David captured it from Hadadezer and sent its treasures to Jerusalem (1 Chron 18:7–9; "Betah" of 2 Sam 8:8). NIV has "Tebah" in both passages.

TIGLATH-PILESER (tĭg'lăth-pĭ-lē'zêr, Assyr. *Tukulti-apil-esharra*, Heb. *tiglath-pil'eser, tilleghath-pilne'ser*). In 745 a usurper took the Assyrian throne and assumed the name Tiglath-Pileser. Tiglath-Pileser III (745–727) injected new vigor into the Assyrian Empire, which had suffered decline after a resurgence of power in the ninth century. He is referred to as "Pul" (2 Kings 15:19; 1 Chron 5:26). His annals list Azariah of Judah among the kings from whom he received tribute; the OT does not relate this account. The annals also mention tribute from Menahem of Samaria, who bought him off (cf. 2 Kings 15:19–20). During the reign of the Judean king Ahaz, Pekah of Israel and Rezin of Syria moved against Judah. Ahaz secured the help of Tiglath-Pileser (2 Kings 16:5–8), who captured Damascus, deported its people, and killed Rezin. He took a number of Israelite cities and exiled the inhabitants to Assyria (2 Kings 15:29).

Campaigns of Tiglath-Pileser

(745–732 B.C.)

Campaign of 738 B.C. ⟹

Campaign of 734 B.C. ·······▸

Campaign of 733 B.C. ────▸

Capture of ─ ─ ─ ─ ▸
Damascus 732 B.C.

Miles 0   20   40
Kms 0   20   40   60

He was also responsible for the deportation of Transjordanian Israelites (1 Chron 5:6, 26). The transfer of peoples to foreign areas was a practical policy designed to reduce the possibility of revolts in conquered regions. Ahaz also requested military aid from him because of invasions by Edomites and Philistines (2 Chron 28:20–21).

TIGRIS (tī'grĭs, Assyr. *Idigalat, arrow*, Heb. *hiddeqel*). One of the two great rivers of the Mesopotamian area. It originates in the Taurus Mountains of Armenia; in its 1,150 miles (1,917 km.) the Tigris flows past famous cities, living and dead: Mosul, Nineveh, Asshur, Samarra, and Baghdad. In the Bible the Tigris is mentioned with the Euphrates and two other streams as rivers that watered the Garden of Eden (Gen 2:14). While standing on the bank of the Tigris, Daniel saw the vision he subsequently recorded (Dan 10:4).

TIKVAH (tĭk'và, Heb. *tiqwah*). 1. The father-in-law of the prophetess Huldah (2 Kings 22:8–14). 2. During the reforms under Ezra a son of another Tikvah was a chief leader (Ezra 10:9–15).

TIKVATH (See TIKVAH)

TILE (Heb. *levēnâh, brick*, Gr. *keramos*). Ancient writing was done with a stylus on blocks of soft clay, which varied in size according to need. Ezekiel used such a tile in drawing a prophetic picture of the doom awaiting Jerusalem (Ezek 4:1–8 KJV; NIV "tablet"). When a permanent record was desired, the inscribed tile was baked in a furnace. So skilled were scribes of the day that many of their tiles remain in perfect condition after 3,000 years.

Roofing tiles (Luke 5:19) refer apparently to clay roofing. Clay tiles were not commonly used as roofing material for houses in Palestine, roofs usually being covered with a mixture of clay and straw.

TILING (See TILE)

TILLER (See OCCUPATIONS AND PROFESSIONS)

TIMAEUS (tĭ-mē'ŭs, Gr. *Timaios*). The father of a blind man whose eyes Jesus opened (Mark 10:46–52), the name Bartimaeus meaning "son of Timaeus."

TIMBREL (see MUSIC AND MUSICAL INSTRUMENTS)

TIME The Roman day began at midnight and had 12 hours (John 11:9). The Hebrew day was reckoned from sunset. There was the cool of the day (Gen 3:8) or twilight (Job 24:15). Mid-morning was when the sun had become hot (1 Sam 11:9). Noon was the heat of the day (Gen 18:1). Night was divided into watches, so that the length of each varied with changing seasons. The first watch came about 3:30 P.M. Midnight was the middle watch (Judg 7:19). Morning watch began about 9:30 A.M. Exod 14:24). It was called cockcrow in NT times (Matt 26:34; Mark 13:35). The watch was so named because of the changing of watchmen and was not a very definite period (Pss 90:4; 119:148; Jer 51:12). Roman influence caused a revision of the watches, so in the days of Christ there were four divisions of the night (Matt 14:25; Mark 6:48), these being marked approximately by 7:00 P.M., 9:30 P.M., midnight, 2:30 A.M., and 5:00 A.M.

In the Scriptures the words translated "time" have varied connotations. A period allotted for a special object, task, or cause was its time (Eccl 3:1; 8:6). A special period of life was "a time," as a period of conception (Gen 18:10, 14) or the days of pregnancy (1 Sam 1:20); any special feast or celebration (Ps 81:3); an occasion for the consummation of divine plans (Job 24:1; Jer 2:27; John 7:6, 8; Acts 3:21; Rom 8:22–23; 1 Tim 6:15); a time for showing affection (Eccl 3:8; Ezek 16:8). The dispensation of grace is the time of salvation (Ps 69:13; Isa 49:8; 2 Cor 6:2). The Greeks' year began on January 1. In Asia Minor the year began with the autumn equinox. Luke's dating of events (1:5; 2:1–2; 3:1) when John the Baptist began his ministry is the only definite fact on which to determine the times of Jesus with any certainty.

The Hebrews used great and well-known events like the Exodus, the Babylonian exile, the building of the temple, and the earthquake (Amos 1:1) as fixed points for indicating the time of other events. In the Maccabean age the beginning of the Seleucid era (312 B.C.) became a starting point.

TIMEUS (See TIMAEUS)

TIMNA (tĭm'nà, Heb. *timna'*, *holding in check*). **1.** A concubine of Esau's son Eliphaz (Gen 36:12). **2.** A Horite woman, sister of Lotan (36:20–22; 1 Chron 1:39). **3.** A chief or clan descended from Esau (Gen 36:40; Timnah KJV). **4.** A son of Eliphaz (1 Chron 1:36).

TIMNAH (tĭm'nà, Heb. *timnāh, thimnāthāh*). **1.** A town on the border of Judah (Josh 15:10), later given to the tribe of Dan and called Thimnathah (19:43 KJV, MOF; Timnah NASB, NIV, RSV). Located at Tibnah, 3 miles (5 km.) SW of Beth Shemesh, it may be the same as Timnah (Judg 14:1–5 KJV, MOF, NEB). **2.** A town in the hill country of Judah (Josh 15:57; Timnath in Gen 38:12–14 KJV, NEB). **3.** A duke (chief) in Edom (1 Chron 1:51). **4.** A town in south Judah (2 Chron 28:18).

TIMNATH (See TIMNAH)

TIMNATH-HERES (See TIMNATH-SERAH)

TIMNATH-SERAH (tĭm'năth-hē'rēz, Heb. *timnath serah*). The same as Timnath Heres (Judg 2:9), a village in Ephraim that Joshua requested as an inheritance (Josh 19:50; cf. 24:30).

TIMOTHEUS (See TIMOTHY)

TIMOTHY (tĭm'ô-thē, Gr. *Timotheos, honoring God*). Paul's spiritual child (1 Tim 1:2; 2 Tim 1:2), later the apostle's fellow-traveler and official representative. His character was a blend of amiability and faithfulness in spite of natural timidity. One must read Philippians 2:19–22 to know how highly the apostle esteemed this young friend. None of Paul's companions is mentioned as often and is with him as constantly as is Timothy. That this relationship was of an enduring nature is clear from 2 Timothy 4:9, 21. Paul knew that he could count on

Timothy. He was the kind of person who in spite of his youth (1 Tim 4:12), his natural reserve and timidity (1 Cor 16:10; 2 Tim 1:7), and his frequent ailments (1 Tim 5:23), was willing to leave his home to accompany the apostle on dangerous journeys, to be sent on difficult errands, and to remain to the very end Christ's faithful servant.

In the popular mind the distinction between Timothy and Titus is not always clear. Both of these men were Paul's worthy fellow workers but in different ways. Titus was more of a leader; Timothy, more of a follower. Titus was resourceful, a man of initiative in a good cause. One finds in him something of the aggressiveness of Paul. (See TITUS.) Timothy, on the other hand, was shy and reserved. Nevertheless, he manifested his complete willingness even when he was required to do things that ran counter to his natural shyness.

Timothy is first mentioned in Acts 16:1, from which passage it may be inferred that he was an inhabitant of Lystra (cf. 20:4). He was the offspring of a mixed marriage: he had a Greek pagan father and a devout Jewish mother, Eunice (Acts 16:1; 2 Tim 1:5). From the days of his childhood Timothy had been instructed in the sacred writings of the OT (3:15). In the manner of devout Israelites his grandmother Lois and mother Eunice had nurtured him (1:5). All three became followers of Christ on Paul's first missionary journey. Timothy knew about the persecutions and sufferings that the missionaries (Paul and Barnabas) had experienced on that first journey (3:11), even before he joined Paul in active missionary labor. Timothy was ordained by the elders, Paul himself taking part in this solemn laying on of hands.

Timothy accompanied the missionaries to Philippi and Thessalonica. He also helped the others in the next place to which they went, Berea. Here he and Silas were left behind to give spiritual support to the infant church, while Paul went on to Athens (Acts 17:10–15). At Paul's request Timothy left Berea and met Paul at Athens. Afterward he was sent back to Thessalonica to strengthen the brothers there (1 Thess 3:1–2). Both Silas and Timothy joined Paul in Corinth (Acts 18:1, 5). On the third missionary journey Timothy was again with the apostle during the lengthy Ephesus ministry. From there he was sent to Macedonia and to Corinth (Acts 19:21–22; 1 Cor 4:17; 16:10). When Paul arrived in Macedonia, Timothy rejoined him (2 Cor 1:1). Afterward he accompanied the apostle to

Corinth (Rom 16:21), was with him on the return to Macedonia (Acts 20:3-4), and was waiting for him at Troas (20:5). He was probably also with Paul in Jerusalem (1 Cor 16:3). During Paul's first imprisonment at Rome the two were again in close contact (Phil 1:1; Col 1:1; Philem 1). When Paul expected to be released in a little while, he told the Philippians that he expected to send Timothy to them soon (Phil 2:19).

Timothy was next found in Ephesus, where the apostle joined him. Paul, on leaving, asked Timothy to remain at this place (1 Tim 1:3). While there, Timothy one day received a letter from Paul, the letter we now call 1 Timothy. Later, in another letter, Paul, writing from Rome as a prisoner facing death, urged his friend to come to him before winter (2 Tim 4:9, 21). Whether the two ever actually saw each other again is not recorded.

TIMOTHY, LETTERS TO (See PASTORAL LETTERS)

TIN (See MINERALS)

TINKLING The sound of small bells that women wore on a chain fastened to anklets. The tinkling (Isa 3:16 JB, KJV, MLB, NASB; jingling NEB, NIV) to) is caused by the affected pose and short, jerky steps. In 1 Corinthians 13:1 the tinkling (KJV; clanging NASB, NEB, NIV, RSV; clashing JB, MLB) is the noise made by a cymbal.

TIPHSAH (tĭf'sà, Heb. *tiphsah*). 1. A town on the northern border of Solomon's kingdom (1 Kings 4:24). It was an important city on the Euphrates River where the caravan route from Egypt and Syria passed en route to countries to the east. 2. A town on the Jordan, apparently not far from Tirzah, whose inhabitants were massacred by Menahem (2 Kings 15:16).

TIRE (Heb. *pe'ēr, headdress*). An ornamental headdress (Ezek 24:17, 23 KJV; NIV "turban") worn by Aaron (Exod 39:28 ASV; NIV "headbands") and women (Isa 3:20 ASV; NIV "headdresses").

TIRHAKAH (tûr'hà-kà, Heb. *tirhāqâh*). An Egyptian king, the third and last king of the 25th, or Ethiopian, Dynasty. There was much confusion in the Egyptian political situation (Isa 19) and Isaiah warned about relying on Egypt. Tirhakah was commander of the army of Shabaka, his uncle and first king of the 25th Dynasty, and he led the Egyptian armies in their initial conflict with Assyria. Isaiah 37:9 and 2 Kings 19:9 state that

Sennacherib, while besieging Judean cities, heard that Tirhakah was coming against him. Sennacherib was successful against Tirhakah, but the loss of his troops forced him back to Assyria (2 Kings 19:35-36; Isa 37:36-37). Tirhakah became king about 689 B.C. and for a number of years was not threatened by the Assyrians, but later he was defeated by Esarhaddon and by Ashurbanipal. Being driven south, he did retain rule of Upper Egypt.

TIRSHATHA (tûr-shā'thà, Heb. *tirshāthā', revered*). In the KJV the title of the governor of Judah under Persia. Zerubbabel (Ezra 2:63; Neh 7:65, 70) and Nehemiah (Neh 8:9; 10:1) bore the title. NIV has "governor."

TIRZAH (tûr'zà, Heb. *tirtsâh*). 1. The youngest daughter of Zelophehad (Num 26:33; Josh 17:3). 2. A town 6 miles (10 km.) east of Samaria captured by Joshua (Josh 12:24). It must have been noted for its beauty, since Solomon compared his beautiful Shulammite woman to the beauty of Tirzah (Song of Songs 6:4). With the division of the kingdom after the death of Solomon, it became the capital of the northern kingdom (1 Kings 14:17). In it reigned Baasha (15:21-33), his son Elah, and Zimri (16:6-15). Omri defeated Tibni and, since Zimri had destroyed the palace in Tirzah (16:18), moved the capital to Samaria (16:23-24). While Uzziah ruled in Judah, Menahem of Tirzah conspired against Shallum of Israel, killed him, and began a ten-year wicked reign (2 Kings 15:16-18).

TISHBITE, TISHBE (tĭsh'bīt, Heb. *tĭshbî*). Elijah is mentioned as a Tishbite in 1 Kings 17:1. The NIV gives a good reading, "Elijah the Tishbite, from Tishbe in Gilead." The place has been identified, with some probability, with the modern el-Istib, a little west of Mahanaim.

TITHE (tīth, Heb. *ma'ăsēr*, Gr. *dekatē, the tenth*). Just when and where the idea arose of making the tenth the rate for paying tribute to rulers and of offering gifts as a religious duty cannot be determined. History reveals that it existed in Babylon in ancient times, as well as in Persia, Egypt, and even China. Abraham knew of it when he migrated from Ur (Gen 14:17-20). Since Melchizedek was a priest of the Most High, it is certain that by Abraham's day the giving of tithes had been recognized as a holy deed (see Heb 7:4). Samuel warned Israel that the king whom they were demanding would exact tithes of their grain and flocks (1 Sam

8:10–18). When Jacob made his covenant with God at Bethel it included payment of tithes (Gen 28:16–22).

It was a long time before definite legal requirements were set on tithing, hence customs in paying it varied. At first the tither was entitled to share his tithe with the Levites (Deut 14:22–23). After the Levitical code had been completed, tithes belonged exclusively to the Levites (Num 18:21). A penalty of 20 percent of the tithe was exacted from one who sold his tithes and refused to use the money to pay for a substitute (Lev 27:31). The Levites in turn gave a tenth to provide for the priests (Num 18:25–32). The temple was the place to which tithes were taken (Deut 12:5–12).

To make sure that no deceit would be practiced regarding tithing, each Hebrew was compelled to make a declaration of honesty before the Lord (Deut 26:13–15). Was there only one tithe each year or was the third-year tithe an extra one? Confusion exists about this, even among Hebrew scholars themselves. As the needs for funds increased with the expansion of the temple service, a third-year tithe (all for the use of the Levites and those in need) was exacted.

By the time of Christ, Roman rule had greatly affected the economic life of Judea, hence it was difficult for people to tithe. But that the laws regarding the tenth were still observed is shown in that the Pharisees tithed even the herbs that were used in seasoning food (Matt 23:23; Luke 11:42).

TITTLE (tĭt'l, Gr. *keraia, a horn*). A small, horn-shaped mark used to indicate accent in Hebrew (Matt 5:18; Luke 16:17 KJV). In Matthew 5:18 it is used with "jot" (Gr. *iōta*) to denote a minute requirement of the law.

TITUS (tī'tŭs, Gr. *Titos*). A convert, friend, and helper of Paul (Titus 1:4), in the NT mentioned only in Paul's letters, especially in 2 Corinthians. He was a Greek, a son of Gentile parents (Gal 2:3). After his conversion he accompanied Paul to Jerusalem, where Paul rejected the demand of the Judaists that Titus be circumcised. Hence, Titus became a person of significance for the principle of Gentile admission to the church solely on the basis of faith in Christ. During Paul's third missionary journey Titus was assigned missions to Corinth to solve its vexing problems (1 Cor 1–6; 2 Cor 2:13; 7:5–16) and to encourage material assistance to the needy at Jerusalem (2 Cor 8). Much later Paul left Titus in Crete to organize its churches (Titus 1:4–5). He

was requested to meet Paul at Nicopolis (3:12). Titus was consecrated, courageous, resourceful. He knew how to handle the quarrelsome Corinthians, the dishonest Cretans, and the belligerent Dalmatians (2 Tim 4:10).

TITUS, LETTER TO (See PASTORAL LETTERS)

TITUS JUSTUS (See TITIUS JUSTUS)

TOAH (tō'à, Heb. *tôah*). An ancestor of Samuel (1 Chron 6:34, Nahath in 6:26). He is called Tohu in 1 Samuel 1:1.

TOB (tŏb, Heb. *tôv*). A fertile district in Syria, extending NE from Gilead. Jephthah took refuge here (Judg 11:1–3). When Ammon was preparing to fight David, they hired 12,000 men of Tob to fight for them (2 Sam 10:6, 8).

TOBIAH (tō-bī'à, Heb. *tôvîyâh, the LORD is good*). **1.** A family among the exiles who returned to Jerusalem under Zerubbabel (Ezra 2:59–60; Neh 7:61–62). **2.** An Ammonite, half Jew, who with Sanballat tried to hinder Nehemiah in repairing Jerusalem (2:10, 19; 13:4ff.).

TOBIJAH (tō-bī'jà, Heb. *tôvîyâh, the LORD is good*). **1.** A Levite whom Jehoshaphat sent to teach the law (2 Chron 17:7–9). **2.** One of the exiles who returned to Jerusalem from Babylon bringing gold and silver (Zech 6:9–15).

TOBIT, BOOK OF (See APOCRYPHA)

TOCHEN (See TOKEN)

TOGARMAH (tō-gàr'mà, Heb. *tôghar-mâh*). A man who appears in two genealogies as a son of Gomer (Gen 10:3; 1 Chron 1:6), who is a descendant of Japheth. Ezekiel 27:14 states that Beth Togarmah traded "work horses, war horses and mules" for Tyrian merchandise. Later the prophet lists among the forces of Gog: "Beth Togarmah from the far north" (Ezek 38:6). Some have equated Togarmah with a province between the Euphrates River and the Antitaurus Mountains. The prophet may refer to a people or nation more distant from Palestine.

TOI (See TOU)

TOKEN (Heb. *'ôth, sign, token*, Gr. *endeigma, endeixis, syssēmon, sēmeion*). A word that in the KJV of the OT is used practically synonymously with "sign" (so NIV) (Exod 13:9, 16). In Numbers 17:10 and Joshua 2:12 it means a memorial of something past. In the NT (KJV) "token" is self-explanatory (Mark 14:44, NIV "signal"; Phil 1:28, NIV "sign";

First century A.D. Jewish ossuary, with incised decoration, in which the bones of the dead were placed after the flesh had decayed. Courtesy Zev Radovan

2 Thess 1:5; 3:17, NIV "evidence," "distinguishing mark").

TOLA (tō'là, Heb. *tôlā'*). **1.** One of Issachar's sons who migrated to Egypt and founded a tribal family (Gen 46:1–13). **2.** Son of Puah, of the tribe of Issachar, who judged Israel 23 years (Judg 10:1–2).

TOMB (Gr. *taphos*). It may mean a chamber, vault, or crypt, either underground or above. It may refer to a pretentious burying place on a special site. It may be a beehive structure where many bodies can be placed. The Hebrews' burials remained simple, most burying sites being unmarked. Some kings were interred in a vault in Jerusalem (1 Kings 2:10; 11:43). Some mention their "father's tomb" (2 Sam 2:32; Neh 2:3).

Tombs of NT times were either caves or they were holes dug into stone cliffs. Since only grave clothes are mentioned in connection with tombs, it seems certain that the Jews used neither caskets nor sarcophagi. Tombs carried no inscriptions, no paintings. Embalming, learned in Egypt (Gen 50:2), was soon a lost art (John 11:39). A general opening gave access to vaults that opened on ledges to provide support for the stone doors. The door to such a grave weighed from one to three tons (.9 to 2.7 metric tons), hence the miracle of the stone being rolled away from Jesus' tomb (Luke 24:2; John 20:1).

TONGS (Heb. *melqāhayim*). The word usually means wicktrimmers (KJV "snuffers," "snuffdish," Exod 25:38; Num 4:9); in Isaiah 6:6 it is "tongs." In 1 Kings 7:49 and 2 Chronicles 4:21 it could be either. In Isaiah 44:12 the KJV

"tongs" is translated "axe" in ASV, "tool" in NIV.

TONGUE (Heb. *lāshôn*, Gr. *glōssa*). **1.** An organ of the body, used sometimes in drinking (lapping) as Gideon's men did (Judg 7:5; see also Ps 68:23; Zech 14:12; Mark 7:33; Rev 16:10). **2.** An organ of speech (Job 27:4; Ps 35:28; Prov 15:2; Mark 7:35). **3.** A language or dialect (Gen 10:5, 20; Deut 28:49; Dan 1:4; Acts 1:19; 2:8; 10:46). **4.** A people or race having a common language (Isa 66:18; Dan 3:4; Rev 5:9; 10:11). **5.** The figurative uses of the word are interesting. The tongue can be sharpened, i.e., made to utter caustic words (Pss 64:3; 140:3). It is a sharp sword (57:4). It is gentle when it uses quieting language (Prov 25:15). Ranting is a rage of tongues (Ps 31:20; Hos 7:16). The tongue is the pen of an eager writer (Ps 45:1), a shrewd antagonist (52:2). The tongue of the just is a treasure (Prov 10:20; 12:18) and a mark of wisdom (Isa 50:4). It is like a bow (Jer 9:3), an arrow (9:8), and a lash (18:18). The miracle at Pentecost included "tongues of fire" (Acts 2:3). The tongue is little but can do great things (James 3:5, 8). In Acts 1:19; 2:8; 21:40; 22:2 the original word is *dialektos*, "dialect," meaning "language."

TONGUES, CONFUSION OF The Tower of Babel presents an answer to an otherwise insoluble mystery and reveals God's anger against human vanity and disobedience (Gen 11:1–9). That there was originally a common language among people becomes more certain as linguistic research progresses. God, who designed the media of speech, in an instant made the modifications in speech that caused such confusion.

TONGUES, GIFT OF A spiritual gift (Mark 16:17; Acts 2:1–13; 10:44–46; 19:6; 1 Cor 12, 14) that appeared on the Day of Pentecost with the outpouring of the Holy Spirit on the assembled believers (Acts 2:1–13). The *external* phenomena heralding the Spirit's coming were followed by the *internal* filling of all those gathered together there. The immediate result was that they "began to speak in other tongues." "Began" implies that the phenomenon recorded was now first imparted and that it was afterward repeated (cf. 8:17–18; 10:44–46; 19:6). The context makes it clear that "other tongues" means languages different from their own, and by implication, previously unknown to the speakers, for the amazement of the crowd, coming from many lands, was caused by the fact that *Galileans* could speak these varied languages; the utterances were praise to God (2:11; 10:46). The gift was not designed merely to facilitate the preaching of the gospel; the message in 2:14–36 was not delivered in more than one language. There is no express NT instance of this gift being used to evangelize others. There is no indication that the 3,000 converts at Pentecost received the gift.

It is not stated that the Samaritans received this gift when the Spirit was imparted to them, but the request of Simon to buy the power to bestow the Spirit indicates that some *external* manifestation did result (Acts 8:14–19). The Pentecostal phenomenon clearly appeared again when the Holy Spirit was poured out on the Gentiles in the house of Cornelius (10:44–46). Here again it served as a miraculous token of the divine approval and acceptance of these Gentile believers (11:15–17; 15:7–9). The appearance of the phenomenon in connection with the 12 disciples at Ephesus (19:6), who dispensationally stood before Pentecost, marked the full incorporation of this group into the church and authenticated Paul's teaching.

The gift of tongues is mentioned by Paul as one of the spiritual gifts so richly bestowed on the Corinthian believers. Their reaction to this gift drew forth Paul's discussion of the varied gifts. They are enumerated, compared, and evaluated by their usefulness to the church. He lists the gifts twice and places tongues and their interpretation at the very bottom of the scale (1 Cor 12:8–10, 28–30), thus rebuking the Corinthians' improper evaluation of this spectacular gift. He emphasized the comparative value of tongues and prophecy by insisting that "five intelligible words" spoken in the church were of more value than "ten thousand words in a tongue" not understood (14:19). Paul felt it necessary to regulate the use of tongues in their assembly; the ideal place for their exercise was in private (14:28). He insisted that not more than two or three speak in tongues, and that they do so in turn, and one should interpret; no one was to speak in tongues if no interpreter was present (14:27–28). Speaking in tongues was not prohibited (14:39), but intelligent preaching in understandable words was vastly superior. He further insisted that women were not to speak in their meetings (14:34).

Two views are held as to the exact nature of the Corinthian "tongues." One view holds that they were foreign languages that the speakers were miraculously enabled to speak without having previously learned them. This view is demanded by Acts 2:1–13, unless it is maintained that the two phenomena are quite distinct. That they were intelligible utterances is urged from the fact that they could be interpreted and were the vehicle of prayer, praise, and thanksgiving (1 Cor 14:14–17).

Modern commentators, however, generally hold that the Corinthian tongues were not identical with the tongues at Pentecost but were ecstatic outbursts of prayer and praise in which the utterances often became abnormal and incoherent and the connection with the speaker's own conscious intellectual activity was suspended. It is held that the utterances were incomprehensible to the speaker as well as to the audience (14:14) and that the resultant edification was emotional only (14:4). But 14:4 may only mean that the person's understanding was "unfruitful" to others. Its advocates further hold that this view is indicated in the fact that interpretation was likewise a special gift (12:10).

From 14:27–28 it is clear that this speaking in tongues was not uncontrollable. It was very different from the religious frenzy that marked some pagan rites in which the worshiper lost control both of reason and the power of will. Any manifestation of tongues that is not under the speaker's control is thereby suspect (14:32).

TONGUES OF FIRE One of the phenomena that occurred at the outpouring of the Holy Spirit on the Day of Pentecost (Acts 2:3) as they were all filled with the Holy Spirit. The tongues of fire were symbolic of the Holy Spirit, who came in power on the church.

TOOLS In the Bible a variety of tools used by the ancients are mentioned. These may be grouped into various categories: **1.** Cutting tools: knife (Gen 22:6, 10; Judg 19:29), saw (Isa 10:15), sickle (Joel 3:13), ax (Deut 19:5; 20:19), reaping hook (Isa 44:12), pruning hook (2:4; 18:5). **2.** Boring tools: the awl (Exod 21:6; Deut 15:17). **3.** Forks and shovels (1 Sam 13:21; 1 Kings 7:40, 45), tongs (Exod 25:38). **4.** Carpentry tools: hammer (Judg 5:26), plane (Isa 44:13), plumb line (Amos 7:8), level (2 Kings 21:13). **5.** Drawing tools: chisel and compass (Isa 44:13). **6.** Measuring tools: line (1 Kings 7:23; 2 Kings 21:13), measuring rod (Ezek 40:3–8; Rev 11:1). **7.** Tilling tools: plowshare and mattock (1 Sam 13:20–21). **8.** Metalworking tools: anvil (Isa 41:7), file (1 Sam

Assyrian men carrying work tools, on relief from the palace of Sennacherib at Nineveh, c. 690 B.C. Reproduced by courtesy of the Trustees of the British Museum

13:21). **9.** Stone-working tools: chisel (Exod 20:25), saw (1 Kings 7:9).

TOOTH (See TEETH)

TOPAZ (See MINERALS)

TOPHETH, TOPHET (tō'phĕth, tō'phĕt, Heb. *tōpheth*). An area in the Valley of Hinnom where human sacrifices were made to Molech (2 Kings 23:10; Jer 7:31). A place of burning was prepared by the Lord for the king of Assyria (Isa 30:33). The name of the place would be changed to the Valley of Slaughter because of the many people who would be killed there (Jer 7:32–33; 19:6). Josiah desecrated this place so that it no longer could be used for idolatrous practices (2 Kings 23:10).

TORAH (tō'rà, Heb. *tôrâh, direction, instruction, law*). The common Hebrew word for "law," appearing over 200 times in the OT. The word is used for human instruction such as takes place between caring parents and beloved children (e.g., Prov 4:1–2 KJV). "Law" is both God's "authoritative imposition" (Deut 6:1–2) and his loving and caring "instruction" of his people.

The division of the Hebrew Scriptures into the Law (*tôrâh*), the Prophets, and the Writings comes from ancient times.

The Samaritans have only the Pentateuch for their Scripture.

TORCH (See LAMP)

TORTOISE (See ANIMALS)

TOU (tō'ū, Heb. *tō'û*). King of Hamath who sent presents to David for conquering their common enemy Hadadezer of Zobah (1 Chron 18:9–10). The variant "Toi" is found in 2 Samuel 8:9–10 KJV.

TOW (Heb. *ne'ōreth*). The coarse and broken part of flax ready for spinning. In the OT it is used as an example of easily inflammable material (Judg 16:9 KJV; NIV "string"; Isa 1:31 KJV; NIV "tinder").

TOWER (Heb. *mighdāl, mighdōl, bāhan, misgāv, pinnâh*, Gr. *pyrgos*). A lofty structure used for purposes of protection or attack: to defend a city wall, particularly at a gate or a corner in the wall (2 Chron 14:7; 26:9); to protect flocks and herds and to safeguard roads (2 Kings 17:9; 2 Chron 26:10; 27:4); to observe and to attack a city (Isa 23:13); to protect a vineyard (Matt 21:33).

TOWN The translation of several words used in the OT: *bānôth*, literally "daughters," always in the plural, refers to the towns surrounding a city. Cities listed as having towns are Heshbon, Jazer (Num 21:25, 32; KJV "villages," NIV "settlements"); Ekron, Ashdod (Josh 15:45–

47); Beth Shan, Ibleam, Dor, Endor, Taanach, Megiddo (17:11; Judg 1:27); Areor (11:26); Jair, Kenath (1 Chron 2:23); Bethel, Gezer, Shechem, Ayyah (7:28); Ono, Lod (8:12); Gath (18:1); Jeshanah, Ephron (2 Chron 13:19); Soco, Timnah, Ginzo (28:18 ASV; KJV and NIV "villages"); Kiriath Arba, Dibon, Jekabzeel, Beersheba, Meconah, Azekah (Neh 11:25–30 ASV, KJV"villages"; NIV "villages" and "settlements"). All the "daughters" of these cities were small towns without walls: *hawwôth*, "village, tent village" (Num 32:41; Josh 13:30; 1 Kings 4:13; 1 Chron 2:23), sometimes in compound names—Havvoth Jair (Deut 3:14; Judg 10:4). These villages may have been the dwelling places of nomads, that is, tent dwellings. *Hâtsēr*, "settled abode, village" in Genesis 25:16 was a village of Ishmaelites, probably a movable one made up of tents; but this word usually means villages without walls around them. *'Ir*, the common Hebrew word for "city," can indicate an unwalled town (Deut 3:5); a town with gates and bars (1 Sam 23:7); "country town" (27:5). Other words used are *qîr*, "wall," once translated "town" (Josh 2:15 KJV; ASV and NIV omit); and *perāzôth*, "open region, hamlet" (Zech 2:4, KJV "towns," ASV "villages," NIV "city"). The latter word denotes villages in the open country in contrast to those located in the mountains.

The only NT word that, strictly speaking, means "town" (*kōmopolis*) denotes a community larger than a village but smaller than a city; it occurs only once (Mark 1:38 KJV, RSV; NIV "village"). Another word, *kōmē*, "village," is rendered "town" ten times in KJV (Matt 10:11; Mark 8:23, 26–27; Luke 5:17; 9:6, 12; John 7:42; 11:1, 30). NIV occasionally follows this but usually, like ASV, prefers "village."

TOWN CLERK (See OCCUPATIONS AND PROFESSIONS)

TRACHONITIS, TRACONITIS (trăk-ō-nī'tĭs, Gr. *Trachōnitis, rough region*). A volcanic region SE of Damascus, the tetrarchy of Philip (Luke 3:1). The "region of Argob" (Deut 3:4), part of the realm of Og of Bashan, probably included this wild, infertile area.

TRADE AND TRAVEL Abraham came from a trading port, Ur of the Chaldees, which stood in those days at the head of the Persian Gulf. The most negotiable route between East and West ran this way. Abraham was rich in gold and silver

Turn-of-the-century photograph of an Arab merchant from Bethlehem traveling on his donkey. Courtesy University Library, Istanbul

as well as in the nomad wealth of flocks and herds (Gen 13:2; 24:22, 53).

Slave trading formed a profitable sideline, and it is significant that Joseph was sold to a company of Ishmaelites carrying myrrh into Egypt (Gen 37:25). The rich imports of the land were balanced by an export trade in corn, and by tribute money from the neighboring spheres of Egyptian dominance. Corn was paid for in weighed silver (41:57; 42:3, 25, 35; 43:11).

The first organized commerce of the Hebrew people was under Solomon, whose farsighted trading ventures were inspired by the Phoenician mercantile cities of Tyre and Sidon. It is possible that the building of the temple first made the Phoenicians aware of the market to be found in their own hinterland, and of the profit to be gained from a partnership with the people who dominated the land route to the Gulf of Aqabah. Cedar for the architectural projects of David and Solomon was collected at Tyre (1 Kings 5:6, 9; 2 Chron 2:16). The partnership thus begun was extended in a joint venture out of Ezion Geber at the head of the Gulf of Aqabah, down the Red Sea to Ophir and India. Hiram king of Tyre supplied the pilots (1 Kings 9:27–28; 10:11). Ophir was in all probability in southern Arabia, but the cargoes mentioned in 1 Kings 10:22 suggest a trading connection with India. A larger type of vessel was used in this ocean-going commerce, the "ships of Tarshish" (10:22 KJV). Tarshish was probably Tartessos in Spain, and for such distant and exacting voyaging the Phoenicians had developed a sturdy type of vessel called by this name. An "Indiaman" or a "China clipper" in the days of more recent ocean commerce did not necessarily journey to the lands mentioned in the title. The text quoted seems to imply that Solomon's traders were speedily throwing off the tutelage of Tyre and venturing forth on their own. Judea supplied Phoenicia with wheat, honey, oil, and balm (1 Kings 5:11).

Tyrian traders brought fish into Jerusalem and distressed Nehemiah by their Sabbath trading (Neh 13:16). The timber trade too continued into postcaptivity days, and Ezra made arrangements similar to those of Solomon to secure his supplies of Lebanese timber (1 Kings 5:6, 9; 2 Chron 2:16; Ezra 3:7). Oil was also exported to Egypt (Hos 12:1), and a small domestic export trade in woven goods from Judea seems to be implied in Proverbs 31:24.

When the Hebrew monarchy fell apart after Solomon's death, it is possible that an interesting commercial situation may have arisen. Israel, the northern kingdom, must have inherited the profitable but seductive alliance with the Phoenician trading towns. Jezebel, daughter of the prince of Sidon, married Ahab to seal this partnership. The southern kingdom, however, lay across communication lines to Aqabah and the Red Sea, and there is every evidence that Judah had reverted, after Solomon, to an agricultural economy with nothing more than petty trading. Apart from a half-hearted attempt by Jehoshaphat to revive it (1 Kings 22:48), the eastern trade seems to have vanished with the king who inspired and ordered it. It may have been at this time that Phoenicians, denied the convenient route down the Red Sea, discovered the sea route to India by way of the Cape of Good Hope. A passage in Herodotus (4:42) seems to imply that the intrepid traders succeeded in this amazing achievement. The prosperity of the Phoenician cities certainly continued, and Ezekiel 27 is an eloquent record of the wide and tireless trading activity of Tyre. Ahab's prosperity is also vouched for by the archaeologists' confirmation of the king's "ivory palace" (1 Kings 22:39).

The commercial consequences of the break with Baal worship and the death of Jezebel is an interesting speculation. Tyre, without great difficulty, could strangle the economic life of Israel. Tyre's dependence on the hinterland for primary produce would provide a strong deterrent, but there is no doubt that the choice on Mt. Carmel with which Elijah confronted the people involved economic as well as theological considerations. The Hebrew kingdoms from this time onward fell into the background as far as commerce was concerned. The Captivity brought vast depopulation, and the restored Israel was a largely agricultural economy. Internal interchange of goods was vigorous enough from earliest times, and provisions in the law stressed fairness of dealing, and honesty in weights and measures (Lev 19:35–36; Deut 25:13–16). The petty trading in the temple, castigated by Christ, was a sample of the seamier side of this internal commerce; but the foreign trade, which invited investment (Eccl 11:1) and brought great wealth, was no more. Palestine at the close of the OT and in the time of Christ was a poor land.

The fascinating account of the last journey of Paul to Rome (Acts 27), first in a ship from Adramyttium and then in an Alexandrian freighter, probably under charter to the Roman government for the transport of Egyptian corn to the capital, gives a firsthand picture of the hazards of trade, and of the navigation, the ships, and the management of Mediterranean commerce.

Certain localities became famous for special commodities. Lydia (Acts 16:14), "a dealer in purple cloth from the city of Thyatira" in Asia Minor, was found at Philippi in Macedonia in pursuit of her trade. Corinthian bronze and the Cilician cloth that was the raw material of Paul's "tentmaking" were probably distributed, locally or abroad, by similar private enterprise (18:3). The imagery of John's apocalyptic letter to Laodicea (Rev 3:14–18) is based partly on the trade and industry of the rich Asian town. An important item of trade in Ephesus, now that the harbor was silting and the port losing its trade and prosperity to Smyrna, was the manufacture of silver shrines of Artemis to sell to the pilgrims and tourists who visited the famous temple.

Ramsay's illuminating research revealed a Laodicean trade in valuable wool garments of various kinds. There is also evidence of a Laodicean eye salve, based probably on the thermal mud of the nearby Hierapolis. Hence the taunt in the letter about "white garments," and the anointing of the eyes of the spirit with a more effective medicine. Another of the seven churches of the Apocalypse was a center of trade and commerce. More trade guilds are named in the records of Thyatira than in those of any other Asian city. Lydia's trade (Acts 16:14) possibly fell under the category of the dyers. They brewed a red dye, perhaps the modern turkey red, from the madder root, which grows abundantly in the district. This "purple" was nearer in color to scarlet than blue, and Lydia's presence in Macedonia, 500 miles (833 km.) away, suggests that the commodity was an important export.

In Ephesus the guild of silversmiths and allied trades exerted enough pressure on authority and public opinion to check the free activities of Paul in the city. The famous letter of Pliny (*Ep.* 10.96), in which the repression of vigorous Christian activity in Bithynia in A.D. 112 is vividly described, is fairly clear indication that the guild of the butchers, alarmed at the falling-off in sales of sacrificial meat, was the ally of the pagan priesthoods in rousing the official persecution of the thriving church. Nor was it easy for a Christian to prosper in his trade or business if he attempted to refrain from membership in the appropriate guild or participation in its activities. Since those activities included periodic feasts in the temple of the god or goddess whose patronage was traditionally acknowledged by the trade or calling concerned, what was the faithful Christian to do? Hence the activities of the "Nicolaitans," the "followers of Balaam" and of "Jezebel" of Thyatira are castigated by Jude, Peter, and John. The simple functions and operations of trade and commerce may thus have proved a source of embarrassment, controversy, and division in the early church.

Trade implied travel, and many of the great journeys of the ancient world were made in the pursuit of commerce and remain unrecorded. Those who pioneered the trade routes from the Euphrates and the Persian Gulf to the Indus civilization and Ceylon must have been intrepid voyagers. Other motives for travel included colonization, exploration, migration, pilgrimage, courier service, and exile.

The necessities of preaching and teaching caused widespread travel in both Greek and Roman times, most strikingly illustrated in the journeys of Paul. It is traditionally believed that Thomas traveled to India, and a large Christian group in that subcontinent is traditionally believed to have descended from his original foundation. Apollos (Acts 18:24–28) had moved about, no doubt on teaching missions, between Alexandria, Corinth, and Ephesus.

Travel was not without its hazards. Paul (2 Cor 11:25–27) spoke of the perils of road and seaway. Luke's superb account of the voyage and wreck of the Alexandrian grain ship is further illustration (Acts 27). In NT times, however, travel was rather safer by land than it has been at most periods in history.

Roads were the great contribution of the Romans to Mediterranean civilization, and roads promoted the rapid movement of travelers and contributed substantially to their safety by facilitating the rapid movement of troops.

Regular passenger services by land or sea were unknown, and there is no evidence that the pattern of procedure changed from OT times to New. Travelers evidently made their own arrangements, attached themselves to official parties, accompanied caravans, and coordinated their movements with those of trade and commerce.

TRADE GUILDS Not trade unions in the modern sense, their functions were primarily social. Records exist of guilds of bakers, bankers, doctors, architects, producers of linen and woolen goods, dyers, workers in metal or stone or clay, builders, carpenters, farmers, pastry cooks, barbers, embalmers, and transport workers. The *collegia* satisfied the need of the humble for the pleasures of social intercourse and the dignity of self-expression. It was apparently the guild of the butchers that precipitated the persecution of A.D. 112 in Bithynia, according to Pliny. The guild banquets, with associated worship of the patron deity and the compromising fellowship involved, were probably the problem of 1 Corinthians. The attempt of certain groups to work out a form of compromise, so essential to the social comfort, and indeed livelihood of many Christians, led to strong reproaches (2 Peter, Jude, Rev 2–3).

TRADITION (Gr. *paradosis, a giving over*, by word of mouth or in writing). This term does not occur in the Hebrew OT. There are three types of tradition mentioned in the NT. First, the most common use, is the kind of tradition handed down by the Jewish fathers or elders that constituted the oral law, regarded by many of the Jews as of equal authority with the revealed law of Moses. Indeed, the Pharisees tended to make these traditions of even greater authority than the Scriptures. The Pharisees were incensed at Christ because he disregarded their traditions and also permitted his disciples to do so (Matt 15:2–6; Mark 7:1–13). Paul refers to his former zeal for the traditions of his fathers (Gal 1:14). Some scholars hold that Colossians 2:8 refers to Judaistic heresies, but the emphasis seems to be on the *human*, not necessarily Jewish, origin of these teachings, thus a second type of tradition. The third type of tradition is the gospel truths that the apostle Paul taught (1 Cor 11:2 ASV; 2 Thess 2:15; 3:6 KJV).

TRAIN 1. Hebrew *hayil*, "army," a much used word that has the meaning of a train or retinue of a monarch, as in the case of the queen of Sheba (1 Kings 10:2 KJV; NIV "caravan"). **2.** Hebrew *shûl*, "skirt" of a robe, best translated "train" (Isa 6:1). **3.** Hebrew *hānak*, "to train up" is used in connection with rearing a child (Prov 22:6). **4.** Greek *sōphronizō*, "to discipline," occurs once in the NT (Titus 2:4).

Drawing of a bust of Trajan, Roman emperor from A.D. 98 to 117. Courtesy Carta, Jerusalem

TRAJAN (trā'jăn). Trajan, Marcus Ulpius Traianus, was emperor from A.D. 98 to 117. Born in Spain in 53, Trajan was adopted by the emperor Nerva as his heir in 97, after a distinguished military career. The choice of the able and popular soldier was a wise one. Trajan began his rule by dealing firmly with the growing menace of the Roman garrison, the Praetorian Guard; and he succeeded in conciliating the senatorial class. Trajan proved an able financial organizer and a vigorous builder. A large program of public works was financed largely from the loot of the Dacian War. During Trajan's reign the Empire reached its widest extent and held its frontiers more firmly than ever

before or after that time. Provincial administration was economical, strict, humane, and progressive.

TRANCE (Gr. *ekstasis, a throwing of the mind out of its normal state*). A mental state in which the senses are partially or wholly suspended and the person is unconscious of the environment while contemplating some extraordinary object (Acts 10:9–16; 22:17–21; cf. Num 24:4, 16; Isa 6:1–13; Ezek 8–11, 40–48; Rev 4–22). Probably every vision recorded in the Bible that came to a person while awake, came when that person was in a trance.

TRANSFIGURATION The name given to that singular event recorded in all the Synoptic Gospels (Matt 17:1–8; Mark 9:2–8; Luke 9:28–36), when Jesus was visibly glorified in the presence of three select disciples. The name is derived from the Latin term used to translate the Greek *metamorphoō*, meaning "to change into another form." Jesus' body assumed properties of the resurrection body.

The place is simply identified as "a high mountain" (Mark 9:2). Tradition has identified it with Mt. Tabor, but Hermon and Jebel Jermuk have also been suggested. Witnessed by Peter, James, and John, the Transfiguration occurred while Jesus "was praying" (Luke 9:29). Its historical reality is also attested by the apostle Peter (2 Peter 1:16–18). The experience gave encouragement to Jesus before the cross. To the shocked disciples it confirmed the necessity of the cross through the conversation of the heavenly visitors, linking the suffering with the glory. It was also an entry for Jesus into the glory in which he would reign (Matt 16:28).

TRANSJORDAN (trăns-jôr'dăn). A region included today in the country of Jordan, which is bordered on the west by Israel, on the north by Syria, on the east by Iraq, and on the south by Egypt and Saudi Arabia. The region is essentially a plateau. In OT times it included the regions of Bashan and Gilead and the peoples of Edom and Moab, as well as the tribes of Reuben, Gad, and half of Manasseh. In NT times it was the area of Perea and the Decapolis.

TRANSLATE (trăns'lāt, Heb. *'āvar, to transfer,* Gr. *metathesis, a transfer, metatithēmi, methistēmi, to remove from one place to another*). The Hebrew word is translated this way once in the OT (2 Sam 3:10 KJV; transfer ASV, NIV). Two Greek words with this same idea occur in

Hebrews 11:5—where it is said that Enoch was translated (KJV; taken, taken away NIV) by faith so that he would not die and that before this translation (KJV; he was taken NIV) he pleased God. *Methistēmi* is used to picture regeneration as the believer passing (translated KJV; brought NIV) from the kingdom of darkness into the kingdom of light (Col 1:13).

TRANSPORTATION (See TRADE AND TRAVEL)

TRAVAIL (trăʹvāl). "Travail" translates several Hebrew and Greek words in the KJV, all of which are translated with related words and meanings in the NIV. In the OT the word *yalādh*, "to bear a child," is used a few times for literal travail (Gen 35:16; 38:27; 1 Sam 4:19), and many times figuratively. Also figuratively for toil or trouble *hûl*, "anguish" (Isa 23:4; 54:1; 66:7–8); *hālâh*, "to be weak or sick" (Jer 4:31); *āmāl*, "toil" (Eccl 4:4, 6; Isa 53:11); *'invan*, "occupation, task" only in Ecclesiastes (1:13; 2:23, 26; 3:10; 4:8; 5:15); *hābal*, "writhe, twist" (Song of Songs 8:5 ASV); *telā'âh*, "weariness, hardship" (Exod 18:8; Num 20:14; Lam 3:5).

The NT uses various words in this connection (none of which is rendered "travail" by NIV): *ōdinō*, "to be in pain" (Gal 4:19; Rev 12:2); *ōdin*, "pain, labor, sorrow" (1 Thess 5:3); *synōdinō*, "to feel pain together" (Rom 8:22); *tiktō*, "to bring forth" (John 16:21); *mochthos*, "toil, labor, weariness" (1 Thess 2:9; 2 Thess 3:8).

TRAVEL (See TRADE AND TRAVEL)

TREASURE A word that signifies a collection of objects of value, including stores of provisions (e.g., Jer 41:8; Ezek 28:4; Dan 11:43). The word *ōtzar* has this meaning in two verses—Job 38:22 (treasures KJV; storehouses NIV, RSV) and Psalm 135:7 (treasuries KJV; storehouses NIV, RSV). The treasure cities (store cities NIV) of Exodus 1:11 were arsenals and depots for provisions (cf. Gen 41:48, 56). Matthew 2:11 and 19:21 refer to the store of precious things, but Matthew 12:35 clearly refers to the storehouses. In Acts 8:27 both notions are incorporated. The word *gaza'* is a Persian word and is used only in this place in the NT. In Matthew 27:6 the word is derived from Hebrew: the chief priests could not put the polluted silver into the *korbanas*, the sacred treasury, into which the *corban* gifts were paid. This seems to be distinguished from the *gazophylakion*, the treasury of the temple, into which general offerings were

cast (Mark 12:41; Luke 21:1). This was simply a collection box. John 8:20 refers to the place where Jesus was teaching in the colonnade, where boxes were placed for the convenient reception of gifts. The metaphorical meaning of treasure is a more common figure of speech in the OT than in the NT (Exod 19:5; Deut 28:12; Ps 17:14; Matt 13:44; Luke 12:21; 2 Cor 4:7).

TREASURER (See OCCUPATIONS AND PROFESSIONS)

TREE (Heb. *'ēts, tree wood,* Gr. *dendron, tree, xylon, timber, wood, tree*). There are over 300 references to trees and wood in the Bible. Over 25 different kinds of trees have been identified as having grown in the Holy Land. Trees identified with the holy places were permitted to flourish. Trees were venerated by pagan people who believed gods inhabited them. Sacrifices were often offered under trees (Deut 12:2; 1 Kings 14:23). Planting a tree near a sacred altar was forbidden (Deut 16:21). Trees identified places (Gen 12:6; Deut 11:30; great tree NIV; plain KJV; oak ASV). Tree limbs were used in celebrating the Feast of Tabernacles (Lev 23:40). See also PLANTS.

TREE OF KNOWLEDGE A special tree in the Garden of Eden, set apart by the Lord as an instrument to test the obedience of Adam and Eve (Gen 2:9, 17). The sin in eating its fruit did not lie in the tree but in the disobedience of the persons who ate.

The phrase "to know good and evil" is used in other places: Infants do not know good and evil (Deut 1:39), nor does an old man of failing mind (2 Sam 19:35); but a king does know good and evil (1 Kings 3:9), as do angels (2 Sam 14:17) and God himself (Gen 3:5, 22).

TREE OF LIFE A special tree in the Garden of Eden (Gen 2:9; 3:22). This tree appears again in Revelation 22:2 as a fruit-bearing tree with leaves. It will have healing in its leaves (22:2). The phrase "tree of life" in Proverbs (3:18; 11:30; 13:12; 15:4) is figurative for an exhilarating experience.

TRENCH The KJV translation (1 Sam 26:5, 7; 17:20; 2 Sam 20:15) of two Hebrew words—*ma'gāl* and *hēl*—which mean "rampart" and "entrenchment." ASV has "the place of the wagons" for *ma'gāl*. A third Hebrew word, *te'ālâh* (1 Kings 18:32, 35, 38), is given as "trench" in NIV, which uses the same English word to translate *haruts* ("rampart") in Daniel 9:25 (trench NIV; wall

Mosaic from Hisham's palace at Jericho that portrays stylized animals eating from the "tree of life." Courtesy Zev Radovan

KJV). The NT uses *charax* ("palisade, rampart") once (Luke 19:43; trench KJV; embankment NIV).

TRESPASS (Heb. *'ashām*, Gr. *paraptōma*). Used in the KJV of the OT to express the rights of others, whether of God or of another person. In Jewish law acknowledged violation of a person's rights required restoration plus one-fifth of the amount or value of the thing involved and the presentation of a guilt offering (KJV "trespass offering"). Unintentional trespass against God, when the guilty person became aware of it, required a guilt offering to remove guilt.

TRESPASS OFFERING (See SACRIFICE AND OFFERINGS)

TRIAL OF JESUS The tumultuous proceedings before the Jewish and Roman authorities resulting in the crucifixion of Jesus. All four Gospels record at least part of the twofold trial (Matt 26:57–27:31; Mark 14:53–15:20; Luke 22:54–23:25; John 18:12–19:16), both marked by great irregularities.

Following his arrest in Gethsemane, Jesus was first brought before the former high priest Annas, who conducted a preliminary examination by questioning Jesus about his disciples and teaching (John 18:12–14, 19–23). Meanwhile the Sanhedrin members had assembled in the palace of Caiaphas, the president of the Sanhedrin, for an illegal night session. Annas sent Jesus to them bound (18:24). The attempt to convict Jesus through false witnesses collected and instructed by the Sanhedrin failed because of their contradictory testimony (Matt 26:59–61; Mark 14:55–59). Caiaphas brushed aside the witnesses and put Jesus under oath to tell the court if he was "the Christ, the Son of God" (Matt 26:63). The answer, in deliberate self-incrimination, was used to condemn Jesus for blasphemy (26:64–66; Mark 14:61–64). The session broke up in disorder, with indignities being heaped on Jesus (Matt 26:67–68; Mark 14:65; Luke

22:63-65). After dawn the Sanhedrin assembled in its council chamber and reenacted their trial by questioning Jesus on his messianic claims and deity (Luke 22:66-71). This meeting was held to give a semblance of legality to the condemnation.

Since the Romans had deprived the Sanhedrin of the power of capital punishment, it was necessary to secure a death sentence from the Roman governor. When Jesus explained to him the nature of his kingdom, Pilate concluded that Jesus was harmless and announced a verdict of acquittal (John 18:33-38). This verdict should have ended the trial, but it only evoked a torrent of further charges against Jesus (Matt 27:12-14). Pilate decided to send Jesus to Herod Antipas. Jesus refused to amuse Herod with a miracle; Herod mocked him and returned him to Pilate uncondemned (Luke 23:2-12).

Pilate reviewed the case before the people hoping to prove the innocence of Jesus, proposing a compromise by offering to scourge Jesus before releasing him (Luke 23:13-16). When the multitude requested the customary release of one prisoner (Mark 15:8), Pilate offered them the choice between the notorious Barabbas and Jesus (Matt 27:17). When asked their choice, the people shouted for Barabbas, demanding that Jesus be crucified (27:20-21; Luke 23:18-19). Further remonstrance by Pilate proved useless (23:20-22).

Pilate had him scourged, allowed the soldiers to stage a mock coronation, and then brought out the pathetic figure before the people, hoping that the punishment would satisfy them. It only intensified their shouts for his crucifixion (John 19:1-6). The Jewish leaders threatened to report Pilate to Caesar if he released Jesus (19:12). When Pilate sought to absolve himself of the guilt of Christ's death by publicly washing his hands, the people voluntarily accepted the responsibility (Matt 27:24-26). Keenly conscious of the gross miscarriage of justice, Pilate yielded by releasing Barabbas and sentencing Jesus to the cross. See also CHRIST, JESUS.

TRIBE (Heb. *matteh, rod, staff, tribe, shēvĕt, rod, scepter, tribe, Gr. phylē, tribe*). With two exceptions (Isa 19:13; Matt 24:30 KJV) these words always denote a tribe (or the tribes) of Israel. Each tribe was made up of all the persons descended from one of the sons of the patriarch Jacob. The clan was composed of kinsmen on the father's side. The heads of the tribes are called "rulers" (KJV) or "leaders" (NIV) (Exod 34:31), "heads" (Num 1:16), or "chiefs" (Gen 36:15ff.).

The 12 tribes of Israel (Jacob's new name given in Gen 32:28) were first mentioned by Jacob in prophecy (49:16, 28). While the Hebrews were in Egypt they were grouped according to their fathers' houses (Exod 6:14). After they left Egypt the whole company was conceived of as the 12 tribes of Israel (24:4). The 12 sons of Jacob were Reuben, Simeon, Levi, Judah, Issachar, Dan, Gad, Asher, Naphtali, Joseph, and Benjamin. Although they all had a common father, they had four mothers, Leah and Rachel, who were full wives, and Bilhah and Zilpah, who were concubines. On the breastplate of the high priest were 12 precious stones arranged in four rows; each stone had the name of a tribe engraved on it (28:21, 29; 39:14).

When the Israelites were counted to find out the number of men of war in each group, the tribe of Levi was left out of this census because the Lord selected them to take care of the keeping and transporting of the tabernacle and its furniture (Num 1). The whole encampment of the Israelites was organized at Sinai and each tribe assigned its place in which to march and to camp (ch. 2). The leadership of Judah among the tribes was prophesied by Jacob (Gen 49:10), and this tribe was assigned first place in the order of marching (Num 2:3; 10:14). Judah also was the first tribe to bring an offering after the setting up of the tabernacle (7:12).

The withdrawal of the Levites from the group of tribes left only 11 tribes. In the list of leaders from each tribe who were to take the census, the children of Joseph are divided between his two sons to make up the tribe of Ephraim and the tribe of Manasseh (Num 1:10), bringing the total number of tribes back up to 12.

Before the Israelites entered the Promised Land, the tribes of Reuben and Gad and half of Manasseh chose to settle on the east side of the Jordan (Num 32:33). After the land of Canaan was subdued, the land was divided among the nine and one-half tribes (Josh 15-19). Judah was given the first lot and received the largest area of land (15:1-62). The tribe of Simeon was assigned territory within Judah (19:1). Part of the tribe of Dan went north and seized some territory just south of Mt. Hermon, thus settling the farthest north of all the Israelites (Judg 18). When Elijah built an altar in the contest with the prophets of Baal on Mt.

Carmel, he used 12 stones to represent the 12 tribes of Israel (1 Kings 18:31). The unity of the tribes had a tendency to be disrupted into two factions. After the death of Saul, David reigned over only Judah at first (2 Sam 2:4) and did not become king of all the tribes until later (5:3). After the death of Solomon this same division occurred again: Judah and Benjamin became one nation, the kingdom of Judah, and all the area north of them became another nation, the kingdom of Israel (1 Kings 12:20). This division continued until both kingdoms went into captivity—Israel in 721 B.C. to Assyria, and Judah in 586 to Babylon.

Jesus says that the apostles of Christ will sit on 12 thrones, judging the 12 tribes of Israel (Matt 19:28; Luke 22:30). The Holy City, the New Jerusalem, will have 12 gates, each bearing the name of one of the tribes of Israel (Rev 21:21).

TRIBULATION, THE GREAT (Heb. *tsar, narrow,* Gr. *thlipsis, pressure*). The Hebrew word for "tribulation" has a large variety of meanings in the OT, but it usually refers to trouble of a general sort (Ps 13:4). Likewise the Greek word refers to tribulation of a general sort (Matt 13:21; John 16:33). Sometimes this suffering is just the natural part of one's life (Rom 12:12; James 1:27), while at other times it is looked on as a definite punishment or chastening from the Lord for misbehavior (Rom 2:9).

The Great Tribulation is a definite period of suffering sent from God on the earth to accomplish several purposes. According to premillennial eschatology, it precedes the millennial reign of Christ. Postmillennial theology places it at the end of the 1,000-year reign of Christ. Amillennial theology places it just before the new heavens and the new earth are brought in. This period of suffering will be unlike any other period in the past or future (Dan 12:1; Matt 24:21 KJV; NIV "distress"). See also ESCHATOLOGY.

TRIBUTE (Heb. *mas, forced laborers, middâh, tribute, toll,* Gr. *kēnsos, tax, census, phoros, tax, burden*). The word *mas* occurs 22 times in the OT and is usually translated "tribute" in the KJV. Solomon conscripted a force of taskworkers consisting of 30,000 men (1 Kings 5:13; 9:15, 21). David, too, had forced laborers (4:6; 5:13). Conquered populations were often compelled to render forced labor (Deut 20:11; Josh 16:10).

TRINITY The one eternal God, the Lord, has disclosed to his people that he is the Father, the Son, and the Holy Spirit. Yet he is not three deities but one Godhead, since all three Persons share the one Deity/Godhead. The biblical teaching of the Trinity is, in a sense, a mystery; and the more we enter into union with God and deepen our understanding of him, the more we recognize how much there is yet to know. Based on the biblical teaching, the traditional Christian confession is that God is One in Three and Three in One.

The OT condemns polytheism and declares that God is one and is to be worshiped and loved as such (Deut 6:4–5; Isa 45:21). And this conviction of the unity of God is continued in the NT (see Mark 10:18; 12:29; Gal 3:20; 1 Cor 8:4; 1 Tim 2:5).

God is the Father of Israel (Isa 64:8; Jer 31:9) and of the anointed king of his people (2 Sam 7:14; Pss 2:7; 89:27). Jesus lived in communion with his heavenly Father, always doing his will and recognizing him as truly and eternally God (Matt 11:25–27; Luke 10:21–22; John 10:25–28; Rom 15:6; 2 Cor 1:3; 11:31). The disciples came to see that Jesus was the long-expected Messiah of Israel (Matt 16:13–20; Mark 8:27–30). Later they understood that to be the Messiah, Jesus must also be God made man (see John 1:1–2, 18; 20:28; Rom 9:5; Titus 2:13; Heb 1:8; 2 Peter 1:1). Thus doxologies were offered to him as God (Heb 13:20–21; 2 Peter 3:18; Rev 1:5–6; 5:13; 7:10).

The apostles, following Jesus, refer to the Holy Spirit as a Person. In Acts, the Spirit inspires Scripture, is lied to, is tempted, bears witness, is resisted, directs, carries someone away, informs, commands, calls, sends, thinks a certain decision is good, forbids, prevents, warns, appoints, and reveals prophetic truth (see Acts 1:16; 5:3, 9, 32; 7:51; 8:29, 39; 10:19; 11:12; 13:2, 4; 15:28; 16:6, 7; 20:23, 28; 28:25). Paul describes the Spirit as bearing witness, speaking, teaching, and acting as guide (Rom 8:14, 16, 26; Gal 4:6; Eph 4:30). The Holy Spirit is another *paraklētos* (John 14:16; 15:26–27; 16:13–15). God, the Lord, is Father, Son, and Holy Spirit. This confession and understanding may be said to be basic to the faith of the writers of the NT, though they rarely express it in precise terms. But in certain passages the doctrine is articulated (Matt 28:19; 1 Cor 12:4–6; 2 Cor 13:14; 2 Thess 2:13–14; 1 Peter 1:2).

TRIUMPH (Gr. *thriambeuō, to lead in triumph*). In the OT the eight Hebrew words for triumph are all used with reference to God. Paul uses the word twice in his letters (2 Cor 2:14; Col 2:15).

In Roman times a triumph was a magnificent procession in honor of a victorious general, the highest military honor he could obtain. He entered the city in a chariot, preceded by the senate and magistrates, musicians, the spoils of his victory, and the captives in chains. Sacrifices were made to Jupiter, and incense was burned by the priests.

TROAS (trō'ăs, Gr. *Trōas*). **1.** The NW corner of Asia Minor, in the district of Mysia and the Roman province of Asia. **2.** Alexandria Troas, some 10 miles (17 km.) from the ruins of ancient Troy. Troas was one of the most important cities of NW Asia (Acts 16:8; 20:5; 2 Cor 2:12).

TROPHIMUS (trŏf'ĭ-mŭs, Gr. *Trophimos, nourishing*). A Gentile Christian of Ephesus (Acts 21:29) and companion of Paul (2 Cor 8:19ff.; cf. Acts 20:4). In Jerusalem he was the innocent cause of the tumult resulting in Paul's imprisonment when hostile Asian Jews hastily "assumed" that Paul had illegally taken him into the temple itself (21:29). He is conjectured to be one of the two brothers sent to Corinth with Titus to complete the collection (2 Cor 8:18–22). Shortly before his final Roman imprisonment Paul left Trophimus sick at Miletus (2 Tim 4:20).

TRUMPET (See MUSIC AND MUSICAL INSTRUMENTS)

TRUMPETS, FEAST OF (See FEASTS)

TRUTH The word "truth," *alētheia* in the NT and a variety of words, chiefly *'emeth* in the OT, always connotes (1) the interrelated consistency of statements and their correspondence with the facts of reality and (2) the facts themselves.
  The biblical use of the word has rich suggestive meanings that go beyond the literal connotations. When Moses (Exod 18:21 KJV) refers to "able men, such as fear God, men of truth, hating covetousness," there is suggested integrity of character—a kind of reliability that goes beyond the literal meaning to include those aspects of personal behavior that seem to be implied by the love of truth. The concept of truth is assumed to be derived from the character of God (Heb 6:18; cf. Exod 18:21; 2 Tim 2:13; Titus 1:2). Jesus refers to the gospel of the grace of God as the truth (John 8:31–32; 17:17).
  One of the saddest scenes in the Bible (John 18:37–38) is the one in which Pilate asks Jesus, "What is truth?" and does not even wait for an answer. Those who disbelieve the gospel are morally reprehensible in the sight of God (3:18–19, 36; 2 Thess 2:10–12). Christ is the truth.

TRYPHENA (trī-fē'nà, Gr. *Tryphaina, dainty*). A Christian woman who live in Rome and was known to Paul. He asked the Roman believers to greet her and Tryphosa, her close relative (Rom 16:12). This name has been found on inscriptions of name plates in the burial places of the servants of the royal household of Rome from the time of Paul.

TRYPHOSA (See TRYPHENA)

TUBAL (tū'bàl, Heb. *tûval*). A tribe descended from Japheth (Gen 10:2). It is mentioned with Javan (Isa 66:19) as trading in the markets of Tyre.

TUMBLEWEED (See PLANTS)

TUNIC (See DRESS)

TUNNEL (See AQUEDUCT)

TURBAN (See DRESS)

TURQUOISE (See MINERALS)

TURTLEDOVE (See BIRDS)

TWELVE, THE (See APOSTLE)

TYCHICUS (tĭk'ĭ-kŭs, Gr. *Tychikos, fortuitous*). An Asian Christian and close friend and valued helper of Paul (Acts 20:4), perhaps a native of Ephesus. As one of the delegates chosen by the churches to bear the collection to the poor in Jerusalem (2 Cor 8:19ff.), he apparently went all the way there with Paul. He was with Paul during the first Roman imprisonment and carried the letters to the Ephesians (Eph 6:21) and the Colossians (Col 4:7–9). Onesimus, returning to his master, accompanied him (Col 4:7–9; Philem). Paul told Titus that he would send either Artemas or Tychicus to replace him in the difficult work on Crete (Titus 3:12). Tychicus was with Paul during his second Roman imprisonment and was sent to Ephesus by him (2 Tim 4:12). Tychicus was a man distinguished for integrity and fidelity; he held the affection and confidence of Paul as an able worker in the service of Christ (Col 4:7).

TYRANNUS (tī-răn'ŭs, Gr. *Tyrannos, tyrant*). According to a well-supported reading of Acts 19:9, Paul taught daily at Ephesus "in the lecture hall of Tyrannus." This could indicate a public building traditionally so named or a school founded by Tyrannus. Another common reading, "in the school of one Tyrannus" (KJV), would refer to the school of a living Ephesian schoolmaster named Tyrannus.

The ruins of Tyre, showing remains of the Roman cemetery. The port city's East Gate is in background. Courtesy Zev Radovan

TYRE (tĭr, Heb. *tsôr, a rock*, Gr. *Tyros*). A Phoenician port south of Sidon and north of Carmel. Isaiah (23:2, 12) implies that Tyre was a colony of Sidon. Joshua assigned Tyre to Asher, but in all probability the city was not occupied (Josh 19:29; 2 Sam 24:7).

Tyre emerges into history again with the name of Hiram, friend of David (2 Sam 5:11). Dynastic troubles followed Hiram's death. A certain Ethbaal emerged victorious after the assassina-

tion of his brother. It was Ethbaal's daughter Jezebel who became Ahab's notorious queen (1 Kings 16:31). Renewed troubles after Ethbaal's death led to the emigration of Elissa, the Dido of Vergil's Aeneid IV, and to the founding of Carthage.

During the 200 years of Assyrian aggression, Tyre suffered with the rest of the Middle East but, owing to the strength of her position and her sea power, maintained a measure of independence over much of the troubled era. She broke free from Nineveh a generation before the last stronghold of the Assyrians fell (606 B.C.). These years were the greatest years of Tyrian glory. Ezekiel's account (Ezek 27–28), set though it is in a context of denunciation and prophecy of ruin, gives a vivid picture of the power and wealth of the great trading port. Ruin eventually came. Babylon succeeded Assyria, and although Tyre seems successfully to have resisted the long siege of Nebuchadnezzar, the strain of her resistance to Babylon and the damage to her commerce brought the city to poverty. She briefly fell under the power of Egypt and then became a dependency of Babylon, a status she held until Babylon fell to Persia. Ezra 3:7 contains an order of Cyrus II to Tyre to supply cedar for the restoration of the temple in Jerusalem. Cambyses II conscripted a Tyrian fleet against Egypt, and Tyrian ships fought on the Persian side against the Greeks at Salamis. In 332, in the course of his conquest of the East, Alexander appeared before Tyre. The island stronghold closed her gates, and Alexander was forced to build a causeway. After long months of frustration, he took the city by costly storming. Tyre was broken, and the causeway still remains, now as a place, as Ezekiel foretold, on which fishermen dry their nets (Ezek 26:5, 14; 47:10).

–U–

The Ulai River, with the ancient mounds of Susa on its bank. The NIV calls it the Ulai Canal, the place Daniel had a vision (Dan 8:2–16). Courtesy The Oriental Institute, University of Chicago

UGARIT (See RAS SHAMRA)

ULAI (ū'lī, Heb. *'ûlāy,* meaning uncertain). A river that Daniel mentions twice (8:2, 16). It ran through the province of Elam and flowed through Susa.

ULAM (ū'lăm, Heb. *'ûlām*). 1. A son of Sheresh from the tribe of Manasseh (1 Chron 7:16–17). 2. A descendant of the Benjamite Eshek (8:39–40).

UNCIAL LETTERS (See TEXTS AND VERSIONS; WRITING)

UNCIRCUMCISED (ŭn-sûr'kŭm-sīzd, Heb. *'ārēl,* Gr. *akrobystia*). Literally, one who has not submitted to the Jewish rite of circumcision. Figuratively, a pagan (Judg 14:3; Rom 4:9), the unresponsive heart (Lev 26:41), and the unhearing ear (Jer 6:10 KJV).

UNCLE (Heb. *dôdh, beloved*). A word used in the OT denoting any kinsman on the father's side (Lev 10:4; Jer 32:7).

UNCLEAN, UNCLEANNESS (Heb. *tūm' âh, uncleanness, defilement, niddâh, separation, impurity, 'erwâh, 'erwath dāvār, unclean things, tamē',*

defiled unclean, tāmē', to make or declare unclean, Gr. *akatharsia, miasmos, pollution, akathartos, unclean, koinoō, to defile, mianō, to defile, molynō, to make filthy, spiloō, phtheirō, to corrupt*). All Israel's restricted foods, unlike those of some other nations, involved the flesh of animals—differentiating the clean from the unclean mammals (Lev 11:1–8, 26–28), sea creatures (11:9–12), birds (11:13–25), and creeping things (11:29–38). Nothing that died of itself was fit for their food, nor were they to eat anything strangled. Blood was a forbidden part of their diet.

A dead person, regardless of the cause of death, made anyone who touched the body unclean (Num 19:22). Likewise anything the body touched (19:22) or the enclosure in which the person died was made unclean (19:14–19). Those who touched the carcass of an animal became unclean (Lev 11:24–28). Certain types of creeping things that died made anything they touched unclean. Some objects thus touched could be cleansed by washing, whereas others had to be destroyed (11:29–37).

Leprosy, being a type of sin, was looked on as unclean whether it was in people, houses, or clothing. God required the person pronounced leprous by the priest to identify himself in a prescribed manner and to separate himself from the rest of the people. Any time anyone drew near to him, he was to cry "Unclean, unclean." Since this disease was also very contagious, detailed instructions were given for dealing with it (Lev 13–15).

Whatever the seminal fluid that issued from the body touched became unclean. This applied also to certain other kinds of issues (Lev 15:1–33). Childbirth made a woman unclean, and special instructions were given for cleansing (ch. 13).

In the NT one notes the cumbersome systems of defilement developed by the scribes and Pharisees, which Jesus condemned. Only four restrictions were placed on the new believers (Acts 15:28–29). In the New Testament era, uncleanness has become moral, not ceremonial.

UNCTION (ŭngk'shŭn, Gr. *chrisma, anointing*). The act of anointing, in the KJV found only in 1 John 2:20. In 1 John 2:27 the Greek is translated "anointing."

UNDEFILED (Heb. *tām, perfect,* Gr. *amiantos, unsullied*). A person or thing untainted with moral evil (KJV Ps 119:1; Song of Songs 5:2; 6:9; Heb 7:26; 13:4; James 1:27; 1 Peter 1:4).

UNICORN (See ANIMALS)

UNITY (Heb. *yāhadh, unitedness,* Gr. *henotēs, oneness*). Used in the OT in the sense of togetherness of persons (Gen 13:6), fellowship (Judg 19:6), and praise (Ps 34:3). Isaiah 11:6–7 tells of a future time when there will be a togetherness among animals. The NT word speaks of the unity of faith that binds together the people of God (Eph 4:13).

UNKNOWN GOD (Gr. *agnōstos theos*). These words occur only in Acts 17:23. This was probably a votive altar erected by some worshiper who did not know what god to thank for some benefit he had received.

UNKNOWN TONGUE (Gr. *glōssa, tongue*). The expression "*unknown* tongue" occurs six times in the KJV (1 Cor 14:2, 4, 13–14, 19, 27) where Paul refers to the charismatic gift of speaking in tongues.

UNLEARNED A word that KJV uses to translate four different Greek words in the NT: (1) *agrammatos* ("lacking technical rabbinical instruction" Acts 4:13), (2) *amathēs* ("ignorant, uninstructed" 2 Peter 3:16), (3) *apaideutos* ("an uneducated person" 2 Tim 2:23), and (4) *idiōtēs* ("private person, nonprofessional" 1 Cor 14:16, 23–24).

UNLEAVENED (Heb. *matstsâh, sweet,* Gr. *azymos*). A word often found in both Testaments, usually in a literal sense. When used literally, it refers to bread made without any fermented dough (yeast, leaven) or to the Passover Feast, when only unleavened bread could be used. When used figuratively, it means "unmixed" (1 Cor 5:7–8 KJV; NIV "without yeast").

UNLEAVENED BREAD, FEAST OF (See FEASTS)

UNNI (ŭn'ī, Heb. *'unnî*, meaning unknown). 1. One of the Levites whom David appointed to play in connection with the tabernacle service (1 Chron 15:18, 20). 2. Another Levite employed in the temple music service following the Captivity (Neh 12:9).

UNPARDONABLE SIN Not a phrase used in the Bible, but the usual way of referring to blasphemy against the Holy Spirit (Matt 12:31–32; Mark 3:28–29; Luke 12:10). There is much difference of opinion as to the meaning of this sin, but one of the most popular and likely views is that the sin involves decisively and finally rejecting the testimony of the Holy Spirit regarding the person and work of Jesus Christ.

UNTEMPERED MORTAR (Heb. *tāphēl*). Mortar made of clay instead of slaked lime. It was smeared on the walls of houses made of small stones or mud bricks so as to prolong the life of the building. Ezekiel (13:10ff. KJV; NIV "whitewash") uses the term symbolically to refer to the flimsiness of the work of the false prophets.

UPHARSIN (See MENE, MENE, TEKEL, PARSIN)

UPHAZ (ū'făz, Heb. *'ûphāz,* meaning unknown). A famous gold-producing region (Jer 10:9; Dan 10:5 KJV).

UPPER CHAMBER, UPPER ROOM (Heb. *'ălîyâh, lofty,* Gr. *anōgeon, a room upstairs, hyperōon, upper*). A room frequently built on the roofs of houses and used in summer because it was cooler than the regular living quarters (Mark 14:15; Luke 22:12; Acts 1:13; 20:8).

URI (ū'rī, Heb. *'ûrî, fiery*). 1. The father of Bezalel (Exod 31:2; 35:30; 38:22;

1 Chron 2:20; 2 Chron 1:5). 2. The father of Geber, one of the 12 provision officers of Solomon (1 Kings 4:19). 3. A porter of the temple (Ezra 10:24).

URIAH, URIAS, URIJAH (ū-rī'à, ū-rī'ăs, ū-rī'jà, Heb. *'ûrîyâh, Jehovah is light*). 1. A Hittite, the husband of Bathsheba (2 Sam 11:3). The fact that he had married a Hebrew wife, his Hebrew name, and his loyalty and devotion as a soldier (11:11) all indicate that he probably was a worshiper of the Lord. When Uriah was killed, David took Bathsheba for his own wife. 2. A priest during the kingship of Ahaz (Isa 8:2) taken by the king to record the matter concerning Maher-Shalal-Hash-Baz. It also seems highly probable that he was the one who carried out the king's command to build in the temple an Assyrian altar that was to be used for sacrifice (2 Kings 16:10–16; KJV "Urijah"). 3. A priest who aided Ezra in carrying on his ministry (Neh 8:4), perhaps the Uriah referred to as the father of Meremoth (Ezra 8:33; Neh 3:4, 21, KJV "Urijah"). 4. A prophet who predicted the destruction of Judah (Jer 26:20). He was apprehended by the king and killed (Jer 26:21–23, KJV "Urijah").

URIEL (ū'rī-ĕl, Heb. *'ûrî'ēl, God is light*). 1. A Levite from the family of Kohath (1 Chron 6:24). 2. A chief of the Kohathites (15:5, 11). 3. The father of Maacah, wife of Rehoboam (2 Chron 13:2).

URIJAH (See URIAH)

URIM AND THUMMIM (ū'rĭm and thŭm'ĭm, Heb. *hā'ûrîm wehatûmmîm, lights and perfections*). Objects not specifically described, perhaps stones, placed in the breastplate of the high priest, which he wore when he went into the presence of the Lord and by which he ascertained the will of God in any important matter affecting the nation (Exod 28:30; Lev 8:8; Num 27:21; Neh 7:65). It is uncertain what they were and what they looked like and how they were used. One theory is that they were used as the lot and cast like dice, the manner of their fall somehow revealing the Lord's will (1 Sam 10:19–22; 14:37–42).

UR OF THE CHALDEANS The early home of Abraham (Gen 11:28, 31; 15:7; Neh 9:7), located in southern Mesopotamia, about 140 miles (233 km.) SE of the site of old Babylon. Education was well developed at Ur, for a school was found there with its array of clay tablets. Students learned to read, write, and do varied forms of arithmetic. Commerce was well developed. Nanna was the

Ruins of the great ziggurat temple at Ur, facing southwest. It is a solid tower with a mud-brick core and a fired-brick shell about 70 feet (21 m.) high and served as a religious center of the moon god. Courtesy University Museum, University of Pennsylvania

moon god worshiped there. The temple, ziggurat, and other buildings used in connection with the worship of this pagan deity have been found; there were idols in private niches in the home walls.

USURY (Heb. *neshekh, interest, nāshakh, to bite, to lend on interest, nāshâh, to remove, nash', lead astray,* Gr. *tokos, interest on money).* Any money that a Jew lent to his brother was to be without interest (Exod 22:25; Deut 23:19). Money could, however, be lent to a stranger with interest (Deut 23:20). The main purpose for lending money among the Israelites was for the relief of the poor for which, according to law, no interest was to be demanded (Lev 25:35-36). During Israel's time in Babylon many abuses arose regarding the lending of money (Ezek 18:8, 17). Because of this, Nehemiah, after the return from exile, took measures to have the practice stopped (Neh 5:10-12). In the NT reasonable rates of interest received for money lent are never condemned (e.g., the parable of the talents).

UTHAI (ū'thī, Heb. *'ûthay,* meaning uncertain). **1.** A descendant of Judah who lived in Jerusalem (1 Chron 9:4). **2.** One of the sons of Bigvai who returned with Ezra (Ezra 8:14).

UZ (ŭz, Heb. *'ûts,* meaning uncertain). **1.** One of Nahor's sons by Milcah (Gen 22:21). He is called "Huz" (KJV). **2.** One of the sons of Aram (10:23), the grandson of Shem (1 Chron 1:17). **3.** One of the sons of Dishan (Gen 36:28). **4.** The country in which Job lived (Job 1:1; Jer 25:20; Lam 4:21). Uz was exposed to attacks by the Chaldeans and Sabeans (Job 1:15, 17).

UZZA (ūz'à, Heb. *'uzzâh, strength).* **1.** The eldest son of Ehud (1 Chron 8:7). **2.** The caretaker of, owner of, or one in whose memory a garden was named (2 Kings 21:18, 26). **3.** One whose children returned under Zerubbabel (Ezra 2:49; Neh 7:51).

UZZAH (ūz'à, Heb., *'uzzâh, strength).* **1.** One who accompanied the ark of the Lord when it was being brought from Kirjath Jearim to Jerusalem. When something caused the ark to shake, Uzzah took hold of it, thus displeasing the Lord. As a result, he met instant death (2 Sam 6:3-8; 1 Chron 13:6-11, KJV "Uzza"). **2.** The son of Shimei (6:29; KJV "Uzza").

UZZI (ŭz'ī, Heb. *'uzzî, strong).* **1.** One of Aaron's descendants (1 Chron 6:6, 51; Ezra 7:4). **2.** Tola's son from the family of Issachar (1 Chron 7:2-3). **3.** Bela's son

Stone plaque marking resting place of bones of King Uzziah (769-733 B.C.). Aramaic inscription reads "Hither were brought the bones of Uzziah, king of Judah. Do not open." Courtesy Israel Museum, Jerusalem. Photo David Harris

from the tribe of Benjamin (7:7). **4.** Another Benjamite, the father of Elah (9:8). **5.** An overseer of the Levites (Neh 11:22). **6.** A priest in the family of Jedaiah (12:19).

UZZIAH (ŭ-zī'à, Heb. *'uzzîyâh, the* LORD *is strength).* **1.** Uzziah, also called Azariah, Judah's tenth king (2 Kings 14:21); he ruled 52 years. His father, because of a military failure, had been killed (14:19). Uzziah was the people's choice as his successor (14:21). He undertook, very early in his career, an expedition against his father's enemies and won battles against the Edomites, Philistines, Arabians, and the Meunites (2 Kings 14:22; 2 Chron 26:1-7). He strayed far from the Lord at the end of his life (2 Chron 26:5). He went into the temple, determined to burn incense to the Lord, a duty to be performed only by the priest. God struck him with leprosy (26:16-21).

2. A Levite descended from Kohath (1 Chron 6:24). **3.** The father of a certain Jonathan (27:25). **4.** One of the sons of Harim (Ezra 10:16-21). **5.** The father of Athaiah (Neh 11:4).

UZZIEL, UZZIELITE (ŭ-zī'ĕl, ŭ-zī'ĕl-īt, Heb. *'uzzî'ēl, God is strength).* **1.** A Levite, son of Kohath (Exod 6:18, 22; Lev 10:4; Num 3:19, 30; 1 Chron 6:2, 18). **2.** A captain from the tribe of Simeon (4:42). **3.** Head of a Benjamite family (7:7). **4.** One of David's musicians (25:4).

5. One of the sons of Jeduthun, a Levite (2 Chron 29:14-19). **6.** The son of Harhaiah, a goldsmith (Neh 3:8).

Anyone who descended from Uzziel the Levite was known as an Uzzielite (Num 3:27; 1 Chron 26:23). During David's day Amminadab was their chief, and those whom he led numbered 112 (15:10).

—V—

VAGABOND (Heb. *nûdh, to wander*). A word used in the curse pronounced on Cain (Gen 4:12, 14 KJV; NIV "wanderer"). The plural form is found in the imprecatory prayer in Psalm 109:10 (KJV; NIV "wandering beggars"). The sorcerers mentioned in Acts 19:13 as "vagabond Jews" were professional exorcists (NIV has "Jews who went around driving out evil spirits").

VALE, VALLEY 1. *Gaye'*, "a gorge." The word is used to describe the place of Moses' burial (Deut 34:6), the Valley of Hinnom (Josh 15:8; 18:16; 2 Kings 23:10; Jer 7:31), a valley of salt (2 Sam 8:13; 1 Chron 18:12; 2 Chron 25:11), the Valley of Hamon Gog (Ezek 39:11, 15), and the great valley formed when Christ returns to the earth to rule (Zech 14:4–5). **2.** *Nahal*, "receiving." Today often translated *wady*. It refers to a valley that is the bed of a brook or river that can be filled quickly by rain (Gen 26:19; Num 13:23; Josh 12:1). **3.** *'Emeq*, "a deep place"— the valleys of Achor (Josh 7:24), Aijalon (10:12), Gibeon (Isa 28:21), Hebron (Gen 37:14), Jehoshaphat (Joel 3:2), Jezreel (Josh 17:16). **4.** *Biq'âh*, "a split," a plain between two hills or mountains (Deut 34:3; Josh 11:17). **5.** *Shephēlâh*, "lowland," the low-lying hills that stretch from Israel's coast up to the mountains (Josh 10:40; Jer 32:44 KJV). **6.** Greek *pharanx*, "a ravine" (Luke 3:5).

VALLEY OF BEN HINNOM (See GEHENNA)

VANITY (Heb. *hevel, 'āwen, shâw'*, Gr. *kenos, mataiotēs*). A word occurring almost 100 times in the KJV, but never in the sense of conceit or undue self-esteem. The word *vanity* is not used in the NIV but the Hebrew and Greek words are translated "emptiness," "worthlessness," "futility." This thought appears most often (37 times) in the Book of Ecclesiastes. Man's natural life (Job 7:3; Ps 39:5–6), all idolatry (1 Sam 12:21; 2 Kings 17:15; Isa 41:29; 44:9), and the proclamation of false prophets (Jer 23:16; Ezek 13:1–23; Zech 10:2) are vanity. In the NT the word *matiotēs* occurs only three times (Rom 8:20; Eph 4:17; 2 Peter 2:18). In the KJV the word "vanity" sometimes means iniquity (Job 15:35; Ps 10:7; Prov 22:8).

VASHNI (văsh'nī, Heb. *washnî, weak*). The name of the firstborn of Samuel (1 Chron 6:28 KJV). Another passage says that Samuel's firstborn was Joel and his second Abijah (1 Sam 8:2).

VASHTI (văsh'tī, Heb. *washtî, beautiful woman, from the Persian*). Xerxes' queen whom he divorced because of her refusal to show herself to the king's guests at a feast. Her place was taken by Esther (Esth 1:11).

VEIL (See DRESS; TEMPLE)

VENGEANCE (Heb. *nāqam, to grudge*). Any punishment meted out in the sense of retribution. The word occurs in 32 OT verses (16 of them in Isa and Jer—e.g., Gen 4:15; Deut 32:35, 41, 43; Pss 94:1; 99:8; Jer 50:15, 28; 51:6, 11, 36). In the NT (KJV) the English word translates three Greek words: in two verses *dikē* is translated "vengeance," in the sense of punishment for wrong done (Acts 28:4; Jude 7), *ekdikēsis* is used in much the same sense (Luke 21:22; Rom 12:19; 2 Thess 1:8; Heb 10:30), and *orgē* is used of God punishing evil in human beings (Rom 3:5).

VENISON (Heb. *tsayidh, tsēdhâh, game of any kind*). Properly the flesh of the deer, but as used in the KJV of Genesis 25:28 and 27:5ff. it could mean any game taken in hunting. NIV "wild game" and "game."

VERMILION (Heb. *shāshār*). A red pigment used for painting walls of palaces (Jer 22:14 KJV, RSV) and for coloring the exotic clothing of the Chaldeans (Ezek 23:14 KJV, RSV). NIV has "red" both times.

VERSIONS OF THE SCRIPTURES (See BIBLE; BIBLE, ENGLISH VERSIONS; TEXTS AND VERSIONS)

VESSEL (Heb. *kelî*, Gr. *skeuos*). A material object that may have one or more uses, whether it be a tool, an implement, a weapon, or a receptacle. KJV translates *kelî* and *skeuos* 146 times by "vessel," but an almost equal number of times they are translated "armor," "artillery," "bag," "carriage," "furniture," "instrument," "jewel," "pot," "sack," "stuff," "thing," "wares," and "weapon." RSV and NIV translate *kelî* and *skeuos* "utensils" where the context seems to indicate a hollow utensil.

In Romans 9:20–24 and 2 Timothy 2:20–21 the term is applied to persons; in 2 Corinthians 4:7 it means the person as an instrument of God's will, and it is used figuratively (1 Thess 4:4) for a man's own

A hoard of household utensils and containers found in the caves of the Judean wilderness. Second century A.D. Courtesy Israel Museum, Jerusalem. Photo David Harris

A group of limestone vessels, including a two-handled cup and one-handled pitcher, characteristic of the Jerusalem area. Dated c. A.D. 70. Courtesy Reuben and Edith Hecht Museum, University of Haifa. Photo Zev Radovan

body (NIV) or for his wife (NIV footnote), more likely the latter. The weaker vessel (1 Peter 3:7 KJV, MLB, NASB; weaker partner NIV; weaker sex RSV) is a man's wife.

VIA DOLOROSA "The sorrowful way," the traditional route that our Lord traveled on the day of his crucifixion from the judgment seat of Pilate (Matt 27:26, 31; Mark 15:20; Luke 23:26; John 19:16) to the place of his crucifixion on Mt. Calvary (Matt 27:33; Mark 15:22; Luke 23:33; John 19:18).

VIAL (Heb. *pakh*, from a root meaning *to pour*, Gr. *phialē*). A hollow vessel used for various purposes. The word occurs 13 times in the KJV (1 Sam 10:1; Rev 5:8; 15:57; 16:1–4, 8, 10, 12, 17; 17:1; 21:9), where other versions have either "vial" or "bottle," "bowl," or "flask."

VICTORY The OT associates victory with the God of power and glory and majesty who is in full control of his creation (1 Chron 29:11). That he gives victory in this life to faithful believers is seen throughout Hebrews 11. Faith is the victory that conquers the world (1 John 5:4–5), and through it Christians continually know the victory because of what God has done in Jesus (1 Cor 15:7; Rev 2:11; 21:1–7).

VICTUAL (See FOOD)

VIGILANCE In Gethsemane a particular occasion for watchfulness was stressed by Jesus (Matt 26:38–41; Mark 14:34, 38). Watchfulness is directed as a general attitude of preparedness in those who await their Lord's return (Matt 24:42;

Jesus' route ("The Sorrowful Road") from Pilate's judgment hall to Golgotha, the place of crucifixion. Courtesy Zev Radovan

Mark 13:33–34, 37; Luke 21:36). The KJV uses "watch" in Paul's letters to the Ephesian elders (Acts 20:31), to the Colossians (Col 4:2), and to the Thessalonians (1 Thess 5:6). It is found also three times in John's writing (Rev 3:2–3; 16:15). NIV reads "Be on guard," "alert," "watchful." The word "vigilant" itself is used by KJV in Peter's call for alertness against the diabolical adversary (1 Peter 5:8). NIV has "alert."

VILLAGE Villages were usually grouped around a fortified town to which the people could flee in time of war. The farmers walk out daily to their fields, some at quite a distance from the village.

VINE, VINEYARD (Heb. gephen, usually the cultivated grapevine, sōrēq, dark grapes, nāzîr, undressed vine, Gr. ampelōn, staphylē, botrys). A vineyard was usually surrounded with a protecting wall of stones or thorny hedges to keep out destructive animals (Num 22:24; Ps 80:8–13; Prov 24:30–31; Isa 5:5). In every vineyard was a tower for the watchman, a winepress hollowed out of a flat rock, and a vat into which the juice flowed from the winepress (Isa 1:8; 5:1–7; Matt 21:33–41).

The treaders of the winepress shouted and sang as they trod the grapes (Judg 9:27; Isa 16:10; Jer 25:30; 48:33). The gleanings were left to the poor (Lev 19:10; Deut 24:21; Judg 8:2). The wine was stored in new goatskin bags (Matt 9:17) or in large pottery containers. Every seventh year the vines were allowed to lie fallow (Exod 23:11; Lev 25:3).

Figuratively, the vine symbolized prosperity and peace among the ancient Hebrews (1 Kings 4:25; Mic 4:4; Zech 3:10). The vine also symbolized the chosen people, who instead of producing outstanding fruit yielded only wild grapes.

VINEGAR (Heb. hōmets, Gr. oxos). With us, generally a sour fluid obtained by fermentation of cider, but in Bible times from wine. The Nazirite was to abstain from drinking it (Num 6:3), and it was used as a condiment on bread (Ruth 2:14; cf. Prov 10:26; 25:20). On the cross Jesus was offered vinegar (NIV "wine") mixed with gall or with myrrh (Matt 27:34; Mark 15:23) in fulfillment of Psalm 69:21, but he refused it. Later he was offered a mixture of water and vinegar on a sponge (Matt 27:48), a drink very popular among the poor and used by Roman soldiers when in camp.

VIPER (See ANIMALS)

VIRGIN Nine times 'almâh is found—four singular (Gen 24:43; Exod 2:8; Prov 30:19; Isa 7:14) and five plural (Ps 46, title, 68:25; Song of Songs 1:3; 6:8). In three passages (Gen 24:43; Exod 2:8; Song of Songs 6:8; probably Prov 30:19), the girl is unquestionably a virgin. So far, then, 'almâh is a virgin.

Turning now to bethûlâh, and leaving aside metaphorical uses (such as references to cities and tribes; e.g., Isa 37:22), there are 14 occurrences that are noncommittal (e.g., Deut 32:25), grouping girls and young men simply as "young people," without any more implying that the young women are married or unmarried than that the young men are bachelors. There are 21 cases where the girls certainly are virgins (e.g., Exod 22:16; Judg 19:24). In three cases bethûlâh was amplified by saying that she had never had sexual intercourse (Gen 24:16; Lev 21:3; Judg 21:12). By comparison, 'almâh is never qualified or amplified.

Genesis 24 is the only passage in which the words occur so as to enable comparison. Abraham's servant uses the term na'arah (24:14). In verse 16 Rebekah arrives and, knowing only what his eyes tell him, she is described as female (na'arah), as of marriageable age (be-

thûlâh), but as unmarried (whom no man had known). If *bethûlâh* necessarily meant "unmarried," no definition would be needed. But in verse 43 the servant, recounting all that has happened, simply describes Rebekah as *'almâh*, i.e., using it as a summary word for all he now knows: female, marriageable, and unmarried.

This conclusion has great bearing on the NT use of *parthenos*, especially as it occurs in Matthew 1:23, and on the virgin birth of the Lord Jesus Christ. See also VIRGIN BIRTH.

VIRGIN BIRTH The teaching that Mary, the mother of Jesus was a virgin both when she conceived and when she gave birth to Jesus, the child who was Immanuel (Matt 1:18-25; Luke 1:26-38; Isa 7:14). Conception by a virgin was the appropriate way for the eternal Son to become a man. As the Holy Spirit had "hovered" over the old creation (Gen 1:2), so now the Holy Spirit is present to superintend the origin of a new creation, of which the Incarnate Son will be the center. The virginal conception points to the unique relation of the Incarnate Son to the human race he came to save: There is a basic continuity with us in that he shares our flesh and was born in the "normal" way. There is a basic discontinuity in that he was conceived in regard to his manhood in a unique way—as a new creation.

VIRTUE (Heb. *hayil, strength, ability*, often involving moral worth, Gr. *aretē*, any excellence of a person or a thing, *dynamis, power, influence*). The phrase "a virtuous woman" found in KJV (Ruth 3:11; Prov 12:4; 31:10) is literally "a woman of worth" (so rendered once by RSV, where NIV has "a woman of noble character"). Sometimes the word is used in its Old English sense of "power" (thus NIV in Mark 5:30; Luke 6:19; 8:46) and "strength" (2 Cor 12:9; Heb 11:11).

VISION (Heb. *hāzôn, hizzāyôn, mar'âh*, Gr. *horama, optasia*). It is impossible to draw a sharp line of demarcation between dreams and visions. They came under various circumstances, in men's waking hours (Dan 10:7; Acts 9:7), by day (10:3) or by night (Gen 46:2). In the OT both "writing" and "nonwriting" prophets were recipients of visions (Isa 1:1; Obad 1; Nah 1:1; and 2 Sam 7:17; 1 Kings 22:17-19; 2 Chron 9:29). With perhaps one exception (Num 24:4), they were given only to holy men in the service of God. In the NT, Luke especially manifests great interest in visions (Luke 1:22; Acts 9:10; 10:3, 10ff.; 18:9). Biblical visions concerned both immediate situations (Gen 15:1-2; Acts 12:7) and more distant ones as seen in the writings of Isaiah, Ezekiel, Hosea, Micah, Daniel, and John. In the OT false prophets feigned visions and were denounced (Jer 14:14; 23:16; Ezek 13:7).

VISITATION (Heb. *pekuddâh*, Gr. *episkopē*). Used in the KJV for a divine visit for the purpose of rewarding or punishing people for their deeds (Jer 10:15, NIV "judgment"; Luke 19:44, NIV "God's coming"; 1 Peter 2:12, NIV "visits").

VOW (Heb. *nedher*, Gr. *euchē*). A voluntary promise to God to perform some service or do something pleasing to him, in return for some hoped-for benefits (Gen 28:20-22; Lev 27:2, 8; Num 30; Judg 11:30); or to abstain from certain things (Num 30:3). In the OT vows were never regarded as a religious duty (Deut 23:22); but once they were made, they were considered sacred and binding (Deut 23:21-23; Judg 11:35; Ps 66:13; Eccl 5:4). Fathers could veto vows made by their daughters, and husbands could veto their wives' vows; but if a husband did not veto a wife's vow and then caused her to break it, the blame was his, not hers (Num 30). A vow had to be uttered to be binding (Deut 23:23). Almost anything—people, possessions, oneself—except what was already the Lord's or was an abomination to the Lord (23:18), could be vowed; and all these things could be redeemed with money, their value to be determined by a priest. Houses, lands, and unclean animals that were redeemed had to have a fifth of their value added to make up the redemption money. Jesus condemned the abuse of vows (Matt 15:4-6; Mark 7:10-13). Paul's vow in Acts 18:18 was probably a temporary Nazirite vow.

VULGATE (See TEXTS AND VERSIONS, OT)

VULTURE (See BIRDS)

–W–

Three courses of "Herodian" stones from the Western ("wailing") Wall in Jerusalem.
Courtesy Israel Government Press Office

WADI (wä′dē). A valley that forms the bed of a stream during the winter but dries up in the hot season (cf. Gen 26:19; Num 34:5; Josh 15:4; 1 Kings 8:65; Isa 27:12; Ezek 47:19).

WAFERS (Heb. *rāqîq, tsappîhith*). Thin cakes. The word in Exodus 16:31 emphasizes the thinness, but elsewhere what is meant is the process of beating that rendered the cakes thin (Exod 29:2; Lev 2:4; 7:12; 8:26; Num 6:15, 19). The same word is translated "cakes" in 1 Chronicles 23:29 KJV.

WAGES (Heb. *hinnām, maskōreth, pe'ullâh, sākhar*, Gr. *misthos, opsōnion*). The earliest mention of wages is in the bargaining between Laban and his nephew Jacob (Gen 29–30). Pharaoh's daughter promised wages to the mother of Moses for acting as his nurse (Exod 2:5–9). In the Mosaic Law a hired servant must be paid at the end of the day (Lev 19:13; Deut 24:14–15), thus implying a hand-to-mouth existence. The same sort of poverty is in the parable of the eleventh-hour laborers (Matt 20:1–16; cf. Luke 3:14; Rom 6:23; 2 Cor 11:8; 1 Tim 5:18).

WAGON (Heb. *'āghālâh*, from ' *aghal*, to be round, to roll). A vehicle with wheels (usually two) used for carrying goods as well as persons. Ancient wagons were covered or uncovered, usually drawn by oxen but sometimes horses. Covered wagons, each drawn by two oxen, were used for moving the tabernacle (Num 7:3–9 KJV, NIV "carts") but not the sacred furniture, which was carried on the shoulders of priests.

WAIL (Heb. *mispēdh, nehî*, Gr. *alalazō, pentheō*). In ancient funeral processions wailing relatives, often accompanied by hired female (sometimes male) mourners and musicians, preceded the body to the grave (Jer 9:17–18; Amos 5:16; Matt 9:23).

WALK More than 12 Hebrew and Greek verbs are translated "walk." Used hundreds of times, the meaning is generally literal but often figurative (e.g., Ps 1:1). In the NT Letters the word is used uniformly in the figurative sense and refers to the whole manner of life and conduct (Rom 4:12; 2 Cor 6:16; 1 John 1:7) or to the observance of laws or customs (Acts 21:21 KJV).

War panel from the "Standard of Ur," c. 2500 B.C., showing the triumph of a king over his enemies. Mosaic made of lapis lazuli, shell, and red limestone set in bitumen on wood. Height: 9 inches (23 cm.); length: 19 inches (48 cm.). Reproduced by courtesy of the Trustees of the British Museum

WALL Stone was used only in a certain few localities. In Palestine houses were constructed of crude brick, although sometimes wood, mud-brick, and stone were used in alternate layers. Every ancient city had enormous walls surrounding it, sometimes containing chambers inside. Josephus tells of stones in the temple of Solomon 60 feet (18 m.) long.

WAR (Heb. *milhāmâh*, from *laham, to fight*, Gr. *polemos*). War had religious significance for Israel. It was customary for priests to accompany Israel's armies into battle (Deut 20:1–4). Campaigns were begun and engagements entered into with sacrificial rites (1 Sam 7:8–10; 13:9) and after consulting the Lord (Judg 20:18ff.; 1 Sam 14:37; 23:2; 28:6; 30:8). Prophets were sometimes asked for guidance before a campaign (1 Kings 22:5; 2 Kings 3:11).

The blowing of a trumpet throughout the land announced the call to arms (Judg 3:27; 1 Sam 13:3; 2 Sam 15:10), and priests sounded an alarm with trumpets (2 Chron 13:12–16). Weapons included slings, spears, javelins, bows and arrows, swords, and battering rams. Strategical movements included the ambush (Josh 8:3ff.), the feint (Judg 20:20ff.), the flank movement (2 Sam 5:22ff.), the surprise attack (Josh 11:1–2), the raid (1 Chron 14:9), the foray (2 Sam 3:22), and foraging to secure supplies (23:11). Victorious armies pillaged the camp of the enemy, robbed the dead (Judg 8:24–26; 1 Sam

31:9; 2 Chron 20:25), and often killed or mutilated prisoners (Josh 8:23, 29; 10:22–27; Judg 1:6). Booty was divided equally between those who had taken part in the battle and those who had been left behind in camp (Num 31:27; Josh 22:8; 1 Sam 30:24–25), but some of the spoils were reserved for the Levites and for the Lord (Num 31:28, 30).

Jesus accepted war as an inevitable part of the present sinful world order (Matt 24:6) but warned that those who take the sword must perish by it (26:52). The Christian is said to be a soldier (2 Tim 2:3; 1 Peter 2:11). The Apocalypse uses the figure of battle and war to describe the final triumph of Christ over Satan (Rev 16:14–16; 17:14; 19:14).

WASHERMAN'S FIELD (See FULLER'S FIELD)

WASHING (Heb. *rāhats, kāvas*, Gr. *niptō, louō, loutron*). Frequent bathing was necessary in the warm climate of the East. In Egypt, Syria, and Palestine people washed the dust from their feet when they entered a house (Gen 18:4; John 13:10). Ceremonial defilement was removed by bathing the body and washing the clothing (Lev 14:8; Num 19:7–8). The priests washed their hands and feet before entering the sanctuary or offering a sacrifice (Exod 30:19–21). In the time of Christ the Jews did much ceremonial washing of hands before eating (Mark

7:3–4) and used public baths as the Greeks and Romans did.

WATCH (Heb. *'ashmurâh, 'ashmōreth,* Gr. *phylakē*). A man or group of men set to guard a city (Neh 4:9; 7:3). Even today in the East, when the crops are ripening in the fields and vineyards, one may see watchmen on guard day and night (Isa 1:8). The Latin word *custodia,* transliterated in Greek, is used three times (Matt 27:65–66; 28:11 NIV "guard," KJV "watch") for the Roman watch that was set to guard our Lord's tomb.

WATCHES OF THE NIGHT The divisions into which the 12 hours of the night were divided. The Jews had a threefold division (Judg 7:19), while the Romans had four watches (Mark 6:48).

WATCHMAN (See OCCUPATIONS AND PROFESSIONS; TIME)

WATER (Heb. *mayim,* Gr. *hydōr*). Because of its scarcity in Palestine, water is much appreciated there. Absence of water was very serious (1 Kings 17:1ff.; Jer 14:3; Joel 1:20), and rain was a sign of God's favor. The rivers of Palestine are mostly small and have little if any water in summer. Consequently in Bible times the country depended on rain as its source of water. Cisterns were a necessity for the storing of water, but if water was stored too long it became brackish and filthy and a menace to health. In the summer there was no rain, so vegetation was dependent on the heavy dews. Irrigation was carried on where there was sufficient water. When water was scarce, as during a time of siege, it had to be rationed. Drinking water, carried in goatskins, was often sold in the streets. Wells and pools were comparatively scarce (Gen 21:19; 24:11; John 4:6; 9:7). Water was used for ceremonial washings before meals and in the Jewish temple ceremony (Lev 11:32; 16:4; Num 19:7). The Bible uses it as a symbol of the cleansing of the soul from sin (Ezek 16:4, 9; 36:25; John 3:5; Eph 5:26; Heb 10:22; 1 John 5:6, 8). See also MINERALS.

WATER HEN (See BIRDS)

WATER OF BITTERNESS; WATER OF JEALOUSY (See JEALOUSY, WATER OF)

WATER OF CLEANSING Water for the removal of impurity (Num 19:9, 13, 20–21; 31:23). KJV has "water of separation"; ASV, "water of impurity."

WATERPOT (Gr. *hydria*). An earthen jar for carrying or holding water, either for drinking (John 4:28) or for purifying purposes (2:6–7). The latter was large, hold-

ing 18 to 20 gallons (69 to 77 l.). NIV has "water jar."

WATERSPOUT (Heb. *tsinnôr*). Mentioned only in Psalm 42:7 where ASV and NIV have "waterfall." It means a large rush of water sent by God, perhaps great floods of rain.

WAVE OFFERING (See SACRIFICE AND OFFERINGS)

WAY There are about 25 Hebrew and Greek words translated "way" in the Bible. It is often used metaphorically to describe the conduct or manner of life, whether of God or of man (Deut 5:33; Ps 1:6; Prov 16:17). In the NT God's plan of salvation is called "the way of the Lord" (Matt 3:3). The term is also used to mean Christianity or Judaism (Acts 9:2; 19:9; 22:4).

WAYFARING MAN (Heb. *'ōrēah, 'āvar, 'ōrah, hālakh-derekh*). One who walks the roads (Judg 19:17; 2 Sam 12:4; Isa 33:8; 35:8); a traveler (so NIV).

WEALTH (Heb. *hôn, hayil, nekhāsîm,* Gr. *euporia*). Abundance of possessions (material, social, or spiritual). In the nomadic civilization of the early Hebrews, wealth consisted largely of flocks and herds, silver and gold, brass, iron, and clothing (Josh 22:8). In the days of Job, his sons had houses, but their wealth consisted largely of camels, donkeys, flocks, and herds, and servants (Job 1:3). Wealth can come from sinful endeavors (Acts 19:25). From the beginning of Israel, God taught his people that he was the giver of their wealth (Deut 8:18). He taught them to be liberal (Prov 11:24). NT teaching goes even further (1 Cor 10:24). Some OT passages give the impression that wealth always went with godliness (Ps 112:3) and that poverty was for the wicked (Prov 13:18), but this outlook can be debated.

WEAN, WEANING (Heb. *gāmal, to complete, wean*). To wean is to accustom a child to depend on other food than his mother's milk. In the East weaning is often deferred for as long as three years (1 Sam 1:22). The weaning of a child was celebrated by a feast (Gen 21:8) and with an offering (1 Sam 1:24).

WEAPON (See ARMS AND ARMOR)

WEASEL (See ANIMALS)

WEATHER There is no Hebrew word corresponding to "weather." At the top of Hermon (9,000 ft. [2,813 m.] above sea level) there is snow on the ground year around. The temperature of much of Palestine is comparable to that of California. From about mid-November to mid-January much rain falls, the "former" or "fall" rain of Scripture (Jer 5:24). In late March, if the land is favored, comes the "later" or "spring" rain (Joel 2:23), thus assuring good crops. In OT times there was a close relationship between the spiritual condition of the people and the weather (1 Kings 8:35–36; Joel 1:17–20). Sin brought physical punishment in famine, plagues of insects, and storms. In the highlands, as at Jerusalem, it became quite cold in winter (Ezra 10:9, 13), especially since the houses were inadequately heated (Jer 36:22).

WEAVING (Heb. *'āragh*). Genesis 4:20 implies that the weaving of tents and the taming of cattle had their beginnings nearly at the same time. Weaving, as a fine art, was in the case of Bezelel and Oholiab a gift from God (Exod 35:30–35); and their woven work for the tabernacle, the curtains and veils may have surpassed in beauty anything previously known in cloth. The virtuous woman (Prov 31:10–31) is acquainted with the work of spinning and weaving, as well as the work of dressmaking; but the heavier work of weaving tentcloth was often done by men (Acts 18:2–3). Isaiah speaks of the wicked as weaving the spider's web (59:5). See also OCCUPATIONS AND PROFESSIONS.

Three Arab women weaving a carpet. Courtesy Zev Radovan

WEDDING (Gr. *gamos*). An event regarded in Scripture as the ceremony by which a man and a woman were joined together as husband and wife and legally entitled to form a separate family unit. The betrothal was a significant, binding, legal commitment for the forthcoming marriage (Deut 20:7), a commitment that could be broken only by death or divorce. At the time of the betrothal, gifts of jewelry would be presented to the girl and sometimes to her mother, and, depending on the society, the bride price, dowry, or contract would also be exchanged. It became increasingly common for gold coins to form part of the betrothal gifts. During the period of the betrothal, which normally lasted for one year, the girl was already deemed to belong to her future husband, and the punishment for any man who violated her sexually was death by stoning.

Often a separate small tent or hut was erected to be used by the bride and groom for the wedding night (2 Sam 16:22; Ps 19:4–5; Song of Songs 1:16–17). For the very poor, who could not afford this privacy, a small section of the groom's parents' tent was partitioned off for the use of the young couple. Tradi-tionally, the bride remained veiled and the tent was kept in darkness until after the marriage was consummated (e.g. Laban substituted Leah for her more attractive sister Rachel; cf. Gen 24:67).

With the passage of time the wedding ceremony became more elaborate, with the entire village participating. Bride and groom would be dressed in clothing of fine linen, while the bride was also groomed with cosmetic preparations and anointed with sweet-smelling perfumes. She also wore an elaborate headdress that was adorned with gold coins, forming part of the bride's dowry. In later biblical times there appear to have been separate processions for bride and groom, where each was accompanied by musicians, dancers, torchbearers, well-wishers, and friends (Jer 7:34; 16:9; 25:10).

Following the example of King Solomon (Song of Songs 3:11), the bride-groom was crowned king of the festival, and apparently from about the same period (900 B.C.) the bride also submitted to a ceremonial crowning (Ezek 16:8–13). Traditionally, the feasting lasted for seven days (Judg 14:12, 17). At an approved point in the ceremonies, she was escorted to the specially prepared bridal chamber, to the cheers, laughter, and enthusiasm of the assembled guests.

WEDGE (Heb. *lāshôn zāhāv, tongue of gold*). The English word occurs only in Joshua 7:21, 24, where the Hebrew word *lashon* ("tongue") indicates the shape. A more accurate translation than "golden wedge" (Isa 13:12 KJV) would be simply "gold" (as in most other versions).

WEEDS (See PLANTS)

WEEK (See CALENDAR)

WEEKS, FEAST OF (See FEASTS)

WEIGHTS AND MEASURES The ancient Hebrews used the terms *pace* (about a yard), *cubit* (the length of the forearm), *span* (length of a hand; about half a cubit), *palm* (hand-breadth; about one-third of a span), and a *finger* (about one-quarter of a palm). In Egypt a similar system was used.

The ordinary cubit is equivalent to about 17½ or 18 inches (45 or 46 cm.). Ezekiel mentions a "long cubit," which he equates with a cubit and a handbreadth (40:5; 43:13; cf. 2 Chron 3:3), roughly equivalent to 20½ inches (53 cm.). The length of Hezekiah's water tunnel underneath Jerusalem is stated by the inscription in the tunnel to be 1,200 cubits. The tunnel is 1,749 feet (547 m.) long according to the most reliable measurement. The cubit length thus arrived at is 17.49 inches (45 cm.). Many ancient buildings have been found on excavation to be measurable in terms of a cubit of about 17 1/2 inches, or in reeds equivalent to 6 such cubits.

The *reed*, mainly an instrument for measuring rather than a unit of measurement, was 6 cubits long (Ezek 40:5). The *fathom* (armstretch; Acts 27:28) was about 6 feet (almost 2 m.).

In OT times distance was usually measured by the length of time necessary to traverse it (Gen 30:36; 31:23). In the NT these terms are used: stadium ("furlong" KJV, Luke 24:13; John 6:19), about 606 feet (189 m.); mile (Matt 5:41), about 4,860 feet (1,519 m.). About the Sabbath day's journey there is some uncertainty. The term, used to indicate the distance one might walk without breaking the Sabbath law, seems to have been an elastic one. Josephus calls it 5 stadia in one place and 6 in another, making it equal 3,000 or 3,600 feet (938 or 1,125 m.). This is about the distance from Jerusalem to the Mt. of Olives (Acts 1:12). Land measurements were indicated in terms of the area that a team of oxen could plow in one day (1 Sam 14:14,

"acre" in Isa 5:10) or the part of a field that could be seeded with barley in one day (Lev 27:16). The *hin* was a pot and the *ephah* a basket. The *omer* was a sheaf and the *homer* a donkey load. The word *bath* means "daughter"; could this jar be the one that one's daughters carried home from the well? (Gen 24:15). The English "measure" may equal a *kōr*, (Luke 16:7), or a *bath*, (16:6). The *firkin* of John 2:6 (KJV) held about 10.3 gallons (40 l.).

The *homer* was the standard dry measure of the OT. *Homer* means "donkey," and therefore a donkey-load, or about 6.25 bushels (208 l.) It is to be equated with the *cor*. The *ephah* (about 3/5 bushel or 20 liters) is the dry equivalent of the liquid measure *bath* (Ezek 45:10). The *lethekh* is mentioned only in Hosea 3:2 and is probably given its correct value in the KJV, which translates it "half homer."

NT dry measures are *bushel* (Matt 5:15), about 7½ dry quarts or slightly less than ½ U.S. bushel; *measure* ("quart," RSV), about 1 dry quart; *pot* (Mark 7:4), about 1 dry pint.

Ezra 2:69 is probably the first mention of coined money in the Bible (drachmas NIV; drams KJV; daries RSV). During most of OT times, barter (e.g., Gen 30:27–34; 31:8; 2 Kings 3:4), value determined by precious metal weighed out, was the means of exchange. The *shekel* is a weight in the OT, not a coin (Ezek 4:10), and the verb *shāqal* means "to weigh out," as in Jeremiah 32:10. Simple balance scales were used, and stones of certain weight (often shekels) were used to determine the weight of the silver or gold involved in the transaction (cf. Prov 16:11).

The Babylonians had 60 shekels in their maneh, but from Exodus 38:25–26 it appears that the Hebrew maneh consisted of only 50. Half a shekel each was paid by 603,550 men, and totaled 100 talents and 1,775 shekels; this means that the talent here equaled 3,000 shekels. Since the talent was almost 60 manehs, the maneh here equals 50 shekels. Ezekiel uses a different system, with 60 shekels to the maneh (45:12).

The *beqa'* or *half-shekel* is the only weight named both in the OT and on discovered weights, and of which the relationship to the shekel is given (Exod 38:26).

WELL (Heb. *be'ēr*, Gr. *phrear*). A pit or hole dug in the earth down to the water table. For both safety and permanence, the well was generally surrounded by a

Turn-of-the-century photograph of Jacob's Well near Shechem, where the Samaritan woman met Jesus (John 4). Courtesy University Library, Istanbul

wall of stone, and in the case of some famous wells, like that of Jacob at Sychar (John 4), the walls were beautifully constructed with dressed stone.

WEST (Heb. *yām, sea, māvô', setting of the sun, ma'ărāv, west*, Gr. *dysmē*). *Yām*, "sea," is the Hebrew word usually used for "west," because the Mediterranean Sea lies to the west of Palestine. The word is sometimes used figuratively with "east" to denote great distance (Ps 103:12).

WHALE (See ANIMALS)

WHEAT (See PLANTS)

WHEEL (Heb. *'ôphan, galgal, gilgal, 'ovnayim, pa'am*, Gr. *trochos*). When the Egyptians with their chariots pursued the Israelites at the Red Sea (Exod 14:24–25), the Lord took off their chariot wheels. In 1 Kings 7:30–33 where the bases of the great "sea" of Solomon's temple are described, reference is made to wheels with their axles, rings, spokes, and hubs, showing that by Solomon's time (c. 1000 B.C.) the wheel was quite developed and was similar to modern wagon wheels. Cart wheels were used for threshing some kinds of grain, but not cummin (Isa 28:27). The word for "pot-

ter's wheel" means literally "two stones" (Jer 18:3). In ancient times two circular stone disks were joined by a short shaft, and so spun. Today, the shaft is longer and the wheels are of wood.

WHIP (Heb. *shôt*). An instrument of punishment or inciting to work; generally a lash attached to a handle. This word was used figuratively by Rehoboam in reference to his father (1 Kings 12:14).

WHIRLWIND (Heb. *sûphâh, se'ārâh, sa'ar*). In biblical usage this does not exactly conform to our modern idea of a violent whirling as at the vortex of a tornado, but rather emphasizes the idea of being tossed about. These Hebrew words are often translated "storm" or "tempest," which is a more accurate translation; and they are used figuratively of swift and terrible destruction (Prov 1:27; Isa 5:28; Jer 4:13; Hos 8:7). Elijah was carried to heaven by a whirlwind (2 Kings 2:1, 11).

WHORE (See PROSTITUTE)

WICKED, WICKEDNESS (Heb. *ra, rasha*, Gr. *ponēros, ponēria*). The KJV often uses these words, but later translations prefer "evil," especially in the NT. The idea is that of a person or thing that is bad, worthless, depraved, and corrupt, and especially of a person or thing that opposes God, his will, his Messiah, and his gospel (e.g., Gen 6:5; Ps 37; Matt 16:4; Acts 2:23; Rom 1:29).

The origin and source of wickedness is to be sought, not in the wicked hearts of mankind, but in the work and wiles of the devil, who is the "wicked" or "evil" one (Matt 13:19; Mark 4:15; Luke 8:12; Eph 6:12). Christians are to have nothing to do with the Wicked One or wickedness (1 John 5:18–19; 2:13) and are to use the shield of faith (Eph 6:16). God permits wickedness in this age but does not condone it, and he will judge those responsible for it (Matt 13:49). See also EVIL; MALICE.

WIDOW (Heb. *'almānâh*, Gr. *chēra*). Widows in the OT are regarded as being under God's special care (Pss 68:5; 146:9; Prov 15:25). From early times they wore a distinctive garb. The Hebrews were commanded to treat them with special consideration and were punished if they did otherwise (Exod 22:22; Deut 14:29; Isa 1:17; Jer 7:6). The church looked after poor widows (Acts 6:1; James 1:27; 1 Tim 5:4); but only those were taken care of who were at least 60 years of age, had been married only once, and had a reputation for good works (5:9–10). In the second and third centuries there was an order of widows in the church. Its members looked after the women of the congregation. This order was abolished by the Synod of Laodicea, A.D. 364.

WIFE (See FAMILY; MARRIAGE)

WILDERNESS Either barren desert or to an uncultivated region suitable for pasturage and occupied by nomads. (1) The most common Hebrew word rendered "wilderness" is *midhbār*, "a place for the driving of cattle" (Num 14:33; Deut 2:8; Judg 1:16 KJV; NIV "desert"). The word may refer to grassy pastures (Ps 65:12; Joel 2:22 KJV; NIV "grasslands") or a wasteland of rock and sand (Deut 32:10; Job 38:26 KJV; NIV "desert"). (2) *Yeshîmôn*, sometimes rendered as a proper name in KJV (Num 21:20), refers to a dry or riverless region (Isa 43:19–20 KJV; NIV "desert"). (3) *'Arāvâh*, "arid, barren" (Isa 33:9; 51:3), when used with the definite article, denotes the plain of the Jordan and Dead Sea (2 Sam 2:29; Ezek 47:8) and is translated "Arabah" in RV and NIV. (4) *Tsiyyâh*, "land of drought" (Hos 2:3) is translated "desert" in NIV. (5) *Tohû*, "empty waste" (Job 12:24; Ps 107:40 KJV; NIV "trackless waste") refers to barren deserts. (6) Greek *erēmos* is a word that, like *midhbār* above, is used with considerable latitude (Matt 14:13, NIV "solitary place"; Heb 11:38, KJV and NIV "desert").

WILD GOAT (See ANIMALS)

WILD GOURD (See PLANTS)

WILD VINE (See PLANTS)

WILLOW (See PLANTS)

WILLOWS, BROOK OF THE A brook on the boundary of Moab (Isa 15:7 KJV, RSV), generally identified with the Zered (Wâdi el-Hesâ), which flows into the southern end of the Dead Sea and forms the boundary between Edom and Moab. NIV reads "Ravine of the Poplars."

WILLS Testaments, oral or written, which law courts put into effect, by which property may be disposed of after death. Covenants between living persons might be bilateral, each party making promises, or unilateral, an agreement by one party that the other may accept or reject but may not alter. Wills grew out of the latter. In early times among the Hebrews as among others, property descended according to the laws of inheritance without wills. The only clear Bible reference to a will is in Hebrews 9:16–17, and its meaning is disputed. The context

seems to assimilate the testament to a unilateral covenant of God with his people: Greek *diathēkē* always primarily meant a will, but was used in the LXX for Hebrew *berîth*, "covenant." In question here is an instrument that is effective only after the death of the one who made it, and this justifies RSV and NIV in translating it as "will."

WINDOW (See HOUSE)

WINDS Wind in Hebrew is usually *rûah*, translated also "breath, spirit"; in Greek *anemos*, always "wind." Greek *pneuma*, "breath, wind, spirit" (John 3:8); *pnoē*, "breath" (Acts 2:2); the verb *pneō*, "to blow" (27:40).

God causes winds, and he created them (Gen 8:1; Exod 10:13; Num 11:31; Pss 107:25; 135:7; 147:18; Jer 10:13; Jonah 1:4). The four winds are limits of distance or direction (Jer 49:36; Ezek 37:9; Dan 7:2; 8:8; 11:4; Zech 2:6; Matt 24:31; Rev 7:1). Of the cardinal directions, the east wind is most often mentioned (Gen 41:6, 23, 27; Exod 10:13; 14:21; Job 15:2; 27:21; 38:24; Pss 48:7; 78:26; Isa 27:8; Jer 18:17; Ezek 17:10; 19:12; 27:26; Hos 12:1; 13:15; Jonah 4:8; Hab 1:9). Sometimes it is stormy, wrecks ships, withers growing things. The north wind brings rain (Prov 25:23), is refreshing (Song of Songs 4:16), or stormy (Ezek 1:4). The south wind is gentle, helps growth (Job 37:17; Ps 78:26; Song of Songs 4:16). The west wind blew away the plague of locusts (Exod 10:19). Winds brought notable storms (1 Kings 18:45; 19:11; Job 1:19; Matt 8:26–27; 14:24, 32; Acts 27:4, 7, 14–15). In Acts the following winds are named: the south wind (Gr. *notos*, 27:13; 28:13), the northwest wind (*chōros*, 27:12), the southwest wind (*lips*, 27:12), and the "nor'easter" (*eurakylon*, 27:14). Wind blows chaff (Job 21:18; Pss 1:4; 35:5; 83:13; Isa 17:13; 41:16; Jer 13:24; Dan 2:35); fulfills God's commands (Pss 104:4; 148:8 RSV, NIV); reveals weakness, transitoriness, worthlessness (Job 15:2; Pss 18:42; 78:39; 103:16; Prov 11:29; 25:14; Eccl 5:16; 11:4; Isa 7:2; 26:18; 41:29; Jer 5:13; 22:22; 49:32); clears the sky (Job 37:21); drives ships (James 3:4). Elisha promises water not brought by wind (2 Kings 3:17). God rides on the wings of the wind (2 Sam 22:11; Ps 104:3). The circulation of the wind is recognized (Eccl 1:6). Wind has a drying effect (Isa 11:15; Jer 4:11–12). Princes are to be a hiding place from the wind (Isa 32:2). Wind has an observable effect on animal life (Jer 2:24). Ezekiel scattered hair in the wind to symbolize the scattering of the people (Ezek 5:2, 10, 12; 12:14; 17:21). Winds can be strong

Wall painting from the tomb of Nakht that depicts the gathering of grapes and the treading and storage of wine in jars with stoppers. Thebes, 18th Dynasty, time of Thutmose IV (?), fourteenth century B.C. Courtesy The Metropolitan Museum of Art (15.5.19e)

and destructive (Jer 51:16; Ezek 13:11, 13; Hos 4:19; 13:15). Wind can represent folly and resulting troubles (Hos 8:7). God controls the force of the wind (Job 28:25). Believers are warned against evil winds of false doctrine (Eph 4:14; Jude 12).

WINE Several Hebrew words occur, of which two are frequent. These two are (1) *yayin*, wine, as a common drink (Gen 14:18); as a drink offering (Lev 23:13); as intoxicating (Gen 9:21); figuratively of wisdom (Prov 9:2, 5), of wrath (Jer 25:15), of love (Song of Songs 1:2; 4:10) and (2) *tîrôsh*, "must," "fresh or sweet wine"; with approval (Gen 27:28; Judg 9:13; 2 Kings 18:32; Zech 9:17) and once with disapproval (Hos 4:11). Priests were forbidden to drink wine on duty (Lev 10:9; Ezek 44:21). Nazirites were not even to touch grapes while under a vow (Num 6:3, 20; Judg 13:4–14; Luke 1:15). Abuse of wine is condemned (Prov 4:17– 31:6; Isa 5:11), but God offers the wine of his Word (55:1).

In the NT, the primary Greek word is *oinos*. The word *gleukos* ("new, sweet wine") occurs only once (Act 2:13), where the disciples in their exuberant enthusiasm appeared intoxicated. New wine fermenting would burst old wineskins (Matt 9:17). Jesus refused the wine offered him on the cross because it was drugged (Mark 15:23). Jesus contrasts himself with John the Baptist (Luke 7:33–34) as one who ate and drank with others. In OT times wine was not diluted. Before NT times the Hellenistic practice of mixing it with much water was common in Palestine. Wine was a disinfectant (10:34) and medicine (1 Tim 5:23). It is right for a Christian not to drink wine if it

causes his brother to stumble (Rom 14:21). Men (1 Tim 3:8) and women (Titus 2:3) church officers were warned against overindulgence. Jesus made water into *oinos* at Cana (John 2:2–11).

At the Last Supper Jesus spoke of "this fruit of the vine" (Matt 26:29; Mark 14:25), as in the Passover liturgy; it may be a studied avoidance of the term "wine," indicating that the drink was unfermented, as the bread was unleavened. Whatever use Jesus or others made of wine is not proof that its use today is wise. The Bible gives more space to danger than to the benefit of wine.

WINEPRESS Hebrew *gath* (Judg 6:11; Neh 13:15; Isa 63:2–3), Greek *lēnos* (Matt 21:33). A "trough," usually of stone, cement-lined, from which juice flowed through a hole near the bottom into a vat (Heb. *yeqev*; Num 18:27, 30; Judg 7:25; Isa 5:2; Gr. *hypolēnion*, Mark 12:1). The grapes were pressed by men treading them, the treaders holding onto ropes suspended overhead. The process is compared to the execution of the wrath of God (Lam 1:15; Rev 14:19–20; 19:15).

WINESKIN (See BOTTLE)

WING (Heb. *kānāph*, Gr. *pteryx*). Birds' wings (Deut 32:11; Job 39:13, 26; Ps 55:6), wings of the cherubim (1 Kings 6:24) or "living creatures" (Ezek 1:5–25; Rev 4:8), and figurative wings (Pss 17:8; 18:10; 55:6; 68:13; 91:4; 139:9; Prov 23:5; Isa 40:31; Mal 4:2; Matt 23:37).

WINNOW (See FARMING)

WINNOWING FORK (Heb. *mizreh*). A fork with two or more prongs used to throw grain into the air after it had been threshed, so that the chaff might be blown away (Jer 15:7; Matt 3:12; Luke 3:17). The work was done toward evening and at night when a wind came in from the sea and carried away the light chaff. Sometimes a shovel was used for the same purpose.

WINTER Hebrew *hōreph*, "harvest time, autumn," and the cold, rainy season following (Gen 8:22; Ps 74:17; Zech 14:8); also the verb "to winter" (Isa 18:6). Hebrew *sethāw*, "winter" (Song of Songs 2:11). Greek *cheimōn*, "winter," the cold, stormy season (Matt 24:20; Mark 13:18; John 10:22; 2 Tim 4:21) and related verbs (Acts 27:12; 28:11; 1 Cor 16:6; Titus 3:12).

WINTER HOUSE (Heb. *bēth ha-hōreph*). Kings and wealthy people had residences for hot seasons and residences for cold seasons (Jer 36:22; Amos 3:15).

WISDOM The commonest OT words for wisdom are Hebrew *hākham* and related forms and Greek *sophia*. In God wisdom is the infinite, perfect comprehension of all that is or might be (Rom 11:33–36). God is the source of wisdom as of power, and wisdom is given to people through the fear of the Lord (Job 28:28; Ps 111:10). In man wisdom is an eminently practical attribute, including technical skill (Exod 28:3; RSV "an able mind"), military prowess (Isa 10:13), and shrewdness for questionable ends (1 Kings 2:6). Wisdom is shown in getting desired ends by effective means. People of the world are often wiser in their generation than the children of light (Luke 16:8). The wisdom of Solomon was far ranging in statesmanship (1 Kings 10:23–24); in understanding of human nature (3:16–25); and in natural history, literature, and popular proverbs (4:29–34). Wisdom is personified (Prov 8) in terms related to the concept of the Word in John 1:1–18, and became one of the names of God the Father and the Son, the Holy Spirit being the Spirit of Wisdom.
    Wisdom is bound up with doing the will of the Lord (Deut 4:6): to forsake his Word is to forfeit one's wisdom (Jer 8:8–9). Although wisdom literature (Prov; Eccl; Job; Pss 19, 37, 104, 107, 147, 148) often seems to equate right with advantage (profit, Eccl 1:5), there is clear evidence of the controlling hand and moral interest of God in human affairs. The sayings of Jesus, largely proverbial and parabolical, are the crown of biblical wisdom (1 Cor 1:24, 30; Col 2:3). When Paul compares the wisdom of people with the wisdom of God (1 Cor 2), he is thinking of the former as that of Greek philosophers rather than OT biblical wisdom. James' letter is wisdom literature at its best, a clear mirror of the teaching of Jesus. See also WISE PERSONS.

WISDOM OF JESUS, SON OF SIRACH (See APOCRYPHA)

WISDOM OF SOLOMON (See APOCRYPHA)

WISE PERSONS The name is often applied to people of understanding and skill in ordinary affairs (Job 15:2; Ps 49:10; Prov 1:5; Eccl 2:14; 1 Cor 1:26; 10:15; James 3:13), to Solomon superlatively (1 Kings 2:9; 5:7; 2 Chron 2:12), to the ladies of Sisera's mother (Judg 5:29), and to court women (2 Sam 14:2; 20:16). In a more specialized sense in Israel, the builders of the tabernacle (Exod 28:3; 35:30–35) and the leaders of the tribes (Deut 1:13, 15) were wise men. Wise, understanding, experienced older men came to be recognized as a distinct class, widely esteemed by the discerning. In pagan nations the wise men, grouped with and identified as magicians, sorcerers, enchanters, astrologers, and Chaldeans, appear in Egypt (Gen 41:8; Exod 7:11), Babylon (Dan 2:12–5:15), and Persia (Esth 1:13). See MAGI.

WITCH, WITCHCRAFT A title commonly linked with those in league with evil spirits and their practices. Hebrew *kāshaph*, "to practice sorcery" is sometimes so translated in NIV, ASV, often in RSV (Exod 22:18; Deut 18:10; 2 Kings 9:22; 2 Chron 33:6; Mic 5:12; Nah 3:4). Hebrew *qesem*, "divination," is once translated "witchcraft" (1 Sam 15:23, KJV, ASV), otherwise "divination." Greek *pharmakeia* (Gal 5:20 ASV; RSV "sorcery") means the use of drugs, charms, or magic words. In Acts 8:9, 11 KJV, "bewitch" is a translation of the Greek *existēmi* (NIV "amazed"). In Galatians 3:1 the Greek *baskainō*, "to use the evil eye on one," is rendered "bewitched." The famous witch of Endor (1 Sam 28:7–25) is not so called in the Bible, but is referred to as a woman who had a "familiar spirit" (KJV, ASV) or who was a "medium" (RSV, NIV). All practices of witchcraft are strictly condemned (Exod 22:18; Deut 18:9–14; 1 Sam 28:3, 9; 2 Kings 23:24; Isa 8:19; Acts 19:18–19). See MAGIC; OCCUPATIONS AND PROFESSIONS: *Sorcerer*.

WITHE (wĭth, wīth, Heb. *yether, bowstring, cord*). A strong, flexible willow or other twig. The "green withs" that Samson was bound with (Judg 16:7–9 KJV) are translated "fresh thongs" by NIV.

WITHERED HAND (See DISEASES)

WITNESS (Heb. *'ēdh* and related forms, Gr. *martys* and related words and combinations). Things may be witnesses: a heap of stones (Gen 31:44–52), a song (Deut 31:19–21), the law (31:26), an altar (Josh 22:27–34), a stone that has "heard" God speak (24:27), an altar and a pillar on the border of Egypt (Isa 19:20). Bearing false witness is condemned (Exod 20:16; 23:2; Deut 5:20) and punished the same as for the crime of which one accused another (19:16–18). True and false witnesses are contrasted (Prov 14:5). Two or three witnesses were required in legal proceedings (Deut 19:15; Matt 18:16; 2 Cor 13:1; 1 Tim 5:19; Heb 10:28). Jeremiah (32:6–25, 44) describes the use of witnesses in a transfer of real estate property. The tabernacle of witness, or testimony (Num 17:7–8; 9:15; 2 Chron 24:6), was so named because the witness of God's presence (the shekinah and the tables of the Law) was in it. God is called on as a witness (Gen 31:50; Job 16:19; Jer 29:23; 42:5; Mic 1:2; Mal 3:5; Rom 1:9; 1 Thess 2:5, 10). On solemn occasions men acknowledged themselves witnesses (Josh 24:22; Ruth 4:9–11). God called his people Israel his witnesses (Isa 43:10, 12; 44:8), and the apostles acknowledged themselves to be such (Luke 24:48; Acts 1:8; 2:32; 3:15; 5:32; 10:39–41; 1 Thess 2:10). Peter thought that Judas must be replaced as a witness (Acts 1:22). Paul had a special appointment as a witness (22:15; 26:16). He reminds Timothy of many witnesses (1 Tim 6:12; 2 Tim 2:2). Peter appeals to his readers as a witness of the sufferings of Christ (1 Peter 5:1). Jesus Christ is the "faithful witness" (Rev 1:5; 3:14). The cloud of witnesses of Hebrews 12:1 are those who by the lives they lived testify that the life of faith is the only truly worthwhile life.

WIZARD (See OCCUPATIONS AND PROFESSIONS)

WOLF (See ANIMALS)

WOMAN (Heb. *'ishshâh*, Gr. *gynē*). The general account of Creation implies the full humanity of Eve (Gen 1:26–27), and the special account of her creation (2:18–24) emphasizes her superiority to all lower animals, Adam's need of her as helper, her intimate relationship to him as a part of his inmost being, and the nature of marriage as a "one flesh" relationship. Though many OT women are not important, three patriarchal wives (Sarah, Rebekah, and Rachel) played significant roles, as did also Moses' sister Miriam (Exod 2:1–9; 15:20; Num 12). Deborah

exercised unusual leadership (Judg 4–5), and the Moabitess Ruth became a chaste blessing to Israel. Hannah (1 Sam 1:1–2:11) illustrates both the despair of a childless woman and the grace of godly motherhood. The advice of Lemuel's mother to her son (Prov 31) pictures an ideal, industrious wife in a prosperous family. Queens, good and bad, and evil women of other classes of society are frankly portrayed in the Bible.

Godly women stand out in Jesus' life and ministry: Elizabeth, mother of his forerunner (Luke 1); the Virgin Mary; Anna (2:36–38); the sinner of Luke 7:36–40; Mary Magdalene; Martha and Mary of Bethany; the women who accompanied the disciples on missionary journeys and who provided for them out of their means (8:3). Women remained at the cross until the burial and were first at the empty tomb. Women joined the men in prayer between the Ascension and Pentecost (Acts 1:14). The disciples in Jerusalem met in the house of Mary, mother of John Mark (12:12). Women were the first converts in Europe, including the prosperous business woman Lydia at Philippi (16:13–15). Phoebe, a deaconess, and many other women were greeted in Romans 16. Paul (1 Cor 11:2–16; 14:34–35) urges subordination for Christian women, but he exalts the believing wife as a type of the church, the bride of Christ (Eph 5:21–33). He sets high standards for the wives of church officers and for women in official positions (1 Tim 3:11; Titus 2:3–5). Likewise, 1 Peter 3:1–6 urges a subordinate but noble role for married women.

WOOL (Heb. *tsemer*, Gr. *erion*). The fleece of sheep and some other animals. The first wool was one of the firstfruits that the people of Israel were to give to the priests (Deut 18:4). Israelites were forbidden to wear mixed woolen and linen clothing (Deut 22:11). Wool symbolizes purity (Isa 1:18). It was used principally for the outside garments. Snow is compared to it (Ps 147:16).

WORD (Heb. *dābhār*, Gr. *logos*). "The Word of the Lord" usually denotes the prophetic word (word from God through the mouth of the prophet); however, it also can refer to the law of God (Ps 147:19ff.) and to the creative activity of God, who speaks and causes to be (Gen 1; Ps 33:6–9). The prophet becomes a mouthpiece for God (Isa 6; Jer 1:4–10; Ezek 1). The word of God is the fundamental aspect of God's self-revelation, for by his word he makes known who he is, what he is like, and what his will is for the world.

In the NT the "word of the Lord" or "word of God" (Acts 4:29; 6:2; 1 Thess 1:8) is primarily good news from God (Acts 15:7). It is the word concerning Jesus Christ and God's kingdom in and through him (16:31–32; 17:13); and it is also the word of the cross (1 Cor 1:18), of reconciliation (2 Cor 5:19), of eternal life (Phil 2:16), and of salvation (Acts 13:26). Christians are told to abide in this word (John 8:31), to keep it (8:51; 14:23), and serve it (Acts 6:4).

The words of Jesus are the words of the heavenly Father, and so to receive and accept them is to receive eternal salvation (John 5:24; 8:51; 12:48; 14:24). Jesus himself is the true Word who has come to earth from heaven (1:1–14).

WORK (See LABOR; OCCUPATIONS AND PROFESSIONS)

WORKS (Heb. *ma'aseh, work, deed, pa'al, a work,* Gr. *ergon, work, erga, works*). Used of deeds done by God out of holy love, and by human beings as God's creatures. In the OT the work/ works of God refer to his creating and preserving the cosmos (Gen 2:2; Ps 8:3) and his deeds of salvation and judgment on behalf of Israel (28:5; Isa 5:12, 19). The godly meditate on God's work and works (Pss 77:12; 143:5) and praise him for them (72:18; 105:1–2). In the NT God is presented as working in and through the Messiah both in creation (John 1:1–3) and in redemption (9:3–4). By his works Jesus reveals his true identity and from whom he comes (Matt 9:2–5; John 5:36; 10:37–38).

What deeds humans perform cannot be isolated from the state of their hearts and their motivation (Ps 28:3–4; Gal 5:19). There is no justification by works (Rom 3:20; Gal 2:16; 2 Tim 1:9). True works, in which God delights, are those that arise from an inward gratitude to God for his goodness and salvation. These spring from faith, the faith that holds to Christ as Savior and Lord (Eph 2:10; Col 1:10; James 2:14ff.).

WORLD The word "world" can mean age (Matt 13:22; Mark 10:30; Luke 18:30; 20:34–35; Eph 1:21), the inhabited earth (Matt 24:14; Luke 4:5; 21:26; Acts 17:31; Rom 10:18; Heb 1:6), the Hellenistic world (Acts 19:27), the Roman Empire (Luke 2:1; Acts 11:28; 24:5), a fallen universe hostile to God (John 8:23; 14:17–22; 15:18–19; 17:9; 18:36; 1 John), human history (John 9:32 KJV),

the human race (Pss 9:8; 96:13; Acts 17:31), and the universe (John 1:10).

WORM (See ANIMALS)

WORMWOOD (See PLANTS)

WORSHIP (Heb. *shāhâh, bow down, prostrate,* Gr. *proskyneō, to prostrate, do obeisance to*). The honor, reverence, and homage paid to superior beings or powers, whether men, angels, or God. The English word means "worthship" and denotes the worthiness of the individual receiving the special honor.

When given to God, worship involves an acknowledgment of divine perfections. It may express itself in the form of direct address, as in adoration or thanksgiving, or in service to God; it may be private, or it may be public.

In patriarchal times there was both the privacy of prayer (e.g., Gen 18) and the public act of setting up an altar (e.g., 12:7). Moses established the basis of the public worship of Israel and gave it its focal point in the tabernacle (e.g., 1 Sam 1:1). The temple ritual, which had its origin in the tabernacle, was led by priests assisted by the Levites. In the synagogues the emphasis was more on instruction than on worship. Jewish Christians continued, as long as they were permitted, to worship in the temple and in the synagogue, though for them the whole ceremonial and sacrificial system ended with the death and resurrection of Jesus. Public Christian worship developed along the lines of the synagogue. It appears that from the first, Christians met in homes for private brotherhood meetings, and the time was the Lord's Day (John 20:19, 26; Acts 20:7; 1 Cor 16:2). Christian public worship consisted of preaching (Acts 20:7; 1 Cor 14:9), reading of Scripture (Col 4:16; James 1:22), prayer (1 Cor 14:14–16), singing (Eph 5:19; Col 3:16), baptism and the Lord's Supper (Acts 2:41; 1 Cor 11:18–34), almsgiving (1 Cor 16:1–2), and sometimes prophesying and speaking in tongues.

WRATH The translation of many Hebrew and Greek words, ranging widely in tone, intensity, and effects (2 Chron 26:19; Esth 1:12; Ps 85:4; Matt 2:16). The first display of human wrath recorded in the Bible (Gen 4:5–6) is followed by numerous accounts of disaster wrought by man's wrath, which never works the righteousness of God (James 1:20) and is never more than tolerated (Eph 4:26; Ps 37:8; Rom 12:19). The wrath of a just, pure, and holy God is dreadful to evildoers (Num 11:1–10; Heb 10:26–31), yet

Proto-Canaanite	South Semitic		Proto-Canaanite	Aramaic (?) (Tell Fakhariya)	Greek	Latin	Phoenician				Hebrew					Samaritan
c. 1500 B.C.	Ancient South Arabic 1st mill. B.C.	Ethiopian	13th cent. B.C.	c. 1000 B.C.(?)	Ancient 8th-7th cent. B.C.	Classic	c. 1000 B.C.	8th-7th cent. B.C.	c. 800 B.C.	7th-1st cent. B.C.	New Punic	c. 1000 B.C.	[Moab.] c. 850 B.C.	7th cent. B.C.	6th cent. B.C.	2nd cent. B.C.	13th cent. A.D.

Chronological chart of the alphabet, Plate A. Courtesy Carta, Jerusalem

God is slow to anger, eager to forgive (Ps 103:8–9) and so should we be (Eph 4:31–32). Less often mentioned in the NT than in the OT, the wrath of God is no less terrible, is revealed most dramatically in the wrath of the Lamb (John 1:29; Rev 6:16), and abides on unbelievers (John 3:36).

WRESTLE The Hebrew *pāthal*, with a root meaning "twist" (Gen 30:8), is used of Rachel's wrestling or struggling (emotional and vocal rather than literal) with Leah, leading Rachel to name her handmaid's son Naphtali, "my wrestlings." Hebrew *'āvaq*, "get dusty, wrestle" (Gen 32:24–25), is used of Jacob's wrestling with the angel (physical effect: the dislocation of Jacob's thigh). Greek *palē*, "wrestling," is used later of any kind of fighting; used of the Christian's spiritual conflict with the powers of evil (Eph 6:12 KJV; NIV "struggle").

WRITING It is generally assumed that the earliest forms of writing were picto-graphic, not phonetic—the ideas were recorded by means of pictures, or sense-symbols, rather than by sound-symbols. Evidently the next stage in the history of writing was the introduction of the *phonogram*—the type of sign that indicates a sound. At first this was achieved by the *rebus* principle, that is, by using objects that have a name sounding like the sound of the word that the writer wishes to convey, even though the meaning of the object portrayed is entirely different. To the Egyptians goes the credit for being the first to develop an alphabetic system of writing. However, they did not see any need to abandon their ideograms, determinative signs, and syllabic characters just because they had alphabetic letters; and so they simply used all four types of sign in the writing out of their language.

The origin of the "Phoenician" alphabet is found in the alphabetic hieroglyphs of the Sinaitic Inscriptions of Serabit el-Khadim (written some time between 1900 and 1500 B.C.—for the scholars' esti-

Chronological chart of the alphabet, Plate B. Courtesy Carta, Jerusalem

mates vary). The idea for their alphabet came from Egypt, but instead of resorting to ideograms and syllabic signs, they contented themselves with alphabetic symbols chosen on the basis of *acrophony*. That is to say, the first sound of the name of the object represented conveyed the alphabetic unit intended.

During the ensuing centuries this Sinaitic type of script (or modifications of it) was cultivated in Canaan, for household objects like daggers, rings, ewers, pots, and plaques have been found with short inscriptions, mostly of very uncertain interpretation. But a totally different form of alphabetic writing assumed great importance during the period (1800–1400 B.C.), namely the cuneiform alphabet associated with Ras Shamra, or Ugarit. Unlike the cuneiform of Babylonia and Assyria, this kind of cuneiform represented an alphabet of about twenty-nine or thirty characters, all of them consonantal (except that three of them indicated the type of vowel occurring after

aleph, whether *a*, *i* [or, *e*], or *u*). This very early dialect of Canaanite (for Ugaritic is much closer to biblical Hebrew than to any other known Semitic language) contained several consonants not appearing in any of the Northwest Semitic scripts.

The inscription on the sarcophagus (stone coffin) of King Ahiram is dated by various authorities from before 1250 to as late as 1000 (the later date being advocated by Dunand, who maintained that the Shaphatbaal inscription was centuries earlier). This writing has the twenty-two-letter alphabet that was to hold the stage from then on in all the northwest Semitic languages (Phoenician, Hebrew, Moabite, Aramaic, and Syriac). The earliest Israelite document that has survived in this script is the Gezer Calendar of about 900 B.C. or a few decades earlier. It is most likely that Moses used a Proto-Phoenician type of script rather than any kind of cuneiform. The next important Hebrew inscription after the Gezer Calendar was the Siloam Inscription, incised on the wall of the underground tunnel dug through to the Pool of Siloam in preparation (probably) for the siege of Jerusalem by Sennacherib in 701 B.C. Here we see a trend toward the more freely flowing style of manuscript writing, rather than the stern angularity of monumental style.

Following the Babylonian exile, the Paleo-Hebrew script (as it is called) was retained for some types of text, such as the books of the Pentateuch, for fragments of Leviticus and Exodus have been discovered in the Qumran Caves, dating from the late fourth century (according to the estimate of some scholars).

It is important to observe that the Greeks received their alphabet from the Phoenicians and Arameans, perhaps through contact with their merchants. The Hellenic tribal groups found written expression for their language through the Phoenician alphabet, which supplied the first twenty-two letters of the Greek alphabet (i.e., *alpha* through *tau*). Those Semitic letters that expressed sounds not used by the Greeks were adapted to express vowels.

This, then, was the writing medium that in the providence of God came to be used to convey the message of redemption that is found in the NT Scriptures. From the Western form of the Greek alphabet the Romans derived their Latin alphabet, omitting from it those letters used by the Eastern Greeks that were unnecessary to express the sounds of the Latin tongue. It is this alphabet, therefore, that has descended to us at the present day, ultimately derived from the Semites of the Holy Land.

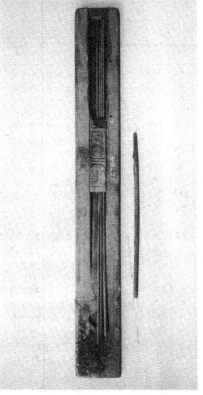

An 18th Dynasty (1550–1350 B.C.) scribe's wooden palette (0.285 m. long) inscribed with the name of Ahmose I (1570–1545 B.C.). Palette is equipped with rushes, which served as pens, and a circular hollow to hold ink or paint. Reproduced by courtesy of the Trustees of the British Museum

- XYZ -

Crown Prince Ahasuerus (see Esth 1:1) standing behind the enthroned king of Persia, Darius I. Limestone relief from Persepolis, 521–486 B.C. Courtesy The Oriental Institute, University of Chicago

XERXES (zŭrk'sēz, Gr. form of Heb. *'ăhashwērôsh*, Persian *Khshayarsha*). 1. The father of Darius the Mede (Dan 9:1). 2. King of Persia, mentioned in the Book of Esther. There seems to be little doubt that he is the well-known historical Xerxes (KJV, Ahasuerus), who reigned from 486 to 465 B.C.

YAHWEH (See YHWH; GOD)

YARN (Heb. *miqweh*). The KJV translation of the Hebrew word in 1 Kings 10:28 and 2 Chronicles 1:16 translated in RSV and NIV by the proper name "Kue," the old Assyrian name given to Cilicia (in the SE portion of Asia Minor).

YEAR (See CALENDAR)

YEARLING (See ANIMALS)

YHWH This is not in reality a word but is known as the "Tetragrammaton," the four consonants standing for the ancient Hebrew name for God commonly referred to as "Jehovah" or "Yahweh." The original Hebrew text was not vocalized. YHWH was considered too sacred to pronounce, so *'adonai* ("my Lord") was substituted in reading. When eventually a vowel system was invented, since the Hebrews had forgotten how to pronounce YHWH, they substituted the vowels for *'adonai*, making "Jehovah," a form first attested at beginning of the 12th century A.D.

YODH (See JOT)

YOKE (Heb. *môtâh, an oxbow, 'ôl, a yoke, tsemedh, yoke of oxen, an acre*, i.e., as much land as a yoke of oxen could plow in a day, Gr. *zeugos, a team* and *zygos, yoke*). In the literal sense, a bar of wood so constructed as to unite two animals, usually oxen, enabling them to work in the fields. Drawing loads and pulling instruments used in farming, such as the plow, were two chief functions the yoke made possible. Also used figuratively in the sense of servitude (Jer 27–28) and "the law of God."

YOKEFELLOW (Gr. *syzygos, yoked together*). A common word among Greek writers referring to those united by close bonds, as in marriage, labor, etc. It is found only once in the NT (Phil 4:3).

YOM KIPPUR (See FEASTS)

ZAANAIM (See ZAANANNIM)

ZAANANNIM (zā'ă-năn'ĭm, Heb. text uncertain). A place on Naphtali's southern border near the spot where Sisera lost his life at the hands of the wife of Heber the Kenite (Josh 19:33; Judg 4:11), about 3 miles (5 km.) NE of Mt. Tabor.

ZABAD (zā'băd, Heb. *zāvādh, the LORD has given*). 1. The son of Nathan (1 Chron 2:36; cf. 11:41). 2. One from the tribe of Ephraim (7:21). 3. The son of

Shimeath, the Ammonitess. He conspired against King Joash (2 Chron 24:26; cf. 25:3–4). 4–6. Three Israelites were given this name, sons of Zattu (Ezra 10:27), Hashum (10:33), and Nebo (10:43). In response to Ezra's plea after the Captivity, they put away their Gentile wives.

ZABBAI (zăb'ā-ī, Heb. *zabbay*, meaning unknown). 1. One of the sons of Bebai who put away his foreign wife (Ezra 10:28). 2. The father of Baruch (Neh 3:20).

ZABBUD (See ZACCUR)

ZABDI (zăb'dī, Heb. *zavdî, he [God] has given*). 1. Achan's grandfather (Josh 7:1, 17 JB, KJV, MLB, MOF, NASB, NEB, RSV; Zimri NIV). 2. A son of Shimei from the tribe of Benjamin (1 Chron 8:19). 3. One of the officers of David (27:27). 4. One of the ancestors of Mattaniah, who aided in worship in the days of Nehemiah (Neh 11:17).

ZABDIEL (zăb'dĭ-ĕl, Heb. *zavdî 'ēl, God has given*). 1. The father of Jashobeam (1 Chron 27:2). 2. A temple overseer (Neh 11:14).

ZABULON (See ZEBULUN)

ZACCHAEUS (ză-kē'ŭs, Gr. *Zakchaios*, from the Hebrew *zakkay, pure*). A "chief" tax collector. When Jesus was passing through Jericho on one occasion, Zacchaeus wished very much to see him. Being short, he climbed a tree by the side of the path. Jesus paused in his journey beneath this very tree and, looking up, urged Zacchaeus to come down, for he had decided to stay at his house (Luke 19:6). Zacchaeus hurried down gladly and invited Jesus to his home. From that day on his life was changed (19:8).

ZACCUR, ZACCHUR (Heb. *zakkûr, remembered*). 1. The father of the Reubenite spy Shammua (Num 13:4). 2. The son of Hamuel, a Simeonite (1 Chron 4:26), Zacchur in AV. 3. One of the sons of Merari (24:27). 4. One of the sons of Asaph set apart by David for musical service (25:1–2; Neh 12:35). 5. The son of Imri who aided in rebuilding the wall of Jerusalem (3:2). 6. One of those who, with Nehemiah, sealed the covenant (10:12). 7. One of the treasurers (13:13). 8. A son of Bigvai (Ezra 8:14 NIV; Zabbud KJV and most versions).

ZACHARIAH, ZACHARIAS (See ZECHARIAH)

ZADOK (ză'dŏk, Heb. *tsādhōq, righteous*). 1. A priest in the time of David (2 Sam 8:17; 1 Chron 12:23–38; 15:11–13). So faithful was he to David that he

accompanied him with the ark when he fled from Jerusalem at the rebellion of Absalom and stayed with him until commanded by David to return to Jerusalem to act as a spy for him (2 Sam 15:24–36; 17:15). When, at the end of David's life, Adonijah aspired to be king, Zadok followed the instructions of King David and anointed Solomon, David's son, king in Gihon (1 Kings 1:8–45; cf. 2:26–35). 2. The son of Ahitub (1 Chron 6:12). 3. Jerusha's father (2 Kings 15:33; 2 Chron 27:1). 4. The son of Baana who aided in the construction of the wall of Jerusalem (Neh 3:4; cf. 10:21). 5. Another priest who shared in rebuilding the Jerusalem walls under Nehemiah (3:29). 6. One appointed by Nehemiah to be a scribe (13:13). He may well be one of the two wall-builders mentioned above.

ZALMON (zăl'mŏn, Heb. *tsalmôn, dark*). 1. A Benjamite who was one of David's mighty men (2 Sam 23:28), also called "Ilai" (1 Chron 11:29). 2. A forest near Shechem (Judg 9:48).

ZALMUNNA (zăl-mŭn'à, Heb. *tsalmunnā', deprived of shade*). One of the two kings of Midian whom Gideon captured and killed during his bold raid on the Midianites (Judg 8:4–21; Ps 83:11).

ZAMZUMMITE, ZAMZUMMIM (zăm-zŭm'ĭt, zăm-zŭm'ĭm, Heb. *zamzummîn, murmurers*). A name found only in Deuteronomy 2:20. It is used of the race of giants, called Rephaim (2 Sam 5:18, 22), who lived east of the Jordan. Later on the Ammonites captured them and occupied their land. They may be the same as the Zuzites (Zuzim) in Genesis 14:5.

ZANOAH (zà-nō'à, Heb. *zānôah, rejected*). 1. A town in the low hills of Judah (Josh 15:34). After the Babylonian captivity some Jews returned to lived there (Neh 11:30) and assisted in the rebuilding of the walls of Jerusalem (3:13). 2. A town located in the mountains of Judah (Josh 15:56), 10 or 12 miles (17 or 20 km.) SW of Hebron. It was built or rebuilt by Jekuthiel, who is called its "father" (1 Chron 4:18).

ZAREAH, ZAREATHITE (See ZORAH)

ZARED (See ZERED)

ZAREDAH (See ZARETHAN)

ZAREPHATH (zăr'ĕ-făth, Heb. *tsārephath, refinement*). An OT town remembered chiefly because Elijah resided there during the latter half of the famine caused by the drought (1 Kings 17:9ff.). Its Greek equivalent "Sarepta" is mentioned in the KJV of Luke 4:26, where it is described as being in the land of Sidon.

ZARETHAN (zăr'ĕ-thăn, Heb. *tsārethān*). A place near Beth Shan and Adam that is mentioned in connection with Israel's crossing of the Jordan (Josh 3:16). It is also spelled Zaretan and Zartanah. Bronze castings for the temple were made there (1 Kings 7:46; cf. 4:12). In 2 Chronicles 4:17 the name is given as Zeredah (ASV, RSV) and Zeredathah (KJV).

ZARETH-SHAHAR (See ZERETH SHAHAR)

ZARHITES (See ZERAH)

ZARTANAH, ZARTHAN (See ZARETHAN)

ZATTU, ZATTHU (ză'tū, Heb. *zattû'*). Head of a large family of children (Ezra 2:8; Neh 7:13; 10:14). Several of his children were among those who put away their Gentile wives (Ezra 10:27).

ZAVAN (See ZAAVAN)

ZEALOT (zĕl'ŭt, Gr. *zēlōtēs, zealous one*). A member of a Jewish patriotic party started in the time of Quirinius to resist Roman aggression. According to Josephus (*War* 4.3.9; 5.1; 7.8.1), the Zealots resorted to violence and assassination in their hatred of the Romans, their fanatical violence eventually provoking the Roman war. Simon the Zealot was distinguished from Simon Peter by this epithet (Luke 6:15; Acts 1:13).

ZEBADIAH (zĕb'à-dī'à, Heb. *zevadhyāhû, Jehovah has bestowed*). 1. A descendant of Benjamin (1 Chron 8:15). 2. Another Benjamite (8:17). 3. A Benjamite who joined David at Ziklag. He used bows and arrows as well as stones and was just as adept with his left as with his right hand (12:1–7). 4. One of the Korahite doorkeepers of David's time (26:2). 5. One of the officers of David's army (27:7). 6. A Levite sent by King Jehoshaphat to teach the law (2 Chron 17:8). 7. Head of the house of Judah in all matters that pertained to King Jehoshaphat (19:11). 8. One of those who returned with Ezra from Babylon (Ezra 8:8). 9. A priest who had married a foreign woman after the return from the Babylonian captivity (10:20).

ZEBAH (zē'bà, Heb. *zevah, sacrifice*). One of the two kings of Midian whom Gideon overthrew, the other being Zalmunna (Judg 8:10, 12; Ps 83:11). Gideon, having heard their personal confession that they had killed some of the Israelites (Judg 8:18–19), ordered them executed.

The son to whom this command was given, only a boy, refused, and when these kings asked Gideon to kill them, he did so (8:19–21).

ZEBEDEE (zĕb'ĕ-dē, Gr. *Zebedaios*, meaning uncertain). A fisherman on the Sea of Galilee (Mark 1:20), the father of James and John (Matt 4:21; Mark 1:19). He was the husband of Salome and in all probability lived in the vicinity of Bethsaida (Matt 27:56).

ZEBIDAH (zē-bī'dà, Heb. *zevûdhâh, given*). Josiah's wife, the daughter of Pedaiah. She was the mother of Jehoiakim the king (2 Kings 23:36).

ZEBOIIM, ZEBOIM (zē-boi'ĭm, zēbō'-ĭm, Heb. *tsevô'ĭm, gazelles, hyena*). 1. One of the five cities in the Valley of Siddim that God destroyed with Sodom and Gomorrah (Gen 10:19; 14:2, 8; Deut 29:23; Hos 11:8). 2. A ravine in Benjamin not far from Micmash (1 Sam 13:18; Neh 11:34).

ZEBUDAH (See ZEBIDAH)

ZEBULUN (zĕb'û-lŭn, Heb. *zevûlûn, habitation*). 1. Jacob's tenth son, the sixth and last son of Leah (Gen 30:19–20). Three sons were born to him in the land of his birth (46:14). 2. One of the 12 tribes of Israel (Num 1:31). The place assigned to this tribe was on the east side of the tabernacle with the standard of Judah (2:7). Zebulun's territory lay between the Sea of Galilee and the Mediterranean. This area included many points at which Christ later carried on his ministry, and Matthew records that he thus fulfilled the ancient prophecy of Isaiah (Isa 9:1–2; Matt 4:12–16). 3. A city, located in the tribe of Asher between Beth Dagon and the Valley of Iphtah El (Josh 19:27). (See map on page 638.)

ZECHARIAH (zĕk'à-rī'à, Heb. *zekharyāhû, Jehovah remembers*). 1. Fourteenth king of Israel, the son of Jeroboam II. In fulfillment of 2 Kings 10:30 he was the last of the house of Jehu. After reigning six months, he was killed by Shallum, his successor (2 Kings 15:8–10). 2. A Reubenite chief (1 Chron 5:7). 3. A Korahite (9:21; 26:2, 14). 4. A Benjamite (9:37). 5. A Levitical doorkeeper in the time of David (15:17–18, 20; 16:5). 6. One of the Davidic priests who was used as a trumpeter to help in bringing the ark from the house of Obed-Edom back to Jerusalem (15:24). 7. A Levite from Uzziel (24:25). 8. A Merarite in David's day (26:11). 9. A Manassite in the time of David (27:21). 10. One of the princes whom Jehoshaphat sent to teach

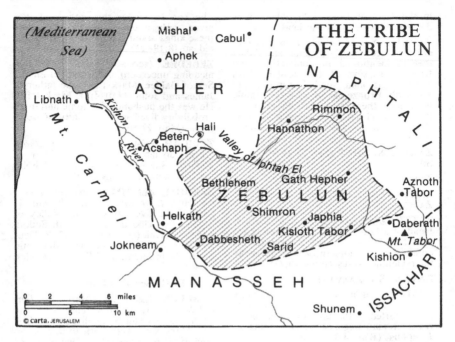

(Mediterranean Sea)

Mishal
Cabul
Aphek

THE TRIBE OF ZEBULUN

A S H E R

N A P H T A L I

Libnath
Kishon
Mt. Carmel

Hali
Beten
Acshaph
Rimmon
Hannathon

Valley of Iphtah El

Bethlehem
Gath Hepher
Z E B U L U N
Aznoth
Tabor

Helkath
Shimron
Japhia
Kisloth Tabor
Daberath
Mt. Tabor

Joknean
Dabbesheth
Sarid
Kishion

M A N A S S E H

0 2 4 6 miles
0 5 10 km
© carta. JERUSALEM

Shunem
ISSACHAR

in the cities of Judah (2 Chron 17:7). **11.** The father of the prophet Jahaziel and son of Benaiah (20:14). **12.** Jehoshaphat's third son, killed by his brother Jehoram (21:2–4). **13.** A son of Jehoiada the high priest, he sought to check the rising tide of idolatry. A conspiracy was formed against him and, on the king's orders, he was stoned (24:20–22). **14.** A prophet whose good influence on King Uzziah was outstanding (26:5). **15.** The father of Abijah (29:1). **16.** A Levite who in King Hezekiah's day assisted in the purification of the temple (29:13). **17.** A Kohathite and one of the overseers who assisted in temple repairs in the days of King Josiah (34:12). **18.** One of the temple administrators in the time of King Josiah (35:8). **19.** One who returned to Jerusalem with Ezra (Ezra 8:3). **20.** The son of Bebai who returned with Ezra (8:11). **21.** One of those who stood by Ezra as he read the Law to the people (Neh 8:4; Ezra 8:15–16). **22.** A son of Elam who at Ezra's suggestion divorced his Gentile wife (10:26). **23.** A man from the tribe of Judah (Neh 11:4). **24.** A descendant of Shelah who lived at Jerusalem (11:5). **25.** One who aided in the work at Jerusalem after the Captivity (11:12). **26.** A priest in the days of Joiakim (12:16; Ezra 5:1; 6:14). **27.** A priest, one of the trumpeters at the dedication of the wall of Jerusalem

under the leadership of Ezra and Nehemiah (Neh 12:35, 41). **28.** A contemporary of Isaiah (Isa 8:1–2). **29.** The next to the last of the 12 minor prophets. He came from a line of priests, being the son of Berekiah and the grandson of Iddo (Zech 1:1). He was a prophet as well as a priest (1:7). He returned from the Babylonian captivity to Jerusalem under the leadership of Zerubbabel. It was during the eighth month of the second year of the Persian king Darius that he began his prophetic ministry (1:1). He was contemporary with Haggai, beginning his ministry just two months after the latter prophet. **30.** The father of John the Baptist (Luke 1:5, 67–69). **31.** The son of Berakiah (Matt 23:35; Luke 11:51) murdered between the altar and the temple.

ZECHARIAH, BOOK OF
I. Historical Background.
Zechariah was the grandson of Iddo, the head of one of the priestly families that returned from the Exile (Neh 12:4, 16). Twenty years after the return, the temple still lay a blackened ruin, and the discouraged people did not see how it could be restored. At this critical moment God raised up the prophets Haggai and Zechariah to encourage the Jews to rebuild the temple. The prophecies of the two men were delivered almost at the

same time Haggai in August 520 B.C. and, soon after, Zechariah (Zech 1:1–6). Haggai finished his recorded prophecies the same year. The following year Zechariah gave a message consisting of eight symbolic visions, with an appendix (1:7–6:15). Two years later he gave a third message in answer to an inquiry by the men of Bethel regarding the observance of a fast. The two prophecies found in chapters 9–14 are not dated and were probably given at a much later period.

II. Contents.

A. Zechariah 1–8. Messages delivered on three separate occasions.

1. Zechariah 1:1–6. A general introduction.

2. Zechariah 1:7–6:15. A series of eight symbolic night visions, followed by a coronation scene. These visions were intended to encourage the Israelites to complete the temple.

3. Zechariah 7–8 were spoken two years later than the series of visions described above and represent Zechariah's answer to the questions put to him by certain visitors as to whether the fasts observed in memory of the destruction of Jerusalem should still be kept. The reply is no; for God demands not fasts, but observance of moral laws. God has come to dwell with his people; and even the heathen will desire to worship God in Jerusalem.

B. Zechariah 9–14. This is made up of two distinct prophecies, without dates.

1. Zechariah 9–11. God will visit the nations in judgment and his people in mercy. The Prince of Peace will come and confound the evil shepherds, but he will be rejected by the flock, and they will consequently again experience suffering.

2. Zechariah 12–14. A prophecy describing the victories of the new age and the coming Day of the Lord. Three apocalyptic pictures are presented: (1) Jerusalem will be saved from a siege by her enemies by the intervention of the Lord. (2) A remnant of Israel will be saved. (3) The nations will come to Jerusalem to share in the joyous Feast of Tabernacles, and all will enjoy the blessings of God's kingdom.

ZEDAD (zē′dăd, Heb. *tsedhādhâh, a siding*). A city located on the ideal northern boundary of Palestine (Num 34:8; Ezek 47:15).

ZEDEKIAH (zĕd′ĕ-kī′à, Heb. *tsidhqîyahû, the LORD is righteous*). 1. The leader and voice for the 400 prophets whom Ahab consulted to learn the outcome of his proposed expedition against Ramoth Gilead (1 Kings 22:5–24; 2 Chron 18:10). 2. The last king of Judah, son of Josiah and Hamutal (2 Kings 24:18). He rebelled against the king of Babylon, and as a result he was taken by Nebuchadnezzar and bound. His sons were killed before his eyes, and his own eyes were put out. He was then taken to Babylon where he died (2 Kings 24–25). Because of his evil he was permitted only 11 years of reign, many details of which are given in Jeremiah 34–37. 3. The son of Jehoiachin (1 Chron 3:16). 4. A false prophet (Jer 29:21–23). 5. A prince of Israel in the reign of Jehoiakim (36:12). 6. A high official who sealed the renewed covenant (Neh 10:1).

ZELAH, ZELA (zē′là, Heb. *tsēla′*). A town in Benjamin probably close to Jerusalem (Josh 18:28; 2 Sam 21:14).

ZELOPHEHAD (zē-lō′fĕ-hăd, Heb. *tselophādh*, meaning unknown). A Manassite who died in the wilderness, leaving five daughters but no sons; in the division of the land, they begged a share in the inheritance (Num 27:1–11). This the Lord granted, and when their tribesmen feared that their property might be alienated from the tribe by marriage (36:1–12), he commanded that they should

Design of the seven-branched lampstand described in the Book of Zechariah (ch. 4).
Courtesy Carta, Jerusalem

marry only within their tribe; and this became a general law regarding heiresses.

ZELOTES (See ZEALOT)

ZEMARAIM (zĕm'à-rā'ĭm, Heb. *tsemārayim*). **1.** An ancient town allotted to the tribe of Benjamin, about 4 miles (7 km.) north of Jericho (Josh 18:22). **2.** A mountain in the hill country of Ephraim on which King Abijah stood and rebuked Jeroboam and Israel for their rebellion against Judah and for their idolatry (2 Chron 13:4ff.). Though Jeroboam's army was twice the size of Abijah's, God gave Abijah victory.

ZEPHANIAH (zĕf'à-nī'à, Heb. *tsephanyâh, hidden of the LORD*). **1.** An ancestor of Samuel (1 Chron 6:36). **2.** The author of the Book of Zephaniah. He was very probably related to the kings of Judah (Zeph 1:1). His principal work seems to have been early in Josiah's reign, like that of his contemporaries Nahum and Habakkuk, and before the greater prophecies of his other contemporary, Jeremiah. **3.** A priest whom Zedekiah sent to inquire of Jeremiah (2 Kings 25:18–21; Jer 21:1). The Babylonian captain of the guard took him to Riblah where Nebuchadnezzar had him executed. **4.** The father of a Josiah in the days of Darius to whom God sent the prophet Zechariah with a message of comfort and encouragement (Zech 6:9–15).

ZEPHANIAH, BOOK OF Dated in the reign of Josiah (Zeph 1:1), this book was probably written early in his reign, before the religious reformation that began around the period from 640 to 622 B.C.

The book is concerned throughout with the Day of the Lord. This prophetic concept refers to any intervention of God in history. The ultimate expression of the Day of the Lord will occur in the end times.

In Zephaniah 1:2–6 the Day of the Lord is seen in its effects on Judah and Jerusalem. It comes as a punishment for the idolatry of the people (1:4–6). In 1:7–13 the prophet pictures the people as though they were coming to a communal sacrifice, but when they arrive, they are suddenly subject to the devastating punishment of God (1:8–9). The punishment is for social crimes as well as for idolatry.

The eschatological Day of the Lord is described in Zephaniah 1:14–18. In chapter 2 the prophet appeals to the humble to return to God, for the Day of the Lord will involve universal destruction. The third chapter continues the same message, but there the prophet includes a message of hope that is centered in a remnant of God's people, who will be kept secure throughout the turmoil predicted by the prophet (3:12–18).

ZEPHO, ZEPHI (zē'fō, zē'fī, Heb. *tsephî, watchtower*). A grandson of Esau through Eliphaz—called Zepho (Gen 36:11, 15) and Zephi (1 Chron 1:36 most versions; Zepho NIV).

ZEPHON, ZIPHION (zē'fŏn, zĭf'ĭ-ŏn, Heb. *tsephôn, watching*). The Gadite ancestor of the Zephonite family—called Zephon (Num 26:15) and Ziphion (Gen 46:16 most versions).

ZEPHONITES (See ZEPHO, ZEPHI)

ZERAH (zē'rà, Heb. *zerah, rising*). **1.** One of twin sons born to Judah (Gen 38:30). Of him came the Zerahite family of Numbers 26:20 (KJV "Zarhites"). He was great-grandfather of Achan (Josh 7). He is named with his brother Perez in the genealogy of Jesus (Matt 1:3; KJV "Zara"). **2.** A cousin of the preceding; son of Simeon (Num 26:13). **3.** A Gershonite Levite (1 Chron 6:21). **4.** Another Gershonite Levite (6:41). **5.** A grandson of Esau (Gen 36:13). He was a chief (36:17; KJV "duke"). **6.** The father of Jobab, the second of the early kings of Edom (36:33). **7.** A king of Cush (2 Chron 14:9) in the latter part of the 10th century B.C. who invaded Judah with an immense army during the reign of Asa, but Asa prayed and the Lord conquered the Cushites and gave Asa victory.

ZERAHIAH (zĕr-à-hī'à, Heb. *zerahyâh, the LORD is risen*). **1.** A Levite in the ancestry of Ezra (1 Chron 6:6, 51). **2.** A leader of 200 men who returned with Ezra (Ezra 8:4).

ZERED (zē'rĕd, Heb. *zeredh*). A valley running northwestward on the border between Moab and Edom and ending at the southern end of the Dead Sea; also the brook that follows the valley. A camping place of Israel at the end of their long wanderings (Num 21:12, KJV "Zared"; Deut 2:13–14). In Isaiah 15:7 it is called "the Ravine of the Poplars"; in Amos 6:14, the "valley of the Arabah."

ZEREDATHAH (See ZARETHAN)

ZERESH (zē'rĕsh, Heb. *zeresh, golden*). The wife of Haman the Agagite, the enemy of the Jews. She advised him to build a gallows for Mordecai, but later saw her error (Esth 5:10, 14; 6:13).

ZERETH SHAHAR (zē'rĕth shā'hàr, Heb. *tsereth hashahar, the glory of dawn*). A city located in the land belonging to Reuben "on the hill in the valley" (Josh 13:19). It ihas not been identified.

ZERUBBABEL (zĕ-rŭb'à-bĕl, Heb. *zerubbavel, shoot of Babylon*). The son of Shealtiel and the grandson of King Jehoiachin (Ezra 3:2; Hag 1:1; Matt 1:13). In 1 Chronicles 3:19 he is declared to be the son of Pedaiah, Shealtiel's brother. The explanation for this apparent discrepancy is very likely that Shealtiel died without issue; and either his nephew was his legal heir and was therefore called his son (Exod 2:10) or else Pedaiah married his brother's widow and thus Zerubbabel became Shealtiel's son by levirate law (Deut 25:5–10). He was heir to the throne of Judah (1 Chron 3:17–19) and is listed in the genealogy of our Lord (Matt 1:13; Luke 3:27).

When Cyrus allowed the Jews to return to their own land, he appointed Zerubbabel governor of the colony (Ezra 1:8, 11; 5:14). Joshua the high priest was the religious leader. When they reached Jerusalem, they first set up the altar of burnt offering, then they proceeded to lay the foundation of the new temple. Soon, however, opposition arose. The adversaries of the Jews made an apparently friendly offer of assistance (Ezra 4), but Zerubbabel and the other leaders rebuffed them; therefore they wrote to the king and succeeded in stopping the work during the reigns of Cambyses (the Ahasuerus [KJV] or Xerxes [NIV] of Ezra 4:6) and the pseudo-Smerdis (the Artaxerxes of Ezra 4:7ff.). In 520 B.C. the work was resumed and was completed four years later. A great celebration was held at the dedication of the new temple (6:16–22).

ZETHAM (zē'thăm, Heb. *zethām, olive tree*). A Gershonite Levite in David's time. He was son of Ladan (1 Chron 23:8; Laadan KJV, NEB) or the son of Jehieli (26:22); perhaps one was actually his grandfather.

ZEUS (zūs, Gr. *Zeus*). The chief of the Olympian gods, corresponding to the Roman Jupiter (see Acts 14:12–13).

ZIBA (zī'bà, Heb. *tsîvā', tsivā', a plant*). A servant or slave of King Saul (2 Sam 9:2). He had 15 sons and 20 servants. David, desiring to show kindness to the house of his departed friend Jonathan, appointed Ziba to work for Mephibosheth, Jonathan's crippled son. When David was in trouble, Ziba brought him supplies (2 Sam 19), but lied and said that Mephibosheth had been disloyal to David. David therefore gave Ziba his master's property; but later (19:24–30)

when Mephibosheth declared his innocence, David altered the decree.

ZIBIAH (zīb'ī-à, Heb. *tsivyāh, gazelle*). A woman of Beersheba who married King Ahaziah and was mother of Joash king of Judah (2 Kings 12:1; 2 Chron 24:1).

ZICRI (zĭk'rī, Heb. *zikhrî*). **1.** A Levite, first cousin of Aaron and Moses (Exod 6:21). **2.** A Benjamite of the family of Shimei (KJV Shimhi; 1 Chron 8:19–21; cf. 8:13, 21). **3.** Another Benjamite, son of Shashak (8:23). **4.** Still another Benjamite (8:27). **5.** A Levite ancestor of Mattaniah, who returned from captivity (9:15, but called "Zabdi" in Neh 11:17). **6.** A descendant of Eliezer, younger son of Moses, in the days of King David (1 Chron 26:25). **7.** The father of Eliezer, ruler of the tribe of Reuben in David's time (27:16). **8.** The father of Amasiah, the leader of 200,000 men of valor of Judah in the time of Jehoshaphat (2 Chron 17:16). **9.** The father of Elishaphat, who covenanted with Jehoiada to put Joash on the throne (23:1). **10.** A mighty man of Ephraim who, in Pekah's war against Judah, killed the son of Ahaz and other leaders (28:7). **11.** The father of Joel, the overseer of the Benjamites under Nehemiah (Neh 11:9). **12.** Head of a family of priests in the days of Joiakim (12:17), a descendant of Abijah.

ZIDKIJAH (See ZEDEKIAH)

ZIDON, ZIDONIANS (See SIDON)

ZIF (See ZIV)

Drawing of the Ziggurat of Anu at Uruk (Erech) in Mesopotamia, crowned by the "white temple" of the Jamdat Nasr period, probably built shortly before 3000 B.C.
Courtesy Carta, Jerusalem

ZIGGURAT (zĭg'ū-răt, Assyr.-Bab. *ziqquratu*, from the verb *zaqaru*, meaning *to be high* or *raised up*; hence the top of a mountain, or a staged tower). A temple tower of the Babylonians, consisting of a lofty structure in the form of a pyramid,

The ziggurat at Choga Zambil, located 37 miles (60 km.) southeast of Susa. One of the best preserved ziggurats found, it measures 492 feet (150 m.) square at the base and was originally 170 feet (52 m.) high. It was built c. 1280 B.C. in honor of the Elamite god In-Shushinak. Courtesy B. Brandl.

built in successive stages, with staircases on the outside and a shrine at the top. These structures are the most characteristic feature of the temple architecture in Mesopotamia, and the locations of more than two dozen are known today. The oldest one known is at Uruk. It measures 140 by 150 feet (44 by 47 m.) and stands about 30 feet (9 m.) high. At the top was the shrine, 65 feet (20 m.) long, 50 feet (16 m.) wide, and built about a narrow court. The ziggurat at Ur was 200 feet (63 m.) long, 150 feet (47 m.) wide, and some 70 feet (22 m.) high. The tower of Babel was a ziggurat (Gen 11:1–9).

ZIIIA (zī'hà, Heb. *tsîhā'*). 1. Head of a family of temple servants, (KJV Nethinim), who returned to Jerusalem with Zerubbabel (Ezra 2:43; Neh 7:46). 2. A ruler of the temple servants in Ophel in the days of Nehemiah (11:21).

ZIKLAG (zĭk'lăg, Heb. *tsiqelagh*). A city in the south of Palestine, given to the tribe of Judah in Joshua's day (Josh 15:31), but subsequently given to or shared by the tribe of Simeon (19:5). Later it was ruled by the Philistines; Achish king of Gath assigned it to David and his men who were fleeing from Saul (1 Sam 27:1–7). During their occupation of the city, David offered to go with Achish against Saul, but the Philistines sent him back. On reaching Ziklag he found that the Amalekites had raided it, burned it, and had carried off the women

and children. David recovered his property, returned to Ziklag, and from there began to recruit men of Judah to take his side when they would be needed. Later Ziklag became the property of the kings of Judah until the Captivity.

ZIKRI (See ZICRI)

ZILLETHAI (zĭl'ē-thī, Heb. *tsillethay, shadow of the LORD*). 1. An early Benjamite, a descendant of Shimei (1 Chron 8:20; Zilthai KJV, NEB). 2. A Manassite captain of a 1,000 (12:20).

ZILPAH (zĭl'pà, Heb. *zilpâh*, meaning uncertain). Handmaid of Leah, given to her by her father Laban. Later through Jacob she became the mother of Gad and Asher (Gen 29:24; 30:9–13).

ZIMMAH (zĭm'à, Heb. *zimmâh*). A Gershonite Levite (1 Chron 6:20, 42–43; and perhaps 2 Chron 29:12).

ZIMRI (zĭm'rī, Heb. *zimrî*). 1. A prince of the tribe of Simeon who shamelessly brought a Midianite woman into the camp of Israel to commit adultery with her, even while God was dealing with Israel for this sin (Num 25:14). Phinehas, grandson of Aaron, killed him and the woman. 2. The fifth king of the northern kingdom. He had been captain of half of the chariots of his master Elah (1 Kings 16:9–20). He assassinated the drunken Elah and reigned for seven days, until he himself was besieged by Omri. He committed suicide by burning the king's house over himself. 3. A grandson of Judah (1 Chron 2:6), possibly the Zimri of Joshua 7:1 (NIV; Zabdi KJV and most versions). 4. A son of Jehoddah or Jarah of the tribe of Benjamin (1 Chron 8:36; 9:42). 5. An unknown tribe in the East (Jer 25:25).

ZIN (zĭn, Heb. *tsin*). A wilderness the Israelites traversed on their way to Canaan. It was close to the borders of Canaan (Num 13:21) and included Kadesh Barnea within its bounds (20:1; 27:14; 33:36). Edom bordered it on the east, Judah on the SE (Josh 15:1-3), and the wilderness of Paran on the south. It was not the same as the wilderness of Sin, Zin and Sin being quite different Hebrew words.

ZINA (See ZIZA)

ZION (zī'ŭn, Heb. *tsîyôn*, Gr. *Siôn*, meaning uncertain, probably *citadel*). One of the hills on which Jerusalem stood. It is first mentioned in the OT as a Jebusite fortress (2 Sam 5:6-9). David captured it and called it the city of David (1 Kings 8:1; 2 Chron 5:2; 32:30; 33:14). David brought the ark to Zion, and the hill henceforth became sacred (2 Sam 6:10-12). When Solomon later moved the ark to the temple on nearby Mt. Moriah, the name Zion was extended to take in the temple (Isa 8:18; 18:7; 24:23; Joel 3:17; Mic 4:7). Zion came to stand for the whole of Jerusalem (2 Kings 19:21; Ps 48; 69:35; 133:3; Isa 1:8). The name is frequently used figuratively for the Jewish church and polity (Pss 126:1; 129:5; Isa 33:14; 34:8; 49:14; 52:8) and for heaven (Heb 12:22; cf. Rev 14:1).

ZIPH (zĭf, Heb. *zîph*, meaning unknown). 1. A city in the Negev given to the tribe of Judah (Josh 15:24). 2. The wilderness named from no. 1, which was in the southern part of Jeshimon (1 Sam 23:14-24; 26:1-2). 3. A city in the western part of Judah (2 Chron 11:8). 4. Possibly the same as no. 1, though mentioned separately in Joshua 15:55. 5. A Calebite family name (1 Chron 2:42). 6. A son of Jehallelel of the tribe of Judah (4:16). In KJV and NEB his father's name is Jehaleleel.

ZIPHIM (See ZIPHITES)

ZIPHION (See ZEPHON, ZIPHION)

ZIPHITES (zĭf'īts, Heb. *zîphî*). The inhabitants of Ziph, whether the name designated the town or the wilderness surrounding it (1 Sam 23:14-23; 26:1-5). Twice, apparently, David hid in their vicinity when being pursued by King Saul.

ZIPPORAH (zĭ-pō'rà, Heb. *tsippōrâh*, *bird*, fem. of *Zippor*). Daughter of Jethro or Reuel, the priest of Midian, who became the first wife of Moses (Exod 2:21). She was the mother of Gershom and Eliezer (18:1-6). Apparently Moses sent her back to her father during the unsettled and troubled times connected with the Exodus, though she had at least started to Egypt with him (cf. 4:20; 18:2).

ZITHER (See MUSIC AND MUSICAL INSTRUMENTS)

ZITHRI (See SITHRI)

ZIV (Heb. *ziw*). The second month of the old Hebrew calendar, corresponding to Iyyar in the later Jewish calendar (1 Kings 6:1, 37; Zif KJV). See also CALENDAR.

ZIZA (zī'zà, Heb. *zîzâ'*, *abundance*). 1. A Simeonite in the days of King Hezekiah, who, with others, drove out the ancient inhabitants of Gedor, SW of Bethlehem, and took their land for pasture (1 Chron 4:37-41). 2. The second son of Shimei, a leading Gershonite Levite in the days of David (1 Chron 23:10-11 MOF, NEB, NIV; Zina in v. 10, Zizah in v. 11—JB, KJV, MLB, NASB, RSV). 3. A son of Rehoboam and brother of Abijah, kings of Judah (2 Chron 11:20).

ZOAN (zō'ăn, Heb. *tsō'an*). An ancient Egyptian city, built on the east part of the Delta seven years after Hebron was built (Num 13:22). The first kings of the Twelfth Dynasty made it their capital; the Hyksos fortified it and changed the name to Avaris. The Egyptian god Seth had a center of worship there. Moses met Pharaoh at Zoan (Ps 78:12, 43), an important city (Isa 19:11, 13; Ezek 30:14). For a time the Assyrians were in control of it. The Greeks called it "Tanis." Eventually it was superseded by the new city of Alexandria.

ZOAR (zō'êr, Heb. *tsō'ar*, *little*). An ancient Canaanite city now probably under the waters of the bay at the SE part of the Dead Sea. Formerly called "Bela" (Gen 14:2), it was saved from immediate destruction with Sodom and Gomorrah in answer to the prayer of Lot (19:20-22). When Moses stood on Mt. Pisgah to view the Promised Land, Zoar was at the southern limit of his view (Deut 34:3). In the "Doom of Moab" (Isa 15) the fleeing Moabites were to go to Zoar (15:5). We read of its later doom in Jeremiah 48:34.

ZOBAH, ZOBA (zō'bà, Heb. *tsôvâh*). A region in central Syria, sometimes under one king (2 Sam 8:3); but in its first occurrence (1 Sam 14:47) Saul of Israel fought against the kings of Zobah, which may indicate more than one kingdom or possibly successive kings. The kings of Zobah were persistent enemies of Israel, not only fighting against Saul, but also against David (2 Sam 8) and Solomon. Solomon captured Hamath Zobah (2 Chron 8:3), and we hear no more of this kingdom. The servants of Hadadezer in the days of David had shields of gold (2 Sam 8:3–12) and a large army, all of which David captured. Later the Ammonites, in warring against David, hired mercenary troops from Zobah, and these too were badly defeated (2 Sam 10). It lay between Hamath and Damascus. It is called Zoba in Hebrew and KJV.

ZOBEBAH (See HAZZOBEBAH)

ZOHAR (zō'hàr, Heb. *tsōhar*). **1.** A noble Hittite, father of Ephron, from whom Abraham purchased the field of Machpelah where he buried the body of Sarah in a cave (Gen 23:8; 25:9). **2.** A son of Simeon (46:10; Exod 6:15). He is also called Zerah (Num 26:13; 1 Chron 4:24). **3.** A man of Judah (4:7 JB, NIV; Izhar ASV, MLB, RSV; Jezoar KJV, NEB).

ZOHELETH (zō'hē-lĕth, Heb. *zōheleth, serpent*). A stone beside En Rogel where Adonijah, fourth son of David and older than Solomon, gathered his conspirators before David's death. He sacrificed sheep and oxen, attempting to make himself king at or before the death of his father. The plot was revealed to David, who had Solomon anointed, and thus the plot was foiled (1 Kings 1, esp. v. 9). The exact site of Zoheleth is unknown.

ZOPHAI (zō'fī, Heb. *tsōphay*). An ancestor of Samuel the prophet (1 Chron 6:26; called Zuph in 6:35).

ZOPHAR (zō'fêr, Heb. *tsōphar*). One of Job's friends who came to comfort him in his affliction (Job 2:11).

ZORAH (zō'rà, Heb. *tsorâh*). A city about 15 miles (25 km.) west of Jerusalem on the border of Judah and Dan (Josh 15:33; 19:41), the home of Manoah, father of Samson (Judg 13:2). Samson was buried near there (16:31). From Zorah the Danites sent spies to seek a new home for their tribe (18:2).

ZOREAH (See ZORAH)

ZUPH (zŭf, Heb. *tsûph, honeycomb*). **1.** An ancestor of the prophet Samuel. He was a Levite descended from Kohath (1 Sam 1:1; 1 Chron 6:35). He is also called Zophai (6:26). **2.** A district in Benjamin near its northern border (1 Sam 9:5).

ZUR (zûr, Heb. *tsûr, rock*). **1.** One of the five kings of the Midianites killed by Israel (Num 25:15; 31:8). Cozbi, his daughter, was killed by Phinehas, grandson of Aaron. **2.** An inhabitant of Gibeon in Benjamin; a son of Jeiel (1 Chron 8:30; 9:36).

ZURISHADDAI (zū'rī-shăd'ī, Heb. *tsûrîshadday, whose rock is the Almighty*). Father of Shelumiel, head of the tribe of Simeon in the wilderness (Num 1:6; 2:12; 7:36, 41; 10:19).

Names Not Listed in the Dictionary

The names of people and places that are found only once in the Bible are not listed in the main dictionary if nothing is known about them beyond the mere mention of the name—quite a few names in the genealogies fall in this category. (In some cases names that are found twice but that are otherwise unknown are also included in this list.) The following is a complete list of these names.

Abagtha Esth 1:10
Abdeel Jer 36:26
Abdiel 1 Chron 5:15
Abel Keramim Judg 11:33
Abel Maim 2 Chron 16:4
Abel Shittim Num 33:49
Abiasaph Exod 6:24
Abihud 1 Chron 8:3
Abimael Gen 10:28; 1 Chron 1:22
Abinoam Judg 4:6; 5:12
Abishur 1 Chron 2:28–29
Abital 2 Sam 3:4; 1 Chron 3:3
Abitub 1 Chron 8:8–11
Abiud Matt 1:13
Abrech Gen 41:43
Abronah Num 33:34–35
Adadah Josh 15:22
Adalia Esth 9:8
Adamah Josh 19:36
Adami Nekeb Josh 19:33
Adbeel Gen 25:13; 1 Chron 1:29
Addar Josh 15:3
Addi Luke 3:28
Adina 1 Chron 11:42
Adino 2 Sam 23:8; 1 Chron 11:11
Adithaim Josh 15:33–36
Adlai 1 Chron 27:29
Admatha Esth 1:14
Adoraim 2 Chron 11:9
Adria Acts 27:27
Agee 1 Sam 23:11
Aharah 1 Chron 8:1
Aharhel 1 Chron 4:8
Ahasbai 2 Sam 23:34
Ahava Ezra 8:15, 21
Ahban 1 Chron 2:29
Aher 1 Chron 7:12
Ahiam 2 Sam 23:33
Ahian 1 Chron 7:19
Ahimoth 1 Chron 6:25
Ahinadab 1 Kings 4:14
Ahiramite Num 26:38
Ahisamach Exod 31:6; 35:34; 38:23
Ahishahar 1 Chron 7:10
Ahishar 1 Kings 4:6
Ahlab Judg 1:31

Ahumai 1 Chron 4:2
Ahuzzam 1 Chron 4:6
Ahzai Neh 11:13
Aiath Isa 10:28
Aija Neh 11:31
Akan Gen 36:27
Akim Matt 1:14
Alcimus 1 Macc 7:9
Allammelech Josh 19:26
Almon Diblathaim Num 33:46–47
Aloth 1 Kings 4:16
Alush Num 33:13–14
Alvah Gen 36:40
Alvan Gen 36:23; 1 Chron 1:40
Amad Josh 19:26
Amal 1 Chron 7:35
Amam Josh 15:26
Amana, Amanah S of S 4:8
Amashsai Neh 11:13
Amasiah 2 Chron 17:16
Ami Ezra 2:57
Amittai 2 Kings 14:25; Jonah 1:1
Ammah 2 Sam 2:24
Ammizabad 1 Chron 27:6
Amok Neh 12:7, 20
Amphipolis Acts 17:1
Ampliatus Rom 16:8
Anab Josh 11:21; 15:50
Anaharath Josh 19:19
Anamites Gen 10:13; 1 Chron 1:11
Anammelech 2 Kings 17:31
Anan Neh 10:26
Anani 1 Chron 3:24
Anath Judg 3:31; 5:6
Andronicus Rom 16:7
Anem 1 Chron 6:73
Aniam 1 Chron 7:19
Anim Josh 15:50
Anthothijah 1 Chron 8:24–25
Antipatris Acts 23:31
Anub 1 Chron 4:8
Apelles Rom 16:10
Aphekah Josh 15:53
Aphiah 1 Sam 9:1
Apollonia Acts 17:1
Appaim 1 Chron 2:30–31

Ara 1 Chron 7:38
Arab Josh 15:52
Aran Gen 26:28; 1 Chron 1:42
Archevites Ezra 4:9
Ardon 1 Chron 2:18
Areli Gen 46:16; Num 26:17
Aridai Esth 9:9
Aridatha Esth 9:8
Arieh 2 Kings 15:25
Arisai Esth 9:9
Armoni 2 Sam 21:8-11
Arnan 1 Chron 3:21
Arubboth 1 Kings 4:10
Arumah Judg 9:41
Arza 1 Kings 16:9
Asarel 1 Chron 4:16
Asarelah 1 Chron 25:2
Ashbea 1 Chron 4:21
Ashbel 1 Chron 8:1
Ashima 2 Kings 17:30
Ashvath 1 Chron 7:33
Asiel 1 Chron 4:35
Asnah Ezra 2:50
Aspatha Esth 9:7
Assos Acts 20:13-14
Asyncritus Rom 16:14
Atad Gen 50:11
Atarah 1 Chron 2:26
Athach 1 Sam 30:30
Athaiah Neh 11:4
Atharim Num 21:1
Athlai Ezra 10:28
Atroth Shophan Num 32:35
Aven Amos 1:5
Avith Gen 36:35
Ayyah 1 Chron 7:28
Azaliah 2 Kings 22:3
Azaniah Neh 10:9
Azaz 1 Chron 5:8
Azbuk Neh 3:16
Aziza Ezra 10:27
Azmon Num 34:4-5; Josh 15:4
Aznoth Tabor Josh 19:34
Azor Matt 1:13-14
Azzan Num 34:26
Baal Hamon S of S 8:11
Baal Hazor 2 Sam 13:23
Baal Shalishah 2 Kings 4:42-44
Baal Tamar Judg 20:33
Baara 1 Chron 8:8
Bakbakkar 1 Chron 9:15
Bamah Ezek 20:29
Barakel Job 32:2, 6
Bariah 1 Chron 3:22
Barkos Ezra 2:53; Neh 7:55
Bath Rabbim S of S 7:4

Bazluth Ezra 2:52; Neh 7:54
Bealiah 1 Chron 12:5
Becorath 1 Sam 9:1
Bedad Gen 36:35; 1 Chron 1:46
Bedeiah Ezra 10:35
Beera 1 Chron 7:37
Beerah 1 Chron 5:6
Beer Elim Isa 15:8
Ben-Abinadab 1 Kings 4:11
Ben-Deker 1 Kings 4:13
Bene Berak Josh 19:45
Bene Jaakan Deut 10:6
Ben-Geber 1 Kings 4:13
Ben-Hail 2 Chron 17:7
Ben-Hanan 1 Chron 4:20
Ben-Hesed 1 Kings 4:10
Ben-Hur 1 Kings 4:8
Beninu Neh 10:13
Beno 1 Chron 24:26-27
Ben-Zoheth 1 Chron 4:20
Beracah, Berachah 1 Chron 12:3
Beraiah 1 Chron 8:21
Beri 1 Chron 7:36
Besai Ezra 2:49; Neh 7:52
Besodeiah Neh 3:6
Beth Anath Josh 19:38; Judg 1:33
Beth Anoth Josh 15:59
Beth Arabah Josh 18:18
Beth Eked 2 Kings 10:12, 14
Beth Emek Josh 19:27
Beth Ezel Mic 1:11
Beth Gamul Jer 48:23
Beth Gilgal Neh 12:27-29
Beth Haggan 2 Kings 9:27
Beth Haram, Beth Haran Num 32:36;
    Josh 13:27
Beth Ophrah Mic 1:10
Beth Pazzez Josh 19:21
Beth Pelet Josh 15:27; Neh 11:26
Beth Rapha 1 Chron 4:12
Beth Shittah Judg 7:22
Beth Tappuah Josh 15:53
Bether S of S 2:17
Betonim Josh 13:26
Bicri 2 Sam 20:1
Bidkar 2 Kings 9:26
Bigtha Esth 1:10
Bileam 1 Chron 6:70
Bilgai Neh 10:8
Bilshan Ezra 2:2; Neh 7:7
Bimhal 1 Chron 7:33
Binea 1 Chron 8:37; 9:43
Birsha Gen 14:2
Birzaith 1 Chron 7:31
Bishlam Ezra 4:7
Bithiah 1 Chron 4:18

Bithron 2 Sam 2:29
Biziothiah Josh 15:28
Biztha Esth 1:10
Blastus Acts 12:20
Bohan Josh 15:6; 18:17
Bokeru 1 Chron 8:38
Bokim Judg 2:1–5
Bozkath Josh 15:39; 2 Kings 22:1
Bubastis Ezek 30:17
Bukkiah 1 Chron 25:4, 13
Bunah 1 Chron 2:25
Buzi Ezek 1:3
Cabbon Josh 15:40
Calno Isa 10:9
Canneh Ezek 27:23
Carcas Esth 1:10
Carpus 2 Tim 4:13
Carshena Esth 1:14
Casiphia Ezra 8:17
Cauda Acts 27:16
Cun 1 Chron 18:8
Cushan-Rishathaim Judg 3:5–11
Dabbesheth Josh 19:10
Dalmatia 2 Tim 4:10
Dalphon Esth 9:6–13
Damaris Acts 17:34
Dan Jaan 2 Sam 24:6
Dannah Josh 15:49
Darkon Ezra 2:56
Diblah Ezek 6:14
Diblaim Hos 1:3
Dibri Lev 24:11–16
Diklah Gen 10:27; 1 Chron 1:21
Dilean Josh 15:38
Dimnah Josh 21:35
Dimon Isa 15:9
Dimonah Josh 15:22
Dinhabah Gen 36:32
Dionysius Acts 17:34
Dishan Gen 36:21
Dizahab Deut 1:1
Dodai 1 Chron 27:4
Dodavahu 2 Chron 20:37
Dophkah Num 33:12
Dura Dan 3:1
Ebez Josh 19:20
Eglaim Isa 15:8
Eker 1 Chron 2:27
Ela 1 Kings 4:18
El Bethel Gen 35:7
Eldaah Gen 25:4
Elead 1 Chron 7:21
Eleadah 1 Chron 7:20
Eleph Josh 18:28
Eliahba 2 Sam 23:32; 1 Chron 11:33
Eliathah 1 Chron 25:4, 27

Elidad Num 34:21
Elienai 1 Chron 8:20
Elihoreph 1 Kings 4:3
Elika 2 Sam 23:25
Eliphal 1 Chron 11:35
Eliphelehu 1 Chron 15:18, 21
Elishaphat 2 Chron 23:1
Elishua 2 Sam 5:15; 1 Chron 14:5
Eliud Matt 1:14–15
Elkosh Nah 1:1
Elmadam, Elmodam Luke 3:28
Elnaam 1 Chron 11:46
Elpaal 1 Chron 8:11–12, 18
Eltekon Josh 15:59
Eluzai 1 Chron 12:15
Emek Keziz Josh 18:21
En Eglaim Ezek 47:10
En Haddah Josh 19:21
En Hakkore Judg 15:19
En Hazor Josh 19:37
En Mishpat Gen 14:7
En Tappuah Josh 17:7–8
Enaim Gen 38:14, 21
Epenetus Rom 16:5
Ephlal 1 Chron 2:37
Eran Num 26:36
Eri Gen 46:16
Esek Gen 26:20
Eshan Josh 15:52
Eshban Gen 36:26; 1 Chron 1:41
Eshek 1 Chron 8:38–40
Eshtemoh Josh 15:50
Eshton 1 Chron 4:11–12
Esli Luke 3:25
Eth Kazin Josh 19:13
Ethbaal 1 Kings 16:31
Ether Josh 15:42
Ethnan 1 Chron 4:7
Ethni 1 Chron 6:41
Eubulus 2 Tim 4:21
Euergetes Luke 22:25
Ezbai 1 Chron 11:37
Ezel 1 Sam 20:19
Ezrah 1 Chron 4:17
Ezrahite 1 Kings 4:31; titles of Pss 88, 89
Ezri 1 Chron 27:26
Fortunatus 1 Cor 16:17
Gabbai Neh 11:8
Gaddi Num 13:11
Gaddiel Num 13:10
Gadi 2 Kings 15:14–20
Gaham Gen 22:24
Gahar Ezra 2:47
Galeed Gen 31:47–48
Gammadim Ezek 27:11
Gamul 1 Chron 24:17

Garmite 1 Chron 4:19
Gazzam Ezra 2:48; Neh 7:51
Ge Harashim 1 Chron 4:14
Gebim Isa 10:31
Geder Josh 12:13
Gederah Josh 15:36, 41
Gederoth Josh 15:41
Gederothaim Josh 15:36
Geliloth Josh 18:17
Gemalli Num 13:12
Genubath 1 Kings 11:20
Geruth Kimham Jer 41:17-18
Geshan 1 Chron 2:47
Gether Gen 10:23; 1 Chron 1:17
Geuel Num 13:15
Giah 2 Sam 2:24
Gibbar Ezra 2:20
Gibea 1 Chron 2:49
Gibeath Haaraloth Josh 5:3
Giddalti 1 Chron 25:4, 29
Gideoni Num 7:60; 10:24
Gidom Judg 20:45
Gilalai Neh 12:36
Gimzo 2 Chron 28:18
Ginath 1 Kings 16:21
Ginnethon Neh 12:4; 10:6
Gispa Neh 11:21
Gizonite 1 Chron 11:34
Goah Jer 31:39
Gob 2 Sam 21:18
Gudgodah Deut 10:7
Gur 2 Kings 9:27
Gur Baal 2 Chron 26:7
Haahashtari 1 Chron 4:6
Habazziniah Jer 35:3
Hacaliah, Hachaliah Neh 1:1; 10:1
Hadashah Josh 15:37
Hadassah Esth 2:7, 15
Hadlai 2 Chron 28:12
Hadrach Zech 9:1
Hagab Ezra 2:46
Hagaba Neh 7:48
Hagabah Neh 7:48; Ezra 2:45
Haggedolim Neh 11:14
Haggi Gen 46:16; Num 26:15
Haggiah 1 Chron 6:30
Hakkatan Ezra 8:12
Hakupha Ezra 2:51; Neh 7:53
Halak Josh 11:17; 12:7
Halhul Josh 15:58
Hali Josh 19:25
Hamath Zobah 2 Chron 8:3
Hammedatha Esth 3:1
Hammoleketh 1 Chron 7:18
Hammoth Dor Josh 21:32
Hammuel 1 Chron 4:26

Hamonah Ezek 39:16
Hamul Gen 46:12
Hanes Isa 30:4
Hannathon Josh 19:14
Hapharaim Josh 19:19
Happizzez 1 Chron 24:15
Hara 1 Chron 5:26
Haradah Num 33:24
Harbona, Harbonah Esth 1:10; 7:9
Hareph 1 Chron 2:51
Harhaiah Neh 3:8
Harhas 2 Kings 22:14
Harhur Ezra 2:51; Neh 7:53
Harmon Amos 4:3
Harnepher 1 Chron 7:36
Harod Judg 7:1
Harodite 2 Sam 23:25
Haroeh 1 Chron 2:52
Harsha Ezra 2:52; Neh 7:54
Harum 1 Chron 4:8
Harumaph Neh 3:10
Haruphite 1 Chron 12:5
Haruz 2 Kings 21:19
Hasadiah 1 Chron 3:20
Hashabnah Neh 10:25
Hashbaddanah Neh 8:4
Hashem 1 Chron 11:34
Hashmonah Num 33:29-30
Hashubah 1 Chron 3:20
Hasrah 2 Chron 34:22
Hassenaah Neh 3:3
Hasupha Ezra 2:43; Neh 7:46
Hathach Esh 4:5 6, 9
Hathath 1 Chron 4:13
Hatipha Ezra 2:54; Neh 7:56
Hatita Ezra 2:42; Neh 7:45
Hattil Ezra 2:57; Neh 7:59
Hazaiah Neh 11:5
Hazar Addar Num 34:4
Hazar Enan Num 34:9-10; Ezek 47:17
Hazar Gaddah Josh 15:27
Hazar Susah Josh 19:5
Hazarmaveth Gen 10:26; 1 Chron 1:20
Hazazon Tamar Gen 14:7
Hazer Hatticon Ezek 47:16
Haziel 1 Chron 23:9
Hazo Gen 22:22
Hazzelelponi 1 Chron 4:3
Hazzobebah 1 Chron 4:8
Helah 1 Chron 4:5, 7
Helam 2 Sam 10:16-17
Helbah Judg 1:31
Helbon Ezek 27:18
Heleb 2 Sam 23:29
Heled 2 Sam 23:29; 1 Chron 11:30
Helek Num 26:30; Josh 17:2

Heleph Josh 19:33
Helkai Neh 12:15
Helkath Hazzurim 2 Sam 2:12-16
Helon Num 1:9
Hemdan Gen 36:26
Heresh 1 Chron 9:15
Hereth 1 Sam 22:5
Hermas Rom 16:14
Hermogenes 2 Tim 1:15
Herodion Rom 16:11
Heshmon Josh 15:27
Hethlon Ezek 47:15; 48:1
Hezion 1 Kings 15:18
Hezro 2 Sam 23:35; 1 Chron 11:37
Hillel Judg 12:13, 15
Hirah Gen 38:1, 12, 20
Hizki 1 Chron 8:17
Hobah Gen 14:15
Hod 1 Chron 7:37
Hodesh 1 Chron 8:9
Hoham Josh 10:3
Horam Josh 10:33
Horem Josh 19:38
Horesh 1 Sam 23:15-19
Hoshama 1 Chron 3:18
Hothir 1 Chron 25:4, 28
Hubbah 1 Chron 7:34
Hukkok Josh 19:34
Hul Gen 10:23; 1 Chron 1:17
Humtah Josh 15:54
Huppah 1 Chron 24:13
Huri 1 Chron 5:14
Hushah 1 Chron 4:4
Husham Gen 36:34-35; 1 Chron 1:45-46
Ibhar 2 Sam 5:15; 1 Chron 14:5
Ibneiah 1 Chron 9:8
Ibnijah 1 Chron 9:8
Ibri 1 Chron 24:27
Ibsam 1 Chron 7:2
Idalah Josh 19:15
Idbash 1 Chron 4:3
Igdaliah Jer 35:4
Ikkesh 2 Sam 23:26; 1 Chron 11:28
Imna 1 Chron 7:35
Imrah 1 Chron 7:36
Iphdeiah 1 Chron 8:25
Iphtah Josh 15:43
Iphtah El Josh 19:14, 27
Ir Nahash 1 Chron 4:12
Irad Gen 4:18
Iram Gen 36:43; 1 Chron 1:54
Irijah Jer 37:13
Iron Josh 19:38
Irpeel Josh 18:27
Iru 1 Chron 4:15
Iscah Gen 11:29

Ishbah 1 Chron 4:17
Ishbak Gen 25:2
Ishbi-Benob 2 Sam 21:16-17
Ishhod 1 Chron 7:18
Ishijah Ezra 10:31
Ishma 1 Chron 4:3-4
Ishmerai 1 Chron 8:18
Ishpah 1 Chron 8:16
Ishpan 1 Chron 8:22
Ishvah Gen 46:17; 1 Chron 7:30
Ismakiah 2 Chron 31:13
Ithlah Josh 19:42
Ithmah 1 Chron 11:46
Ithnan Josh 15:23
Ithream 2 Sam 3:5; 1 Chron 3:3
Iye Abarim Num 33:44
Izliah 1 Chron 8:18
Izrahiah 1 Chron 7:3
Izrahite 1 Chron 27:8
Izzian Ezra 10:25
Jaakobah 1 Chron 4:36
Jaala, Jallah Ezra 2:56
Jaar Ps 132:6
Jaare-Oregim 2 Sam 21:19
Jaareshiah 1 Chron 8:27
Jaasiel 1 Chron 27:21; 11:47
Jaasu Ezra 10:16-19, 37
Jaaziah 1 Chron 24:26-27
Jaaziel 1 Chron 15:18
Jacan 1 Chron 5:13
Jada 1 Chron 2:26, 28
Jaddai Ezra 10:43
Jadon Neh 3:7
Jagur Josh 15:21
Jahdai 1 Chron 2:46-47
Jahdiel 1 Chron 5:24
Jahdo 1 Chron 5:14
Jahleel Gen 46:14; Num 26:26
Jahmai 1 Chron 7:1-2
Jahzeiah Ezra 10:15
Jahzerah 1 Chron 9:12
Jalam Gen 36:2, 5, 18
Jalon 1 Chron 4:17
Jamlech 1 Chron 4:34
Janai 1 Chron 5:12
Janim Josh 15:53
Jannai Luke 3:23-24
Japhlet 1 Chron 7:32
Japhletites, Japhleti Josh 16:1-3
Japho Josh 19:46
Jared Gen 5:18-20
Jaroah 1 Chron 5:14
Jashubi Lehem 1 Chron 4:22
Jathniel 1 Chron 26:2
Jaziz 1 Chron 27:31
Jearim Josh 15:10

Jeatherai 1 Chron 6:21
Jeberekiah Isa 8:2
Jecoliah 2 Kings 15:2; 2 Chron 26:3
Jedidah 2 Kings 22:1
Jedidiah 2 Sam 12:24–25
Jegar Sahadutha Gen 31:47
Jehezkel 1 Chron 24:16
Jehiah 1 Chron 15:24
Jehieli 1 Chron 26:21–22
Jehizkiah 2 Chron 28:12
Jehoaddin, Jehoaddan 2 Chron 25:1
Jehucal Jer 37:3
Jehud Josh 19:45
Jehudi Jer 36:14, 21
Jekabzeel Neh 11:25
Jekameam 1 Chron 23:19; 24:23
Jekuthiel 1 Chron 4:18
Jemimah Job 42:14
Jerah Gen 10:26; 1 Chron 1:20
Jeribai 1 Chron 11:46
Jeriel 1 Chron 7:2
Jerioth 1 Chron 2:18
Jeruel 2 Chron 20:16
Jesarelah 1 Chron 25:14
Jeshanah 2 Chron 13:19
Jeshebeab 1 Chron 24:13
Jesher 1 Chron 2:18
Jeshishai 1 Chron 5:14
Jeshohaiah 1 Chron 4:36
Jesimiel 1 Chron 4:36
Jetheth Gen 36:40; 1 Chron 1:51
Jeuz 1 Chron 8:10
Jeziel 1 Chron 12:3
Jezrahiah Neh 12:42
Jidlaph Gen 22:22
Joahaz 2 Chron 34:8
Joanan Luke 3:27
Joda Luke 3:26
Joed Neh 11:7
Joelah 1 Chron 12:7
Joezer 1 Chron 12:6
Jogbehah Num 32:35; Judg 8:11
Jogli Num 34:22
Joiakim Neh 12:10, 12, 26
Jokdeam Josh 15:56
Jokim 1 Chron 4:22
Jokmeam 1 Chron 6:68
Jokneam Josh 12:22; 21:34
Jokshan Gen 25:2–3
Jonam Luke 3:30
Jorah Ezra 2:18
Jorai 1 Chron 5:13
Jorim Luke 3:29
Jorkeam 1 Chron 2:44
Jose Luke 3:29
Josech Luke 3:26

Joshah 1 Chron 4:34
Joshaviah 1 Chron 11:46
Joshbekashah 1 Chron 25:4, 24
Josheb-Basshebeth 2 Sam 23:8
Joshibiah 1 Chron 4 ٰٮ
Josiphiah Ezra 8:10
Jotbathah, Jotbath Num 33:33–34; Deut 10:7
Jubal Gen 4:21
Judith Gen 26:34
Julia Rom 16:15
Julias, Junia Rom 16:7
Jushab-Hesed 1 Chron 3:20
Kabzeel Josh 15:21; 2 Sam 23:20
Kadmonites Gen 15:18–21
Kallai Neh 12:20
Kamon Judg 10:5
Kareah 2 Kings 25:23
Karka Josh 15:3
Karkor Judg 8:10
Kartah Josh 21:34
Kartan Josh 21:32
Kattath Josh 19:15
Kedemah Gen 25:15
Kehelathah Num 33:22–23
Kelaiah Ezra 10:23
Kelal Ezra 10:30
Keluhi Ezra 10:35
Kenani Neh 9:4
Kephar Ammoni Josh 18:24
Keran Gen 36:26; 1 Chron 1:41
Keren-Happuch Job 42:14–15
Keros Ezra 2:44; Neh 7:47
Kerub Ezra 2:59; Neh 7:61
Kesalon Josh 15:10
Kesed Gen 22:22
Kesil Josh 15:30
Kesulloth Josh 19:18
Kezlah, Kezia Job 42:12
Kezib Gen 38:5
Kibzaim Josh 21:22
Kidon 1 Chron 13:9
Kilion Ruth 1:2–5; 4:9–10
Kilmad Ezek 27:23
Kinah Josh 15:21–22
Kios Acts 20:15
Kishi 1 Chron 6:44
Kislon Num 34:21
Kisloth Tabor Josh 19:12
Kitlish Josh 15:40
Kitron Judg 1:30
Koa Ezek 23:23
Koz 1 Chron 4:8
Kue 1 Kings 10:28; 2 Chron 1:16
Kushaiah 1 Chron 15:17
Laadah 1 Chron 4:21

Lael Num 3:24
Lahad 1 Chron 4:2
Lahmas, Lahmam Josh 15:40
Lahmi 1 Chron 20:5
Lakkum, Lakum Josh 19:33
Lappidoth Judg 4:4
Lasea Acts 27:8
Lasha Gen 10:19
Lasharon Josh 12:18
Lebana Neh 7:48
Lebanah Ezra 2:45
Leb Kamai Jer 51:1
Lebonah Judg 21:19
Lecah 1 Chron 4:21
Lehi Judg 15:9, 14
Leshem Josh 19:47; 1 Sam 3:20
Letushites Gen 25:3
Leummites Gen 25:3
Likhi 1 Chron 7:19
Linus 2 Tim 4:21
Lod 1 Chron 8:12
Lo Debar 2 Sam 9:1–13; 17:27ff.
Luhith Isa 15:5; Jer 48:5
Maadai Ezra 10:34
Maadiah Neh 12:5
Maai Neh 12:36
Maarath Josh 15:59
Maasai 1 Chron 9:12
Maath Luke 3:26
Maaz 1 Chron 2:27
Macbannai 1 Chron 12:13
Macbenah 1 Chron 2:49
Macnadebai Ezra 10:40
Madai Gen 10:2; 1 Chron 1:5
Madmenah Isa 10:31
Madon Josh 11:1; 12:19
Magbish Ezra 2:30
Magdiel Gen 36:43; 1 Chron 1:54
Magor-Missabib Jer 20:3
Magpiash Neh 10:20
Mahavite 1 Chron 11:46
Mahazioth 1 Chron 25:4, 30
Mahol 1 Kings 4:31
Makaz 1 Kings 4:9
Makheloth Num 33:25–26
Maki Num 13:15
Makkedah Josh 10:16ff.; 15:41
Malchus John 18:10
Malkiram 1 Chron 3:18
Mallothi 1 Chron 25:4, 26
Manaen Acts 13:1
Mara Ruth 1:20
Maralah Josh 19:10–11
Maroth Mic 1:21
Marsena Esth 1:10–14
Massa Gen 25:14; 1 Chron 1:30

Matri 1 Sam 10:21
Mattanah Num 21:18
Mattatha Luke 3:31
Mattathah Ezra 10:33
Mattathias Luke 3:25–26
Matthan Matt 1:15
Matthat Luke 3:24, 29
Meconah Neh 11:28
Medan Gen 25:2; 1 Chron 1:32
Mehida Ezra 2:52; Neh 7:54
Mehir 1 Chron 4:11
Meholah, Meholathite 1 Sam 18:19; 2 Sam 21:8
Mehujael Gen 4:18
Mehuman Esth 1:10
Mekerathite 1 Chron 11:36
Melatiah Neh 3:7
Melea Luke 3:31
Melech 1 Chron 8:35; 9:41
Memucan Esth 1:13–22
Menna Luke 3:31
Meonothai 1 Chron 4:13–14
Mephaath Josh 13:18; 21:37
Meraiah Neh 12:12
Merathaim Jer 50:21
Mered 1 Chron 4:17–18
Meres Esth 1:14
Merib-Baal 1 Chron 8:34; 9:40
Meshobab 1 Chron 4:34
Meshullemeth 2 Kings 21:19
Metheg Ammah 2 Sam 8:1
Methu Shael Gen 4:18
Me-Zahab Gen 36:39; 1 Chron 1:50
Mezobaite 1 Chron 11:47
Mibhar 1 Chron 11:38
Mibzar Gen 36:42
Micmethath Josh 16:6; 17:7
Micri 1 Chron 9:8
Middin Josh 15:61
Migdal El Josh 19:38
Migdal Gad Josh 15:37
Mikneiah 1 Chron 15:18, 21
Milalai Neh 12:36
Minni Jer 51:27
Mirmah 1 Chron 8:10
Misgab Jer 48:1
Misham 1 Chron 8:12
Mishmannah 1 Chron 12:10
Mishraites 1 Chron 2:53
Mispereth Neh 7:7
Mithcah Num 33:28–29
Mithnite 1 Chron 11:43
Mizar Ps 42:6
Mizzah Gen 36:13, 17
Mnason Acts 21:16
Molid 1 Chron 2:29

Moreh Judg 7:1
Moresheth Gath Mic 1:14
Moserah Deut 10:6; Num 33:30
Mozah Josh 18:26
Naam 1 Chron 4:15
Naamites Num 26:40
Naarai 1 Chron 11:37
Naaran 1 Chron 7:28
Naggai, Nagge Luke 3:25
Nahaliel Num 21:19
Naham 1 Chron 4:19
Nahamani Neh 7:6-7
Naharai, Nahari 2 Sam 23:37; 1 Chron 11:39
Nahbi Num 13:14
Naphtuhites, Naphtuhim Gen 10:13; 1 Chron 1:11
Narcissus Rom 16:11
Neah Josh 19:13
Nebai Neh 10:19
Neballat Neh 11:34
Nebat 1 Kings 12:15
Nebo-Sarsekim Jer 39:3
Nebushazban Jer 39:11-14
Nedabaiah 1 Chron 3:18
Nehelamite Jer 29:24, 31-32
Nehiloth Psalm 5 (title)
Nehum Ezra 2:2; Neh 7:7
Neiel Josh 19:27
Nephtoah Josh 15:9; 18:15
Nephussim, Nephishesim Ezra 2:50; Neh 7:52
Nereus Rom 16:15
Neri Luke 3:27
Netaim 1 Chron 4:23
Neziah Ezra 2:54; Neh 7:56
Nezib Josh 15:43
Nibhaz 2 Kings 17:31
Nibshan Josh 15:62
Nicanor Acts 6:5
Nicolas, Nicolaus Acts 6:5
Nicopolis Titus 3:12
Niger Acts 13:1-3
Nimrim Isa 15:6; Jer 48:34
Nimshi 1 Kings 19:16; 2 Kings 9:2, 14
Nod Gen 4:16; Ps 56:8
Nodab 1 Chron 5:19
Nogah 1 Chron 3:7; 14:6
Nohah 1 Chron 8:2
Nophah Num 21:30
Nympha Col 4:15
Obil 1 Chron 27:30
Oboth Num 21:10-11; 33:43
Ocran, Ochran Num 1:13; 7:72
Ohad Gen 46:10; Exod 6:15
Ohel 1 Chron 3:20

Oholiab Exod 31:6
Olympas Rom 16:15
Omar Gen 36:11, 15
Ophni Josh 18:24
Oren 1 Chron 2:25
Othni 1 Chron 26:7
Ozni Num 26:16
Padon Ezra 2:44; Neh 7:47
Pagiel Num 7:72
Palal Neh 3:25
Palti Num 13:9
Parah Josh 18:23
Parmashta Esth 9:9
Parmenas Acts 6:5
Parnach Num 34:25
Parshandatha Esth 9:7
Paruah 1 Kings 4:17
Parvaim 2 Chron 3:6
Pasach 1 Chron 7:33
Patara Acts 21:1-2
Patrobas Rom 16:14
Pedahel Num 34:28
Pedahzur Num 1:10; 2:20
Pekod Jer 50:21; Ezek 23:23
Pelaliah Neh 11:12
Pelonite 1 Chron 11:27, 36
Peninnah 1 Sam 1:2-7
Perazim, Mount 2 Sam 5:20; 1 Chron 14:11
Peres Dan 5:28
Peresh 1 Chron 7:16
Perez Uzzah 2 Sam 6:8; 1 Chron 13:11
Perida Neh 7:57
Persis Rom 16:12
Pethor Num 22:5; Deut 23:4
Pethuel Joel 1:1
Peullethai 1 Chron 26:5
Phanuel Luke 2:36
Pharpar 2 Kings 5:12
Philologus Rom 16:15
Phlegon Rom 16:14
Phoenix Acts 27:12
Pildash Gen 22:22
Pilha Neh 10:24
Piltai Neh 12:17
Pinon Gen 36:40-41; 1 Chron 1:52
Piram Josh 10:1-11
Pispah 1 Chron 7:38
Pithon 1 Chron 8:35; 9:41
Pokereth-Hazzebaim Ezra 2:57; Neh 7:59
Poratha Esth 9:8
Potter's Gate Jer 19:2
Procorus, Prochorus Acts 6:5
Pudens 2 Tim 4:21
Punon Num 33:42-43
Purah Judg 7:10-11

Puthites 1 Chron 2:50, 53
Putiel Exod 6:25
Pyrrhus Acts 20:4
Quartus Rom 16:23
Raamiah Neh 7:7; Ezra 2:2
Rabbith Josh 19:20
Rab-Mag Jer 39:3
Racal 1 Sam 30:29
Raddai 1 Chron 2:14
Ragau Luke 3:35
Raham 1 Chron 2:44
Rakem 1 Chron 7:16
Rakkath Josh 19:35
Rakkon Josh 19:46
Ramath Lehi Judg 15:17
Ramiah Ezra 10:25
Raphah 1 Chron 8:37
Raphu Num 13:9
Reba Num 31:8; Josh 13:21
Recah, Reca 1 Chron 4:12
Reelaiah Ezra 2:2; Neh 7:7
Regem 1 Chron 2:47
Regem-Melech Zech 7:2
Rei 1 Kings 1:8
Remaliah 2 Kings 15:25
Rephael 1 Chron 26:7–12
Rephah 1 Chron 7:23–25
Rephan Acts 7:37–50
Resen Gen 10:8–12
Resheph 1 Chron 7:25
Reu Gen 11:10–19
Reumah Gen 22:20–24
Rezeph 2 Kings 19:8–12; Isa 37:12
Rhegium Acts 28:13
Rhesa Luke 3:27
Rimmon Perez Num 33:16–19
Rinnah 1 Chron 4:20
Riphath Gen 10:3; 1 Chron 1:6
Rissah Num 33:21
Rithmah Num 33:18
Rohgah 1 Chron 7:34
Romamti-Ezer 1 Chron 25:4, 31
Rumah Judg 9:41; Josh 15:52
Sabta, Sabtah Gen 10:7; 1 Chron 1:9
Sabteca, Sabtecah Gen 10:5–7; 1 Chron 1:9
Sakia 1 Chron 8:10
Sallai Neh 11:8
Salma 1 Chron 2:51, 54
Salmone Acts 27:7
Salt, City of Josh 15:62
Salu Num 25:14
Samlah Gen 36:36–37; 1 Chron 1:47–48
Saraph 1 Chron 4:22
Sarid Josh 19:10, 12
Sarsechim Jer 39:3

Seba Gen 10:7
Secacah Josh 15:61
Secu 1 Sam 19:22
Secundus Acts 20:4
Seirah, Seirath Judg 3:26
Sela Hammahlekoth 1 Sam 23:28
Seled 1 Chron 2:30
Semakiah 1 Chron 26:7
Semein, Semei Luke 3:26
Seneh 1 Sam 14:4–5
Seorim 1 Chron 24:1–8
Sephar Gen 10:30
Sepharad Obad 20
Sered Gen 46:14; Num 26:26
Seredite Gen 46:14; Num 26:26
Sethur Num 13:2–3, 13
Shaalabbin Josh 19:42
Shaalim 1 Sam 9:4
Shaashgaz Esth 2:14
Shagee, Shage 1 Chron 11:34
Shaharaim 1 Chron 8:8–11
Shahazumah, Shahazimah Josh 19:22
Shalisha, Shalishah 1 Sam 9:4
Shalleketh Gate 1 Chron 26:13–16
Shalmai Ezra 2:46
Shalman Hosea 10:14
Shama 1 Chron 11:44
Shamma 1 Chron 7:37
Shamsherai 1 Chron 8:26
Shapham 1 Chron 5:12
Shaphir Mic 1:10–15
Sharai Ezra 10:10, 40, 44
Sharar 2 Sam 23:33
Sharonite 1 Chron 27:29
Shashai Ezra 10:40
Shashak 1 Chron 8:14–15, 22–25
Shaveh, Valley of Gen 14:17
Shaveh Kiriathaim Gen 14:5
Sheal Ezra 10:29
Sheariah 1 Chron 8:38; 9:44
Shebah Gen 26:31 33
Sheber 1 Chron 2:48
Sheep Gate Neh 3:1, 32; 12:39
Sheerah 1 Chron 7:24; 2 Chron 8:5
Shehariah 1 Chron 8:26
Sheleph Gen 10:26
Shelesh 1 Chron 7:35
Shelomi Num 34:27
Shelumiel Num 1:6; 7:36
Shemaah 1 Chron 12:3
Shemeber Gen 14:2
Shemed 1 Chron 8:12
Shemidaites Num 26:32; Josh 17:2
Shen 1 Sam 7:12
Shenazzar 1 Chron 3:18
Shepham Num 34:10–11

Shepher Num 33:23
Sheresh 1 Chron 7:16
Shethar Esth 1:41
Shethar-Bozenai, Shethar-Boznai Ezra 5:3, 6
Shigionoth Hab 3:1
Shihor Libnath Josh 19:26
Shikkeron Josh 15:11
Shilhi 1 Kings 22:42
Shilhim Josh 15:32
Shilshah 1 Chron 7:37
Shimeath 2 Chron 24:26; 2 Kings 12:21
Shimeathites 1 Chron 2:55
Shimeon Ezra 10:31
Shimite Num 3:21
Shimon 1 Chron 4:20
Shimrath 1 Chron 8:21
Shimron Meron Josh 12:20
Shimshai Ezra 4:8
Shinab Gen 14:2
Shion Josh 19:19
Shiphi 1 Chron 4:37
Shiphmite 1 Chron 27:27
Shiphrah Exod 1:15–21
Shiphtan Num 34:24
Shitrai 1 Chron 27:29
Shiza 1 Chron 11:42
Shoa Ezek 23:23
Shobai Ezra 2:42; Neh 7:45
Shobek Neh 10:24
Shobi 2 Sam 17:27
Shoham 1 Chron 24:27
Shumathites 1 Chron 2:53
Shuni, Shunite Gen 46:16; Num 26:15
Shupham Num 26:39
Shuppim 1 Chron 26:16
Shuppites 1 Chron 7:12, 15
Shur Gen 16:7–14; 20:1
Sia, Siaha Neh 7:47, Ezra 2:44
Sibraim Ezek 47:16
Silla 2 Kings 12:20
Sin (city) Ezek 30:15–16
Sinim Isa 49:12
Sinites Gen 10:17; 1 Chron 1:15
Siphmoth 1 Sam 30:28
Sippai 1 Chron 20:4
Sirah 2 Sam 3:26
Sirion Deut 3:9
Sismai, Sisamai 1 Chron 2:40
Sithri Exod 6:22
Sitnah Gen 26:21
Sodi Num 13:10
Sophereth, Sophoreth Ezra 2:55
Sotai Ezra 2:55; Neh 7:57
Stachys Rom 16:9
Suah 1 Chron 7:36

Sucathites 1 Chron 2:55
Succoth Benoth 2 Kings 17:24–30
Sukkites, Sukkiim 2 Chron 12:3
Susanna Luke 8:1–3
Susi Num 13:11
Sychar John 4:5
Syrtis Acts 27:17
Taanath Shiloh Josh 16:6
Tabaliah 1 Chron 26:11
Tabbaoth Ezra 2:43; Neh 7:46
Tabbath Judg 7:22
Tabrimmon 1 Kings 15:18
Tahash Gen 22:24
Tahkemonite 2 Sam 23:8
Tahpenes 1 Kings 11:14–22
Talitha Koum Mark 5:41
Tanhumeth 2 Kings 25:23; Jer 40:8
Taphath 1 Kings 4:11
Taralah Josh 18:27
Tarea 1 Chron 8:35
Tarpelites Ezra 4:9–10
Tartak 2 Kings 17:31
Tehinnah 1 Chron 4:12
Tekel Dan 5:25
Tel Assar Isa 37:12
Tel Aviv, Tel Abib Ezek 3:15
Tel Harsha Ezra 2:59; Neh 7:61
Tel Melah Ezra 2:59; Neh 7:61
Temah Ezra 2:53; Neh 7:55
Temani, Temanites Gen 36:34
Temeni 1 Chron 4:6
Teresh Esth 2:21
Terrace 2 Chron 9:11
Tertius Rom 16:22
Theudas Acts 5:36–37
Thimnathah Josh 19:43
Three Taverns Acts 28:15
Tibni 1 Kings 16:15–21
Tidal Gen 14:1, 9
Tilon 1 Chron 4:20
Timaeus Mark 10:46–52
Timnite Judg 15:3–6
Timon Acts 6:5
Tiras Gen 10:2; 1 Chron 1:5
Tirathite 1 Chron 2:55
Tirhanah 1 Chron 2:48
Tiria 1 Chron 4:16
Titius Justus Acts 18:7
Tizite 1 Chron 11:45
Tob-Adonijah 2 Chron 17:7–9
Tohu 1 Sam 1:1
Tolad 1 Chron 4:29
Tophel Deut 1:1
Tripolis Ezra 4:9
Trogyllium Acts 20:15
Tryphena Rom 16:12

Tubal-Cain Gen 4:22
Ucal Prov 30:1
Uel Ezra 10:34
Ulla 1 Chron 7:39
Ummah Josh 19:30
Ur 1 Chron 11:35
Urbanus Rom 16:9
Uzai Neh 3:25
Uzal Gen 10:27; 1 Chron 1:21
Uzza, Garden of 2 Kings 21:18, 26
Uzzen Sheerah 1 Chron 7:24
Uzzia 1 Chron 11:44
Vaizatha, Vajezatha Esth 9:9
Valley Gate Neh 2:13; 3:13
Vaniah Ezra 10:36
Vineyards, Plain of the Judg 11:33
Vophsi Num 13:14
Zaanan Mic 1:11
Zaavan Gen 36:27; 1 Chron 1:42
Zabud 1 Kings 4:5
Zaccai Ezra 2:9; Neh 7:14
Zaham 2 Chron 11:19
Zair 2 Kings 8:21
Zalaph Neh 3:30
Zalmonah Num 33:41-42
Zaphenath-Paneah Gen 41:45
Zaphon Josh 13:27
Zara Matt 1:3
Zaza 1 Chron 2:33
Zebidah 2 Kings 23:36
Zebina Ezra 10:43
Zebul Judg 9:28, 30, 38
Zeeb Judg 7:25ff.

Zeker 1 Chron 8:31
Zemarites Gen 10:18; 1 Chron 1:16
Zemirah 1 Chron 7:8
Zenan Josh 15:37
Zenas Titus 3:13
Zephath Judg 1:17
Zephathah 2 Chron 14:9-12
Zer Josh 19:35
Zeredah, Zereda 1 Kings 11:26
Zererah Judg 7:22
Zereth Shahar Josh 13:19
Zeri 1 Chron 25:3
Zeror 1 Sam 9:1
Zeruah 1 Kings 11:26
Zeruiah 2 Sam 17:25
Zethan 1 Chron 7:10
Zethar Esth 1:10
Zia 1 Chron 5:13
Zibeon Gen 36:2, 14
Zibia 1 Chron 8:9
Ziddim Josh 19:35
Zillah Gen 4:19-22
Zimran Gen 25:2; 1 Chron 1:32
Zior Josh 15:54
Ziphron Num 34:9
Zippor Num 22:3-4
Ziz 2 Chron 20:16-17
Zoheth 1 Chron 4:20
Zophah 1 Chron 7:35-36
Zophim Num 23:14
Zorathites 1 Chron 4:2
Zorites 1 Chron 2:54
Zuar Num 1:8; 2:5

Topical Index

For most of the main (boldface) entries in this index there is a general article in the dictionary proper. In some cases, however, there is no general article; this is indicated by brackets around the main entry. For example, there is a general article on agriculture, but, as indicated by the brackets around the entry below, the dictionary does not contain an article on the alphabet as a whole, only articles about specific letters of the Hebrew alphabet (aleph, beth, etc.).

AGRICULTURE (*see also* Occupations; Tools)
Chaff
Farming
Field
Fodder
Glean
Graft
Granary
Harrow
Harvest
Irrigation
Mowing
Reaping
Seed
Sheaf
Stubble
Threshing
Threshing Floor
Vine, Vineyard
Water
Winepress
Winnowing Fork
Yoke

[ALPHABET]
Aleph
Beth
Caph
He
Jot

AMMONITES
Rabbah, Rabbath

ANIMALS (*see also* Birds)
Dragon
Flock
Herd
Lamb
Ram Skins
Red Heifer
Saddle
Sheep Pen, Sheepfold
Snare
Speckled
Stall
Unclean, Uncleanness
Wool
Yoke

ANGEL (*see also* Demons; Satan)
Angel of the Lord

Cherub, Cherubim
Gabriel
Living Creatures
Mediator
Michael
Minister
Seraphs, Seraphim
Sons of God
Wing

APOCALYPTIC LITERATURE
Apocrypha
Daniel, Book of
Enoch, Books of
Ezekiel
Jubilees, Book of
Revelation, Book of the
Symbol
Zechariah

ARCHAEOLOGY
Amarna, Tell El
Beth Shan
Dead Sea Scrolls
Habiru
Hittites
Jerusalem
Moabite Stone
Nazareth Decree
Ostraca
Palace
Ras Shamra
Rosetta Stone
Siloam
Tell

ARCHITECTURE, BUILDINGS (*see also* Building Materials; House)
Antonia, Tower of
Appian Way
Appius, Forum of
Beam
Castle
Fort, Fortress
Gate
Machaerus
Palace
Pillar
Pinnacle
Porch
Post
Solomon's Colonnade
Stairs, Stairway, Steps

Prophet
Propitiation and Expiation
Resurrection of Jesus Christ
Revelation
Righteousness
Savior
Servant of Jehovah
Seven Words from the Cross
Son of God
Son of Man
Transfiguration
Trial of Jesus
Virgin Birth

[CHRISTIAN DOCTRINES] (see also Redemption)
Assurance
Atonement
Confession
Conversion
Conviction
Faith
Forgiveness
Grace
Guilt
Hope
Impute
Justification
Propitiation and Expiation
Reconciliation
Regeneration
Repentance
Resurrection
Salvation
Sanctification

[CHRISTIAN RELIGIOUS PRACTICES] (see also Sacrament)
Alms
Anoint
Binding and Loosing
Consecration
Dedication
Excommunication
Fasting
Laying on of Hands
Ordain, Ordination
Power of the Keys
Prayer
Religion
Sprinkling
Worship

[CHRISTIAN VIRTUES] (see also Self-discipline)
Agape
Charity
Faithfulness
Gentleness
Godliness
Goodness
Grace
Holy
Hospitality
Humility

Joy
Longsuffering
Love
Meekness
Mercy
Patience
Peace
Perseverance
Pity
Righteousness

CHURCH (see also Prophets; Sacraments; Worship)
Apostle
Binding and Loosing
Bishop
Deacon, Deaconess
Disciple
Elder
Eleven, The
Evangelist
Excommunication
Fellowship
Holy
Martyr
Member
Minister
Ordain, Ordination
Power of the Keys
Presbytery
Prophetess
Prophets
Sacrament
Saint
Worship

[CIVIL LAW] (see also Law; Legal System; Punishment)
Adoption
Appeal
Council
Court
Debts
Firstborn
Inheritance
Interest
Marriage
Pledge
Usury
Wages
Witness

[CIVIL LEADERS]
Deputy
Duke
Governor
Judges, The
King
Magistrate
Officer
Potentate
Presidents
Prince, Princess
Proconsul
Procurator

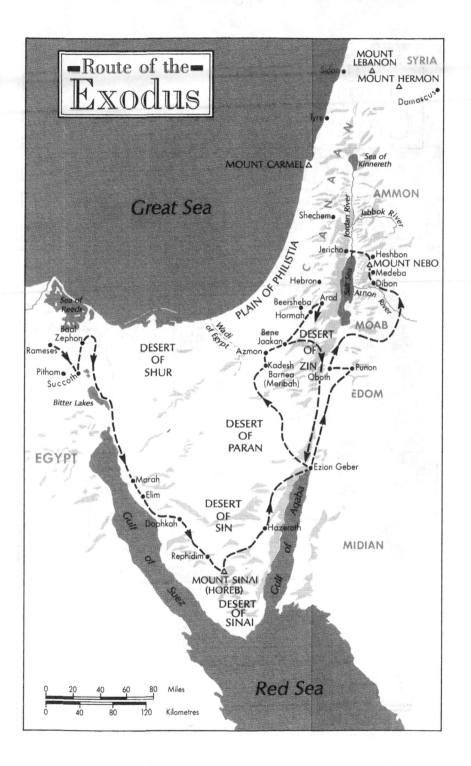

Route of the Exodus

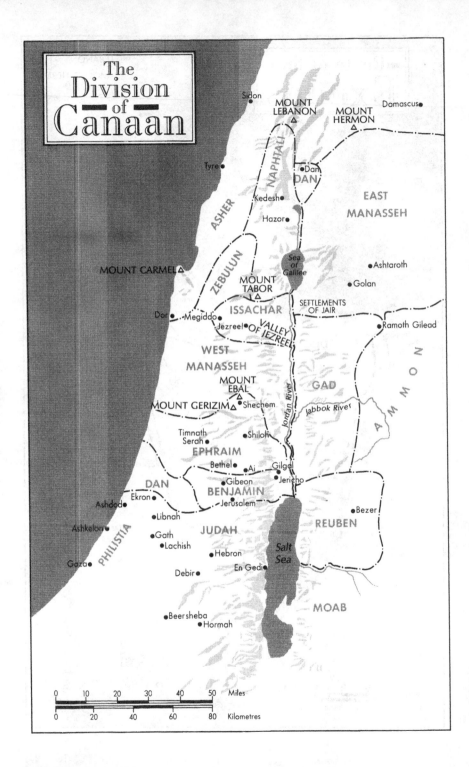

The Division of Canaan

Sidon

MOUNT LEBANON △

MOUNT HERMON △

Damascus●

Tyre●

NAPHTALI

Dan

DAN

EAST MANASSEH

Kedesh●

ASHER

Hazor●

Sea of Galilee

Ashtaroth●

MOUNT CARMEL △

ZEBULUN

MOUNT TABOR △

Golan●

SETTLEMENTS OF JAIR

ISSACHAR

Dor● ●Megiddo

Jezreel● VALLEY OF JEZREEL

Ramoth Gilead●

WEST MANASSEH

Jordan River

GAD

MOUNT EBAL △

A M M O N

MOUNT GERIZIM △ ●Shechem

Jabbok River

Timnath Serah● ●Shiloh

EPHRAIM

Bethel● ●Ai Gilgal●

DAN ●Gibeon ●Jericho

Ekron● BENJAMIN

Ashdod●

Ashkelon● PHILISTIA ●Libnah Jerusalem●

●Gath JUDAH

Bezer●

REUBEN

●Lachish ●Hebron Salt Sea

Gaza● Debir● En Gedi●

MOAB

●Beersheba
●Hormah

| 0 | 10 | 20 | 30 | 40 | 50 | Miles |

| 0 | 20 | 40 | 60 | 80 | Kilometres |

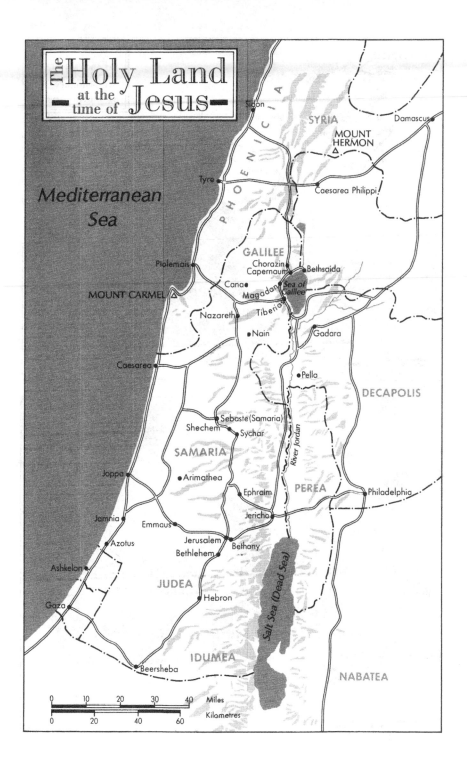

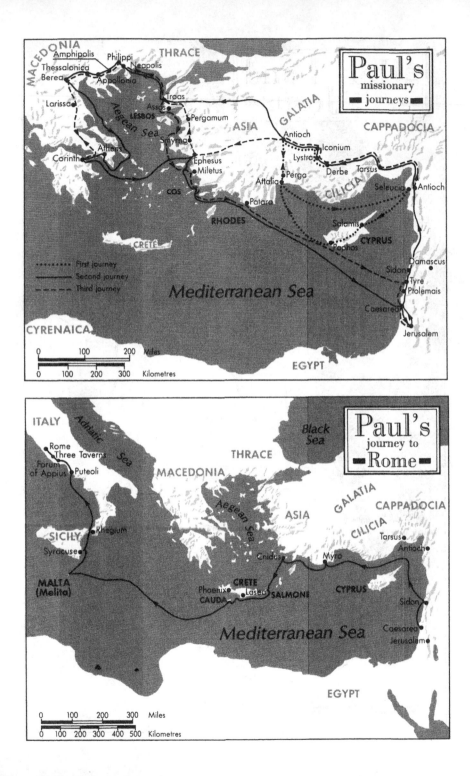